ADO.NET 3.5 Cookbook™

SECOND EDITION

ADO.NET 3.5 Cookbook™

Bill Hamilton

O'REILLY®

Beijing · Cambridge · Farnham · Köln · Paris · Sebastopol · Taipei · Tokyo

ADO.NET 3.5 Cookbook™, Second Edition
by Bill Hamilton

Published by O'Reilly Media, Inc., 1005 Gravenstein Highway North, Sebastopol, CA 95472.

O'Reilly books may be purchased for educational, business, or sales promotional use. Online editions are also available for most titles (*safari.oreilly.com*). For more information, contact our corporate/institutional sales department: (800) 998-9938 or *corporate@oreilly.com*.

Editor: John Osborn

Production Editor: Rachel Monaghan

Copyeditor: Colleen Gorman

Proofreader: Nancy Reinhardt

Indexer: Ellen Troutman Zaig

Cover Designer: Karen Montgomery

Interior Designer: David Futato

Illustrator: Jessamyn Read

Printing History:

September 2003:	First Edition.
March 2008:	Second Edition.

ISBN: 978-0-596-10140-4

[C]

Table of Contents

Preface

Microsoft ADO.NET 3.5 is the latest data access technology from Microsoft. ADO.NET is a collection of classes that are part of the .NET Framework, and is designed to provide consistent access to data in loosely coupled *n*-tier application architectures such as web services. ADO.NET can be used to access a variety of data sources including databases such as Microsoft SQL Server, Oracle, and Microsoft Access, as well as XML, OLE DB, and ODBC data sources.

ADO.NET separates data access from manipulation. Connected classes available in .NET data providers connect to a data source, execute commands, and retrieve results. Disconnected classes let you access and manipulate data offline and later synchronize changes with the underlying data source. XML support is tightly integrated with ADO.NET, allowing you to load, access, and manipulate data using XML as well as the disconnected classes simultaneously.

ADO.NET is very different from its predecessor ADO. With the increasing popularity of .NET and ADO.NET, there are many questions from developers about how to solve specific problems and how to implement solutions most efficiently. This book is a reference containing solutions and techniques that make using ADO.NET easier and more productive. You may have already encountered some of these problems; others you may never see. Some of the solutions are responses to problems that have been posted in various discussion groups, while others are real problems encountered while building applications.

This book is organized into chapters, with each chapter containing solutions (stated as recipes) to a specific problem category. Each recipe consists of a single question and its solution followed by a discussion. The question-answer format provides complete solutions to problems, making it easy to read and use. Every recipe contains a complete, documented code sample showing you how to solve the specific problem, as well as a discussion of how the underlying technology works and a discussion of alternatives, limitations, and other considerations when appropriate.

What's New in the Second Edition

A lot has changed since the first edition of this book. ADO.NET has had two significant releases—versions 2.0 and 3.5. SQL Server has also had two major releases with SQL Server 2005 and SQL Server 2008. The .NET Framework has had three major releases with versions 2.0, 3.0, and 3.5. And Visual Studio has had two major releases with Visual Studio 2005 and 2008. This book is updated for the latest version of all of these technologies.

This book is a significant revision from the first edition. In addition to the obvious reason for revising this book in order to cover technology changes, I wanted to improve on the first edition in a number of important ways. First, I wanted to make the book easier to use and more accessible. In addition to updating and adding recipes to cover new or changed technology and tools, the recipes have been reorganized and new recipes added to fill in gaps that I and others saw. A number of new recipes in the early chapters address core concepts in depth. The second change that I made was to rewrite most of the solutions as Windows console applications. While the Windows Forms solutions in the first edition had a certain elegance, I felt that the additional code required and the complexity in both building and presenting the solutions distracted from the core objective of demonstrating solutions to ADO.NET problems. It also made it difficult to show output from the solutions. Windows and Web Forms solutions are presented as necessary, especially when demonstrating how to use ADO.NET controls. I've also rewritten code to focus on and highlight the solution and to programmatically explore key concepts rather than relying on the reader running and interacting with the solution. Third, I wanted to make the book more usable as a standalone resource—that is, without loading code samples. Sample output has been included for each solution. And finally, I wanted to make the book more useful and readable in many small ways—I've clarified and expanded (and in some cases reduced) explanations, increased consistency in the way solutions are presented, and of course fixed a few errors along the way.

Who This Book Is For

You don't have to be an experienced .NET developer to use this book; it is designed for users of all levels. This book provides solutions to problems that developers face every day. Reference or tutorial books can teach general concepts but do not usually provide help solving real-world problems. This book teaches by example, the natural way for most people to learn.

Although some of the samples in this book use advanced techniques, the problems they address are frequently faced by developers with all levels of experience. The code samples are all complete, well commented, and thoroughly explained to help you apply them and solve your own problems quickly, easily, and efficiently.

At the same time, you will understand exactly how and why the solution works, the requirements, trade-offs, and drawbacks. This book is designed to move you up the learning curve quickly.

This book presents code together with output so that you can use book without loading the actual code. Code generated automatically by Visual Studio is not shown. You don't need to retype the code in this book since it is available in both C# and Visual Basic on the O'Reilly web site (*http://www.oreilly.com/catalog/9780596101404*). T-SQL and PL/SQL code is also available for download.

What You Need to Use This Book

To run the samples in this book, you will need a computer running Windows 2000 or later. The Web Forms solutions require Microsoft Internet Information Server (IIS) version 5.1 or later.

The solutions in this book were written using Microsoft Visual Studio 2008. Most solutions will work with Visual Studio 2005. Many of the samples will run on Microsoft SQL Server 2000. Others require SQL Server 2005 and a few require SQL Server 2008. Oracle 10g is used to build the Oracle solutions, although Oracle 8*i* version 3 (release 8.1.7) or later is all you need.

How This Book Is Organized

This book is organized into 12 chapters, each of which focuses on a particular topic in creating ADO.NET solutions. Each recipe consists of a specific problem, stated as a question, followed by a solution and discussion. Here is a summary of each chapter:

Chapter 1, *Connecting to Data*
> The solutions in this chapter show how to connect to a variety of data sources from ADO.NET. Connecting to data sources involves connections strings, security-related issues including storing connection strings and how to use them, the different authentication methods available, and how to enable the user to build a connection string at runtime. Solutions show how to set up, monitor, and optimize connection pooling, and how to use transactions with pooled connection.

Chapter 2, *Working with Disconnected Data Objects*
> ADO.NET includes both connected and disconnected classes. The solutions in this chapter explain how to work with the ADO.NET disconnected classes— `DataColumn`, `DataTable`, `DataSet`, unique constraint, primary key, foreign key, and `DataRelation`. You will also learn about `DataRow` arrays, how to access data in them, and how to convert between a `DataRow` array and `DataTable`. Finally, you will learn about strongly typed `DataSet` objects, how to create them, and how to customize aspects of them.

Chapter 3, *Querying and Retrieving Data*

The solutions in this chapter show how to retrieve data and schemas using SQL statements, parameterized SQL statements, parameterized stored procedures, and batched queries, into both untyped and strongly typed DataSet objects, and DataReader objects, and how to access the data in those objects. You'll learn how to work with commands that return multiple result sets. Solutions show how to retrieve and navigate hierarchical data in both untyped and strongly typed DataSet objects. You'll understand how to retrieve data using scalar-valued and table-valued functions. Solutions show how to query a DataSet using LINQ and how to query a data source using LINQ. Solutions also show how to retrieve data from a text file and from an Excel workbook. Finally, you will learn how to query data asynchronously using message queuing.

Chapter 4, *Searching and Analyzing Data*

The solutions in this chapter focus on searching for, finding, and filtering records in views and tables, calculating values based on values in the same or other tables, and navigating data relations between tables. Solutions show alternate techniques to retrieve hierarchical data, including the COMPUTE BY and SHAPE clauses. You'll learn how to use Common Table Expressions (CTEs) including recursive queries, and how to retrieve ranked result sets, random result sets, and pivot and unpivot tables. Finally, a solution shows how to invoke a function for each row in a result set.

Chapter 5, *Adding and Modifying Data*

This chapter focuses on issues related to inserting and updating data, and using messaging to update data. You'll learn how to manage autoincrement columns with SQL Server and sequences with Oracle. Solutions show how to add and modify data in Excel files and text files. You'll see how to retrieve and work with DBMS update errors. Solutions show how to change primary keys and how to use GUID primary keys, as well as how to work with master-detail data and how to update a DataSet with many to many relationships. A solution shows how to insert multiple rows using T-SQL row constructors introduced in SQL Server 2008. And you'll also learn how to capture changes made to data in a SQL Server 2008 database.

Chapter 6, *Copying and Transferring Data*

This chapter focuses on copying data between ADO.NET disconnected classes, converting between ADO.NET disconnected classes and between ADO and ADO.NET classes, serializing and deserializing data, merging data, encrypting data, and securing login credentials.

Chapter 7, *Maintaining Database Integrity*

The solutions in this chapter show how to use manual and automatic transactions and DBMS transactions from ADO.NET. You'll learn how to identify and handle concurrency errors, set isolation levels, use SQL Server pessimistic concurrency with locking hints, update master-detail data without concurrency errors, and resolve data conflicts.

Chapter 8, *Programmatically Working with Data in .NET Windows and Web Forms User Interfaces*

This chapter focuses on programmatically binding simple and complex data to Web Forms and Windows Forms. You'll learn how to manage master-detail data in Windows and Web Forms, update complex data, and data-bind images. You'll understand how to use globalization and localization to create applications for multiple cultures.

Chapter 9, *Working with XML Data*

The solutions in this chapter show how to use XML with ADO.NET. You'll learn how to load schema and data from XML into a DataSet, and about the DiffGram format and how to use it to determine what changes were made to a DataSet. Solutions show how to work with XML in a database and how to work with XML data and the SQL Server xml data type. You'll learn how to read XML data directly from a SQL Server using FOR XML. Solutions show how to use XPath queries, control the format of XML output, and use XML template queries to fill a DataSet. Optimizing update performance by batching data updates with OpenXML is also illustrated.

Chapter 10, *Optimizing .NET Data Access*

This chapter shows how to improve application performance and responsiveness with asynchronous processing as well as how to cancel those processes, how to cache data to improve performance while retrieving data, and how to use custom paging to improve performance over automatic paging. Solutions show how to work with BLOB data in SQL Server and Oracle and work with SQL Server user-defined types. You'll learn how to optimize loading data into a SQL Server using bulk loading and batch DataAdapter updates. You'll also learn how to effectively debug SQL Server stored procedures using Visual Studio. Solutions show how to automatically refresh data using polling and SQL Server Notifications. Last, you'll learn how to write both provider- and database-independent ADO.NET code.

Chapter 11, *Enumerating and Maintaining Database Objects*

This chapter shows how to get schema information and metadata from databases, manage database objects, and enumerate installed .NET providers, OLE DB providers, and ODBC drivers using SQL Server Management Objects (SSO), DDL, catalog views, information schema views, and system stored procedures. You'll learn how to use ADOX to create a Microsoft Access database and tables within that database. A solution shows how to get a SQL Server query execution plan. You'll also learn to programmatically change a SQL Server user password.

Chapter 12, *SQL Server CLR Integration*

This chapter provides an overview of CLR routines in SQL Server and shows you how to build each type of CLR routine: stored procedure, scalar-valued function, table-valued function, aggregate function, user-defined type, DML trigger, and DDL trigger.

Finally, Appendix A discusses changes made to ADO.NET since version 1.0, covering both ADO.NET 2.0 and ADO.NET 3.5.

What Was Left Out

The primary objective of this book is not to be a reference or a primer about ADO.NET. This second edition is expanded to include more recipes about fundamental ADO.NET concepts and an improved arrangement of recipes that can help you get up to speed quickly on ADO.NET. The MSDN Library is an invaluable resource. It is included with Visual Studio and available online at *http://msdn2.microsoft.com/en-us/library/default.aspx*. SQL Server Books Online, installed with Microsoft SQL Server and available in MSDN Library Online, is an excellent reference to SQL Server. This is not a book about how to use Visual Studio to build, compile, and deploy applications or how to use Visual Studio IDE functionality related to ADO.NET and data access in general.

Conventions Used in This Book

This book uses the following typographic conventions:

Italic

> Used for example URLs, names of directories and files, options, and occasionally for emphasis.

Constant width

> Used for program listings. Also used within paragraphs to refer to program elements such as namespaces, classes, and method and database names.

Constant width italic

> Used for text that should be replaced with user-supplied values.

Constant width bold

> Used to highlight portions of code.

> This icon indicates a tip, suggestion, or general note.

> This icon indicates a warning or caution.

About the Code

This book contains Visual Studio projects that demonstrate complete solutions to problems. Most of the projects are console applications used because they most simply and clearly demonstrate the solution with minimal overhead and additional code. In some cases, Windows Forms and Web Forms projects are used to demonstrate solutions where user interface elements are involved. Multiple solutions to problems are sometimes presented. Where appropriate, one alternative will be recommended;

in other cases, alternatives are equivalent; make your choice based on your specific application requirements.

All of the code examples in the book use C# as a programming language. Listing Visual Basic solutions would have made the book less readable, added hundreds of pages to its length, and increased both the cover price and weight. Visual Basic code for all solutions in addition to C# code is available on the book's web site, *http://www.oreilly.com/catalog/9780596101404*.

The code in the book shows how to accomplish ADO.NET programming tasks as clearly and concisely as possible. As a result, the code is not production quality in some aspects. My top three examples are:

1. Exception handling is not included for most solutions. Omitting exception handling makes solutions easier to understand by focusing on the key concepts. Exception handling is included and explained thoroughly when it is a key part of the solution. Always include good exception handling in your applications— MSDN has excellent coverage about this topic.

2. Inconsistent use of *using blocks*. I've been forced to leave them out in most cases because they add an extra level of indent to the code that causes significant formatting problems because of line shortening. I strongly encourage their use to guarantee disposition of resources.

3. Assigning string literal database connection strings to variables. I do this in nearly every solution and while it makes the solutions clear, it is terrible practice in real-world applications. Chapter 1 discusses more suitable approaches for storing and accessing connection strings.

Many solutions using a SQL Server database use the AdventureWorks sample database. Some solutions require modifying data or the use of additional tables, stored procedures, or other database objects—in these cases, a database named AdoDotNet35Cookbook is used so that your version of AdventureWorks is not affected. T-SQL statements and batches for creating database objects are presented in the solution. Oracle solutions use either sample databases installed with Oracle, or, in some cases where those are inadequate, a custom database named AdoDotNet35Cookbook. As with SQL Server, PL/SQL statements and scripts for creating any additional Oracle database objects are presented in the solution.

Some solutions require stored procedures. Most are written for Microsoft SQL Server; however, in some cases Oracle is used because the recipe solves a problem specific to Oracle—identity columns in SQL Server versus sequences in Oracle, for example. SQL Server's T-SQL is somewhat similar to Oracle's PL/SQL; Oracle users, or users familiar with other procedural extensions to SQL, should have little difficulty understanding or adapting these stored procedures. The disconnected parts of the ADO.NET are database-independent and are, for the most part, portable without modification regardless of the underlying data source.

Using Code Examples

This book is here to help you get your job done. In general, you may use the code in this book in your programs and documentation. You do not need to contact us for permission unless you're reproducing a significant portion of the code. For example, writing a program that uses several chunks of code from this book does not require permission. Selling or distributing a CD-ROM of examples from O'Reilly books *does* require permission. Answering a question by citing this book and quoting example code does not require permission. Incorporating a significant amount of example code from this book into your product's documentation *does* require permission.

We appreciate, but do not require, attribution. An attribution usually includes the title, author, publisher, and ISBN. For example: *"ADO.NET 3.5 Cookbook,* Second Edition, by Bill Hamilton. Copyright 2008 O'Reilly Media, Inc., 978-0-596-10140-4."

If you feel your use of code examples falls outside fair use or the permission given above, feel free to contact us at *permissions@oreilly.com.*

Comments and Questions

We at O'Reilly have tested and verified the information in this book to the best of our ability, but mistakes and oversights do occur. Please let us know about errors you may find, as well as your suggestions for future editions, by writing to:

O'Reilly Media, Inc.
1005 Gravenstein Highway North
Sebastopol, CA 95472
800-998-9938 (in the U.S. or Canada)
707-829-0515 (international or local)
707-829-0104 (fax)

To ask technical questions or comment on the book, send email to:

bookquestions@oreilly.com

We have a web site for this book where examples, errata, and any plans for future editions are listed. You can access this site at:

http://www.oreilly.com/catalog/9780596101404

For more information about this book and others, see the O'Reilly web site:

http://www.oreilly.com

Safari® Books Online

 When you see a Safari® Books Online icon on the cover of your favorite technology book, that means the book is available online through the O'Reilly Network Safari Bookshelf.

Safari offers a solution that's better than e-books. It's a virtual library that lets you easily search thousands of top tech books, cut and paste code samples, download chapters, and find quick answers when you need the most accurate, current information. Try it for free at *http://safari.oreilly.com*.

Acknowledgments

The decision to write the second edition of this book was made in early 2007. Rather than just adding new recipes to cover additions and changes since ADO.NET 1.0, I came up with an ambitious plan that among other things involved writing new recipes to fill gaps, making it easier to read and use the book without a computer nearby, reorganizing the book to improve continuity, and rewriting all of the code to clarify solutions. The result is a book that has more than 50 additional recipes and is over 50 percent longer than the original. It's been a long effort that wouldn't have been possible without the efforts and support of many people.

Colleen Gorman edited the second edition of this book, and I thank her for a careful review and many thoughtful suggestions and corrections. Thanks also to Brian Jepson, who was editor for the first version of this book—a big job for him because it was also my first book. Brian's encouragement, support, and constructive criticism helped create a successful book and made me a better writer in many ways. And thanks to Rachel Monaghan, production editor, and the entire production team at O'Reilly for turning the manuscript into this book.

John Osborn, executive editor, conceived the original idea for the first edition of this book. His support throughout that project contributed to the success of the first edition and made this sequel possible. John is representative of O'Reilly and its employees. Together, they make the difficult and often tedious task of writing a book much easier with their support, fairness, directness, professionalism, and honesty. I write for O'Reilly because I believe this publisher is truly dedicated to creating a high-quality book that provides great value for the reader. A big plus is that they have a low-bureaucracy environment—contracts, for example, are short and written in plain English, allowing me to understand them without legal advice.

I had the privilege and benefit of working with four outstanding and committed technical reviewers for this version of the book—Lou Franco, Tim Lentine, Zoiner Tejada, and Shawn Wildermuth. I'd like to thank them for reviewing this book so carefully and for providing valuable feedback. I've done enough technical reviews to understand and appreciate the effort it takes to do this well. The four of them pointed out where explanations needed clarification, where more detail was needed, and also fixed some mistakes I made along the way. This book is better because of their contributions.

Thanks to the members of the .NET programming community who happily and cooperatively share what they know. I began working with .NET in Beta 1 and together with this community learned how to be productive with ADO.NET. With the help of these people, most of whom I don't know and am unlikely to meet, I was able to understand ADO.NET well enough to write books about it. I hope this book helps you get through the challenges that I remember well and admittedly still face from time to time.

Thanks to my friends and family for their encouragement and support. They are always there when I need to take my mind off work—sometimes too often for my own good.

And finally, I'd like to thank Nicole. She perfectly balances being both very supportive and very distracting. I think a smart, funny, and beautiful girl deserves better—I'm glad she doesn't think so. I love you, doll.

CHAPTER 1

Connecting to Data

1.0   Introduction

This chapter shows how to connect to a variety of data sources from ADO.NET; how to handle security-related issues including storing connection strings and using different authentication methods; and how to set up, monitor, and optimize connection pooling.

ADO.NET Overview

ADO.NET is the part of the .NET Framework that connects applications to data sources and lets you retrieve and update the contained data. ADO.NET supports a variety of different data sources, including relational databases such as Microsoft SQL Server, Oracle, and Microsoft Access, as well as other data sources such as Microsoft Excel, Outlook, and text files.

A .NET Framework data provider is used to connect to a data source, execute commands, and retrieve results. The .NET Framework ships with the data providers shown in Table 1-1.

Table 1-1. Data providers included in the .NET Framework

.NET Framework data provider	Data source access
SQL Server	Microsoft SQL Server version 7.0 or later
OLE DB	Data sources using OLE DB
ODBC	Data sources using ODBC
Oracle	Oracle client software version 8.1.7 or later

Other providers are also available; for example, Oracle has developed its own .NET data provider. Data providers also exist for databases such as Sybase and MySQL. Database-specific providers usually access the underlying data store directly and offer the best performance, broadest functionality, and support for database-specific features. Since a data provider needs only to implement a core set of standard interfaces, the capabilities and performance of data providers for the same data source can differ significantly.

In addition to database-specific providers, the OLE DB .NET data provider allows access to most OLE DB data sources through OLE DB providers. Similarly, the ODBC .NET data provider uses the ODBC drivers to access most ODBC data sources. You can also develop your own data provider to access proprietary data sources or to meet special requirements.

ADO.NET is fundamentally different from ADO despite sharing a similar name. ADO.NET is based on a disconnected architecture with tight XML integration and is designed specifically to facilitate development of loosely coupled solutions.

ADO.NET code is forward-compatible—ADO.NET code written using .NET Framework 1.1 or later will run on later versions of the .NET Framework.

ADO.NET has both connected and disconnected classes. The connected classes let you retrieve and update data in underlying data sources. The disconnected classes let you access and manipulate offline the data you retrieved using the connected classes and later synchronize it with the underlying data source using the connected class.

Each data provider is responsible for implementing the connected classes. A brief description of each follows:

Connection

> A unique session with the data source. A Connection specifies necessary authentication information needed to connect to a data source. The Connection object is specific to the type of data source—for example, the .NET Framework data provider for SQL Server includes the SqlConnection class.

Command

> Issues database commands against the data source using an established Connection. The CommandText property of the Command class contains the SQL statement, stored procedure name, or table name executed at the data source. The Command object is specific to the type of data source—for example, the .NET Framework data provider for SQL Server includes the SqlCommand object.

DataReader

> Retrieves a forward-only, read-only data stream from a data source. The DataReader object is specific to the type of data source—for example, the .NET Framework data provider for SQL Server includes the SqlDataReader object.

DataAdapter

> Bridges the connected classes with the disconnected classes by retrieving data from a data source and filling a (disconnected) DataSet. The DataAdapter also updates the data source with changes made to a disconnected DataSet. The DataAdapter uses the Connection object to connect the data source and up to four Command objects to retrieve data from and resolve changes (i.e., update, insert, and delete rows) to the data source. The DataAdapter object is specific to the type of data source—for example, the .NET Framework data provider for SQL Server includes the SqlDataAdapter object.

The disconnected classes are part of the ADO.NET classes in the .NET Framework. They provide a consistent programming model regardless of the data source or data provider. The disconnected classes include:

DataSet

> An in-memory cache of data retrieved from the data source. The DataSet exhibits similar properties to an in-memory relational database—for example, data is organized into multiple tables using DataTable objects, tables can be related using DataRelation objects, and data integrity can be enforced using the constraint objects UniqueConstraint and ForeignKeyConstraint.

> The DataSet retains no information about the source of the data used to fill it with data. It maintains both current and original versions of data allowing the data source to be updated with changes at some future time. Disconnected data classes (DataSet and DataTable) are serializable. This supports transport-independent marshaling between application tiers and across a distributed application. You can also use these classes to persist data independently of a database.

DataTable

> A single table of in-memory data that can exist independently or as part of a collection of DataTable objects in a DataSet.

DataColumn

> The schema of a column in a DataTable.

DataRow

> A row of data in the DataTable.

DataView

> A data-bindable view of a DataTable used for custom sorting, filtering, searching, editing, and navigation.

DataRelation

> A parent/child relationship between two DataTable objects in a DataSet.

Constraint

> A constraint on one or more columns in a DataTable used to maintain data integrity. A constraint is either a UniqueConstraint that ensures that a column or collection of Column objects are unique within a DataTable or a ForeignKeyConstraint that represents an action restriction on one or more columns in a relationship in a DataTable when a value or row is either updated or deleted.

ADO.NET and XML converge in .NET. You can save the DataSet as an XML document, or fill it from an XML document. You can access and modify data simultaneously using both the DataSet classes and XML classes.

Connections, Connection Strings, and Connection Pooling

Database connections are a critical and limited resource. Connections must be managed to ensure that an application performs well and is scalable. SQL Server and Oracle data providers provide connection pooling, while the OLE DB and ODBC providers use the pooling provided by OLE DB or ODBC, respectively.

Connections should be opened as late as possible and closed as soon as possible using the Close( )method. Alternatively, you can create the connection in a using block to ensure that the system disposes of the connection when the code exits the block. The connection should be used as briefly as possible, meaning that connections should not last longer than a method call. Connections should not be passed between methods—in addition to creating performance problems and limiting scalability, this can lead to security vulnerabilities.

Data providers use a connection string containing a collection of attribute/value pairs to establish the connection with the database. You specify connection strings using ConnectionString property of a Connection object. The DBConnectionStringBuilder class or the strongly typed version for each specific .NET data provider is used to build connection strings programmatically.

1.1   Storing Connection Strings

Problem

You need to choose the best place to store connection strings that you need in your application to increase maintainability, simplify future modifications, and eliminate the need to recompile the application when it is modified.

Solution

Solutions include storing the connection string in an application configuration file or the Windows registry, hardcoding the connection string in your application, representing it using a Universal Data Link (UDL) file, and storing it in a custom file. Some of these techniques are better than others, and some are completely inadvisable. This solution explores and discusses the alternatives.

The .NET Framework 2.0 introduced protected configuration as a mechanism for encrypting stored connection strings used by ASP.NET applications. It also introduced the connectionStrings configuration element to specify a collection of database strings. In prior versions, connection strings were stored in the appSettings element.

Discussion

A connection string is made up of a semicolon delimited collection of attribute/value pairs that define how to connect a data source. Although connection strings tend to look similar, the available and required attributes are different depending on the data provider and on the underlying data source. There are a variety of options providing differing degrees of flexibility and security.

Persist Security Info

The Persist Security Info connection string attribute specifies whether the data source can hang on to, or *persist*, sensitive information such as user authentication credentials. Its value should be kept at the default false. If its value is true, the connection information—including the password—can be obtained by querying the connection, allowing an untrusted party to have access to sensitive information when a Connection is passed or persisted to a disk. This is an issue only when passing connected objects such as Connection or DataAdapter; disconnected objects such as DataSet and DataTable do not store information about the original source of their data.

Before a data source object is initialized for the first time, sensitive information can be retrieved from it regardless of the setting of the Persist Security Info property. Avoid passing uninitialized data source objects.

The Persist Security Info connection string attribute is supported by the SQL Server, OLE DB, and Oracle .NET Framework data providers. Although not supported by the ODBC .NET Framework data provider, its behavior is as if Persist Security Info is false and cannot be changed. Check the documentation for other data providers to determine specific implementation details.

Connecting to a database server requires passing credentials—username and password—to the server in a connection string. These credentials, together with the data source name, need to be kept private to protect unauthorized access to the data source. There are three approaches for obtaining these credentials:

- Prompting for connection credentials at runtime
- Storing predetermined connection credentials on the server and using them at runtime to connect to the database server
- Using integrated security, which passes current credentials to the server

Often, it is not practical to prompt for connection credentials because of disadvantages including:

Security

Transferring connection information from the client to the server can expose connection credentials if they are not encrypted.

Connection pooling

The server must recognize each user separately. This results in different connection strings for each user and prevents using connection pooling, which in turn limits application scalability. For more on connection pooling, see Recipe 1.17.

Single sign-on

It is difficult to integrate with single sign-on strategies, which are becoming increasingly important in enterprise environments (for example, where numerous applications are aggregated into portals).

Server-based applications

Cannot be used by applications that otherwise have no user interface, such as an XML web service.

There are a number of techniques that you can use to store predetermined connection credentials. These, together with their advantages and drawbacks, are discussed in the following subsections.

Here are a few tips:

- Always configure predetermined accounts with the minimum permissions required.
- Use integrated security whenever possible.
- Always encrypt stored credentials and carefully control access to the associated encryption keys.
- Never use sa or any other administrative account.
- Never use blank or weak passwords.

Application configuration file

An application configuration file is an XML-based text file that is used to store application-specific settings used at runtime by the application. The naming convention for and deployment location of the file depend on the type of application:

Executable application

The name of the configuration file is the name of the application executable with a *.config* extension—for example, *myApplication.exe.config*. It is located in the same directory as the executable file.

ASP.NET application

A web application can have multiple configuration files all named *web.config*. Each configuration file supplies configuration settings for its directory and all of its child directories; it also overrides any configuration settings inherited from parent directories.

The machine configuration file—*machine.config*, located in the *CONFIG* subdirectory of the .NET runtime installation—contains configuration information that applies to the computer. The *machine.config* file is checked for configuration settings before the application configuration file is checked.

It is best to put application settings in the application configuration file both to facilitate deployment and to keep the machine configuration file manageable and secure.

The `<connectionStrings>` element of the application configuration file is used to store a collection of connection strings as name/value pairs. You can store a connection string as shown:

```
<configuration>
    <connectionStrings>
        <add key="ConnectionString"
value="Data Source=(local);Initial Catalog=AdventureWorks;
User ID=sa;password=;"
        />
    </connectionStrings>
</configuration>
```

The ConnectionStrings property of the System.Configuration class is used to retrieve the value for a specific key within the connectionStrings element; the System.Configuration class cannot be used to write settings to a configuration file.

Application configuration files facilitate deployment because the files are simply installed alongside other application files. One drawback is that application configuration files are not inherently secure since they store information as clear text in a file that is accessible through the filesystem. Encrypt the connection and other sensitive information within the configuration file and ensure that NTFS file permissions are set to restrict access to the file. Recipe 6.11 shows techniques to encrypt data.

 Make sure you name the application configuration file for a Windows Forms application *App.config*—this is the default. At build time, this file is automatically copied into the startup directory by Visual Studio .NET with the name *applicationName.exe.config*.

If you name the application configuration file *applicationName.exe.config* within your solution, you will have to copy it to the startup directory each time you modify it and each time you build the solution; the build process deletes it from the startup directory.

1. Create a new C# console application named StoredConnectionStringConfig.

2. In the Solution Explorer pane, right-click the project and select Add → New Item from the context menu to open the Add New Item dialog. Select the Application Configuration File template, accept the default name *App.config*, and click the Add button to add the configuration file.

3. Add a SQL Server connection string within a connectionStrings element in the file *App.config* as shown in Example 1-1.

Example 1-1. File: App.config

```
<?xml version="1.0" encoding="utf-8" ?>
<configuration>
    <connectionStrings>
        <add name="AdventureWorks"
         providerName="System.Data.SqlClient"
         connectionString="Data Source=(local);
          Integrated security=SSPI;Initial Catalog=AdventureWorks;" />
    </connectionStrings>
</configuration>
```

4. Add a reference to the System.Configuration assembly.

The C# code in *Program.cs* in the project StoreConnectionStringConfig is shown in Example 1-2.

Example 1-2. File: Program.cs for StoreConnectionStringConfig solution

```
using System;
using System.Data;
using System.Data.SqlClient;
using System.Configuration;

namespace StoreConnectionStringConfig
{
    class Program
    {
        static void Main(string[] args)
        {
            // Enumerate connection strings
            Console.WriteLine("---Connection string enumeration---");
            foreach (ConnectionStringSettings css in
                ConfigurationManager.ConnectionStrings)
            {
                Console.WriteLine(css.Name);
                Console.WriteLine(css.ProviderName);
                Console.WriteLine(css.ConnectionString);
            }

            // Retrieve a connection string and open/close it
            Console.WriteLine("\n---Using a connection string---");
            Console.WriteLine("-> Retrieving connection string AdventureWorks");
            string sqlConnectString =
                ConfigurationManager.ConnectionStrings[
                "AdventureWorks"].ConnectionString;
            SqlConnection connection = new SqlConnection(sqlConnectString);
            Console.WriteLine("-> Opening connection string.");
            connection.Open();
            Console.WriteLine("Connection string state = {0}", connection.State);
            connection.Close();
            Console.WriteLine("-> Closing connection string.");
            Console.WriteLine("Connection string state = {0}", connection.State);

            Console.WriteLine("\nPress any key to continue.");
            Console.ReadKey();
        }
    }
}
```

The output is shown in Figure 1-1.

Protected configuration

You can use protected configuration to encrypt sensitive information, including database connection strings in a web application configuration file. Values are saved in encrypted form rather than as clear text. The .NET Framework decrypts the information when the configuration file is processed and makes it available to your application. Protected configuration requires IIS 6.0 or later. For more information about using protected configuration, search for "Protected Configuration" in MSDN.

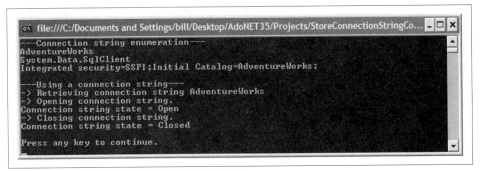

Figure 1-1. Output for StoreConnectionStringConfig solution

Hardcode in the application

An obvious, but poor, technique for storing connection strings is hardcoding them into the application. Although this approach results in the good performance, it has poor flexibility; the application needs to be recompiled if the connection string needs to be changed for any reason. Security is poor. The code can be disassembled to expose connection string information. Caching techniques together with external storage techniques eliminate nearly all performance benefits of hardcoding over external storage techniques.

Hardcoding connection string information is not advised; external server-side storage is preferred in nearly all cases because of the increased flexibility, security, and configuration ease. A discussion of available external storage options follows.

Universal data link (UDL) file

The OLE DB .NET data providers support UDL filenames in its connection string. The UDL file is a resource external to the application that encapsulates connection properties in a separate file. It must be protected using NTFS security to prevent connection information from being exposed or altered. The SQL Server .NET data provider does not support UDL files in its connection string. UDL files are not encrypted; cryptography cannot be used to increase security. NTFS directory and file encryption can secure a UDL file so that even if unauthorized access is gained to the file or the physical disk is stolen, the user ID and password of the user who encrypted the file would still be required to access its contents.

Windows registry

You can store connection strings in the Windows registry as a subkey of HKEY_LOCAL_MACHINE\SOFTWARE. You can encrypt these settings within the registry subkey and restrict access to the subkey to increase the security of this technique. This technique is easy to use because of programmatic support for registry access in .NET classes Registry and RegistryKey in the Microsoft.Win32 namespace.

NTFS Encryption

NTFS was enhanced in Windows 2000 with the Encrypted File System (EFS) that provides file- and directory-level encryption. Actually, EFS encrypts only files—directories are simply marked so that new files in the directory are encrypted. Encryption and decryption of files is both automatic and transparent for the user who set the encryption.

Encrypted files are visible to any user who can access the system but the *contents* of the encrypted files can only be viewed by the user who set the encryption. If necessary, standard NT security methods can hide directories and files from the view of specific users and user groups.

EFS is a separate mechanism that is used together with the standard security subsystem.

Storing connection strings in the registry is usually discouraged because of deployment issues; the registry settings must be deployed with the application, defeating benefits of *xcopy* deployment. Application code can also be restricted in its access to the registry, further complicating deployment.

Custom file

A custom file is any file that is used to for proprietary storage of application settings that are typically used at runtime. There is generally no particular advantage to using a custom file to store connection information so the technique is not recommended. The approach requires extra coding and forces concurrency and other issues to be explicitly addressed.

1.2   Building a Connection String

Problem

You need to programmatically construct a connection string.

Solution

Use a connection string builder class.

The solution uses `SqlConnectionStringBuilder` to programmatically construct a connection string for SQL Server that connects to the `AdventureWorks` database using integrated security.

The C# code in *Program.cs* in the project `BuildConnectionString` is shown in Example 1-3.

Example 1-3. File: Program.cs for BuildConnectionString solution

```csharp
using System;
using System.Data.SqlClient;

namespace BuildConnectionString
{
    class Program
    {
        static void Main(string[] args)
        {
            // Create a connection string builder
            SqlConnectionStringBuilder csb = new SqlConnectionStringBuilder( );

            // Define connection string attributes using three techniques
            csb.DataSource = "(local)";
            csb.Add("Initial Catalog", "AdventureWorks");
            csb["Integrated Security"] = true;

            // Output the connection string from the connection string builder
            Console.WriteLine("Connection string:\n{0}", csb.ConnectionString);

            // Create a connection string from the connection string builder
            SqlConnection connection = new SqlConnection(csb.ConnectionString);
            // Open and close the connection
            connection.Open( );
            Console.WriteLine("\nConnectionState = {0}", connection.State);
            connection.Close( );
            Console.WriteLine("ConnectionState = {0}", connection.State);

            Console.WriteLine("\nPress any key to continue.");
            Console.ReadKey( );
        }
    }
}
```

The output is shown in Figure 1-2.

Figure 1-2. Output for BuildConnectionString solution

Discussion

.NET Framework 2.0 introduced connection string builders—helper classes used to construct provider-specific connection strings. You supply the connection string name-value pairs using properties of the connection string builder, the Add( ) method, or the indexer. You retrieve and use the connection string using the ConnectionString property.

Connection string builders are included for SQL Server, Oracle, OLE DB, and ODBC. These strongly typed connection string builders inherit from the DbConnectionStringBuilder-based class that can be used to create applications that are portable across databases. You have to ensure when using DbConnectionStringBuilder that the name/value pairs you create are supported by the target database. Unlike the strongly typed connection string builders, DbConnectionString builder allows you to create invalid connection strings.

1.3   Connecting to SQL Server

Problem

You want to connect to a SQL Server database.

Solution

You can connect to an SQL Server database using the SQL Server .NET data provider, the OLE DB .NET data provider, or the ODBC .NET data provider.

The solution creates and opens a connection to an SQL Server database using the SQL Server .NET data provider, OLE DB .NET data provider, and ODBC.NET data provider in turn. In each case, information about the connection is displayed from the properties of the connection object.

The C# code in *Program.cs* in the project ConnectSqlServer is shown in Example 1-4.

Example 1-4. File: Program.cs for ConnectSqlServer solution

```
using System;
using System.Data.SqlClient;
using System.Data.OleDb;
using System.Data.Odbc;

namespace ConnectSqlServer
{
    class Program
    {
        static void Main(string[] args)
        {
```

Example 1-4. File: Program.cs for ConnectSqlServer solution (continued)

```csharp
// Connect using .NET data provider for SQL Server and integrated
// security
string sqlConnectString1 = "Data Source=(local);" +
    "Integrated security=SSPI;Initial Catalog=AdventureWorks;";

using (SqlConnection connection = new SqlConnection(sqlConnectString1))
{
    connection.Open( );

    // Return some information about the server.
    Console.WriteLine("---.NET data provider for SQL Server " +
        "with Windows Authentication mode---");
    Console.WriteLine("ConnectionString = {0}\n", sqlConnectString1);
    Console.WriteLine("State = {0}", connection.State);
    Console.WriteLine("DataSource = {0}", connection.DataSource);
    Console.WriteLine("ServerVersion = {0}", connection.ServerVersion);
}

// Connect using .NET data provider for SQL Server and SQL Server
// authentication
string sqlConnectString2 = "Data Source=(local);" +
    "User Id=sa;Password=password;Initial Catalog=AdventureWorks;";

using (SqlConnection connection = new SqlConnection(sqlConnectString2))
{
    connection.Open( );

    // Return some information about the server.
    Console.WriteLine("\n---.NET data provider for SQL Server " +
        "with SQL Server Authentication mode---");
    Console.WriteLine("ConnectionString = {0}\n", sqlConnectString2);
    Console.WriteLine("State = {0}", connection.State);
    Console.WriteLine("DataSource = {0}", connection.DataSource);
    Console.WriteLine("ServerVersion = {0}", connection.ServerVersion);
}

// Connect using .NET data provider for OLE DB.
string oledbConnectString = "Provider=SQLOLEDB;Data Source=(local);" +
    "Initial Catalog=AdventureWorks;User Id=sa;Password=password;";

using (OleDbConnection connection =
    new OleDbConnection(oledbConnectString))
{
    connection.Open( );

    // Return some information about the server.
    Console.WriteLine("\n---.NET data provider for OLE DB---");
    Console.WriteLine("ConnectionString = {0}\n", oledbConnectString);
    Console.WriteLine("State = {0}", connection.State);
    Console.WriteLine("DataSource = {0}", connection.DataSource);
    Console.WriteLine("ServerVersion = {0}", connection.ServerVersion);
}
```

Example 1-4. File: Program.cs for ConnectSqlServer solution (continued)

```
        // Connect using .NET data provider for ODBC.
        string odbcConnectString = "Driver={SQL Native Client};" +
            "Server=(local);Database=AdventureWorks;uid=sa;pwd=password;";

        using (OdbcConnection connection =
            new OdbcConnection(odbcConnectString))
        {
            connection.Open( );

            // Return some information about the server.
            Console.WriteLine("\n---.NET data provider for ODBC---");
            Console.WriteLine("ConnectionString = {0}\n", odbcConnectString);
            Console.WriteLine("State = {0}", connection.State);
            Console.WriteLine("DataSource = {0}", connection.DataSource);
            Console.WriteLine("ServerVersion = {0}", connection.ServerVersion);
        }

        Console.WriteLine("\nPress any key to continue.");
        Console.ReadKey( );
    }
  }
}
```

The output is shown in Figure 1-3.

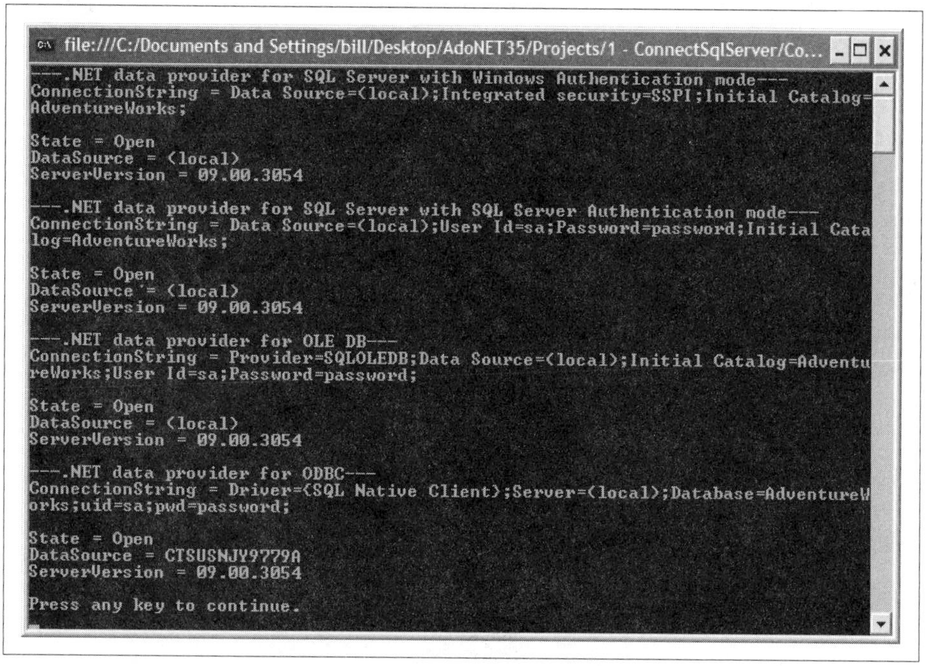

Figure 1-3. Output for ConnectSqlServer solution

Discussion

You can access a SQL Server database using three different provider types: native SQL Server, OLE DB, and ODBC. These alternatives are discussed in the following subsections.

Native SQL Server

The Microsoft SQL Server .NET data provider accesses SQL Server databases beginning with version 7.0 using an internal protocol. The classes are located in the `System.Data.SqlClient` namespace. An example of a connection string using integrated security is shown in the following snippet:

```
Data Source=(local);Integrated security=SSPI;Initial Catalog=AdventureWorks;
```

Without integrated security, the connection string is:

```
Data Source=(local);User Id=sa;Password=password;Initial Catalog=AdventureWorks;
```

Native providers generally perform better than OLE DB or ODBC providers because they are built specifically for the database and because they remove a layer of indirection from the application to the database.

OLE DB

You can use the OLE DB .NET data provider with the SQL Server OLE DB provider (SQL Server or SQL Native Client) to access SQL Server. An example of the connection string is shown here:

```
Provider=SQLOLEDB;Data Source=(local);Initial Catalog=AdventureWorks;
User Id=sa;Password=password;
```

The OLE DB provider should be used primarily as a bridge from applications that already use OLE DB. Use a native SQL Server .NET data provider where practical.

ODBC

Finally, the ODBC .NET data provider can connect to an SQL Server database. An example of the connection string is shown here:

```
Driver={SQL Native Client};Server=(local);Database=AdventureWorks;
uid=sa;pwd=password;
```

The ODBC .NET data provider should be used primarily as a bridge from applications that already use ODBC. Use a native SQL Server .NET data provider where possible.

1.4   Connecting to a Named Instance of SQL Server

Problem

You want to connect to a named instance of a SQL Server or SQL Server Express.

Solution

You need to understand what a SQL Server or SQL Server Express named instance is and how to connect to one.

The solution creates and opens a connection to a named instance of a SQL Server Express. Information about the SQL Server is displayed from the properties of the SqlConnection object.

The C# code in *Program.cs* in the project ConnectSqlServerNamedInstance is shown in Example 1-5.

Example 1-5. File: Program.cs for ConnectSqlServerNamedInstance solution

```
using System;
using System.Data.SqlClient;

namespace ConnectSqlServerNamedInstance
{
    class Program
    {
        static void Main(string[] args)
        {
            string sqlConnectString = @"Data Source=(local)\SQLExpress;" +
                "Integrated security=SSPI;Initial Catalog=master;";

            using (SqlConnection connection = new SqlConnection(sqlConnectString))
            {
                connection.Open();

                // Return some information about the server.
                Console.WriteLine("ConnectionString = {0}\n", sqlConnectString);
                Console.WriteLine("State = {0}", connection.State);
                Console.WriteLine("DataSource = {0}", connection.DataSource);
                Console.WriteLine("ServerVersion = {0}", connection.ServerVersion);
            }

            Console.WriteLine("\nPress any key to continue.");
            Console.ReadKey();
        }
    }
}
```

The output is shown in Figure 1-4.

Figure 1-4. Output for ConnectSqlServerNamedInstance solution

Discussion

SQL Server 2000 introduced the ability to install multiple copies of SQL Server on a single computer. Only one copy can function as the default instance at any time; it is identified by the network name of the computer on which it is running. All other copies are named instances and are identified by the network name of the computer plus an instance name. The format is *<computerName>**<instanceName>*. This format is used in the connection string to specify the Data Source attribute for a named instance.

Each instance operates independently of the other instances installed on the same computer. Each instance has its own set of system and user databases that are not shared between instances and it runs within its own security context. The maximum number of instances of the Enterprise Edition of SQL Server 2005 and later is 50. The maximum number of instances of other versions of SQL Server 2005 and later is 16. The maximum number of instances supported on SQL Server 2000 is 16. The Microsoft Distributed Transaction Coordinator (DTC) and the Microsoft Search services are installed and used simultaneously by every installed instance of SQL Server. Client tools such as SQL Server Management Studio and Query Analyzer are also shared.

The System.Data.SqlClient class cannot automatically discover the port number of a named instance of SQL Server listening on a port other than the default 1433. To connect to a named instance of SQL Server listening on a custom port, specify the port number following the instance name in the connection string separated by a comma. For example, if the named instance SQLExpress was set up to listen on port 1450, the following connection string might be used:

```
Data Source=(local)\SQLExpress,1450;Integrated security=SSPI;
    Initial Catalog=AdventureWorks
```

1.5   Connecting to SQL Server Using an IP Address

Problem

You want to connect to a SQL Server using its IP address instead of its server name.

Solution

Use the Network Address and Network Library attributes of the connection string.

The solution creates and opens a connection to a SQL Server using its IP address. Information about the SQL Server is displayed from the properties of the SqlConnection object.

The C# code in *Program.cs* in the project ConnectIPAddressSqlServer is shown in Example 1-6.

Example 1-6. File: Program.cs for ConnectIPAddressSqlServer solution

```csharp
using System;
using System.Data.SqlClient;

namespace ConnectIPAddressSqlServer
{
    class Program
    {
        static void Main(string[] args)
        {
            string connectString =
                "Network Library=dbmssocn;Network Address=127.0.0.1;" +
                "Integrated security=SSPI;Initial Catalog=AdventureWorks";

            using (SqlConnection connection = new SqlConnection(connectString))
            {
                connection.Open( );

                // Return some information about the server.
                Console.WriteLine(
                    "ConnectionState = {0}\nDataSource = {1}\nServerVersion = {2}",
                    connection.State, connection.DataSource,
                    connection.ServerVersion);
            }

            Console.WriteLine("\nPress any key to continue.");
            Console.ReadKey( );
        }
    }
}
```

The output is shown in Figure 1-5.

Figure 1-5. Output for ConnectIPAddressSqlServer solution

Discussion

SQL Server network libraries are dynamic-link libraries (DLLs) that perform network operations required for client computers and SQL Server computers to communicate. A server can monitor multiple libraries simultaneously; the only requirement is that each network library to be monitored is installed and configured.

Available network protocols for SQL Server include:

Shared Memory
> Connects to SQL Server instances running on the same computer as the client. Shared memory protocol is used primarily for troubleshooting. This protocol cannot be used on clients that use MDAC 2.8 or earlier—these clients are automatically switched to the named pipes protocol.

TCP/IP
> Uses the TCP/IP protocol for communication.

Named Pipes
> Interprocess communication (IPC) mechanism provided by SQL Server for communication between clients and servers.

VIA
> Virtual Interface Adapter (VIA) protocol is used with VIA hardware.

As of SQL Server 2005, the following network protocols are no longer supported:

AppleTalk ADSP
> Allows Apple Macintosh to communicate with SQL Server using native AppleTalk protocol.

Banyan VINES
> Supports Banyan VINES Sequenced Packet Protocol (SPP) across Banyan VINES IP network protocol.

Multiprotocol
> Automatically chooses the first available network protocol to establish a connection generally with performance comparable to using a native network library. TCP/IP Sockets, NWLink IPX/SPX, and Named Pipes are supported.

NWLink IPX/SPX
> The native protocol of Novell Netware networks.

For more information about configuring network protocols, see Microsoft SQL Server Books Online.

The use of the SQL Server TCP/IP Sockets improves performance and scalability with high volumes of data. It avoids some security issues associated with named pipes. As with any protocol, the client and the server must be configured to use TCP/IP.

Do this through SQL Server Configuration Manager by expanding the SQL Server Network Configuration node and enabling TCP/IP in the Protocols subnode. You will need to restart SQL Server for the change to take effect.

To connect to SQL Server using an IP address, the TCP/IP network library must be used to connect to the SQL Server. This is done by specifying the library in the connection string as either the attribute Net or Network Library with a value of *dbmssocn*. Specify the IP address using the Data Source, Server, Address, Addr, or Network Address parameter. The following connection string demonstrates using an IP address to specify the data source:

```
"Network Library=dbmssocn;Network Address=127.0.0.1;" +
    "Integrated security=SSPI;Initial Catalog=AdventureWorks";
```

In the example, the IP address 127.0.0.1 is the IP address for the local machine. This could also be specified as (local). To specify a SQL Server other than a local instance, specify the IP address of the computer on which SQL Server is installed.

Default instances of SQL Server listen on port 1433. Named instances of SQL Server dynamically assign a port number when they are first started. The example above does not specify the port number and therefore uses the default port 1433. If the SQL Server is configured to listen on another port, specify the port number following the IP address specified by the Network Address attribute separated by a comma as shown in the following snippet, which connects to a local SQL Server listening on port 1450:

```
Network Address=(local),1450
```

1.6   Connecting to SQL Server Using Integrated Security from ASP.NET

Problem

You want to coordinate Windows security accounts between an ASP.NET application and SQL Server.

Solution

Connect to SQL Server from ASP.NET using Windows Authentication in SQL Server:

1. Begin by creating a new ASP.NET Web Application project.

2. Add the following elements to the *Web.config* file within the <system.web> element:

```
<authentication mode="Windows" />
<identity impersonate="true" />
```

3. Add a connection string to AdventureWorks on the local machine to the configuration file *Web.config* by updating the <connectionStrings> element within the <configuration> element as follows:

```
<connectionStrings>
    <add name="AdventureWorks" providerName="System.Data.SqlClient"
        connectionString="Data Source=(local);
        Integrated security=SSPI;Initial Catalog=AdventureWorks;"/>
</connectionStrings>
```

The C# code in *Default.aspx.cs* in the project IntegratedSecurityFromAspNet is shown in Example 1-7.

Example 1-7. File: Default.aspx.cs for IntegratedSecurityFromAspNet solution

```csharp
using System;
using System.Data;
using System.Data.SqlClient;
using System.Configuration;

namespace IntegratedSecurityFromAspNet
{
    public partial class _Default : System.Web.UI.Page
    {
        protected void Page_Load(object sender, EventArgs e)
        {
            string sqlText = "SELECT TOP 10 * FROM Person.Contact";
            string connectString =
                ConfigurationManager.ConnectionStrings[
                "AdventureWorks"].ConnectionString;
            DataTable dt = new DataTable();
            SqlDataAdapter da = new SqlDataAdapter(sqlText, connectString);
            da.Fill(dt);

            foreach (DataRow row in dt.Rows)
                Response.Write(row["ContactID"] + " - " + row["LastName"] +
                    ", " + row["FirstName"] + "<br/>");
        }
    }
}
```

The output is shown in Figure 1-6.

Discussion

Connecting to a SQL Server database provides two different authentication modes:

Windows Authentication
    Uses the current security identity from the Windows user account to provide authentication information. It does not expose the user ID and password and is the recommended method for authenticating a connection.

SQL Server Authentication
    Uses a SQL Server login account providing a user ID and password.

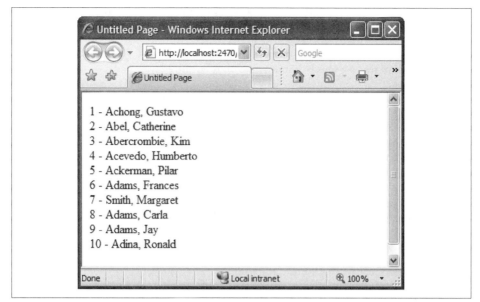

Figure 1-6. Output for IntegratedSecurityFromAspNet solution

Integrated security requires that all application users are on the same domain so that their credentials are available to IIS. The following areas of the application need to be configured:

- Configure the ASP.NET application so that Integrated Windows Authentication is enabled and Anonymous Access is disabled.

- The *web.config* file establishes the authentication mode that the application uses and that the application will run as or impersonate the user. Add the following elements to the *web.config* file within the <system.web> element:

  ```
  <authentication mode="Windows" />
  <identity impersonate="true" />
  ```

- The connection string must contain attributes that tell the SQL Server that integrated security is used. Use the Integrated Security=SSPI attribute-and-value pair instead of the User ID and Password attributes in the connection string. The older attribute-and-value pair Trusted_Connection=Yes is also supported.

- Add users and groups from the domain and set their access permissions as required.

By default, ASP.NET applications run in the context of a local user ASPNET on IIS. The account has limited permissions and is local to the IIS computer and therefore not recognized as a user on remote computers. To use SQL Server on a different computer than IIS, run the web application in the context of a domain user recognized on both IIS and SQL Server computers.

In addition to the areas identified where IIS and SQL Server are on the same computer, the following additional items must be configured if the SQL Server is on a different domain:

- Ensure that the mapped domain user has required privileges to run the web application.
- Configure the web application to impersonate the domain user. Add the following elements to the *web.config* file for the web application:

```
<authentication mode="Windows" />
<identity impersonate="true" userName="domain\username"
        password="myPassword" />
```

1.7 Connecting to an Oracle Database

Problem

You want to connect to an Oracle database.

Solution

You can connect to an Oracle database using the Oracle .NET data provider, the OLE DB .NET data provider, or the ODBC .NET data provider.

The solution creates and opens a connection to an Oracle database using the Oracle .NET data provider, OLE DB .NET data provider, and ODBC .NET data provider in turn. In each case, information about the connection is displayed from the properties of the connection object.

The solution requires a reference to the System.Data.OracleClient assembly.

The C# code in *Program.cs* in the project ConnectOracle is shown in Example 1-8.

Example 1-8. File: Program.cs for ConnectOracle solution

```csharp
using System;
using System.Data.OracleClient;
using System.Data.OleDb;
using System.Data.Odbc;

namespace ConnectOracle
{
    class Program Interprocess communication (IPC)
    {
        static void Main(string[] args)
        {
            // Connect using .NET data provider for Oracle
            string oracleConnectString =
                "Data Source=ORCL;User Id=hr;Password=password;";

            using (OracleConnection connection =
                new OracleConnection(oracleConnectString))
```

Example 1-8. File: Program.cs for ConnectOracle solution (continued)

```csharp
{
    connection.Open( );

    // Return some information about the server.
    Console.WriteLine("---Microsoft .NET Provider for Oracle---");
    Console.WriteLine("ConnectionString = {0}\n", oracleConnectString);
    Console.WriteLine("State = {0}", connection.State);
    Console.WriteLine("DataSource = {0}", connection.DataSource);
    Console.WriteLine("ServerVersion = {0}", connection.ServerVersion);
}

// Connect using .NET data provider for OLE DB.
string oledbConnectString =
    "Provider=MSDAORA;Data Source=ORCL;User Id=hr;Password=password;";

using (OleDbConnection connection =
    new OleDbConnection(oledbConnectString))
{
    connection.Open( );

    // Return some information about the server.
    Console.WriteLine("\n---Microsoft .NET Provider for OLE DB---");
    Console.WriteLine("ConnectionString = {0}\n", oledbConnectString);
    Console.WriteLine("State = {0}", connection.State);
    Console.WriteLine("DataSource = {0}", connection.DataSource);
    Console.WriteLine("ServerVersion = {0}", connection.ServerVersion);
}

// Connect using .NET data provider for ODBC
string odbcConnectString = "Driver={Oracle in OraDb10g_home1};" +
    "Server=ORCL;uid=hr;pwd=password;";

using (OdbcConnection connection =
    new OdbcConnection(odbcConnectString))
{
    connection.Open( );

    // Return some information about the server.
    Console.WriteLine("\n---Microsoft .NET Provider for ODBC---");
    Console.WriteLine("ConnectionString = {0}\n", odbcConnectString);
    Console.WriteLine("State = {0}", connection.State);
    Console.WriteLine("DataSource = {0}", connection.DataSource);
    Console.WriteLine("ServerVersion = {0}", connection.ServerVersion);
}

Console.WriteLine("\nPress any key to continue.");
Console.ReadKey( );
        }
    }
}
```

The output is shown in Figure 1-7.

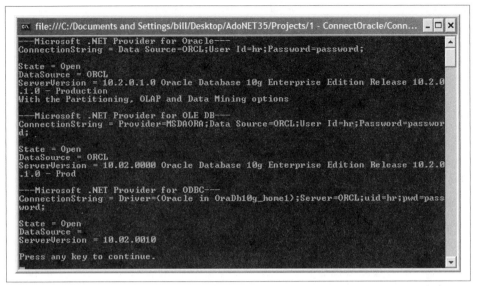

```
ox  file:///C:/Documents and Settings/bill/Desktop/AdoNET35/Projects/1 - ConnectOracle/Conn...  _ □ ×
---Microsoft .NET Provider for Oracle---
ConnectionString = Data Source=ORCL;User Id=hr;Password=password;

State = Open
DataSource = ORCL
ServerVersion = 10.2.0.1.0 Oracle Database 10g Enterprise Edition Release 10.2.0
.1.0 - Production
With the Partitioning, OLAP and Data Mining options

---Microsoft .NET Provider for OLE DB---
ConnectionString = Provider=MSDAORA;Data Source=ORCL;User Id=hr;Password=passwor
d;

State = Open
DataSource = ORCL
ServerVersion = 10.02.0000 Oracle Database 10g Enterprise Edition Release 10.2.0
.1.0 - Prod

---Microsoft .NET Provider for ODBC---
ConnectionString = Driver={Oracle in OraDb10g_home1};Server=ORCL;uid=hr;pwd=pass
word;

State = Open
DataSource =
ServerVersion = 10.02.0010

Press any key to continue.
```

Figure 1-7. Output for ConnectOracle solution

Discussion

You can access an Oracle database using three different provider types: native Oracle, OLE DB, and ODBC. These alternatives are discussed in the following subsections.

Native Oracle

The Microsoft Oracle .NET data provider accesses an Oracle database using the Oracle Call Interface (OCI) through Oracle client connectivity software. The provider can access Oracle 7.3.4 or later and requires Oracle 8*i* Release 3 (8.1.7) or later client software. The classes are located in the System.Data.OracleClient namespace. An example of a connection string using integrated security is shown in the following snippet:

```
Data Source=ORCL;Integrated Security=yes;
```

Without integrated security, the connection string is:

```
Data Source=ORCL;User Id=hr;Password=password;
```

The Microsoft Oracle .NET data provider is included with .NET Framework version 1.1. It is not included with the .NET Framework version 1.0, but you can download it from *http://msdn.microsoft.com/downloads*. The Oracle .NET data provider can access Oracle8 Release 8.0 or later and requires the Oracle9*i* Client Release 2 (9.2) or later.

Native providers generally perform better than OLE DB or ODBC providers because they are built specifically for the database and because they remove a layer of indirection from the application to the database.

OLE DB

You can use the OLE DB .NET data provider with the Oracle OLE DB provider (MSDAORA) to access Oracle data. An example of the connection string is shown here:

```
Provider=MSDAORA;Data Source=myOracleDb;User Id=hr;Password=password;
```

The OLE DB provider should be used primarily as a bridge from applications that already use OLE DB. Use a native Oracle .NET data provider where practical.

ODBC

Finally, the ODBC .NET data provider can connect to an Oracle database. An example of the connection string using the Oracle 10g driver from Oracle is shown here:

```
"Driver={Oracle in OraDb10g_home1};Server=ORCL;uid=hr;pwd=password;";
```

The ODBC .NET data provider should be used primarily as a bridge from applications that already use ODBC. Use a native Oracle .NET data provider where possible.

TNSNAMES.ORA

Oracle uses a configuration file named *TNSNAMES.ORA* to locate the Oracle database and determine how to connect to it based on the Data Source or Database attribute in the connection string.

An example of an entry in the *TNSNAMES.ORA* file for the alias ORCL follows:

```
ORCL =
  (DESCRIPTION =
    (ADDRESS = (PROTOCOL = TCP)(HOST = 192.168.1.100)(PORT = 1521))
    (CONNECT_DATA =
      (SERVER = DEDICATED)
      (SERVICE_NAME = orcl)
    )
  )
```

In this simple example, the connection to the alias ORLC uses TCP/IP on port 1521 (the default).

1.8   Connecting to an OLE DB Data Source

Problem

You want to access your data source using an OLE DB provider from your .NET application.

Solution

Use the OLE DB .NET data provider to access data exposed through an OLE DB driver.

The solution creates an OleDbDataReader and uses it to output the FirstName and LastName columns from the first five rows in the Person.Contact table in the AdventureWorks sample database.

The C# code in *Program.cs* in the project ConnectOleDbDataSource is shown in Example 1-9.

Example 1-9. File: Program.cs for ConnectOleDbDataSource solution

```
using System;
using System.Data.OleDb;

namespace ConnectOleDbDataSource
{
    class Program
    {
        static void Main(string[] args)
        {
            string oledbConnectString = "Provider=SQLOLEDB;Data Source=(local);" +
                "Initial Catalog=AdventureWorks;Integrated Security=SSPI";

            string sqlSelect = "SELECT TOP 5 Title, FirstName, LastName " +
                "FROM Person.Contact";

            // Create an ODBC Connection
            using (OleDbConnection connection =
                new OleDbConnection(oledbConnectString))
            {
                OleDbCommand command = new OleDbCommand(sqlSelect, connection);

                // Execute the DataReader
                connection.Open( );
                OleDbDataReader reader = command.ExecuteReader( );

                // Output the data from the DataReader to the console

                while (reader.Read( ))
                    Console.WriteLine("{0} {1}", reader[0], reader[1]);
            }
```

Example 1-9. File: Program.cs for ConnectOleDbDataSource solution (continued)

```
            Console.WriteLine("\nPress any key to continue.");
            Console.ReadKey( );
        }
    }
}
```

The output is shown in Figure 1-8.

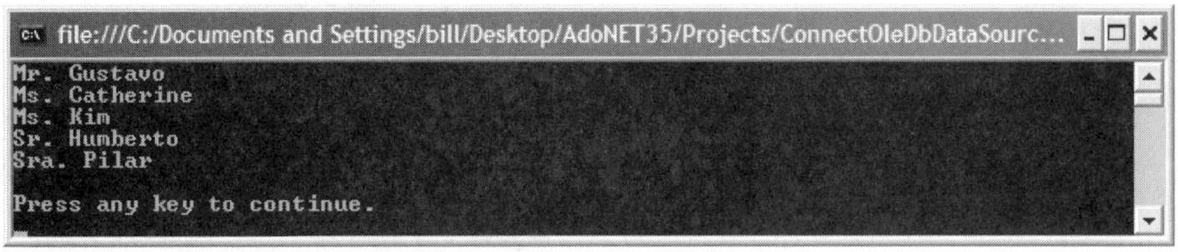

Figure 1-8. Output for ConnectOleDbDataSource solution

Discussion

An OLE DB provider is a set of COM objects that serves tabular data from a data source to the client in response to interface calls. The .NET Framework data provider for OLE DB is a collection of managed classes that lets you access an OLE DB data source. OLE DB providers exist for virtually every database as well as for many other data sources including Active Directory Service, Microsoft Exchange, and Microsoft Indexing Service. `System.Data.OleDb` is the namespace for the .NET Framework data provider for OLE DB.

The .NET Framework data provider for OLE DB connects to an OLE DB data sources through the `OleDbConnection` object. The OLE DB provider connection string is specified using the `ConnectionString` property of the `OleDbConnection` object. This property specifies all settings needed to establish the connection to the data source and matches the OLE DB connection string format with an added `Provider` key-value pair specifying the OLE DB provider is required.

1.9 Connecting to an ODBC Data Source

Problem

You want to access your data source using an ODBC provider from your .NET application.

Solution

Use the ODBC .NET data provider to access data exposed through an ODBC driver.

The solution creates an OdbcDataReader and uses it to output the FirstName and LastName columns from the first five rows in the Person.Contact table in the AdventureWorks sample database.

The C# code in *Program.cs* in the project ConnectOdbcDataSource is shown in Example 1-10.

Example 1-10. File: Program.cs for ConnectOdbcDataSource solution

```csharp
using System;
using System.Data.Odbc;

namespace ConnectOdbcDataSource
{
    class Program
    {
        static void Main(string[] args)
        {
            string odbcConnectString = "DRIVER={SQL Server};SERVER=(local);" +
                "DATABASE=AdventureWorks;Trusted_Connection=yes;";

            string sqlSelect = "SELECT TOP 5 Title, FirstName, LastName " +
                "FROM Person.Contact";

            // Create an ODBC Connection
            using (OdbcConnection connection =
                new OdbcConnection(odbcConnectString))
            {
                OdbcCommand command = new OdbcCommand(sqlSelect, connection);

                // Execute the DataReader
                connection.Open();
                OdbcDataReader reader = command.ExecuteReader();

                // Output the data from the DataReader to the console

                while (reader.Read())
                    Console.WriteLine("{0} {1}", reader[0], reader[1]);
            }

            Console.WriteLine("\nPress any key to continue.");
            Console.ReadKey();
        }
    }
}
```

The output is shown in Figure 1-9.

Figure 1-9. Output for ConnectOdbcDataSource solution

Discussion

The ODBC .NET data provider uses the native ODBC Driver Manager to access data. The following ODBC providers are guaranteed to be compatible with the ODBC.NET data provider:

- Microsoft SQL Server ODBC Driver
- Microsoft ODBC Driver for Oracle
- Microsoft Access (Jet) ODBC Driver

The .NET data provider for ODBC connects to ODBC data sources through the OdbcConnection object. The ODBC driver connection string is specified using the ConnectionString property of the OdbcConnection object. This property specifies all settings needed to establish the connection to the data source and matches the ODBC connection string format. You can also specify an ODBC data source name (DSN) or file DSN by setting the ConnectionString attribute "DSN=myDSN" or "FileDSN=myFileDSN".

The .NET ODBC data provider requires MDAC 2.6 or later with MDAC 2.8 SP1 recommended.

The .NET ODBC data provider requires a reference to the System.Data.Odbc namespace in .NET Framework version 1.1 and later. In version 1.0, the namespace is Microsoft.Data.Odbc. Add a reference to the Microsoft.Data.Odbc assembly for a .NET Framework version 1.0 project.

The .NET ODBC .NET data provider ships with .NET Framework version 1.1 and later. The data provider can be downloaded from *http://msdn.microsoft.com/downloads* for .NET Framework version 1.0.

1.10 Connecting to a Microsoft Access Database

Problem

You want to connect to a Microsoft Access database.

Solution

Use the OLE DB .NET data provider.

The solution creates and opens a connection to a Microsoft Access database using the OLE DB .NET data provider. Information about the connection is displayed.

The C# code in *Program.cs* in the project ConnectAccessDatabase is shown in Example 1-11.

Example 1-11. File: Program.cs for ConnectAccessDatabase solution

```
using System;
using System.Data;
using System.Data.OleDb;

namespace ConnectAccessDatabase
{
    class Program
    {
        static void Main(string[] args)
        {
            string oledbConnectString =
                "Provider=Microsoft.ACE.OLEDB.12.0;Data Source=" +
                @"C:\Documents and Settings\bill\My Documents\" +
                "Northwind 2007.accdb;";

            using (OleDbConnection connection =
                new OleDbConnection(oledbConnectString))
            {
                connection.Open();

                // Output some connection and database information.
                Console.WriteLine("Connection State: {0}", connection.State);
                Console.WriteLine("OLE DB Provider: {0}", connection.Provider);
                Console.WriteLine("Server Version: {0}", connection.ServerVersion);
            }

            Console.WriteLine("\nPress any key to continue.");
            Console.ReadKey();
        }
    }
}
```

The output is shown in Figure 1-10.

Figure 1-10. Output for ConnectAccessDatabase solution

Discussion

You can connect to a Microsoft Access database using the OLE DB .NET data provider. The OLE DB connection uses the Microsoft.ACE.OLEDB.12.0, which is the new Access database engine OLE DB driver that can also read previous formats. The Jet OLE DB driver cannot access Microsoft Access 2007 databases.

1.11 Connecting to a Password-Protected Microsoft Access Database

Problem

You want to connect to a Microsoft Access database that has a database password.

Solution

Use the Jet OLEDB:Database Password attribute in the connection string to specify the password.

The solution creates and opens a connection to a password-secured Microsoft Access database using the OLE DB .NET data provider. Information about the connection is displayed from the properties of the OleDbConnection object.

The C# code in *Program.cs* in the project ConnectPasswordAccessDatabase is shown in Example 1-12.

Example 1-12. File: Program.cs for ConnectPasswordAccessDatabase solution

```
using System;
using System.Data;
using System.Data.OleDb;

namespace ConnectAccessDatabase
{
    class Program
    {
        static void Main(string[] args)
        {
            string oledbConnectString =
                "Provider=Microsoft.ACE.OLEDB.12.0;Data Source=" +
```

Example 1-12. File: Program.cs for ConnectPasswordAccessDatabase solution (continued)

```
                @"C:\Documents and Settings\bill\My Documents\" +
                "Northwind 2007.accdb;" +
                "Jet OLEDB:Database Password=password;";

            using (OleDbConnection connection =
                new OleDbConnection(oledbConnectString))
            {
                connection.Open( );

                // Output some connection and database information.
                Console.WriteLine("Connection State: {0}", connection.State);
                Console.WriteLine("OLE DB Provider: {0}", connection.Provider);
                Console.WriteLine("Server Version: {0}", connection.ServerVersion);
            }

            Console.WriteLine("\nPress any key to continue.");
            Console.ReadKey( );
        }
    }
}
```

The output is shown in Figure 1-11.

Figure 1-11. Output for ConnectPasswordAccessDatabase solution

Discussion

A Microsoft Access database password requires that users enter a password to obtain access to the database and database objects. This is also known as share-level security. A password does not allow groups or users to have distinct levels of access or permissions. Anyone with the password has unrestricted access to the database.

The Set Database command from the Tools → Security menu is used to set up a database password.

The OLE DB provider for the Microsoft Access database engine has several provider-specific connection string attributes in addition to those defined by ADO.NET. To open a database secured by a Microsoft Access database password, use the Jet OLEDB:Database Password attribute in the connection string to specify the password. This corresponds to the OLE DB property DBPROP_JETOLEDB_DATABASEPASSWORD.

A Microsoft Access database password does not provide strong security and should only be used as a simple deterrent.

1.12 Connecting to a Microsoft Access Database from ASP.NET

Problem

You know your connection string is correct, but still can't connect to your Microsoft Access database from your ASP.NET application. What are the differences between connecting from a Windows Forms .NET application and an ASP.NET application?

Solution

You must grant the necessary file permissions for accessing a Microsoft Access database engine to the default user account used by ASP.NET.

1. Begin by creating a new ASP.NET Web Application project named ConnectMSAccessDataAspNet.

2. Add the following elements to the *Web.config* file within the `<system.web>` element:

   ```
   <authentication mode="Windows" />
   <identity impersonate="true" />
   ```

3. Add a connection string to *Northwind 2007.accdbs* on the local machine to the configuration file *Web.config* by adding the following `<connectionStrings>` element within the `<configuration>` element:

   ```
   <connectionStrings>
       <add name="Northwind2007" providerName="System.Data.OleDb"
           connectionString="Provider=Microsoft.ACE.OLEDB.12.0;
               Data Source=C:\Documents and Settings\bill\My Documents\
               Northwind 2007.accdb;"/>
   </connectionStrings>
   ```

The C# code *Default.aspx.cs* in the project ConnectMSAccessDataAspNet is shown in Example 1-13.

Example 1-13. File: Default.aspx.cs for ConnectMSAccessDataAspNet solution

```
using System;
using System.Data;
using System.Data.OleDb;
using System.Configuration;

namespace ConnectMSAccessDataAspNet
{
```

Example 1-13. File: Default.aspx.cs for ConnectMSAccessDataAspNet solution (continued)

```
public partial class _Default : System.Web.UI.Page
{
    protected void Page_Load(object sender, EventArgs e)
    {
        string sqlText = "SELECT TOP 10 * FROM Customers";
        string connectString =
            ConfigurationManager.ConnectionStrings[
            "Northwind2007"].ConnectionString;
        DataTable dt = new DataTable();
        OleDbDataAdapter da =
            new OleDbDataAdapter(sqlText, connectString);
        da.Fill(dt);

        foreach (DataRow row in dt.Rows)
            Response.Write(row["ID"] + " - " + row["Last Name"] +
                ", " + row["First Name"] + "<br/>");
    }
}
```

The output is shown in Figure 1-12.

Figure 1-12. Output for ConnectMSAccessAspNet solution

Discussion

When a user retrieves a page from an ASP.NET web site, code runs on the server to generate and deliver the page. By default, IIS (Internet Information Server) uses the system account to provide the security context for all processes. This account can access the IIS computer, but is not allowed to access network shares on other computers.

To allow an ASP.NET application to connect to a Microsoft Access database, IIS must be configured to use an account other than the system account. The new account must be configured to have permission to access all files and folders needed to use the Access database. If the Access database is on a remote computer, the account also requires access to that computer.

The following sections describe how to configure the IIS Server and the Access computer to allow ASP.NET to connect to an Access database.

Configure IIS

The system account cannot authenticate across a network. Enable impersonation in the *web.config* file for a given ASP.NET application so that ASP.NET impersonates an account on the Microsoft Access computer with the required access permissions to the Access database. For example:

```
<identity impersonate="true" userName="domain\username"
    password="myPassword" />
```

This method stores the username and password in clear text on the server. Ensure that IIS is configured to prevent users of the web site from viewing the contents of the *web.config* file—this is the default configuration.

The Microsoft Access database engine uses the *TEMP* folder on the IIS computer that is accessing the Access database. The user identity requires NTFS (Windows NT File System) full-control permissions on the *TEMP* folder. Ensure that the TEMP and TMP environment variables are properly configured.

Configure the Access computer

On the Access computer, the user account that is used to access the database requires Read, Write, Execute, and Change permissions on the database file. The user identity needs Read, Write, Execute, Delete, and Change permissions on the folder containing the database files. The user account requires permissions to access the share that contains the database file and folders.

The user account must be recognized by the Access computer. For a domain user account, add it to the permissions list on both computers. For a user account local to the IIS computer, create a duplicate account on the Access computer with the same name and password.

Grant the user account "Log on Locally and Access this Computer from the Network" permission to access the computer in the local security policy. These permissions are assigned within the Security Settings\Local Policies\User Rights Assignment node in the Local Security Policy tool.

1.13   Connecting to a Microsoft Excel Workbook

Problem

You want to connect to a Microsoft Excel workbook.

Solution

Use the OLE DB .NET data provider.

The solution creates and opens a connection to a Microsoft Excel workbook using the OLE DB .NET data provider. Information about the connection is displayed.

The Excel 2007 workbook in this solution is shown in Figure 1-13.

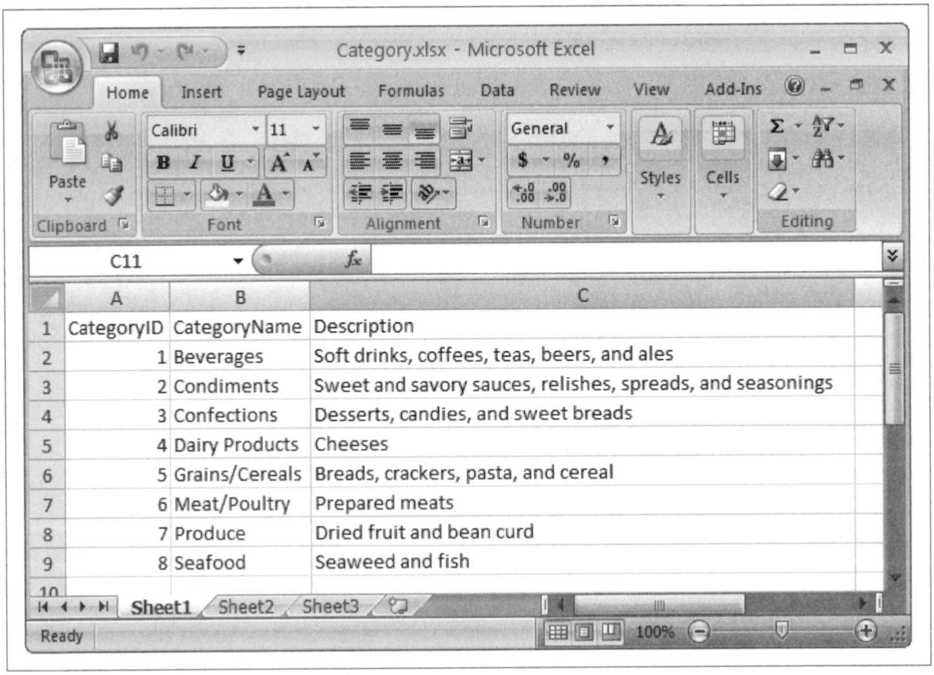

Figure 1-13. Excel workbook Category.xlsx

The Excel 2003 workbook used in this solution is identical.

The C# code in *Program.cs* in the project ConnectExcel is shown in Example 1-14.

Example 1-14. File: Program.cs for ConnectExcel solution

```csharp
using System;
using System.Data;
using System.Data.OleDb;

namespace ConnectExcel
{
    class Program
    {
        static void Main(string[] args)
        {
            // Define connection strings for both default
            // Excel .xlsx format and Excel 97-2003 .xls format
            string[] oledbConnectString = new string[]
            {
                "Provider=Microsoft.ACE.OLEDB.12.0;" +
                @"Data Source=..\..\..\Category.xlsx;" +
                "Extended Properties=\"Excel 12.0;HDR=YES\";",

                "Provider=Microsoft.ACE.OLEDB.12.0;" +
                @"Data Source=..\..\..\Category.xls;" +
                "Extended Properties=\"Excel 8.0;HDR=YES\";"
            };

            foreach (string connectString in oledbConnectString)
            {
                // Define and open the connection
                OleDbConnection connection =
                    new OleDbConnection(connectString);
                connection.Open();

                // Output some connection properties to the console
                Console.WriteLine("---CONNECTION---");
                Console.WriteLine("Connection.String = {0}\n",
                    connectString);
                Console.WriteLine("Connection.State = {0}",
                    connection.State);
                Console.WriteLine("Connection.Provider = {0}",
                    connection.Provider);
                Console.WriteLine("Connection.ServerVersion = {0}",
                    connection.ServerVersion);

                connection.Close();

                Console.WriteLine();
            }

            Console.WriteLine("Press any key to continue.");
            Console.ReadKey();
        }
    }
}
```

The output is shown in Figure 1-14.

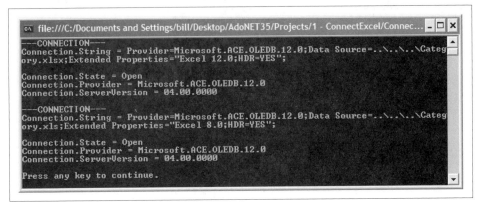

Figure 1-14. Output for ConnectExcel solution

Discussion

You can connect to a Microsoft Excel workbook using the OLE DB .NET data provider. The OLE DB connection uses the Microsoft.ACE.OLEDB.12.0, which is the new Access database engine OLE DB driver that can also read previous versions of Microsoft Excel workbooks. The Jet OLE DB driver cannot access Microsoft Excel 2007 workbooks.

1.14 Connecting to a Text File

Problem

You want to use ADO.NET to access data stored in a text file.

Solution

Use the OLE DB .NET data provider.

The solution creates and opens a connection to a text file using the OLE DB .NET data provider. Information about the connection is displayed.

The C# code in *Program.cs* in the project `ConnectTextFile` is shown in Example 1-15.

Example 1-15. File: Program.cs for ConnectTextFile solution

```
using System;
using System.Data;
using System.Data.OleDb;

namespace ConnectTextFile
{
    class Program
    {
```

Example 1-15. File: Program.cs for ConnectTextFile solution (continued)

```
        static void Main(string[] args)
        {
            string connectString = "Provider=Microsoft.ACE.OLEDB.12.0;" +
                @"Data Source=..\..\..\;" +
                "Extended Properties=\"text;HDR=yes;FMT=Delimited\";";

            OleDbConnection connection = new OleDbConnection(connectString);
            connection.Open( );

            // Output some connection properties to the console
            Console.WriteLine("Connection.String = {0}\n",
                connectString);
            Console.WriteLine("Connection.State = {0}",
                connection.State);
            Console.WriteLine("Connection.Provider = {0}",
                connection.Provider);
            Console.WriteLine("Connection.ServerVersion = {0}",
                connection.ServerVersion);

            connection.Close( );

            Console.WriteLine("\nPress any key to continue.");
            Console.ReadKey( );
        }
    }
}
```

The output is shown in Figure 1-15.

Figure 1-15. Output for ConnectTextFile solution

Discussion

The .NET OLE DB provider can read records from and insert records into a text file data source using the Microsoft Access database engine (ACE) driver. The ACE driver can access other database file formats through Indexed Sequential Access Method (ISAM) drivers specified in the Extended Properties attribute of the connection. Text files are supported with the text source database type as shown in the following example:

```
"Provider=Microsoft.ACE.OLEDB.12.0;Data Source=..\..\..\;
Extended Properties="text;HDR=yes;FMT=Delimited";
```

Notice that only the directory for the text file is specified in the connection string. The filename of the text file is specified in the T-SQL commands that access data in the text file, similar to a table name in a database.

The `Extended Properties` attribute can, in addition to the ISAM version property, specify whether tables include headers as field names in the first row of a range using an HDR attribute.

It is not possible to define all characteristics of a text file through the connection string. You can access files that use nonstandard text delimiters and fixed-width text files by creating a *schema.ini* file in the same directory as the text file. A text file, *Category.txt*, is shown in Figure 1-16.

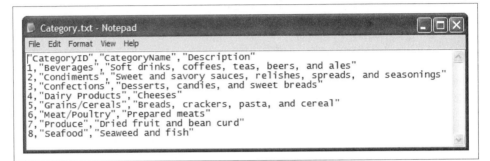

Figure 1-16. Text file Category.Txt

A possible *schema.ini* file for the *Category.txt* file is:

```
[Category.txt]
Format=CSVDelimited
ColNameHeader=True
MaxScanRows=0
Character=OEM
Col1=CategoryID Long Width 4
Col2=CategoryName Text Width 15
Col3=Description Text Width 100
```

The *schema.ini* file provides this schema information about the data in the text file:

- Filename
- File format
- Field names, widths, and data types
- Character set
- Special data type conversions

The first entry in the *schema.ini* file is the text filename enclosed in square brackets. For example:

```
[Category.txt]
```

The `Format` option specifies the text file format. Table 1-2 describes the options.

Table 1-2. Schema.ini format options

Format	Description
CSV Delimited	Fields are delimited with commas: `Format=CSVDelimited` This is the default value.
Custom Delimited	Fields are delimited with a custom character. You can use any single character except the double quotation mark (") as a delimiter: `Format=Delimited(customCharacter)`
Fixed Length	Fields are fixed length: `Format=FixedLength` If the `ColumnNameHeader` option is `True`, the first line containing the column names must be comma-delimited.
Tab Delimited	Fields are delimited with tabs: `Format=TabDelimited`

You can specify the fields in the text file in two ways:

- Include the field names in the first row of the text file and set the `ColNameHeader` option to `True`.
- Identify each column using the format `ColN` (where `N` is the one-based column number) and specify the name, width, and data type for each column.

The `MaxScanRows` option indicates how many rows should be scanned to automatically determine column type. A value of `0` indicates that all rows should be scanned.

The `ColN` entries specify the name, width, and data type for each column. This entry is required for fixed-length formats and optional for character-delimited formats. The syntax of the `ColN` entry is:

```
ColN=columnName dataType [Width n]
```

The parameters in the entry are:

columnName

    The name of the column. If the column name contains spaces, it must be enclosed in double quotation marks.

dataType

    The data type of the column. This value can be `Bit`, `Byte`, `Currency`, `DateTime`, `Double`, `Long`, `Memo`, `Short`, `Single`, or `Text`.

    `DateTime` values must be in one of the following formats: `dd-mmm-yy`, `mm-dd-yy`, `mmm-dd-yy`, `yyyy-mm-dd`, or `yyyy-mmm-dd`, where `mm` is the month number and `mmm` are the characters specifying the month.

`Width` *n*

    The literal value `Width` followed by the integer value specifying the column width.

The `Character` option specifies the character set; you can set it to either `ANSI` or `OEM`.

1.15   Changing the Database for an Open Connection

Problem

You want to change the database that a connection uses without recreating the connection.

Solution

Use the ChangeDatabase( ) method to change the database for a connection.

The solution creates a Connection to the AdventureWorks database using the SQL Server .NET data provider. The database for the connection is then changed to use the ReportServer database. Finally, the connection is explicitly closed.

The C# code in *Program.cs* in the project ChangeConnectionDatabase is shown in Example 1-16.

Example 1-16. File: Program.cs for ChangeConnectionDatabase solution

```
using System;
using System.Data.SqlClient;

namespace ChangeConnectionDatabase
{
    class Program
    {
        static void Main(string[] args)
        {
            string sqlConnectString = "Data Source=(local);" +
                "Integrated security=SSPI;Initial Catalog=AdventureWorks;";

            using (SqlConnection connection = new SqlConnection(sqlConnectString))
            {
                Console.WriteLine("ConnectionString = {0}\n",
                    connection.ConnectionString);

                // Open the connection
                connection.Open( );
                Console.WriteLine("=> Connection opened.\n");

                Console.WriteLine("Connection.State = {0}", connection.State);
                Console.WriteLine("Database = {0}\n", connection.Database);

                // Change the database.
                connection.ChangeDatabase("ReportServer");
                Console.WriteLine("=> Database changed to ReportServer.\n");

                Console.WriteLine("Connection.State = {0}", connection.State);
                Console.WriteLine("Database = {0}\n", connection.Database);
```

```
            // Close the connection
            connection.Close();
            Console.WriteLine("=> Connection closed.\n");

            Console.WriteLine("Connection.State = {0}", connection.State);
            Console.WriteLine("Database = {0}", connection.Database);
        }

        Console.WriteLine("\nPress any key to continue.");
        Console.ReadKey();
      }
    }
}
```

The output is shown in Figure 1-17.

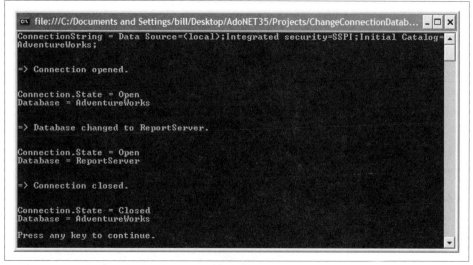

Figure 1-17. Output for ChangeConnectionDatabase solution

Discussion

The ChangeDatabase() method is defined in the IDbConnection interface that represents a connection to a data source and is implemented by .NET data providers. The ChangeDatabase() method changes the current database for an open connection. It takes a single parameter that specifies the name of the database to use in place of the current database. The name of the database must be valid or an ArgumentException will be raised. If the connection is not open when the method is called, an InvalidOperationException is raised. A provider-specific exception (e.g., SqlException for SQL Server data provider) is raised if the database cannot be changed for any reason.

The Database property of the Connection object is updated dynamically and returns the current database for an open connection or the name of a database that will be used by a closed connection when it is opened.

When the Connection is closed after ChangeDatabase( ) is called, the database is reset to that specified in the original connection string.

1.16   Setting Connection Pooling Options

Problem

You need to know the different connection pooling options and how you can control them.

Solution

Use the connection string to control connection pooling for the SQL Server, OLE DB .NET, Oracle, or ODBC .NET data provider. Note that connection pooling does not work in the debugger regardless of whether build configuration is set to Debug or Release.

The solution creates two connection strings, each with different connection pooling options. Each connection is opened and closed. In each case, an event handler is attached to the StateChange event to monitor changes in connection state.

The C# code in *Program.cs* in the project SetConnectionPoolingOptions is shown in Example 1-17.

Example 1-17. File: Program.cs for SetConnectionPoolingOptions solution

```
using System;
using System.Data;
using System.Data.SqlClient;

namespace SetConnectionPoolingOptions
{
    class Program
    {
        static void Main(string[] args)
        {
            string sqlConnectString = "Data Source=(local);" +
                "Integrated security=SSPI;Initial Catalog=AdventureWorks;";

            SqlConnection connection = new SqlConnection( );

            // Set up the event handler to detect connection state change
            connection.StateChange +=
                new StateChangeEventHandler(connection_StateChange);
```

Example 1-17. File: Program.cs for SetConnectionPoolingOptions solution (continued)

```
        // Set the connection string with pooling options
        connection.ConnectionString = sqlConnectString +
            "Connection Timeout=15;Connection Lifetime=0;" +
            "Min Pool Size=0;Max Pool Size=100;Pooling=true;";

        // Output the connection string and open/close the connection
        Console.WriteLine("Connection string = {0}",
            connection.ConnectionString);
        Console.WriteLine("-> Open connection.");
        connection.Open( );
        Console.WriteLine("-> Close connection.");
        connection.Close( );

        // Set the connection string with new pooling options
        connection.ConnectionString = sqlConnectString +
            "Connection Timeout=30;Connection Lifetime=0;" +
            "Min Pool Size=0;Max Pool Size=200;Pooling=true;";

        // Output the connection string and open/close the connection
        Console.WriteLine("\nConnection string = {0}",
            connection.ConnectionString);
        Console.WriteLine("-> Open connection.");
        connection.Open( );
        Console.WriteLine("-> Close connection.");
        connection.Close( );

        Console.WriteLine("\nPress any key to continue.");
        Console.ReadKey( );
    }

    static void connection_StateChange(object sender, StateChangeEventArgs e)
    {
        Console.WriteLine("\tConnection.StateChange event occurred.");
        Console.WriteLine("\tOriginalState = {0}", e.OriginalState.ToString( ));
        Console.WriteLine("\tCurrentState = {0}", e.CurrentState.ToString( ));
    }
  }
}
```

The output is shown in Figure 1-18.

Discussion

The following subsections describe how to control connection pooling for SQL Server, Oracle, OLE DB, and ODBC .NET data providers.

SQL Server

The connection string attributes that control connection pooling for the SQL Server .NET data provider are described in Table 1-3.

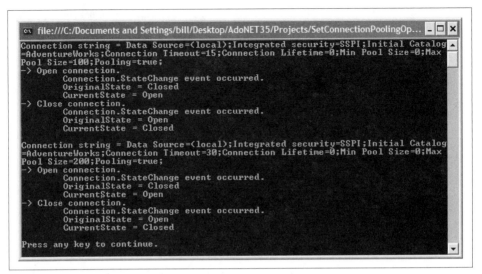

Figure 1-18. Output for SetConnectionPoolingOptions solution

Table 1-3. SQL Server connection string pooling attributes

Attribute	Description
Connection Lifetime	Length of time in seconds after creation after which a connection is destroyed. The default is 0, indicating that connection will have the maximum timeout.
Connection Reset	Specifies whether the connection is reset when removed from the pool. The default is `true`.
Enlist	Specifies whether the connection is automatically enlisted in the current transaction context of the creation thread if that transaction context exists. The default is `true`.
Load Balance Timeout	Length of time in seconds that a connection can remain idle in a connection pool before being removed.
Max Pool Size	Maximum number of connections allowed in the pool. The default is 100.
Min Pool Size	Minimum number of connections maintained in the pool. The default is 0.
Pooling	Specifies whether the connection is drawn from a pool or, when necessary, created and added to a pool. The default is `true`.

Oracle

The connection string attributes that control connection pooling for the Oracle .NET data provider are described in Table 1-4.

Table 1-4. Oracle connection string pooling attributes

Attribute	Description
Connection Lifetime	Length of time in seconds after creation after which a connection is destroyed. The default is 0, indicating that connection will have the maximum timeout.
Enlist	Specifies whether the connection is automatically enlisted in the current transaction context of the creation thread if that transaction context exists. The default is `true`.

Table 1-4. Oracle connection string pooling attributes (continued)

Attribute	Description
Max Pool Size	Maximum number of connections allowed in the pool. The default is 100.
Min Pool Size	Minimum number of connections maintained in the pool. The default is 0.
Pooling	Specifies whether the connection is drawn from a pool or, when necessary, created and added to a pool. The default is `true`.

OLE DB

The OLE DB .NET data provider uses resource-pooling support provided by the OLE DB Service component. You can override the default OLE DB provider services by specifying a value for the OLE DB Services attribute in the connection string. For more information, see Recipe 1.17, next.

OLE DB Resource pooling configuration is controlled using registry entries. There is no user interface to configure these entries—the registry must be edited directly. The registry entries are identified by the `<Provider's CLSID>`. CLSID values for some Microsoft OLE DB providers are:

- SQLOLEDB (SQL Server):

    `HKEY_CLASSES_ROOT\CLSID\{0C7FF16C-38E3-11d0-97AB-00C04FC2AD98}`

- Microsoft.Jet.OLEDB.4.0 (Jet):

    `HKEY_CLASSES_ROOT\CLSID\{dee35070-506b-11cf-b1aa-00aa00b8de95}`

- MSDAORA (Oracle):

    `HKEY_CLASSES_ROOT\CLSID\{e8cc4cbe-fdff-11d0-b865-00a0c9081c1d}`

- MSDASQL (OLE DB Provider for ODBC):

    `HKEY_CLASSES_ROOT\CLSID\{c8b522cb-5cf3-11ce-ade5-00aa0044773d}`

An OLE DB provider configuration option set by registry entries is:

`HKEY_CLASSES_ROOT\CLSID\<Provider's CLSID>\SPTimeout`

The session pooling timeout is the number of seconds that an unused session remains in the pool before timing out and being closed. This is a DWORD value with a default of 60 if the registry entry is not specified.

The following registry entries are global to all providers:

`HKEY_LOCAL_MACHINE\SOFTWARE\Microsoft\DataAccess\Session Pooling\Retry Wait`
> The amount of time that the service component will wait until attempting to contact the server again in the event of a failed connection attempt. This is a DWORD value with a default of 64 if no registry value is present.

`HKEY_LOCAL_MACHINE\SOFTWARE\Microsoft\DataAccess\Session Pooling\ExpBackOff`
> Determines the factor by which the service components will wait between reconnect attempts in the event of a failed connection attempt. This is a DWORD value with a default of 2 if no registry value is present.

`HKEY_CLASSES_ROOT\CLSID\{2206CDB0-19C1-11D1-89E0-00C04FD7A829}`
A `DWORD` value that specifies the maximum lifetime in seconds of a pooled connection. The default is 600. The CLSID is for the MSDAINITIALIZE component, which is the OLE DB service component manager that is used to parse OLE DB connection strings and initialize the appropriate provider.

ODBC

The ODBC .NET data provider uses the connection pooling support provided by the ODBC Driver Manager (DM). Connection pooling is supported by version 3.0 or later of the ODBC DM; the version of the ODBC driver does not matter.

The following two registry settings control ODBC connection pooling:

`Wait Retry`
The time in seconds that that the pool is blocked when the server is not responding. This setting affects all applications using the ODBC driver. The registry key specifies a REG_SZ value:

> `HKEY_LOCAL_MACHINE\SOFTWARE\ODBC\ODBCINST.INI\<Driver_Name>\CPTimeout`

`CPTimeout`
The time in seconds that unused connections remain in the pool. This setting affects all ODBC drivers on the system. The registry key specifies a REG_SZ value:

> `HKEY_LOCAL_MACHINE\SOFTWARE\ODBC\ODBCINST.INI\ODBC Connection Pooling`

You can control ODBC connection pooling in three ways:

- Using the `ODBC Data Source Administrator` to enable or disable pooling for the entire driver, and to control the `CPTimeout` and `Wait Retry` settings.
- Using the ODBC API to control pooling options from an ODBC application. For more information about the ODBC API, see the ODBC Programmer's Reference in the MSDN Library.
- Editing the registry settings described previously.

1.17   Taking Advantage of Connection Pooling

Problem

You need to understand connection pooling and make sure that your applications use it.

Solution

To effectively use connection pooling, you need to understand the concepts underlying connection pooling, how connection pooling is implemented by the major .NET data providers, and how to ensure that connection pooling is used by an application.

Discussion

Connection pooling allows an application to reuse connections from a pool instead of repeatedly creating and destroying new connections. Connection pooling can significantly improve the performance and scalability of applications by allowing a smaller number of connections to service the connection requirements of an application and because the overhead of establishing a new connection is eliminated.

A connection pool is created for each unique connection string. An algorithm associates items in the pool based on an exact match with the connection string; this includes capitalization, order of name/value pairs, and even spaces between name/value pairs. Dynamically generated connection strings must be identical so that connection pooling is used. If delegation is used, there will be one pool per delegate user. When transactions are used, one pool is created per transaction context. (For more information, see Recipe 1.18, next.) When the connection pool is created, connection objects are created and added to the pool to satisfy the minimum pool size specified.

When a connection is requested by an application and the maximum pool size has been reached, the request is queued. The request is satisfied by reallocating a connection that is released back to the pool when the Connection is closed or disposed. The connection pool manager removes expired connections and connections that have had their connection with the server severed from the pool.

The Connection object should be closed as soon as it is no longer needed so that it is added to or returned to the connection pool. This is done by calling either the Close( ) or Dispose( ) method of the Connection. Connections that are not explicitly closed might not be added to or returned to the connection pool.

 The DataAdapter automatically opens and closes a Connection as required if it is not already open when a method such as Fill( ), FillSchema( ), or Update( ) is called. The Connection must be explicitly closed if it is already open prior to the DataAdapter operation.

The following subsections detail connection pooling for specific .NET Framework data providers.

SQL Server and Oracle

The .NET data providers for SQL Server and Oracle provide efficient, transaction-aware support for connection pooling. Pools are created for each process and not destroyed until the process ends. Connection pooling is enabled by default.

Controlling SQL Server and Oracle .NET data provider connection pooling with connection string attribute/value pairs is discussed in Recipe 1.16.

OLE DB

The OLE DB .NET data provider pools connections by using resource pooling provided by the OLE DB core components.

The default OLE DB services that are enabled for a provider are specified by the value for the registry HKEY_CLASSES_ROOT\CLSID\<Provider's CLSID>\OLE_DBSERVICES DWORD value. Table 1-5 describes the alternatives.

Table 1-5. OLE DB services enabled values

OLE_DBSERVICES value	Description
0xffffffff	All services (default).
0xfffffffe	All services except pooling.
0xfffffffc	All services except pooling and automatic transaction enlistment.
0xfffffffb	All services except Client Cursor Engine.
0xfffffff8	All services except pooling, automatic transaction enlistment, and Client Cursor Engine.
0000000003	Pooling and automatic transaction enlistment, session-level aggregation only.
0x00000000	No services.
missing value	No aggregation. All services are disabled.

You can override the default OLE DB provider services by specifying a value for the OLE DB Services attribute in the connection string. Table 1-6 describes possible values.

Table 1-6. OLE DB services connection string values

OLE DB services attribute value	Default services enabled
−1	All services (default)
−4	All services except pooling and automatic transaction enlistment.
−5	All services except Client Cursor Engine.
−8	All services except pooling, automatic transaction enlistment, and Client Cursor Engine.
3	Pooling and automatic transaction enlistment, session-level aggregation only.
0	No services.

The following three configurable settings control OLE DB connection pooling:

SPTimeout
> The length of time in seconds that an unused connection remains in the pool before it is released. This can be configured for each provider and defaults to 60 seconds.

Retry Wait
> The length of time in seconds before an attempt to acquire a connection is reattempted when the server is not responding. This is global to all providers and defaults to 64 seconds.

ExpBackOff

The factor by which the retry wait time is increased when a connection attempt fails before reattempting the connection. This is global to all providers and defaults to a factor of 2.

OLE DB connection pooling is enabled by default; you can control it in three different ways:

- Specify a value for the OLE DB Services attribute in the connection string.
- Edit the registry to enable or disable pooling for an individual provider or globally by changing registry values. For more information, see Recipe 1.16.
- Use the OLE DB API from an application to enable or disable connection pooling. The SPTimeout and Retry Wait can be configured programmatically only by manipulating the registry entries. For more information about the OLE DB API, see the OLE DB Programmer's Reference in MSDN Library.

ODBC

The ODBC .NET data provider pools connections by using the connection pooling provided by the ODBC Driver Manager (DM). Pooling parameters for an ODBC driver affect all applications that use that driver, unless changed from within a native ODBC application.

The following two configurable settings control ODBC connection pooling:

CPTimeout

The length of time in seconds that an unused connection remains in the pool before it is released.

Wait Retry

The length of time before an attempt to acquire a connection is reattempted when the server is not responding.

Connection pooling is enabled by default. You can enable, disable, and configure it in three ways:

- Use the ODBC Data Source Administrator, introduced with ODBC 3.5 (MDAC 1.5), to enable or disable pooling for the entire driver and to control the CPTimeout and Wait Retry settings.
- Use the ODBC API from an application to limit the scope of pooling to the environment handler or to the driver, and to configure other pooling options. For more information about the ODBC API, see the ODBC Programmer's Reference in the MSDN Library.
- Edit the registry. For more information, see Recipe 1.16.

1.18   Using Transactions with Pooled Connections

Problem

You want to use connection pooling with transactions in your .NET application to maximize performance.

Solution

Use connection pooling with transactions.

Discussion

Connections participating in transactions are drawn from the connection pool and assigned based on an exact match with the transaction context of the requesting thread and with the connection string.

Each connection pool is divided into a subdivision for connections without a transaction context and zero or more subdivisions for connections associated with a particular transaction context. Each of these subdivisions, whether associated with a transaction context or not, uses connection pooling based on exact matching of the connection string as described in Recipe 1.17.

When a thread associated with a particular transaction context requests a connection, one from the appropriate pool enlisted with that transaction is automatically returned.

When a connection is closed, it is returned to the appropriate subdivision in the connection pool based on the transaction context. This allows a connection to be closed without generating an error even if a distributed transaction is still pending. The transaction can be committed or aborted later.

1.19   Displaying a Connection Property Dialog Box

Problem

You want to display a dialog box from an application that lets users create database connections using a Properties dialog box similar to that in the Visual Studio IDE.

Solution

Use a PropertyGrid control.

Follow these steps to create the solution:

1. Create a C# Windows Forms application, DisplayConnectionPropertyDialog.

2. Add a PropertyGrid control. Accept all default properties including the name propertyGrid1. Add an event handler named onPropertyValueChanged() for the PropertyValueChanged event.

3. Add a Label control below the PropertyGrid control. Set its Text property to Connection String:.

4. Add a TextBox control below the Label control. Name it connectString. Set the ReadOnly property to true. Set the Multiline property to true. Size the control to accommodate about four lines of text.

5. The C# code in *Form1.cs* in the project DisplayConnectionPropertyDialog is shown in Example 1-18. You need to add the highlighted code.

Example 1-18. File: Program.cs for DisplayConnectionPropertyDialog solution

```
using System;
using System.Windows.Forms;
using System.Data.SqlClient;

namespace DisplayConnectionPropertyDialog
{
    public partial class Form1 : Form
    {
        SqlConnectionStringBuilder scsb =
            new SqlConnectionStringBuilder( );

        public Form1( )
        {
            InitializeComponent( );

            propertyGrid1.SelectedObject = scsb;
        }

        private void onPropertyValueChanged(
            object s, PropertyValueChangedEventArgs e)
        {
            connectString.Text = scsb.ConnectionString;
        }
    }
}
```

Run the solution and set the DataSource, Initial Catalog, and Integrated Security properties in the property grid. The output is shown in Figure 1-19.

Discussion

The PropertyGrid control provides a user interface for browsing the properties of an object. Set the SelectedObject property of the PropertyGrid class to the object to display properties for—a SqlConnectionStringBuilder, in this case. The PropertyValueChanged event occurs when a property is changed. In the solution, the event handler displays the updated connection string when a property is changed.

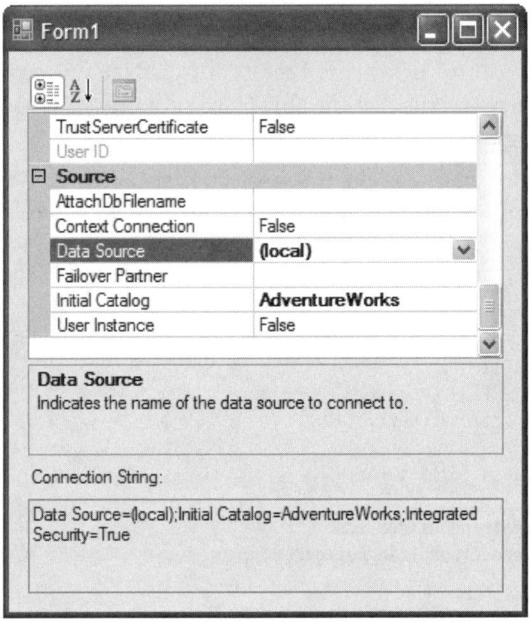

Figure 1-19. Output for DisplayConnectionPropertyDialog solution

1.20 Displaying the Data Link Properties Dialog Box

Problem

You want to display the Data Link Properties dialog box from an application so that users can create their own database connections.

Solution

Use COM interop with the OLE DB Service Component to display the Data Link Properties dialog box.

You'll need a reference to the Primary Interop Assembly (PIA) for ADO provided in the file *ADODB.DLL*; select adodb from the .NET tab in Visual Studio .NET's Add Reference Dialog. You'll also need a reference to the Microsoft OLE DB Service Component 1.0 Type Library from the COM tab in Visual Studio .NET's Add Reference Dialog.

The solution creates and displays a Data Link Properties dialog box using the Microsoft OLE DB Service Component through COM Interop. Follow these steps:

1. Create a C# Windows Forms application, DisplayDataLinkPropertiesDialog.

2. Add a TextBox control. Name it connectString. Set the MultiLine property = true.

3. Add a Button control. Name it openDialog.

4. Double-click the button to add a Click event handler named openDialog_Click.

The C# code in *Form1.cs* shown in the project DisplayDataLinkPropertiesDialog is shown in Example 1-19.

Example 1-19. File: Form1.cs for DisplayDataLinkPropertiesDialog solution

```
using System;
using System.Windows.Forms;

namespace DisplayDataLinkPropertiesDialog
{
    public partial class Form1 : Form
    {
        public Form1( )
        {
            InitializeComponent( );
        }

        private void openDialog_Click(object sender, EventArgs e)
        {
            ADODB.Connection adodbConnection = new ADODB.Connection( );
            object connection = (object)adodbConnection;

            MSDASC.DataLinks dlg = new MSDASC.DataLinks( );
            dlg.PromptEdit(ref connection);

            connectString.Text = adodbConnection.ConnectionString;
        }
    }
}
```

Execute the application.

Click the Display Dialog button. In the Data Link Properties dialog, select SQL Native Client on the Provider tab. Select the Connection tab. Set the Data Source to (local), select the Use Windows NT Integrated security radio button, and click the OK button to create the connection string. The completed Data Link Properties dialog is shown in Figure 1-20.

The output is shown in Figure 1-21.

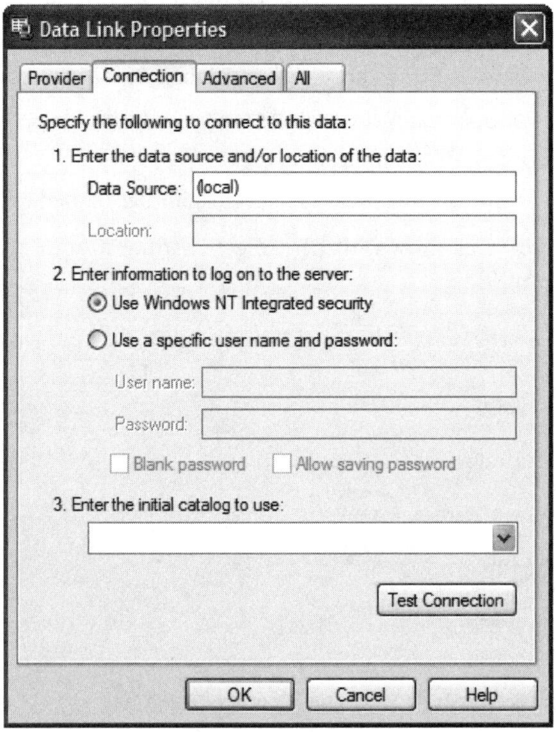

Figure 1-20. Data Link Properties dialog

Figure 1-21. Output for DisplayDataLinkPropertiesDialog solution

Discussion

You can use COM Interop to open a Data Link Properties dialog box that lets a user select an OLE DB provider and set its properties. You can use the results programmatically to construct the connection string for an ADO.NET connection object at runtime.

1.21 Monitoring Connections

Problem

You want to monitor the opening and closing of connections and the number of connections in the connection pool while an application is running.

Solution

Use the Windows Performance Monitor and the SQL Profiler to monitor connections and connection pooling. See Recipe 1.17 for more information on connection pooling.

Discussion

The following subsections discuss monitoring connection pooling for SQL Server and ODBC .NET Framework data providers.

SQL Server

You can monitor SQL Server connections and connection pooling using the SQL Server Profiler or the Windows Performance Monitor as described in the following subsections.

SQL Server Profiler. To use the SQL Server Profiler to monitor connection pooling:

1. Start the Profiler using one of the following methods:
   - From Windows desktop: Start → All Programs → Microsoft SQL Server → Performance Tools → SQL Server Profiler.
   - From SQL Server Management Studio: Tools → SQL Server Profiler.
2. When the SQL Server Profiler appears, select File → New Trace.
3. Supply connection details and click Connect. The Trace Properties dialog box will appear.

4. Select the Events Selection tab of the Trace Properties dialog box.

5. In the Selected Events list box, ensure that the `Audit Login` and `Audit Logout` events appear beneath the Security Audit node. Remove all other events from the list. Click the Run button to start the trace.

6. The new Profiler window will display a table containing `Audit Login` events when connections are established and `Audit Logout` events when connections are closed.

7. Figure 1-22 shows the result of the trace after a database connection is opened and closed.

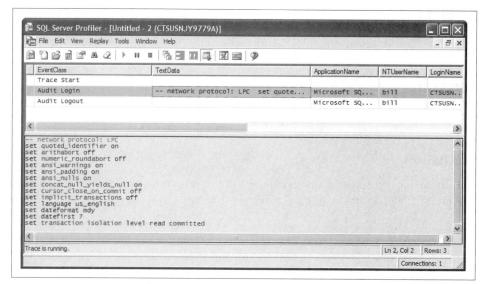

Figure 1-22. SQL Server Profiler trace

Windows Performance Monitor. To use the Windows Performance Monitor to monitor connection pooling:

1. Start Performance Monitor by selecting Start → All Programs → Administrative Tools → Performance.

2. Right-click the graph and select Properties from the context menu to open the System Monitor Properties dialog. Select the Graph tab and set the "Vertical scale maximum" to 2. This will make the results easier to see. Click OK to close the dialog.

3. Add performance counters to monitor connection pooling with one of the following methods:

   - Right-click the graph and select Add Counters from the pop-up menu.
   - Click the Add button above the graph.

   Both of these actions open the Add Counters dialog shown in Figure 1-23.

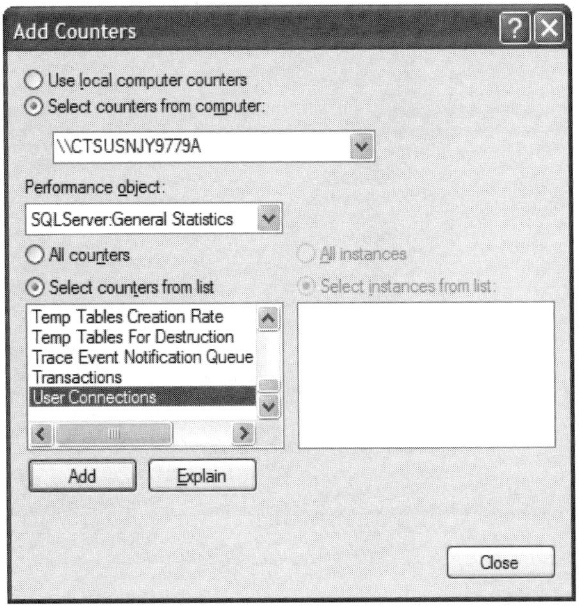

Figure 1-23. Add Counters dialog

4. In the "Performance object" drop-down list, select SQLServer:General Statistics.

   Performance counters can help tune connection pooling and troubleshoot pooling problems. To get an explanation for a counter, select the counter and click the Explain button.

5. Select the User Connections counter from the list and click the Add button. Click the Close button.

6. Figure 1-24 shows the Performance Monitor as a user connects to and disconnects from SQL Server.

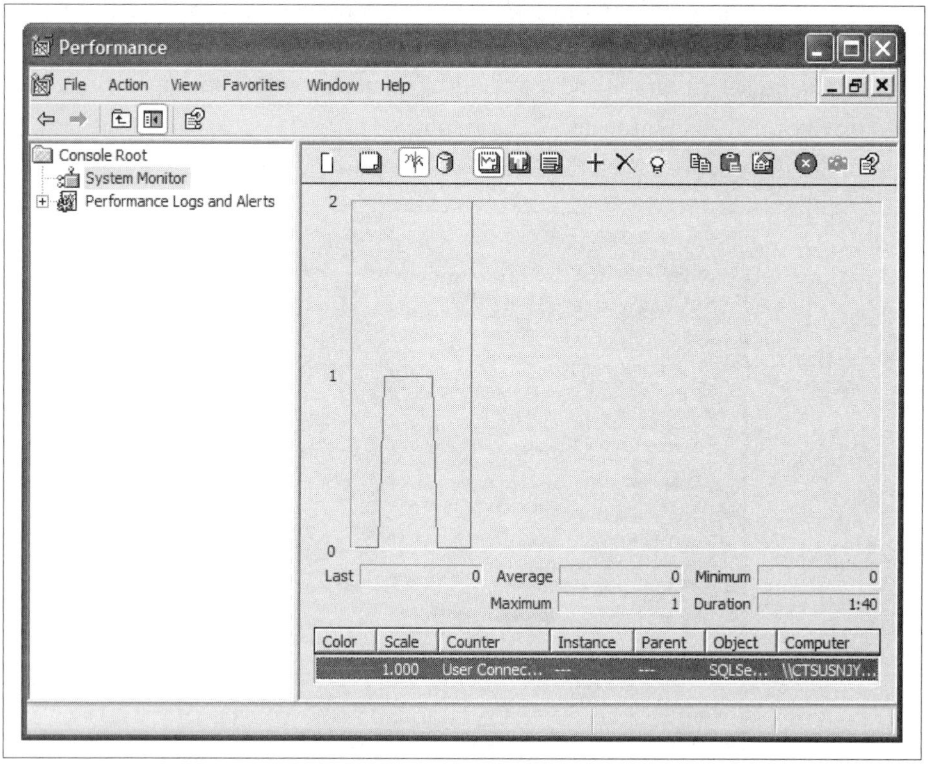

Figure 1-24. Performance Monitor display of user connections

ODBC

To enable ODBC performance monitoring:

1. Open the ODBC Data Source Administrator by selecting Start → All Programs → Administrative Tools → Data Sources (ODBC) as shown in Figure 1-25.

2. Select the Connection Pooling tab.

3. Ensure that the PerfMon Enable checkbox is checked. Click OK to close the dialog.

4. Start Performance Monitor by selecting Start → All Programs → Administrative Tools → Performance.

5. Add performance counters to monitor connection pooling with one of the following methods:

   • Right-click the graph and select Add Counters from the pop-up menu.

   • Click the Add button above the graph.

   Both of these actions open the Add Counters dialog shown in Figure 1-26.

6. In the "Performance object" drop-down list, select ODBC Connection Pooling. Table 1-7 describes the available ODBC connection pooling counters.

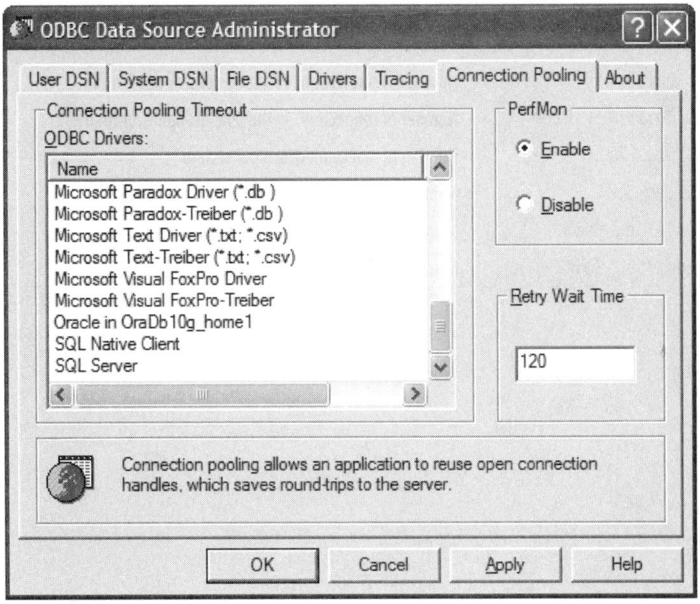

Figure 1-25. ODBC Data Source Administrator dialog

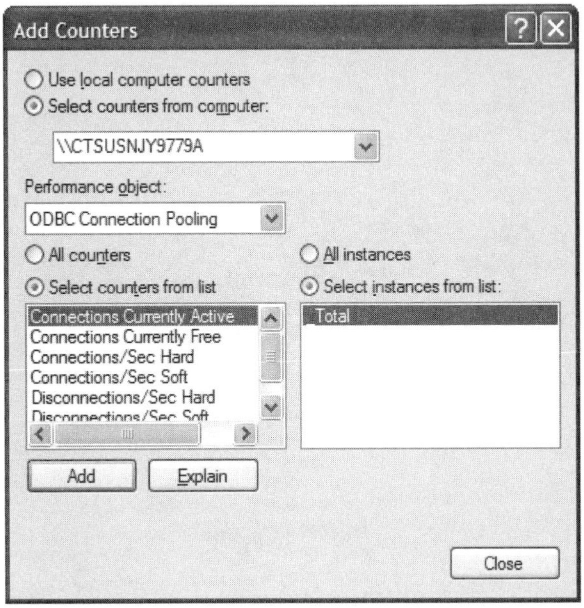

Figure 1-26. Add Counters dialog

Table 1-7. ODBC connection pooling counters

Counter	Description
Connections Currently Active	Number of connections currently used by applications
Connections Currently Free	Number of connections in the pool available for requests
Connections/Sec Hard	Number of real connections per second
Connections/Sec Soft	Number of connections from the pool per second
Disconnections/Sec Hard	Number of real disconnects per second
Disconnections/Sec Soft	Number of disconnects from the pool per second

CHAPTER 2

Working with Disconnected Data Objects

2.0 Introduction

ADO.NET has both connected and disconnected classes. Connected classes let you retrieve and update data in underlying data sources. They include the Connection, Command, DataReader, and DataAdapter classes. Each data provider is responsible for implementing the connected classes. Disconnected classes let you access and manipulate offline the data you retrieved using the connected classes and later synchronize it with the underlying data source using the connected classes. The disconnected classes include the DataSet, DataTable, DataColumn, DataRow, DataView, DataRelation, and Constraint classes. The disconnected classes are part of the ADO.NET classes in the .NET Framework. The recipes in this chapter discuss creating, working with, and managing the ADO.NET disconnected objects.

The DataSet is a disconnected, in-memory relational database that provides sophisticated navigational capabilities. It acts as a container for other objects, including DataTable, DataColumn, DataRow, and DataRelation. You can work with the data in these objects programmatically or you can data bind DataSet and DataTable objects to a variety of Windows Forms and Web Forms controls.

The DataSet and DataTable objects are data source-independent. Within these objects, .NET Framework data types are used to define column data types within tables. These data types are not the same as .NET provider native data types—provider data types are mapped to .NET Framework data types. Recipe 2.4 shows the mappings for SQL Server, Oracle, OLE DB, and ODBC .NET data providers to .NET Framework data types.

You can define DataSet object schemas programmatically or infer them from a database schema using the FillSchema( ) method of the DataAdapter class. Automatically retrieving schema information from the database has its limitations. For example, data relations cannot be created in a DataSet from the database schema and some column metadata such as default values and column lengths are not or are only partly available.

ADO.NET supports strongly typed DataSet objects, which are a collection of classes that inherit from and extend the DataSet, DataTable, and DataRow classes, providing additional properties, methods, and events, and making them easier to use. Because they are typed, you'll get type mismatch and other errors at compilation rather than at runtime (also, strongly typed DataSets work with Visual Studio .NET's IntelliSense). They are, however, slightly slower than untyped DataSet objects because of extra overhead. Because they are typed, they can make maintaining interfaces in distributed applications more complicated and difficult to administer. Recipe 2.16 discusses the different ways to create and use a strongly typed DataSet. Recipes 2.17 and 2.18 show how to override the default naming used by and behavior of a strongly typed DataSet.

You load a query result set into a DataTable or DataSet using the Fill( ) method of the DataAdapter. The DataAdapter automatically maps names when retrieving and updating data. The DataAdapter can also map table and column names in the database to tables and columns with different names in a DataTable. This allows the application to use different column and table names than are used by the database. The Update( ) method of the DataAdapter updates changes in a DataSet or DataTable to offline to a data source such as a database. The DataSet maintains both current and original versions of its data. Although data *appears* to be changed, it is not permanently changed until the AcceptChanges( ) method is called either explicitly or implicitly to commit the changes.

2.1 Creating a DataColumn and Adding It to a DataTable

Problem

You need to create a column and add it to a DataTable.

Solution

Use the Add( ) or AddRange( ) method of the DataColumnCollection of the DataTable exposed through its Columns property.

The solution creates, configures, and adds a column to a DataTable using four different techniques:

- Adds a DataColumn to a DataTable and configures the column

- Creates and configures a DataColumn and adds it to a DataTable

- Adds a DataColumn to a DataTable and configures it using the Add( ) method of the ColumnCollection of the DataTable exposed through the Columns property

- Creates multiple DataColumn objects, configures them, and adds them to the DataTable using the AddRange( ) method of the ColumnCollection of the DataTable

---

The C# code in *Program.cs* in the project CreateDataColumnAddDataTable is shown in Example 2-1.

Example 2-1. File: Program.cs for CreateDataColumnAddDataTable solution

```
using System;
using System.Data;

namespace CreateDataColumnAddDataTable
{
    class Program
    {
        static void Main(string[] args)
        {
            DataTable dt = new DataTable( );

            // Add the column to the DataTable to create
            DataColumn col1 = dt.Columns.Add( );
            // Configure the column -- integer with a default = 0 that
            // does not allow nulls
            col1.ColumnName= "Column-1";
            col1.DataType = typeof(int);
            col1.DefaultValue = 0;
            col1.Unique = true;
            col1.AllowDBNull = false;

            // Create and configure the column
            DataColumn col2 = new DataColumn( );
            // Configure the column -- string with max length = 50
            col2.ColumnName = "Column-2";
            col2.DataType = typeof(string);
            col2.MaxLength = 50;
            // Add the column to the DataTable
            dt.Columns.Add(col2);

            // Add a column directly using an overload of the Add( )
            // method of the DataTable.Columns collection -- the column
            // is a string with max length = 50
            dt.Columns.Add("Column-3", typeof(string)).MaxLength = 50;

            // Add multiple existing columns to the DataTable
            DataColumn col4 = new DataColumn("Column-4");
            // ... configure column 4
            DataColumn col5 = new DataColumn("Column-5", typeof(int));
            // Add columns 4 and 5 to the DataTable
            dt.Columns.AddRange(new DataColumn[] { col4, col5 });

            // Output the columns in the DataTable to the console
            Console.WriteLine("DataTable has {0} DataColumns named:",
                dt.Columns.Count);
            foreach (DataColumn col in dt.Columns)
                Console.WriteLine("\t{0}", col.ColumnName);
```

Example 2-1. File: Program.cs for CreateDataColumnAddDataTable solution (continued)

```
        Console.WriteLine("\nPress any key to continue.");
        Console.ReadKey( );
    }
  }
}
```

The output is shown in Figure 2-1.

Figure 2-1. Output for CreateDataColumnAddDataTable solution

Discussion

You add DataColumn objects to a DataTable to define the table schema.

The DataColumn constructor has five overloads:

```
DataColumn( )
DataColumn(string columnName)
DataColumn(string columnName, Type dataType)
DataColumn(string columnName, Type dataType, string expression)
DataColumn(string columnName, Type dataType, string expression,
    MappingType mappingType)
```

Where:

columnName

Name of the column to be created.

dataType

Column data type, from supported members of the Type class.

expression

Expression used to create the column.

mappingType

Specifies how columns are mapped to elements or attributes when transformed to an XML document. The MappingType enumeration lets you specify Element, Attribute, SimpleContent, or Hidden.

The DataColumn class exposes properties used to configure the column, as described in Table 2-1.

Table 2-1. DataColumn configuration properties

Property	Description
AllowDbNull	Gets or sets whether null values are permitted.
AutoIncrement	Gets or sets whether the column automatically increments the column value for new rows.
AutoIncrementSeed	Gets or sets the starting value for autoincrementing columns.
AutoIncrementStep	Gets or sets the increment value for each new row in an autoincrementing column.
ColumnMapping	Gets or sets how columns are mapped to elements or attributes when transformed to an XML document. The MappingType enumeration lets you specify Element, Attribute, SimpleContent, or Hidden.
ColumnName	Gets or sets the name of the column.
DataType	Gets or sets column data type from supported members of the Type class.
DateTimeMode	Gets or sets the DateTimeMode for the column from the DataSetDateTime enumeration. This specifies how DateTime columns in the DataSet are serialized.
DefaultValue	Gets or sets the default value for the column when creating new rows.
Expression	Gets or sets the expression to calculate the value of, or an aggregate value for, the column.
ExtendedProperties	Gets or sets user custom information associated with the column.
MaxLength	Gets or sets the maximum length of text type columns.
Namespace	Gets or sets the namespace of the column when reading and writing XML documents from DataTable or DataSet objects containing the column.
Ordinal	Gets or sets the position of the column in a DataColumnCollection collection.
Prefix	Gets or sets the XML prefix that aliases the XML namespace of the column when reading and writing XML documents from DataTable or DataSet objects containing the column.
ReadOnly	Gets or sets whether the column allows changes once a row is added to a DataTable.
Unique	Gets or sets whether each row of the column must be unique.

The DataColumnCollection collection contains a collection of DataColumn objects. The DataTable has a DataColumnCollection object accessed through the Columns property of the DataTable object—you use this property to access and manage the columns in the DataTable. The DataColumnCollection has members that are used to manage the columns in the collection. The key methods and properties are described in Tables 2-2 and 2-3.

Table 2-2. DataColumnCollection key methods

Method	Description
Add( )	Adds a DataColumn to the DataColumnCollection. This method has five overloads: Add( ) Add(DataColumn *dataColumn*) Add(string *columnName*) Add(string *columnName*, Type *dataType*) Add(string *columnName*, Type *dataType*, string *expression*) Where: *dataColumn* The DataColumn object to add to the collection. *columnName* The name of the column to create and add to the collection. *dataType* The data type of the column to create and add to the collection. *expression* The expression of the column to create and add to the collection. All of the overloads except the second both create a DataColumn and add it to the DataColumnCollection.
AddRange( )	Copies members of a DataColumn array to the end of a DataColumnCollection.
CanRemove( )	Returns whether a DataColumn can be removed from a DataColumnCollection.
Clear( )	Clears the DataColumnCollection of all columns.
Contains( )	Returns whether a DataColumnCollection contains a DataColumn with a specified ColumnName.
CopyTo( )	Copies all elements of the DataColumnCollection to a one-dimensional DataColumn array.
IndexOf( )	Returns the zero-based index of the first occurrence of a DataColumn specified by a ColumnName or a DataColumn object. –1 is returned if the column does not exist in the collection.
Remove( )	Removes a DataColumn specified by the ColumnName or by a DataColumn object from the DataColumnCollection.
RemoveAt( )	Removes a DataColumn at the specified index from the DataColumnCollection.

Table 2-3. DataColumnCollection key properties

Property	Description
Count	Gets the number of columns in the collection.
indexer	Gets the DataColumn object specified by an ordinal or ColumnName value.

2.2 Creating a DataTable and Adding It to a DataSet

Problem

You need to create a table and add it to a DataSet.

Solution

Use the Add( ) or AddRange( ) method of the DataTableCollection of the DataSet, which is exposed through its Tables property.

The solution creates, configures, and adds a column to a DataTable using three different techniques:

- Add a DataTable to a DataSet and configure the DataTable.
- Creates and configures a DataTable and adds it to a DataSet.
- Creates multiple DataTable objects, configures them, and adds them to the DataSet using the AddRange( ) method of the DataTableCollection of the DataSet.

The C# code in *Program.cs* in the project CreateDataTableAddDataSet is shown in Example 2-2.

Example 2-2. File: Program.cs for CreateDataTableAddDataSet solution

```
using System;
using System.Data;

namespace CreateDataTableAddDataSet
{
    class Program
    {
        static void Main(string[] args)
        {
            DataSet ds = new DataSet();

            // Add a DataTable named Table-1 directly
            DataTable dt1 = ds.Tables.Add("Table-1");
            // ... Configure the DataTable -- add some columns, etc.

            // Add a DataTable named Table-2 by creating the table
            // and adding it to the DataSet
            DataTable dt2 = new DataTable("Table-2");
            // ... Configure the DataTable -- add some columns, etc.
            ds.Tables.Add(dt2);
```

```
        // Add multiple DataTables to the DataSet
        DataTable dt3 = new DataTable("Table-3");
        DataTable dt4 = new DataTable("Table-4");
        // ... Configure the DataTable -- add some columns, etc.
        ds.Tables.AddRange(new DataTable[] { dt3, dt4 });

        // Output the tables in the DataSet to the console.
        Console.WriteLine("DataSet has {0} DataTables named: ",
            ds.Tables.Count);
        foreach (DataTable dt in ds.Tables)
            Console.WriteLine("\t{0}", dt.TableName);

        Console.WriteLine("\nPress any key to continue.");
        Console.ReadKey();
    }
  }
}
```

The output is shown in Figure 2-2.

Figure 2-2. Output for CreateDataTableAddDataSet solution

Discussion

The DataTable constructor has four overloads:

```
DataTable( )
DataTable(string tableName)
DataTable(SerializationInfo, serializationInfo, StreamingContext, streamingContext)
DataTable(string tableName, string namespace)
```

Where:

tableName
> Name of the table to be created.

serializationInfo
> Stores data needed to serialize or deserialize a DataTable with custom serialization behavior.

streamingContext
> Source and destination of the serialized stream.

namespace
> Namespace for the XML representation of the data in the DataTable.

The `DataTable` class exposes properties used to configure the table, as described in Table 2-4.

Table 2-4. DataColumn configuration properties

Property	Description
CaseSensitive	Gets or sets whether string comparisons within the table are case-sensitive. The default is set to the parent DataSet object's CaseSensitive value or false if the DataTable is not contained in a DataSet.
ExtendedProperties	Gets or sets user custom information associated with the table.
Locale	Gets or sets locale information used for string comparisons within the table.
MinimumCapacity	Gets or sets the initial starting size of the table.
Namespace	Gets or sets the namespace for the XML representation of the table.
Prefix	Gets or sets the XML prefix that aliases the XML namespace for the XML representation of the table.
RemotingFormat	Gets or sets the serialization format of the table.
TableName	Gets or sets the name of the table.

The `DataTableCollection` collection contains a collection of `DataTable` objects. The `DataSet` has a `DataTable` collection accessed through the `Tables` property of the `DataSet` object—you use this property to access and manage the tables in the `DataSet`. The `DataTableCollection` has members that are used to manage the tables in the collection. The key methods and properties are described in Tables 2-5 and 2-6.

Table 2-5. DataTableCollection key methods

Method	Description

Add( )	Adds a DataTable to the DataTablesCollection. This method has four overloads:
	
	Add( )
	Add(DataTable *dataTable*)
	Add(string *tableName*)
	Add(string *tableName*, string *namespace*)
	
	Where:
	
	dataTable
	  The DataTable object to add to the collection.
	tableName
	  The name of the table to create and add to the collection.
	namespace
	  The namespace of the table to create and add to the collection.
	
	All of the overloads except the second both create a DataTable and add it to the DataTableCollection.

AddRange( )	Copies members of a DataTable array to the end of a DataTableCollection.
CanRemove( )	Returns whether a DataTable can be removed from a DataTableCollection.
Clear( )	Clears the DataTableCollection of all tables.
Contains( )	Returns whether a DataTableCollection contains a DataTable with a specified TableName.

Table 2-5. DataTableCollection key methods (continued)

Method	Description
CopyTo( )	Copies all elements of the DataTableCollection to a one-dimensional DataTable array.
IndexOf( )	Returns the zero-based index of the first occurrence of a DataTable specified by a TableName or a DataTable object. –1 is returned if the table does not exist in the collection.
Remove( )	Removes a DataTable specified by the TableName or by a DataTable object from the DataTableCollection.
RemoveAt( )	Removes a DataTable at the specified index from the DataTableCollection.

Table 2-6. DataTableCollection key properties

Property	Description
Count	Gets the number of tables in the collection.
indexer	Gets the DataTable object specified by an ordinal or TableName value.

2.3 Mapping Table and Column Names Between a Data Source and DataSet

Problem

You want to control the names assigned to tables and columns when you fill a DataSet using a DataAdapter.

Solution

Use DataTableMapping and DataColumnMapping objects to map the names of database tables and columns in the data source to different names in a DataSet filled using a DataAdapter.

The solution defines a SQL statement to retrieve the Title, FirstName, and LastName columns from the Person.Contact table in AdventureWorks. A DataAdapter is created with a DataTableMapping object to map the DataSet default table name Table to the name mappedContact. Three DataColumnMapping objects are created to map the database column names to different names in the table in the DataSet. The DataAdapter is used to fill a new DataSet. The table and column names are output together with the result set to the console.

The C# code in *Program.cs* in the project MappingTableAndColumnNames is shown in Example 2-3.

Example 2-3. File: Program.cs for MappingTableAndColumnNames solution

```
using System;
using System.Data;
using System.Data.Common;
using System.Data.SqlClient;
```

Example 2-3. File: Program.cs for MappingTableAndColumnNames solution (continued)

```csharp
namespace MappingTableAndColumnNames
{
    class Program
    {
        static void Main(string[] args)
        {
            // Create the connection
            string sqlConnectString = "Data Source=(local);" +
                "Integrated security=SSPI;Initial Catalog=AdventureWorks;";

            string sqlSelect = "SELECT TOP 5 Title, FirstName, LastName " +
                "FROM Person.Contact";

            SqlDataAdapter da =
                new SqlDataAdapter(sqlSelect, sqlConnectString);

            // Create the table mapping to map the default table name 'Table'.
            DataTableMapping dtm =
                da.TableMappings.Add("Table", "mappedContact");

            // Create column mappings
            dtm.ColumnMappings.Add("Title", "mappedTitle");
            dtm.ColumnMappings.Add("FirstName", "mappedFirstName");
            dtm.ColumnMappings.Add("LastName", "mappedLastName");

            // Create and fill the DataSet
            DataSet ds = new DataSet();
            da.Fill(ds);

            Console.WriteLine("DataTable name = {0}",
                ds.Tables[0].TableName);

            foreach(DataColumn col in ds.Tables["mappedContact"].Columns)
            {
                Console.WriteLine("\tDataColumn {0} name = {1}",
                    col.Ordinal, col.ColumnName);
            }

            Console.WriteLine();

            foreach(DataRow row in ds.Tables["mappedContact"].Rows)
            {
                Console.WriteLine(
                    "Title = {0}, FirstName = {1}, LastName = {2}",
                    row["mappedTitle"], row["mappedFirstName"],
                    row["mappedLastName"]);
            }

            Console.WriteLine("\nPress any key to continue.");
            Console.ReadKey();
        }
    }
}
```

The output is shown in Figure 2-3.

Figure 2-3. Output for MappingTableAndColumnNames solution

Discussion

When the Fill( ) method of the DataAdapter is used to fill a DataSet, the column names used in the DataSet default to the column names defined in the data source.

A DataAdapter has a collection of DataTableMapping objects in its DataTableMappingCollection accessed through its TableMappings property. These objects map the name of a table in the data source to a DataTable with a different name in the DataSet. When a batch query is used to fill multiple tables within a DataSet, the table names default to Table, Table1, Table2, and so on. You can also use an overload of the Fill( ) method to specify a source table name other than the default Table—in that case, the numbering works the same way. You can use table mapping to rename tables created within the DataSet to match the table names in the data source or to map the tables returned from a batch query to DataTable objects that already exist within the DataSet.

Each table mapping object has a collection of DataColumnMapping objects in its DataColumnMappingCollection that are accessed through its ColumnMappings property. These objects map the name of a column in the data source to a column with a different name in the DataSet for the table associated with the containing table mapping object.

The Fill( ) method of the DataAdapter always uses mapping information (if present) to retrieve data from a data source. The FillSchema( ) method accepts an argument specifying whether to use mapping information when retrieving schema information from a data source. Like the Fill( ) method, the Update( ) method always uses mapping information (if present) when submitting DataSet changes back to the data source.

In the solution, the Person.Contact table retrieved by the query is mapped to a table in the DataSet called mappedContact with the following code:

```
DataTableMapping dtm = da.TableMappings.Add("Table", "mappedContact");
```

Without the table mapping, a table named Table will be created when the Fill() method is called. For a query returning a single table, the table mapping can also be specified by using an overload of the Fill() method as shown:

```
da.Fill(ds, "mappedContact");
```

For batch SQL queries, add multiple table mappings to control the table names used for the DataTable objects in the DataSet.

The solution also maps the three column names returned by the query, Title, FirstName, and LastName using the following code:

```
dtm.ColumnMappings.Add("Title", "mappedTitle");
dtm.ColumnMappings.Add("FirstName", "mappedFirstName");
dtm.ColumnMappings.Add("LastName", "mappedLastName");
```

This code adds column mapping objects to the table mapping object for the table containing the columns to be mapped.

2.4   Mapping .NET Data Provider Data Types to .NET Framework Data Types

Problem

You want to convert between .NET provider data types and .NET Framework data types.

Solution

You need to understand the .NET Framework data types; their mappings to SQL Server, OLE DB, ODBC, and Oracle data types; and how to properly cast them. The .NET Framework typed accessors and .NET Framework provider-specific typed accessors for use with the DataReader class are also important.

The solution shows how to cast a value from a DataReader to a .NET Framework data type and how to use the .NET Framework typed accessor and the SQL Server-specific typed accessor.

The C# code in *Program.cs* in the project MappingDataTypes is shown in Example 2-4.

Example 2-4. File: Program.cs for MappingDataTypes solution

```
using System;
using System.Data.SqlClient;
using System.Data.SqlTypes;

namespace MappingDataTypes
{
    class Program
    {
```

Example 2-4. File: Program.cs for MappingDataTypes solution (continued)

```
static void Main(string[] args)
{
    string sqlConnectString = "Data Source=(local);" +
        "Integrated security=SSPI;Initial Catalog=AdventureWorks;";

    string sqlSelect = "SELECT TOP 5 ContactID, FirstName, MiddleName, " +
        "LastName FROM Person.Contact";

    int contactID;
    string firstName, middleName, lastName;

    // Create the connection and the command.
    SqlConnection connection = new SqlConnection(sqlConnectString);
    SqlCommand command = new SqlCommand(sqlSelect, connection);

    // Open the connection and build the DataReader.
    connection.Open();

    using (SqlDataReader dr = command.ExecuteReader())
    {
        Console.WriteLine("---Cast value retrieved by ordinal---");
        // Get values from the DataReader and cast to int.
        while (dr.Read())
        {
            contactID = Convert.ToInt32(dr[0]);
            firstName = Convert.ToString(dr[1]);
            middleName = Convert.ToString(dr[2]);
            lastName = Convert.ToString(dr[3]);

            Console.WriteLine("{0}\t{1}, {2} {3}",
                contactID, lastName, firstName, middleName);
        }
    }

    using (SqlDataReader dr = command.ExecuteReader())
    {
        // Get values from the DataReader using generic typed accessors.
        Console.WriteLine("\n---Generic typed accessors---");
        while (dr.Read())
        {
            contactID = dr.GetInt32(0);
            firstName = dr.GetString(1);
            middleName = dr.IsDBNull(2) ? null : dr.GetString(2);
            lastName = dr.GetString(3);

            Console.WriteLine("{0}\t{1}, {2} {3}",
                contactID, lastName, firstName, middleName);
        }
    }

    using (SqlDataReader dr = command.ExecuteReader())
    {
```

Example 2-4. File: Program.cs for MappingDataTypes solution (continued)

```
                // Get values from the DataReader using SQL Server
                // specific typed accessors.
                Console.WriteLine("\n---SQL Server specific typed accessors---");
                while (dr.Read( ))
                {
                    contactID = (int)dr.GetSqlInt32(0);
                    firstName = (string)dr.GetSqlString(1);
                    middleName = dr.IsDBNull(2) ? null :
                        (string)dr.GetSqlString(2);
                    lastName = (string)dr.GetSqlString(3);

                    Console.WriteLine("{0}\t{1}, {2} {3}",
                        contactID, lastName, firstName, middleName);
                }
            }

            Console.WriteLine("\nPress any key to continue.");
            Console.ReadKey( );
        }
    }
}
```

The output is shown in Figure 2-4.

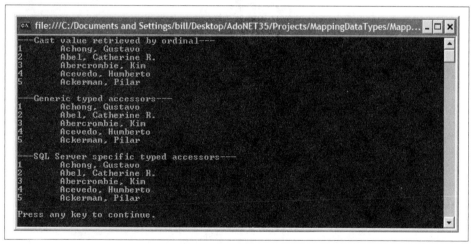

Figure 2-4. Output for MappingDataTypes solution

Discussion

The ADO.NET DataSet and contained objects are data source-independent. The DataAdapter is used to retrieve data into the DataSet and to reconcile modifications made to the data to the data source at some later time. The implication is that data in the DataTable objects contained in the DataSet are .NET Framework data types rather than data types specific to the underlying data source or the .NET data provider used to connect to that data source.

While the `DataReader` object for a data source is specific to the .NET data provider used to retrieve the data, the values in the `DataReader` are stored in variables with .NET Framework data types.

The .NET Framework data type is inferred from the .NET data provider used to fill the `DataSet` or build the `DataReader`. The `DataReader` has typed accessor methods that improve performance by returning a value as a specific .NET Framework data type when the data type is known, thereby eliminating the need for additional type conversion. For more information about using typed accessors with a `DataReader`, see Recipe 10.11.

Some `DataReader` classes expose data source-specific accessor methods as well. For example, the `SqlDataReader` exposes accessor methods that return SQL Server data types as objects of `System.Data.SqlType`.

In all cases, a null value for a .NET Framework data type is represented by `System.DBNull.Value`.

Table 2-7 lists the inferred .NET Framework data type, the .NET Framework typed accessor for the `DataReader`, and the SQL Server-specific typed accessor for each SQL Server data type.

Table 2-7. Data types and accessors for SQL Server .NET data provider

SQL Server data type	.NET Framework data type	.NET Framework typed accessor	SQLType typed accessor
bigint	Int64	GetInt64( )	GetSqlInt64( )
binary	Byte[]	GetBytes( )	GetSqlBinary( )
bit	Boolean	GetBoolean( )	GetSqlBit( )
char	String Char[]	GetString( ) GetChars( )	GetSqlString( )
datetime	DateTime	GetDateTime( )	GetSqlDateTime( )
decimal	Decimal	GetDecimal( )	GetSqlDecimal( )
float	Double	GetDouble( )	GetSqlDouble( )
image	Byte[]	GetBytes( )	GetSqlBinary( )
int	Int32	GetInt32( )	GetSqlInt32( )
money	Decimal	GetDecimal( )	GetSqlMoney( )
nchar	String Char[]	GetString( ) GetChars( )	GetSqlString( )
ntext	String Char[]	GetString( ) GetChars( )	GetSqlString( )
numeric	Decimal	GetDecimal( )	GetSqlDecimal( )
nvarchar	String Char[]	GetString( ) GetChars( )	GetSqlString( )
real	Single	GetFloat( )	GetSqlSingle( )
smalldatetime	DateTime	GetDateTime( )	GetSqlDateTime( )
smallint	Int16	GetInt16( )	GetSqlInt16( )

SQL Server data type	.NET Framework data type	.NET Framework typed accessor	SQLType typed accessor
smallmoney	Decimal	GetDecimal( )	GetSqlDecimal( )
sql_variant	Object	GetValue( )	GetSqlValue( )
text	String Char[]	GetString( ) GetChars( )	GetSqlString( )
timestamp	Byte[]	GetBytes( )	GetSqlBinary( )
tinyint	Byte	GetByte( )	GetSqlByte( )
uniqueidentifier	Guid	GetGuid( )	GetSqlGuid( )
varbinary	Byte[]	GetBytes( )	GetSqlBinary( )
varchar	String Char[]	GetString( ) GetChars( )	GetSqlString( )

Table 2-8 lists the inferred .NET Framework data type, the .NET Framework typed accessor for the DataReader for each OLE DB type, and the corresponding ADO type.

Table 2-8. Data types and accessors for OLE DB .NET data provider

OLE DB data type	ADO type	.NET Framework data type	.NET Framework typed accessor
DBTYPE_BOOL	adBoolean	Boolean	GetBoolean( )
DBTYPE_BSTR	adBSTR	String	GetString( )
DBTYPE_BYTES	adBinary	Byte[]	GetBytes( )
DBTYPE_CY	adCurrency	Decimal	GetDecimal( )
DBTYPE_DATE	adDate	DateTime	GetDateTime( )
DBTYPE_DBDATE	adDBDate	DateTime	GetDateTime( )
DBTYPE_DBTIME	adDBTime	DateTime	GetDateTime( )
DBTYPE_DBTIMESTAMP	adDBTimeStamp	DateTime	GetDateTime( )
DBTYPE_DECIMAL	adDecimal	Decimal	GetDecimal( )
DBTYPE_ERROR	adError	ExternalException	GetValue( )
DBTYPE_FILETIME	adFileTime	DateTime	GetDateTime( )
DBTYPE_GUID	adGUID	Guid	GetGuid( )
DBTYPE_HCHAPTER	adChapter	[a]	GetValue( )
DBTYPE_I1	adTinyInt	Byte	GetByte( )
DBTYPE_I2	adSmallInt	Int16	GetInt16( )
DBTYPE_I4	adInteger	Int32	GetInt32( )
DBTYPE_I8	adBigInt	Int64	GetInt64( )
DBTYPE_IDISPATCH2	adIDispatch	Object[b]	GetValue( )
DBTYPE_IUNKNOWN2	adIUnknown	Object	GetValue( )
DBTYPE_NUMERIC	adNumeric	Decimal	GetDecimal( )
DBTYPE_PROPVARIANT	adPropVariant	Object	GetValue( )
DBTYPE_R4	adSingle	Single	GetFloat( )

Table 2-8. Data types and accessors for OLE DB .NET data provider (continued)

OLE DB data type	ADO type	.NET Framework data type	.NET Framework typed accessor
DBTYPE_R8	adDouble	Double	GetDouble( )
DBTYPE_STR	adChar	String	GetString( )
DBTYPE_UI1	adUnsignedTinyInt	Byte	GetByte( )
DBTYPE_UI2	adUnsignedSmallInt	UInt16	GetValue( )
DBTYPE_UI4	adUnsignedInt	UInt32	GetValue( )
DBTYPE_UI8	adUnsignedBigInt	UInt64	GetValue( )
DBTYPE_UDT	adUserDefined	Not supported	Not supported
DBTYPE_VARIANT	adVariant	Object	GetValue( )
DBTYPE_VARNUMERIC	adVarNumeric	Not supported	Not supported
DBTYPE_WSTR	adWChar	String	GetString( )

[a] Supported using the DataReader. For more information, see Recipe 3.19.
[b] The object reference is a marshaled representation of the pointer.

Table 2-9 lists the inferred .NET Framework data type and the .NET Framework typed accessor for the DataReader for each ODBC data type.

Table 2-9. Data types and accessors for ODBC .NET data provider

ODBC data type	.NET Framework data type	.NET Framework typed accessor
SQL_BIGINT	Int64	GetInt64( )
SQL_BINARY	Byte[]	GetBytes( )
SQL_BIT	Boolean	GetBoolean( )
SQL_CHAR	StringChar[]	GetString( )GetChars( )
SQL_DECIMAL	Decimal	GetDecimal( )
SQL_DOUBLE	Double	GetDouble( )
SQL_GUID	Guid	GetGuid( )
SQL_INTEGER	Int32	GetInt32( )
SQL_LONG_VARCHAR	StringChar[]	GetString( )GetChars( )
SQL_LONGVARBINARY	Byte[]	GetBytes( )
SQL_NUMERIC	Decimal	GetDecimal( )
SQL_REAL	Single	GetFloat( )
SQL_SMALLINT	Int16	GetInt16( )
SQL_TINYINT	Byte	GetByte( )
SQL_TYPE_TIMES	DateTime	GetDateTime( )
SQL_TYPE_TIMESTAMP	DateTime	GetDateTime( )
SQL_VARBINARY	Byte[]	GetBytes( )
SQL_WCHAR	StringChar[]	GetString( )GetChars( )
SQL_WLONGVARCHAR	StringChar[]	GetString( )GetChars( )
SQL_WVARCHAR	StringChar[]	GetString( )GetChars( )

Table 2-10 lists the inferred .NET Framework data type, the .NET Framework typed accessor for the `DataReader`, and the Oracle-specific typed accessor for each Oracle data type.

Table 2-10. Data types and accessors for Oracle .NET data provider

Oracle data type	.NET Framework data type	.NET Framework typed accessor	OracleType typed accessor
BFILE	Byte[]	GetBytes()	GetOracleBFile()
BINARY_DOUBLE	Double	GetDouble()	GetOracleNumber()
BINARY_FLOAT	float	GetFloat()	GetOracleNumber()
BINARY_INTEGER	Int64	GetInt64()	GetOracleNumber()
BLOB	Byte[]	GetBytes()	GetOracleLob()
CHAR	StringChar[]	GetString() GetChars()	GetOracleString()
CLOB	StringChar[]	GetString() GetChars()	GetOracleLob()
DATE	DateTime	GetDateTime()	GetOracleDateTime()
FLOAT	Decimal	GetDecimal()	GetOracleNumber()[a]
INTERVAL YEAR TO MONTH[b]	Int32	GetInt32()	GetOracleMonthSpan()
INTERVAL DAY TO SECOND[b]	TimeSpan	GetTimeSpan()	GetOracleTimeSpan()
LONG	StringChar[]	GetString() GetChars()	GetOracleString()
LONG RAW	Byte[]	GetBytes()	GetOracleBinary()
NCHAR	StringChar[]	GetString() GetChars()	GetOracleString()
NCLOB	StringChar[]	GetString() GetChars()	GetOracleLob()
NUMBER	Decimal	GetDecimal()	GetOracleNumber()[a]
NVARCHAR2	StringChar[]	GetString() GetChars()	GetOracleString()
RAW	Byte[]	GetBytes()	GetOracleBinary()
REF CURSOR	N/A	N/A	N/A
ROWID	StringChar[]	GetString() GetChars()	GetOracleString()
TIMESTAMP[b]	DateTime	GetDateTime()	GetOracleDateTime()
TIMESTAMP WITH LOCAL TIME ZONE[b]	DateTime	GetDateTime()	GetOracleDateTime()
TIMESTAMP WITH TIME ZONE[b]	DateTime	GetDateTime()	GetOracleDateTime()
VARCHAR2	StringChar[]	GetString() GetChars()	GetOracleString()

[a] The Oracle NUMBER type has a maximum of 38 significant digits while the .NET Framework decimal type has a maximum of 28. An OverflowException will be raised if the Oracle NUMBER type has more than 28 significant digits.
For details about inferred .NET Framework data types, .NET Framework typed accessors for the DataReader, and provider-specific typed accessors for other .NET data providers, consult the documentation for the specific .NET data provider.
[b] Available only when using Oracle 9*i* or later client and server software.

2.5   Adding a Calculated Column to a DataTable

Problem

You need to display a calculated value for each row in a DataTable.

Solution

Add an expression column to the table and display it.

The solution creates a DataTable containing the top five rows from the Sales.SalesOrderDetail table from AdventureWorks. An expression column calculating the extended price for each record is added to the table. The results are output to the console.

The C# code in *Program.cs* in the project AddCalculatedColumnDataTable is shown in Example 2-5.

Example 2-5. File: Program.cs for AddCalculatedColumnDataTable solution

```
using System;
using System.Data;
using System.Data.SqlClient;

namespace AddCalculatedColumnDataTable
{
    class Program
    {
        static void Main(string[] args)
        {
            string sqlConnectString = "Data Source=(local);" +
                "Integrated security=SSPI;Initial Catalog=AdventureWorks;";

            string sqlSelect = "SELECT TOP 5 * FROM Sales.SalesOrderDetail";

            // Use a DataAdapter to fill a DataTable
            SqlDataAdapter da = new SqlDataAdapter(sqlSelect, sqlConnectString);
            DataTable dt = new DataTable();
            da.Fill(dt);

            // Add an expression column to the table.
            dt.Columns.Add(new DataColumn("ExtendedPrice", typeof(Decimal),
                "UnitPrice * (1 - UnitPriceDiscount) * OrderQty"));

            foreach (DataRow row in dt.Rows)
                Console.WriteLine("ID = {0}, UnitPrice = {1}, " +
                    "Disc = {2}, Qty = {3}, Total = {4}",
                    row["SalesOrderDetailID"], row["UnitPrice"],
                    row["UnitPriceDiscount"], row["OrderQty"],
                    row["ExtendedPrice"]);

            Console.WriteLine("\nPress any key to continue.");
            Console.ReadKey();
        }
```

Example 2-5. File: Program.cs for AddCalculatedColumnDataTable solution (continued)

```
    }
}
```

The output is shown in Figure 2-5.

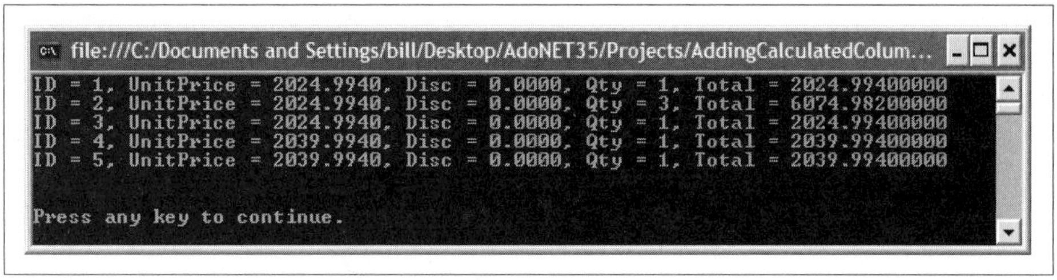

Figure 2-5. Output for AddCalculatedColumnDataTable solution

Discussion

An expression column contains a value that is calculated from other column values in the same row, or from an aggregate of rows in the table or in a related table. The DataType of the column must be compatible with the return value of the expression. For information about expression syntax, see the "DataColumn.Expression Property" topic in the MSDN Library.

An expression column is added to a table either through one of the DataColumn constructors that take the expression for the column as the third argument (the technique used in the solution) or by setting the Expression property of the column to the expression.

In the solution, an expression column named ExtendedPrice is created with a data type of Decimal. The column calculates the extended price for the column using the expression UnitPrice * (1 – UnitPriceDiscount) * OrderQty.

After the column is added to the table, the RowFilter and Sort properties of a DataView bound to the table with the expression column can sort or filter data in the same way as they can on any other column. This is discussed in more detail in Recipes 4.3 and 4.5.

2.6   Creating a Unique Constraint

Problem

You need to ensure that values for a column are unique for each row in a table.

Solution

Use the System.Data.UniqueConstraint class.

The solution creates a DataTable with two columns and adds a unique constraint to one of the columns. Rows are added including a row that violates the constraint. The results are output to the console.

The C# code in *Program.cs* in the project CreateUniqueConstraint is shown in Example 2-6.

Example 2-6. File: Program.cs for CreateUniqueConstraint solution

```csharp
using System;
using System.Data;

namespace CreateUniqueConstraint
{
    class Program
    {
        static void Main(string[] args)
        {
            // Create a table
            DataTable dt = new DataTable("Table-1");
            // Add two columns
            dt.Columns.Add("Id", typeof(int));
            dt.Columns.Add("Field1", typeof(string)).MaxLength = 50;
            // Create a unique constraint on Field1
            UniqueConstraint uc1 =
                new UniqueConstraint("UniqueConstraint", dt.Columns["Field1"]);
            // Add the constraint to the table
            dt.Constraints.Add(uc1);
            // Output the properties of the table constraint added
            OutputConstraintProperties(dt);

            // Verify the unique constraint by adding rows
            try
            {
                AddRow(dt, 1, "Value 1");
                AddRow(dt, 2, "Value 2");
                AddRow(dt, 3, "Value 2");
            }
            catch (Exception ex)
            {
                Console.WriteLine("Error: {0}", ex.Message);
            }

            Console.WriteLine("\nPress any key to continue.");
            Console.ReadKey();
        }

        private static void OutputConstraintProperties(DataTable dt)
        {
            Console.WriteLine("DataTable {0} => Constraint properties: ",
                dt.TableName);
            Console.WriteLine("\tName = ", dt.Constraints[0].ConstraintName);
```

```
        Console.WriteLine("\tIsPrimaryKey = {0}",
            ((UniqueConstraint)dt.Constraints[0]).IsPrimaryKey);
        Console.WriteLine("\tColumns: ");
        foreach (DataColumn col in
            ((UniqueConstraint)dt.Constraints[0]).Columns)
        {
            Console.WriteLine("\t\t{0}", col.ColumnName);
        }
    }

    private static void AddRow(DataTable dt, int id, string field1)
    {
        Console.WriteLine("\nAdding row: {0}, {1}", id, field1);
        dt.Rows.Add(new object[] { id, field1 });
        Console.WriteLine("Row added.");
    }
    }
}
```

The output is shown in Figure 2-6.

Figure 2-6. Output for CreateUniqueConstraint solution

Discussion

A unique constraint is a restriction on a column that forces all values in a collection of the columns to be unique.

The System.Data.Constraint class is an abstract class that is the base class for the two .NET Framework built-in constraint classes:

System.Data.UniqueConstraint

Ensures that all data in the specified column or columns in the row is unique within the collection of columns, generally in a table. Defining a primary key for a DataTable by setting the PrimaryKey property automatically creates a unique constraint for the specified column or columns.

`System.Data.ForeignKeyConstraint`

Enforces rules about how updates of values in rows or row deletions are propagated to related tables through the `DeleteRule` and `UpdateRule` properties, which define the action to be taken.

By default, a `UniqueConstraint` is created on the parent table and a `ForeignKeyConstraint` is created on the child table when a `DataRelation` object is created relating the two tables. Constraints are only enforced if the `EnforceConstraints` property of the `DataSet` is true. For more information about foreign key constraints, see Recipe 2.9.

The `UniqueConstraint` constructor has nine overloads:

```
UniqueConstraint(DataColumn col)
UniqueConstraint(DataColumn[] cols)
UniqueConstraint(DataColumn col, bool isPrimaryKey)
UniqueConstraint(DataColumn[] cols, bool isPrimaryKey)
UniqueConstraint(string name, DataColumn col)
UniqueConstraint(string name, DataColumn[] cols)
UniqueConstraint(string name, DataColumn col, bool isPrimaryKey)
UniqueConstraint(string name, DataColumn[] cols, bool isPrimaryKey)
UniqueConstraint(string name, string[] columnNames, bool isPrimaryKey)
```

Where:

col

The `DataColumn` that is uniquely constrained.

cols

The array of `DataColumn` objects that are uniquely constrained.

name

The name of the unique constraint.

isPrimaryKey

Specifies whether the unique constraint is a primary key.

columnNames

An array of column names that are uniquely constrained.

The `UniqueConstraint` class exposes properties used to configure the constraint as described in Table 2-11.

Table 2-11. UniqueConstraint configuration properties

Property	Description
`Columns`	Gets the array of `DataColumn` objects that are constrained.
`ConstraintName`	Gets or sets the name of the constraint.
`ExtendedProperties`	Gets or sets user custom information associated with the constraint.
`IsPrimaryKey`	Gets whether the constraint is on a primary key.
`Table`	Gets the `DataTable` to which the constraint belongs.

The `ConstraintCollection` collection contains a collection of constraints for a DataTable, both `UniqueConstraint` and `ForeignKeyConstraint` objects. The `DataTable` has a Constraint collection accessed through the Constraints property of the DataTable object—you use this property to access and manage the constraints for the DataTable. The `ConstaintCollection` has members that are used to manage the constraints in the collection. The key methods and properties are described in Tables 2-12 and 2-13.

Table 2-12. ConstraintCollection key methods

Method	Description
Add( )	Adds a `Constraint` to the `ConstraintCollection`. This method has five overloads used to add constraints to the collection.
	The first overload adds a `Constraint` object to the constraint collection:
	`Add(Constraint constraint)`
	The next two methods create and add unique constraints to the constraint collection:
	`Add(string name, DataColumn col, bool isPrimaryKey)` `Add(string name, DataColumn[] cols, bool isPrimaryKey)`
	Where:
	name The name of the unique constraint.
	col The column that is uniquely constrained.
	cols The array of columns that are uniquely constrained.
	isPrimaryKey Specifies whether the column or columns represent the primary key for the table.
	The last two methods create and add foreign key constraints to the constraint collection:
	`Add(string name, DataColumn parentCol, DataColumn childCol)` `Add(string name, DataColumn[] parentCols, DataColumn[] childCols)`
	Where:
	name The name of the foreign key constraint.
	parentCol The primary key (parent) column.
	childCol The foreign key (child) column.
	parentCols The array of primary key (parent) columns.
	childCols The array of foreign key (child) columns.
AddRange( )	Copies members of a `Constraint` array to the end of a `ConstraintCollection`.
CanRemove( )	Returns whether a `Constraint` can be removed from a `ConstraintCollection`.
Clear( )	Clears the `ConstraintCollection` of all constraints, both unique and foreign key.
Contains( )	Returns whether a `ConstraintCollection` contains a `Constraint` with a specified `ConstraintName`.

Table 2-12. ConstraintCollection key methods (continued)

Method	Description
CopyTo( )	Copies all elements of the ConstraintCollection to a one-dimensional Constraint array or to an Array object.
IndexOf( )	Returns the zero-based index the Constraint specified by a ConstraintName or a Constraint object. –1 is returned if the column does not exist in the collection.
Remove( )	Removes a Constraint specified by the ConstraintName or by a Constraint object from the ConstraintCollection.
RemoveAt( )	Removes a Constraint at the specified index from the ConstraintCollection.

Table 2-13. ConstraintCollection key properties

Property	Description
Count	Gets the number of constraints in the collection.
indexer	Gets the Constraint object specified by an ordinal or ConstraintName value.

2.7   Creating Single- and Multi-Column Primary Keys

Problem

You need to add a primary key to a table.

Solution

Either set the PrimaryKey property of the DataTable or add a primary key UniqueConstraint to the table.

The solution shows three techniques:

- Adding a one-column primary key by setting the PrimaryKey property of the DataTable.

- Adding a one-column primary key by creating a primary key UniqueConstraint and adding it to the constraints collection of the DataTable.

- Adding a two-column primary key by creating and adding a primary key UniqueConstraint directly to the DataTable.

In each case, information about the added primary key is output to the console.

The C# code in *Program.cs* in the project CreatePrimaryKey is shown in Example 2-7.

Example 2-7. File: Program.cs for CreatePrimaryKey solution

```
using System;
using System.Data;

namespace CreatePrimaryKey
{
    class Program
```

Example 2-7. File: Program.cs for CreatePrimaryKey solution (continued)

```csharp
{
    static void Main(string[] args)
    {
        // Create a table that will have a single-column constraint
        DataTable dt1 = new DataTable("Table-1");
        // Add two columns
        DataColumn pkCol = dt1.Columns.Add("Id", typeof(int));
        dt1.Columns.Add("Field1", typeof(string)).MaxLength = 50;
        // Set the primary key using the PrimaryKey
        dt1.PrimaryKey = new DataColumn[] { pkCol };
        // Output the properties of the table constraint added
        OutputConstraintProperties(dt1);
        Console.WriteLine();

        // Create a table that will have a single-column constraint
        DataTable dt2 = new DataTable("Table-2");
        // Add two columns
        dt2.Columns.Add("Id", typeof(int));
        dt2.Columns.Add("Field1", typeof(string)).MaxLength = 50;
        // Create the constraint
        UniqueConstraint uc =
            new UniqueConstraint("PrimaryKey-2", dt2.Columns["Id"], true);
        // Add the constraint to the table
        dt2.Constraints.Add(uc);
        // Output the properties of the table constraint added
        OutputConstraintProperties(dt2);
        Console.WriteLine();

        // Create a table that will have a multi-column constraint
        DataTable dt3 = new DataTable("Table-3");
        // Add two columns
        dt3.Columns.Add("Id1", typeof(int));
        dt3.Columns.Add("Id2", typeof(int));
        dt3.Columns.Add("Field1", typeof(string)).MaxLength = 50;
        // Add a constraint directly to the table
        dt3.Constraints.Add("PrimaryKey-3",
            new DataColumn[] { dt3.Columns["Id1"], dt3.Columns["Id2"] },
            true);
        // Output the properties of the table constraint added
        OutputConstraintProperties(dt3);

        Console.WriteLine("\nPress any key to continue.");
        Console.ReadKey();
    }

    private static void OutputConstraintProperties(DataTable dt)
    {
        Console.WriteLine("DataTable {0} => Constraint properties: ",
            dt.TableName);
        Console.WriteLine("\tName = ", dt.Constraints[0].ConstraintName);
        Console.WriteLine("\tIsPrimaryKey = {0}",
            ((UniqueConstraint)dt.Constraints[0]).IsPrimaryKey);
```

Example 2-7. File: Program.cs for CreatePrimaryKey solution (continued)

```
            Console.WriteLine("\tColumns: ");
            foreach (DataColumn col in
                ((UniqueConstraint)dt.Constraints[0]).Columns)
            {
                Console.WriteLine("\t\t{0}", col.ColumnName);
            }
        }
    }
}
```

The output is shown in Figure 2-7.

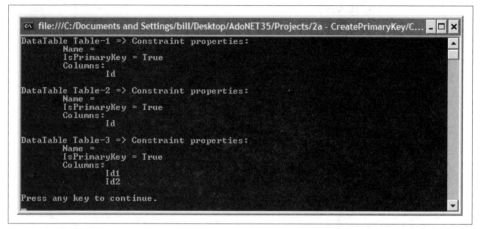

Figure 2-7. Output for CreatePrimaryKey solution

Discussion

The `PrimaryKey` property of the `DataTable` is used to set or get the primary key for a table as shown in the following examples.

```
DataColumn[] pka = DataTable.PrimaryKey;    // get
DataTable.PrimaryKey = pka;                 // set
```

Where:

pka

    An array of columns making up the primary key.

Setting the `PrimaryKey` property creates a `UniqueConstraint` on the column or columns specified within the `DataTable`.

Alternatively, and as the solution shows, you can create a primary key by adding a `UniqueConstraint` with `IsPrimaryKey` property true to a `DataTable`. For more information about unique constraints, see Recipe 2.6.

2.8   Creating an Autoincrementing Primary Key

Problem

You need to create a primary key on a single column in a table that increments its value automatically for each new row.

Solution

Create a primary key and set the `AutoIncrement`, `AutoIncrementSeed`, and `AutoIncrementStep` properties of the column.

The solution creates a table with two columns. The first column is made of the primary key that increments automatically as rows are added, starting with 100 and incrementing by 10 for each new record. Records are added to the table and the contents of the table are output to the console.

The C# code in *Program.cs* in the project `CreateAutoIncrementColumn` is shown in Example 2-8.

Example 2-8. File: Program.cs for CreateAutoIncrementColumn solution

```
using System;
using System.Data;

namespace CreateAutoIncrementColumn
{
    class Program
    {
        static void Main(string[] args)
        {
            // Create a table and add two columns
            DataTable dt = new DataTable( );
            DataColumn pkCol = dt.Columns.Add("Id", typeof(int));
            dt.Columns.Add("Field1", typeof(string)).MaxLength = 50;

            // Make the Id column the primary key
            dt.PrimaryKey = new DataColumn[] {dt.Columns["Id"]};

            // Make the primary key autoincrementing starting at 100
            // and incrementing by 10 with each new record added
            pkCol.AutoIncrement = true;
            pkCol.AutoIncrementSeed = 100;
            pkCol.AutoIncrementStep = 10;

            // Add five rows to the table
            for (int i = 1; i <= 5; i++)
                dt.Rows.Add(new object[] {null, "Value " + i });
```

Example 2-8. File: Program.cs for CreateAutoIncrementColumn solution (continued)

```
            // Output the table rows to the console
            foreach (DataRow row in dt.Rows)
                Console.WriteLine("Id = {0}\tField1 = {1}",
                    row["Id"], row["Field1"]);

            Console.WriteLine("\nPress any key to continue.");
            Console.ReadKey( );
        }
    }
}
```

The output is shown in Figure 2-8.

Figure 2-8. Output for CreateAutoIncrementColumn solution

Discussion

A `DataColumn` object has three properties that manage its autoincrementing properties. These are shown in Table 2-14.

Table 2-14. DataColumn properties for managing autoincrement

Property	Description
AutoIncrement	Gets or sets whether the column automatically increments its value with each new row added.
AutoIncrementSeed	Gets or sets the starting value for an autoincrementing column.
AutoIncrementStep	Gets or sets the increment from the previous value for each new value of an autoincrementing column.

Notice that when adding rows with an autoincrementing column, you pass `null` as the column when adding a row to the table using the `Add( )` method of the `DataRowCollection`:

```
    dt.Rows.Add(new object[] {null, "Value " + i });
```

The value assigned to the autoincrement column is available in the `DataRow` object row returned by the `Add( )` method. The above line of code could be rewritten:

```
    DataRow newRow;
    newRow = dt.Rows.Add(new object[] {null, "Value " + i });
```

You can now access the autoincrement value for a row by accessing `row["Id"]`.

See Recipe 5.1 for information about using and synchronizing autoincrementing columns with underlying data sources.

2.9   Creating a Foreign Key Constraint

Problem

You need to create a foreign key constraint on one or more columns in a table to implement referential integrity between parent and child tables.

Solution

Use the System.Data.ForeignConstraint class.

The solution creates a DataSet containing two tables and adds a foreign key constraint. Rows are added to both parent and child tables, including a row that violates the constraint. The results are output to the console.

The C# code in *Program.cs* in the project CreateForeignKeyConstraint is shown in Example 2-9.

Example 2-9. File: Program.cs forCreateForeignKeyConstraint solution

```
using System;
using System.Data;

namespace CreateForeignKeyConstraint
{
    class Program
    {
        static void Main(string[] args)
        {
            DataSet ds = new DataSet( );

            // Create the parent table and add to the DataSet
            DataTable dt1 = new DataTable("Table-1");
            dt1.Columns.Add("Id1", typeof(int));
            dt1.Columns.Add("Field1", typeof(string)).MaxLength = 50;
            ds.Tables.Add(dt1);

            // Create the child table and add to the DataSet
            DataTable dt2 = new DataTable("Table-2");
            dt2.Columns.Add("Id2", typeof(int));
            dt2.Columns.Add("Id1", typeof(int));
            dt2.Columns.Add("Field2", typeof(string)).MaxLength = 50;
            ds.Tables.Add(dt2);

            // Create the foreign key constraint and add to the
            // child table
            ForeignKeyConstraint fk = new ForeignKeyConstraint(
                "ForeignKey", dt1.Columns["Id1"], dt2.Columns["Id1"]);
            dt2.Constraints.Add(fk);

            try
            {
```

Example 2-9. File: Program.cs forCreateForeignKeyConstraint solution (continued)

```
                AddParentRecord(dt1, 1, "Value 1.1");
                AddParentRecord(dt1, 2, "Value 1.2");

                AddChildRecord(dt2, 10, 1, "Value 2.10");
                AddChildRecord(dt2, 11, 2, "Value 2.11");
                AddChildRecord(dt2, 12, 3, "Value 2.12");
            }
            catch (Exception ex)
            {
                Console.WriteLine("Error: {0}\n", ex.Message);
            }

            Console.WriteLine("Press any key to continue.");
            Console.ReadKey( );
        }

        private static void AddParentRecord(
            DataTable dt, int id1, string field1)
        {
            Console.WriteLine("Adding parent record: {0}, {1}",
                id1, field1);
            dt.Rows.Add(new object[] { id1, field1 });
            Console.WriteLine("Done.\n");
        }

        private static void AddChildRecord(
            DataTable dt, int id2, int id1, string field2)
        {
            Console.WriteLine("Add child record: {0}, {1}, {2}",
                id2, id1, field2);
            dt.Rows.Add(new object[] { id2, id1, field2 });
            Console.WriteLine("Done.\n");
        }
    }
}
```

The output is shown in Figure 2-9.

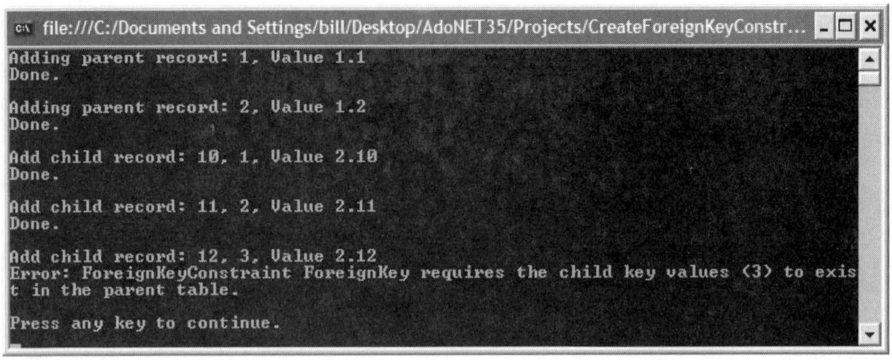

Figure 2-9. Output for CreateForeignKeyConstraint solution

Discussion

A foreign key constraint is a restriction on a set of columns in a primary/foreign key relationship when rows are added to, updated, or deleted.

The `System.Data.Constraint` class is an abstract class that is the base class for the two .NET Framework built-in constraint classes:

`System.Data.UniqueConstraint`

> Ensures that all data in the specified column or columns in the row is unique within the collection of columns, generally in a table. Defining a primary key for a `DataTable` by setting the `PrimaryKey` property automatically creates a unique constraint for the specified column or columns.

`System.Data.ForeignKeyConstraint`

> Enforces rules about how updates of values in rows or row deletions are propagated to related tables through the `DeleteRule` and `UpdateRule` properties, which define the action to be taken.

By default, a `UniqueConstraint` is created on the parent table and a `ForeignKeyConstraint` is created on the child table when a `DataRelation` object relating the two tables is created. Constraints are only enforced if the `EnforceConstraints` property of the `DataSet` is true, which is the default value. For more information about unique constraints, see Recipe 2.6. For more information about data relations, see Recipe 2.10.

The `ForeignKeyConstraint` constructor has six overloads:

```
ForeignKeyConstraint(DataColumn parentCol, DataColumn childCol)
ForeignKeyConstraint(DataColumn[] parentCols, DataColumn[] childCols)
ForeignKeyConstraint(string constraintName, DataColumn parentCol,
    DataColumn childCol)
ForeignKeyConstraint(string constraintName, DataColumn[] parentCols,
    DataColumn[] childCols)
ForeignKeyConstraint(string constraintName, string parentTableName,
    String[] parentColumnNames, string[] childColumnNames,
    AcceptRejectRule acceptRejectRule, Rule deleteRule, Rule updateRule)
ForeignKeyConstraint(string constraintName, string parentTableName,
    String parentTableNamespace,
    String[] parentColumnNames, string[] childColumnNames,
    AcceptRejectRule acceptRejectRule, Rule deleteRule, Rule updateRule)
```

Where:

parentCol

> The parent column in the constraint.

childCol

> The child column in the constraint.

parentCols

> The array of parent columns in the constraint.

childCols

The array of child columns in the constraint.

constraintName

The name of the constraint.

parentTableName

The name of the table containing the parent columns.

parentColumnNames

The array of column names in the parent table.

childColumnNames

The array of column names in the child table.

parentTableNamespace

The namespace of the parent table.

acceptRejectRule

A value that determines the action that occurs when the AcceptChanges( ) or RejectChanges( ) method is called on a table with a foreign key constraint. One of either None or Cascade. The default is None.

deleteRule

A rule that is applied when a row is deleted. One of either Cascade, None, SetDefault, or SetNull. The default is Cascade.

updateRule

A rule that is applied when a row is updated. One of either Cascade, None, SetDefault, or SetNull. The default is Cascade.

The ForeignKeyConstraint class exposes properties used to configure the constraint as described in Table 2-15.

Table 2-15. ForeignKey configuration properties

Property	Description
AcceptRejectRule	Gets or sets the action that occurs when the AcceptChanges( ) or RejectChanges( ) method is called on a table with a foreign key constraint. One of either None or Cascade from the AcceptRejectRule enumeration.
Columns	Gets the child columns of the constraint as an array of DataColumn objects.
ConstraintName	Gets or sets the name of the constraint.
DeleteRule	Gets or sets the rule that is applied when a row is deleted. One of either Cascade, None, SetDefault, or SetNull from the Rule enumeration. The default is Cascade.
ExtendedProperties	Gets or sets user custom information associated with the constraint.
RelatedColumns	Gets the parent columns of the constraint as an array of DataColumn objects.
RelatedTable	Gets the parent table of the constraint as a DataTable object.
Table	Gets the child table of the constraint as a DataTable object.
UpdateRule	Gets or sets the rule that is applied when a row is updated. One of either Cascade, None, SetDefault, or SetNull from the Rule enumeration. The default is Cascade.

The `ConstraintCollection` collection contains a set of constraints for a `DataTable`, both `UniqueConstraint` and `ForeignKeyConstraint` objects. The `DataTable` has a constraint collection accessed through the `Constraints` property of the `DataTable` object—you use this property to access and manage the constraints for the `DataTable`. The `ConstaintCollection` has members that are used to manage the constraints in the collection. The key methods and properties are described in Tables 2-11 and 2-12 in Recipe 2.6.

2.10   Creating a Data Relation

Problem

You need to create a parent/child relation between two tables.

Solution

Use the `System.Data.DataRelation` class.

The solution creates a `DataSet` with two tables. A data relation is added to the `DataSet` establishing a parent/child relationship between the tables. Rows are added to both parent and child tables, including a row that violates the constraint. The results are output to the console.

The C# code in *Program.cs* in the project `CreateDataRelation` is shown in Example 2-10.

Example 2-10. File: Program.cs forCreateDataRelation solution

```
using System;
using System.Data;

namespace CreateDataRelation
{
    class Program
    {
        static void Main(string[] args)
        {
            DataSet ds = new DataSet( );

            // Create the parent table and add to the DataSet
            DataTable dt1 = new DataTable("Table-1");
            dt1.Columns.Add("Id1", typeof(int));
            dt1.Columns.Add("Id2", typeof(int));
            dt1.Columns.Add("Field1", typeof(string)).MaxLength = 50;
            ds.Tables.Add(dt1);

            // Create the child table and add to the DataSet
            DataTable dt2 = new DataTable("Table-2");
            dt2.Columns.Add("Id3", typeof(int));
            dt2.Columns.Add("Id1", typeof(int));
```

Example 2-10. File: Program.cs forCreateDataRelation solution (continued)

```csharp
        dt2.Columns.Add("Id2", typeof(int));
        dt2.Columns.Add("Field2", typeof(string)).MaxLength = 50;
        ds.Tables.Add(dt2);

        // Create the data relation and add to the DataSet
        DataRelation dr = new DataRelation("DataRelation",
            new DataColumn[] { dt1.Columns["Id1"], dt1.Columns["Id2"] },
            new DataColumn[] { dt2.Columns["Id1"], dt2.Columns["Id2"] },
            true);
        ds.Relations.Add(dr);

        try
        {
            AddParentRecord(dt1, 1,10, "Value 1.1");
            AddParentRecord(dt1, 2,20, "Value 1.2");

            AddChildRecord(dt2, 100, 1,10, "Value 2.100");
            AddChildRecord(dt2, 101, 2,20, "Value 2.101");
            AddChildRecord(dt2, 102, 3,30, "Value 2.102");
        }
        catch (Exception ex)
        {
            Console.WriteLine("Error: {0}\n", ex.Message);
        }

        Console.WriteLine("Press any key to continue.");
        Console.ReadKey();
    }

    private static void AddParentRecord(
        DataTable dt, int id1, int id2, string field1)
    {
        Console.WriteLine("Adding parent record: {0}, {1}, {2}",
            id1, id2, field1);
        dt.Rows.Add(new object[] { id1, id2, field1 });
        Console.WriteLine("Done.\n");
    }

    private static void AddChildRecord(
        DataTable dt, int id3, int id1, int id2, string field2)
    {
        Console.WriteLine("Add child record: {0}, {1}, {2}, {3}",
            id3, id1, id2, field2);
        dt.Rows.Add(new object[] { id3, id1, id2, field2 });
        Console.WriteLine("Done.\n");
    }
  }
}
```

The output is shown in Figure 2-10.

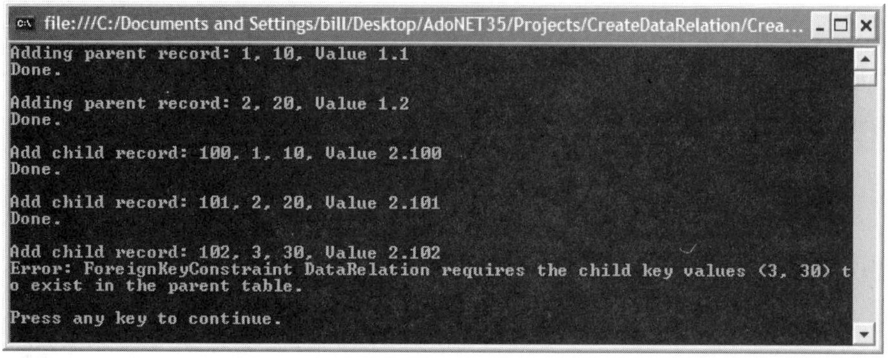

Figure 2-10. Output for CreateDataRelation solution

Discussion

A data relation represents a parent/child relationship between two tables.

The `System.Data.DataRelation` class relates two `DataTable` objects in a `DataSet` through `DataColumn` objects in the parent and child tables. The data values for columns in the matching columns in the parent and child tables must be of identical data types. Data relationships can be used to cascade changes from the parent to the child by specifying the `DeleteRule`, `UpdateRule`, and `AcceptRejectRule` of the `ForeignKeyConstraint` that is accessed through the `ChildConstraint` property of the `DataRelation`.

By default, a `UniqueConstraint` is created on the parent table and a `ForeignKeyConstraint` is created on the child table when a `DataRelation` object relating the two tables is created. You change this behavior by setting the Boolean `createConstraints` argument to `false` in the `DataRelation` constructor.

The `DataRelation` constructor has six overloads:

```
DataRelation(string relationName, DataColumn parentCol, DataColumn childCol)
DataRelation(string relationName, DataColumn[] parentCols, DataColumn[] childCols)
DataRelation(string relationName, DataColumn parentCol, DataColumn childCol, bool
createConstraints)
DataRelation(string relationName, DataColumn[] parentCols, DataColumn[] childCols,
bool createConstraints)
DataRelation(string relationName, string parentTableName, string childTableName,
string[] parentColumnNames, string[] childColumnNames, bool isNested)
DataRelation(string relationName, string parentTableName, string
parentTableNamespace, string childTableName, string childTableNamespace, string[]
parentColumnNames, string[] childColumnNames, bool isNested)
```

Where:

relationName
> The name of the data relation.

parentCol
> The parent DataColumn in the relationship.

childCol
> The child DataColumn in the relationship.

parentCols
> The array of parent DataColumn objects in the relationship.

childCols
> The array of child DataColumn objects in the relationship.

createConstraints
> Indicates whether to automatically create a UniqueConstraint on the parent table and a ForeignKeyConstraint on the child table when the DataRelation object is created.

parentTableName
> The name of the parent table in the relationship

childTableName
> The name of the child table in the relationship.

parentColumnNames
> An array of names of parent columns in the relationship.

childColumnNames
> An array of names of child columns in the relationship.

isNested
> Indicates whether relationships are nested.

parentTableNamespace
> The namespace of the parent table in the relationship.

childTableNamespace
> The namespace of the child table in the relationship.

The DataRelationCollection is a collection that contains a set of data relations. The DataSet has a DataRelationCollection that is accessed through the DataRelations property of the DataSet. The DataRelationCollection has members that are used to manage the data relations in the collection. The key methods and properties are discussed in Tables 2-16 and 2-17.

Table 2-16. DataRelationCollection key methods

Method	Description
Add( )	Adds a DataRelation to the DataRelationCollection. This method has the following overloads used to add data relations to the collection:
	Add(DataRelation *dataRelation*) Add(DataColumn *parentCol*, DataColumn *childCol*) Add(DataColumn[] *parentCols*, DataColumn *childCols*) Add(string *name*, DataColumn *parentCol*, DataColumn *childCol*) Add(string *name*, DataColumn[] *parentCols*, DataColumn *childCols*) Add(string *name*, DataColumn *parentCol*, DataColumn *childCol*, bool *createConstraints*) Add(string *name*, DataColumn[] *parentCols*, DataColumn *childCols*, bool *createConstraints*)
	Where:
	dataRelation A DataRelation object.
	parentCol The parent column in the data relationship.
	childCol The child column in the data relationship.
	parentCols The array of parent columns in the data relationship.
	childCols The array of child columns in the data relationship.
	name The name of the data relationship.
	createConstraints Indicates whether to create constraints.
AddRange( )	Copies members of a DataRelation array to the end of a DataRelationCollection.
CanRemove( )	Returns whether a DataRelation can be removed from a DataRelationCollection.
Clear( )	Clears the DataRelationCollection of all data relations.
Contains( )	Returns whether a DataRelationCollection contains a DataRelation with a specified RelationName.
CopyTo( )	Copies all elements of the DataRelationCollection to a one-dimensional DataRelation array or to an Array object.
IndexOf( )	Returns the zero-based index the DataRelation specified by a RelationName or a DataRelation object. –1 is returned if the column does not exist in the collection.
Remove( )	Removes a DataRelation specified by the RelationName or by a DataRelation object from the DataRelationCollection.
RemoveAt( )	Removes a DataRelation at the specified index from the DataRelationCollection.

Table 2-17. DataRelationCollection key properties

Property	Description
Count	Gets the number of data relations in the collection.
indexer	Gets the DataRelation object specified by an ordinal or RelationName value.

2.11   Building a DataSet Programmatically

Problem

You want to build a DataSet programmatically—including adding tables, columns, primary keys, and relations—from a schema that you have designed.

Solution

The following example shows how to build a complex DataSet programmatically, including how to build and add tables, columns, primary key constraints, relations, and column mappings. Use this as a template for building your own DataSet.

The solution creates a DataSet. A DataTable object containing sales order header data is created. Columns are added, including the autoincrement primary key, to the table. The table is added to the DataSet. The process is repeated for a DataTable containing sales order detail data. A DataRelation is created relating the two tables. Finally, the tables are filled with data from the Sales.SalesOrderHeader and Sales.SalesOrderDetail data from the AdventureWorks database using a DataAdapter. Data from the DataSet is output to the console.

The C# code in *Program.cs* in the project BuildDataSetProgrammatically is shown in Example 2-11.

Example 2-11. File: Program.cs for BuildDataSetProgramatically solution

```
using System;
using System.Data;
using System.Data.SqlClient;

namespace BuildDataSetProgrammatically
{
    class Program
    {
        static void Main(string[] args)
        {
            DataSet ds = new DataSet("SalesOrders");

            // Build the SaleOrderHeader (parent) table
            DataTable dtHeader = new DataTable("SalesOrderHeader");

            // Get the collection of columns for the parent table
            DataColumnCollection cols = dtHeader.Columns;
```

Example 2-11. File: Program.cs for BuildDataSetProgramatically solution (continued)

```
// Add the identity field.
DataColumn col = cols.Add("SalesOrderID", typeof(System.Int32));
col.AutoIncrement = true;
col.AutoIncrementSeed = -1;
col.AutoIncrementStep = -1;
// Add other fields
cols.Add("OrderDate", typeof(System.DateTime)).AllowDBNull = false;
cols.Add("SalesOrderNumber", typeof(System.String)).MaxLength = 25;
cols.Add("TotalDue", typeof(System.Decimal));
// Set the primary key.
dtHeader.PrimaryKey = new DataColumn[] {cols["SalesOrderID"]};
// Add the SalesOrderHeader table to the DataSet.
ds.Tables.Add(dtHeader);

// Build the Order Details (child) table.
DataTable dtDetail = new DataTable("SalesOrderDetail");

cols = dtDetail.Columns;
// Add the PK fields.
cols.Add("SalesOrderID", typeof(System.Int32)).AllowDBNull = false;

col = cols.Add("SalesOrderDetailID", typeof(System.Int32));
col.AutoIncrement = true;
col.AutoIncrementSeed = -1;
col.AutoIncrementStep = -1;
// Add the other fields.
cols.Add("UnitPrice", typeof(System.Decimal)).AllowDBNull = false;
cols.Add("OrderQty", typeof(System.Int16)).AllowDBNull = false;
cols.Add("LineTotal", typeof(System.Decimal));
// Set the primary key.
dtDetail.PrimaryKey = new DataColumn[]
    { cols["OrderID"], cols["ProductID"] };
// Add the Order Details table to the DataSet.
ds.Tables.Add(dtDetail);

// Add the relation between header and detail tables
ds.Relations.Add("SalesOrderHeader_SalesOrderDetail",
    dtHeader.Columns["SalesOrderID"], dtDetail.Columns["SalesOrderID"]);

// Fill the DataSet
string sqlConnectString = "Data Source=(local);" +
    "Integrated security=SSPI;Initial Catalog=AdventureWorks;";

string sqlSelect =
    @"SELECT SalesOrderID, OrderDate, SalesOrderNumber, TotalDue
    FROM Sales.SalesOrderHeader
    SELECT SalesOrderID, SalesOrderDetailID, UnitPrice, OrderQty, LineTotal
    FROM Sales.SalesOrderDetail;";

SqlDataAdapter da = new SqlDataAdapter(sqlSelect, sqlConnectString);
da.TableMappings.Add("Table", "SalesOrderHeader");
da.TableMappings.Add("Table1", "SalesOrderDetail");
da.Fill(ds);
```

Example 2-11. File: Program.cs for BuildDataSetProgramatically solution (continued)

```csharp
// Output the first three orders with detail for each
for (int i = 0; i < 3; i++)
{
    DataRow row = ds.Tables["SalesOrderHeader"].Rows[i];
    Console.WriteLine("{0}\t{1}\t{2}\t{3}",
        row[0], row[1], row[2], row[3]);

    foreach (DataRow rowChild
        in row.GetChildRows("SalesOrderHeader_SalesOrderDetail"))
    {
        Console.WriteLine("\t{0}\t{1}\t{2}\t{3}\t{4}",
            rowChild[0], rowChild[1], rowChild[2], rowChild[3], rowChild[4]);
    }
}

Console.WriteLine("\nPress any key to continue.");
Console.ReadKey();
```

The output is shown in Figure 2-11.

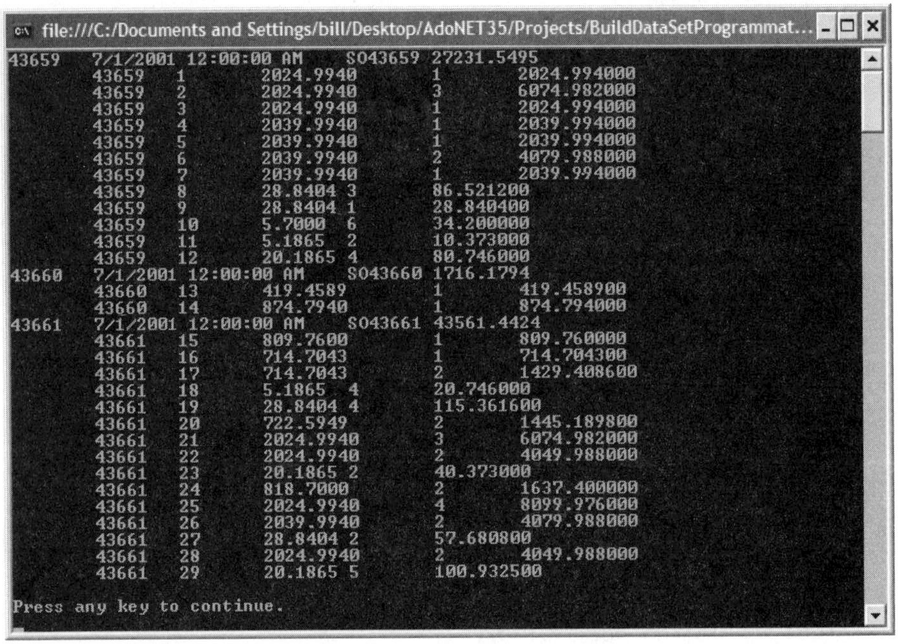

Figure 2-11. Output for BuildDataSetProgrammatically solution

Discussion

The steps to build a complex `DataSet` programmatically, as shown in the code for the solution, are:

1. Design the `DataSet` identifying the tables, columns, indexes, constraints, and data relations that need to be created.

2. Create a new `DataSet`, naming it in the constructor.

3. Create a new `DataTable`, naming it in the constructor.

4. Add a column to the `ColumnCollection` of the table using the `Add( )` method exposed by the `Columns` property of the `DataTable` specifying the name and data type of the column. If the column is a character-type column, define its maximum length. If the column is an autoincrement column, set the `AutoIncrement` property to `true` and set both the `AutoIncrementSeed` and `AutoIncrementStep` properties of the column to `-1`. (For more information about using autoincrement columns, see Recipe 5.1). Repeat Step 4 for each column in the table.

5. Define the primary key for the table by setting the `PrimaryKey` property of the `DataTable` to the array of primary key `DataColumn` objects.

6. Add the new table to the `DataSet` using the `Add( )` method of the `DataTableCollection` exposed by the `Tables` property of the `DataSet`.

7. Repeat Steps 3–6 for each table in the `DataSet`.

8. Create a data relationship between two related tables in the `DataSet` by using the `Add( )` method of the `DataRelationCollection` exposed by the `Relations` property of the `DataSet`. Specify the relationship name, the related columns, and whether constraints are to be created when calling the `Add( )` method. Repeat Step 8 for each data relationship in the `DataSet`.

The steps continue, demonstrating how to fill the new `DataSet`:

1. To fill the `DataSet` with data from the data source, create a `DataAdapter` defining the batch SQL `SELECT` statement and the connection string in the constructor.

2. Add table mappings to the `DataAdapter`.

3. Execute the `Fill( )` method of the `DataAdapter` to fill the `DataSet` with the result sets.

See Recipe 3.15 for information about how to fill related tables from the data source without raising constraint violation errors. Details about batch T-SQL queries and column mappings are described in Recipes 2.3 and 3.13.

Details about creating and using specific disconnected ADO.NET objects used in this solution are described in detail in previous sections of this chapter.

2.12 Adding a Column to a Child DataTable That Displays Data from the Parent Table

Problem

You want to add a column to a DataTable that displays a value from a row in a related table in the DataSet.

Solution

Use expression columns to retrieve lookup values based on DataRelation objects.

The solution creates a new DataSet containing the Sales.SalesOrderHeader and Sales.SalesOrderDetail tables from AdventureWorks. A DataRelation is created between the tables. A column is added to the Sales.SalesOrderDetail table that gets the CustomerID from the parent Sales.SalesOrderHeader table using the relation between the tables. Parent and child rows are output to the console.

The C# code in *Program.cs* in the project AddParentColumnDataTable is shown in Example 2-12.

Example 2-12. File: Program.cs for AddParentColumnDataTable solution

```
using System;
using System.Data;
using System.Data.SqlClient;

namespace AddParentColumnDataTable
{
    class Program
    {
        static void Main(string[] args)
        {
            string sqlConnectString = "Data Source=(local);" +
                "Integrated security=SSPI;Initial Catalog=AdventureWorks;";

            string sqlSelect = @"SELECT * FROM Sales.SalesOrderHeader;
                SELECT * FROM Sales.SalesOrderDetail;";

            DataSet ds = new DataSet();

            // Fill the DataSet
            SqlDataAdapter da = new SqlDataAdapter(sqlSelect, sqlConnectString);
            da.TableMappings.Add("Table", "SalesOrderHeader");
            da.TableMappings.Add("Table1", "SalesOrderDetail");
            da.Fill(ds);

            // Relate the Header and Order tables in the DataSet
            DataRelation dr = new DataRelation("SalesOrderHeader_SalesOrderDetail",
                ds.Tables["SalesOrderHeader"].Columns["SalesOrderID"],
                ds.Tables["SalesOrderDetail"].Columns["SalesOrderID"]);
            ds.Relations.Add(dr);
```

Example 2-12. File: Program.cs for AddParentColumnDataTable solution (continued)

```
        // Add the CustomerID column from SalesOrderHeader to
        // the SalesOrderDetail table
        ds.Tables["SalesOrderDetail"].Columns.Add("CustomerID", typeof(int),
            "Parent(SalesOrderHeader_SalesOrderDetail).CustomerID");

        // Output fields from first three header rows with detail
        for (int i = 0; i < 3; i++)
        {
            DataRow rowHeader = ds.Tables["SalesOrderHeader"].Rows[i];
            Console.WriteLine("HEADER: OrderID = {0}, CustomerID = {1}",
                rowHeader["SalesOrderID"], rowHeader["CustomerID"]);

            foreach (DataRow rowDetail in rowHeader.GetChildRows(dr))
            {
                Console.WriteLine("\tDETAIL: OrderID = {0}, DetailID = {1}, " +
                    "CustomerID = {2}",
                    rowDetail["SalesOrderID"], rowDetail["SalesOrderDetailID"],
                    rowDetail["CustomerID"]);
            }
        }

        Console.WriteLine("\nPress any key to continue.");
        Console.ReadKey( );
    }
}
}
```

The output is shown in Figure 2-12.

Discussion

An expression column creates a calculated column that displays information from a related record. You can refer to a column in a parent record by appending the prefix Parent. to the beginning of the name of the column in the parent table. If there are multiple parent records because of multiple data relations, the name of the DataRelation is specified within parentheses and the prefix Parent(*DataRelationName*). is appended to the name of the column in the parent table.

The solution creates a calculated column in the Sales.SalesOrderDetail table retrieving the CustomerID from the parent Sales.SalesOrderHeader record for each detail record:

```
ds.Tables["SalesOrderDetail"].Columns.Add("CustomerID", typeof(int),
    "Parent(SalesOrderHeader_SalesOrderDetail).CustomerID");
```

It is not necessary to specify the data relation SalesOrderHeader_SalesOrderDetail since there is only one data relation making the parent unambiguous. The data relation name is included to show how it would be written when there is more than one parent table. The code could be rewritten:

```
ds.Tables["SalesOrderDetail"].Columns.Add("CustomerID", typeof(int),
    "Parent.CustomerID");
```

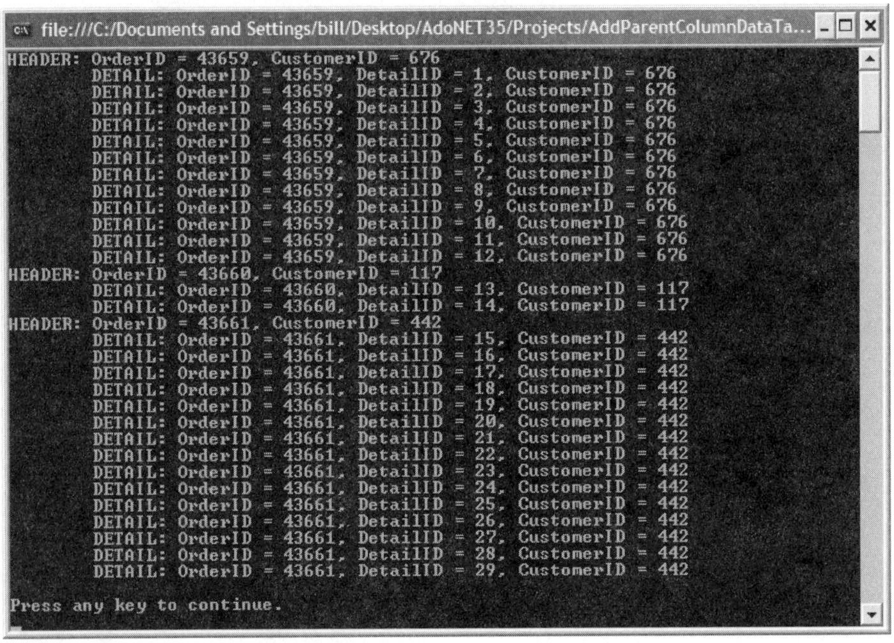

Figure 2-12. Output for AddParentColumnDataTable solution

2.13 Adding a Column to a Parent DataTable That Aggregates a Child Table's Column Values

Problem

You want to add summary information such as averages, sums, and counts to a table based on related child rows.

Solution

Use expression columns to retrieve lookup values based on `DataRelation` objects.

The solution creates a new `DataSet` containing the `Sales.SalesOrderHeader` and `Sales.SalesOrderDetail` tables from `AdventureWorks`. A `DataRelation` is created between the tables. An expression column is added to the `Sales.SalesOrderHeader` table that gets the sum of the related `LineTotal` from the child `Sales.SalesOrderDetail` table. Parent and child rows are output to the console.

The C# code in *Program.cs* in the project `AddAggregateChildColumnDataTable` is shown in Example 2-13.

Example 2-13. File: Program.cs for AddAggregateChildColumnDataTable solution

```csharp
using System;
using System.Data;
using System.Data.SqlClient;

namespace AddAggregateChildColumnDataTable
{
    class Program
    {
        static void Main(string[] args)
        {
            string sqlConnectString = "Data Source=(local);" +
                "Integrated security=SSPI;Initial Catalog=AdventureWorks;";

            string sqlSelect = @"SELECT * FROM Sales.SalesOrderHeader;
                SELECT * FROM Sales.SalesOrderDetail;";

            DataSet ds = new DataSet();

            // Fill the DataSet
            SqlDataAdapter da = new SqlDataAdapter(sqlSelect, sqlConnectString);
            da.TableMappings.Add("Table", "SalesOrderHeader");
            da.TableMappings.Add("Table1", "SalesOrderDetail");
            da.Fill(ds);

            // Relate the Header and Order tables in the DataSet
            DataRelation dr = new DataRelation("SalesOrderHeader_SalesOrderDetail",
                ds.Tables["SalesOrderHeader"].Columns["SalesOrderID"],
                ds.Tables["SalesOrderDetail"].Columns["SalesOrderID"]);
            ds.Relations.Add(dr);

            // Add a column to the SalesOrderHeader table summing all
            // LineTotal values in SalesOrderDetail
            ds.Tables["SalesOrderHeader"].Columns.Add("SumDetailLineTotal",
                typeof(decimal), "SUM(Child.LineTotal)");

            // Output fields from first three header rows with detail
            for (int i = 0; i < 3; i++)
            {
                DataRow rowHeader = ds.Tables["SalesOrderHeader"].Rows[i];
                Console.WriteLine("HEADER: OrderID = {0}, CustomerID = {1}, " +
                    "SumDetailLineTotal = {2}", rowHeader["SalesOrderID"],
                    rowHeader["CustomerID"], rowHeader["SumDetailLineTotal"]);

                foreach (DataRow rowDetail in rowHeader.GetChildRows(dr))
                {
                    Console.WriteLine("\tDETAIL: OrderID = {0}, DetailID = {1}, " +
                        "LineTotal = {2}",
                        rowDetail["SalesOrderID"], rowDetail["SalesOrderDetailID"],
                        rowDetail["LineTotal"]);
                }
            }
```

Example 2-13. File: Program.cs for AddAggregateChildColumnDataTable solution (continued)

```
            Console.WriteLine("\nPress any key to continue.");
            Console.ReadKey( );
        }
    }
}
```

The output is shown in Figure 2-13.

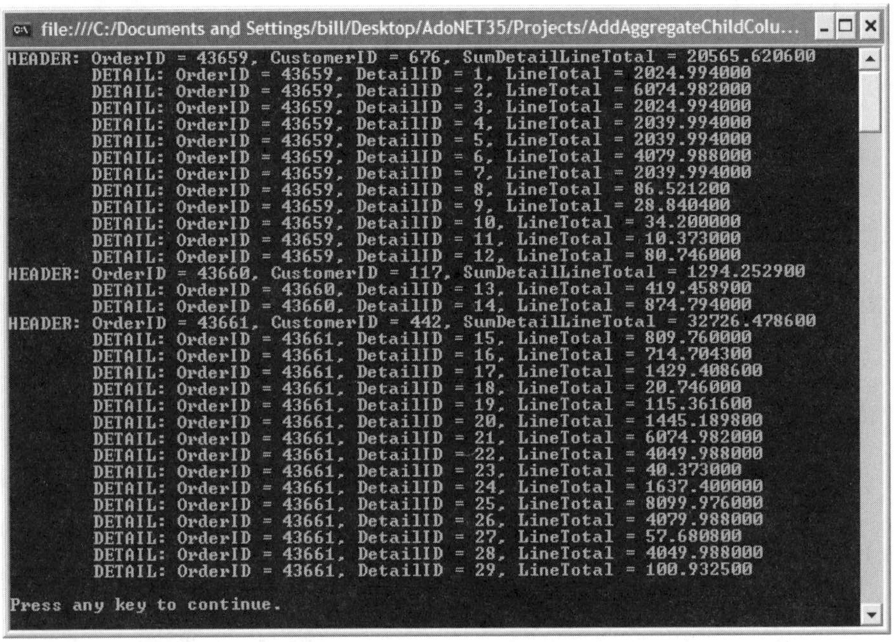

Figure 2-13. Output for AddAggregateChildColumnDataTable solution

Discussion

You can create aggregate columns within a table to display summary information for related child records. When a `DataRelation` exists between a parent and child table in a `DataSet`, you can refer to a child record by appending the prefix `Child.` to the column name in the child table. In the solution, `SUM(Child.LineTotal)` returns the sum of line total of all child `Sales.SalesOrderDetail` records in the parent `Sales.SalesOrderHeader` record. Expression columns support aggregate functions as shown in Table 2-18.

Table 2-18. Aggregate functions supported by expression columns

Function	Description
AVG	Average of all values
COUNT	Number of values
MAX	Largest value
MIN	Smallest value
STDEV	Statistical standard deviation of all values
SUM	Sum of all values
VAR	Statistical variance of all values

If the parent table has more than one child table, the relationship must be specified in the aggregate function. The fully qualified syntax to access the sum of LineTotal values for child Sales.SalesOrderDetail records would be:

```
SUM(Child("SalesOrderHeader_SalesOrderDetail").LineTotal)
```

The solution creates a calculated column in the Orders table that sums the line total for all order detail items with the following code:

```
ds.Tables["SalesOrderHeader"].Columns.Add("SumDetailLineTotal",
    typeof(decimal), "SUM(Child.LineTotal)");
```

Note that the DataRelation name is omitted in this case because only one DataRelation exists making it unnecessary.

If the parent record has no child records, the aggregate function returns a null reference in C# or Nothing in Visual Basic.

2.14 Converting Between a DataTable and a DataRow Array

Problem

You need to convert between a DataTable object and an array of DataRow objects.

Solution

Use the CopyTo( ) method of the DataRowCollection for the DataTable to convert from a DataTable to an array of DataRow objects.

Use the CopyToDataTable( ) method of the DataRow array to copy elements from a DataRow array to a DataTable.

The solution creates and fills a DataTable from the Person.Contact table in AdventureWorks. A DataRow array is created from the rows in the DataTable. Two DataTable objects are created from the DataRow array using different overloads of the CopyToDataTable( ) method of the DataRow array. Results are output to the console.

The C# code in *Program.cs* in the project ConvertBetweenDataTableAndDataRowArray is shown in Example 2-14.

Example 2-14. File: Program.cs for ConvertBetweenDataTableAndDataRowArray solution

```
using System;
using System.Data;
using System.Data.SqlClient;

namespace ConvertBetweenDataTableAndDataRowArray
{
    class Program
    {
        static void Main(string[] args)
        {
            string sqlConnectString = "Data Source=(local);" +
                "Integrated security=SSPI;Initial Catalog=AdventureWorks;";

            string sqlSelect =
                "SELECT ContactID, FirstName, LastName FROM Person.Contact " +
                "WHERE ContactID BETWEEN 10 AND 13";

            // Create a data adapter
            SqlDataAdapter da = new SqlDataAdapter(sqlSelect, sqlConnectString);

            // Fill a DataTable using DataAdapter
            DataTable dt1 = new DataTable( );
            da.Fill(dt1);

            // Output the rows from the table
            Console.WriteLine(
                "---foreach loop over DataRowCollection (DataTable 1)---");
            foreach (DataRow row in dt1.Rows)
            {
                Console.WriteLine(
                    "ContactID = {0}\tFirstName = {1}\tLastName = {2}",
                    row["ContactID"], row["FirstName"], row["LastName"]);
            }

            // Create and fill the DataRow array
            DataRow[] dra = new DataRow[dt1.Rows.Count];
            dt1.Rows.CopyTo(dra, 0);

            Console.WriteLine("\n---for loop over DataRow array---");
            for (int i = 0; i < dra.Length; i++)
```

Example 2-14. File: Program.cs for ConvertBetweenDataTableAndDataRowArray solution (continued)

```
        {
            Console.WriteLine(
                "ContactID = {0}\tFirstName = {1}\tLastName = {2}",
                dra[i].Field<int>("ContactID"), dra[i].Field<string>("FirstName"),
                dra[i].Field<string>("LastName"));
        }

        // Filling a DataTable from the DataRow array using CopyToDataTable()
        DataTable dt2 = dra.CopyToDataTable();
        // Output the rows from the table
        Console.WriteLine(
            "\n---foreach loop over DataRowCollection (DataTable 2)---");
        foreach (DataRow row in dt2.Rows)
        {
            Console.WriteLine(
                "ContactID = {0}\tFirstName = {1}\tLastName = {2}",
                row["ContactID"], row["FirstName"], row["LastName"]);
        }

        // Filling a DataTable from the DataRow array using
        // CopyToDataTable(DataTable, LoadOption)
        DataTable dt3 = dt1.Clone();
        dra.CopyToDataTable(dt3, LoadOption.Upsert);
        Console.WriteLine(
            "\n---foreach loop over DataRowCollection (DataTable 3)---");
        foreach (DataRow row in dt3.Rows)
        {
            Console.WriteLine(
                "ContactID = {0}\tFirstName = {1}\tLastName = {2}",
                row["ContactID"], row["FirstName"], row["LastName"]);
        }

        Console.WriteLine("\nPress any key to continue.");
        Console.ReadKey();
    }
  }
}
```

The output is shown in Figure 2-14.

Discussion

The CopyTo() method of the DataRowCollection object copies all DataRow objects from the collection into a specified array starting at the specified index. The method has two overloads:

```
CopyTo(Array array, int index)
CopyTo(DataRow[] dataRows, int index)
```

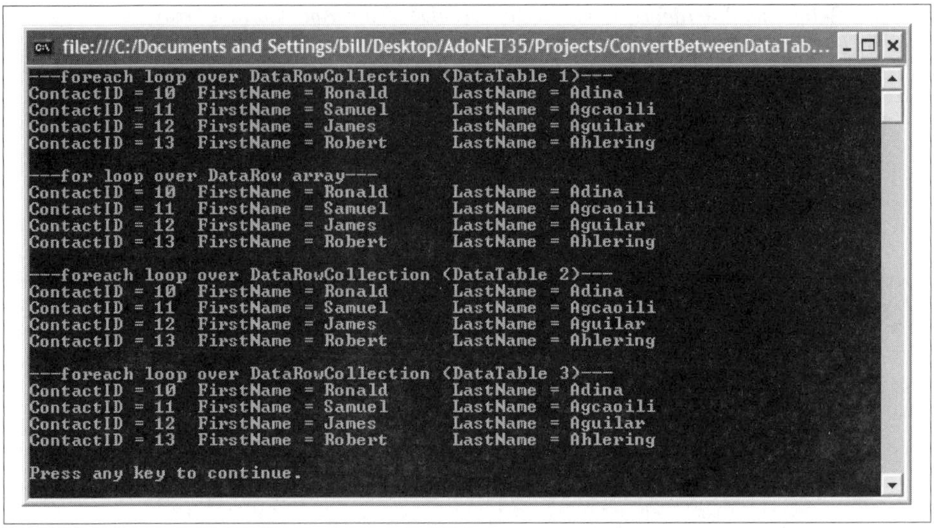

Figure 2-14. Output for ConvertBetweenDataTableAndDataRowArray solution

Where:

array
> A one-dimensional array that is the destination of the copy from the data row collection.

index
> The zero-based index in the array at which copying begins.

dataRows
> A one-dimensional array of DataRow objects that is the destination of the copy from the data row collection.

The CopyToDataTable( ) method is a member of the DataTableExtensions class—a static class that defines extension methods to the DataTable class. The method returns a DataTable containing copies of DataRow objects from an input IEnumerable<T> object, where the generic parameter T is of type DataRow. The CopyToDataTable( ) method has two overloads.

```
CopyToDataTable<T>(IEnumerable<T>)
CopyToDataTable<T>(IEnumerable<T>, DataTable dataTable, LoadOption loadOption)
```

Where:

dataTable
> Destination table.

loadOption
> Specifies how values from the source are applied to the destination. This is a value from the LoadOptions enumeration as described in Table 2-19.

Table 2-19. LoadOption enumeration

Value	Description
OverwriteChanges	The new values for the row are written to both the current and original versions of the data for each column.
PreserveChanges	The new values for the row are written to the original versions of the data for each column. This is the default.
Upsert	The new values for the row are written to the current versions of the data for each column.

The solution shows how to use both methods. The relevant code is:

```
DataTable dt2 = dra.CopyToDataTable();
```

Which uses the first method to copy the DataRow array *dra* to a new DataTable *dt2* using an assignment of the return value of the method:

```
dra.CopyToDataTable(dt3, LoadOption.Upsert);
```

Which uses the second method to copy the DataRow array dra to the DataTable *dt3* passed in as an argument to the function. The load option is specified as Upsert in this case, for no particular reason.

2.15 Accessing Data Values in a DataRow Array

Problem

You need to access the values in a DataRow array.

Solution

The solution shows five ways to access the data in a DataRow array:

- Using a column ordinal.
- Using a column name.
- Using the strongly typed accessor Field<T> with a column ordinal.
- Using the strongly typed accessor Field<T> with a column name.
- Using the strongly typed accessor Field<T> with a column name and a data row version.

The solution creates and fills a DataTable from the Person.Contact table in AdventureWorks. The DataTable is copied to a DataRow array. The value of the FirstName field for the third row is output to the console using each of the five techniques.

The C# code in *Program.cs* in the project RetrieveValuesDataRowArray is shown in Example 2-15.

Example 2-15. File: Program.cs for RetrieveValuesDataRowArray solution

```
using System;
using System.Data;
using System.Data.SqlClient;

namespace RetrieveValuesDataRowArray
{
    class Program
    {
        static void Main(string[] args)
        {
            string sqlConnectString = "Data Source=(local);" +
                "Integrated security=SSPI;Initial Catalog=AdventureWorks;";

            string sqlSelect =
                "SELECT ContactID, FirstName, LastName FROM Person.Contact " +
                "WHERE ContactID BETWEEN 10 AND 13";

            // Create a data adapter
            SqlDataAdapter da = new SqlDataAdapter(sqlSelect, sqlConnectString);

            // Fill a DataTable using DataAdapter
            DataTable dt = new DataTable( );
            da.Fill(dt);

            // Create and fill the DataRow array
            DataRow[] dra = new DataRow[dt.Rows.Count];
            dt.Rows.CopyTo(dra, 0);

            // Access DataRow array FirstName value in row 3
            // using different techniques
            Console.WriteLine("FirstName = {0}", dra[2][1]);
            Console.WriteLine("FirstName = {0}", dra[2]["FirstName"]);
            Console.WriteLine("FirstName = {0}",
                dra[2]["FirstName", DataRowVersion.Default]);
            Console.WriteLine("FirstName = {0}", dra[2].Field<string>(1));
            Console.WriteLine("FirstName = {0}",
                dra[2].Field<string>("FirstName"));
            Console.WriteLine("FirstName = {0}",
                dra[2].Field<string>("FirstName", DataRowVersion.Default));

            Console.WriteLine("\nPress any key to continue.");
            Console.ReadKey( );
        }
    }
}
```

The output is shown in Figure 2-15.

Figure 2-15. Output for RetrieveValuesDataRowArray solution

Discussion

The `Field<T>()` method from the `DataRowExtensions` class provides strongly typed access to column values in a `DataRow`. The method has six overloads:

```
Field<T>(DataRow row, DataColumn col)
Field<T>(DataRow row, int columnOrdinal)
Field<T>(DataRow row, string columnName)
Field<T>(DataRow row, DataColumn col, DataRowVersion version)
Field<T>(DataRow row, int columnOrdinal, DataRowVersion version)
Field<T>(DataRow row, string columnName, DataRowVersion version)
```

Where:

row

The input `DataRow` object.

col

The input `DataColumn` object that specifies the column for which to return a value.

columnOrdinal

The index of the column for which to return a value.

columnName

The name of the column for which to return a value.

version

The version of the `DataRow` for which to return a value. This is a value from the `DataRowVersion` enumeration—one of `Original`, `Current`, `Proposed`, or `Default`.

2.16   Creating a Strongly Typed DataSet

Problem

You want to create a strongly typed object wrapper around a `DataSet`.

Solution

Use either the Visual Studio .NET IDE or a command line approach to create a strongly typed DataSet. The solution shows both techniques in the following subsections.

Using the Visual Studio .NET IDE to generate a typed DataSet

The first and easiest method uses Visual Studio .NET following these steps:

1. Open the Visual Studio .NET IDE.

2. Create a new Visual C# Console Application named CreateStronglyTypedDataSet.

3. Right-click on the project in Solution Explorer and click Add → New Item to open the Add New Item dialog. Select DataSet from the Visual Studio installed templates. Name the DataSet *AdventureWorks.xsd*. The completed dialog is shown in Figure 2-16. Click the Add button to create the DataSet and close the dialog.

   The DataSet is added to Solution Explorer and the DataSet Designer is opened.

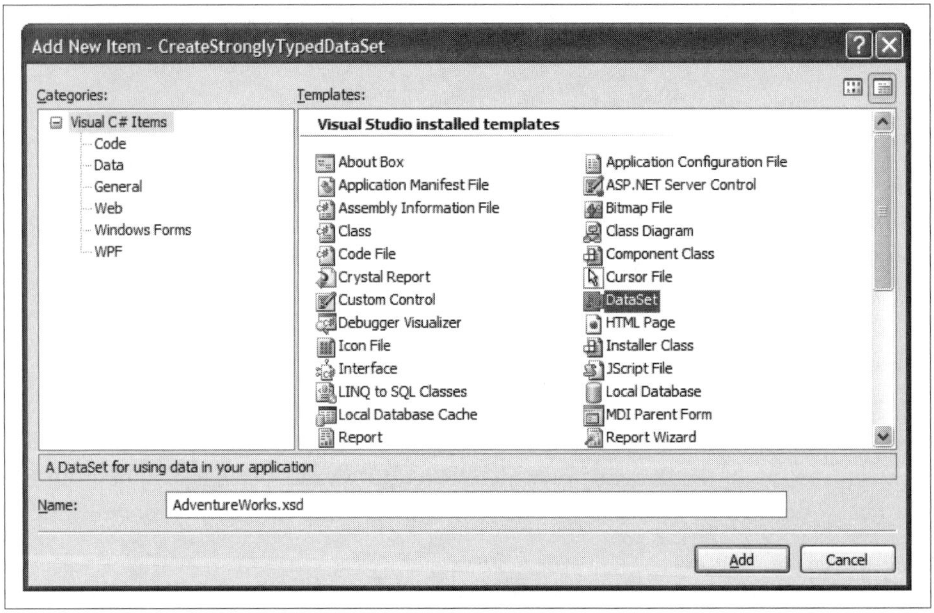

Figure 2-16. Add New Item dialog

4. Next, add database objects to the DataSet using a Database Connection. If you do not already have an AdventureWorks Database Connection, create one: Open Server Explorer by selecting View → Server Explorer from the main menu. Right-click on the Data Connections node and select Add Connection from the context menu to Open the Add Connection dialog. In the Add Connection dialog, select the SQL Server with the AdventureWorks database, leave log on mode as Windows Authentication, and select the AdventureWorks database from the Connect to a database drop down. The completed dialog is shown in Figure 2-17. Click the OK button to create the connection and close the dialog.

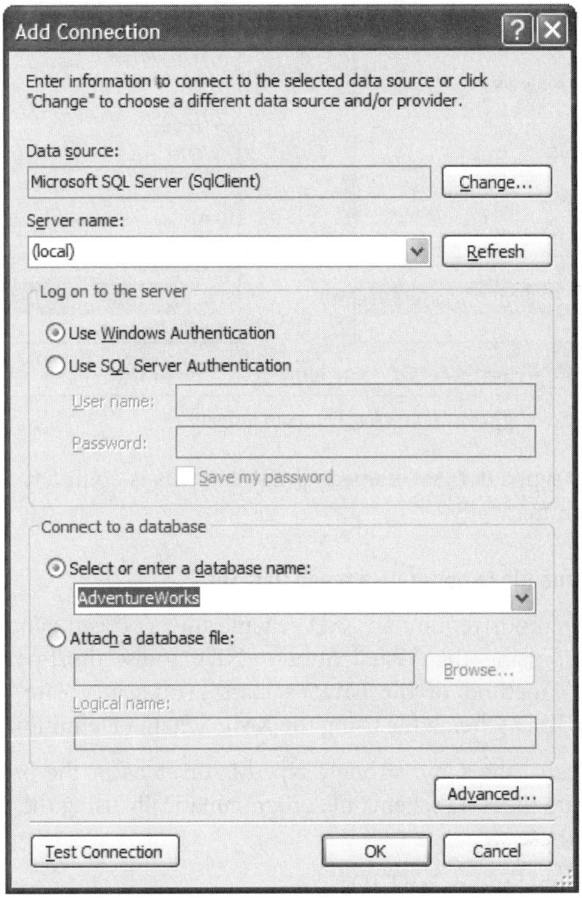

Figure 2-17. Add Connection dialog

5. Expand the Tables node in Server Explorer for the Data Connection that you just added. Select the SalesOrderHeader (Sales) and SalesOrderDetail (Sales) tables and drag them onto the DataSet Designer surface. This adds both tables to the strongly typed DataSet. If you don't want all of the columns in a table, expand a table and drag just the columns you need onto the design surface. The designer now shows the two tables together with the data relation between the tables as shown in Figure 2-18.

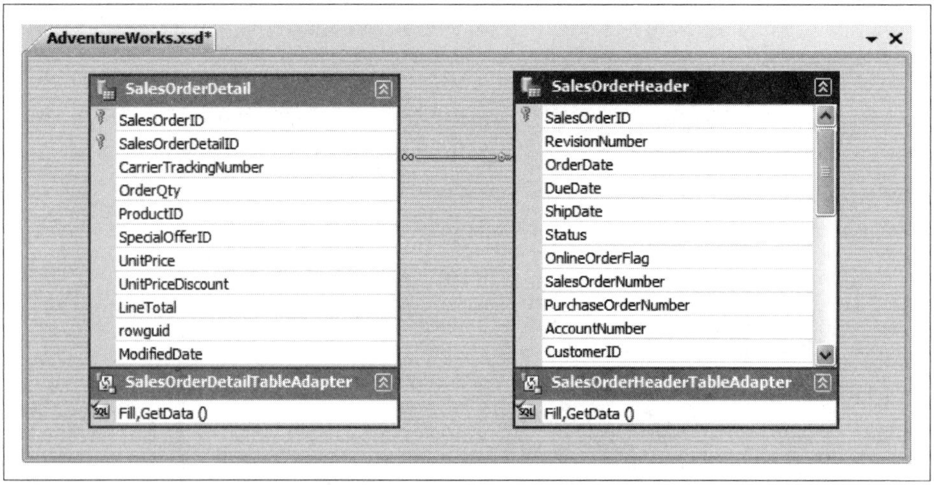

Figure 2-18. CreateStronglyTypedDataSet_DataSetDesigner

6. The strongly typed DataSet named AdventureWorks is complete and you can now use it programmatically.

Using an XSD schema file to generate a typed DataSet

The other two methods require an XSD schema file. You can generate this file in a number of ways: using the Visual Studio .NET tools, third-party tools, or the WriteXmlSchema() method of the DataSet class. You can create a strongly typed DataSet from the XSD schema file using the XML Schema Definition Tool (XSD.exe).

This solution creates the same strongly typed DataSet as in the preceding example. First, we will create the XSD schema file programmatically using the WriteXmlSchema() method. Follow these steps:

1. Open the Visual Studio .NET IDE.
2. Create a new C# Console Application named CreateStronglyTypedDataSetXsd.
3. The C# code in *Program.cs* in the project CreateStronglyTypedDataSetXsd is shown in Example 2-16.

Example 2-16. File: Program.cs for CreateStronglyTypedDataSetXsd solution

```
using System;
using System.Data;
using System.Data.SqlClient;

namespace CreateStronglyTypedDataSetXsd
{
    class Program
    {
        static void Main(string[] args)
        {
            string xsdFileName = @"..\..\AdventureWorks.xsd";

            string sqlConnectString = "Data Source=(local);" +
                "Integrated security=SSPI;Initial Catalog=AdventureWorks;";

            string sqlText = "SELECT * FROM Sales.SalesOrderHeader;" +
                "SELECT * FROM Sales.SalesOrderDetail;";

            // Create and fill a DataSet schema using a data adapter
            SqlDataAdapter da = new SqlDataAdapter(sqlText, sqlConnectString);
            da.TableMappings.Add("Table", "SalesOrderHeader");
            da.TableMappings.Add("Table1", "SalesOrderDetail");
            DataSet ds = new DataSet("AdventureWorks");
            da.FillSchema(ds, SchemaType.Mapped);
            // Add the data relation
            ds.Relations.Add("SalesOrderHeader_SalesOrderDetail",
                ds.Tables["SalesOrderHeader"].Columns["SalesOrderID"],
                ds.Tables["SalesOrderDetail"].Columns["SalesOrderID"]);

            // Output the XSD schema for the DataSet
            ds.WriteXmlSchema(xsdFileName);

            Console.WriteLine("File: {0} created.", xsdFileName);

            Console.WriteLine("\nPress any key to continue.");
            Console.ReadKey();
        }
    }
}
```

4. Execute the project to create the XSD schema file *AdventureWorks.xsd*.

Next, generate a strongly typed DataSet using the XML Schema Definition Tool (*XSD.exe*) found in the .NET Framework SDK *bin* directory. Follow these steps:

1. Open the Visual Studio Command Prompt by selecting Start → All Programs → Microsoft Visual Studio 2008 → Visual Studio Tools → Visual Studio 2008 Command Prompt.

2. Switch to the directory containing the XSD schema file *AdventureWorks.xsd* generated in the preceding steps.

3. Issue the following command to generate the strongly typed DataSet class file from the XSD schema file:

```
xsd AdventureWorks.xsd /d /l:CS
```

The /d switch specifies that source code for a strongly typed DataSet should be created.

The /l:CS switch specifies that the utility should use the C# language, which is the default if not specified. For VB.NET, use the switch /l:VB.

The XML Schema Definition Tool offers other options. For more information, see the .NET Framework SDK documentation or the MSDN Library.

Close the command prompt dialog.

4. The XML Schema Definition Tool generates the class file for the strongly typed DataSet and names it using the DataSet name in the XSD schema and with the extension corresponding to the programming language: *.cs* for C# and *.vb* for VB.NET—in our example *AdventureWorks.cs*.

5. Add the strongly typed DataSet class can to the project by right-clicking the project in Solution Explorer and selecting Add → Existing Item from the context menu. If the strongly typed DataSet file is not visible as a child node of the XSD Schema in the Solution Explorer window, select Show All Files from the Project menu.

Discussion

A strongly typed DataSet is a collection of classes that inherit from and extend the DataSet, DataTable, and DataRow classes, and provide additional properties, methods, and events based on the DataSet schema. You can use all of the functionality in classes from which the strongly typed classes inherit in the same way as with untyped classes.

A strongly typed DataSet class contains, in addition to a single class extending the DataSet class, three classes for each table in the DataSet extending each of the DataTable, DataRow, and DataRowChangeEvent classes. This solution describes these classes and discusses their commonly used methods and properties.

There is a class named *TableName*DataTable for each table in the strongly typed DataSet. It has the base class DataTable. Table 2-20 lists commonly used methods of this class specific to the strongly typed DataSet.

Table 2-20. TableNameDataTable methods

Method	Description
AddTableNameRow( )	Adds a row to the table. The method has two overloads: one takes a *TableName*Row object as the argument, while the other takes a set of arguments containing the column values.
FindByPrimaryKeyField1 ... PrimaryKeyFieldN( )	Takes *N* arguments, which are the values of the primary key fields of the row to find. Returns a *TableName*Row object, if found.
NewTableNameRow( )	Takes no arguments and returns a new *TableName*Row object with the same schema as the table to be used for adding new rows to the table in the strongly typed DataSet.

There is a class named *TableName*Row for each table in the strongly typed DataSet. It has the base class DataRow and represents a row of data in the table. Table 2-21 lists commonly used properties and methods of this class specific to the strongly typed DataSet.

Table 2-21. TableNameRow class properties and methods

Property/method	Description
Typed accessor	Sets and gets the value of a column. The typed accessor is exposed as a property having the same name as the underlying data column.
Is*ColumnName*Null( )	Returns a Boolean value indicating whether the field contains a null value.
Set*ColumnName*Null( )	Sets the value of the underlying field to a null value.
Get*ChildTableName*Rows( )	Returns the rows for the table as an array of *ChildTableName*Row objects.
*ParentTableName*Row( )	Returns the parent row as an object of type *ParentTableName*Row.

There is a class named *TableName*RowChangeEvent for each table in the strongly typed DataSet. It has the base class EventArgs. Table 2-22 describes the properties of this class.

Table 2-22. TableNameRowChangeEvent properties

Property	Description
Action	A value from the System.Data.DataRowAction enumeration that describes the action performed on a row that caused the event to be raised.
Row	The *TableName*Row object for which the event was raised.

A strongly typed DataSet has some advantages over using an untyped DataSet:

- The schema information is contained within the strongly typed DataSet resulting in a performance over retrieving schema information at runtime. The schema of an untyped DataSet can also be defined programmatically, as discussed in Recipe 3.15, resulting in similar performance.
- Programming is more intuitive and code is easier to maintain. Table, column, and other object names are accessed through properties with names based on the underlying data source object names rather than by using index or delimited string arguments. The Visual Studio .NET IDE provides autocomplete functionality for strongly typed DataSet names.
- Type mismatch errors and errors resulting from misspelled or out of bounds arguments used with DataSet objects can be detected during compilation, rather than at runtime.

The disadvantages of a strongly typed DataSet object include:

- Additional overhead when executing, resulting in a small performance penalty.
- A strongly typed DataSet must be regenerated when the structure of the underlying data source changes. Applications using these strongly typed DataSet objects will need to be rebuilt with a reference to the new strongly typed DataSet.

2.17 Controlling the Names Used in a Strongly Typed DataSet

Problem

You want to assign your own names to the classes and properties for strongly typed DataSet classes.

Solution

Use annotations in the XML schema to control the names of classes and properties in strongly typed DataSet classes.

Use the Visual Studio .NET IDE to create the strongly typed DataSet object based on the HumanResources.Department table in AdventureWorks that you will annotate. For more details about creating a strongly typed DataSet using the Visual Studio .NET IDE, see Recipe 2.16. Follow these steps:

1. Create a Visual C# Console Application named AnnotateStronglyTypedDataSet.

2. Right-click on the project in Solution Explorer and click Add → New Item to open the Add New Item dialog shown in the following figure. Select DataSet from the Visual Studio installed templates. Name the DataSet *AnnotatedDepartment.xsd*. Click the Add button to create the DataSet and close the dialog. The DataSet is added to Solution Explorer and the DataSet Designer is opened.

3. Next, add database objects to the DataSet using a Database Connection. If you do not already have an AdventureWorks Database Connection, create one: Open Server Explorer by selecting View → Server Explorer from the main menu. Right-click on the Data Connections node and select Add Connection from the context menu to Open the Add Connection dialog. In the Add Connection dialog, select the SQL Server with the AdventureWorks database, leave log on mode as Windows Authentication, and select the AdventureWorks database from the Connect to a database drop down. Click the OK button to create the connection and close the dialog.

4. Expand the Tables node in Server Explorer for the Data Connection that you just added. Select the Department (HumanResources) table and drag it onto the DataSet Designer surface. This adds the table to the strongly typed DataSet AnnotatedDepartment.

Add annotations to the XML schema to control the names of classes and properties in strongly typed DataSet class.

1. Right-click on the *AnnotatedDepartment.xsd* file in Solution Explorer and select Open With → XML Editor from the context menu. The XSD schema for the strongly typed DataSet opens in the Designer.

2. Add the following reference to the XSD schema, as shown in Figure 2-19:

```
xmlns:codegen="urn:schemas-microsoft-com:xml-msprop"
```

Figure 2-19. AnnotatedDepartment.xsd file

3. Annotate the "Department" element (subnode of the AnnotatedDepartment element) with the codegen:typedPlural="Depts" attribute so that you can access the collection of Department rows using the Depts property of the DataSet rather than the default DepartmentDataTable property. Figure 2-20 shows the change.

4. Annotate the "Department" element (subnode of the AnnotatedDepartment element) with the codegen:typedName="Dept" attribute so that you can access a row in the Department table using the Dept property of the AnnotatedDepartment class rather than the default DepartmentRow property. Figure 2-20 shows the change.

Figure 2-20. AnnotatedDepartment.xsd file with typedPlural and typedName annotations for Deaprtment table

5. Annotate the "DepartmentID" element with the codegen:typedName="ID" attribute so that you can access the DepartmentID column using the ID property of the row rather than the default DepartmentID property. This is shown in Figure 2-21.

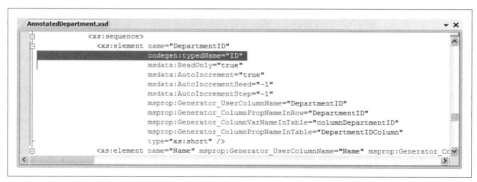

Figure 2-21. AnnotatedDepartment.xsd file with typedName annotation for DepartmentID column

Finally, the solution makes use of the annotations. The C# code in *Program.cs* in the project AnnotateStronglyTypedDataSet is shown in Example 2-17.

Example 2-17. File: Program.cs for AnnotateStronglyTypedDataSet solution

```
using System;
using System.Data;
using System.Data.SqlClient;

namespace AnnotateStronglyTypedDataSet
{
    class Program
    {
        static void Main(string[] args)
        {
            string sqlConnectString = "Data Source=(local);" +
                "Integrated security=SSPI;Initial Catalog=AdventureWorks;";
            string sqlText = "SELECT TOP 5 * FROM HumanResources.Department";

            SqlDataAdapter da = new SqlDataAdapter(sqlText, sqlConnectString);
            AnnotatedDepartment ad = new AnnotatedDepartment();
            da.Fill(ad, "Department");

            foreach (AnnotatedDepartment.Dept row in ad.Depts)
                Console.WriteLine("DepartmentID = {0}\tName = {1}",
                    row.ID, row.Name);

            Console.WriteLine("\nPress any key to continue.");
            Console.ReadKey();
        }
    }
}
```

The output is shown in Figure 2-22.

Figure 2-22. Output for AnnotateStronglyTypedDataSet solution

Discussion

Annotations are modifications to the XSD schema used to generate a strongly typed DataSet that allows the names of elements in the strongly typed DataSet to be customized without changing the underlying schema. This allows more meaningful element names to be used, resulting in code that is easier to read, use, and maintain. Table 2-23 lists available annotations.

Table 2-23. Available XSD schema annotations

Annotation	Description
typedChildren	Name of the method that returns objects from a child data relation.
typedName	Name of the object. This can be set from the UI using ADO.NET 2.0 or later.
typedParent	Name of the method that returns an object from a parent data relation.
typedPlural	Name of the collection of objects.
nullValue	Value or behavior if the underlying value is DBNull. Table 2-17 lists possible values for this annotation. The default value is _throw. This can be set from the UI using ADO.NET 2.0 or later.

Table 2-24 describes possible values for the nullValue annotation.

Table 2-24. Values for nullValue annotation

nullValue	Description
Replacement Value	A value having the same type as the element to be returned.
_empty	Return String.Empty for a String. Return an object created from an empty constructor for other objectsThrow, an exception for primitive types.
_null	Return a null reference for objectsThrow, an exception for primitive types.
_throw	Raise an exception.

Table 2-25 lists the different objects in a strongly typed DataSet and the default names and available annotations for each.

Table 2-25. *Default values and available annotations for elements of strongly typed DataSet objects*

Element	Default name	Annotation
DataTable	*TableName*DataTable	typedPlural
DataTable methods	New*TableName*Row	typedName
	Add*TableName*Row	
	Remove*TableName*Row	
DataRowCollection	*TableName*	typedPlural
DataRow	*TableName*Row	typedName
DataColumn	DataTable.*ColumnName*	typedName
	ColumnDataRow.*ColumnName*	
Property	*PropertyName*	typedName
Child accessor	Get*ChildTableName*Rows	typedChildren
Parent accessor	*TableName*Row	typedParent
DataSet events	*TableName*RowChangeEvent	typedName
	*TableName*RowChangeEventHandler	

The use annotations, a reference to the codegen namespace, must be included in the XSD schema, as shown:

```
xmlns:codegen="urn:schemas-microsoft-com:xml-msprop"
```

The codegen namespace allows the names of methods, properties, relations, constraints, and events in the strongly typed DataSet to be customized.

2.18 Replacing Null Values in a Strongly Typed DataSet

Problem

When a column has a null value, you want the value in the strongly typed DataSet to be a string indicating that no value is available.

Solution

Use annotations in the XML schema to control the handling of null values.

Use the Visual Studio .NET IDE to create the strongly typed DataSet object based on the HumanResources.Department table in AdventureWorks that you will annotate. For more details about creating a strongly typed DataSet using the Visual Studio .NET IDE, see Recipe 2.16. Follow these steps:

1. Create a Visual C# Console Application, `ReplaceNullValueStronglyTypedDataSet`.

2. Right-click on the project in Solution Explorer and click Add → New Item to open the Add New Item dialog shown in the following figure. Select `DataSet` from the Visual Studio installed templates. Name the `DataSet` *ReplaceNullValueDepartment.xsd*. Click the Add button to create the `DataSet` and close the dialog. The `DataSet` is added to Solution Explorer and the `DataSet` Designer is opened.

3. Next, add database objects to the `DataSet` using a Database Connection. If you do not already have an `AdventureWorks` Database Connection, create one: Open Server Explorer by selecting View → Server Explorer from the main menu. Right-click on the Data Connections node and select Add Connection from the context menu to Open the Add Connection dialog. In the Add Connection dialog, select the SQL Server with the `AdventureWorks` database, leave log on mode as Windows Authentication, and select the `AdventureWorks` database from the Connect to a database drop down. Click the OK button to create the connection and close the dialog.

4. Expand the Tables node in Server Explorer for the Data Connection that you just added. Select the `Department` (`HumanResources`) table and drag it onto the DataSet Designer surface. This adds the table to the strongly typed `DataSet` `ReplaceNullValueDepartment`.

5. The `Name` field in the `Department` table does not allow null values. Change this by selecting the `Name` field and setting the `AllowDBNull` property to `true` in the Properties pane.

Add annotations to the XML schema to handle a null value in the `Name` field in the `Department` table in the strongly typed `DataSet` class. There are two ways you can do this. First, there's the easy way, which you can use if you have created the `DataSet` using the Visual Studio .NET IDE:

1. Select the `Name` field in the `Department` table in the DataSet Designer and set the `NullValue` property to `- no name available -`.

Or you can follow the more difficult way, described in the next three steps:

1. Right-click on the *ReplaceNullValueDepartment.xsd* file in Solution Explorer and select Open With → XML Editor from the context menu. The XSD schema for the strongly typed `DataSet` opens in the Designer.

2. Add the following reference to the XSD schema as shown in Figure 2-23:

       xmlns:codegen="urn:schemas-microsoft-com:xml-msprop"

3. Annotate the `"Name"` element (subnode of the `Department` element which is in turn a subnode of the `ReplaceNullValueDepartment` element) with the `codegen:nullValue="- no name available -"` attribute so that null `Name` values are replaced with the string `- no name available -`. Figure 2-23 shows the change.

```
ReplaceNullVal...Department.xsd                                        ▼ ✕
  <xs:element name="ReplaceNullValueDepartment" msdata:IsDataSet="true" msdata:UseCurren
    <xs:complexType>
      <xs:choice minOccurs="0" maxOccurs="unbounded">
        <xs:element name="Department" msprop:Generator_UserTableName="Department" msprop
          <xs:complexType>
            <xs:sequence>
              <xs:element name="DepartmentID" msdata:ReadOnly="true" msdata:AutoIncremen
              <xs:element name="Name"
                          msprop:Generator_UserColumnName="Name"
                          msprop:Generator_ColumnPropNameInRow="Name"
                          msprop:Generator_ColumnVarNameInTable="columnName"
                          msprop:Generator_ColumnPropNameInTable="NameColumn"
                          codegen:nullValue="- no name available -">
                <xs:simpleType>
                  <xs:restriction base="xs:string">
                    <xs:maxLength value="50" />
                  </xs:restriction>
                </xs:simpleType>
              </xs:element>
              <xs:element name="GroupName" msprop:Generator_UserColumnName="GroupName"
```

Figure 2-23. Department.xsd with nullValue annotation for Name column

Finally, the solution makes use of the annotations. The C# code in *Program.cs* in the project ReplaceNullValueStronglyTypedDataSet is shown in Example 2-18.

Example 2-18. File: Program.cs for ReplaceNullValueStronglyTypedDataSet solution

```csharp
using System;
using System.Data;
using System.Data.SqlClient;

namespace ReplaceNullValueStronglyTypedDataSet
{
    class Program
    {
        static void Main(string[] args)
        {
            string sqlConnectString = "Data Source=(local);" +
                "Integrated security=SSPI;Initial Catalog=AdventureWorks;";
            string sqlText = "SELECT TOP 5 * FROM HumanResources.Department";

            // Use a data adapter to fill the strongly typed DataSet
            SqlDataAdapter da = new SqlDataAdapter(sqlText, sqlConnectString);
            ReplaceNullValueDepartment ds = new ReplaceNullValueDepartment();
            da.Fill(ds, "Department");

            // Add a row with a null value for the name field
            ds.Department.AddDepartmentRow(null, "A Group Name", DateTime.Now);

            // Output the DataSet to show the effect of the null annotation
            foreach (ReplaceNullValueDepartment.DepartmentRow row in ds.Department)
                Console.WriteLine("DepartmentID = {0}\tName = {1}",
                    row.DepartmentID, row.Name);
```

Example 2-18. File: Program.cs for ReplaceNullValueStronglyTypedDataSet solution (continued)

```
        Console.WriteLine("\nPress any key to continue.");
        Console.ReadKey( );
    }
  }
}
```

The output is shown in Figure 2-24.

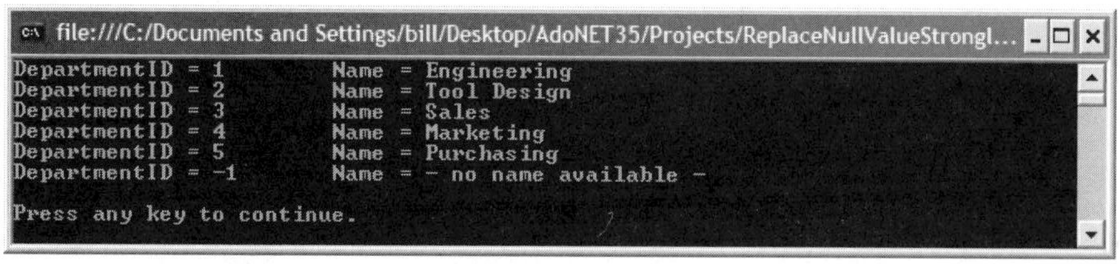

Figure 2-24. Output for ReplaceNullValueStronglyTypedDataSet solution

Discussion

Annotations to XSD schemas used to generate strongly typed DataSet objects are discussed in detail in Recipe 2.17.

CHAPTER 3

Querying and Retrieving Data

3.0   Introduction

ADO.NET has both connected and disconnected classes. Disconnected classes let you access and manipulate offline the data you retrieved using the connected classes and later synchronize it with the underlying data source using the connected classes. The disconnected classes include the DataSet, DataTable, DataColumn, DataRow, DataView, DataRelation, and Constraint classes. The disconnected classes are part of the ADO.NET classes in the .NET Framework. Connected classes let you retrieve and update data in underlying data sources. These classes include the Connection, Command, DataReader, and DataAdapter classes. Each data provider is responsible for implementing the connected classes. The recipes in this chapter discuss creating, working with, and managing the ADO.NET connected objects—this includes executing queries, retrieving results, and retrieving and navigating results sets.

A Connection object is a unique session with the data source. A Connection specifies necessary authentication information needed to connect to a data source. The Connection object is specific to the type of data source—for example, the .NET Framework data provider for SQL Server includes the SqlConnection class.

A Command executes SQL statements and stored procedures against the data source using an established Connection. The CommandText property of the Command class contains the SQL statement executed against the data source. The Command object is specific to the type of data source—for example, the .NET Framework data provider for SQL Server includes the SqlCommand object.

A DataReader provides forward-only, read-only access to a result set. The DataReader offers the best performance for accessing data by avoiding the overhead associated with the DataSet. You create a DataReader by executing the ExecuteReader( ) method of the Command class. The schema of a DataReader object is inferred from the database schema.

The Connection object for a DataReader remains open and cannot be used for any other purpose while data is being accessed. This makes the DataReader unsuitable for communicating data remotely between application tiers, or interacting with the data dynamically. Since the DataReader reads a result set stream directly from a connection, there is no way to know the number of records in a DataReader. Recipe 3.12 demonstrates techniques that simulate a record count for a DataReader and discusses limitations of the techniques.

A DataAdapter bridges the connected classes with the disconnected classes by retrieving data from a data source and filling a (disconnected) DataSet. The DataAdapter also updates the data source with changes made to a disconnected DataSet. The DataAdapter uses the Connection object to connect the data source and the Command object to retrieve data from and resolve changes to the data source. The DataAdapter object is specific to the type of data source—for example, the .NET Framework data provider for SQL Server includes the SqlDataAdapter object.

In addition to recipes for executing queries and retrieving results using the connected classes—DataAdapter, Connection, Command, and DataReader—this chapter covers using SQL Server and Oracle parameterized statements and stored procedures to retrieve result sets and as well as using input and output parameters, and return values.

3.1 Executing a Query That Does Not Return a Result Set

Problem

You need to execute a query or command that does not return a result set.

Solution

Use the ExecuteNonQuery( ) method of the Command object.

The T-SQL statement to create the table ExecuteQueryNoResultSet used in this solution is shown in Example 3-1.

Example 3-1. Stored Procedure: Create table ExecuteQueryNoResultSet

```
USE AdoDotNet35Cookbook
GO
CREATE TABLE ExecuteQueryNoResultSet(
    Id int NOT NULL PRIMARY KEY,
    Field1 nvarchar(50) NOT NULL,
    Field2 nvarchar(50) NOT NULL,
)
```

And here is the T-SQL statement to add sample data to the table ExecuteQueryNoResultSet:

```
USE AdoDotNet35Cookbook
GO
INSERT INTO ExecuteQueryNoResultSet
    VALUES (1, 'Field 1.1', 'Field 2.1');
INSERT INTO ExecuteQueryNoResultSet
    VALUES (2, 'Field 1.2', 'Field 2.2');
INSERT INTO ExecuteQueryNoResultSet
    VALUES (3, 'Field 1.3', 'Field 2.3');
```

The solution creates a connection and executes a T-SQL statement using the ExecuteNonQuery( ) method to delete a single row from the table ExecuteQueryNoResultSet. The number of rows affected is output to the console.

The C# code in *Program.cs* in the project ExecuteQueryNoResultSet is shown in Example 3-2.

Example 3-2. File: Program.cs for ExecuteQueryNoResultSet solution

```
using System;
using System.Data;
using System.Data.SqlClient;

namespace ExecuteQueryNoResultSet
{
    class Program
    {
        static void Main(string[] args)
        {
            string sqlConnectString =
                "Data Source=(local);Integrated security=SSPI;" +
                "Initial Catalog=AdoDotNet35Cookbook;";

            string sqlDelete = "DELETE FROM ExecuteQueryNoResultSet " +
                "WHERE Id = 2";

            // Create and execute a command to delete the record with
            // Id = 2 from the table ExecuteQueryNoResultSet
            SqlConnection connection =
                new SqlConnection(sqlConnectString);
            SqlCommand command = new SqlCommand(sqlDelete, connection);
            connection.Open( );
            int rowsAffected = command.ExecuteNonQuery( );
            Console.WriteLine("{0} row(s) affected.", rowsAffected);
            Console.WriteLine("Record with Id = 2 deleted.");
            connection.Close( );

            Console.WriteLine("\nPress any key to continue.");
            Console.ReadKey( );
        }
    }
}
```

The output is shown in Figure 3-1.

Figure 3-1. Output for ExecuteQueryNoResultSet solution

Discussion

The `ExecuteNonQuery( )` method of the `Command` object executes a T-SQL statement. The number of rows affected is returned for `UPDATE`, `INSERT`, and `DELETE` statements. All other statements return –1. You can use the `ExecuteNonQuery( )` method to execute T-SQL DDL statements such as `CREATE TABLE` or execute T-SQL commands that affect data such as `INSERT`, `UPDATE`, and `DELETE`. You don't have to store or use the return value—for example, the command in the solution could have been written:

```
command.ExecuteNonQuery( );
```

Although the `ExecuteNonQuery( )` does not return rows, output and return values mapped to parameters are returned.

3.2   Executing a Query That Returns a Single Value

Problem

You want to execute a query that returns a single value.

Solution

Use the `ExecuteScalar( )` method of the `Command` object to return a single value from a query.

The solution uses the `ExecuteScalar( )` method to get the number of records in the `Person.Contact` table in `AdventureWorks`. The number of records is output to the console.

The C# code in *Program.cs* in the project `RetrieveSingleValueFromQuery` is shown in Example 3-3.

Example 3-3. File: Program.cs for RetrieveSingleValueFromQuery solution

```
using System;
using System.Data;
using System.Data.SqlClient;

namespace RetrieveSingleValueFromQuery
{
    class Program
```

```
{
    static void Main(string[] args)
    {
        string sqlConnectString = "Data Source=(local);" +
            "Integrated security=SSPI;Initial Catalog=AdventureWorks;";

        string sqlSelect = "SELECT COUNT(*) FROM Person.Contact";

        SqlConnection connection = new SqlConnection(sqlConnectString);

        // Create the scalar command and open the connection
        SqlCommand command = new SqlCommand(sqlSelect, connection);
        connection.Open();

        // Execute the scalar SQL statement and store results.
        int count = Convert.ToInt32(command.ExecuteScalar());
        connection.Close();

        Console.WriteLine("Record count in Person.Contact = {0}", count);

        Console.WriteLine("\nPress any key to continue.");
        Console.ReadKey();
    }
}
}
```

The output is shown in Figure 3-2.

Figure 3-2. Output for RetrieveSingleValueFromQuery solution

Discussion

The ExecuteScalar( ) method of the Command object returns a single value from the data source rather than a collection of records as a table or data stream. While the ExecuteScalar( ) method does improve performance when compared to retrieving a single value using an output parameter or using a DataReader, it allows that single value to be returned with the least code and may therefore improve readability and maintainability of your code.

If the query returns a result set rather than a single value, the first column of the first row is returned as a scalar value. A null reference is returned if the result set is empty or if the result set is a Ref Cursor when using the Oracle .NET data provider.

3.3   Retrieving a Result Set Stream Using a DataReader

Problem

You need to return a result set as a forward-only stream of rows.

Solution

Use the ExecuteReader( ) method of the Command object to create a DataReader that retrieves a result set.

The solution creates a Connection, Command, and DataReader that return a subset of rows from the Person.Contact table in AdventureWorks. Result set values from the DataReader are output to the console.

The C# code in *Program.cs* in the project RetrieveDataUsingDataReader is shown in Example 3-4.

Example 3-4. File: Program.cs for RetrieveDataUsingDataReader solution

```
using System;
using System.Data.SqlClient;

namespace RetrieveDataUsingDataReader
{
    class Program
    {
        static void Main(string[] args)
        {
            string sqlConnectString = "Data Source=(local);" +
                "Integrated security=SSPI;Initial Catalog=AdventureWorks;";

            string sqlSelect =
                "SELECT ContactID, FirstName, LastName FROM Person.Contact " +
                "WHERE ContactID BETWEEN 10 AND 14";

            SqlConnection connection = new SqlConnection(sqlConnectString);

            // Create the command and open the connection
            SqlCommand command = new SqlCommand(sqlSelect, connection);
            connection.Open( );

            // Create the DataReader to retrieve data
            using (SqlDataReader dr = command.ExecuteReader( ))
            {
                while (dr.Read( ))
                {
```

Example 3-4. File: Program.cs for RetrieveDataUsingDataReader solution (continued)

```
                    // Output fields from DataReader row
                    Console.WriteLine(
                        "ContactID = {0}\tFirstName = {1}\tLastName = {2}",
                        dr["ContactID"], dr["LastName"], dr["FirstName"]);
                }
            }

            connection.Close( );

            Console.WriteLine("\nPress any key to continue.");
            Console.ReadKey( );
        }
    }
}
```

The output is shown in Figure 3-3.

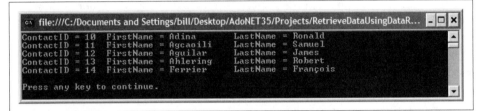

Figure 3-3. Output for RetrieveDataUsingDataReader solution

Discussion

A DataReader provides a way of reading a forward-only stream of rows from a data source. You create a DataReader by calling the ExecuteReader( ) method of the Command object. The method has two overloads that both return DataReader objects:

```
ExecuteReader( )
ExecuteReader(CommandBehavior behavior)
```

Where:

behavior

Specifies the results returned by the query—this is a value from the CommandBehavior enumeration described in Table 3-1. Bitwise combinations of multiple CommandBehavior values can be specified.

Table 3-1. CommandBehavior enumeration

Behavior	Description
Default	The query can return one or more result sets. Execution of the query can affect the database state.
SingleResult	The query returns one result set.
SchemaOnly	The query returns column information only—no data is returned.

Table 3-1. CommandBehavior enumeration (continued)

Behavior	Description
KeyInfo	The query returns column and primary key information only—no data is returned.
SingleRow	The query returns a single row. Specifying this behavior can improve performance. If the query contains multiple result sets, one row is returned for each result set.
SequentialAccess	The query returns each row as a stream. This mechanism lets you handle rows that return large binary values by letting you use GetBytes( ) or GetChars( ) methods to limit the data returned for those values.
CloseConnection	The connection is closed when the last row in the result set is read.

3.4   Accessing Data Values in a DataReader

Problem

You need to access the data values in a DataReader.

Solution

Use one of the techniques shown in this solution.

The solution creates a DataReader that returns rows from the Person.Contact table in AdventureWorks. Values from the result set are output to the console using a variety of techniques.

The C# code in *Program.cs* in the project RetrieveValuesDataReader is shown in Example 3-5.

Example 3-5. File: Program.cs for RetrieveValuesDataReader solution

```
using System;
using System.Data;
using System.Data.SqlClient;

namespace RetrieveValuesDataReader
{
    class Program
    {
        static void Main(string[] args)
        {
            string sqlConnectString = "Data Source=(local);" +
                "Integrated security=SSPI;Initial Catalog=AdventureWorks;";

            string sqlSelect = @"SELECT ContactID, NameStyle, Title,
                FirstName, MiddleName, LastName, Suffix, EmailAddress,
                EmailPromotion, Phone, PasswordHash, PasswordSalt
                FROM Person.Contact";

            SqlConnection connection = new SqlConnection(sqlConnectString);
```

Example 3-5. File: Program.cs for RetrieveValuesDataReader solution (continued)

```
    // Create the command and open the connection
    SqlCommand command = new SqlCommand(sqlSelect, connection);
    connection.Open( );

    SqlDataReader dr = command.ExecuteReader( );
    dr.Read( );

    // Output fields from the first DataRow reader using different
    // techniques
    Console.WriteLine("ContactID = {0}", dr[0]);
    Console.WriteLine("Title = {0}", dr["Title"]);
    Console.WriteLine("FirstName = {0}",
        dr.IsDBNull(3) ? "NULL" : dr.GetString(3));
    Console.WriteLine("MiddleName = {0}",
        dr.IsDBNull(4) ? "NULL" : dr.GetSqlString(4));
    Console.WriteLine("LastName = {0}",
        dr.IsDBNull(5) ? "NULL" : dr.GetSqlString(5).Value);
    Console.WriteLine("EmailAddress = {0}", dr.GetValue(7));
    Console.WriteLine("EmailPromotion = {0}",
        int.Parse(dr["EmailPromotion"].ToString( )));

    // Get the column ordinal for the Phone attribute and use it to
    // output the column
    int coPhone = dr.GetOrdinal("Phone");
    Console.WriteLine("Phone = {0}", dr[coPhone]);

    // Get the column name for the PasswordHash attribute
    // and use it to output the column
    string cnPasswordHash = dr.GetName(10);
    Console.WriteLine("PasswordHash = {0}", dr[cnPasswordHash]);

    // Create an object array and load the row into it
    object[] o = new object[dr.FieldCount];
    // Output the PasswordSalt attribute from the object array
    dr.GetValues(o);
    Console.WriteLine("PasswordSalt = {0}", o[11].ToString( ));

    Console.WriteLine("\nPress any key to continue.");
    Console.ReadKey( );
    }
    }
}
```

The output is shown in Figure 3-4.

Discussion

The indexer of the DataReader (Item property in Visual Basic) lets you access a column value in the current row of a DataReader in its native format. You can specify the column using a zero-based column index or using a column name.

Figure 3-4. Output for RetrieveValuesDataReader solution

The DataReader exposes a set of methods that return the value of a column as a .NET Framework data type—these methods are described in Table 3-2. You specify the column using its zero-based index. The data retrieved isn't converted and an exception is raised if the column data type is not compatible with the method invoked.

Table 3-2. DataReader methods that return values as .NET Framework data types

Method	Description
GetBoolean( )	Returns the column value as a bool.
GetByte( )	Returns the column value as a byte.
GetBytes( )	Reads a stream of bytes from the specified column into a buffer as a byte[ ] starting at the specified buffer offset.
GetChar( )	Returns the column value as a char.
GetChars( )	Reads a stream of characters from the specified column into a buffer as a char[ ] starting at the specified buffer offset.
GetDateTime( )	Returns the column value as a DateTime object.
GetDateTimeOffset( )	Returns the column value as a DateTimeOffset object.
GetDecimal( )	Returns the column value as a decimal.
GetDouble( )	Returns the column value as a double.
GetFloat( )	Returns the column value as a float.
GetGuid( )	Returns the column value as a Guid object.
GetInt16( )	Returns the column value as a short.
GetInt32( )	Returns the column value as a int.
GetInt64( )	Returns the column value as a long.
GetString( )	Returns the column value as a string.
GetTimeSpan( )	Returns the column value as a TimeSpan object.

Each DataReader exposes a set of methods that return the value of a column as data source data type—the methods for the SQL Server DataReader (SqlDataReader) are described in Table 3-3. You specify the column using its zero-based index.

The data retrieved isn't converted and an exception is raised if the column data type does not match the method.

Table 3-3. DataReader methods that return values as SQL Server data types

Method	Description
GetSqlBinary( )	Returns the column value as a SqlBinary object.
GetSqlBoolean( )	Returns the column value as a SqlBoolean object.
GetSqlByte( )	Returns the column value as a SqlByte object.
GetSqlBytes( )	Returns the column value as a SqlBytes object.
GetSqlChars( )	Returns the column value as a SqlChars object.
GetSqlDateTime( )	Returns the column value as a SqlDateTime object.
GetSqlDecimal( )	Returns the column value as a SqlDecimal object.
GetSqlDouble( )	Returns the column value as a SqlDouble object.
GetSqlGuid( )	Returns the column value as a SqlGuid object.
GetSqlInt16( )	Returns the column value as a SqlInt16 object.
GetSqlInt32( )	Returns the column value as a SqlInt32 object.
GetSqlInt64( )	Returns the column value as a SqlInt64 object.
GetSqlMoney( )	Returns the column value as a SqlMoney object.
GetSqlSingle( )	Returns the column value as a SqlSingle object.
GetSqlString( )	Returns the column value as a SqlString object.
GetSqlXml( )	Returns the column value as a SqlXml object.

The DataReader methods described in Table 3-4 can help you retrieve values from a DataReader row.

Table 3-4. DataReader methods for accessing row values

Method	Description
GetName( )	Returns the column name for a column specified by its zero-based column ordinal.
GetOrdinal( )	Returns the zero-based ordinal for a column specified by its name.
GetProviderSpecificFieldType( )	Returns an object representing the provider-specific data type for the column specified by its zero-based column ordinal.
GetProviderSpecificValue( )	Returns an object representing the provider-specific data value for the column specified by its zero-based column ordinal.
GetProviderSpecificValues( )	Returns an object[ ] representing the provider-specific data values for the current row.
GetValue( )	Returns an object representing the value of the column in its native format for a column specified by its zero-based column ordinal.
GetValues( )	Returns an object[ ] representing the value of all columns in their native format for the current row.

3.5 Retrieving a Result Set Using a DataTable or a DataSet

Problem

You want to fill a DataTable or DataSet with a result set.

Solution

Use the Fill( ) method of the DataAdapter object to load the result set into a DataTable or into a DataSet.

The solution fills both a DataTable and a DataSet with data from the Person.Contact table in AdventureWorks. Results are output to the console.

The C# code in *Program.cs* in the project RetrieveDataIntoDataTable is shown in Example 3-6.

Example 3-6. File: Program.cs for RetrieveDataIntoDataTable solution

```
using System;
using System.Data;
using System.Data.SqlClient;

namespace RetrieveDataIntoDataTable
{
    class Program
    {
        static void Main(string[] args)
        {
            string sqlConnectString = "Data Source=(local);" +
                "Integrated security=SSPI;Initial Catalog=AdventureWorks;";

            string sqlSelect =
                "SELECT TOP 5 FirstName, LastName FROM Person.Contact";

            // Create a data adapter
            SqlDataAdapter da =
                new SqlDataAdapter(sqlSelect, sqlConnectString);

            // Fill a DataTable using DataAdapter and output to console
            DataTable dt = new DataTable( );
            da.Fill(dt);

            Console.WriteLine("---DataTable---");
            foreach (DataRow row in dt.Rows)
                Console.WriteLine("{0} {1}", row[0], row["LastName"]);

            // Fill a DataSet using DataAdapter and output to console
            DataSet ds = new DataSet( );
            da.Fill(ds, "Contact");
```

```
        Console.WriteLine("\n---DataSet; DataTable count = {0}---",
            ds.Tables.Count);
        Console.WriteLine("[TableName = {0}]", ds.Tables[0].TableName);
        foreach (DataRow row in ds.Tables["Contact"].Rows)
            Console.WriteLine("{0} {1}", row[0], row[1]);

        Console.WriteLine("\nPress any key to continue.");
        Console.ReadKey( );
    }
  }
}
```

The output is shown in Figure 3-5.

Figure 3-5. Output for RetrieveDataIntoDataTable solution

Discussion

The Fill( ) method of the DataAdapter adds or refreshes rows in a DataTable or in a DataSet and returns the number of rows successfully added or refreshed as an int. The Fill( ) method has 11 overloads:

```
Fill(DataSet ds)
Fill(DataTable dt)
Fill(DataSet ds, string srcTableName)
Fill(DataTable dt, IDataReader dr)
Fill(DataTable dt, IDbCommand command, CommandBehavior behavior)
Fill(int startRecord, int maxRecords, DataTable[] dts)
Fill(DataSet ds, int startRecord, int maxRecords, string srcTableName)
Fill(DataTable[] dts, IDataReader dr, int startRecord, int maxRecords)
Fill(DataSet ds, string srcTableName, IDataReader dr, int startRecord,
    int maxRecords)
Fill(DataTable[] dts, int startRecord, int maxRecords, IDbCommand command,
    CommandBehavior behavior)
Fill(DataSet ds, int startRecord, int maxRecords, string srcTableName,
    IDbCommand command, CommandBehavior behavior)
```

Where:

ds
> The DataSet to fill with records.

dt
> The DataTable to fill with records.

srcTableName
> The name of the source table to use for table mapping.

dr
> The DataReader that is the source of the records.

command
> The SQL SELECT statement used to retrieve records from the data source.

behavior
> Specifies the results returned by the query—this is a value from the CommandBehavior enumeration described in Table 3-1. Bitwise combinations of multiple CommandBehavior values can be specified.

startRecord
> The zero-based record to start with.

maxRecords
> The maximum number of records to retrieve.

dts
> The array of DataTable objects to fill with records.

When you use the Fill( ) method to refresh records in subsequent calls, the SQL statement must match the one initially used to populate the DataSet or DataTable and each table object must have a primary key so that duplicate rows can be reconciled.

3.6   Accessing Data Values in a DataTable or DataSet

Problem

You need to access values in a DataTable or DataSet.

Solution

Use one of the techniques shown in this solution.

The C# code in *Program.cs* in the project RetrieveValuesDataTable is shown in Example 3-7.

Example 3-7. File: Program.cs for RetrieveValuesDataTable solution

```
using System;
using System.Data;
using System.Data.SqlClient;
```

```
namespace RetrieveValuesDataTable
{
    class Program
    {
        static void Main(string[] args)
        {
            string sqlConnectString = "Data Source=(local);" +
                "Integrated security=SSPI;Initial Catalog=AdventureWorks;";

            string sqlSelect =
                "SELECT ContactID, FirstName, LastName FROM Person.Contact " +
                "WHERE ContactID BETWEEN 10 AND 14";

            // Create a data adapter
            SqlDataAdapter da = new SqlDataAdapter(sqlSelect, sqlConnectString);

            // Fill a DataTable using DataAdapter and output to console
            DataTable dt = new DataTable( );
            da.Fill(dt);

            // Accessing rows using indexer
            Console.WriteLine("---Index loop over DataRowCollection---");
            for (int i = 0; i < 5; i++)
            {
                DataRow row = dt.Rows[i];
                Console.WriteLine("Row = {0}\tContactID = {1}\tFirstName = {2}" +
                    "\tLastName = {3}", i, row[0], row["FirstName"],
                    row[2, DataRowVersion.Default]);
            }

            // Accessing rows using foreach loop
            Console.WriteLine("\n---foreach loop over DataRowCollection---");
            int j = 0;
            foreach (DataRow row in dt.Rows)
            {
                j++;
                Console.WriteLine("Row = {0}\tContactID = {1}\tFirstName = {2}" +
                    "\tLastName = {3}", j, row[0], row["FirstName"],
                    row["LastName", DataRowVersion.Default]);
            }

            // Accessing DataTable values directly
            Console.WriteLine("\n---Accessing FirstName value in row 3 " +
                "(ContactID = 12) directly---");
            Console.WriteLine("FirstName = {0}", dt.Rows[2][1]);
            Console.WriteLine("FirstName = {0}", dt.Rows[2]["FirstName"]);
            Console.WriteLine("FirstName = {0}",
                dt.Rows[2]["FirstName", DataRowVersion.Default]);
            Console.WriteLine("FirstName = {0}", dt.Rows[2][dt.Columns[1]]);
            Console.WriteLine("FirstName = {0}",
                dt.Rows[2][dt.Columns["FirstName"]]);
```

Example 3-7. File: Program.cs for RetrieveValuesDataTable solution (continued)

```
        Console.WriteLine("FirstName = {0}",
            dt.Rows[2].Field<string>(1));
        Console.WriteLine("FirstName = {0}",
            dt.Rows[2].Field<string>("FirstName"));
        Console.WriteLine("FirstName = {0}",
            dt.Rows[2].Field<string>("FirstName", DataRowVersion.Default));
        Console.WriteLine("FirstName = {0}",
            dt.Rows[2].Field<string>(dt.Columns[1]));
        Console.WriteLine("FirstName = {0}",
            dt.Rows[2].Field<string>(dt.Columns["FirstName"]));

        Console.WriteLine("\nPress any key to continue.");
        Console.ReadKey( );
    }
  }
}
```

The output is shown in Figure 3-6.

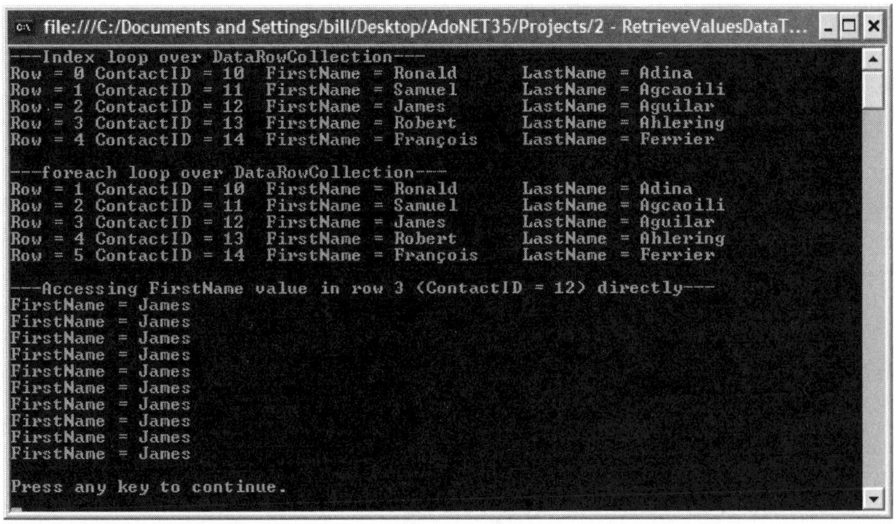

Figure 3-6. Output for RetrieveValuesDataTable solution

Discussion

A DataTable has a collection of rows that can be accessed through its DataRows property, which returns a DataRowCollection object. You access specific rows using the indexer (Item property in Visual Basic) of the DataRowCollection. You specify the row using a zero-based index. For example, dt.Rows[3] refers to the third row in a DataTable object, named dt.

Alternatively, you can iterate over the collection of DataRow objects in the DataRowCollection—the solution shows how to do this with a foreach loop.

The indexer of the DataRow lets you get or set a column value in the row. You specify the column using a zero-based column index or using a column name. The indexer has six overloads:

```
this[DataColumn col]
this[int columnIndex]
this[string columnName]
this[DataColumn col, DataRowVersion version]
this[int columnIndex, DataRowVersion version]
this[string columnName, DataRowVersion version]
```

Where:

col

> The DataColumn object to get or set.

columnIndex

> The zero-based ordinal of the column to get or set.

columnName

> The name of the column to get or set.

version

> The version of the row to retrieve—one of Original, Current, Proposed, or Default from the DataRowVersion enumeration.

The solution shows how to retrieve data values from a DataTable. Retrieving values from a DataSet is similar except that you need to specify the DataTable within the DataSet using an indexer on its Tables property with either the zero-based DataTable ordinal or the DataTable name. For example, the following code fragment refers to the value in the column named columnName in the second row of the DataTable named dataTable.

```
dataTable.Rows[1]["columnName"]
```

If a DataTable named dataTableName is in a DataSet named dataSet, the value is accessed using the following code fragment:

```
dataset.Tables["dataTable"].Rows[1]["columnName"]
```

3.7 Working with Data in a Strongly Typed DataSet

Problem

You have retrieved data into a strongly typed DataSet and you need to access the data.

Solution

The solution demonstrates how to fill a strongly typed DataSet and how to read, insert, update, delete, and work with null data using strongly typed DataSet methods.

Follow these steps:

1. The solution uses a single table AccessTypedDS in the AdoDotNet35Cookbook database. Execute the following T-SQL statement to create the table:

```
USE AdoDotNet35Cookbook
GO
CREATE TABLE AccessTypedDSTable(
    ID int NOT NULL PRIMARY KEY,
    StringField nvarchar(50) NULL,
    DateField datetime NULL,
    MoneyField money NULL )
```

2. The solution needs some sample data in the table. Execute the following T-SQL batch to add sample data to the table AccessTypedDSTable:

```
USE AdoDotNet35Cookbook
GO
INSERT INTO AccessTypedDSTable VALUES (1, 'String1', '11/15/2007', 22.95)
INSERT INTO AccessTypedDSTable VALUES (2, 'String2', '11/16/2007', 85.99)
INSERT INTO AccessTypedDSTable VALUES (3, 'String3', '11/17/2007', 7.63)
```

3. Create a C# Windows console application, AccessValuesStronglyTypedDataSetXsd. This solution creates the XSD file that will be used to create the strongly typed DataSet class. The C# code in *Program.cs* is shown in Example 3-8.

Example 3-8. File: Program.cs for AccessValuesStronglyTypedDataSetXsd solution

```csharp
using System;
using System.Data;
using System.Data.SqlClient;

namespace AccessValuesStronglyTypedDataSetXsd
{
    class Program
    {
        static void Main(string[] args)
        {
            string xsdFileName = @"..\..\AccessTypedDS.xsd";

            string sqlConnectString = "Data Source=(local);" +
                "Integrated security=SSPI;Initial Catalog=AdoDotNet35Cookbook;";

            string sqlText = "SELECT * FROM AccessTypedDSTable";

            // Create and fill a DataSet schema using a data adapter
            SqlDataAdapter da = new SqlDataAdapter(sqlText, sqlConnectString);
            da.TableMappings.Add("Table", "AccessTypedDSTable");
            DataSet ds = new DataSet("AccessTypedDS");
            da.FillSchema(ds, SchemaType.Mapped);

            // Output the XSD schema for the DataSet
            ds.WriteXmlSchema(xsdFileName);

            Console.WriteLine("File: {0} created.", xsdFileName);
```

```
        Console.WriteLine("\nPress any key to continue.");
        Console.ReadKey( );
    }
}
}
```

4. Build and execute the solution to create the schema file *AccessTypedDS.xsd*, shown in Example 3-9.

Example 3-9. File: AccessTypedDS.xsd

```xml
<?xml version="1.0" standalone="yes"?>
<xs:schema id="AccessTypedDS" xmlns="" xmlns:xs=http://www.w3.org/2001/XMLSchema
  xmlns:msdata="urn:schemas-microsoft-com:xml-msdata">
  <xs:element name="AccessTypedDS" msdata:IsDataSet="true"
    msdata:UseCurrentLocale="true">
    <xs:complexType>
      <xs:choice minOccurs="0" maxOccurs="unbounded">
        <xs:element name="AccessTypedDSTable">
          <xs:complexType>
            <xs:sequence>
              <xs:element name="ID" type="xs:int" />
              <xs:element name="StringField" minOccurs="0">
                <xs:simpleType>
                  <xs:restriction base="xs:string">
                    <xs:maxLength value="50" />
                  </xs:restriction>
                </xs:simpleType>
              </xs:element>
              <xs:element name="DateField" type="xs:dateTime" minOccurs="0" />
              <xs:element name="MoneyField" type="xs:decimal" minOccurs="0" />
            </xs:sequence>
          </xs:complexType>
        </xs:element>
      </xs:choice>
    </xs:complexType>
    <xs:unique name="Constraint1" msdata:PrimaryKey="true">
      <xs:selector xpath=".//AccessTypedDSTable" />
      <xs:field xpath="ID" />
    </xs:unique>
  </xs:element>
</xs:schema>
```

5. Open the Visual Studio Command Prompt, switch to the directory containing the schema file *AccessTypedDS.xsd*, and execute the XML Schema Definition Tool (xsd.exe) to create the strongly typed DataSet class file named *AccessTypedDS.xsd*:

```
xsd AccessTypedDS.xsd /d /l:CS
```

For more information about xsd.exe, see Recipe 2.16.

Close the Visual Studio Command Prompt once the strongly typed DataSet class file is built.

6. Create a C# Windows console application, `AccessValuesStronglyTypedDataSet`, that will demonstrate how to work with data values in a strongly typed `DataSet`.

7. Copy the strongly typed `DataSet` class file *AccessTypedDS.cs* (created in Step 4) to the project folder—the folder that contains the file *AccessValuesStronglyTypedDataSet.csproj*.

8. Add the strongly typed `DataSet` class file to the project. Right-click on the project in Solution Explorer. Select Add → Existing Item to open the Add Existing Item dialog. Select the *AccessTypedDS.cs* file and click Add. You can now use the strongly typed `DataSet` `AccessTypedDS` in your project.

9. The C# code in *Program.cs* in the project is shown in Example 3-10.

Example 3-10. File: Program.cs for AccessValuesStronglyTypedDataSet solution

```csharp
using System;
using System.Data;
using System.Data.SqlClient;
using System.Data.SqlTypes;

namespace AccessValuesStronglyTypedDataSet
{
    class Program
    {
        private static AccessTypedDS atds;

        static void Main(string[] args)
        {
            string sqlConnectString = "Data Source=(local);" +
                "Integrated security=SSPI;Initial Catalog=AdoDotNet35Cookbook;";

            string sqlSelect = "SELECT * FROM AccessTypedDSTable";

            // Create an instance of the strongly typed DataSet
            atds = new AccessTypedDS( );

            // Create a DataAdapter to fill the DataSet
            SqlDataAdapter da = new SqlDataAdapter(sqlSelect, sqlConnectString);
            // Add a command builder
            SqlCommandBuilder cb = new SqlCommandBuilder(da);
            // Add table mapping
            da.TableMappings.Add("Table", "AccessTypedDSTable");
            // Fill the strongly typed DataSet
            da.Fill(atds);

            OutputDataSet("READ [INITIAL]");

            // Add a row
            AccessTypedDS.AccessTypedDSTableRow row1 =
                atds.AccessTypedDSTable.NewAccessTypedDSTableRow( );
            row1.ID = 4;
            row1.StringField = "String4";
            row1.DateField = new DateTime(2007, 11, 18);
            row1.MoneyField = 115.44M;
```

```
        atds.AccessTypedDSTable.AddAccessTypedDSTableRow(row1);

        // Add another row
        atds.AccessTypedDSTable.AddAccessTypedDSTableRow(
            5, "String5", new DateTime(2007, 11, 19), .66M);

        OutputDataSet("INSERT");

        // Update the last row added (ID = 5)
        AccessTypedDS.AccessTypedDSTableRow row2 =
            atds.AccessTypedDSTable.FindByID(5);
        row2.StringField += "(new)";
        row2.DateField = row2.DateField.AddDays(1);
        row2.SetMoneyFieldNull();

        OutputDataSet("UPDATE");

        // Delete the last row added (ID = 5)
        atds.AccessTypedDSTable.FindByID(5).Delete();

        OutputDataSet("DELETE");

        // Update to databsae
        da.Update(atds);
        Console.WriteLine("\n=> Database updated with changes.");

        // Clear and reload the strongly typed DataSet
        atds.Clear();
        da.Fill(atds);
        Console.WriteLine("\n=> DataSet cleared and loaded.");

        // Output the strongly typed DataSet after updating database
        OutputDataSet("READ [FINAL]");

        Console.WriteLine("\nPress any key to continue.");
        Console.ReadKey();
    }

    static void OutputDataSet(string headerText)
    {
        Console.WriteLine("\n---{0}---", headerText);
        Console.WriteLine("ID\tStringField\t\tDateField\tMoneyField");
        Console.WriteLine("--\t-----------\t\t---------\t----------");
        foreach (AccessTypedDS.AccessTypedDSTableRow row in
            atds.AccessTypedDSTable.Rows)
        {
            Console.WriteLine("{0}\t{1}\t\t{2}\t{3}", row.ID,
                row.StringField.PadRight(12),
                row.DateField.ToShortDateString(),
                row.IsMoneyFieldNull() ? "[null]" : row.MoneyField.ToString("C"));
```

Example 3-10. File: Program.cs for AccessValuesStronglyTypedDataSet solution (continued)

```
            }
        }
    }
}
```

The output is shown in Figure 3-7.

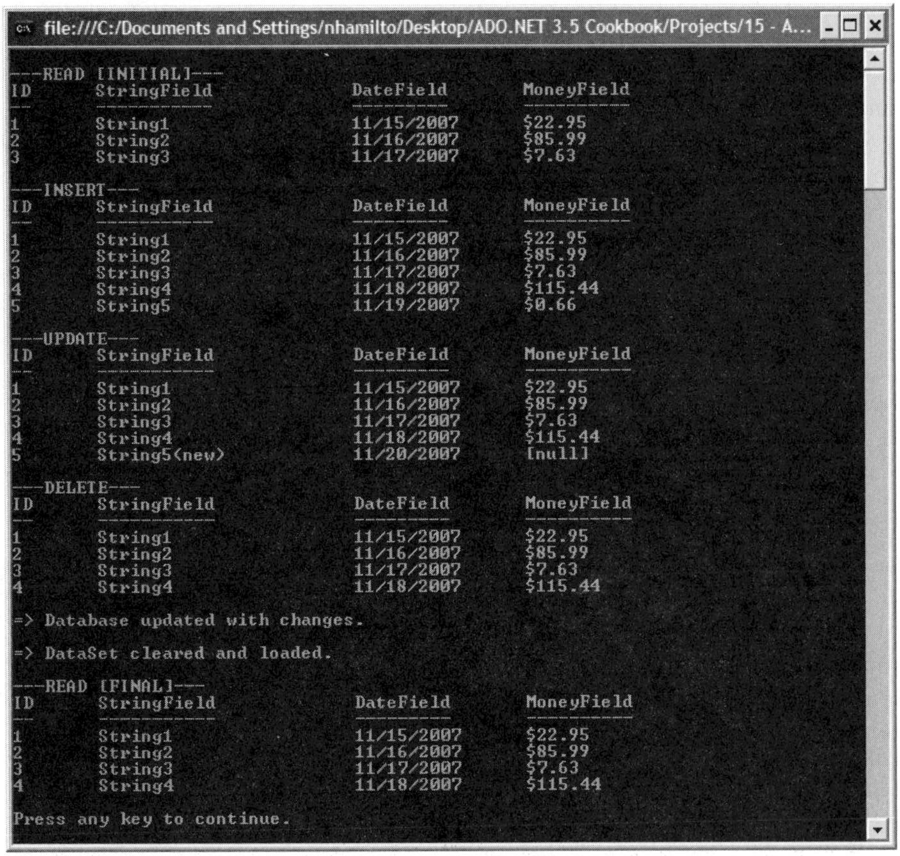

Figure 3-7. Output for AccessValuesStronglyTypedDataSet solution

Discussion

The strongly typed DataSet exposes a number of methods and properties that make it easier to access and work with the data in the DataSet. A description of the commonly used methods and properties follows.

The strongly typed `DataTable` has two methods for manipulating rows.

New{*table_name*}Row
Creates a new strongly typed row object {*strongly_typed_table_name*}TableRow.

Add{*table_name*}Row
Adds a strongly typed row {*strongly_typed_table_name*}TableRow to the table.

The `DataRow` in the strongly typed `DataSet` lets you get and set field value through a property of the strongly typed `DataRow` with the same name as the field in the data source. For example, the field `StringValue` is a property of the strongly typed `DataRow` `AccessTypedDSTableRow` and accesses the value in the database field with the same name—`StringValue`.

The strongly typed `DataSet` facilitates working with null values with two methods:

Set{*field_name*}Null
Sets the values of the specified field to `null`.

Is{*field_name*}Null
Returns a Boolean value indicating whether the field value is `null`.

3.8   Working with Parent-Child Relations in a Strongly Typed DataSet

Problem

You have retrieved data into related tables in a strongly typed `DataSet` and you need to navigate the hierarchy and retrieve data values.

Solution

The solution shows how to work with related data tables in a strongly typed `DataSet`.

Follow these steps:

1. Create a new C# Windows Console application, and name it `AccessValuesStronglyTypedDataSet`.

2. The solution needs the strongly typed `DataSet` class file *AdventureWorks.cs* created in the second half of Recipe 2.16. Copy this file to the project folder—the folder that contains the file *AccessValuesStronglyTypedDataSet.csproj*.

3. Add the strongly typed `DataSet` class to the project. Right-click on the project in Solution Explorer. Select Add → Existing Item to open the Add Existing Item dialog. Select the *AdventureWorks.cs* file and click Add. You can now use the strongly typed `DataSet` `AdventureWorks` in your project.

   The C# code in *Program.cs* in the project `DataRelationStronglyTypedDataSet` is shown in Example 3-11.

Example 3-11. File: Program.cs for DataRelationStronglyTypedDataSet solution

```
using System;
using System.Data;
using System.Data.SqlClient;

namespace DataRelationStronglyTypedDataSet
{
    class Program
    {
        static void Main(string[] args)
        {
            string sqlConnectString = "Data Source=(local);" +
                "Integrated security=SSPI;Initial Catalog=AdventureWorks;";

            string sqlSelect = "SELECT * FROM Sales.SalesOrderHeader;" +
                "SELECT * FROM Sales.SalesOrderDetail;";

            AdventureWorks awds = new AdventureWorks();

            // Create a DataAdapter to fill the DataSet
            SqlDataAdapter da = new SqlDataAdapter(sqlSelect, sqlConnectString);
            // Add a command builder
            SqlCommandBuilder cb = new SqlCommandBuilder(da);
            // Add table mapping
            da.TableMappings.Add("Table", "SalesOrderHeader");
            da.TableMappings.Add("Table1", "SalesOrderDetail");
            // Fill the strongly typed DataSet
            da.Fill(awds);

            int rowCount = 0;
            // output the first three header records
            foreach (AdventureWorks.SalesOrderHeaderRow hRow in
                awds.SalesOrderHeader.Rows)
            {
                Console.WriteLine("SalesOrderID = {0}\tOrderDate = {1}\tTotalDue = {2}",
                    hRow.SalesOrderID, hRow.OrderDate.ToShortDateString(),
                    hRow.TotalDue);

                // output the detail records for the header
                foreach (AdventureWorks.SalesOrderDetailRow dRow
                    in hRow.GetSalesOrderDetailRows())
                {
                    Console.WriteLine(
                        "\tSalesOrderDetailID = {0}\tLineTotal = {1}\tPO # = {2}",
                        dRow.SalesOrderDetailID, dRow.LineTotal,
                        dRow.SalesOrderHeaderRow.PurchaseOrderNumber);
                }

                if (++rowCount >= 3)
                    break;
            }

            Console.WriteLine("\nPress any key to continue.");
            Console.ReadKey();
```

Example 3-11. File: Program.cs for DataRelationStronglyTypedDataSet solution (continued)

```
        }
    }
}
```

The output is shown in Figure 3-8.

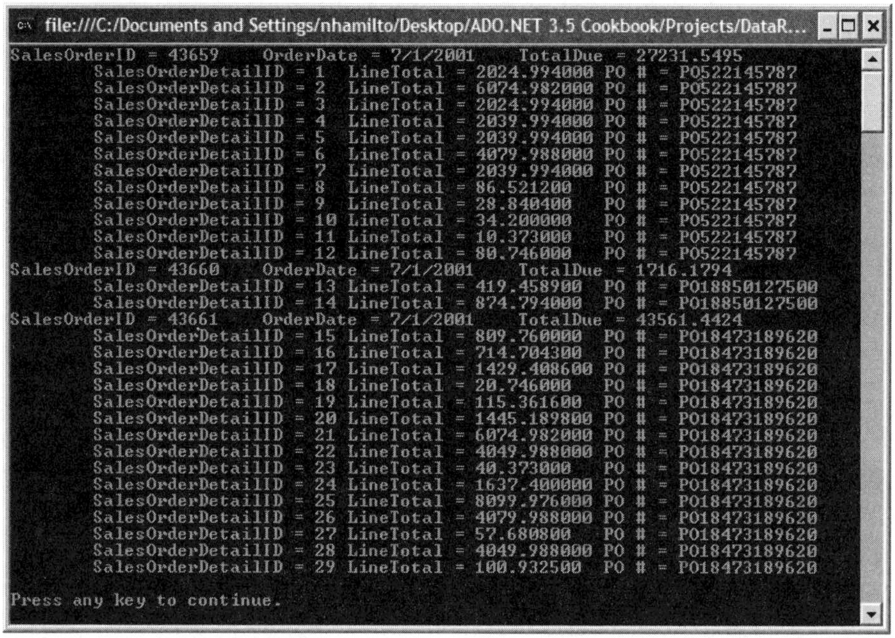

Figure 3-8. Output for DataRelationStronglyTypedDataSet solution

Discussion

The strongly typed DataSet exposes a number of methods and properties that make it easier to work with related tables and the data contained in them. A description of the commonly used methods and properties follows.

The strongly typed DataRow exposes two properties:

Get{*child_table_name*}Rows

Returns a strongly typed DataRow array of child rows for the specified row. The row will have one property for each data relation where the row contains the primary key value.

{*parent_table_name*}Row

Returns a strongly typed parent DataRow—the row in the parent table whose parent key matches the foreign key for the row. The row will have one property for each data relation where the row contains the foreign key value.

3.9 Using a DataView with a Strongly Typed DataSet

Problem

When using a DataView to find rows in a typed DataSet, you want to convert the rows you find to typed DataRow objects with all the properties and methods defined in your typed DataSet.

Solution

Cast the DataRow object returned by the Row property of a DataView to a typed DataRow.

The solution creates the strongly typed DataSet AdventureWorks and fills it from the Sales.SalesOrderHeader and Sales.SalesOrderDetail tables in AdventureWorks. A DataView is created of the Sales.SalesOrderHeader records where the TotalDue amount is greater than 175,000.The solution iterates over the collection of rows in the DataView, casting each to the strongly types AdventureWorks.SalesOrderHeaderRow row and uses the properties of the strongly typed row to output column values to the console.

The C# code in *Program.cs* in the project DataViewStronglyTypedDataSet is shown in Example 3-12.

Example 3-12. File: Program.cs for DataViewStronglyTypedDataSet solution

```
using System;
using System.Data;
using System.Data.SqlClient;

namespace DataViewStronglyTypedDataSet
{
    class Program
    {
        static void Main(string[] args)
        {
            string sqlConnectString = "Data Source=(local);" +
                "Integrated security=SSPI;Initial Catalog=AdventureWorks;";

            string sqlSelect = "SELECT * FROM Sales.SalesOrderHeader;" +
                "SELECT * FROM Sales.SalesOrderDetail;";

            AdventureWorks awds = new AdventureWorks();

            // Create a DataAdapter to fill the DataSet
            SqlDataAdapter da = new SqlDataAdapter(sqlSelect, sqlConnectString);
            // Add a command builder
            SqlCommandBuilder cb = new SqlCommandBuilder(da);
            // Add table mapping
            da.TableMappings.Add("Table", "SalesOrderHeader");
            da.TableMappings.Add("Table1", "SalesOrderDetail");
```

Example 3-12. File: Program.cs for DataViewStronglyTypedDataSet solution (continued)

```
            // Fill the strongly typed DataSet
            da.Fill(awds);

            DataView dv = new DataView(awds.SalesOrderHeader,
                "TotalDue > 175000", null, DataViewRowState.CurrentRows);
            for(int i = 0; i < dv.Count; i++)
            {
                AdventureWorks.SalesOrderHeaderRow typedRow =
                    (AdventureWorks.SalesOrderHeaderRow)dv[i].Row;

                Console.WriteLine("{0}:\tSalesOrderID = {1}\tOrderDate = {2}" +
                    " \tTotalDue = {3}",
                    i, typedRow.SalesOrderID, typedRow.OrderDate.ToShortDateString( ),
                    typedRow.TotalDue);
            }

            Console.WriteLine("\nPress any key to continue.");
            Console.ReadKey( );
        }
    }
}
```

The output is shown in Figure 3-9.

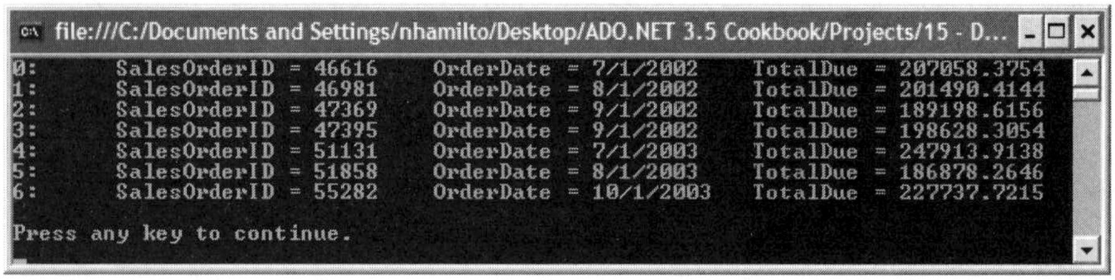

Figure 3-9. Output for DataViewStronglyTypedDataSet solution

Discussion

The DataView indexer in C# or Item property in Visual Basic allows access to the DataRowView objects in the DataView. The DataRowView object in turn exposes a Row property that is a reference to the underlying DataRow object. Just as DataTable objects contain DataRow objects, DataView objects contain DataRowView objects. The Row property of the DataRowView object is used to return the underlying DataRow object. The typed DataSet classes—including the DataTable, DataColumn, and DataRow objects—inherit from the ADO.NET disconnected classes, letting you cast the DataRow to the strongly typed row, as in this solution.

3.10 Testing Whether a Query Returns an Empty Result Set

Problem

You need to determine whether any records were returned from a query that you just executed.

Solution

Use the `DataRowCollection.Count` property, the `DataReader.HasRows` property, or the `DataReader.Read( )` method.

Using both nonempty and empty result sets, the solution creates and fills a `DataTable` and uses the `Count` property of the `DataRowCollection` to determine whether the query used to create the table returned any rows. Next, a `DataReader` is created and both the `HasRows` property and the `Read( )` method are used to determine whether the query used to create the `DataReader` returned any rows.

The C# code in *Program.cs* in the project `TestQueryReturnEmptyResultSet` is shown in Example 3-13.

Example 3-13. File: Program.cs for TestQueryReturnEmptyResultSet solution

```
using System;
using System.Data;
using System.Data.SqlClient;

namespace TestQueryReturnEmptyResultSet
{
    class Program
    {
        static void Main(string[] args)
        {
            string sqlConnectString = "Data Source=(local);" +
                "Integrated security=SSPI;Initial Catalog=AdventureWorks;";

            string sqlSelect = "SELECT * FROM Person.Contact";
            string sqlSelectEmpty =
                "SELECT * FROM Person.Contact WHERE ContactID = 0";

            Console.WriteLine("---QUERY RETURNS NON-EMPTY RESULT SET---");
            SqlDataAdapter da = new SqlDataAdapter(sqlSelect, sqlConnectString);
            DataTable dt = new DataTable( );
            da.Fill(dt);
            Console.WriteLine("DataTable has records = {0}", dt.Rows.Count > 0);
```

Example 3-13. File: Program.cs for TestQueryReturnEmptyResultSet solution (continued)

```csharp
using (SqlConnection connection = new SqlConnection(sqlConnectString))
{
    SqlCommand command = new SqlCommand(sqlSelect, connection);
    connection.Open( );
    SqlDataReader dr = command.ExecuteReader( );

    Console.WriteLine(
        "DataReader has records using HasRows property = {0}",
        dr.HasRows);

    Console.WriteLine(
        "DataReader has records using Read( ) method = {0}",
        dr.Read( ));

    dr.Close( );
}

Console.WriteLine( );
Console.WriteLine("---QUERY RETURNS EMPTY RESULT SET---");
da = new SqlDataAdapter(sqlSelectEmpty, sqlConnectString);
dt = new DataTable( );
da.Fill(dt);
Console.WriteLine("DataTable has records = {0}", dt.Rows.Count > 0);

using (SqlConnection connection = new SqlConnection(sqlConnectString))
{
    SqlCommand command = new SqlCommand(sqlSelectEmpty, connection);
    connection.Open( );
    SqlDataReader dr = command.ExecuteReader( );

    Console.WriteLine(
        "DataReader has records using HasRows property = {0}",
        dr.HasRows);

    Console.WriteLine(
        "DataReader has records using Read( ) method = {0}",
        dr.Read( ));

    dr.Close( );
}

Console.WriteLine("\nPress any key to continue.");
Console.ReadKey( );
            }
        }
}
```

The output is shown in Figure 3-10.

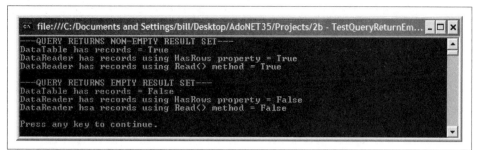

Figure 3-10. Output for TestQueryReturnEmptyResultSet solution

Discussion

The DataTable contains a DataRowCollection object that is accessed through the Rows property and contains all DataRow objects in the table. The DataRowCollection has a Count property that returns the number of rows in the table. The Count property for an empty table has the value 0.

The HasRows property of the DataReader returns a Boolean value indicating whether the DataReader has any records.

Another way is to use the Read( ) method to advance the DataReader to the next record. This returns a value of true if a record is available and false otherwise. The first call to the Read( ) method will indicate whether any records were returned by the DataReader. This was the only way to determine whether the DataReader contained any records prior to the introduction of the HasRows property in .NET Framework 1.1.

3.11   Counting Records Meeting Criteria

Problem

You want to determine how many rows that meet certain criteria are in a table.

Solution

Use the ExecuteScalar( ) method of the Command object to determine the number of records in the table.

The solution executes the COUNT function on the results of a query returning rows from the Person.Contact table in the AdventureWorks sample database, where the last name starts with *A*.

The C# code in *Program.cs* in the project CountRecordsMeetingCriteria is shown in Example 3-14.

Example 3-14. File: Program.cs for CountRecordsMeetingCriteria solution

```
using System;
using System.Data;
using System.Data.SqlClient;

namespace CountRecordsMeetingCriteria
{
    class Program
    {
        static void Main(string[] args)
        {
            string sqlConnectString = "Data Source=(local);" +
                "Integrated security=SSPI;Initial Catalog=AdventureWorks;";

            // Create the connection.
            SqlConnection connection = new SqlConnection(sqlConnectString);

            // Build the query to count including criteria.
            string selectText = "SELECT COUNT(*) FROM Person.Contact " +
                "WHERE LastName LIKE 'A%'";

            // Create the command to count the records.
            SqlCommand command = new SqlCommand(selectText, connection);
            // Execute the command, storing the results.
            connection.Open();
            int recordCount = (int)command.ExecuteScalar();
            connection.Close();

            Console.WriteLine("Person.Contact records starting with 'A' = {0}",
                recordCount);

            Console.WriteLine("\nPress any key to continue.");
            Console.ReadKey();
        }
    }
}
```

The output is shown in Figure 3-11.

Figure 3-11. Output for CountRecordsMeetingCriteria solution

Discussion

The ExecuteScalar() method of the Command object returns a single value from a query rather than a table or a data stream. If the query returns a result set, this method returns the value of the first column of the first row.

The number of records matching certain criteria can be determined by executing a SQL statement that returns the COUNT(*) aggregate function and includes a WHERE clause that specifies the criteria. Use the ExecuteScalar( ) method to execute the statement and return the count. Cast the result to an int data type.

This technique can also be used with other aggregate functions to determine values such as averages or sums. For more information about aggregate functions, see Microsoft SQL Server Books Online.

3.12 Determining the Number of Records Returned in a DataReader

Problem

You want to determine how many records there are in a DataReader.

Solution

Use one of the following three techniques:

- Issue a COUNT(*) query as part of a batch query. Note that not all data sources support batch queries. If not, execute the statements separately one after the other for a similar result.

- Iterate over the rows in the DataReader and use a counter.

- Use the @@ROWCOUNT function in a stored procedure to return the number or rows in a DataReader after the DataReader has been closed. This technique is SQL Server-specific.

The solution uses a single stored procedure:

Person.GetContacts

> Returns a result set containing all records in the Person.Contact table in AdventureWorks. Also, the stored procedure returns the @@ROWCOUNT value for the query in an output parameter. The stored procedure is shown in Example 3-15.

Example 3-15. Stored procedure: Person.GetContacts

```
CREATE PROCEDURE Person.GetContacts
    @RowCount int OUTPUT
AS
    SET NOCOUNT ON

    SELECT * FROM Person.Contact

    set @RowCount = @@ROWCOUNT

    RETURN @RowCount
```

The C# code in *Program.cs* in the project DataReaderRowCount is shown in Example 3-16.

Example 3-16. File: Program.cs for DataReaderRowCount solution

```
using System;
using System.Data;
using System.Data.SqlClient;

namespace DataReaderRowCount
{
    class Program
    {
        static void Main(string[] args)
        {
            string sqlConnectString = "Data Source=(local);" +
                "Integrated security=SSPI;Initial Catalog=AdventureWorks;";

            // Batch query to retrieve the COUNT of records and
            // all of the records in the Person.Contact table as two result sets.
            string sqlSelect =
                "SELECT COUNT(*) FROM Person.Contact; " +
                "SELECT * FROM Person.Contact;";

            // Create the connection.
            using (SqlConnection connection = new SqlConnection(sqlConnectString))
            {
                // Create the command
                SqlCommand command = new SqlCommand(sqlSelect, connection);

                // Create a DataReader on the first result set.
                connection.Open( );
                SqlDataReader dr = command.ExecuteReader( );

                // Get and output the record count from the
                // SELECT COUNT(*) statement.
                dr.Read( );
                Console.WriteLine("Record count, using COUNT(*)= {0}",
                    dr.GetInt32(0));

                // Move to the next result set in the batch.
                dr.NextResult( );

                int count = 0;
                // Iterate over the records in the DataReader.
                while (dr.Read( ))
                {
                    count++;

                    // ... do something interesting with the data here.
                }
                Console.WriteLine(
                    "Record count, iterating over results = {0}", count);
```

```
                    // Close the DataReader.
                    dr.Close( );

                    // Create the stored procedure to use in the DataReader.
                    command = new SqlCommand("Person.GetContacts", connection);
                    command.CommandType = CommandType.StoredProcedure;
                    // Create the output paramter to return @@ROWCOUNT.
                    command.Parameters.Add("@RowCount", SqlDbType.Int).Direction =
                        ParameterDirection.Output;

                    // Create a DataReader for the result set returned by
                    // the stored procedure.
                    dr = command.ExecuteReader( );

                    //  ... process the data in the DataReader.

                    // Close the DataReader.
                    dr.Close( );
                    // The output parameter containing the row count is now available.

                    Console.WriteLine("Record count, using @@ROWCOUNT = {0}",
                        command.Parameters["@RowCount"].Value);
                }

            Console.WriteLine("\nPress any key to continue.");
            Console.ReadKey( );
        }
    }
}
```

The output is shown in Figure 3-12.

Figure 3-12. Output for DataReaderRowCount solution

Discussion

The DataReader provides forward-only, read-only access to a stream of rows from a data source. It is optimized for performance by reading data directly from a connection to a data source. As a result, there is no way to determine the number of records in the result set for the DataReader without iterating through all of the records using Read( ) method, and counting each record. Additionally, because the DataReader is forward-only, you cannot move backward in DataReader, so when iterating, you must process data at the same time.

A second technique demonstrated in the solution counts the records using the T-SQL COUNT aggregate function. This technique can have discrepancies with the number of records actually in the DataReader because of the timing lag between issuing the COUNT function and creating and using the DataReader.

The solution also demonstrates using the SQL Server @@ROWCOUNT variable, which returns the number of rows affected by the previous statement, to return the number of records in the result set used to create the DataReader. The count is returned as an output parameter and is therefore not available until the DataReader is closed. Although this does not improve the availability of the record count, centralizing the count in the stored procedure is less prone to coding errors than the counting approach. For more information about output parameters, see Recipe 3.23.

The HasRows( ) method of the DataReader was introduced in version 1.1 of the .NET Framework. It returns a Boolean value indicating whether the DataReader contains at least one row.

There is also no way to determine the number of result sets in a DataReader built using a batch query without iterating over the result sets using the NextResult( ) method.

3.13 Executing a Query That Returns Multiple Result Sets

Problem

You have a batch SQL query that returns multiple result sets and you need to work with the result sets in ADO.NET.

Solution

Use the techniques shown in this solution to use a batch query with both a DataSet and with a DataReader.

The solution defines a SQL batch query statement that selects the top three rows of each Sales.SalesOrderHeader and Sales.SalesOrderDetails from AdventureWorks.

A DataAdapter is used to load the multiple result sets into a DataSet. The data values in the DataSet are accessed through the collection of DataTable objects in the DataSet and output to the console.

The NextResult( ) method of the DataReader is used to iterate through and the multiple result sets that the batch query returns. The DataReader values are output to the console.

The C# code in *Program.cs* in the project ExecuteBatchQuery is shown in Example 3-17.

Example 3-17. File: Program.cs for ExecuteBatchQuery solution

```csharp
using System;
using System.Data;
using System.Data.SqlClient;

namespace ExecuteBatchQuery
{
    class Program
    {
        static void Main(string[] args)
        {
            string sqlConnectString = "Data Source=(local);" +
                "Integrated security=SSPI;Initial Catalog=AdventureWorks;";

            string sqlSelect = "SELECT TOP 3 * FROM Sales.SalesOrderHeader;" +
                "SELECT TOP 3 * FROM Sales.SalesOrderDetail";

            int rsNumber;

            // SQL batch using a DataSet
            Console.WriteLine("---DataSet---");

            // Fill the DataSet with the results of the batch query.
            SqlDataAdapter da = new SqlDataAdapter(sqlSelect, sqlConnectString);
            DataSet ds = new DataSet( );
            da.Fill(ds);

            rsNumber = 0;
            // Iterate over the result sets in the DataTable collection
            foreach (DataTable dt in ds.Tables)
            {
                Console.WriteLine("Result set: {0}", ++rsNumber);

                foreach (DataRow row in dt.Rows)
                {
                    // Output the first three fields for each record
                    Console.WriteLine("{0}, {1}, {2}", row[0], row[1], row[2]);
                }

                Console.WriteLine(Environment.NewLine);
            }

            using (SqlConnection connection = new SqlConnection(sqlConnectString))
            {
                // SQL batch using a DataReader
                Console.WriteLine("---DataReader---");

                // Create the DataReader from the batch query
                SqlCommand command = new SqlCommand(sqlSelect, connection);
                connection.Open( );
                SqlDataReader dr = command.ExecuteReader( );
```

Example 3-17. File: Program.cs for ExecuteBatchQuery solution (continued)

```
                rsNumber = 0;
                //Iterate over the result sets using the NextResult( ) method
                do
                {
                    Console.WriteLine("Result set: {0}", ++rsNumber);

                    // Iterate over the rows in the DataReader.
                    while (dr.Read( ))
                    {
                        // Output the first three fields for each record
                        Console.WriteLine("{0}, {1}, {2}", dr[0], dr[1], dr[2]);
                    }

                    Console.WriteLine(Environment.NewLine);
                } while (dr.NextResult( ));
            }

            Console.WriteLine("Press any key to continue.");
            Console.ReadKey( );
        }
    }
}
```

The output is shown in Figure 3-13.

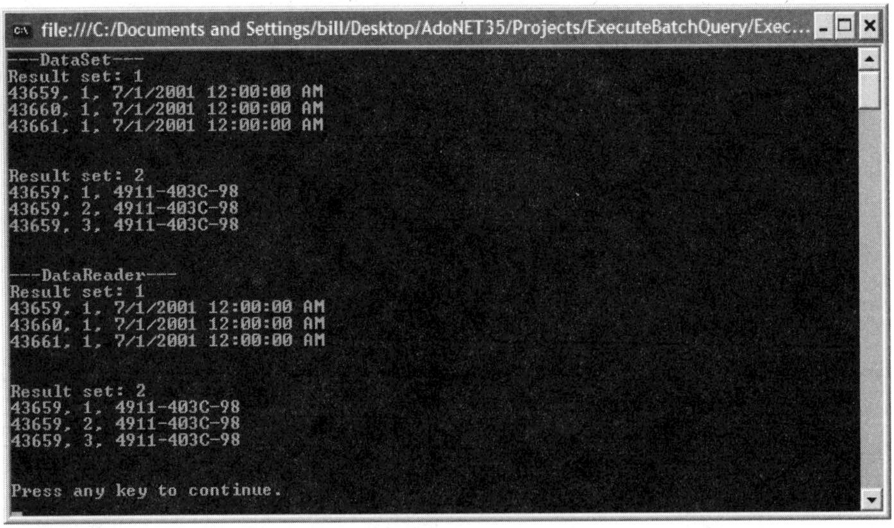

Figure 3-13. Output for ExecuteBatchQuery solution

Discussion

A batch command is a group of SQL statements sent to a database server at the same time for execution. In T-SQL, these statements are separated by semicolons. When SQL Server receives a batch, it compiles the statements into a single execution plan. The statements within the execution plan are then executed one at a time. A compile error in the batch prevents the execution plan from being compiled—no statements in the batch are executed. Most runtime errors in a batch stop execution at the current statement and for all successive statements. A few runtime errors such as constraint violations stop only the current statement—execution resumes with the statements that follow.

A batch command can be used to fill a DataSet or to build a DataReader. Working with the results is different for each of these scenarios, as described in the following sections.

The batch command can also be contained within a stored procedure. Everything is the same as for the example where the SQL batch command is defined in the code once the Command is executed.

 The Oracle .NET data provider does not support batch SQL statements. To execute a batch query against an Oracle database it is necessary to use an Oracle package that returns multiple REF CURSOR output parameters. For more information, see the solution in Recipe 3.19.

DataSet

The Fill( ) method of the DataAdapter adds multiple result sets from a batch query to a DataSet. One table is created in the DataSet for each result set. By default, these tables will be named Table, Table1, Table2, and so on. You can make these names more meaningful by specifying table mappings in the TableMappings collection of the DataAdapter. For more information about using table mappings, see Recipe 2.3.

Data relationships between the tables added with a batch query must be created programmatically. As with nonbatch queries, you can define the relations and foreign key constraints for the tables prior to filling them with the results of the batch query.

When using the Fill( ) method of the DataAdapter with a batch fill operation, if one of the result sets contains an error, all subsequent processing is skipped and result sets are not added to the DataSet.

When using the FillSchema( ) method of the DataAdapter with a batch query and the OLE DB data provider, the schema is returned for only the first query. To retrieve the schema for all result sets, use the Fill( ) method with the MissingSchemaAction argument set to AddWithKey.

DataReader

As with a single statement command, a batch command is used to build a DataReader by calling the ExecuteReader( ) method of the Command object. The NextResult( ) method of the DataReader is used to advance to the next result set where the method returns true if there is another result set.

Initially, the DataReader is positioned on the first result set. After NextResult( ) is called there is no way to return to a previous result set.

3.14   Retrieving Schema and Constraints for a DataSet

Problem

You need to retrieve schema and constraint information from the data source into a DataSet or DataTable.

Solution

Use the FillSchema( ) method of the DataAdapter or set the MissingSchemaAction property of the DataAdapter to AddWithKey before calling the Fill( ) method of the DataAdapter.

The solution loads a DataSet with the first five records from the Person.Contact table from AdventureWorks and outputs the schema for the DataSet when calling Fill( ) without and with calling FillSchema( ).

The C# code in *Program.cs* in the project AddExistingConstraints is shown in Example 3-18.

Example 3-18. File: Program.cs for AddExistingConstraints solution

```
using System;
using System.Data;
using System.Data.SqlClient;

namespace AddingExistingConstraints
{
    class Program
    {
        static void Main(string[] args)
        {
            string sqlConnectString = "Data Source=(local);" +
                "Integrated security=SSPI;Initial Catalog=AdventureWorks;";

            string sqlSelect = "SELECT TOP 5 ContactID," +
                "FirstName, LastName FROM Person.Contact";
```

Example 3-18. File: Program.cs for AddExistingConstraints solution (continued)

```
        // Create a data adapter
        SqlDataAdapter da =
            new SqlDataAdapter(sqlSelect, sqlConnectString);

        // Fill a DataSet without schema
        DataSet ds = new DataSet();
        da.Fill(ds, "Contact");

        Console.WriteLine("---WITHOUT SCHEMA--", ds.Tables.Count);
        Console.WriteLine("GetXmlSchema() = {0}", ds.GetXmlSchema());

        // Fill a DataSet with schema using FillSchema()
        DataSet dsSchema = new DataSet();
        da.FillSchema(dsSchema, SchemaType.Source, "Person.Contact");
        da.Fill(dsSchema, "Contact");
        Console.WriteLine("\n---WITH SCHEMA using FillSchema()--",
            dsSchema.Tables.Count);
        Console.WriteLine(
            "GetXmlSchema() = {0}", dsSchema.GetXmlSchema());

        Console.WriteLine("\nPress any key to continue.");
        Console.ReadKey();
    }
  }
}
```

The output is shown in Figure 3-14.

Discussion

By default, the Fill() method of the DataAdapter loads a DataSet with only tables and columns from a data source without other schema information. You can add primary key and unique constraints together with the AllowDBNull, AutoIncrement (but not AutoIncrementStep or AutoIncrementSeed), MaxLength, ReadOnly, and Unique column properties by using the FillSchema() method of the DataAdapter or by setting the MissingSchemaAction property of the DataAdapter to AddWithKey before calling the Fill() method.

The solution uses the FillSchema() method:

```
    da.FillSchema(dsSchema, SchemaType.Source, "Person.Contact");
```

You can achieve similar results by setting the MissingSchemaAction property:

```
    da.MissingSchemaAction = MissingSchemaAction.AddWithKey;
```

Either technique requires extra processing at the data source to determine primary key information. Explicitly setting primary key information at design time will optimize performance by eliminating the extra processing.

Figure 3-14. Output for AddExistingConstraints solution

The FillSchema( ) method has the following overloads:

```
FillSchema(DataSet ds, SchemaType schemaType)
FillSchema(DataTable dt, SchemaType schemaType)
FillSchema(DataSet ds, SchemaType schemaType, string sourceTableName)
FillSchema(DataTable dt, SchemaType schemaType, IDataReader dr)
FillSchema(DataSet ds, SchemaType schemaType, string sourceTableName,
    IDataReader dr)
FillSchema(DataTable dt, SchemaType schemaType, IDbCommand command,
    CommandBehavior behavior)
```

Where:

ds
> The DataSet into which to insert the schema.

dt
> The DataTable into which to insert the schema.

schemaType
> Specifies how to insert the schema. A value—Source or Mapped—from the SchemaType enumeration.

sourceTableName
> The name of the source table to use for table mapping.

dr
> The DataReader to use as the schema source.

command
> The SQL SELECT statement used as the schema source.

behavior
> Specifies the results returned by the query—this is a value from the CommandBehavior enumeration described in Table 3-1. Bitwise combinations of multiple CommandBehavior values can be specified.

3.15   Retrieving Hierarchical Data

Problem

You want to fill a DataSet with parent and related child data, even if the DataSet already has a schema that includes the relationship.

Solution

The solution shows how to load parent and child data into a DataSet using both multiple SQL SELECT queries and a batch SQL query.

The solution creates a DataSet and loads it with both schema and data from the Sales.SalesOrderHeader and Sales.SalesOrderDetail tables in AdventureWorks. A DataRelation object is created relating the two tables. The first three rows from the SalesOrderHeader table is output together with the related SalesOrderDetail rows for each.

The C# code in *Program.cs* in the project RetrieveHierarchicalDataSet is shown in Example 3-19.

Example 3-19. File: Program.cs for RetrieveHierarchicalDataSet solution

```
using System;
using System.Data;
using System.Data.SqlClient;

namespace RetrieveHierarchicalDataSet
{
    class Program
    {
        static void Main(string[] args)
        {
            string sqlConnectString = "Data Source=(local);" +
                "Integrated security=SSPI;Initial Catalog=AdventureWorks;";

            string sqlSelectHeader = "SELECT * FROM Sales.SalesOrderHeader";
            string sqlSelectDetail = "SELECT * FROM Sales.SalesOrderDetail";

            DataSet ds = new DataSet();
            SqlDataAdapter da;

            // Fill the Header table in the DataSet
            da = new SqlDataAdapter(sqlSelectHeader, sqlConnectString);
            da.FillSchema(ds, SchemaType.Source, "SalesOrderHeader");
            da.Fill(ds, "SalesOrderHeader");

            // Fill the Detail table in the DataSet
            da = new SqlDataAdapter(sqlSelectDetail, sqlConnectString);
            da.FillSchema(ds, SchemaType.Source, "SalesOrderDetail");
            da.Fill(ds, "SalesOrderDetail");

            // Relate the Header and Order tables in the DataSet
            DataRelation dr = new DataRelation("SalesOrderHeader_SalesOrderDetail",
                ds.Tables["SalesOrderHeader"].Columns["SalesOrderID"],
                ds.Tables["SalesOrderDetail"].Columns["SalesOrderID"]);
            ds.Relations.Add(dr);

            // Output fields from first three header rows with detail
            for (int i = 0; i < 3; i++)
            {
                DataRow rowHeader = ds.Tables["SalesOrderHeader"].Rows[i];
                Console.WriteLine(
                    "HEADER: OrderID = {0}, Date = {1}, TotalDue = {2}",
                    rowHeader["SalesOrderID"], rowHeader["OrderDate"],
                    rowHeader["TotalDue"]);

                foreach (DataRow rowDetail in rowHeader.GetChildRows(dr))
                {
                    Console.WriteLine("\tDETAIL: OrderID = {0}, DetailID = {1}, " +
                        "LineTotal = {2}",
                        rowDetail["SalesOrderID"], rowDetail["SalesOrderDetailID"],
                        rowDetail["LineTotal"]);
                }
            }
```

Example 3-19. File: Program.cs for RetrieveHierarchicalDataSet solution (continued)

```
        Console.WriteLine("\nPress any key to continue.");
        Console.ReadKey( );
    }
  }
}
```

The output is shown in Figure 3-15.

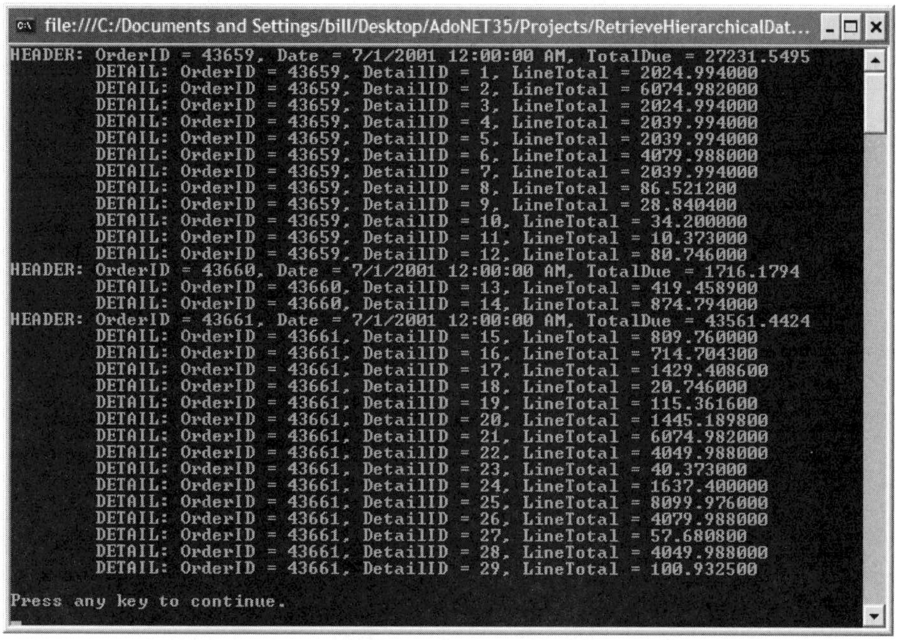

Figure 3-15. Output for RetrieveHierarchicalDataSet solution

You can also load a hierarchical DataSet using a batch SQL query. The code is similar; however, notice that two DataTableMapping objects are added to the DataTableMappings collection for the DataAdapter to make the names of the DataTable names in the DataSet more usable.

The batch solution is generally a better practice because it reduces the number of roundtrips to the database. Additionally, the batch solution uses the MissingSchemaAction property of the DataAdapter to retrieve schema information— this eliminates the roundtrip required by the FillSchema( ) method in the non-batch solution. The MissingSchemaAction still results in the additional processing time required to retrieve the schema information.

The C# code in *Program.cs* in the project RetrieveHierarchicalDataSetBatch and is shown in Example 3-20.

Example 3-20. File: Program.cs for RetrieveHierarchicalDataSetBatch solution

```
using System;
using System.Data;
using System.Data.SqlClient;

namespace RetrieveHierarchicalDataSetBatch
{
    class Program
    {
        static void Main(string[] args)
        {
            string sqlConnectString = "Data Source=(local);" +
                "Integrated security=SSPI;Initial Catalog=AdventureWorks;";

            string sqlSelect = "SELECT * FROM Sales.SalesOrderHeader;" +
                "SELECT * FROM Sales.SalesOrderDetail";

            DataSet ds = new DataSet();
            SqlDataAdapter da;

            // Fill the DataSet with Header and Detail,
            // mapping the default table names
            da = new SqlDataAdapter(sqlSelect, sqlConnectString);
            da.TableMappings.Add("Table", "SalesOrderHeader");
            da.TableMappings.Add("Table1", "SalesOrderDetail");
            da.MissingSchemaAction = MissingSchemaAction.AddWithKey;
            da.Fill(ds);

            // Relate the Header and Order tables in the DataSet
            DataRelation dr = new DataRelation("SalesOrderHeader_SalesOrderDetail",
                ds.Tables["SalesOrderHeader"].Columns["SalesOrderID"],
                ds.Tables["SalesOrderDetail"].Columns["SalesOrderID"]);
            ds.Relations.Add(dr);

            // Output fields from first three header rows with detail
            for (int i = 0; i < 3; i++)
            {
                DataRow rowHeader = ds.Tables["SalesOrderHeader"].Rows[i];
                Console.WriteLine(
                    "HEADER: OrderID = {0}, Date = {1}, TotalDue = {2}",
                    rowHeader["SalesOrderID"], rowHeader["OrderDate"],
                    rowHeader["TotalDue"]);

                foreach (DataRow rowDetail in rowHeader.GetChildRows(dr))
                {
                    Console.WriteLine(
                        "\tDETAIL: OrderID = {0}, DetailID = {1}, " +
                        "LineTotal = {2}", rowDetail["SalesOrderID"],
                        rowDetail["SalesOrderDetailID"], rowDetail["LineTotal"]);
                }
            }
```

```
        Console.WriteLine("\nPress any key to continue.");
        Console.ReadKey( );
    }
  }
}
```

The output is identical to Example 3-19 and is shown in Figure 3-15.

Discussion

The DataRelation class represents a parent/child relationship between two DataTable objects.

By default, a DataRelation is created with constraints as in the example; however, an overloaded constructor can override this behavior if necessary. If constraints are created, it is important that each record in the child table refers to a valid parent record; otherwise, a ConstraintException is raised. Two techniques can be used to load parent and related child data without error into a DataSet with a schema that includes data relations defined:

- Load data from the parent tables before loading data from the child table. This ensures that each record in the child table refers to a valid parent record.

- The EnforceConstraints property of the DataSet indicates whether constraint rules are followed when data is added to or modified in the DataSet. Turn constraints off by setting the EnforceConstraints property to false prior to loading the data and back to true once the data is loaded. With this approach, the sequence in which the data is loaded is not important. If one or more constraints cannot be enforced when EnforceConstraints is set back to true, a ConstraintException will be raised and EnforceConstraints stay set to false.

See Recipe 2.10 for more information about data relations.

3.16 Navigating Between Parent and Child Tables in an Untyped DataSet

Problem

You want to navigate between the parent and child records in a hierarchical DataSet.

Solution

Use a DataRelation to find the child rows for a parent row in a related table, or to find the parent row for a child row in a related table.

The solution begins by creating a DataSet containing the Sales.SalesOrderHeader and Sales.SalesOrderDetail tables from AdventureWorks and creating a relation between them. The code then iterates over the SalesOrderHeader DataTable and uses the relation to output all child rows in the SalesOrderDetail DataTable to the console. The solution retrieves the CustomerID field for each child row from the parent row, and outputs it to the console.

The C# code in *Program.cs* in the project NavigatingParentChildTables is shown in Example 3-21.

Example 3-21. File: Program.cs for NavigatingParentChildTables solution

```
using System;
using System.Data;
using System.Data.SqlClient;

namespace NavigatingParentChildTables
{
    class Program
    {
        static void Main(string[] args)
        {
            string sqlConnectString = "Data Source=(local);" +
                "Integrated security=SSPI;Initial Catalog=AdventureWorks;";

            string sqlSelect = @"SELECT * FROM Sales.SalesOrderHeader;
                SELECT * FROM Sales.SalesOrderDetail;";

            DataSet ds = new DataSet();
            SqlDataAdapter da;

            // Fill the Header and Detail table in the DataSet
            da = new SqlDataAdapter(sqlSelect, sqlConnectString);
            da.MissingSchemaAction = MissingSchemaAction.AddWithKey;
            da.TableMappings.Add("Table", "SalesOrderHeader");
            da.TableMappings.Add("Table1", "SalesOrderDetail");
            da.Fill(ds);

            // Relate the Header and Order tables in the DataSet
            DataRelation dr = new DataRelation("SalesOrderHeader_SalesOrderDetail",
                ds.Tables["SalesOrderHeader"].Columns["SalesOrderID"],
                ds.Tables["SalesOrderDetail"].Columns["SalesOrderID"]);
            ds.Relations.Add(dr);

            // Iterate over the first two header rows
            for (int i = 0; i < 2; i++)
            {
                // Display data from the SalesOrderHeader record
                DataRow rowHeader = ds.Tables["SalesOrderHeader"].Rows[i];
                Console.WriteLine("HEADER: OrderID = {0}, CustomerID = {1}",
                    rowHeader["SalesOrderID"],rowHeader["CustomerID"]);
```

```
                // Iterate over the SalesOrderDetail records for the
                // SalesOrderHeader
                foreach (DataRow rowDetail in rowHeader.GetChildRows(dr))
                {
                    Console.WriteLine("\tDETAIL: OrderID = {0}, DetailID = {1}, " +
                        "CustomerID = {3}",
                        rowDetail["SalesOrderID"], rowDetail["SalesOrderDetailID"],
                        rowDetail["LineTotal"],
                        rowDetail.GetParentRow(dr)["CustomerID"]);
                }
            }

            Console.WriteLine("\nPress any key to continue.");
            Console.ReadKey();
        }
    }
}
```

The output is shown in Figure 3-16.

```
file:///C:/Documents and Settings/bill/Desktop/AdoNET35/Projects/NavigatingParentChildTa...
HEADER: OrderID = 43659, CustomerID = 676
        DETAIL: OrderID = 43659, DetailID = 1, CustomerID = 676
        DETAIL: OrderID = 43659, DetailID = 2, CustomerID = 676
        DETAIL: OrderID = 43659, DetailID = 3, CustomerID = 676
        DETAIL: OrderID = 43659, DetailID = 4, CustomerID = 676
        DETAIL: OrderID = 43659, DetailID = 5, CustomerID = 676
        DETAIL: OrderID = 43659, DetailID = 6, CustomerID = 676
        DETAIL: OrderID = 43659, DetailID = 7, CustomerID = 676
        DETAIL: OrderID = 43659, DetailID = 8, CustomerID = 676
        DETAIL: OrderID = 43659, DetailID = 9, CustomerID = 676
        DETAIL: OrderID = 43659, DetailID = 10, CustomerID = 676
        DETAIL: OrderID = 43659, DetailID = 11, CustomerID = 676
        DETAIL: OrderID = 43659, DetailID = 12, CustomerID = 676
HEADER: OrderID = 43660, CustomerID = 117
        DETAIL: OrderID = 43660, DetailID = 13, CustomerID = 117
        DETAIL: OrderID = 43660, DetailID = 14, CustomerID = 117

Press any key to continue.
```

Figure 3-16. Output for NavigatingParentChildTables solution

Discussion

The GetChildRows( ) method of a row in the parent table returns the child rows as an array of DataRow objects for a specified DataRelation. The method takes an optional second argument that you can use to specify the version of the data to retrieve as one of the DataRowVersion enumeration values: Current, Default, Original, or Proposed.

Similarly, the GetParentRow( ) method of a row in the child table returns the parent row as a DataRow object for a specified DataRelation. Again, an optional second argument allows a specific version of the data to be returned.

The `GetParentRows( )` method can also be called on a row in the child table to return parent rows in situations where the child row can have multiple parents. This method returns an array of `DataRow` objects. Few commercial database products support many-to-many relationships between parent and child records. Many-to-many relationships are decomposed into two one-to-many relationships through an intermediate table in relational database management systems (RDBMS).

3.17   Executing a Parameterized Query

Problem

You want to create and execute a SQL statement with parameters that are set dynamically.

Solution

Add parameters to the `Command` object's `Parameters` collection.

The solution begins by creating a parameterized SQL statement that retrieves records from the `Sales.SalesOrderHeader` table in `AdventureWorks` where the `TotalDue` field is greater than a parameterized amount. A `Command` is built from the statement and the single parameter, `@TotalDue`, is created and set to 200,000. A `DataAdapter` uses the `Command` to fill a `DataTable`. Several columns for all rows in the result set are written to the console. The solution shows how to create and execute a parameterized query using both the SQL Server data provider and the OLE DB data provider. Results are output to the console.

The C# code in *Program.cs* in the project `ExecutingParameterizedQuery` is shown in Example 3-22.

Example 3-22. File: Program.cs for ExecutingParameterizedQuery solution

```
using System;
using System.Data;
using System.Data.SqlClient;
using System.Data.OleDb;

namespace ExecutingParameterizedQuery
{
    class Program
    {
        static void Main(string[] args)
        {
            // SQL Server parameterized query
            Console.WriteLine("---Data Provider for SQL Server");

            string sqlConnectString = "Data Source=(local);" +
                "Integrated security=SSPI;Initial Catalog=AdventureWorks;";
```

```csharp
string sqlSelect = "SELECT * FROM Sales.SalesOrderHeader " +
    "WHERE TotalDue > @TotalDue";

SqlConnection sqlConnection = new SqlConnection(sqlConnectString);
SqlCommand sqlCommand = new SqlCommand(sqlSelect, sqlConnection);

// Add the TotalDue parameter to the command
sqlCommand.Parameters.Add("@TotalDue", SqlDbType.Money);

// Set the value of the TotalDue paramter
sqlCommand.Parameters["@TotalDue"].Value = 200000;

// Use a DataAdapter to retrieve the result set into a DataTable
SqlDataAdapter sqlDa = new SqlDataAdapter(sqlCommand);
DataTable sqlDt = new DataTable( );
sqlDa.Fill(sqlDt);

foreach (DataRow row in sqlDt.Rows)
{
    Console.WriteLine
        ("SalesOrderID = {0}, OrderDate = {1}, TotalDue = {2}",
        row["SalesOrderID"], row["OrderDate"], row["TotalDue"]);
}

Console.WriteLine( );

// OLE DB parameterized query
Console.WriteLine("---Data Provider for OLE DB");

string oledbConnectString = "Provider=SQLOLEDB; Data Source=(local);" +
    "Integrated security=SSPI;Initial Catalog=AdventureWorks;";

string oledbSelect = "SELECT * FROM Sales.SalesOrderHeader " +
    "WHERE TotalDue > ?";

OleDbConnection oledbConnection =
    new OleDbConnection(oledbConnectString);
OleDbCommand oledbCommand =
    new OleDbCommand(oledbSelect, oledbConnection);

// Add the TotalDue parameter to the command
oledbCommand.Parameters.Add("@TotalDue", OleDbType.Currency);

// Set the value of the TotalDue paramter
oledbCommand.Parameters["@TotalDue"].Value = 200000;

// Use a DataAdapter to retrieve the result set into a DataTable
OleDbDataAdapter oledbDa = new OleDbDataAdapter(oledbCommand);
DataTable oledbDt = new DataTable( );
oledbDa.Fill(oledbDt);
```

Example 3-22. File: Program.cs for ExecutingParameterizedQuery solution (continued)

```
            foreach (DataRow row in oledbDt.Rows)
            {
                Console.WriteLine
                    ("SalesOrderID = {0}, OrderDate = {1}, TotalDue = {2}",
                    row["SalesOrderID"], row["OrderDate"], row["TotalDue"]);
            }

            Console.WriteLine("\nPress any key to continue.");
            Console.ReadKey( );
        }
    }
}
```

The output is shown in Figure 3-17.

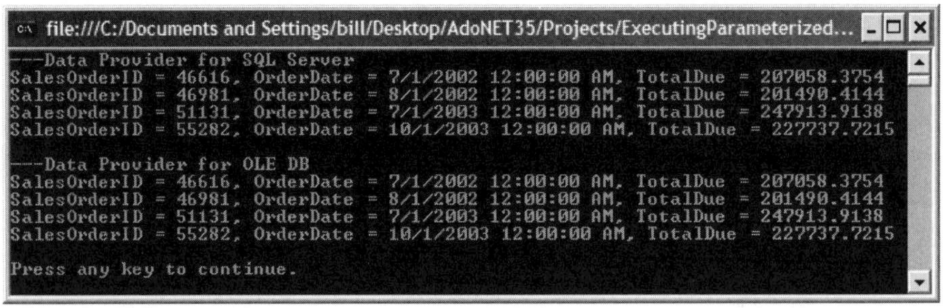

Figure 3-17. Output for ExecutingParameterizedQuery solution

Discussion

Parameterized queries are queries with one or more parameters that are replaced at runtime. Using parameterized queries is both easier and less prone to errors than dynamically building queries. You're not responsible for creating delimiters such as single quotes around strings and pound signs around dates. In ADO.NET, parameters are specified using `Parameter` objects in the `ParameterCollection` class of a `Command` object.

The SQL Server data provider uses named parameters in a query; parameter names must be unique and the order they are added to the `ParameterCollection` is not important. The OLE DB data provider uses positional parameter markers—the question mark (?)—and they must be added to the `ParameterCollection` in the same order as they appear in the query.

3.18   Retrieving Data Using a SQL Server Stored Procedure

Problem

You need to execute a SQL Server stored procedure to retrieve a result set.

Solution

Use a SqlCommand object with its CommandType property set to StoredProcedure.

The solution executes the stored procedure dbo.uspGetEmployeeManagers, stores the result set in a DataTable, and outputs the values in the DataTable to the console.

The C# code in *Program.cs* in the project RetreiveDataSqlServerStoredProcedure is shown in Example 3-23.

Example 3-23. File: Program.cs for RetrieveDataSqlServerStoredProcedure solution

```
using System;
using System.Data;
using System.Data.SqlClient;

namespace RetrieveDataSqlServerStoredProcedure
{
    class Program
    {
        static void Main(string[] args)
        {
            string sqlConnectString = "Data Source=(local);" +
                "Integrated security=SSPI;Initial Catalog=AdventureWorks;";

            string sqlSelect = "uspGetEmployeeManagers";

            // Create a connection
            SqlConnection connection = new SqlConnection(sqlConnectString);
            // Create the store procedure command
            SqlCommand command = new SqlCommand(sqlSelect, connection);
            command.CommandType = CommandType.StoredProcedure;
            // Add the parameter and set its value to 100
            command.Parameters.Add("@EmployeeID", SqlDbType.Int).Value = 100;

            // Create a DataTable and fill it using the stored procedure
            DataTable dt = new DataTable();
            SqlDataAdapter da = new SqlDataAdapter(command);
            da.Fill(dt);
```

Example 3-23. File: Program.cs for RetrieveDataSqlServerStoredProcedure solution (continued)

```
            // Output the result set to the console
            foreach (DataRow row in dt.Rows)
            {
                Console.WriteLine("[{0}] {1} {2}, {3} -> {4} {5}, {6}",
                    row["RecursionLevel"], row["EmployeeID"], row["LastName"],
                    row["FirstName"], row["ManagerID"], row["ManagerLastName"],
                    row["ManagerFirstName"]);
            }

            Console.WriteLine("\nPress any key to continue.");
            Console.ReadKey();
        }
    }
}
```

The output is shown in Figure 3-18.

Figure 3-18. Output for RetrieveDataSqlServerStoredProcedure solution

Discussion

The CommandType property of the Command object specifies how the CommandText property of the command is interpreted. The CommandType property takes one of three values from the CommandTypeEnumeration, as described in Table 3-5.

Table 3-5. CommandType enumeration

Value	Description
StoredProcedure	Stored procedure.
TableDirect	Name of a table. All rows and columns are returned for TableDirect queries. You can access a join of multiple tables by creating a comma-delimited list of table names without spaces.
	TableDirect is only supported by the OLE DB data provider. You cannot access multiple tables when CommandType is set to TableDirect.
Text	A SQL text command. This is the default.

3.19 Retrieving Multiple Result Sets Using the Oracle Provider

Problem

You have an Oracle package that returns multiple result sets for related tables as REF CURSOR data types. You want to load the data into a DataSet.

Solution

Use the data type OracleType.Cursor.

The solution creates a Command for an Oracle package CURSPKG that takes an EMPLOYEE_ID input parameter. The package calls a stored procedure that returns two result sets—HR.EMPLOYEES and HR.JOB_HISTORY for the specified employee—as Oracle REF CURSOR output parameters.

A DataAdapter is created from the Command, retrieves the result sets, and loads them into a DataSet. A relation is created between the tables. Results are output to the console.

The Oracle package used in the solution is shown in Example 3-24, and the package body is shown in Example 3-25.

Example 3-24. Package: CURSPKG

```
CREATE OR REPLACE PACKAGE CURSPKG
AS
  TYPE T_CURSOR IS REF CURSOR;
  PROCEDURE GetEmployeeWithJobHistory (
    pEmployeeID IN NUMBER,
    rcEmployees OUT T_CURSOR,
    rcJobHistory OUT T_CURSOR);
END CURSPKG;
```

Example 3-25. Package body: CURSPKG

```
CREATE OR REPLACE PACKAGE BODY CURSPKG
AS
  PROCEDURE GetEmployeeWithJobHistory
  (
    pEmployeeID IN NUMBER,
    rcEmployees OUT T_CURSOR,
    rcJobHistory OUT T_CURSOR
  )
  IS
    V_CURSOR1 T_CURSOR;
    V_CURSOR2 T_CURSOR;
```

Example 3-25. Package body: CURSPKG (continued)

```
  BEGIN
    OPEN V_CURSOR1 FOR
    SELECT * FROM EMPLOYEES
    WHERE EMPLOYEE_ID = pEmployeeID;

    OPEN V_CURSOR2 FOR
    SELECT * FROM JOB_HISTORY
    WHERE EMPLOYEE_ID IN
      (SELECT EMPLOYEE_ID FROM EMPLOYEES WHERE
      EMPLOYEE_ID = pEmployeeID);

    rcEmployees := V_CURSOR1;
    rcJobHistory := V_CURSOR2;
  END GetEmployeeWithJobHistory;
END CURSPKG;
```

You need to add a reference to System.Data.Oracle client to the project.

The C# code in *Program.cs* in the project RetrieveDataOraclePackage is shown in Example 3-26.

Example 3-26. File: Program.cs for RetrieveDataOraclePackage solution

```csharp
using System;
using System.Data;
using System.Data.OracleClient;

namespace RetrieveDataOraclePackage
{
    class Program
    {
        static void Main(string[] args)
        {
            string oracleConnectString =
                "Data Source=ORCL;User Id=HR;Password=password;";

            OracleConnection connection =
                new OracleConnection(oracleConnectString);

            // Create the command for the Oracle package.
            OracleCommand command = new OracleCommand();
            command.Connection = connection;
            command.CommandType = CommandType.StoredProcedure;
            command.CommandText = "CURSPKG.GetEmployeeWithJobHistory";
            // Add the parameters, and the EmployeeID value for the input paramter.
            command.Parameters.Add("pEmployeeID", OracleType.Number);
            command.Parameters.Add("rcEmployees", OracleType.Cursor).Direction =
                ParameterDirection.Output;
            command.Parameters.Add("rcJobHistory", OracleType.Cursor).Direction =
                ParameterDirection.Output;
            command.Parameters["pEmployeeID"].Value = 200;
```

Example 3-26. File: Program.cs for RetrieveDataOraclePackage solution (continued)

```
// Create the DataAdapter and table mappings.
OracleDataAdapter da = new OracleDataAdapter(command);
da.TableMappings.Add("Table", "EMPLOYEES");
da.TableMappings.Add("Table1", "JOB_HISTORY");
// Fill the DataSet from the Oracle package.
DataSet ds = new DataSet( );
da.Fill(ds);

// Create a relation.
ds.Relations.Add("FK_EMPLOYEES_JOBHISTORY",
    ds.Tables["EMPLOYEES"].Columns["EMPLOYEE_ID"],
    ds.Tables["JOB_HISTORY"].Columns["EMPLOYEE_ID"]);

// Output to the console.
DataRow eRow = ds.Tables["EMPLOYEES"].Rows[0];
Console.WriteLine("EmployeeID = {0}; Name = {1}, {2};  HireDate = {3}",
    eRow["EMPLOYEE_ID"], eRow["LAST_NAME"], eRow["FIRST_NAME"],
    eRow["HIRE_DATE"]);
foreach (DataRow jhRow in eRow.GetChildRows("FK_EMPLOYEES_JOBHISTORY"))
    Console.WriteLine("Start = {0}; End = {1}; JobID = {2}",
        jhRow["START_DATE"], jhRow["END_DATE"], jhRow["JOB_ID"]);


Console.WriteLine("\nPress any key to continue.");
Console.ReadKey( );
        }
    }
}
```

The output is shown in Figure 3-19.

Figure 3-19. Output for RetrieveDataOraclePackage solution

Discussion

You cannot use a collection of SQL statements as a batch query within an Oracle stored procedure. Instead, you must use an Oracle package, that is, a container that groups stored procedures and functions. An Oracle package consists of a header and a body. The package header defines the name of the package and provides method signatures for each procedure or function in the package. The package body contains the code for the stored procedures and functions defined in the package header.

A REF CURSOR is an Oracle data type that points into a result set returned by a query. A REF CURSOR differs from a normal cursor in that while a cursor points to a specific result set, a REF CURSOR is a variable that can point to different result sets—a reference to a cursor—and can be assigned at execution time.

A REF CURSOR is typically used to pass result sets from a stored procedure to a client.

You can access a result using an output parameter that references an Oracle REF CURSOR. The parameter name must match the name of the REF CURSOR and it must have the data type OracleType.Cursor.

If the package returns more than one REF CURSOR parameter, an OracleDataAdapter loads them into a DataSet in the order that they appear in the parameters collection. An OracleDataReader also accesses the results sets in the order that they were added to the parameters collection and uses its NextResult( ) method to advance to the next REF CURSOR.

3.20   Passing a Null Value to a Query Parameter

Problem

You need to pass a null value to a query parameter.

Solution

Use the System.DbNull.Value static value.

The solution uses a single stored procedure shown in Example 3-27.

Example 3-27. Stored procedure: PassNullParameter

```
CREATE PROCEDURE PassNullParameter
    @ValueIn int
AS
    IF @ValueIn IS NULL
        SELECT 1 AS IsParameterNull
    ELSE
        SELECT 0 AS IsParameterNull

    RETURN 0
```

The stored procedure accepts a single parameter and returns a one-row result set containing a single value indicating whether that input parameter was null.

The solution creates a stored procedure command for the stored procedure PassNullParameter and defines the single input parameter. The input parameter is set to both null and System.DbNull.Value. The stored procedure is executed in each case using the ExecuteScalar( ) method. In each case, output to the console indicates whether the input parameter to the stored procedure is null.

The C# code in *Program.cs* in the project PassNullValueToStoredProcedureParameter is shown in Example 3-28.

Example 3-28. File: Program.cs for PassNullValueToStoredProcedureParameter solution

```
using System;
using System.Data;
using System.Data.SqlClient;

namespace PassNullValueToStoredProcedureParameter
{
    class Program
    {
        static void Main(string[] args)
        {
            // Create the connection
            string sqlConnectString = "Data Source=(local);" +
                "Integrated security=SSPI;Initial Catalog=AdventureWorks;";

            bool isNullParameter;

            using (SqlConnection connection = new SqlConnection(sqlConnectString))
            {
                // Create the stored procedure command.
                SqlCommand command =
                    new SqlCommand("PassNullParameter", connection);
                command.CommandType = CommandType.StoredProcedure;

                // Define the parameter.
                command.Parameters.Add("@ValueIn", SqlDbType.Int);

                // Set the parameter value to 1 and execute the stored procedure
                command.Parameters[0].Value = 1;
                Console.WriteLine("Parameter value = 1");
                connection.Open( );
                isNullParameter = Convert.ToBoolean(command.ExecuteScalar( ));
                Console.WriteLine(
                    "Input parameter is null = {0}", isNullParameter);
                Console.WriteLine( );

                // Set the parameter value to null and execute the stored procedure
                // in a try...catch block
                command.Parameters[0].Value = null;
                Console.WriteLine("Parameter value = null");
```

```
            try
            {
                isNullParameter = Convert.ToBoolean(command.ExecuteScalar());
                Console.WriteLine(
                    "Input parameter is null = {0}", isNullParameter);
            }
            catch (Exception ex)
            {
                Console.WriteLine("ERROR: {0}", ex.Message);
            }
            Console.WriteLine();

            // Set the parameter value to System.DBNull.Value and execute the
            // stored procedure
            command.Parameters[0].Value = System.DBNull.Value;
            Console.WriteLine("Parameter value = System.DBNull.Value");
            isNullParameter = Convert.ToBoolean(command.ExecuteScalar());
            Console.WriteLine(
                "Input parameter is null = {0}", isNullParameter);
            Console.WriteLine();
        }

        Console.WriteLine("Press any key to continue.");
        Console.ReadKey();
    }
  }
}
```

The output is shown in Figure 3-20.

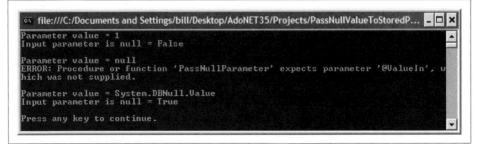

Figure 3-20. Output for PassNullValueToStoredProcedureParameter solution

Discussion

System.DBNull is not the same as null in C# or Nothing in Visual Basic. System.DBNull represents a nonexistent data value, typically in a database field, while null and Nothing indicate that an object or variable has not yet been initialized or doesn't have a reference to an object.

Passing a null parameter value into a query is not very different than passing any other parameter value. Construct the parameter using either the `Parameter` constructor or the `Add( )` method of the `ParameterCollection` for the `Command` object. The value is set by passing `System.DBNull.Value` for the value argument when constructing the parameter or by setting the `Value` property of the `Parameter` object to `System.DBNull.Value`.

To test for a null value, the `IsDBNull( )` method returns a Boolean value that indicates whether an object expression evaluates to `System.DBNull`. This is the same as comparing an object to the `System.DBNull.Value` using an equality operator.

If the stored procedure accepts optional parameters—parameters for which a default value is specified—you can set these parameters to `null` in C# or `Nothing` in Visual Basic. This is not the same as setting the parameter value to `System.DBNull.Value` but rather causes the parameter to be set to its default value.

3.21   Using Table-Valued Types As Parameters

Problem

You need to pass data to a stored procedure table-valued parameter.

Solution

Use the `AddWithValue( )` method of the `ParameterCollection` for the `Command` to assign a value to the table-value parameter and specify the `SqlDbType` of the parameter as `Structured` from the `SqlDbType` enumeration.

The solution needs a table named `TVPTable` in the `AdoDotNet35Cookbook` database. Execute the following T-SQL statement to create the table:

```
USE AdoDotNet35Cookbook
GO
CREATE TABLE TVPTable(
    Id int NOT NULL PRIMARY KEY,
    Field1 nvarchar(50) NULL,
    Field2 nvarchar(50) NULL )
```

Execute the following T-SQL statement to create the user-defined table type named TVPType used in this solution:

```
USE AdoDotNet35Cookbook
GO
CREATE TYPE TVPType AS TABLE (
    Id int,
    Field1 nvarchar(50),
    Field2 nvarchar(50))
```

The solution also uses a stored procedure named `InsertTVPTable` that takes a table-valued parameter and adds the records in it to the table `TVPTable`. Execute the following T-SQL statement to create the stored procedure:

```
USE AdoDotNet35Cookbook
GO
CREATE PROCEDURE InsertTVPTable (
    @tvp TVPType READONLY)
AS
    SET NOCOUNT ON

    INSERT INTO TVPTable
    SELECT Id, Field1, Field2 FROM @tvp
```

The solution creates a DataTable named dvTVP that is used to pass a table value into a parameter into the stored procedure InsertTVPTable that inserts a record into the table TVPTable in the AdoDotNet35Cookbook database. A Command object is created for the stored procedure InsertTVPTable and the value of the table-valued parameter is set using the AddWithValue( ) method of the Parameter object in the ParameterCollection of the Command. The stored procedure is executed using the ExecuteNonQuery( ) method of the Command object. The contents of the TVPTable table are loaded into a DataTable and output to the console before and after the stored procedure InsertTVPTable is executed.

The C# code in *Program.cs* in the project TableValuedParameter is shown in Example 3-29.

Example 3-29. File: Program.cs for TableValuedParameter solution

```
using System;
using System.Data;
using System.Data.SqlClient;

namespace TableValuedParameter
{
    class Program
    {
        static void Main(string[] args)
        {
            string sqlConnectString = @"Data Source=(local);
                Integrated security=SSPI;Initial Catalog=AdoDotNet35Cookbook;";

            string sqlSelect = "SELECT * FROM TVPTable";

            // Output the contents of the table in the database
            SqlDataAdapter da = new SqlDataAdapter(sqlSelect, sqlConnectString);
            DataTable dt = new DataTable( );
            da.Fill(dt);
            Console.WriteLine("---INITIAL---");
            foreach (DataRow row in dt.Rows)
            {
                Console.WriteLine("ID = {0}\tField1 = {1}\tField2 = {2}",
                    row["ID"], row["Field1"], row["Field2"]);
            }
```

Example 3-29. File: Program.cs for TableValuedParameter solution (continued)

```
            // Create the DataTable that will be used to pass a table
            // into the table-valued parameter
            DataTable dtTVP = new DataTable( );
            dtTVP.Columns.Add("Id", typeof(int));
            dtTVP.Columns.Add("Field1", typeof(string)).MaxLength = 50;
            dtTVP.Columns.Add("Field2", typeof(string)).MaxLength = 50;
            // Add data to the DataTable
            dtTVP.Rows.Add(new object[] { 1, "Field1.1", "Field2.1" });
            dtTVP.Rows.Add(new object[] { 2, "Field1.2", "Field2.2" });
            dtTVP.Rows.Add(new object[] { 3, "Field1.3", "Field2.3" });

            SqlConnection connection = new SqlConnection(sqlConnectString);
            SqlCommand command = new SqlCommand("InsertTVPTable", connection);
            command.CommandType = CommandType.StoredProcedure;
            SqlParameter param = command.Parameters.AddWithValue("@tvp", dtTVP);
            param.SqlDbType = SqlDbType.Structured;
            connection.Open( );
            command.ExecuteNonQuery( );
            connection.Close( );
            Console.WriteLine("\n=> Stored procedure with TVP executed.");

            // Output the contents of the table in the database
            dt.Clear( );
            da.Fill(dt);
            Console.WriteLine("\n---FINAL---");
            foreach (DataRow row in dt.Rows)
            {
                Console.WriteLine("ID = {0}\tField1 = {1}\tField2 = {2}",
                    row["ID"], row["Field1"], row["Field2"]);
            }

            Console.WriteLine("\nPress any key to continue.");
            Console.ReadKey( );
        }
    }
}
```

The output is shown in Figure 3-21.

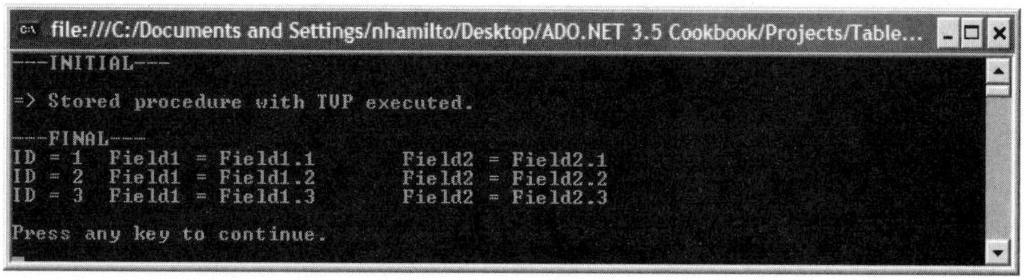

Figure 3-21. Output for TableValuedParameter solution

Discussion

SQL Server 2008 introduces the table-valued parameter type declared using user-defined table types. You can use table-valued parameters to send multiple rows of data to a T-SQL statement, stored procedure, or function.

Use `DataTable`, `DbDataReader`, or `System.Collection.Generic.IList<SqlDataRecord>` objects to populate table parameters. Use the `AddWithValue( )` method of the `Command` object to create the table-valued parameter and set its value. Specify the `SqlDbType` of the parameter as `Structured` from the `SqlDbType` enumeration. Execute the `Command` object in the same way as any other command.

3.22 Retrieving a Return Value from a Stored Procedure

Problem

You are using a stored procedure and need to get the return value.

Solution

Use a parameter defined with a `ParameterDirection` property of `ReturnValue` and access the return value.

The solution uses a single stored procedure:

Person.GetContacts

Returns a result set containing all records in the `Person.Contact` table in `AdventureWorks`. Also, the stored procedure returns the `@@ROWCOUNT` value for the query in an output parameter. The stored procedure is shown in Example 3-30.

Example 3-30. Stored procedure: Person.GetContacts

```
CREATE PROCEDURE Person.GetContacts
    @RowCount int OUTPUT
AS
    SET NOCOUNT ON

    SELECT * FROM Person.Contact

    SET @RowCount = @@ROWCOUNT

    RETURN @RowCount
```

The solution creates a DataReader from the stored procedure command. The stored procedure returns the count of records in the return result set—in this case, all records from the Person.Contact table in AdventureWorks. The code displays the value of the return parameter at five different stages of working with the result set in the DataReader:

- Before the DataReader is created
- Immediately after the DataReader is created
- After all rows in the DataReader have been read
- After the DataReader is closed
- After the Connection is closed

The C# code in *Program.cs* in the project StoredProcedureReturnValueDataReader is shown in Example 3-31.

Example 3-31. File: Program.cs for StoredProcedureReturnValueDataReader solution

```csharp
using System;
using System.Data;
using System.Data.SqlClient;

namespace StoredProcedureReturnValueDataReader
{
    class Program
    {
        static void Main(string[] args)
        {
            string sqlConnectString = "Data Source=(local);" +
                "Integrated security=SSPI;Initial Catalog=AdventureWorks;";

            using (SqlConnection connection = new SqlConnection(sqlConnectString))
            {
                // Create the stored procedure to use in the DataReader.
                SqlCommand command =
                    new SqlCommand("Person.GetContacts", connection);
                command.CommandType = CommandType.StoredProcedure;
                // Create the output parameter
                command.Parameters.Add("@RowCount", SqlDbType.Int).Direction =
                    ParameterDirection.Output;
                // Create the return parameter
                SqlParameter retParam =
                    command.Parameters.Add("@RetVal", SqlDbType.Int);
                retParam.Direction = ParameterDirection.ReturnValue;

                Console.WriteLine(
                    "Before execution, return value = {0}", retParam.Value);
```

Example 3-31. File: Program.cs for StoredProcedureReturnValueDataReader solution (continued)

```
            // Create a DataReader for the result set returned by
            // the stored procedure.
            connection.Open( );
            SqlDataReader dr = command.ExecuteReader( );
            Console.WriteLine(
                "After execution, return value = {0}", retParam.Value);

            // Iterate over the records for the DataReader.
            int rowCount = 0;
            while (dr.Read( ))
            {
                rowCount++;

                // Code to process result set in DataReader.
            }

            Console.WriteLine(
                "After reading all {0} rows, return value = {1}",
                rowCount, retParam.Value);

            // Close the DataReader
            dr.Close( );

            Console.WriteLine(
                "After DataReader.Close( ), return value = {0}",
                retParam.Value);

            connection.Close( );

            Console.WriteLine(
                "After Connection.Close( ), return value = {0}",
                retParam.Value);
        }

        Console.WriteLine("\nPress any key to continue.");
        Console.ReadKey( );
    }
}
}
```

The output is shown in Figure 3-22.

Figure 3-22. Output for StoredProcedureReturnValueDataReader solution

---

Discussion

Every stored procedure returns an integer value to the caller. If the value for the return code is not explicitly set, it defaults to 0. The return value is accessed from ADO.NET through a parameter that represents it. The parameter is defined with a `ParameterDirection` property of `ReturnValue`. The data type of the `ReturnValue` parameter must be an integer. Table 3-6 describes all values in the `ParameterDirection` enumeration.

Table 3-6. ParameterDirection enumeration

Value	Description
Input	The parameter is an input parameter allowing the caller to pass a data value to the stored procedure.
InputOutput	The parameter is both an input and output parameter, allowing the caller to pass a data value to the stored procedure and the stored procedure to pass a data value back to the caller.
Output	The parameter is an output parameter allowing the stored procedure to pass a data value back to the caller.
ReturnValue	The parameter represents the value returned from the stored procedure.

Return parameters from the stored procedure used to build a `DataReader` are not available until the `DataReader` is closed by calling the `Close( )` method or until `Dispose( )` is called on the `DataReader`. You do not have to read any of records in the `DataReader` to obtain a return value. If you have used the `Fill( )` method of a `DataAdapter` to fill a `DataTable`, the return value is available immediately after the `Fill( )` method is called.

3.23   Retrieving a Stored Procedure Output Parameter

Problem

You want to access an output parameter returned by a stored procedure.

Solution

Add a parameter to a Command's `ParameterCollection` and specify the `ParameterDirection` as either `Output` or `InputOutput`.

The example uses a single stored procedure, shown in Example 3-32:

Person.GetContacts

> Returns a result set containing all records in the `Person.Contact` table in `AdventureWorks`. Also, the stored procedure returns the `@@ROWCOUNT` value for the query in an output parameter.

Example 3-32. Stored procedure: Person.GetContacts

```
CREATE PROCEDURE Person.GetContacts
    @RowCount int OUTPUT
AS
    SET NOCOUNT ON

    SELECT * FROM Person.Contact

    SET @RowCount = @@ROWCOUNT

    RETURN @RowCount
```

The solution creates a DataReader based on the stored procedure. The stored procedure returns a single output parameter containing the count of records in the return result set—in this case, all records from the Person.Contact table in AdventureWorks. The code displays the value of the output parameter at five different stages of working with the result set in the DataReader:

- Before the DataReader is created
- Immediately after the DataReader is created
- After all rows in the DataReader have been read
- After the DataReader is closed
- After the Connection is closed

The C# code in *Program.cs* in the project StoredProcedureOutputValueDataReader is shown in Example 3-33.

Example 3-33. File: Program.cs for StoredProcedureOutputValueDataReader solution

```
using System;
using System.Data;
using System.Data.SqlClient;

namespace StoredProcedureOutputValueDataReader
{
    class Program
    {
        static void Main(string[] args)
        {
            string sqlConnectString = "Data Source=(local);" +
                "Integrated security=SSPI;Initial Catalog=AdventureWorks;";

            using (SqlConnection connection = new SqlConnection(sqlConnectString))
            {
                // Create the stored procedure to use in the DataReader.
                SqlCommand command =
                    new SqlCommand("Person.GetContacts", connection);
                command.CommandType = CommandType.StoredProcedure;
                // Create the output parameter
                command.Parameters.Add("@RowCount", SqlDbType.Int).Direction =
                    ParameterDirection.Output;
```

```csharp
            Console.WriteLine("Before execution, @RowCount = {0}",
                command.Parameters["@RowCount"].Value);

            // Create a DataReader for the result set returned by
            // the stored procedure.
            connection.Open( );
            SqlDataReader dr = command.ExecuteReader( );
            Console.WriteLine("After execution, @RowCount = {0}",
                command.Parameters["@RowCount"].Value);

            // Iterate over the records for the DataReader.
            int rowCount = 0;
            while (dr.Read( ))
            {
                rowCount++;

                // Code to process result set in DataReader.
            }

            Console.WriteLine("After reading all {0} rows, @RowCount = {1}",
                rowCount, command.Parameters["@RowCount"].Value);

            // Close the DataReader
            dr.Close( );

            Console.WriteLine("After DataReader.Close( ), @RowCount = {0}",
                command.Parameters["@RowCount"].Value);

            connection.Close( );

            Console.WriteLine("After Connection.Close( ), @RowCount = {0}",
                command.Parameters["@RowCount"].Value);
        }

        Console.WriteLine("\nPress any key to continue.");
        Console.ReadKey( );
    }
  }
}
```

The output is shown in Figure 3-23.

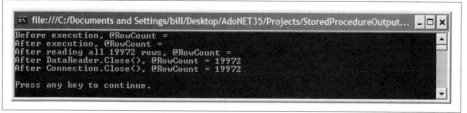

Figure 3-23. Output for StoredProcedureOutputValueDataReader solution

Discussion

Output parameters allow a stored procedure to pass a data value or cursor variable back to the caller. To use an output parameter with a DataReader, add the output parameter to the ParameterCollection for the Command object used to create the DataReader. Specify the ParameterDirection property of the Parameter as Output or InputOutput. Table 3-6 describes all values in the ParameterDirection enumeration. Once all parameters are defined, build the DataReader using the ExecuteReader( ) method of the Command object.

Output parameters from the stored procedure used to build a DataReader are not available until the DataReader is closed by calling the Close( ) method or until Dispose( ) is called on the DataReader. You do not have to read any of records in the DataReader to obtain an output value.

3.24   Raising and Handling Stored Procedure Errors

Problem

You want to catch and handle an error raised from a stored procedure.

Solution

Use a try...catch block to catch serious errors. Use the SqlConnection.InfoMessage event handler to catch informational and warning messages.

The example uses a single stored procedure, shown in Example 3-34:

SP0210_Raiserror

>   Accepts two input parameters specifying the severity and the state of an error and raises an error with the specified severity and state.

Example 3-34. Stored procedure: RaiseError

```
CREATE PROCEDURE RaiseError
    @Severity int,
    @State int = 1
AS
    IF @Severity <=18
        RAISERROR ('Error of severity %d raised from stored procedure RaiseError.',
            @Severity, @State, @Severity)
    ELSE
        RAISERROR ('Error of severity %d raised from stored procedure RaiseError.',
            @Severity, @State, @Severity) WITH LOG

    RETURN
```

The solution creates a connection and attaches a handler named SqlMessageEventHandler() for warning and information messages from the SQL Server. A Command is created for the RaiseError stored procedure and the input parameters are defined. The stored procedure is called for error severity levels from −1 through 26 and results are output to the console demonstrating how errors of different severities are handled.

The C# code in *Program.cs* in the project RaiseAndHandleStoredProcedureError is shown in Example 3-35.

Example 3-35. File: Program.cs for RaiseAndHandleStoredProcedureError solution

```
using System;
using System.Data;
using System.Data.SqlClient;

namespace RaiseAndHandleStoredProcedureError
{
    class Program
    {
        static void Main(string[] args)
        {
            string sqlConnectString = "Data Source=(local);" +
                "Integrated security=SSPI;Initial Catalog=AdventureWorks;";

            using (SqlConnection connection = new SqlConnection(sqlConnectString))
            {
                // Attach handler for SqlInfoMessage events.
                connection.InfoMessage +=
                    new SqlInfoMessageEventHandler(SqlMessageEventHandler);

                // Create the stored procedure
                SqlCommand command = new SqlCommand("RaiseError", connection);
                command.CommandType = CommandType.StoredProcedure;
                // Create the input parameters for error severity and state
                command.Parameters.Add("@Severity", SqlDbType.Int);
                command.Parameters.Add("@State", SqlDbType.Int);

                for(int severity = -1; severity <= 26; severity++)
                {
                    // Set the value for the stored procedure parameters.
                    command.Parameters["@Severity"].Value = severity;
                    command.Parameters["@State"].Value = 0;

                    // Open the connection.
                    connection.Open();
                    try
```

```
            {
                // Try to execute the stored procedure.
                command.ExecuteNonQuery( );
            }
            catch (System.Data.SqlClient.SqlException ex)
            {
                // Catch SqlException errors.
                Console.WriteLine("ERROR: {0}", ex.Message);
            }
            catch (Exception ex)
            {
                // Catch other errors.
                Console.WriteLine("OTHER ERROR: {0}", ex.Message);
            }
            finally
            {
                // Close the connection.
                connection.Close( );
            }
        }
    }

    Console.WriteLine("\nPress any key to continue.");
    Console.ReadKey( );
}

private static void SqlMessageEventHandler(object sender,
    SqlInfoMessageEventArgs e)
{
    Console.WriteLine("MESSAGE: {0}", e.Message);
}
    }
}
```

The output is shown in Figure 3-24.

Discussion

Errors and messages are returned from a SQL Server stored procedure to a calling application using the RAISERROR (note the spelling) function. The error message severity levels are listed in Table 3-7.

Table 3-7. RAISERROR error message severity levels

Severity level	Description
0–10	Informational
11–16	Error which can be corrected by the user
17–19	Resource or system error
20–25	Fatal error indicating a system problem

```
file:///C:/Documents and Settings/bill/Desktop/AdoNET35/Projects/RaiseAndHandleStoredPr...

MESSAGE: Error of severity -1 raised from stored procedure RaiseError.
MESSAGE: Error of severity 0 raised from stored procedure RaiseError.
MESSAGE: Error of severity 1 raised from stored procedure RaiseError.
MESSAGE: Error of severity 2 raised from stored procedure RaiseError.
MESSAGE: Error of severity 3 raised from stored procedure RaiseError.
MESSAGE: Error of severity 4 raised from stored procedure RaiseError.
MESSAGE: Error of severity 5 raised from stored procedure RaiseError.
MESSAGE: Error of severity 6 raised from stored procedure RaiseError.
MESSAGE: Error of severity 7 raised from stored procedure RaiseError.
MESSAGE: Error of severity 8 raised from stored procedure RaiseError.
MESSAGE: Error of severity 9 raised from stored procedure RaiseError.
MESSAGE: Error of severity 10 raised from stored procedure RaiseError.
ERROR: Error of severity 11 raised from stored procedure RaiseError.
ERROR: Error of severity 12 raised from stored procedure RaiseError.
ERROR: Error of severity 13 raised from stored procedure RaiseError.
ERROR: Error of severity 14 raised from stored procedure RaiseError.
ERROR: Error of severity 15 raised from stored procedure RaiseError.
ERROR: Error of severity 16 raised from stored procedure RaiseError.
ERROR: Error of severity 17 raised from stored procedure RaiseError.
ERROR: Error of severity 18 raised from stored procedure RaiseError.
ERROR: Error of severity 19 raised from stored procedure RaiseError.
ERROR: Error of severity 20 raised from stored procedure RaiseError.
Process ID 53 has raised user error 50000, severity 20. SQL Server is terminatin
g this process.
A severe error occurred on the current command.  The results, if any, should be
discarded.
ERROR: Error of severity 21 raised from stored procedure RaiseError.
Process ID 53 has raised user error 50000, severity 21. SQL Server is terminatin
g this process.
A severe error occurred on the current command.  The results, if any, should be
discarded.
ERROR: Error of severity 22 raised from stored procedure RaiseError.
Process ID 53 has raised user error 50000, severity 22. SQL Server is terminatin
g this process.
A severe error occurred on the current command.  The results, if any, should be
discarded.
ERROR: Error of severity 23 raised from stored procedure RaiseError.
Process ID 53 has raised user error 50000, severity 23. SQL Server is terminatin
g this process.
A severe error occurred on the current command.  The results, if any, should be
discarded.
ERROR: Error of severity 24 raised from stored procedure RaiseError.
Process ID 53 has raised user error 50000, severity 24. SQL Server is terminatin
g this process.
A severe error occurred on the current command.  The results, if any, should be
discarded.
ERROR: Error of severity 25 raised from stored procedure RaiseError.
Process ID 53 has raised user error 50000, severity 25. SQL Server is terminatin
g this process.
A severe error occurred on the current command.  The results, if any, should be
discarded.
ERROR: Error of severity 26 raised from stored procedure RaiseError.
Process ID 53 has raised user error 50000, severity 25. SQL Server is terminatin
g this process.
A severe error occurred on the current command.  The results, if any, should be
discarded.

Press any key to continue.
```

Figure 3-24. Output for RaiseAndHandleStoredProcedureError solution

Severity levels greater than 20 result in the connection being closed.

Since severity levels 10 or less are considered to be informational, they raise a SqlInfoMessageEvent rather than an error. This is handled by subscribing a SqlInfoMessageEventHandler to the InfoMessage event of the SqlConnection object.

If the error has severity level 11 or greater, a SqlException is thrown by the SQL Server .NET data provider.

For more information about the RAISERROR function, look up RAISERROR in SQL Server Books Online.

3.25   Executing a SQL Server Scalar-Valued Function

Problem

Your SQL Server database includes a user-defined function that returns a scalar value. You want to retrieve the value from this function using ADO.NET.

Solution

Invoke the function as you would a query or stored procedure.

The solution uses a single SQL Server function, shown in Example 3-36:

ExtendedPrice
>   Calculates and returns the extended price for an order line item based on the unit price, quantity, and discount.

Example 3-36. SQL Server scalar-valued function: ExtendedPrice

```
CREATE FUNCTION ExtendedPrice
(
    @UnitPrice money,
    @Quantity smallint,
    @Discount real
)
RETURNS money
AS

BEGIN
    RETURN (@UnitPrice * (1 - @Discount)* @Quantity)
END
```

The solution defines a SQL statement that uses the ExtendedPrice user-defined scalar-valued function. The statement is used by a DataAdapter to fill a DataTable with the first five records from the Sales.SalesOrderDetail table in AdventureWorks together with the extended price for the record calculated using the scalar-valued function for each record. The value calculated by the scalar-valued function is the same as that calculated by the computed field LineTotal in the Sales.SalesOrderDetail table.

The C# code in *Program.cs* in the project ExecuteUserDefinedScalarValuedFunction is shown in Example 3-37.

Example 3-37. File: Program.cs for ExecuteUserDefinedScalarValuedFunction solution

```csharp
using System;
using System.Data;
using System.Data.SqlClient;

namespace ExecuteUserDefinedScalarValuedFunction
{
    class Program
    {
        static void Main(string[] args)
        {
            string sqlConnectString = "Data Source=(local);" +
                "Integrated security=SSPI;Initial Catalog=AdventureWorks;";

            string sqlSelect = "SELECT TOP 5 *, " +
                "dbo.ExtendedPrice(UnitPrice, OrderQty, UnitPriceDiscount) " +
                "ExtendedPrice FROM Sales.SalesOrderDetail";

            SqlDataAdapter da = new SqlDataAdapter(sqlSelect, sqlConnectString);
            DataTable dt = new DataTable( );
            da.Fill(dt);

            foreach (DataRow row in dt.Rows)
                Console.WriteLine("SalesOrderDetailID = {0}, LineTotal = {1}, " +
                    "ExtendedPrice = {2}", row["SalesOrderDetailID"],
                    row["LineTotal"], row["ExtendedPrice"]);

            Console.WriteLine("\nPress any key to continue.");
            Console.ReadKey( );
        }
    }
}
```

The output is shown in Figure 3-25.

```
file:///C:/Documents and Settings/bill/Desktop/AdoNET35/Projects/2b - ExecuteUserDefined...
SalesOrderDetailID = 1, LineTotal = 2024.994000, ExtendedPrice = 2024.9940
SalesOrderDetailID = 2, LineTotal = 6074.982000, ExtendedPrice = 6074.9819
SalesOrderDetailID = 3, LineTotal = 2024.994000, ExtendedPrice = 2024.9940
SalesOrderDetailID = 4, LineTotal = 2039.994000, ExtendedPrice = 2039.9940
SalesOrderDetailID = 5, LineTotal = 2039.994000, ExtendedPrice = 2039.9940

Press any key to continue.
```

Figure 3-25. Output for ExecuteUserDefinedScalarValuedFunction solution

Discussion

A user-defined scalar-valued function is a SQL routine that accepts one or more scalar input parameters and returns a single value. A user-defined scalar-valued function is invoked from a query or executed like a stored procedure using an EXECUTE statement.

You can invoke scalar-valued functions where scalar expressions can be used. To invoke a scalar-valued function, use the following syntax:

```
[databaseName.]ownerName.functionName([argument1][, . . . ])
```

In the example, the ExtendedPrice function is called by the following part of the SQL SELECT statement:

```
dbo.ExtendedPrice(UnitPrice, Quantity, Discount)
```

This calculates the extended price for each row in the Sales.SalesOrderDetail table based on the UnitPrice, OrderQty, and UnitPriceDiscount values. The result is returned in the result set in a column named ExtendedPrice.

3.26   Executing a SQL Server Table-Valued Function

Problem

Your SQL Server database includes a table-valued function that returns a table. You want to retrieve the table from this function using ADO.NET.

Solution

Execute a SQL SELECT command to retrieve records from the table returned by the table-valued function.

The solution fills a DataTable using a DataAdapter with a SQL SELECT command that retrieves records using the table-valued function dbo.ufnGetContactInformation in AdventureWorks. The values in the DataTable are output to the console.

The C# code in *Program.cs* in the project ExecuteTableValuedFunction is shown in Example 3-38.

Example 3-38. File: Program.cs for ExecuteTableValuedFunction solution

```
using System;
using System.Data;
using System.Data.SqlClient;

namespace ExecuteTableValuedFunction
{
    class Program
```

Example 3-38. File: Program.cs for ExecuteTableValuedFunction solution (continued)

```
{
    static void Main(string[] args)
    {
        string sqlConnectString = "Data Source=(local);" +
            "Integrated security=SSPI;Initial Catalog=AdventureWorks;";

        // Select all fields from all records returned by the
        // table-valued function for ContactID = 10.
        string sqlSelect = "SELECT * FROM dbo.ufnGetContactInformation(10)";

        // Fill a DataTable with the result set from the table-valued function
        SqlDataAdapter da = new SqlDataAdapter(sqlSelect, sqlConnectString);
        DataTable dt = new DataTable( );
        da.Fill(dt);

        // Output the row count and result set to the console
        Console.WriteLine("{0} rows retrieved.\n", dt.Rows.Count);
        foreach (DataColumn col in dt.Columns)
        {
            Console.WriteLine("{0} = {1}",
                col.ColumnName, dt.Rows[0][col.Ordinal]);
        }

        Console.WriteLine("\nPress any key to continue.");
        Console.ReadKey( );
    }
}
}
```

The output is shown in Figure 3-26.

Figure 3-26. Output for ExecuteTableValuedFunction solution

Discussion

A table-valued function returns a table data type. You retrieve records returned by a table-valued function in the same way you access records from any database table object: using a SQL SELECT command.

3.27 Querying a DataSet Using LINQ

Problem

You need to query a DataSet using a LINQ query.

Solution

Use LINQ to DataSet as shown in this solution.

The solution fills two DataTable objects in a DataSet with all records from the Production.Product and Production.ProductInventory tables in the AdoDotNet35Cookbook database. A relationship is created between the tables on the ProductID column. A LINQ query that retrieves joined data from both columns in the DataSet is created and executed and the results are output to the console.

The C# code in *Program.cs* in the project LinqToDataSetQuery is shown in Example 3-39.

Example 3-39. File: Program.cs for LinqToDataSetQuery solution

```
using System;
using System.Data;
using System.Data.SqlClient;
using System.Linq;

namespace LinqToDataSetQuery
{
    class Program
    {
        static void Main(string[] args)
        {
            string connectString = "Data Source=(local);" +
                "Integrated security=SSPI;Initial Catalog=AdventureWorks;";

            string sqlSelect = "SELECT * FROM Production.Product; " +
                "SELECT * FROM Production.ProductInventory;";

            // Create the data adapter to retrieve data from the database
            SqlDataAdapter da = new SqlDataAdapter(sqlSelect, connectString);
            // Create table mappings
            da.TableMappings.Add("Table", "Product");
            da.TableMappings.Add("Table1", "ProductInventory");
            // Create and fill the DataSet
            DataSet ds = new DataSet();
            da.Fill(ds);

            // Create the relationship between the Product and
            // ProductInventory tables
            DataRelation dr = ds.Relations.Add("Product_ProductInventory",
                        ds.Tables["Product"].Columns["ProductID"],
                        ds.Tables["ProductInventory"].Columns["ProductID"]);
```

Example 3-39. File: Program.cs for LinqToDataSetQuery solution (continued)

```
            DataTable product = ds.Tables["Product"];
            DataTable inventory = ds.Tables["ProductInventory"];

            var query = from p in product.AsEnumerable( )
                        join i in inventory.AsEnumerable( )
                        on p.Field<int>("ProductID") equals
                        i.Field<int>("ProductID")
                        where p.Field<int>("ProductID") < 100
                        select new
                        {
                            ProductID = p.Field<int>("ProductID"),
                            Name = p.Field<string>("Name"),
                            LocationID = i.Field<short>("LocationID"),
                            Quantity = i.Field<short>("Quantity")
                        };

            foreach (var q in query)
            {
                Console.WriteLine("{0} - {1}: LocationID = {2} => Quantity = {3}",
                    q.ProductID, q.Name, q.LocationID, q.Quantity);
            }

            Console.WriteLine("\nPress any key to continue.");
            Console.ReadKey( );
        }
    }
}
```

The output is shown in Figure 3-27.

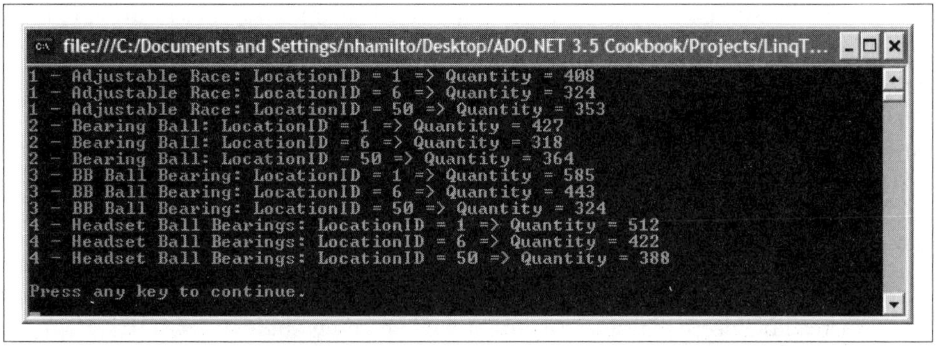

Figure 3-27. Output for LinqToDataSetQuery solution

Discussion

Language-Integrated Query (LINQ) is a technology introduced in .NET Framework 3.5 that lets you express queries directly in programming languages rather than as string literals in the application code. C# 3.0 and Visual Basic 9.0 introduce language extensions that implement LINQ—compilers for these languages ship with .NET Framework 3.5.

LINQ provides standard query and update mechanisms that can potentially support any type of data store, thereby unifying the syntax for querying any data source. LINQ creates a unified programming model for working with objects, relational data, and XML data with LINQ providers that let you access these data sources with LINQ.

LINQ to Objects

Provides query capabilities over in-memory data collection objects that implement IEnumerable or IEnumerable<T> including user-defined Lists, Arrays, Dictionaries, and .NET collections.

LINQ to ADO.NET

Provides query capabilities over any enumerable ADO.NET object. LINQ to ADO.NET consists of two related LINQ technologies:

- LINQ to DataSet provides LINQ query capabilities into DataSet objects.
- LINQ to SQL manages relational data as objects by mapping and brokering the data models of a relational database to the object model of a programming language.

LINQ to XML

Provides query and document modification capabilities for XML data. It provides similar functionality to XPath queries and the document modifications capabilities of the Document Object Model (DOM) in a more strongly typed manner.

The following subsections provide a brief overview of LINQ queries, description of LINQ to ADO.NET, and a discussion of the solution.

LINQ queries

A query is an expression that retrieves data from or updates data in a data store. Different query languages have been developed for different types of data stores— for example, SQL for relational databases and XQuery for XML. LINQ simplifies creating queries for different data stores by providing a common model for accessing data in different data stores and formats. You write query expressions using a declarative syntax introduced in C# 3.0 and in Visual Basic 9.0. The same coding pattern is used to query and transform data in diverse stores including relational databases, ADO.NET DataSet objects, XML data, and .NET collections.

Although a LINQ query looks somewhat like a SQL statement, it is structured differently. Instead of specifying the fields to return like you would with a SQL statement, you specify the data source first in a LINQ query. This isn't arbitrary—in C# and Visual Basic it is necessary to declare a variable before it is used. This ordering also lets Intellisense work with LINQ queries.

A LINQ query operation requires three steps: obtain a data source, create a query, and execute the query. A brief introduction to LINQ query operators used to create a LINQ query follows.

- You specify the data source using a from clause in C# (From clause in Visual Basic). The from clause is called a generator. In addition to the data source, the generator specifies a range variable that serves the same purpose as the iterator in a foreach loop (although no iteration actually takes place). The compiler can infer the type of the range variable from the context so there is no need to specify type explicitly.

- The join clause in C# (Join clause in Visual Basic) is used to combine multiple data sources into a single source for a query—similar to an INNER JOIN in T-SQL. In addition to explicitly using a LINQ join clause, you can access related items through collections exposed as properties of foreign keys.

- The where clause in C# (Where clause in Visual Basic) is used to filter the results returned by a LINQ query—similar to a WHERE clause in T-SQL. The filter takes the form of a Boolean expression that uses optional OR (||) and ADD (&&) operators to exclude non-non-matching elements from the source.

- The orderby clause in C# (Order By clause in Visual Basic) is used to sort the data returned by the LINQ query—similar to the ORDER BY clause in T-SQL. The orderby clause specifies a comma-delimited list of fields to sort by. The default comparator for each field is used as the basis of the sort. The default ascending clause is used to sort the results in the normal order while the descending clause is used to sort the results in the reverse order.

- The group clause in C# (Group By in Visual Basic) groups the results returned based on a specified key—similar to the GROUP BY clause in T-SQL. The group clause specifies a comma-separated list of fields to group by. The results are returned as a set of nested lists corresponding to the grouping specified.

- The select clause in C# (Select in Visual Basic) specifies the elements that the query returns from the data source—similar to the T-SQL SELECT statement. You can select multiple elements from a source object in one of two ways—define a named type, and create and initialize it within the select clause or create and initialize an anonymous type in the select clause.

A simple example follows that uses LINQ to query a string array. The example creates a string array containing seven colors, executes a LINQ query over the array to locate colors that are five or fewer characters long, and outputs the resulting colors in ascending order to the console:

```
using System;
using System.Linq;

class Program
{
    static void Main(string[] args)
    {
        string[] colors = {"Red", "Orange", "Yellow", "Green",
                    "Blue", "Indigo", "Violet"};
```

```
var colorQuery = from color in colors
                 where color.Length <= 5
                 orderby color
                 select color;

foreach (string s in colorQuery)
    Console.WriteLine(s);

Console.WriteLine("\nPress any key to continue.");
Console.ReadKey();
    }
}
```

The results are shown in Figure 3-28.

Figure 3-28. Output for LinqQueryStringArray solution

The first line sets up the data source—a string array of colors. The array implicitly supports IEnumerable<T>, allowing it to be used as a data source for a LINQ query.

The second line creates the query. This query has four clauses—from, orderby, where, and select. The from clause specifies that the data source is the array colors and that the color is the range variable representing each successive element in the source as it is traversed. The query is stored to a query variable named colorQuery. The query variable and range variable are strongly typed—in this case, the compiler infers the types from the data source. In the case of the query variable, the var keyword indicates an anonymous type and instructs the compiler to infer the type of the query variable at compile time. The where clause uses the Length property of the color range variable to select only colors where the length of the colors array element <= 5 characters. The orderby clause sorts the result set in ascending order. Finally the select clause instructs the query to return the range variable color. You could return the uppercase of the colors by rewriting the select clause as select color.ToUpper().

The third line uses a foreach loop to execute the query. A query variable stores the query and not the result set returned by the query—the query is not actually executed until you iterate over the query variable using either a foreach loop (or by calling the MoveNext() method of the query). The results of the query are returned through the iteration variable of the foreach loop—in this case s. The third line iterates over the query colorQuery to execute it, the results are returned in the foreach loop iterator s, and each value of s is written to the console.

LINQ to ADO.NET lets you query over enumerable ADO.NET objects using the LINQ programming model. As mentioned previously, LINQ to ADO.NET is made up of two technologies: LINQ to DataSet and LINQ to SQL. The following sections discuss LINQ to DataSet. Recipe 3.28 discusses and demonstrates LINQ to SQL.

LINQ to DataSet

The DataSet is the standard object used in ADO.NET to work with disconnected data from a variety of data sources and optionally update the data source at a later time with changes made while working in disconnected mode. Despite its extensive capabilities, the DataSet object has limited query capabilities—these capabilities include basic filtering and sorting through the Select( ) method of the DataSet. Other methods can be used to navigate the hierarchy of related parent and child tables within the database. Evaluating complex queries requires you to either create a new DataSet or use complex programming that performs poorly, tends to be error-prone, and frequently results in business logic being hardcoded in layers of the application where it does not belong.

LINQ to DataSet lets you query DataSet objects using LINQ queries. Additionally, Visual Studio developers benefit from Intellisense and compile-syntax checking. LINQ to DataSet also lets you easily flexible solutions to support tasks such as generic reporting and analysis.

Solution

The first step in every LINQ query is to obtain a data source. With LINQ to DataSet this means that you need to fill a DataSet object from the data source. You do this using the DataAdapter object (the only way before LINQ) or by using LINQ to SQL discussed in the next section. In this solution, the DataSet is filled with the Production.Product and Production.ProductInventory tables from AdventureWorks and a relationship is created between the tables.

The second step is to create a LINQ query. This example uses a cross-table query—a query against two related tables. In LINQ, this done using join clause to specify the elements being related. The select clause returns four fields—ProductID, Name, LocationID, and Quantity—in the result set.

The example sets up a relationship between the Product and ProductInventory tables in the DataSet. This lets you eliminate the join clause in the query. The query in the following code is equivalent to that shown in the preceding example. The query eliminates the explicit join clause and adds a nested from clause. The GetChildRows( ) method of the range variable p accesses the related records in the ProductInventory table:

```
var query = from p in product.AsEnumerable( )
            where p.Field<int>("ProductID") < 100
            from i in p.GetChildRows("Product_ProductInventory")
            select new
```

```
                    {
                        ProductID = p.Field<int>("ProductID"),
                        Name = p.Field<string>("Name"),
                        LocationID = i.Field<short>("LocationID"),
                        Quantity = i.Field<short>("Quantity")
                    };
```

The final step uses a foreach loop to execute the query:

```
foreach (var q in query)
{
    Console.WriteLine("{0} - {1}: LocationID = {2} => Quantity = {3}",
        q.ProductID, q.Name, q.LocationID, q.Quantity);
}
```

As mentioned, a query variable stores the query and not the result set returned by the query—the query is executed when you iterate over the query variable using either a foreach loop (or by calling the MoveNext( ) method of the query). The results of the query are returned through the iteration variable of the foreach loop—in this case, q. The loop outputs the four fields in the query result set to the console.

3.28   Querying a SQL Server Database Using LINQ

Problem

You need to query a SQL Server database using a LINQ query.

Solution

Use LINQ to SQL as shown in this solution.

You first need to create a LINQ object model. Follow these steps to use the O/R Designer to generate a simple C# object model:

1. Open Visual Studio and create a console application named LinqToSql.

2. Right-click the project in the Solution Explorer pane and select Add → New Item... from the context menu to open the Add New Item dialog. Select the LINQ to SQL file template in the Data category. Change the Name to *MyDataClasses.dbml*. Click the Add button to close the Add New Item dialog. The empty design surface for the new *dbml* file appears representing the DataContext that you will configure next. LINQ to SQL files have the extension *.dbml*.

3. In Server Explorer, right-click on the Data Connections node and select Add Connection from the context menu to open the Add Connection dialog. Complete the dialog to create a connection to the AdventureWorks database on your SQL Server. Click OK to close the dialog and create the connection.

4. Expand the new data connection in the Data Connections node. Drag the Product (Production) table from the table subnode onto the O/R Designer design surface to create the entity class Product—the new class contains properties corresponding to columns in the Product table. Next, drag the ProductInventory (Production) table onto the design surface to create the entity class ProductInventory. Notice that an association (relationship) is automatically created between the two entities based on the database metadata. The design surface is shown in Figure 3-29.

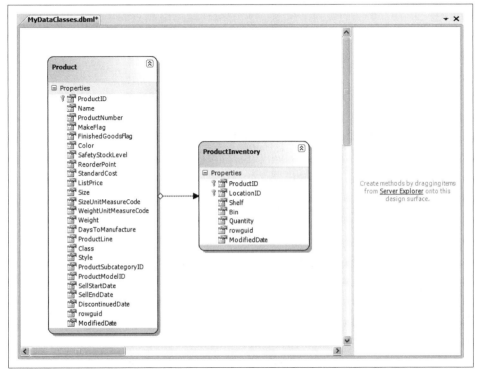

Figure 3-29. Linq to SQL O/R design surface

5. Build the project.

6. Open the Data Sources pane by selecting Data → Show Data Sources from the main menu. Click the Add New Data Source link to open the Data Source Configuration Wizard dialog. Select Object as the data source type. Click Next.

7. Expand the LinqToSql node. Navigate to and select the Product class. Click Next. Click Finish to confirm that you want to add the Product entity class. The Product and its related ProductInventory classes are added to the Data Sources pane as shown in Figure 3-30.

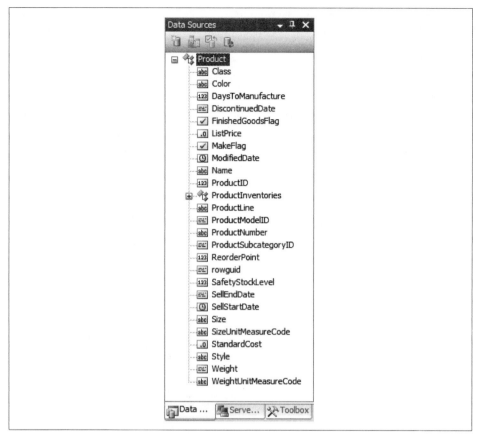

Figure 3-30. Linq To SQL Data Sources pane

The solution uses the object model to execute four LINQ queries against the SQL server database:

1. The first query in the method, Query1( ), instantiates an instance of MyDataClassesDataContext. This class inherits from DataContext—the LINQ to SQL class that contains methods and properties that connect the database to the LINQ to SQL entity classes mapped to the database. The LINQ query retrieves all of the rows in the Product table where the ProductID < 100 into the query variable products. The ProductID and Name fields are output to the console.

2. The second query in the method, Query2( ), returns a type from the query that contains a subset of the data in each row. The query in the following code snippet returns a type containing the ProductID and Name. These are output in the foreach loop, which iterates over the inferred type variable p—the output is the same as in the first query.

3. The third query in the method, Query3( ), uses the association created by the O/R Designer to navigate to the related ProductInventory records for each Product. These records are accessed through the ProductInventories property of Product that exposes the related collection for each Product record. This is shown in the foreach loop shown in the following code. The parent and child data is output to the console.

4. The fourth query in the method, Query4( ), explicitly joins tables in a LINQ query using the join clause. The Products entity class is joined to the ProductInventories entity class on the ProductID. The select clause returns a new type (inferred by the compiler) containing a Product and the associated (related) ProductInventory objects. The foreach loop performs a nested iteration over the query variable to return and output the same results as with the third query.

The C# code in *Program.cs* in the project LinqToSql is shown in Example 3-40.

Example 3-40. File: Program.cs for LinqToSql solution

```
using System;
using System.Linq;

namespace LinqToSql
{
    class Program
    {
        private static MyDataClassesDataContext dc;

        static void Main(string[] args)
        {
            dc = new MyDataClassesDataContext();

            // Execute the queries and output results
            Query1();
            Query2();
            Query3();
            Query4();

            Console.WriteLine("\nPress any key to continue.");
            Console.ReadKey();
        }

        private static void Query1()
        {
            Console.WriteLine("---QUERY 1---");

            var products = from row in dc.Products
                           where row.ProductID < 100
                           select row;
```

Example 3-40. File: Program.cs for LinqToSql solution (continued)

```
        foreach (Product p in products)
            Console.WriteLine(p.ProductID + ": " + p.Name);
    }

    private static void Query2( )
    {
        Console.WriteLine("\n---QUERY 2---");

        var products = from row in dc.Products
                       where row.ProductID < 100
                       select new
                       {
                           ProductID = row.ProductID,
                           ProductName = row.Name
                       };

        foreach (var p in products)
            Console.WriteLine(p.ProductID + ": " + p.ProductName);
    }

    private static void Query3( )
    {
        Console.WriteLine("\n---QUERY 3---");

        var products = from row in dc.Products
                       where row.ProductID < 100
                       select row;

        foreach (var p in products)
        {
            Console.WriteLine("{0}: {1}", p.ProductID, p.Name);
            // iterate over the collection of ProductInventory records
            foreach (var pi in p.ProductInventories)
                Console.WriteLine("    {0} = {1}", pi.LocationID, pi.Quantity);
        }
    }

    private static void Query4( )
    {
        Console.WriteLine("\n---QUERY 4---");

        var query = from p in dc.Products
                    join pi in dc.ProductInventories
                      on p.ProductID equals pi.ProductID into pis
                    where p.ProductID < 100
                    select new { Product = p, Inventories = pis };

        foreach (var q in query)
```

Example 3-40. File: Program.cs for LinqToSql solution (continued)

```
            {
                Console.WriteLine("{0}: {1}", q.Product.ProductID, q.Product.Name);
                // iterate over the collection of ProductInventory records
                foreach (var pi in q.Inventories)
                    Console.WriteLine("    {0} = {1}", pi.LocationID, pi.Quantity);
            }
        }
    }
}
```

The output is shown in Figure 3-31.

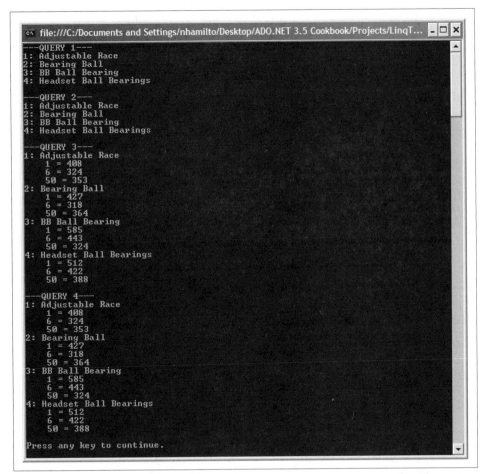

Figure 3-31. Output for LinqToSql solution

Discussion

LINQ to SQL provides a runtime infrastructure that lets you manage relational data as objects. In LINQ to SQL you set object properties and execute object methods instead of issuing database commands. LINQ to SQL translates LINQ to SQL objects to SQL queries and sends them to the database for processing. Once processed, LINQ to SQL translates the results back to LINQ objects that you can work with programmatically.

The first step to use LINQ to SQL is to create an object model that represents the database in terms of the programming language. You can create an object model using the Object Relational Designer (O/R Designer), which is a graphical tool hosted in Visual Studio or using the SQLMetal Tool, which is a command-line utility. This discussion is limited to the O/R Designer. For more information about SQLMetal, see Microsoft Visual Studio documentation.

The O/R Designer generates a LINQ to SQL object model from a relational database. It provides a visual design surface for creating LINQ entity classes (tables and columns) and associations (relationships) from the objects in a database. The O/R Designer can also map stored procedures and functions to DataContext methods. The O/R Designer supports only 1:1 mapping from an entity class to a database table or view.

The O/R Designer generates either C# or Visual Basic source code that you add that to your Visual Studio project. Alternatively, you can generate an external XML file—this approach keeps mapping metadata separate from your application code.

For more information about LINQ and LINQ queries, see Recipe 3.27.

3.29   Retrieving Data from a Text File

Problem

You want to use ADO.NET to access data stored in a text file.

Solution

Use the Microsoft Access Database Engine OLE DB provider to access data in a text file.

The solution creates an OleDbDataAdapter that loads the text file *Category.txt*, shown in Example 3-41, from the directory containing the solution file *ReadTextFileData.sln* into a DataTable and outputs the contents of the DataTable to the console.

Example 3-41. File: Category.txt

```
"CategoryID","CategoryName","Description"
1,"Beverages","Soft drinks, coffees, teas, beers, and ales"
2,"Condiments","Sweet and savory sauces, relishes, spreads, and seasonings"
3,"Confections","Desserts, candies, and sweet breads"
4,"Dairy Products","Cheeses"
5,"Grains/Cereals","Breads, crackers, pasta, and cereal"
6,"Meat/Poultry","Prepared meats"
7,"Produce","Dried fruit and bean curd"
8,"Seafood","Seaweed and fish"
```

The C# code in *Program.cs* in the project ReadTextFileData is shown in Example 3-42.

Example 3-42. File: Program.cs for ReadTextFileData solution

```csharp
using System;
using System.Data;
using System.Data.OleDb;

namespace ReadTextFileData
{
    class Program
    {
        static void Main(string[] args)
        {
            string sqlSelect = "SELECT * FROM [Category.txt]";
            string connectString = "Provider=Microsoft.ACE.OLEDB.12.0;" +
                @"Data Source=..\..\..\;" +
                "Extended Properties=\"text;HDR=yes;FMT=Delimited\";";

            // Create and fill a DataTable.
            OleDbDataAdapter da =
                new OleDbDataAdapter(sqlSelect, connectString);
            DataTable dt = new DataTable("Categories");
            da.Fill(dt);

            Console.WriteLine("CategoryID; CategoryName; Description\n");
            foreach (DataRow row in dt.Rows)
            {
                Console.WriteLine("{0}; {1}; {2}", row["CategoryID"],
                    row["CategoryName"], row["Description"]);
            }

            Console.WriteLine("\nPress any key to continue.");
            Console.ReadKey();
        }
    }
}
```

The output is shown in Figure 3-32.

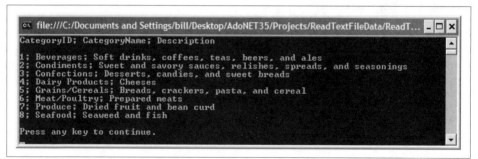

Figure 3-32. Output for ReadTextFileData solution

Discussion

The Microsoft Access Database Engine OLE DB provider can read records from and insert records into a text file data source. The provider can also access other database file formats through Indexed Sequential Access Method (ISAM) drivers specified in the Extended Properties attribute of the connection. Text files are supported with the text source database type, as shown in the following example:

```
"Provider=Microsoft.ACE.OLEDB.12.0;Data Source=..\..\..\;
    Extended Properties=\"text;HDR=yes;FMT=Delimited\";
```

The Extended Properties attribute can, in addition to the ISAM version property, specify whether or not tables include headers as field names in the first row of a range using an HDR attribute.

Notice that only the directory containing the text file is specified in the connection string. The filename is specified in the query—in a SELECT statement in the solution, for example:

```
SELECT * FROM [Category.txt]
```

It is not possible to define all characteristics of a text file through the connection string. You can access files that use nonstandard text delimiters and fixed-width text files by creating a *schema.ini* file in the same directory as the text file. As an example, a possible *schema.ini* file for the *Category.txt* file used in this solution is:

```
[Category.txt]
Format=CSVDelimited
ColNameHeader=True
MaxScanRows=0
Character=OEM
Col1=CategoryID Long Width 4
Col2=CategoryName Text Width 15
Col3=Description Text Width 100
```

The *schema.ini* file provides the following schema information about the data in the text file:

- Filename
- File format
- Field names, widths, and data types
- Character set
- Special data type conversions

The first entry in the *schema.ini* file is the text filename enclosed in square brackets. For example:

```
[Category.txt]
```

The `Format` option specifies the text file format. Table 3-8 describes the different options.

Table 3-8. Schema.ini format options

Format	Description
CSV Delimited	Fields are delimited with commas: `Format=CSVDelimited` This is the default value.
Custom Delimited	Fields are delimited with a custom character. You can use any single character except the double quotation mark (") as a delimiter: `Format=Delimited(customCharacter)`
Fixed Length	Fields are fixed length: `Format=FixedLength` If the `ColumnNameHeader` option is `True`, the first line containing the column names must be comma-delimited.
Tab Delimited	Fields are delimited with tabs: `Format=TabDelimited`

You can specify the fields in the text file in two ways:

1. Include the field names in the first row of the text file and set the `ColNameHeader` option to `True`.

2. Identify each column using the format `ColN` (where *N* is the one-based column number) and specify the name, width, and data type for each column.

The `MaxScanRows` option indicates how many rows should be scanned to automatically determine column type. A value of `0` indicates that all rows should be scanned.

The `ColN` entries specify the name, width, and data type for each column. This entry is required for fixed-length formats and optional for character-delimited formats. The syntax of the `ColN` entry is:

```
ColN=columnName dataType [Width n]
```

The parameters in the entry are:

columnName
> The name of the column. If the column name contains spaces, it must be enclosed in double quotation marks.

dataType
> The data type of the column. This value can be Bit, Byte, Currency, DateTime, Double, Long, Memo, Short, Single, or Text.
>
> DateTime values must be in one of the following formats: dd-mmm-yy, mm-dd-yy, mmm-dd-yy, yyyy-mm-dd, or yyyy-mmm-dd, where mm is the month number and mmm are the characters specifying the month.

Width *n*
> The literal value Width followed by the integer value specifying the column width.

The Character option specifies the character set; you can set it to either ANSI or OEM.

3.30 Retrieving Data from a Microsoft Excel Workbook

Problem

You want to access data stored in a Microsoft Excel workbook.

Solution

Use the Microsoft Access Database Engine OLE DB provider to create, access, and modify data stored in an Excel workbook.

The solution creates an OleDbDataAdapter that loads the Excel workbook *Category.xlsx*, shown in Figure 3-33, into a DataTable and outputs the contents of the DataTable to the console.

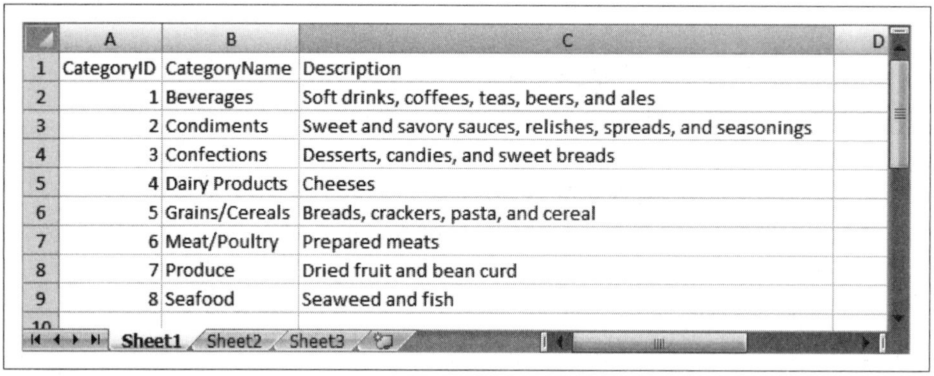

	A	B	C	D
1	CategoryID	CategoryName	Description	
2	1	Beverages	Soft drinks, coffees, teas, beers, and ales	
3	2	Condiments	Sweet and savory sauces, relishes, spreads, and seasonings	
4	3	Confections	Desserts, candies, and sweet breads	
5	4	Dairy Products	Cheeses	
6	5	Grains/Cereals	Breads, crackers, pasta, and cereal	
7	6	Meat/Poultry	Prepared meats	
8	7	Produce	Dried fruit and bean curd	
9	8	Seafood	Seaweed and fish	

Figure 3-33. Excel workbook Category.xlsx

The C# code in *Program.cs* in the project ReadExcelData is shown in Example 3-43.

Example 3-43. File: Program.cs for ReadExcelData solution

```csharp
using System;
using System.Data;
using System.Data.OleDb;

namespace ReadExcelData
{
    class Program
    {
        static void Main(string[] args)
        {
            string oledbConnectString =
                "Provider=Microsoft.ACE.OLEDB.12.0;" +
                @"Data Source=..\..\..\Category.xlsx;" +
                "Extended Properties=\"Excel 12.0;HDR=YES\";";

            string commandText = "SELECT CategoryID, CategoryName, " +
                "Description FROM [Sheet1$]";

            Console.WriteLine("---CONNECTION---");
            Console.WriteLine(oledbConnectString);

            OleDbConnection connection =
                new OleDbConnection(oledbConnectString);

            OleDbCommand command =
                new OleDbCommand(commandText, connection);
            connection.Open();
            OleDbDataReader dr = command.ExecuteReader();
            Console.WriteLine("\nID Name            Description");
            while (dr.Read())
            {
                Console.WriteLine("{0}  {1} {2}", dr["CategoryID"],
                    dr["CategoryName"].ToString().PadRight(14),
                    dr["Description"]);
            }
            connection.Close();

            Console.WriteLine("\nPress any key to continue.");
            Console.ReadKey();
        }
    }
}
```

The output is shown in Figure 3-34.

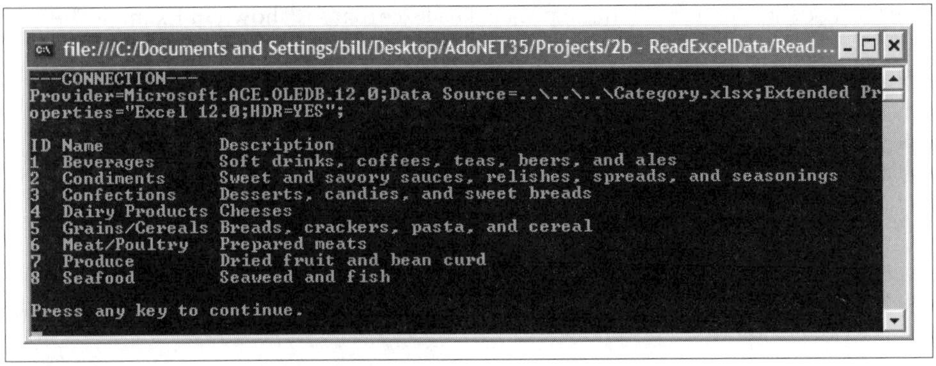

Figure 3-34. Output for ReadExcelData solution

Discussion

You can use the Microsoft Access Database Engine OLE DB provider to access Microsoft Excel as a data source. The provider can access other database file formats through Indexed Sequential Access Method (ISAM) drivers specified in the Extended Properties attribute of the connection. Excel files are supported with the Excel 12.0 source database type as shown in the following example:

```
Provider=Microsoft.ACE.OLEDB.12.0;Data Source=..\..\..\Category.xlsx;
    Extended Properties=\"Excel 12.0;HDR=YES\";
```

The Extended Properties attribute can, in addition to the ISAM version property, specify whether or not tables include headers as field names in the first row of a range using an HDR attribute.

There are three ways in which you can reference Excel workbook data within a SQL statement:

- Specify the worksheet name followed by a dollar sign to access the entire range used in the worksheet:

    ```
    SELECT * FROM [MySheet$]
    ```

- Specify a range explicitly using cells:

    ```
    SELECT * FROM [MySheet$A1:E5]
    ```

- Specify a range with a defined name, as shown in the solution:

    ```
    SELECT * FROM MyRange
    ```

The following subsections discuss how to use Excel as an ADO.NET data source.

Create table

The CREATE TABLE command will create a table in an Excel workbook. The workbook for the connection will be created if it does not exist. For example:

```
CREATE TABLE MySheet (Field1 char(10), Field2 float, Field3 date)
```

Create data

You can use the INSERT command, either static or parameterized, to insert data into a worksheet or range:

```
INSERT INTO [MySheet$]  (Field1, Field2, Field3)
VALUES ('testdata', 1.234, '09/28/1979');
```

Retrieve data

Use either a DataAdapter or a DataReader to retrieve data from an Excel workbook. Create a SQL SELECT statement referencing a worksheet or a range in an Excel workbook and execute the statement to fill a DataSet using a DataAdapter or to create a DataReader. For example:

```
SELECT * FROM [MySheet$]
```

Update data

The UPDATE command, either static or parameterized, can update data in a worksheet or range. For example:

```
UPDATE [MySheet$]
SET Field2 = '2.345',
    Field3 = '10/18/1964'
WHERE
    Field1 = 'testdata'
```

Delete data

The Microsoft Access Database Engine OLE DB provider does not allow DELETE operations in an Excel file. An error will be raised if an attempt is made to execute a DELETE statement affecting one or more records.

3.31 Querying Data Asynchronously with Message Queuing

Problem

You want to asynchronously retrieve data from a system that is not always connected.

Solution

You must:

- Use message queuing to construct and send a data request from the client.
- Access and process the requesting message at the server.
- Compose and send a response message containing the result set to the client.
- Retrieve the response at the client and deserialize it into a DataSet.

The solution creates query and result message queues if they do not exist. A message is sent to the query queue containing the query. The message is retrieved from the message queue and the query is parsed from it. The query is processed and the results are sent to the result queue. Finally the message is received from the result queue, cast to a DataSet, and the result set is output to the console.

This project needs a reference to the System.Messaging assembly.

The C# code in *Program.cs* in the project AsynchronousQueryMSMQ is shown in Example 3-44.

Example 3-44. File: Program.cs for AsynchronousQueryMSMQ solution

```csharp
using System;
using System.Data;
using System.Data.SqlClient;
using System.Messaging;

namespace AsynchronousQueryMSMQ
{
    class Program
    {
        private static string queueNameQuery =
            @".\Private$\AdoNet35Cookbook_AsynchronousQuery";
        private static string queueNameResult =
            @".\Private$\AdoNet35Cookbook_AsynchronousResult";
        private static int contactID = 10;

        static void Main(string[] args)
        {
            // Create the query queue if it does not exist.
            if (!MessageQueue.Exists(queueNameQuery))
            {
                MessageQueue.Create(queueNameQuery);
                Console.WriteLine("Query queue {0} created.", queueNameQuery);
            }
            else
                Console.WriteLine("Query queue {0} found.", queueNameQuery);

            // Create the result queue if it does not exist.
            if (!MessageQueue.Exists(queueNameResult))
            {
                MessageQueue.Create(queueNameResult);
                Console.WriteLine("Result queue {0} created.", queueNameResult);
            }
            else
                Console.WriteLine("Result queue {0} found.", queueNameResult);

            // Create an object to access the query queue for sending.
            using (MessageQueue mqQueryOut = new MessageQueue(queueNameQuery))
            {
                mqQueryOut.Formatter =
                    new XmlMessageFormatter(new Type[] { typeof(String) });
```

```csharp
        // Send a message containing the contact ID to query for.
        string body = "ContactID=" + contactID;
        mqQueryOut.Send(body);
        Console.WriteLine(
            "\nQuery for ContactID = {0} sent to query queue.", contactID);
    }

    // Create an object to access the query queue for receiving.
    int queryContactID;
    using (MessageQueue mqQueryIn = new MessageQueue(queueNameQuery))
    {
        mqQueryIn.Formatter =
            new XmlMessageFormatter(new Type[] { typeof(String) });

        // Retrieve the query message from the queue
        Message msg = mqQueryIn.Receive(new TimeSpan(0, 0, 1));
        Console.WriteLine("\nQuery message {0} received.", msg.Id);

        // Get the contact ID from the message body.
        queryContactID = int.Parse(msg.Body.ToString().Substring(10));
        Console.WriteLine("Query ContactID = {0} retrieved from message.",
            queryContactID);
    }

    // Retrieve data for the specified contact using a DataAdapter.
    string sqlConnectString = "Data Source=(local);" +
        "Integrated security=SSPI;Initial Catalog=AdventureWorks;";
    String sqlText = "SELECT * FROM Person.Contact WHERE ContactID=" +
        queryContactID;
    SqlDataAdapter da = new SqlDataAdapter(sqlText,sqlConnectString);
    // Fill the Customer table in the DataSet with customer data.
    DataSet ds = new DataSet();
    da.FillSchema(ds, SchemaType.Source);
    da.Fill(ds);
    Console.WriteLine("Result set created.");

    // Create an object to access the result queue for sending.
    using (MessageQueue mqResultOut = new MessageQueue(queueNameResult))
    {
        mqResultOut.Formatter =
            new XmlMessageFormatter(new Type[] { typeof(DataSet) });

        // Write the result message to the queue
        mqResultOut.Send(ds, "ContactID=" + queryContactID);
        Console.WriteLine(
            "Result message ContactID = {0} sent to result queue.",
            queryContactID);
    }

    // Create an object to access the result queue for receiving.
    DataSet dsResult;
    using (MessageQueue mqResultIn = new MessageQueue(queueNameResult))
```

```
        {
            mqResultIn.Formatter =
                new XmlMessageFormatter(new Type[] { typeof(DataSet) });

            Message msg = mqResultIn.Receive(new TimeSpan(0, 0, 1));
            Console.WriteLine("\nResult message {0} received.", msg.Id);

            // Create the customer DataSet from the message body.
            dsResult = (DataSet)msg.Body;
        }

        //Output the results to the console
        Console.WriteLine("\n---RESULT SET---");
        foreach (DataColumn col in dsResult.Tables[0].Columns)
            Console.WriteLine("{0} = {1}",
                col.ColumnName, dsResult.Tables[0].Rows[0][col.Ordinal]);

        Console.WriteLine("\nPress any key to continue.");
        Console.ReadKey();
    }
  }
}
```

The output is shown in Figure 3-35.

Figure 3-36 shows the query and result queues that the application created.

Discussion

Microsoft Message Queuing (MSMQ) provides an inter-application messaging infra-structure that allows messages to be sent between disconnected applications. MSMQ provides for message transport, queuing, transactional message support, error hand-ling, and auditing, and makes available a variety of Application Programming Inter-faces to interact with MSMQ programmatically. The System.Messaging namespace contains the .NET classes that support MSMQ.

To send a message using MSMQ, perform the following actions:

- Create a connection to the message queue to which you want to send the message.

- Specify a formatter—an object that controls the type of data that can be sent in the message body and how it is persisted—for the data that you want to send. Table 3-9 describes the different formatters available.

- Call the Send( ) method of the MessageQueue to write the Message to the queue. The object to be sent is passed as an argument to the method.

Figure 3-35. Output for AsynchronousQueryMSMQ solution

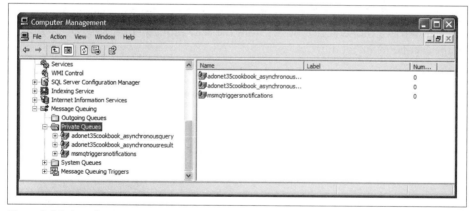

Figure 3-36. Asynchronous Query message queues

Table 3-9. .NET predefined formatters

Formatter	Description
ActiveXMessageFormatter	Serializes or deserializes primitive data types and other objects using a format compatible with MSMQ ActiveX Component to allow interoperability with previous versions of MSMQ. It is fast and produces a compact serialization.
BinaryMessageFormatter	Serializes or deserializes an object or an object graph using a binary format. It is fast and produces a compact serialization.
XMLMessageFormatter	Serializes or deserializes objects and primitive data types into XML based on an XSD schema. This is the default formatter for MessageQueue components.

When the Send( ) method of the MessageQueue is called, the body of the message is serialized using the XMLMessageFormatter if the Formatter property is not specified.

To read a message and recreate the serialized body, formatter properties must be set before reading the message. The properties that must be set are specific to the formatter:

ActiveXMessageFormatter
No properties must be set.

BinaryMessageFormatter
Specify the format of the root object and the type descriptions either in the constructor or by explicitly setting the TopObjectFormat and TypeFormat properties.

XmlMessageFormatter
Specify the target types or target type names either in the constructor or by explicitly setting the TargetTypes or TargetTypeNames property.

The message can now be read by using the Receive( ) method of the MessageQueue. You can retrieve the serialized object from the Body property of the Message returned by the Receive( ) method.

For more information about Microsoft Message Queue (MSMQ), see the MSDN Library.

CHAPTER 4

Searching and Analyzing Data

4.0 Introduction

This chapter focuses on searching for records in views and tables, calculating values based on values in those or other tables, and navigating data relations between tables.

The DataView is a data-bindable view of a DataTable that presents data with different sort orders and filters. You can create multiple views for each table; every table has a default data view. The DataViewManager class helps to manage the default data views for tables in a DataSet. Recipe 4.5 shows how to use the DataView to filter and sort data in a DataSet. Recipe 4.6 shows how to filter a data view for rows that have null values.

The DataTable and DataView classes both provide several ways to locate records from specified criteria. Searching an existing table or view saves a roundtrip to the database server. Although the DataView is created from a DataTable, searching is done differently in each. Recipe 4.4 shows how to find rows in a DataTable and in a DataView. Recipe 4.7 shows how to access deleted rows in DataTable.

ADO.NET does not provide a way to compare two DataSet objects with identical schemas to determine the data differences between the two. Recipe 4.1 creates a method GetDataSetDifference( ) that returns the differences as a DiffGram, which is an XML format that identifies original and current versions of data and is used by .NET to serialize and persist the DataSet.

In addition to recipes about the DataRelation, DataSet, DataTable, and DataView classes, this chapter covers topics including:

- ADO.NET does not provide a way to get the TOP N rows from a DataTable based on the value of a column in the table. Recipe 4.8 shows how to build a filter on the DataView at runtime to return the TOP N rows.

- Queries sometimes need to be based on data from more than one data source. Recipe 4.2 shows how to return a result set from a query based on more than one table using *ad hoc connector names* that allow data from heterogeneous data sources to be accessed by providing the connection information in the SQL statement.

- The COMPUTE BY clause returns both summary and detail data in a single result set from a single SELECT statement. Recipe 4.9 shows how to execute a COMPUTE BY statement and how to navigate the result set.
- The Shape language uses Data Shaping Services for OLE DB as an alternative to JOIN and GROUP BY syntax to generate hierarchical result sets. Recipe 4.10 shows how to use the Shape language to get a hierarchical result set from SQL Server using the OLE DB .NET data provider, and how to navigate the result set.
- Executing Common Table Expression (CTE) and recursive queries and working with the returned result sets is demonstrated and discussed in Recipes 4.12 and 4.13.

Retrieving random samples of data, retrieving ranked result sets, working with pivot tables, and invoking functions for each row in a result set are also the topics of recipes in this chapter.

4.1   Determining the Differences in Data Between Two DataSet Objects

Problem

You have two DataSet objects with the same schema but containing different data and need to determine the difference between the data in the two.

Solution

Compare the two DataSet objects with the GetDataSetDifference( ) method in this solution and return the differences between the data as a DiffGram.

The solution creates two DataSet objects each containing a different subset of records from the HumanResources.Department table in AdventureWorks. The GetDataSetDifference( ) method takes two DataSet objects with identical schemas as arguments and returns a DiffGram of the differences between the data in the two.

The C# code in *Program.cs* in the project DetermineDataDifferenceDataSets is shown in Example 4-1.

Example 4-1. File: Program.cs for DetermineDataDifferenceDataSets solution

```
using System;
using System.Data;
using System.Data.SqlClient;
using System.IO;

namespace DetermineDataDifferenceDataSets
{
    class Program
    {
        {
```

```csharp
static void Main(string[] args)
{
    string sqlConnectString = "Data Source=(local);" +
        "Integrated security=SSPI;Initial Catalog=AdventureWorks;";

    // Fill DataSet A
    string sqlSelectA = "SELECT * FROM HumanResources.Department " +
        "WHERE DepartmentID BETWEEN 1 AND 5";
    DataSet dsA = new DataSet();
    SqlDataAdapter da = new SqlDataAdapter(sqlSelectA, sqlConnectString);
    da.TableMappings.Add("Table", "TableA");
    da.FillSchema(dsA, SchemaType.Source);
    da.Fill(dsA);
    // Set the primary key
    dsA.Tables["TableA"].PrimaryKey =
        new DataColumn[] { dsA.Tables["TableA"].Columns["DepartmentID"] };

    // Fill DataSet B
    string sqlSelectB = "SELECT * FROM HumanResources.Department " +
        "WHERE DepartmentID BETWEEN 4 AND 8";
    DataSet dsB = new DataSet();
    da = new SqlDataAdapter(sqlSelectB, sqlConnectString);
    da.TableMappings.Add("Table", "TableB");
    da.FillSchema(dsB, SchemaType.Source);
    da.Fill(dsB);
    // Set the primary key
    dsB.Tables["TableB"].PrimaryKey =
        new DataColumn[] { dsB.Tables["TableB"].Columns["DepartmentID"] };

    Console.WriteLine(GetDataSetDifference(dsA, dsB));

    Console.WriteLine("\nPress any key to continue.");
    Console.ReadKey();
}

private static string GetDataSetDifference(DataSet ds1, DataSet ds2)
{
    // Accept any edits within the DataSet objects.
    ds1.AcceptChanges();
    ds2.AcceptChanges();

    // Create a DataSet to store the differences.
    DataSet ds = new DataSet();

    DataTable dt1Copy = null;
    // Iterate over the collection of tables in the first DataSet.
    for (int i = 0; i < ds1.Tables.Count; i++)
    {
        DataTable dt1 = ds1.Tables[i];
        DataTable dt2 = ds2.Tables[i];

        // Create a copy of the table in the first DataSet.
        dt1Copy = dt1.Copy();
```

```
// Iterate over the collection of rows in the
// copy of the table from the first DataSet.
foreach (DataRow row1 in dt1Copy.Rows)
{
    DataRow row2 = dt2.Rows.Find(row1["DepartmentID"]);
    if (row2 == null)
    {
        // Delete rows not in table 2 from table 1.
        row1.Delete( );
    }
    else
    {
        // Modify table 1 rows that are different from
        // table 2 rows.
        for (int j = 0; j < dt1Copy.Columns.Count; j++)
        {
            if (row2[j] == DBNull.Value)
            {
                // Column in table 2 is null,
                // but not null in table 1
                if (row1[j] != DBNull.Value)
                    row1[j] = DBNull.Value;
            }
            else if (row1[j] == DBNull.Value)
            {
                // Column in table 1 is null,
                // but not null in table 2
                row1[j] = row2[j];
            }
            else if (row1[j].ToString( ) !=
                row2[j].ToString( ))
            {
                // Neither column in table 1 nor
                // table 2 is null, and the
                // values in the columns are
                // different.
                row1[j] = row2[j];
            }
        }
    }
}

foreach (DataRow row2 in dt2.Rows)
{
    DataRow row1 =
        dt1Copy.Rows.Find(row2["DepartmentID"]);
    if (row1 == null)
```

```
            {
                // Insert rows into table 1 that are in table 2
                // but not in table 1.
                dt1Copy.LoadDataRow(row2.ItemArray, false);
            }
        }

        // Add the table to the difference DataSet.
        ds.Tables.Add(dt1Copy);
    }

    // Write a XML DiffGram with containing the differences between tables.
    StringWriter sw = new StringWriter( );
    ds.WriteXml(sw, XmlWriteMode.DiffGram);

    return sw.ToString( );
    }
  }
}
```

The output is shown in Figure 4-1.

Discussion

A DiffGram is an XML format used to specify original and current values for the data elements in a DataSet. It does not include any schema information. The DiffGram is used by .NET Framework applications as the serialization format for the contents of a DataSet including changes made to the DataSet.

A DiffGram is XML-based, which makes it platform- and application-independent. It is not, however, widely used or understood outside of Microsoft .NET applications.

The DiffGram format is divided into three sections: current, original, and errors. The original and current data in the DiffGram can also be used to report the differences between data in two DataSet objects. For more information about the DiffGram XML format, see Recipe 9.4.

The solution contains a method GetDataSetDifference( ) that takes two DataSet objects with the same schema as arguments and returns a DiffGram containing the differences in data when the second DataSet is compared to the first. Table 4-1 describes how the differences between the DataSet objects appear in the DiffGram.

Figure 4-1. Output for DetermineDataDifferenceDataSets solution

Table 4-1. DiffGram representation of DataSet differences

Condition	DiffGram representation
Row is the same in both DataSet 1 and DataSet 2	Row data appears only in the current data section of the DiffGram without a diffgr:haschanges attribute. (In the example, rows with DepartmentID of 4 and 5 appear.)
Row is in both DataSet 1 and DataSet 2 but the rows do not contain the same data	Row data appears in the current data section of the DiffGram. The row element contains the attribute diffgr:hasChanges with a value of *"modified"*. The data in the current section is the updated data. The original data appears in the original <diffgr:before> block of the DiffGram.

Table 4-1. DiffGram representation of DataSet differences (continued)

Condition	DiffGram representation
Row is in DataSet 2 but not in DataSet 1	Row data appears in the current data section of the DiffGram. The row element contains the attribute diffgr: hasChanges with a value of "inserted". (In the example, rows with DepartmentID between 6 and 8 appear.)
Row is DataSet 1 but not in DataSet 2	Row data appears only in the original <diffgr:before> block of the DiffGram. (In the example, rows with DepartmentID between 1 and 3 appear.)

The sample begins by loading two different subsets of data from the HumanResources. Department table into separate DataSet objects. In this example, the DataSet objects both contain just a single table. To determine the difference between the DataSet objects, the tables within the DataSet objects are compared as described next and changes are applied to the data in a copy of the first DataSet until it matches the second DataSet. Once all differences in all tables are processed, the DiffGram of the copy of the first DataSet contains the difference in the second DataSet when compared to the first DataSet.

More specifically, a copy of each table is made as it is processed. The data in the copy of the first table is modified to make it consistent with the data in the second table. The modified copy of the first table is then added to the DataSet containing the differences between the two DataSet objects.

The process of modifying the data in the copy of the first table to match the data in second table involves several steps:

- Rows that are in the copy of the first table but not in the second table (based on the primary key value) are deleted from the copy of the first table.

- If the row is found in the second table, the columns are compared and any differences in the columns in the second table are changed in the column in the first table.

- Rows that are in the second table but not in the copy of the first table are inserted into the copy of the first table without accepting changes.

4.2   Combining Data from Heterogeneous Data Sources

Problem

You want to create a report based on data from tables in more than one data source.

Solution

Use ad hoc connector names in SQL statements.

The solution retrieves data from both a SQL Server table and a Microsoft Access table to create a single result set. Specifically, Sales.SalesOrderHeader data is retrieved from AdventureWorks in SQL Server and joined to Sales.SalesOrderDetail data retrieved from Microsoft Access.

You must enable OPENROWSET support in SQL Server to run this example. To do this, open SQL Server Surface Area Configuration tool from the SQL Server Configuration Tools folder. Select Surface Area Configuration for Features. Select the Ad Hoc Remote Queries component and check the "Enable OPENROWSET and OPENDATASOURCE support" checkbox as shown in Figure 4-2.

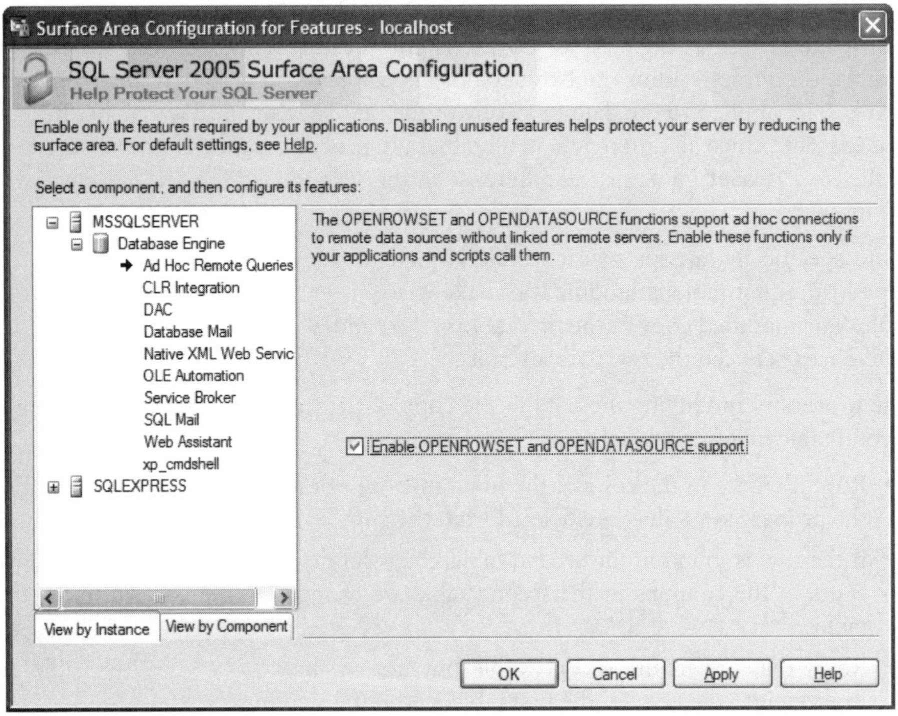

Figure 4-2. Surface Area Configuration for Features dialog

Click the OK button to apply the changes. Close the Surface Area Configuration main window.

You also need to create a Microsoft Access file (named *AdventureWorks.accdb* in this example) and import the Sales.SalesOrderDetail table into it from AdventureWorks in SQL Server. Set the filename variable accessFileName in the example to match the location and name of your Microsoft Access file. Ensure that the Microsoft Access database is closed before running the example.

The C# code in *Program.cs* in the project CombineHeterogeneousData is shown in Example 4-2.

Example 4-2. File: Program.cs for CombineHeterogeneousData solution

```
using System;
using System.Data;
using System.Data.SqlClient;

namespace CombineHeterogeneousData
{
    class Program
    {
        static void Main(string[] args)
        {
            string sqlConnectString = "Data Source=(local);" +
                "Integrated security=SSPI;Initial Catalog=AdventureWorks;";

            string accessFileName =
                @"C:\Documents and Settings\bill\My Documents\AdventureWorks.accdb";

            string sqlSelect =
                "SELECT TOP 20 h.SalesOrderID, h.CustomerID, h.OrderDate, " +
                "d.ProductID, d.OrderQty, d.LineTotal " +
                "FROM Sales.SalesOrderHeader h INNER JOIN " +
                "OPENROWSET('Microsoft.ACE.OLEDB.12.0','" + accessFileName +
                "';'admin';'',Sales_SalesOrderDetail) AS d " +
                "ON h.SalesOrderID = d.SalesOrderID " +
                "ORDER BY h.SalesOrderID, d.ProductID";

            SqlDataAdapter da = new SqlDataAdapter(sqlSelect, sqlConnectString);
            DataTable dt = new DataTable( );
            da.Fill(dt);

            Console.WriteLine("OrderID\tCustID\tOrderDate\t\tProdID\t" +
                "Qty\tLineTotal");
            foreach (DataRow row in dt.Rows)
                Console.WriteLine("{0}\t{1}\t{2}\t{3}\t{4}\t{5}",
                    row["SalesOrderID"], row["CustomerID"], row["OrderDate"],
                    row["ProductID"], row["OrderQty"], row["LineTotal"]);

            Console.WriteLine("\nPress any key to continue.");
            Console.ReadKey( );
        }
    }
}
```

The output is shown in Figure 4-3.

Discussion

Microsoft SQL Server 2000 and later supports two methods to access data from heterogeneous data sources through OLE DB: ad hoc connector names and linked servers.

```
file:///C:/Documents and Settings/bill/Desktop/AdoNET35/Projects/CombineHeterogeneousD...
OrderID CustID  OrderDate            ProdID Qty    LineTotal
43659   676     7/1/2001 12:00:00 AM  709    6     34.200000
43659   676     7/1/2001 12:00:00 AM  711    4     80.746000
43659   676     7/1/2001 12:00:00 AM  712    2     10.373000
43659   676     7/1/2001 12:00:00 AM  714    3     86.521200
43659   676     7/1/2001 12:00:00 AM  716    1     28.840400
43659   676     7/1/2001 12:00:00 AM  771    1     2039.994000
43659   676     7/1/2001 12:00:00 AM  772    1     2039.994000
43659   676     7/1/2001 12:00:00 AM  773    2     4079.988000
43659   676     7/1/2001 12:00:00 AM  774    1     2039.994000
43659   676     7/1/2001 12:00:00 AM  776    1     2024.994000
43659   676     7/1/2001 12:00:00 AM  777    3     6074.982000
43659   676     7/1/2001 12:00:00 AM  778    1     2024.994000
43660   117     7/1/2001 12:00:00 AM  758    1     874.794000
43660   117     7/1/2001 12:00:00 AM  762    1     419.458900
43661   442     7/1/2001 12:00:00 AM  708    5     100.932500
43661   442     7/1/2001 12:00:00 AM  711    2     40.373000
43661   442     7/1/2001 12:00:00 AM  712    4     20.746000
43661   442     7/1/2001 12:00:00 AM  715    4     115.361600
43661   442     7/1/2001 12:00:00 AM  716    2     57.680800
43661   442     7/1/2001 12:00:00 AM  741    2     1637.400000

Press any key to continue.
```

Figure 4-3. Output for CombineHeterogeneousData solution

Ad hoc connector names allow data from heterogeneous data sources to be accessed without setting up linked servers by providing the information required to connect to each data source in the SQL statement. This is done using either the OPENROWSET or the OPENDATASOURCE function to open the row set from the OLE DB data source. Both functions take arguments containing all connection information required to access the data source. The functions allow the row sets to be subsequently referenced like any other table in SQL statements.

For more information about OPENROWSET and OPENDATASOURCE functions, see Microsoft SQL Server Books Online.

Add linked servers using the Server Objects → Linked Servers node in Object Explorer in SQL Server Management Studio or using system stored procedures. Refer to linked servers in SQL statements using a four-part name comprised of the names of the linked server, the catalog, the schema within the catalog, and the data object, separated using periods. Access to linked servers has better performance than access using ad hoc connector names. For more information about using linked servers, see Microsoft SQL Server Books Online.

4.3   Filtering Rows in a DataTable or DataView

Problem

You need to filter a DataTable or DataView for rows meeting certain criteria.

Solution

Use one of the two techniques shown in the solution to locate data in the table meeting user-specified criteria.

The solution creates a DataTable containing data from the Person.Contacts table in AdventureWorks. The solution uses two different techniques—the DataTable.Select( ) method and the DataView.RowFilter property—to filter and display rows.

The C# code in *Program.cs* in the project FilterRows is shown in Example 4-3.

Example 4-3. File: Program.cs for FilterRows solution

```csharp
using System;
using System.Data;
using System.Data.SqlClient;

namespace FilterRows
{
    class Program
    {
        static void Main(string[] args)
        {
            string sqlConnectString = "Data Source=(local);" +
                "Integrated security=SSPI;Initial Catalog=AdventureWorks;";

            string sqlSelect = "SELECT * FROM Person.Contact";

            DataTable dt = new DataTable( );
            SqlDataAdapter da = new SqlDataAdapter(sqlSelect, sqlConnectString);
            da.Fill(dt);

            string filter = "LastName LIKE 'AG*'";

            // Filter the rows using Select( ) method of DataTable
            DataRow[] rows = dt.Select(filter);

            Console.WriteLine("---Filtering using DataTable.Select( )---");
            foreach (DataRow row in rows)
                Console.WriteLine("{0}\t{1}, {2}",
                    row["ContactID"], row["LastName"], row["FirstName"]);

            Console.WriteLine( );

            // Filter the rows using RowFilter property of a DataView
            DataView dv = dt.DefaultView;
            dv.RowFilter = filter;
            Console.WriteLine("---Filtering using DataView.RowFilter---");
            foreach (DataRowView row in dv)
                Console.WriteLine("{0}\t{1}, {2}",
                    row["ContactID"], row["LastName"], row["FirstName"]);

            Console.WriteLine("\nPress any key to continue.");
            Console.ReadKey( );
        }
    }
}
```

The output is shown in Figure 4-4.

Figure 4-4. Output for FilterRows solution

Discussion

There are two ways to filter a result set in a DataTable or DataView:

- Use the Select( ) method of the DataTable to return an array of DataRow objects matching the specified filter criteria. By default, the rows in the array are ordered by the primary key or, lacking a primary key, by the order in which the rows were added to the table. A sort order can be specified in an optional argument. The Select( ) method also takes an optional argument that can also be used to select records matching a specified row state from the DataViewRowState enumeration.

- Use the RowFilter property of a DataView to specify the expression used to filter which rows are viewed. The expression is similar to a T-SQL WHERE clause—the name of a column followed by an operator and filter criteria. For details about expression syntax, see the topic "DataColumn.Property" in MSDN.

4.4   Finding Rows in a DataTable or DataView

Problem

You need to find rows meeting certain criteria in a DataTable or DataView.

Solution

Choose from the three techniques shown in the solution to find data in the table meeting user-specified criteria.

The solution creates a DataTable containing data from the Person.Contact table in AdventureWorks. The solution uses three different techniques—the DataRowCollection.Find( ) method, the DataView.Find( ) method, and the DataView.FindRows( ) method—to find rows.

The C# code in *Program.cs* in project FindRows is shown in Example 4-4.

Example 4-4. File: Program.cs for FindRows solution

```csharp
using System;
using System.Data;
using System.Data.SqlClient;

namespace FindRows
{
    class Program
    {
        static void Main(string[] args)
        {
            string sqlConnectString = "Data Source=(local);" +
                "Integrated security=SSPI;Initial Catalog=AdventureWorks;";

            string sqlSelect = "SELECT * FROM Person.Contact";

            // Fill the DataTable with schema and data
            DataTable dt = new DataTable();
            SqlDataAdapter da = new SqlDataAdapter(sqlSelect, sqlConnectString);
            da.FillSchema(dt, SchemaType.Source);
            da.Fill(dt);

            // Find a row matching a primary key (ContactID) value (429)
            Console.WriteLine("---Finding rows using DataTable.Rows.Find( )---");
            DataRow row = dt.Rows.Find(new object[] { 429 });
            if (row != null)
                Console.WriteLine("{0}\t{1}, {2}",
                    row["ContactID"], row["LastName"], row["FirstName"]);
            else
                Console.WriteLine("Row not found.");

            Console.WriteLine( );

            DataView dv = dt.DefaultView;

            // Find a row matching a primary key (ContactID) value (429)
            Console.WriteLine("---Finding a row using DataView.Find( )---");
            dv.Sort = "ContactID";
            int rowIndex = dv.Find(new object[] { 429 });
            if (rowIndex != -1)
                Console.WriteLine("{0}\t{1}, {2}",
                    dv[rowIndex]["ContactID"], dv[rowIndex]["LastName"],
                    dv[rowIndex]["FirstName"]);
            else
                Console.WriteLine("Row not found.");

            Console.WriteLine( );

            // Find rows matching the sort field LastName in a DataView
            dv.Sort = "LastName";
            DataRowView[] drv = dv.FindRows(new object[] {"Jacobson"});
```

Example 4-4. File: Program.cs for FindRows solution (continued)

```
        Console.WriteLine("---Finding rows using DataView.FindRows( )---");
        foreach (DataRowView dvrow in drv)
            Console.WriteLine("{0}\t{1}, {2}",
                dvrow["ContactID"], dvrow["LastName"], dvrow["FirstName"]);

        Console.WriteLine("\nPress any key to continue.");
        Console.ReadKey( );
    }
  }
}
```

The output is shown in Figure 4-5.

Figure 4-5. Output for FindRows solution

Discussion

The Find( ) method of the DataRowCollection of a DataTable returns a row or rows matching the primary key value or key values passed as an object argument or an array of object arguments. The DataTable to which the DataRowCollection belongs must have a primary key defined, otherwise a MissingPrimaryKeyException is raised. If the primary key does not exist in the DataRowCollection, the method returns null.

The Find( ) and FindRows( ) methods of the DataView search for rows in a DataView using its sort key values. The search values must match the sort key values exactly to return a result; wild card matches are not possible.

The primary difference between the Find( ) and FindRows( ) methods is that Find( ) returns the zero-based index of the first row that matches the search criteria (or –1 if no match is found) while FindRows( ) returns a DataRowView array of all matching rows (or an empty array if no match is found).

Before the Find( ) or FindRows( ) method of the DataView class can be used, a sort order must be specified. You can do this in two ways:

- Set the `ApplyDefaultSort` property of the `DataView` to true. This automatically creates an ascending sort order based on the primary column or columns of the table. The default sort can be applied only when the `Sort` property of the `DataView` is a null reference or an empty string and when the underlying `DataTable` has a primary key defined. By default, the `AutoDefaultSort` property is set to false, so it must be explicitly set.
- Set the `Sort` property of the `DataView` to a string containing one or more column names followed by nothing, or `ASC` for an ascending sort, or by `DESC` for a descending sort. Use commas to separate multiple sort column names.

Both the `Find()` and `FindRows()` methods take a single input argument. This is an object value if the `DataView` is sorted on a single column or an array of objects containing values for all of the columns defined by the `Sort` property in the same order as specified by the `Sort` property.

The `Find()` and `FindRows()` methods perform better than the `RowFilter` property when a result set from the `DataView` matching specific criteria is required rather than a dynamic view on the subset of data. This is because setting the `RowFilter` property of the `DataView` causes the index for the `DataView` to be rebuilt, while the `Find()` and `FindRows()` methods use the existing index.

4.5 Filtering and Sorting Data in a DataTable

Problem

You have a `DataTable` filled with data, but you need to work with only a subset of the records and also to sort them. You need a way to both filter and sort the records in your `DataTable` without requerying the data source.

Solution

Use either the `Sort` and `RowFilter` properties of the `DataView` or the `Select()` method of the `DataTable`.

Choose from the two techniques shown in the solution to filter and sort records from table according to user-specified criteria.

The solution creates a `DataSet` containing data from the `Production.Product` table in AdventureWorks. Solutions are presented to illustrate how to use two different techniques—the `RowFilter` property of the `DataView` and the `DataTable.Select()` method—to filter and sort records.

The C# code in *Program.cs* in the project `FillSortData` that uses the `Sort` and `RowFilter` properties of the `DataView` is shown in Example 4-5.

Example 4-5. File: Program.cs for FillSortData solution

```
using System;
using System.Data;
using System.Data.SqlClient;

namespace FilterSortData
{
    class Program
    {
        static void Main(string[] args)
        {
            string sqlConnectString = "Data Source=(local);" +
                "Integrated security=SSPI;Initial Catalog=AdventureWorks;";

            string sqlSelect = "SELECT * FROM Production.Product";

            // Fill the DataSet, mapping the default table name
            SqlDataAdapter da = new SqlDataAdapter(sqlSelect, sqlConnectString);
            da.TableMappings.Add("Table", "Product");
            DataSet ds = new DataSet();
            da.Fill(ds);

            DataView dv = ds.Tables["Product"].DefaultView;
            dv.RowFilter = "DaysToManufacture >= 4";
            dv.Sort = "Name";

            foreach (DataRowView dvr in dv)
                Console.WriteLine(
                    "ProductID = {0}, Name = {1}, DaysToManufacture = {2}",
                    dvr["ProductID"], dvr["Name"], dvr["DaysToManufacture"]);

            Console.WriteLine("\nPress any key to continue.");
            Console.ReadKey();
        }
    }
}
```

Partial output is shown in Figure 4-6.

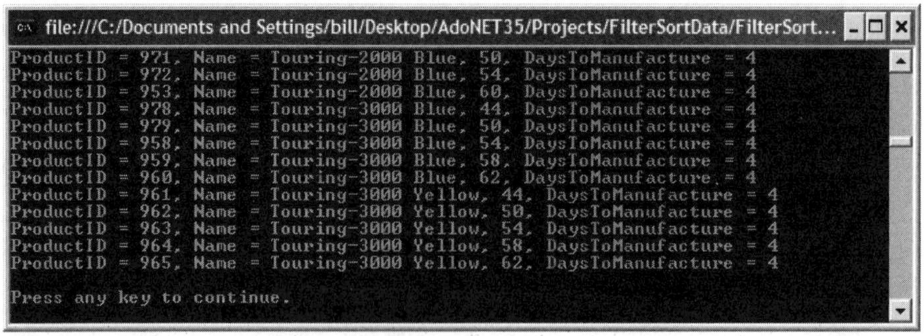

Figure 4-6. Output for FilterSortData solution

The C# code in *Program.cs* in the project FillSortDataSelect that uses the DataTable.Select( ) method is shown in Example 4-6.

Example 4-6. File: Program.cs for FillSortDataSelect solution

```csharp
using System;
using System.Data;
using System.Data.SqlClient;

namespace FilterSortDataSelect
{
    class Program
    {
        static void Main(string[] args)
        {
            string sqlConnectString = "Data Source=(local);" +
                "Integrated security=SSPI;Initial Catalog=AdventureWorks;";

            string sqlSelect = "SELECT * FROM Production.Product";

            // Fill the DataSet, mapping the default table name
            SqlDataAdapter da = new SqlDataAdapter(sqlSelect, sqlConnectString);
            da.TableMappings.Add("Table", "Product");
            DataSet ds = new DataSet();
            da.Fill(ds);

            // Filter and sort using the Select() method of the DataTable
            string rowFilter = "DaysToManufacture >= 4";
            string sort = "Name";
            DataRow[] rows = ds.Tables["Product"].Select(rowFilter, sort);

            foreach (DataRow row in rows)
                Console.WriteLine(
                    "ProductID = {0}, Name = {1}, DaysToManufacture = {2}",
                    row["ProductID"], row["Name"], row["DaysToManufacture"]);

            Console.WriteLine("\nPress any key to continue.");
            Console.ReadKey();
        }
    }
}
```

The output is the same as for the previous solution and is shown in Figure 4-6.

Discussion

The DataView filters and sorts the data in DataTable objects in the DataSet. The RowFilter property of the DataView accesses the expression that filters the view. The Sort property of the DataView sorts the view on single or multiple columns in either ascending or descending order.

The `DataViewManager` can simplify working with multiple views within a `DataSet`, but is not required. The `DataViewManager` object exposes a `DataViewSettingCollection` object through the `DataViewSettings` property. The collection contains a single `DataViewSetting` object for each table in the `DataSet`. The object is accessed using the name or ordinal of the table by using an indexer in C# or by using the `Item()` property in VB.NET. The `DataViewSetting` object allows access to the `ApplyDefaultSort`, `RowFilter`, `RowStateFilter`, and `Sort` properties of a `DataView` created from the `DataViewManager` for the table. Accessing these properties is identical to accessing the same properties directly through the `DataView`.

The `Select()` method of the `DataTable` class has an overload that takes two arguments specifying the filter criteria and sort order and returns an array of matching `DataRow` objects. The filter criteria argument's syntax corresponds to a T-SQL WHERE clause while the sort order argument syntax corresponds to a T-SQL ORDER BY clause. For information about converting a `DataRow` array to a `DataTable`, see Recipe 2.14.

4.6 Filtering Null Field Values in a DataTable

Problem

You want to filter a `DataTable` or `DataView` for rows that have null field values.

Solutions

Choose from the two techniques shown in the solution to find data in the table with null field values.

The solution creates a `DataTable` containing data from the `Person.Contact` table in AdventureWorks. The solution uses two different techniques—the `Sort` property of the `DataView` class or the `DataTable.Select()` method—to filter records containing null values for user-specified fields.

The C# code in *Program.cs* in project `FilterNullValues` is shown in Example 4-7.

Example 4-7. File: Program.cs for FilterNullValues solution

```
using System;
using System.Data;
using System.Data.SqlClient;

namespace FilterNullValues
{
    class Program
    {
        static void Main(string[] args)
        {
            string sqlConnectString = "Data Source=(local);" +
                "Integrated security=SSPI;Initial Catalog=AdventureWorks;";
```

Example 4-7. File: Program.cs for FilterNullValues solution (continued)

```csharp
        string sqlSelect = "SELECT * FROM Person.Contact";

        string filter = "Title IS NULL";

        DataTable dt = new DataTable( );
        SqlDataAdapter da = new SqlDataAdapter(sqlSelect, sqlConnectString);
        da.Fill(dt);

        // Filter the rows using Select( ) method of DataTable
        DataRow[] rows = dt.Select(filter);

        // Output the top 5 rows
        Console.WriteLine("---DataTable.Select( )---");
        for (int i = 0; i <= 5; i++)
        {
            Console.WriteLine("{0}\tTitle = '{1}'\t{2}, {3}",
                rows[i]["ContactID"], rows[i]["Title"],
                rows[i]["LastName"], rows[i]["FirstName"]);
        }

        // Filter the rows using the Filter property of the DataView
        DataView dv = dt.DefaultView;
        dv.RowFilter = filter;

        // Output the top 5 rows
        Console.WriteLine("\n---Filter property of DataView---");
        for (int i = 0; i <= 5; i++)
        {
            Console.WriteLine("{0}\tTitle = '{1}'\t{2}, {3}",
                dv[i]["ContactID"], dv[i]["Title"],
                dv[i]["LastName"], dv[i]["FirstName"]);
        }

        Console.WriteLine("\nPress any key to continue.");
        Console.ReadKey( );
    }
  }
}
```

The output is shown in Figure 4-7.

Discussion

Every DataTable has a default DataView associated with it that can filter a table for records meeting specific criteria. In the solution, the RowFilter property of the DefaultView is filtered for rows containing a null Title field. The result of applying the filter is immediately reflected in any controls bound to the DataView object in addition to any operations performed on the records within the DataView.

Alternatively, you can use the Select( ) method on the DataTable underlying the DataView to retrieve an array of DataRow objects containing only rows with a null Title field using the same filter expression.

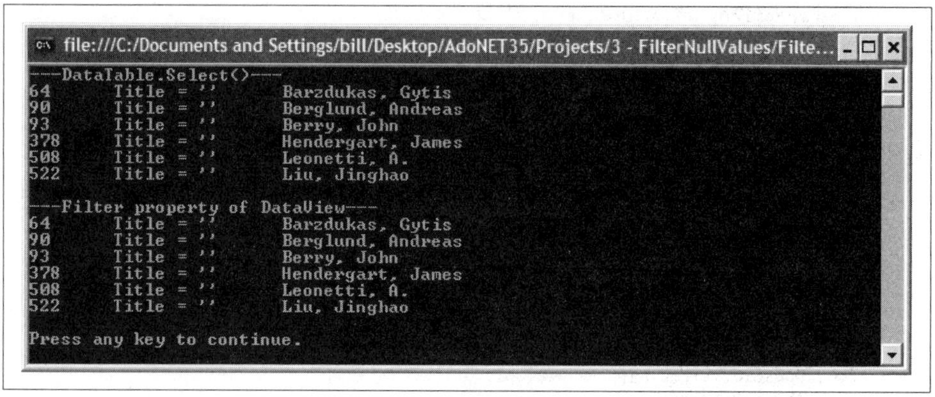

Figure 4-7. Output for FilterNullValues solution

4.7 Accessing Deleted Rows in a DataTable

Problem

When you delete rows from a DataSet they are really marked for deletion until changes are committed by calling AcceptChanges( ) either directly or indirectly. You want to access the rows that you have deleted from a DataTable.

Solution

Use one of the four techniques demonstrated in this solution.

The solution fills a DataSet with the TOP 3 records from the Person.Contact table in the AdventureWorks database. The second row is deleted. The deleted row is accessed and written to the console using the following techniques:

- Iterating over the records in the DataTable, identifying the deleted rows as having their RowState property being set to DataRowState.Deleted, and accessing the original values for the deleted row using the field accessor of the DataRow that takes a second argument and specifying it as DataRowVersion.Original.

- Creating a DataView of only deleted records in the table using an overload of the DataView constructor with the row state argument set to DataViewRowState.Deleted.

- Creating a DataView based on the table and filtering only deleted records by setting the RowStateFilter property of the DataView to DataViewRowState.Deleted.

- Using the Select( ) method with the row state set to DataViewRowState.Deleted to get a DataRow array of deleted records from the DataTable and accessing the values for the deleted rows through their original values by specifying a row state of DataRowVersion.Original in the DataRow field accessor.

The C# code in *Program.cs* in the project AccessDeletedDataRows is shown in Example 4-8.

Example 4-8. File: Program.cs for AccessDeletedDataRows solution

```
using System;
using System.Data;
using System.Data.SqlClient;

namespace AccessDeletedDataRows
{
    class Program
    {
        static void Main(string[] args)
        {
            string sqlConnectString = "Data Source=(local);" +
                "Integrated security=SSPI;Initial Catalog=AdventureWorks;";

            string sqlSelect = "SELECT TOP 3 ContactID, FirstName, LastName " +
                "FROM Person.Contact";

            // Fill the DataSet with the results of the batch query.
            SqlDataAdapter da = new SqlDataAdapter(sqlSelect, sqlConnectString);
            DataTable dt = new DataTable();
            da.Fill(dt);

            // Output the rows in the DataTable
            Console.WriteLine("---ORIGINAL DATATABLE---");
            foreach (DataRow row in dt.Rows)
                Console.WriteLine("{0}, {1}, {2}", row[0], row[1], row[2]);
            Console.WriteLine();

            // Delete row 2
            dt.Rows[1].Delete();

            // Output the rows in the DataTable
            Console.WriteLine("---AFTER ROW 2 DELETED---");
            foreach (DataRow row in dt.Rows)
            {
                if (row.RowState == DataRowState.Deleted)
                {
                    Console.WriteLine("{0}:\t {1}, {2}, {3}",
                        row.RowState, row[0, DataRowVersion.Original],
                        row[1, DataRowVersion.Original], row[2, DataRowVersion.Original]);
                }
                else
                {
                    Console.WriteLine("{0}:\t {1}, {2}, {3}", row.RowState,
                        row[0], row[1], row[2]);
                }
            }
            Console.WriteLine();

            Console.WriteLine("---USING DATAVIEW CONSTRUCTOR TO ACCESS DELETED ROW---");
            DataView dv = new DataView(dt, null, null, DataViewRowState.Deleted);
            foreach (DataRowView row in dv)
                Console.WriteLine("{0}, {1}, {2}", row[0], row[1], row[2]);
```

```
Console.WriteLine("\n---USING DATAVIEW FILTER TO ACCESS DELETED ROWS---");
dv = new DataView(dt);
dv.RowStateFilter = DataViewRowState.Deleted;
foreach (DataRowView row in dv)
    Console.WriteLine("{0}, {1}, {2}", row[0], row[1], row[2]);

Console.WriteLine("\n---USING DATATABLE.SELECT( )---");
// Get the DataRow array of deleted items
DataRow[] dra = dt.Select(null, null, DataViewRowState.Deleted);
// Iterate over the array and display the original version of each
// deleted row
for (int i = 0; i < dra.Length; i++)
{
    Console.WriteLine("{0}, {1}, {2}", dra[i][0, DataRowVersion.Original],
        dra[i][1, DataRowVersion.Original],
        dra[i][2, DataRowVersion.Original]);
}

Console.WriteLine("\nPress any key to continue.");
Console.ReadKey( );
        }
    }
}
```

The output is shown in Figure 4-8.

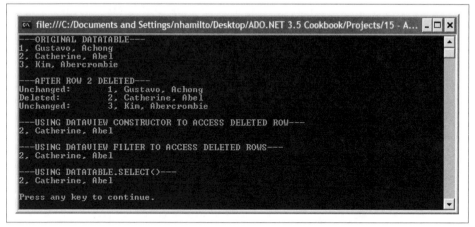

Figure 4-8. Output for AccessDeletedDataRows solution

Discussion

ADO.NET manages the state of the rows while they are being modified. Rows are assigned a state from the DataRowState enumeration described in Table 4-2.

Table 4-2. DataRowState enumeration

Value	Description
Added	The row has been added to the collection of rows in the table but AcceptChanges( ) has not been called.
Deleted	The row has been deleted from the collection of rows in the table but AcceptChanges( ) has not been called.
Detached	The row does not belong to the collection of rows in a DataTable.
Modified	The data in the row has been changed but AcceptChanges( ) has not been called.
Unchanged	The data in the row has not been changed since it was loaded or since AcceptChanges( ) was last called.

When AcceptChanges( ) is called on the DataSet, DataTable, or DataRow, either explicitly or implicitly by calling the Update( ) method of the DataAdapter, the following occurs:

- All rows with a row state of Deleted are removed.
- All other rows are assigned a row state of Unchanged and the Original row version values are overwritten with the Current version values.

When RejectChanges( ) is called on the DataSet, DataTable, or DataRow, the following occurs:

- All rows with a row state of Added are removed.
- All other rows are assigned a row state of Unchanged and the Current row version values are overwritten with the Original row version values.

Each DataRow has a RowState property that returns the current state of the row.

ADO.NET maintains several versions of the data in each row while it is being modified to allow the disconnected to be later reconciled with the data source. Table 4-3 describes the DataRowVersion enumeration values.

Table 4-3. DataRowVersion enumeration

Value	Description
Current	Current value. This version does not exist for rows with a state of Deleted.
Default	Default value as determined by the DataRowState: • The Current version for rows with Added, Modified, or Unchanged state • The Original version for rows with Deleted state • The Proposed value for rows with Detached state
Original	Original value. This version does not exist for rows with a state of Added.
Proposed	Proposed value. This value exists during a row edit operation started either implicitly or explicitly with the BeginEdit( ) method and for Detached rows.

The HasVersion( ) method of the DataRow object checks whether a particular row version exists.

The DataViewRowState enumeration is used to retrieve a particular version of data or to determine whether a version exists. It is used for this purpose by both the Select( ) method of the DataTable and by the RowStateFilter property of the DataView. You can retrieve more than one version by using a Boolean OR of DataViewRowState values. Table 4-4 describes the DataViewRowState enumeration values.

Table 4-4. DataViewRowState enumeration

Value	Description
Added	The Current version of all Added rows.
CurrentRows	The Current version of all Unchanged, Added, and Modified rows. This is the default value.
Deleted	The Original version of all Deleted rows.
ModifiedCurrent	The Current version of all Modified rows.
ModifiedOriginal	The Original version of all Modified rows.
None	No rows.
OriginalRows	The Original version of Unchanged, Modified, and Deleted rows.
Unchanged	The Current version of all Unchanged rows.

The Current version of each row is retrieved by default when accessing rows in a DataTable or in a DataView. The solution demonstrates an approach for getting Deleted rows from both a DataTable and a DataView. Deleted rows include only those marked for deletion using the Delete( ) method of the DataRow or the DataView, not the Remove( ) or RemoveAt( ) methods of the DataRowCollection, which instead immediately remove the specified DataRow from the collection.

The solution demonstrates two techniques for retrieving the deleted rows.

To get the Deleted rows from the DataTable, use an overload of the Select( ) method of the DataTable to return an array of deleted DataRow objects. The overload accepts an argument having a DataViewRowState enumeration value. To retrieve deleted rows, pass a value of Deleted as the argument. To access their values, use the original version of the row by specifying DataRowVersion.Original in the overloaded field accessor of the DataRow. You cannot access the values of a deleted row directly.

To get the Deleted rows from the DataView, set the RowStateFilter property of the DataView to Deleted—you can do this using the fourth argument in the DataView constructor.

4.8   Selecting the Top N Rows in a DataTable

Problem

You want to select the top 10 rows in a DataTable, based on the values in one or more of the columns, without requerying the data source.

Solution

Use an appropriate sort order with a DataView filter.

The solution creates a DataTable containing data from the HumanResources. EmployeePayHistory table in AdventureWorks and uses the Filter and Sort properties of the default DataView to select exactly four rows with the top Rate values.

The C# code in *Program.cs* in the project SelectTopNRowsDataTable is shown in Example 4-9.

Example 4-9. File: Program.cs for SelectTopNRowsDataTable solution

```
using System;
using System.Data;
using System.Data.SqlClient;
using System.Text;

namespace SelectTopNRowsDataTable
{
    class Program
    {
        private static int topN = 4;

        static void Main(string[] args)
        {
            string sqlConnectString = "Data Source=(local);" +
                "Integrated security=SSPI;Initial Catalog=AdventureWorks;";

            string sqlSelect = "SELECT * FROM Sales.SalesTaxRate";

            // Fill the DataTable with Sales.SalesOrderHeader schema and data
            DataTable dt = new DataTable( );
            SqlDataAdapter da = new SqlDataAdapter(sqlSelect, sqlConnectString);
            da.FillSchema(dt, SchemaType.Source);
            da.Fill(dt);

            // Sort the default view on the TaxRate field
            DataView dv = dt.DefaultView;
            dv.Sort = "TaxRate DESC";

            // Output the top 10 records from the DataView
            Console.WriteLine("---First 10 records from DataView---");
            for (int i = 0; i < 10; i++)
                Console.WriteLine("Record = {0}\t{1}\t{2}\tTaxRate = {3}", i + 1,
                    dv[i]["SalesTaxRateID"], dv[i]["StateProvinceID"],
                    dv[i]["TaxRate"]);

            // Create a filter for all records with a value <= the nth.
            StringBuilder filter = new StringBuilder("SalesTaxRateID >=" +
                dv[topN - 1]["SalesTaxRateID"]);
            dv.RowFilter = filter.ToString( );
```

Example 4-9. File: Program.cs for SelectTopNRowsDataTable solution (continued)

```
        // Handle where there is more than one record with the nth value.
        // Eliminate enough rows from the bottom of the dv using a filter on
        // the primary key to return the correct number (top N) of values.
        bool refilter = false;
        // Iterate over all records in the view after the nth.
        for (int i = dv.Count; i > topN; i--)
        {
            // Exclude the record using a filter on the primary key
            filter.Append(" AND SalesTaxRateID <> " + dv[i - 1]["SalesTaxRateID"]);
            refilter = true;
        }

        // Reapply the view filter if necessary.
        if (refilter)
            dv.RowFilter = filter.ToString( );

        // Output all of the records from the filtered DataView
        int record = 1;
        Console.WriteLine("\n---Top {0} records using filtered DataView---", topN);
        foreach (DataRowView row in dv)
            Console.WriteLine("Record: {0}\t{1}\t{2}\tTaxRate = {3}", record++,
                row["SalesTaxRateID"], row["StateProvinceID"], row["TaxRate"]);

        Console.WriteLine("\nPress any key to continue.");
        Console.ReadKey( );
    }
  }
}
```

The output is shown in Figure 4-9.

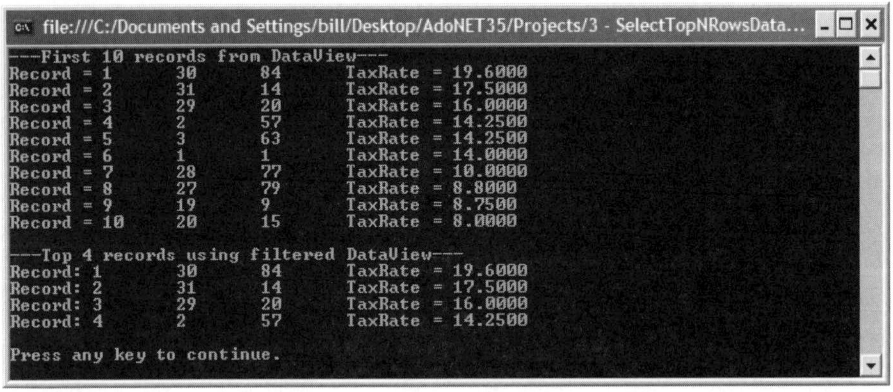

Figure 4-9. Output for SelectTopNRowsDataTable solution

Discussion

While it is possible to locate, sort, and filter records in a DataTable or DataView, there is no method in either class to select the top *n* rows.

Several steps are needed to get the top *n* rows based on the TaxRate value. First, use the Sort property of the DataView to sort the DataView on the TaxRate field in descending order; this places the top *n* records at the top of the view. Next, get the TaxRate value for the *n*th record and set the DataView filter to contain only rows with a TaxRate value greater than or equal to that value. Add the appropriate delimiters when making nonnumeric comparisons in the filter expression.

At this point, we are done unless there is more than one instance of the value in the *n*th record, as is the case with the TaxRate 14.25 in this example. In this case, iterate over the records following the *n*th record and add criteria to a copy of the DataView filter to exclude them from the view. Use either the primary key or a unique column or combination of columns to identify the row to be excluded in each case. Apply the new filter to the view. If the view is ordered on the primary key or unique columns in addition to the top *n* columns, this can be used in the initial DataView filter to limit returned records in cases where there might be duplicate values in the *n*th record. This would be used instead of the technique just outlined. However, the technique shown requires no sort other than on the top *n* column.

The solution can be extended with little change to handle multiple column top *n* criteria as well as ascending sorts.

Finally, the T-SQL TOP clause limits the number of rows returned by an SQL statement from the data source. This might be a more appropriate solution in most cases, especially when the disconnected table does not already exist. For more information, look up "TOP clause" in Microsoft SQL Server Books Online.

4.9 Executing Queries That Use COMPUTE BY

Problem

The SQL Server .NET data provider does not support the COMPUTE BY clause but you want to execute a COMPUTE BY statement using ADO.NET.

Solution

Use the COMPUTE BY statement from the Command object of the OLE DB .NET data provider.

The solution defines a COMPUTE BY statement and executes it using the ExecuteReader( ) method of the OleDbCommand object. Multiple result sets are returned by the DataReader, which are then displayed.

The C# code in *Program.cs* in the project ExecuteComputeByQuery is shown in Example 4-10.

Example 4-10. File: Program.cs for ExecuteComputeByQuery solution

```csharp
using System;
using System.Data;
using System.Data.OleDb;

namespace ExecuteComputeByQuery
{
    class Program
    {
        static void Main(string[] args)
        {
            string oledbConnectString = "Provider=SQLOLEDB;Data Source=(local);" +
                "Integrated Security=SSPI;Initial Catalog=AdventureWorks;";

            string sqlSelect = "SELECT SalesOrderID, ProductID, OrderQty " +
                "FROM Sales.SalesOrderDetail " +
                "WHERE SalesOrderID BETWEEN 43683 AND 43699 " +
                "ORDER BY ProductID " +
                "COMPUTE SUM(OrderQty) BY ProductID";

            using (OleDbConnection connection
                = new OleDbConnection(oledbConnectString))
            {
                OleDbCommand command = new OleDbCommand(sqlSelect, connection);
                connection.Open();
                OleDbDataReader dr = command.ExecuteReader();

                do
                {
                    // Output the detail result set.
                    Console.WriteLine("Order\tProduct\tQuantity");
                    while (dr.Read())
                        Console.WriteLine("{0}\t{1}\t{2}",
                            dr.GetInt32(0), dr.GetInt32(1), dr.GetInt16(2));

                    Console.WriteLine();

                    // Output the sum result set.
                    dr.NextResult();
                    dr.Read();
                    Console.WriteLine("SUM:\t\t{0}\n", dr.GetInt32(0));

                } while (dr.NextResult());
            }
```

Example 4-10. File: Program.cs for ExecuteComputeByQuery solution (continued)

```
            Console.WriteLine("\nPress any key to continue.");
            Console.ReadKey( );
        }
    }
}
```

Partial output is shown in Figure 4-10.

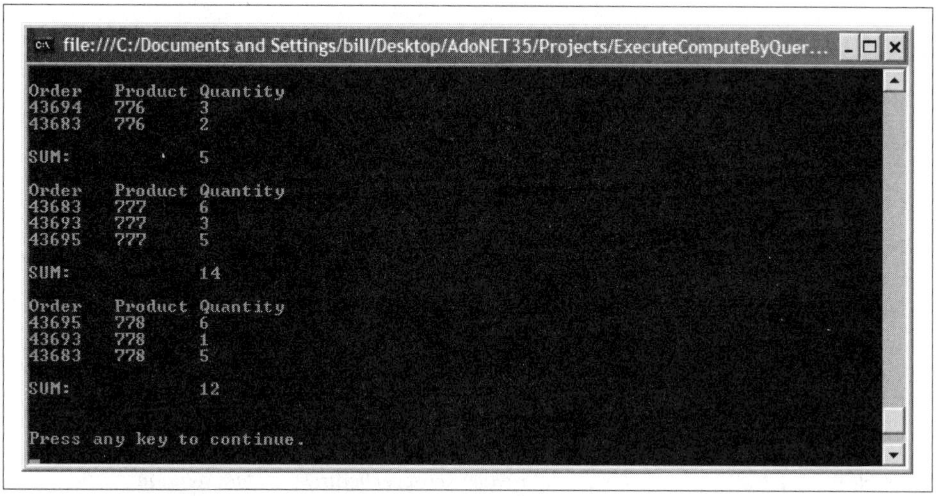

Figure 4-10. Output for ExecuteComputeByQuery solution

Discussion

The SQL Server .NET data provider does not support the COMPUTE BY clause, but the OLE DB .NET data provider does. The results are returned as multiple pairs of result sets, the first of which contains the selected details; the second contains the results of the aggregate functions specified (the sum of the quantity ordered for the product in this example) in the COMPUTE BY clause. This pattern is repeated for the remaining pairs of result sets.

Microsoft states that the COMPUTE and COMPUTE BY clauses are provided in SQL Server 7.0 and later versions for backward compatibility. The ROLLUP operator provides similar functionality and is recommended instead. The main difference is that ROLLUP returns a single result set instead of multiple result sets and is supported by the SQL Server .NET data provider. For more information about the ROLLUP operator, see Microsoft SQL Server Books Online.

4.10 Using the Shape Language to Retrieve Hierarchical Data

Problem

You want to use the Shape language with ADO.NET to retrieve hierarchical data from a SQL Server.

Solution

Execute the SHAPE command using the OLE DB provider.

The solution defines a SHAPE query to retrieve the TOP 2 Sales.SalesorderHeader records from AdventureWorks and the Sales.SalesOrderDetail records for each. A DataReader based on the query is created. The code iterates over the rows in the DataReader displaying the data for each Sales.SalesorderHeader row. If the value for the column can be cast to the IDataReader interface, it is a DataReader containing the Sales.SalesOrderDetail for the Sales.SalesorderHeader row. The value for the column is cast to a DataReader and the collection of records is iterated over and displayed.

The C# code in *Program.cs* in the project ShapeProviderRetrieveHierarchicalData is shown in Example 4-11.

Example 4-11. File: Program.cs for ShapeProviderRetrieveHierarchicalData solution

```
using System;
using System.Data;
using System.Data.OleDb;

namespace ShapeProviderRetrieveHierarchicalData
{
    class Program
    {
        static void Main(string[] args)
        {
            string oledbConnectString = "Provider=MSDataShape;" +
                "Data Provider=SQLOLEDB;Data Source=(local);" +
                "Initial Catalog=AdventureWorks;Integrated Security=SSPI;";

            // SHAPE SQL to retrieve TOP two orders and associated details.
            string shapeText =
                "SHAPE {SELECT TOP 2 * from Sales.SalesOrderHeader} AS Header " +
                "APPEND ({SELECT * from Sales.SalesOrderDetail} AS Detail " +
                "RELATE SalesOrderID TO SalesOrderID)";

            // Create the connection.
            OleDbConnection connection = new OleDbConnection(oledbConnectString);

            // Create a command and fill a DataReader with the
            // SHAPE result set.
            OleDbCommand command = new OleDbCommand(shapeText, connection);
            connection.Open();
```

Example 4-11. File: Program.cs for ShapeProviderRetrieveHierarchicalData solution (continued)

```csharp
        OleDbDataReader dr = command.ExecuteReader( );

        // Iterate over the collection of rows in the DataReader.
        while (dr.Read( ))
        {
            Console.WriteLine("---ORDER---");
            // Iterate over the collection of Order columns in the DataReader.
            for (int colOrder = 0; colOrder < dr.FieldCount; colOrder++)
            {
                if (dr[colOrder] is IDataReader)
                {
                    // The column is an IDataReader interface.
                    Console.WriteLine("\n\t---{0} result set---",
                        dr.GetName(colOrder).ToUpper( ));

                    // Create a DataReader for the Order Detail from the
                    // IDataReader interface column.
                    OleDbDataReader orderDetailDR =
                        (OleDbDataReader)dr.GetValue(colOrder);
                    // Iterate over records in the Order Detail DataReader.
                    while (orderDetailDR.Read( ))
                    {
                        // Iterate over the Order Detail columns
                        // in the Data Reader.
                        for (int colOrderDetail = 0;
                            colOrderDetail < orderDetailDR.FieldCount;
                            colOrderDetail++)
                        {
                            Console.WriteLine("\t{0}: {1}",
                                orderDetailDR.GetName(colOrderDetail),
                                orderDetailDR[colOrderDetail]);
                        }
                        Console.WriteLine( );
                    }
                }
                else
                {
                    Console.WriteLine("{0}: {1}", dr.GetName(colOrder),
                        dr[colOrder]);
                }
            }
        }

        dr.Close( );
        connection.Close( );

        Console.WriteLine("\nPress any key to continue.");
        Console.ReadKey( );
    }
  }
}
```

Partial output is shown in Figure 4-11.

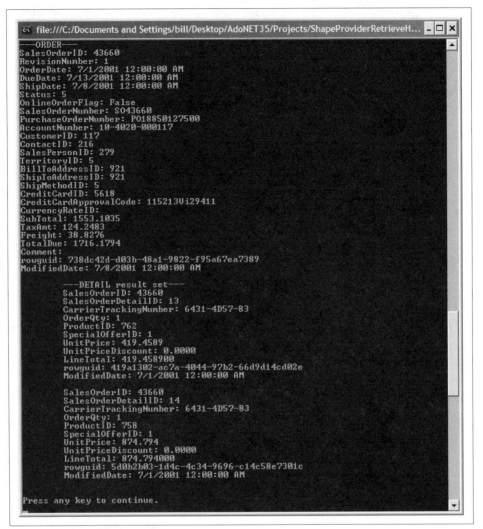

Figure 4-11. Output for ShapeProviderRetrieveHierarchicalData solution

Discussion

You can retrieve hierarchical result sets or *chapters* (OLE DB type `DBTYPE_HCHAPTER`) from SQL Server using the OLE DB .NET data provider. The chapter is returned as a field in the data reader with a data type of `Object`, which is a `DataReader`.

Hierarchical result sets combine the results for multiple queries into a single structure. They are generated using the Data Shaping Service for OLE DB first introduced in ADO 2.0. This provider supports the Shape language, allowing the result set hierarchies to be constructed. Shaping is an alternative to `JOIN` and `GROUP BY` syntax that you can use to access parent/child data and associated summary data.

The connection string using data shaping is shown here:

```
Provider=MSDataShape;Data Provider=SQLOLEDB;Data Source=(local);
    Initial Catalog=AdventureWorks;Integrated Security=SSPI;
```

For more information about data shaping or the MSDataShape provider, see "Data Shaping Service for OLE DB" in the MSDN library.

4.11   Retrieving a Random Sample of Records

Problem

You want to retrieve a result set containing a random sample of records from a result set using SQL Server 2005 or later.

Solution

Use either the TABLESAMPLE T-SQL clause or a custom method. The solution shows how to use both techniques to return a random sample of 10 percent of records from the Person.Contact table in AdventureWorks. In either case, the top 10 sampled rows are returned.

The C# code in *Program.cs* in the project RetrieveRandomSampleRecords is shown in Example 4-12.

Example 4-12. File: Program.cs for RetrieveRandomSampleRecords solution

```
using System;
using System.Data;
using System.Data.SqlClient;

namespace RetrieveRandomSampleRecords
{
    class Program
    {
        static void Main(string[] args)
        {
            string sqlConnectString = "Data Source=(local);" +
                "Integrated security=SSPI;Initial Catalog=AdventureWorks;";

            string sqlSelect;
            DataTable dt;
            SqlDataAdapter da;

            // Get the count of records in Person.Contact.
            sqlSelect = "SELECT COUNT(*) FROM Person.Contact";
            int recCount;
            using (SqlConnection connection = new SqlConnection(sqlConnectString))
            {
                SqlCommand command = new SqlCommand(sqlSelect, connection);
                connection.Open( );
```

```
        recCount = (int)command.ExecuteScalar( );
    }
    Console.WriteLine("Person.Contact record count = {0}\n", recCount);

    // Fill the DataTable with Person.Contact data
    sqlSelect = "SELECT * FROM Person.Contact TABLESAMPLE (10 PERCENT)";
    dt = new DataTable( );
    da = new SqlDataAdapter(sqlSelect, sqlConnectString);
    da.Fill(dt);

    // Output the top 10 rows using TABLESAMPLE
    Console.WriteLine("---{0} rows retrieved using TABLESAMPLE. " +
        "Displaying top 10 rows.---", dt.Rows.Count);
    for (int i = 0; i < 10; i++)
        Console.WriteLine("ID = {0}\t{1}, {2}",
            dt.Rows[i]["ContactID"], dt.Rows[i]["LastName"],
            dt.Rows[i]["FirstName"]);

    // Fill the DataTable with Person.Contact data
    sqlSelect = "SELECT * FROM Person.Contact WHERE " +
        "0.1 >= CAST(CHECKSUM(NEWID( ), ContactID) & 0x7fffffff AS float) " +
        "/ CAST(0x7fffffff AS int)";
    dt = new DataTable( );
    da = new SqlDataAdapter(sqlSelect, sqlConnectString);
    da.Fill(dt);

    // Output top 10 rows using custom method
    Console.WriteLine("\n---{0} rows retrieved using custom method. " +
        "Displaying top 10 rows.---", dt.Rows.Count);
    for (int i = 0; i < 10; i++)
        Console.WriteLine("ID = {0}\t{1}, {2}",
            dt.Rows[i]["ContactID"], dt.Rows[i]["LastName"],
            dt.Rows[i]["FirstName"]);

    Console.WriteLine("\nPress any key to continue.");
    Console.ReadKey( );
    }
  }
}
```

The output is shown in Figure 4-12.

Discussion

The TABLESAMPLE clause, introduced in SQL Server 2005, quickly returns a random, representative sample of the table expressed as either an approximate number of rows or a percentage of the total rows. Unlike the TOP clause, TABLESAMPLE returns a result set containing a sampling of rows from all rows processed by the query. As you can see from the results in Figure 4-12, the TABLESAMPLE clause does not return a truly random sample at the individual row level.

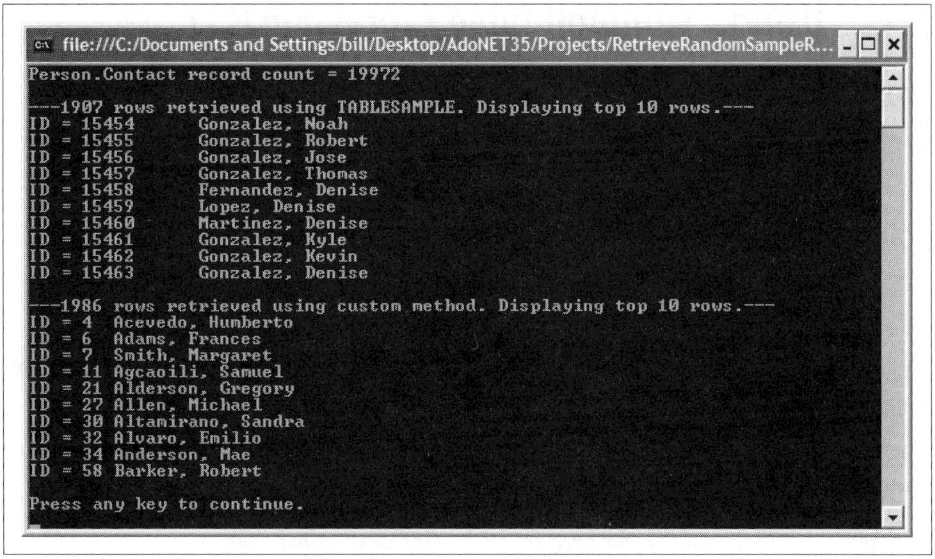

Figure 4-12. Output for RetrieveRandomSampleRecords solution

The TABLESAMPLE clause syntax is:

```
TABLESAMPLE [SYSTEM] (sample_number [PERCENT | ROWS])
    [REPEATABLE (repeat_seed)]
```

Where:

SYSTEM

An ANSI SQL keyword that specifies a database server-dependent sampling method. Although other databases support additional sampling methods that are database server-independent (e.g., DB2 supports BERNOULLI), SYSTEM is the only method supported by SQL Server and the default value if not specified.

sample_number [PERCENT | ROWS])

A numeric expression that specifies the number of rows to return or the percentage of rows in the result set to return.

REPEATABLE (repeat_seed)

The seed used to select rows to be returned in the sample. REPEATABLE indicates that the selected sample can be returned more than once. If the same seed is used, the same rows will be returned each time the query is run as long as no changes have been made to the data in the table.

The TABLESAMPLE clause cannot be used with views or in an inline table-valued function.

The custom technique calculates a CHECKSUM based on a NEWID( ) and the ContactID value for each row and scales it to a value between 0 and 1. This value is compared to 0.1 to select the top 10 percent of rows.

4.12 Using a Common Table Expression (CTE)

Problem

You need to create and access a temporary result set during the execution of a SELECT statement.

Solution

Use a Common Table Expression (CTE).

The solution uses a CTE to retrieve and display the number of employees directly reporting to each manager in the Employee table in AdventureWorks, where the ManagerID <= 25.

The C# code in *Program.cs* in the project ExecuteCommonTableExpression is shown in Example 4-13.

Example 4-13. File: Program.cs for ExecuteCommonTableExpression solution

```
using System;
using System.Data;
using System.Data.SqlClient;

namespace ExecuteCommonTableExpression
{
    class Program
    {
        static void Main(string[] args)
        {
            string sqlConnectString = "Data Source=(local);" +
                "Integrated security=SSPI;Initial Catalog=AdventureWorks;";

            string sqlSelect =
                "WITH ManagerEmployees(ManagerID, EmployeesPerManager) AS " +
                "( SELECT ManagerID, COUNT(*) " +
                "FROM HumanResources.Employee " +
                "WHERE ManagerID <= 25 " +
                "GROUP BY ManagerID ) " +
                "SELECT ManagerID, EmployeesPerManager " +
                "FROM ManagerEmployees " +
                "ORDER BY ManagerID";

            // Fill the DataTable
            DataTable dt = new DataTable( );
            SqlDataAdapter da = new SqlDataAdapter(sqlSelect, sqlConnectString);
            da.Fill(dt);

            Console.WriteLine("ManagerID\tEmployeesPerManager");
            foreach (DataRow row in dt.Rows)
                Console.WriteLine("{0}\t\t{1}", row["ManagerID"],
                    row["EmployeesPerManager"]);
```

Example 4-13. File: Program.cs for ExecuteCommonTableExpression solution (continued)

```
        Console.WriteLine("\nPress any key to continue.");
        Console.ReadKey();
      }
    }
}
```

The output is shown in Figure 4-13.

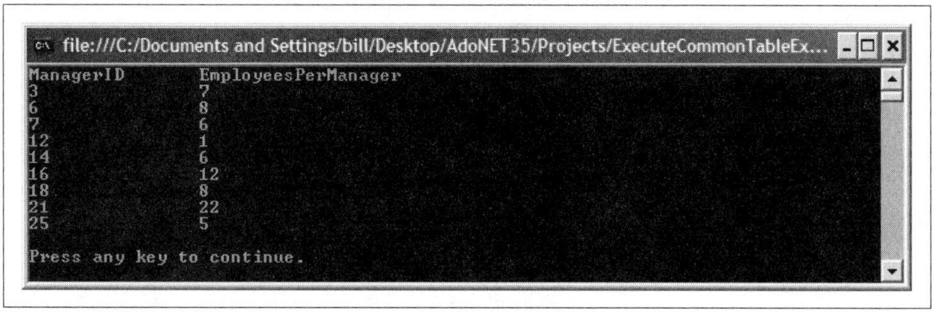

Figure 4-13. Output for ExecuteCommonTableExpression solution

Discussion

A common table expression (CTE), introduced in SQL Server 2005, is a temporary named result set derived from a simple query within the scope of a SELECT, INSERT, DELETE, UPDATE, or CREATE VIEW statement. A CTE can reference itself to create a recursive CTE. A CTE is not stored and lasts only for the duration of its containing query.

The CTE syntax is:

```
[WITH <common_table_expression> [ , ...n]]
<common_table_expression>::=
expression_name [(column_name [ , ...n])]
AS
(query_definition)
```

Where:

expression_name
: Specifies the name of the CTE.

column_name
: Specifies the column name in the CTE, unique within the definition. The number of column names must match the number of columns returned by the CTE query *query_definition*. The list of column names is optional if distinct names are returned for all columns in the CTE query.

query_definition
: Specifies the SELECT statement that populates the CTE.

The solution in this recipe can be accomplished without a CTE; however, it is useful to illustrate the basic syntax of a CTE and how to execute a query that uses a CTE.

4.13   Executing a Recursive Query

Problem

You need to execute a recursive query—that is a query that references itself.

Solution

Use a recursive Common Table Expression (CTE).

This solution uses a recursive CTE to return a list of employees and their managers from the HumanResources.Employee table in AdventureWorks. The top 20 records are displayed.

The C# code in *Program.cs* in the project ExecuteRecursiveQuery is shown in Example 4-14.

Example 4-14. File: Program.cs for ExecuteRecursiveQuery solution

```
using System;
using System.Data;
using System.Data.SqlClient;

namespace ExecuteRecursiveQuery
{
    class Program
    {
        static void Main(string[] args)
        {
            string sqlConnectString = "Data Source=(local);" +
                "Integrated security=SSPI;Initial Catalog=AdventureWorks;";

            string sqlSelect =
                "WITH DirectReports( " +
                "ManagerID, EmployeeID, Title, FirstName, LastName, EmployeeLevel) AS " +
                "(SELECT e.ManagerID, e.EmployeeID, e.Title, c.FirstName, c.LastName, " +
                "0 AS EmployeeLevel " +
                "FROM HumanResources.Employee e " +
                "JOIN Person.Contact AS c ON e.ContactID = c.ContactID " +
                "WHERE ManagerID IS NULL " +
                "UNION ALL " +
                "SELECT e.ManagerID, e.EmployeeID, e.Title, c.FirstName, c.LastName, " +
                "EmployeeLevel + 1 " +
                "FROM HumanResources.Employee e " +
                "INNER JOIN DirectReports d ON e.ManagerID = d.EmployeeID " +
                "JOIN Person.Contact AS c ON e.ContactID = c.ContactID) " +
```

Example 4-14. File: Program.cs for ExecuteRecursiveQuery solution (continued)

```
            "SELECT TOP 20 * " +
            "FROM DirectReports";

        // Fill the DataTable
        DataTable dt = new DataTable( );
        SqlDataAdapter da = new SqlDataAdapter(sqlSelect, sqlConnectString);
        da.Fill(dt);

        Console.WriteLine("MgrID\tEmpID\tTitle\t\t\tLevel\tName");
        foreach (DataRow row in dt.Rows)
            Console.WriteLine("{0}\t{1}\t{2}\t{3}\t{4}, {5}",
                row["ManagerID"],row["EmployeeID"],
                row["Title"].ToString( ).PadRight(23).Substring(0,23),
                row["EmployeeLevel"], row["LastName"], row["FirstName"]);

        Console.WriteLine("\nPress any key to continue.");
        Console.ReadKey( );
    }
}
}
```

The output is shown in Figure 4-14.

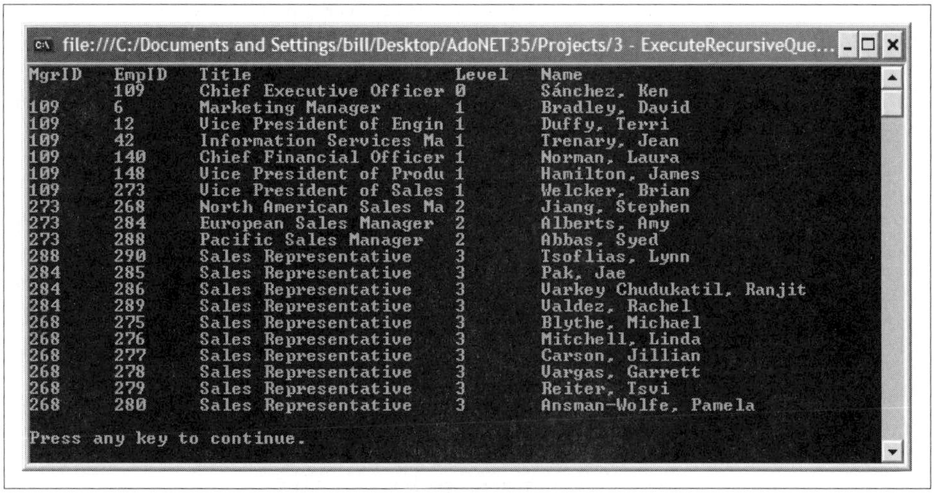

Figure 4-14. Output for ExecuteRecursiveQuery solution

Discussion

A recursive CTE must contain at least two CTE query definitions—an anchor member and a recursive member. The UNION ALL operator combines the anchor member with the recursive member. You can limit the number of recursions by specifying a MAXRECURSION query hint.

The first SELECT statement in the solution retrieves all top-level employees—that is, employees without a manager (ManagerID IS NULL). The second SELECT statement after the UNION ALL operator recursively retrieves the employees for each manager (employee) until all employee records have been processed. Finally, the last SELECT statement retrieves all the records from the recursive CTE, which is named DirectReports.

For more information about Common Table Expressions, see Recipe 4.12.

4.14   Retrieving a Ranked Result Set

Problem

You need to rank records in a result set based on the values in one or more fields.

Solution

Two solutions are presented. The first solution uses the ROW_NUMBER( ) ranking function to rank records from the Person.Contact table in AdventureWorks based on the LastName and FirstName values. The top 10 records are output.

The C# code in *Program.cs* in the project RetrieveRankedResultSet is shown in Example 4-15.

Example 4-15. File: Program.cs for RetrieveRankedResultSet solution

```
using System;
using System.Data;
using System.Data.SqlClient;

namespace RetrieveRankedResultSet
{
    class Program
    {
        static void Main(string[] args)
        {
            string sqlConnectString = "Data Source=(local);" +
                "Integrated security=SSPI;Initial Catalog=AdventureWorks;";

            string sqlSelect = "SELECT TOP 10 ROW_NUMBER( ) " +
                "OVER(ORDER BY LastName, FirstName) Rank, " +
                "ContactID, FirstName, LastName " +
                "FROM Person.Contact";

            // Fill the DataTable
            DataTable dt = new DataTable( );
            SqlDataAdapter da = new SqlDataAdapter(sqlSelect, sqlConnectString);
            da.Fill(dt);
```

Example 4-15. File: Program.cs for RetrieveRankedResultSet solution (continued)

```
        Console.WriteLine("Rank\tID\tName");
        foreach (DataRow row in dt.Rows)
            Console.WriteLine("{0}\t{1}\t{2}, {3}",
                row["Rank"], row["ContactID"], row["LastName"], row["FirstName"]);

        Console.WriteLine("\nPress any key to continue.");
        Console.ReadKey();
    }
  }
}
```

The output is shown in Figure 4-15.

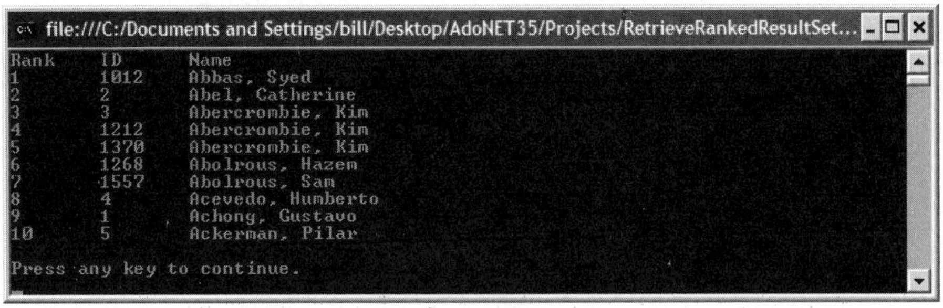

Figure 4-15. Output for RetrieveRankedResultSet solution

The second solution uses the ROW_NUMBER( ) ranking function and the PARTITION BY clause to rank records from the Person.Contact table in AdventureWorks within each ManagerID based on the LastName and FirstName values. The top 20 records are output.

The C# code in *Program.cs* in the project RetrieveRankedPartitionedResultSet is shown in Example 4-16.

Example 4-16. File: Program.cs for RetrieveRankedPartitionedResultSet solution

```
using System;
using System.Data;
using System.Data.SqlClient;

namespace RetrieveRankedPartitionedResultSet
{
    class Program
    {
        static void Main(string[] args)
        {
            string sqlConnectString = "Data Source=(local);" +
                "Integrated security=SSPI;Initial Catalog=AdventureWorks;";

            string sqlSelect = "SELECT TOP 20 ManagerID, ROW_NUMBER( ) " +
                "OVER(PARTITION BY ManagerID ORDER BY LastName, FirstName) Rank, " +
```

Example 4-16. File: Program.cs for RetrieveRankedPartitionedResultSet solution (continued)

```
                "e.ContactID, FirstName, LastName " +
                "FROM HumanResources.Employee e " +
                " LEFT JOIN Person.Contact c " +
                " ON e.ContactID = c.ContactID";

            // Fill the DataTable
            DataTable dt = new DataTable( );
            SqlDataAdapter da = new SqlDataAdapter(sqlSelect, sqlConnectString);
            da.Fill(dt);

            Console.WriteLine("MgrID\tRank\tID\tName");
            foreach (DataRow row in dt.Rows)
                Console.WriteLine("{0}\t{1}\t{2}\t{3}, {4}",
                    row["ManagerID"], row["Rank"], row["ContactID"],
                    row["LastName"], row["FirstName"]);

            Console.WriteLine("\nPress any key to continue.");
            Console.ReadKey( );
        }
    }
}
```

The output is shown in Figure 4-16.

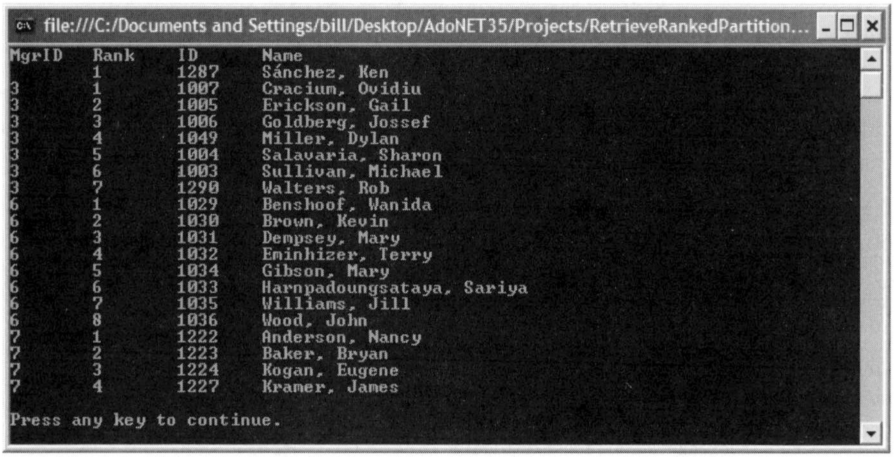

Figure 4-16. Output for RetrieveRankedPartitionedResultSet solution

Discussion

SQL Server 2005 introduced three new ranking functions: ROW_NUMBER( ), DENSE_RANK( ), and NTILE( ). This is in addition to the RANK( ) function available in SQL Server 2000. These are discussed in the following subsections.

ROW_NUMBER( )

The ROW_NUMBER( ) function returns the number of a row within a result set starting with 1 for the first row. The ROW_NUMBER( ) function does not execute until after a WHERE clause is used to select the subset of data.

The ROW_NUMBER( ) function syntax is:

```
ROW_NUMBER( ) OVER ([<partition_by_clause>] <order_by_clause>)
```

Where:

<partition_by_clause>

Divides the result set into groups to which the ROW_NUMBER( ) function is applied. The function is applied to each partition separately; computation restarts for each partition.

<order_by_clause>

Specifies the order in which the sequential ROW_NUMBER( ) values are assigned.

RANK( )

The RANK( ) function returns the rank of each row in a result set starting with 1. If two or more rows ties for rank, the same value is assigned to each tied row with numbering continuing normally (i.e., leaving a gap) with the non-tied row.

The RANK( ) function syntax is:

```
RANK( ) OVER ([<partition_by_clause>] <order_by_clause>)
```

Where:

<partition_by_clause>

Divides the result set into groups to which the RANK( ) function is applied. The function is applied to each partition separately; computation restarts for each partition.

<order_by_clause>

Specifies the order in which the sequential RANK( ) values are assigned.

DENSE_RANK( )

The DENSE_RANK( ) function returns the rank of rows in a result set without gaps in the ranking. This is similar to the RANK( ) function, except in cases where more than one row receives the same ranking. In this case, the rank value for a row following a group of rows with the same rank is the rank value for the rows in the group plus 1 rather than the next row number. For example, if the values a, b, b, c, d, e were being ranked, RANK( ) would return 1, 2, 2, 4, 5 while DENSE_RANK( ) would return 1, 2, 2, 3, 4.

The DENSE_RANK( ) function syntax is:

    DENSE_RANK( ) OVER ([<partition_by_clause>] <order_by_clause>)

Where:

<partition_by_clause>
Divides the result set into groups to which the DENSE_RANK( ) function is applied. The function is applied to each partition separately; computation restarts for each partition.

<order_by_clause>
Specifies the order in which the sequential DENSE_RANK( ) values are assigned.

NTILE( )

The NTILE( ) function returns the group in which a row belongs within an ordered distribution of groups. Group numbering starts with 1.

The NTILE( ) function syntax is:

    NTILE(n) OVER ([<partition_by_clause>] <order_by_clause>)

Where:

n
Specifies the number of groups that each partition should be divided into.

<partition_by_clause>
Divides the result set into groups to which the NTILE( ) function is applied. The function is applied to each partition separately; computation restarts for each partition.

<order_by_clause>
Specifies the column used to define the groups to which the NTILE( ) function is applied.

4.15 Retrieving a Pivot and Unpivot Table

Problem

You need to take rows in a result set and put (pivot) them into columns or take columns in a result set and put (unpivot) them into rows.

Solution

Use the T-SQL PIVOT and UNPIVOT operators.

Two solutions are presented. The first solution sums the total orders by employee in the Purchasing.PurchaseOrderHeader table in AdventureWorks for the years 2002, 2003, and 2004; pivots the total amount by year; and sorts the result set by employee ID.

The C# code in *Program.cs* in the project RetrievePivotTable is shown in Example 4-17.

Example 4-17. File: Program.cs for RetrievePivotTable solution

```
using System;
using System.Data;
using System.Data.SqlClient;

namespace RetrievePivotTable
{
    class Program
    {
        static void Main(string[] args)
        {
            string sqlConnectString = "Data Source=(local);" +
                "Integrated security=SSPI;Initial Catalog=AdventureWorks;";

            string sqlSelect = "SELECT EmployeeID, [2002] Y2002, " +
                "[2003] Y2003, [2004] Y2004 FROM " +
                "(SELECT YEAR(OrderDate) OrderYear, EmployeeID, TotalDue " +
                "FROM Purchasing.PurchaseOrderHeader) poh " +
                "PIVOT (SUM(TotalDue) FOR OrderYear IN " +
                "([2002], [2003], [2004])) pvt " +
                "WHERE EmployeeID BETWEEN 200 AND 300 " +
                "ORDER BY EmployeeID";

            // Fill the DataTable
            DataTable dt = new DataTable( );
            SqlDataAdapter da = new SqlDataAdapter(sqlSelect, sqlConnectString);
            da.Fill(dt);

            Console.WriteLine("Employee ID\t2002\t\t2003\t\t2004");
            Console.WriteLine("-----------\t----\t\t----\t\t----");
            foreach (DataRow row in dt.Rows)
                Console.WriteLine("{0}\t\t{1}\t{2}\t{3}", row["EmployeeID"],
                    row["Y2002"], row["Y2003"], row["Y2004"]);

            Console.WriteLine("\nPress any key to continue.");
            Console.ReadKey( );
        }
    }
}
```

The output is shown in Figure 4-17.

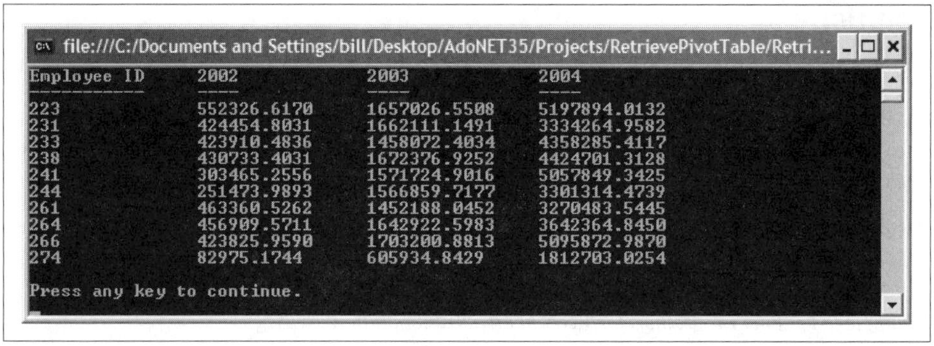

Figure 4-17. Output for RetrievePivotTable solution

The second solution unpivots the result set in the first solution to recreate the original result set.

The C# code in *Program.cs* in the project `RetrieveUnpivotTable` is shown in Example 4-18.

Example 4-18. File: Program.cs for RetrieveUnpivotTable solution

```csharp
using System;
using System.Data;
using System.Data.SqlClient;

namespace RetrieveUnpivotTable
{
    class Program
    {
        static void Main(string[] args)
        {
            string sqlConnectString = "Data Source=(local);" +
                "Integrated security=SSPI;Initial Catalog=AdventureWorks;";

            string sqlSelect = "SELECT EmployeeID, OrderYear, TotalDue FROM " +
                "(SELECT EmployeeID, [2002] Y2002, " +
                "[2003] Y2003, [2004] Y2004 FROM " +
                "(SELECT YEAR(OrderDate) OrderYear, EmployeeID, TotalDue " +
                "FROM Purchasing.PurchaseOrderHeader) poh " +
                "PIVOT (SUM(TotalDue) FOR OrderYear IN " +
                "([2002], [2003], [2004])) pvt " +
                "WHERE EmployeeID BETWEEN 200 AND 300) pvtTable " +
                "UNPIVOT " +
                "(TotalDue FOR OrderYear IN (Y2002, Y2003, Y2004)) unpvt " +
                "ORDER BY EmployeeID, OrderYear";

            // Fill the DataTable
            DataTable dt = new DataTable();
            SqlDataAdapter da = new SqlDataAdapter(sqlSelect, sqlConnectString);
            da.Fill(dt);
```

Example 4-18. File: Program.cs for RetrieveUnpivotTable solution (continued)

```
            Console.WriteLine("EmployeeID\tOrderYear\tTotalDue");
            foreach (DataRow row in dt.Rows)
                Console.WriteLine("{0}\t\t{1}\t\t{2}",
                    row["EmployeeID"], row["OrderYear"], row["TotalDue"]);

            Console.WriteLine("\nPress any key to continue.");
            Console.ReadKey( );
        }
    }
}
```

The output is shown in Figure 4-18.

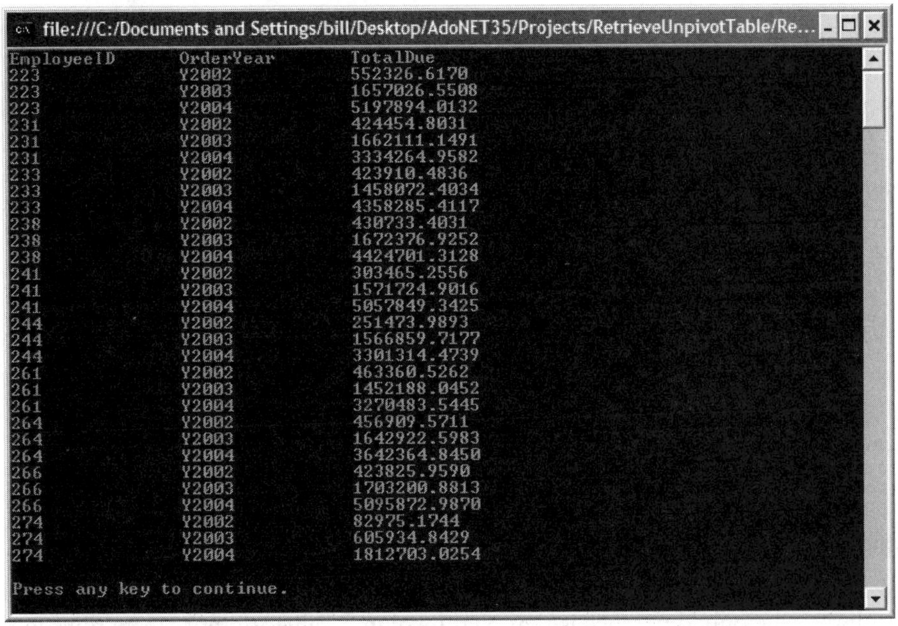

Figure 4-18. Output for RetrieveUnpivotTable solution

Discussion

The PIVOT and UNPIVOT operators introduced in SQL Server 2005 manipulate a table-valued expression into another table. These operators are essentially opposites of each other—PIVOT takes rows and puts them into columns, whereas UNPIVOT takes columns and puts them into rows.

PIVOT

The PIVOT operator rotates unique values in one column into multiple columns in a result set. The syntax of the PIVOT operator is:

```
<pivoted_table> ::=
    table_source PIVOT <pivot_clause> table_alias
<pivot_clause> ::=
    ( aggregate_function ( value_column )
        FOR pivot_column
        IN ( <column_list>)
    )
<column_list> ::=
    column_name [, ...]
```

Where:

table_source
> The table, view, or derived table to use in the T-SQL statement.

table_alias
> An alias for table_source—this is required for PIVOT operators.

aggregate_function
> A system- or user-defined aggregate function. COUNT(*) is not allowed.

value_column
> The column containing the pivoted value.

pivot_column
> The column containing the values into which the *value_column* aggregate values are grouped. These values are the pivot columns.

<column_list>
> The pivot column names of the output table.

UNPIVOT

UNPIVOT does the opposite of PIVOT, rotating multiple column values into rows in a result set. The only difference is that NULL column values do not create rows in the UNPIVOT result set. The syntax of the UNPIVOT operator is:

```
<unpivoted_table> ::=
    table_source UNPIVOT <unpivot_clause> table_alias
<unpivot_clause> ::=
    ( value_column FOR pivot_column IN ( <column_list> ) )
<column_list> ::=
    column_name [, ...]
```

The arguments are the same as those for the PIVOT operator.

4.16   Invoking a Function for Each Row in a Result Set

Problem

You need to invoke a table-valued function to return additional information for each row in a result set.

Solution

Use the APPLY operator.

The solution uses the APPLY operator to retrieve the FirstName, LastName, JobTitle, and ContactType using the table-valued function ufnGetContactInformation for records in the HumanResources.Employee table in AdventureWorks where the ContactID is between 1285 and 1290.

The C# code in *Program.cs* in the project InvokeFunctionForEachRowResultSet is shown in Example 4-19.

Example 4-19. File: Program.cs for InvokeFunctionForEachRowResultSet solution

```
using System;
using System.Data;
using System.Data.SqlClient;

namespace InvokeFunctionForEachRowResultSet
{
    class Program
    {
        static void Main(string[] args)
        {
            string sqlConnectString = "Data Source=(local);" +
                "Integrated security=SSPI;Initial Catalog=AdventureWorks;";

            string sqlSelect = "SELECT e.ContactID, " +
                "c.FirstName, c.LastName, c.JobTitle, c.ContactType " +
                "FROM HumanResources.Employee e " +
                "CROSS APPLY ufnGetContactInformation(e.ContactID) c " +
                "WHERE e.ContactID BETWEEN 1285 AND 1290 " +
                "ORDER BY e.ContactID";

            // Fill the DataTable
            DataTable dt = new DataTable();
            SqlDataAdapter da = new SqlDataAdapter(sqlSelect, sqlConnectString);
            da.Fill(dt);
```

Example 4-19. File: Program.cs for InvokeFunctionForEachRowResultSet solution (continued)

```
            Console.WriteLine("ID\tType\t\tName\t\tJobTitle");
            Console.WriteLine("--\t----\t\t----\t\t--------");
            foreach (DataRow row in dt.Rows)
                Console.WriteLine("{0}\t{1}\t{2}, {3}\t{4}",
                    row["ContactID"], row["ContactType"], row["LastName"],
                    row["FirstName"], row["JobTitle"]);

            Console.WriteLine("\nPress any key to continue.");
            Console.ReadKey();
        }
    }
}
```

The output is shown in Figure 4-19.

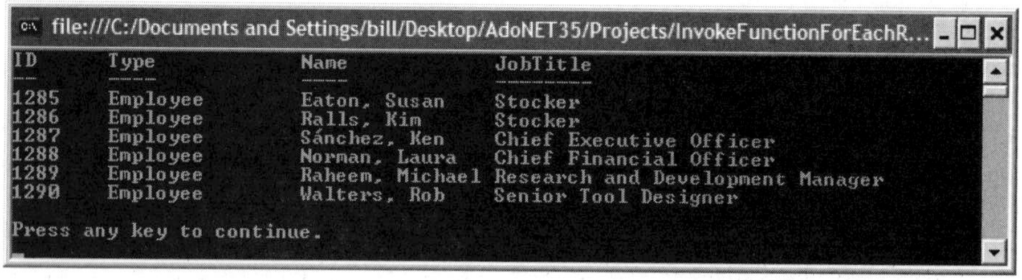

Figure 4-19. Output for InvokeFunctionForEachRowResultSet solution

Discussion

The APPLY operator introduced in SQL Server 2005 invokes a table-valued function for each row returned by an outer table expression of a query. The table-valued function is evaluated for each row in the result set and can take its parameters from the row.

There are two forms of the APPLY operator—CROSS and OUTER. CROSS APPLY returns only the rows from the outer table where the table-value function returns a result set. OUTER APPLY returns all rows, returning null values for rows where the table-valued function does not return a result set.

The syntax for the APPLY operator is:

```
{CROSS | OUTER} APPLY {table_value_function}
```

Where:

table_value_function
    Specifies the name of a table-valued function.

CHAPTER 5

Adding and Modifying Data

5.0   Introduction

This chapter focuses on issues related to adding and editing, and persisting data changes to the data source. An overview of some of the topics in this chapter follows.

ADO.NET provides an autoincrementing column type that generates a unique value for each new row. There is no mechanism to ensure that the values are unique from the values produced by other users. Recipe 5.1 shows how to use autoincrementing columns to ensure that the values generated by different users do not conflict.

SQL Server has an identity column that is also an autoincrementing column type. This value is used rather than the ADO.NET autoincrement column type when adding new records; there is no automatic way to keep these values synchronized after new rows in a DataTable have been inserted into a SQL Server table. Recipe 5.2 shows you how to synchronize the DataTable to the values in the database. Recipe 5.3 shows you how to synchronize these values with a Microsoft Access database.

Oracle does not support autoincrement columns but rather uses a *sequence*, that is, a procedure that generates a series of unique values. Recipe 5.4 shows how to synchronize autoincrementing columns in a DataTable with Oracle sequence values after a row has been inserted into an Oracle database.

Recipe 5.8 shows how to add master-detail records to a DataSet where the primary key of the parent table is an autoincrementing column.

A Globally Unique Identifier (GUID) is a 128-bit integer that is statistically unique. Recipe 5.9 shows how to add records to a DataSet containing master-detail records with both parent and child tables having a GUID primary key.

Changing the primary key value in a database is a little more complicated than changing it in a DataTable and updating it to the database. When the primary key is changed in the DataTable, the default update behavior is to look for a row matching the modified value for the primary key rather than the original. Recipe 5.12 demonstrates how to change the primary key in a database.

In a relational database, many-to-many relationships use a junction table to join two other tables. Recipe 5.14 shows how to update changes made to the tables and relationships between the rows without causing referential integrity errors.

A DataSet keeps no connection or data source information about its data source. This allows a DataSet to be loaded with data from one data source and updated back to another data source, perhaps for auditing or logging purposes. Recipe 5.11 shows how this is done.

A CommandBuilder can quickly and easily generate update logic for a DataAdapter in small or test applications. A CommandBuilder cannot generate valid update logic if the table or column names contain special characters or spaces. Recipe 5.17 shows how to make the CommandBuilder delimit table and column names to overcome this problem.

Although of questionable usefulness in a production environment, ADO.NET allows you to retrieve stored procedure parameters information at runtime. SQL Server also lets you do the same thing using a system stored procedure. Recipe 5.13 shows you both techniques.

Messaging allows applications running on disparate platforms to communicate whether they are connected or disconnected. Recipe 5.15 shows how to use messaging to update a database.

Recipe 5.16 shows how to use a DataView to control editing, deleting, and inserting data.

SQL Server 2008 introduces Change Data Capture (CDC) that lets you automatically log all changes made to data in a database table or to selected columns in a database table. Recipe 5.18 shows you how to use this new feature.

5.1 Using Autoincrementing Columns Without Causing Conflicts

Problem

You want to use an AutoIncrement column in a table without producing values that may be duplicated at the data source in records added by other users.

Solution

Use the AutoIncrementSeed and AutoIncrementStep properties of the AutoIncrement column.

The solution creates a DataTable and uses a DataAdapter to load schema and data from the HumanResources.Department table in AdventureWorks. The AutoIncrementSeed and AutoIncrementStep property values are both set to –1 for the AutoIncrement primary key column DepartmentID. Two new records are added to the DataTable. The contents of the DataTable are written to the console.

The C# code in *Program.cs* in the project AutoIncrementWithoutConflict is shown in Example 5-1.

Example 5-1. File: Program.cs for AutoIncrementWithoutConflict solution

```csharp
using System;
using System.Data;
using System.Data.SqlClient;

namespace AutoIncrementWithoutConflict
{
    class Program
    {
        static void Main(string[] args)
        {
            string sqlConnectString = "Data Source=(local);" +
                "Integrated security=SSPI;Initial Catalog=AdventureWorks;";

            string sqlSelect = "SELECT * FROM HumanResources.Department";

            // Create and fill a DataTable with schema and data
            DataTable dt = new DataTable();
            SqlDataAdapter da = new SqlDataAdapter(sqlSelect, sqlConnectString);
            da.FillSchema(dt, SchemaType.Source);
            // Configure the primary key column DepartmentID
            dt.Columns["DepartmentID"].AutoIncrementSeed = -1;
            dt.Columns["DepartmentID"].AutoIncrementStep = -1;
            dt.PrimaryKey = new DataColumn[] { dt.Columns["DepartmentID"] };
            da.Fill(dt);

            // Add two records
            dt.Rows.Add(new object[] {null, "Test Name 1", "Test Group 1",
                System.DateTime.Now});
            dt.Rows.Add(new object[] { null, "Test Name 2", "Test Group 2",
                System.DateTime.Now });

            foreach (DataRow row in dt.Rows)
                Console.WriteLine("ID = {0}\tName = {1}, GroupName = {2}",
                    row["DepartmentID"], row["Name"], row["GroupName"]);

            Console.WriteLine();
            Console.WriteLine("Press any key to continue.");
            Console.ReadKey();
        }
    }
}
```

The output is shown in Figure 5-1.

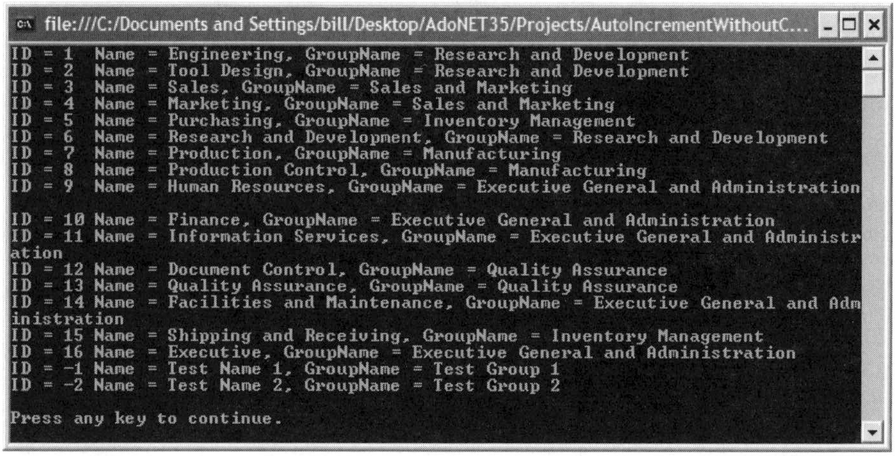

Figure 5-1. Output for AutoIncrementWithoutConflict solution

Discussion

An `AutoIncrement` column generates a series of values beginning with the `AutoIncrementSeed` value and incremented by the `AutoIncrementStep` value for each new value. This lets you easily generate unique values for integer-type columns.

A potential problem exists when new rows are being inserted into an existing table for an identity field (in SQL Server) where the generated values conflict with existing values in the table because of, perhaps, new records added to the data source by other users. In this case, instead of being interpreted as new records by the data source, these records are incorrectly interpreted as updates of existing records.

The problem can be avoided by setting the `AutoIncrementSeed` value to –1 and the `AutoIncrementStep` value to –1, thereby generating a sequence of negative values that does not conflict with the values generated by the data source, as long as the data source does not generate negative sequence values. When the disconnected data is reconciled with the underlying data (see Recipe 5.2), the data source correctly identifies the records that have negative `AutoIncrement` field values as new records, adds them to the data source, and in the process generates new values for the `AutoIncrement` field. Recipe 5.2 discusses synchronizing these data source-generated values with the disconnected data.

5.2 Getting an Identity Column Value from SQL Server

Problem

When you add a row into a SQL Server table that has an identity column, the value assigned to the column in the DataTable is replaced by a value generated by the database. You need to retrieve the new value to keep the DataTable synchronized with the database.

Solution

There are two ways to synchronize identity values generated by the data source: use either the first returned record or the output parameters of a stored procedure. This solution demonstrates both approaches.

The solution uses one table named GetSqlServerIdentityValue with the schema shown in Figure 5-2. The Id column is an identity column with a seed of 1 and an increment of 1.

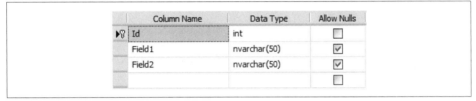

	Column Name	Data Type	Allow Nulls
▶🔑	Id	int	☐
	Field1	nvarchar(50)	☑
	Field2	nvarchar(50)	☑
			☐

Figure 5-2. Schema of table GetSqlServerIdentityValue

The T-SQL DDL to create the table GetSqlServerIdentityValue is shown in Example 5-2.

Example 5-2. Create table GetSqlServerIdentityValue

```
USE AdoDotNet35Cookbook
GO
CREATE TABLE GetSqlServerIdentityValue (
    Id int IDENTITY(1,1) NOT NULL,
    Field1 nvarchar(50) NULL,
    Field2 nvarchar(50) NULL,
  CONSTRAINT PK_GetSqlServerIdentityValue PRIMARY KEY CLUSTERED
    ( Id ASC )
)
```

For the purposes of this example, a single record is added to the GetSqlServerIdentityValue table. The T-SQL to add the initial record into the table GetSqlServerIdentityValue is shown in Example 5-3.

Example 5-3. Insert initial records into table GetServerIdentityValue

```
USE AdoDotNet35Cookbook
GO
DELETE FROM GetSqlServerIdentityValue;
INSERT INTO GetSqlServerIdentityValue VALUES ('field 1.1', 'field 2.1');
```

The solution uses a single stored procedure that inserts a record into the
GetSqlServerIdentityValueTable and returns the identity value from SQL Server
using both an output parameter and as a result set containing a single value. The T-SQL
to create the stored procedure InsertGetSqlServerIdentityValue is shown in
Example 5-4.

Example 5-4. Stored procedure: InsertGetSqlServerIdentityValue

```
CREATE PROCEDURE InsertGetSqlServerIdentityValue
    @Id int output,
    @Field1 nvarchar(50),
    @Field2 nvarchar(50)
AS
    SET NOCOUNT ON

    INSERT GetSqlServerIdentityValue(Field1, Field2)
    VALUES ( @Field1, @Field2)

    IF @@ROWCOUNT=0
        RETURN 1

    SET @Id = SCOPE_IDENTITY( )

    SELECT SCOPE_IDENTITY( ) Id
```

The solution creates a DataAdapter and sets its insert command to the stored procedure InsertGetSqlServerIdentityValue. Next, a DataTable is created, its schema is
filled from the GetSqlServerIdentityValue table, the AutoIncrementSeed and
AutoIncrementStep properties for the Id column are both set to –1, and the DataTable
is filled from the database. The initial content of the DataTable is output to the console. Three rows are added using different techniques to retrieve the new value of the
identity value from SQL Server. Records from the DataTable are output to the console before and after updating the table in the SQL Server database to show the
effects of the different identity value retrieval approaches.

The C# code in *Program.cs* in the project GetSqlServerIdentityValue is shown in
Example 5-5.

Example 5-5. File: Program.cs for GetSqlServerIdentityValue solution

```
using System;
using System.Data;
using System.Data.SqlClient;
```

Example 5-5. File: Program.cs for GetSqlServerIdentityValue solution (continued)

```csharp
namespace GetSqlServerIdentityValue
{
    class Program
    {
        static void Main(string[] args)
        {
            string sqlConnectString = "Data Source=(local);" +
                "Integrated security=SSPI;Initial Catalog=AdoDotNet35Cookbook;";
            string sqlSelect = "SELECT * FROM GetSqlServerIdentityValue";

            // Create a DataAdapter, setting the insert command to the
            // stored procedure
            SqlDataAdapter da = new SqlDataAdapter(sqlSelect, sqlConnectString);
            da.InsertCommand = new SqlCommand("InsertGetSqlServerIdentityValue",
                da.SelectCommand.Connection);
            da.InsertCommand.CommandType = CommandType.StoredProcedure;
            SqlParameter param = da.InsertCommand.Parameters.Add("@Id",
                SqlDbType.Int, 0, "Id");
            param.Direction = ParameterDirection.Output;
            da.InsertCommand.Parameters.Add("@Field1", SqlDbType.NVarChar,
                50, "Field1");
            da.InsertCommand.Parameters.Add("@Field2", SqlDbType.NVarChar,
                50, "Field2");

            // Use a DataAdapter to fill schema and data of a DataTable
            DataTable dt = new DataTable( );
            da.FillSchema(dt, SchemaType.Source);
            // Set autoincrement properties to avoid collision with existing records
            dt.Columns["Id"].AutoIncrementSeed = -1;
            dt.Columns["Id"].AutoIncrementStep = -1;
            da.Fill(dt);

            //Output the initial DataTable to the console.
            Console.WriteLine("---INITIAL RESULT SET---");
            foreach (DataRow row in dt.Rows)
                Console.WriteLine("Id = {0}\tField1 = {1}\tField2 = {2}\tRowState = {3}",
                    row["Id"], row["Field1"], row["Field2"], row.RowState);

            // Add rows and display results of different UpdateRowSource values
            AddRow(1, da, dt, UpdateRowSource.FirstReturnedRecord);
            AddRow(2, da, dt, UpdateRowSource.OutputParameters);
            AddRow(3, da, dt, UpdateRowSource.None);

            // Clear the DataTable reload
            dt.Clear( );
            da.Fill(dt);

            //Output the final DataTable to the console.
            Console.WriteLine("\n---FINAL RESULT SET---");
            foreach (DataRow row in dt.Rows)
                Console.WriteLine("Id = {0}\tField1 = {1}\tField2 = {2}\tRowState = {3}",
                    row["Id"], row["Field1"], row["Field2"], row.RowState);
```

```
        Console.WriteLine("\nPress any key to continue.");
        Console.ReadKey();
    }

    private static void AddRow(int n, SqlDataAdapter da, DataTable dt,
        UpdateRowSource urs)
    {
        // Add a row to the DataTable
        dt.Rows.Add(new object[] { null, "field 1." + (n + 1),
            "field 2." + (n + 1) });
        Console.WriteLine("\n=> Row added");

        // Output the interim DataTable to the console.
        Console.WriteLine("\n---INTERIM RESULT SET {0}---", n);
        foreach (DataRow row in dt.Rows)
            Console.WriteLine("Id = {0}\tField1 = {1}\tField2 = {2}\tRowState = {3}",
                row["Id"], row["field1"], row["field2"], row.RowState);

        // Set the UpdateRowSource to first returned record
        da.InsertCommand.UpdatedRowSource = urs;
        da.Update(dt);
        Console.WriteLine("\n=> DataTable.Update()");

        // Output the DataTable to the console.
        Console.WriteLine(
            "\n---UpdateRowSource.{0} RESULT SET AFTER DataAdapter.Update()---",
            urs.ToString());
        foreach (DataRow row in dt.Rows)
            Console.WriteLine("Id = {0}\tField1 = {1}\tField2 = {2}\tRowState = {3}",
                row["Id"], row["field1"], row["field2"], row.RowState);
    }
}
}
```

The output is shown in Figure 5-3.

Discussion

As discussed in Recipe 5.1, the AutoIncrementSeed and AutoIncrementStep property values for the AutoIncrement column should both be set to -1 to prevent conflict with the positive identity values generated by the data source.

The values created for an AutoIncrement column will have new identity values generated by the data source when they are updated back to the data source. There are two ways in which the data source-generated value can be retrieved and this solution demonstrates both. The UpdatedRowSource property of the Command object specifies how results from calling the Update() method of the DataAdapter are applied to the DataRow. Table 5-1 lists possible values.

```
file:///C:/Documents and Settings/bill/Desktop/AdoNET35/Projects/GetSqlServerIdentityVal...
----INITIAL RESULT SET----
Id = 1   Field1 = field 1.1       Field2 = field 2.1       RowState = Unchanged

=> Row added

----INTERIM RESULT SET 1----
Id = 1   Field1 = field 1.1       Field2 = field 2.1       RowState = Unchanged
Id = -1  Field1 = field 1.2       Field2 = field 2.2       RowState = Added

=> DataTable.Update()

----UpdateRowSource.FirstReturnedRecord RESULT SET AFTER DataAdapter.Update()----
Id = 1   Field1 = field 1.1       Field2 = field 2.1       RowState = Unchanged
Id = 2   Field1 = field 1.2       Field2 = field 2.2       RowState = Unchanged

=> Row added

----INTERIM RESULT SET 2----
Id = 1   Field1 = field 1.1       Field2 = field 2.1       RowState = Unchanged
Id = 2   Field1 = field 1.2       Field2 = field 2.2       RowState = Unchanged
Id = -2  Field1 = field 1.3       Field2 = field 2.3       RowState = Added

=> DataTable.Update()

----UpdateRowSource.OutputParameters RESULT SET AFTER DataAdapter.Update()----
Id = 1   Field1 = field 1.1       Field2 = field 2.1       RowState = Unchanged
Id = 2   Field1 = field 1.2       Field2 = field 2.2       RowState = Unchanged
Id = 3   Field1 = field 1.3       Field2 = field 2.3       RowState = Unchanged

=> Row added

----INTERIM RESULT SET 3----
Id = 1   Field1 = field 1.1       Field2 = field 2.1       RowState = Unchanged
Id = 2   Field1 = field 1.2       Field2 = field 2.2       RowState = Unchanged
Id = 3   Field1 = field 1.3       Field2 = field 2.3       RowState = Unchanged
Id = -3  Field1 = field 1.4       Field2 = field 2.4       RowState = Added

=> DataTable.Update()

----UpdateRowSource.None RESULT SET AFTER DataAdapter.Update()----
Id = 1   Field1 = field 1.1       Field2 = field 2.1       RowState = Unchanged
Id = 2   Field1 = field 1.2       Field2 = field 2.2       RowState = Unchanged
Id = 3   Field1 = field 1.3       Field2 = field 2.3       RowState = Unchanged
Id = -3  Field1 = field 1.4       Field2 = field 2.4       RowState = Unchanged

----FINAL RESULT SET----
Id = 1   Field1 = field 1.1       Field2 = field 2.1       RowState = Unchanged
Id = 2   Field1 = field 1.2       Field2 = field 2.2       RowState = Unchanged
Id = 3   Field1 = field 1.3       Field2 = field 2.3       RowState = Unchanged
Id = 4   Field1 = field 1.4       Field2 = field 2.4       RowState = Unchanged

Press any key to continue.
```

Figure 5-3. Output for GetSqlServerIdentityValue solution

Table 5-1. Values for the UpdateRowSource enumeration

Value	Description
Both	Both the data in the first returned row and the output parameters are mapped to the DataSet row that has been inserted or updated. This is the default value unless the command is generated by a CommandBuilder.
FirstReturnedRecord	The data in the first returned row is mapped to the DataSet row that has been inserted or updated.
None	Return values and parameters are ignored. This is the default value if the command is generated by a CommandBuilder.
OutputParameters	Output parameters are mapped to the DataSet row that has been inserted or updated.

The stored procedure InsertCategories has a single output parameter @CategoryId that is used to return the value of the data source-generated identity value. The value is set to the new identity value by the stored procedure statement:

```
SET @Id = SCOPE_IDENTITY( )
```

The column to be updated in the row is identified by the source column of the Parameter object, in this case, the fourth argument in the constructor.

The stored procedure also returns a result set containing a single row with a single value—CategoryId—containing the new identity value generated by the data source. The result set is returned by the stored procedure statement:

```
SELECT SCOPE_IDENTITY( ) Id
```

The columns are updated from the data source to the row matching column names, taking into account any column mappings that might be in place.

You can also apply the FirstReturnedRecord when using a batch SQL statement. Replace the InsertCommand command constructor for the DataAdapter with the following code:

```
// Create the insert command for the DataAdapter.
string sqlText="INSERT GetSqlServerIdentityValue(Field1, Field2) VALUES" +
    "(@Field1, @Field2);" +
    "SELECT SCOPE_IDENTITY( ) Id";
da.InsertCommand = new SqlCommand(sqlText, da.SelectCommand.Connection);
da.InsertCommand.CommandType = CommandType.Text;
```

Batch SQL commands do not support output parameters, so only the FirstReturnedRecord method will work with a batch SQL command.

 The SCOPE_IDENTITY( ) function was introduced in SQL Server 2000 to make it easier to work with identity values. While SCOPE_IDENTITY( ) and @@IDENTITY both return the last identity value generated in any column in the current session, SCOPE_IDENTITY( ) returns values inserted within the current scope while @@IDENTITY is not limited to the current scope. This means that these functions can return different values under certain conditions leading to unexpected results. Use the SCOPE_IDENTITY( ) function unless you are certain that you need the @@IDENTITY function. For more information, see Microsoft SQL Server Books Online.

5.3 Getting an AutoNumber Value from Microsoft Access

Problem

If you add a row into a Microsoft Access table that has an AutoNumber column, the value assigned to the column in the DataTable is replaced by a value generated by the database. You need to retrieve the new value to keep the DataTable synchronized with the database.

Solution

Use the RowUpdated event handler to retrieve the new AutoNumber value generated by Microsoft Access using the @@IDENTITY function.

The solution creates a DataAdapter and sets its insert command to a parameterized query. An event handler is created for the RowUpdated event of the DataAdapter—when a row is inserted, the event handler retrieves the AutoNumber value from Access using the @@IDENTITY function and stores it to the ID value in the row that raised the event. Next, a DataTable is created, its schema filled from the Customers table, the AutoIncrementSeed and AutoIncrementStep values both set to -1, and the DataTable loaded with the data in the Customers table. A new row is added to the DataTable and the autoincrement ID value is output to the console. The Update( ) method of the DataAdapter is used to update the Access database with the inserted row. The OnRowUpdated( ) method is called in response to the RowUpdated event that this raises, the AutoNumber value for the ID column is retrieved from Access using the @@IDENTITY function, and the inserted row is updated with that value. Finally, the updated row is output to the console.

The C# code in *Program.cs* in the project AccessAutoNumberValue is shown in Example 5-6.

Example 5-6. File: Program.cs for AccessAutoNumberValue solution

```
using System;
using System.Data;
using System.Data.OleDb;

namespace AccessAutoNumberValue
{
    class Program
    {
        static OleDbDataAdapter da;

        static void Main(string[] args)
        {
            string oledbConnectString =
                "Provider=Microsoft.ACE.OLEDB.12.0;Data Source=" +
                @"C:\Northwind 2007.accdb;";

            string sqlSelect = "SELECT * FROM Customers";
            da = new OleDbDataAdapter(sqlSelect, oledbConnectString);

            // Create the insert command for the DataAdapter.
            // (most fields omitted for brevity)
            string sqlInsert = "INSERT INTO Customers " +
                "([Last Name], [First Name]) VALUES (?, ?)";
```

```csharp
        da.InsertCommand = new OleDbCommand(sqlInsert,
            da.SelectCommand.Connection);
        da.InsertCommand.Parameters.Add("@LastName", OleDbType.Char,
            50, "Last Name");
        da.InsertCommand.Parameters.Add("@FirstName", OleDbType.Char,
            50, "First Name");

        // Handle this event to retrieve the autonumber value.
        da.RowUpdated += new OleDbRowUpdatedEventHandler(OnRowUpdated);

        // Create DataTable and fill with schema and data
        DataTable dt = new DataTable();
        da.FillSchema(dt, SchemaType.Source);
        // Set these values before adding rows to the DataTable with Fill()
        dt.Columns["ID"].AutoIncrementSeed = -1;
        dt.Columns["ID"].AutoIncrementStep = -1;
        da.Fill(dt);

        // Create the new row, setting a few fields and leaving the rest null
        DataRow row = dt.NewRow();
        row["First Name"] = "Bill";
        row["Last Name"] = "Hamilton";
        // Add the row the the DataTable
        dt.Rows.Add(row);

        Console.WriteLine("ID AutoNumber value in new row before update = {0}",
            row["ID"]);

        // Persist the changes (new row) to the database
        da.Update(dt);
        Console.WriteLine("\nID AutoNumber value in new row after update = {0}",
            row["ID"]);

        Console.WriteLine("\nPress any key to continue.");
        Console.ReadKey();
    }

    private static void OnRowUpdated(object Sender,
        OleDbRowUpdatedEventArgs args)
    {
        // Retrieve autonumber value for inserts only.
        if (args.StatementType == StatementType.Insert)
        {
            Console.WriteLine("\nOnRowUpdate() called for StatementType.Insert.");

            // SQL command to retrieve the identity value created
            OleDbCommand cmd = new OleDbCommand("SELECT @@IDENTITY",
                da.SelectCommand.Connection);

            // Store the new identity value to the ID in the table.
            args.Row["ID"] = (int)cmd.ExecuteScalar();
        }
```

Example 5-6. File: Program.cs for AccessAutoNumberValue solution (continued)

```
        }
    }
}
```

The output is shown in Figure 5-4.

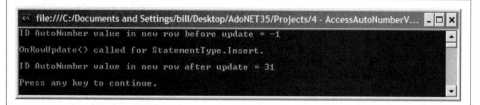

Figure 5-4. Output for AccessAutoNumberValue solution

Discussion

Microsoft Access does not support stored procedures or batch command processing. It is therefore not possible to map returned stored procedure output parameters, or a result set, back to the row being inserted or updated, as is possible for Microsoft SQL server (see Recipe 5.2). Microsoft Access 2000 and later does support @@IDENTITY function, which allows the last AutoNumber value generated to be retrieved.

To use @@IDENTITY, attach a handler to the OnRowUpdated event of the DataAdapter. The OnRowUpdated event will be called after any update to the row is made in the data source. The AutoNumber is only generated for rows that are inserted, so check that the update type of the event has a StatementType of Insert. Next, retrieve the new AutoNumber value by executing the following command:

```
SELECT @@IDENTITY
```

Finally, store the AutoNumber value generated by Microsoft Access to the AutoIncrement column in the DataRow.

This solution will only work using the Jet 4.0 OLE DB provider or later or the Access Database Engine (ACE) 12.0 OLE DB provider or later.

5.4   Getting a Sequence Value from Oracle

Problem

When you add a row into an Oracle table that uses a sequence to generate the value for a primary key column, the value assigned to the column in the DataTable is replaced by a value generated by the database. You need to retrieve the new value to keep the DataTable synchronized with the database.

Solution

Use the `CURRVAL` keyword to return the sequence value in the output parameter of an Oracle stored procedure.

The solution executes a stored procedure to insert a record into an Oracle table and uses the output parameter of the stored procedure to return the sequence value generated for the primary key column. The sequence value for the new record is displayed.

The solution uses one table named `OracleSequenceValue` with the schema shown in Figure 5-5.

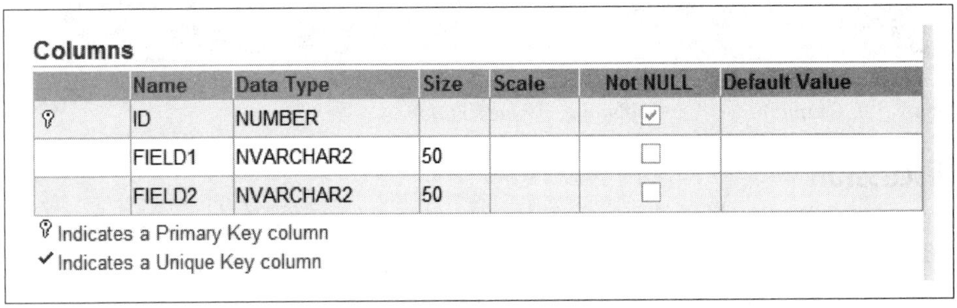

Columns

	Name	Data Type	Size	Scale	Not NULL	Default Value
🔑	ID	NUMBER			☑	
	FIELD1	NVARCHAR2	50		☐	
	FIELD2	NVARCHAR2	50		☐	

🔑 Indicates a Primary Key column
✔ Indicates a Unique Key column

Figure 5-5. Schema for table OracleSequenceValue

The PL/SQL DDL to create the table `OracleSequenceValue` is shown in Example 5-7.

Example 5-7. DDL to create the table OracleSequenceValue

```
CREATE TABLE "ADODOTNET35COOKBOOK"."ORACLESEQUENCEVALUE" (
    "ID" NUMBER,
    "FIELD1" NVARCHAR2(50),
    "FIELD2" NVARCHAR2(50),
    PRIMARY KEY ("ID") VALIDATE )
TABLESPACE "ADODOTNET35COOKBOOK" PCTFREE 10 INITRANS 1 MAXTRANS 255
    STORAGE ( INITIAL 64K BUFFER_POOL DEFAULT) LOGGING
```

The solution uses a single stored procedure that inserts a record into the table `OracleSequenceValue` and returns the sequence value generated by the Oracle sequence `OracleSequenceValue_Sequence` in the output parameter pID. The PL/SQL to create the stored procedure `Insert_OracleSequenceValue` is shown in Example 5-8.

Example 5-8. Stored procedure: Insert_OracleSequenceValue

```
CREATE PROCEDURE "ADODOTNET35COOKBOOK"."INSERT_ORACLESEQUENCEVALUE" (
    pID out number,
    pFIELD1 nvarchar2,
    pFIELD2 nvarchar2
)
as

begin
```

Example 5-8. Stored procedure: Insert_OracleSequenceValue (continued)

```
INSERT INTO OracleSequenceValue (
    ID,
    FIELD1,
    FIELD2)
VALUES (
    OracleSequenceValue_SEQUENCE.NEXTVAL,
    pFIELD1,
    pFIELD2
);

SELECT OracleSequenceValue_SEQUENCE.CURRVAL INTO pID FROM DUAL;
end;
```

The solution uses a single sequence OracleSequenceValue_Sequence to generate unique, sequential values for the primary key field ID in the table OracleSequenceValue. The PL/SQL used to create the Oracle sequence is shown in Example 5-9.

Example 5-9. Sequence: OracleSequenceValue_Sequence

```
CREATE SEQUENCE "ADODOTNET35COOKBOOK"."ORACLESEQUENCEVALUE_SEQUENCE"
NOCYCLE
NOORDER
CACHE 20
NOMAXVALUE
MINVALUE 1
INCREMENT BY 1
START WITH 1
```

The solution creates a stored procedure command for the stored procedure Insert_OracleSequenceValue. The stored procedure parameters are set and the command is executed. The sequence value is retrieved from the output parameter pID and is output to the console.

The solution needs a reference to the assembly Sequence.Data.OracleClient.

The C# code in *Program.cs* in the project OracleSequenceValue is shown in Example 5-10.

Example 5-10. File: Program.cs for OracleSequenceValue solution

```
using System;
using System.Data;
using System.Data.OracleClient;

namespace OracleSequenceValue
{
    class Program
    {
        static void Main(string[] args)
        {
```

```
        string oracleConnectString =
            "Data Source=ORCL;User Id=ADODOTNET35COOKBOOK;Password=password;";

        // Create the connection.
        OracleConnection connection =
            new OracleConnection(oracleConnectString);

        // Create the command for the insert stored procedure.
        OracleCommand command = new OracleCommand( );
        command.Connection = connection;
        command.CommandText = "Insert_OracleSequenceValue";
        command.CommandType = CommandType.StoredProcedure;
        // Add the parameters and set values for them.
        command.Parameters.Add("pID", OracleType.Int32).Direction =
            ParameterDirection.Output;
        command.Parameters.Add("pField1", OracleType.NVarChar, 50);
        command.Parameters.Add("pField2", OracleType.NVarChar, 50);
        command.Parameters["pField1"].Value = "Field1 test value 1";
        command.Parameters["pField2"].Value = "Field2 test value 1";

        // Execute the insert query.
        connection.Open( );
        command.ExecuteNonQuery( );
        connection.Close( );

        // Retrieve and display the sequence value.
        int sequenceValue = (int)command.Parameters["pID"].Value;
        Console.WriteLine("Inserted record with ID = {0}", sequenceValue);

        Console.WriteLine("\nPress any key to continue.");
        Console.ReadKey( );
    }
  }
}
```

The output is shown in Figure 5-6.

Figure 5-6. Output for OracleSequenceValue solution

The inserted record in the table OracleSequenceValue with the sequence value in the ID field is shown in Figure 5-7.

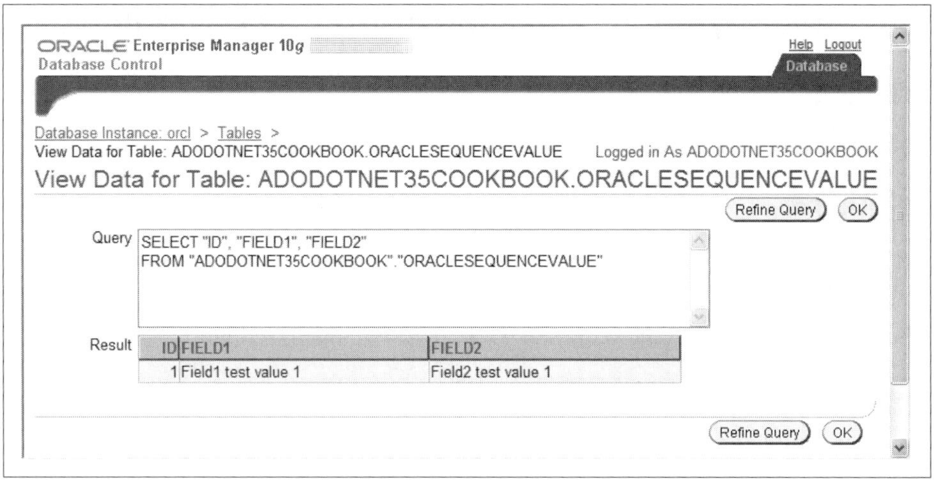

Figure 5-7. Data in table OracleSequenceValue

Discussion

Oracle does not support autoincrement fields in the same way that SQL Server does. Instead, Oracle uses a sequence generator, which is a database object that is used to generate a sequence of unique values for a primary key column, but is not related to the table containing the column. As a result, a sequence generator can generate unique values for more than one table.

The SQL command CREATE SEQUENCE is used to create a new sequence as shown in the previous sample. The increment, start value, maximum value, cycling, and caching can be specified when creating the sequence.

Oracle stores the definition of sequences for a database in a single data dictionary table in the SYSTEM table namespace. As a result, all sequence definitions are always available.

A sequence is referenced in SQL statements using the NEXTVAL and CURRVAL keywords. NEXTVAL generates and returns the next sequence number while CURRVAL can be used to refer to that value as needed.

Oracle does not support batch queries to return data as SQL Server does. You can, however, return the sequence value by setting the return value of a stored procedure. The sample demonstrates using the NEXTVAL and CURRVAL keywords to generate the new sequence value when inserting a row using a stored procedure and subsequently setting the stored procedure's return value.

5.5   Modifying Data in a Microsoft Excel Workbook

Problem

You need to modify the contents of a Microsoft Excel workbook.

Solution

Use an OLE DB DataAdapter together with parameterized SQL insert and update statements.

The solution uses the Excel workbook *Category.xlsx* shown in Figure 5-8.

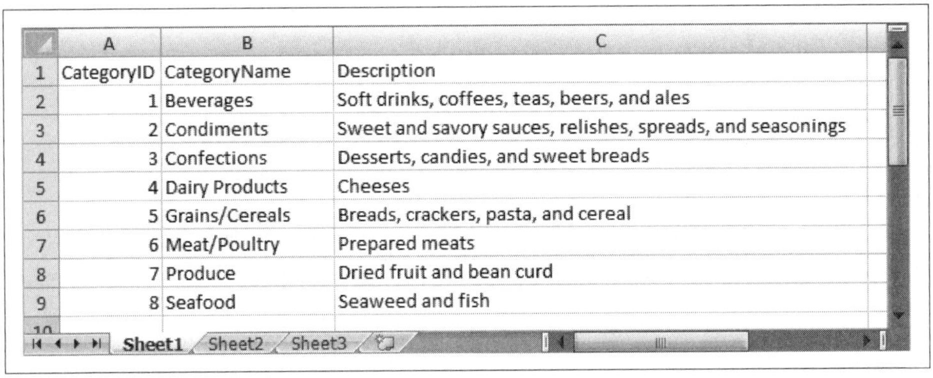

	A	B	C
1	CategoryID	CategoryName	Description
2	1	Beverages	Soft drinks, coffees, teas, beers, and ales
3	2	Condiments	Sweet and savory sauces, relishes, spreads, and seasonings
4	3	Confections	Desserts, candies, and sweet breads
5	4	Dairy Products	Cheeses
6	5	Grains/Cereals	Breads, crackers, pasta, and cereal
7	6	Meat/Poultry	Prepared meats
8	7	Produce	Dried fruit and bean curd
9	8	Seafood	Seaweed and fish

Figure 5-8. Excel workbook Category.xlsx

The solution creates a DataAdapter and creates parameterized insert and update SQL statements. A DataSet is created and filled from the Excel workbook using the DataAdapter. The initial contents are output to the console. Next, a new row is added and the Update( ) method of the DataAdapter is called to update the Excel workbook. The DataSet is reloaded and its contents output to the console. Finally, a row is updated and the Update( ) method of the DataAdapter is called to update the Excel workbook. The DataSet is reloaded and its contents output to the console.

The C# code in *Program.cs* in the project ModifyExcelData is shown in Example 5-11.

Example 5-11. File: Program.cs for ModifyExcelData solution

```
using System;
using System.Data;
using System.Data.OleDb;

namespace ModifyExcelData
{
    class Program
    {
        static void Main(string[] args)
```

Example 5-11. File: Program.cs for ModifyExcelData solution (continued)

```
{
    string oledbConnectString =
        "Provider=Microsoft.ACE.OLEDB.12.0;" +
        @"Data Source=..\..\..\Category.xlsx;" +
        "Extended Properties=\"Excel 12.0;HDR=YES\";";

    string commandText =
        "SELECT CategoryID, CategoryName, Description " +
        "FROM [Sheet1$]";

    // Create the connection
    OleDbConnection connection =
        new OleDbConnection(oledbConnectString);

    // Create the DataAdapter.
    OleDbDataAdapter da = new OleDbDataAdapter( );
    da.SelectCommand = new OleDbCommand(commandText, connection);

    // Create the INSERT command.
    string insertSql = "INSERT INTO [Sheet1$] " +
        "(CategoryID, CategoryName, Description) VALUES (?, ?, ?)";
    da.InsertCommand =
        new OleDbCommand(insertSql, connection);
    da.InsertCommand.Parameters.Add(
        "@CategoryID", OleDbType.Integer, 0, "CategoryID");
    da.InsertCommand.Parameters.Add(
        "@CategoryName", OleDbType.Char, 15, "CategoryName");
    da.InsertCommand.Parameters.Add(
        "@Description", OleDbType.VarChar, 100, "Description");

    // Create the UPDATE command.
    string updateSql = "UPDATE [Sheet1$] " +
        "SET CategoryName=?, Description=? WHERE CategoryID=?";
    da.UpdateCommand =
        new OleDbCommand(updateSql, connection);
    da.UpdateCommand.Parameters.Add(
        "@CategoryName", OleDbType.Char, 15, "CategoryName");
    da.UpdateCommand.Parameters.Add(
        "@Description", OleDbType.VarChar, 100, "Description");
    da.UpdateCommand.Parameters.Add(
        "@CategoryID", OleDbType.Integer, 0, "CategoryID");

    // Fill a DataSet from the Excel workbook
    DataSet ds = new DataSet( );
    da.Fill(ds, "[Sheet1$]");

    // Output the initial data from the Excel workbook
    Console.WriteLine("---INITIAL---");
    Console.WriteLine("ID Name             Description");
    foreach (DataRow row in ds.Tables["[Sheet1$]"].Rows)
    {
        Console.WriteLine("{0}  {1} {2}", row["CategoryID"],
```

Example 5-11. File: Program.cs for ModifyExcelData solution (continued)

```
                    row["CategoryName"].ToString( ).PadRight(18),
                    row["Description"]);
        }

        // Add a new row and update the Excel workbook
        ds.Tables["[Sheet1$]"].Rows.Add(
            new object[] { 9, "Name 9", "Description 9" });
        Console.WriteLine("\n=> Insert record into Excel WorkBook.");
        da.Update(ds, "[Sheet1$]");

        // Clear the DataSet and reload from the Excel workbook
        ds.Clear( );
        da.Fill(ds, "[Sheet1$]");
        // Output the data from the Excel workbook
        Console.WriteLine("\n---AFTER INSERT---");
        Console.WriteLine("ID Name               Description");
        foreach (DataRow row in ds.Tables["[Sheet1$]"].Rows)
        {
            Console.WriteLine("{0}  {1} {2}", row["CategoryID"],
                row["CategoryName"].ToString( ).PadRight(18),
                row["Description"]);
        }

        // Modify the row just added and udpate the Excel workbook
        ds.Tables["[Sheet1$]"].Rows[8]["CategoryName"] = "Name 9.2";
        ds.Tables["[Sheet1$]"].Rows[8]["Description"] =
            "Description 9.2";
        Console.WriteLine("\n=> Modify record in Excel WorkBook.");
        da.Update(ds, "[Sheet1$]");

        // Clear the DataSet and reload from the Excel workbook
        ds.Clear( );
        da.Fill(ds, "[Sheet1$]");
        // Output the data from the Excel workbook
        Console.WriteLine("\n---AFTER UPDATE---");
        Console.WriteLine("ID Name               Description");
        foreach (DataRow row in ds.Tables["[Sheet1$]"].Rows)
        {
            Console.WriteLine("{0}  {1} {2}", row["CategoryID"],
                row["CategoryName"].ToString( ).PadRight(18),
                row["Description"]);
        }

        Console.WriteLine("\nPress any key to continue.");
        Console.ReadKey( );
    }
  }
}
```

The output is shown in Figure 5-9.

```
file:///C:/Documents and Settings/bill/Desktop/AdoNET35/Projects/ModifyExcelData/ModifyE...  _ □ ×
---INITIAL---
ID Name              Description
1  Beverages         Soft drinks, coffees, teas, beers, and ales
2  Condiments         Sweet and savory sauces, relishes, spreads, and seasonings

3  Confections        Desserts, candies, and sweet breads
4  Dairy Products     Cheeses
5  Grains/Cereals     Breads, crackers, pasta, and cereal
6  Meat/Poultry       Prepared meats
7  Produce            Dried fruit and bean curd
8  Seafood            Seaweed and fish

=> Insert record into Excel WorkBook.

---AFTER INSERT---
ID Name              Description
1  Beverages          Soft drinks, coffees, teas, beers, and ales
2  Condiments         Sweet and savory sauces, relishes, spreads, and seasonings

3  Confections        Desserts, candies, and sweet breads
4  Dairy Products     Cheeses
5  Grains/Cereals     Breads, crackers, pasta, and cereal
6  Meat/Poultry       Prepared meats
7  Produce            Dried fruit and bean curd
8  Seafood            Seaweed and fish
9  Name 9             Description 9

=> Modify record in Excel WorkBook.

---AFTER UPDATE---
ID Name              Description
1  Beverages          Soft drinks, coffees, teas, beers, and ales
2  Condiments         Sweet and savory sauces, relishes, spreads, and seasonings

3  Confections        Desserts, candies, and sweet breads
4  Dairy Products     Cheeses
5  Grains/Cereals     Breads, crackers, pasta, and cereal
6  Meat/Poultry       Prepared meats
7  Produce            Dried fruit and bean curd
8  Seafood            Seaweed and fish
9  Name 9.2           Description 9.2

Press any key to continue.
```

Figure 5-9. Output for ModifyExcelData solution

Discussion

Parameterized INSERT and UPDATE commands are required because the OleDbDataAdapter does not supply key/index information for Excel workbooks; without key/index fields, the CommandBuilder cannot automatically generate the commands for you.

Although the Access Database Engine (ACE) OLE DB driver allows you to insert and update records in an Excel workbook, it does not allow DELETE operations.

For more information about connecting to a Microsoft Excel workbook, see Recipe 1.13.

5.6   Modifying Data in a Text File

Problem

You need to modify the contents of a text file.

Solution

Use an OLE DB DataAdapter together with parameterized SQL insert and update statements.

The solution uses the text file *Category.txt* shown in Figure 5-10.

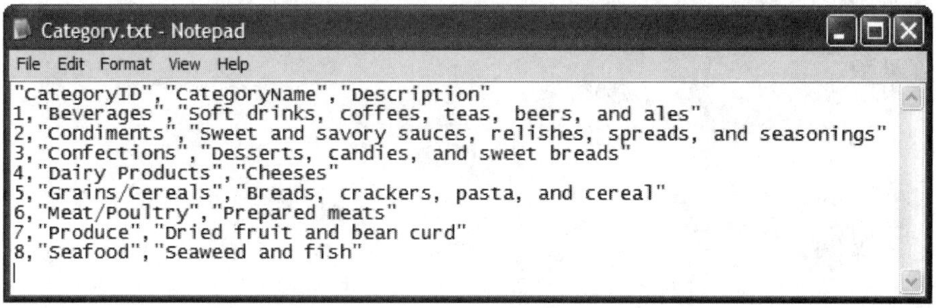

Figure 5-10. Text file Category.txt

The solution creates a DataAdapter and creates parameterized insert and update SQL statements. A DataSet is created and filled from the text file using the DataAdapter. The initial contents are output to the console. Next, a new row is added and the Update( ) method of the DataAdapter is called to update the text file. The DataSet is reloaded and its contents output to the console. Finally, a row is updated and the Update( ) method of the DataAdapter is called to update the text file. The DataSet is reloaded and its contents output to the console.

The C# code in *Program.cs* in the project ModifyTextFileData is shown in Example 5-12.

Example 5-12. File: Program.cs for ModifyTextFileData solution

```
using System;
using System.Data;
using System.Data.OleDb;

namespace ModifyTextFileData
{
    class Program
    {
        static void Main(string[] args)
        {
            string oledbConnectString =
                "Provider=Microsoft.ACE.OLEDB.12.0;" +
                @"Data Source=..\..\..\;" +
                "Extended Properties=\"text;HDR=yes;FMT=Delimited\";";

            string sqlSelect = "SELECT * FROM [Category.txt]";
```

```csharp
// Create the connection
OleDbConnection connection =
    new OleDbConnection(oledbConnectString);

// Create the DataAdapter
OleDbDataAdapter da =
    new OleDbDataAdapter(sqlSelect, connection);

// Create the INSERT command.
string insertSql = "INSERT INTO [Category.txt] " +
    "(CategoryID, CategoryName, Description) " +
    "VALUES (?, ?, ?)";
da.InsertCommand =
    new OleDbCommand(insertSql, connection);
da.InsertCommand.Parameters.Add(
    "@CategoryID", OleDbType.Integer, 0, "CategoryID");
da.InsertCommand.Parameters.Add(
    "@CategoryName", OleDbType.Char, 15, "CategoryName");
da.InsertCommand.Parameters.Add(
    "@Description", OleDbType.VarChar, 100, "Description");

// Create the UPDATE command.
string updateSql = "UPDATE [Category.txt] " +
    "SET CategoryName=?, Description=? WHERE CategoryID=?";
da.UpdateCommand =
    new OleDbCommand(updateSql, connection);
da.UpdateCommand.Parameters.Add(
    "@CategoryName", OleDbType.Char, 15, "CategoryName");
da.UpdateCommand.Parameters.Add(
    "@Description", OleDbType.VarChar, 100, "Description");
da.UpdateCommand.Parameters.Add(
    "@CategoryID", OleDbType.Integer, 0, "CategoryID");

// Fill the DataTable from the text file
DataTable dt = new DataTable( );
da.Fill(dt);

// Output the initial data from the text file
Console.WriteLine("---INITIAL---");
Console.WriteLine("CategoryID; CategoryName; Description\n");
foreach (DataRow row in dt.Rows)
    Console.WriteLine("{0}; {1}; {2}", row["CategoryID"],
        row["CategoryName"], row["Description"]);

// Add a new row and update the text file
dt.Rows.Add(new object[] { 9, "Name 9", "Description 9" });
Console.WriteLine("\n=> Insert record into text file.");
da.Update(dt);

// Clear the DataTable and reload from the text file
dt.Clear( );
da.Fill(dt);
```

Example 5-12. File: Program.cs for ModifyTextFileData solution (continued)

```
                // Output the data from the text file
                Console.WriteLine("\n---AFTER INSERT---");
                Console.WriteLine("CategoryID; CategoryName; Description\n");
                foreach (DataRow row in dt.Rows)
                    Console.WriteLine("{0}; {1}; {2}", row["CategoryID"],
                        row["CategoryName"], row["Description"]);

                // Modify the row just added and udpate the text file
                dt.Rows[8]["CategoryName"] = "Name 9.2";
                dt.Rows[8]["Description"] = "Description 9.2";
                Console.WriteLine("\n=> Modify record in text file.");
                try
                {
                    da.Update(dt);
                }
                catch (Exception ex)
                {
                    Console.WriteLine("\nERROR: {0}", ex.Message);
                }

                // Clear the DataSet and reload from the text file
                dt.Clear();
                da.Fill(dt);
                // Output the data from the text file
                Console.WriteLine("\n---AFTER UPDATE---");
                Console.WriteLine("CategoryID; CategoryName; Description\n");
                foreach (DataRow row in dt.Rows)
                    Console.WriteLine("{0}; {1}; {2}", row["CategoryID"],
                        row["CategoryName"], row["Description"]);

                Console.WriteLine("\nPress any key to continue.");
                Console.ReadKey();
            }
        }
}
```

The output is shown in Figure 5-11.

Discussion

Parameterized INSERT and UPDATE commands are required because the OleDbDataAdapter does not supply key/index information for text files; without key/index fields, the CommandBuilder cannot automatically generate the commands for you.

Although the Access Database Engine (ACE) OLE DB driver allows you to insert and update records in an text file, it does not allow DELETE operations.

For more information about connecting to a text file, see Recipe 1.14.

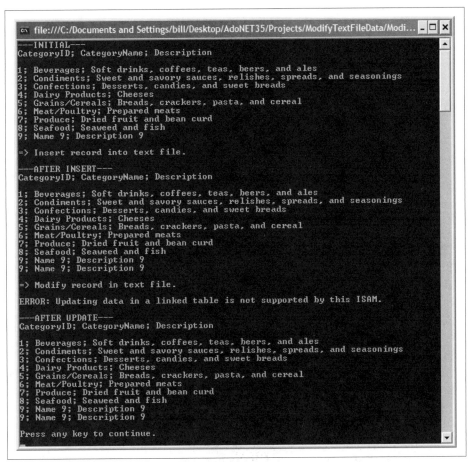

```
file:///C:/Documents and Settings/bill/Desktop/AdoNET35/Projects/ModifyTextFileData/Modi...

---INITIAL---
CategoryID; CategoryName; Description

1; Beverages; Soft drinks, coffees, teas, beers, and ales
2; Condiments; Sweet and savory sauces, relishes, spreads, and seasonings
3; Confections; Desserts, candies, and sweet breads
4; Dairy Products; Cheeses
5; Grains/Cereals; Breads, crackers, pasta, and cereal
6; Meat/Poultry; Prepared meats
7; Produce; Dried fruit and bean curd
8; Seafood; Seaweed and fish
9; Name 9; Description 9

=> Insert record into text file.

---AFTER INSERT---
CategoryID; CategoryName; Description

1; Beverages; Soft drinks, coffees, teas, beers, and ales
2; Condiments; Sweet and savory sauces, relishes, spreads, and seasonings
3; Confections; Desserts, candies, and sweet breads
4; Dairy Products; Cheeses
5; Grains/Cereals; Breads, crackers, pasta, and cereal
6; Meat/Poultry; Prepared meats
7; Produce; Dried fruit and bean curd
8; Seafood; Seaweed and fish
9; Name 9; Description 9
9; Name 9; Description 9

=> Modify record in text file.

ERROR: Updating data in a linked table is not supported by this ISAM.

---AFTER UPDATE---
CategoryID; CategoryName; Description

1; Beverages; Soft drinks, coffees, teas, beers, and ales
2; Condiments; Sweet and savory sauces, relishes, spreads, and seasonings
3; Confections; Desserts, candies, and sweet breads
4; Dairy Products; Cheeses
5; Grains/Cereals; Breads, crackers, pasta, and cereal
6; Meat/Poultry; Prepared meats
7; Produce; Dried fruit and bean curd
8; Seafood; Seaweed and fish
9; Name 9; Description 9
9; Name 9; Description 9

Press any key to continue.
```

Figure 5-11. Output for ModifyTextFileData solution

5.7 Retrieving Update Errors

Problem

You want to access all of the error information available after an update fails.

Solution

Use one of the available properties (such as HasErrors) and methods (such as GetErrors( )) to obtain the error information.

The solution uses a table named RetrieveUpdateErrors in the AdoDotNet35Cookbook database. Execute the following T-SQL to create the table:

```
USE AdoDotNet35Cookbook
GO

CREATE TABLE RetrieveUpdateErrors(
    UniqueId int NOT NULL,
    NumericField int NOT NULL,
    StringNoNullsField nvarchar(50) NOT NULL,
    ConstrainedNegativeField int NOT NULL,
  CONSTRAINT PK_RetrieveUpdateErrors PRIMARY KEY CLUSTERED
    ( UniqueId ASC ),
  CONSTRAINT CK_ConstrainedNegativeField CHECK
    ( ConstrainedNegativeField < 0)
)
```

The schema of table RetrieveUpdateErrors is shown in Table 5-2.

Table 5-2. RetrieveUpdateErrors table schema

Column name	Data type	Length	Allow nulls?
UniqueId	int	4	No
NumericField	int	4	No
StringNoNullsField	nvarchar	50	No
ConstrainedNegativeField	int	4	No

The solution creates a table to demonstrate error information retrieval, using a DataAdapter to fill it with sample data, and adding it to a DataSet. The ContinueUpdateOnError property of the DataAdapter is set to true so that an exception is not raised if an error is encountered during an update. Finally, the default view of the table is bound to the data grid on the form.

Specifically, the solution creates one good row and two rows with errors. For each, an error description is set for the column in error using the SetColumnError() method. The Update() method of the DataAdapter is called to update changes that the user has made to the data back to the database.

After the update, the HasErrors property of the DataTable is tested to see if the table has any errors. The collection of DataRow objects in the table with errors are accessed using the GetErrors() method on the table. For each row in error, the HasErrors property is checked to determine if the row has any errors and the RowError property of a row having errors is accessed to get the text describing the error. The collection of DataColumn objects in the row with errors are accessed using the row's GetColumnsInError() method. For each column with an error, the row's GetColumnError() method is used to output the error description for the column.

The C# code in *Program.cs* in the project RetrieveUpdateErrors is shown in Example 5-13.

Example 5-13. File: Program.cs for RetrieveUpdateErrors solution

```csharp
using System;
using System.Data;
using System.Data.SqlClient;

namespace RetrieveUpdateErrors
{
    class Program
    {
        static void Main(string[] args)
        {
            string sqlConnectString = "Data Source=(local);" +
                "Integrated security=SSPI;Initial Catalog=AdoDotNet35Cookbook;";

            string sqlSelect = "SELECT * FROM RetrieveUpdateErrors";

            // Create the DataAdapter and CommandBuilder.
            SqlDataAdapter da = new SqlDataAdapter(sqlSelect, sqlConnectString);
            da.ContinueUpdateOnError = true;
            SqlCommandBuilder cb = new SqlCommandBuilder(da);

            // Create and load a DataTable
            DataTable dt = new DataTable();
            dt.Columns.Add("UniqueId", typeof(int));
            dt.Columns.Add("NumericField");
            dt.Columns.Add("StringNoNullsField", typeof(string));
            dt.Columns.Add("ConstrainedNegativeField", typeof(int));
            da.Fill(dt);

            DataRow row;
            // Create one good row
            row = dt.Rows.Add(new object[] { 1, 11, "test string 1", -111 });
            row.SetColumnError("UniqueID", "All field values are valid.");
            // Create two bad rows, together with column error information
            row = dt.Rows.Add(new object[] { 2, 22, null, -222 });
            row.SetColumnError("StringNoNullsField","Field cannot be null.");
            row = dt.Rows.Add(new object[] { 3, 33, "test string 3", 333 });
            row.SetColumnError("ConstrainedNegativeField",
                "Field must be negative.");

            // Send the updates to the database
            da.Update(dt);

            // Display the results of the database update
            Console.WriteLine("DataTable.HasErrors = {0}\n", dt.HasErrors);
            for (int i = 0; i < dt.Rows.Count; i++)
            {
                Console.WriteLine("\n---UPDATE RESULTS---");
                Console.WriteLine("Row = {0}\nHasError = {1}\nRowError = {2}\n",
                    i, dt.Rows[i].HasErrors, dt.Rows[i].RowError);
```

Example 5-13. File: Program.cs for RetrieveUpdateErrors solution (continued)

```
            Console.WriteLine("---Row Values---");
            for (int j = 0; j < dt.Columns.Count; j++)
                Console.WriteLine("{0} = {1}; ColumnError = {2}",
                    dt.Columns[j].ColumnName, dt.Rows[i][j],
                    dt.Rows[i].GetColumnError(j));
        }

        Console.WriteLine("\nPress any key to continue.");
        Console.ReadKey( );
    }
  }
}
```

The output is shown in Figure 5-12.

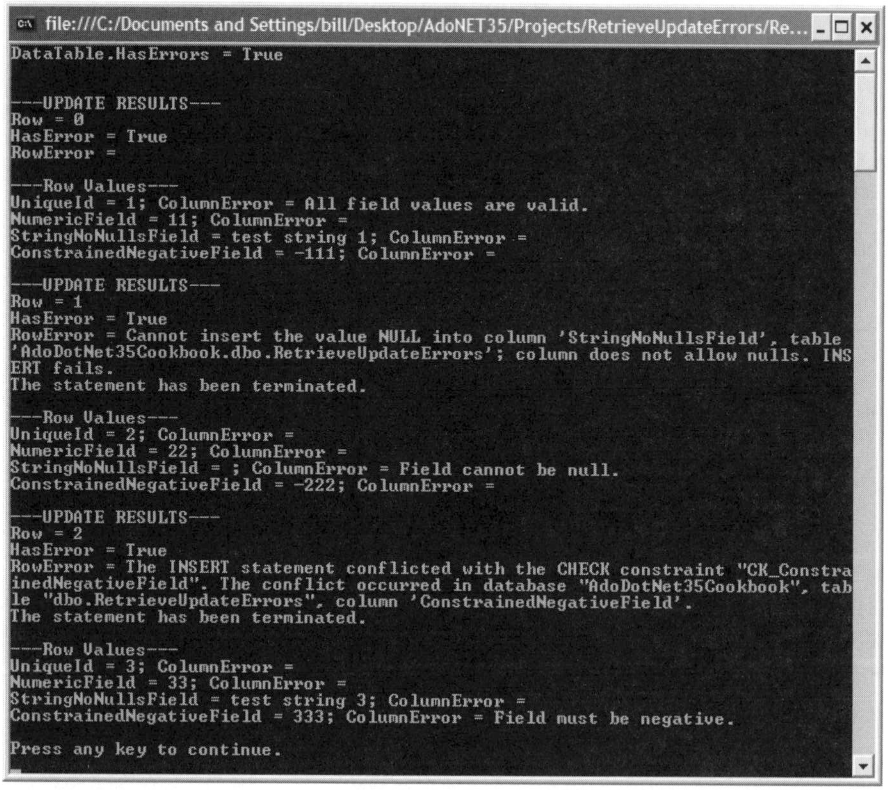

Figure 5-12. Output for RetrieveUpdateErrors solution

Discussion

The `Update()` method of the `DataAdapter` is used to reconcile changes made to a `DataSet` back to the underlying data source. If errors occur during the reconciliation, the `ContinueUpdateOnError` property of the `DataAdapter` specifies whether the update continues with remaining rows or stops processing:

- If `ContinueUpdateOnError` is true and an error is encountered during the update, the `RowError` property of the `DataRow` causing the error is set to the error message that would have been raised, the update of the row is skipped, and updating continues with subsequent rows. No exception is raised.

- If `ContinueUpdateOnError` is false, the `DataAdapter` raises a `DBConcurrencyException` when a row update attempt fails.

Once the update has completed, there are a number of properties and methods you can use to investigate errors in the `DataSet`, `DataTable`, `DataRow`, and `DataColumn` objects:

`HasErrors`

> This property exists for the `DataSet`, `DataTable`, and `DataRow` objects. It returns a Boolean value indicating whether there are any errors within the object. Checking the `HasErrors` property for an object before calling specific error retrieval methods can improve performance by eliminating unnecessary calls to the more time-consuming error retrieval methods.

`GetErrors()`

> This method of the `DataTable` returns an array of `DataRow` objects having errors.

`RowError`

> This property of the `DataRow` returns the custom error description for the row.

`GetColumnsInError()`

> This method of the `DataRow` returns an array of columns containing errors. Rather than iterating over the collection of columns in a row and checking each for an error, this method reduces error processing by returning only those columns having an error.

`GetColumnError()`

> This method of the `DataRow` returns the error description for a column. Column errors are set using the `SetColumnError()` method of the `DataRow`; errors for individual columns are not set by the `DataAdapter`.

`ClearErrors()`

> This method of the `DataRow` clears all errors for a row including both the `RowError` and errors set using the `SetColumnError()` method. The `SetColumnError()` method of the `DataRow` sets an error description for a specified column.

The solution code demonstrates how to use these error-checking methods and properties when updates are made with user-specified data.

5.8   Adding Parent/Child Rows with Autoincrementing Keys

Problem

You want to insert related parent/child records into a DataSet where the primary key of the parent table is an automatically incrementing value.

Solution

Use the DataColumn object's AutoIncrementSeed and AutoIncrementStep properties.

The solution uses two tables, ParentAutoincrementKey and ChildAutoincrementKey, related on the ParentId column in each table. The tables are shown in Figures 5-13 and 5-14. The primary key in each table is an identity column with a seed of 1 and an increment of 1.

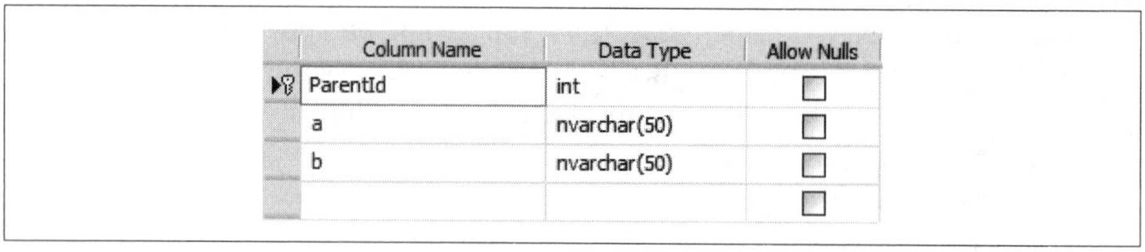

Figure 5-13. Schema for table ParentAutoincrementKey

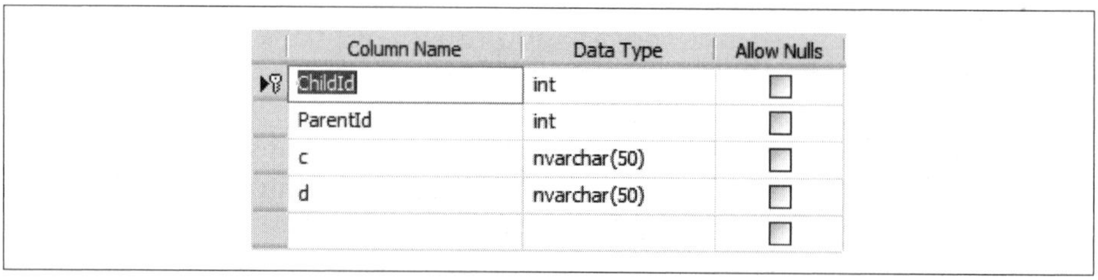

Figure 5-14. Schema for table ChildAutoincrementKey

The T-SQL DDL code to create the parent and child tables together with the relationship between them is shown in Example 5-14.

Example 5-14. Create tables ParentAutoincrementKey and ChildAutoincrementKey

```
USE AdoDotNet35Cookbook
GO

CREATE TABLE ParentAutoincrementKey(
    ParentId int IDENTITY(1,1) NOT NULL PRIMARY KEY,
    a nvarchar(50) NOT NULL,
    b nvarchar(50) NOT NULL
)
```

```
GO

CREATE TABLE ChildAutoincrementKey(
    ChildId int IDENTITY(1,1) NOT NULL PRIMARY KEY,
    ParentId int NOT NULL,
    c nvarchar(50) NOT NULL,
    d nvarchar(50) NOT NULL )
GO

ALTER TABLE ChildAutoincrementKey WITH CHECK ADD
  CONSTRAINT FK_ChildAutoincrementKey_ParentAutoincrementKey
  FOREIGN KEY(ParentId)
  REFERENCES ParentAutoincrementKey (ParentId)
```

The solution creates a DataSet containing a parent and child DataTable. Each DataTable has an primary key that is an autoincrement column—the example sets the AutoIncrementSeed and AutoIncrementStep for each to –1. A relation is created between the parent and child table. Several rows are added to the both parent and child tables demonstrating how to propagate the autoincrementing ParentId column in the parent table to the ParentId foreign key in the child table. The DataSet is output to the console.

The C# code in *Program.cs* in the project AddParentChildAutoincrementKey is shown in Example 5-15.

Example 5-15. File: Program.cs for AddParentChildAutoincrementKey solution

```
using System;
using System.Data;
using System.Data.SqlClient;

namespace AddParentChildRowsAutoincrementKey
{
    class Program
    {
        static void Main(string[] args)
        {
            string sqlConnectString = "Data Source=(local);" +
                "Integrated security=SSPI;Initial Catalog=AdoDotNet35Cookbook;";
            string sqlSelect = "SELECT * FROM ParentAutoincrementKey;" +
                "SELECT * FROM ChildAutoincrementKey";

            // Load the DataSet with the schemas
            DataSet ds = new DataSet();
            SqlDataAdapter da = new SqlDataAdapter(sqlSelect, sqlConnectString);
            da.TableMappings.Add("Table", "Parent");
            da.TableMappings.Add("Table1", "Child");
            da.FillSchema(ds, SchemaType.Mapped);

            // Set the autoincrement properties for parent and child PKs
            ds.Tables["Parent"].Columns["ParentId"].AutoIncrementSeed = -1;
```

```
        ds.Tables["Parent"].Columns["ParentId"].AutoIncrementStep = -1;
        ds.Tables["Child"].Columns["ChildId"].AutoIncrementSeed = -1;
        ds.Tables["Child"].Columns["ChildId"].AutoIncrementStep = -1;

        // Add the relation
        ds.Relations.Add("FK_Child_Parent",
            ds.Tables["Parent"].Columns["ParentId"],
            ds.Tables["Child"].Columns["ParentId"]);

        // Add 2 records to the parent table
        for (int i = 1; i <= 2; i++)
        {
            DataRow parentRow = ds.Tables["Parent"].NewRow( );
            parentRow["a"] = "a." + i;
            parentRow["b"] = "b." + i;
            ds.Tables["Parent"].Rows.Add(parentRow);

            // Add 3 records to the child table
            for (int j = 1; j <= 3; j++)
            {
                ds.Tables["Child"].Rows.Add(new object[]
                    { null, parentRow["ParentId"], "c." + j, "d." + j });
            }
        }

        // Output the tables
        Console.WriteLine("---Parent table---");
        foreach (DataRow row in ds.Tables["Parent"].Rows)
            Console.WriteLine("ParentId = {0}\ta = {1}\t\tb = {2}",
                row["ParentId"], row["a"], row["b"]);

        Console.WriteLine("\n---Child table---");
        foreach (DataRow row in ds.Tables["Child"].Rows)
            Console.WriteLine("ChildId = {0}\tParentId = {1}\tc = {2}\t\td = {3}",
                row["ChildId"], row["ParentId"], row["c"], row["d"]);

        Console.WriteLine("\nPress any key to continue.");
        Console.ReadKey( );
        }
    }
}
```

The output is shown in Figure 5-15.

Discussion

The example adds two rows to the parent table and three rows to the child table for each parent record. The autoincrement primary key of the parent table is used as the foreign key value when constructing the records added to the child table.

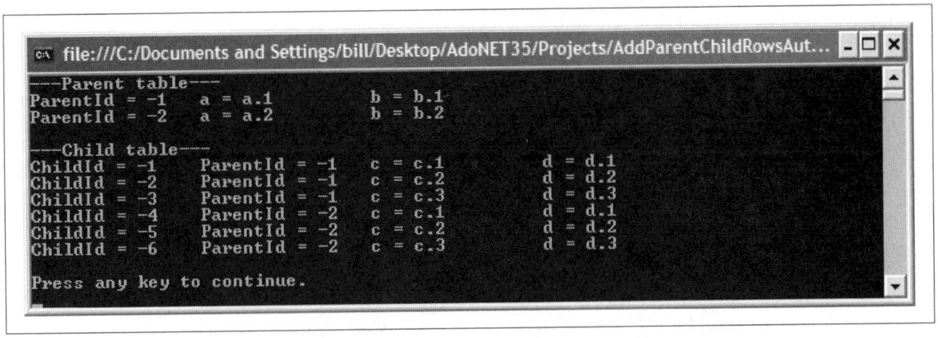

Figure 5-15. Output for AddParentChildRowsAutoincrementKey solution

When a record is added to the parent table or the child table, a new primary key value is generated starting in the sequence –1, –2, –3, and so on, because of the auto-increment properties of the column. The AutoIncrementSeed and AutoIncrementStep properties are both set to –1 to ensure that when the DataSet is ultimately resolved to the data source, the values do not conflict with values within the data source (this assumes that the data source uses positive integers for the primary key values). For more information about avoiding conflicts when using AutoIncrement columns, see Recipe 5.1.

5.9   Adding Records with a GUID Primary Key

Problem

You want to add records to a DataTable that uses a GUID as its primary key.

Solution

Use the DataTable.RowChanging event handler to generate new GUID values for each row.

The solution creates a DataTable that has a GUID primary key column Id with the DefaultValue set to a new GUID. An event handler is added for the RowChanging event of the DataTable. The RowChanging event handler sets the default value of the primary key column in the DataTable to a new GUID value when a new row is added.

The C# code in *Program.cs* in the project AddRecordGuidPrimaryKey is shown in Example 5-16.

Example 5-16. File: Program.cs for AddRecordGuidPrimaryKey solution

```
using System;
using System.Data;
using System.Data.SqlClient;

namespace AddRecordGuidPrimaryKey
```

Example 5-16. File: Program.cs for AddRecordGuidPrimaryKey solution (continued)

```csharp
{
    class Program
    {
        static void Main(string[] args)
        {
            // Build the data table
            DataTable dt = new DataTable();
            // The Id column is a GUID; set the default value to a new GUID
            dt.Columns.Add("Id", typeof(Guid)).DefaultValue = Guid.NewGuid();
            dt.Columns.Add("Field1", typeof(string)).MaxLength = 50;
            dt.Columns.Add("Field2", typeof(string)).MaxLength = 50;

            // event handler sets the default value of Id to a new GUID value
            dt.RowChanging += new DataRowChangeEventHandler(dt_RowChanging);

            // Add five rows to the table
            for (int i = 1; i <= 5; i++)
            {
                // Create the new row
                DataRow row = dt.NewRow();
                row.SetField<string>("Field1", "field 1." + i);
                row.SetField<string>("Field2", "field 2." + i);
                dt.Rows.Add(row);
            }

            foreach (DataRow row in dt.Rows)
                Console.WriteLine("Id={0}; Field1={1}; Field2={2}",
                    row["Id"], row["Field1"], row["Field2"]);

            Console.WriteLine("\nPress any key to continue.");
            Console.ReadKey();
        }

        static void dt_RowChanging(object sender, DataRowChangeEventArgs e)
        {
            // Set the default column value to a new GUID when a row is added
            if (e.Action == DataRowAction.Add)
                e.Row.Table.Columns["Id"].DefaultValue = Guid.NewGuid();
        }
    }
}
```

The output is shown in Figure 5-16.

Discussion

A Globally Unique Identifier (GUID) is a 128-bit integer that is statistically unique; you can use it wherever a unique identifier is needed. The System.Guid type is a .NET structure that contains members to facilitate working with GUIDs.

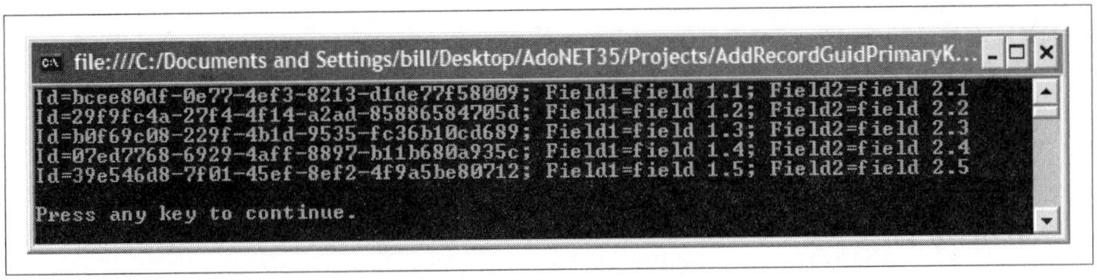

Figure 5-16. Output for AddRecordGuidPrimaryKey solution

The RowChanging event of the DataTable is raised when a DataRow is changing. The action that occurred on the row can be determined by the Action property of the DataRowChangingEventArgs argument of the event handler. The Action property is set to one of the DataRowAction values detailed in Table 5-3.

Table 5-3. DataRowAction enumeration

Value	Description
Add	The row has been added to the table.
Change	The row has been changed.
Commit	The changes made to the row have been committed.
Delete	The row has been deleted from the table.
Nothing	The row has not been changed.
Rollback	The changes made to the row have been rolled back.

The DefaultValue of the GUID primary key column in the DataTable is set to a new GUID using the NewGuid( ) method of the Guid structure when the DataTable is created. This causes a new GUID value to be assigned to the primary key when the first row is added. Because the DefaultValue for the column is calculated once when the property is set rather than as each new row is added, it must be changed after each row is added to the table so that each row has a different GUID primary key value. This is done by handling the RowChanging event for the DataTable. When a row has been added, that is, the Action property of the DataRowChangingEventArgs argument is Add, indicating that a row is being added, the DefaultValue for the primary key column is set to a new GUID.

5.10 Inserting Multiple Rows into a Database Table Using T-SQL Row Constructors

Problem

You need to insert multiple rows into a table in a SQL Server 2008 database using a single T-SQL statement.

Solution

Use T-SQL row constructors.

The solution needs a table named RowConstructor in the AdoDotNet35Cookbook database. Execute the following T-SQL statement to create the table:

```
USE AdoDotNet35Cookbook
GO
CREATE TABLE RowConstructor(
    ID int NOT NULL PRIMARY KEY,
    Field1 nvarchar(50) NULL,
    Field2 nvarchar(50) NULL )
```

The solution creates a T-SQL INSERT statement that inserts three records into the RowConstructor table in the AdoDotNet35Cookbook database. The contents of that table are loaded into a DataTable before and after the insert operation and the contents output to the console.

The C# code in *Program.cs* in the project InsertMultipleRows is shown in Example 5-17.

Example 5-17. File: Program.cs for InsertMultipleRows solution

```csharp
using System;
using System.Data;
using System.Data.SqlClient;

namespace InsertMultipleRows
{
    class Program
    {
        static void Main(string[] args)
        {
            string sqlConnectString = @"Data Source=(local);
                Integrated security=SSPI;Initial Catalog=AdoDotNet35Cookbook;";

            string sqlSelect = "SELECT * FROM RowConstructor";

            string sqlInsert = @"INSERT INTO RowConstructor VALUES
                (1, 'Field1.1', 'Field2.1'),
                (2, 'Field1.2', 'Field2.2'),
                (3, 'Field1.3', 'Field2.3')";

            SqlDataAdapter da = new SqlDataAdapter(sqlSelect, sqlConnectString);
            DataTable dt = new DataTable();
            da.Fill(dt);

            Console.WriteLine("---INITIAL---");
            foreach (DataRow row in dt.Rows)
            {
                Console.WriteLine("ID = {0}\tField1 = {1}\tField2 = {2}",
                    row["ID"], row["Field1"], row["Field2"]);
            }
```

Example 5-17. File: Program.cs for InsertMultipleRows solution (continued)

```
using(SqlConnection connection = new SqlConnection(sqlConnectString))
{
    SqlCommand command = new SqlCommand(sqlInsert, connection);
    connection.Open( );

    int rowsAff = command.ExecuteNonQuery( );
    Console.WriteLine(
        "\n=> Row constructor insert executed. {0} rows affected.",
        rowsAff);
}

dt.Clear( );
da.Fill(dt);
Console.WriteLine("\n---FINAL---");
foreach (DataRow row in dt.Rows)
{
    Console.WriteLine("ID = {0}\tField1 = {1}\tField2 = {2}",
        row["ID"], row["Field1"], row["Field2"]);
}

Console.WriteLine("\nPress any key to continue.");
Console.ReadKey( );
        }
    }
}
```

The output is shown in Figure 5-17.

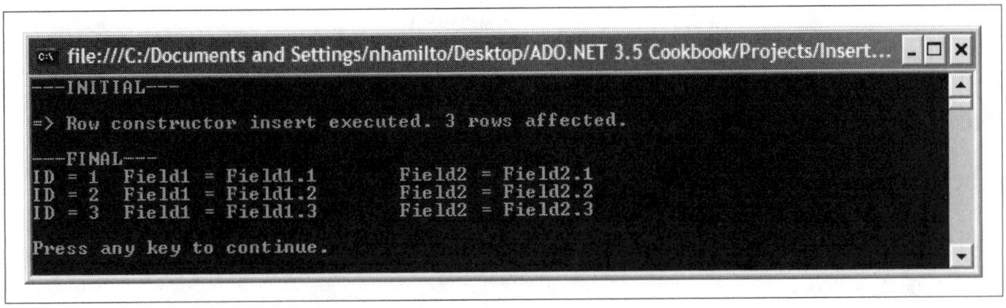

Figure 5-17. Output for InsertMultipleRows solution

Discussion

SQL Server 2008 introduces new capability in the T-SQL INSERT statement that lets you insert multiple rows into a table using a single INSERT statement. Simply delimit each set of values to be inserted using a comma as shown in the T-SQL INSERT statement in the solution:

```
INSERT INTO RowConstructor VALUES
    (1, 'Field1.1', 'Field2.1'),
    (2, 'Field1.2', 'Field2.2'),
    (3, 'Field1.3', 'Field2.3')
```

The values must either be in the same order as the columns in the table and have a value for each column in the table or explicitly specify the columns to store each incoming value.

5.11 Updating a Data Source with Data from a Different Data Source

Problem

You want to update a data source using changes made to another data source for data replication or auditing purposes.

Solution

Use the GetChanges( ) method of the DataSet to identify changes made to a DataSet and replicate these changes into a different data source.

The solution uses a table named UpdateDifferentDataSource in each database—SQL Server source database and SQL Server Express destination database—with the schema shown in Figure 5-18.

	Column Name	Data Type	Allow Nulls
▶⫚	Id	int	☐
	Field1	nvarchar(50)	☑
	Field2	nvarchar(50)	☑
			☐

Figure 5-18. Schema for table UpdateDifferentDataSource

The T-SQL DDL to create the table in each data source is shown in Example 5-18.

Example 5-18. Create table UpdateDifferentDataSource

```
USE AdoDotNet35Cookbook
GO
CREATE TABLE UpdateDifferentDataSource (
    Id int NOT NULL,
    Field1 nvarchar(50) NULL,
    Field2 nvarchar(50) NULL,
  CONSTRAINT PK_UpdateDifferentDataSource PRIMARY KEY CLUSTERED
    ( Id ASC )
)
```

The solution also requires some data in the table UpdateDifferentDataSource in both the SQL Server and SQL Server Express databases. Initially these tables will both contain identical data. The T-SQL to add three initial records to the table UpdateDifferentDataSource is shown in Example 5-19.

Example 5-19. Insert initial records into table UpdateDifferentDataSource

```
USE AdoDotNet35Cookbook
GO
DELETE FROM UpdateDifferentDataSource;
INSERT INTO UpdateDifferentDataSource VALUES (1, 'field 1.1', 'field 2.1');
INSERT INTO UpdateDifferentDataSource VALUES (2, 'field 1.2', 'field 2.2');
INSERT INTO UpdateDifferentDataSource VALUES (3, 'field 1.3', 'field 2.3');
```

The solution creates two DataSet objects each containing a single DataTable. The first table is filled with the source UpdateDifferentDataSources table in a SQL Server database; the second is filled with the destination UpdateDifferentSources table in a SQL Server Express database. A change is made to a record in the source DataTable. A delta DataSet containing only the changes made is created. The SQL Server source database is updated using the DataAdapter. The SQL Server Express database is updated using the delta DataSet.

The C# code in *Program.cs* in the project UpdateDifferentDataSource is shown in Example 5-20.

Example 5-20. File: Program.cs for UpdateDifferentDataSource solution

```csharp
using System;
using System.Data;
using System.Data.SqlClient;

namespace UpdateDifferentDataSource
{
    class Program
    {
        static void Main(string[] args)
        {
            string sqlConnectStringSource = "Data Source=(local);" +
                "Integrated security=SSPI;Initial Catalog=AdoDotNet35Cookbook;";
            string sqlConnectStringDest = @"Data Source=(local)\SQLExpress;" +
                "Integrated security=SSPI;Initial Catalog=AdoDotNet35Cookbook;";

            // Create the DataAdapter for the source records.
            SqlDataAdapter daSource =
                new SqlDataAdapter("SELECT * FROM UpdateDifferentDataSource",
                sqlConnectStringSource);
            SqlCommandBuilder cbSource = new SqlCommandBuilder(daSource);
            DataSet dsSource = new DataSet();
            // Get the data for the source.
            daSource.FillSchema(dsSource, SchemaType.Source);
            daSource.Fill(dsSource);
            Console.WriteLine("Loaded source DataSet.");

            // Create the DataAdapter for the destination records.
            SqlDataAdapter daDest =
                new SqlDataAdapter("SELECT * FROM UpdateDifferentDataSource",
                sqlConnectStringDest);
            SqlCommandBuilder cbDest = new SqlCommandBuilder(daDest);
            DataSet dsDest = new DataSet();
```

Example 5-20. File: Program.cs for UpdateDifferentDataSource solution (continued)

```
                // Get the data for the destination.
                daDest.FillSchema(dsDest, SchemaType.Source);
                daDest.Fill(dsDest);
                Console.WriteLine("Loaded destination DataSet.");

                //Output the destination result set to the console
                Console.WriteLine("\n---INITIAL DESTINATION RESULT SET---");
                foreach (DataRow row in dsDest.Tables[0].Rows)
                    Console.WriteLine("Id = {0}\tField1 = {1}\tField2 = {2}",
                        row["Id"], row["Field1"], row["Field2"]);

                //Update the row where Id = 2
                int updateRowId = 2;
                dsSource.Tables[0].Rows.Find(
                    new object[] { updateRowId }).SetField<string>
                    ("Field1", "Field 1.2 new");
                Console.WriteLine("\nSource row with Id = {0} changed.", updateRowId);

                // Create a DataSet of the added, modified, and deleted records.
                // Note that this is the same as simply using GetChanges()
                // and is meant to illustrate using the GetChanges() overload that
                // accepts row states from the DataRowState enumeration
                DataSet dsDelta = dsSource.GetChanges(DataRowState.Added |
                    DataRowState.Modified | DataRowState.Deleted);

                // Update the source
                daSource.Update(dsSource);
                Console.WriteLine("\nSource data source updated.");

                // Update the destination using the delta DataSet.
                daDest.Update(dsDelta);
                Console.WriteLine("\nDestination data source updated.");

                // Reload the destination DataSet.
                dsDest.Clear();
                daDest.Fill(dsDest);

                //Output the destination result set to the console
                Console.WriteLine("\n---FINAL DESTINATION RESULT SET---");
                foreach (DataRow row in dsDest.Tables[0].Rows)
                    Console.WriteLine("Id = {0}\tField1 = {1}\tField2 = {2}",
                        row["Id"], row["Field1"], row["Field2"]);

                Console.WriteLine("\nPress any key to continue.");
                Console.ReadKey();
            }
        }
    }
```

The output is shown in Figure 5-19.

```
file:///C:/Documents and Settings/bill/Desktop/AdoNET35/Projects/UpdateDifferentDataSou...

Loaded source DataSet.
Loaded destination DataSet.

---INITIAL DESTINATION RESULT SET---
Id = 1   Field1 = field 1.1        Field2 = field 2.1
Id = 2   Field1 = field 1.2        Field2 = field 2.2
Id = 3   Field1 = field 1.3        Field2 = field 2.3

Source row with Id = 2 changed.

Source data source updated.

Destination data source updated.

---FINAL DESTINATION RESULT SET---
Id = 1   Field1 = field 1.1        Field2 = field 2.1
Id = 2   Field1 = field 1.2 new    Field2 = field 2.2
Id = 3   Field1 = field 1.3        Field2 = field 2.3

Press any key to continue.
```

Figure 5-19. Output for UpdateDifferentDataSource solution

Discussion

The ADO.NET DataSet holds data and schema information within its contained objects, but not information about the provider that was used to retrieve the data or the original source of the data. The DataSet tracks changes made to data by maintaining multiple versions of each row, allowing the data to be reconciled later to a data source using a DataAdapter. The data source to which the DataSet is reconciled is usually, but does not have to be, the original data source.

The GetChanges( ) method of the DataSet creates a copy of the DataSet containing all changes that have been made to it since it was last retrieved from the data source or since AcceptChanges( ) was last called.

To replicate the changes made to the first data source into the second data source, the GetChanges( ) method of the first DataSet is called to retrieve a subset of rows that have been added, modified, or deleted. This is the subset returned if the DataRowState filter argument is not specified. Next, the Update( ) method of the destination DataAdapter is called using the DataSet containing the changes as the data object argument; this applies the changes to the destination data source. The destination DataSet is then cleared and reloaded to reflect the applied changes. Finally, the changes are applied to the first data source.

The technique demonstrated in this example relies on the changes made to a DataSet and can therefore be used only to keep a second data source synchronized to a data source that is being modified. This is one-way replication. The destination data source server does not have to be the same as the source database server, so an Oracle table could be synchronized to reflect all changes made to a SQL Server table. In fact, the data sources do not even have to be databases. If the destination data is not identical to the source data or if the destination is updated outside of this synchronizing application, primary key violations will occur if records with the same primary key as the source are inserted into the destination. Concurrency errors will result if records are modified within or deleted from the destination source. You can use application-specific logic to handle the DataAdapter.RowUpdating to resolve these concurrency errors. For more information about the RowUpdating event, see the Discussion section in Recipe 7.7.

The technique demonstrated in this example requires only slight modification to create an audit trail of changes made to a DataSet. Instead of using the update logic generated by the CommandBuilder for the destination DataAdapter, create custom update logic to write the changes made to the source data, along with any other required audit information such as a user ID or the date and time of the change, to the data destination. One or more values from the DataRowState enumeration can be used to filter the changes returned by the GetChanges( ) method to further control the logging.

5.12   Updating a Primary Key Value

Problem

You changed a primary key value in a DataTable and updated the change back to the underlying data source, but the value in the data source remained unchanged. You need to update a primary key value in the data source underlying the DataTable.

Solution

Use the SourceVersion property of SqlParameter to update the primary key value in the data source.

The solution uses a single table named UpdatePrimaryKey with the schema shown in Figure 5-20.

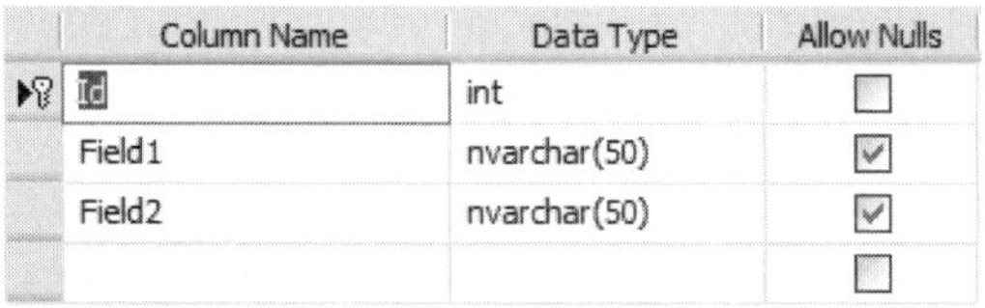

	Column Name	Data Type	Allow Nulls
🔑	Id	int	☐
	Field1	nvarchar(50)	☑
	Field2	nvarchar(50)	☑
			☐

Figure 5-20. Schema for table UpdatePrimaryKey

The T-SQL DDL to create the table is shown in Example 5-21.

Example 5-21. Create table UpdatePrimaryKey

```
USE AdoDotNet35Cookbook
GO
CREATE TABLE UpdatePrimaryKey (
    Id int NOT NULL,
    Field1 nvarchar(50) NULL,
    Field2 nvarchar(50) NULL,
```

Example 5-21. Create table UpdatePrimaryKey (continued)

```
  CONSTRAINT PK_UpdatePrimaryKey PRIMARY KEY CLUSTERED
    ( Id ASC )
)
```

The solution requires some initial data in the UpdatePrimaryKey table. The T-SQL to add three records to the table UpdatePrimaryKey is shown in Example 5-22.

Example 5-22. Insert initial records into table UpdatePrimaryKey

```
USE AdoDotNet35Cookbook
GO
DELETE FROM UpdatePrimaryKey;
INSERT INTO UpdatePrimaryKey VALUES (1, 'field 1.1', 'field 2.1');
INSERT INTO UpdatePrimaryKey VALUES (2, 'field 1.2', 'field 2.2');
INSERT INTO UpdatePrimaryKey VALUES (3, 'field 1.3', 'field 2.3');
```

The solution creates a DataTable containing an integer primary key called Id and two string fields called Field1 and Field2. A DataAdapter is created and the select, delete, insert, and update commands are defined for it. Finally, the DataTable is filled from the UpdatePrimaryKey table using a DataAdapter and its contents are output to the console. The primary key for a record is changed and the data source is update. The DataTable is reloaded to show the result set from the data source with the updated primary key value.

The C# code in *Program.cs* in the project UpdatePrimaryKey is shown in Example 5-23.

Example 5-23. File: Program.cs for UpdatePrimaryKey solution

```
using System;
using System.Data;
using System.Data.SqlClient;

namespace UpdatePrimaryKey
{
    class Program
    {
        static void Main(string[] args)
        {
            string sqlConnectString = "Data Source=(local);" +
                "Integrated security=SSPI;Initial Catalog=AdoDotNet35Cookbook;";

            // Define the table.
            DataTable dtOld = new DataTable( );
            DataColumnCollection cols;
            cols = dtOld.Columns;
            DataColumn col = cols.Add("Id", typeof(int));
            dtOld.PrimaryKey = new DataColumn[] { col };
            cols.Add("Field1", typeof(string)).MaxLength = 50;
            cols.Add("Field2", typeof(string)).MaxLength = 50;
```

Example 5-23. File: Program.cs for UpdatePrimaryKey solution (continued)

```
// Create the DataAdapter and connection.
SqlDataAdapter da = new SqlDataAdapter( );
SqlConnection conn = new SqlConnection(sqlConnectString);

// Build the select command.
string sqlSelect = "SELECT Id, Field1, Field2 FROM UpdatePrimaryKey";
da.SelectCommand = new SqlCommand(sqlSelect, conn);

// Build the delete command.
string sqlDelete = "DELETE FROM UpdatePrimaryKey WHERE Id=@Id";
SqlCommand deleteCommand = new SqlCommand(sqlDelete, conn);
deleteCommand.Parameters.Add("@Id", SqlDbType.Int, 0, "Id");
da.DeleteCommand = deleteCommand;

// Build the insert command.
string sqlInsert = "INSERT UpdatePrimaryKey (Id, Field1, Field2) " +
    "VALUES (@Id, @Field1, @Field2)";
SqlCommand insertCommand = new SqlCommand(sqlInsert, conn);
insertCommand.Parameters.Add("@Id", SqlDbType.Int, 0, "Id");
insertCommand.Parameters.Add("@Field1", SqlDbType.NVarChar, 50,
    "Field1");
insertCommand.Parameters.Add("@Field2", SqlDbType.NVarChar, 50,
    "Field2");
da.InsertCommand = insertCommand;

// Build the update command.
string sqlUpdate = "UPDATE UpdatePrimaryKey SET " +
    "Id=@Id, Field1=@Field1, Field2=@Field2 WHERE Id=@IdOriginal";
SqlCommand updateCommand = new SqlCommand(sqlUpdate, conn);
updateCommand.Parameters.Add("@Id", SqlDbType.Int, 0, "Id");
updateCommand.Parameters.Add("@Field1", SqlDbType.NVarChar, 50,
    "Field1");
updateCommand.Parameters.Add("@Field2", SqlDbType.NVarChar, 50,
    "Field2");
updateCommand.Parameters.Add("@IdOriginal", SqlDbType.Int, 0, "Id");
updateCommand.Parameters["@IdOriginal"].SourceVersion =
    DataRowVersion.Original;
da.UpdateCommand = updateCommand;

// Fill the table from the data source.
da.Fill(dtOld);

Console.WriteLine("---Original DataTable---");
foreach(DataRow row in dtOld.Rows)
    Console.WriteLine("Id = {0}\tField1 = {1}\tField2 = {2}",
        row["Id"], row["Field1"], row["Field2"]);
```

Example 5-23. File: Program.cs for UpdatePrimaryKey solution (continued)

```
        // Update the row with Id = 2
        int oldId = 2;
        int newId = 4;
        Console.WriteLine("\n=> Updating Id in row with Id = {0}", oldId);
        dtOld.Rows.Find(new object[] { oldId })["Id"] = newId;
        Console.WriteLine("=> Id set to {0}", newId);
        da.Update(dtOld);

        // Retrieve and output the updated DataTable
        DataTable dtNew = new DataTable( );
        da.Fill(dtNew);

        Console.WriteLine("\n---Updated DataTable---");
        foreach (DataRow row in dtNew.Rows)
            Console.WriteLine("Id = {0}\tField1 = {1}\tField2 = {2}",
                row["Id"], row["Field1"], row["Field2"]);

        Console.WriteLine("\nPress any key to continue.");
        Console.ReadKey( );
    }
  }
}
```

The output is shown in Figure 5-21.

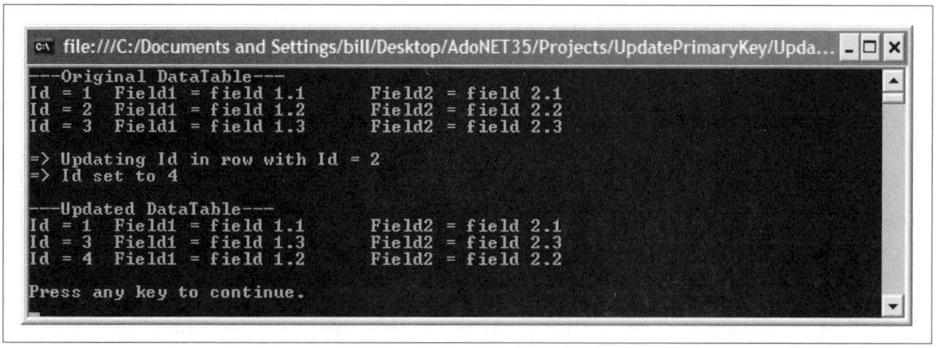

Figure 5-21. Output for UpdatePrimaryKey solution

Discussion

ADO.NET maintains up to three versions of each DataRow in a DataTable: the current, original, and proposed. The current version is accessed by default. All versions can be accessed using an overloaded DataRow indexer (C#) or an overload of the Item( ) property (Visual Basic). Table 5-4 describes the different values of the DataRowVersion enumeration.

Table 5-4. DataRowVersion enumeration

Value	Description
Current	The current values in the row, representing the latest edits. This value is always available.
Default	The default row version. If the row is being edited, this is the Proposed version; otherwise it is the Current version.
Original	The original values for the row. Not available for rows that have been added since data was last retrieved from data source or since AcceptChanges( ) was last called.
Proposed	The proposed values for the row. Only available after BeginEdit( ) is called for the DataRow( ) until EndEdit( ) or CancelEdit( ) is called.

To change the primary key in the table in the database, the UpdateCommand of the DataAdapter needs to locate the row based on the original primary key and update the primary key value with the current value of the primary key, in addition to updating the other row values with their current values. In the sample, this is done using the following SQL update command:

```
string sqlUpdate = "UPDATE UpdatePrimaryKey SET " +
    "Id=@Id, Field1=@Field1, Field2=@Field2 WHERE Id=@IdOriginal";
```

The primary key—Id field—is updated with the current value of the Id field, where the Id field of the row matches the original value of the Id field.

The current value for the Id field is set with the following code:

```
updateCommand.Parameters.Add("@Id", SqlDbType.Int, 0, "Id");
```

The original value for the Id field is set by the following two lines of code in the sample:

```
updateCommand.Parameters.Add("@IdOriginal", SqlDbType.Int, 0, "Id");
updateCommand.Parameters["@IdOriginal"].SourceVersion = DataRowVersion.Original;
```

The second line sets the SourceVersion property of the parameter so that the original value for the Id field is used when setting the value of the @IdOriginal parameter. The UpdateCommand correctly identifies the row in the data source to be updated based on the original value of the Id field and updates that row with the current Id value.

Updating the primary key in a database is not normally necessary. Some RDBMSs do not support updating the primary key. Additionally, if a data relation is based on the primary key, related foreign key fields in the child tables will have to be updated to maintain referential integrity.

5.13   Getting Stored Procedure Parameter Information at Runtime

Problem

You want to get information about the parameters for a stored procedure at runtime.

Solution

Use the DeriveParameters() method of the CommandBuilder class. With Microsoft SQL Server, you can also use system stored procedures, catalog views, and information schema views.

The solution demonstrates each of these techniques. In each case, information about the stored procedure parameters is output to the console.

The C# code in *Program.cs* in the project GetStoredProcedureParameterInformation is shown in Example 5-24.

Example 5-24. File: Program.cs for GetStoredProcedureParameterInformation solution

```
using System;
using System.Data;
using System.Data.SqlClient;

namespace GetStoredProcedureParameterInformation
{
    class Program
    {
        static void Main(string[] args)
        {
            string sqlConnectString = "Data Source=(local);" +
                "Integrated security=SSPI;Initial Catalog=AdventureWorks;";
            SqlDataAdapter da;
            DataTable dt;

            using (SqlConnection connection = new SqlConnection(sqlConnectString))
            {
                // Get parameter information using CommandBuilder
                SqlCommand command =
                    new SqlCommand("uspGetBillOfMaterials", connection);
                command.CommandType = CommandType.StoredProcedure;

                // Get the parameters.
                connection.Open();
                SqlCommandBuilder.DeriveParameters(command);
                connection.Close();

                // Output the results
                Console.WriteLine("---Using CommandBuilder---");
                foreach (SqlParameter param in command.Parameters)
                    Console.WriteLine("ParameterName = {0}\tDirection = {1}" +
                        "\tSqlDbType = {2}",
                        param.ParameterName, param.Direction.ToString(),
                        param.SqlDbType.ToString());
                Console.WriteLine();

                // Get parameter information using sp_sproc_columns
                command = new SqlCommand("sp_sproc_columns", connection);
                command.CommandType = CommandType.StoredProcedure;
```

Example 5-24. File: Program.cs for GetStoredProcedureParameterInformation solution (continued)

```csharp
SqlParameter param1 = command.Parameters.Add("@procedure_name",
    SqlDbType.NVarChar, 390);
param1.Value = "uspGetBillOfMaterials";

// Fill the results table.
da = new SqlDataAdapter(command);
dt = new DataTable();
da.Fill(dt);

// Output the results
Console.WriteLine("---Using sp_proc_columns---");
foreach (DataRow row in dt.Rows)
    Console.WriteLine("ParameterName = {0}\tDirection = {1}" +
        "\tSqlDbType = {2}",
        row["COLUMN_NAME"], row["COLUMN_TYPE"], row["DATA_TYPE"]);
Console.WriteLine();

// Get parameter information using catalog views
string sqlCV = "SELECT sys.schemas.*, sys.parameters.* " +
    "FROM sys.procedures JOIN sys.parameters " +
    "    ON sys.procedures.object_id = sys.parameters.object_id " +
    " JOIN sys.schemas " +
    "    ON sys.procedures.schema_id = sys.schemas.schema_id " +
    "WHERE sys.schemas.name = 'dbo' AND " +
    "    sys.procedures.name = 'uspGetBillOfMaterials'";
command = new SqlCommand(sqlCV, connection);
da = new SqlDataAdapter(command);
dt = new DataTable();
da.Fill(dt);

// Output the results
Console.WriteLine("---Using catalog views---");
foreach (DataRow row in dt.Rows)
    Console.WriteLine("ParameterName = {0}\tis_output = {1}" +
        "\tsystem_type_id = {2}",
        row["name1"], row["is_output"], row["system_type_id"]);
Console.WriteLine();

// Get parameter information using information schema views
string sqlISV = "SELECT * FROM INFORMATION_SCHEMA.PARAMETERS " +
    "WHERE SPECIFIC_SCHEMA = 'dbo' AND " +
    "    SPECIFIC_NAME = 'uspGetBillOfMaterials'";
command = new SqlCommand(sqlISV, connection);
da = new SqlDataAdapter(command);
dt = new DataTable();
da.Fill(dt);

// Output the results
Console.WriteLine("---Using information schema views---");
foreach (DataRow row in dt.Rows)
    Console.WriteLine("ParameterName = {0}\tis_output = {1}" +
        "\tsystem_type_id = {2}",
```

```
                          row["PARAMETER_NAME"], row["PARAMETER_MODE"],
                          row["DATA_TYPE"]);

            }

            Console.WriteLine("\nPress any key to continue.");
            Console.ReadKey( );
        }
    }
}
```

The output is shown in Figure 5-22.

```
file:///C:/Documents and Settings/bill/Desktop/AdoNET35/Projects/4 - GetStoredProcedure...
----Using CommandBuilder----
ParameterName = @RETURN_VALUE    Direction = ReturnValue SqlDbType = Int
ParameterName = @StartProductID Direction = Input       SqlDbType = Int
ParameterName = @CheckDate       Direction = Input       SqlDbType = DateTime

----Using sp_proc_columns----
ParameterName = @RETURN_VALUE    Direction = 5   SqlDbType = 4
ParameterName = @StartProductID Direction = 1   SqlDbType = 4
ParameterName = @CheckDate       Direction = 1   SqlDbType = 11

----Using catalog views----
ParameterName = @StartProductID is_output = False       system_type_id = 56
ParameterName = @CheckDate       is_output = False       system_type_id = 61

----Using information schema views----
ParameterName = @StartProductID is_output = IN  system_type_id = int
ParameterName = @CheckDate       is_output = IN  system_type_id = datetime

Press any key to continue.
```

Figure 5-22. Output for GetStoredProcedureParameterInformation solution

Discussion

This solution demonstrates four techniques to retrieve information about parameters for a stored procedure. These techniques are described in the following subsections.

DeriveParameters( ) method

The first technique uses the static `DeriveParameters( )` method of the `CommandBuilder` object to populate the `Parameters` collection of the `Command` object with the parameter information for the stored procedure specified by the `Command`. Any existing information in the `Parameters` collection is overwritten.

The example demonstrates creating a stored procedure `Command` object. The name of the stored procedure and the `Connection` object are both specified in the `Command` constructor. The `Connection` is opened and the `DeriveParameters( )` method is called to retrieve the information about the parameters for the stored procedure into a `Parameters` collection. The collection is iterated over to extract information about the parameters, which is subsequently displayed.

If the stored procedure specified does not exist, an `InvalidOperationException` is raised.

The `DeriveParameters()` method incurs a performance penalty because it requires an extra round trip between the application and the data server to retrieve parameter metadata. It is more efficient to populate the parameters collection explicitly if the parameter information is known. As a result, the `DeriveParameters()` method is not recommended for use in production environments. The method exists primarily for design-time or ad hoc use.

Microsoft SQL Server System stored procedure: sp_sproc_columns

The second technique is specific to Microsoft SQL Server. The system stored procedure `sp_sproc_columns` returns parameter information for one or more stored procedures. Unlike the `DeriveParameters()` method, you cannot use it to automatically populate a `Parameters` collection with parameter information. It does, however, return more information than the `DeriveParameters()` method, and you can use it to return results for more than one stored procedure at a time. It also supports filtering options and does not require a stored procedure `Command` object. Executing this procedure returns a result set in which the rows correspond to stored procedure columns. For more information about the parameter information returned, see SQL Server Books Online.

The example demonstrates retrieving information about parameters for only a single stored procedure by specifying the name of the stored procedure in the `@procedure_name` parameter. See SQL Server Books Online for other parameters that you can use to filter the information returned.

Catalog views

The `sys.parameters` catalog view returns a row for each parameter in a database object that accepts parameters. That view is joined to the `sys.procedures` catalog view, which returns a row for each procedure (`sys.objects.type` = `P`, `X`, `RF`, and `PC`) on the `object_id` field. The `sys.procedures` catalog view is used to filter the parameters retrieved to those for a specific procedure. The `sys.parameters` catalog view is joined to the `sys.schemas` catalog view to specify the schema for the stored procedure. The query that retrieves stored procedure parameter information for the stored procedure `dbo.uspGetBillOfMaterials` using catalog views is:

```
SELECT sys.schemas.*, sys.parameters.*
FROM sys.procedures JOIN sys.parameters
    ON sys.procedures.object_id = sys.parameters.object_id
JOIN sys.schemas
    ON sys.procedures.schema_id = sys.schemas.schema_id
WHERE sys.schemas.name = 'dbo' AND
    sys.procedures.name = 'uspGetBillOfMaterials'
```

For more information about catalog views, see the discussion in Recipe 11.3.

Information schema views

The `INFORMATION_SCHEMA.PARAMETERS` information schema view returns a row for each user-defined function or stored procedure that can be accessed by the user in the current database. A row is also returned for function return values. Here is the query that retrieves stored procedure parameter information for the stored procedure `dbo.uspGetBillOfMaterials` using information schema views:

```
SELECT *
FROM INFORMATION_SCHEMA.PARAMETERS
WHERE SPECIFIC_SCHEMA = 'dbo' AND
    SPECIFIC_NAME = 'uspGetBillOfMaterials'
```

For more information about information schema views, see the discussion in Recipe 11.3.

5.14   Updating a DataSet with a Many-to-Many Relationship

Problem

You have a `DataSet` that contains two tables that have a many-to-many relationship between them using a third junction table. You get referential integrity errors when you try to update changes to the data in this `DataSet` back to the data source.

Solution

Use the techniques described in the discussion.

The solution uses three tables: `ParentUpdateManyMany`, `JunctionUpdateManyMany`, and `ChildUpdateManyMany` shown in Figures 5-23, 5-24, and 5-25.

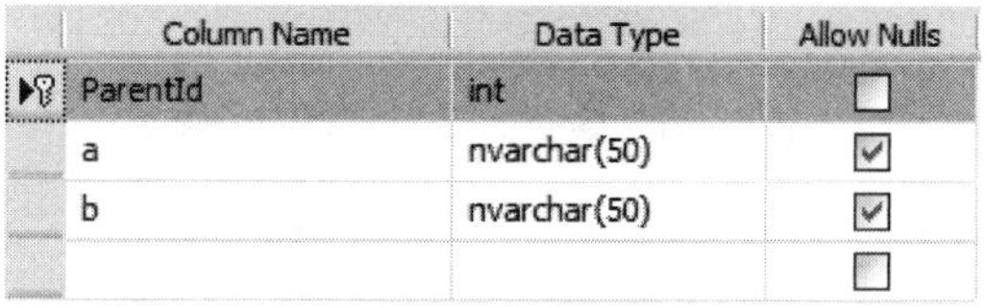

	Column Name	Data Type	Allow Nulls
▶🔑	ParentId	int	☐
	a	nvarchar(50)	☑
	b	nvarchar(50)	☑
			☐

Figure 5-23. Schema for table ParentUpdateManyMany

	Column Name	Data Type	Allow Nulls
▶🔑	ParentId	int	☐
🔑	ChildId	int	☐
			☐

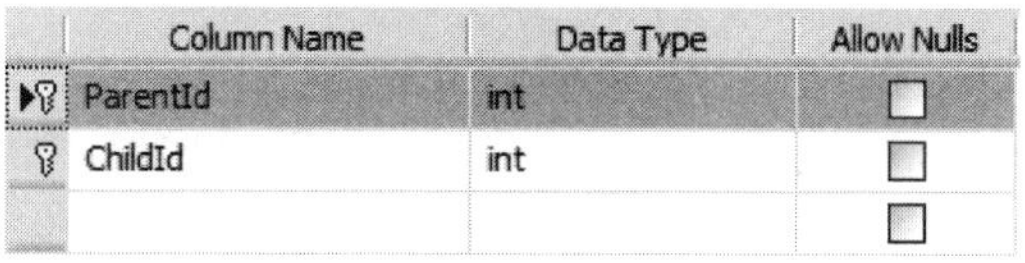

Figure 5-24. Schema for table JunctionUpdateManyMany

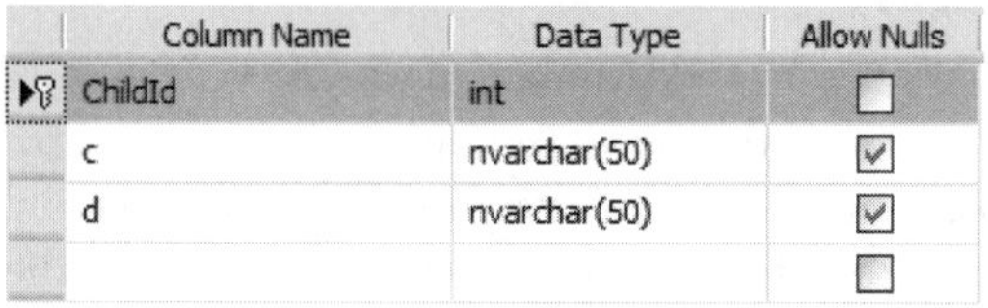

Column Name	Data Type	Allow Nulls
ChildId	int	☐
c	nvarchar(50)	☑
d	nvarchar(50)	☑
		☐

Figure 5-25. Schema for table ChildUpdateManyMany

The T-SQL to create the three tables is shown in Example 5-25.

Example 5-25. Create tables

```
USE AdoDotNet35Cookbook
GO

CREATE TABLE ParentUpdateManyMany(
    ParentId int IDENTITY(1,1) NOT NULL PRIMARY KEY,
    a nvarchar(50),
    b nvarchar(50)
)
GO

CREATE TABLE JunctionUpdateManyMany(
    ParentId int NOT NULL,
    ChildId int NOT NULL,
  CONSTRAINT PK_JunctionUpdateManyMany PRIMARY KEY (ParentId, ChildId)
)
GO

CREATE TABLE ChildUpdateManyMany(
    ChildId int IDENTITY(1,1) NOT NULL PRIMARY KEY,
    c nvarchar(50),
    d nvarchar(50)
)
GO

ALTER TABLE JunctionUpdateManyMany  WITH CHECK
  ADD  CONSTRAINT FK_JunctionUpdateManyMany_ChildUpdateManyMany
  FOREIGN KEY(ChildId)
  REFERENCES ChildUpdateManyMany (ChildId)
GO

ALTER TABLE JunctionUpdateManyMany  WITH CHECK
  ADD  CONSTRAINT FK_JunctionUpdateManyMany_ParentUpdateManyMany
  FOREIGN KEY(ParentId)
  REFERENCES ParentUpdateManyMany (ParentId)
```

The solution uses 11 stored procedures, as described in Table 5-5.

Table 5-5. Stored procedures for solution in Example 5-25

Name	Description
InsertParentUpdateManyMany	Adds a new parent record. The stored procedure returns the ParentId value generated by the data source as both an output parameter and in the first returned record.
GetParentUpdateManyMany	Gets the parent record corresponding to the ParentId specified or returns all parent records if no ParentId is specified.
UpdateParentUpdateManyMany	Updates the parent record matching the specified ParentId.
DeleteParentUpdateManyMany	Deletes the parent record specified by the ParentId input parameter.
InsertChildUpdateManyMany	Adds a new child record. The stored procedure returns the ChildId value generated by the data source as both an output parameter and in the first returned record.
GetChildUpdateManyMany	Gets the child record corresponding to the ChildId specified or returns all child records if no ChildId is specified.
UpdateChildUpdateManyMany	Updates the child record matching the specified ChildId.
DeleteChildUpdateManyMany	Deletes the child record specified by the ChildId input parameter.
InsertJunctionUpdateManyMany	Adds a new junction record.
GetJunctionUpdateManyMany	Gets the junction records corresponding to the ParentId specified or returns all junction records if no ParentId is specified.
DeleteJunctionUpdateManyMany	Deletes the junction record specified by the ParentId and ChildId input parameters.

The T-SQL to create the stored procedures that insert, retrieve, update, and delete records of the ParentUpdateManyMany table is shown in Example 5-26.

Example 5-26. T-SQL to create stored procedures for ParentUpdateManyMany table

```
USE AdoDotNet35Cookbook
GO

CREATE PROCEDURE InsertParentUpdateManyMany
    @ParentId int OUTPUT,
    @a nvarchar(50)=NULL,
    @b nvarchar(50)=NULL
AS
    SET NOCOUNT ON

    INSERT ParentUpdateManyMany(a, b)
    VALUES (@a, @b)

    IF @@ROWCOUNT=0
        RETURN 1
```

```
    SET @ParentId=SCOPE_IDENTITY( )
    SELECT @ParentId ParentId
    RETURN 0
GO


CREATE PROCEDURE GetParentUpdateManyMany
    @ParentId int=null
AS
    SET NOCOUNT ON

    IF @ParentId IS NOT NULL
    BEGIN
        SELECT ParentId, a, b
        FROM ParentUpdateManyMany
        WHERE ParentId=@ParentId

        RETURN 0
    END

    SELECT ParentId, a, b
    FROM ParentUpdateManyMany

    RETURN 0
GO


CREATE PROCEDURE UpdateParentUpdateManyMany
    @ParentId int,
    @a nvarchar(50)=NULL,
    @b nvarchar(50)=NULL
AS
    SET NOCOUNT ON

    UPDATE ParentUpdateManyMany
    SET a=@a, b=@b
    WHERE ParentId=@ParentId

    IF @@ROWCOUNT=0
        RETURN 1

    RETURN 0
GO


CREATE PROCEDURE DeleteParentUpdateManyMany
    @ParentId int
AS
    SET NOCOUNT ON

    DELETE FROM ParentUpdateManyMany
    WHERE ParentId=@ParentId

    RETURN 0
```

The T-SQL to create the stored procedures that insert, retrieve, update, and delete records of the ChildUpdateManyMany table is shown in Example 5-27.

Example 5-27. T-SQL to create stored procedures for ChildUpdateManyMany table

```
USE AdoDotNet35Cookbook
GO

CREATE PROCEDURE InsertChildUpdateManyMany
    @ChildId int OUTPUT,
    @c nvarchar(50)=NULL,
    @d nvarchar(50)=NULL
AS
    SET NOCOUNT ON

    INSERT ChildUpdateManyMany(c, d)
    VALUES (@c, @d)

    IF @@ROWCOUNT=0
        RETURN 1

    SET @ChildId=SCOPE_IDENTITY( )
    SELECT @ChildId ChildId
    RETURN 0
GO

CREATE PROCEDURE GetChildUpdateManyMany
    @ChildId int=NULL
AS
    SET NOCOUNT ON

    IF @ChildId IS NOT NULL
    BEGIN
        SELECT
            ChildID, c, d
        FROM
            ChildUpdateManyMany
        WHERE
            ChildId=@ChildId

        RETURN 0
    END

    SELECT ChildId, c, d
    FROM ChildUpdateManyMany

    RETURN 0
GO

CREATE PROCEDURE UpdateChildUpdateManyMany
    @ChildId int,
    @c nvarchar(50)=NULL,
    @d nvarchar(50)=NULL
```

```
AS
    SET NOCOUNT ON

    UPDATE ChildUpdateManyMany
    SET c=@c, d=@d
    WHERE ChildId=@ChildId

    IF @@ROWCOUNT=0
        RETURN 1

    RETURN 0
GO

CREATE PROCEDURE DeleteChildUpdateManyMany
    @ChildId int
AS
    SET NOCOUNT ON

    DELETE FROM ChildUpdateManyMany
    WHERE ChildId=@ChildId

    RETURN 0
```

The T-SQL to create the stored procedures that insert, retrieve, and delete records of the JunctionUpdateManyMany table is shown in Example 5-28.

Example 5-28. T-SQL to create stored procedures for JunctionUpdateManyMany table

```
USE AdoDotNet35Cookbook
GO

CREATE PROCEDURE InsertJunctionUpdateManyMany
    @ParentId int,
    @ChildId int
AS
    SET NOCOUNT ON

    INSERT JunctionUpdateManyMany(ParentId, ChildId)
    VALUES (@ParentId, @ChildId)

    IF @@ROWCOUNT=0
        RETURN 1

    RETURN 0
GO

CREATE PROCEDURE GetJunctionUpdateManyMany
    @ParentId int=NULL
```

```
AS
    IF @ParentId IS NOT NULL
    BEGIN
        SELECT ParentId, ChildID
        FROM JunctionUpdateManyMany
        WHERE ParentId=@ParentId

        RETURN 0
    END

    SELECT ParentId, ChildID
    FROM JunctionUpdateManyMany

    RETURN 0
GO

CREATE PROCEDURE DeleteJunctionUpdateManyMany
    @ParentId int,
    @ChildId int
AS
    SET NOCOUNT ON

    DELETE FROM JunctionUpdateManyMany
    WHERE
        ParentId=@ParentId AND
        ChildId=@ChildId

    RETURN 0
```

The solution creates a DataSet and loads the schemas for the parent, junction, and child tables. The AutoIncrementSeed and AutoIncrementStep properties of the parent and child primary key columns (ParentID and ChildID) are both set to -1. DataRelation objects are created relating parent and child tables through the junction table.

A DataAdapter is created for each of the parent, child, and junction tables. The select, insert, update, and delete commands are set to the appropriate stored procedure described earlier in this solution.

The DataSet is loaded from the data source. All of the data in the DataSet is deleted and updated back to the data source. Next, related example data is created in parent and child tables and updated back to the data source. Finally, this data is randomly modified and again updated back to the data source. The contents of the DataSet are output to the console at each stage.

The solution uses five methods:

CreateData( )

> Creates random data in both the parent and child tables and randomly creates relationships between them by adding records to the junction table.

ModifyData( )

> Makes random changes to the data in the DataSet:
>
> - Rows from the parent and child table are deleted or have values in their fields modified.
> - Parent/child relationships are eliminated by deleting records from the junction table.
> - The CreateData( ) method is called to create new data.

DeleteData( )

> Deletes all data from the parent, child, and junction tables.

UpdateData( )

> Updates all changes in the DataSet to the data source by calling the Update( ) methods of the DataAdapter object for subsets of the data in each of the parent, child, and junction tables in the correct order.

OutputData( )

> Outputs all data from the parent, child, and junction table to the console.

The C# code in *Program.cs* in the project UpdateManyManyRelationship is shown in Example 5-29.

Example 5-29. File: Program.cs for UpdateManyManyRelationship solution

```
using System;
using System.Data;
using System.Data.SqlClient;

namespace UpdateManyManyRelationship
{
    class Program
    {
        static void Main(string[] args)
        {
            string sqlConnectString = "Data Source=(local);" +
                "Integrated security=SSPI;Initial Catalog=AdoDotNet35Cookbook;";

            string sqlSelect = "SELECT * FROM ParentUpdateManyMany;" +
                "SELECT * FROM JunctionUpdateManyMany;" +
                "SELECT * FROM ChildUpdateManyMany;";

            // Fill the DataSet schema
            DataSet ds = new DataSet();
            SqlDataAdapter da = new SqlDataAdapter(sqlSelect, sqlConnectString);
            da.TableMappings.Add("Table", "Parent");
            da.TableMappings.Add("Table1", "Junction");
```

Example 5-29. File: Program.cs for UpdateManyManyRelationship solution (continued)

```
da.TableMappings.Add("Table2", "Child");
da.FillSchema(ds, SchemaType.Mapped);
// Set the parent and child autoincrement seeds and steps
ds.Tables["Parent"].Columns["ParentID"].AutoIncrementSeed = -1;
ds.Tables["Parent"].Columns["ParentID"].AutoIncrementStep = -1;
ds.Tables["Child"].Columns["ChildID"].AutoIncrementSeed = -1;
ds.Tables["Child"].Columns["ChildID"].AutoIncrementStep = -1;
// Add relations
ds.Relations.Add(new DataRelation("Parent_Junction",
    ds.Tables["Parent"].Columns["ParentId"],
    ds.Tables["Junction"].Columns["ParentId"], true));
ds.Relations.Add(new DataRelation("Child_Junction",
    ds.Tables["Child"].Columns["ChildId"],
    ds.Tables["Junction"].Columns["ChildId"], true));

// Create the parent DataAdapter
SqlDataAdapter daParent =
    new SqlDataAdapter("GetParentUpdateManyMany", sqlConnectString);
daParent.SelectCommand.CommandType = CommandType.StoredProcedure;

// Build the parent delete command.
SqlCommand deleteCommand = new SqlCommand("DeleteParentUpdateManyMany",
    daParent.SelectCommand.Connection);
deleteCommand.CommandType = CommandType.StoredProcedure;
deleteCommand.Parameters.Add("@ParentId", SqlDbType.Int, 0,
    "ParentId");
daParent.DeleteCommand = deleteCommand;

// Build the parent insert command.
SqlCommand insertCommand = new SqlCommand("InsertParentUpdateManyMany",
    daParent.SelectCommand.Connection);
insertCommand.CommandType = CommandType.StoredProcedure;
insertCommand.Parameters.Add("@ParentId", SqlDbType.Int, 0,
    "ParentId");
insertCommand.Parameters.Add("@a", SqlDbType.NVarChar, 50, "a");
insertCommand.Parameters.Add("@b", SqlDbType.NVarChar, 50, "b");
daParent.InsertCommand = insertCommand;

// Build the parent update command.
SqlCommand updateCommand = new SqlCommand("UpdateParentUpdateManyMany",
    daParent.SelectCommand.Connection);
updateCommand.CommandType = CommandType.StoredProcedure;
updateCommand.Parameters.Add("@ParentId", SqlDbType.Int, 0,
    "ParentId");
updateCommand.Parameters.Add("@a", SqlDbType.NVarChar, 50, "a");
updateCommand.Parameters.Add("@b", SqlDbType.NVarChar, 50, "b");
daParent.UpdateCommand = updateCommand;

// Create the child DataAdapter.
SqlDataAdapter daChild = new SqlDataAdapter("GetChildUpdateManyMany",
    sqlConnectString);
daChild.SelectCommand.CommandType = CommandType.StoredProcedure;
```

Example 5-29. File: Program.cs for UpdateManyManyRelationship solution (continued)

```csharp
// Build the child delete command.
deleteCommand = new SqlCommand("DeleteChildUpdateManyMany",
    daChild.SelectCommand.Connection);
deleteCommand.CommandType = CommandType.StoredProcedure;
deleteCommand.Parameters.Add("@ChildId", SqlDbType.Int, 0,
    "ChildId");
daChild.DeleteCommand = deleteCommand;

// Build the child insert command.
insertCommand = new SqlCommand("InsertChildUpdateManyMany",
    daChild.SelectCommand.Connection);
insertCommand.CommandType = CommandType.StoredProcedure;
insertCommand.Parameters.Add("@ChildId", SqlDbType.Int, 0,
    "ChildId");
insertCommand.Parameters.Add("@c", SqlDbType.NVarChar, 50,
    "c");
insertCommand.Parameters.Add("@d", SqlDbType.NVarChar, 50,
    "d");
daChild.InsertCommand = insertCommand;

// Build the child update command.
updateCommand = new SqlCommand("UpdateChildUpdateManyMany",
    daChild.SelectCommand.Connection);
updateCommand.CommandType = CommandType.StoredProcedure;
updateCommand.Parameters.Add("@ChildId", SqlDbType.Int, 0,
    "ChildId");
updateCommand.Parameters.Add("@c", SqlDbType.NVarChar, 50,
    "c");
updateCommand.Parameters.Add("@d", SqlDbType.NVarChar, 50,
    "d");
daChild.UpdateCommand = updateCommand;

// Create the junction DataAdapter.
SqlDataAdapter daJunction =
    new SqlDataAdapter("GetJunctionUpdateManyMany", sqlConnectString);
daJunction.SelectCommand.CommandType = CommandType.StoredProcedure;

// Build the junction delete command.
deleteCommand = new SqlCommand("DeleteJunctionUpdateManyMany",
    daJunction.SelectCommand.Connection);
deleteCommand.CommandType = CommandType.StoredProcedure;
deleteCommand.Parameters.Add("@ParentId", SqlDbType.Int, 0,
    "ParentId");
deleteCommand.Parameters.Add("@ChildId", SqlDbType.Int, 0,
    "ChildId");
daJunction.DeleteCommand = deleteCommand;

// Build the junction insert command.
insertCommand = new SqlCommand("InsertJunctionUpdateManyMany",
    daJunction.SelectCommand.Connection);
insertCommand.CommandType = CommandType.StoredProcedure;
insertCommand.Parameters.Add("@ParentId", SqlDbType.Int, 0,
    "ParentId");
```

```
    insertCommand.Parameters.Add("@ChildId", SqlDbType.Int, 0,
        "ChildId");
    daJunction.InsertCommand = insertCommand;

    // Fill the DataSet.
    daParent.Fill(ds, "Parent");
    daChild.Fill(ds, "Child");
    daJunction.Fill(ds, "Junction");

    // Delete all data, update the source, and output to console
    DeleteData(ds);
    UpdateData(ds, daParent, daJunction, daChild);
    Console.WriteLine("=> Data cleared.");
    OutputData(ds);

    // Create some data, update the source, and output to console
    CreateData(ds, 4, 4);
    UpdateData(ds, daParent, daJunction, daChild);
    Console.WriteLine("\n=> Data created.");
    OutputData(ds);

    // Modify some data, update the source, and output to console
    ModifyData(ds);
    UpdateData(ds, daParent, daJunction, daChild);
    Console.WriteLine("\n=> Data modified.");
    OutputData(ds);

    Console.WriteLine("\nPress any key to continue.");
    Console.ReadKey();
}

private static void CreateData(DataSet ds, int parentRows, int childRows)
{
    // Create some data update the data source with it.
    for (int iParent = 0; iParent < parentRows; iParent++)
    {
        DataRow parentRow = ds.Tables["Parent"].NewRow();
        parentRow["a"] = Guid.NewGuid().ToString();
        parentRow["b"] = Guid.NewGuid().ToString();
        ds.Tables["Parent"].Rows.Add(parentRow);
    }

    for (int iChild = 0; iChild < childRows; iChild++)
    {
        DataRow childRow = ds.Tables["Child"].NewRow();
        childRow["c"] = Guid.NewGuid().ToString();
        childRow["d"] = Guid.NewGuid().ToString();
        ds.Tables["Child"].Rows.Add(childRow);
    }

    // Randomly create the parent-child relationships.
    Random r = new Random((int)DateTime.Now.Ticks);
```

Example 5-29. File: Program.cs for UpdateManyManyRelationship solution (continued)

```
        foreach (DataRow rowParent in ds.Tables["Parent"].Rows)
        {
            if (rowParent.RowState != DataRowState.Deleted)
            {
                foreach (DataRow rowChild in
                    ds.Tables["Child"].Rows)
                {
                    if (rowChild.RowState != DataRowState.Deleted &&
                        r.Next(2) == 1)
                    {
                        // Check to see that row doesn't exist
                        // before adding.
                        if (ds.Tables["Junction"].Rows.Find(new object[]
                                {rowParent["ParentId"],
                                rowChild["ChildId"]}) == null)
                        {
                            ds.Tables["Junction"].Rows.Add(new object[]
                                    {rowParent["ParentId"],
                                    rowChild["ChildId"]});
                        }
                    }
                }
            }
        }
    }

    private static void ModifyData(DataSet ds)
    {
        Random r = new Random((int)DateTime.Now.Ticks);

        // Randomly leave, delete, or modify rows from the child and parent rows.
        for (int i = ds.Tables["Child"].Rows.Count; i > 0; i--)
        {
            DataRow childRow = ds.Tables["Child"].Rows[i - 1];

            switch (r.Next(3))
            {
                case 0:     // do nothing
                    break;
                case 1:     // modify
                    childRow["c"] = Guid.NewGuid().ToString();
                    childRow["d"] = Guid.NewGuid().ToString();
                    break;
                case 2:     // delete
                    childRow.Delete();
                    break;
            }
        }
```

Example 5-29. File: Program.cs for UpdateManyManyRelationship solution (continued)

```
    for (int i = ds.Tables["Parent"].Rows.Count; i > 0; i--)
    {
        DataRow parentRow = ds.Tables["Parent"].Rows[i - 1];

        switch (r.Next(3))
        {
            case 0:     // do nothing
                break;
            case 1:     // modify
                parentRow["a"] = Guid.NewGuid( ).ToString( );
                parentRow["b"] = Guid.NewGuid( ).ToString( );
                break;
            case 2:
                parentRow.Delete( );
                break;
        }
    }

    // Randomly delete m-n parent/child relationships.
    for (int i = ds.Tables["Junction"].Rows.Count; i > 0; i--)
    {
        DataRow parentChildRow = ds.Tables["Junction"].Rows[i - 1];

        if (r.Next(2) == 0)      // 0 = delete, 1 = do nothing
            parentChildRow.Delete( );
    }

    // Insert random 1 to 3 rows into Parent, Child, and random ParentChild.
    CreateData(ds, r.Next(1, 3), r.Next(1, 3));
}

private static void DeleteData(DataSet ds)
{
    ds.Tables["Junction"].Clear( );
    ds.Tables["Parent"].Clear( );
    ds.Tables["Child"].Clear( );
}

private static void UpdateData(DataSet ds, SqlDataAdapter daParent,
    SqlDataAdapter daJunction, SqlDataAdapter daChild)
{
    daJunction.Update(ds.Tables["Junction"].Select(
        null, null, DataViewRowState.Deleted));
    daChild.Update(ds.Tables["Child"].Select(
        null, null, DataViewRowState.Deleted));
    daParent.Update(ds.Tables["Parent"].Select(
        null, null, DataViewRowState.Deleted));
    daParent.Update(ds.Tables["Parent"].Select(
        null, null, DataViewRowState.ModifiedCurrent));
    daParent.Update(ds.Tables["Parent"].Select(
        null, null, DataViewRowState.Added));
```

```
        daChild.Update(ds.Tables["Child"].Select(
            null, null, DataViewRowState.ModifiedCurrent));
        daChild.Update(ds.Tables["Child"].Select(
            null, null, DataViewRowState.Added));
        daJunction.Update(ds.Tables["Junction"].Select(
            null, null, DataViewRowState.Added));
    }

    private static void OutputData(DataSet ds)
    {
        // Output data for the parent, junction, and child tables
        Console.WriteLine("\n---DATASET---");
        Console.WriteLine("---Parent table---");
        foreach (DataRow row in ds.Tables["Parent"].Rows)
            Console.WriteLine("ParentId = {0}\ta = {1}\tb={2}",
                row["ParentId"], row["a"].ToString( ).Substring(0, 13),
                row["b"].ToString( ).Substring(0, 13));

        Console.WriteLine("\n---Junction table---");
        foreach (DataRow row in ds.Tables["Junction"].Rows)
            Console.WriteLine("ParentId = {0}\tChildId = {1}",
                row["ParentId"], row["ChildId"]);

        Console.WriteLine("\n---Child table---");
        foreach (DataRow row in ds.Tables["Child"].Rows)
            Console.WriteLine("ChildId = {0}\tc = {1}\td={2}",
                row["ChildId"], row["c"].ToString( ).Substring(0, 13),
                row["d"].ToString( ).Substring(0, 13));
    }
}
}
```

The output is shown in Figure 5-26.

Discussion

To avoid referential integrity problems when updating a data source with changes in a DataSet having tables related with a many-to-many relationship (through a junction table), update the rows in the following order:

1. Deleted junction rows
2. Deleted child rows
3. Deleted parent rows
4. Updated parent rows
5. Inserted parent rows
6. Updated child rows
7. Inserted child rows
8. Inserted junction rows

```
=> Data cleared.

---DATASET---
---Parent table---

---Junction table---

---Child table---
=> Data created.

---DATASET---
---Parent table---
ParentId = 124    a = 8b3dbda1-cf7e        b=10e0e6a8-eb44
ParentId = 125    a = 023a1dec-18a4        b=30037956-a043
ParentId = 126    a = cac534c4-c2d2        b=119767fc-b26a
ParentId = 127    a = 05a2cce0-bf7f        b=9b6843b3-8dd7

---Junction table---
ParentId = 124    ChildId = 108
ParentId = 125    ChildId = 107
ParentId = 125    ChildId = 108
ParentId = 126    ChildId = 107
ParentId = 127    ChildId = 105
ParentId = 127    ChildId = 106

---Child table---
ChildId = 105     c = d5615eb5-5b18        d=2b15a452-cc7a
ChildId = 106     c = 775133b1-4169        d=ee896ed9-d600
ChildId = 107     c = c15b70dd-c2db        d=82819b1d-2972
ChildId = 108     c = 8dde27cc-3387        d=cf23c60c-e8e5
=> Data modified.

---DATASET---
---Parent table---
ParentId = 124    a = 8b3dbda1-cf7e        b=10e0e6a8-eb44
ParentId = 125    a = 45316afd-90a5        b=0bae3d29-4773
ParentId = 127    a = 016c3060-9a87        b=06f3b15f-327f
ParentId = 128    a = a3a161b5-4359        b=acabad24-b3d6

---Junction table---
ParentId = 125    ChildId = 107
ParentId = 124    ChildId = 108
ParentId = 124    ChildId = 109
ParentId = 125    ChildId = 105
ParentId = 127    ChildId = 105
ParentId = 127    ChildId = 108
ParentId = 128    ChildId = 105

---Child table---
ChildId = 105     c = 22cfc34d-ee07        d=5987f22b-6ae2
ChildId = 107     c = c15b70dd-c2db        d=82819b1d-2972
ChildId = 108     c = 8dde27cc-3387        d=cf23c60c-e8e5
ChildId = 109     c = db53c1e8-a8bc        d=fa2c9ee0-9d7f

Press any key to continue.
```

Figure 5-26. Output for UpdateManyManyRelationship solution

The following code accomplishes this within the solution:

```
daJunction.Update(ds.Tables["Junction"].Select(null, null,
    DataViewRowState.Deleted));
daChild.Update(ds.Tables["Child"].Select(null, null, DataViewRowState.Deleted));
daParent.Update(ds.Tables["Parent"].Select(null, null, DataViewRowState.Deleted));
daParent.Update(ds.Tables["Parent"].Select(null, null,
    DataViewRowState.ModifiedCurrent));
daParent.Update(ds.Tables["Parent"].Select(null, null, DataViewRowState.Added));
daChild.Update(ds.Tables["Child"].Select(null, null,
    DataViewRowState.ModifiedCurrent));
daChild.Update(ds.Tables["Child"].Select(null, null, DataViewRowState.Added));
daJunction.Update(ds.Tables["Junction"].Select(null, null, DataViewRowState.Added));
```

Pass DataViewRowState.Deleted into the Select( ) method of the DataTable object to get the subset of deleted rows from a table. Similarly, pass DataViewRowState.Added to obtain inserted rows and DataViewRowState.ModifiedCurrent to obtain modified rows.

There are three related tables—parent, child, and junction—and one DataAdapter for each table. An overload of the Select( ) method of the DataTable is used to retrieve the subset of rows identified by the state argument containing a value from the DataViewRowState enumeration:

Added
> To get the subset of inserted rows

Deleted
> To get the subset of deleted rows

ModifiedCurrent
> To get the subset of modified rows

A few more considerations involving the primary key:

- If the primary key cannot be modified once it's added, the updated and inserted rows can be processed in the same statement. Pass a bitwise combination into the select method as shown here:

```
daParent.Update(ds.Tables["Parent"].Select(null, null,
    DataViewRowState.Added | DataViewRowState.ModifiedCurrent));
```

- If the primary key can be modified, the database must cascade the updated primary key values to the child records; otherwise, a referential integrity violation will occur. If the foreign key is used as part of the concurrency handling process, the UpdateCommand property of child tables must accept either its Original or the Current value.

- If the primary key is an AutoIncrement value and its value is generated by the database, the InsertCommand must return the primary key value from the data source and use it to update the value in the DataSet. The DataSet will then automatically cascade this new value to the child records.

5.15 Updating Data Asynchronously Using Message Queuing

Problem

You need to asynchronously update data in a database on a system that is not always connected.

Solution

Use message queuing and a XML DiffGrams to:

- Construct and send an MSMQ message containing a DiffGram to the server.
- Extract the DiffGram from the message and use it to update the data source at the server.
- Construct and send a message containing the latest DataSet to the client.
- Retrieve the response at the client and deserialize it into a DataSet.

The solution performs the following steps:

- Creates three message queues, if they do not already exist—one each for the query command (AdoNet35Cookbook_queueNameUpdateQuery), the query results (AdoNet35Cookbook_queueNameUpdateResult), and the update command (AdoNet35Cookbook_AsynchronousUpdateCommand). In this example, the query and update commands are issued from the same computer that processes the query and update—in a real situation, these tasks would be processed on different computers that might not always be connected.
- Creates a query message and sends it to the query command queue.
- Gets and deserializes the query message from the query command queue, creates and executes the query, and sends the result set to the result queue.
- Gets the result set from the result queue and creates the result DataSet by deserializing the message body.
- Outputs the result set in the DataSet to the console.
- Updates the row in the first (only) DataSet table with Id = 2.
- Creates a DiffGram containing the changes made to the DataSet and sends it to the update command queue.
- Gets and deserializes the update message from the update command queue and applies the updates to the data source using a DataAdapter together with the DiffGram containing the changes.

The solution uses one table named AsynchronousUpdateMSMQ with the schema shown in Figure 5-27.

Column Name	Data Type	Allow Nulls
Id	int	☐
Field1	nvarchar(50)	☑
Field2	nvarchar(50)	☑
		☐

Figure 5-27. Schema for table AsynchronousUpdateMSMQ

The T-SQL to create the table AsynchronousUpdateMSMQ is shown in Example 5-30.

Example 5-30. Create table AsynchronousUpdateMSMQ

```
USE AdoDotNet35Cookbook
GO
CREATE TABLE AsynchronousUpdateMSMQ (
    Id int NOT NULL,
    Field1 nvarchar(50) NULL,
    Field2 nvarchar(50) NULL,
  CONSTRAINT PK_AsynchronousUpdateMSMQ PRIMARY KEY CLUSTERED
    ( Id ASC )
)
```

The T-SQL to add the initial records to the table AsynchronousUpdateMSMQ is shown in Example 5-31.

Example 5-31. Insert initial records into table AsnchronousUpdateMSMQ

```
USE AdoDotNet35Cookbook
GO
DELETE FROM AsynchronousUpdateMSMQ;
INSERT INTO AsynchronousUpdateMSMQ VALUES (1, 'field 1.1', 'field 2.1');
INSERT INTO AsynchronousUpdateMSMQ VALUES (2, 'field 1.2', 'field 2.2');
INSERT INTO AsynchronousUpdateMSMQ VALUES (3, 'field 1.3', 'field 2.3');
```

The C# code in *Program.cs* in the project AsynchronousUpdateMSMQ is shown in Example 5-32.

Example 5-32. File: Program.cs for AsynchronousUpdateMSMQ solution

```
using System;
using System.Data;
using System.Data.SqlClient;
using System.Messaging;

namespace AsynchronousUpdateMsmq
{
    class Program
    {
        private static string queueNameUpdateQuery =
            @".\Private$\AdoNet35Cookbook_AsynchronousUpdateQuery";
        private static string queueNameUpdateResult =
            @".\Private$\AdoNet35Cookbook_AsynchronousUpdateResult";
        private static string queueNameUpdateCommand =
            @".\Private$\AdoNet35Cookbook_AsynchronousUpdateCommand";

        static void Main(string[] args)
        {
            // The Id for which to retrieve records. * is all.
            string id = "*";

            // Create the MSMQ queues, if necessary
            CreateQueue(queueNameUpdateQuery);
            CreateQueue(queueNameUpdateResult);
            CreateQueue(queueNameUpdateCommand);
```

Example 5-32. File: Program.cs for AsynchronousUpdateMSMQ solution (continued)

```csharp
// Create an object to access the update query queue for sending.
using (MessageQueue mqQueryOut = new MessageQueue(queueNameUpdateQuery))
{
    mqQueryOut.Formatter =
        new XmlMessageFormatter(new Type[] { typeof(String) });

    // Send a message containing the contact ID to query for.
    string body = "Id=" + id;
    mqQueryOut.Send(body);
    Console.WriteLine(
        "\nQuery for id = {0} sent to query queue.", id);
}

// Create an object to access the update query queue for receiving.
string queryId;
using (MessageQueue mqQueryIn = new MessageQueue(queueNameUpdateQuery))
{
    mqQueryIn.Formatter =
        new XmlMessageFormatter(new Type[] { typeof(String) });

    // Retrieve the query message from the queue
    Message msg = mqQueryIn.Receive(new TimeSpan(0, 0, 1));
    Console.WriteLine("\nQuery message {0} received.", msg.Id);

    // Get the Id from the message body.
    queryId = msg.Body.ToString( ).Substring(3);
    Console.WriteLine("Query Id = {0} retrieved from message.",
        queryId);
}

// Retrieve data for the specified contact using a DataAdapter.
string sqlConnectString = "Data Source=(local);" +
    "Integrated security=SSPI;Initial Catalog=AdoDotNet35Cookbook;";
string sqlText;
if (queryId == "*")
    sqlText = "SELECT * FROM AsynchronousUpdateMSMQ";
else
    sqlText = "SELECT * FROM AsynchronousUpdateMSMQ WHERE Id = " +
        queryId;
SqlDataAdapter da1 = new SqlDataAdapter(sqlText, sqlConnectString);
// Fill the Customer table in the DataSet with customer data.
DataSet ds = new DataSet( );
da1.FillSchema(ds, SchemaType.Source);
da1.Fill(ds);
Console.WriteLine("Result set created.");

// Create an object to access the update result queue for sending.
using (MessageQueue mqResultOut = new MessageQueue(queueNameUpdateResult))
{
    mqResultOut.Formatter =
        new XmlMessageFormatter(new Type[] { typeof(DataSet) });
```

```csharp
            // Write the result message to the queue
            mqResultOut.Send(ds, "id=" + queryId);
            Console.WriteLine(
                "Result message id = {0} sent to result queue.",
                queryId);
        }

        // Create an object to access the update result queue for receiving.
        DataSet dsResult;
        using (MessageQueue mqResultIn = new MessageQueue(queueNameUpdateResult))
        {
            mqResultIn.Formatter =
                new XmlMessageFormatter(new Type[] { typeof(DataSet) });

            Message msg = mqResultIn.Receive(new TimeSpan(0, 0, 1));
            Console.WriteLine("\nResult message {0} received.", msg.Id);

            // Create the customer DataSet from the message body.
            dsResult = (DataSet)msg.Body;
        }

        // Output the results to the console
        Console.WriteLine("\n---INITIAL RESULT SET---");
        foreach (DataRow row in dsResult.Tables[0].Rows)
            Console.WriteLine("Id = {0}\tField1 = {1}\tField2 = {2}",
                row["Id"], row["Field1"], row["Field2"]);

        // Update the row where Id = 2
        int updateRowId = 2;
        ds.Tables[0].Rows.Find(new object[]
            { updateRowId }).SetField<string>("Field1", "Field 1.2 new");
        Console.WriteLine("\nRow with Id = {0} updated.", updateRowId);

        // Create an object to access the update command queue for sending.
        using (MessageQueue mqUpdateCommandOut =
            new MessageQueue(queueNameUpdateCommand))
        {
            mqUpdateCommandOut.Formatter =
                new XmlMessageFormatter(new Type[] { typeof(DataSet) });

            // Create the changes (DiffGram) message body
            mqUpdateCommandOut.Send(ds.GetChanges());
            Console.WriteLine(
                "DataSet updates (DiffGram) sent to update command queue.");
        }

        // Create an object to access the update result queue for receiving.
        DataSet dsUpdateDelta;
        using (MessageQueue mqUpdateCommandIn =
            new MessageQueue(queueNameUpdateCommand))
```

Example 5-32. File: Program.cs for AsynchronousUpdateMSMQ solution (continued)

```
        {
            mqUpdateCommandIn.Formatter =
                new XmlMessageFormatter(new Type[] { typeof(DataSet) });

            Message msg = mqUpdateCommandIn.Receive(new TimeSpan(0, 0, 1));
            Console.WriteLine("\nUpdate command message {0} received.", msg.Id);

            // Parse the delta DataSet (DiffGram) from the message body.
            dsUpdateDelta = (DataSet)msg.Body;
            Console.WriteLine("Update command (DiffGram) parsed from message.");
        }

        // Create the DataAdapter and CommandBuilder to update.
        SqlDataAdapter da2 =
            new SqlDataAdapter("SELECT * FROM AsynchronousUpdateMSMQ",
            sqlConnectString);
        SqlCommandBuilder cb2 = new SqlCommandBuilder(da2);

        // Process the updates.
        da2.Update(dsUpdateDelta, "Table");
        Console.WriteLine("Update successfully applied.");

        Console.WriteLine("\nPress any key to continue.");
        Console.ReadKey( );
    }

    private static void CreateQueue(string queueName)
    {
        // Create the queue if it does not exist.
        if (!MessageQueue.Exists(queueName))
        {
            MessageQueue.Create(queueName);
            Console.WriteLine("Queue {0} created.", queueName);
        }
        else
            Console.WriteLine("Queue {0} found.", queueName);
    }
  }
}
```

The output is shown in Figure 5-28.

The contents of the table after the update are shown in Figure 5-29.

The message queues created in this solution are shown in Figure 5-30.

Discussion

The discussion in Recipe 3.31 provides an overview of Microsoft Message Queuing (MSMQ).

For more information about DiffGrams, see Recipe 9.4.

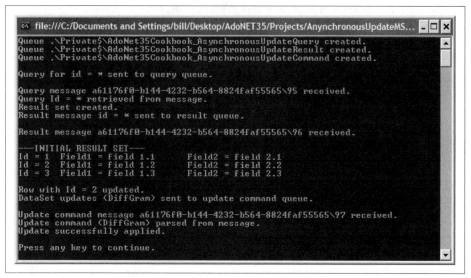

Figure 5-28. Output for AsynchronousUpdateMSMQ solution

	Id	Field1	Field2
▶	1	field 1.1	field 2.1
	2	Field 1.2 new	field 2.2
	3	field 1.3	field 2.3
*	NULL	NULL	NULL

Figure 5-29. Data in table UpdateMSMQResult after update

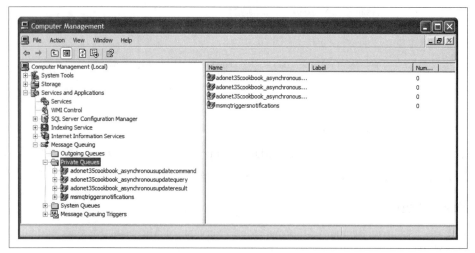

Figure 5-30. Message queues created by AsynchronousUpdateMSMQQueues solution

5.16 Controlling Edits, Deletions, or Additions to Data with a DataView

Problem

You need to programmatically prevent users from editing, deleting, or adding data to a DataTable or DataView.

Solution

Use the AllowDelete, AllowEdit, and AllowInsert properties of a DataView.

The solution uses a table named ControlDataModification in the AdoDotNet35Cookbook database. Execute the following T-SQL statement to create the table:

```
USE AdoDotNet35Cookbook
GO
CREATE TABLE ControlDataModification (
    Id int NOT NULL PRIMARY KEY,
    Field1 nvarchar(50) NULL,
    Field2 nvarchar(50) NULL )
```

The solution needs some sample data in the table ControlDataModification. Create the data by executing the following T-SQL batch:

```
USE AdoDotNet35Cookbook
GO
INSERT INTO ControlDataModification VALUES (1, 'Field1.1', 'Field2.1')
INSERT INTO ControlDataModification VALUES (2, 'Field1.2', 'Field2.2')
INSERT INTO ControlDataModification VALUES (3, 'Field1.3', 'Field2.3')
```

This solution fills a DataTable with the ControlDataModification table in the AdoDotNet35Cookbook database. A DataView is created from the default DataView for the table. The AllowDelete, AllowEdit, and AllowNew properties of the DataView are set to false. An attempt is made to delete, edit, and insert a record using the DataView. Next, the AllowDelete, AllowEdit, and AllowNew properties of the DataView are set to true and another attempt is made to delete, edit, and insert a record. Successes, failures, and the data in the DataView at different stages are written to the console.

The C# code in *Program.cs* in the project ControlDataModification is shown in Example 5-33.

Example 5-33. File: Program.cs for ControlDataModification solution

```
using System;
using System.Data;
using System.Data.SqlClient;

namespace ControlDataModification
```

Example 5-33. File: Program.cs for ControlDataModification solution (continued)

```csharp
{
    class Program
    {
        static void Main(string[] args)
        {
            string sqlConnectString = @"Data Source=(local);
                Integrated security=SSPI;Initial Catalog=AdoDotNet35Cookbook;";

            string sqlSelect = "SELECT * FROM ControlDataModification";

            // Load data into a DataTable
            SqlDataAdapter da = new SqlDataAdapter(sqlSelect, sqlConnectString);
            DataTable dt = new DataTable( );
            da.Fill(dt);

            // Get the default DataView from the DataTable
            DataView dv = dt.DefaultView;
            dv.Sort = "Id";

            OutputData("INITIAL", dv);

            // Prevent insert, edit, and delete
            dv.AllowDelete = false;
            dv.AllowEdit = false;
            dv.AllowNew = false;
            Console.WriteLine("\n=> Disabled modifications.");

            // Try to delete the row with Id = 1
            Console.WriteLine("\n=> Attempting to delete row with Id = 1.");
            try
            {
                dv[dv.Find(1)].Delete( );
            }
            catch (Exception ex)
            {
                Console.WriteLine("Exception: {0}", ex.Message);
            }

            // Try to modify the row with Id = 2
            Console.WriteLine("\n=> Attempting to edit row with Id = 2.");
            try
            {
                dv[dv.Find(2)]["Field1"] = "Field1.2 (new)";
            }
            catch (Exception ex)
            {
                Console.WriteLine("Exception: {0}", ex.Message);
            }

            // Try to insert a new row
            Console.WriteLine("\n=> Attempting to add a new row.");
```

Example 5-33. File: Program.cs for ControlDataModification solution (continued)

```csharp
            try
            {
                DataRowView drv1 = dv.AddNew( );
            }
            catch (Exception ex)
            {
                Console.WriteLine("Exception: {0}", ex.Message);
            }

            OutputData("POST MODIFICATIONS: NOT ALLOWED", dv);

            // Allow insert, edit, and delete
            dv.AllowDelete = true;
            dv.AllowEdit = true;
            dv.AllowNew = true;
            Console.WriteLine("\n=> Enabled modifications.");

            // Delete the row with Id = 1
            dv[dv.Find(1)].Delete( );
            Console.WriteLine("\n=> Deleted row with Id = 1.");

            // Try to modify the row with Id = 2
            dv[dv.Find(2)]["Field1"] = "Field1.2 (new)";
            Console.WriteLine("\n=> Edited row with Id = 2.");

            // Try to insert a new row
            Console.WriteLine("\n=> Added a new row.");
            DataRowView drv2 = dv.AddNew( );
            drv2["Id"] = 4;
            drv2["Field1"] = "Field1.4";
            drv2["Field2"] = "Field2.4";

            OutputData("POST MODIFICATIONS: ALLOWED", dv);

            Console.WriteLine("\nPress any key to continue.");
            Console.ReadKey( );
        }

        private static void OutputData(string caption, DataView dv)
        {
            Console.WriteLine("\n---{0}---", caption);
            foreach (DataRowView drv in dv)
            {
                Console.WriteLine("{0}\t{1}\t{2}",
                    drv["Id"], drv["Field1"], drv["Field2"]);
            }
        }
    }
}
```

The output is shown in Figure 5-31.

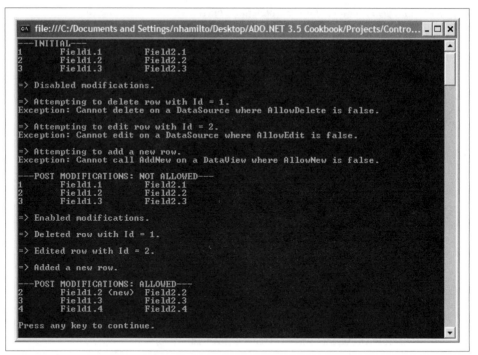

```
file:///C:/Documents and Settings/nhamilto/Desktop/ADO.NET 3.5 Cookbook/Projects/Contro...
---INITIAL---
1       Field1.1        Field2.1
2       Field1.2        Field2.2
3       Field1.3        Field2.3

=> Disabled modifications.

=> Attempting to delete row with Id = 1.
Exception: Cannot delete on a DataSource where AllowDelete is false.

=> Attempting to edit row with Id = 2.
Exception: Cannot edit on a DataSource where AllowEdit is false.

=> Attempting to add a new row.
Exception: Cannot call AddNew on a DataView where AllowNew is false.

---POST MODIFICATIONS: NOT ALLOWED---
1       Field1.1        Field2.1
2       Field1.2        Field2.2
3       Field1.3        Field2.3

=> Enabled modifications.

=> Deleted row with Id = 1.

=> Edited row with Id = 2.

=> Added a new row.

---POST MODIFICATIONS: ALLOWED---
2       Field1.2 (new)  Field2.2
3       Field1.3        Field2.3
4       Field1.4        Field2.4

Press any key to continue.
```

Figure 5-31. Output for ControlDataModification solution

Discussion

The DataView class can be used to add, edit, or delete records in the underlying DataTable. The properties described in Table 5-6 control the data modification permitted in a DataView.

Table 5-6. DataView properties

Property	Description
AllowDelete	Gets or sets a Boolean value indicating whether deletes are allowed.
AllowEdit	Gets or sets a Boolean value indicating whether edits are allowed.
AllowNew	Gets or sets a Boolean value indicating whether new rows can be added.

If AllowNew is true, the record is not added until the EndEdit( ) method is called either explicitly or implicitly. The CancelEdit( ) method of the DataRowView can be called to discard the row before it is added.

If AllowEdit is true, the changes to the row are not committed until the EndEdit( ) method is called either explicitly or implicitly. Only one row can be edited at a time. The CancelEdit( ) method of the DataRowView can be called to discard the row before it is added.

If the `AddNew( )` or `BeginEdit( )` method of the `DataRowView` is called, `EndEdit( )` is called implicitly on the pending row; this applies the changes to the row in the underlying `DataTable`. In data controls that allow editing multiple records, `EndEdit( )` is called implicitly when the current row is changed.

5.17   Overcoming Keyword Conflicts When Using a CommandBuilder

Problem

Your data includes table and column names that conflict with SQL keywords. You can overcome this with brackets or quotes in `SELECT` statements that you write, but the `CommandBuilder` creates illegal update statements. You need to know how to use the `CommandBuilder` with your data.

Solution

Use the `QuotePrefix` and `QuoteSuffix` properties of the `CommandBuilder` object to delimit database server object names containing spaces or other illegal characters.

The solution displays the default database object name delimiters; the delete, insert, and update commands using the default delimiters; and the delete, insert, and update commands using explicitly specified delimiters through the `QuotePrefix` and `QuoteSuffix` properties for both the OLE DB and SQL Server .NET data providers.

The C# code in *Program.cs* in the project `ResolveCommandBuilderKeywordConflict` is shown in Example 5-34.

Example 5-34. File: Program.cs for ResolveCommandBuilderKeywordConflict solution

```
using System;
using System.Data;
using System.Data.SqlClient;
using System.Data.OleDb;

namespace ResolveCommandBuilderKeywordConflict
{
    class Program
    {
        static void Main(string[] args)
        {
            string sqlConnectString = "Data Source=(local);" +
                "Integrated security=SSPI;Initial Catalog=AdventureWorks;";

            string oledbConnectString = "Provider=SQLOLEDB;Data Source=(local);" +
                "Integrated Security=SSPI;Initial Catalog=AdventureWorks;";

            string sqlSelect = "SELECT ContactID, FirstName, LastName " +
                "FROM Person.Contact";
```

```csharp
// Create a SQL Server data adapter and command builder
SqlDataAdapter daSql =
    new SqlDataAdapter(sqlSelect, sqlConnectString);
SqlCommandBuilder cbSql = new SqlCommandBuilder(daSql);

// Output the default prefix and suffix
Console.WriteLine("---Default SQL Server quote prefix and suffix---");
Console.WriteLine("Quote_Prefix = {0}", cbSql.QuotePrefix);
Console.WriteLine("Quote_Suffix = {0}", cbSql.QuoteSuffix);
Console.WriteLine();

// Output the default delete, insert, and update statements
Console.WriteLine("---SQL Server CommandBuilder default---");
Console.WriteLine("DeleteCommand = {0}\n",
    cbSql.GetDeleteCommand().CommandText);
Console.WriteLine("InsertCommand = {0}\n",
    cbSql.GetInsertCommand().CommandText);
Console.WriteLine("UpdateCommand = {0}",
    cbSql.GetUpdateCommand().CommandText);
Console.WriteLine();

// Set the quote quote prefix and suffix
cbSql = new SqlCommandBuilder(daSql);
cbSql.QuotePrefix = "\"";
cbSql.QuoteSuffix = "\"";
Console.WriteLine("\n=> Set QuotePrefix to {0}", cbSql.QuotePrefix);
Console.WriteLine("=> Set QuoteSuffix to {0}", cbSql.QuoteSuffix);

// Output the delete, insert, and update statements
Console.WriteLine(
    "\n---SQLServer CommandBuilder with prefix and suffix---");
Console.WriteLine("DeleteCommand = {0}\n",
    cbSql.GetDeleteCommand().CommandText);
Console.WriteLine("InsertCommand = {0}\n",
    cbSql.GetInsertCommand().CommandText);
Console.WriteLine("UpdateCommand = {0}",
    cbSql.GetUpdateCommand().CommandText);
Console.WriteLine();

// Retrieve the OLEDB quote prefix and suffix from the server.
DataTable dtOleDBSchema;
using (OleDbConnection connection =
    new OleDbConnection(oledbConnectString))
{
    connection.Open();
    dtOleDBSchema = connection.GetOleDbSchemaTable(
        OleDbSchemaGuid.DbInfoLiterals, new object[] { });
}
```

```
            // Set the primary key to enable find on LiteralName column.
            dtOleDBSchema.PrimaryKey =
                new DataColumn[] { dtOleDBSchema.Columns["LiteralName"] };

            // Output the default prefix and suffix from
            // the OleDbLiteral enumeration.
            Console.WriteLine("---Default OLEDB quote prefix and suffix---");
            Console.WriteLine("Quote_Prefix = {0}",
                dtOleDBSchema.Rows.Find("Quote_Prefix")["LiteralValue"]);
            Console.WriteLine("Quote_Suffix = {0}",
                dtOleDBSchema.Rows.Find("Quote_Suffix")["LiteralValue"]);
            Console.WriteLine( );

            // Create an OLE DB data adapter and command builder
            OleDbDataAdapter daOleDB =
                new OleDbDataAdapter(sqlSelect, oledbConnectString);
            OleDbCommandBuilder cbOleDB = new OleDbCommandBuilder(daOleDB);

            // Output the default delete, insert, and update statements
            Console.WriteLine("---OLEDB CommandBuilder default---");
            Console.WriteLine("DeleteCommand = {0}\n",
                cbOleDB.GetDeleteCommand( ).CommandText);
            Console.WriteLine("InsertCommand = {0}\n",
                cbOleDB.GetInsertCommand( ).CommandText);
            Console.WriteLine("UpdateCommand = {0}",
                cbOleDB.GetUpdateCommand( ).CommandText);
            Console.WriteLine( );

            // Set the quote prefix and suffix
            cbOleDB = new OleDbCommandBuilder(daOleDB);
            cbOleDB.QuotePrefix = "[";
            cbOleDB.QuoteSuffix = "]";
            Console.WriteLine("\n=> Set QuotePrefix to {0}", cbOleDB.QuotePrefix);
            Console.WriteLine("=> Set QuoteSuffix to {0}", cbOleDB.QuoteSuffix);

            // Output the delete, insert, and update statements
            Console.WriteLine("\n---OLEDB CommandBuilder with prefix and suffix---");
            Console.WriteLine("DeleteCommand = {0}\n",
                cbOleDB.GetDeleteCommand( ).CommandText);
            Console.WriteLine("InsertCommand = {0}\n",
                cbOleDB.GetInsertCommand( ).CommandText);
            Console.WriteLine("UpdateCommand = {0}",
                cbOleDB.GetUpdateCommand( ).CommandText);

            Console.WriteLine("\nPress any key to continue.");
            Console.ReadKey( );
        }
    }
}
```

The output is shown in Figure 5-32.

```
---Default SQL Server quote prefix and suffix---
Quote_Prefix = [
Quote_Suffix = ]

---SQL Server CommandBuilder default---
DeleteCommand = DELETE FROM [Person].[Contact] WHERE (([ContactID] = @p1) AND ([
FirstName] = @p2) AND ([LastName] = @p3))

InsertCommand = INSERT INTO [Person].[Contact] ([FirstName], [LastName]) VALUES
(@p1, @p2)

UpdateCommand = UPDATE [Person].[Contact] SET [FirstName] = @p1, [LastName] = @p
2 WHERE (([ContactID] = @p3) AND ([FirstName] = @p4) AND ([LastName] = @p5))


=> Set QuotePrefix to "
=> Set QuoteSuffix to "

---SQLServer CommandBuilder with prefix and suffix---
DeleteCommand = DELETE FROM "Person"."Contact" WHERE (("ContactID" = @p1) AND ("
FirstName" = @p2) AND ("LastName" = @p3))

InsertCommand = INSERT INTO "Person"."Contact" ("FirstName", "LastName") VALUES
(@p1, @p2)

UpdateCommand = UPDATE "Person"."Contact" SET "FirstName" = @p1, "LastName" = @p
2 WHERE (("ContactID" = @p3) AND ("FirstName" = @p4) AND ("LastName" = @p5))

---Default OLEDB quote prefix and suffix---
Quote_Prefix = "
Quote_Suffix = "

---OLEDB CommandBuilder default---
DeleteCommand = DELETE FROM AdventureWorks.Person.Contact WHERE ((ContactID = ?)
 AND (FirstName = ?) AND (LastName = ?))

InsertCommand = INSERT INTO AdventureWorks.Person.Contact (FirstName, LastName)
VALUES (?, ?)

UpdateCommand = UPDATE AdventureWorks.Person.Contact SET FirstName = ?, LastName
 = ? WHERE ((ContactID = ?) AND (FirstName = ?) AND (LastName = ?))

=> Set QuotePrefix to [
=> Set QuoteSuffix to ]

---OLEDB CommandBuilder with prefix and suffix---
DeleteCommand = DELETE FROM [AdventureWorks].[Person].[Contact] WHERE (([Contact
ID] = ?) AND ([FirstName] = ?) AND ([LastName] = ?))

InsertCommand = INSERT INTO [AdventureWorks].[Person].[Contact] ([FirstName], [L
astName]) VALUES (?, ?)

UpdateCommand = UPDATE [AdventureWorks].[Person].[Contact] SET [FirstName] = ?,
[LastName] = ? WHERE (([ContactID] = ?) AND ([FirstName] = ?) AND ([LastName] =
?))

Press any key to continue.
```

Figure 5-32. Output for ResolveCommandBuilderConflict solution

Discussion

The QuotePrefix and QuoteSuffix properties of the CommandBuilder object specify the
beginning and ending characters used to delimit database server object names, such
as tables and columns in the delete, insert, and update commands generated by the
CommandBuilder. This is necessary when the object names contain special characters
or reserved tokens; otherwise, the commands will fail when executed.

For example, in SQL Server 7.0 and later, database object names can contain any valid Microsoft Windows NT/2000/XP character, including spaces and punctuation marks. T-SQL is more restrictive with identifiers that can be used without delimiters. You can use QuotePrefix and QuoteSuffix to delimit the SQL Server object names when required by T-SQL.

The QuotePrefix and QuoteSuffix values have no effect on the CommandText of SelectCommand. Valid delimiters, if required, must be specified in CommandText for the SelectCommand of the DataAdapter that the CommandBuilder is based on.

The QuotePrefix and QuoteSuffix properties are not validated to ensure that they can be used as delimiters.

An InvalidOperationException will be raised if you attempt to change the QuotePrefix or QuoteSuffix property after an insert, update, or delete command has been generated.

The example demonstrates using QuotePrefix and QuoteSuffix with both the OLE DB and SQL Server CommandBuilder objects. As you can see, they function nearly identically.

 The CommandBuilder makes it easy to update the data source with changes made to the DataSet. Update logic is created automatically, so no understanding is required of how to code the actual delete, insert, and update SQL statements. The CommandBuilder drawbacks include slower performance because of the time that it takes to request metadata and construct the updating logic, updates that are limited to simple single-table scenarios, and a lack of support for stored procedures. Because of these drawbacks, the CommandBuilder is seldom used in enterprise application development.

The example also demonstrates retrieving the default quote prefix and suffix. With SQL Server, it's as simple as retrieving the QuotePrefix and QuoteSuffix properties from the CommandBuilder object. With the OLE DB provider, the GetOleDbSchemaTable( ) method of the OleDbConnection object returns schema information from a data source based on a GUID argument indicating one of the OleDbSchemaGuid values. The value DbInfoLiterals returns a list of provider-specific literals used in text commands. The literals are returned as a table of rows. Within this table, there is a column named LiteralName. The rows containing the default values for the quote prefix and suffix are identified by a LiteralName value of Quote_Prefix and Quote_Suffix, respectively. The actual values are stored in the LiteralValue column.

5.18 Capturing Changes to Data in a SQL Server Database

Problem

You need to automatically capture changes made to data in a table in a SQL Server 2008 database.

Solution

Use change data capture as shown in this solution.

The solution uses a table named CaptureDataChanges in the AdoDotNet35Cookbook database. Execute the following T-SQL statement to create the table:

```
USE AdoDotNet35Cookbook
GO
CREATE TABLE CaptureDataChanges (
    Id int NOT NULL PRIMARY KEY,
    Field1 nvarchar(50) NULL,
    Field2 nvarchar(50) NULL )
```

The solution needs some sample data in the table CaptureDataChanges. Create the data by executing the following T-SQL batch:

```
USE AdoDotNet35Cookbook
GO
INSERT INTO CaptureDataChanges VALUES (1, 'Field1.1', 'Field2.1')
INSERT INTO CaptureDataChanges VALUES (2, 'Field1.2', 'Field2.2')
INSERT INTO CaptureDataChanges VALUES (3, 'Field1.3', 'Field2.3')
```

You need to enable change data capture on the database that you want to monitor. Do this by executing the stored procedure sys.sp_cdc_enable_db_change_data_capture in the database. For the AdoDotNet35Cookbook database used in this solution, execute the following command:

```
USE AdoDotNet35Cookbook
GO
sys.sp_cdc_enable_db_change_data_capture
```

Once CDC is enabled on the database, a new user cdc is created, a new user role cdc_admin is created, and five CDC tables are created in the database:

- cdc.captured_columns
- cdc.change_tables
- cdc.ddl_history
- cdc.index_columns
- cdc.lsn_time_mapping

Verify that data capture is enabled on the database by querying the sys.databases catalog view and examining the value the is_cdc_enabled column. Execute the following query:

```
SELECT is_cdc_enabled FROM sys.databases WHERE name='AdoDotNet35Cookbook'
```

A value of 1 indicates that data capture is enabled for the database. Otherwise the value of is_cdc_enabled is 0. You cannot enable data capture on system databases or distribution databases.

Next, you need to enable change data capture on the table. SQL Server Agent needs to be running—start it if it is not either by right-clicking on SQL Server Agent object in the SQL Server Management Studio object tree view and selecting Start from the context menu, or by selecting the SQL Services node in SQL Server Configuration Manager, right-clicking on SQL Server Agent, and selecting Start from the context menu.

Next, execute the stored procedure sys.sp_cdc_enable_table_change_data_capture to enable change data capture for the CaptureDataChanges table. Execute the following T-SQL statement:

```
USE AdoDotNet35Cookbook
GO
EXECUTE sys.sp_cdc_enable_table_change_data_capture
    @source_schema = N'dbo',
    @source_name = N'CaptureDataChanges',
    @role_name = N'cdc_admin';
```

When the stored procedure executes successfully, you will see the output in Figure 5-33. Two SQL Server Agent jobs have been created and started.

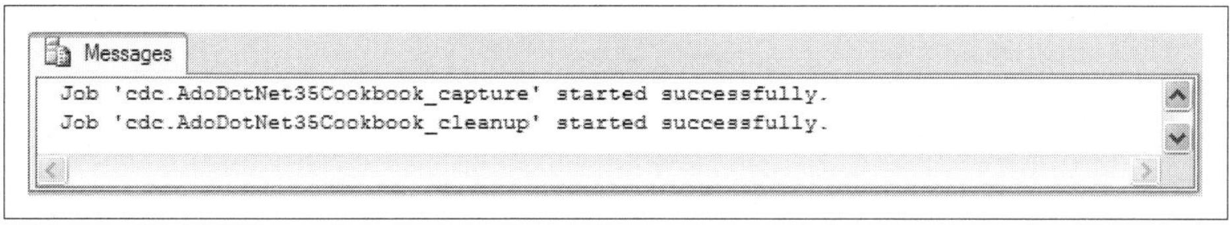

Figure 5-33. Output for executing stored procedure sys.sp_cdc_enable_table_change_data_capture

After you have executed this procedure, the table cdc.dbo_CaptureChangeData_CT is created that holds the change data and information for the table CaptureChangeData.

You can confirm that the table has been enabled for change data capture by querying the sys.tables catalog view and examining the value of the is_tracked_by_cdc column. Execute the following query:

```
SELECT is_tracked_by_cdc FROM sys.tables WHERE name = 'CaptureDataChanges'
```

A value of 1 indicates that the tables are enabled for change data capture. Otherwise, the value of is_tracked_by_cdc is 0.

You can disable change data tracking on a table by executing the sys.sp_cdc_disable_table_change_data_capture stored procedure as shown in the following code:

```
USE AdoDotNet35Cookbook
GO

sys.sp_cdc_disable_table_change_data_capture
    @source_schema = 'dbo',
    @source_name = 'CaptureDataChanges',
    @capture_instance = 'all'
```

The solution retrieves data into a DataTable from the CaptureDataChanges table in the AdoDotNet35Cookbook database and outputs the DataTable to the console. An update, delete, and insert operation is performed in the DataTable and updated to the database. A small delay is executed to give the capture change data a chance to update and then the change capture data in the table cdc.dbo_CaptureDataChanges_CT is retrieved into a DataTable and output to the console. The ending contents of the CaptureDataChanges table are loaded into a DataTable from the database and output to the console.

The C# code in *Program.cs* in the project CaptureDataChanges is shown in Example 5-35.

Example 5-35. File: Program.cs for CaptureDataChanges solution

```
using System;
using System.Data;
using System.Data.SqlClient;
using System.Data.SqlTypes;

namespace CaptureDataChanges
{
    class Program
    {
        static void Main(string[] args)
        {
            string sqlConnectString = @"Data Source=(local);
                Integrated security=SSPI;Initial Catalog=AdoDotNet35Cookbook;";

            string sqlSelect = "SELECT * FROM CaptureDataChanges";
            string sqlSelectCDC =
                @"SELECT __$operation, Id, Field1, Field2
                FROM cdc.dbo_CaptureDataChanges_CT";

            // Retrieve the table from the database and output to console
            SqlDataAdapter da = new SqlDataAdapter(sqlSelect, sqlConnectString);
            SqlCommandBuilder cb = new SqlCommandBuilder(da);
            DataTable dt = new DataTable();
            da.FillSchema(dt, SchemaType.Source);
            da.Fill(dt);
```

```csharp
        Console.WriteLine("---CaptureDataChanges table (Initial)---");
        foreach (DataRow row in dt.Rows)
        {
            Console.WriteLine("ID = {0}\tField1 = {1}\tField2 = {2}",
                row["ID"], row["Field1"], row["Field2"]);
        }

        // Get the start time for changes
        DateTime beginTime = DateTime.Now;

        // Change the data in the DataTable -- modify, delete, and insert
        dt.Rows.Find(2)["Field2"] += " (new)";
        dt.Rows.Find(3).Delete();
        dt.Rows.Add(new object[] {4, "Field1.4", "Field2.4"});

        // Update the data source with the changes
        da.Update(dt);

        // Wait for the CDC table to reflect the changes
        using (SqlConnection connection = new SqlConnection(sqlConnectString))
        {
            SqlCommand command = new SqlCommand("WAITFOR DELAY '00:00:02'",
                connection);
            connection.Open();
            command.ExecuteNonQuery();
        }

        // Get the changes logged by change data capture
        SqlDataAdapter daCDC = new SqlDataAdapter(sqlSelectCDC, sqlConnectString);
        DataTable dtCDC = new DataTable();
        daCDC.Fill(dtCDC);

        Console.WriteLine("\n---Change data capture records---");
        foreach (DataRow row in dtCDC.Rows)
        {
            Console.WriteLine(
                "__$operation = {0}\tID = {1}\tField1 = {2}\tField2 = {3}",
                row["__$operation"], row["ID"], row["Field1"], row["Field2"]);
        }

        // Retrieve the table from the database and output to console
        dt.Clear();
        da.Fill(dt);
        Console.WriteLine("\n---CaptureDataChanges table (Final)---");
        foreach (DataRow row in dt.Rows)
        {
            Console.WriteLine("ID = {0}\tField1 = {1}\tField2 = {2}",
                row["ID"], row["Field1"], row["Field2"]);
        }
```

Example 5-35. File: Program.cs for CaptureDataChanges solution (continued)

```
            Console.WriteLine("\nPress any key to continue.");
            Console.ReadKey();
        }
    }
}
```

The output is shown in Figure 5-34.

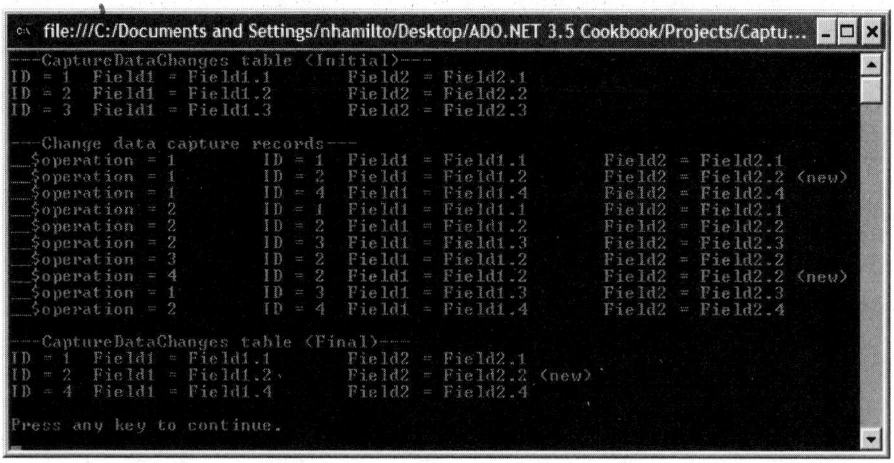

Figure 5-34. Output for CaptureDataChanges solution

Discussion

SQL Server 2008 introduces Change Data Capture (CDC) that records inserts, updates, and deletes to SQL Server tables. The solution discusses how to enable and manage change tracking for a database and shows how to view the change track data logged by CDC.

CDC logs changes to a capture instance to a SQL Server table named cdc.<*capture_ instance_schema*>_<*capture_instance*>_CT. The change table contains five columns and a column for each field in the capture instance table. Table 5-7 describes the additional columns.

Table 5-7. Change data capture table columns

Column name	Data type	Description
__$start_lsn	binary(10)	Log sequence number (LSN) for one or more changes within the same committed transaction.
__$end_lsn	binary(10)	Not supported. Always null.
__$seqval	binary(10)	Sequence value used to order rows within a committed transaction (i.e., same LSN).
__$operation	int	The DML operation associated with the change. One of the following values: • 1 = delete • 2 = insert • 3 = update (original values) • 4 = update (new values) • 5 = merge
__$update_mask	varbinary(128)	Bit mask based on the column ordinals of the capture instance table identifying the columns that were changed.
capture instance columns		Columns identified for capture. If no columns were identified, all columns from the capture instance are included.

Two functions query change data:

- cdc.fn_cdc_get_all_changes_*<capture_instance>* returns all changes within a specified interval.
- cdc.fn_cdc_get_net_changes_*<capture_instance>* returns final changes within a specified interval. Only one change per row is returned regardless of the number of actual changes made within the interval.

For more information about these functions and change data capture, see SQL Server Books Online.

CHAPTER 6

Copying and Transferring Data

6.0 Introduction

This chapter focuses on copying data between ADO.NET classes and between ADO and ADO.NET classes, serializing and deserializing data, and encrypting data and login credentials to build secure applications.

Copying rows from one `DataTable` to another and copying tables from one `DataSet` to another are operations performed frequently in data-centric applications. Recipes 6.1 and 6.2 show different ways to copy data and discuss the advantages, limitations, and disadvantages of the different approaches.

The `DataReader` provides connected forward-only, read-only access to a data stream, while the `DataSet` provides disconnected access to data stored as an in-memory relational database. Recipes 6.3, 6.4, 6.5, and 6.6 show how it's done.

In addition, this chapter covers:

Serializing and deserializing data

Serialization allows data conversion to a format that can be persisted or transported. The .NET framework supports serialization and deserialization with the `System.Runtime.Serialization` namespace. Support for binary, XML, and SOAP formats is built in and serialization can easily be customized if required. Recipes 6.7 and 6.8 show how to serialize and deserialize data.

As well as copying data, ADO.NET supports merging disconnected data in `DataTable` or `DataSet` objects into each other. Recipe 6.9 shows how merging works and how to use the arguments that control the merge operation.

Security and encryption

The .NET Framework provides extensive support for encryption in the `System.Security.Cryptography` namespace. The classes in the namespace are both easy and intuitive to use. You can use the cryptography classes to encrypt a disconnected data class such as a `DataSet` prior to transmission. Encrypting the data allows it to be transmitted securely using nonencrypted protocols such as HTTP.

Recipe 6.11 explores cryptographic algorithms, public keys, private keys, and demonstrates encryption solutions using symmetric and asymmetric keys.

ASP.NET uses the classes in the System.Web.Security namespace to implement security in web service applications. Securing authentication credentials—usually a username and password—during transmission and storage in a database is critical to building secure distributed applications. Recipe 6.12 demonstrates how to protect credentials using a hash algorithm with password salt.

ADO

The OLE DB DataAdapter supports importing ADO Recordset or Record objects into a DataTable or DataSet. This is a one-way operation: changes made to the DataTable or DataSet can't be updated back to ADO using the data adapter. ADO.NET does not, however, provide a way to convert a DataTable or DataSet to an ADO Recordset; therefore, Recipe 6.16 shows how to do this.

During the evolution of ADO to ADO.NET, a few functions got lost along the way. Recipes 6.13 and 6.14 re-create the ADO Recordset GetString( ) and GetRows( ) methods in ADO.NET.

6.1   Copying Rows from One DataTable to Another

Problem

You have records in a DataTable that you need to copy to another DataTable.

Solution

Use the ImportRow( ) method of the DataTable to copy DataRow objects from one DataTable to another. Three techniques for selecting the records to copy are demonstrated in the following example:

- Use the Rows property to access rows in the DataRowCollection of the DataTable using the row index.
- Use the Select( ) method of the DataTable.
- Use the RowFilter property of a DataView for the DataTable.

The solution creates a source DataTable containing the Person.Contact table from AdventureWorks. The Clone( ) method is used to create a second empty destination DataTable with the same schema as the source. Each of the three selection techniques is used together with ImportRows( ) to copy records from the source table to the destination.

The C# code in *Program.cs* in the project CopyRowsFromOneDataTableToAnother is shown in Example 6-1.

Example 6-1. File: Program.cs for CopyRowsFromOneDataTableToAnother solution

```
using System;
using System.Data;
using System.Data.SqlClient;

namespace CopyRowsFromOneDataTableToAnother
{
    class Program
    {
        static void Main(string[] args)
        {
            string sqlConnectString = "Data Source=(local);" +
                "Integrated security=SSPI;Initial Catalog=AdventureWorks;";

            string sqlSelect = "SELECT ContactID, FirstName, LastName " +
                "FROM Person.Contact";

            // Create a data adapter
            SqlDataAdapter da = new SqlDataAdapter(sqlSelect, sqlConnectString);

            // Fill a DataTable using DataAdapter and output to console
            DataTable dtSource = new DataTable();
            da.Fill(dtSource);

            // Clone the schema to the copy table.
            DataTable dtCopy = dtSource.Clone();

            // Use DataTable.ImportRow() indexer method to import first 3 rows.
            for (int i = 0; i < 3; i++)
                dtCopy.ImportRow(dtSource.Rows[i]);

            Console.WriteLine("---Using DataTable.ImportRow() indexer---");
            foreach (DataRow row in dtCopy.Rows)
                Console.WriteLine("ID = {0}\tFirstName = {1}\tLastName = {2}",
                    row["ContactID"], row["FirstName"], row["LastName"]);

            // Use DataTable.Select() method.
            dtCopy.Rows.Clear();
            foreach (DataRow row in dtSource.Select("ContactID <= 3"))
                dtCopy.ImportRow(row);

            Console.WriteLine("\n---Using ImportRow() and DataTable.Select()---");
            foreach (DataRow row in dtCopy.Rows)
                Console.WriteLine("ID = {0}\tFirstName = {1}\tLastName = {2}",
                    row["ContactID"], row["FirstName"], row["LastName"]);
```

```
            // Copy using result of filtered DataView.
            dtCopy.Rows.Clear( );
            DataView dv = dtSource.DefaultView;
            dv.RowFilter = "ContactID <= 3";
            for (int i = 0; i < dv.Count; i++)
                dtCopy.ImportRow(dv[i].Row);

            Console.WriteLine("\n---Using ImportRow( ) and RowFilter---");
            foreach (DataRow row in dtCopy.Rows)
                Console.WriteLine("ID = {0}\tFirstName = {1}\tLastName = {2}",
                    row["ContactID"], row["FirstName"], row["LastName"]);

            Console.WriteLine("\nPress any key to continue.");
            Console.ReadKey( );
        }
    }
}
```

The output is shown in Figure 6-1.

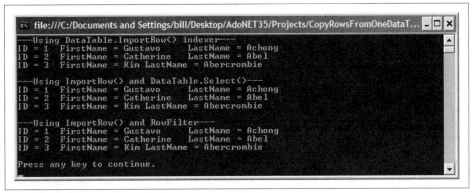

Figure 6-1. Output for CopyRowsFromOneDataTableToAnother solution

Discussion

You can copy rows between tables using the `ImportRow( )` methods of the `DataTable` object. The `ImportRow( )` method copies a `DataRow` into a `DataTable`, preserving original and current values as well as property settings. Unlike `NewRow( )`, which sets the `DataRowState` to `Added` when it adds a row using the existing table schema, `ImportRow( )` leaves the `DataRowState` unchanged from the source.

The `ImportRow()` method requires that both the source and destination tables have the same schema. In this example, the `Clone()` method of the `DataTable` creates a table with identical structure, but any technique that creates a table with an identical structure can be used.

You can also use the `Copy()` method of the `DataTable` object to create a new `DataTable` having the same structure and data as the original as shown in the following code sample:

```
// Create the source table.
DataTable dtSource = new DataTable("Source");

// . . . Fill the source table with data.

// Create the destination table and copy the source table.
DataTable dtDest = new DataTable("Dest");
dtDest = dtSource.Copy();
```

6.2   Copying Tables from One DataSet to Another

Problem

You need to copy an existing schema and data from one `DataSet` to another.

Solution

Use one of the following techniques:

- Use the `Copy()` method of the `DataTable` when all of the data for a table needs to be copied.
- Use the `Clone()` method of the `DataTable` to create the schema for each table in the destination `DataSet` when only a subset of the data needs to be copied. You can then use the `ImportRows()` method of the `DataTable` to copy the subset of rows from the source to the destination table as demonstrated in Recipe 6.1.

Once the destination tables are created and the data is copied into them, the example shows how to create the source `DataRelation` objects in the destination `DataSet`.

The solution creates a `DataSet` containing the `Sales.SalesOrderHeader` and `Sales.SalesOrderDetail` tables from `AdventureWorks`, and a relation between the two tables. The schema, both complete and subset data, and relationships are copied from the source `DataSet` into the destination `DataSet`. Results are output to the console.

The C# code in *Program.cs* in Project `CopyTablesFromOneDataSetToAnother` is shown in Example 6-2.

Example 6-2. File: Program.cs for CopyTablesFromOneDataSetToAnother solution

```csharp
using System;
using System.Data;
using System.Data.SqlClient;

namespace CopyTablesFromOneDataSetToAnother
{
    class Program
    {
        static void Main(string[] args)
        {
            string sqlConnectString = "Data Source=(local);" +
                "Integrated security=SSPI;Initial Catalog=AdventureWorks;";

            string sqlSelect = "SELECT * FROM Sales.SalesOrderHeader;" +
                "SELECT * FROM Sales.SalesOrderDetail;";

            DataSet dsSource = new DataSet( );
            DataSet dsDest = new DataSet( );

            // Fill the source DataSet with the header and detail tables
            SqlDataAdapter da = new SqlDataAdapter(sqlSelect, sqlConnectString);
            da.TableMappings.Add("Table", "Header");
            da.TableMappings.Add("Table1", "Detail");
            da.FillSchema(dsSource, SchemaType.Mapped);
            da.Fill(dsSource);

            // Create a relation between the tables.
            DataRelation dr = dsSource.Relations.Add("Header_Detail",
                dsSource.Tables["Header"].Columns["SalesOrderID"],
                dsSource.Tables["Detail"].Columns["SalesOrderID"],
                true);

            // Create the destination DataSet into which to copy tables
            dsDest = new DataSet( );

            // Copy all tables, all rows
            foreach (DataTable sourceTable in dsSource.Tables)
                dsDest.Tables.Add(sourceTable.Copy( ));

            // Add relations from source into destination
            AddRelations(dsSource, dsDest);

            // Output fields from first three header rows with detail
            Console.WriteLine("---Copy all parent and child rows---");
            for (int i = 0; i < 3; i++)
            {
                DataRow rowHeader = dsDest.Tables["Header"].Rows[i];
                Console.WriteLine("HEADER: OrderID = {0}, Date = {1}, TotalDue = {2}",
                    rowHeader["SalesOrderID"], rowHeader["OrderDate"],
                    rowHeader["TotalDue"]);
```

```
            foreach (DataRow rowDetail in
                rowHeader.GetChildRows(dsDest.Relations["Header_Detail"]))
            {
                Console.WriteLine("\tDETAIL: OrderID = {0}, DetailID = {1}, " +
                    "LineTotal = {2}",
                    rowDetail["SalesOrderID"], rowDetail["SalesOrderDetailID"],
                    rowDetail["LineTotal"]);
            }
        }
        Console.WriteLine( );

        // Second technique: can be used to import subset
        dsDest = new DataSet( );
        foreach (DataTable dtSource in dsSource.Tables)
            dsDest.Tables.Add(dtSource.Clone( ));

        // Copy rows for selected SalesOrderHeader.
        string sqlWhere = "SalesOrderID=43661";
        foreach (DataRow parentRow in
            dsSource.Tables["Header"].Select(sqlWhere))
        {
            dsDest.Tables["Header"].ImportRow(parentRow);

            // Copy the Order Details for the Order.
            foreach (DataRow childRow in parentRow.GetChildRows("Header_Detail"))
                dsDest.Tables["Detail"].ImportRow(childRow);
        }

        // Add relations from source into destination
        AddRelations(dsSource, dsDest);

        // Output fields from all header rows with detail
        Console.WriteLine("---Copy select parent and child rows---");
        foreach (DataRow rowHeader in dsDest.Tables["Header"].Rows)
        {
            Console.WriteLine("HEADER: OrderID = {0}, Date = {1}, TotalDue = {2}",
                rowHeader["SalesOrderID"], rowHeader["OrderDate"],
                rowHeader["TotalDue"]);

            foreach (DataRow rowDetail in
                rowHeader.GetChildRows(dsDest.Relations["Header_Detail"]))
            {
                Console.WriteLine("\tDETAIL: OrderID = {0}, DetailID = {1}, " +
                    "LineTotal = {2}",
                    rowDetail["SalesOrderID"], rowDetail["SalesOrderDetailID"],
                    rowDetail["LineTotal"]);
            }
        }

        Console.WriteLine("\nPress any key to continue.");
        Console.ReadKey( );
    }
```

Example 6-2. File: Program.cs for CopyTablesFromOneDataSetToAnother solution (continued)

```
    private static void AddRelations(DataSet dsSource, DataSet dsDest)
    {
        // Create the relations in the destination DataSet.
        // Iterate over the collection of relations in the source.
        foreach (DataRelation sourceRelation in dsSource.Relations)
        {
            // Get the name of the parent and child table for the relation.
            String parentTableName = sourceRelation.ParentTable.TableName;
            String childTableName = sourceRelation.ChildTable.TableName;

            // Get the number of parent columns for the source relation.
            int nCol = sourceRelation.ParentColumns.Length;

            // Create an array of parent columns in the destination.
            DataColumn[] parentCols = new DataColumn[nCol];
            for (int i = 0; i < nCol; i++)
                parentCols[i] = dsDest.Tables[parentTableName].Columns[
                    sourceRelation.ParentColumns[i].Ordinal];

            // Create an array of child columns in the destination.
            DataColumn[] childCols = new DataColumn[nCol];
            for (int i = 0; i < nCol; i++)
                childCols[i] = dsDest.Tables[childTableName].Columns[
                    sourceRelation.ChildColumns[i].Ordinal];

            // Create the relation in the destination DataSet.
            dsDest.Relations.Add(
                new DataRelation(sourceRelation.RelationName,
                parentCols, childCols, false));
        }

        // Set the enforce constraints flag to match the source DataSet.
        dsDest.EnforceConstraints = dsSource.EnforceConstraints;
    }
}
}
```

The output is shown in Figure 6-2.

Discussion

This solution demonstrates two scenarios for copying tables from one DataSet to another.

In the first scenario, all of the data and tables in the source DataSet are copied to the destination. This is accomplished by iterating over the collection of tables in the source DataSet and using the Copy( ) method of each DataTable object to copy both the schema and data for each table into the destination DataSet.

In the second scenario, only a subset of the data in the source DataSet is copied to the destination. Since there is a relation in place between the Orders and Order

```
cs   file:///C:/Documents and Settings/bill/Desktop/AdoNET35/Projects/CopyTablesFromOneData...  _ □ ×
----Copy all parent and child rows----
HEADER:  OrderID = 43659, Date = 7/1/2001 12:00:00 AM, TotalDue = 27231.5495
         DETAIL: OrderID = 43659, DetailID = 1, LineTotal = 2024.994000
         DETAIL: OrderID = 43659, DetailID = 2, LineTotal = 6074.982000
         DETAIL: OrderID = 43659, DetailID = 3, LineTotal = 2024.994000
         DETAIL: OrderID = 43659, DetailID = 4, LineTotal = 2039.994000
         DETAIL: OrderID = 43659, DetailID = 5, LineTotal = 2039.994000
         DETAIL: OrderID = 43659, DetailID = 6, LineTotal = 4079.988000
         DETAIL: OrderID = 43659, DetailID = 7, LineTotal = 2039.994000
         DETAIL: OrderID = 43659, DetailID = 8, LineTotal = 86.521200
         DETAIL: OrderID = 43659, DetailID = 9, LineTotal = 28.840400
         DETAIL: OrderID = 43659, DetailID = 10, LineTotal = 34.200000
         DETAIL: OrderID = 43659, DetailID = 11, LineTotal = 10.373000
         DETAIL: OrderID = 43659, DetailID = 12, LineTotal = 80.746000
HEADER:  OrderID = 43660, Date = 7/1/2001 12:00:00 AM, TotalDue = 1716.1794
         DETAIL: OrderID = 43660, DetailID = 13, LineTotal = 419.458900
         DETAIL: OrderID = 43660, DetailID = 14, LineTotal = 874.794000
HEADER:  OrderID = 43661, Date = 7/1/2001 12:00:00 AM, TotalDue = 43561.4424
         DETAIL: OrderID = 43661, DetailID = 15, LineTotal = 809.760000
         DETAIL: OrderID = 43661, DetailID = 16, LineTotal = 714.704300
         DETAIL: OrderID = 43661, DetailID = 17, LineTotal = 1429.408600
         DETAIL: OrderID = 43661, DetailID = 18, LineTotal = 20.746000
         DETAIL: OrderID = 43661, DetailID = 19, LineTotal = 115.361600
         DETAIL: OrderID = 43661, DetailID = 20, LineTotal = 1445.189800
         DETAIL: OrderID = 43661, DetailID = 21, LineTotal = 6074.982000
         DETAIL: OrderID = 43661, DetailID = 22, LineTotal = 4049.988000
         DETAIL: OrderID = 43661, DetailID = 23, LineTotal = 40.373000
         DETAIL: OrderID = 43661, DetailID = 24, LineTotal = 1637.400000
         DETAIL: OrderID = 43661, DetailID = 25, LineTotal = 8099.976000
         DETAIL: OrderID = 43661, DetailID = 26, LineTotal = 4079.988000
         DETAIL: OrderID = 43661, DetailID = 27, LineTotal = 57.680800
         DETAIL: OrderID = 43661, DetailID = 28, LineTotal = 4049.988000
         DETAIL: OrderID = 43661, DetailID = 29, LineTotal = 100.932500

----Copy select parent and child rows----
HEADER:  OrderID = 43661, Date = 7/1/2001 12:00:00 AM, TotalDue = 43561.4424
         DETAIL: OrderID = 43661, DetailID = 15, LineTotal = 809.760000
         DETAIL: OrderID = 43661, DetailID = 16, LineTotal = 714.704300
         DETAIL: OrderID = 43661, DetailID = 17, LineTotal = 1429.408600
         DETAIL: OrderID = 43661, DetailID = 18, LineTotal = 20.746000
         DETAIL: OrderID = 43661, DetailID = 19, LineTotal = 115.361600
         DETAIL: OrderID = 43661, DetailID = 20, LineTotal = 1445.189800
         DETAIL: OrderID = 43661, DetailID = 21, LineTotal = 6074.982000
         DETAIL: OrderID = 43661, DetailID = 22, LineTotal = 4049.988000
         DETAIL: OrderID = 43661, DetailID = 23, LineTotal = 40.373000
         DETAIL: OrderID = 43661, DetailID = 24, LineTotal = 1637.400000
         DETAIL: OrderID = 43661, DetailID = 25, LineTotal = 8099.976000
         DETAIL: OrderID = 43661, DetailID = 26, LineTotal = 4079.988000
         DETAIL: OrderID = 43661, DetailID = 27, LineTotal = 57.680800
         DETAIL: OrderID = 43661, DetailID = 28, LineTotal = 4049.988000
         DETAIL: OrderID = 43661, DetailID = 29, LineTotal = 100.932500
Press any key to continue.
```

Figure 6-2. Output for CopyAllTablesFromOneDataSetToAnother solution

Details tables, only the child records related to the selected parent records are copied to the destination.

Once the data has been copied, the DataRelation objects are copied by iterating over the collection of DataRelation objects in the source DataSet, and adding them to the destination DataSet. This involves creating an array of parent and source columns for the destination DataRelation from the parent and child column ordinals in the source DataRelation. This information, together with the name of the source DataRelation, is used to create the DataRelation in the destination DataSet. Finally, the EnforceConstraints property in the destination DataRelation is set to match the source.

6.3   Converting a DataReader to a DataTable

Problem

You need to transfer data from a DataReader to a DataTable.

Solution

Use either the Load( ) method of the DataTable class or programmatically create a
DataTable from the DataReader metadata schema and load the data from the
DataReader into the DataTable. The solution demonstrates both approaches.

To show the first approach, a DataReader is created returning all records in the
Person.Contact table in AdventureWorks. The Load( ) method of the DataTable is used
to load the DataReader into a DataTable. The first five rows from the DataTable are
output to the console.

To show the second approach, a DataReader is created, returning all records in the
Person.Contact table in AdventureWorks. Next, a DataTable schema is created in the destination DataSet using the schema information returned by the GetSchemaTable( )
method of the DataReader. Then, the GetData( ) method of the DataReader loads each
row of data into an array of objects, and adds it to the DataTable using the Add( )
method of the contained DataRowCollection. The first five rows from the DataTable
are output to the console.

The C# code in *Program.cs* in the project ConvertDataReaderToDataTable is shown in
Example 6-3.

Example 6-3. File: Program.cs for ConvertDataReaderToDataTable solution

```
using System;
using System.Data;
using System.Data.SqlClient;
using System.Collections.Generic;

namespace ConvertDataReaderToDataTable
{
    class Program
    {
        static void Main(string[] args)
        {
            string sqlConnectString = "Data Source=(local);" +
                "Integrated security=SSPI;Initial Catalog=AdventureWorks;";

            string sqlSelect = "SELECT * FROM Person.Contact";

            SqlDataReader dr;
            SqlConnection connection = new SqlConnection(sqlConnectString);
            SqlCommand command = new SqlCommand(sqlSelect, connection);
```

Example 6-3. File: Program.cs for ConvertDataReaderToDataTable solution (continued)

```csharp
connection.Open( );
dr = command.ExecuteReader( );

// Create the DataTable using the overloaded DataTable.Load( )
// method
Console.WriteLine("---DataTable.Load( )---");
DataTable dtDest1 = new DataTable( );
dtDest1.Load(dr);
// Output the first five rows from the DataTable
for (int i = 0; i < 5; i++)
{
    DataRow row = dtDest1.Rows[i];
    Console.WriteLine("ID = {0}\tFirstName = {1}\tLastName = {2}",
        row["ContactID"], row["FirstName"], row["LastName"]);
}

// Use DataReader metadata to create the DataTable
// and load the data from the DataReader
Console.WriteLine("\n---Programmatic approach---");
DataTable dtDest2 = new DataTable( );
dr = command.ExecuteReader(CommandBehavior.KeyInfo);
DataTable dtSchema = dr.GetSchemaTable( );
if (dtSchema != null)
{
    List<DataColumn>pkCols = new List<DataColumn>( );

    foreach (DataRow schemaRow in dtSchema.Rows)
    {
        DataColumn col = new DataColumn( );
        col.ColumnName = schemaRow["ColumnName"].ToString( );
        col.DataType = (Type)schemaRow["DataType"];

        // set the length of the field for string types only
        if (schemaRow["DataType"].ToString( ) == "System.String")
            col.MaxLength = (Int32)schemaRow["ColumnSize"];
        col.Unique = (bool)schemaRow["IsUnique"];
        col.AllowDBNull = (bool)schemaRow["AllowDBNull"];
        col.AutoIncrement = (bool)schemaRow["IsAutoIncrement"];

        // If part of the key, add the column name to the
        // array of columns comprising the primary key.
        if ((bool)schemaRow["IsKey"])
            pkCols.Add(col);

        dtDest2.Columns.Add(col);
    }

    // Add the primary key to the table.
    dtDest2.PrimaryKey = pkCols.ToArray( );
```

Example 6-3. File: Program.cs for ConvertDataReaderToDataTable solution (continued)

```
            object[] aData = new object[dtDest2.Columns.Count];
            // Read all rows from the DataReader.
            while (dr.Read( ))
            {
                // Read the row from the DataReader into an array.
                dr.GetValues(aData);
                // Add the row from the array to the DataTable.
                dtDest2.Rows.Add(aData);
            }
        }

        // Output the first five rows from the DataTable
        for (int i = 0; i < 5; i++)
        {
            DataRow row = dtDest2.Rows[i];
            Console.WriteLine("ID = {0}\tFirstName = {1}\tLastName = {2}",
                row["ContactID"], row["FirstName"], row["LastName"]);
        }

        Console.WriteLine("\nPress any key to continue.");
        Console.ReadKey( );
    }
  }
}
```

The output is shown in Figure 6-3.

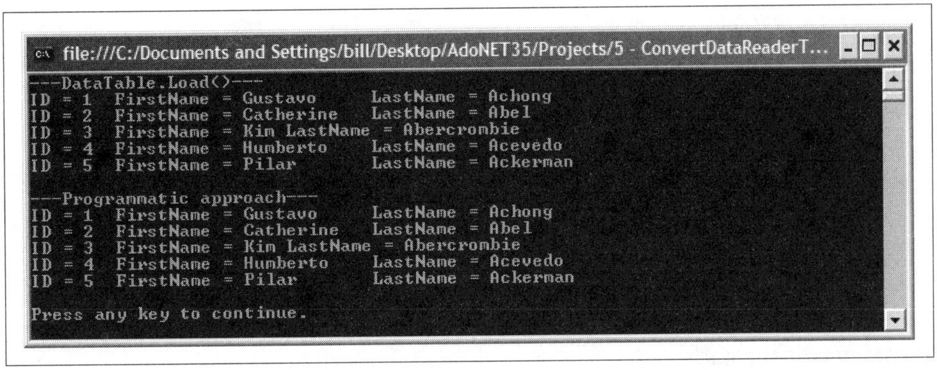

Figure 6-3. Output for ConvertDataReaderToDataTable solution

Discussion

Two approaches are discussed in the following subsections. The first uses the `Load( )` method of the `DataTable` class introduced in ADO.NET 2.0. The second approach programmatically uses the `DataReader` metadata together with the data.

The DbDataAdapter class—from which DataAdapter classes in .NET providers for relational databases inherit—defines an overload of the Fill() method that converts a DataReader to a DataSet; this method is declared protected and cannot be accessed (unless you write a custom DataAdapter). The Load() method of the DataTable class loads the contents of a DataReader into a DataTable.

DataTable.Load() approach

ADO.NET 2.0 adds a Load() method to the DataTable that converts a DataReader to a DataTable. If the DataReader has multiple result sets, only the first is converted to a DataTable. The Load() method has three overloads:

```
Load(IDataReader dataReader)
Load(IDataReader dataReader, LoadOption loadOption)
Load(IDataReader dataReader, LoadOption loadOption,
    FillErrorEventHandler fillErrorEventHandler)
```

Where:

dataReader
> The DataReader that is the source of the rows loaded into the DataTable.

loadOption
> Controls how the values from the data source are applied when the source has existing data. The options are described in Table 6-1.

Table 6-1. LoadOption enumeration

LoadOption value	Description
OverwriteChanges	Incoming values are written to both current and original versions of data for each column.
PreserveChanges	Incoming values are written only to the original version of data for each column.
Upsert	Incoming values are written only to the current version of data for each column.

fillErrorEventHandler
> The method that will handle a FillError event.

Programmatic approach

This solution demonstrates how this can be done programmatically.

Both the SQL Server and OLE DB DataReader expose a GetSchemaTable() method that returns a table containing the column metadata of the DataReader. You can use this table in turn to define the DataTable object, into which the DataReader data will be copied.

The GetSchemaTable() method returns the metadata described in Table 6-2 for each column.

Table 6-2. DataReader GetSchemaTable( ) metadata

Column name	Description
ColumnName	The name of the column.
ColumnOrdinal	The zero-based ordinal of the column.
ColumnSize	The maximum length of a column value. This is the data size of fixed-length data types.
NumericPrecision	The maximum precision of numeric data type columns. Null for non-numeric data type columns.
NumericScale	The number of digits to the right of the decimal for DBTYPE_DECIMAL or DBTYPE_NUMERIC data type columns. Otherwise, null.
IsUnique	Indicates whether the value in the column must be unique within all records.
IsKey	Indicates whether the column is part of the primary key or a unique key uniquely identifying the record.
BaseServerName	The instance name of the data server used by the DataReader.
BaseCatalogName	The name of the catalog in the data store.
BaseColumnName	The name of the column in the data store.
BaseSchemaName	The name of the schema in the data store.
BaseTableName	The name of the table in the data store.
DataType	The .NET Framework data type of the column.
AllowDBNull	Indicates whether null values are allowed in the column.
ProviderType	The .NET data provider data type of the column.
IsAliased	Indicates whether the column name is an alias.
IsExpression	Indicates whether the column is an expression.
IsIdentity	Indicates whether the column is an identity column.
IsAutoIncrement	Indicates whether values for the columns are automatically in fixed increments for each new row.
IsRowVersion	Indicates whether the column is a read-only persistent row identifier.
IsHidden	Indicates whether the column is hidden.
IsLong	Indicates whether the column contains a Binary Long Object (BLOB).
IsReadOnly	Indicates whether the column value cannot be modified.
DataTypeName	A string representation of the data type of the column.
XmlSchemaCollectionBase	The database where the schema collection for the XML instance is located.
XmlSchemaCollectionOwningSchema	The owning relational schema where the schema collection for the XML instance is located.
XmlSchemaCollectionName	The name of the schema collection for the XML instance.

Make sure that you set the behavior parameter of the ExecuteReader( ) method of the Command object to CommandBehavior.KeyInfo so that the metadata columns return the correct information. Note that the CommandBehavior.KeyInfo behavior executes the query with the FOR BROWSE option in SQL Server.

The conversion process uses the GetSchemaData( ) method to retrieve metadata as described in Table 6-2 about the columns in the result set of the DataReader and into a DataTable—each row in the DataTable corresponds to a column in the result set. A target DataTable is created to hold the result set in the DataReader. The solution iterates over the rows in the schema DataTable and uses the metadata to construct a DataColumn in the target DataTable for each column in the DataReader.

If the DataReader contain multiple result sets, iterate over the collection of result sets using the NextResult( ) method. Load each into result set into a separate DataTable in the DataSet, following the instructions in the previous paragraph. If the DataReader returns multiple result sets, there will not be information in the DataReader to create relationships between the tables. Create them programmatically if they are needed.

6.4   Converting a DataReader to a DataSet

Problem

You need to transfer data from a DataReader to a DataSet.

Solution

Use the Load( ) method of the DataSet class.

A DataReader is created returning the top five records in the HumanResources.Department and in the Person.Contact tables in AdventureWorks. The Load( ) method of the DataSet is used to load the DataReader into a DataSet. Records from the DataSet are output to the console together with some DataSet metadata.

The C# code in *Program.cs* in the CovertDataReaderToDataSet project is shown in Example 6-4.

Example 6-4. File: Program.cs for ConvertDataReaderToDataSet solution

```
using System;
using System.Data;
using System.Data.SqlClient;

namespace ConvertDataReaderToDataSet
{
    class Program
    {
        static void Main(string[] args)
        {
            string sqlConnectString = "Data Source=(local);" +
                "Integrated security=SSPI;Initial Catalog=AdventureWorks;";

            string sqlSelect = "SELECT TOP 5 DepartmentID, Name, GroupName " +
                "FROM HumanResources.Department;" +
                "SELECT TOP 5 ContactID, FirstName, LastName " +
                "FROM Person.Contact;";
```

Example 6-4. File: Program.cs for ConvertDataReaderToDataSet solution (continued)

```
            SqlDataReader dr;
            SqlConnection connection = new SqlConnection(sqlConnectString);
            SqlCommand command = new SqlCommand(sqlSelect, connection);
            connection.Open( );
            dr = command.ExecuteReader( );

            // Create the DataSet using the DataSet.Load( ) method
            DataSet ds = new DataSet( );
            ds.Load(dr, LoadOption.OverwriteChanges,
                new string[] {"Department", "Contact"});

            int tableCount = 0;
            foreach(DataTable dt in ds.Tables)
            {
                Console.WriteLine("Table {0}; Name = {1}", tableCount++,
                    dt.TableName);
                foreach(DataRow row in dt.Rows)
                {
                    for(int i = 0; i < dt.Columns.Count; i++)
                        Console.Write("{0} = {1};", dt.Columns[i].ColumnName,
                            row[i]);
                    Console.WriteLine( );
                }
                Console.WriteLine( );
            }

            Console.WriteLine("Press any key to continue.");
            Console.ReadKey( );
        }
    }
}
```

The output is shown in Figure 6-4.

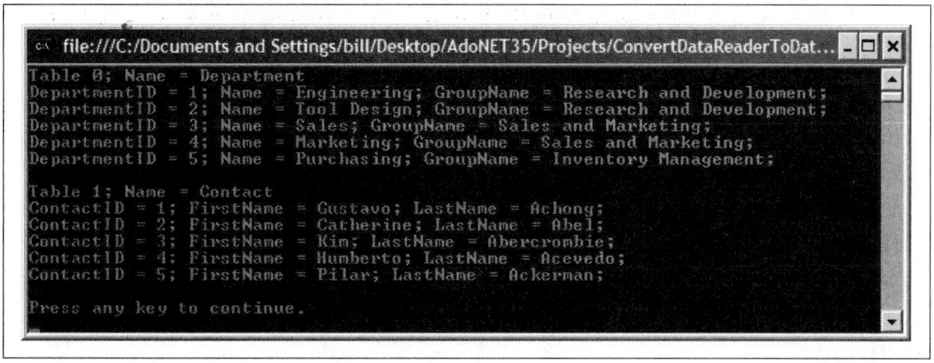

Figure 6-4. Output for ConvertDataReaderToDataSet solution

Discussion

ADO.NET 2.0 adds a Load( ) method to the DataSet that converts the result sets in a DataReader to a DataSet. This method uses an overload of the Load( ) method that has a string array parameter that specifies the names of the tables created in the DataSet—these are shown in the output from the example. The Load( ) method has three overloads:

```
Load(IDataReader dataReader, LoadOption loadOption, DataTable[] dataTables)
Load(IDataReader dataReader, LoadOption loadOption, string[] tableNames)
Load(IDataReader dataReader, LoadOption loadOption,
    FillErrorEventHandler fillErrorEventHandler, DataTable[] dataTables)
```

Where:

dataReader
> The DataReader to convert.

loadOption
> Controls how the values from the data source are applied when the source has existing data. The options are described in Table 6-3.

Table 6-3. LoadOption enumeration

LoadOption value	Description
OverwriteChanges	Incoming values are written to both current and original versions of data for each column.
PreserveChanges	Incoming values are written only to the original version of data for each column.
Upsert	Incoming values are written only to the current version of data for each column.

fillErrorEventHandler
> The method that will handle a FillError event.

dataTables
> Schema and namespace information for the tables created in the DataSet.

tableNames[]
> The names of the tables created in the DataSet.

6.5   Converting a DataTable to a DataReader

Problem

You need to access the data in a DataTable using DataReader mechanisms.

Solution

Use the CreateDataReader( ) method of the DataTable object.

The solution uses a DataAdapter to fill a DataTable with data from the first five rows in the Person.Contact in AdventureWorks. The CreateDataReader() method of the DataTable is used to convert the DataTable to a DataTableReader. The contents of the DataTableReader are output to the console.

The C# code in *Program.cs* in the project ConvertingDataTableToDataReader is shown in Example 6-5.

Example 6-5. File: Program.cs for ConvertingDataTableToDataReader solution

```csharp
using System;
using System.Data;
using System.Data.SqlClient;

namespace ConvertingDataTableToDataReader
{
    class Program
    {
        static void Main(string[] args)
        {
            string sqlConnectString = "Data Source=(local);" +
                "Integrated security=SSPI;Initial Catalog=AdventureWorks;";

            string sqlSelect = "SELECT TOP 5 ContactID, FirstName, LastName " +
                "FROM Person.Contact";

            // Create a data adapter
            SqlDataAdapter da = new SqlDataAdapter(sqlSelect, sqlConnectString);

            // Fill a DataTable using DataAdapter and output to console
            DataTable dt = new DataTable();
            da.Fill(dt);

            // Create a DataTableReader
            DataTableReader dtr = dt.CreateDataReader();
            // Iterate over the rows in the DataTableReader and output
            // the ID, first name, and last name for each person
            while (dtr.Read())
                Console.WriteLine("{0}\t{1}, {2}",
                dtr["ContactID"], dtr["LastName"], dtr["FirstName"]);

            Console.WriteLine("\nPress any key to continue.");
            Console.ReadKey();
        }
    }
}
```

The output is shown in Figure 6-5.

Figure 6-5. Output for ConvertingDataTableToDataReader solution

Discussion

The CreateDataReader( ) method of the DataTable returns a DataTableReader object corresponding to the data in the DataReader. A DataTableReader object exposes the contents of one or more DataTable objects as read-only, forward-only result sets similar to any other DataReader object. A DataTableReader iterates over the rows in a DataTable rather than in a data source. If you modify the data in the underlying DataTable while the DataTableReader is active, the reader automatically maintains its position.

6.6   Converting a DataSet to a DataReader

Problem

You need to access the data in a DataSet using DataReader mechanisms.

Solution

Use the CreateDataReader( ) method of the DataSet object.

The solution uses a DataAdapter to fill a DataSet with two result sets—the first five rows from HumanResources.Department and the first five rows in the Person.Contact in AdventureWorks. First, the CreateDataReader( ) method of the DataSet is used to convert the DataSet to a DataTableReader. Some metadata for the DataTableReader is output to the console. Next, the overloaded CreateDataReader(DataTable[]) method is used to convert only the Person.Contact DataTable to a DataTableReader. Metadata is again output to the console to show the effect of using the overloaded method.

The C# code in *Program.cs* in the project ConvertDataSetToDataReader is shown in Example 6-6.

Example 6-6. File: Program.cs for ConvertDataSetToDataReader solution

```
using System;
using System.Data;
using System.Data.SqlClient;
```

```csharp
namespace ConvertingDataSetToDataReader
{
    class Program
    {
        static void Main(string[] args)
        {
            string sqlConnectString = "Data Source=(local);" +
                "Integrated security=SSPI;Initial Catalog=AdventureWorks;";

            string sqlSelect = "SELECT TOP 5 DepartmentID, Name, GroupName " +
                "FROM HumanResources.Department;" +
                "SELECT TOP 5 ContactID, FirstName, LastName FROM " +
                "Person.Contact";

            // Create a data adapter
            SqlDataAdapter da = new SqlDataAdapter(sqlSelect, sqlConnectString);
            da.TableMappings.Add("Table", "Department");
            da.TableMappings.Add("Table1", "Contact");

            // Fill a DataSet using DataAdapter and output to console
            DataSet ds = new DataSet();
            da.Fill(ds);

            // Output information about the DataSet
            Console.WriteLine("---Source DataSet---");
            int tableIndex = 0;
            foreach (DataTable dt in ds.Tables)
            {
                Console.WriteLine("Result set {0} ({1}) columns: ",
                    tableIndex, dt.TableName);
                foreach (DataColumn col in dt.Columns)
                    Console.WriteLine("  {0}", col.ColumnName);
                tableIndex++;
            }

            // Create a DataTableReader
            Console.WriteLine("\n---DataTableReader using CreateDataReader---");
            DataTableReader dtr1 = ds.CreateDataReader();
            // Output information about the DataTableReader
            int result1Index = 0;
            do
            {
                result1Index++;
                Console.WriteLine("Result set: {0}", result1Index);
                for (int i = 0; i < dtr1.FieldCount; i++)
                    Console.WriteLine("  {0}", dtr1.GetName(i));
            } while (dtr1.NextResult());

            // Create a DataTableReader
            Console.WriteLine(
                "\n---DataTableReader using CreateDataReader(DataTable())---");
```

Example 6-6. File: Program.cs for ConvertDataSetToDataReader solution (continued)

```
DataTableReader dtr2 =
    ds.CreateDataReader(new DataTable[] {ds.Tables[1]});
// Output information about the DataTableReader
int result2Index = 0;
do
{
    result2Index++;
    Console.WriteLine("Result set: {0}", result2Index);
    for (int i = 0; i < dtr2.FieldCount; i++)
        Console.WriteLine("  {0}", dtr2.GetName(i));
} while (dtr2.NextResult());

Console.WriteLine("\nPress any key to continue.");
Console.ReadKey();
        }
    }
}
```

The output is shown in Figure 6-6.

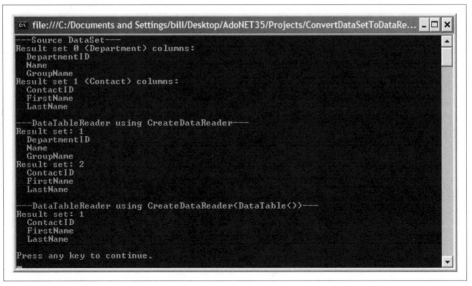

Figure 6-6. Output for ConvertDataSetToDataReader solution

Discussion

The CreateDataReader( ) method of the DataSet class returns a DataTableReader that contains one result set for each table in the DataSet in the same sequence that the tables appear in the Tables collection. An empty result set is created for tables that don't contain any records. A DataTableReader object returns the contents of one or more DataTable objects as read-only, forward-only result sets similar to any other DataReader object. A DataTableReader iterates over the rows in a DataTable rather than in a data source. This lets you update data using a DataTableReader.

An overload of the CreateDataReader( ) method of the DataSet class takes a DataTable array as a parameter and returns a DataTableReader object that exposes one result set for each DataTable in the array, in the same sequence that the DataTable objects appear in the input array.

6.7 Serializing Data

Problem

You need to serialize the contents of a DataSet so that you can store the data on a disk or transfer it across a network.

Solution

You can serialize a DataSet or DataTable into XML, binary, or SOAP formats and save the serialized DataSet to a stream (such as a file or network stream).

The solution creates a DataSet containing the Production.Product and Production.ProductInventory tables from AdventureWorks and a relation between the two tables. A file stream is created and the DataSet is serialized to XML, SOAP, and binary formats.

You need to add references to the System.Runtime.Serialization.Formatters.Soap assembly to build the solution.

The C# code in *Program.cs* in the project SerializeData is shown in Example 6-7.

Example 6-7. File: Program.cs for SerializeData solution

```
using System;
using System.Data;
using System.Data.SqlClient;
// Namespaces used for serialization
using System.IO;
using System.Xml.Serialization;
using System.Runtime.Serialization.Formatters.Soap;
using System.Runtime.Serialization.Formatters.Binary;

namespace SerializeData
{
    class Program
    {
        static void Main(string[] args)
        {
            string fileName = @"..\..\..\SerializedDataSet";
            Stream stream;
```

Example 6-7. File: Program.cs for SerializeData solution (continued)

```csharp
string sqlConnectString = "Data Source=(local);" +
    "Integrated security=SSPI;Initial Catalog=AdventureWorks;";

string sqlSelect = "SELECT * FROM Production.Product;" +
    "SELECT * FROM Production.ProductInventory";

DataSet ds = new DataSet( );
SqlDataAdapter da;

// Fill the Header table in the DataSet
da = new SqlDataAdapter(sqlSelect, sqlConnectString);
da.TableMappings.Add("Table", "Product");
da.TableMappings.Add("Table1", "ProductInventory");
da.FillSchema(ds, SchemaType.Mapped);
da.Fill(ds);

// Relate the Header and Order tables in the DataSet
DataRelation dr = new DataRelation("Product_ProductInventory",
    ds.Tables["Product"].Columns["ProductID"],
    ds.Tables["ProductInventory"].Columns["ProductID"]);
ds.Relations.Add(dr);

// Serialize using DataSet.WriteXml( )
using (stream = File.Open(fileName + "_1.xml", FileMode.Create,
    FileAccess.Write))
{
    ds.WriteXml(stream, XmlWriteMode.WriteSchema);
    Console.WriteLine(
        "DataSet serialized using DataSet.WriteXml( ) to {0}_1.xml",
        fileName);
}

// Serialize using XmlSerializer
using (stream = File.Open(fileName + "_2.xml", FileMode.Create,
    FileAccess.Write))
{
    XmlSerializer xs = new XmlSerializer(typeof(DataSet));
    xs.Serialize(stream, ds);
    Console.WriteLine(
        "DataSet serialized using XmlSerializer to {0}_2.xml",
        fileName);
}

// Serialize using SoapFormatter
using (stream = File.Open(fileName + ".soap", FileMode.Create,
    FileAccess.Write))
{
    SoapFormatter sf = new SoapFormatter( );
    sf.Serialize(stream, ds);
    Console.WriteLine(
        "DataSet serialized using SoapFormatter to {0}.soap",
        fileName);
}
```

Example 6-7. File: Program.cs for SerializeData solution (continued)

```
// Serialize using BinaryFormatter
using (stream = File.Open(fileName + ".bin", FileMode.Create,
    FileAccess.Write))
{
    BinaryFormatter bf = new BinaryFormatter( );
    bf.Serialize(stream, ds);
    Console.WriteLine(
        "DataSet serialized using BinaryFormatter to {0}.bin",
        fileName);
}

Console.WriteLine("\nPress any key to continue.");
Console.ReadKey( );
            }
        }
}
```

The output is shown in Figure 6-7.

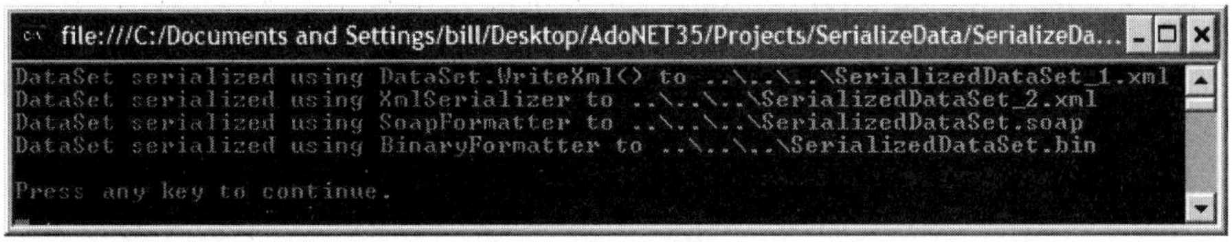

Figure 6-7. Output for SerializeData solution

Discussion

Serialization converts an object into a stream of data that can be transported or saved as a file. Deserialization reconstructs the original object from the file.

The most basic data serialization is done by writing the contents of the DataSet object to XML using the WriteXml( ) or GetXml( ) methods. The contents are then deserialized with the ReadXml( ) method. These methods, unlike the others shown in this solution, are limited to serializing and deserializing DataTable and DataSet objects and provide little control over serialization format.

The XmlSerializer class serializes and deserializes objects into XML classes. It performs *shallow* serialization: only the read-write property values of the class are serialized, not the underlying data. The XML stream generated by the XmlSerializer class is compliant with the World Wide Web Consortium (*http://www.w3.org*) XML Schema Definition (XSD) language 1.0 recommendations. The XmlSerializer object can serialize to any object that inherits from System.IO.Stream. When constructing the XmlSerializer object, you must specify the type of object that can be serialized by the instance.

You can also use the XmlSerializer class to serialize an object into a SOAP XML stream that conforms to Section 5 of the World Wide Web Consortium document "Simple Object Access Protocol (SOAP) 1.1." To do this, use the overloaded constructor that accepts the XmlTypeMapping argument.

The IFormatter interface provides functionality for formatting serialized objects. The class to be serialized must be marked with the SerializableAttribute attribute; otherwise, a SerializationException will be raised. A class can implement the ISerializable interface to override the default serialization behavior.

The System.Runtime.Serialization.Formatter class provides base functionality for the serialization formatters:

System.Runtime.Serialization.Formatters.Binary
    This namespace contains the BinaryFormatter class that can serialize and deserialize objects in binary format.

System.Runtime.Serialization.Formatters.Soap
    This namespace contains the SoapFormatter classes that can serialize and deserialize objects in SOAP format.

The BinaryFormatter and SoapFormatter both perform *deep* serialization: the values in the object's variables are serialized. If the object holds references to other objects, they will be serialized as well. The NonSerializedAttribute attribute can exclude a variable from the serialization process.

Both the BinaryFormatter and SoapFormatter implement the IFormatter and IRemotingFormatter interfaces, which provide functionality for formatting serialized objects and for sending and receiving remote procedure calls (RPC), respectively. The methods for serialization and deserialization in both interfaces are called Serialize( ) and Deserialize( ). Overloaded versions determine whether the call is a remote call.

The Serialize( ) method of the IFormatter interface serializes the object to a Stream object. This includes all classes that have the base class System.IO.Stream, such as:

- System.IO.BufferedStream
- System.IO.FileStream
- System.IO.MemoryStream
- System.Net.Sockets.NetworkStream
- System.Security.Cryptography.CryptoStream

Once the serialization object has been created, serialization is accomplished by calling the Serialize( ) method of the serializing object with arguments referencing the destination stream and the object to be serialized.

The `Deserialize()` method of the `IFormatter` interface deserializes the specified `Stream` object to recreate the object graph that was previously serialized. For more information about deserializing data, see Recipe 6.8, next.

6.8 Deserializing Data

Problem

You have a `DataSet` that has been serialized and written to a file. You want to re-create the `DataSet` from this file.

Solution

Deserialize the file contents and cast the result to a `DataSet` object.

The solution loads a file stream containing a previously serialized `DataSet` in XML, SOAP, and binary formats and deserializes it to recreate the original `DataSet`. Specifically, the solution uses the files created in the solution for Recipe 6.7. Copy these files to the directory that contains the solution file *DeserializeData.sln*.

You need to add references to the `System.Runtime.Serialization.Formatters.Soap` assembly to build the solution.

The C# code in *Program.cs* in the project `DeserializeDate` is shown in Example 6-8.

Example 6-8. File: Program.cs for DeserializeData solution

```
using System;
using System.Data;
using System.Data.SqlClient;
// Namespaces used for deserialization
using System.IO;
using System.Xml.Serialization;
using System.Runtime.Serialization.Formatters.Soap;
using System.Runtime.Serialization.Formatters.Binary;

namespace DeserializeData
{
    class Program
    {
        static void Main(string[] args)
        {
            string fileName = @"..\..\..\SerializedDataSet";

            Stream stream;
            DataSet ds;
```

Example 6-8. File: Program.cs for DeserializeData solution (continued)

```csharp
            // Deserialize using DataSet.ReadXml( )
            using (stream = File.Open(fileName + "_1.xml", FileMode.Open,
                FileAccess.Read))
            {
                ds = new DataSet( );
                ds.ReadXml(stream);
            }
            Console.WriteLine("{0} deserialized using DataSet.ReadXml( ).",
                fileName + "_1.xml");
            OutputDataSetInfo(ds);

            // Deserialize using XmlSerializer
            using (stream = File.Open(fileName + "_2.xml", FileMode.Open,
                FileAccess.Read))
            {
                XmlSerializer xs = new XmlSerializer(typeof(DataSet));
                ds = (DataSet)xs.Deserialize(stream);
            }
            Console.WriteLine("\n{0} deserialized using XmlSerializer.",
                fileName + "_2.xml");
            OutputDataSetInfo(ds);

            // Deserialize using SoapFormatter
            using (stream = File.Open(fileName + ".soap", FileMode.Open,
                FileAccess.Read))
            {
                SoapFormatter sf = new SoapFormatter( );
                ds = (DataSet)sf.Deserialize(stream);
            }
            Console.WriteLine("\n{0} deserialized using SoapFormatter.",
                fileName + ".soap");
            OutputDataSetInfo(ds);

            // Deserialize using BinaryFormatter
            using (stream = File.Open(fileName + ".bin", FileMode.Open,
                FileAccess.Read))
            {
                BinaryFormatter bf = new BinaryFormatter( );
                ds = (DataSet)bf.Deserialize(stream);
            }
            Console.WriteLine("\n{0} deserialized using BinaryFormatter.",
                fileName + ".bin");
            OutputDataSetInfo(ds);

            Console.WriteLine("\nPress any key to continue.");
            Console.ReadKey( );
        }

        private static void OutputDataSetInfo(DataSet ds)
```

Example 6-8. File: Program.cs for DeserializeData solution (continued)

```
    {
        foreach(DataTable dt in ds.Tables)
            Console.WriteLine("\tTable {0} contains {1} records.",
                dt.TableName, dt.Rows.Count);
    }
  }
}
```

The output is shown in Figure 6-8.

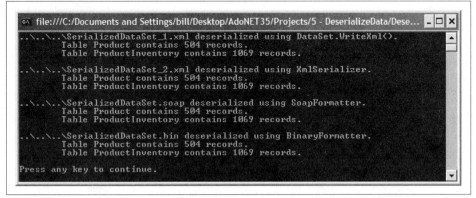

Figure 6-8. Output for DeserializeData solution

Discussion

This solution deserializes each of the serialized DataSet objects created in the solution for Recipe 6.7.

The appropriate serializing object is created for each file and in the case of the XmlSerializer object, its type is specified in the constructor. The Deserialize( ) method of the serializer object is then used to deserialize the file stream into an object graph. This is then cast to a DataSet to complete the deserialization.

See the discussion in Recipe 6.7 for more information about the serialization and the formatter classes that can serialize ADO.NET objects.

6.9   Merging Data in Two DataSet Objects

Problem

You have two DataSet objects with the same schema, each containing different data. You need to combine data from these two DataSet objects, merging the changes and without creating duplicate rows.

Solution

Use the DataSet.Merge() method with the appropriate MissingSchemaAction enumeration values.

The solution creates two DataSet objects each with a single DataTable containing a different subset of data from the Person.Contact table in AdventureWorks. The content of each is output to the console. Both DataSet objects are merged into a third DataSet using the Merge() method. The content of the merged DataSet is output to the console.

The C# code in *Program.cs* in the project MergeDataSets is shown in Example 6-9.

Example 6-9. File: Program.cs for MergeDataSets solution

```csharp
using System;
using System.Data;
using System.Data.SqlClient;

namespace MergeDataSets
{
    class Program
    {
        static void Main(string[] args)
        {
            string sqlConnectString = "Data Source=(local);" +
                "Integrated security=SSPI;Initial Catalog=AdventureWorks;";

            string sqlSelect1 = "SELECT ContactID, FirstName, LastName " +
                "FROM Person.Contact WHERE ContactID BETWEEN 1 AND 4";
            string sqlSelect2 = "SELECT ContactID, FirstName, LastName " +
                "FROM Person.Contact WHERE ContactID BETWEEN 5 AND 8";

            // Fill the first DataSet and output
            DataSet ds1 = new DataSet();
            SqlDataAdapter da1 = new SqlDataAdapter(sqlSelect1, sqlConnectString);
            da1.TableMappings.Add("Table", "Contact");
            da1.FillSchema(ds1, SchemaType.Source);
            da1.Fill(ds1);

            Console.WriteLine("---DataSet 1---");
            foreach (DataRow row in ds1.Tables["Contact"].Rows)
                Console.WriteLine("{0}\t{1}, {2}",
                    row["ContactID"], row["LastName"], row["FirstName"]);

            // Fill the second DataSet and output
            DataSet ds2 = new DataSet();
            SqlDataAdapter da2 = new SqlDataAdapter(sqlSelect2, sqlConnectString);
            da2.TableMappings.Add("Table", "Contact");
            da2.FillSchema(ds2, SchemaType.Source);
            da2.Fill(ds2);

            Console.WriteLine("\n---DataSet 2---");
```

Example 6-9. File: Program.cs for MergeDataSets solution (continued)

```
        foreach (DataRow row in ds2.Tables["Contact"].Rows)
            Console.WriteLine("{0}\t{1}, {2}",
                row["ContactID"], row["LastName"], row["FirstName"]);

        //Create the merged DataSet
        DataSet dsM = new DataSet();
        dsM.Merge(ds1);
        dsM.Merge(ds2);

        Console.WriteLine("\n---Merged DataSet---");
        foreach (DataRow row in dsM.Tables["Contact"].Rows)
            Console.WriteLine("{0}\t{1}, {2}",
                row["ContactID"], row["LastName"], row["FirstName"]);

        Console.WriteLine("\nPress any key to continue.");
        Console.ReadKey();
    }
  }
}
```

The output is shown in Figure 6-9.

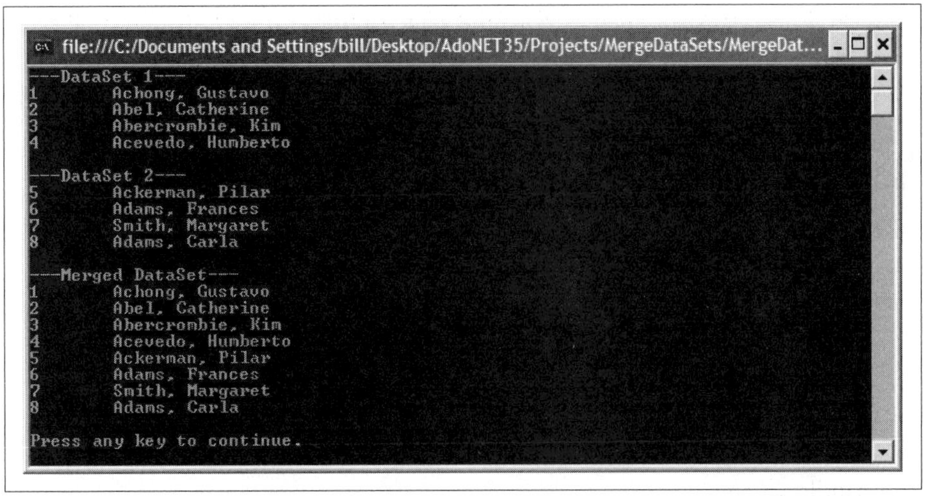

Figure 6-9. Output for MergeDataSets solution

Discussion

The Merge( ) method of the DataSet object can merge a DataRow array, a DataTable, or a DataSet into an existing DataSet. If the existing DataSet has a primary key defined, the incoming data is matched to rows with the same primary key values. Where matches are found, the existing row is updated with the new values. Otherwise, rows are appended to the existing table.

The DataTable has a similar Merge( ) method that can merge a DataRow array or a DataTable. The Merge( ) method of the DataTable object merges only the original table and not related child tables that might be defined through a relationship.

There are two arguments that can be optionally specified in the overloaded Merge( ) methods.

The first, preserveChanges, is a Boolean value that indicates whether incoming values will overwrite changes made to the existing DataSet. If preserveChanges is false, the default, both the Current and Original row are overwritten with incoming values and the RowState of the row is set to the RowState of the incoming row. Exceptions are shown in Table 6-4.

Table 6-4. Exceptions to PreserveChanges argument when PreserveChanges = false

Incoming RowState	Existing RowState	New RowState
Unchanged	Modified, Deleted, or Added	Modified
Added	Unchanged, Modified, or Deleted	Modified. Also, data in the Original version of the existing row is not overwritten because the Original version of the incoming row does not exist.

If preserveChanges is specified as true, the values in the Current version of the existing row are maintained while values in the Original version of the existing row are overwritten with the Original values for the incoming row. The RowState of the existing row is set to Modified. Exceptions are shown in Table 6-5.

Table 6-5. Exceptions to PreserveChanges argument when PreserveChanges = true

Incoming RowState	Existing RowState	New RowState
Any	Deleted	Deleted
Added	Any	Modified. Data in the Original version of the row is not overwritten because the Original version of the incoming row does not exist.

The second argument is the missingSchemaAction argument, which accepts a value from the MissingSchemaAction enumeration that specifies how the Merge( ) method will handle schema elements in the incoming data that are not part of the existing DataSet. Table 6-6 describes the values in the MissingSchemaAction enumeration.

Table 6-6. MissingSchemaAction enumeration

Value	Decription
Add	Add the new schema information and populate the new schema with incoming values. This is the default value.
AddWithKey	Add the new schema and primary key information and populate the new schema with incoming values.
Error	Throw an exception if the incoming schema does not match the schema of the existing DataSet.
Ignore	Ignore new schema information.

6.10   Merging Data in Two Database Tables

Problem

You need to merge the data in two SQL Server 2008 database tables.

Solution

Use the T-SQL MERGE statement.

The solution needs a table named MergeTable in the AdoDotNet35Cookbook database. Execute the following T-SQL statement to create the table:

```
USE AdoDotNet35Cookbook
GO
CREATE TABLE MergeTable(
    ID int NOT NULL PRIMARY KEY,
    Field1 nvarchar(50) NULL,
    Field2 nvarchar(50) NULL )
```

The solution needs some sample data in the table MergeTable. Create the data by executing the following T-SQL batch:

```
USE AdoDotNet35Cookbook
GO
INSERT INTO MergeTable VALUES (1, 'Field1.1', 'Field2.1')
INSERT INTO MergeTable VALUES (2, 'Field1.2', 'Field2.2')
INSERT INTO MergeTable VALUES (3, 'Field1.3', 'Field2.3')
```

The solution needs a second table named MergeTableDelta. Execute the following T-SQL statement to create the table:

```
USE AdoDotNet35Cookbook
GO
CREATE TABLE MergeTableDelta(
    ID int NOT NULL PRIMARY KEY,
    Field1 nvarchar(50) NULL,
    Field2 nvarchar(50) NULL )
```

The solution needs some sample data in the table MergeTableDelta. Create the data by executing the following T-SQL batch:

```
USE AdoDotNet35Cookbook
GO
INSERT INTO MergeTableDelta VALUES (2, 'Field1.2', 'Field2.2 (new)')
INSERT INTO MergeTableDelta VALUES (4, 'Field1.4', 'Field2.4')
INSERT INTO MergeTableDelta VALUES (5, 'Field1.5', 'Field2.5')
```

The solution fills a DataTable with data from the destination merge table named MergeTable in the AdoDotNet35Cookbook database and output to the console. A second DataTable is filled with the merge data from the table named MergeTableDelta in the AdoDotNet35Cookbook database and output to the console. The T-SQL MERGE statement is executed merging the records in MergeTableDelta into the table named MergeTable.

After the MERGE operation completes, a DataTable is filled with the data from the destination merge table and output to the console showing the effects of the merge.

The C# code in *Program.cs* in the project MergeTables is shown in Example 6-10.

Example 6-10. File: Program.cs for MergeTables solution

```csharp
using System;
using System.Data;
using System.Data.SqlClient;

namespace MergeTables
{
    class Program
    {
        static void Main(string[] args)
        {
            string sqlConnectString = @"Data Source=(local);
                Integrated security=SSPI;Initial Catalog=AdoDotNet35Cookbook;";

            string sqlSelect = "SELECT * FROM MergeTable";
            string sqlSelectDelta = "SELECT * FROM MergeTableDelta";

            string sqlMerge = @"MERGE MergeTable AS m
                USING MergeTableDelta AS d
                ON (m.ID = d.ID)
                WHEN MATCHED AND m.Field1 <> d.Field1 OR m.Field2 <> d.Field2
                    THEN UPDATE SET m.Field1 = d.Field1, m.Field2 = d.Field2
                WHEN NOT MATCHED THEN
                    INSERT (ID, Field1, Field2)
                        VALUES (d.ID, d.Field1, d.Field2);";

            SqlDataAdapter da = new SqlDataAdapter(sqlSelect, sqlConnectString);
            DataTable dt = new DataTable( );
            da.Fill(dt);
            Console.WriteLine("---MergeTable (Initial)---");
            foreach (DataRow row in dt.Rows)
            {
                Console.WriteLine("ID = {0}\tField1 = {1}\tField2 = {2}",
                    row["ID"], row["Field1"], row["Field2"]);
            }

            SqlDataAdapter daDelta =
                new SqlDataAdapter(sqlSelectDelta, sqlConnectString);
            DataTable dtDelta = new DataTable( );
            daDelta.Fill(dtDelta);
            Console.WriteLine("\n---MergeTableDelta---");
            foreach (DataRow row in dtDelta.Rows)
            {
                Console.WriteLine("ID = {0}\tField1 = {1}\tField2 = {2}",
                    row["ID"], row["Field1"], row["Field2"]);
            }
```

Example 6-10. File: Program.cs for MergeTables solution (continued)

```
using (SqlConnection connection = new SqlConnection(sqlConnectString))
{
    SqlCommand command = new SqlCommand(sqlMerge, connection);
    connection.Open( );

    int rowsAff = command.ExecuteNonQuery( );
    Console.WriteLine("\n=> Merge executed. {0} rows affected.", rowsAff);
}

dt.Clear( );
da.Fill(dt);
Console.WriteLine("\n---MergeTable (After Merge)---");
foreach (DataRow row in dt.Rows)
{
    Console.WriteLine("ID = {0}\tField1 = {1}\tField2 = {2}",
        row["ID"], row["Field1"], row["Field2"]);
}

Console.WriteLine("\nPress any key to continue.");
Console.ReadKey( );
        }
    }
}
```

The output is shown in Figure 6-10.

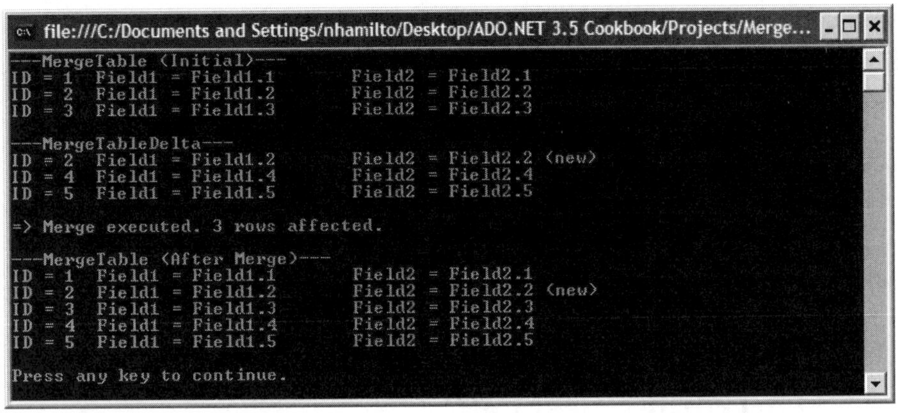

Figure 6-10. Output for MergeTables solution

Discussion

SQL Server 2008 introduces the T-SQL MERGE statement that lets you perform INSERT, UPDATE, and DELETE operations in a single statement. The MERGE statement lets you join a source of merge data to a destination table and perform those actions based on the results of the JOIN.

The solution uses the following MERGE statement to perform both inserts and updates:

```
MERGE MergeTable AS m
USING MergeTableDelta AS d
ON (m.ID = d.ID)
WHEN MATCHED AND m.Field1 <> d.Field1 OR m.Field2 <> d.Field2
    THEN UPDATE SET m.Field1 = d.Field1, m.Field2 = d.Field2
WHEN NOT MATCHED THEN
    INSERT (ID, Field1, Field2)
        VALUES (d.ID, d.Field1, d.Field2)
```

The MERGE statement syntax has four clauses:

- The MERGE clause specifies the table or view that is the destination for the INSERT, UPDATE, and DELETE operations using the records in the merge source table specified by the USING clause.

- The USING clause specifies the source of the data to be merged into the destination.

- The ON clause specifies the JOIN conditions that matches records in destination destination and merge data.

- The WHEN clause specifies the INSERT, UPDATE, and DELETE actions to take during the merge operation.

The WHEN MATCHED AND...THEN clause specifies the action to take when record in the target and merge source tables match based on the join specified in the ON clause and the optional criteria specified. The WHEN NOT MATCHED THEN clause specifies the action to take when a record in the merge source has no matching record in the merge destination based on the join specified in the ON clause.

The example inserts and deletes records into the destination based on the merge source data. You can process tables that exist in the original table and not in the merge table by using the WHEN SOURCE clause. For example, to delete rows from the merge source table when they do not exist in the merge destination table, use the following T-SQL clause:

```
WHEN SOURCE NOT MATCHED THEN DELETE;
```

You can use the @@ROWCOUNT function after executing a MERGE statement to return the number of rows inserted, deleted, and updated by the MERGE statement.

6.11   Encrypting a DataSet

Problem

You need to encrypt and write a DataSet to a file for storage or transmission. You also need to decrypt the file and reconstruct the DataSet.

Solution

Encrypt and decrypt the DataSet using the .NET cryptographic services, and serialize and save the encrypted DataSet to a stream (such as a file or network stream).

The solution creates a DataSet that contains a subset of data from the Person.Contact table in AdventureWorks. The contents of the DataSet are output to the console.

Next, the DataSet is encrypted to a file named *symmetric.dat* in the same directory as the solution file *EncryptDataSet.sln* and decrypted using a (symmetric) DES algorithm. The contents of the decrypted DataSet are output to the console.

Finally, the DataSet is encrypted to a file named *asymmetric.dat* in the same directory as the solution file *EncryptDataSet.sln* and decrypted using both a (symmetric) RC2 algorithm and an (asymmetric) RSA algorithm. The contents of the decrypted DataSet are output to the console.

The C# code in *Program.cs* in the project EncryptDataSet is shown in Example 6-11.

Example 6-11. File: Program.cs for EncryptDataSet solution

```
using System;
using System.Data;
using System.Data.SqlClient;
using System.Security.Cryptography;
using System.IO;
using System.Runtime.Serialization;
using System.Runtime.Serialization.Formatters.Binary;
using System.Xml;

namespace EncryptDataSet
{
    [Serializable()]
    internal class EncryptedMessage
    {
        public byte[] Body;        // RC2 encrypted
        public byte[] Key;         // RSA encrypted RC2 key
        public byte[] IV;          // RC2 initialization vector
    }

    class Program
    {
        private enum Algorithm { DES, RC2, Rijndael, TripleDES };

        private const string symmetricFileName = @"..\..\..\symmetric.dat";
        private const string asymmetricFileName = @"..\..\..\asymmetric.dat";
        private const int keySize = 128;
        private static RSACryptoServiceProvider rSAReceiver =
            new RSACryptoServiceProvider();
        private static int symmetricAlgorithm = (int)Algorithm.DES;
```

Example 6-11. File: Program.cs for EncryptDataSet solution (continued)

```csharp
// DES key and IV
private static Byte[] dESKey =
    new Byte[] { 0x01, 0x02, 0x03, 0x04, 0x05, 0x06, 0x07, 0x08 };
private static Byte[] dESIV =
    new Byte[] { 0x11, 0x12, 0x13, 0x14, 0x15, 0x16, 0x17, 0x18 };
// RC2 key and IV
private static Byte[] rC2Key = new Byte[]
    {0x00, 0x01, 0x02, 0x03, 0x04, 0x05, 0x06, 0x07,
     0x08, 0x09, 0x0A, 0x0B, 0x0C, 0x0D, 0x0E, 0x0F};
private static Byte[] rC2IV = new Byte[]
    {0x10, 0x11, 0x12, 0x13, 0x14, 0x15, 0x16, 0x17,
     0x18, 0x19, 0x1A, 0x1B, 0x1C, 0x1D, 0x1E, 0x1F};
// Rijndael key and IV
private static Byte[] rijndaelKey = new Byte[]
    {0x20, 0x21, 0x22, 0x23, 0x24, 0x25, 0x26, 0x27,
     0x28, 0x29, 0x2A, 0x2B, 0x2C, 0x2D, 0x2E, 0x2F};
private static Byte[] rijndaelIV = new Byte[]
    {0x30, 0x31, 0x32, 0x33, 0x34, 0x35, 0x36, 0x37,
     0x38, 0x39, 0x3A, 0x3B, 0x3C, 0x3D, 0x3E, 0x3F};
// triple DES key and IV
private static Byte[] tDESKey = new Byte[]
    {0x00, 0x01, 0x02, 0x03, 0x04, 0x05, 0x06, 0x07,
     0x08, 0x09, 0x0A, 0x0B, 0x0C, 0x0D, 0x0E, 0x0F,
     0x10, 0x11, 0x12, 0x13, 0x14, 0x15, 0x16, 0x17};
private static Byte[] tDESIV = new Byte[]
    {0x20, 0x21, 0x22, 0x23, 0x24, 0x25, 0x26, 0x27,
     0x28, 0x29, 0x2A, 0x2B, 0x2C, 0x2D, 0x2E, 0x2F,
     0x30, 0x31, 0x32, 0x33, 0x34, 0x35, 0x36, 0x37};

static void Main(string[] args)
{
    string sqlConnectString = "Data Source=(local);" +
        "Integrated security=SSPI;Initial Catalog=AdventureWorks;";

    string sqlSelect = "SELECT ContactID, FirstName, LastName " +
        "FROM Person.Contact WHERE ContactID BETWEEN 10 AND 13";

    DataSet dsSource = new DataSet( );
    SqlDataAdapter da;

    // Fill the table in the DataSet
    da = new SqlDataAdapter(sqlSelect, sqlConnectString);
    da.FillSchema(dsSource, SchemaType.Source);
    da.Fill(dsSource);

    // Output the source DataSet to the console
    Console.WriteLine("---Source DataSet---");
    foreach (DataRow row in dsSource.Tables[0].Rows)
        Console.WriteLine("ContactID = {0}\tFirstName = {1}\tLastName = {2}",
            row["ContactID"], row["FirstName"], row["LastName"]);
```

Example 6-11. File: Program.cs for EncryptDataSet solution (continued)

```
        // Encrypt the DataSet
        SymmetricEncryptDataSet(dsSource, symmetricFileName);

        // Decrypt the DataSet
        DataSet dsSymmetric = SymmetricDecryptDataSet(symmetricFileName);

        // Output the symmetric decrypted DataSet to the console
        Console.WriteLine("\n---Symmetric Decryption---");
        foreach (DataRow row in dsSymmetric.Tables[0].Rows)
            Console.WriteLine("ContactID = {0}\tFirstName = {1}\tLastName = {2}",
                row["ContactID"], row["FirstName"], row["LastName"]);

        // Encrypt the DataSet
        AsymmetricEncryptDataSet(dsSource, asymmetricFileName);

        // Decrypt the DataSet
        DataSet dsAsymmetric = AsymmetricDecryptDataSet(asymmetricFileName);

        // Output the asymmetric decrypted DataSet to the console
        Console.WriteLine("\n---Asymmetric Decryption---");
        foreach (DataRow row in dsAsymmetric.Tables[0].Rows)
            Console.WriteLine("ContactID = {0}\tFirstName = {1}\tLastName = {2}",
                row["ContactID"], row["FirstName"], row["LastName"]);

        Console.WriteLine("\nPress any key to continue.");
        Console.ReadKey();
    }

    private static void SymmetricEncryptDataSet(DataSet dsSource, string fileName)
    {
        // symmetric algorithms
        SymmetricAlgorithm sa = null;
        byte[] key = null;
        byte[] iV = null;

        switch (symmetricAlgorithm)
        {
            case (int)Algorithm.DES:
                sa = new DESCryptoServiceProvider();
                key = dESKey;
                iV = dESIV;
                break;
            case (int)Algorithm.RC2:
                sa = new RC2CryptoServiceProvider();
                sa.KeySize = keySize;
                key = rC2Key;
                iV = rC2IV;
                break;
            case (int)Algorithm.Rijndael:
                sa = new RijndaelManaged();
                key = rijndaelKey;
                iV = rijndaelIV;
                break;
```

Example 6-11. File: Program.cs for EncryptDataSet solution (continued)

```
            case (int)Algorithm.TripleDES:
                sa = new TripleDESCryptoServiceProvider( );
                key = tDESKey;
                iV = tDESIV;
                break;
        }

        FileStream fsWrite =
            new FileStream(fileName, FileMode.Create, FileAccess.Write);
        CryptoStream cs = new CryptoStream(fsWrite,
            sa.CreateEncryptor(key, iV), CryptoStreamMode.Write);

        dsSource.WriteXml(cs, XmlWriteMode.WriteSchema);
        cs.Close( );
        fsWrite.Close( );
    }

    private static DataSet SymmetricDecryptDataSet(string fileName)
    {
        FileStream fsRead =
            new FileStream(symmetricFileName, FileMode.Open, FileAccess.Read);

        SymmetricAlgorithm sa = null;
        byte[] key = null;
        byte[] iV = null;

        switch (symmetricAlgorithm)
        {
            case (int)Algorithm.DES:
                sa = new DESCryptoServiceProvider( );
                key = dESKey;
                iV = dESIV;
                break;
            case (int)Algorithm.RC2:
                sa = new RC2CryptoServiceProvider( );
                sa.KeySize = keySize;
                key = rC2Key;
                iV = rC2IV;
                break;
            case (int)Algorithm.Rijndael:
                sa = new RijndaelManaged( );
                key = rijndaelKey;
                iV = rijndaelIV;
                break;
            case (int)Algorithm.TripleDES:
                sa = new TripleDESCryptoServiceProvider( );
                key = tDESKey;
                iV = tDESIV;
                break;
        }
```

Example 6-11. File: Program.cs for EncryptDataSet solution (continued)

```
        CryptoStream cs =
            new CryptoStream(fsRead, sa.CreateDecryptor(key, iV),
                CryptoStreamMode.Read);

        DataSet ds = new DataSet();
        ds.ReadXml(cs, XmlReadMode.ReadSchema);
        cs.Close();
        fsRead.Close();

        return ds;
    }

    private static void AsymmetricEncryptDataSet(DataSet ds, string fileName)
    {
        // Asymmetric algorithm
        EncryptedMessage em = new EncryptedMessage();

        // RC2 symmetric algorithm to encode the DataSet
        RC2CryptoServiceProvider rC2 = new RC2CryptoServiceProvider();
        rC2.KeySize = keySize;
        // Generate RC2 Key and IV.
        rC2.GenerateKey();
        rC2.GenerateIV();

        // Get the receiver's RSA public key.
        RSACryptoServiceProvider rSA = new RSACryptoServiceProvider();
        rSA.ImportParameters(rSAReceiver.ExportParameters(false));
        // Encrypt the RC2 key and IV with the receiver's RSA public key.
        em.Key = rSA.Encrypt(rC2.Key, false);
        em.IV = rSA.Encrypt(rC2.IV, false);

        // Use the CryptoStream to write the encrypted DataSet to the
        // MemoryStream.
        MemoryStream ms = new MemoryStream();
        CryptoStream cs = new CryptoStream(ms, rC2.CreateEncryptor(),
            CryptoStreamMode.Write);
        ds.WriteXml(cs, XmlWriteMode.WriteSchema);
        cs.FlushFinalBlock();
        em.Body = ms.ToArray();

        cs.Close();
        ms.Close();

        // Serialize the encrypted message to a file.
        Stream s = File.Open(fileName, FileMode.Create);
        BinaryFormatter bf = new BinaryFormatter();
        bf.Serialize(s, em);
        s.Close();
    }
```

Example 6-11. File: Program.cs for EncryptDataSet solution (continued)

```
        private static DataSet AsymmetricDecryptDataSet(string fileName)
        {
            // Asymmetric algorithm

            // Deserialize the encrypted message from a file.
            Stream s = File.Open(fileName, FileMode.Open);

            BinaryFormatter bf = new BinaryFormatter( );
            EncryptedMessage em = (EncryptedMessage)bf.Deserialize(s);
            s.Close( );

            // RC2 symmetric algorithm to decode the DataSet
            RC2CryptoServiceProvider rC2 = new RC2CryptoServiceProvider( );
            rC2.KeySize = keySize;

            // Decrypt the RC2 key and IV using the receiver's RSA private
            // key.
            rC2.Key = rSAReceiver.Decrypt(em.Key, false);
            rC2.IV = rSAReceiver.Decrypt(em.IV, false);

            // Put the message body into the MemoryStream.
            MemoryStream ms = new MemoryStream(em.Body);
            // Use the CryptoStream to read the encrypted DataSet from the
            // MemoryStream.
            CryptoStream cs = new CryptoStream(ms, rC2.CreateDecryptor( ),
                CryptoStreamMode.Read);
            DataSet ds = new DataSet( );
            ds.ReadXml(cs, XmlReadMode.ReadSchema);
            cs.Close( );

            return ds;
        }
    }
}
```

The output is shown in Figure 6-11.

Discussion

Cryptography protects data from being viewed or modified and provides security when transmitting or serializing the data in environments that are otherwise not secure. The data can be encrypted, transmitted, or serialized in its encrypted state, and later decrypted. If the data is intercepted in its encrypted state, it is much more difficult to access the data because it is necessary to first decrypt it.

Encryption algorithms are of two types: *symmetric key* and *asymmetric key*. A brief overview follows.

Symmetric key algorithms use a secret key to both encrypt and decrypt the data. Because the same key is used both to encrypt and decrypt the data, it must be kept secret. Symmetric algorithms are also known as *secret key* algorithms.

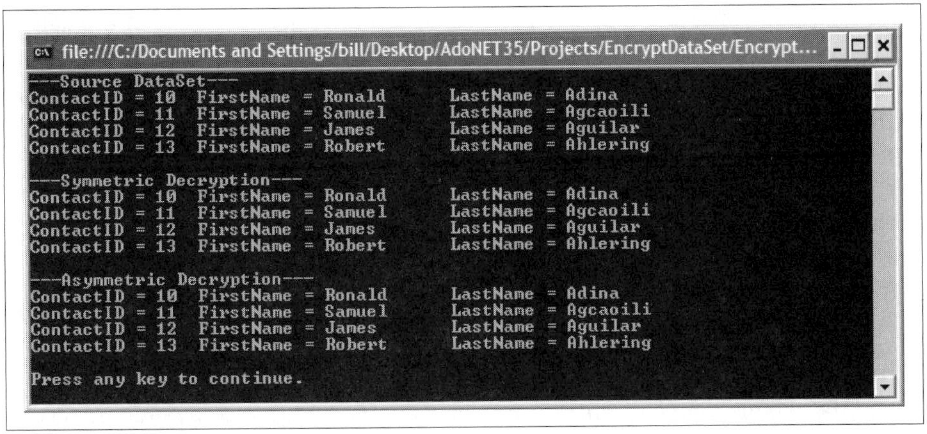

Figure 6-11. Output for EncryptDataSet solution

Symmetric key algorithms are very fast compared to asymmetric algorithms and are therefore suitable for encrypting large amounts of data. The .NET Framework classes that implement symmetric key algorithms are:

- `DESCryptoServiceProvider`
- `RC2CryptoServiceProvider`
- `RijndaelManaged`
- `TripleDESCryptoServiceProvider`

The symmetric key algorithms provided in these classes use an initialization vector (IV) in addition to the key so that an identical plain-text message produces different cipher-text when using the same key with a different IV. It is good practice to use a different IV with each encryption.

Asymmetric key algorithms use both a private key that must be kept secret and a public key that can be made available to anyone. These key pairs are used to both encrypt data (data encrypted with the public key can only be decrypted with the private key) and sign data (data signed with the private key can only be verified with the public key). The public key is used to encrypt data that is being sent to the owner of the private key while the private key is used to digitally sign data to allow the origin of communication to be verified and to ensure that those communications have not been altered. While more secure, asymmetric key algorithms are much slower than symmetric algorithms. The .NET Framework classes that implement asymmetric key algorithms are:

- `DSACryptoServiceProvider`
- `RSACryptoServiceProvider`

To overcome the performance limitations of asymmetric key algorithms with large amounts of data and still benefit from the much stronger security they provide, only a symmetric key is encrypted, which is in turn used to encrypt the data.

Here's how it works: a public key is obtained from the person to whom the data is being sent. A symmetric key is generated by the sender and subsequently encrypted using the public key received from the recipient. The data is then encrypted using the symmetric key; this is much faster than using the public key. The encrypted key and data are then sent to the owner of the public/private key pair. The recipient uses the private key to decrypt the symmetric key and can then use the symmetric key to decrypt the data.

In the solution, both the encryption and decryption use the key and IV values defined using variable initializers only as a convenience. While the same key and IV values must be used when encrypting and decrypting data, these values will normally be set according to the specific requirements of the application.

When the symmetric algorithm is used, the solution creates a cryptographic service provider, sets the key and IV, and uses a CryptoStream object to encrypt the XML representation of the DataSet, which is then written to the specified file. To decrypt the file, a CryptoStream object is used to decrypt the contents of the file into an XML representation of the DataSet, which is subsequently used to re-create the DataSet.

When the asymmetric (RSA) algorithm is used, the solution generates both an RC2 (symmetric) key and an IV. The receiver RSACryptoServiceProvider object is created in the constructor and because the default constructor is used, a new public/private key pair is generated for the receiver each time the application is run. This means that for this example, an asymmetric encryption of the DataSet can only be decrypted during the same run of the console application. Once the application exits, restarting it will re-create the public/private key pair for the receiver. The ExportParameters() method is used to get only the public key information as an RSAParameters object from the receiver. This is imported into a new RSACryptoServiceProvider object using the ImportParameters() method. The Encrypt() method of the RSACryptoServiceProvider is then called to encrypt both the RC2 key and the IV and store them to the appropriate variables of an EncryptedMessage object, defined as an internal class. Next, the CryptoStream object is used to write the XML representation of the DataSet, encrypted using the RC2 key and IV, to a MemoryStream object, which is then stored in the Body variable of the EncryptedMessage object. Finally, the EncryptedMessage is serialized to a file.

The decryption of the encrypted file is just the reverse of the encryption process. The file is deserialized to an EncryptedMessage object. The Decrypt() method of the receiver RSACryptoServiceProvider object is used to decrypt the RC2 key and IV using the receiver's private key. The CryptoStream object is then used to decrypt the XML for the DataSet stored in the Body variable of the EncryptedMessage object. The DataSet is recreated from the XML.

Although this example demonstrates serializing the encrypted DataSet to a file, you can use the same technique to serialize the DataSet to a stream so that it can be transmitted securely in an environment that is otherwise not secure.

6.12 Securing Login Credentials

Problem

You need to protect login credentials during transmission over the network and when they are stored within a database.

Solution

Use password *hashing* and *salting* with the .NET `FormsAuthentication` class to control user authentication and access to the application.

The solution creates and displays a salt of data type GUID. The hash of the password concatenated with the salt is generated and output to the console. The username, password hash, and salt are inserted into a `DataTable` that simulates a database in this solution.

Next, login is simulated with both an incorrect password and a correct password. In each case, the salt and the hash of the password and salt are retrieved from the `DataTable` for the username. The password is concatenated with the retrieved salt and the hash is generated. If the hash matches the hash retrieved from the database, the user is authenticated. The login attempt details and success status are output to the console for both incorrect and correct login attempts.

This solution requires a reference to the `System.Web` assembly.

The C# code in *Program.cs* in the project `SecureLoginCredentials` is shown in Example 6-12.

Example 6-12. File: Program.cs for SecureLoginCredentials solution

```
using System;
using System.Data;
using System.Data.SqlClient;
using System.Web.Security;

namespace SecureLoginCredentials
{
    class Program
    {
        private static string userName = "User1";
        private static string password = "MyPassword123";

        static void Main(string[] args)
        {
            // Create a DataTable to holder user login information (simulate database)
            DataTable dtLogin = new DataTable("UserLogin");
            dtLogin.Columns.Add("UserName", typeof(string)).MaxLength = 50;
            dtLogin.Columns.Add("PasswordSalt", typeof(string)).MaxLength = 50;
            dtLogin.Columns.Add("PasswordHash", typeof(string)).MaxLength = 50;
            dtLogin.PrimaryKey = new DataColumn[] { dtLogin.Columns["UserName"] };
```

```
// Simulate password secure storage to database
Console.WriteLine("---SECURE PASSWORD STORAGE---\n");
// Display the password
Console.WriteLine("Password = {0}", password);

// Create and display the password salt.
string passwordSalt1 = Guid.NewGuid( ).ToString( );
Console.WriteLine("Password salt = {0}", passwordSalt1);

// Create and display the password hash.
String passwordHash1 =
    FormsAuthentication.HashPasswordForStoringInConfigFile(
    password + passwordSalt1, "md5");
Console.WriteLine("Password hash = {0}", passwordHash1);

// Add the user with password hash and salt to the user login DataTable
dtLogin.Rows.Add(new object[] { userName, passwordSalt1, passwordHash1 });

Console.WriteLine("\n---Save: user and password information to DataTable---");
foreach (DataRow row in dtLogin.Rows)
{
    Console.WriteLine(
        "UserName = {0}\nPasswordSalt = {1}\nPasswordHash = {2}",
        row["UserName"], row["PasswordSalt"],row["PasswordHash"]);
}

// Simulate login
Console.WriteLine("\n---LOGIN SIMULATION---");
DataRow loginRow = dtLogin.Rows.Find(userName);

// Get and output user name and password salt and hash from database
string userNameDB = loginRow.Field<string>("UserName");
string passwordSaltDB = loginRow.Field<string>("PasswordSalt");
string passwordHashDB = loginRow.Field<string>("PasswordHash");

Console.WriteLine(
    "\n---Login: user and password information from DataTable---");
Console.WriteLine("UserName = {0}\nPasswordSalt = {1}\nPasswordHash = {2}",
    userNameDB, passwordSaltDB, passwordHashDB);

// Login attempt with the incorrect password
Console.WriteLine("\n---Login attempt 1---");
string loginPassword1 = "WrongPassword123";
Console.WriteLine("Password = {0}", loginPassword1);
// Calcuate whether hash of the password entered and the password salt
// from the database matches the password hash in the database to
// determine if the user is authenticated
bool isAuthenticated1 =
    (FormsAuthentication.HashPasswordForStoringInConfigFile(
    loginPassword1 + passwordSaltDB, "md5") == passwordHashDB);
Console.WriteLine("IsAuthenticated = {0}", isAuthenticated1);
```

```
            // Login attempt with the correct password
            Console.WriteLine("\n---Login attempt 2---");
            string loginPassword2 = "MyPassword123";
            Console.WriteLine("Password = {0}", loginPassword2);
            // Calcuate whether hash of the password entered and the password salt
            // from the database matches the password hash in the database to
            // determine if the user is authenticated
            bool isAuthenticated2 =
                (FormsAuthentication.HashPasswordForStoringInConfigFile(
                loginPassword2 + passwordSaltDB, "md5") == passwordHashDB);
            Console.WriteLine("IsAuthenticated = {0}", isAuthenticated2);

            Console.WriteLine("\nPress any key to continue.");
            Console.ReadKey();
        }
    }
}
```

The output is shown in Figure 6-12.

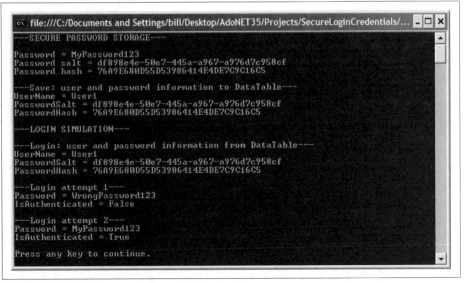

Figure 6-12. Output for SecureLoginCredentials solution

Discussion

Persisting a user's password can be made more secure by first hashing the password. This means that an algorithm is applied to the password to generate a one-way transformation—or *hash*—of the password, making it statistically infeasible to re-create the password from the hash.

A hash algorithm creates a small binary value of fixed length from a larger binary value of an arbitrary length. The hash value is a statistically unique compact representation of the original data. A hash value can be created for and transmitted together with data. The hash can be re-created at a later time and compared to the original hash to ensure that the data has not been altered. To prevent the message from being intercepted and replaced along with a new hash, the hash is encrypted using the private key of an asymmetric key algorithm. This allows the hash to be authenticated as having come from the sender. For more information about symmetric and asymmetric key algorithms, see the discussion in Recipe 6.11. The .NET Framework classes that implement hash algorithms are:

- HMACSHA1
- MACTripleDES
- MD5CryptoServiceProvider
- SHA1Managed
- SHA256Managed
- SHA384Managed
- SHA512Managed

In the solution, the user enters his password, the password is hashed, and then the combination of user ID and password hash are compared to values stored persistently such as in a database table. If the pairs match, the user is authenticated, without comparing the actual password. Because the hash algorithm is a one-way algorithm, the user's password cannot be re-created even if unauthorized access is gained to the persistent store where the user's password hash is stored.

The .NET Framework, as part of the FormsAuthentication class, provides the method HashPasswordForStoringInConfigFile( ) that can hash a password using either SHA1 or MD5 algorithms. The method is easy to call. It takes two arguments, the password and the hash algorithm, and returns a string containing the password hash.

Security is never perfect and this technique is no exception. It can be compromised by a dictionary attack where hash values for most commonly used passwords are generated. When these values are compared with the hash of the password and a match is found, the password is then known. To thwart the dictionary attack, a random string referred to as *salt* is concatenated with the original password before generating the hash value. This makes a dictionary attack much more difficult to perform.

The most secure technique is useless if the password policy does not prevent users from choosing easy-to-guess passwords, or if security is compromised by users who write passwords down on notes attached to their computer monitors, for example.

6.13   Exporting the Results of a Query As a String

Problem

You need to export the results of a query to a string in a manner similar to the GetString( ) method of the ADO Recordset.

Solution

Use a routine that mimics the functionality of the ADO Recordset GetString( ) method.

The solution creates a DataTable containing data from the Person.Contact table in AdventureWorks. The custom GetString( ) method in this solution is called to convert the DataTable into a string similar to one that is generated by the GetString( ) method of the ADO Recordset. The string is output to the console.

The GetString( ) method mimics the functionality of the GetString( ) method of the ADO Recordset. The method iterates over the collection of rows and columns in the table appending the field values to a string. Null values are replaced as specified and column and row delimiters are applied.

The C# code in *Program.cs* in the project ExportQueryResultsString is shown in Example 6-13.

Example 6-13. File: Program.cs for ExportQueryResultsString solution

```
using System;
using System.Data;
using System.Data.SqlClient;
using System.Text;

namespace ExportQueryResultsString
{
    class Program
    {
        static void Main(string[] args)
        {
            string sqlConnectString = "Data Source=(local);" +
                "Integrated security=SSPI;Initial Catalog=AdventureWorks;";

            string sqlSelect = "SELECT ContactID, Title, FirstName, LastName " +
                "FROM Person.Contact";

            // Create a data adapter
            SqlDataAdapter da = new SqlDataAdapter(sqlSelect, sqlConnectString);

            // Fill a DataTable using DataAdapter and output to console
            DataTable dt = new DataTable( );
            da.Fill(dt);
```

```
        // Call method to convert the DataTable to a string.
        Console.WriteLine(dt.GetString(5, null, null, null));

        Console.WriteLine("\nPress any key to continue.");
        Console.ReadKey();
    }
}


// DataTable extension method
static class DataTableStringExt
{
    public static string GetString(this DataTable dt, int numRows,
        string columnDelimiter, string rowDelimiter, string nullExpr)
    {
        if (numRows < 0)
            // Negative number of rows returns all rows
            numRows = dt.Rows.Count;
        else
            // Set number of rows to the lesser of the user entered
            // number of rows and the number of rows in the table.
            numRows = Math.Min(numRows, dt.Rows.Count);

        // Column delimiter defaults to TAB
        if (columnDelimiter == null)
            columnDelimiter = "\t";

        // Row delimiter defaults to NEW LINE
        if (rowDelimiter == null)
            rowDelimiter = "\n";

        // Null expression defaults to empty string
        if (nullExpr == null)
            nullExpr = "";

        StringBuilder sb = new StringBuilder();

        // Iterate over the collection of rows.
        for (int i = 0; i < numRows; i++)
        {
            // Iterate over the collection of columns.
            foreach (object col in dt.Rows[i].ItemArray)
            {
                // Replace null values as they occur.
                String colString = (col == System.DBNull.Value) ?
                    nullExpr : col.ToString();

                // Add the column value to the string.
                sb.Append(colString + columnDelimiter);
            }
            // Remove the column delimiter on last field.
            sb.Remove(sb.Length - columnDelimiter.Length,
                columnDelimiter.Length);
```

Example 6-13. File: Program.cs for ExportQueryResultsString solution (continued)

```
                // Append row delimiter.
                sb.Append(rowDelimiter);
            }

            return sb.ToString();
        }
    }
}
```

The output is shown in Figure 6-13.

Figure 6-13. Output for ExportQueryResultsString solution

Discussion

ADO.NET does not contain a method that is equivalent to the GetString( ) method of the ADO Recordset or a method that converts the Recordset to a string.

This solution presents an extension method of the DataTable class called GetString( ), which duplicates the functionality of the ADO GetString( ) method. The prototype for the ADO.NET method is:

```
string GetString(this DataTable dt, Integer numRows, string columnDelimiter,
    string rowDelimiter, string nullExpr);
```

Parameters

`<return value>`

> A string corresponding to the rows selected from the table.

`dt`

> The DataTable to convert to a string.

`numRows`

> The number of rows in the table to convert. If this number is negative, all rows in the table are converted. If a number larger than the number of records in the table is specified, all records are converted without error.

`columnDelimiter`

> The character or characters that separate columns. The default value is the Tab character.

rowDelimiter

The character or characters that separate rows. The default value is the newline character.

nullExpr

A string that is substituted for null column values in the table. The default value is an empty string.

Extension methods were introduced in C# 3.0 and let you extend class functionality even when you don't have access to the code for those classes. In this solution, extension methods let you call GetString() method as a method of the DataTable class as shown in this highlighted snippet from the solution:

```
Console.WriteLine(dt.GetString(5, null, null, null));
```

Without using extension methods, you would have to pass the DataTable as an argument of the GetString() method as shown in the following snippet:

```
Console.WriteLine(GetString(dt, 5, null, null, null));
```

This can make the code much more readable and in certain cases perform complex tasks much more easily.

You need to follow four simple rules to create an extension method:

1. The extension method must be static.
2. The extension method must be defined in a static class.
3. The extension method must be public.
4. The this keyword must precede the first parameter of the method, which in turn becomes the class that the method extends.

6.14   Exporting the Results of a Query to an Array

Problem

You need to export the results of a query to an array in a manner similar to the GetRows() method of the ADO Recordset.

Solution

Use a routine that mimics the functionality of the ADO Recordset's GetRows() method.

The solution creates a DataTable that contains data from the Person.Contact table in AdventureWorks. The custom GetRows() method in this solution is called to convert the DataTable into an array similar to one that is generated by the GetRows() method of the ADO Recordset. The contents of the array are output to the console.

The GetRows() method mimics the functionality of the GetRows() method of the ADO Recordset. First, an object array is created to hold the rows and columns in the table. The number of columns in the array is set to hold either all of the columns in the table or the subset of columns defined by the optional string array of column names. The number of rows in the table is set to hold either all of the rows in the table or the subset defined by the optional start row and row count arguments. The method then iterates over the collection of rows and columns in the table and sets the values in the array to the field values.

The C# code in *Program.cs* in the project ConvertQueryResultsArray is shown in Example 6-14.

Example 6-14. File: Program.cs for ConvertQueryResultsArray solution

```
using System;
using System.Data;
using System.Data.SqlClient;
using System.Text;

namespace ConvertQueryResultsArray
{
    class Program
    {
        static void Main(string[] args)
        {
            string sqlConnectString = "Data Source=(local);" +
                "Integrated security=SSPI;Initial Catalog=AdventureWorks;";

            string sqlSelect = "SELECT ContactID, Title, FirstName, LastName " +
                "FROM Person.Contact";

            // Create a data adapter
            SqlDataAdapter da = new SqlDataAdapter(sqlSelect, sqlConnectString);

            // Fill a DataTable using DataAdapter and output to console
            DataTable dt = new DataTable();
            da.Fill(dt);

            // Call method to convert the DataTable to an Array.
            Array a = dt.GetRows(5, -1, null);

            // Iterate over the rows of the array storing cells to a StringBuilder
            StringBuilder sb = new StringBuilder();
            for (int iRow = 0; iRow < a.GetLength(0); iRow++)
            {
                // Iterate over the columns of the array.
                for (int iCol = 0; iCol < a.GetLength(1); iCol++)
                {
                    sb.Append(a.GetValue(iRow, iCol).ToString() + "\t");
                }
            }
```

```
                sb.Remove(sb.Length - 1, 1);
                sb.Append(Environment.NewLine);
            }

            Console.Write(sb.ToString());

            Console.WriteLine("\nPress any key to continue.");
            Console.ReadKey();
        }
    }

    // DataTable extension method
    static class DataTableExt
    {
        public static Array GetRows(this DataTable dt, int rowCount, int startRow,
            string[] colName)
        {
            // If column names are specified, ensure that they exist in the table.
            if (colName != null)
            {
                for (int i = 0; i < colName.Length; i++)
                {
                    if (!dt.Columns.Contains(colName[i]))
                        throw (new ArgumentException("The column " +
                            colName[i] +
                            " does not exist in the table."));
                }
            }

            // If no columns were specified, set the number of columns to the
            // number of columns in the table; otherwise, set the number of
            // columns to the number of items in the specified columns array.
            int nCols = (colName == null) ? dt.Columns.Count : colName.Length;

            // The table row to start exporting
            // Set to 1 if less than 1 is specified.
            startRow = (startRow < 1) ? 1 : startRow;

            // The number of rows to export calculated as the number of rows in
            // the table less the starting row number
            // If the starting row is specified as greater than the number of
            // rows in the table, set the number of rows to 0.
            int nRows = Math.Max((dt.Rows.Count - startRow) + 1, 0);
            // If the number of rows to export is specified as greater than 0,
            // set the number of rows to export as the lesser of the number
            // specified and the number of rows calculated in the table
            // starting with the specified row.
            if (rowCount >= 0)
                nRows = Math.Min(nRows, rowCount);

            // Create an object array to hold the data in the table.
            Array a = Array.CreateInstance(typeof(object), nRows, nCols);
```

Example 6-14. File: Program.cs for ConvertQueryResultsArray solution (continued)

```
            // Iterate over the collection of rows in the table.
            for (int iRow = startRow - 1; iRow < startRow - 1 + nRows; iRow++)
            {
                if (colName == null)
                {
                    // Iterate over the collection of columns in the table.
                    for (int iCol = 0; iCol < dt.Columns.Count; iCol++)
                    {
                        // Set the cell in the array.
                        a.SetValue(dt.Rows[iRow][iCol], iRow, iCol);
                    }
                }
                else
                {
                    for (int i = 0; i < colName.Length; i++)
                    {
                        // Set the cell in the array.
                        a.SetValue(dt.Rows[iRow][colName[i]],
                            iRow - startRow + 1, i);
                    }
                }
            }

            return a;
        }
    }
}
```

The output is shown in Figure 6-14.

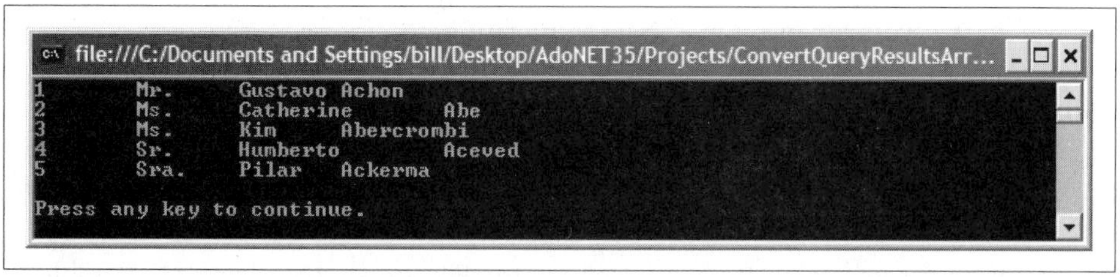

Figure 6-14. Output for ConvertQueryResultsArray solution

Discussion

There is no ADO.NET `DataTable` method that works like the `GetRows()` method of the ADO `Recordset` or method that converts the `Recordset` into a two-dimensional array.

This solution presents an extension method of the `DataTable` class called `GetRows()`, which duplicates the functionality of the ADO `GetRows()` method. The prototype for the ADO.NET method is:

```
Array GetRows(this DataTable dt, int rowCount, int startRow,
    string[] colName);
```

Parameters

<return value>
> A two-dimensional array of field values corresponding to the values in the columns and rows selected from the table.

dt
> The DataTable to convert to the array.

rowCount
> The number of rows to export to the array.

startRow
> The row number of the first row to export.

colName
> A string array containing the names of the columns to export. If this parameter is null, all columns are exported.

Unlike the ADO method, columns cannot be specified by their ordinal values. An overloaded GetRows( ) method that accepts the column ordinals rather than names could be written to do this.

See the solution for Recipe 6.13 for more information about extension methods.

6.15   Loading an ADO Recordset into a DataSet

Problem

You want to convert an ADO Recordset generated within a legacy application to a DataSet so that you can use it in a .NET application.

Solution

Use the Fill( ) method of the OLE DB data provider DataAdapter.

Add a reference to the adodb assembly from the .NET tab in the Add Reference dialog.

The solution creates an ADO Recordset for the HumanResources.Department table in AdventureWorks. The Fill( ) method of the OleDbDataAdapter is used to load the Recordset into a DataTable.

The C# code in *Program.cs* in the project LoadAdoRecordsetIntoDataSet is shown in Example 6-15.

Example 6-15. File: Program.cs for LoadAdoRecordsetIntoDataSet solution

```
using System;
using System.Data;
using System.Data.OleDb;
```

Example 6-15. File: Program.cs for LoadAdoRecordsetIntoDataSet solution (continued)

```
namespace LoadAdoRecordsetIntoDataSet
{
    class Program
    {
        static void Main(string[] args)
        {
            string adodbConnectString = "Provider=SQLOLEDB;" +
                "Data Source=(local);Initial Catalog=AdventureWorks;";

            string sqlSelect = "SELECT * FROM Person.Contact";

            // Open an ADO connection.
            ADODB.Connection connection = new ADODB.Connection();
            connection.Open(adodbConnectString, "sa", "password", 0);

            // Create an ADO recordset.
            ADODB.Recordset rs = new ADODB.Recordset();
            rs.Open(sqlSelect, connection,
                ADODB.CursorTypeEnum.adOpenForwardOnly,
                ADODB.LockTypeEnum.adLockReadOnly, 0);

            // Create and fill a dt from the ADO recordset.
            DataTable dt = new DataTable();
            (new OleDbDataAdapter()).Fill(dt, rs);
            connection.Close();

            // Output 5 records from DataTable loaded from ADO recordset
            for (int i = 0; i < 5; i++)
            {
                DataRow row = dt.Rows[i];
                Console.WriteLine("{0} {1}, {2} {3}", row["ContactID"],
                    row["LastName"], row["FirstName"], row["MiddleName"]);
            }

            Console.WriteLine("\nPress any key to continue.");
            Console.ReadKey();
        }
    }
}
```

The output is shown in Figure 6-15.

Figure 6-15. Output for LoadAdoRecordsetIntoDataSet solution

Discussion

One of the overloads of the OLE DB .NET DataAdapter.Fill( ) method accepts an ADO Recordset or Record object as the data source used to fill the DataTable.

While the data can be loaded into a DataSet in this way, there is no way to automatically reconcile the changes made to the data in the DataSet with the data source underlying the ADO object—i.e., propagate changes made to the DataTable back to the source ADO Recordset. If you need this functionality, you need to write the code to do this.

There is no FillSchema( ) method that allows the schema of an ADO Recordset to be retrieved into a DataSet.

6.16 Converting a DataSet to an ADO Recordset

Problem

You need to convert a DataSet to an ADO Recordset so that you can use it in a legacy application.

Solution

Persist the DataSet to XML, transform it to an ADO Recordset schema, and load it into an ADO Recordset.

The solution converts the DataSet to an ADO Recordset using the following steps:

1. A shell XML document for the ADO Recordset is created.

2. A DataReader accesses the schema information for the data to convert using the GetSchemaTable( ) method. This information is mapped to and added to the ADO Recordset XML document.

3. The DataSet is loaded with data for a single DataTable. The XML document for the DataSet is transformed and written into the ADO Recordset XML document.

4. An ADO Recordset object is created and loaded with the ADO Recordset XML document. This completes the conversion.

5. The ADO Recordset is loaded into a DataTable using the OleDbDataAdapter. The default view for the table is bound to the data grid on the form to display the results of the conversion.

The GetDataTypeInfo( ) method maps SQL Server specific types to data type attributes for the ds and rs namespaces used to serialize an ADO Rowset.

The solution uses one XSLT stylesheet *Department.xslt* to transform the XML document output by the DataSet into an ADO Recordset XML document.

The XSLT file is shown in Example 6-16.

Example 6-16. File: Department.xslt

```
<?xml version="1.0" ?>
<xsl:stylesheet xmlns:xsl="http://www.w3.org/1999/XSL/Transform"
    xmlns:rs="urn:schemas-microsoft-com:rowset"
    xmlns:z="#RowsetSchema"
    xmlns:msxsl="urn:schemas-microsoft-com:xslt"
    xmlns:wxh="http://element14.com/wxhnamespace"
    version="1.0">
    <msxsl:script language="CSharp" implements-prefix="wxh">
        <![CDATA[
            public string GetShortTime(String longDateTime)
            {
                return longDateTime.Substring(0,19);
            }
        ]]>
    </msxsl:script>

    <xsl:output method="xml" indent="yes" />
    <xsl:template match="NewDataSet">
        <rs:data>
            <xsl:apply-templates select="Department" />
        </rs:data>
    </xsl:template>
    <xsl:template match="Department">
        <z:row>
            <xsl:apply-templates select="@DepartmentID" />
            <xsl:apply-templates select="@Name" />
            <xsl:apply-templates select="@GroupName" />
            <xsl:apply-templates select="@ModifiedDate" />
        </z:row>
    </xsl:template>
    <xsl:template match="@ModifiedDate">
        <xsl:attribute name="ModifiedDate">
            <xsl:value-of select="wxh:GetShortTime(.)" />
        </xsl:attribute>
    </xsl:template>
    <xsl:template match="@*">
        <xsl:copy-of select="." />
    </xsl:template>
</xsl:stylesheet>
```

You need to add a reference to the adodb assembly in the .NET tab in the Add Reference dialog to this solution.

The C# code in *Program.cs* in the project ConvertDataSetAdoRecordset is shown in Example 6-17.

Example 6-17. File: Program.cs for ConvertDataSetAdoRecordset solution

```csharp
using System;
using System.Data;
using System.Data.SqlClient;
using System.Data.OleDb;
using System.Xml;
using System.Xml.Xsl;
using System.Text;
using System.IO;

namespace ConvertDataSetAdoRecordset
{
    class Program
    {
        static void Main(string[] args)
        {
            string adoXmlFileName = @"..\..\..\ADO_Department.xml";
            string xsltFileName = @"..\..\Department.xslt";
            string adoConnectString = @"Provider = SQLOLEDB;Data Source=(local);" +
                "Initial Catalog=AdventureWorks";

            string schemaName = "HumanResources";
            string tableName = "Department";
            string sqlConnectString = "Data Source=(local);" +
                "Integrated security=SSPI;Initial Catalog=AdventureWorks;";
            string sqlSelect = "SELECT * FROM " + schemaName + "." + tableName;

            // Create the connection.
            SqlConnection conn = new SqlConnection(sqlConnectString);
            // Create the command to load all records.
            SqlCommand cmd = new SqlCommand(sqlSelect, conn);
            conn.Open();
            // Create a DataReader from the command.
            SqlDataReader dr = cmd.ExecuteReader(
                CommandBehavior.SchemaOnly | CommandBehavior.KeyInfo);
            // Create a table of the schema for the DataReader.
            DataTable schemaTable = dr.GetSchemaTable();

            // Create an XML document.
            XmlDocument xmlDoc = new XmlDocument();
            // Add ADO namespace and schema definition tags to the XML document.
            string adoXml =
                "<xml xmlns:s = 'uuid:BDC6E3F0-6DA3-11d1-A2A3-00AA00C14882' " +
                "xmlns:dt = 'uuid:C2F41010-65B3-11d1-A29F-00AA00C14882' " +
                "xmlns:rs = 'urn:schemas-microsoft-com:rowset' " +
                "xmlns:z = '#RowsetSchema'>" +
                "<s:Schema id = 'RowsetSchema'>" +
                "<s:ElementType name = 'row' content = 'eltOnly'>" +
                "</s:ElementType>" +
                "</s:Schema>" +
                "</xml>";
            xmlDoc.LoadXml(adoXml);
```

Example 6-17. File: Program.cs for ConvertDataSetAdoRecordset solution (continued)

```
// Create a namespace manager for the XML document.
XmlNamespaceManager nm = new XmlNamespaceManager(xmlDoc.NameTable);
// Add ADO prefixes.
nm.AddNamespace("s", "uuid:BDC6E3F0-6DA3-11d1-A2A3-00AA00C14882");
nm.AddNamespace("dt", "uuid:C2F41010-65B3-11d1-A29F-00AA00C14882");
nm.AddNamespace("rs", "urn:schemas-microsoft-com:rowset");
nm.AddNamespace("z", "#RowsetSchema");

// Select the s:ElementType node.
XmlNode curNode = xmlDoc.SelectSingleNode("//s:ElementType", nm);

XmlElement xe = null;
XmlAttribute xa = null;
// Iterate through the schema records for the DataReader.
foreach (DataRow sr in schemaTable.Rows)
{
    // Create an 'AttributeType' element for the schema record.
    xe = xmlDoc.CreateElement("s", "AttributeType",
        "uuid:BDC6E3F0-6DA3-11d1-A2A3-00AA00C14882");

    // Get the data type.
    SqlDbType sqlDbType = (SqlDbType)sr["ProviderType"];

    // Create the 'name' attribute.
    xa = xmlDoc.CreateAttribute("", "name", "");
    xa.Value = sr["ColumnName"].ToString();
    xe.SetAttributeNode(xa);

    // Create the 'number' attribute.
    xa = xmlDoc.CreateAttribute("rs", "number",
        "urn:schemas-microsoft-com:rowset");
    xa.Value = ((int)sr["ColumnOrdinal"] + 1).ToString();
    xe.SetAttributeNode(xa);

    // Add attribute if null values are allowed in the column.
    if ((bool)sr["AllowDBNull"])
    {
        xa = xmlDoc.CreateAttribute("rs", "nullable",
            "urn:schemas-microsoft-com:rowset");
        xa.Value = sr["AllowDBNull"].ToString().ToLower();
        xe.SetAttributeNode(xa);
    }

    // Add 'writeunknown' attribute.
    xa = xmlDoc.CreateAttribute("rs", "writeunknown",
        "urn:schemas-microsoft-com:rowset");
    xa.Value = "true";
    xe.SetAttributeNode(xa);

    // Create a 'datatype' element for the column within the
    // 'AttributeType'.
```

```csharp
XmlElement dataele = xmlDoc.CreateElement("s", "datatype",
    "uuid:BDC6E3F0-6DA3-11d1-A2A3-00AA00C14882");
String typeName, dbTypeName;
GetDataTypeInfo(sqlDbType, out typeName, out dbTypeName);

// Add a 'type' attribute specifying the data type.
xa = xmlDoc.CreateAttribute("dt", "type",
    "uuid:C2F41010-65B3-11d1-A29F-00AA00C14882");
xa.Value = typeName;
dataele.SetAttributeNode(xa);

// Add a 'dbtype' attribute, if necessary.
if (dbTypeName != "")
{
    xa = xmlDoc.CreateAttribute("rs", "dbtype",
        "urn:schemas-microsoft-com:rowset");
    xa.Value = dbTypeName;
    dataele.SetAttributeNode(xa);
}

// Add the 'maxlength' attribute.
xa = xmlDoc.CreateAttribute("dt", "maxLength",
    "uuid:C2F41010-65B3-11d1-A29F-00AA00C14882");
xa.Value = sr["ColumnSize"].ToString();
dataele.SetAttributeNode(xa);

// Add 'scale' and 'precision' attributes, if appropriate.
if (sr["DataType"].ToString() != "System.String")
{
    if (Convert.ToByte(sr["NumericScale"]) != 255)
    {
        xa = xmlDoc.CreateAttribute("rs", "scale",
            "urn:schemas-microsoft-com:rowset");
        xa.Value = sr["NumericScale"].ToString();
        dataele.SetAttributeNode(xa);
    }

    xa = xmlDoc.CreateAttribute("rs", "precision",
        "urn:schemas-microsoft-com:rowset");
    xa.Value = sr["NumericPrecision"].ToString();
    dataele.SetAttributeNode(xa);
}

// Add a 'fixedlength' attribute, if appropriate.
if (sqlDbType != SqlDbType.VarChar &&
    sqlDbType != SqlDbType.NVarChar)
{
    xa = xmlDoc.CreateAttribute("rs", "fixedlength",
        "urn:schemas-microsoft-com:rowset");
    xa.Value = "true";
    dataele.SetAttributeNode(xa);
}
```

```
        // Add a 'maybe' null attribute, if appropriate.
        if (!(bool)sr["AllowDBNull"])
        {
            xa = xmlDoc.CreateAttribute("rs", "maybenull",
                "urn:schemas-microsoft-com:rowset");
            xa.Value = sr["AllowDBNull"].ToString( ).ToLower( );
            dataele.SetAttributeNode(xa);
        }

        // Add the 'datatype' element to the 'AttributeType'.
        xe.AppendChild(dataele);

        // Add the 'AttributeType' element to the 'ElementType'
        // attribute.
        curNode.AppendChild(xe);
    }

    // Add the 'extends' element with attribute 'type" of 'rs:rowbase'.
    xe = xmlDoc.CreateElement("s", "extends",
        "uuid:BDC6E3F0-6DA3-11d1-A2A3-00AA00C14882");
    xa = xmlDoc.CreateAttribute("", "type", "");
    xa.Value = "rs:rowbase";
    xe.SetAttributeNode(xa);
    curNode.AppendChild(xe);

    // Close the reader and connection.
    dr.Close( );
    conn.Close( );

    // Load the data into a table in a DataSet.
    DataSet ds = new DataSet( );
    SqlDataAdapter da = new SqlDataAdapter(sqlSelect, sqlConnectString);
    da.Fill(ds, tableName);

    // Output the DataTable
    Console.WriteLine("---ADO.NET DataSet---");
    foreach(DataRow row in ds.Tables[tableName].Rows)
        Console.WriteLine("DepartmentID = {0}; Name = {1}; ModifiedDate = {2}",
            row["DepartmentID"], row["Name"],
            DateTime.Parse(row["ModifiedDate"].ToString( )).ToShortDateString( ));

    // Write the column data as attributes.
    foreach (DataColumn dc in ds.Tables[tableName].Columns)
        dc.ColumnMapping = MappingType.Attribute;
    // Write the DataSet to an XML document.
    XmlDataDocument xmlTable = new XmlDataDocument(ds);

    // Load the XML transformation.
    XslTransform xslt = new XslTransform( );
    xslt.Load(xsltFileName);
```

```csharp
// Transform the XML document.
XmlReader xr = xslt.Transform(xmlTable, null, (XmlResolver)null);

// Load the transformed document into an XML document.
XmlDocument resultXmlDoc = new XmlDocument( );
resultXmlDoc.Load(xr);
xr.Close( );

StringBuilder sb = new StringBuilder(xmlDoc.OuterXml);
// Insert the data before the closing </xml> tag.
sb.Insert(sb.Length - 6, resultXmlDoc.InnerXml.Remove(8,
    resultXmlDoc.InnerXml.IndexOf(">") - 8));
// Make the <z:row> elements self closing
// (ADO import doesn't work otherwise).
sb.Replace("></z:row>", "/>");

// Write the data to a file as ADO XML format.
using (StreamWriter sw = new StreamWriter(adoXmlFileName))
{
    sw.Write(sb.ToString( ));
}
Console.WriteLine("\n=> ADO Recordset serialized to XML document {0}",
    adoXmlFileName);

// Create and open an ADO connection.
ADODB.Connection adoConn = new ADODB.Connection( );
adoConn.Open(adoConnectString, "sa", "password", 0);

// Create the ADO recordset.
ADODB.Recordset rs = new ADODB.Recordset( );
try
{
    // Load the XML into the ADO recordset.
    rs.Open(adoXmlFileName,
        adoConn,
        ADODB.CursorTypeEnum.adOpenStatic,
        ADODB.LockTypeEnum.adLockBatchOptimistic,
        (int)ADODB.CommandTypeEnum.adCmdFile);

    Console.WriteLine("=> ADO Recordset created.");
}
catch (System.Exception ex)
{
    Console.WriteLine(ex.Message);
    adoConn.Close( );

    return;
}
```

Example 6-17. File: Program.cs for ConvertDataSetAdoRecordset solution (continued)

```
        // Output the ADO Recordset
        Console.WriteLine("\n---ADO Recordset---");
        rs.MoveFirst();
        while (!rs.EOF)
        {
            Console.WriteLine("DepartmentID = {0}; Name = {1}; ModifiedDate = {2}",
                rs.Fields[0].Value, rs.Fields[1].Value,
                DateTime.Parse(rs.Fields[3].Value.ToString()).ToShortDateString());
            rs.MoveNext();
        }

        // Close the ADO connection
        adoConn.Close();

        Console.WriteLine("\nPress any key to continue.");
        Console.ReadKey();
    }

    private static void GetDataTypeInfo(SqlDbType sqlDbType,
        out String type, out String dbtype)
    {
        type = "";
        dbtype = "";

        // Convert the SqlDbType to type attributes in the dt and rs namespaces.
        switch (sqlDbType)
        {
            case SqlDbType.BigInt:
                type = "i8";
                break;
            case SqlDbType.Binary:
                type = "bin.hex";
                break;
            case SqlDbType.Bit:
                type = "Boolean";
                break;
            case SqlDbType.Char:
                type = "string";
                dbtype = "str";
                break;
            case SqlDbType.DateTime:
                type = "dateTime";
                dbtype = "variantdate";
                break;
            case SqlDbType.Decimal:
                type = "number";
                dbtype = "decimal";
                break;
            case SqlDbType.Float:
                type = "float";
                break;
```

```
            case SqlDbType.Image:
                type = "bin.hex";
                break;
            case SqlDbType.Int:
                type = "int";
                break;
            case SqlDbType.Money:
                type = "i8";
                dbtype = "currency";
                break;
            case SqlDbType.NChar:
                type = "string";
                break;
            case SqlDbType.NText:
                type = "string";
                break;
            case SqlDbType.NVarChar:
                type = "string";
                break;
            case SqlDbType.Real:
                type = "r4";
                break;
            case SqlDbType.SmallDateTime:
                type = "dateTime";
                break;
            case SqlDbType.SmallInt:
                type = "i2";
                break;
            case SqlDbType.SmallMoney:
                type = "i4";
                dbtype = "currency";
                break;
            case SqlDbType.Text:
                type = "string";
                dbtype = "str";
                break;
            case SqlDbType.Timestamp:
                type = "dateTime";
                dbtype = "timestamp";
                break;
            case SqlDbType.TinyInt:
                type = "i1";
                break;
            case SqlDbType.UniqueIdentifier:
                type = "uuid";
                break;
            case SqlDbType.VarBinary:
                type = "bin.hex";
                break;
```

Example 6-17. File: Program.cs for ConvertDataSetAdoRecordset solution (continued)

```
                case SqlDbType.VarChar:
                    type = "string";
                    dbtype = "str";
                    break;
                case SqlDbType.Variant:
                    type = "string";
                    break;
            }
        }
    }
}
```

The output is shown in Figure 6-16.

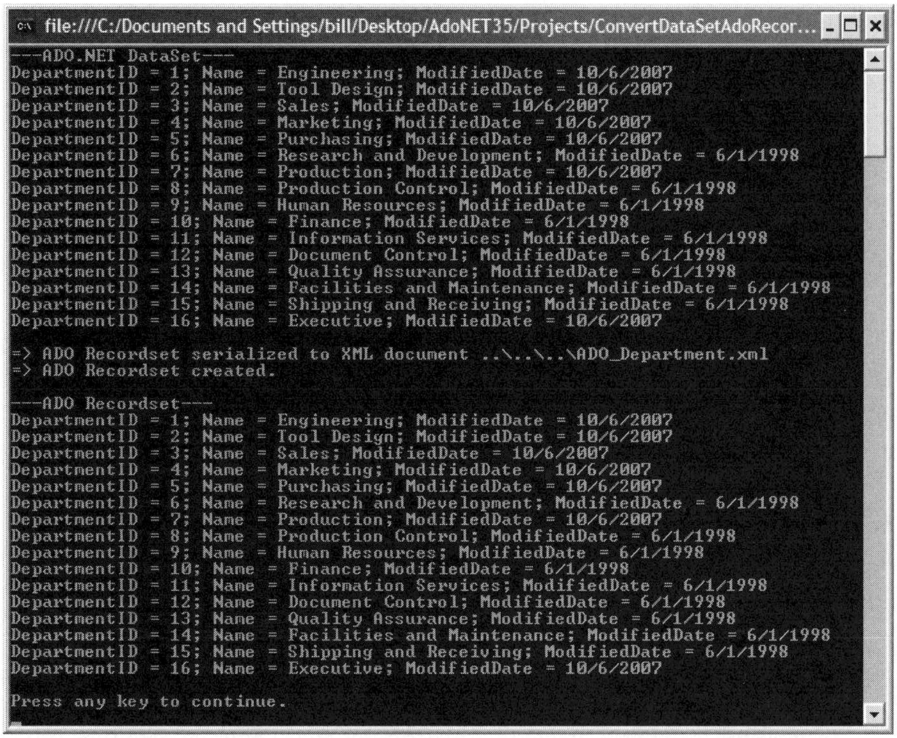

Figure 6-16. Output for ConvertDataSetAdoRecordset solution

Discussion

ADO uses UTF-8 encoding when it persists data as an XML stream. The XML persistence format used by ADO has four namespaces as described in Table 6-7.

Table 6-7. Namespaces for a serialized Rowset

Namespace URI	Prefix	Description
urn:schemas-microsoft-com: rowset	rs	OLE DB Persistence Provider Rowset, which are the elements and attributes specific to ADO Recordset properties and attributes.
uuid:BDC6E3F0-6DA3-11d1-A2A3-00AA00C14882	s	XML Data Reduced, which is the XML-Data namespace that contains elements and attributes defining the schema of the current ADO Recordset.
uuid:C2F41010-65B3-11d1-A29F-00AA00C14882	dt	XML Data Reduced (XDR) Datatypes, which are the data type definition specifications.
#RowsetSchema	z	Contains the actual data for the RecordSet using the schema defined by the s namespace.

The ADO XML format has three parts: the namespace declarations, followed by the schema section and the data section. The schema section is required and contains detailed metadata about each column in the table. The data section contains an element for each row. Column data is stored as attribute-value pairs according to the schema section definitions. For an empty row set, the data section can be empty, but the <rs:data> tags must be present.

Use the dt:type attribute to specify a data type for a column. The data type can be specified directly on the column definition or on the s:datatype nested element of the column definition. ADO adopts the latter approach. If the dt:type attribute is omitted from the column definition, the column type will default to a variable length string.

The solution converts the HumanResources.Department table in AdventureWorks to an ADO Recordset. The solution begins by getting a DataTable containing the table schema using the GetSchemaTable( ) method of the DataReader. As mentioned earlier, the ADO XML format has three sections, and this schema information will be used to define the schema section.

The solution defines the shell of the ADO XML document for the table containing the namespace declarations and the nested row elements that will contain the column definition elements.

The code iterates over the rows in the schema table and adds a child s:AttributeType column element to the s:ElementType row element. The name of the column, as well as properties shown in Table 6-8, are defined as attributes of this column, while an s:datatype nested element is created with attributes specifying the data type properties described in Table 6-9.

Table 6-8. Attributes for s:AttributeType element

Attribute	Description
Name	Column name.
rs:name	Column name in the Recordset. This value defaults to the value for the name attribute. This only need to be explicitly specified if a name other than the Recordset column name is used for the value of the name attribute.
rs:number	Column ordinal.
rs:nullable	Indicates whether the column can contain a null value.
rs:writeunknown	Indicates whether a value can be written to the column.

Table 6-9. Attributes for s:datatype Element

Attribute	Description
dt:type	XML column data type.
rs:dbtype	Database column data type.
dt:maxLength	The maximum length of the column.
rs:scale	The numeric scale of the column.
rs:precision	The precision of the column.
rs:fixedlength	Indicates whether the column has a fixed length.
rs:maybenull	Indicates whether the column can contain a null value.

Having defined the schema inline, the solution loads the table into a DataSet. The MappingType is set so that the column values are written as attributes rather than nested elements. The DataSet is then serialized to an XmlDataDocument object. The XML transformation *Department.xslt* (see Example 6-16) is then applied to the XML document and the results are output to an XmlReader. The stylesheet transforms the XML format for the data in the DataSet to the format required for the ADO XML data section. The namespace declarations are removed from the <rs:data> element and the document is inserted into the ADO XML document for the table, immediately before the closing </xml> tag as the data section. Finally, the </z:row> closing tags for the <z:row> elements are removed and the <z:row> elements are made self-closing, since the ADO import only imports the first row, otherwise. The ADO XML document for the table is saved to the file *ADO_Department.xml* shown in Figure 6-17.

Finally, the XML file is loaded into an ADO Recordset object and the contents are output to the console.

Figure 6-17. XML file loaded into Department ADO Recordset

CHAPTER 7

Maintaining Database Integrity

7.0   Introduction

Transactions allow a system to maintain integrity when interacting with multiple data sources. If an update to one data source fails, all changes are rolled back to a known good state. This chapter focuses on using transactions from ADO.NET, maintaining database integrity, and resolving conflicts and concurrency problems.

.NET supports both manual and automatic transactions with classes in the System.Transaction namespace. Manual transactions use the transactional capabilities of the data source. The Microsoft Distributed Transaction Coordinator (DTC) manages automatic transactions.

In a manual transaction, a transaction object is associated with a connection to a data source. Multiple commands against the data source can be associated with the transaction, grouping the commands together as a single transaction. Manual transactions can also be controlled using SQL commands in a stored procedure. Manual transactions are significantly faster than automatic transactions because they do not require interprocess communication (IPC) with the DTC. Manual transactions are limited to performing transactions against a single data source. Recipe 7.2 shows how to work with manual transactions.

Automatic transactions are easier to program, can span multiple data sources, and can use multiple resource managers. They are significantly slower than manual transactions. Distributed transactions are demonstrated in Recipe 7.1.

Concurrency problems occur when multiple users attempt to modify unlocked data. Possible problems include lost updates, dirty reads, nonrepeatable reads, and phantom reads. Isolation levels specify transaction locking behavior. Locking data ensures database consistency by controlling how changes made to data within an uncommitted transaction can be used by concurrent transactions. Higher isolation levels increase data accuracy at the expense of data availability. Recipe 7.11 shows how to use transaction isolation levels. Recipe 7.12 shows how to use pessimistic concurrency implemented using SQL Server database locks.

Even in well-designed applications, concurrency violations often occur by design. The ADO.NET DataAdapter raises events that can be handled programmatically to resolve concurrency violations as required by application requirements. Recipe 7.9 shows how to use a timestamp to check for concurrency violations, while Recipe 7.10 shows how to resolve concurrency violations with DataAdapter event handlers.

A DataSet can contain both foreign key and unique constraints as well as relationships between tables to define and maintain data and referential integrity. The order in which DataRow changes from a DataSet containing hierarchical data are updated back to the data source is important to avoid referential integrity errors during the update process. ADO.NET allows data changes of a certain type—inserts, deletes, and updates—to be identified so that they can be processed separately as required. Recipe 7.6 shows how to update a DataSet containing hierarchical data back to the data source.

7.1 Using Distributed Transactions

Problem

You need to create a *distributed transaction*—a transaction that spans two or more data sources.

Solution

Use the TransactionScope class within the System.Transactions namespace.

The solution uses a table named SystemTransaction in the AdoDotNet35Cookbook database. Create the database in the AdoDotNet35Cookbook database in both SQL Server and SQL Server Express instances by executing the following T-SQL statement.

```
USE AdoDotNet35Cookbook
GO
CREATE TABLE SystemTransaction(
    Id int NOT NULL PRIMARY KEY,
    Field1 nvarchar(50) NULL,
    Field2 nvarchar(50) NULL )
```

You need to configure the Microsoft Distributed Transaction Coordinator (MS DTC) in Windows to let applications enlist resources in a distributed transaction.

Follow these steps to fully enable MS DTC:

1. Select Control Panel → Administrative Tools → Component Services to open the Component Services dialog.

2. Expand Console Root → Component Services → Computers → My Computer in the tree view.

3. Right-click My Computer and select Properties from the context menu.

4. Select the MSDTC tab in the My Computer Properties dialog.

5. Click the Security Configuration button to open the Security Configuration dialog.

6. Ensure that all of the checkboxes are checked.

7. Ensure that the DTC Logon Account name is NT Authority\ NetworkService.

8. Click OK to close the Security Configuration dialog.

9. Click OK to close the My Computer Properties dialog.

10. Close the Component Services dialog.

The solution successfully inserts a record into the SystemTransaction table in the AdoDotNet35Cookbook database in both a SQL Server and SQL Server Express instance. The Complete( ) method of the TransactionScope class is called in the try block to indicate that all operations within the transaction completed successfully. Next, the solution attempts to insert a record into the SystemTransaction table in the AdoDotNet35Cookbook database in both a SQL Server and SQL Server Express instance. The second insert into the SQL Server Express table fails because of a duplicate primary key. The error is written to the console in the catch block and the transaction is closed once the TransactionScope object is closed when its using block ends. The contents of the SystemTransaction table are output to the console at the beginning and after each transaction.

The solution needs a reference to the System.Transactions assembly.

The C# code in *Program.cs* in the project SystemTransaction is shown in Example 7-1.

Example 7-1. File: Program.cs for SystemTransaction solution

```
using System;
using System.Data;
using System.Data.SqlClient;
using System.Transactions;

namespace SystemTransaction
{
    class Program
    {
        private static string sqlConnectString1 = "Data Source=(local);" +
            "Integrated security=SSPI;Initial Catalog=AdoDotNet35Cookbook;";

        private static string sqlConnectString2 = @"Data Source=(local)\SQLExpress;" +
            "Integrated security=SSPI;Initial Catalog=AdoDotNet35Cookbook;";

        static void Main(string[] args)
        {
            OutputData( );

            // Insert records into both SQL Server and SQL Server Express databases
            string sqlInsert1 = "INSERT INTO SystemTransaction " +
                "VALUES (1, 'Field1.1a', 'Field2.1a')";
            string sqlInsert2 = "INSERT INTO SystemTransaction " +
                "VALUES (1, 'Field1.1b', 'Field2.1b')";
            using (TransactionScope ts = new TransactionScope( ))
            {
                try
                {
                    Console.WriteLine("\n=> Execute: {0}", sqlInsert1);
                    SqlConnection connection1 = new SqlConnection(sqlConnectString1);
                    SqlCommand command1 = new SqlCommand(sqlInsert1, connection1);
                    connection1.Open( );
                    int rowsAff1 = command1.ExecuteNonQuery( );
                    connection1.Close( );

                    Console.WriteLine("=> Execute: {0}", sqlInsert2);
                    SqlConnection connection2 = new SqlConnection(sqlConnectString2);
                    SqlCommand command2 = new SqlCommand(sqlInsert2, connection2);
                    connection2.Open( );
                    int rowsAff2 = command2.ExecuteNonQuery( );
                    connection2.Close( );

                    Console.WriteLine("\nTransactionScope.Complete( )");
                    ts.Complete( );
                }
                catch (Exception ex)
                {
                    Console.WriteLine("\nEXCEPTION: {0}", ex.Message);
                }
            }
```

Example 7-1. File: Program.cs for SystemTransaction solution (continued)

```csharp
        OutputData( );

        // Insert records into both SQL Server and SQL Server Express databases
        sqlInsert1 = "INSERT INTO SystemTransaction " +
            "VALUES (2, 'Field1.2a', 'Field2.2a')";
        // Insert to Express has an "error" in -- Id value 1 already exists
        sqlInsert2 = "INSERT INTO SystemTransaction " +
            "VALUES (1, 'Field1.2b', 'Field2.2b')";
        using (TransactionScope ts = new TransactionScope( ))
        {
            try
            {
                Console.WriteLine("\n=> Execute: {0}", sqlInsert1);
                SqlConnection connection1 = new SqlConnection(sqlConnectString1);
                SqlCommand command1 = new SqlCommand(sqlInsert1, connection1);
                connection1.Open( );
                int rowsAff1 = command1.ExecuteNonQuery( );
                connection1.Close( );

                Console.WriteLine("=> Execute: {0}", sqlInsert2);
                SqlConnection connection2 = new SqlConnection(sqlConnectString2);
                SqlCommand command2 = new SqlCommand(sqlInsert2, connection2);
                connection2.Open( );
                int rowsAff2 = command2.ExecuteNonQuery( );
                connection2.Close( );

                Console.WriteLine("\nTransactionScope.Complete( )");
                ts.Complete( );
            }
            catch (Exception ex)
            {
                Console.WriteLine("\nEXCEPTION: {0}", ex.Message);
            }
        }

        OutputData( );

        Console.WriteLine("\nPress any key to continue.");
        Console.ReadKey( );
    }

    static void OutputData( )
    {
        // Output data from table in each SQL Server and SQL Server Express
        string sqlSelect1 = "SELECT * FROM SystemTransaction";
        SqlDataAdapter da1 = new SqlDataAdapter(sqlSelect1, sqlConnectString1);
        DataTable dt1 = new DataTable( );
        da1.Fill(dt1);
```

Example 7-1. File: Program.cs for SystemTransaction solution (continued)

```
string sqlSelect2 = "SELECT * FROM SystemTransaction";
SqlDataAdapter da2 = new SqlDataAdapter(sqlSelect2, sqlConnectString2);
DataTable dt2 = new DataTable();
da2.Fill(dt2);

Console.WriteLine("\n---{0}---", da1.SelectCommand.Connection.DataSource);
Console.WriteLine("Id\tField1\t\tField2");
Console.WriteLine("--\t------\t\t------");
if (dt1.Rows.Count == 0)
    Console.WriteLine("[Empty]");
else
    foreach (DataRow row in dt1.Rows)
    {
        Console.WriteLine("{0}\t{1}\t{2}",
            row["Id"], row["Field1"], row["Field2"]);
    }

Console.WriteLine("\n---{0}---", da2.SelectCommand.Connection.DataSource);
Console.WriteLine("Id\tField1\t\tField2");
Console.WriteLine("--\t------\t\t------");
if (dt2.Rows.Count == 0)
    Console.WriteLine("[Empty]");
else
    foreach (DataRow row in dt2.Rows)
    {
        Console.WriteLine("{0}\t{1}\t{2}",
            row["Id"], row["Field1"], row["Field2"]);
    }
        }
    }
}
```

The output is shown in Figure 7-1.

Discussion

The System.Transaction namespace introduced in .NET Framework 2.0 contains classes that let you create and participate in a local or distributed transaction. Transactions initiated in SQL Server, ADO.NET, MSMQ, and MSDTC are supported. It provides an explicit programming model based on the Transaction class and an explicit programming model based on the TransactionScope class. Transactions using the TransactionScope class are automatically managed.

A transaction scope is automatically started when a TransactionScope object is created. Call the Complete() method of the TransactionScope object to inform the transaction manager that the transaction should be committed. Failing to call the Complete() method aborts and rolls back the transaction.

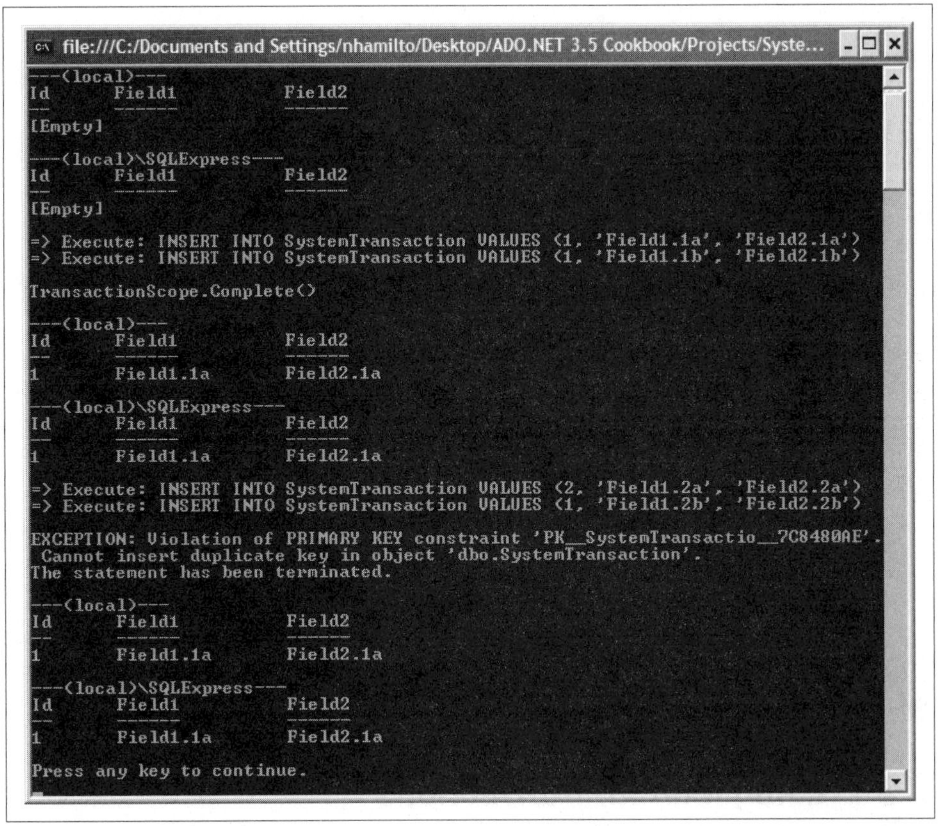

Figure 7-1. Output for SystemTransaction solution

The TransactionScope class provides eight overloaded constructors that define behavior of the transaction:

```
TransactionScope( )
TransactionScope(Transaction trans)
TransactionScope(TransactionScopeOption transScopeOption)
TransactionScope(Transaction trans, TimeSpan timeSpan)
TransactionScope(TransactionScopeOption transScopeOption,
    TimeSpan timeSpan)
TransactionScope(TransactionScopeOption transScopeOption,
    TransactionOptions transOptions)
TransactionScope(Transaction trans, TimeSpan timeSpan,
    EnterpriseServicesInteropOption enterpriseServicesInteropOption)
TransactionScope(TransactionScopeOption transScopeOption,
    TransactionOptions transOptions,
    EnterpriseServicesInteropOption enterpriseServicesInteropOption)
```

Where:

trans
> Transaction to be used.

transScopeOption
> A value from the TransactionScopeOptions enumeration specifying transaction requirements for the transaction scope. One of Required, RequiresNew, or Suppress.

timeSpan
> Time after which the transaction scope times out and aborts.

transOptions
> Transaction options to use if a new transaction is created. The TransactionOptions structure encapsulates timeout and isolation level parameters as a simple way to pass these parameters into a transaction.

enterpriseServicesInteropOption
> A value from the EnterpriseServicesInteropOption enumeration that specifies how the transaction interacts with COM+ transactions. One of None, Automatic, or Full.

For more information about using the TransactionScope to implement implicit transactions, see "Implementing Implicit Transactions using Transaction Scope" in MSDN.

7.2   Using Manual Transactions

Problem

You need to explicitly begin, control, and end a transaction from within a .NET application.

Solution

Use the Connection object with structured exceptions (try-catch-finally).

The solution uses a table named ManualTransaction in the AdoDotNet35Cookbook database. Execute the T-SQL in Example 7-2 to create the table.

Example 7-2. Create table ManualTransaction

```
USE AdoDotNet35Cookbook
GO
CREATE TABLE ManualTransaction (
    Id int NOT NULL PRIMARY KEY,
    Field1 nvarchar(50) NULL,
    Field2 nvarchar(50) NULL )
```

The solution starts a transaction, executes two commands that successfully insert records into the ManualTransaction table, and commits the transaction within a try block. Next, the solution starts a transaction and executes two commands that insert records into the ManualTransaction table. The second insert fails because the Id value is null and the transaction is rolled back within a catch block. The contents of the ManualTransaction table are output to the console after both transactions are completed.

The C# code in *Program.cs* in the project ManualTransaction is shown in Example 7-3.

Example 7-3. File: Program.cs for ManualTransaction solution

```
using System;
using System.Data;
using System.Data.SqlClient;

namespace ManualTransaction
{
    class Program
    {
        static void Main(string[] args)
        {
            string sqlConnectString = "Data Source=(local);" +
                "Integrated security=SSPI;Initial Catalog=AdoDotNet35Cookbook;";

            string sqlSelect = "SELECT * FROM ManualTransaction";
            string sqlInsert = "INSERT INTO ManualTransaction VALUES " +
                "(@Id, @Field1, @Field2)";

            // Create and open a connection
            SqlConnection connection = new SqlConnection(sqlConnectString);
            connection.Open( );

            // Create the parameterized insert command
            SqlCommand command = new SqlCommand(sqlInsert, connection);
            command.Parameters.Add("@Id", SqlDbType.Int);
            command.Parameters.Add("@Field1", SqlDbType.NVarChar, 50);
            command.Parameters.Add("@Field2", SqlDbType.NVarChar, 50);
            // Begin a new transaction and assign it to the command
            SqlTransaction tran = connection.BeginTransaction( );
            command.Transaction = tran;

            // try...catch block that succeeds
            try
            {
                Console.WriteLine("=> Add row with Id = 1");
                command.Parameters["@Id"].Value = 1;
                command.Parameters["@Field1"].Value = "field 1.1";
                command.Parameters["@Field2"].Value = "field 2.1";
                command.ExecuteNonQuery( );
```

Example 7-3. File: Program.cs for ManualTransaction solution (continued)

```
                    Console.WriteLine("=> Add row with Id = 2");
                    command.Parameters["@Id"].Value = 2;
                    command.Parameters["@Field1"].Value = "field 1.2";
                    command.Parameters["@Field2"].Value = "field 2.2";
                    command.ExecuteNonQuery();

                    // If OK to here, commit the transaction.
                    tran.Commit();
                    Console.WriteLine("\nTRANSACTION COMMIT.\n");
                }
                catch (Exception ex)
                {
                    tran.Rollback();
                    Console.WriteLine("\nTRANSACTION ROLLBACK.\n{0}\n", ex.Message);
                }

                // Begin a new transaction and assign it to the command
                tran = connection.BeginTransaction();
                command.Transaction = tran;

                // try...catch block that fails
                try
                {
                    Console.WriteLine("=> Add row with Id = 3");
                    command.Parameters["@Id"].Value = 3;
                    command.Parameters["@Field1"].Value = "field 1.3";
                    command.Parameters["@Field2"].Value = "field 2.3";
                    command.ExecuteNonQuery();

                    Console.WriteLine("=> Add row with Id = null");
                    command.Parameters["@Id"].Value = DBNull.Value;
                    command.Parameters["@Field1"].Value = "field 1.4";
                    command.Parameters["@Field2"].Value = "field 2.4";
                    command.ExecuteNonQuery();

                    // If OK to here, commit the transaction.
                    tran.Commit();
                    Console.WriteLine("\nTRANSACTION COMMIT.\n");
                }
                catch (Exception ex)
                {
                    tran.Rollback();
                    Console.WriteLine("\nTRANSACTION ROLLBACK.\n{0}\n", ex.Message);
                }

                connection.Close();

                // Retrieve and output the contents of the table
                SqlDataAdapter da = new SqlDataAdapter(sqlSelect, sqlConnectString);
                DataTable dt = new DataTable();
                da.Fill(dt);
                Console.WriteLine("---TABLE ManualTransaction---");
                foreach (DataRow row in dt.Rows)
```

Example 7-3. File: Program.cs for ManualTransaction solution (continued)

```
            Console.WriteLine("Id = {0}\tField1 = {1}\tField2 = {2}",
                row["Id"], row["Field1"], row["Field2"]);

        Console.WriteLine("\nPress any key to continue.");
        Console.ReadKey();
    }
  }
}
```

The output is shown in Figure 7-2.

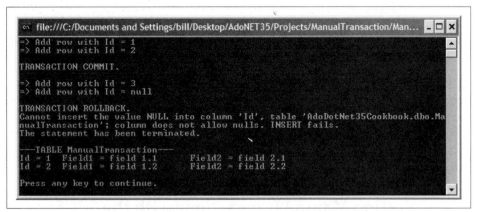

Figure 7-2. Output for ManualTransaction solution

Discussion

Manual transactions allow control over the transaction boundary through explicit commands to start and end the transaction. There is no built-in support for distributed transactions spanning multiple resources with manual transactions.

.NET data providers make available objects to enable manual transactions. The Connection object has a BeginTransaction( ) method that is used to start a transaction. If successful, the method returns a Transaction object that is used to perform all subsequent actions associated with the transaction, such as committing or aborting. Calling the BeginTransaction( ) method does not implicitly cause all subsequent commands to execute within the transaction. The Transaction property of the Command object must be set to a transaction that has already been started for the command to execute within the transaction.

Once started, the transaction remains in a pending state until it is explicitly committed or rolled back using the Commit( ) or Rollback( ) methods of the Transaction object. The Commit( ) method of the Transaction is used to commit the database transaction. The Rollback( ) method of the Transaction is used to roll back a database transaction from a pending state. An InvalidOperationException will be raised if Rollback( ) is called after Commit( ) has been called.

The isolation level of the transaction can be specified through an overload of the `BeginTransaction( )` method and if it is not specified, the default isolation level `ReadCommitted` is used.

Unlike automatic transactions, manual transactions must be explicitly committed or rolled back using the `Commit( )` or `Rollback( )` method. If possible, use the .NET data provider transaction management exclusively; avoid using other transaction models, such as the one provided by SQL Server. If this is necessary for any reason, Recipe 7.3 discusses using the SQL Server transaction model together with the .NET SQL Server data provider transaction management.

The `IDbTransaction` interface is implemented by .NET data providers that access relational databases. Applications create an instance of the class implementing the `IDbTransaction` interface rather than creating an instance of the interface directly. Classes that inherit `IDbTransaction` must implement the inherited members and typically define provider-specific functionality by adding additional members.

The SQL .NET data provider allows *savepoints* to be defined allowing a transaction to be partially rolled back to a point in the transaction other than its beginning. The OLE DB .NET data provider allows nested transactions to be started within the parent transaction; the parent transaction cannot commit until all of its nested transactions have committed.

7.3   Nesting Manual Transactions with the SQL Server .NET Data Provider

Problem

You need to create a nested transaction using the SQL Server .NET data provider, but the `Begin( )` command that you need is only available with the OLE DB .NET data provider. The SQL Server data provider appears to provide no built-in support for nested transactions. You want to nest transactions when using it.

Solution

Simulate nested transactions with savepoints when using the SQL Server .NET data provider, manage and control the lifetime of the `SqlTransaction` class, and create the required exception handling.

The solution requires a table named `NestManualTransaction` in the `AdoDotNet35Cookbook` database. Execute the T-SQL code in Example 7-4 to create the table.

Example 7-4. Create table NestManualTransaction

```
USE AdoDotNet35Cookbook
GO
CREATE TABLE NestManualTransaction (
    Id int NOT NULL,
    Field1 nvarchar(50) NULL,
    Field2 nvarchar(50) NULL,
  CONSTRAINT PK_NestManualTransaction PRIMARY KEY CLUSTERED
    ( Id ASC )
)
```

The solution creates a parameterized insert command that inserts a single record into the NestManualTransaction table. A transaction is started and a record inserted with Id = 1. A savepoint named SavePoint1 is created. Next, an attempt is made to insert two records with Id = 2 and Id = null within a try-catch block. The insert of the Id = null record fails and the transaction is rolled back to SavePoint1 in a catch block and the transaction is committed. The contents of the NestManualTransaction table are retrieved and output to the console, showing the inserted record with Id = 1.

The C# code in *Program.cs* in the project NestManualTransaction is shown in Example 7-5.

Example 7-5. File: Program.cs for NestManualTransaction solution

```
using System;
using System.Data;
using System.Data.SqlClient;

namespace NestManualTransaction
{
    class Program
    {
        private static string savePointName = "SavePoint1";

        static void Main(string[] args)
        {
            string sqlConnectString = "Data Source=(local);" +
                "Integrated security=SSPI;Initial Catalog=AdoDotNet35Cookbook;";

            string sqlSelect = "SELECT * FROM NestManualTransaction";
            string sqlInsert = "INSERT INTO NestManualTransaction VALUES " +
                "(@Id, @Field1, @Field2)";

            // Create and open a connection
            SqlConnection connection = new SqlConnection(sqlConnectString);
            connection.Open();
            // Begin a new transaction
            SqlTransaction tran = connection.BeginTransaction();
```

```
// Create the parameterized insert command
SqlCommand command = new SqlCommand(sqlInsert, connection, tran);
command.Parameters.Add("@Id", SqlDbType.Int);
command.Parameters.Add("@@Field1", SqlDbType.NVarChar, 50);
command.Parameters.Add("@@Field2", SqlDbType.NVarChar, 50);

try
{
    Console.WriteLine("=> Add row with Id = 1");
    command.Parameters["@Id"].Value = 1;
    command.Parameters["@Field1"].Value = "field 1.1";
    command.Parameters["@Field2"].Value = "field 2.1";
    command.ExecuteNonQuery( );
}
catch (Exception ex)
{
    // Exception occurred. Roll back the transaction.
    tran.Rollback( );
    Console.WriteLine("\nTRANSACTION ROLLBACK.\n{0}", ex.Message);
    connection.Close( );

    Console.WriteLine("\nPress any key to continue.");
    Console.ReadKey( );
    return;
}

// Create a SavePoint
tran.Save(savePointName);
Console.WriteLine("\nSavePoint [{0}] created.\n", savePointName);

try
{
    Console.WriteLine("=> Add row with Id = 2");
    command.Parameters["@Id"].Value = 2;
    command.Parameters["@Field1"].Value = "field 1.2";
    command.Parameters["@Field2"].Value = "field 2.2";
    command.ExecuteNonQuery( );

    Console.WriteLine("=> Add row with Id = null");
    command.Parameters["@Id"].Value = DBNull.Value;
    command.Parameters["@Field1"].Value = "field 1.4";
    command.Parameters["@Field2"].Value = "field 2.4";
    command.ExecuteNonQuery( );

    // If OK to here, commit the transaction.
    tran.Commit( );
    Console.WriteLine("\nTRANSACTION COMMIT.\n");
}
catch (Exception ex)
{
    // Rollback to the SavePoint
    tran.Rollback(savePointName);
```

```
                Console.WriteLine("\nTRANSACTION ROLLBACK to {0}.\n{1}\n",
                    savePointName, ex.Message);
                // Commit the transaction up to the SavePoint
                tran.Commit();
            }

            connection.Close();

            // Retrieve and output the contents of the table
            SqlDataAdapter da = new SqlDataAdapter(sqlSelect, sqlConnectString);
            DataTable dt = new DataTable();
            da.Fill(dt);
            Console.WriteLine("---TABLE NestManualTransaction---");
            foreach (DataRow row in dt.Rows)
                Console.WriteLine("Id = {0}\tField1 = {1}\tField2 = {2}",
                    row["Id"], row["Field1"], row["Field2"]);

            Console.WriteLine("\nPress any key to continue.");
            Console.ReadKey();
        }
    }
}
```

The output is shown in Figure 7-3.

Figure 7-3. Output for NestManualTransaction solution

Discussion

The OLE DB .NET data provider's transaction class OleDbTransaction has a Begin()
method that is used to initiate a nested transaction. A nested transaction allows part
of a transaction to be rolled back without rolling back the entire transaction. An
InvalidOperationException is raised if the OLE DB data source does not support
nested transactions.

The SQL Server .NET data provider's transaction class SqlTransaction does not have a Begin( ) method to initiate a nested transaction. Instead, it has a Save( ) method that creates a savepoint in the transaction that can later be used to roll back a portion of the transaction—to the savepoint rather than rolling back to the start of the transaction. The savepoint is named using the only argument of the Save( ) method. An overload of the Rollback( ) method of the SqlTransaction class accepts an argument that you can use to specify the name of the savepoint to roll back to.

7.4 Using ADO.NET and SQL Server DBMS Transactions Together

Problem

You need to use a DBMS transaction within a SQL Server stored procedure from an ADO.NET transaction with the SQL Server .NET data provider.

Solution

Use error-checking within a try-catch block as shown in Example 7-5.

The solution uses a table named SimultaneousTransaction in the database AdoDotNet35Cookbook. Execute the following T-SQL to create the table:

```
USE AdoDotNet35Cookbook
GO
CREATE TABLE SimultaneousTransaction(
    Id int IDENTITY(1,1) NOT NULL PRIMARY KEY,
    Field1 nvarchar(50) NULL,
    Field2 nvarchar(50) NULL )
```

The solution uses a single stored procedure named InsertSimultaneousTransaction that inserts a single record into the SimultaneousTransaction table within a DBMS transaction. If the record insert fails, the transaction is rolled back; otherwise, the transaction is committed. The solution takes an argument named @RollbackFlag that causes the DBMS transaction to be rolled back simulating a failure. Create the stored procedure by executing the T-SQL code in Example 7-6.

Example 7-6. Stored procedure: InsertSimultaneousTransaction

```
USE AdoDotNet35Cookbook
GO

CREATE PROCEDURE InsertSimultaneousTransaction
    @Id int output,
    @Field1 nvarchar(50),
    @Field2 nvarchar(50),
    @RollbackFlag bit = 0
```

Example 7-6. Stored procedure: InsertSimultaneousTransaction (continued)

```
AS
    SET NOCOUNT ON

    BEGIN TRAN

    INSERT SimultaneousTransaction(
        Field1,
        Field2)
    VALUES (
        @Field1,
        @Field2)

    IF @@ERROR <> 0 OR @@ROWCOUNT = 0 OR @RollbackFlag = 1
    BEGIN
        ROLLBACK TRAN
        SET @Id = -1
        RETURN 1
    END

    COMMIT TRAN

    SET @ID = SCOPE_IDENTITY( )

    SELECT @Id Id

    RETURN 0
```

The solution fills a `DataTable` with the `SimultaneousTransaction` table from the `AdoDotNet35Cookbook` database. The method `InsertRecord( )` is called to insert two records—the second record causes a DBMS rollback. The `InsertRecord( )` method creates a command that calls the stored procedure `InsertSimultaneousTransaction` in a try-catch block, which shows how to handle the `SqlException` that indicates a DBMS rollback.

The C# code in *Program.cs* in the project `SimultaneousTransaction` is shown in Example 7-7.

Example 7-7. File: Program.cs for SimultaneousTransaction solution

```
using System;
using System.Data;
using System.Data.SqlClient;

namespace SimultaneousTransaction
{
    class Program
    {
        static void Main(string[] args)
        {
            string sqlConnectString = "Data Source=(local);" +
                "Integrated security=SSPI;Initial Catalog=AdoDotNet35Cookbook;";
```

Example 7-7. File: Program.cs for SimultaneousTransaction solution (continued)

```csharp
        string sqlText = "SELECT Id, Field1, Field2 " +
            "FROM SimultaneousTransaction";

        // Fill the table
        SqlDataAdapter da = new SqlDataAdapter(sqlText, sqlConnectString);
        DataTable dt = new DataTable( );
        da.FillSchema(dt, SchemaType.Source);
        da.Fill(dt);

        InsertRecord(da, dt, sqlConnectString, "Field1.a", "Field2.a", false);
        InsertRecord(da, dt, sqlConnectString, "Field1.b", "Field2.b", true);

        Console.WriteLine("\nPress any key to continue.");
        Console.ReadKey( );
    }

    static void InsertRecord(SqlDataAdapter da, DataTable dt,
        string sqlConnectString, string field1, string field2, bool rollbackFlag)
    {
        Console.WriteLine(
            "\nINSERT: Field1 = {0}, Field2 = {1}, RollbackFlag = {2}",
            field1, field2, rollbackFlag);

        // Create the connection.
        SqlConnection connection = new SqlConnection(sqlConnectString);
        // Create the transaction.
        connection.Open( );
        SqlTransaction tran = connection.BeginTransaction( );
        Console.WriteLine("\n=> SqlConnection.BeginTransaction( )");

        // Create command in the transaction with parameters.
        SqlCommand command =
            new SqlCommand("InsertSimultaneousTransaction", connection, tran);
        command.CommandType = CommandType.StoredProcedure;
        command.Parameters.Add("@Id", SqlDbType.Int).Direction =
            ParameterDirection.Output;
        command.Parameters.Add("@Field1", SqlDbType.NVarChar, 50);
        command.Parameters.Add("@Field2", SqlDbType.NVarChar, 50);
        command.Parameters.Add("@RollbackFlag", SqlDbType.Bit);

        try
        {
            // Set the parameters to the user-entered values.
            // Set Field1 and Field2 to DBNull if empty.
            if (field1.Trim( ).Length == 0)
                command.Parameters["@Field1"].Value = DBNull.Value;
            else
                command.Parameters["@Field1"].Value = field1;
            if (field2.Trim( ).Length == 0)
                command.Parameters["@Field2"].Value = DBNull.Value;
            else
                command.Parameters["@Field2"].Value = field1;
            command.Parameters["@RollbackFlag"].Value = rollbackFlag;
```

Example 7-7. File: Program.cs for SimultaneousTransaction solution (continued)

```csharp
            // Attempt to insert the record.
            command.ExecuteNonQuery( );

            // Success. Commit the transaction.
            tran.Commit( );

            Console.WriteLine("=> SqlTransaction.Commit( )." );
        }
        catch (SqlException ex)
        {
            bool spRollback = false;
            foreach (SqlError err in ex.Errors)
            {
                // Check if transaction rolled back in the
                // stored procedure.
                if (err.Number == 266)
                {
                    Console.WriteLine(
                        "\nDBMS transaction rolled back in " +
                        "stored procedure.\nEXCEPTION: {0}", ex.Message);
                    spRollback = true;
                    break;
                }
            }

            if (!spRollback)
            {
                // transaction was not rolled back by the DBMS
                // SqlException error. Roll back the transaction.
                tran.Rollback( );
                Console.WriteLine("\n=> SqlTransaction.Rollback( )" );
                Console.WriteLine("\nEXCEPTION: {0}", ex.Message);
            }
        }
        catch (Exception ex)
        {
            // Other Exception. Roll back the transaction.
            tran.Rollback( );
            Console.WriteLine("\n=> SqlTransaction.Rollback( )" );
            Console.WriteLine("\nEXCEPTION: {0}", ex.Message);
        }
        finally
        {
            connection.Close( );
        }

        // Refresh the data.
        da.Fill(dt);
    }
}
}
```

The output is shown in Figure 7-4.

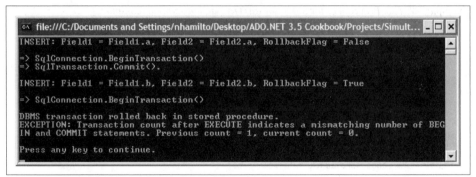

Figure 7-4. Output for SimultaneousTransaction solution

Discussion

SQL Server returns error 266 if a stored procedure exits with a transaction count that is not the same as when the stored procedure was entered. The count is returned by the function @@TRANCOUNT. The error simply sends a message to the client and does not affect execution of the stored procedure. It doesn't mean that the DBMS transaction in the stored procedure could not be started, completed, or terminated properly.

When calling a stored procedure from a .NET manual transaction, the transaction count entering the stored procedure is 1. Using the SQL BEGIN TRAN command in the stored procedure creates a nested transaction, increasing the transaction count to 2. If the stored procedure transaction is subsequently committed with the COMMIT TRAN command, the transaction count is decremented back to 1. Keep in mind commits of inner transactions don't free resources or make modifications permanent, and don't affect outer transactions. If ROLLBACK is called, all inner transactions to the outermost transaction are rolled back and the transaction count is decremented to 0. Error 266 is returned by the rolled-back stored procedure since the transaction count entering the stored procedure is 1 while the count when exiting is 0. Attempting to commit or roll back the transaction from .NET after it has been rolled back in the stored procedure will cause an InvalidOperationException because the transaction has already been rolled back.

The solution catches exceptions raised while executing a stored procedure and checks if they correspond to SQL Server error 266, which is the mismatch between the starting and exiting stored procedure transaction count values as a result of the stored procedure rolling back the transaction. If the stored procedure has rolled back the transaction, it is not rolled back by the .NET code. All other errors raised while executing the stored procedure are rolled back by the .NET code.

7.5 Using a Transaction with a DataAdapter

Problem

You need to use a transaction when updating a data source using a DataAdapter.

Solution

Associate a Transaction with the Command object for the DataAdapter.

The solution uses a table named DataAdapterTransaction in the AdoDotNet35Cookbook database. Execute the T-SQL in Example 7-8 to create the table.

Example 7-8. Create table DataAdapterTransaction

```
USE AdoDotNet35Cookbook
GO
CREATE TABLE DataAdapterTransaction (
    Id int NOT NULL PRIMARY KEY,
    Field1 nvarchar(50) NULL,
    Field2 nvarchar(50) NULL )
```

The solution creates a DataAdapter that loads a DataTable with the DataAdapterTransaction table in the AdoDotNet35Cookbook database. The method InsertRecords( ) adds records to a DataTable and updates the DataAdapterTransaction table using a transaction to rollback the update if all records cannot be added. A CommandBuilder is used to generate the updating logic. A Transaction object on the Connection of the SelectCommand of the DataAdapter is created. The Transaction is associated with the Connection objects for the update commands generated for the DataAdapter by the CommandBuilder. The Update( ) method of the DataAdapter is called to update DataTable changes to the Orders table. If no errors are encountered, the transaction is committed; otherwise, all changes made are rolled back. The InsertRecords( ) method is called twice. The first call successfully adds two records. The second call fails to add two records because the Id of the second record is null. The contents of the DataAdapterTransaction table is output to the console after both insert attempts.

The C# code in *Program.cs* in the project DataAdapterTransaction is shown in Example 7-9.

Example 7-9. File: Program.cs for DataAdapterTransaction solution

```
using System;
using System.Data;
using System.Data.SqlClient;
```

Example 7-9. File: Program.cs for DataAdapterTransaction solution (continued)

```
namespace DataAdapterTransaction
{
    class Program
    {
        private static string sqlConnectString = "Data Source=(local);" +
            "Integrated security=SSPI;Initial Catalog=AdoDotNet35Cookbook;";

        private static string sqlSelect = "SELECT * FROM DataAdapterTransaction";

        static void Main(string[] args)
        {
            object[,] o1 = {{ "1", "field 1.1", "field 2.1" },
                           { "2", "field 1.2", "field 2.2" }};
            InsertRecords(o1);

            object[,] o2 = {{ "3", "field 1.3", "field 2.3" },
                           { null, "field 1.4", "field 2.4" }};
            InsertRecords(o2);

            // Retrieve and output the contents of the table
            SqlDataAdapter daRead = new SqlDataAdapter(sqlSelect, sqlConnectString);
            DataTable dtRead = new DataTable( );
            daRead.Fill(dtRead);
            Console.WriteLine("---TABLE DataAdapterTransaction---");
            foreach (DataRow row in dtRead.Rows)
                Console.WriteLine("Id = {0}\tField1 = {1}\tField2 = {2}",
                    row["Id"], row["Field1"], row["Field2"]);

            Console.WriteLine("\nPress any key to continue.");
            Console.ReadKey( );
        }

        static void InsertRecords(object[,] o)
        {
            DataTable dt = new DataTable( );
            SqlTransaction tran;

            SqlConnection connection = new SqlConnection(sqlConnectString);

            // Create a DataAdapter
            SqlDataAdapter da = new SqlDataAdapter(sqlSelect, connection);
            // Stop updating when an error is encountered for roll back.
            da.ContinueUpdateOnError = false;
            // Create CommandBuilder and generate updating logic.
            SqlCommandBuilder cb = new SqlCommandBuilder(da);
            // Create and fill a DataTable with schema and data
            da.Fill(dt);
            // Open the connection
            connection.Open( );
            // Begin a new transaction and assign it to the DataAdapter
            tran = connection.BeginTransaction( );
            da.SelectCommand.Transaction = tran;
```

```
                // Add two rows that will succeed update
                for (int i = 0; i <= o.GetUpperBound(0); i++)
                {
                    dt.Rows.Add(new object[] { o[i, 0], o[i, 1], o[i, 2] });
                    Console.WriteLine(
                        "=> Row with [Id = {0}] added to DataTable.", o[i, 0]);
                }

                Console.WriteLine("=> Updating data source using DataAdapter.");
                try
                {
                    da.Update(dt);
                    tran.Commit( );

                    Console.WriteLine("\nTRANSACTION COMMIT.\n");
                }
                catch (Exception ex)
                {
                    tran.Rollback( );
                    Console.WriteLine("\nTRANSACTION ROLLBACK.\n{0}\n", ex.Message);
                }
                finally
                {
                    connection.Close( );
                }
            }
        }
}
```

The output is shown in Figure 7-5.

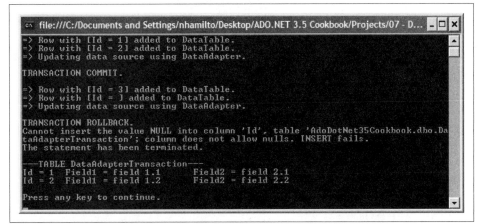

Figure 7-5. Output for DataAdapterTransaction solution

Discussion

You can use a transaction with a DataAdapter to roll back updates made by the DataAdapter before an error.

If, as in the solution, a CommandBuilder is used to generate the update logic for the DataAdapter, associate the Transaction with the SelectCommand of the DataAdapter as shown in the solution code:

```
da.SelectCommand.Transaction = tran;
```

If custom update logic is used for the DataAdapter, the Transaction must be associated with the DeleteCommand, InsertCommand, and UpdateCommand of the DataAdapter, but not the SelectCommand, as shown in the following code:

```
da.DeleteCommand.Transaction = tran;
da.InsertCommand.Transaction = tran;
da.UpdateCommand.Transaction = tran;
```

7.6 Avoiding Referential Integrity Problems when Updating Data in Related Tables

Problem

You sometimes get referential integrity errors when you update a DataSet that contains related parent, child, and grandchild records back to the underlying data source, but want to perform the update without errors.

Solution

Use one DataAdapter for each DataTable to update the deleted, updated, and inserted rows as shown in the following example.

The solution uses three tables named Parent, Child, and Grandchild. Execute the following T-SQL batch to create the tables:

```
USE AdoDotNet35Cookbook
GO

CREATE TABLE Parent (
    ParentId int NOT NULL IDENTITY (1, 1) PRIMARY KEY,
    Field1 nvarchar(50) NOT NULL,
    Field2 nvarchar(50) NOT NULL
);

CREATE TABLE Child (
    ChildId int NOT NULL IDENTITY (1, 1) PRIMARY KEY,
    ParentId int NOT NULL,
    Field3 nvarchar(50) NOT NULL,
    Field4 nvarchar(50) NOT NULL
);
```

```
CREATE TABLE Grandchild (
    GrandchildId int NOT NULL IDENTITY (1, 1) PRIMARY KEY,
    ChildId int NOT NULL,
    Field5 nvarchar(50) NOT NULL,
    Field6 nvarchar(50) NOT NULL
);

ALTER TABLE Child WITH CHECK
ADD CONSTRAINT FK_Child_Parent FOREIGN KEY(ParentId)
REFERENCES Parent (ParentId)
GO

ALTER TABLE Grandchild WITH CHECK
ADD CONSTRAINT FK_Grandchild_Child FOREIGN KEY(ChildId)
REFERENCES Child (ChildId)
GO
```

The schema of table Parent used in this solution is shown in Table 7-1.

Table 7-1. Parent table schema

Column name	Data type	Length	Allow nulls?
ParentId	int	4	No
Field1	nvarchar	50	Yes
Field2	nvarchar	50	Yes

The schema of table Child used in this solution is shown in Table 7-2.

Table 7-2. Child table schema

Column name	Data type	Length	Allow nulls?
ChildId	int	4	No
ParentId	int	4	No
Field3	nvarchar	50	Yes
Field4	nvarchar	50	Yes

The schema of table Grandchild used in this solution is shown in Table 7-3.

Table 7-3. Grandchild table schema

Column name	Data type	Length	Allow nulls?
GrandchildId	int	4	No
ChildId	int	4	No
Field5	nvarchar	50	Yes
Field6	nvarchar	50	Yes

The solution uses 12 stored procedures:

GetParent

> Used to retrieve a single record from the Parent table if the optional @ParentId parameter is specified or all Parent records if it is not.

DeleteParent

> Used to delete the record specified by the @ParentId parameter from the Parent table.

InsertParent

> Used to insert a record into the Parent table and return the *ParentId* identity value for the new record.

UpdateParent

> Used to update all field values for the record in the Parent table specified by the @ParentId input parameter.

GetChild

> Used to retrieve a single record from the Child table if the optional @ChildId parameter is specified or all Child records if it is not.

DeleteChild

> Used to delete the record specified by the @ChildId parameter from the Child table.

InsertChild

> Used to insert a record into the Child table and return the *ChildId* identity value for the new record.

UpdateChild

> Used to update all field values for the record in the Child table specified by the @ChildId input parameter.

GetGrandchild

> Used to retrieve a single record from the Grandchild table if the optional @GrandchildId parameter is specified or all Grandchild records if it is not.

DeleteGrandchild

> Used to delete the record specified by the @GrandchildId parameter from the Grandchild table.

InsertGrandchild

> Used to insert a record into the Grandchild table and return the GrandchildId identity value for the new record.

UpdateGrandchild

> Used to update all field values for the record in the Grandchild table specified by the @GrandchildId input parameter.

The 12 stored procedures are shown in Examples 7-10 through 7-21.

Example 7-10. Stored procedure: GetParent

```
CREATE PROCEDURE GetParent
    @ParentId int = NULL
AS
    SET NOCOUNT ON

    IF @ParentId IS NOT NULL
    BEGIN
        SELECT ParentId, Field1, Field2
        FROM Parent
        WHERE ParentId = @ParentId

        RETURN 0
    END

    SELECT ParentId, Field1, Field2
    FROM Parent

    RETURN 0
```

Example 7-11. Stored procedure: DeleteParent

```
CREATE PROCEDURE DeleteParent
    @ParentId int
AS
    SET NOCOUNT ON

    DELETE FROM  Parent
    WHERE ParentId = @ParentId

    RETURN 0
```

Example 7-12. Stored procedure: InsertParent

```
CREATE PROCEDURE InsertParent
    @ParentId int OUTPUT,
    @Field1 nvarchar(50) = NULL,
    @Field2 nvarchar(50) = NULL
AS
    SET NOCOUNT ON

    INSERT Parent(Field1, Field2)
    VALUES (@Field1, @Field2)

    IF @@ROWCOUNT=0
        RETURN 1

    SET @ParentId = SCOPE_IDENTITY( )

    SELECT @ParentId ParentId

    RETURN 0
```

Example 7-13. Stored procedure: UpdateParent

```
CREATE PROCEDURE UpdateParent
    @ParentId int,
    @Field1 nvarchar(50) = NULL,
    @Field2 nvarchar(50) = NULL
AS
    SET NOCOUNT ON

    UPDATE Parent
    SET
        Field1 = @Field1,
        Field2 = @Field2
    WHERE
        ParentId = @ParentId

    IF @@ROWCOUNT=0
        RETURN 1

    RETURN 0
```

Example 7-14. Stored procedure: GetChild

```
CREATE PROCEDURE GetChild
    @ChildId int = NULL
AS
    SET NOCOUNT ON

    IF @ChildId IS NOT NULL
    BEGIN
        SELECT ChildId, ParentId, Field3, Field4
        FROM Child
        WHERE ChildId = @ChildId

        RETURN 0
    END

    SELECT ChildId, ParentId, Field3, Field4
    FROM Child

    RETURN 0
```

Example 7-15. Stored procedure: DeleteChild

```
CREATE PROCEDURE DeleteChild
    @ChildId int
AS
    SET NOCOUNT ON

    DELETE FROM Child
    WHERE ChildId = @ChildId

    RETURN 0
```

Example 7-16. Stored procedure: InsertChild

```
CREATE PROCEDURE InsertChild
    @ChildId int OUTPUT,
    @ParentId int,
    @Field3 nvarchar(50) = NULL,
    @Field4 nvarchar(50) = NULL
AS
    SET NOCOUNT ON

    INSERT Child(ParentId, Field3, Field4)
    VALUES (@ParentId, @Field3, @Field4)

    IF @@ROWCOUNT = 0
        RETURN 1

    SET @ChildId = SCOPE_IDENTITY( )

    SELECT @ChildId ChildId

    RETURN 0
```

Example 7-17. Stored procedure: UpdateChild

```
CREATE PROCEDURE UpdateChild
    @ChildId int,
    @ParentId int,
    @Field3 nvarchar(50) = NULL,
    @Field4 nvarchar(50) = NULL
AS
    SET NOCOUNT ON

    UPDATE
        Child
    SET
        ParentId = @ParentId,
        Field3 = @Field3,
        Field4 = @Field4
    WHERE
        ChildId = @ChildId

    if @@ROWCOUNT=0
        RETURN 1

    RETURN 0
```

Example 7-18. Stored procedure: GetGrandchild

```
CREATE PROCEDURE GetGrandchild
    @GrandchildId int = null
AS
    SET NOCOUNT ON
```

Example 7-18. Stored procedure: GetGrandchild (continued)

```
IF @GrandchildId IS NOT NULL
BEGIN
    SELECT GrandchildId, ChildId, Field5, Field6
    FROM Grandchild
    WHERE GrandchildId = @GrandchildId

    RETURN 0
END

SELECT GrandchildId, ChildId, Field5, Field6
FROM Grandchild

RETURN 0
```

Example 7-19. Stored procedure: DeleteGrandchild

```
CREATE PROCEDURE DeleteGrandchild
    @GrandchildId int
AS
    SET NOCOUNT ON

    DELETE FROM Grandchild
    WHERE GrandchildId = @GrandchildId

    return 0
```

Example 7-20. Stored procedure: InsertGrandchild

```
CREATE PROCEDURE InsertGrandchild
    @GrandchildId int OUTPUT,
    @ChildId int,
    @Field5 nvarchar(50) = null,
    @Field6 nvarchar(50) = null
AS
    SET NOCOUNT ON

    INSERT Grandchild(ChildId, Field5, Field6)
    VALUES (@ChildId, @Field5, @Field6)

    IF @@ROWCOUNT=0
        RETURN 1

    SET @GrandchildId = SCOPE_IDENTITY( )

    SELECT @GrandchildId GrandchildId

    RETURN 0
```

Example 7-21. Stored procedure: UpdateGrandchild

```
CREATE PROCEDURE UpdateGrandchild
    @GrandchildId int,
    @ChildId int,
    @Field5 nvarchar(50) = NULL,
    @Field6 nvarchar(50) = NULL
AS
    SET NOCOUNT ON

    UPDATE
        Grandchild
    SET
        ChildId = @ChildId,
        Field5 = @Field5,
        Field6 = @Field6
    WHERE
        GrandchildId=@GrandchildId

    IF @@ROWCOUNT=0
        RETURN 1

    RETURN 0
```

The solution creates a DataSet containing the Parent, Child, and Grandchild
DataTable objects. DataRelation objects are created relating the tables. DataAdapter
objects are created for each DataTable and the select, delete, insert, and update
Command objects are specified for each using the custom logic in the 12 stored procedures used by this solution. The DataAdapter objects are used to fill the tables in the
DataSet. The solution creates random data, randomly modifies the data including the
relationships, and deletes all data—each time the data source is updated by calling
the UpdateData( ) method, which calls the Update( ) method of the DataAdapter for
each table in the correct order so that referential integrity do not occur when the
tables in the database are updated. The contents of the data source are output after
each output.

The C# code in *Program.cs* in the project AvoidReferentialIntegrityProblems is
shown in Example 7-22.

Example 7-22. File: Program.cs for AvoidReferentialIntegrityProblem solution

```
using System;
using System.Data;
using System.Data.SqlClient;
```

Example 7-22. File: Program.cs for AvoidReferentialIntegrityProblem solution (continued)

```
namespace AvoidReferentialIntegrityProblems
{
    class Program
    {
        static void Main(string[] args)
        {
            string sqlConnectString = "Data Source=(local);" +
                "Integrated security=SSPI;Initial Catalog=AdoDotNet35Cookbook;";

            DataColumnCollection cols;
            DataColumn col;

            // Build the parent table.
            DataTable dtParent = new DataTable("Parent");
            cols = dtParent.Columns;
            col = cols.Add("ParentId", typeof(int));
            col.AutoIncrement = true;
            col.AutoIncrementSeed = -1;
            col.AutoIncrementStep = -1;
            cols.Add("Field1", typeof(string)).MaxLength = 50;
            cols.Add("Field2", typeof(string)).MaxLength = 50;

            // Build the child table.
            DataTable dtChild = new DataTable("Child");
            cols = dtChild.Columns;
            col = cols.Add("ChildId", typeof(int));
            col.AutoIncrement = true;
            col.AutoIncrementSeed = -1;
            col.AutoIncrementStep = -1;
            cols.Add("ParentId", typeof(int)).AllowDBNull = false;
            cols.Add("Field3", typeof(string)).MaxLength = 50;
            cols.Add("Field4", typeof(string)).MaxLength = 50;

            // Build the grandchild table.
            DataTable dtGrandchild = new DataTable("Grandchild");
            cols = dtGrandchild.Columns;
            col = cols.Add("GrandchildId", typeof(int));
            col.AutoIncrement = true;
            col.AutoIncrementSeed = -1;
            col.AutoIncrementStep = -1;
            cols.Add("ChildId", typeof(int)).AllowDBNull = false;
            cols.Add("Field5", typeof(string)).MaxLength = 50;
            cols.Add("Field6", typeof(string)).MaxLength = 50;

            // Create the DataSet and add tables to it
            DataSet ds = new DataSet();
            ds.Tables.Add(dtParent);
            ds.Tables.Add(dtChild);
            ds.Tables.Add(dtGrandchild);

            // Create the data relations in the DataSet
            ds.Relations.Add("FK_Child_Parent",
                dtParent.Columns["ParentId"], dtChild.Columns["ParentId"]);
```

```
ds.Relations.Add("FK_Grandchild_Child",
    dtChild.Columns["ChildId"], dtGrandchild.Columns["ChildId"]);

// Create a connection
SqlConnection connection = new SqlConnection(sqlConnectString);

// Create the DataAdapter objects for the tables.
SqlDataAdapter daParent = new SqlDataAdapter();
SqlDataAdapter daChild = new SqlDataAdapter();
SqlDataAdapter daGrandchild = new SqlDataAdapter();

// Build the parent select command.
SqlCommand selectCommand = new SqlCommand("GetParent", connection);
selectCommand.CommandType = CommandType.StoredProcedure;
daParent.SelectCommand = selectCommand;

// Build the parent delete command.
SqlCommand deleteCommand = new SqlCommand("DeleteParent",
    daParent.SelectCommand.Connection);
deleteCommand.CommandType = CommandType.StoredProcedure;
deleteCommand.Parameters.Add("@ParentId", SqlDbType.Int, 0,
    "ParentId");
daParent.DeleteCommand = deleteCommand;

// Build the parent insert command.
SqlCommand insertCommand = new SqlCommand("InsertParent",
    daParent.SelectCommand.Connection);
insertCommand.CommandType = CommandType.StoredProcedure;
insertCommand.Parameters.Add("@ParentId", SqlDbType.Int, 0,
    "ParentId");
insertCommand.Parameters.Add("@Field1", SqlDbType.NVarChar, 50,
    "Field1");
insertCommand.Parameters.Add("@Field2", SqlDbType.NVarChar, 50,
    "Field2");
daParent.InsertCommand = insertCommand;

// Build the parent update command.
SqlCommand updateCommand = new SqlCommand("UpdateParent",
    daParent.SelectCommand.Connection);
updateCommand.CommandType = CommandType.StoredProcedure;
updateCommand.Parameters.Add("@ParentId", SqlDbType.Int, 0,
    "ParentId");
updateCommand.Parameters.Add("@Field1", SqlDbType.NVarChar, 50,
    "Field1");
updateCommand.Parameters.Add("@Field2", SqlDbType.NVarChar, 50,
    "Field2");
daParent.UpdateCommand = updateCommand;

// Build the child select command.
selectCommand = new SqlCommand("GetChild", connection);
selectCommand.CommandType = CommandType.StoredProcedure;
daChild.SelectCommand = selectCommand;
```

```csharp
// Build the child delete command.
deleteCommand = new SqlCommand("DeleteChild",
    daChild.SelectCommand.Connection);
deleteCommand.CommandType = CommandType.StoredProcedure;
deleteCommand.Parameters.Add("@ChildId", SqlDbType.Int, 0,
    "ChildId");
daChild.DeleteCommand = deleteCommand;

// Build the child insert command.
insertCommand = new SqlCommand("InsertChild",
    daChild.SelectCommand.Connection);
insertCommand.CommandType = CommandType.StoredProcedure;
insertCommand.Parameters.Add("@ChildId", SqlDbType.Int, 0,
    "ChildId");
insertCommand.Parameters.Add("@ParentId", SqlDbType.Int, 0,
    "ParentId");
insertCommand.Parameters.Add("@Field3", SqlDbType.NVarChar, 50,
    "Field3");
insertCommand.Parameters.Add("@Field4", SqlDbType.NVarChar, 50,
    "Field4");
daChild.InsertCommand = insertCommand;

// Build the child update command.
updateCommand = new SqlCommand("UpdateChild",
    daChild.SelectCommand.Connection);
updateCommand.CommandType = CommandType.StoredProcedure;
updateCommand.Parameters.Add("@ChildId", SqlDbType.Int, 0,
    "ChildId");
updateCommand.Parameters.Add("@ParentId", SqlDbType.Int, 0,
    "ParentId");
updateCommand.Parameters.Add("@Field3", SqlDbType.NVarChar, 50,
    "Field3");
updateCommand.Parameters.Add("@Field4", SqlDbType.NVarChar, 50,
    "Field4");
daChild.UpdateCommand = updateCommand;

// Build the grandchild select command.
selectCommand = new SqlCommand("GetGrandchild", connection);
selectCommand.CommandType = CommandType.StoredProcedure;
daGrandchild.SelectCommand = selectCommand;

// Build the grandchild delete command.
deleteCommand = new SqlCommand("DeleteGrandchild",
    daGrandchild.SelectCommand.Connection);
deleteCommand.CommandType = CommandType.StoredProcedure;
deleteCommand.Parameters.Add("@GrandchildId", SqlDbType.Int, 0,
    "GrandchildId");
daGrandchild.DeleteCommand = deleteCommand;

// Build the grandchild insert command.
insertCommand = new SqlCommand("InsertGrandchild",
    daGrandchild.SelectCommand.Connection);
```

```
        insertCommand.CommandType = CommandType.StoredProcedure;
        insertCommand.Parameters.Add("@GrandchildId", SqlDbType.Int, 0,
            "GrandchildId");
        insertCommand.Parameters.Add("@ChildId", SqlDbType.Int, 0,
            "ChildId");
        insertCommand.Parameters.Add("@Field5", SqlDbType.NVarChar, 50,
            "Field5");
        insertCommand.Parameters.Add("@Field6", SqlDbType.NVarChar, 50,
            "Field6");
        daGrandchild.InsertCommand = insertCommand;

        // Build the grandchild update command.
        updateCommand = new SqlCommand("UpdateGrandchild",
            daGrandchild.SelectCommand.Connection);
        updateCommand.CommandType = CommandType.StoredProcedure;
        updateCommand.Parameters.Add("@GrandchildId", SqlDbType.Int, 0,
            "GrandchildId");
        updateCommand.Parameters.Add("@ChildId", SqlDbType.Int, 0,
            "ChildId");
        updateCommand.Parameters.Add("@Field5", SqlDbType.NVarChar, 50,
            "Field5");
        updateCommand.Parameters.Add("@Field6", SqlDbType.NVarChar, 50,
            "Field6");
        daGrandchild.UpdateCommand = updateCommand;

        // Fill the DataSet.
        daParent.Fill(ds, "Parent");
        daChild.Fill(ds, "Child");
        daGrandchild.Fill(ds, "Grandchild");

        // Create some data, update the source, and output to console
        CreateData(ds, 3, 3, 3);
        UpdateData(ds, daParent, daChild, daGrandchild);
        Console.WriteLine("=> Data created.");
        OutputData(ds);

        // Modufy some data, update the source, and output to console
        ModifyData(ds);
        UpdateData(ds, daParent, daChild, daGrandchild);
        Console.WriteLine("\n=> Data modified.");
        OutputData(ds);

        // Delete all data, update the source, and output to console
        DeleteData(ds);
        UpdateData(ds, daParent, daChild, daGrandchild);
        Console.WriteLine("\n=> Data deleted.");
        OutputData(ds);

        Console.WriteLine("\nPress any key to continue.");
        Console.ReadKey();
    }
```

```csharp
static void CreateData(DataSet ds, int parentRows, int childRows,
    int grandchildRows)
{
    // Generate some data into each of the related tables.
    for (int iParent = 0; iParent < parentRows; iParent++)
    {
        // Generate parentRows of data in the parent table.
        DataRow parentRow = ds.Tables["Parent"].NewRow( );
        parentRow["Field1"] = Guid.NewGuid( ).ToString( );
        parentRow["Field2"] = Guid.NewGuid( ).ToString( );
        ds.Tables["Parent"].Rows.Add(parentRow);

        for (int iChild = 0; iChild < childRows; iChild++)
        {
            // Generate childRows of data in the child table.
            DataRow childRow = ds.Tables["Child"].NewRow( );
            childRow["ParentId"] =
                (int)parentRow["ParentId"];
            childRow["Field3"] = Guid.NewGuid( ).ToString( );
            childRow["Field4"] = Guid.NewGuid( ).ToString( );
            ds.Tables["Child"].Rows.Add(childRow);

            for (int iGrandchild = 0; iGrandchild < grandchildRows;
                iGrandchild++)
            {
                // Generate grandchildRows of data in the
                // grandchild table.
                DataRow grandchildRow =
                    ds.Tables["Grandchild"].NewRow( );
                grandchildRow["ChildId"] =
                    (int)childRow["ChildId"];
                grandchildRow["Field5"] =
                    Guid.NewGuid( ).ToString( );
                grandchildRow["Field6"] =
                    Guid.NewGuid( ).ToString( );
                ds.Tables["Grandchild"].Rows.Add(
                    grandchildRow);
            }
        }
    }
}

static void ModifyData(DataSet ds)
{
    // Randomly delete or modify rows from the grandchild, child, and
    // parent rows.
    Random r = new Random((int)DateTime.Now.Ticks);

    // Modify grandchild rows.
    for (int i = ds.Tables["Grandchild"].Rows.Count; i > 0; i--)
    {
        DataRow grandchildRow =
            ds.Tables["Grandchild"].Rows[i - 1];
```

```
        if (r.Next(2) == 0)
        {
            grandchildRow["Field5"] = Guid.NewGuid( ).ToString( );
            grandchildRow["Field6"] = Guid.NewGuid( ).ToString( );
        }
        else
            grandchildRow.Delete( );
    }

    // Modify or delete child rows.
    for (int i = ds.Tables["Child"].Rows.Count; i > 0; i--)
    {
        DataRow childRow = ds.Tables["Child"].Rows[i - 1];

        if (r.Next(2) == 0)
        {
            childRow["Field3"] = Guid.NewGuid( ).ToString( );
            childRow["Field4"] = Guid.NewGuid( ).ToString( );
        }
        else
            childRow.Delete( );
    }

    // Modify or delete parent rows.
    for (int i = ds.Tables["Parent"].Rows.Count; i > 0; i--)
    {
        DataRow parentRow = ds.Tables["Parent"].Rows[i - 1];

        if (r.Next(2) == 0)
        {
            parentRow["Field1"] = Guid.NewGuid( ).ToString( );
            parentRow["Field2"] = Guid.NewGuid( ).ToString( );
        }
        else
            parentRow.Delete( );

    }

    // Insert two rows into parent, child, and grandchild.
    CreateData(ds, 2, 2, 2);
}

static void DeleteData(DataSet ds)
{
    foreach (DataRow row in ds.Tables["Grandchild"].Rows)
        row.Delete( );

    foreach (DataRow row in ds.Tables["Child"].Rows)
        row.Delete( );

    foreach (DataRow row in ds.Tables["Parent"].Rows)
        row.Delete( );
}
```

```csharp
static void UpdateData(DataSet ds, SqlDataAdapter daParent,
    SqlDataAdapter daChild, SqlDataAdapter daGrandchild)
{
    daGrandchild.Update(ds.Tables["Grandchild"].Select(
        null, null, DataViewRowState.Deleted));
    daChild.Update(ds.Tables["Child"].Select(
        null, null, DataViewRowState.Deleted));
    daParent.Update(ds.Tables["Parent"].Select(
        null, null, DataViewRowState.Deleted));
    daParent.Update(ds.Tables["Parent"].Select(
        null, null, DataViewRowState.ModifiedCurrent));
    daParent.Update(ds.Tables["Parent"].Select(
        null, null, DataViewRowState.Added));
    daChild.Update(ds.Tables["Child"].Select(
        null, null, DataViewRowState.ModifiedCurrent));
    daChild.Update(ds.Tables["Child"].Select(
        null, null, DataViewRowState.Added));
    daGrandchild.Update(ds.Tables["Grandchild"].Select(
        null, null, DataViewRowState.ModifiedCurrent));
    daGrandchild.Update(ds.Tables["Grandchild"].Select(
        null, null, DataViewRowState.Added));
}

static void OutputData(DataSet ds)
{
    // Output data for the parent, junction, and child tables
    Console.WriteLine("\n---DATASET---");

    if (ds.Tables["Parent"].Rows.Count == 0)
        Console.WriteLine("[Empty]");
    else
    {
        foreach (DataRow rowParent in ds.Tables["Parent"].Rows)
        {
            Console.WriteLine("ParentId = {0}\tField1 = {1}\tField2 = {2}",
                rowParent["ParentId"],
                rowParent["Field1"].ToString().Substring(0, 13),
                rowParent["Field2"].ToString().Substring(0, 13));

            foreach (DataRow rowChild in
                rowParent.GetChildRows("FK_Child_Parent"))
            {
                Console.WriteLine("++ChildId = {0}\tField3 = {1}\tField4 = {2}",
                    rowChild["ChildId"],
                    rowChild["Field3"].ToString().Substring(0, 13),
                    rowChild["Field4"].ToString().Substring(0, 13));

                foreach (DataRow rowGrandchild in
                    rowChild.GetChildRows("FK_Grandchild_Child"))
                {
                    Console.WriteLine(
```

Example 7-22. File: Program.cs for AvoidReferentialIntegrityProblem solution (continued)

```
                        "++++GrandchildId = {0}\tField5 = {1}\tField6 = {2}",
                        rowGrandchild["GrandchildId"],
                        rowGrandchild["Field5"].ToString( ).Substring(0, 13),
                        rowGrandchild["Field6"].ToString( ).Substring(0, 13));
                }
            }
        }
    }
}
}
```

The output is shown in Figure 7-6.

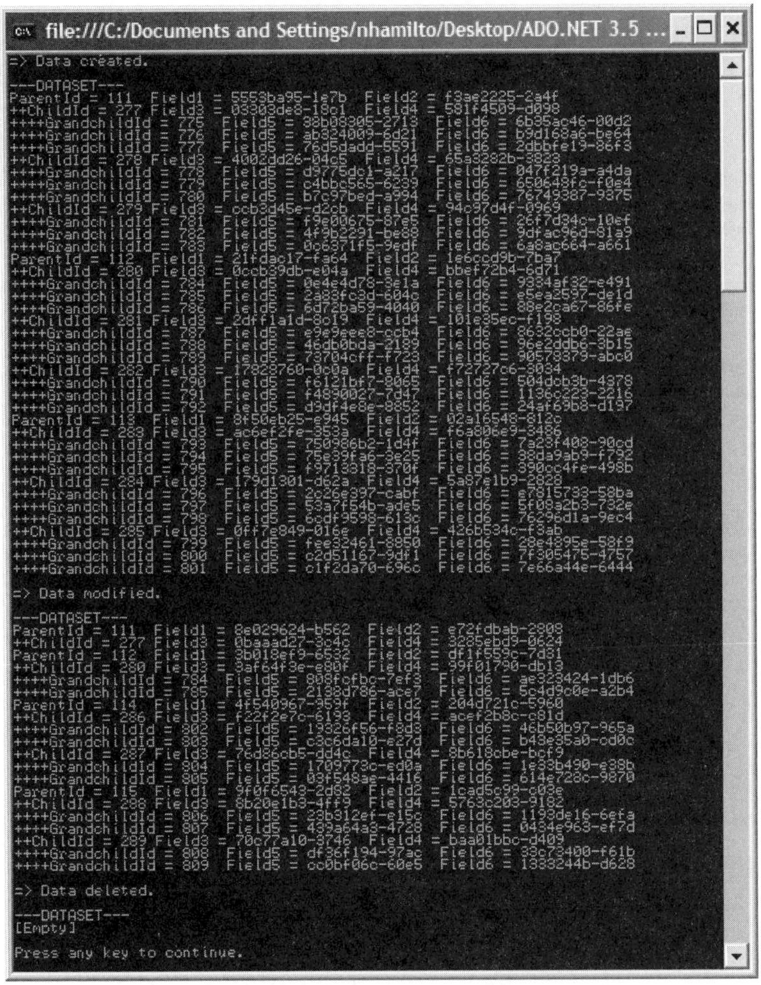

Figure 7-6. Output for AvoidReferentialIntegrityProblems solution

Discussion

To avoid referential integrity problems when updating the data source from a DataSet containing related tables, use one DataAdapter for each DataTable to update the deleted, updated, and inserted rows in the following order:

1. Deleted grandchild rows

2. Deleted child rows

3. Deleted parent rows

4. Updated parent rows

5. Inserted parent rows

6. Updated child rows

7. Inserted child rows

8. Updated grandchild rows

9. Inserted grandchild rows

In the solution, this is done using the following code:

```
daGrandchild.Update(ds.Tables["Grandchild"].Select(
    null, null, DataViewRowState.Deleted));
daChild.Update(ds.Tables["Child"].Select(
    null, null, DataViewRowState.Deleted));
daParent.Update(ds.Tables["Parent"].Select(
    null, null, DataViewRowState.Deleted));
daParent.Update(ds.Tables["Parent"].Select(
    null, null, DataViewRowState.ModifiedCurrent));
daParent.Update(ds.Tables["Parent"].Select(
    null, null, DataViewRowState.Added));
daChild.Update(ds.Tables["Child"].Select(
    null, null, DataViewRowState.ModifiedCurrent));
daChild.Update(ds.Tables["Child"].Select(
    null, null, DataViewRowState.Added));
daGrandchild.Update(ds.Tables["Grandchild"].Select(
    null, null, DataViewRowState.ModifiedCurrent));
daGrandchild.Update(ds.Tables["Grandchild"].Select(
    null, null, DataViewRowState.Added));
```

There are three related tables—parent, child, and grandparent—and one DataAdapter for each table. An overload of the Select( ) method of the DataTable is used to retrieve the subset of rows identified by the state argument containing a value from the DataViewRowState enumeration:

- Added to get the subset of inserted rows

- Deleted to get the subset of deleted rows

- ModifiedCurrent to get the subset of modified rows

There are a few other considerations involving the primary key:

- If the primary key cannot be modified once added, the updated and inserted rows can be processed together in the same statement.

- If the primary key can be modified after it has been added, the database must cascade the updated primary key values to the child records or else a referential integrity violation will occur. The UpdateCommand property of child tables must accept either the Original or the Current value of the foreign key if it is used in the concurrency check.

- If the primary key for the DataTable is an autoincrement value and the primary key value is generated by the data source, the InsertCommand must return the primary key value from the data source and use it to update the value in the DataSet. The DataSet can automatically cascade this new value to the foreign keys in the related child records.

7.7   Enforcing Business Rules with Column Expressions

Problem

You need to enforce a business rule based on multiple columns in a table.

Solution

Use expression-based columns to enforce business rules at the user interface tier. The business rule for this solution is that the sum of Field1 and Field2 for a row in the table must be 10.

The solution uses a table named EnforceBusinessRulesColumnExpressions in the AdoDotNet35Cookbook database. Execute the T-SQL statement in Example 7-23 to create the table.

Example 7-23. Create table EnforceBusinessRulesColumnExpressions

```
USE AdoDotNet35Cookbook
GO
CREATE TABLE EnforceBusinessRulesColumnExpressions (
    Id int NOT NULL PRIMARY KEY,
    Field1 int NOT NULL,
    Field2 int NOT NULL
)
```

The solution creates a DataTable and creates a schema for it matching the EnforceBusinessRulesColumnExpressions table in the database. An expression column is added to the table that returns a Boolean value indicating whether the sum of Field1 and Field2 is equal to 10. A DataAdapter is created and an event handler is attached to handle its RowUpdating event. A CommandBuilder is used to supply the updating logic. Four rows are added to the DataTable—two are valid and two are invalid based on the expression. The Update( ) method of the DataAdapter is called to update the table in the database. For each row being updated or inserted, the handler for the RowUpdating event of the DataAdapter checks whether the value of the expression column is false indicating that the data is invalid according to the business rule defined by the expression column. If the business rule has not been met, an error is set on the row and the update for the row is skipped. The contents of the DataTable and the table in the database are output to the console.

The C# code in *Program.cs* in the project EnforceBusinessRulesColumnExpressions is shown in Example 7-24.

Example 7-24. File: Program.cs for EnforceBusinessRulesColumnExpressions solution

```
using System;
using System.Data;
using System.Data.SqlClient;

namespace EnforceBusinessRulesColumnExpressions
{
    class Program
    {
        static void Main(string[] args)
        {
            string sqlConnectString = "Data Source=(local);" +
                "Integrated security=SSPI;Initial Catalog=AdoDotNet35Cookbook;";
            string sqlSelect = "SELECT * FROM EnforceBusinessRulesColumnExpressions";

            // Build the table.
            DataTable dt = new DataTable( );
            DataColumnCollection cols = dt.Columns;
            cols.Add("Id", typeof(int));
            cols.Add("Field1", typeof(int));
            cols.Add("Field2", typeof(int));
            // add the primary key
            dt.PrimaryKey = new DataColumn[] { cols["Id"] };
            // Expression whether the sum of Field1 and Field2 equals 10
            cols.Add("CK_Expression", typeof(Boolean), "Field1 + Field2 = 10");

            // Create the DataAdapter, handling the RowUpdating event.
            SqlDataAdapter da = new SqlDataAdapter(sqlSelect, sqlConnectString);
            da.RowUpdating += new SqlRowUpdatingEventHandler(da_RowUpdating);
            SqlCommandBuilder cb = new SqlCommandBuilder(da);
```

```
        // Add some rows to the DataTable
        dt.Rows.Add(new object[] { 1, 7, 3 }); //Valid
        dt.Rows.Add(new object[] { 2, 5, 2 }); //Invalid
        dt.Rows.Add(new object[] { 3, 5, 5 }); //Valid
        dt.Rows.Add(new object[] { 4, 1, 1 }); //Inalid

        // Output the DataTable
        Console.WriteLine("---DATATABLE BEFORE DATAADAPTER.UPDATE( )---");
        foreach (DataRow row in dt.Rows)
            Console.WriteLine(
                "Id = {0}\tField1 = {1}\tField2 = {2}\tRowError = {3}",
                row["Id"], row["Field1"], row["Field2"], row.RowError);

        // Update the data source using the DataAdapter
        da.Update(dt);
        Console.WriteLine("\n=> DataAdapter.Update( )");

        Console.WriteLine("\n---DATATABLE AFTER DATAADAPTER.UPDATE( )---");
        foreach (DataRow row in dt.Rows)
            Console.WriteLine(
                "Id = {0}\tField1 = {1}\tField2 = {2}\tRowError = {3}",
                row["Id"], row["Field1"], row["Field2"], row.RowError);

        //Load the Datatable from the data source and output
        dt.Clear();
        da.Fill(dt);
        Console.WriteLine("\n---DATA SOURCE AFTER DATAADAPTER.UPDATE( )---");
        foreach (DataRow row in dt.Rows)
            Console.WriteLine("Id = {0}\tField1 = {1}\tField2 = {2}",
                row["Id"], row["Field1"], row["Field2"]);

        Console.WriteLine("\nPress any key to continue.");
        Console.ReadKey( );
    }

    static void da_RowUpdating(object sender, SqlRowUpdatingEventArgs e)
    {
        // For insert or update statements, check that the
        // calculated constraint column is true.
        if ((e.StatementType == StatementType.Insert ||
            e.StatementType == StatementType.Update) &&
            !(bool)e.Row["CK_Expression"])
        {
            // Constraint has not been met.
            // Set an error on the row and skip it.
            e.Row.RowError = "Constraint error.";
            e.Status = UpdateStatus.SkipCurrentRow;
        }
    }
}
}
```

The output is shown in Figure 7-7.

Figure 7-7. Output for EnforceBusinessRulesColumnExpressions solution

Discussion

The RowUpdating event of the DataAdapter occurs during the Update( ) method before the command to update a row is executed against the data source. The event fires with each row update attempt.

The RowUpdating event handler receives an argument of type RowUpdatingEventArgs that provides information specifically related to the event as described in Table 7-4.

Table 7-4. RowUpdatingEventArgs properties

Property	Description
Command	Gets the Command to execute during the Update( ) method.
Errors	Gets errors generated by the .NET data provider when the Command was executed.
Row	Gets the DataRow to send through the Update( ) method.
StatementType	Gets the type of SQL statement to execute. This is one of the following values from the StatementType enumeration: Select, Insert, Update, or Delete.
Status	Gets or sets the action to take with the current and remaining rows during the Update( ) method. This is a value from the UpdateStatus enumeration (described in Table 7-5).
TableMapping	Gets the DataTableMapping to send through the Update( ) method.

Table 7-5 describes the values in the UpdateStatus enumeration used by the Status property of the RowUpdatingEventArgs object.

Table 7-5. UpdateStatus enumeration

Value	Description
Continue	Continue processing the rows. This is the default value.
ErrorsOccurred	The event handler reports that the update should be treated as an error.

Table 7-5. UpdateStatus enumeration (continued)

Value	Description
SkipAllRemainingRows	Do not update the current row and skip updating the remaining rows.
SkipCurrentRow	Do not update the current row and continue updating with the subsequent row.

The Update( ) method of the DataAdapter raises two events for every row in the data source that is updated. The order of the events is:

1. The values in the DataRow are moved to parameter values.

2. The OnRowUpdating event is raised.

3. The update command executes against the row in the data source.

4. If the UpdatedRowSource property of the Command is set to FirstReturnedRecord or Both, the first returned result is placed in the DataRow.

5. If the UpdateRowSource property of the Command is set to OutputParameters or Both, the output parameters are placed in the DataRow.

6. The OnDataRowUpdated event is raised.

7. AcceptChanges( ) is called.

If zero rows are affected, the DBConcurrencyException is raised during the update operation on a row. This usually indicates a concurrency violation.

The solution uses the RowUpdating event of the DataAdapter to check whether the expression column in the DataTable is true, indicating that the business rule has been satisfied, before a database record is updated. If the expression if false, an error is set on the row and the Status is set to SkipCurrentRow, preventing the record in the database from being updated and continuing the processing with the next row.

7.8   Retrieving Constraints from a SQL Server Database

Problem

You need to programmatically retrieve the constraint information that is defined in a SQL Server database.

Solution

Use the SQL Server Management Objects (SMO), catalog views, or INFORMATION_SCHEMA views to get information about primary key, foreign key, and check constraints. The solution shows how to use all three techniques to retrieve constraint information and output it to the console.

This solution needs a reference to the `Microsoft.SqlServer.ConnectionInfo`, `Microsoft.SqlServer.Smo`, and `Microsoft.SqlServer.SqlEnum` assemblies.

The C# code in *Program.cs* in the project RetrieveConstraintsSqlServer is shown in Example 7-25.

Example 7-25. File: Program.cs for RetrieveConstraintsSqlServer solution

```csharp
using System;
using System.Data;
using System.Data.SqlClient;
using Microsoft.SqlServer.Management.Smo;

namespace RetrieveConstraintsSqlServer
{
    class Program
    {
        static void Main(string[] args)
        {
            string sqlConnectString = "Data Source=(local);" +
                "Integrated security=SSPI;Initial Catalog=AdventureWorks;";

            // ---Use SMO---
            Console.WriteLine("---SMO---");
            Server server = new Server("(local)");
            Database db = server.Databases["AdventureWorks"];
            Console.WriteLine("---Primary key constraints---");
            Console.WriteLine("Row 1:");
            bool pkFlag = false;
            int pkCount = 0;
            // Iterate over table collection
            foreach (Table table in db.Tables)
            {
                // Iterate over index collection
                foreach (Index index in table.Indexes)
                {
                    // Count the primary keys
                    if (index.IndexKeyType == IndexKeyType.DriPrimaryKey)
                    {
                        pkCount++;
                        // Output details about the first primary index
                        if (!pkFlag)
                        {
                            Console.WriteLine("\tConstraintName = {0}", index.Name);
                            Console.WriteLine("\tTableName = {0}", table.Name);
                            Console.WriteLine("\tColumnCount = {0}",
                                index.IndexedColumns.Count);
                            pkFlag = true;
                        }
                    }
                }
            }
            Console.WriteLine("Total = {0}", pkCount);
```

```csharp
Console.WriteLine("\n---Foreign key constraints---");
Console.WriteLine("Row 1:");
bool fkFlag = false;
int fkCount = 0;
// Iterate over table collection
foreach (Table table in db.Tables)
{
    // Iterate over the foreign key collection
    foreach (ForeignKey fk in table.ForeignKeys)
    {
        // Count the foreign keys
        fkCount++;
        // Output details about the first foreign key
        if (!fkFlag)
        {
            Console.WriteLine("\tConstraintName = {0}", fk.Name);
            Console.WriteLine("\tUpdateRule = {0}", fk.UpdateAction);
            Console.WriteLine("\tDeleteRule = {0}", fk.DeleteAction);
            Console.WriteLine("\tParentTable = {0}", table.Name);
            Console.WriteLine("\tChildTable = {0}", fk.ReferencedTable);
            Console.WriteLine("\tColumnCount = {0}", fk.Columns.Count);
            fkFlag = true;
        }
    }
}
Console.WriteLine("Total = {0}", fkCount);

Console.WriteLine("\n---Check constraints---");
Console.WriteLine("Row 1:");
bool ccFlag = false;
int ccCount = 0;
// Iterate over table collection
foreach (Table table in db.Tables)
{
    // Iterate over index collection
    foreach (Check cc in table.Checks)
    {
        // Count the check constraints
        ccCount++;
        // Output details about the first check constraint
        if (!ccFlag)
        {
            Console.WriteLine("\tTableName = {0}", table.Name);
            Console.WriteLine("\tConstraintName = {0}", cc.Name);
            Console.WriteLine("\tCheckClause = {0}", cc.Text);
            ccFlag = true;
        }
    }
}
Console.WriteLine("Total = {0}", ccCount);
```

```
// ---Use catalog views---
Console.WriteLine("\n---CATALOG VIEWS---");
// Get primary key constraints
string cvGetPrimaryKeyConstraints =
    "SELECT i.name PKName, t.name TableName, " +
    "COUNT(c.column_id) ColumnCount "+
    "FROM sys.indexes i " +
    "JOIN sys.tables t ON i.object_id = t.object_id " +
    "JOIN sys.index_columns c ON i.index_id = c.index_id AND " +
    "    t.object_id = c.object_id " +
    "WHERE is_primary_key = 1 " +
    "GROUP BY i.name, t.name " +
    "ORDER BY t.name, i.name";
SqlDataAdapter daCvPKC =
    new SqlDataAdapter(cvGetPrimaryKeyConstraints, sqlConnectString);
DataTable dtCvPKC = new DataTable( );
daCvPKC.Fill(dtCvPKC);

Console.WriteLine("---Primary key constraints---");
Console.WriteLine("Row 1:");
foreach (DataColumn col in dtCvPKC.Columns)
    Console.WriteLine("\t{0} = {1}",
        col.ColumnName, dtCvPKC.Rows[0][col.Ordinal]);
Console.WriteLine("Total = {0}", dtCvPKC.Rows.Count);

// Get foreign key constraints
string cvGetForeignKeyConstraints =
    "SELECT fk.name ConstraintName, " +
    "MIN(fk.update_referential_action_desc) UpdateRule, " +
    "MIN(fk.delete_referential_action_desc) DeleteRule, " +
    "MIN(pt.name) ParentTable, MIN(ct.name) ChildTable, " +
    "COUNT(fkc.constraint_column_id) " +
    "FROM sys.foreign_keys fk " +
    "JOIN sys.tables pt ON fk.referenced_object_id = pt.object_id " +
    "JOIN sys.tables ct ON fk.parent_object_id = ct.object_id " +
    "JOIN sys.foreign_key_columns fkc ON " +
    "    fk.object_id = fkc.constraint_object_id " +
    "GROUP BY fk.name " +
    "ORDER BY fk.name ";
SqlDataAdapter daCvFKC =
    new SqlDataAdapter(cvGetForeignKeyConstraints, sqlConnectString);
DataTable dtCvFKC = new DataTable();
daCvFKC.Fill(dtCvFKC);

Console.WriteLine("\n---Foreign key constraints---");
Console.WriteLine("Row 1:");
foreach (DataColumn col in dtCvFKC.Columns)
    Console.WriteLine("\t{0} = {1}",
        col.ColumnName, dtCvFKC.Rows[0][col.Ordinal]);
Console.WriteLine("Total = {0}", dtCvFKC.Rows.Count);
```

```csharp
    // Get check constraints
    string cvGetCheckConstraints =
        "SELECT t.name TableName, cc.name ConstraintName, " +
        "cc.definition CheckClause " +
        "FROM sys.check_constraints cc " +
        "JOIN sys.tables t on cc.parent_object_id = t.object_id " +
        "ORDER BY TableName, ConstraintName";
    SqlDataAdapter daCvCC =
        new SqlDataAdapter(cvGetCheckConstraints, sqlConnectString);
    DataTable dtCvCC = new DataTable( );
    daCvCC.Fill(dtCvCC);

    Console.WriteLine("\n---Check constraints---");
    Console.WriteLine("Row 1:");
    foreach (DataColumn col in dtCvCC.Columns)
        Console.WriteLine("\t{0} = {1}",
            col.ColumnName, dtCvCC.Rows[0][col.Ordinal]);
    Console.WriteLine("Total = {0}", dtCvCC.Rows.Count);

    // ---Use information schema views---
    Console.WriteLine("\n---INFORMATION SCHEMA VIEWS---");
    // Get primary key constraints
    string isvGetPrimaryKeyConstraints =
        "SELECT tc.CONSTRAINT_NAME, tc.TABLE_NAME, " +
        "COUNT(kcu.COLUMN_NAME) ColumnCount " +
        "FROM INFORMATION_SCHEMA.TABLE_CONSTRAINTS tc " +
        "JOIN INFORMATION_SCHEMA.KEY_COLUMN_USAGE kcu ON " +
        "tc.CONSTRAINT_NAME=kcu.CONSTRAINT_NAME " +
        "WHERE tc.CONSTRAINT_TYPE='PRIMARY KEY' " +
        "GROUP BY tc.CONSTRAINT_NAME, tc.TABLE_NAME " +
        "ORDER BY tc.TABLE_NAME, tc.CONSTRAINT_NAME;";
    SqlDataAdapter daIsvPKC =
        new SqlDataAdapter(isvGetPrimaryKeyConstraints, sqlConnectString);
    DataTable dtIsvPKC = new DataTable( );
    daIsvPKC.Fill(dtIsvPKC);

    Console.WriteLine("---Primary key constraints---");
    Console.WriteLine("Row 1:");
    foreach (DataColumn col in dtIsvPKC.Columns)
        Console.WriteLine("\t{0} = {1}",
            col.ColumnName, dtIsvPKC.Rows[0][col.Ordinal]);
    Console.WriteLine("Total = {0}", dtIsvPKC.Rows.Count);

    // Get foreign key constraints
    string isvGetForeignKeyConstraints =
        "SELECT rc.CONSTRAINT_NAME, MIN(rc.UPDATE_RULE) UpdateRule, " +
        "MIN(rc.DELETE_RULE) DeleteRule, " +
        "MIN(kcuP.TABLE_NAME) ParentTable, " +
        "MIN(kcuC.TABLE_NAME) ChildTable, " +
        "COUNT(kcuP.COLUMN_NAME) ColumnCount " +
        "FROM INFORMATION_SCHEMA.REFERENTIAL_CONSTRAINTS rc " +
        "LEFT JOIN INFORMATION_SCHEMA.KEY_COLUMN_USAGE kcuP ON " +
```

```
                    "rc.UNIQUE_CONSTRAINT_NAME=kcuP.CONSTRAINT_NAME " +
                    "LEFT JOIN INFORMATION_SCHEMA.KEY_COLUMN_USAGE kcuC ON " +
                    "rc.CONSTRAINT_NAME=kcuC.CONSTRAINT_NAME AND " +
                    "kcuP.ORDINAL_POSITION=kcuC.ORDINAL_POSITION " +
                    "GROUP BY rc.CONSTRAINT_NAME " +
                    "ORDER BY rc.CONSTRAINT_NAME";
                SqlDataAdapter daIsvFKC =
                    new SqlDataAdapter(isvGetForeignKeyConstraints, sqlConnectString);
                DataTable dtIsvFKC = new DataTable();
                daIsvFKC.Fill(dtIsvFKC);

                Console.WriteLine("\n---Foreign key constraints---");
                Console.WriteLine("Row 1:");
                foreach (DataColumn col in dtIsvFKC.Columns)
                    Console.WriteLine("\t{0} = {1}",
                        col.ColumnName, dtIsvFKC.Rows[0][col.Ordinal]);
                Console.WriteLine("Total = {0}", dtIsvFKC.Rows.Count);

                // Get check constraints
                string isvGetCheckConstraints =
                    "SELECT tc.TABLE_NAME, tc.CONSTRAINT_NAME, cc.CHECK_CLAUSE " +
                    "FROM INFORMATION_SCHEMA.TABLE_CONSTRAINTS tc " +
                    "JOIN INFORMATION_SCHEMA.CHECK_CONSTRAINTS cc ON " +
                    "tc.CONSTRAINT_NAME=cc.CONSTRAINT_NAME " +
                    "WHERE CONSTRAINT_TYPE='CHECK' " +
                    "ORDER BY tc.TABLE_NAME, cc.CONSTRAINT_NAME";
                SqlDataAdapter daIsvCC =
                    new SqlDataAdapter(isvGetCheckConstraints, sqlConnectString);
                DataTable dtIsvCC = new DataTable();
                daIsvCC.Fill(dtIsvCC);

                Console.WriteLine("\n---Check constraints---");
                Console.WriteLine("Row 1:");
                foreach (DataColumn col in dtIsvCC.Columns)
                    Console.WriteLine("\t{0} = {1}",
                        col.ColumnName, dtIsvCC.Rows[0][col.Ordinal]);
                Console.WriteLine("Total = {0}", dtIsvCC.Rows.Count);

                Console.WriteLine("\nPress any key to continue.");
                Console.ReadKey();
            }
        }
    }
}
```

The output is shown in Figure 7-8.

Discussion

The following subsections discuss the three approaches demonstrated in the solution—SQL Management Objects (SMO), catalog views, and information schema views.

Figure 7-8. Output for RetrieveConstraintsSqlServer solution

SQL Server Management Objects

SMO is supported in .NET Framework 2.0 and later and is compatible with SQL Server 7.0 and later. SMO is a collection of objects designed for programming SQL Server management tasks. SMO is used to create databases, perform backups, create jobs, configure SQL Server, configure security, and many other administrative tasks.

The SMO Server class represents an instance of SQL Server and determines the connection to the physical SQL Server installation. The Server object is the topmost object in the SMO instance object hierarchy. A connection to a SQL Server instance is created when a Server object is instantiated.

The SMO Database class represents a SQL Server database, either system- or user-defined, on the SQL Server instance specified by the Server parameter in the Database class constructor and by the Parent property. In the solution, the AdventureWorks database is specified in the constructor.

A Database object has a TableCollection object that represents all tables defined in the database as a collection of Table objects. The Tables property accesses the collection. The Table class gives you access to the different constraints.

A Table object has an IndexCollection object that represents all indexes defined on the table as a collection of Index objects. The Indexes property accesses the collection. The Index object has an IndexKeyType property, which takes a value from the IndexKeyType enumeration—one of DriPrimaryKey, DriUniqueKey, or None—that specifies the type of key on which the index is created. The solution accesses properties for the first primary key and outputs that information to the console. Information about unique key constraints is accessed similarly. The number of primary key constraints on all of the tables in the database is output to the console.

A Table object has a ForeignKeyCollection object that represents all foreign keys defined on the table as a collection of ForeignKey objects. The ForeignKeys property accesses the collection. The solution accesses properties for the first foreign key and outputs that information to the console. The number of foreign key constraints on all of the tables in the database is output to the console.

A Table object has a CheckCollection object that represents all check constraints defined on a table as a collection of Check objects. The Checks property accesses the collection. The solution accesses properties for the first check constraint and outputs that information to the console. The number of check constraints on all of the tables in the database is output to the console.

Catalog views

Catalog views were introduced in SQL Server 2005 and return metadata used by the SQL Server Database Engine. Microsoft recommends using catalog views because they provide the most general interface to catalog metadata and the most efficient way to get and present this information. All user-available catalog metadata is exposed through catalog views. Catalog views don't expose information about replication, backup, Database Maintenance Plan, or SQL Server Agent.

Catalog views are defined within each database in a schema named sys. The metadata returned is limited to that which the user has permission to view. To access a catalog view, simply specify the fully qualified view name. For more information about catalog views, see Recipe 11.3 and SQL Server Books Online.

The solution uses six catalog views to retrieve information about constraints in the database.

sys.check_constraints
> A row for each check constraint in the current database.

sys.foreign_keys
> A row for each foreign key in the current database.

sys.foreign_key_columns
> A row for each column or set of columns that make up a foreign key.

sys.index_columns
> A row for each column that is part of an index.

sys.indexes
> A row for each index in the current database.

sys.tables
> A row for each table in the current database.

Primary key information is obtained by querying the sys.indexes, sys.index_columns, and sys.tables catalog views. The result set returns the primary key name, table name, and the number of columns in the primary key for each primary key in the database, sorted by primary key name and table name.

```
SELECT
    i.name PKName,
    t.name TableName,
    COUNT(c.column_id) ColumnCount
FROM sys.indexes i
    JOIN sys.tables t ON i.object_id = t.object_id
    JOIN sys.index_columns c ON i.index_id = c.index_id AND t.object_id = c.object_id
WHERE is_primary_key = 1
GROUP BY i.name, t.name
ORDER BY t.name, i.name
```

Information about foreign keys is obtained by querying the sys.foreign_keys, sys.foreign_key_columns, and sys.tables catalog views. The result set returns the foreign key name, update rule, delete rule, parent table, child table, and the number of columns in the constraint for each foreign key constraint in the database sorted by the foreign key name.

```
SELECT
    fk.name ConstraintName,
    MIN(fk.update_referential_action_desc) UpdateRule,
    MIN(fk.delete_referential_action_desc) DeleteRule,
    MIN(pt.name) ParentTable,
    MIN(ct.name) ChildTable,
    COUNT(fkc.constraint_column_id)
FROM sys.foreign_keys fk
    JOIN sys.tables pt ON fk.referenced_object_id = pt.object_id
    JOIN sys.tables ct ON fk.parent_object_id = ct.object_id
    JOIN sys.foreign_key_columns fkc ON fk.object_id = fkc.constraint_object_id
GROUP BY fk.name
ORDER BY fk.name
```

Check constraint information is obtained by querying the sys.check_constraints and sys.tables catalog views. The results set returns the table name, constraint name, and check clause for each check constraint in the database.

```
SELECT
    t.name TableName,
    cc.name ConstraintName,
    cc.definition CheckClause
FROM sys.check_constraints cc
    JOIN sys.tables t on cc.parent_object_id = t.object_id
ORDER BY TableName, ConstraintName
```

Information schema views

Information schema views were first available in SQL Server 7.0 and later. They provide system-table independent access to SQL Server metadata. The views are based on system tables and provide a layer of abstraction that allows applications to continue to work properly if the system tables change in future releases of SQL Server. Information schema views provide an alternative to using system stored procedures that were previously and are still available. The INFORMATION_SCHEMA views conform to the SQL-92 standard.

Information schema views are defined within each database in a schema named INFORMATION_SCHEMA. To access the views, specify the fully qualified view name. In the solution, for example, the view containing metadata about the tables in the database is accessed using the following syntax:

```
INFORMATION_SCHEMA.TABLES
```

The metadata returned is limited to that which the user has permission to view. Like any other views, information schema views can also be joined in queries or participate in complex queries to extract specific information. For more information about information schema views, see Recipe 11.3 and SQL Server Books Online.

The solution uses four information schema views to retrieve information about constraints in the database:

INFORMATION_SCHEMA.CHECK_CONSTRAINTS
    A row for each CHECK constraint in the current database.

INFORMATION_SCHEMA.KEY_COLUMN_USAGE
    A row for each column that is constrained as a key in the current database.

INFORMATION_SCHEMA.REFERENTIAL_CONSTRAINTS
    A row for each foreign key constraint in the current database.

INFORMATION_SCHEMA.TABLE_CONSTRAINTS
    A row for each table constraint in the current database.

Information about primary keys is obtained by querying the TABLE_CONSTRAINTS and KEY_COLUMN_USAGE information schema views. The views are joined on the CONSTRAINT_NAME field and restricted to constraints with a CONSTRAINT_TYPE of Primary Key. The result set is sorted on the TABLE_NAME, COLUMN_NAME, and ORDINAL_POSITION fields:

```
SELECT
    tc.CONSTRAINT_NAME,
    tc.TABLE_NAME,
    kcu.COLUMN_NAME,
    kcu.ORDINAL_POSITION
FROM
    INFORMATION_SCHEMA.TABLE_CONSTRAINTS tc JOIN
    INFORMATION_SCHEMA.KEY_COLUMN_USAGE kcu ON
        tc.CONSTRAINT_NAME = kcu.CONSTRAINT_NAME
WHERE
    tc.CONSTRAINT_TYPE = 'PRIMARY KEY'
ORDER BY
    tc.TABLE_NAME,
    kcu.COLUMN_NAME,
    kcu.ORDINAL_POSITION
```

Foreign key information is obtained by querying the REFERENTIAL_CONSTRAINTS and KEY_COLUMN_USAGE information schema views. The REFERENTIAL_CONSTRAINTS view is joined to the KEY_COLUMN_USAGE view on the UNIQUE_CONSTRAINT_NAME column to return information about the parent table and its columns. The REFERENTIAL_CONSTRAINTS view is joined again to the KEY_COLUMN_USAGE view on the CONSTRAINT_NAME, matching the ORDINAL_POSITION of the parent column to return information about the child table and its columns. The result set is sorted in ascending order on the parent TABLE_NAME, child TABLE_NAME, and parent constraint column ORDINAL_POSITION:

```
SELECT
    rc.CONSTRAINT_NAME,
    rc.UPDATE_RULE,
    rc.DELETE_RULE,
    kcuP.TABLE_NAME ParentTable,
    kcuC.TABLE_NAME ChildTable,
    kcuP.COLUMN_NAME ParentColumn,
    kcuC.COLUMN_NAME ChildColumn
FROM
    INFORMATION_SCHEMA.REFERENTIAL_CONSTRAINTS rc LEFT JOIN
    INFORMATION_SCHEMA.KEY_COLUMN_USAGE kcuP ON
    rc.UNIQUE_CONSTRAINT_NAME = kcuP.CONSTRAINT_NAME LEFT JOIN
    INFORMATION_SCHEMA.KEY_COLUMN_USAGE kcuC ON
    rc.CONSTRAINT_NAME = kcuC.CONSTRAINT_NAME AND
    kcuP.ORDINAL_POSITION = kcuC.ORDINAL_POSITION
ORDER BY
    kcuP.TABLE_NAME,
    kcuC.TABLE_NAME,
    kcuP.ORDINAL_POSITION;
```

Check constraint information is obtained by querying the TABLE_CONSTRAINTS and CHECK_CONSTRAINTS information schema views. The views are joined on the CONSTRAINT_NAME field and restricted to constraints with a CONSTRAINT_TYPE of CHECK. The result set is sorted on the TABLE_NAME and CONSTRAINT_NAME fields:

```
SELECT
    tc.TABLE_NAME,
    tc.CONSTRAINT_NAME,
    cc.CHECK_CLAUSE
FROM
    INFORMATION_SCHEMA.TABLE_CONSTRAINTS tc JOIN
    INFORMATION_SCHEMA.CHECK_CONSTRAINTS cc ON
    tc.CONSTRAINT_NAME = cc.CONSTRAINT_NAME
WHERE
    CONSTRAINT_TYPE = 'CHECK'
ORDER BY
    tc.TABLE_NAME,
    cc.CONSTRAINT_NAME
```

7.9   Checking for Concurrency Violations

Problem

You need to check for concurrency violations while using optimistic concurrency.

Solution

Use a timestamp data type column to manage data concurrency violations.

The solution uses a single table named ConcurrencyViolation in the AdoDotNet35Cookbook database. Execute the following T-SQL statement to create the table:

```
USE AdoDotNet35Cookbook
GO
CREATE TABLE ConcurrencyViolation(
    Id int NOT NULL PRIMARY KEY,
    Field1 nvarchar(50) NULL,
    Version timestamp NOT NULL)
```

Execute the following T-SQL batch to create sample data needed by the solution:

```
USE AdoDotNet35Cookbook
GO
INSERT INTO ConcurrencyViolation VALUES (1, 'Field1.1', null);
INSERT INTO ConcurrencyViolation VALUES (2, 'Field1.2', null);
INSERT INTO ConcurrencyViolation VALUES (3, 'Field1.3', null);
```

The solution creates a DataTable named TableA and fills it with the schema and data from the ConcurrencyViolation table in the AdoDotNet35Cookbook database.

The timestamp column is made read-only. An event handler named da_RowUpdated is created for the RowUpdated event of the DataAdapter. The event handler da_RowUpdated checks that an error did not occur (Status = Continue) and that a row was either inserted or updated. For those rows, the current value of the timestamp column is retrieved from the ConcurrencyViolaton in the database and used to update the row in the DataTable TableA. The parameterized update command is created for the DataAdapter—the WHERE clause of the update command matches both the Id (primary key used to locate the record) field and the Version field (timestamp column used to determine whether the data has been changed since last read and control concurrency violations).

The solution creates a DataTable named TableB and fills and configures it in exactly the same way as TableA in the preceding paragraph. Together DataTable objects TableA and TableB simulate two users simultaneously interacting with the same data.

The contents of DataTable objects TableA and TableB are output to the console to show the initial state.

The record with Id = 2 in DataTable TableA is modified, updated to table ConcurrencyViolation, and output to the console to show the effect of the change. The RowUpdated event handler da_RowUpdated retrieves the updated value for the timestamp field and updates the value in the updated DataTable row.

The record with Id = 2 in DataTable TableB is modified. An attempt is made to update the modification to the table ConcurrencyViolation. The update command of the DataAdapter cannot find a matching record for both the Id and timestamp field because of the previous update by DataTable TableA. The RowUpdated handler does not process the timestamp update logic for the row because the Status is ErrorsOccurred rather than Continue. It might make sense in some situations to update the contents of DataTable TableB at this point. The catch block for the Update( ) method of the DataAdapter outputs the error to the console. The contents of DataTable objects TableA and TableB are output to the console.

The C# code in *Program.cs* in the project CheckConcurrencyViolation is shown in Example 7-26.

Example 7-26. File: Program.cs for CheckConcurrencyViolation solution

```
using System;
using System.Data;
using System.Data.SqlClient;

namespace CheckConcurrencyViolation
{
    class Program
    {
        private static string sqlConnectString = "Data Source=(local);" +
            "Integrated security=SSPI;Initial Catalog=AdoDotNet35Cookbook;";
```

```csharp
private static DataTable dtA;
private static DataTable dtB;
private static SqlDataAdapter daA;
private static SqlDataAdapter daB;

static void Main(string[] args)
{
    // Build SELECT and UPDATE statement; DELETE and INSERT not
    // required for the solution, but would need to be supplied
    string selectText = "SELECT Id, Field1, Version FROM " +
        "ConcurrencyViolation";
    string updateText = "UPDATE ConcurrencyViolation " +
        "SET Field1 = @Field1 " +
        "WHERE Id = @Id AND Version = @Version";

    // Create table A and fill it with the schema.
    dtA = new DataTable("TableA");
    daA = new SqlDataAdapter(selectText, sqlConnectString);
    daA.RowUpdated += new SqlRowUpdatedEventHandler(da_RowUpdated);
    daA.FillSchema(dtA, SchemaType.Source);
    dtA.Columns["Version"].ReadOnly = false;
    daA.Fill(dtA);

    // Create the update command and define the parameters.
    daA.UpdateCommand = new SqlCommand(updateText,
        daA.SelectCommand.Connection);
    daA.UpdateCommand.CommandType = CommandType.Text;
    daA.UpdateCommand.Parameters.Add("@Id", SqlDbType.Int, 0, "Id");
    daA.UpdateCommand.Parameters["@Id"].SourceVersion =
        DataRowVersion.Original;
    daA.UpdateCommand.Parameters.Add("@Field1", SqlDbType.NVarChar, 50,
        "Field1");
    daA.UpdateCommand.Parameters["@Field1"].SourceVersion =
        DataRowVersion.Current;
    daA.UpdateCommand.Parameters.Add("@Version", SqlDbType.Timestamp, 0,
        "Version");
    daA.UpdateCommand.Parameters["@Version"].SourceVersion =
        DataRowVersion.Original;

    // Create table B and fill it with the schema.
    dtB = new DataTable("TableB");
    daB = new SqlDataAdapter(selectText, sqlConnectString);
    daB.RowUpdated += new SqlRowUpdatedEventHandler(da_RowUpdated);
    daB.FillSchema(dtB, SchemaType.Source);
    dtB.Columns["Version"].ReadOnly = false;
    daB.Fill(dtB);

    // Create the update command and define the parameters.
    daB.UpdateCommand = new SqlCommand(updateText,
        daB.SelectCommand.Connection);
    daB.UpdateCommand.CommandType = CommandType.Text;
    daB.UpdateCommand.Parameters.Add("@Id", SqlDbType.Int, 0, "Id");
```

```csharp
        daB.UpdateCommand.Parameters["@Id"].SourceVersion =
            DataRowVersion.Original;
        daB.UpdateCommand.Parameters.Add("@Field1", SqlDbType.NVarChar, 50,
            "Field1");
        daB.UpdateCommand.Parameters["@Field1"].SourceVersion =
            DataRowVersion.Current;
        daB.UpdateCommand.Parameters.Add("@Version", SqlDbType.Timestamp, 0,
            "Version");
        daB.UpdateCommand.Parameters["@Version"].SourceVersion =
            DataRowVersion.Original;

        // Output the tables
        Console.WriteLine("---INITIAL---");
        OutputTable(dtA);
        OutputTable(dtB);

        // Update table A
        dtA.Rows.Find(2)["Field1"] += " (new.A)";
        UpdateTable(daA, dtA);

        // Output the tables
        Console.WriteLine("\n---AFTER TABLE A UPDATE---");
        OutputTable(dtA);
        OutputTable(dtB);

        // Update table B
        dtB.Rows.Find(2)["Field1"] += " (new.B)";
        UpdateTable(daB, dtB);

        // Output the tables
        Console.WriteLine("\n---AFTER TABLE B UPDATE---");
        OutputTable(dtA);
        OutputTable(dtB);

        Console.WriteLine("\nPress any key to continue.");
        Console.ReadKey( );
    }

    static void OutputTable(DataTable dt)
    {
        Console.WriteLine("\n---{0}---", dt.TableName);
        foreach (DataRow row in dt.Rows)
        {
            Console.WriteLine("{0}\t{1}\t{2}",
                row["Id"], row["Field1"],
                Convert.ToBase64String(row.Field<byte[]>("Version")));
        }
    }

    static void UpdateTable(SqlDataAdapter da, DataTable dt)
    {
        Console.WriteLine("\n=> Update({0})", dt.TableName);
```

Example 7-26. File: Program.cs for CheckConcurrencyViolation solution (continued)

```
        try
        {
            da.Update(dt);
            Console.WriteLine("=> Update succeeded.");
        }
        catch (DBConcurrencyException ex)
        {
            // Error if timestamp does not match
            Console.WriteLine("=> EXCEPTION: {0}", ex.Message);
            dt.RejectChanges();
        }
    }

    static void da_RowUpdated(object sender, SqlRowUpdatedEventArgs e)
    {
        Console.WriteLine("=> DataAdapter.RowUpdated event. Status = {0}.",
            e.Status);

        // Check if an insert or update operation is being performed.
        if (e.Status == UpdateStatus.Continue &&
            (e.StatementType == StatementType.Insert ||
            e.StatementType == StatementType.Update))
        {
            // Build a command object to retrieve the updated timestamp.
            String sqlGetRowVersion = "SELECT Version FROM " +
                "ConcurrencyViolation WHERE Id = " + e.Row["Id"];
            SqlConnection conn = new SqlConnection(sqlConnectString);
            SqlCommand cmd = new SqlCommand(sqlGetRowVersion, conn);

            // Set the timestamp to the new value in the data source and
            // call accept changes.
            conn.Open();
            e.Row["Version"] = (Byte[])cmd.ExecuteScalar();
            conn.Close();
            e.Row.AcceptChanges();
        }
    }
  }
}
```

The output is shown in Figure 7-9.

Discussion

The timestamp data type automatically generates an eight-byte binary value guaranteed to be unique within the database. It tracks row versions within a database and has no relation to clock time. To record the time of record inserts and updates, define a datetime column in the table and create update and insert triggers to set its value.

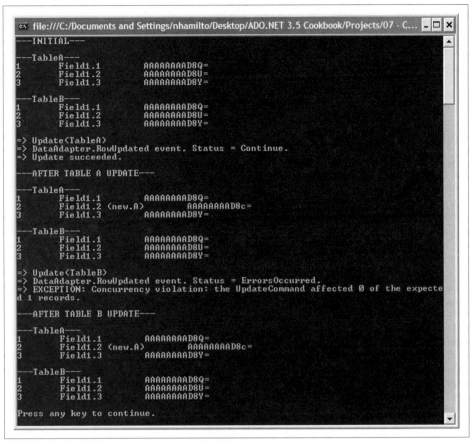

```
file:///C:/Documents and Settings/nhamilto/Desktop/ADO.NET 3.5 Cookbook/Projects/07 - C...

----INITIAL----

----TableA----
1       Field1.1            AAAAAAAD8Q=
2       Field1.2            AAAAAAAD8U=
3       Field1.3            AAAAAAAD8Y=

----TableB----
1       Field1.1            AAAAAAAD8Q=
2       Field1.2            AAAAAAAD8U=
3       Field1.3            AAAAAAAD8Y=

=> Update(TableA)
=> DataAdapter.RowUpdated event. Status = Continue.
=> Update succeeded.

----AFTER TABLE A UPDATE----

----TableA----
1       Field1.1            AAAAAAAD8Q=
2       Field1.2 (new.A)         AAAAAAAD8c=
3       Field1.3            AAAAAAAD8Y=

----TableB----
1       Field1.1            AAAAAAAD8Q=
2       Field1.2            AAAAAAAD8U=
3       Field1.3            AAAAAAAD8Y=

=> Update(TableB)
=> DataAdapter.RowUpdated event. Status = ErrorsOccurred.
=> EXCEPTION: Concurrency violation: the UpdateCommand affected 0 of the expecte
d 1 records.

----AFTER TABLE B UPDATE----

----TableA----
1       Field1.1            AAAAAAAD8Q=
2       Field1.2 (new.A)         AAAAAAAD8c=
3       Field1.3            AAAAAAAD8Y=

----TableB----
1       Field1.1            AAAAAAAD8Q=
2       Field1.2            AAAAAAAD8U=
3       Field1.3            AAAAAAAD8Y=

Press any key to continue.
```

Figure 7-9. Output for CheckConcurrencyViolation solution

The T-SQL timestamp data type is not the same as the timestamp data type defined in the SQL-92 standard. The timestamp data type defined by the SQL-92 standard is equivalent to the T-SQL datetime data type.

A table can have only one timestamp column. Its value is updated with the current database row version each time a row with a timestamp column is inserted or updated.

The rowversion data type is a synonym for the timestamp data type.

7.10 Resolving Data Conflicts

Problem

You need to effectively resolve data conflicts and prevent overwriting of existing data when attempting to update changes in a DataSet to a database where the underlying data has changed.

Solution

Handle the DBConcurrencyException within the RowUpdated event of the DataAdapter.

The solution uses a table named ResolveDataConflict in the database AdoDotNet35Cookbook. Execute the following T-SQL statement to create the table:

```
USE AdoDotNet35Cookbook
GO
CREATE TABLE ResolveDataConflict(
    Id int NOT NULL PRIMARY KEY,
    Field1 nvarchar(50) NULL,
    Field2 nvarchar(50) NULL )
```

The schema of table ResolveDataConflict is shown in Table 7-6.

Table 7-6. ResolveDataConflict table schema

Column name	Data type	Length	Allow nulls?
Id	int	4	No
Field1	nvarchar	50	Yes
Field2	nvarchar	50	Yes

Execute the following T-SQL statement to create some sample data for the solution:

```
USE AdoDotNet35Cookbook
GO
INSERT INTO ResolveDataConflict VALUES (1, 'Field1.1', 'Field2.1');
INSERT INTO ResolveDataConflict VALUES (2, 'Field1.2', 'Field2.2');
INSERT INTO ResolveDataConflict VALUES (3, 'Field1.3', 'Field2.3');
```

The solution creates a DataTable named User 1 and fills it with the schema and data in the table ResolveDataConflict in the AdoDotNet35Cookbook database. The ContinueUpdateOnError property of the DataAdapter is set to true. A handler named daUser1_RowUpdated is assigned to the RowUpdated event of the DataAdapter. A CommandBuilder object is created to generate the updating logic for the DataAdapter.

The daUser1_RowUpdated( ) event handler checks to see if a concurrency error occurred when updating the row in the DataTable named User 1 to table ResolveDataConflict in the database. If an error occurred during the deletion of a row, the RejectChanges( ) method is used to cancel the delete. For all rows with a concurrency error, the Id for the row is retrieved from the row and used with the

DataAdapter for the conflict table to try to get the original data for the row from the table ResolveDataConflict. An error is set on the row in the conflict table indicating whether it was changed (the row in error was retrieved from the database) or deleted (a row in error could not be retrieved from the database).

A DataTable named User 1 Conflict is created to store the original row data for a row when a concurrency error is encountered while updating a row from the DataTable named User 1 back to the ResolveDataConflict table in the database. A DataAdapter is created that uses a parameterized SQL SELECT statement to retrieve the original row. The schema for the conflict table is loaded from the ResolveDataConflict table using the DataAdapter.

A DataTable named User 2 and a DataTable named User 2 Conflict and their associated DataAdapter objects are created in the same way as for the DataTable named User 1 and the DataTable named User 1 Conflict and described in the preceding three paragraphs.

The DataTable objects User 1 and User 2 are filled using their DataAdapter objects and their contents output to the console.

In the DataTable named User 1, the row with Id = 2 is modified and the row with Id = 3 is deleted. The UpdateTable( ) method is called, which clears the DataTable named User 1 Conflict, updates the changes in the DataTable named User 1 back to the ResolveDataConflict table in the database using the Update( ) method of the DataAdapter, and outputs the number of rows affected by the update and whether the update had errors. In this case, both rows successfully update back to the database and no rows have errors updating. The contents of the DataTable objects User 1 and User 1 Conflict are output to the console.

In the DataTable named User 2, the row with Id = 1 is modified, the row with Id = 2 is modified, and the row with Id = 3 is modified. The UpdateTable( ) method is called, which clears the DataTable named User 2 Conflict, updates the changes in the DataTable named User 2 back to the ResolveDataConflict table in the database using the Update( ) method of the DataAdapter, and outputs the number of rows affected by the update and whether the update had errors. In this case, one row is successful updated. The row with Id = 1 is updated successfully because it had not been changed previously. The attempted update of the row with Id = 2 raises a concurrency violation because it has been modified by the earlier update of the User 1 DataTable. The attempted update of the row with Id = 3 raises a concurrency violation because it has been deleted by the earlier update of the User 1 DataTable. The contents of the DataTable objects User 1 and User 1 Conflict are output to the console. The User 1 conflict table shows additional details about the rows that could not be updated back to the database.

The C# code in *Program.cs* in the project ResolveDataConflict is shown in Example 7-27.

Example 7-27. File: Program.cs for ResolveDataConflict solution

```csharp
using System;
using System.Data;
using System.Data.SqlClient;

namespace ResolveDataConflict
{
    class Program
    {
        private static SqlDataAdapter daUser1Conflict;
        private static SqlDataAdapter daUser2Conflict;
        private static DataTable dtUser1;
        private static DataTable dtUser2;
        private static DataTable dtUser1Conflict;
        private static DataTable dtUser2Conflict;

        static void Main(string[] args)
        {
            string sqlConnectString = "Data Source=(local);" +
                "Integrated security=SSPI;Initial Catalog=AdoDotNet35Cookbook;";

            string sqlText = "SELECT * FROM ResolveDataConflict";

            // Create the DataAdapter for user 1 table.
            SqlDataAdapter daUser1 = new SqlDataAdapter(sqlText, sqlConnectString);
            daUser1.ContinueUpdateOnError = true;
            // Handle the RowUpdated event.
            daUser1.RowUpdated += new SqlRowUpdatedEventHandler(daUser1_RowUpdated);
            // Get the schema and data for user 1 table.
            dtUser1 = new DataTable("User 1");
            daUser1.FillSchema(dtUser1, SchemaType.Source);
            daUser1.Fill(dtUser1);
            // Create the command builder.
            SqlCommandBuilder cbUser1 = new SqlCommandBuilder(daUser1);

            // Create a DataAdapter to retrieve original rows
            // for conflicts when updating user 1 table.
            daUser1Conflict =
                new SqlDataAdapter(sqlText + " WHERE Id = @Id", sqlConnectString);
            daUser1Conflict.SelectCommand.Parameters.Add("@Id", SqlDbType.Int);
            // Create a DataSet with the conflict table schema.
            dtUser1Conflict = new DataTable("User 1 Conflicts");
            daUser1.FillSchema(dtUser1Conflict, SchemaType.Source);

            // Create the DataAdapter for user 2 table.
            SqlDataAdapter daUser2 = new SqlDataAdapter(sqlText, sqlConnectString);
            daUser2.ContinueUpdateOnError = true;
            // Handle the RowUpdated event.
            daUser2.RowUpdated += new SqlRowUpdatedEventHandler(daUser2_RowUpdated);
            // Get the schema and data for user 2 table.
```

```csharp
        dtUser2 = new DataTable("User 2");
        daUser2.FillSchema(dtUser2, SchemaType.Source);
        daUser2.Fill(dtUser2);
        // Create the command builder.
        SqlCommandBuilder cbB = new SqlCommandBuilder(daUser2);

        // Create a DataAdapter to retrieve original rows
        // for conflicts when updating user 2 table.
        daUser2Conflict =
            new SqlDataAdapter(sqlText + " WHERE Id = @Id", sqlConnectString);
        daUser2Conflict.SelectCommand.Parameters.Add("@Id", SqlDbType.Int);
        // Create a DataSet with the conflict table schema.
        dtUser2Conflict = new DataTable("User 2 Conflicts");
        daUser2.FillSchema(dtUser2Conflict, SchemaType.Source);

        // Fill and output tables for both user 1 and user 2
        Console.WriteLine("---INITIAL---");
        daUser1.Fill(dtUser1);
        OutputTable(dtUser1);
        daUser2.Fill(dtUser2);
        OutputTable(dtUser2);

        // Modify row with Id = 2 and delete row with Id = 3
        // in User 1 table, and update
        dtUser1.Rows.Find(2)["Field2"] += " (new1)";
        dtUser1.Rows.Find(3).Delete( );

        Console.WriteLine("\n---AFTER USER 1 TABLE UPDATES---");
        UpdateTable(daUser1, dtUser1, dtUser1Conflict);
        OutputTable(dtUser1);
        OutputTable(dtUser1Conflict);

        // Update rows 1, 2, and 3 in User 2 table, and update
        dtUser2.Rows.Find(1)["Field1"] += " (new2)";
        dtUser2.Rows.Find(2)["Field1"] += " (new2)";
        dtUser2.Rows.Find(3)["Field2"] += " (new2)";

      Console.WriteLine("\n---AFTER USER 2 TABLE UPDATES---");
       UpdateTable(daUser2, dtUser2, dtUser2Conflict);
       OutputTable(dtUser2);
       OutputTable(dtUser2Conflict);

       Console.WriteLine("\nPress any key to continue.");
       Console.ReadKey( );
    }

    static void OutputTable(DataTable dt)
    {
```

```csharp
        Console.WriteLine("\nTABLE: {0}", dt.TableName);
        Console.WriteLine("ID\tField1\t\tField2\t\tRowError");
        Console.WriteLine("--\t------\t\t------\t\t--------");
        if (dt.Rows.Count == 0)
            Console.WriteLine("[EMPTY]");
        else
            foreach (DataRow row in dt.Rows)
            {
                if (row.RowState != DataRowState.Deleted)
                {
                    Console.WriteLine("{0}\t{1}\t{2}\tRowError = {3}",
                        row["Id"], row["Field1"], row["Field2"],
                        row.RowError);
                }
            }
    }

    static void UpdateTable(SqlDataAdapter da, DataTable dt, DataTable dtConflict)
    {
        // clear the conflict table
        dtConflict.Clear();

        // update the table
        int rows = da.Update(dt);

        // output update stats
        Console.WriteLine(
            "\n=> Table '{0}' udpated. RowsAffected = {1}, HasErrors = {2}",
            dt.TableName, rows, dt.HasErrors);
    }

    static void daUser1_RowUpdated(object sender, SqlRowUpdatedEventArgs e)
    {
        // Check if a concurrency exception occurred.
        if (e.Status == UpdateStatus.ErrorsOccurred &&
            e.Errors.GetType() == typeof(DBConcurrencyException))
        {
            // If the row was deleted, reject the delete.
            if (e.Row.RowState == DataRowState.Deleted)
                e.Row.RejectChanges();

            // Get the row ID.
            int id = e.Row.Field<int>("Id");
            daUser1Conflict.SelectCommand.Parameters["@Id"].Value = id;
            // Get the row from the data source for the conflicts table.
            if (daUser1Conflict.Fill(dtUser1Conflict) == 1)
                dtUser1Conflict.Rows.Find(e.Row["Id"]).RowError =
                    "Row changed in database.";
            else
            {
```

```
                    // Add a row for the deleted row
                    dtUser1Conflict.ImportRow(e.Row);
                    dtUser1Conflict.Rows.Find(id).RowError =
                        "Row deleted from database.";
                }
            }
        }

        static void daUser2_RowUpdated(object sender, SqlRowUpdatedEventArgs e)
        {
            // Check if a concurrency exception occurred.
            if (e.Status == UpdateStatus.ErrorsOccurred &&
                e.Errors.GetType( ) == typeof(DBConcurrencyException))
            {
                // If the row was deleted, reject the delete.
                if (e.Row.RowState == DataRowState.Deleted)
                    e.Row.RejectChanges( );

                // Get the row ID.
                int id = e.Row.Field<int>("Id");
                daUser2Conflict.SelectCommand.Parameters["@Id"].Value = id;
                // Get the row from the data source for the conflicts table.
                if (daUser2Conflict.Fill(dtUser2Conflict) == 1)
                    dtUser2Conflict.Rows.Find(e.Row["Id"]).RowError =
                        "Row changed in database.";
                else
                {
                    // Add a row for the deleted row
                    dtUser2Conflict.ImportRow(e.Row);
                    dtUser2Conflict.Rows.Find(id).RowError =
                        "Row deleted from database.";
                }
            }
        }
    }
}
```

The output is shown in Figure 7-10.

Discussion

The RowUpdated event of the DataAdapter occurs during the Update( ) method after the command to update a row is executed against the data source. The event fires with each row update attempt.

The RowUpdated event handler receives an argument of type RowUpdatedEventArgs that provides information specifically related to the event as described in Table 7-7.

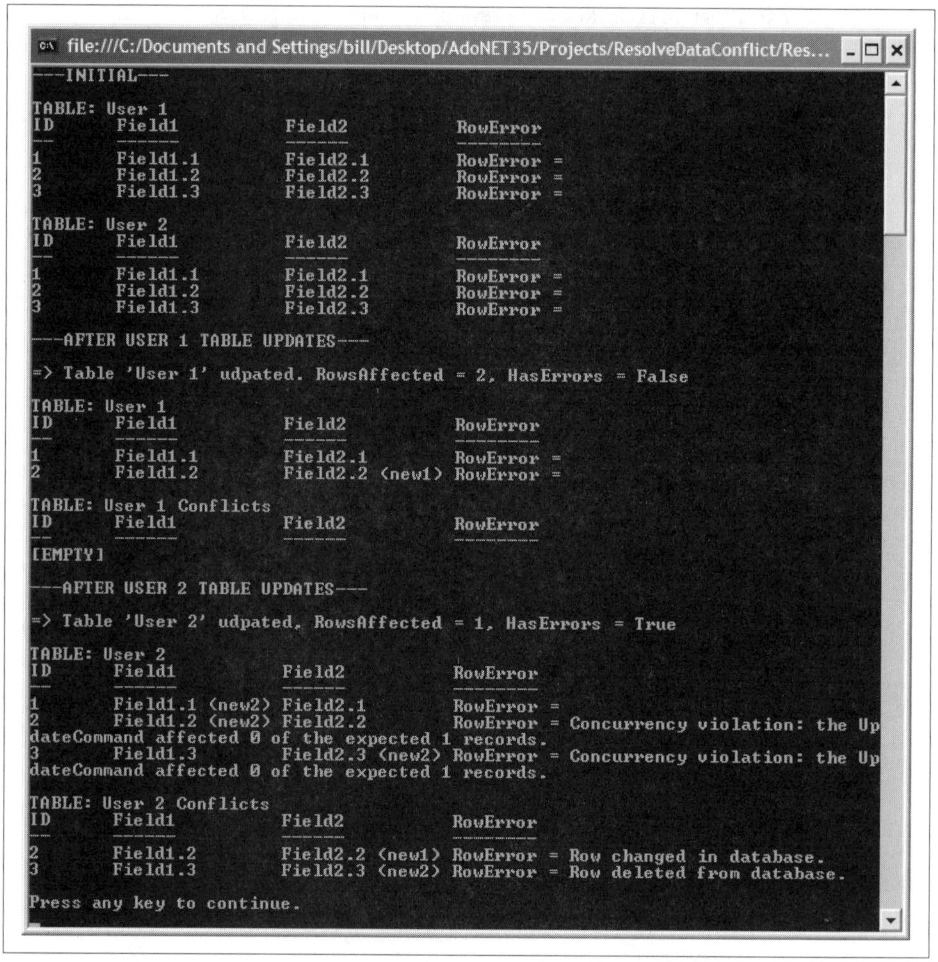

Figure 7-10. Output for ResolveDataConflict solution

Table 7-7. RowUpdatedEventArgs properties

Property	Description
Command	Gets or sets the Command executed when the Update( ) method is called.
Errors	Gets errors generated by the .NET data provider when the Command was executed.
RecordsAffected	Gets the number of rows changed, inserted, or deleted by the execution of the Command.
Row	Gets the DataRow sent through the Update( ) method.
StatementType	Gets the type of SQL statement executed. This is one of the following values from the StatementType enumeration: Select, Insert, Update, or Delete.
Status	Gets or sets the action to take with the current and remaining rows during the Update( ) method. This is a value from the UpdateStatus enumeration described in Table 7-5.
TableMapping	Gets the DataTableMapping sent through the Update( ) method.

Table 7-8 describes the values in the UpdateStatus enumeration used by the Status property of the RowUpdatedEventArgs object.

Table 7-8. UpdateStatus enumeration

Value	Description
Continue	Continue processing the rows. This is the default value.
ErrorsOccurred	The event handler reports that the update should be treated as an error.
SkipAllRemainingRows	Do not update the current row and skip updating the remaining rows.
SkipCurrentRow	Do not update the current row and continue updating with the subsequent row.

The Update( ) method of the DataAdapter raises two events for every row in the data source that is updated. The order of the events is:

1. The values in the DataRow are moved to parameter values.
2. The OnRowUpdating event is raised.
3. The update command executes against the row in the data source.
4. If the UpdatedRowSource property of the Command is set to FirstReturnedRecord or Both, the first returned result is placed in the DataRow.
5. If the UpdateRowSource property of the Command is set to OutputParameters or Both, the output parameters are placed in the DataRow.
6. The OnDataRowUpdated event is raised.
7. AcceptChanges( ) is called.

The DBConcurrencyException is raised during the update operation on a row if zero rows are affected. This usually indicates a concurrency violation.

7.11   Using Transaction Isolation Levels to Protect Data

Problem

You want to effectively use transaction isolation levels to ensure data consistency for a range of data rows.

Solution

Use the Begin( ) method of the Transaction object to control isolation level.

The solution uses a table named TransactionIsolationLevel in the AdoDotNet35Cookbook database. Execute the following T-SQL statement to create the table:

```
USE AdoDotNet35Cookbook
GO
CREATE TABLE TransactionIsolationLevel(
    Id int NOT NULL PRIMARY KEY,
    Field1 nvarchar(50) NULL,
    Field2 nvarchar(50) NULL )
```

Create the test data the solution needs by executing the following T-SQL batch:

```
USE AdoDotNet35Cookbook
GO
INSERT INTO TransactionIsolationLevel VALUES (1, 'Field1.1', 'Field2.1');
INSERT INTO TransactionIsolationLevel VALUES (2, 'Field1.2', 'Field2.2');
INSERT INTO TransactionIsolationLevel VALUES (3, 'Field1.3', 'Field2.3');
```

The solution uses *snapshot isolation*. Enable snapshot isolation in the AdoDotNet35Cookbook database by executing the following T-SQL statement:

```
ALTER DATABASE AdoDotNet35Cookbook SET ALLOW_SNAPSHOT_ISOLATION ON
```

The solution outputs the contents of the TransactionIsolationLevel table to the console. Next, a Connection is opened and a transaction started with the isolation level SnapShot. An attempt is made to insert two records into the TransactionIsolationLevel table within the transaction. The TransactionIsolationLevel table is read into a DataTable and output to the console between the two insert commands showing the data as it was before the first insert. The transaction is committed after the second insert and the contents of TransactionIsolationLevel is output to the console showing the new records.

The C# code in *Program.cs* in the project TransactionIsolationLevel is shown in Example 7-28.

Example 7-28. File: Program.cs for TransactionIsolationLevel solution

```
using System;
using System.Data;
using System.Data.SqlClient;

namespace TransactionIsolationLevel
{
    class Program
    {
        private static string sqlConnectString = "Data Source=(local);" +
            "Integrated security=SSPI;Initial Catalog=AdoDotNet35Cookbook;";

        static void Main(string[] args)
        {
            string sqlInsert1 = "INSERT INTO TransactionIsolationLevel " +
                "VALUES (4, 'Field1.4', 'Field2.4')";
            string sqlInsert2 = "INSERT INTO TransactionIsolationLevel " +
                "VALUES (5, 'Field1.5', 'Field2.5')";

            OutputData("Initial");
```

Example 7-28. File: Program.cs for TransactionIsolationLevel solution (continued)

```
    // Open a connection.
    using (SqlConnection connection = new SqlConnection(sqlConnectString))
    {
        connection.Open( );

        // Start a transaction.
        SqlTransaction tran =
            connection.BeginTransaction(IsolationLevel.Snapshot);
        Console.WriteLine("\nTransaction started: IsolationLevel = {0}",
            tran.IsolationLevel);

        try
        {
            // Insert two records by executing sqlInsert1 and sqlInsert2
            Console.WriteLine("\n=> Executing SQL:\n    {0}", sqlInsert1);
            SqlCommand command1 = new SqlCommand(sqlInsert1, connection, tran);
            command1.ExecuteNonQuery( );

            // Output the data from the database
            OutputData("During transaction");

            Console.WriteLine("\n=> Executing SQL:\n    {0}", sqlInsert2);
            SqlCommand command2 = new SqlCommand(sqlInsert2, connection, tran);
            command2.ExecuteNonQuery( );

            Console.WriteLine("\nTransaction committed");
            tran.Commit( );
        }
        catch(Exception ex)
        {
            Console.WriteLine("\nException: {0}", ex.Message);

            tran.Rollback( );
            Console.WriteLine("\nTransaction rolled back.");
        }
    }

    // Output the data from the database
    OutputData("After transaction");

    Console.WriteLine("\nPress any key to continue.");
    Console.ReadKey( );
}

static void OutputData(string s)
{
    string sqlSelect = "SELECT * FROM TransactionIsolationLevel";

    SqlDataAdapter da = new SqlDataAdapter(sqlSelect, sqlConnectString);
    DataTable dt = new DataTable( );
    da.Fill(dt);
```

```
        Console.WriteLine("\n---TransactionIsolationLevel table: {0}", s);
        foreach (DataRow row in dt.Rows)
        {
            Console.WriteLine("Id = {0}\tField1 = {1}\tField2 = {2}",
                row["Id"], row["Field1"], row["Field2"]);
        }
    }
}
}
```

The output is shown in Figure 7-11.

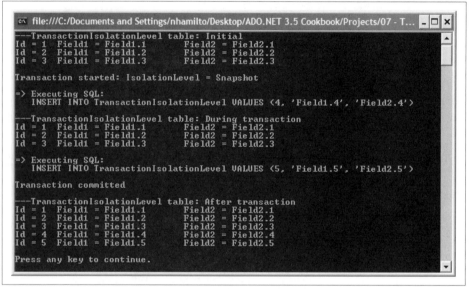

Figure 7-11. Output for TransactionIsolationLevel solution

Discussion

The *isolation level* specifies the transaction locking behavior for a connection. It determines what changes made to data within a transaction are visible outside of the transaction while the transaction is uncommitted.

Concurrency violations occur when multiple users or processes attempt to modify the same data in a database at the same time without locking. Table 7-9 describes concurrency problems.

Table 7-9. Concurrency problems

Condition	Description
Lost update	Two or more transactions select the same row and subsequently update that row. Data is lost because the transactions are unaware of each other and over-write each other's updates.
Uncommitted dependency (dirty read)	A second transaction selects a row that has been updated, but not committed, by another transaction. The first transaction makes more changes to the data or rolls back the changes already made resulting in the second transaction having invalid data.
Inconsistent analysis (nonrepeatable read)	A second transaction reads different data each time that the same row is read. Another transaction has changed and committed the data between the reads.
Phantom read	An insert or delete is performed for a row belonging to a range of rows being read by a transaction. The rows selected by the transaction are missing the inserted rows and still contain the deleted rows that no longer exist.

Isolation level defines the degree to which one transaction must be isolated from other transactions. A higher isolation level increases data correctness but decreases concurrent access to data. Table 7-10 describes the different isolations levels supported by ADO.NET. The first four levels are listed in order of increasing isolation.

Table 7-10. IsolationLevel enumeration

Name	Description
Unspecified	A different isolation level than the one specified is being used, but that level cannot be determined.
Chaos	Pending changes from more highly isolated transactions cannot be overwritten. This isolation level is not supported by SQL Server.
ReadUncommitted	No shared locks are issued. Exclusive locks are not honored. A dirty read is possible.
ReadCommitted	Shared locks are held while data is being read by the transaction. Dirty reads are not possible. Nonrepeatable reads or phantom rows can still occur because data can be changed prior to being committed.
RepeatableRead	Shared locks are placed on all data used by the query. Other users are prevented from updating the data. Nonrepeatable reads are prevented, but phantom reads are still possible.
Serializable	A range lock—covering individual records and the ranges between them—is placed on the data preventing other users from updating or inserting rows until the transaction is complete. Phantom reads are prevented.
SnapShot	Stores a version of the data that can be read by other applications while an application is modifying the same data—this reduces blocking. The changes made during the transaction cannot be seen by other applications until committed.

In ADO.NET, the isolation level can be set by creating the transaction using an overload of the BeginTransaction( ) method of the Command or by setting the IsolationLevel property of an existing Transaction object. The default isolation level is ReadCommitted.

Parallel transactions are not supported, so the isolation level applies to the entire transaction. It can be changed programmatically at any time. If the isolation level is changed within a transaction, the new level applies to all statements remaining in the transaction.

7.12 Specifying Locking Hints in a SQL Server Database

Problem

You need to explicitly control locking behavior a T-SQL transaction.

Solution

Use SQL Server locking hints from ADO.NET.

The solution uses a table named LockingHint in the AdoDotNet35Cookbook database. Execute the following T-SQL statement to create the table:

```
USE AdoDotNet35Cookbook
GO
CREATE TABLE LockingHint(
    Id int NOT NULL PRIMARY KEY,
    Field1 nvarchar(50) NULL,
    Field2 nvarchar(50) NULL )
```

Execute the following T-SQL batch to create the sample data this solution uses:

```
USE AdoDotNet35Cookbook
GO
INSERT INTO LockingHint VALUES (1, 'Field1.1', 'Field2.1');
INSERT INTO LockingHint VALUES (2, 'Field1.2', 'Field2.2');
INSERT INTO LockingHint VALUES (3, 'Field1.3', 'Field2.3');
INSERT INTO LockingHint VALUES (4, 'Field1.4', 'Field2.4');
```

The solution creates a DataTable and fills it with records with Id = 2 and Id = 3 from the table LockingHint in the AdoDotNet35Cookbook database. The contents of the DataTable are output to the console. The select statement that retrieves the records locks uses an update lock (UPDLOCK). The UpdateRow( ) method is called twice to modify and update rows with Id = 1 and Id = 3. The row with Id = 1 updates successfully, but the row with Id = 3 times out because of the update lock on rows with Id = 2 and Id = 3. The contents of the table LockingHint are output to the console at the end of the solution to confirm the results of the update on the database.

The C# code in *Program.cs* in the project SpecifyLockingHints is shown in Example 7-29.

Example 7-29. File: Program.cs for SpecifyLockingHints solution

```csharp
using System;
using System.Data;
using System.Data.SqlClient;

namespace SpecifyLockingHints
{
    class Program
    {
        private static string sqlConnectString = "Data Source=(local);" +
            "Integrated security=SSPI;Initial Catalog=AdoDotNet35Cookbook;";

        static void Main(string[] args)
        {
            // SQL query with pessimistic locking.
            string sqlSelect = "SELECT * FROM LockingHint " +
                "WITH (UPDLOCK) WHERE Id BETWEEN 2 AND 3";

            // Start the transaction and create the command.
            SqlConnection connection = new SqlConnection(sqlConnectString);
            connection.Open();
            SqlTransaction tran = connection.BeginTransaction();
            SqlCommand command = new SqlCommand(sqlSelect, connection, tran);

            // Create the DataAdapter and CommandBuilder.
            SqlDataAdapter da = new SqlDataAdapter(command);
            SqlCommandBuilder cb = new SqlCommandBuilder(da);

            // Fill table using the DataAdapter.
            DataTable dt = new DataTable();
            da.Fill(dt);

            // Output the result set
            Console.WriteLine("---RESULT SET FROM LOCKINGHINT TABLE (UPDLOCK)---");
            foreach (DataRow row in dt.Rows)
            {
                Console.WriteLine("Id = {0}\tField1 = {1}\tField2 = {2}",
                    row["Id"], row["Field1"], row["Field2"]);
            }

            // Update 2 rows
            UpdateRow(1);
            UpdateRow(3);

            // Commit the transaction and close the connection.
            tran.Commit();
            connection.Close();

            // Output the table after the updates
            dt.Clear();
            da = new SqlDataAdapter("SELECT * FROM LockingHint", sqlConnectString);
            da.Fill(dt);
```

```csharp
        Console.WriteLine("\n---LOCKINGHINT TABLE (AFTER UPDATE)---");
        foreach (DataRow row in dt.Rows)
        {
            Console.WriteLine("Id = {0}\tField1 = {1}\tField2 = {2}",
                row["Id"], row["Field1"], row["Field2"]);
        }

        Console.WriteLine("\nPress any key to continue.");
        Console.ReadKey( );
    }

    static void UpdateRow(int id)
    {
        Console.WriteLine("\n=> Updating row with Id = {0}.", id);

        string sqlUpdate = "UPDATE LockingHint SET " +
            "Field1 = 'Field1." + id + " (new)' WHERE Id = " + id;

        SqlConnection connection = new SqlConnection(sqlConnectString);
        connection.Open( );
        SqlCommand command2 = new SqlCommand(sqlUpdate, connection);

        // try the update
        try
        {
            command2.ExecuteNonQuery( );
            Console.WriteLine("=> Update successful.");
        }
        catch (Exception ex)
        {
            Console.WriteLine("=> Update failed.");
            Console.WriteLine("=> EXCEPTION: {0}", ex.Message);
        }
        finally
        {
            connection.Close( );
        }
    }
}
}
```

The output is shown in Figure 7-12.

Discussion

A *lock* is an object indicating that a user has a dependency on a resource. Locks ensure transactional integrity and database consistency by preventing other users from changing data being read by a user and preventing users from reading data being changed by another user. A lock indicates that a user has a dependency on a resource.

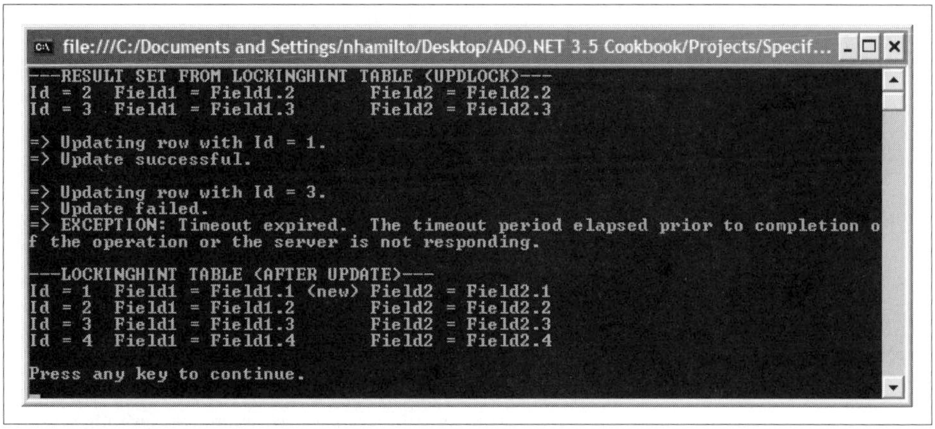

Figure 7-12. Output for SpecifyLockingHints solution

It prevents other users from performing operations that would adversely affect the locked resources. Locks are acquired and released by user actions; they are managed internally by database software.

A locking hint can be specified with SELECT, INSERT, DELETE, and UPDATE statements to instruct SQL Server as to the type of lock to use. You can use locking hints when you need control over locks acquired on objects. The SQL Server Optimizer automatically determines correct locking; hints should be used only when necessary. Locking hints override the current transaction isolation level for the session.

A locking hint is specified following the FROM clause using a WITH clause. The hint is specified within parentheses and multiple hints are separated by commas. For example, the query in the solution specifies update locks with the clause WITH (UPDLOCK).

Table 7-11 describes the different locking hints that you can use.

Table 7-11. SQL Server locking hints for isolation level

Locking hint	Description
HOLDLOCK	Hold a shared lock until a transaction is completed instead of releasing it as soon as the required table or data is no longer needed. HOLDLOCK is equivalent to SERIALIZABLE.
NOLOCK	Allow dirty reads—do not issue shared locks and do not recognize exclusive locks. Applies only to the SELECT statement. Equivalent to READUNCOMMITTED.
PAGLOCK	Use page locks where an individual lock on a row or key or a single table lock would normally be taken.
READCOMMITTED	Read operations comply with rules for a transaction with an isolation level of READ COMMITTED by using either locking or row versioning.
READCOMMITTEDLOCK	Read operations comply with rules for a transaction with an isolation level of READ COMMITTED by using locking.

Table 7-11. SQL Server locking hints for isolation level (continued)

Locking hint	Description
READPAST	Skip locked rows that would ordinarily appear in the result set rather than blocking the transaction by waiting for other transactions to release locks on those rows. Applies only to transactions with an isolation level of READ COMMITTED or REPEATABLE READ. Applies only to the SELECT statement.
READUNCOMMITTED	Allow dirty reads—do not issue shared locks and do not recognize exclusive locks. Applies only to the SELECT statement. Equivalent to NOLOCK.
REPEATABLEREAD	Use the same locking semantics as a transaction with an isolation level of REPEATABLE READ.
ROWLOCK	Use row-level locks instead of page-level and table-level locks.
SERIALIZABLE	Hold a shared lock until a transaction is completed instead of releasing it as soon as the required table or data is no longer needed. SERIALIZABLE is equivalent to HOLDLOCK.
TABLOCK	Use a shared lock on the table instead of using row-level and page-level locking. By default, the lock is held until the end of the statement.
TABLOCKX	Use an exclusive lock on the table preventing other users from reading or updating the table. By default, the lock is held until the end of the statement.
UPDLOCK	Use update locks instead of shared locks when reading a table. This allows you to read data and later update it with a guarantee that it has not changed since you last read it while other users are not blocked from reading the data.
XLOCK	Use an exclusive lock that is held until the end of the transaction on all data processed by the statement. Can be specified with ROWLOCK, PAGLOCK, or TABLOCK granularity. Cannot be used with either NOLOCK or UPDLOCK.

There are a number ways to get information about database locks:

- The dynamic management view sys.dm_tran_locks returns a result set containing currently active lock manager resources.

- The system stored procedure sp_lock returns a result set containing all active locks in the sessions currently active in the database engine instance. Two stored procedure arguments let you narrow the scope of the result set. This feature is provided for backward compatibility—Microsoft recommends you use the sys.dm_tran_locks dynamic management view.

- The syslockinfo table in the master database contains information about all granted, converting, and waiting lock requests. It is a denormalized view of the data structures used internally by the lock manager. This table is included for backward compatibility as of SQL Server 2000.

- The SQL Server Profiler can be used to monitor and record locking information.

- The Windows Performance Monitor has a SQL Server Locks Object counter that can be used to monitor lock activity.

For more information about database locks, using locking hints, or monitoring database locks, see Microsoft SQL Server Books Online.

Programmatically Working with Data in .NET Windows and Web Forms User Interfaces

8.0 Introduction

This chapter discusses and demonstrates programmatically binding controls to data sources in both Web Forms and Windows Forms.

Web Forms are an ASP.NET—a web application platform—feature used to create user interfaces for web applications. You can use the ASP.NET page framework to create browser- and client device-independent Web Forms that run on a web server and are used to dynamically create web pages. In addition to traditional HTML elements, Web Forms pages acts as a container for server-side controls that implement rich web user interface (UI) functionality in reusable controls.

Windows Forms is the .NET platform for Windows application development providing classes that enable rich user interfaces to be constructed. Windows forms act as a container for reusable controls that implement rich functionality.

Windows and Web Form controls allow data to be displayed by binding to data sources. Data binding is typically used for such purposes as displaying lookup or master-detail data, reporting, and data entry. There are two types of data binding: simple and complex. *Simple data binding* binds a control to a single data element such as the value of a field in a row of a result set. Simple binding is used by controls such as the TextBox and Label. *Complex data binding* binds the control to more than one data element—typically one or more columns from multiple rows in a result set. Controls capable of complex binding include ListBox, DataList, and DataGrid controls.

Although conceptually similar, the differences between Web Forms and Windows Forms architecture results in differences in data binding data sources to controls between the platforms. Recipes 8.1 through 8.10 show solutions for binding data to Web Forms controls—this includes solutions for simple data binding, complex data binding with updating, binding master-detail data, and data binding images. Recipes 8.11 through 8.19 show solutions for binding data to Windows Forms controls, which include solutions for simple data binding, complex data binding, binding master-detail data, and data binding images from SQL Server and Microsoft Access databases. Recipe 8.20 shows how to add search capabilities to the DataGridView control.

8.1 Loading Data into and Binding a Field to a Web Forms Control

Problem

You need to load a data value into a server-side control.

Solution

Load the value directly with an assignment or use a `DataBinder` object.

Follow these steps:

1. Create a C# ASP.NET web application named `LoadDataWebFormControl`.
2. Add the following controls to the *Default.aspx* design surface:
   - `TextBox` named `departmentIDTextBox`
   - `TextBox` named `departmentNameTextBox1`
   - `TextBox` named `departmentNameTextBox2`
   - `Button` named `getNameButton` with `Text` property = `Get Name`

   Add HTML text in front of each text box describing the text boxes.

   The completed layout of the Web Form page *Default.aspx* is shown in Figure 8-1.

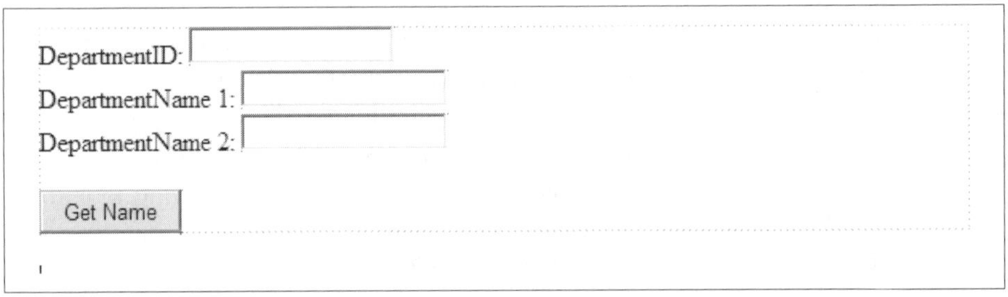

Figure 8-1. Layout for Default.aspx in LoadDataWebFormControl solution

The code in *Default.aspx* in the project `LoadDataWebFormControl` is shown in Example 8-1.

Example 8-1. File: Default.aspx for LoadDataWebFormControl solution

```
<%@ Page Language="C#" AutoEventWireup="true" CodeBehind="Default.aspx.cs"
    Inherits="LoadDataWebFormControl._Default" %>

<!DOCTYPE html PUBLIC "-//W3C//DTD XHTML 1.0 Transitional//EN"
    "http://www.w3.org/TR/xhtml1/DTD/xhtml1-transitional.dtd">
```

Example 8-1. File: Default.aspx for LoadDataWebFormControl solution (continued)

```
<html xmlns="http://www.w3.org/1999/xhtml" >
<head runat="server">
    <title>Untitled Page</title>
</head>
<body>
    <form id="form1" runat="server">
    <div>
        DepartmentID:
        <asp:TextBox ID="departmentIDTextBox" runat="server"></asp:TextBox>
        <br />
        DepartmentName 1:
        <asp:TextBox ID="departmentNameTextBox1" runat="server"></asp:TextBox>
        <br />
        DepartmentName 2:
        <asp:TextBox ID="departmentNameTextBox2" runat="server"></asp:TextBox>
        <br />
        <br />
    </div>
    <asp:Button ID="getNameButton" runat="server" Text="Get Name"
        onclick="getNameButton_Click" />
    </form>
</body>
</html>
```

The C# code-behind code in *Default.aspx.cs* in the project LoadDataWebFormControl
is shown in Example 8-2. The solution loads the HumanResources.Department table
into a DataTable and stores the default view to the session in an object named
DepartmentDataView. The solution displays the department name for the user-
specified DepartmentID by assigning a value to the Text property of TextBox control departmentNameTextBox1 and by using a DataBinder to bind the TextBox
departmentNameTextBox2 to a field in a DataRowView.

Example 8-2. File: Default.aspx.cs for LoadDataWebFormControl solution

```
using System;
using System.Data;
using System.Data.SqlClient;
using System.Web.UI;

namespace LoadDataWebFormControl
{
    public partial class _Default : System.Web.UI.Page
    {
        protected DataRowView drv;

        protected void Page_Load(object sender, EventArgs e)
        {
            if (!Page.IsPostBack)
            {
                LoadDepartmentData();
```

Example 8-2. File: Default.aspx.cs for LoadDataWebFormControl solution (continued)

```
            // set the output text boxes as read only
            departmentNameTextBox1.ReadOnly = true;
            departmentNameTextBox2.ReadOnly = true;
    }
}

protected void LoadDepartmentData( )
{
    // return a DataView containing all records from the
    // HumanResource.Department table
    string sqlConnectString = @"Data Source=(local);
        Integrated security=SSPI;Initial Catalog=AdventureWorks;";

    string sqlSelect = "SELECT * FROM HumanResources.Department";

    SqlDataAdapter da = new SqlDataAdapter(sqlSelect, sqlConnectString);
    DataTable dt = new DataTable( );

    da.Fill(dt);

    DataView dv = dt.DefaultView;
    dv.Sort = "DepartmentID";

    Session["DepartmentDataView"] = dv;
}

protected void getNameButton_Click(object sender, EventArgs e)
{
    int departmentID;

    // Update the text boxes displaying the department name
    if (int.TryParse(departmentIDTextBox.Text, out departmentID))
    {
        DataView departmentDV = (DataView)Session["DepartmentDataView"];
        int rowIndex = departmentDV.Find(departmentID);

        if (rowIndex != -1)
        {
            DataRowView drv = departmentDV[rowIndex];
            departmentNameTextBox1.Text = drv["Name"].ToString( );
            departmentNameTextBox2.Text =
                DataBinder.Eval(drv, "[Name]").ToString( );
        }
        else
        {
            departmentNameTextBox1.Text = "";
            departmentNameTextBox2.Text = "";
        }
    }
    else
```

Example 8-2. File: Default.aspx.cs for LoadDataWebFormControl solution (continued)

```
            {
                departmentNameTextBox1.Text = "---Invalid Department ID---";
                departmentNameTextBox2.Text = "---Invalid Department ID---";
            }
        }
    }
}
```

The output is shown in Figure 8-2.

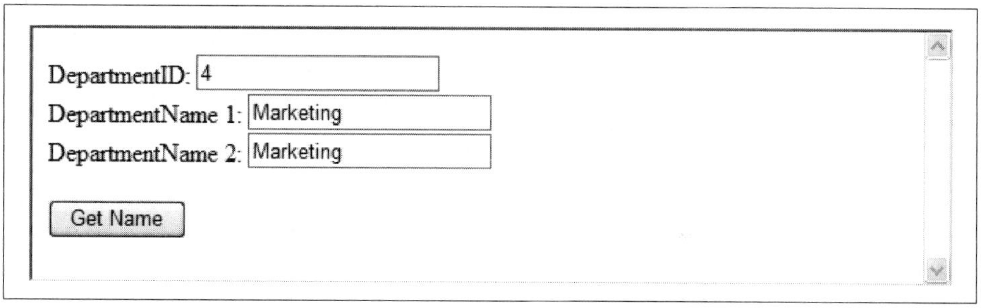

Figure 8-2. Output for LoadDataWebFormControl solution

Discussion

Simple data binding binds an ASP.NET web control property to a single value in a data source. The values can be determined at runtime. Although most commonly used to set control properties to display data, any property of the control can be bound—for example, the background color or size of the control.

The Visual Studio .NET `Properties` window provides a tool to create data binding expressions. It is accessed by clicking the ellipsis (...) in the `(DataBindings)` property.

To simple-bind a control, set the property of the control to a data binding expression that resolves to a single value. The data binding expression is delimited with `<%#` and `#>`. For more information about data binding expressions, see the MSDN Library.

The static `Eval( )` method of the `DataBinder` class can be used to simplify data binding when the value to bind is derived from a data source. The `DataBinder` class helps to extract data from a data source and makes it available to a control property. The `Eval( )` method takes two arguments:

- A reference to the data source object. This is usually a `DataSet`, `DataTable`, or `DataView`.
- A string specifying the navigation path to the specific value in the data source. This usually references a row and a column in that row.

The syntax to retrieve the company name from the first row in a DataTable using the Eval( ) method instead of using a data binding expression might be:

```
Text="<%# DataBinder.Eval(departmentDataTable, '[0]. Name') %>
```

For more information about the DataBinder class and the syntax of the Eval( ) method, see the topic "Data-Binding Expressions for Web Forms Pages" in the MSDN Library.

Data binding expressions must be resolved at runtime to provide the values to which the controls bind. This can be done explicitly by calling the DataBind( ) method of the control:

```
departmentNameTextBox2.DataBind( );
```

The DataBind( ) method of the Page class can be called to data bind all controls on the form.

8.2 Binding Data to a Web Forms Control

Problem

You want to bind multiple columns in a result set to an ASP.NET control.

Solution

Set the control's advanced properties before calling DataBind( ).

Follow these steps:

1. Create a C# ASP.NET web application named BindWebFormSimpleControl.

2. Add the following controls to the *Default.aspx* design surface:

   - ListBox named departmentListBox
   - TextBox named selectedItemTextBox

   The completed layout of the Web Form page *Default.aspx* is shown in Figure 8-3.

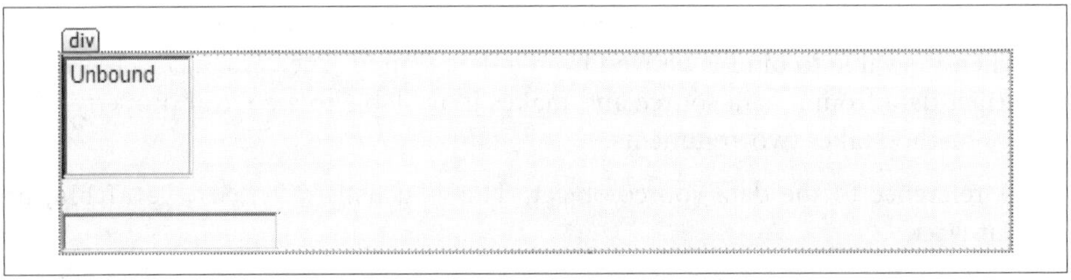

Figure 8-3. Layout for Default.aspx in BindWebFormSimpleControl solution

The code in *Default.aspx* in the project BindWebFormSimpleControl is shown in Example 8-3.

Example 8-3. File: Default.aspx for BindWebFormsSimpleControl solution

```
<%@ Page Language="C#" AutoEventWireup="true" CodeBehind="Default.aspx.cs"
    Inherits="BindWebFormSimpleControl._Default" %>
<!DOCTYPE html PUBLIC "-//W3C//DTD XHTML 1.0 Transitional//EN"
    "http://www.w3.org/TR/xhtml1/DTD/xhtml1-transitional.dtd">
<html xmlns="http://www.w3.org/1999/xhtml" >
<head runat="server">
    <title>Untitled Page</title>
</head>
<body>
    <form id="form1" runat="server">
    <div>
        <asp:ListBox ID="departmentListBox" runat="server"
            onselectedindexchanged="departmentListBox_SelectedIndexChanged">
        </asp:ListBox>
        <br /><br />
        <asp:TextBox ID="selectedItemTextBox" runat="server"></asp:TextBox>
    </div>
    </form>
</body>
</html>
```

3. Create the C# code-behind in *Default.aspx.cs* in the project BindWebFormSimpleControl, as shown in Example 8-4.

   The code-behind fills a DataTable with the DepartmentID and Name the HumanResources.Department table AdventureWorks. The ListBox server control is bound to the DataTable—specifically, the value field is bound to the DepartmentID column and the text field is bound to the Name column.

Example 8-4. File: Default.aspx.cs for BindWebFormSimpleControl solution

```
using System;
using System.Data;
using System.Data.SqlClient;

namespace BindWebFormSimpleControl
{
    public partial class _Default : System.Web.UI.Page
    {
        protected void Page_Load(object sender, EventArgs e)
        {
            if (!Page.IsPostBack)
            {
                // Set properties of and bind data to list box
                departmentListBox.AutoPostBack = true;

                departmentListBox.DataSource = LoadDepartmentData();
                departmentListBox.DataValueField = "DepartmentID";
                departmentListBox.DataTextField = "Name";
                departmentListBox.DataBind();
            }
        }
```

Example 8-4. File: Default.aspx.cs for BindWebFormSimpleControl solution (continued)

```
    protected DataView LoadDepartmentData( )
    {
        // Return a DataTable with a containing all departments from
        // the HumanResources.Department table
        string sqlConnectString = @"Data Source=(local);
            Integrated security=SSPI;Initial Catalog=AdventureWorks;";

        string sqlSelect = "SELECT DepartmentID, Name FROM HumanResources.Department";

        SqlDataAdapter da = new SqlDataAdapter(sqlSelect, sqlConnectString);
        DataTable dt = new DataTable( );

        da.Fill(dt);

        return dt.DefaultView;
    }

    protected void departmentListBox_SelectedIndexChanged(object sender, EventArgs e)
    {
        // Update the text box when a different item is selected in the
        // list box
        selectedItemTextBox.Text = departmentListBox.SelectedItem.Value + ": " +
            departmentListBox.SelectedItem.Text;
    }
  }
}
```

The output is shown in the Figure 8-4.

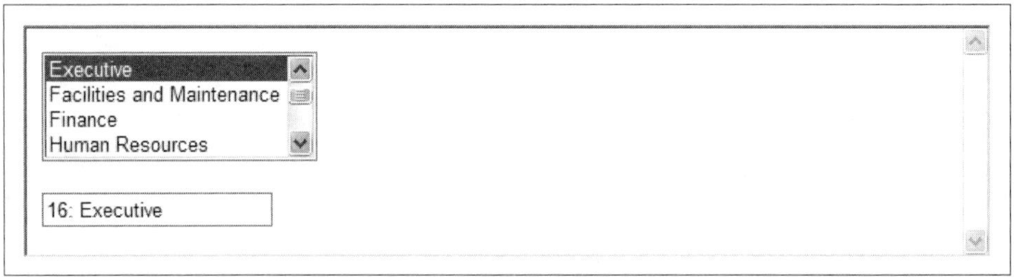

Figure 8-4. Output for BindWebFormSimpleControl solution

Discussion

Complex data binding describes binding a multirecord control to multiple records in a data source. The GridView, DataList, and ListView controls are examples of controls that support complex data binding.

Each control that supports complex data binding exposes a set of properties, slightly different for each control, which control the binding. These properties are described in Table 8-1.

Table 8-1. Data binding properties

Property	Description
DataSource	Gets or sets the data source that the control is displaying data for. Valid data sources include DataTable, DataView, DataSet, DataViewManager, or any object that implements the IEnumerable interface.
DataMember	Gets or sets the table in the data source to bind to the control. You can use this property if the data source contains more than one table—a DataSet, for example.
DataKeyField	Gets or sets the key field in the data source. This allows the key field for a listing control to be stored and later accessed without displaying it in the control.
DataValueField	Gets or sets the field in the data source that provides the value for the control when an item is selected.
DataTextField	Gets or sets the field in the data source that provides the display value for the control when an item is selected.

After the properties appropriate to the control are set, call the DataBind( ) method of the control or of the Page to bind the data source to the server control.

8.3   Binding Data to a Web Forms DetailsView Control

Problem

You need to bind a result set to a Web Forms DetailsView control and page through its records.

Solution

Set the DataSource property of the DetailsView control and then call the DataBind( ) method. Handle the PageIndexChanging event.

Follow these steps:

1. Create a C# ASP.NET web application named BindWebFormDetailsView.
2. Add the following control to the *Default.aspx* design surface:
   - DetailsView named departmentDetailsView

   The completed layout of the Web Form page *Default.aspx* is shown in Figure 8-5.

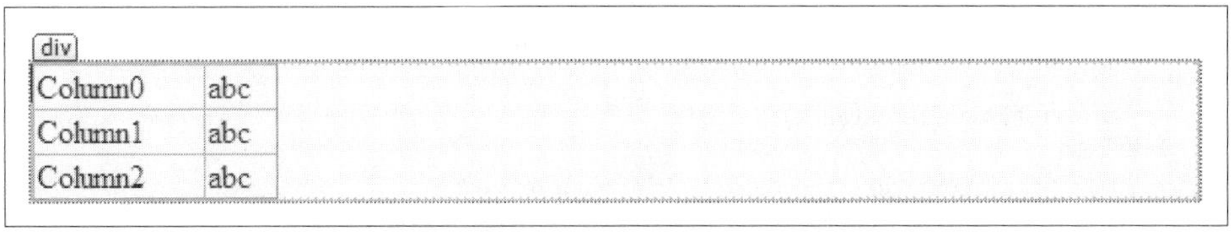

Figure 8-5. Layout for Default.aspx in BindWebFormDetailsView solution

The code in *Default.aspx* in the project BindWebFormDetailsView is shown in Example 8-5.

Example 8-5. File: Default.aspx for BindWebFormDetailsView solution

```
<%@ Page Language="C#" AutoEventWireup="true" CodeBehind="Default.aspx.cs"
    Inherits="BindWebFormDetailsView._Default" %>

<!DOCTYPE html PUBLIC "-//W3C//DTD XHTML 1.0 Transitional//EN"
    "http://www.w3.org/TR/xhtml1/DTD/xhtml1-transitional.dtd">

<html xmlns="http://www.w3.org/1999/xhtml" >
<head runat="server">
    <title>Untitled Page</title>
</head>
<body>
    <form id="form1" runat="server">
    <div>
        <asp:DetailsView ID="departmentDetailsView" runat="server" Height="50px"
            Width="125px"
            onpageindexchanging="departmentDetailsView_PageIndexChanging">
        </asp:DetailsView>
    </div>
    </form>
</body>
</html>
```

The C# code-behind code in *Default.aspx.cs* in the project BindWebFormDetailsView is shown in Example 8-6. The solution fills a DataTable with the HumanResource.Department table in AdventureWorks and stores its default view to the Session object. The default view is bound to the DetailsView control. The event handler for the PageIndexChanging event of the DetailsView sets the new page index, sets the data source of the DetailsView to the DataView in the Session object, and binds the DetailsView control.

Example 8-6. File: Default.aspx.cs for BindWebFormDetailsView solution

```
using System;
using System.Data;
using System.Data.SqlClient;
using System.Web.UI.WebControls;

namespace BindWebFormDetailsView
{
    public partial class _Default : System.Web.UI.Page
    {
        protected void Page_Load(object sender, EventArgs e)
        {
            if (!Page.IsPostBack)
            {
                // configure the details view controls
                departmentDetailsView.Width = Unit.Pixel(500);
                departmentDetailsView.AllowPaging = true;
                departmentDetailsView.PagerSettings.Mode = PagerButtons.Numeric;
```

Example 8-6. File: Default.aspx.cs for BindWebFormDetailsView solution (continued)

```
                // load and bind data into the details view control
                departmentDetailsView.DataSource = LoadData( );
                departmentDetailsView.DataBind( );
            }
        }

        protected DataView LoadData( )
        {
            // return a DataView containing all records from the
            // HumanResource.Department table
            string sqlConnectString = @"Data Source=(local);
                Integrated security=SSPI;Initial Catalog=AdventureWorks;";

            string sqlSelect = "SELECT * FROM HumanResources.Department";

            SqlDataAdapter da = new SqlDataAdapter(sqlSelect, sqlConnectString);
            DataTable dt = new DataTable( );

            da.Fill(dt);

            Session["DepartmentDataView"] = dt.DefaultView;

            return dt.DefaultView;
        }

        protected void departmentDetailsView_PageIndexChanging(
            object sender, DetailsViewPageEventArgs e)
        {
            // update the details view for the selected page
            departmentDetailsView.PageIndex = e.NewPageIndex;
            departmentDetailsView.DataSource = (DataView)Session["DepartmentDataView"];
            departmentDetailsView.DataBind( );
        }
    }
}
```

The output is shown in Figure 8-6.

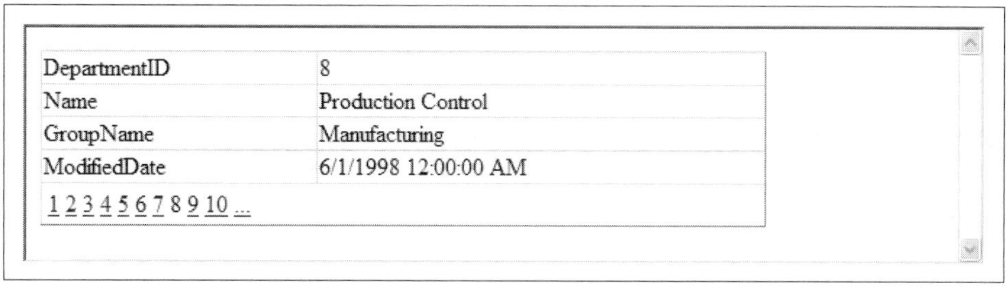
DepartmentID
8
Name
Production Control
GroupName
Manufacturing
ModifiedDate
6/1/1998 12:00:00 AM
1 2 3 4 5 6 7 8 9 10 ...

Figure 8-6. Output for BindWebFormDetailsView solution

Discussion

The DetailsView control displays values for a single record from a data source. You bind data to the DetailsView control specifying the DataSource and DataMember properties. Each field in a data source record is displayed as a row in a table. The DetailsView control lets you delete, insert, and edit records. You configure the control to display Delete, Insert, and New buttons. These function similarly to the corresponding functionality in the DataList and GridView controls.

You customize the appearance of the DetailsView control by setting style properties including HeaderStyle, RowStyle, AlternatingRowStyle, FooterStyle, and PagerStyle. You can use custom templates to further customize the rendering.

The DetailsView control raises events listed in Table 8-2 when the current record is displayed or changed.

Table 8-2. DataView events

Event	Description
PageIndexChanging	Raised when a pager button is clicked, before the DetailsView performs the paging operation.
PageIndexChanged	Raised when a pager button is clicked, after the DetailsView performs the paging operation.
ItemCommand	Raised when a button in the DetailsView is clicked.
ItemCreated	Raised when a record is created in the DetailsView control.
ItemDeleting	Raised when a Delete button is clicked, before the delete operation.
ItemDeleted	Raised when a Delete button is clicked, after the delete operation.
ItemInserting	Raised when an Insert button is clicked, before the insert operation.
ItemInserted	Raised when an Insert button is clicked, after the insert operation.
ItemUpdating	Raised when an Update button is clicked, before the update operation.
ItemUpdated	Raised when an Update button is clicked, after the update operation.
ModeChanging	Raised when the DetailsView attempts to change between edit, insert, and read-only modes, before the CurrentMode property is updated.
ModeChanged	Raised when the DetailsView attempts to change between edit, insert, and read-only modes, after the CurrentMode property is updated.
DataBound	Raised after the DetailsView has finished binding to the data source.

8.4   Binding Data to a Web Forms Repeater Control

Problem

You need to bind a result set to a Web Forms Repeater control.

Solution

Set the control's advanced properties before calling DataBind( ).

Follow these steps:

1. Create a C# ASP.NET web application named BindWebFormRepeater.

2. Add the following control to the *Default.aspx* design surface:

   - Repeater named departmentRepeater. Use the smart tag panel to configure its formatting.

The completed layout of the Web Form page *Default.aspx* is shown in Figure 8-7.

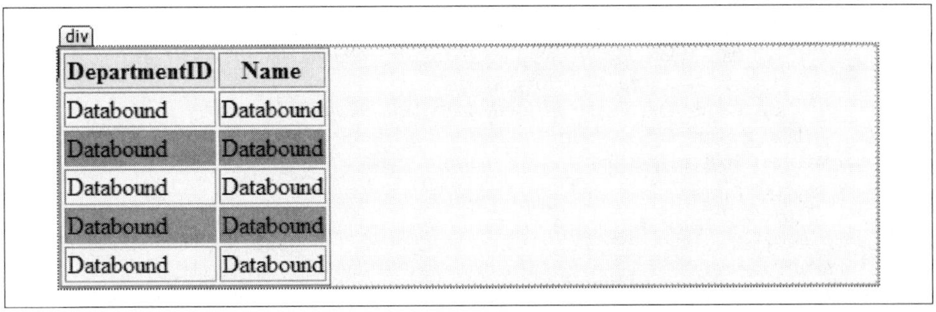

Figure 8-7. Layout for Default.aspx in BindWebFormRepeater solution

The code in *Default.aspx* in the project BindWebFormRepeater is shown in Example 8-7.

Example 8-7. File: Default.aspx for BindWebFormRepeater solution

```
<%@ Page Language="C#" AutoEventWireup="true" CodeBehind="Default.aspx.cs"
    Inherits="BindWebFormRepeater._Default" %>

<!DOCTYPE html PUBLIC "-//W3C//DTD XHTML 1.0 Transitional//EN"
    "http://www.w3.org/TR/xhtml1/DTD/xhtml1-transitional.dtd">

<html xmlns="http://www.w3.org/1999/xhtml" >
<head runat="server">
    <title>Untitled Page</title>
</head>
<body>
    <form id="form1" runat="server">
    <div>
        <asp:Repeater ID="departmentRepeater" runat="server">
        <HeaderTemplate>
          <table border=1>
            <tr>
              <th style="background-color:Yellow">
                DepartmentID</th>
              <th style="background-color:Yellow">
                Name</th>
            </tr>
        </HeaderTemplate>
```

Example 8-7. File: Default.aspx for BindWebFormRepeater solution (continued)

```
          <ItemTemplate>
            <tr>
              <td>
                <%# DataBinder.Eval(Container.DataItem, "DepartmentID") %></td>
              <td>
                <%# DataBinder.Eval(Container.DataItem, "Name") %></td>
            </tr>
          </ItemTemplate>
          <AlternatingItemTemplate>
            <tr>
              <td style="background-color: Silver">
                <%# DataBinder.Eval(Container.DataItem, "DepartmentID") %></td>
              <td style="background-color: Silver">
                <%# DataBinder.Eval(Container.DataItem, "Name") %></td>
            </tr>
          </AlternatingItemTemplate>
          <FooterTemplate>
            </table>
          </FooterTemplate>
          </asp:Repeater>
      </div>
      </form>
</body>
</html>
```

The C# code-behind code in *Default.aspx.cs* in the project BindWebFormRepeater is shown in Example 8-8. The solution fills a DataTable with the HumanResource.Department table in AdventureWorks. The DataTable is bound to the Repeater control.

Example 8-8. File: Default.aspx.cs for BindWebFormRepeater solution

```
using System;
using System.Data;
using System.Data.SqlClient;

namespace BindWebFormRepeater
{
    public partial class _Default : System.Web.UI.Page
    {
        protected void Page_Load(object sender, EventArgs e)
        {
            if (!Page.IsPostBack)
            {
                // load and bind data into the repeater control
                departmentRepeater.DataSource = LoadData();
                DataBind();
            }
        }
```

Example 8-8. File: Default.aspx.cs for BindWebFormRepeater solution (continued)

```
        protected DataTable LoadData( )
        {
            string sqlConnectString = @"Data Source=(local);
                Integrated security=SSPI;Initial Catalog=AdventureWorks;";
            string sqlSelect =
                @"SELECT DepartmentID, Name FROM HumanResources.Department
                ORDER BY DepartmentID";

            // retrieve a DataTable containing all department records in
            // HumanResources.Department
            SqlDataAdapter da = new SqlDataAdapter(sqlSelect, sqlConnectString);
            DataTable dt = new DataTable( );

            da.Fill(dt);

            return dt;
        }
    }
}
```

The output is shown in Figure 8-8.

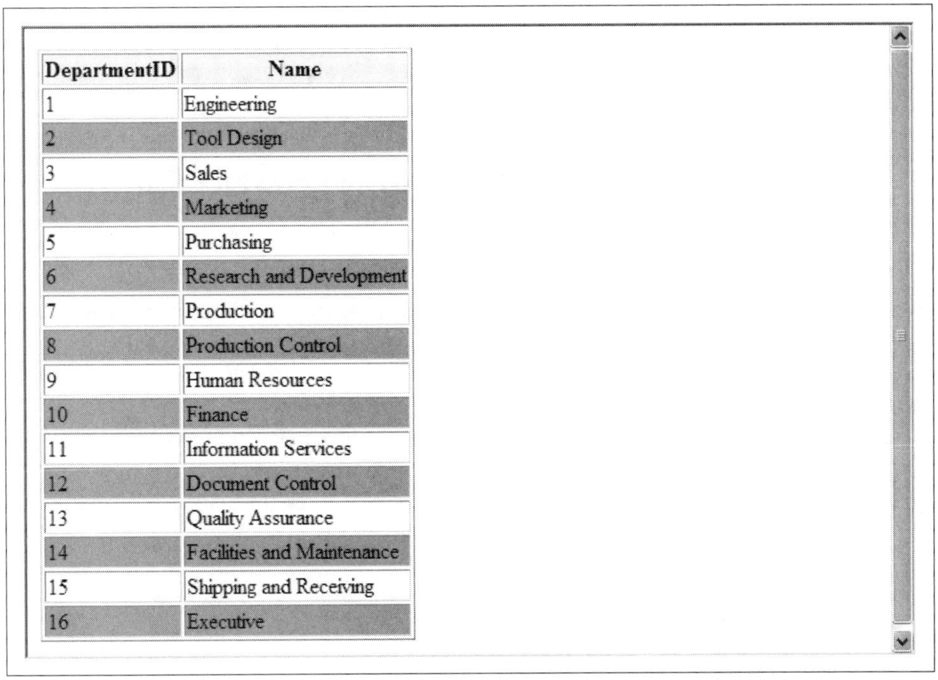

DepartmentID	Name
1	Engineering
2	Tool Design
3	Sales
4	Marketing
5	Purchasing
6	Research and Development
7	Production
8	Production Control
9	Human Resources
10	Finance
11	Information Services
12	Document Control
13	Quality Assurance
14	Facilities and Maintenance
15	Shipping and Receiving
16	Executive

Figure 8-8. Output for BindWebFormRepeater solution

Discussion

The Repeater control is a container control that renders a list of items from the data to which it is bound. You use templates similarly to the DataList or GridView controls to control the formatting of the output. The Repeater control loops through the data and uses the templates to render the results. The Repeater control supports the templates listed in Table 8-3.

Table 8-3. Repeater Templates

Template	Description
ItemTemplate	HTML markup and controls that are rendered for each item in the data source.
AlternatingItemTemplate	HTML markup and controls that are rendered for every other item in the data source.
HeaderItemTemplate	HTML markup and controls that are rendered at the beginning of the data list.
FooterTemplate	HTML markup and controls that are rendered at the end of the data list.
SeparatorTemplate	HTML markup and control that are rendered between each item in the data list.

You need to bind the Repeater to a data control such as a SqlDataSource or ObjectDataSource. You can also bind a Repeater to classes including DataReader, DataSet, DataTable, or DataView—any class that implements the IEnumerable interface can be bound. The easiest way to create a Repeater control is to drag the Repeater control onto the web page design surface.

8.5   Binding Data to a Web Forms DataList Control

Problem

You need to bind the result set from a query to a DataList control and update the data source with changes, deletions, and new records using the DataList.

Solution

Follow the techniques demonstrated by this solution:

1. The solution uses a table named DataList in the AdoDotNet35Cookbook database. Execute the following T-SQL statement to create the table:

```
USE AdoDotNet35Cookbook
GO
CREATE TABLE DataList(
    Id int NOT NULL PRIMARY KEY,
    IntField int NULL,
    StringField nvarchar(50) NULL )
```

The schema of table DataList that is used in the solution is shown in Table 8-4.

Table 8-4. DataList table schema

Column name	Data type	Length	Allow nulls?
Id	int	4	No
IntField	int	4	Yes
StringField	nvarchar	50	Yes

2. Execute the following T-SQL batch to create the sample data needed for the solution.

```
USE AdoDotNet35Cookbook
GO
INSERT INTO DataList VALUES (1, 10, 'StringValue1')
INSERT INTO DataList VALUES (2, 20, 'StringValue2')
INSERT INTO DataList VALUES (3, 30, 'StringValue3')
INSERT INTO DataList VALUES (4, 40, 'StringValue4')
```

3. Create a C# ASP.NET web application named BindWebFormDataList.

4. Add the following controls to the *Default.aspx* design surface:

- DataList named dataList
- Button named insertButton with Text property = Insert

The competed layout of the Web Form page *Default.aspx* is shown in Figure 8-9.

Figure 8-9. Layout for Default.aspx in BindWebFormDataList solution

The code in *Default.aspx* in the project BindWebFormDataList is shown in Example 8-9. *Default.aspx* defines the DataList control and the three templates—SelectedItemTemplate, ItemTemplate, and EditItemTemplate—which control the display of data for selected items, unselected items, and items being edited. The static Eval( ) method of the DataBinder class is used to fill the field values in each template. Container.DataItem specifies the container argument for the method which when used in a list in a template resolves to DataListItem.DataItem.

Example 8-9. File: Default.aspx for BindWebFormDataList solution

```
<%@ Page Language="C#" AutoEventWireup="true" CodeBehind="Default.aspx.cs"
    Inherits="BindWebFormDataList._Default" %>

<!DOCTYPE html PUBLIC "-//W3C//DTD XHTML 1.0 Transitional//EN"
    "http://www.w3.org/TR/xhtml1/DTD/xhtml1-transitional.dtd">
<html xmlns="http://www.w3.org/1999/xhtml">
<head runat="server">
    <title>Untitled Page</title>
</head>
<body>
    <form id="form1" runat="server">
    <div>
        <asp:DataList ID="dataList" runat="server"
            OnItemCommand="dataList_ItemCommand"
            oncancelcommand="dataList_CancelCommand"
            ondeletecommand="dataList_DeleteCommand"
            oneditcommand="dataList_EditCommand"
            onupdatecommand="dataList_UpdateCommand" CellPadding="4"
            ForeColor="#333333">
            <selecteditemstyle backcolor="#C5BBAF" font-bold="True" forecolor="#333333" />
            <headerstyle backcolor="#1C5E55" font-bold="True" forecolor="White" />
            <SelectedItemTemplate>
                <asp:Button ID="editButton" runat="server" Text="Edit" CommandName="Edit">
                </asp:Button>
                <b>
                    <%# DataBinder.Eval(Container.DataItem, "Id") %>;
                    <%# DataBinder.Eval(Container.DataItem, "IntField") %>;
                    <%# DataBinder.Eval(Container.DataItem, "StringField") %></b>
            </SelectedItemTemplate>
            <ItemTemplate>
                <asp:Button ID="selectButton" runat="server" Text="Select"
                CommandName="Select"></asp:Button>
                <%# DataBinder.Eval(Container.DataItem, "Id") %>;
                <%# DataBinder.Eval(Container.DataItem, "IntField") %>;
                <%# DataBinder.Eval(Container.DataItem, "StringField") %>
            </ItemTemplate>
            <footerstyle backcolor="#1C5E55" font-bold="True" forecolor="White" />
            <alternatingitemstyle backcolor="White" />
            <itemstyle backcolor="#E3EAEB" />
            <EditItemTemplate>
                <asp:Button ID="updateButton" runat="server" Text="Update"
                CommandName="Update"></asp:Button>
                <asp:Button ID="deleteButton" runat="server" Text="Delete"
                CommandName="Delete"></asp:Button>
                <asp:Button ID="cancelButton" runat="server" Text="Cancel"
                CommandName="Cancel"></asp:Button>
                <br>
                <asp:Label ID="Label1" runat="server">ID: </asp:Label>
                <asp:TextBox ID="idTextBox" runat="server" Width="96px" ReadOnly="True"
                    Text='<%# DataBinder.Eval(Container.DataItem, "Id") %>'>
                </asp:TextBox>
                <br>
```

```
                <asp:Label ID="Label2" runat="server">IntField: </asp:Label>
                <asp:TextBox ID="intFieldTextBox" runat="server"
                    Text='<%# DataBinder.Eval(Container.DataItem, "IntField") %>'>
                </asp:TextBox>
                <br>
                <asp:Label ID="Label3" runat="server">StringField: </asp:Label>
                <asp:TextBox ID="stringFieldTextBox" runat="server"
                    Text='<%# DataBinder.Eval(Container.DataItem, "StringField") %>'>
                </asp:TextBox>
            </EditItemTemplate>
        </asp:DataList>
    </div>
    <br />
    <asp:Button ID="insertButton" runat="server" Text="Insert"
        onclick="insertButton_Click" />
    </form>
</body>
</html>
```

The C# code-behind code in *Default.aspx.cs* in the project `BindWebFormDataList` is shown in Example 8-10. The solution loads a `DataTable` with the schema and data from the table `DataList` in the `AdoDotNet35Cookbook` database and caches it to the `Session` object. The `DataTable` is assigned as the `DataSource` for the `DataList` control.

The code-behind contains the following event handlers and methods:

`UpdateDataSource( )`

This method creates a `DataAdapter` and uses it together with updating logic generated by a `CommandBuilder` to update the data source with changes made to the cached `DataTable`. The updated `DataTable` is stored to the `Session` variable, which is used to cache the data source for the `DataList`.

`BindDataList( )`

This method gets the cached data from the `Session` variable and binds its default view to the `DataList`.

`dataList_ItemCommand`

Checks whether the Select button was pressed. If it was, the index of the item being edited is set to -1 to cancel its editing. The index of the selected item is then set to the index of the row corresponding to the Select button to put that row into select mode. Finally, `BindDataList( )` is called to refresh the list.

`dataList_CancelCommand`

Sets the index of the item being edited to -1 to cancel any current editing and calls `BindDataList( )` to refresh the list.

`dataList_DeleteCommand`

Finds and deletes the specified row from the data cached in the `Session` variable and calls the `UpdateDataSource( )` method to persist the change back to the data source. `BindDataList( )` is called to refresh the list.

dataList_EditCommand

Sets the index of the selected item to -1 to cancel its selection. The index of the item being edited is then set to the index of the row corresponding to the Edit button putting that row into edit mode. BindDataList( ) is called to refresh the list.

dataList.UpdateCommand

Finds and updates the specified row in the data cached in the Session variable and calls the UpdateDataSource( ) method to persist the change back to the data source. BindDataList( ) is called to refresh the list.

insertButton_Click

Creates a new row and adds it to the DataTable that is the data source of the DataList control. The Id field is set to one larger than the largest Id value in the DataList.

Example 8-10. File: Default.aspx.cs for BindWebFormDataList solution

```
using System;
using System.Data;
using System.Data.SqlClient;
using System.Web.UI.WebControls;
using System.Web.UI;

namespace BindWebFormDataList
{
    public partial class _Default : System.Web.UI.Page
    {
        private string sqlConnectString = @"Data Source=(local);
            Integrated security=SSPI;Initial Catalog=AdoDotNet35Cookbook;";
        private string sqlSelect =
            "SELECT Id, IntField, StringField FROM DataList";

        protected void Page_Load(object sender, EventArgs e)
        {
            if (!Page.IsPostBack)
            {
                dataList.DataSource = LoadData( );
                dataList.DataKeyField = "Id";
                DataBind( );
            }
        }

        protected DataTable LoadData( )
        {
            // Load data in the table DataList into a DataTable
            SqlDataAdapter da = new SqlDataAdapter(sqlSelect, sqlConnectString);
            DataTable dt = new DataTable( );

            da.FillSchema(dt, SchemaType.Source);
            da.Fill(dt);
```

```
        // Store data in session variable to store data between
        // posts to server.
        Session["DataSource"] = dt;

        return dt;
    }

    private DataTable UpdateDataSource(DataTable dt)
    {
        // Create a DataAdapter for the update.
        SqlDataAdapter da = new SqlDataAdapter(sqlSelect, sqlConnectString);
        // Create a CommandBuilder to generate update logic.
        SqlCommandBuilder cb = new SqlCommandBuilder(da);

        // Update the data source with changes to the table.
        da.Update(dt);

        // Store updated data in session variable to store data between
        // posts to server.
        Session["DataSource"] = dt;

        return dt;
    }

    private void BindDataList()
    {
        // Get data from session variable and bind to the data list.
        dataList.DataSource = ((DataTable)Session["DataSource"]);
        dataList.DataBind();
    }

    protected void dataList_ItemCommand(object source, DataListCommandEventArgs e)
    {
        // Check if the "select" button is pressed.
        if (e.CommandName == "Select")
        {
            // Set the index of the item being edited out of range.
            dataList.EditItemIndex = -1;
            // Set the index of the selected item to the current record.
            dataList.SelectedIndex = e.Item.ItemIndex;

            BindDataList();
        }
    }

    protected void dataList_CancelCommand(object source, DataListCommandEventArgs e)
    {
        // Set the index of the item being edited out of range.
        dataList.EditItemIndex = -1;

        BindDataList();
    }
```

```csharp
protected void dataList_DeleteCommand(object source, DataListCommandEventArgs e)
{
    // Get the data from the session variable.
    DataTable dt = (DataTable)Session["DataSource"];

    // Get the ID of the row to delete.
    int id = (int)dataList.DataKeys[e.Item.ItemIndex];

    // Delete the row from the table.
    dt.Rows.Find(id).Delete();

    // Update the data source with the changes to the table.
    UpdateDataSource(dt);

    // Set the index of the item being edited out of range.
    dataList.EditItemIndex = -1;

    BindDataList();
}

protected void dataList_EditCommand(object source, DataListCommandEventArgs e)
{
    // Set the index of the selected item out of range.
    dataList.SelectedIndex = -1;
    // Set the index of the item being edited to the current record.
    dataList.EditItemIndex = e.Item.ItemIndex;

    BindDataList();
}

protected void dataList_UpdateCommand(object source, DataListCommandEventArgs e)
{
    // Get the data from the session variable.
    DataTable dt = (DataTable)Session["DataSource"];

    // Get the ID of the row to update.
    int id = (int)dataList.DataKeys[e.Item.ItemIndex];

    // Get the DataRow to update using the ID.
    DataRow dr = dt.Rows.Find(id);

    // Get the column values for the current record from the DataList.
    int intField;
    if (int.TryParse(((TextBox)e.Item.FindControl("intFieldTextBox")).Text,
        out intField))
    {
        dr["IntField"] = intField;
    }
    dr["StringField"] =
        ((TextBox)e.Item.FindControl("stringFieldTextBox")).Text;
```

Example 8-10. File: Default.aspx.cs for BindWebFormDataList solution (continued)

```
            // Update the data source with the changes to the table.
            UpdateDataSource(dt);

            // Set the index of the item being edited out of range.
            dataList.EditItemIndex = -1;

            BindDataList( );
        }

        protected void insertButton_Click(object sender, EventArgs e)
        {
            int newItemIndex = dataList.Items.Count;
            int id = ((DataTable)Session["DataSource"])
                .Rows[newItemIndex - 1].Field<int>("Id") + 1;

            // Get the data from the session variable.
            DataTable dt = (DataTable)Session["DataSource"];

            dt.Rows.Add(new object[] { id, null, null });

            UpdateDataSource(dt);

            // Set the index of the item being edited out of range.
            dataList.EditItemIndex = newItemIndex;

            BindDataList( );
        }
    }
}
```

The output is shown in Figure 8-10.

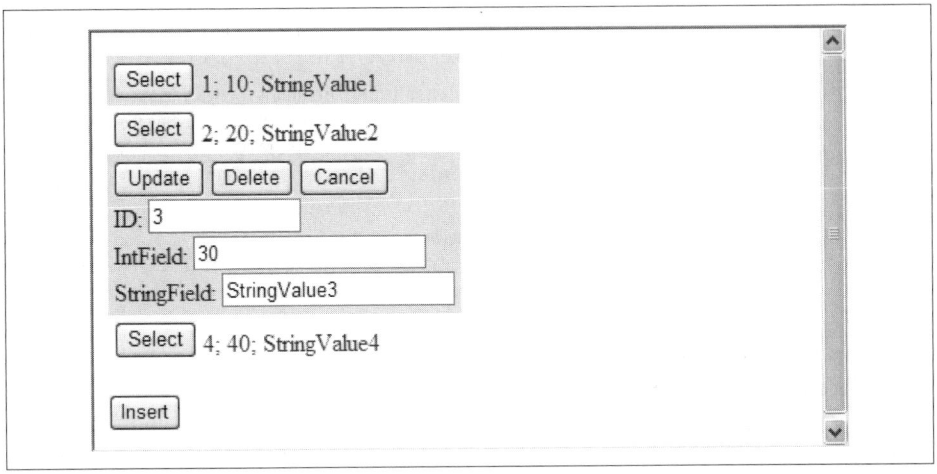

Figure 8-10. Output for BindWebFormDataList solution

Discussion

The DataList Web Forms control displays tabular data from a data source and controls the formatting using templates and styles. The DataList must be bound to a data source control such as a SqlDataSource or ObjectDataSource. You can also bind a DataList to classes including DataReader, DataSet, DataTable, or DataView—any class that implements the IEnumerable interface can be bound. The easiest way to create a DataList control is to drag the DataList control onto the web page design surface.

The DataList Web Form control uses templates to display items, control layout, and provide functional capabilities. Table 8-5 describes the different templates for the DataList.

Table 8-5. DataList templates

Template	Description
AlternatingItemTemplate	Elements to render for every other row in the control. This is normally used to specify a different display style for alternating rows. This template is defined within the <AlternatingItemTemplate> and </AlternatingItemTemplate> tags.
EditItemTemplate	Elements to render when an item is put into edit mode. This template is invoked for the row specified in the EditItemIndex property; setting the EditItemIndex property to -1 cancels the edit mode. This template is defined within the <EditItemTemplate> and </EditItemTemplate> tags.
FooterTemplate	Elements to render at the bottom of the control. The footer template cannot be data bound. This template is defined within the <FooterTemplate> and </FooterTemplate> tags.
HeaderTemplate	Elements to render at the top of the control. The header template cannot be data bound. This template is defined within the <HeaderTemplate> and </HeaderTemplate> tags.
ItemTemplate	Elements to render for each row in the data source. This template is defined within the <ItemTemplate> and </ItemTemplate> tags.
SelectedItemTemplate	Elements to render when an item in the control is selected. This template is invoked for the row specified by the SelectedIndex property; setting the SelectedIndex property to -1 cancels the select mode. This template is defined within the <SelectedItemTemplate> and </SelectedItemTemplate> tags.
SeparatorTemplate	Elements to render between each item. The SeparatorTemplate cannot be data bound. This template is defined within the <SeparatorTemplate> and </SeparatorTemplate> tags.

To format the templates, right-click on the DataList control on the design surface and select one of the three editing submenus of the Edit Template menu. To end editing, right-click the DataList control and select End Template Editing. Templates can also be customized by editing the HTML directly. One of the item templates must contain a data bound control for the DataList control to render at runtime.

A Button, LinkButton, or ImageButton web server control can be added to the control templates. These buttons can let the user switch between the different item modes, for example. The buttons bubble their events to the containing DataList control. The events that the DataList raises in response to button clicks are described in Table 8-6.

Table 8-6. DataList Button click events

Event	Description
CancelCommand	Raised when the Cancel button is clicked for an item in the control.
DeleteCommand	Raised when the Delete button is clicked for an item in the control.
EditCommand	Raised when the Edit button is clicked for an item in the control.
ItemCommand	Raised when any button is clicked for an item in the control. The button clicked can be determined by reading the CommandName property of the DataListCommandEventArgs object in the ItemCommand event handler. This property contains the value of CommandName property of the button that was clicked.
UpdateCommand	Raised when the Update button is clicked for an item in the control.

After the properties appropriate to the control are set, call the DataBind( ) method of the control or of the page to bind the data source to the server control.

8.6   Binding Data to a Web Forms GridView Control

Problem

You want to bind the result set from a query to a GridView control and page through and sort the data.

Solution

Set the advanced properties of the GridView control and bind the data to the control. Handle the PageIndexChanging and Sorting events.

Follow these steps:

1. Create a C# ASP.NET web application named BindWebFormGridView.
2. Add the following control to the *Default.aspx* design surface:
    - GridView named contactGridView

The completed layout of the Web Form page *Default.aspx* is shown in Figure 8-11.

The code in *Default.aspx* in the project BindWebFormGridView is shown in Example 8-11.

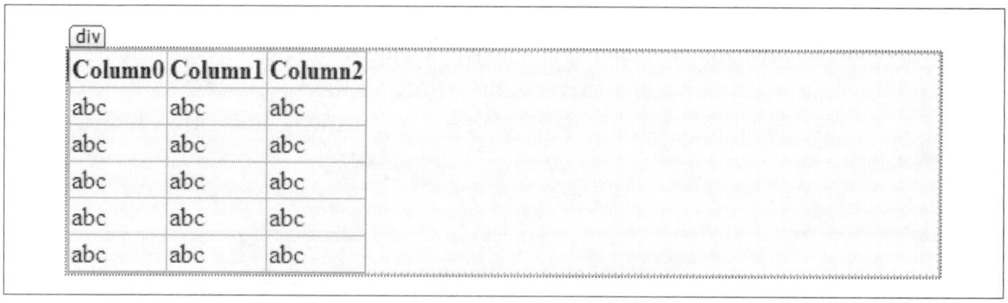

Figure 8-11. Layout for Default.aspx in BindWebFormGridView solution

Example 8-11. File: Default.aspx for BindWebFormGridView solution

```
<%@ Page Language="C#" AutoEventWireup="true" CodeBehind="Default.aspx.cs"
    Inherits="BindWebFormGridView._Default" %>
<!DOCTYPE html PUBLIC "-//W3C//DTD XHTML 1.0 Transitional//EN"
    "http://www.w3.org/TR/xhtml1/DTD/xhtml1-transitional.dtd">

<html xmlns="http://www.w3.org/1999/xhtml" >
<head runat="server">
    <title>Untitled Page</title>
</head>
<body>
    <form id="form1" runat="server">
    <div>
        <asp:GridView ID="contactGridView" runat="server"
            onpageindexchanging="contactGridView_PageIndexChanging"
            onsorting="contactGridView_Sorting">
        </asp:GridView>
    </div>
    </form>
</body>
</html>
```

The C# code-behind code in *Default.aspx.cs* in the project BindWebGridView is shown in Example 8-12. The solution fills a DataTable with the top 50 records from the Person.Contact table in AdventureWorks and stores the default view of the DataTable to the Session object. The data source of the GridView named contactGridView is set to the DataView. The GridView PageIndexChanged event handler updates the CurrentPageIndex of the GridView, gets the cached data from the Session variable, and binds that data to the grid view. The GridView Sorting event handler sets the sort expression of the DataView cached in the view state, and binds the cached data to the grid view.

Example 8-12. File: Default.aspx.cs for BindWebFormGridView solution

```
using System;
using System.Data;
using System.Data.SqlClient;
using System.Web.UI.WebControls;
```

```csharp
namespace BindWebFormGridView
{
    public partial class _Default : System.Web.UI.Page
    {
        protected void Page_Load(object sender, EventArgs e)
        {
            if (!Page.IsPostBack)
            {
                ViewState["SortExpression"] = "ContactID";
                ViewState["SortDirection"] = SortDirection.Ascending;

                contactGridView.AllowPaging = true;
                contactGridView.AllowSorting = true;
                contactGridView.DataSource = LoadData();
                contactGridView.DataKeyNames = new string[] {"ContactID"};
                contactGridView.DataBind();
            }
        }

        protected DataView LoadData()
        {
            string sqlConnectString = @"Data Source=(local);
                Integrated security=SSPI;Initial Catalog=AdventureWorks;";

            string sqlSelect =
                "SELECT TOP 50 ContactID, FirstName, LastName FROM Person.Contact";

            SqlDataAdapter da = new SqlDataAdapter(sqlSelect, sqlConnectString);
            DataTable dt = new DataTable();

            da.Fill(dt);

            Session["ContactDataView"] = dt.DefaultView;

            return dt.DefaultView;
        }

        protected void contactGridView_PageIndexChanging(
            object sender, GridViewPageEventArgs e)
        {
            contactGridView.PageIndex = e.NewPageIndex;
            contactGridView.DataSource = (DataView)Session["ContactDataView"];
            contactGridView.DataBind();
        }

        protected void contactGridView_Sorting(object sender, GridViewSortEventArgs e)
        {
            DataView dv = (DataView)Session["ContactDataView"];

            if (e.SortExpression == (string)ViewState["SortExpression"])
```

Example 8-12. File: Default.aspx.cs for BindWebFormGridView solution (continued)

```
            {
                dv.Sort = e.SortExpression + " " +
                    ((SortDirection)ViewState["SortDirection"] == SortDirection.Ascending
?
                    "DESC" : "ASC");
            }
            else
            {
                dv.Sort = e.SortExpression + " ASC";
            }

            ViewState["SortExpression"] = e.SortExpression;
            ViewState["SortDirection"] = e.SortDirection;

            contactGridView.DataSource = dv;
            contactGridView.DataBind( );
        }
    }
}
```

The output is shown in Figure 8-12.

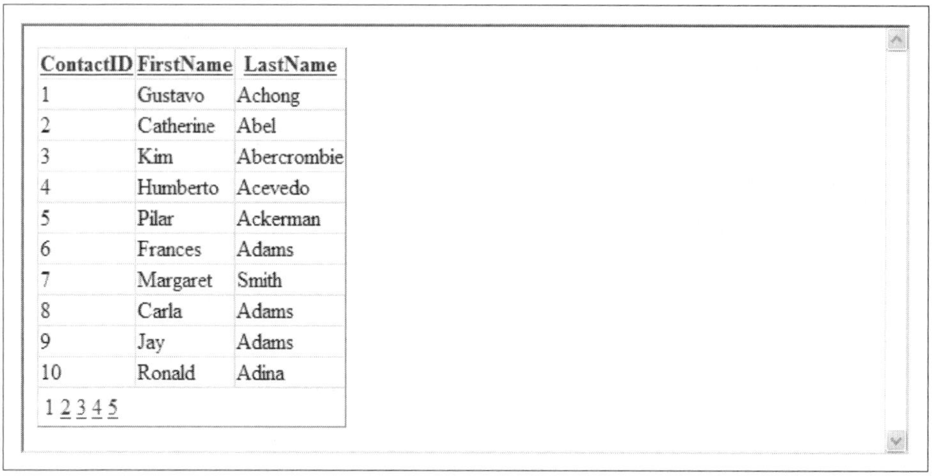

ContactID	FirstName	LastName
1	Gustavo	Achong
2	Catherine	Abel
3	Kim	Abercrombie
4	Humberto	Acevedo
5	Pilar	Ackerman
6	Frances	Adams
7	Margaret	Smith
8	Carla	Adams
9	Jay	Adams
10	Ronald	Adina
1 2 3 4 5		

Figure 8-12. Output for BindWebFormGridView solution

Discussion

The `GridView` Web Form control retrieves tabular information from a data source and renders it in a web page. The control supports functionality for selecting, editing, deleting, sorting, and navigating the data.

The `GridView` must be bound to a data source such as a `SqlDataSource` or `ObjectDataSource`. You can also bind a `GridView` to classes including `DataReader`, `DataSet`, `DataTable`, or `DataView`. Any class that implements the `IEnumerable` interface can be bound. The easiest way to create a `GridView` control is to drag the `GridView` control onto the web page design surface.

The `GridView` control uses templates to display items, control layout, and provide functional capabilities similar to the `DataList` as described in Recipe 8.5. The differences are:

- Item templates are created for columns in the grid rather for the entire grid.
- `GridView` columns don't have a `SelectedItemTemplate` or a `SeparatorItemTemplate`.

Specify columns for and format the `GridView` using the smart tag panel. Right-click on the `GridView` control on the design surface and select Show Smart Tag from the context menu. Alternately, click the small arrow at the top left of the control. The `GridView` can also be customized by editing the HTML directly.

A variety of `GridView` columns can be specified—by default columns are automatically generated based on the fields in the data source. The `GridView` supports the column types described in Table 8-7. The columns are derived from the `DataControlField` class.

Table 8-7. GridView column types

Column type	Description
BoundField	Displays a field value from a data source.
ButtonField	A command button in the grid that invokes custom logic when clicked.
CheckBoxField	Displays a check box. Commonly used to display fields with Boolean values.
CommandField	Displays predefined command buttons for operations such as select, edit, and delete.
HyperlinkColumn	Displays the field value as a hyperlink.
ImageField	Displays an image.
TemplateColumn	A custom layout based on a combination of HTML and Web Server controls in a specified template.

Among the events that the `GridView` supports are those designed to help implement common data editing and manipulation functionality. These events are described in Table 8-8.

Table 8-8. GridView events for editing and navigation

Event	Description
RowCommand	Raised when a button is clicked in the `GridView`.
PageIndexChanging	Raised when a pager button for a row is clicked, before the `GridView` performs the paging operation.
PageIndexChanged	Raised when a pager button for a row is clicked, after the `GridView` performs the paging operation.
SelectedIndexChanging	Raised when the `Select` button for a row is clicked, before the `GridView` performs the select operation.

Table 8-8. GridView events for editing and navigation (continued)

Event	Description
SelectedIndexChanged	Raised when the Select button for a row is clicked, after the GridView performs the select operation.
Sorting	Raised when the sort hyperlink for a row is clicked, before the GridView performs the sorts operation.
Sorted	Raised when the sort hyperlink for a row is clicked, after the GridView performs the sorts operation.
DataRowBound	Raised when a row in the GridView is bound to a data record.
RowCreated	Raised when a new row is created in the GridView.
RowDeleting	Raised when the Delete button for a row is clicked, before the GridView deletes the row.
RowDeleted	Raised when the Delete button for a row is clicked, after the GridView deletes the row.
RowEditing	Raised when the Edit button for a row is clicked, before the GridView enters edit mode for the row.
RowCancelingEdit	Raised when the Cancel button for a row is clicked, before the GridView exits edit mode.
RowUpdating	Raised when the Update button for a row is clicked, before the GridView updates the row.
RowUpdated	Raised when the Update button for a row is clicked, after the GridView updates the row.
DataBound	Raised after the GridView has finished binding to the data source.

The GridView does not inherently support editing, paging, sorting, or updating functionality. Instead, it exposes the events listed in Table 8-8, allowing the functionality to be added using event handling code.

After the properties appropriate to the control are set, call the DataBind( ) method of the control or of the page to bind the data source to the server control.

8.7 Modifying and Updating Data in a Web Forms GridView Control

Problem

You need to edit data using a GridView control and update the database with the changes made.

Solution

Bind the results of a database query to a DataGrid control and update the database with changes made in the DataGrid using a data adapter.

Follow these steps:

1. The solution uses a table named `GridView` in the `AdoDotNet35Cookbook` database. Execute the following T-SQL statement to create the table:

```
USE AdoDotNet35Cookbook
GO
CREATE TABLE GridView(
    Id int NOT NULL PRIMARY KEY,
    IntField int NULL,
    StringField nvarchar(50) NULL )
```

The schema of table `GridView` used in this solution is shown in Table 8-9.

Table 8-9. GridView table schema

Column name	Data type	Length	Allow nulls?
Id	int	4	No
IntField	int	4	Yes
StringField	nvarchar	50	Yes

2. Execute the following T-SQL batch to create the sample data required by the solution:

```
USE AdoDotNet35Cookbook
GO
INSERT INTO GridView VALUES (1, 10, 'Field1.1')
INSERT INTO GridView VALUES (2, 20, 'Field1.2')
INSERT INTO GridView VALUES (3, 30, 'Field1.3')
INSERT INTO GridView VALUES (4, 40, 'Field1.4')
```

3. Create a C# ASP.NET web application named `UpdateDataWebFormGridView`.

4. Add the following control to the *Default.aspx* design surface:

   - `GridView` named gridView

The completed layout of the Web Form page *Default.aspx* is shown in Figure 8-13.

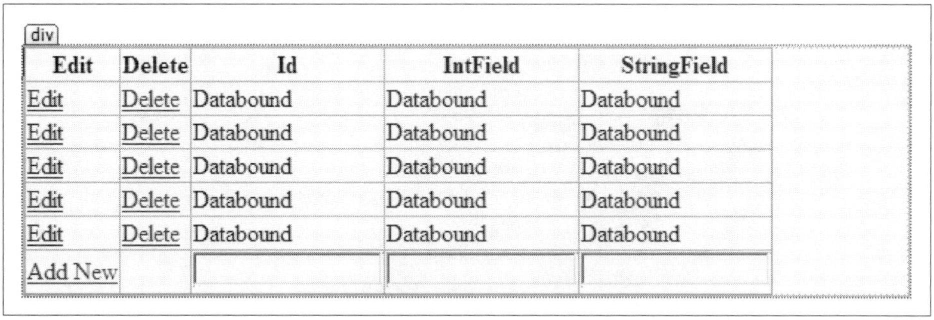

Figure 8-13. Layout for Default.aspx in UpdateDataWebFormGridView solution

The code in *Default.aspx* in the project UpdateDataWebFormGridView is shown in Example 8-13. The Web Forms page solution defines the GridView control with the five columns that it contains—Edit or Update/Cancel button, Delete button, Id field, IntField field, StringField field—and the two templates controlling the appearance of data depending on whether the column is being edited: EditItemTemplate or ItemTemplate. The FooterTemplate is used to add new rows—it contains an add new button and the three fields. The static Eval( ) method of the DataBinder class is used to fill the field values in each template.

Example 8-13. File: Default.aspx for UpdateDataWebFormGridView solution

```
<%@ Page Language="C#" AutoEventWireup="true" CodeBehind="Default.aspx.cs"
    Inherits="UpdateDataWebFormGridView._Default" %>
<!DOCTYPE html PUBLIC "-//W3C//DTD XHTML 1.0 Transitional//EN"
    "http://www.w3.org/TR/xhtml1/DTD/xhtml1-transitional.dtd">

<html xmlns="http://www.w3.org/1999/xhtml" >
<head runat="server">
    <title>Untitled Page</title>
</head>
<body>
    <form id="form1" runat="server">
    <div>

        <asp:GridView ID="gridView" runat="server"
            onrowediting="gridView_RowEditing"
            onrowcancelingedit="gridView_RowCancelingEdit"
            onrowcommand="gridView_RowCommand"
            onrowdeleting="gridView_RowDeleting"
            ShowFooter="True" AutoGenerateColumns="False"
            onrowupdating="gridView_RowUpdating">
            <Columns>
                <asp:TemplateField HeaderText="Edit" ShowHeader="False">
                    <EditItemTemplate>
                        <asp:LinkButton ID="LinkButton1" runat="server"
                            CausesValidation="True"
                            Text="Update" CommandName="Update" >
                        </asp:LinkButton>
                        <asp:LinkButton ID="LinkButton2" runat="server"
                            CausesValidation="False"
                            Text="Cancel" CommandName="Cancel">
                        </asp:LinkButton>
                    </EditItemTemplate>
                    <ItemTemplate>
                        <asp:LinkButton ID="LinkButton1" runat="server"
                            CausesValidation="False"
                            Text="Edit" CommandName="Edit">
                        </asp:LinkButton>
                    </ItemTemplate>
                    <FooterTemplate>
                        <asp:LinkButton ID="LinkButton1" runat="server"
                            CausesValidation="False"
```

```
                    CommandName="AddNew" Text="Add New">
            </asp:LinkButton>
        </FooterTemplate>
    </asp:TemplateField>
    <asp:CommandField HeaderText="Delete" ShowDeleteButton="True"
        ShowHeader="True" />

    <asp:TemplateField HeaderText="Id">
        <ItemTemplate>
            <asp:Label ID="Label1" runat="server"
                Text='<%# DataBinder.Eval(Container, "DataItem.Id") %>'>
            </asp:Label>
        </ItemTemplate>
        <EditItemTemplate>
            <asp:TextBox runat="server" id="idTextBox" ReadOnly="true"
                BackColor=silver
                Text='<%# DataBinder.Eval(Container, "DataItem.Id") %>'>
            </asp:TextBox>
        </EditItemTemplate>
        <FooterTemplate>
            <asp:TextBox runat="server" id="NewIdTextBox">
            </asp:TextBox>
        </FooterTemplate>
    </asp:TemplateField>

    <asp:TemplateField HeaderText="IntField">
        <ItemTemplate>
            <asp:Label runat="server"
                Text='<%# DataBinder.Eval(Container, "DataItem.IntField") %>'>
            </asp:Label>
        </ItemTemplate>
        <EditItemTemplate>
            <asp:TextBox runat="server" id="intFieldTextBox"
                Text='<%# DataBinder.Eval(Container, "DataItem.IntField") %>'>
            </asp:TextBox>
        </EditItemTemplate>
        <FooterTemplate>
            <asp:TextBox runat="server" id="NewIntFieldTextBox">
            </asp:TextBox>
        </FooterTemplate>
    </asp:TemplateField>

    <asp:TemplateField HeaderText="StringField">
        <ItemTemplate>
            <asp:Label runat="server"
                Text='<%# DataBinder.Eval(Container,
                    "DataItem.StringField") %>'>
            </asp:Label>
        </ItemTemplate>
```

```
                    <EditItemTemplate>
                        <asp:TextBox runat="server"
                            id="stringFieldTextBox"
                            Text='<%# DataBinder.Eval(Container,
                                "DataItem.StringField") %>'>
                        </asp:TextBox>
                    </EditItemTemplate>
                    <FooterTemplate>
                        <asp:TextBox runat="server" id="NewStringFieldTextBox">
                        </asp:TextBox>
                    </FooterTemplate>
                </asp:TemplateField>
            </Columns>
        </asp:GridView>
    </div>
    </form>
</body>
</html>
```

The C# code-behind code in *Default.aspx.cs* in the project UpdateDataWebFormGridView is shown in Example 8-14. The solution fills a DataTable with records from the GridView table in the LoadData( ) method and stores the DataTable to the Session object. The DataTable is bound to the GridView.

The code-behind file contains the following methods and event handlers:

UpdateDataSource( )
> This method creates a DataAdapter and uses it with updating logic generated by a CommandBuilder to update the data source with changes made to the cached DataTable. The updated DataTable is stored to the Session variable used to cache the data source for the DataList.

BindDataGrid( )
> This method gets the cached data from the Session variable and binds it to the DataGrid.

RowCancelingEdit
> Sets the index of the item being edited to -1 to cancel any current editing and calls BindDataGrid( ) to refresh the grid.

RowCommand
> If the AddNew button is clicked, a new row is inserted into the data cached in the Session variable and the UpdateDataSource( ) method is called to persist the change back to the data source. BindDataGrid( ) is called to refresh the grid.

RowDeleting
> Finds and deletes the specified row from the data cached in the Session variable using the RowIndex property of the event and calls the UpdateDataSource( ) method to persist the change back to the data source. BindDataGrid( ) is called to refresh the grid.

RowEditing

Sets the index of the item being edited to the index of the row corresponding to the Edit button using the NewEditIndex property of the event. This puts that row into edit mode and calls BindDataGrid( ) to refresh the grid.

RowUpdating

Finds and updates the specified row in the data cached in the Session variable and calls the UpdateDataSource( ) method to persist the change back to the data source. BindDataGrid( ) is called to refresh the grid.

Example 8-14. File: Default.aspx.cs for UpdateDataWebFormGridView solution

```csharp
using System;
using System.Data;
using System.Data.SqlClient;
using System.Web.UI.WebControls;

namespace UpdateDataWebFormGridView
{
    public partial class _Default : System.Web.UI.Page
    {
        private string sqlConnectString = @"Data Source=(local);
                Integrated security=SSPI;Initial Catalog=AdoDotNet35Cookbook;";
        private string sqlSelect = "SELECT Id, IntField, StringField FROM GridView";

        protected void Page_Load(object sender, EventArgs e)
        {
            if (!Page.IsPostBack)
            {
                // configure and bind data to GridView control
                gridView.DataSource = LoadData();
                gridView.DataKeyNames = new string[] { "Id" };
                gridView.DataBind();
            }
        }

        protected DataTable LoadData()
        {
            // return a DataTable containing all records from GridView table
            // in the AdoDotNet35Cookbook database
            SqlDataAdapter da = new SqlDataAdapter(sqlSelect, sqlConnectString);

            DataTable dt = new DataTable();
            da.FillSchema(dt, SchemaType.Source);
            da.Fill(dt);

            Session["GridViewDataTable"] = dt;

            return dt;
        }

        private void UpdateDataSource(DataTable dt)
        {
```

Example 8-14. File: Default.aspx.cs for UpdateDataWebFormGridView solution (continued)

```
        // Update the data source with changes to the table.
        SqlDataAdapter da = new SqlDataAdapter(sqlSelect, sqlConnectString);
        SqlCommandBuilder cb = new SqlCommandBuilder(da);
        da.Update(dt);

        // Store updated data in session variable to store data between
        // posts to server.
        Session["GridViewDataTable"] = dt;
    }

    private void BindDataGrid()
    {
        // Get the data from the session variable.
        DataTable dt = ((DataTable)Session["GridViewDataTable"]);

        // Bind the data view to the data grid.
        gridView.DataSource = dt;
        gridView.DataBind();
    }

    protected void gridView_RowCancelingEdit(object sender,
        System.Web.UI.WebControls.GridViewCancelEditEventArgs e)
    {
        // Set the index of the item being edited out of range.
        gridView.EditIndex = -1;

        BindDataGrid();
    }

    protected void gridView_RowCommand(object sender,
        System.Web.UI.WebControls.GridViewCommandEventArgs e)
    {
        if (e.CommandName.Equals("AddNew"))
        {
            // Get the data from the session variable.
            DataTable dt = (DataTable)Session["GridViewDataTable"];

            // Add the new row.
            DataRow dr = dt.NewRow();

            dr["Id"] =
                ((TextBox)gridView.FooterRow.FindControl("NewIdTextBox")).Text;
            dr["IntField"] =
                ((TextBox)gridView.FooterRow.FindControl("NewIntFieldTextBox")).Text;
            dr["StringField"] =
                ((TextBox)gridView.FooterRow.FindControl(
                "NewStringFieldTextBox")).Text;

            dt.Rows.Add(dr);
```

```csharp
            // Update the data source with the changes to the table.
            UpdateDataSource(dt);

            BindDataGrid();
        }
    }

    protected void gridView_RowDeleting(object sender,
        System.Web.UI.WebControls.GridViewDeleteEventArgs e)
    {
        // Get the data from the session variable.
        DataTable dt = (DataTable)Session["GridViewDataTable"];

        // Get the ID of the row to delete.
        int id = (int)gridView.DataKeys[e.RowIndex].Value;

        // Delete the row from the table.
        dt.Rows.Find(id).Delete();

        // Update the data source with the changes to the table.
        UpdateDataSource(dt);

        BindDataGrid();
    }

    protected void gridView_RowEditing(object sender,
        System.Web.UI.WebControls.GridViewEditEventArgs e)
    {
        // Set the row being edited
        gridView.EditIndex = e.NewEditIndex;

        BindDataGrid();
    }

    protected void gridView_RowUpdating(object sender, GridViewUpdateEventArgs e)
    {
        // Get the data from the session variable.
        DataTable dt = (DataTable)Session["GridViewDataTable"];

        // Update data for edits
        DataRow row =
            dt.Rows.Find(((TextBox)gridView.Rows[e.RowIndex].FindControl(
            "idTextBox")).Text);
        row["IntField"] =
            ((TextBox)gridView.Rows[e.RowIndex].FindControl(
            "intFieldTextBox")).Text;
        row["StringField"] =
            ((TextBox)gridView.Rows[e.RowIndex].FindControl(
            "stringFieldTextBox")).Text;
```

Example 8-14. File: Default.aspx.cs for UpdateDataWebFormGridView solution (continued)

```
            // Update the data source with the changes to the table.
            UpdateDataSource(dt);

            gridView.EditIndex = -1;

            BindDataGrid( );
        }
    }
}
```

The output is shown in Figure 8-14.

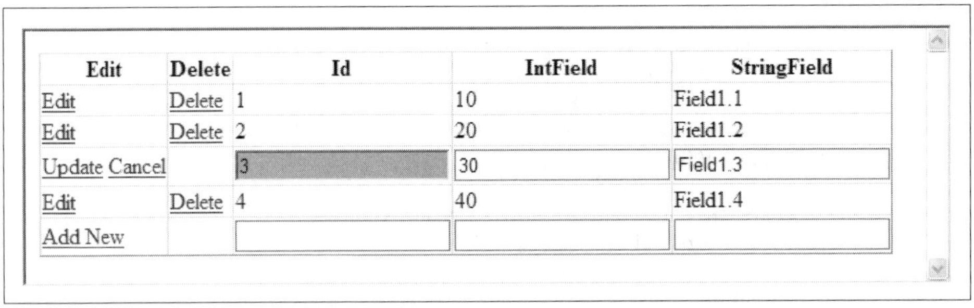
Edit
Delete
Id
IntField
StringField
Edit
Delete
1
10
Field1.1
Edit
Delete
2
20
Field1.2
Update
Cancel
3
30
Field1.3
Edit
Delete
4
40
Field1.4
Add New

Figure 8-14. Output for UpdateDataWebFormGridView solution

Discussion

While Recipe 8.6 looks at the fundamentals of binding and displaying data using a Web Forms `GridView` control, this recipe shows how to delete, edit, change, and insert data into the `DataGrid` control and how to update the data source with the changes made.

By default, the `GridView` displays tabular data in read-only mode. With in-place editing configured, the runtime `GridView` displays two additional link button columns—`Edit` and `Delete`—for each row. When the `Delete` button is clicked, the row is deleted from the data source for the data grid. If the `Edit` button is clicked, it is replaced with `Update` and `Cancel` buttons, and the row is put into edit mode where text boxes appear in the cells allowing the values for the row to be edited. When the `Cancel` button is pressed, the row returns to the default appearance with an `Edit` button. When `Update` is pressed, the data source is updated with the changes made to the row and the row returns to the default appearance.

The `GridView` supports automatic default editing for certain data sources such as the `SqlDataSource` and `ObjectDataSource` control. Other data sources (such as the one in this example) do not automatically support in-place editing, and require some coding.

Use the smart tag panel to set up a GridView for in-place editing for these data sources by adding the required editing buttons to templates. Event handlers must then to be added to handle DataGrid events to enable in-place editing. Table 8-10 describes the events and associated generic event-handling code.

Table 8-10. DataGrid event handler responses

Event	Handler response
RowCancelingEdit	Cancel button for the row in edit mode is clicked.
RowCommand	A button is clicked in the GridView control.
RowDeleting	Delete button for a row is clicked.
RowEditing	Edit button for a row is clicked.
RowUpdating	Update button for a row in edit mode is clicked.

The example code for the solution shows actual implementations for these handlers.

The Web Forms GridView does not automatically support batch updates. To batch the updates, persist the changes to the Session variable with the following code when each change is made, rather than calling the UpdateDataSource( ) method:

```
// Store updated data in session variable to store data between
// posts to server.
Session["DataSource"] = dt;
```

Then call the UpdateDataSource( ) method when you want to update the data source with all changes made.

The Web Forms GridView does not natively support inserting records. The example shows one way to insert a record outside of the GridView and add it to the GridView.

8.8   Binding Data to a Web Forms FormView Control

Problem

You need to bind a result set to a FormView control and page through the data.

Solution

Follow these steps:

1. The solution uses a table named FormView in the AdoDotNet35Cookbook database. Execute the following T-SQL statement to create the table:

```
USE AdoDotNet35Cookbook
GO
CREATE TABLE FormView(
    Id int NOT NULL PRIMARY KEY,
    IntField int NULL,
    StringField nvarchar(50) NULL )
```

2. Execute the following T-SQL batch to create the sample data required by the solution:

```
USE AdoDotNet35Cookbook
GO
INSERT INTO FormView VALUES (1, 10, 'StringValue1')
INSERT INTO FormView VALUES (2, 20, 'StringValue2')
INSERT INTO FormView VALUES (3, 30, 'StringValue3')
INSERT INTO FormView VALUES (4, 40, 'StringValue4')
```

3. Create a C# ASP.NET web application named BindWebFormFormView.

4. Add the following controls to the *Default.aspx* design surface:

   • FormView named formView. Select Auto Format → Classic from the smart tag panel.

The completed layout of the Web Form page *Default.aspx* is shown in Figure 8-15.

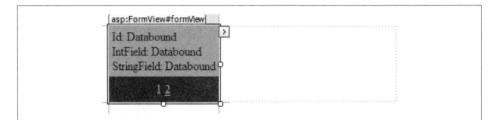

Figure 8-15. Layout for Default.aspx in BindWebFormFormView solution

Example 8-15 shows the code in *Default.aspx* in the project BindWebFormFormView.

Example 8-15. File: Default.aspx for BindWebFormFormView solution

```
<%@ Page Language="C#" AutoEventWireup="true" CodeBehind="Default.aspx.cs"
    Inherits="BindWebFormFormView._Default" %>
<!DOCTYPE html PUBLIC "-//W3C//DTD XHTML 1.0 Transitional//EN"
    "http://www.w3.org/TR/xhtml1/DTD/xhtml1-transitional.dtd">

<html xmlns="http://www.w3.org/1999/xhtml" >
<head runat="server">
    <title>Untitled Page</title>
</head>
<body>
    <form id="form1" runat="server">
    <div>
    <asp:FormView ID="formView" runat="server" CellPadding="4" ForeColor="#333333"
        AllowPaging="True" onpageindexchanging="formView_PageIndexChanging">
        <footerstyle backcolor="#507CD1" font-bold="True" forecolor="White" />
        <rowstyle backcolor="#EFF3FB" />
        <itemtemplate>
            Id: <%# DataBinder.Eval(Container.DataItem, "Id") %><br />
            IntField: <%# DataBinder.Eval(Container.DataItem, "IntField") %><br />
            StringField: <%# DataBinder.Eval(Container.DataItem, "StringField") %>
        </itemtemplate>
```

```
        <pagerstyle backcolor="#2461BF" forecolor="White" horizontalalign="Center" />
        <headerstyle backcolor="#507CD1" font-bold="True" forecolor="White" />
        <editrowstyle backcolor="#2461BF" />
    </asp:FormView>
    </div>
    </form>
</body>
</html>
```

The C# code-behind code in *Default.aspx.cs* in the project BindWebFormFormView is shown in Example 8-16. The solution fills a DataTable with the FormView table in the AdoDotNt35Cookbook database and stores it to the Session object. The DataTable is bound to the FormView control. The event handler for the PageIndexChanging event of the FormView sets the new page index, sets the data source of the FormView to the DataTable in the Session object, and binds the FormView control.

Example 8-16. File: Default.aspx.cs for BindWebFormFormView solution

```
using System;
using System.Data;
using System.Data.SqlClient;

namespace BindWebFormFormView
{
    public partial class _Default : System.Web.UI.Page
    {
        private string sqlConnectString = @"Data Source=(local);
            Integrated security=SSPI;Initial Catalog=AdoDotNet35Cookbook;";
        private string sqlSelect = "SELECT Id, IntField, StringField FROM FormView";

        protected void Page_Load(object sender, EventArgs e)
        {
            formView.DataSource = LoadData();
            formView.DataKeyNames = new string[] { "Id" };
            DataBind();
        }

        protected DataTable LoadData()
        {
            SqlDataAdapter da = new SqlDataAdapter(sqlSelect, sqlConnectString);
            DataTable dt = new DataTable();

            da.FillSchema(dt, SchemaType.Source);
            da.Fill(dt);

            // Store data in session variable to store data between
            // posts to server.
            Session["DataSource"] = dt;

            return dt;
        }
```

```
protected void formView_PageIndexChanging(object sender,
    System.Web.UI.WebControls.FormViewPageEventArgs e)
{
    formView.PageIndex = e.NewPageIndex;
    formView.DataSource = (DataTable)Session["DataSource"];
    formView.DataBind();
}
}
}
```

The output is shown in Figure 8-16.

Figure 8-16. Output for BindWebFormFormView solution

Discussion

The FormView control displays a single record from a data source a flexible, highly configurable format. You use templates similarly to the DataList or GridView controls to control the formatting of the output. The FormView control loops through the fields in the data record and uses the templates to render the results. The FormView control supports the templates listed in Table 8-11.

Table 8-11. FormView templates

Template	Description
ItemTemplate	HTML markup and controls that are rendered for a data row in read-only mode.
InsertItemTemplate	HTML markup and controls that are rendered for new data row.
EditItemTemplate	HTML markup and controls that are rendered for a data row in edit mode.

The FormView control raises the events listed in Table 8-12 when the current record is displayed or changed.

Table 8-12. FormView events

Event	Description
PageIndexChanging	Raised when a pager button is clicked, before the FormView performs the paging operation.
PageIndexChanged	Raised when a pager button is clicked, after the FormView performs the paging operation.
ItemCommand	Raised when a button in the FormView is clicked.

Table 8-12. FormView events (continued)

Event	Description
ItemCreated	Raised after all `FormViewRow` objects are created in the `FormView` control.
ItemDeleting	Raised when a `Delete` button is clicked, before the `FormView` deletes the record.
ItemDeleted	Raised when a `Delete` button is clicked, after the `FormView` deletes the record.
ItemInserting	Raised when an `Insert` button is clicked, before the `FormView` inserts the record.
ItemInserted	Raised when an `Insert` button is clicked, after the `FormView` inserts the record.
ItemUpdating	Raised when an `Update` button is clicked, before the `FormView` updates the record.
ItemUpdated	Raised when an `Update` button is clicked, after the `FormView` updates the record.
ModeChanging	Raised before the `FormView` control changes modes between edit, insert, and read-only.
ModeChanged	Raised after the `FormView` control changes modes between edit, insert, and read-only.
DataBound	Raised after the `FormView` has finished binding to the data source.

You need to bind the FormView to a data control such as a SqlDataSource or ObjectDataSource. You can also bind a FormView to classes including DataReader, DataSet, DataTable, or DataView—any class that implements the IEnumerable interface can be bound. The easiest way to create a FormView control is to drag the FormView control onto the web page design surface.

8.9   Synchronizing Master-Detail Data in a Web Forms Application

Problem

You need to create a master-detail pair of GridView controls and synchronize them so that when you select a record in the master, the child grid is updated with the corresponding records.

Solution

Fill a DataSet with results from both tables, and create the master-detail relation before binding the GridView controls to the DataSet. Handle the SelectedIndexChanged event in the parent GridView and set the source for the child GridView to the set of related child records using the CreateChildView( ) method.

Follow these steps:

1. Create a C# ASP.NET web application named MasterDetailWebFormDataGrid.

2. Add the following controls to the *Default.aspx* design surface:
   - GridView named headerGridView
   - GridView named detailGridView

The completed layout of the Web Form page *Default.aspx* is shown in Figure 8-17.

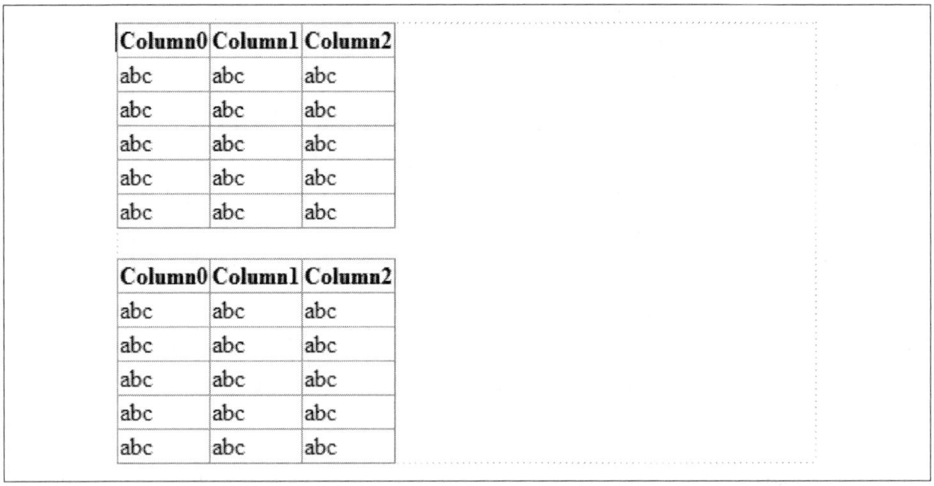

Column0	Column1	Column2
abc	abc	abc
abc	abc	abc
abc	abc	abc
abc	abc	abc
abc	abc	abc

Column0	Column1	Column2
abc	abc	abc
abc	abc	abc
abc	abc	abc
abc	abc	abc
abc	abc	abc

Figure 8-17. Layout for Default.aspx in MasterDetailWebFormDataGrid solution

The code in *Default.aspx* in the project `MasterDetailWebFormDataGrid` is shown in Example 8-17.

Example 8-17. File: Default.aspx for MasterDetailWebFormDataGrid solution

```
<%@ Page Language="C#" AutoEventWireup="true" CodeBehind="Default.aspx.cs"
    Inherits="MasterDetailWebFormDataGrid._Default" %>
<!DOCTYPE html PUBLIC "-//W3C//DTD XHTML 1.0 Transitional//EN"
    "http://www.w3.org/TR/xhtml1/DTD/xhtml1-transitional.dtd">

<html xmlns="http://www.w3.org/1999/xhtml" >
<head runat="server">
    <title>Untitled Page</title>
</head>
<body>
    <form id="form1" runat="server">
    <div>
        <asp:GridView ID="headerGridView" runat="server"
            onselectedindexchanged="headerGridView_SelectedIndexChanged">
        </asp:GridView>
        <br />
        <asp:GridView ID="detailGridView" runat="server">
        </asp:GridView>
    </div>
    </form>
</body>
</html>
```

The C# code-behind code in *Default.aspx.cs* in the project MasterDetailWebFormDataGrid is shown in Example 8-18. The solution creates a DataSet that contains a subset of Sales.SalesOrderHeader and Sales.SalesOrderDetail records from the AdventureWorks database. A data relationship is created between the two DataTable objects in the DataSet. The DataSet is stored to the Session object. The DataSource for the header grid view is set to the default view of the SalesOrderHeader DataTable.

The SelectedIndexChanged handler for the header grid view sets the source for the child GridView to the set of related child records using the CreateChildView( ) method whenever the selected row is changed in the header grid view.

Example 8-18. File: Default.aspx.cs for MasterDetailWebFormDataGrid solution

```
using System;
using System.Data;
using System.Data.SqlClient;

namespace MasterDetailWebFormDataGrid
{
    public partial class _Default : System.Web.UI.Page
    {
        protected void Page_Load(object sender, EventArgs e)
        {
            if (!Page.IsPostBack)
            {
                headerGridView.AutoGenerateSelectButton = true;
                headerGridView.SelectedRowStyle.BackColor = System.Drawing.Color.Gray;

                DataSet ds = LoadData( );

                // Bind the SalesOrderHeader GridView.
                headerGridView.DataSource = ds.Tables["SalesOrderHeader"].DefaultView;
                headerGridView.DataKeyNames = new string[] { "SalesOrderID" };

                Page.DataBind( );
            }
        }

        protected DataSet LoadData( )
        {
            string sqlConnectString = @"Data Source=(local);
                Integrated security=SSPI;Initial Catalog=AdventureWorks;";

            string sqlSelect =
                @"SELECT SalesOrderID, OrderDate, SalesOrderNumber, TotalDue
                FROM Sales.SalesOrderHeader
                WHERE SalesOrderID BETWEEN 43660 AND 43669;
                SELECT SalesOrderID, SalesOrderDetailID, OrderQty, ProductID, LineTotal
                FROM Sales.SalesOrderDetail
                WHERE SalesOrderID BETWEEN 43660 AND 43669;";
```

```
            SqlDataAdapter da = new SqlDataAdapter(sqlSelect, sqlConnectString);
            da.TableMappings.Add("Table", "SalesOrderHeader");
            da.TableMappings.Add("Table1", "SalesOrderDetail");
            DataSet ds = new DataSet();
            da.Fill(ds);

            // Add a relation between parent and child table.
            ds.Relations.Add("FK_SalesOrderDetail_SalesOrderHeader",
                ds.Tables["SalesOrderHeader"].Columns["SalesOrderID"],
                ds.Tables["SalesOrderDetail"].Columns["SalesOrderID"]);

            // Store data in session variable to store data between
            // posts to server.
            Session["SalesOrderDataSet"] = ds;

            return ds;
        }

        protected void headerGridView_SelectedIndexChanged(object sender, EventArgs e)
        {
            if (headerGridView.SelectedIndex != -1)
            {
                int salesOrderID =
                    (int)headerGridView.DataKeys[headerGridView.SelectedIndex].Value;

                // Get the SalesOrderHeader data view from the session variable.
                DataView headerDV =
                    ((DataSet)Session["SalesOrderDataSet"]).
                    Tables["SalesOrderHeader"].DefaultView;

                // Get the selected DataRowView from the SalesOrderHeader table.
                headerDV.Sort = "SalesOrderID";
                DataRowView headerDRV = headerDV[headerDV.Find(salesOrderID)]; ;

                // Bind the child view to the Order Details data grid.
                detailGridView.DataSource =
                    headerDRV.CreateChildView("FK_SalesOrderDetail_SalesOrderHeader");
            }
            else
            {
                detailGridView.DataSource = null;
            }

            detailGridView.DataBind();
        }
    }
}
```

The output is shown in Figure 8-18.

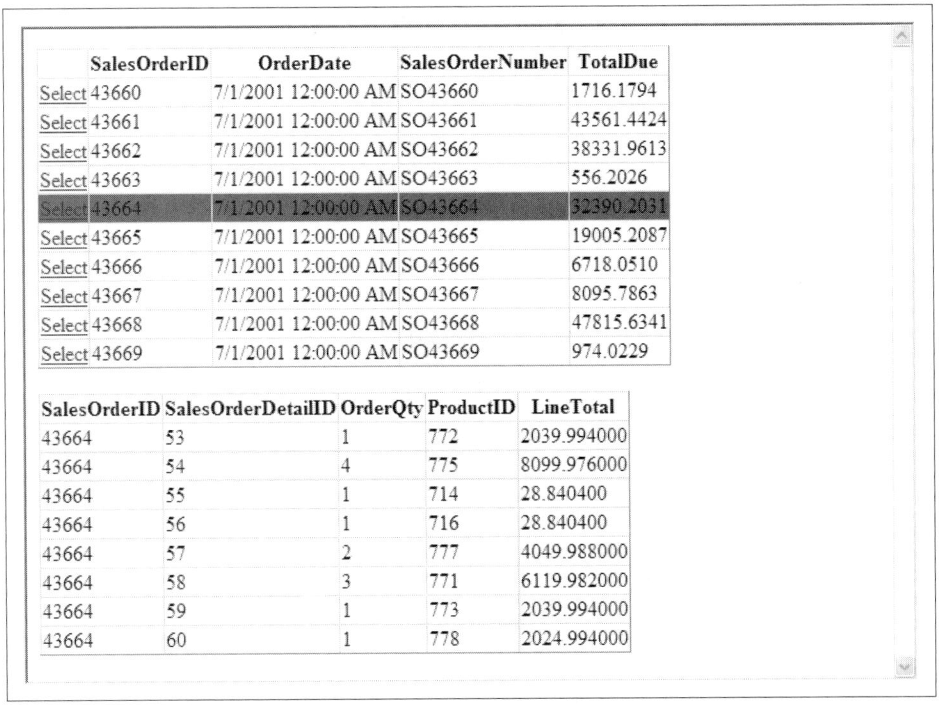

	SalesOrderID	OrderDate	SalesOrderNumber	TotalDue
Select	43660	7/1/2001 12:00:00 AM	SO43660	1716.1794
Select	43661	7/1/2001 12:00:00 AM	SO43661	43561.4424
Select	43662	7/1/2001 12:00:00 AM	SO43662	38331.9613
Select	43663	7/1/2001 12:00:00 AM	SO43663	556.2026
Select	43664	7/1/2001 12:00:00 AM	SO43664	32390.2031
Select	43665	7/1/2001 12:00:00 AM	SO43665	19005.2087
Select	43666	7/1/2001 12:00:00 AM	SO43666	6718.0510
Select	43667	7/1/2001 12:00:00 AM	SO43667	8095.7863
Select	43668	7/1/2001 12:00:00 AM	SO43668	47815.6341
Select	43669	7/1/2001 12:00:00 AM	SO43669	974.0229

SalesOrderID	SalesOrderDetailID	OrderQty	ProductID	LineTotal
43664	53	1	772	2039.994000
43664	54	4	775	8099.976000
43664	55	1	714	28.840400
43664	56	1	716	28.840400
43664	57	2	777	4049.988000
43664	58	3	771	6119.982000
43664	59	1	773	2039.994000
43664	60	1	778	2024.994000

Figure 8-18. Output for MasterDetailWebFormDataGrid solution

Discussion

The Web Forms GridView control does not inherently support master-detail views of data. You must use two Web Forms GridView controls and programmatically synchronize them.

The master and child data GridView controls in this solution each display one DataTable from a DataSet. Displaying and paging through the data in each of the grids is the same as shown in Recipe 8.6.

The SelectedIndexChanged event handler keeps the two data grids synchronized. When a new item is selected in the header GridView, the details data is retrieved from the cached data in the Session variable. The SalesOrderID is obtained from the DataKeys collection for the selected row and used to create a child DataView of the SalesOrderDetail records that is then bound to the sales order details GridView.

8.10 Displaying an Image from a Database in a Web Forms Control

Problem

You need to display an image from a database field in an ASP.NET control.

Solution

Fill an ASP.NET Image control from a database field by pointing the ImageUrl property of an Image control to a second web page that retrieves the image from the database and streams it back to the caller.

Follow these steps:

1. Create a C# ASP.NET web application named BindWebFormSimpleControl.

2. Add the following control to the *Default.aspx* design surface:

   - Image control named productPhotoImage

The completed layout of the Web Form page *Default.aspx* is shown in Figure 8-19.

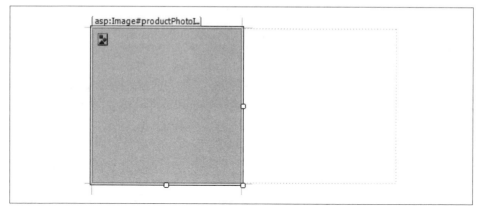

Figure 8-19. Layout for Default.aspx in LoadImageIntoWebFormControl solution

The code in *Default.aspx* in the project LoadImageIntoWebFormControl is shown in Example 8-19.

Example 8-19. File: Default.aspx for LoadImageIntoWebFormControl solution

```
<%@ Page Language="C#" AutoEventWireup="true" CodeBehind="Default.aspx.cs"
    Inherits="LoadImageIntoWebFormControl._Default" %>
<!DOCTYPE html PUBLIC "-//W3C//DTD XHTML 1.0 Transitional//EN"
    "http://www.w3.org/TR/xhtml1/DTD/xhtml1-transitional.dtd">
```

Example 8-19. File: Default.aspx for LoadImageIntoWebFormControl solution (continued)

```
<html xmlns="http://www.w3.org/1999/xhtml" >
<head runat="server">
    <title>Untitled Page</title>
</head>
<body>
    <form id="form1" runat="server">
    <div>
        <asp:Image ID="productPhotoImage" runat="server" Height="200px" Width="200px" />
    </div>
    </form>
</body>
</html>
```

3. Create the C# code-behind code in *Default.aspx.cs* in the project
   LoadImageIntoWebFormControl is shown in Example 8-20. The code sets the
   ImageUrl property of the productPhotoImage Image control to the web page that
   serves the image—a parameter passed in the URL indicates the employee ID to
   retrieve.

Example 8-20. File: Default.aspx.cs for LoadImageIntoWebFormControl solution

```
using System;
using System.Web.UI.WebControls;

namespace LoadImageIntoWebFormControl
{
    public partial class _Default : System.Web.UI.Page
    {
        protected void Page_Load(object sender, EventArgs e)
        {
            productPhotoImage.Width = Unit.Pixel(240);
            productPhotoImage.Height = Unit.Pixel(149);

            // Set the image URL to the page containing just the image.
            productPhotoImage.ImageUrl = "RetrieveImage.aspx?productPhotoID=100";
        }
    }
}
```

4. Add a new Web Form to the project. Name the Web Form *RetrieveImage.aspx*.

5. Create the C# code-behind code in *RetrieveImage.aspx.cs* in the project
   LoadImageIntoWebFormControl is shown in Example 8-21. The code retrieves the
   image from the database for the specified product photo ID. The image is served
   by setting the HTTP MIME type of the output stream to *image/gif* and writing the
   image to the stream.

Example 8-21. File: RetrieveImage.aspx.cs

```
using System;
using System.Data;
using System.Data.SqlClient;

namespace LoadImageIntoWebFormControl
{
    public partial class RetrieveImage : System.Web.UI.Page
    {
        protected void Page_Load(object sender, EventArgs e)
        {
            string sqlConnectString = @"Data Source=(local);
                Integrated security=SSPI;Initial Catalog=AdventureWorks;";

            // Set the query to retrieve the image for the specified
            // ProductPhotoID
            string sqlSelect = @"SELECT LargePhoto FROM Production.ProductPhoto
                WHERE ProductPhotoID = " + Request.QueryString["productPhotoId"];

            // Retrieve the specified image using ExecuteScalar()
            SqlConnection connection = new SqlConnection(sqlConnectString);
            SqlCommand command = new SqlCommand(sqlSelect, connection);
            connection.Open();
            byte[] largePhoto = (byte[])command.ExecuteScalar();
            connection.Close();

            // Set the response content type type.
            Response.ContentType = "image/gif";
            // Stream the binary image data in the response.
            Response.BinaryWrite(largePhoto);
        }
    }
}
```

The output is shown in Figure 8-20.

Figure 8-20. Output for LoadImageIntoWebFormControl solution

Discussion

Rendering an image from a database in a Web Forms Image control is easy to do, but not straightforward. Fortunately, it is much simpler with ASP.NET than it was in ASP.

Two web pages are required: one that contains the user interface that the client sees and one that retrieves the required image from the database and serves it to the Image control on the web page that the client sees. The following steps outline the required tasks:

1. Create a web page that outputs a binary stream containing the image from the database.

2. Create a SQL statement to retrieve the required image from the database and retrieve the image using a DataReader. A DataTable or DataSet filled using a DataAdapter can also be used.

3. Set the ContentType property of the HttpResponse object to the MIME type of the image in the database. The ContentType property of the HttpResponse object gets or sets the MIME type of the output stream. The default value is *text/html*, but other types can be specified to output:

   ```
   Response.ContentType = "image/gif";
   ```

4. Use the BinaryWrite( ) method of the HttpResponse object to output the image as a binary stream. The BinaryWrite( ) method of the HttpResponse object writes a stream of binary characters to the HTTP output stream rather than a textual stream:

   ```
   Response.BinaryWrite(largePhoto);
   ```

The ImageUrl property of the Image control gets or sets the location of the image to display in the control. The location can be specified as either an absolute or relative URL. Set the ImageUrl property of the Image control in the web page that the client sees to the web page that outputs the image from the database as a binary stream.

8.11 Localizing Client-Side Data in a Web Forms Application

Problem

You need to format dates and currency values according to the culture of the client rather than the server.

Solution

Use client culture and encoding to return data to the client formatted according to the client's localization settings rather than the server's settings.

Follow these steps:

1. Create a C# ASP.NET web application named `LocalizeWebFormsApplication`.

2. Add the following controls to the *Default.aspx* design surface:

   - `RadioButtonList` named `cultureRadioButton`. Add four members: en-US, en-CA, ja-JP, and fr-FR.

   - `Label` named `cultureNameLabel`. Add the text `CultureName:` in front of the label control as the description.

   - `Label` named `cultureEnglishNameLabel`. Add the text `CultureEnglishName:` in front of the label control as the description.

   - `Label` named `cultureNativeNameLabel`. Add the text `CultureNativeName:` in front of the label as the description.

   - `Label` named `dateLabel:`. Add the text `Date:` in front of the label as the description.

   - `Label` named `shortDateLabel:`. Add the text `ShortDate:` in front of the label as the description.

   - `Label` named `numberLabel:`. Add the text `Number:` in front of the label as the description.

   - `Label` named `currencyLabel:`. Add the text `Currency:` in front of the label as the description.

The completed layout of the Web Form page *Default.aspx* is shown in Figure 8-21.

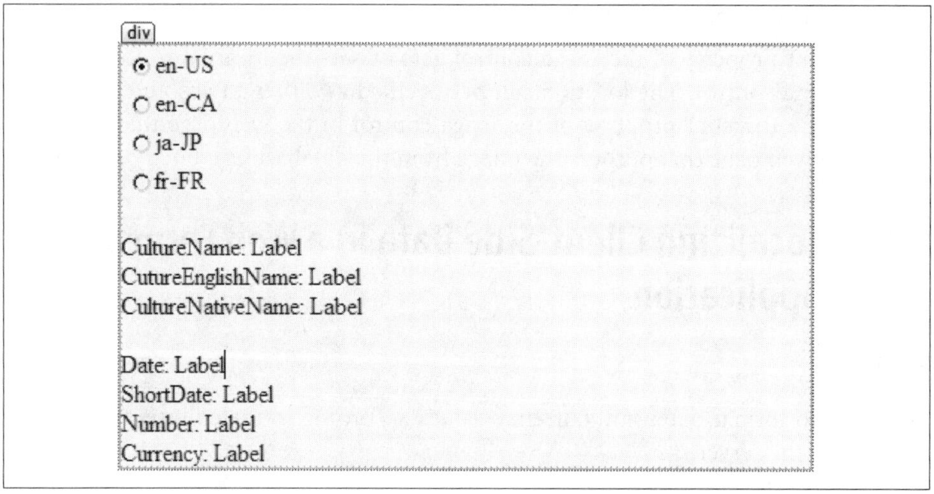

Figure 8-21. Layout for Default.aspx in LocalizeWebFormApplication solution

The code in *Default.aspx* in the project `LocalizeWebFormApplication` is shown in Example 8-22.

Example 8-22. File: Default.aspx for LocalizeWebFormApplication solution

```
<%@ Page Language="C#" AutoEventWireup="true" CodeBehind="Default.aspx.cs"
    Inherits="LocalizeWebFormApplication._Default" %>
<!DOCTYPE html PUBLIC "-//W3C//DTD XHTML 1.0 Transitional//EN"
    "http://www.w3.org/TR/xhtml1/DTD/xhtml1-transitional.dtd">

<html xmlns="http://www.w3.org/1999/xhtml" >
<head runat="server">
    <title>Untitled Page</title>
</head>
<body>
    <form id="form1" runat="server">
    <div>
        <asp:RadioButtonList ID="cultureRadioButton" runat="server">
            <asp:ListItem Selected="True" Value="en-US">en-US</asp:ListItem>
            <asp:ListItem Value="en-CA"></asp:ListItem>
            <asp:ListItem Value="ja-JP"></asp:ListItem>
            <asp:ListItem Value="fr-FR"></asp:ListItem>
        </asp:RadioButtonList>
        <br />
        CultureName:
        <asp:Label ID="cultureNameLabel" runat="server" Text="Label"></asp:Label>
        <br />
        CutureEnglishName:
        <asp:Label ID="cultureEnglishNameLabel" runat="server" Text="Label"></asp:Label>
        <br />
        CultureNativeName:
        <asp:Label ID="cultureNativeNameLabel" runat="server" Text="Label"></asp:Label>
        <br />
        <br />
        Date:
        <asp:Label ID="dateLabel" runat="server" Text="Label"></asp:Label>
        <br />
        ShortDate:
        <asp:Label ID="shortDateLabel" runat="server" Text="Label"></asp:Label>
        <br />
        Number:
        <asp:Label ID="numberLabel" runat="server" Text="Label"></asp:Label>
        <br />
        Currency:
        <asp:Label ID="currencyLabel" runat="server" Text="Label"></asp:Label>
        </div>
    </form>
</body>
</html>
```

The C# code-behind code in *Default.aspx.cs* in the project
LocalizeWebFormApplication is shown in Example 8-23. The code creates the
CultureInformation object based on the user's settings. The RefreshData( ) method
sets the CurrentCulture for the current thread and demonstrates the effect on output
of different data types.

Example 8-23. File: Default.aspx.cs for LocalizeWebFormApplication solution

```
using System;
using System.Data;
using System.Globalization;
using System.Threading;

namespace LocalizeWebFormApplication
{
    public partial class _Default : System.Web.UI.Page
    {
        private CultureInfo ci;

        protected void Page_Load(object sender, EventArgs e)
        {
            if (!Page.IsPostBack)
            {
                cultureRadioButton.AutoPostBack = true;
            }

            // Set the culture info as specified by the user-selected
            // radio button
            ci = new CultureInfo(cultureRadioButton.SelectedItem.Value);

            RefreshData();
        }

        protected void RefreshData()
        {
            if (ci != null)
            {
                // Set the culture for the current thread.
                Thread.CurrentThread.CurrentCulture = ci;

                // Retrieve details about the culture.
                cultureNameLabel.Text = CultureInfo.CurrentCulture.Name +
                    " (" + Thread.CurrentThread.CurrentCulture.Name + ")";
                cultureEnglishNameLabel.Text =
                    CultureInfo.CurrentCulture.EnglishName;
                cultureNativeNameLabel.Text =
                    CultureInfo.CurrentCulture.NativeName;
            }

            // Sample data that might come from a database
            // displayed according to culture set by user.
            dateLabel.Text = DateTime.Now.ToString("D");
            shortDateLabel.Text = DateTime.Now.ToString("d");

            Double d = 12345.678;
            numberLabel.Text = d.ToString();

            currencyLabel.Text = d.ToString("c");
```

Example 8-23. File: Default.aspx.cs for LocalizeWebFormApplication solution (continued)

```
        }
    }
}
```

The output is shown in Figure 8-22.

```
    ○ en-US
    ○ en-CA
    ○ ja-JP
    ◉ fr-FR

    CultureName: fr-FR (fr-FR)
    CutureEnglishName: French (France)
    CultureNativeName: français (France)

    Date: lundi 3 décembre 2007
    ShortDate: 03/12/2007
    Number: 12345,678
    Currency: 12 345,68 €
```

Figure 8-22. Output for LocalizeWebFormApplication solution

Discussion

In a globally accessible application, a server can be processing requests for users around the world. Culture information for each user must be stored and made available to the server when it is processing each request from the user so that culture-specific operations are performed properly.

There are many ways to store the culture information for a user. You can store it persistently on the client in a cookie. Or you can store it in a database on the server and store it to a session variable when the client logs in or on an ad-hoc basis. No matter how the culture information is stored, it needs to be made available to the server as the client navigates through the site. For example, you can do this using session variables, the URL, or hidden fields. Once the server knows the culture of the user, it can use this information in culture-specific operations. Fortunately, .NET provides a collection of classes that makes this relatively easy.

The `System.Globalization` namespace contains classes that specify culture-related information. These classes are useful in writing globalized applications. Within this namespace, the `CultureInfo` class represents information about a specific culture and is used in culture-specific operations such as formatting numbers, currencies, and dates.

The CultureInfo class has four constructor overloads, each allowing the culture to be specified differently. The solution uses the constructor that takes the culture name in the format {*languagecode2*}-{*country | regioncode2*}, in which:

languagecode2
> Is the lowercase two-letter code derived from ISO 639-1.

country
> Is the uppercase two-letter code derived from ISO 3166. If *country* is not available, the *regioncode2* is used.

regioncode2
> Is the three-letter code derived from ISO-639-2. *regioncode2* is used when *country* is not available.

For example, the culture name for U.S. English is en-US.

Once the CultureInfo object is instantiated, you can assign it to the CurrentCulture property of the current thread by code with a SecurityPermission that has the ControlThread flag set. Setting the CurrentCulture property affects subsequent culture-specific operations; setting it to the culture of the current user results in output specific to the user's culture.

8.12 Loading Data into and Binding a Field to a Windows Forms Control

Problem

You need to load a value from a field in a result set into a Windows Forms control.

Solution

Directly assign the value to one of the control properties or add a DataBinding to the control. This solution demonstrates both techniques.

Follow these steps:

1. Create a C# Windows Forms application named LoadDataWindowsFormControl.
2. Add the following controls to the Form1 design surface:
   - Label with the Text property = DepartmentID:
   - TextBox named departmentIDTextBox
   - Label with the Text property = DepartmentName1:
   - TextBox named departmentNameTextBox1
   - Label with the Text property = DepartmentName2:
   - TextBox named departmentNameTextBox2
   - Button named getNameButton with Text property = Get Name

The completed layout of the Windows Form named Form1 is shown in Figure 8-23.

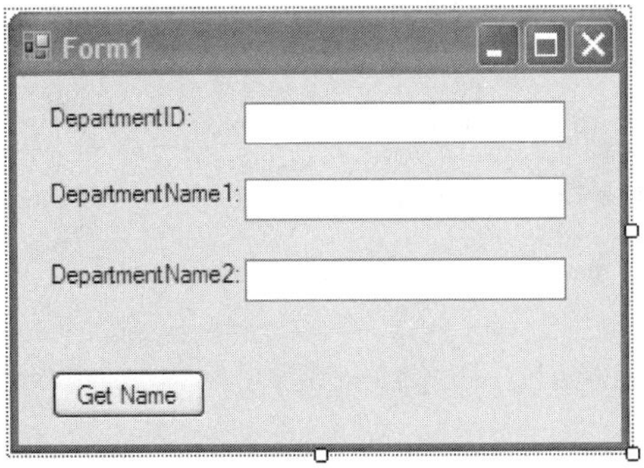

Figure 8-23. Layout for Form1 in LoadDataWindowsFormControl solution

The C# code in *Form1.cs* in the project LoadDataWindowsFormControl is shown in Example 8-24. The solution loads a DataTable with records from the HumanResources.Department table in AdventureWorks. A DataView is created from the DataTable and it sort order is set to the DepartmentID field. A BindingManager object named bm is set to the BindingContext of the DataView. A DataBinding is added to the TextBox named departmentTextBox2, binding it to the Name field in the DataView. Both department name text boxes are initialized to the Name of the first record in the DataView.

The OnClick event handler for the Button named getNameButton validates the value in the TextBox named departmentID where the user enters the DepartmentID to lookup. If it is valid, the GetDepartmentName( ) method is called. The Find( ) method of the DataView is used to locate the row in the DataView with the DepartmentID specified by the user. If it is found, the TextBox named departmentNameTextBox1 is filled directly with the name value in the DataView row and BindingManager is positioned to that record in the DataView to automatically update the value in the TextBox named departmentNameTextBox2.

Example 8-24. File: Form1.cs for LoadDataWindowsFormControl solution

```
using System;
using System.Data;
using System.Data.SqlClient;
using System.Windows.Forms;

namespace LoadDataWindowsFormControl
{
    public partial class Form1 : Form
    {
        private DataView dv = new DataView( );
        private BindingManagerBase bm;
```

```
public Form1()
{
    InitializeComponent();

    // configure the department name text boxes
    departmentNameTextBox1.ReadOnly = true;
    departmentNameTextBox2.ReadOnly = true;

    this.Load += new EventHandler(Form1_Load);
}

void Form1_Load(object sender, EventArgs e)
{
    string sqlConnectString = @"Data Source=(local);
        Integrated security=SSPI;Initial Catalog=AdventureWorks;";
    string sqlSelect = "SELECT DepartmentID, Name FROM HumanResources.Department";

    // Fill a DataTable with the Department table data
    SqlDataAdapter da = new SqlDataAdapter(sqlSelect, sqlConnectString);
    DataTable dt = new DataTable();
    da.Fill(dt);

    // Create a DataView from the table and set the sort order
    dv = dt.DefaultView;
    dv.Sort = "DepartmentID";

    // create the binding context
    bm = BindingContext[dv];

    // add a databinding for text box 2
    departmentNameTextBox2.DataBindings.Add("Text", dv, "Name");

    // initialize the text boxes
    departmentIDTextBox.Text = "1";
    GetDepartmentName(1);
}

private void GetDepartmentName(int departmentID)
{
    // Find the row in the data view with the specified department ID
    int rowIndex = dv.Find(departmentID);
    if (rowIndex == -1)
    {
        MessageBox.Show("Invalid DepartmentID", "Error",
            MessageBoxButtons.OK, MessageBoxIcon.Error);
    }
    else
    {
        departmentNameTextBox1.Text = (string)dv[rowIndex]["Name"];
        bm.Position = rowIndex;
    }
}
```

Example 8-24. File: Form1.cs for LoadDataWindowsFormControl solution (continued)

```
        private void getNameButton_Click(object sender, EventArgs e)
        {
            int departmentID;

            // Try parsing the department ID text box and get the name if success
            if (int.TryParse(departmentIDTextBox.Text, out departmentID))
            {
                GetDepartmentName(departmentID);
            }
            else
            {
                MessageBox.Show("Invalid DepartmentID", "Error",
                    MessageBoxButtons.OK, MessageBoxIcon.Error);
            }
        }
    }
}
```

The output is shown in Figure 8-24.

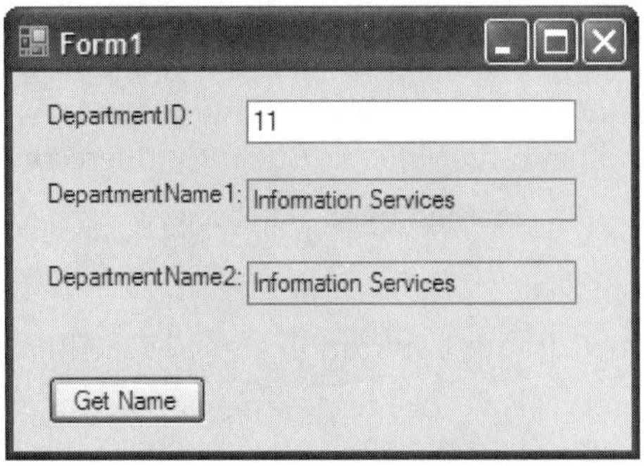

Figure 8-24. Output for LoadDataWindowsFormControl solution

Discussion

The abstract `BindingManagerBase` class synchronizes all Windows Forms controls (i.e., `Binding` objects) that are bound to the same data source so that they display information from the object within the data source, such as a row in a `DataTable`.

The `BindingContext` class is used to instantiate a `BindingManagerBase` object and either a `CurrencyManager` or `PropertyManager` object is returned, depending on the type of data source.

The `CurrencyManager` class inherits from the `BindingManagerBase` class and maintains a pointer for the current item in a data source that implements `IList`, `IListSource`, or `IBindingList`. Data sources do not necessarily support a current-item pointer. The `CurrencyManager` notifies all data-bound controls if the current item changes so that they can refresh their data.

The PropertyManager class inherits from the BindingManagerBase class and maintains the current property of an object, rather than an object in a list.

The Position property is a zero-based index that gets or sets the current position in the underlying data source list. The Count property returns the number of items in the list. The Current property returns the current object in the list, which must be cast to the type of object in the underlying data source before it can be used.

8.13   Binding Data to a Windows Forms Control

Problem

You need to populate a ComboBox from a database and bind a field in a database to the ComboBox so you can select its corresponding value.

Solution

You need to:

- Fill a ComboBox from a database (pay attention to the difference between the SelectedIndex and SelectedValue).
- Bind a ComboBox to a field in a result set so that the value is selected in the ComboBox corresponding to the value in a field for the record displayed.
- Use the selection events returned by the ComboBox.

Follow these steps:

1. Create a C# Windows Forms application named BindWindowsFormSimpleControl.
2. Add the following controls to the Form1 design surface:
    - Label with Text property = Department:
    - ComboBox named departmentComboBox

The completed layout of the Windows Form named Form1 is shown in Figure 8-25.

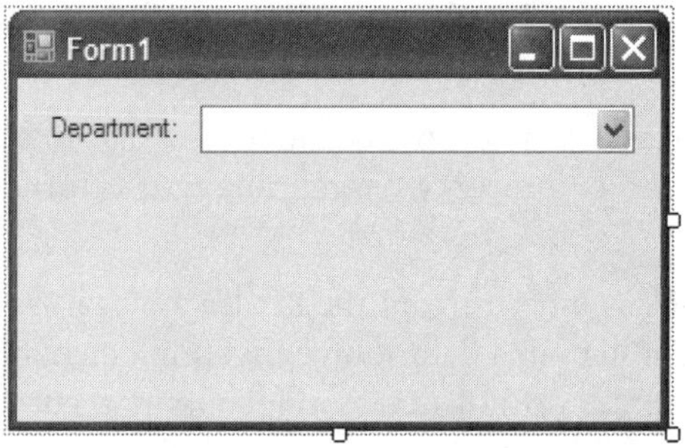

Figure 8-25. Layout for Form1 in BindWindowsFormSimpleControl solution

The C# code in *Form1.cs* in the project BindWindowsFormSimpleControl is shown in Example 8-25. The solution binds a DataView containing the DepartmentID and Name for all records in the HumanResources.Department table in AdventureWorks to the ComboBox. The handler for the SelectedIndexChanged event of the ComboBox control displays the values for the SelectedValue and SelectedText properties of the ComboBox after its selected item has changed.

Example 8-25. File: Form1.cs for BindWindowsFormSimpleControl solution

```csharp
using System;
using System.Data;
using System.Data.SqlClient;
using System.Windows.Forms;

namespace BindWindowsFormSimpleControl
{
    public partial class Form1 : Form
    {
        public Form1( )
        {
            InitializeComponent( );

            // Bind the combobox to a DataTable containing all DepartmentID and
            // Name values
            departmentComboBox.DataSource = LoadDepartmentData( );
            departmentComboBox.ValueMember = "DepartmentID";
            departmentComboBox.DisplayMember = "Name";
        }

        private DataView LoadDepartmentData( )
        {
            string sqlConnectString = @"Data Source=(local);
                Integrated security=SSPI;Initial Catalog=AdventureWorks;";
            string sqlSelect = "SELECT DepartmentID, Name FROM HumanResources.Department";

            // Fill and return a DataTable containing all DepartmentID and Name
            // values
            SqlDataAdapter da = new SqlDataAdapter(sqlSelect, sqlConnectString);
            DataTable dt = new DataTable( );
            da.Fill(dt);

            return dt.DefaultView;
        }

        private void departmentComboBox_SelectedIndexChanged(object sender, EventArgs e)
        {
            // Output the DeparmentID and name for the selected item
            string message = "Selected: [" + departmentComboBox.SelectedValue + "] " +
                ((DataRowView)departmentComboBox.Items[
                departmentComboBox.SelectedIndex])["Name"];

            MessageBox.Show(message);
```

Example 8-25. File: Form1.cs for BindWindowsFormSimpleControl solution (continued)

```
      }
   }
}
```

The output is shown in Figure 8-26.

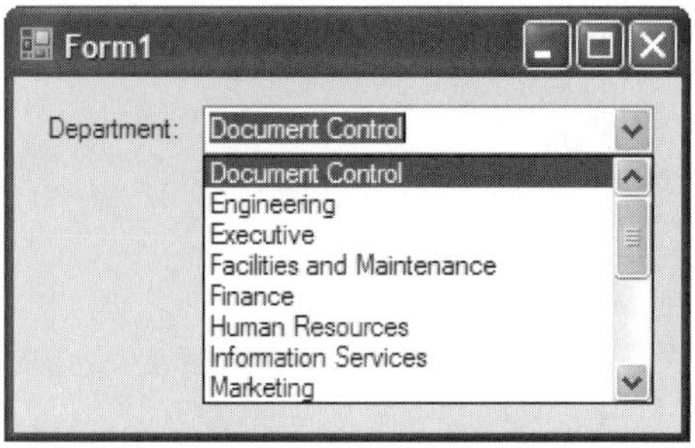

Figure 8-26. Output for BindWindowsFormSimpleControl solution

Discussion

Combo boxes are most commonly used to browse data, enter new data, or edit existing data in a data source.

There are two ways to fill a ComboBox: either use the Add( ) method or bind the ComboBox to a data source. The Windows Forms ComboBox control has three properties that are used to control data binding to an ADO.NET data source. These are described in Table 8-13.

Table 8-13. ComboBox properties for data binding

Property	Description
DataSource	Gets or sets the data source for the control. This can be a DataTable, DataView, or any class that implements the IList interface.
DisplayMember	Gets or sets the property of the data source that is displayed in the control. In a DataTable or DataView, this is the name of a column.
ValueMember	Gets or sets the property of the data source that supplies the value for the control. In a DataTable or DataView, this is the name of a column. The default is an empty string.

The SelectionIndexChange event raised by the ComboBox occurs when the item selected is changed. The event handler receives an EventArgs argument. You can use the handler for the event to get the new value of the ComboBox once it has been changed.

8.14   Binding Data to a Windows Forms DataGridView Control

Problem

You need to bind a result set to a tabular Windows Form control.

Solution

Use the DataGridView control as shown in this solution.

Follow these steps:

1. Create a C# Windows Forms application named BindWindowsFormDataGridView.
2. Add the following control to the Form1 design surface:

   • DataGridView named contactDataGridView

   The completed layout of the Windows Form named Form1 is shown in Figure 8-27.

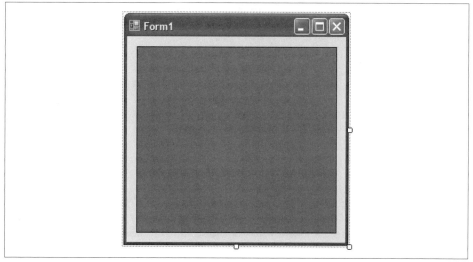

Figure 8-27. Layout for Form1 in BindWindowsFormDataGridView solution

The C# code in *Form1.cs* in the project BindWindowsFormDataGridView is shown in Example 8-26. The code creates a DataTable that contains the top 50 records from the Person.Contact table in AdventureWorks and binds it to the DataGridView control named contactDataGridView by setting its DataSource property to the DataTable.

Example 8-26. File: Form1.cs for BindWindowsFormDataGridView solution

```csharp
using System;
using System.Data;
using System.Data.SqlClient;
using System.Windows.Forms;

namespace BindWindowsFormDataGridView
{
    public partial class Form1 : Form
    {
        public Form1()
        {
            InitializeComponent();

            // Configure the data grid view
            contactDataGridView.Anchor = AnchorStyles.Left | AnchorStyles.Right |
                AnchorStyles.Top | AnchorStyles.Bottom;
            contactDataGridView.ReadOnly = true;
            contactDataGridView.AllowUserToAddRows = false;
            contactDataGridView.AllowUserToDeleteRows = false;
            contactDataGridView.AutoSizeColumnsMode =
                DataGridViewAutoSizeColumnsMode.AllCells;

            this.Width = 500;

            this.Load += new EventHandler(Form1_Load);
        }

        void Form1_Load(object sender, EventArgs e)
        {
            // Set the data source of the data grid view to the DataTable containing
            // details about the TOP 50 contacts
            contactDataGridView.DataSource = LoadData();
        }

        private DataTable LoadData()
        {
            string sqlConnectString = @"Data Source=(local);
                Integrated security=SSPI;Initial Catalog=AdventureWorks;";
            string sqlSelect = @"SELECT TOP 50 ContactID, FirstName, LastName
            FROM Person.Contact";

            // Retrieve and return a DataTable containing details about the TOP 50 contact
            SqlDataAdapter da = new SqlDataAdapter(sqlSelect, sqlConnectString);
            DataTable dt = new DataTable();
            da.Fill(dt);

            return dt;
        }
    }
}
```

The output is shown in Figure 8-28.

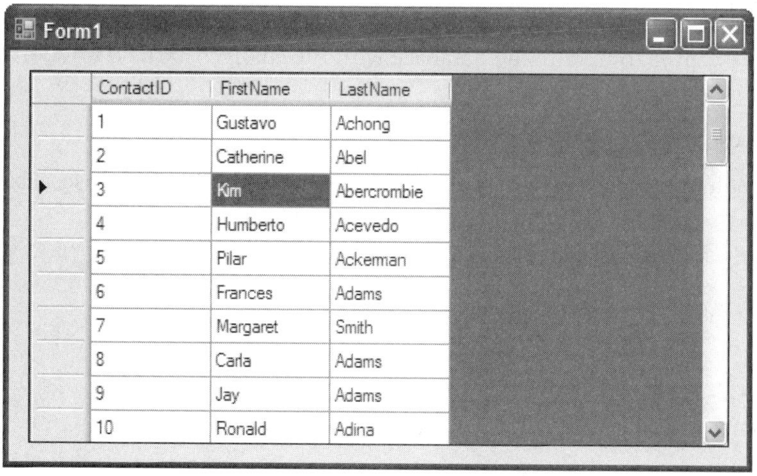

Figure 8-28. Output for BindWindowsFormDataGridView solution

Discussion

The DataGridView is a highly configurable and extensible control that displays tabular data from a variety of data sources—any class that implements the IList, IListSource, IBindingList, or IBindingListSource interface. You can also use the DataGridView in unbound mode—that is, without specifying a data source.

You bind a DataGridView control by setting its DataSource and DataMember properties at either design time or runtime. The DataMember specifies the list or table when the DataSource contains multiple lists of tables. Valid data sources for the DataGrid include DataTable, DataSet, DataView, and DataViewManager objects.

The DataGridView control dynamically reflects any changes made to the data source. If the ReadOnly property of the DataGridView is set to false, the data source is updated when changes are made to data in the DataGridView. This automatic update happens when the field being edited changes or when the EndEdit( ) method is called on the data source for the DataGridView. The data object that is bound to the DataGridView can be used to update the underlying data source.

8.15   Modifying and Updating Data in a Windows Forms DataGridView Control

Problem

You need to update a database with changes that you have made to data in a DataGridView control.

Solution

Use a DataAdapter to update the database with the changes in the data source for the DataGridView control.

Follow these steps:

1. The solution uses a table named DataGridView in the AdoDotNet35Cookbook database. Execute the following T-SQL statement to create the table:

   ```
   USE AdoDotNet35Cookbook
   GO
   CREATE TABLE DataGridView(
       Id int NOT NULL PRIMARY KEY,
       IntField int NULL,
       StringField nvarchar(50) NULL )
   ```

2. Execute the following T-SQL batch to create the sample data required by the solution:

   ```
   USE AdoDotNet35Cookbook
   GO
   INSERT INTO DataGridView VALUES (1, 10, 'Field1.1')
   INSERT INTO DataGridView VALUES (2, 20, 'Field1.2')
   INSERT INTO DataGridView VALUES (3, 30, 'Field1.3')
   INSERT INTO DataGridView VALUES (4, 40, 'Field1.4')
   ```

3. Create a C# Windows Forms application, UpdateDataWindowsFormDataGridView.

4. Add the following controls to the Form1 design surface:

   - DataGridView named dataGridView
   - Button named saveButton with Text property = Save

The completed layout of the Windows Form named Form1 is shown in Figure 8-29.

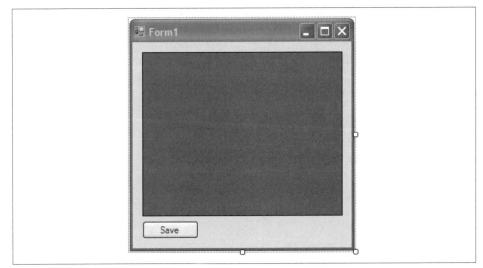

Figure 8-29. Layout for Form1 in UpdateDataWindowsFormDataGridView solution

The C# code in *Form1.cs* in the project UpdateDataWindowsFormDataGridView is shown in Example 8-27. The code creates a DataTable that contains records from the DataGridView table in the AdoDotNet35Cookbook database and binds it to the DataGridView control named dataGridView by setting its DataSource property to the DataTable. Set the Click event handler for the Button named saveButton to the saveButton_Click( ) method. This handler calls the Update( ) method of the data adapter with the DataTable that is the data source of the DataGridView control to update the database with changes made in the DataGridView.

Example 8-27. File: Form1.cs for UpdateDataWindowsFormDataGridView solution

```
using System;
using System.Data;
using System.Data.SqlClient;
using System.Windows.Forms;

namespace UpdateDataWindowsFormDataGridView
{
    public partial class Form1 : Form
    {
        private SqlDataAdapter da;
        private DataTable dt;

        public Form1( )
        {
            InitializeComponent( );

            // Configure display characteristics of the data grid view
            dataGridView.Anchor = AnchorStyles.Left | AnchorStyles.Right |
                AnchorStyles.Top | AnchorStyles.Bottom;
            this.Width = 500;

            this.Load += new EventHandler(Form1_Load);
        }

        void Form1_Load(object sender, EventArgs e)
        {
            // Set the data source of the data grid view
            dataGridView.DataSource = LoadData( );
        }

        private DataTable LoadData( )
        {
            string sqlConnectString = @"Data Source=(local);
                Integrated security=SSPI;Initial Catalog=AdoDotNet35Cookbook;";

            string sqlSelect = "SELECT Id, IntField, StringField FROM DataGridView";

            // Create a data adapter and command builder
            da = new SqlDataAdapter(sqlSelect, sqlConnectString);
            SqlCommandBuilder cb = new SqlCommandBuilder(da);
```

Example 8-27. File: Form1.cs for UpdateDataWindowsFormDataGridView solution (continued)

```
            // Load a DataTable with schema and data from table DataGridView
            dt = new DataTable( );
            da.FillSchema(dt, SchemaType.Source);
            da.Fill(dt);

            return dt;
        }

        private void saveButton_Click(object sender, EventArgs e)
        {
            // Call the Update( ) method of the DataAdapter to update the database
            da.Update(dt);
            MessageBox.Show("Changes saved.", "DataGridView",
                MessageBoxButtons.OK, MessageBoxIcon.Information);
        }
    }
}
```

The output is shown in Figure 8-30.

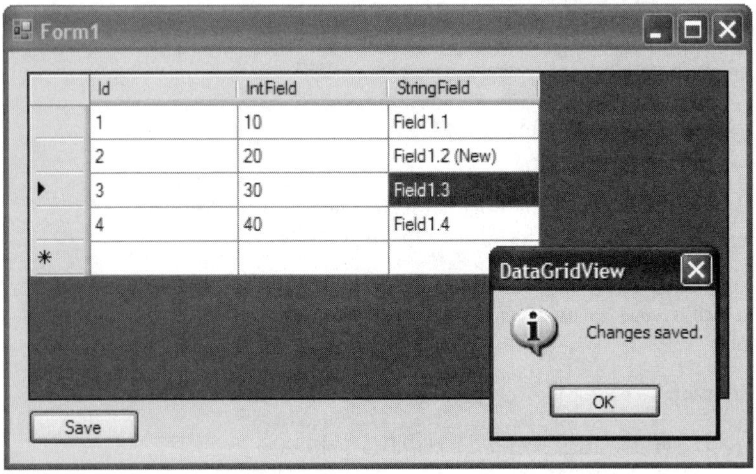

Figure 8-30. Output for UpdateDataWindowsFormDataGridView solution

Discussion

A DataGridView control does not contain any data—it is bound to a data source. The data source can be any class that implements the IList, IListSource, IBindingList, or IBindingListSource interface. If the ReadOnly property of the DataGridView is set to false, the data source is updated when changes are made to data in the DataGridView.

This automatic update happens when the field being edited changes or when the EndEdit( ) method is called on the data source for the DataGridView. The data object that is bound to the DataGridView can be used to update the underlying data source. In the solution, the bound DataTable is used as the argument of the update method of a DataAdapter to update the database with the changes made in the DataGridView control.

8.16   Using Windows Forms BindingNavigator and BindingSource Controls

Problem

You want an easy way to navigate and interact with records in a result set.

Solution

Use a BindingNavigator control that is bound to a BindingSource component. Bind the data controls to the BindingSource component by adding DataBinding objects.

Follow these steps:

1. Create a C# Windows Forms application, BindWindowsFormBindingNavigator.
2. Add the following controls to the Form1 design surface:
   - BindingNavigator named departmentBindingNavigator
   - BindingSource named departmentBindingSource
   - Label with Text property = DepartmentID:
   - TextBox named departmentIDTextBox
   - Label with Text property = DepartmentName
   - TextBox named departmentNameTextBox

   The completed layout of the Windows Form named Form1 is shown in Figure 8-31.

The C# code in *Form1.cs* in the project BindWindowsFormBindingNavigator is shown in Example 8-28. The solution fills a DataTable from the HumanResources.Department table in AdventureWorks and binds it to the data source of the BindingSource control. The BindingSource property of the BindingNavigator is set to the BindingSource control. The TextBox controls—departmentIDTextBox and departmentNameTextBox—are bound to the BindingSource control.

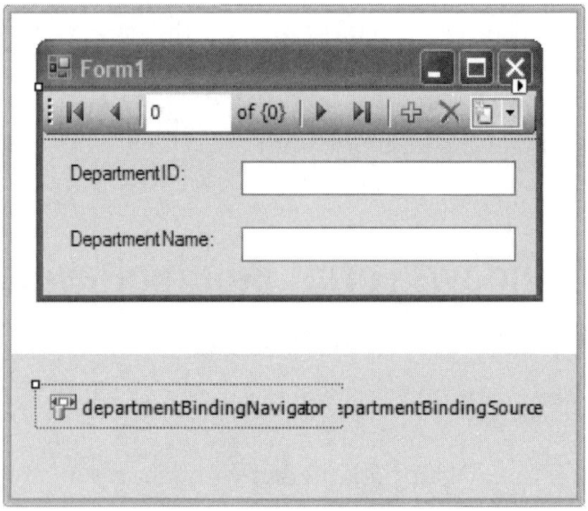

Figure 8-31. Layout for Form1 in BindWindowsFormBindingNavigator solution

Example 8-28. File: Form1.cs for BindWindowsFormBindingNavigator solution

```
using System;
using System.Data;
using System.Data.SqlClient;
using System.Windows.Forms;

namespace BindWindowsFormBindingNavigator
{
    public partial class Form1 : Form
    {
        public Form1( )
        {
            InitializeComponent( );

            this.Load += new EventHandler(Form1_Load);

        }

        void Form1_Load(object sender, EventArgs e)
        {
            // set the data source of the binding source
            departmentBindingSource.DataSource = LoadDepartmentData( );
            // set the binding source of the binding navigator to the binding
            // source
            departmentBindingNavigator.BindingSource = departmentBindingSource;

            // bind the text boxes to the binding source
            departmentIDTextBox.DataBindings.Add(
                "Text", departmentBindingSource, "DepartmentID");
            departmentNameTextBox.DataBindings.Add(
                "Text", departmentBindingSource, "Name");
        }
```

Example 8-28. File: Form1.cs for BindWindowsFormBindingNavigator solution (continued)

```
        private DataTable LoadDepartmentData( )
        {
            string sqlConnectString = @"Data Source=(local);
                Integrated security=SSPI;Initial Catalog=AdventureWorks;";
            string sqlSelect = "SELECT DepartmentID, Name FROM HumanResources.Department";

            // Fill and return a DataTable with Department data
            SqlDataAdapter da = new SqlDataAdapter(sqlSelect, sqlConnectString);
            DataTable dt = new DataTable( );
            da.Fill(dt);

            return dt;
        }
    }
}
```

The output is shown in Figure 8-32.

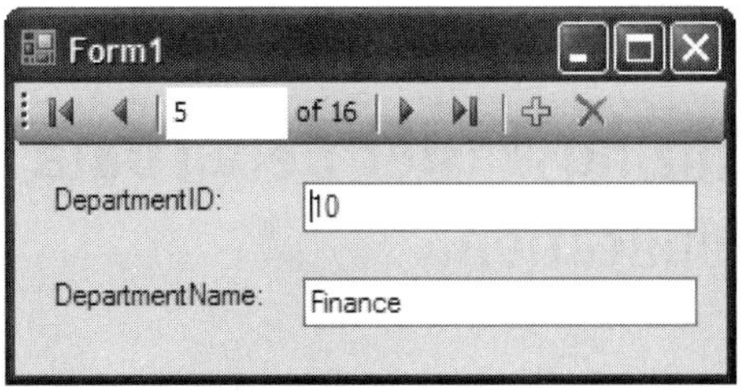

Figure 8-32. Output for BindWindowsFormBindingNavigator solution

Discussion

The `BindingSource` component simplifies binding to an underlying data source. It lets you bind all Windows Forms controls to data sources through a consistent interface. The `BindingSource` provides currency and position management services within the underlying data source. You set the underlying data source for `BindingSource` using the `DataSource` and `DataMember` properties—the `DataMember` property is needed when the underlying data source contains more than one data object.

The `BindingSource` provides properties and methods for accessing and manipulating data, as described in Table 8-14.

Table 8-14. BindingSource members for accessing and manipulating data

Member	Description
`Current`	Gets the current item of the data source.
`Filter`	Gets or sets the expression to filter the rows in the list that are viewed.
`List`	Gets the list specified by the `DataSource` and `DataMember` properties.

Table 8-14. BindingSource members for accessing and manipulating data (continued)

Member	Description
Position	Gets or sets the current position in the underlying data list.
Sort	Gets or sets the column name and sort order information used for sorting the data list.
AddNew( )	Adds a new item to the data list.
CancelEdit( )	Cancels the current edit operation.
EndEdit( )	Ends the current edit operation and applies pending changes.
Insert( )	Inserts an item into the data list at the specified index.
RemoveCurrent( )	Removes the current item from the data list.

The BindingNavigator control provides a standard way to search, navigate, and change data bound to a Windows Form. The BindingNavigator is a toolstrip that has a collection of items that automatically performs common data-related actions including add, delete, insert, and navigation. Set the DataSource property of the BindingNavigator control to a BindingSource component to interact with its underlying data.

8.17   Synchronizing Master-Detail Data in a Windows Forms Application

Problem

You need to bind both a parent table and child table within a DataSet to a pair of DataGridView controls so that the child data is displayed when a parent is selected.

Solution

Create a BindingSource for both the parent and detail DataGridView controls. Set the DataSource and DataMember properties of the parent BindingSource to specify the parent result set. Set the DataSource of the child BindingSource to the parent BindingSource and DataMember of the child BindingSource to the name of the data relation between the parent and child tables.

Follow these steps:

1. Create a C# Windows Forms application, MasterDetailWindowsFormDataGrid.

2. Add the following controls to the Form1 design surface:
   - DataGridView named headerDataGridView
   - DataGridView named detailDataGridView

   The completed layout of the Windows Form named Form1 is shown in Figure 8-33.

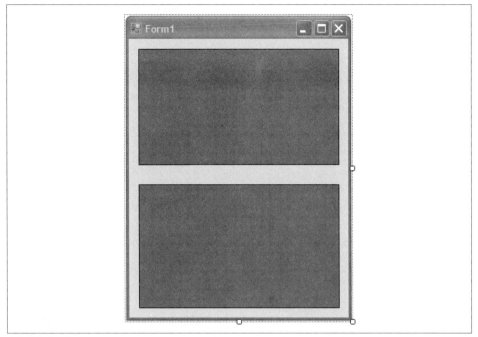

Figure 8-33. Layout for Form1 in MasterDetailWindowsFormDataGrid solution

The C# code in *Form1.cs* in the project `MasterDetailWindowsFormDataGrid` is shown in Example 8-29. The solution creates a `DataSet` containing a subset of the `Sales.SalesOrderHeader` and `Sales.SalesOrderDetail` records from `AdventureWorks` and a `DataRelation` named `FK_SalesOrderDetail_SalesOrderHeader` relating the two tables. A `BindingSource` is created for both the parent and detail `DataGridView` controls named `headerBindingSource` and `detailBindingSource`, respectively. The `DataSource` and `DataMember` properties of the parent `BindingSource` are set to specify the parent result set `SalesOrderHeader` in the `DataSet ds`. The `DataSource` of the child `BindingSource` is set to the parent `BindingSource parentBindingSource` and the `DataMember` of the child `BindingSource` to the name of the data relation `FK_SalesOrderDetail_SalesOrderHeader` between the parent and child tables.

Example 8-29. File: Form1.cs for MasterDetailWindowsFormDataGrid solution

```
using System;
using System.Data;
using System.Data.SqlClient;
using System.Windows.Forms;

namespace MasterDetailWindowsFormDataGrid
{
    public partial class Form1 : Form
    {
```

```
public Form1( )
{
    InitializeComponent( );

    // Configure the layout properties of the header grid
    headerDataGridView.Anchor = AnchorStyles.Left | AnchorStyles.Right |
        AnchorStyles.Top;
    headerDataGridView.ReadOnly = true;
    headerDataGridView.AllowUserToAddRows = false;
    headerDataGridView.AllowUserToDeleteRows = false;
    headerDataGridView.MultiSelect = false;
    headerDataGridView.AutoSizeColumnsMode =
        DataGridViewAutoSizeColumnsMode.AllCells;
    headerDataGridView.SelectionMode = DataGridViewSelectionMode.FullRowSelect;

    // Configure layout properties of the detail grid
    detailDataGridView.Anchor = AnchorStyles.Left | AnchorStyles.Right |
        AnchorStyles.Top;
    detailDataGridView.ReadOnly = true;
    detailDataGridView.AllowUserToAddRows = false;
    detailDataGridView.AllowUserToDeleteRows = false;
    detailDataGridView.MultiSelect = false;
    detailDataGridView.SelectionMode = DataGridViewSelectionMode.FullRowSelect;
    detailDataGridView.AutoSizeColumnsMode =
        DataGridViewAutoSizeColumnsMode.AllCells;

    this.Width = 600;

    this.Load += new EventHandler(Form1_Load);
}

void Form1_Load(object sender, EventArgs e)
{
    // Retrieve a DataSet containing sales order header and detail data in
    // two related DataTable objects
    DataSet ds = LoadData( );

    // Create and assign a BindingSource for each data grid
    BindingSource headerBindingSource = new BindingSource( );
    headerDataGridView.DataSource = headerBindingSource;
    BindingSource detailBindingSource = new BindingSource( );
    detailDataGridView.DataSource = detailBindingSource;

    // Set the data source of the header grid to the SalesOrderHeader table
    headerBindingSource.DataSource = ds;
    headerBindingSource.DataMember = "SalesOrderHeader";
    // Set the data source of the detail grid to the related SalesOrderDetail
    // records
```

```
        detailBindingSource.DataSource = headerBindingSource;
        detailBindingSource.DataMember = "FK_SalesOrderDetail_SalesOrderHeader";
    }

    protected DataSet LoadData( )
    {
        string sqlConnectString = @"Data Source=(local);
            Integrated security=SSPI;Initial Catalog=AdventureWorks;";

        string sqlSelect =
            @"SELECT SalesOrderID, OrderDate, SalesOrderNumber, TotalDue
            FROM Sales.SalesOrderHeader
            WHERE SalesOrderID BETWEEN 43660 AND 43669;
            SELECT SalesOrderID, SalesOrderDetailID, OrderQty, ProductID, LineTotal
            FROM Sales.SalesOrderDetail
            WHERE SalesOrderID BETWEEN 43660 AND 43669;";

        // Fill and return a DataSet containing sales order header and sales order
        // detail DataTable objects that are related on the SalesOrderID field
        SqlDataAdapter da = new SqlDataAdapter(sqlSelect, sqlConnectString);
        da.TableMappings.Add("Table", "SalesOrderHeader");
        da.TableMappings.Add("Table1", "SalesOrderDetail");
        DataSet ds = new DataSet( );
        da.Fill(ds);

        // Add a relation between parent and child table.
        ds.Relations.Add("FK_SalesOrderDetail_SalesOrderHeader",
            ds.Tables["SalesOrderHeader"].Columns["SalesOrderID"],
            ds.Tables["SalesOrderDetail"].Columns["SalesOrderID"]);

        return ds;
    }
    }
}
```

The output is shown in Figure 8-34.

Discussion

The DataGridView provides a user interface for tabular data as well as formatting and editing capabilities. Unlike the DataGrid control in .NET 1.1, the DataGridView control cannot display hierarchical data.

Binding the BindingSource for the child table to the parent BindingSource and setting its DataMember property to the name of the data relation between the tables causes the related detail for the current parent record to be retrieved and displayed in the child DataGridView.

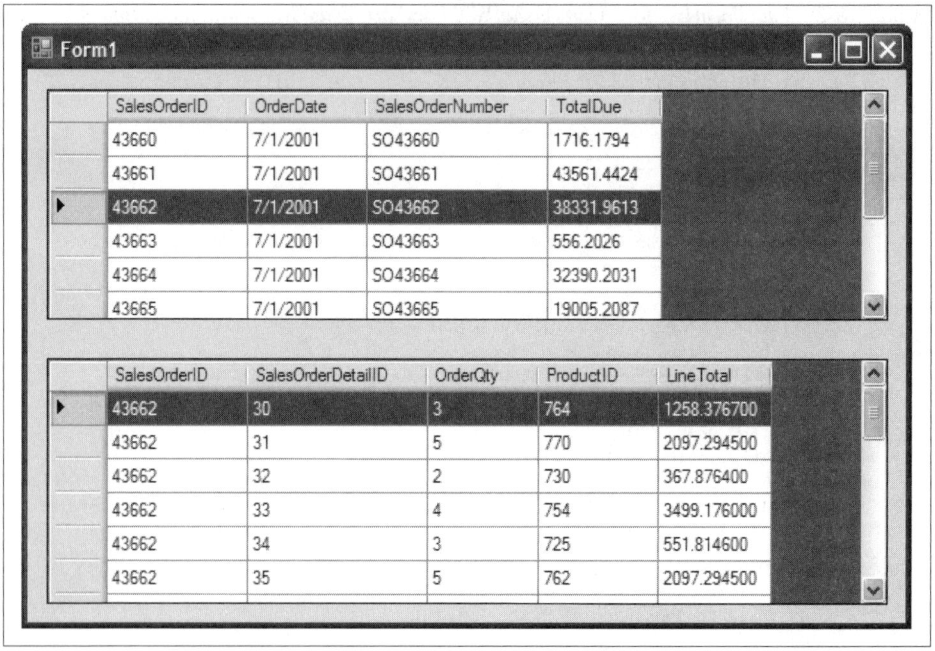

Figure 8-34. Output for MasterDetailWindowsFormDataGrid solution

8.18   Displaying an Image from a Database in a Windows Forms Control

Problem

You need to display an image from a database in a Windows Forms control.

Solution

Read the image into a byte array and load it directly into a PictureBox control using a MemoryStream.

Follow these steps:

1. Create a C# Windows Forms application, LoadImageIntoWindowsFormControl.

2. Add the following control to the Form1 design surface:

   • PictureBox named productPhotoPictureBox

   The completed layout of the Windows Form named Form1 is shown in Figure 8-35.

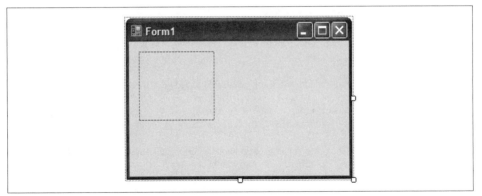

Figure 8-35. Layout for Form1 in LoadImageIntoWindowsFormControl solution

The C# code in *Form1.cs* in the project `LoadImageIntoWindowsFormControl` is shown in Example 8-30. The solution retrieves the `LargePhoto` binary field from the `Production.ProductPhoto` table in `AdventureWorks` for `ProductPhotoID = 100` into a byte array. A `MemoryStream` object is created from the byte array. The static `FromStream( )` method of the `System.Drawing.Image` class is used to load the image into the `PictureBox` from the `MemoryStream`.

Example 8-30. File: Form1.cs for LoadImageIntoWindowsFormControl solution

```
using System;
using System.Data;
using System.Data.SqlClient;
using System.IO;
using System.Windows.Forms;
using System.Drawing;

namespace LoadImageIntoWindowsFormControl
{
    public partial class Form1 : Form
    {
        public Form1( )
        {
            InitializeComponent( );

            productPhotoPictureBox.SizeMode = PictureBoxSizeMode.AutoSize;

            this.Load += new EventHandler(Form1_Load);
        }

        void Form1_Load(object sender, EventArgs e)
        {
            // Load the product photo to a memory stream and assign that
            // to the picture box using the FromStream( ) method of the Image class
```

Example 8-30. File: Form1.cs for LoadImageIntoWindowsFormControl solution (continued)

```
        MemoryStream ms = new MemoryStream(LoadProductPhoto(100));
        productPhotoPictureBox.Image = Image.FromStream(ms);
    }

    public byte[] LoadProductPhoto(int productPhotoId)
    {
        string sqlConnectString = @"Data Source=(local);
            Integrated security=SSPI;Initial Catalog=AdventureWorks;";

        string sqlSelect = @"SELECT LargePhoto FROM Production.ProductPhoto
            WHERE ProductPhotoID = " + productPhotoId;

        // Retrieve and return the product photo for the specified product as
        // a byte array
        SqlConnection connection = new SqlConnection(sqlConnectString);
        SqlCommand command = new SqlCommand(sqlSelect, connection);
        connection.Open( );
        byte[] largePhoto = (byte[])command.ExecuteScalar( );
        connection.Close( );

        return largePhoto;
    }
  }
}
```

The output is shown in Figure 8-36.

Figure 8-36. Output for LoadImageIntoWindowsFormControl solution

Discussion

The Windows Forms PictureBox control displays bitmap, JPEG, GIF, metafile, and icon images.

In the solution, the image stored as a BLOB in the database is retrieved into a byte array, which is in turn copied into a System.IO.MemoryStream object. The static FromStream( ) method of the Image class creates an Image object that is loaded into the PictureBox.

8.19 Binding a Group of Radio Buttons to a Windows Forms Data Field

Problem

You need to bind a field in a database to a radio button and update the database with the radio button selected.

Solution

Use a hidden TextBox to retrieve and update the field value that corresponds to the radio button group. Use the Tag property of each RadioButton control to hold its corresponding data field value.

Follow these steps:

1. The solution uses a table named BindRadioButton in the AdoDotNet35Cookbook database. Execute the following T-SQL statement to create the table:

```
USE AdoDotNet35Cookbook
GO
CREATE TABLE BindRadioButton(
    Id int NOT NULL PRIMARY KEY,
    RadioButtonItemId int NOT NULL,
    Field1 nvarchar(50) NULL )
```

The schema of table BindRadioButton used in this solution is shown in Table 8-15.

Table 8-15. BindRadioButton table schema

Column name	Data type	Length	Allow nulls?
Id	int	4	No
RadioButtonItemId	int	4	No
Field1	nvarchar	50	Yes

2. Execute the following T-SQL batch to create the sample data required by the solution:

```
USE AdoDotNet35Cookbook
GO
INSERT INTO BindRadioButton VALUES (1, 10, 'Field1.1')
INSERT INTO BindRadioButton VALUES (2, 20, 'Field1.2')
INSERT INTO BindRadioButton VALUES (3, 30, 'Field1.3')
INSERT INTO BindRadioButton VALUES (4, 40, 'Field1.4')
```

3. Create a C# Windows Forms application named DataBindWindowsFormRadioButton.

4. Add the following controls to the `Form1` design surface:

- `BindingNavigator` named `bindingNavigator`
- `Button` named `saveToolStripButton` on the `BindingNavigator` control with its Text property = Save
- `BindingSource` named `bindingSource`
- `Label` with Text property = Id:
- `TextBox` named `idTextBox`
- `GroupBox` named `radioButtonItemIdGroupBox` with the Text property = `RadioButtonItemId`
- `RadioButton` named `radioButton1` (in `GroupBox` control `radioButtonItemIdGroupBox`) with Tag property = 10 and Text property = Value of 10
- `RadioButton` named `radioButton2` (in `GroupBox` control `radioButtonItemIdGroupBox`) with Tag property = 20 and Text property = Value of 20
- `RadioButton` named `radioButton3` (in `GroupBox` control `radioButtonItemIdGroupBox`) with Tag property = 30 and Text property = Value of 30
- `RadioButton` named `radioButton4` (in `GroupBox` control `radioButtonItemIdGroupBox`) with Tag property = 40 and Text property = Value of 40
- `TextBox` named `radioButtonItemIdTextBox` (positioned to the right of the GroupBox in this example)
- `Label` with Text property = Field1:
- `TextBox` named `field1TextBox`

The completed layout of the Windows Form named `Form1` is shown in Figure 8-37.

The C# code in *Form1.cs* in the project `DataBindWindowsFormRadioButton` is shown in Example 8-31. The solution loads a `DataTable` with schema and data from the table `BindRadioButton` in the database `AdoDotNet35Cookbook` and binds the `DataTable` to the `BindingSource` control named `bindingSource`. The three `TextBox` controls—`idTextBox`, `radioButtonIdTextBox`, and `field1TextBox`—are bound to the `BindingSource` control and the `BindingSource` is positioned at the first record. When a radio button is checked, an event handler sets the Text property of the bound hidden text box named `radioButtonItemIdTextBox` to the Tag property of the checked radio button that contains the radio button value. Similarly when the user moves to a different record using the `BindingNavigator` control, the `BindingSource` control raises a `PositionChanged` event.

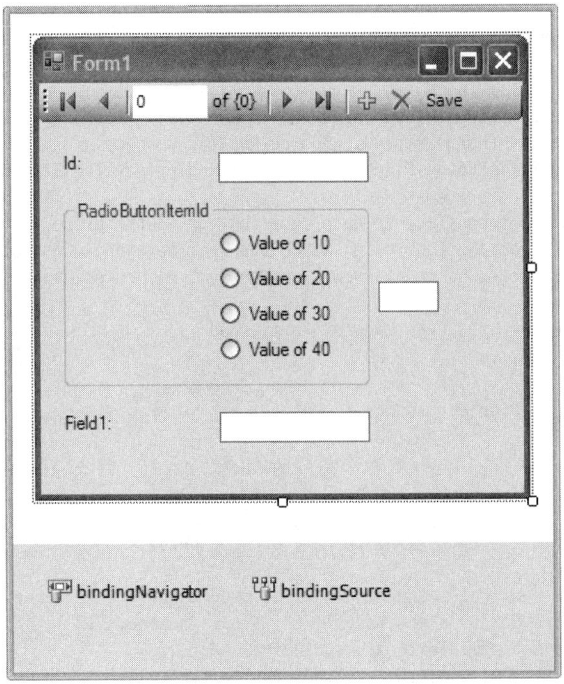

Figure 8-37. Layout for Form1 in DataBindWindowsFormRadioButton solution

The event handler for the PositionChanged event checks the radio button with the same Tag as the Text property of the hidden bound text box radioButtonItemIdTextBox. The event handler for the Save button click event uses the Update( ) method of the DataAdapter with the bound DataTable as an argument to update the database.

Example 8-31. File: Form1.cs for DataBindWindowsFormRadioButton solution

```
using System;
using System.Data;
using System.Data.SqlClient;
using System.Windows.Forms;

namespace DataBindWindowsFormRadioButton
{
    public partial class Form1 : Form
    {
        private SqlDataAdapter da;
        private DataTable dt;

        public Form1( )
        {
            InitializeComponent( );
```

```
    // "hide" the text box used to check the correct radio button
    radioButtonItemIdTextBox.Top = -100;

    bindingSource.PositionChanged +=
        new EventHandler(bindingSource_PositionChanged);
    saveToolStripButton.Click += new EventHandler(saveToolStripButton_Click);

    // Add event handlers to each radio button in the group
    foreach (RadioButton rb in radioButtonItemIdGroupBox.Controls)
        rb.CheckedChanged += new EventHandler(rb_CheckedChanged);

    this.Load += new EventHandler(Form1_Load);
}

void Form1_Load(object sender, EventArgs e)
{
    // Set the data source of the binding source to the BindRadioButton DataTable
    bindingSource.DataSource = LoadData();
    // Set the binding source of the navigator
    bindingNavigator.BindingSource = bindingSource;

    // Bind text boxes and hidden field used to check the correct radio button
    idTextBox.DataBindings.Add("Text", bindingSource, "Id");
    radioButtonItemIdTextBox.DataBindings.Add(
        "Text", bindingSource, "radioButtonItemId");
    field1TextBox.DataBindings.Add("Text", bindingSource, "Field1");

    // Set the radio button for the first record
    bindingSource_PositionChanged(null, null);
}

void rb_CheckedChanged(object sender, EventArgs e)
{
    // Update the hidden text box when a new radio button is checked
    UpdateRadioButtonItemIdTextBox();
}

private DataTable LoadData()
{
    string sqlConnectString = @"Data Source=(local);
        Integrated security=SSPI;Initial Catalog=AdoDotNet35Cookbook;";
    string sqlSelect =
        "SELECT Id, RadioButtonItemId, Field1 FROM BindRadioButton";

    // Create a data adapter and command builder
    da = new SqlDataAdapter(sqlSelect, sqlConnectString);
    SqlCommandBuilder cb = new SqlCommandBuilder(da);

    // Fill a DataTable with schema and data from the BindRadioButton table
    // and return to the caller
```

Example 8-31. File: Form1.cs for DataBindWindowsFormRadioButton solution (continued)

```csharp
            dt = new DataTable( );
            da.FillSchema(dt, SchemaType.Source);
            da.Fill(dt);

            return dt;
        }

        private void SaveData( )
        {
            // Call the data adapter Update( ) method to update the database
            da.Update(dt);
        }

        private void UpdateRadioButtonItemIdTextBox( )
        {
            // Set the value of the hidden text box based on the checked radio button
            // in the group
            foreach (RadioButton rb in radioButtonItemIdGroupBox.Controls)
            {
                if (rb.Checked)
                {
                    radioButtonItemIdTextBox.Text = rb.Tag.ToString( );
                    break;
                }
            }
        }

        private void bindingSource_PositionChanged(object sender, EventArgs e)
        {
            // Refresh the checked radio button when the current record changes.
            foreach (RadioButton rb in radioButtonItemIdGroupBox.Controls)
            {
                if (rb.Tag.ToString( ) == radioButtonItemIdTextBox.Text)
                {
                    rb.Checked = true;
                    break;
                }
            }
        }

        private void saveToolStripButton_Click(object sender, EventArgs e)
        {
            // Update data when the Save button is clicked
            UpdateRadioButtonItemIdTextBox( );

            SaveData( );
        }
    }
}
```

The output is shown in Figure 8-38.

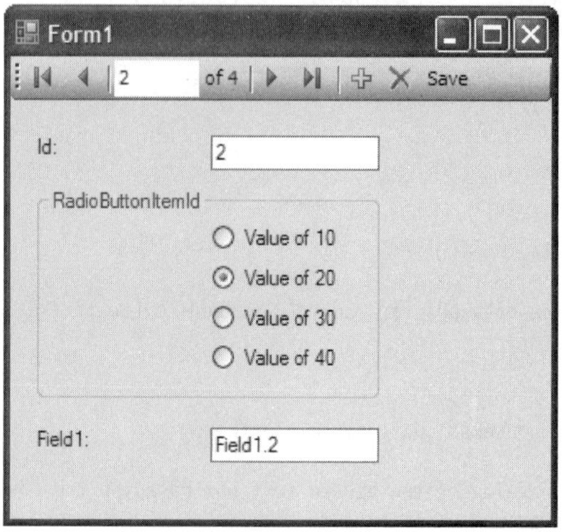

Figure 8-38. Output for DataBindWindowsFormRadioButton solution

Discussion

Although a RadioButton control can be set to simple-bind to data, there is no way to bind a group of RadioButton controls to a data source. Binding a single radio button to a data source isn't a particularly common requirement—nor is it particularly useful—since radio buttons are normally used in groups to allow an option to be selected from a group of mutually exclusive options.

Web Forms provides a RadioButtonList control that works as a parent control to a collection of radio button list items. It inherits from the ListControl class and as a result works similarly to the ListBox and DropDownList controls. There is no RadioButtonList control available for Windows Forms applications.

Radio button data binding can be simulated in a Windows Form application by following these steps:

1. Add the RadioButton controls to the form. For each radio button, set its Tag property to the data value that corresponds to the selection of the radio button.

2. Create a hidden TextBox control to take the value of the selected RadioButton from the group.

3. Bind the Text property of the TextBox to the data source:

```
radioButtonItemIdTextBox.DataBindings.Add("Text", bindingSource,
"radioButtonItemId");
```

4. Attach an event handler for the PositionChanged event of a BindingSource control. This event indicates that the selected row in the DataTable has changed.

```
bindingSource.PositionChanged +=
    new EventHandler(bindingSource_PositionChanged);
```

5. Create the event handler for the PositionChanged event. In the handler, iterate over the collection of radio buttons. Check the radio button that has a Tag matching the hidden TextBox that is bound to the data. This will select the radio button corresponding to the column value for the current row in the DataTable.

6. Create the handler for the CheckedChanged event for the RadioButton control and attach it to each radio button.

```
foreach (RadioButton rb in radioButtonItemIdGroupBox.Controls)
    rb.CheckedChanged += new EventHandler(rb_CheckedChanged);
```

The handler iterates over the collection of radio buttons and transfers the Tag value of the checked radio button to the hidden bound TextBox.

8.20 Searching a Windows Forms DataGridView Control

Problem

You need to use a search criteria specified by a user to locate a record displayed in a DataGridView without executing a query against the database.

Solution

Use the Find( ) method of the DataView bound to the DataGridView to locate a record in the sorted column of the DataGrid and reposition to that row in the DataGridView.

Follow these steps:

1. Create a C# Windows Forms application named SearchWindowsFormsDataGridView.

2. Add the following controls to the Form1 design surface:

   - DataGridView named contactDataGridView
   - TextBox named findTextBox
   - Button named findButton with Text property = Find

   The completed layout of the Windows Form named Form1 is shown in Figure 8-39.

The C# code in *Form1.cs* in the project SearchWindowsFormsDataGridView is shown in Example 8-32. The solution creates a DataTable and filled with the Person.Contact table from AdventureWorks. A DataView is created based on the default view of the DataTable, its sort key is set to the ContactID (first) column, and it is bound to the DataGridView. Finally, a CurrencyManager is created from the DataView.

The event handler for the Find button uses the Find( ) method of the DataView to locate a record with the user-specified value in the DataView sort column. If a match is found, the CurrencyManager is used to select the matching record in the DataGridView.

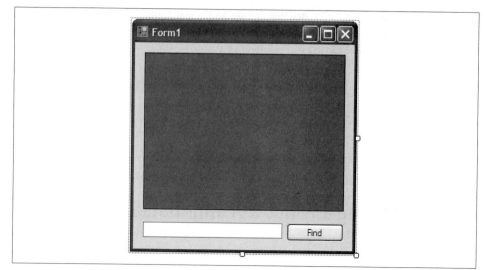

Figure 8-39. Layout for Form1 in SearchWindowsFormsDataGridView solution

Example 8-32. File: Form1.cs for SearchWindowsFormsDataGridView solution

```
using System;
using System.Data;
using System.Data.SqlClient;
using System.Windows.Forms;

namespace SearchWindowsFormsDataGridView
{
    public partial class Form1 : Form
    {
        private DataView dv;
        private CurrencyManager cm;

        public Form1( )
        {
            InitializeComponent( );

            // Set display properties of the data grid view, find text box,
            // and find button
            contactDataGridView.AutoSize = true;
            contactDataGridView.Anchor = AnchorStyles.Left | AnchorStyles.Top |
                AnchorStyles.Right | AnchorStyles.Bottom;
            contactDataGridView.ReadOnly = true;
            contactDataGridView.AllowUserToAddRows = false;
            contactDataGridView.AllowUserToDeleteRows = false;
            contactDataGridView.SelectionMode = DataGridViewSelectionMode.FullRowSelect;

            findTextBox.Anchor = AnchorStyles.Left | AnchorStyles.Right |
                AnchorStyles.Bottom;

            findButton.Anchor = AnchorStyles.Bottom | AnchorStyles.Right;
```

Example 8-32. File: Form1.cs for SearchWindowsFormsDataGridView solution (continued)

```
        this.Width = 500;

        this.Load += new EventHandler(Form1_Load);

    }

    void Form1_Load(object sender, EventArgs e)
    {
        // Get the DataView of some fields in the Contact table in AdventureWorks
        dv = GetDataView( );

        // Bind the DataView to the DataGridView
        contactDataGridView.DataSource = dv;

        // Create a currency manager
        cm = (CurrencyManager)contactDataGridView.BindingContext[dv];
    }

    private DataView GetDataView( )
    {
        string sqlConnectString = @"Data Source=(local);
            Integrated security=SSPI;Initial Catalog=AdventureWorks;";

        string sqlSelect = @"SELECT ContactID, FirstName, LastName
            FROM Person.Contact";

        // Fill a DataTable with data from the Contact table in AdventureWorks
        SqlDataAdapter da = new SqlDataAdapter(sqlSelect, sqlConnectString);
        DataTable dt = new DataTable( );
        da.Fill(dt);

        // Create a data view and set the sort column
        DataView dv = new DataView(dt);
        dv.Sort = dt.Columns[0].ColumnName;

        return dv;
    }

    private void findButton_Click(object sender, EventArgs e)
    {
        if (findTextBox.Text != "")
        {
            bool parseStatus = false;
            switch (contactDataGridView.SortedColumn.Index)
            {
                case 0:
                    // if the sort is on the first column, need to ensure that the
                    // search value is an integer
                    int j;
                    parseStatus = int.TryParse(findTextBox.Text, out j);
                    break;
                case 1:
                case 2:
```

Example 8-32. File: Form1.cs for SearchWindowsFormsDataGridView solution (continued)

```
                    // the second and third columns are strings so the search value
                    // does not need to be checked for validity
                    parseStatus = true;
                    break;
            }

            if (parseStatus)
            {
                // Find the contact.
                int i = dv.Find(findTextBox.Text);
                if (i < 0)
                    // A match was not found.
                    MessageBox.Show("No matching records found.", "Find",
                        MessageBoxButtons.OK,
                        MessageBoxIcon.Information);
                else
                    // Reposition the grid record using the CurrencyManager.
                    cm.Position = i;
            }
            else
            {
                MessageBox.Show("Data type of search value must match sort column.",
                    "Find", MessageBoxButtons.OK, MessageBoxIcon.Exclamation);
                findTextBox.Focus();
            }
        }
        else
        {
            MessageBox.Show("Enter find criteria.", "Find",
                MessageBoxButtons.OK, MessageBoxIcon.Question);
            findTextBox.Focus();
        }
    }
}
}
```

The output is shown in Figure 8-40.

Discussion

The Find( ) method of the DataView locates a row matching a specified sort key value. The Sort property gets or sets the column or columns that the DataView is sorted on. The Sort property is a string that contains the column name, or multiple column names separated by commas, followed by an optional ASC or DESC clause specifying sort direction.

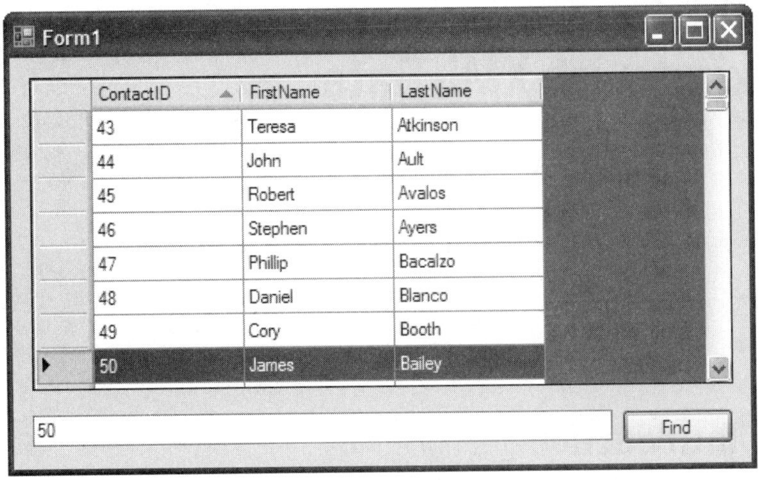

Figure 8-40. Output for SearchWindowsFormsDataGridView solution

There are two methods that you can use to locate records in a `DataView`:

Find( )
> This method of the `DataView` returns the index of the first row matching the specified sort key value or an array of sort key values, for sort keys based on multiple columns. If no records match, it returns –1.

FindRows( )
> This method of the `DataView` returns an array of rows matching the specified sort key value or array of sort key values. It returns an empty array if the sort key value does not exist.

The `Find( )` and `FindRows( )` methods use the current index of the `DataView` without requiring the index to be rebuilt.

Both methods take an argument that is an object array of values whose length matches the number of columns in the sort order of the `DataView`. The order of columns in the array must match the order of columns specified in the `Sort` property. A single value can be passed instead of an array if the sort is based on a single column. The sort key value must match exactly in order to return a result. The `RowFilter` property can be used to locate records matching an expression. For an example, see Recipe 4.5.

The sort order must be specified either by setting the `ApplyDefaultSort` property of the `DataView` to true or by setting the `Sort` property explicitly; otherwise, an exception is thrown. The case-sensitivity of the search is controlled by the `CaseSensitive` property of the underlying `DataTable`.

CHAPTER 9

Working with XML Data

9.0 Introduction

ADO.NET and XML classes are tightly integrated in the .NET Framework. The DataSet can be filled with data or a schema from an XML stream or document. The DataSet can persist or serialize its data or schema to an XML stream or document. You can simultaneously work with the same data in a DataSet and with its XML representation. This chapter focuses on XML support in ADO.NET and in SQL Server.

The XML support in .NET is provided by classes in six namespaces:

System.Xml
  Contains classes that provide standards-based support for processing XML.

System.Xml.Linq
  Contains classes that provide support for LINQ to XML.

System.Xml.Schema
  Contains classes that provide standards-based support for XML Schema Definition (XSD) language schemas.

System.Xml.Serialization
  Contains classes that serialize objects into XML documents or streams.

System.Xml.XPath
  Contains classes that parse and evaluate XPath.

System.Xml.Xsl
  Contains classes that support Extensible Stylesheet Language (XSL) transformations.

.NET Framework classes support saving and loading both XML data and schema from and to ADO.NET disconnected classes. Recipe 9.1 shows how to load XML data into a DataSet or DataTable and how to save data in a DataSet or DataTable to an XML file. Recipe 9.2 shows how to load an XML schema into a DataSet and how to save the schema of a DataSet as an XML schema file. Recipe 9.3 shows how to customize the format of XML data saved from a DataSet.

The DiffGram is an XML format that identifies current and original versions of data allowing the contents of a DataSet to be recreated accurately. The DiffGram allows you to identify the changes made to a DataSet since it was filled. The DataSet uses the DiffGram format to persist and to serialize its contents for transport across a network. Recipe 9.4 shows how to create a DiffGram of changes made to a DataSet.

The .NET Framework allows real-time, synchronous access to both a DataSet and its XML representation in an XmlDataDocument object. The synchronized DataSet and XmlDataDocument classes work with a single set of data—changes to one are reflected immediately in the other. Recipe 9.5 shows how to simultaneously work with ADO.NET and XML representations of the same synchronized data.

Recipe 9.6 shows you how to save and retrieve XML in a database column that is not xml data typed. Recipe 9.7 shows how to save and retrieve data stored in an xml data type column introduced in SQL Server 2005.

ADO.NET supports XPath queries against a DataSet. Recipe 9.8 shows you how.

SQL Server supports retrieving the results of queries in XML format using the FOR XML clause. The XmlReader provides direct forward-only, read-only access to the XML result set stream from the SQL Server. Recipe 9.9 shows how to use the FOR XML clause to retrieve XML-format data from a SQL Server using an XmlReader.

The SQLXML managed classes expose SQLXML functionality that allows .NET applications to access XML data from SQL Server, process the XML data, and update the SQL Server using an XML DiffGram representation of the data. SQLXML classes support *template queries*, an XML document containing one or more SQL queries or stored procedures, to execute. Recipe 9.11 shows how to use template queries.

OPEN XML allows an XML document to be used in a SQL statement in the same way a table or view is used. Recipe 9.12 shows how to use OPEN XML from ADO.NET.

9.1   Using an XML File to Save and Load a DataSet or a DataTable

Problem

You need to save a DataSet or DataTable as an XML file and create a DataSet or DataTable from an XML file.

Solution

Use the XmlTextWriter and XmlTextReader classes together with the WriteXml( ) and ReadXml( ) methods of the DataSet and DataTable classes.

The solution creates a DataSet containing a subset of data from the Person.Contact table in AdventureWorks. The XML schema and data for the DataSet is written to a file named ContactDataset.xml. Next, the solution creates a DataSet and reads in schema and data from the XML file ContactDataSet.xml. Finally, the contents of the DataSet are written to the console.

The C# code in *Program.cs* in the project SaveLoadDataSetXml is shown in Example 9-1.

Example 9-1. File: Program.cs for SaveLoadDataSetXml solution

```
using System;
using System.Data;
using System.Data.SqlClient;
using System.IO;
using System.Xml;
using System.Text;

namespace SaveLoadDataSetXml
{
    class Program
    {
        private const string fileName = @"..\..\..\ContactDataSet.xml";

        static void Main(string[] args)
        {
            string sqlConnectString = "Data Source=(local);" +
                "Integrated security=SSPI;Initial Catalog=AdventureWorks;";

            string sqlSelect = "SELECT ContactID, FirstName, LastName " +
                "FROM Person.Contact WHERE ContactID BETWEEN 10 AND 13";

            // Fill the DataSet using a DataAdapter
            DataSet dsSource = new DataSet("ContactDataSet");
            SqlDataAdapter da = new SqlDataAdapter(sqlSelect, sqlConnectString);
            da.TableMappings.Add("Table", "Contact");
            da.FillSchema(dsSource, SchemaType.Source);
            da.Fill(dsSource);

            // Output the DataSet to the console
            Console.WriteLine("---Source DataSet---");
            foreach (DataRow row in dsSource.Tables["Contact"].Rows)
                Console.WriteLine("ContactID = {0}\tFirstName = {1}\tLastName = {2}",
                    row["ContactID"], row["FirstName"], row["LastName"]);

            // Write the XSD schema and data to a file.
            FileStream fsOut =
                new FileStream(fileName, FileMode.Create, FileAccess.Write);
            // Create an XmlTextWriter using the file stream.
            XmlTextWriter xtw = new XmlTextWriter(fsOut, Encoding.Unicode);
            // Write the XML to the file.
            dsSource.WriteXml(xtw, XmlWriteMode.WriteSchema);
            xtw.Close();
```

Example 9-1. File: Program.cs for SaveLoadDataSetXml solution (continued)

```
            Console.WriteLine("\nXML file written.");

            // Read the XML file into a new DataSet
            FileStream fsIn =
                new FileStream(fileName, FileMode.Open, FileAccess.Read);
            // Create an XmlTextReader using the file stream.
            XmlTextReader xtr = new XmlTextReader(fsIn);
            DataSet dsDest = new DataSet( );
            dsDest.ReadXml(xtr, XmlReadMode.ReadSchema);

            // Output the DataSet to the console.
            Console.WriteLine("\nXML file loaded into DataSet.");
            Console.WriteLine("\n---Destination DataSet---");
            foreach (DataRow row in dsDest.Tables["Contact"].Rows)
                Console.WriteLine("ContactID = {0}\tFirstName = {1}\tLastName = {2}",
                    row["ContactID"], row["FirstName"], row["LastName"]);

            Console.WriteLine("\nPress any key to continue.");
            Console.ReadKey( );
        }
    }
}
```

The output is shown in Figure 9-1.

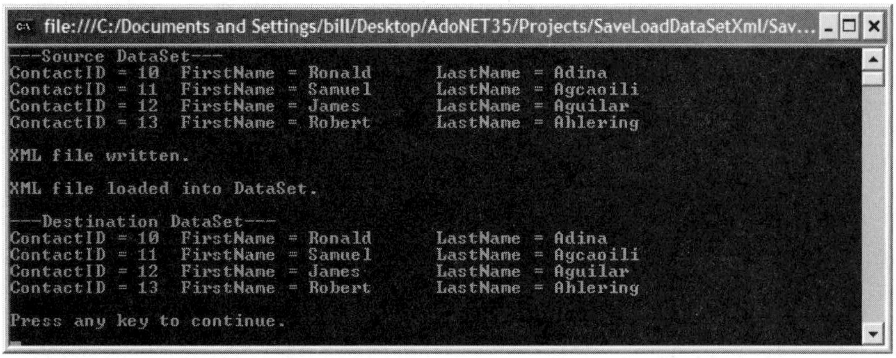

Figure 9-1. Output for SaveLoadDataSetXml solution

Discussion

The solution uses the `XmlTextWriter` and `XmlTextReader` classes to write and read the XML data for the `DataSet`. The `XmlTextWriter` class provides a forward-only mechanism for generating XML streams or files containing XML data. The `XmlTextReader` class provides forward-only access to XML data in streams or files. The `XmlTextReader` does not validate the XML—for validation, use the `XmlValidatingReader` class. Both the `XmlTextWriter` and `XmlTextReader` classes conform to the W3C XML 1.0 and the namespaces in XML recommendations.

The XML file encoding used by the XmlTextWriter is specified in an argument to the constructor as one of the values from the System.Text.Encoding enumeration described in Table 9-1.

Table 9-1. System.Text.Encoding enumeration

Encoding	Description
ASCII	ASCII (7 bit) character set
BigEndianUnicode	Unicode format in big-endian byte order
Default	Encoding for system's current ANSI code page
Unicode	Unicode format in little-endian byte order
UTF7	UTF-7 format
UTF8	UTF-8 format (this is the default)

The WriteXml( ) and ReadXml( ) methods of the DataSet and DataTable classes are used to write and read XML for objects of those types. The WriteXml( ) method takes an optional argument that specifies a value from the XmlWriteMode enumeration described in Table 9-2.

Table 9-2. XmlWriteMode enumeration

Value	Description
DiffGram	The DataSet is written as a DiffGram, which is an XML format used by .NET to persist and serialize a DataSet. A DiffGram includes all information required to re-create the DataSet, including original and current values, row errors, and row order. A DiffGram does not include information about the DataSet schema.
IgnoreSchema	The DataSet is written without inline schema information. This is the default.
WriteSchema	The DataSet is written with an inline XSD schema for the relational structure of the DataSet.

If an in-line schema is not written, the ReadXml( ) method can still be used to read the data into a DataSet or DataTable, but the method will not be able to completely re-create the schema.

The XmlRead( ) method takes an optional argument that specifies a value from the XmlReadMode enumeration described in Table 9-3.

Table 9-3. XmlReadMode enumeration

Value	Description
Auto	Uses the most appropriate of the following settings: <ul><li>DiffGram if the data is a DiffGram</li><li>ReadSchema if the DataSet already has a schema or the XML document contains an inline schema</li><li>InferSchema if the DataSet does not already have a schema and the XML document does not contain an inline schema</li></ul>Auto is the default.

Table 9-3. XmlReadMode enumeration (continued)

Value	Description
DiffGram	Reads a DiffGram applying the changes to the DataSet. The target DataSet must have the same schema as the DataSet from which the WriteXml( ) method created the DiffGram. Otherwise, an exception is raised.
Fragment	Reads an XML document such as one generated by queries with the FOR XML clause.
IgnoreSchema	Ignores any inline schema and reads data from the XML document into the existing DataSet schema. Data not matching the existing schema is discarded.
InferSchema	Ignores any inline schema, infers the schema from the data, and loads the data into the DataSet. The DataSet schema is extended by adding new tables and columns as required.
InferTypedSchema	Ignores any inline schema, infers the schema from the data, and loads the data into the DataSet. The data is interpreted as string data if the type cannot be inferred. The DataSet schema is extended by adding tables or columns if the DataSet already contains a schema. An exception is raised if inferred columns conflict with existing columns or if inferred tables already exist with a different namespace.
ReadSchema	Reads any inline schema and loads the data into the DataSet. If the DataSet already contains tables, new tables will be added but an exception will be raised if any tables defined by the inline schema already exist in the DataSet.

Example 9-2 shows the XML file *ContactDataSet.xml*, which includes an inline schema, written by this solution.

Example 9-2. File: ContactDataSet.xml

```
<ContactDataSet>
  <xs:schema id="ContactDataSet" xmlns="" xmlns:xs=http://www.w3.org/2001/XMLSchema
    xmlns:msdata="urn:schemas-microsoft-com:xml-msdata">
    <xs:element name="ContactDataSet" msdata:IsDataSet="true"
      msdata:UseCurrentLocale="true">
      <xs:complexType>
        <xs:choice minOccurs="0" maxOccurs="unbounded">
          <xs:element name="Table">
            <xs:complexType>
              <xs:sequence>
                <xs:element name="ContactID" msdata:ReadOnly="true"
                  msdata:AutoIncrement="true" type="xs:int" />
                <xs:element name="FirstName">
                  <xs:simpleType>
                    <xs:restriction base="xs:string">
                      <xs:maxLength value="50" />
                    </xs:restriction>
                  </xs:simpleType>
                </xs:element>
                <xs:element name="LastName">
                  <xs:simpleType>
                    <xs:restriction base="xs:string">
                      <xs:maxLength value="50" />
                    </xs:restriction>
                  </xs:simpleType>
```

Example 9-2. File: ContactDataSet.xml (continued)

```
              </xs:element>
            </xs:sequence>
          </xs:complexType>
        </xs:element>
        <xs:element name="Contact">
          <xs:complexType>
            <xs:sequence>
              <xs:element name="ContactID" type="xs:int" minOccurs="0" />
              <xs:element name="FirstName" type="xs:string" minOccurs="0" />
              <xs:element name="LastName" type="xs:string" minOccurs="0" />
            </xs:sequence>
          </xs:complexType>
        </xs:element>
      </xs:choice>
    </xs:complexType>
    <xs:unique name="Constraint1" msdata:PrimaryKey="true">
      <xs:selector xpath=".//Table" />
      <xs:field xpath="ContactID" />
    </xs:unique>
  </xs:element>
</xs:schema>
<Contact>
  <ContactID>10</ContactID>
  <FirstName>Ronald</FirstName>
  <LastName>Adina</LastName>
</Contact>
<Contact>
  <ContactID>11</ContactID>
  <FirstName>Samuel</FirstName>
  <LastName>Agcaoili</LastName>
</Contact>
<Contact>
  <ContactID>12</ContactID>
  <FirstName>James</FirstName>
  <LastName>Aguilar</LastName>
</Contact>
<Contact>
  <ContactID>13</ContactID>
  <FirstName>Robert</FirstName>
  <LastName>Ahlering</LastName>
</Contact>
</ContactDataSet>
```

Use the `WriteXmlSchema( )` and `ReadXmlSchema( )` methods of the `DataSet` and `DataTable` classes to write and read just XSD schema information.

9.2 Using XSD Schema Files to Save and Load a DataSet Structure

Problem

You need to create an XSD schema from a DataSet or DataTable and to define the schema of a DataSet or DataTable from an XSD schema.

Solution

Use the XmlTextWriter and XmlTextReader classes together with the WriteXmlSchema( ) and ReadXmlSchema( ) methods of the DataSet and DataTable classes.

The solution creates a DataSet containing the schema and data for the Sales. SalesOrderHeader and Sales.SalesOrderDetail tables in AdventureWorks. A data relation for the tables is created in the DataSet. The XML schema for the DataSet is written to a file named *Schema.xsd* in the same directory as the solution file *LoadSaveDataSetXsdSchema.sln*. Next, the solution creates a DataSet and reads in schema from the XML file *Schema.xsd*. Finally, metadata about the DataSet schema are written to the console.

The C# code in *Program.cs* in the project LoadSaveDataSetXsdSchema is shown in Example 9-3.

Example 9-3. File: Program.cs for LoadSaveDataSetXsdSchema solution

```
using System;
using System.Data;
using System.Data.SqlClient;
using System.IO;
using System.Xml;
using System.Text;

namespace LoadSaveDataSetXsdSchema
{
    class Program
    {
        private const string fileName = @"..\..\..\Schema.xsd";

        static void Main(string[] args)
        {
            string sqlConnectString = "Data Source=(local);" +
                "Integrated security=SSPI;Initial Catalog=AdventureWorks;";

            string sqlSelect = "SELECT * FROM Sales.SalesOrderHeader;" +
                "SELECT * FROM Sales.SalesOrderDetail";
```

```
DataSet dsSource = new DataSet("SaleOrders");
SqlDataAdapter da;

// Fill the DataSet with Header and Detail, mapping the default table names
da = new SqlDataAdapter(sqlSelect, sqlConnectString);
da.TableMappings.Add("Table", "SalesOrderHeader");
da.TableMappings.Add("Table1", "SalesOrderDetail");
da.FillSchema(dsSource, SchemaType.Mapped);
da.Fill(dsSource);

// Relate the Header and Order tables in the DataSet
DataRelation dr = new DataRelation("SalesOrderHeader_SalesOrderDetail",
    dsSource.Tables["SalesOrderHeader"].Columns["SalesOrderID"],
    dsSource.Tables["SalesOrderDetail"].Columns["SalesOrderID"]);
dsSource.Relations.Add(dr);

// Output information about the source DataSet
Console.WriteLine("---Source DataSet---");
Console.WriteLine("DataSetName = {0}", dsSource.DataSetName);
foreach (DataTable dt in dsSource.Tables)
    Console.WriteLine("TableName = {0}\tColumns.Count = {1}",
        dt.TableName, dt.Columns.Count);
foreach (DataRelation relation in dsSource.Relations)
    Console.WriteLine("RelationName = {0}", relation.RelationName);

// Write the XSD schema to a file.
FileStream fsOut = new FileStream(fileName, FileMode.Create,
    FileAccess.Write);
// Create an XmlTextWriter using the file stream.
XmlTextWriter xtw = new XmlTextWriter(fsOut, Encoding.Unicode);
// Write the XSD schema to the file.
Console.WriteLine("\n-> Writing schema to file.");
dsSource.WriteXmlSchema(xtw);
fsOut.Close();

FileStream fsIn = new FileStream(fileName, FileMode.Open,
    FileAccess.Read);
// Create an XmlTextReader using the file stream.
XmlTextReader xtr = new XmlTextReader(fsIn);
// Read the schema into the DataSet.
DataSet dsDest = new DataSet();
Console.WriteLine("\n-> Reading schema into destination DataSet.");
dsDest.ReadXmlSchema(xtr);
fsIn.Close();

// Output information about the source DataSet
Console.WriteLine("\n---Destination DataSet---");
Console.WriteLine("DataSetName = {0}", dsDest.DataSetName);
foreach (DataTable dt in dsSource.Tables)
    Console.WriteLine("TableName = {0}\tColumns.Count = {1}",
        dt.TableName, dt.Columns.Count);
```

```
        foreach (DataRelation relation in dsDest.Relations)
            Console.WriteLine("RelationName = {0}", relation.RelationName);

        Console.WriteLine("\nPress any key to continue.");
        Console.ReadKey();
    }
  }
}
```

The output is shown in Figure 9-2.

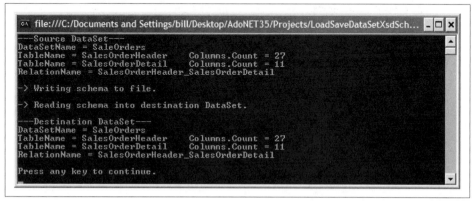

Figure 9-2. Output for LoadSaveDataSetXsdSchema solution

Discussion

The solution uses the XmlTextWriter and XmlTextReader classes to write and read the XML schema for the DataSet. The XmlTextWriter class provides a forward-only mechanism for generating XML streams or files containing XML data. The XmlTextReader class provides forward-only access to XML data in streams or files. The XmlTextReader does not validate the XML—for validation, use the XmlValidatingReader class. Both the XmlTextWriter and XmlTextReader classes conform to the W3C XML 1.0 and the Namespaces in XML recommendations. The XML file encoding used by the XmlTextWriter is specified in an argument to the constructor as one of the values from the System.Text.Encoding enumeration described in Table 9-1.

The WriteXmlSchema() and ReadXmlSchema() methods of the DataSet and DataTable classes are used to write and read the XSD schema for the XML data. The schema is written using the XSD standard and includes tables, relations, and constraint definitions. Example 9-4 shows the XSD file, *Schema.xsd*, created by this solution.

Example 9-4. File: Schema.xsd

```
<?xml version="1.0" encoding="utf-16"?>
  <xs:schema id="SaleOrders" xmlns="" xmlns:xs=http://www.w3.org/2001/XMLSchema
    xmlns:msdata="urn:schemas-microsoft-com:xml-msdata">
    <xs:element name="SaleOrders" msdata:IsDataSet="true"
      msdata:UseCurrentLocale="true">
      <xs:complexType>
        <xs:choice minOccurs="0" maxOccurs="unbounded">
          <xs:element name="SalesOrderHeader">
            <xs:complexType>
              <xs:sequence>
                <xs:element name="SalesOrderID" msdata:ReadOnly="true"
                  msdata:AutoIncrement="true" type="xs:int" />
                <xs:element name="RevisionNumber" type="xs:unsignedByte" />
                <xs:element name="OrderDate" type="xs:dateTime" />
                <xs:element name="DueDate" type="xs:dateTime" />
                <xs:element name="ShipDate" type="xs:dateTime" minOccurs="0" />
                <xs:element name="Status" type="xs:unsignedByte" />
                <xs:element name="OnlineOrderFlag" type="xs:boolean" />
                <xs:element name="SalesOrderNumber" msdata:ReadOnly="true"
                  minOccurs="0">
                  <xs:simpleType>
                    <xs:restriction base="xs:string">
                      <xs:maxLength value="25" />
                    </xs:restriction>
                  </xs:simpleType>
                </xs:element>
                <xs:element name="PurchaseOrderNumber" minOccurs="0">
                  <xs:simpleType>
                    <xs:restriction base="xs:string">
                      <xs:maxLength value="25" />
                    </xs:restriction>
                  </xs:simpleType>
                </xs:element>
                <xs:element name="AccountNumber" minOccurs="0">
                  <xs:simpleType>
                    <xs:restriction base="xs:string">
                      <xs:maxLength value="15" />
                    </xs:restriction>
                  </xs:simpleType>
                </xs:element>
                <xs:element name="CustomerID" type="xs:int" />
                <xs:element name="ContactID" type="xs:int" />
                <xs:element name="SalesPersonID" type="xs:int" minOccurs="0" />
                <xs:element name="TerritoryID" type="xs:int" minOccurs="0" />
                <xs:element name="BillToAddressID" type="xs:int" />
                <xs:element name="ShipToAddressID" type="xs:int" />
                <xs:element name="ShipMethodID" type="xs:int" />
                <xs:element name="CreditCardID" type="xs:int" minOccurs="0" />
                <xs:element name="CreditCardApprovalCode" minOccurs="0">
                  <xs:simpleType>
                    <xs:restriction base="xs:string">
                      <xs:maxLength value="15" />
```

Example 9-4. File: Schema.xsd (continued)

```
            </xs:restriction>
          </xs:simpleType>
        </xs:element>
        <xs:element name="CurrencyRateID" type="xs:int" minOccurs="0" />
        <xs:element name="SubTotal" type="xs:decimal" />
        <xs:element name="TaxAmt" type="xs:decimal" />
        <xs:element name="Freight" type="xs:decimal" />
        <xs:element name="TotalDue" msdata:ReadOnly="true" type="xs:decimal"
          minOccurs="0" />
        <xs:element name="Comment" minOccurs="0">
          <xs:simpleType>
            <xs:restriction base="xs:string">
              <xs:maxLength value="128" />
            </xs:restriction>
          </xs:simpleType>
        </xs:element>
        <xs:element name="rowguid" msdata:DataType="System.Guid, mscorlib,
          Version=2.0.0.0, Culture=neutral, PublicKeyToken=b77a5c561934e089"
          type="xs:string" />
        <xs:element name="ModifiedDate" type="xs:dateTime" />
      </xs:sequence>
    </xs:complexType>
  </xs:element>
  <xs:element name="SalesOrderDetail">
    <xs:complexType>
      <xs:sequence>
        <xs:element name="SalesOrderID" type="xs:int" />
        <xs:element name="SalesOrderDetailID" msdata:ReadOnly="true"
          msdata:AutoIncrement="true" type="xs:int" />
        <xs:element name="CarrierTrackingNumber" minOccurs="0">
          <xs:simpleType>
            <xs:restriction base="xs:string">
              <xs:maxLength value="25" />
            </xs:restriction>
          </xs:simpleType>
        </xs:element>
        <xs:element name="OrderQty" type="xs:short" />
        <xs:element name="ProductID" type="xs:int" />
        <xs:element name="SpecialOfferID" type="xs:int" />
        <xs:element name="UnitPrice" type="xs:decimal" />
        <xs:element name="UnitPriceDiscount" type="xs:decimal" />
        <xs:element name="LineTotal" msdata:ReadOnly="true" type="xs:decimal"
          minOccurs="0" />
        <xs:element name="rowguid" msdata:DataType="System.Guid, mscorlib,
          Version=2.0.0.0, Culture=neutral, PublicKeyToken=b77a5c561934e089"
          type="xs:string" />
        <xs:element name="ModifiedDate" type="xs:dateTime" />
      </xs:sequence>
    </xs:complexType>
  </xs:element>
</xs:choice>
</xs:complexType>
```

Example 9-4. File: Schema.xsd (continued)

```
    <xs:unique name="Constraint1" msdata:PrimaryKey="true">
      <xs:selector xpath=".//SalesOrderHeader" />
      <xs:field xpath="SalesOrderID" />
    </xs:unique>
    <xs:unique name="SalesOrderDetail_Constraint1"
      msdata:ConstraintName="Constraint1" msdata:PrimaryKey="true">
      <xs:selector xpath=".//SalesOrderDetail" />
      <xs:field xpath="SalesOrderID" />
      <xs:field xpath="SalesOrderDetailID" />
    </xs:unique>
    <xs:keyref name="SalesOrderHeader_SalesOrderDetail" refer="Constraint1">
    <xs:selector xpath=".//SalesOrderDetail" />
    <xs:field xpath="SalesOrderID" />
  </xs:keyref>
 </xs:element>
</xs:schema>
```

Use the `WriteXml( )` and `ReadXml( )` methods of the `DataSet` and `DataTable` classes to write and read the XML data in addition to the schema information.

9.3   Formatting Column Values When Saving Data As XML

Problem

You need to save some of the columns in a `DataTable` as attributes instead of elements when you write out the data as XML.

Solution

Use the `ColumnMapping` property of the `DataColumn` class.

The solution creates a `DataSet` containing three fields from the first two records of the `Person.Contact` table in `AdventureWorks`. The solution changes the `ColumnMapping` property on different columns and illustrates the effect by outputting the XML to the console.

The C# code in *Program.cs* in the project `FormatXmlColumnValues` is shown in Example 9-5.

Example 9-5. File: Program.cs for FormatXmlColumnValues solution

```
using System;
using System.Data;
using System.Data.SqlClient;

namespace FormatXmlColumnValues
{
```

Example 9-5. File: Program.cs for FormatXmlColumnValues solution (continued)

```
class Program
{
    static void Main(string[] args)
    {
        string sqlConnectString = "Data Source=(local);" +
            "Integrated security=SSPI;Initial Catalog=AdventureWorks;";

        string sqlSelect =
            "SELECT TOP 2 ContactID, FirstName, LastName " +
            "FROM Person.Contact";

        SqlDataAdapter da = new SqlDataAdapter(sqlSelect, sqlConnectString);
        DataSet ds = new DataSet( );
        da.TableMappings.Add("Table", "Contact");
        da.Fill(ds);
        DataTable dt = ds.Tables["Contact"];

        // Output default XML
        Console.WriteLine("---Default---");
        Console.WriteLine(ds.GetXml( ));

        // Set the column mappings and output XML
        dt.Columns["ContactID"].ColumnMapping = MappingType.Attribute;
        dt.Columns["FirstName"].ColumnMapping = MappingType.Element;
        dt.Columns["LastName"].ColumnMapping = MappingType.Element;
        Console.WriteLine(
            "\n---ContactID:Attribute; FirstName:Element; LastName:Element---");
        Console.WriteLine(ds.GetXml( ));

        // Set the column mappings and output XML
        dt.Columns["ContactID"].ColumnMapping = MappingType.Attribute;
        dt.Columns["FirstName"].ColumnMapping = MappingType.Attribute;
        dt.Columns["LastName"].ColumnMapping = MappingType.Attribute;
        Console.WriteLine(
            "\n---ContactID:Attribute; FirstName:Attribute; LastName:Attribute---");
        Console.WriteLine(ds.GetXml( ));

        // Set the column mappings and output XML
        dt.Columns["ContactID"].ColumnMapping = MappingType.Hidden;
        Console.WriteLine(
            "\n---ContactID:Hidden; FirstName:Attribute; LastName:Attribute---");
        Console.WriteLine(ds.GetXml( ));

        Console.WriteLine("\nPress any key to continue.");
        Console.ReadKey( );
    }
}
}
```

The output is shown in Figure 9-3.

```
file:///C:/Documents and Settings/bill/Desktop/AdoNET35/Projects/FormatXmlColumnValue...    _ □ ×
---Default---
<NewDataSet>
  <Contact>
    <ContactID>1</ContactID>
    <FirstName>Gustavo</FirstName>
    <LastName>Achong</LastName>
  </Contact>
  <Contact>
    <ContactID>2</ContactID>
    <FirstName>Catherine</FirstName>
    <LastName>Abel</LastName>
  </Contact>
</NewDataSet>

---ContactID:Attribute; FirstName:Element; LastName:Element---
<NewDataSet>
  <Contact ContactID="1">
    <FirstName>Gustavo</FirstName>
    <LastName>Achong</LastName>
  </Contact>
  <Contact ContactID="2">
    <FirstName>Catherine</FirstName>
    <LastName>Abel</LastName>
  </Contact>
</NewDataSet>

---ContactID:Attribute; FirstName:Attribute; LastName:Attribute---
<NewDataSet>
  <Contact ContactID="1" FirstName="Gustavo" LastName="Achong" />
  <Contact ContactID="2" FirstName="Catherine" LastName="Abel" />
</NewDataSet>

---ContactID:Hidden; FirstName:Attribute; LastName:Attribute---
<NewDataSet>
  <Contact FirstName="Gustavo" LastName="Achong" />
  <Contact FirstName="Catherine" LastName="Abel" />
</NewDataSet>
Press any key to continue.
```

Figure 9-3. Output for FormatXmlColumnValues solution

Discussion

The ColumnMapping property of the DataColumn specifies how the value of a column will be written when the DataSet is output as an XML document with the GetXml( ) method or WriteXml( ) method. The property value is one of the MappingType enumeration values described in Table 9-4.

Table 9-4. MappingType enumeration

Value	Description
Attribute	The value is written as an XML attribute. For example:
	`<MyRow MyColumn="my column value" />`
Element	The value is written as an XML element. For example:

	`<MyRow>`
	`    <MyColumn>my column value</MyColumn>`
	`</MyRow>`

	This is the default.
Hidden	The value is not written in the XML output.
SimpleContent	The value is written as text in the XML element for its row. For example:
	`<MyRow>my column value</MyRow>`
	This value can only be used if the table has neither Element columns nor nested relations.

There is no way to set the ColumnMapping property for all columns in a DataTable or DataSet at once. Each column must be set individually.

9.4 Creating an XML File That Shows Changes Made to a DataSet

Problem

When you use the GetXML( ) method of the DataSet, you may see only the current values in the DataSet. You want to get the original values and see which rows were added, edited, or deleted.

Solution

Create an XML DiffGram, which is a document that details the modifications made to a DataSet.

The solution loads the TOP three rows for the HumanResources.Department table in AdventureWorks into a DataSet and displays the DiffGram for the DataSet before modification. The solution then deletes the first row, modifies the second row, and adds a row to the end of the Department DataTable. The DiffGram for the DataSet after the changes is output to the console.

The C# code in *Program.cs* in the project CreateXmlDataSetChanges is shown in Example 9-6.

Example 9-6. File: Program.cs for CreateXmlDataSetChanges solution

```
using System;
using System.Data;
using System.Data.SqlClient;
using System.IO;
using System.Text;

namespace CreateXmlDataSetChanges
{
    class Program
    {
        static void Main(string[] args)
        {
            string sqlConnectString = "Data Source=(local);" +
                "Integrated security=SSPI;Initial Catalog=AdventureWorks;";
            string sqlSelect =
                "SELECT TOP 3 DepartmentID, Name, GroupName, ModifiedDate " +
                "FROM HumanResources.Department";

            SqlDataAdapter da = new SqlDataAdapter(sqlSelect, sqlConnectString);
            DataSet ds = new DataSet();
            da.TableMappings.Add("Table", "Department");
            da.FillSchema(ds, SchemaType.Mapped);
```

```
                ds.Tables["Department"].Columns["DepartmentID"].AutoIncrementSeed = -1;
                ds.Tables["Department"].Columns["DepartmentID"].AutoIncrementStep = -1;
                da.Fill(ds);

                // Display the DiffGram before changes
                Console.WriteLine("---DiffGram before data changes---");
                DisplayDiffGram(ds);

                // Make changes to the data
                DataTable dt = ds.Tables["Department"];

                // Delete the first row.
                dt.Rows[0].Delete();

                // Modify the Name field in the second row.
                dt.Rows[1]["Name"] += " [New]";

                // Add a row.
                DataRow row = dt.NewRow();
                row.SetField<string>("Name", "new Name");
                row.SetField<string>("GroupName", "new GroupName");
                row.SetField<DateTime>("ModifiedDate", DateTime.Now);
                dt.Rows.Add(row);

                // Display the DiffGram after changes
                Console.WriteLine("\n---DiffGram after data changes---");
                DisplayDiffGram(ds);

                Console.WriteLine("\nPress any key to continue.");
                Console.ReadKey();
            }

            private static void DisplayDiffGram(DataSet ds)
            {
                // Write the XML diffgram to a memory stream.
                MemoryStream ms = new MemoryStream();
                ds.WriteXml(ms, XmlWriteMode.DiffGram);

                // Display the XML DiffGram.
                byte[] result = ms.ToArray();
                ms.Close();
                Console.WriteLine(Encoding.UTF8.GetString(result, 0, result.Length));
            }
        }
    }
}
```

The output is shown in Figure 9-4.

Figure 9-4. Output for CreateXmlDataSetChanges solution

Discussion

A DiffGram is an XML format used to specify both the original and current values for the contents of a DataSet. It does not include any schema information. The DiffGram is also the primary serialization format used by the .NET Framework to persist and serialize a DataSet. The DiffGram format is XML-based, making it platform and application independent. It is not, however, widely used or understood outside of Microsoft .NET applications.

The DiffGram format is divided into three sections—current, original, and errors—as shown in the following example:

```xml
<?xml version="1.0"?>
<diffgr:diffgram
    xmlns:msdata="urn:schemas-microsoft-com:xml-msdata"
    xmlns:diffgr="urn:schemas-microsoft-com:xml-diffgram-v1">

    <DataInstanceName>
        . . .
    </DataInstanceName>

    <diffgr:before>
        . . .
    </diffgr:before>

    <diffgr:errors>
        . . .
    </diffgr:errors>
</diffgr:diffgram>
```

Here are descriptions of the three DiffGram sections:

<DataInstanceName>

The DataInstanceName is the name of the DataSet or DataTable. This block contains the current version of the data containing all modifications. Modified elements are identified with the diffgr:hasChanges="modified" annotation, while new elements are identified with the diffgr:hasChanges="inserted" annotation. Deleted elements are not annotated, rather, they appear only in the <diffgr:before> section.

<diffgr:before>

This section contains the original version of the elements that have been modified or deleted. Elements in this section are matched to elements in the *<DataInstanceName>* section using the diffgr:id annotation with matching values.

<diffgr:errors>

This section contains error information for an element in the *<DataInstanceName>* section. Elements in this section are matched to elements in the *<DataInstanceName>* section using the diffgr:id annotation with matching values.

The example shows a subset of fields for the top three rows of the HumanResources.Department table in AdventureWorks into a DataTable called Department in a DataSet. The first row is deleted, the second is modified, and a row is added to the end of the DataTable. After these modifications, the DiffGram for the DataSet output is as shown in Figure 9-4.

The DiffGram contains both the annotation indicating inserted and modified records. The <diffgr:before> section contains the original records for both the deleted record with DepartmentID = 1 and the modified record with DepartmentID = 2. The current section of the DiffGram shows the updated record with DepartmentID = 2, the unchanged record with DepartmentID = 3, and the new record with DepartmentID = -1.

As shown in the example, a DiffGram is written for a DataSet by specifying an XmlWriteMode of DiffGram when calling the WriteXml() method of the DataSet. The GetXml() method cannot be used to generate a DiffGram. A DataSet can be loaded from an XML DiffGram by specifying an XmlReadMode of DiffGram when calling the ReadXml() method.

9.5   Synchronizing a DataSet and an XML Document

Problem

You need to simultaneously work with both a DataSet and its XML representation, keeping them automatically synchronized with any changes made.

Solution

Use a DataSet and XmlDataDocument together as demonstrated in the three approaches.

The solution loads a DataSet with a subset of the Production.Product and Production.Location tables in the AdventureWorks database and creates a data relation between them on the ProductID column. The solution demonstrates three methods to create a synchronized DataSet and XML document, as described in the discussion section. DataSet and XML document metrics are output throughout to show the effect of the various aspects of the synchronization for each of the three approaches.

The C# code in *Program.cs* in the project file SynchronizeDataWithXmlDocument is shown in Example 9-7.

Example 9-7. File: Program.cs for SynchronizeDataWithXmlDocument solution

```
using System;
using System.Data;
using System.Data.SqlClient;
using System.Xml;

namespace SynchronizeDataSetWithXmlDocument
{
    class Program
    {
        static void Main(string[] args)
        {
            string xmlFileName = @"..\..\..\ProductInventory.xml";

            DataSet ds;
            XmlDataDocument xd;

            Console.WriteLine("---Fill DataSet with schema and data; " +
                "Get XmlDataDocument based on DataSet---");
```

```
        ds = null;
        xd = null;
        // Fill the DataSet with schema and data
        ds = FillDataSet(true);
        OutputInfo(ds, xd);
        // Synchronize the XmlDataDocument to the DataSet
        xd = new XmlDataDocument(ds);
        OutputInfo(ds, xd);

        Console.WriteLine("\n---Fill DataSet with schema; " +
            "Fill DataSet data from XML document---");
        ds = null;
        xd = null;
        // Fill the DataSet with schema only
        ds = FillDataSet(false);
        OutputInfo(ds, xd);
        // Get the XML document for the DataSet.
        xd = new XmlDataDocument(ds);
        OutputInfo(ds, xd);
        // Load the data into the XML document from the XML file.
        xd.Load(xmlFileName);
        OutputInfo(ds, xd);

        Console.WriteLine("\n---Fill DataSet schema from XML document; " +
            "Fill DataSet data from XML document--");
        ds = null;
        xd = null;
        // Create an XML document.
        xd = new XmlDataDocument( );
        OutputInfo(ds, xd);
        // Get the DataSet for the XML document.
        ds = xd.DataSet;
        OutputInfo(ds, xd);
        // Get schema for the DataSet from the XSD inline schema.
        ds.ReadXmlSchema(xmlFileName);
        OutputInfo(ds, xd);
        // Load the data into the XML document from the XML file.
        xd.Load(xmlFileName);
        OutputInfo(ds, xd);

        Console.WriteLine("\nPress any key to continue.");
        Console.ReadKey( );
    }

    private static DataSet FillDataSet(bool includeData)
    {
        string sqlConnectString = "Data Source=(local);" +
            "Integrated security=SSPI;Initial Catalog=AdventureWorks;";
```

```
        string sqlSelect = "SELECT ProductID, Name, ProductNumber " +
            "FROM Production.Product WHERE ProductID BETWEEN 1 AND 3;" +
            "SELECT ProductID, LocationID, Shelf, Bin, Quantity " +
            "FROM Production.ProductInventory WHERE ProductID BETWEEN 1 AND 3;";

        // Create the data adapter and table name mappings
        SqlDataAdapter da = new SqlDataAdapter(sqlSelect, sqlConnectString);
        da.TableMappings.Add("Table", "Product");
        da.TableMappings.Add("Table1", "Inventory");

        // Create the DataSet and fill with schema and optionally data
        DataSet ds = new DataSet("ProductInventory");
        da.FillSchema(ds, SchemaType.Mapped);
        if(includeData)
            da.Fill(ds);

        // Add the data relation between Product and Inventory table
        ds.Relations.Add("Product_Inventory",
            ds.Tables["Product"].Columns["ProductID"],
            ds.Tables["Inventory"].Columns["ProductID"]);

        return ds;
    }

    private static void OutputInfo(DataSet ds, XmlDataDocument xd)
    {
        string dsInfo = (ds == null) ? "DataSet = null" :
            "DataSet tables = " + ds.Tables.Count + "; " +
            "DataSet rows = " +
            ((ds.Tables.Count == 0) ? "0" :
            (ds.Tables["Product"].Rows.Count +
            ds.Tables["Inventory"].Rows.Count).ToString());
        string xdInfo = (xd == null) ? "XmlDataDocument = null" :
            "XmlDataDocument length = " +
            xd.InnerXml.Length.ToString();
        Console.WriteLine("{0}; {1}", dsInfo, xdInfo);
    }
  }
}
```

The output is shown in Figure 9-5.

Discussion

The .NET Framework allows real-time, synchronous access to both a DataSet and its XML representation in an XmlDataDocument object. The synchronized DataSet and XmlDataDocument classes work with a single set of data—changes to one are reflected immediately in the other.

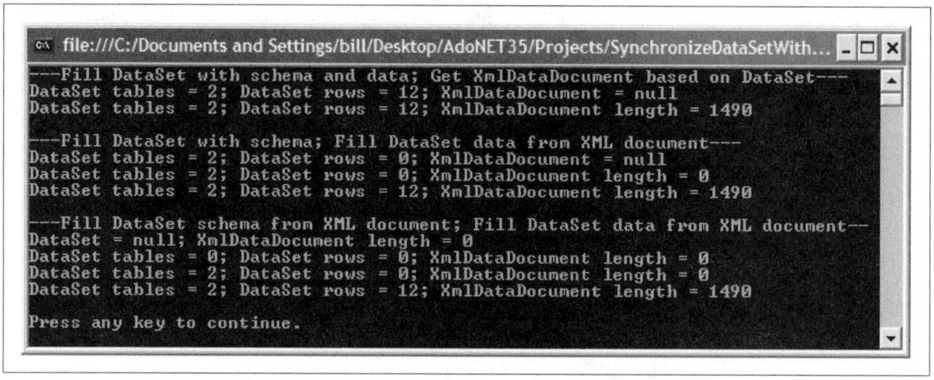

Figure 9-5. Output for SyncronizeDataSetWithXmlDocument solution

The solution shows three ways to synchronize a DataSet with an XmlDataDocument:

Method 1

Populate a DataSet with both schema and data. Synchronize it with a new XmlDataDocument, initializing it with the DataSet in the constructor.

Method 2

Populate a DataSet with a schema but no data. Synchronize it with a new XmlDataDocument, initializing it with the DataSet in the constructor. Load an XML document into the XmlDataDocument. The table and column names in the DataSet schema to be synchronized must match those in the XmlDataDocument.

Method 3

Create a new XmlDataDocument and access its DataSet through the DataSet property. Populate the schema for the DataSet. In the example, the schema is read from the XSD inline schema in the XML document. If the XML document does not have an inline schema, it might be possible to infer the schema using the InferSchema( ) method. Otherwise, the entire DataSet schema must be defined programmatically. Next, load the XML document into the synchronized XmlDataDocument. The table and column names in the DataSet schema to be synchronized must match those in the XmlDataDocument.

Example 9-8 shows the XML file *ProductInventory.xml* used in this solution.

Example 9-8. File: ProductInventory.xml

```
<ProductInventory>
  <Product>
    <ProductID>1</ProductID>
    <Name>Adjustable Race</Name>
    <ProductNumber>AR-5381</ProductNumber>
  </Product>
```

Example 9-8. File: ProductInventory.xml (continued)

```
<Product>
  <ProductID>2</ProductID>
  <Name>Bearing Ball</Name>
  <ProductNumber>BA-8327</ProductNumber>
</Product>
<Product>
  <ProductID>3</ProductID>
  <Name>BB Ball Bearing</Name>
  <ProductNumber>BE-2349</ProductNumber>
</Product>
<Inventory>
  <ProductID>1</ProductID>
  <LocationID>1</LocationID>
  <Shelf>A</Shelf>
  <Bin>1</Bin>
  <Quantity>408</Quantity>
</Inventory>
<Inventory>
  <ProductID>1</ProductID>
  <LocationID>6</LocationID>
  <Shelf>B</Shelf>
  <Bin>5</Bin>
  <Quantity>324</Quantity>
</Inventory>
<Inventory>
  <ProductID>1</ProductID>
  <LocationID>50</LocationID>
  <Shelf>A</Shelf>
  <Bin>5</Bin>
  <Quantity>353</Quantity>
</Inventory>
<Inventory>
  <ProductID>2</ProductID>
  <LocationID>1</LocationID>
  <Shelf>A</Shelf>
  <Bin>2</Bin>
  <Quantity>427</Quantity>
</Inventory>
<Inventory>
  <ProductID>2</ProductID>
  <LocationID>6</LocationID>
  <Shelf>B</Shelf>
  <Bin>1</Bin>
  <Quantity>318</Quantity>
</Inventory>
<Inventory>
  <ProductID>2</ProductID>
  <LocationID>50</LocationID>
  <Shelf>A</Shelf>
  <Bin>6</Bin>
  <Quantity>364</Quantity>
</Inventory>
```

Example 9-8. File: ProductInventory.xml (continued)

```
  <Inventory>
    <ProductID>3</ProductID>
    <LocationID>1</LocationID>
    <Shelf>A</Shelf>
    <Bin>7</Bin>
    <Quantity>585</Quantity>
  </Inventory>
  <Inventory>
    <ProductID>3</ProductID>
    <LocationID>6</LocationID>
    <Shelf>B</Shelf>
    <Bin>9</Bin>
    <Quantity>443</Quantity>
  </Inventory>
  <Inventory>
    <ProductID>3</ProductID>
    <LocationID>50</LocationID>
    <Shelf>A</Shelf>
    <Bin>10</Bin>
    <Quantity>324</Quantity>
  </Inventory>
</ProductInventory>
```

9.6   Storing and Retrieving XML with a Non-XML Data Type Column

Problem

You need to store XML to a database column that does not directly support XML.

Solution

Store the contents of the InnerXml of the XmlDocument to the database. You can later load this into an empty XmlDocument with LoadXml( ).

Example 9-9 shows the T-SQL statement that creates the StoreXmlDatabaseField table used in this solution.

Example 9-9. T-SQL statement: Create table StoreXmlDatabaseField

```
USE AdoDotNet35Cookbook
GO
CREATE TABLE StoreXmlDatabaseField(
    Id int NOT NULL PRIMARY KEY,
    XmlField nvarchar(max) NULL)
```

The T-SQL statement creates a table with the schema shown in Table 9-5.

Table 9-5. StoreXmlDatabaseField schema

Column name	Data type	Length	Allow nulls?
Id	int	4	No
XmlField	nvarchar	MAX	Yes

The solution uses the XML file *Department.xml* shown in Example 9-10. This file contains the XML representation of the first three records in the HumanResources.Department table in AdventureWorks.

Example 9-10. File: Department.xml

```xml
<?xml version="1.0" standalone="yes"?>
<DocumentElement>
  <Department>
    <DepartmentID>1</DepartmentID>
    <Name>Engineering</Name>
    <GroupName>Research and Development</GroupName>
    <ModifiedDate>2007-10-06T19:15:31.803-04:00</ModifiedDate>
  </Department>
  <Department>
    <DepartmentID>2</DepartmentID>
    <Name>Tool Design</Name>
    <GroupName>Research and Development</GroupName>
    <ModifiedDate>2007-10-06T18:52:47.04-04:00</ModifiedDate>
  </Department>
  <Department>
    <DepartmentID>3</DepartmentID>
    <Name>Sales</Name>
    <GroupName>Sales and Marketing</GroupName>
    <ModifiedDate>2007-10-06T21:39:39.85-04:00</ModifiedDate>
  </Department>
</DocumentElement>
```

The solution creates a DataTable and uses a data adapter to fill it with both data and schema from the StoreXmlDatabaseField table. A command builder is created for the data adapter. The Department.xml file is loaded into an XmlDocument. A new row is created in the DataTable. The InnerText property of the XmlDocument is stored to a text-type field named XmlField. The change is updated to the data source using the data adapter. The DataTable is refreshed by clearing it and reloading it with data, including loading the XML field into an XmlDocument from the database. The content of the XML field is output to the console from the XmlDocument.

The C# code in *Program.cs* in the project StoreXmlDatabaseField is shown in Example 9-11.

Example 9-11. File: Program.cs for StoreXmlDatabaseField solution

```csharp
using System;
using System.Data;
using System.Data.SqlClient;
using System.Xml;

namespace StoreXmlDatabaseField
{
    class Program
    {
        static void Main(string[] args)
        {
            string sqlConnectString = "Data Source=(local);" +
                "Integrated security=SSPI;Initial Catalog=AdoDotNet35Cookbook;";

            string selectText = "SELECT Id, XmlField FROM StoreXmlDatabaseField";

            // Create the data adapter and command builder
            SqlDataAdapter da = new SqlDataAdapter(selectText, sqlConnectString);
            SqlCommandBuilder cb = new SqlCommandBuilder(da);

            // Create DataTable and get both schema and data
            DataTable dt = new DataTable( );
            da.FillSchema(dt, SchemaType.Source);
            da.Fill(dt);

            // Load the department XML from a file into an XmlDocument
            string departmentFileName = @"..\..\..\Department.xml";
            XmlDocument xdSource = new XmlDocument( );
            xdSource.Load(departmentFileName);
            // Create a new row from the XML document
            DataRow rowSource = dt.NewRow( );
            rowSource["Id"] = 1;
            rowSource["XmlField"] = xdSource.InnerXml;
            dt.Rows.Add(rowSource);

            // Update the database
            da.Update(dt);

            // Clear the DataTable
            dt.Clear( );

            // Read the DataTable from the database
            da.Fill(dt);

            // Load the XmlField for DataRow with Id = 1 into an XML document
            DataRow rowDest = dt.Rows.Find(1);
            XmlDocument xdDest = new XmlDocument( );
            xdDest.LoadXml(rowDest.Field<string>("XmlField"));

            // Output the XmlDocument to the console
            Console.WriteLine(xdDest.InnerXml);
```

```
        Console.WriteLine("\nPress any key to continue.");
        Console.ReadKey();
    }
  }
}
```

The output is shown in Figure 9-6.

Figure 9-6. Output for StoreXmlDatabaseField solution

Discussion

The solution demonstrates how to store XML data in a text-type field of a database table and subsequently read it into an XmlDocument using the LoadXml( ) method. Standard database access techniques using a DataAdapter and DataTable are used.

9.7 Working with a SQL Server XML Data Type Column

Problem

You need to store an XML document to an xml data type in SQL Server and subsequently retrieve that data as an XML document.

Solution

Example 9-12 shows the T-SQL statement that creates the table TableWithXmlDataType used in this solution.

Example 9-12. T-SQL statement: Create table TableWithXmlDataType

```
USE AdoDotNet35Cookbook
GO
CREATE TABLE TableWithXmlDataType(
    Id int NOT NULL PRIMARY KEY,
    XmlField xml NULL)
```

The T-SQL statement creates a table with the schema shown in Table 9-6.

Table 9-6. TableWithXmlDataType schema

Column name	Data type	Allow nulls?
Id	int	No
XmlField	xml	Yes

The solution executes a T-SQL insert command to insert a row into the table TableWithXmlDataType with the xml data type field XmlField set to a simple XML fragment <MyElement>MyValue</MyElement>. A data adapter is created and used to fill a DataTable with the values TableWithXmlDataType—the newly added row. The contents of the DataTable are output to the console, including the string representation of the value in the field XmlField. A data reader is used to retrieve the value of XmlField as an XmlDocument object and the results are output to the console.

The C# code in *Program.cs* in the project TableWithXmlDataType is shown in Example 9-13.

Example 9-13. File: Program.cs for TableWithXmlDataType solution

```csharp
using System;
using System.Data;
using System.Data.SqlClient;
using System.Xml;
using System.Data.SqlTypes;

namespace TableWithXmlDataType
{
    class Program
    {
        static void Main(string[] args)
        {
            string sqlConnectString = "Data Source=(local);" +
                "Integrated security=SSPI;Initial Catalog=AdoDotNet35Cookbook;";

            // Define T-SQL statements for SELECT and INSERT
            string sqlSelect = "SELECT Id, xmlField FROM TableWithXmlDataType";
            string sqlInsert = "INSERT INTO TableWithXmlDataType VALUES " +
                @"(1, '<MyElement>MyValue</MyElement>')";

            // Create a connection
            SqlConnection connection = new SqlConnection(sqlConnectString);

            // Insert row with simple XML value in an XML data type column
            SqlCommand command1 = new SqlCommand(sqlInsert, connection);
            connection.Open( );
            int rowsAdded = command1.ExecuteNonQuery( );
            connection.Close( );
            Console.WriteLine("{0} row added to database.", rowsAdded);
```

Example 9-13. File: Program.cs for TableWithXmlDataType solution (continued)

```
// Retrieve the XML data as a string data type using a DataAdapter
SqlDataAdapter da = new SqlDataAdapter(sqlSelect, sqlConnectString);
DataTable dt = new DataTable( );
da.Fill(dt);
Console.WriteLine(
    "\n---RETURN XML DATA TYPE AS STRING USING DATAADAPTER---");
foreach (DataRow row in dt.Rows)
{
    Console.WriteLine("Id = {0}, XmlField = {1}",
        row["Id"], row["XmlField"]);
}

// Retrieve data as XML using an SqlDataReader
SqlCommand command2 = new SqlCommand(sqlSelect, connection);
connection.Open( );
SqlDataReader dr = command2.ExecuteReader( );
Console.WriteLine("\n---RETURN XML DATA TYPE AS XML USING DATAREADER---");
while (dr.Read( ))
{
    // Load the XML data type field into a XmlDataDocument
    XmlDocument xdXmlField = new XmlDocument( );
    xdXmlField.Load(dr.GetSqlXml(1).CreateReader( ));

    // Output the record to the console
    Console.WriteLine("Id = {0}, XmlField = {1}",
        dr.GetSqlInt32(0), xdXmlField.InnerXml);
}
connection.Close( );

Console.WriteLine("\nPress any key to continue.");
Console.ReadKey( );
        }
    }
}
```

The output is shown in Figure 9-7.

Figure 9-7. Output for TableWithXmlDataType solution

Discussion

The xml data type was introduced in SQL Server 2005; it supports storing both XML documents and fragments in the database. An XML fragment is an XML instance that does not have a single top-level (root) element. You can create columns, parameters, and variables of the new xml type and store XML instances in them. xml data type instances have a maximum size of 2 GB.

An XML schema collection can be associated with a column, parameter, or variable of an xml data type. An xml data type with an associated schema is referred to as being *typed*. The XML schema validates xml data type instances against constraints and provides data type information about the elements and attributes in the instance. The schema also helps SQL Server optimize data storage. The XML schema collection must be registered with SQL Server before it can be used to create typed xml instances.

9.8   Using an XPath Query to Retrieve Data

Problem

You need to use an XPath expression to extract certain rows from a DataSet.

Solution

Use the SelectSingleNode() and the SelectNodes() method of the XmlDataDocument class.

The solution creates a DataSet and fills it with schema and a subset of data from the Sales.SalesOrderHeader and Sales.SalesOrderDetail tables in AdventureWorks. A nested data relation is created between the tables. An XPath query is used to select the node for the SalesOrderHeader where the SalesOrderID = 43664 using the SelectSingleNode() method of the XmlDataDocument class for the DataSet. The related SalesOrderDetail nodes are selected from the XmlDataDocument using the SelectNodes() method of the XmlDataDocument. The query results are output to the console.

The C# code in *Program.cs* in the project XPathQueryDataSet is shown in Example 9-14.

Example 9-14. File: Program.cs for XPathQueryDataSet solution

```
using System;
using System.Data;
using System.Data.SqlClient;
using System.Xml;
```

Example 9-14. File: Program.cs for XPathQueryDataSet solution (continued)

```csharp
namespace XPathQueryDataSet
{
    class Program
    {
        static void Main(string[] args)
        {
            int salesOrderId = 43664;

            string sqlConnectString = "Data Source=(local);" +
                "Integrated security=SSPI;Initial Catalog=AdventureWorks;";

            string sqlSelect = "SELECT * FROM Sales.SalesOrderHeader " +
                "WHERE SalesOrderID < 43670;" +
                "SELECT * FROM Sales.SalesOrderDetail " +
                "WHERE SalesOrderID < 43670;";

            // Create and fill the DataSet
            SqlDataAdapter da = new SqlDataAdapter(sqlSelect, sqlConnectString);
            da.TableMappings.Add("Table", "SalesOrderHeader");
            da.TableMappings.Add("Table1", "SalesOrderDetail");
            DataSet ds = new DataSet("SalesOrder");
            da.Fill(ds);

            // Create a nested relation between header and detail
            ds.Relations.Add(
                ds.Tables["SalesOrderHeader"].Columns["SalesOrderID"],
                ds.Tables["SalesOrderDetail"].Columns["SalesOrderID"]
                ).Nested = true;

            // Use an XPath query to select the order.
            String xPathQuery =
                "/SalesOrder/SalesOrderHeader[SalesOrderID = " +
                salesOrderId + "]";
            XmlNode xmlNode =
                (new XmlDataDocument(ds)).SelectSingleNode(xPathQuery);

            if (xmlNode != null)
            {
                // Retrieve the query results for the Order.
                Console.WriteLine("SalesOrderHeader:");
                Console.WriteLine("  SalesOrderID = {0}",
                    xmlNode.ChildNodes[0].InnerText);
                Console.WriteLine("  OrderDate = {0}",
                    xmlNode.ChildNodes[2].InnerText);
                Console.WriteLine("  CustomerId = {0}",
                    xmlNode.ChildNodes[10].InnerText);

                // Retrieve the query results for the Order Details.
                Console.WriteLine("\n  SalesOrderDetails:");
                XmlNodeList xmlNodeList = xmlNode.SelectNodes("SalesOrderDetail");
                for (int i = 0; i < xmlNodeList.Count; i++)
```

Example 9-14. File: Program.cs for XPathQueryDataSet solution (continued)

```
                {
                    Console.WriteLine(
                        "\tSalesOrderDetailID = {0}\tProductID = {1}\tOrderQty = {2}",
                        xmlNodeList[i].ChildNodes[0].InnerText,
                        xmlNodeList[i].ChildNodes[4].InnerText,
                        xmlNodeList[i].ChildNodes[3].InnerText);
                }
            }
            else
            {
                Console.WriteLine("No data found for SalesOrderID = " + salesOrderId);
            }

            Console.WriteLine("\nPress any key to continue.");
            Console.ReadKey( );
        }
    }
}
```

The output is shown in Figure 9-8.

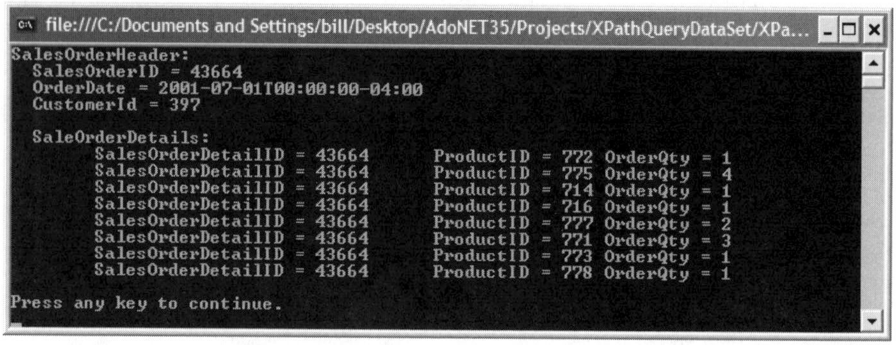

Figure 9-8. Output for XPathQueryDataSet solution

Discussion

The W3C XML Path Language (XPath) is a navigation language used to select nodes from an XML Document. It is defined by W3 as a standard navigation language. The specification can be found at *http://www.w3.org/TR/xpath*. SQL Server implements a subset of the language as described in SQL Server Books Online.

In .NET, the `DataSet` is synchronized with the `XmlDataDocument`. As a result, in some cases XML services can be used to access the `XmlDataDocument` to perform certain functionality more conveniently than by using the `DataSet` directly. To execute an XPath query against the contents of a `DataSet`, call the `SelectSingleNode( )` method of the `XmlDataDocument` for the `DataSet`, passing the XPath query as an argument:

```
XmlNode xmlNode = (new XmlDataDocument(ds)).SelectSingleNode(xPathQuery);
```

The example iterates over the SalesOrderDetail for the SalesOrderHeader by accessing the XmlNodeList containing that data within the XmlNode retrieved by the XPath query:

```
XmlNodeList xmlNodeList = xmlNode.SelectNodes("SalesOrderDetail");
```

This technique works in this example because the Nested property of the DataRelation object is set to true for the DataRelation relating the tables containing the SalesOrderHeader and SalesOrderDetail data. Setting the Nested property to true causes the child rows to be nested within the parent row elements when output as XML data or accessed using the XmlDataDocument for the DataSet. The Nested property is false by default. If the Nested property were false, you'd have to use a second XPath query to retrieve the Order Details data from the XmlDataDocument for the DataSet.

9.9 Reading XML Data Directly from SQL Server

Problem

You need to read XML data directly from the SQL Server.

Solution

Use the FOR XML clause in the stored procedure or SQL statement.

The C# code in *Program.cs* in the project ReadXmlDirectlyFromSqlServer is shown in Example 9-15.

Example 9-15. File: Program.cs for ReadXmlDirectlyFromSqlServer solution

```
using System;
using System.Data;
using System.Data.SqlClient;
using System.Xml;

namespace ReadXmlDirectlyFromSqlServer
{
    class Program
    {
        static void Main(string[] args)
        {
            string sqlConnectString = "Data Source=(local);" +
                "Integrated security=SSPI;Initial Catalog=AdventureWorks;";
            string sqlSelect = "SELECT ContactID, FirstName, LastName " +
                "FROM Person.Contact WHERE ContactID BETWEEN 15 AND 20 " +
                "FOR XML AUTO, XMLDATA";

            DataSet ds = new DataSet();
            using (SqlConnection connection = new SqlConnection(sqlConnectString))
            {
                // Create the command.
                SqlCommand command = new SqlCommand(sqlSelect, connection);
```

Example 9-15. File: Program.cs for ReadXmlDirectlyFromSqlServer solution (continued)

```
                // Read the XML data into a XML reader.
                connection.Open( );
                XmlReader xr = command.ExecuteXmlReader( );

                // Read the data from the XML reader into the DataTable.
                ds.ReadXml(xr, XmlReadMode.Fragment);
                xr.Close( );
            }

            Console.WriteLine("ContactID\tFirstName\tLastName");
            Console.WriteLine("---------\t---------\t--------");
            foreach (DataRow row in ds.Tables[0].Rows)
                Console.WriteLine("{0}\t\t{1}\t\t{2}",
                    row["ContactID"], row["FirstName"], row["LastName"]);

            Console.WriteLine("\nPress any key to continue.");
            Console.ReadKey( );
        }
    }
}
```

The output is shown in Figure 9-9.

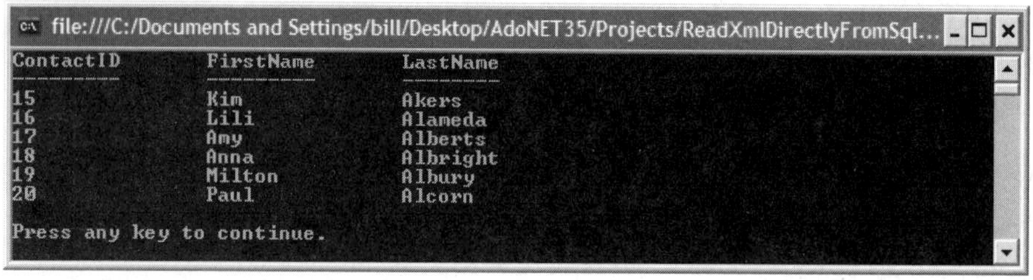

Figure 9-9. Output for ReadXmlDirectlyFromSqlServer solution

Discussion

SQL Server 2000 introduced support for retrieving data in XML format using the FOR XML clause. The .NET SQL Server data provider SqlCommand object has an ExecuteXmlReader( ) that allows you to retrieve an XML value directly from SQL Server. The method returns an XmlReader, which contains the XML value that is the result of the SQL query. The ExecuteXmlReader( ) method returns a single XML value and can only be used with SQL statements that return XML data: SQL statements with a FOR XML clause, ntext or nvarchar data type fields containing valid XML, or xml data type fields.

For more information about the FOR XML clause, see Microsoft SQL Server Books Online.

9.10 Transforming a DataSet Using XSLT

Problem

You need to use an XSLT stylesheet to transform the contents of a DataSet.

Solution

Create an XslTransform object and call the Transform( ) method.

The solution uses a single XSLT stylesheet to transform the XML for the HumanResources.Contact table in the AdventureWorks database into HTML displaying the contact data in an HTML table.

The XSLT stylesheet *Contact.xslt* used to transform the data into HTML is shown in Example 9-16. The solution assumes the stylesheet is in the same directory as the project file *TransformDataSetXslt.csproj*.

Example 9-16. File: Contact.xslt

```
<?xml version="1.0" encoding="UTF-8" ?>
<xsl:stylesheet version="1.0" xmlns:xsl="http://www.w3.org/1999/XSL/Transform">
<xsl:template match="/">
<html>
<body>
    <table>
        <tr bgcolor="#AAAAAA">
            <td>Contact ID</td>
            <td>First Name</td>
            <td>Last Name</td>
        </tr>

        <xsl:for-each select="/ContactDS/Contact">
            <tr>
                <td>
                    <xsl:value-of select="ContactID" />
                </td>
                <td>
                    <xsl:value-of select="FirstName" />
                </td>
                <td>
                    <xsl:value-of select="LastName" />
                </td>
            </tr>
        </xsl:for-each>
    </table>
</body>
</html>
</xsl:template>
</xsl:stylesheet>
```

The solution fills a DataSet with a several fields from the TOP 10 rows of the Person.Contact table in the AdventureWorks database. The XSLT transformation is created from the stylesheet *Contact.xslt* and used to transform the DataSet into a HTML file named *Contact.html* written to the same directory as the solution file *TransformDataSetXslt.sln*.

The C# code in *Program.cs* in the project TransformDataSetXslt is shown in Example 9-17.

Example 9-17. File: Program.cs for TransformDataSetXslt solution

```
using System;
using System.Data;
using System.Data.SqlClient;
using System.Xml;
using System.Xml.Xsl;
using System.Text;

namespace TransformDataSetXslt
{
    class Program
    {
        static void Main(string[] args)
        {
            string xsltFileName = @"..\..\Contact.xslt";
            string htmlFileName = @"..\..\..\Contact.html";

            string sqlConnectString = "Data Source=(local);" +
                "Integrated security=SSPI;Initial Catalog=AdventureWorks;";

            string sqlSelect =
                "SELECT TOP 10 ContactID, FirstName, LastName " +
                "FROM Person.Contact";

            SqlDataAdapter da =
                new SqlDataAdapter(sqlSelect, sqlConnectString);
            DataSet ds = new DataSet("ContactDS");
            da.Fill(ds, "Contact");
            Console.WriteLine("=> DataSet loaded.");

            // Apply the XML transformation storing results to StringWriter.
            XslCompiledTransform xslt = new XslCompiledTransform();
            xslt.Load(xsltFileName);
            Console.WriteLine("=> XSLT stylesheet {0} loaded and compiled.",
                xsltFileName);
            XmlTextWriter xw =
                new XmlTextWriter(htmlFileName, Encoding.UTF8);
            xslt.Transform(new XmlDataDocument(ds), xw);
            Console.WriteLine("=> DataSet transformed to HTML in file {0}",
                htmlFileName);
```

Example 9-17. File: Program.cs for TransformDataSetXslt solution (continued)

```
        Console.WriteLine("\nPress any key to continue.");
        Console.ReadKey();
    }
}
}
```

The output is shown in Figure 9-10.

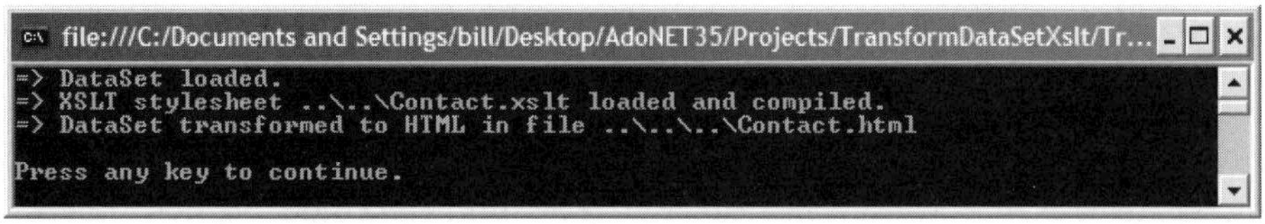

Figure 9-10. Output for TransformDataSetXslt solution

Figure 9-11 shows the transformation result file *Contact.html* opened in a web browser.

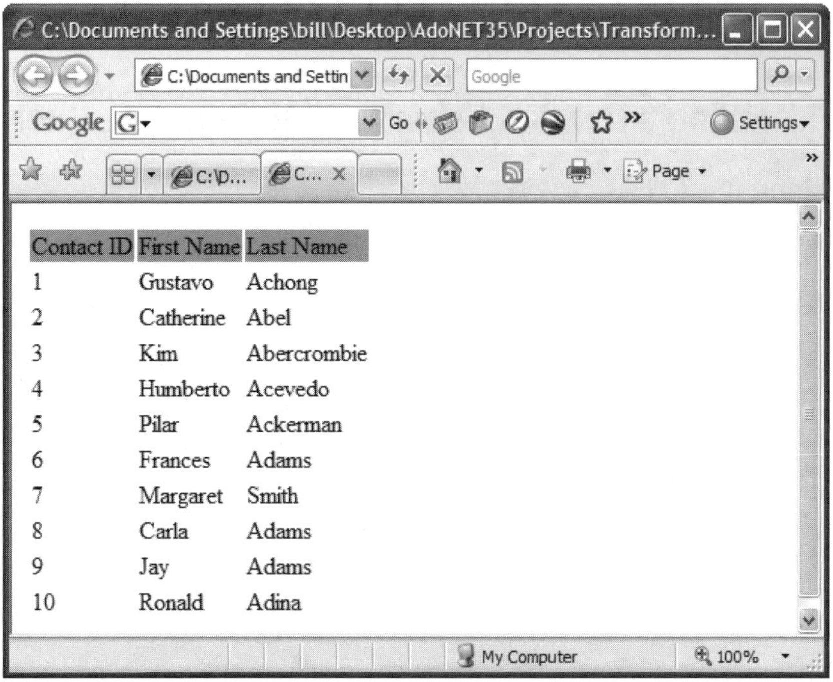

Figure 9-11. HTML output for TransformDataSetXslt

Discussion

Extensible Stylesheet Langauge Transformations (XSLT) evolved from the Extensible Stylesheet Language (XSL). XSLT defines a standard for XML data transformation— parsing an input XML document and converting it into a result document. A common use for XSLT is to transform XML data returned from a middle tier component into one or more result documents (often HTML) to support different user interface or device requirements. For more information about XSLT, see Microsoft's MSDN Library.

In .NET, the DataSet is synchronized with the XmlDataDocument. As a result, in some cases, XML services can be used to access the XmlDataDocument to perform certain functionality more conveniently than could be accomplished using the DataSet directly. To use XSLT to transform the contents of a DataSet, create an XslCompiledTransform object and call the Transform( ) method on that object, as shown in this example:

```
XslCompiledTransform xslt = new XslCompiledTransform( );
xslt.Load(xsltFileName);
XmlTextWriter xw = new XmlTextWriter(htmlFileName, Encoding.UTF8);
xslt.Transform(new XmlDataDocument(ds), xw);
```

The results of the transformation can be sent to a variety of output formats using overloaded versions of the Transform( ) method.

9.11   Filling a DataSet Using an XML Template Query

Problem

You need to fill a DataSet using an XML template query.

Solution

Use the SQL XML Managed classes to use an XML template query to fill a DataSet.

The solution uses one XML file named *GetContactQuery.xml*, shown in Example 9-18. The solution assumes the file is in the same directory as the solution file *FillDataSetXmlTemplateQuery.sln*.

Example 9-18. File: GetContactQuery.xml

```
<?xml version="1.0" encoding="utf-8" ?>
<ROOT xmlns:sql='urn:schemas-microsoft-com:xml-sql'>
    <sql:header>
        <sql:param name="ContactID" />
    </sql:header>
    <sql:query>
        SELECT
            ContactID, FirstName, LastName
        FROM
            Person.Contact
```

Example 9-18. File: GetContactQuery.xml (continued)

```
        WHERE
            ContactID = @ContactID
        FOR XML AUTO
    </sql:query>
</ROOT>
```

The solution creates a `SqlXmlCommand` template query and its single `SqlXmlParameter` object. The parameter is set to the user-specified value. A `SqlXmlDataAdapter` object is created and executed to fill a new `DataSet` based on the template query. The result set in the `DataSet` is output to the console.

The project needs a reference to the assembly `Microsoft.Data.SqlXml`. If this assembly is not installed on your computer, you can download it from Microsoft Download Center—the URL is *http://www.microsoft.com/downloads/details.aspx?FamilyID=51d4a154-8e23-47d2-a033-764259cfb53b&DisplayLang=en* as of the writing of this book.

The C# code in *Program.cs* in the project `FillDataSetXmlTemplateQuery` is shown in Example 9-19.

Example 9-19. File: Program.cs for FillDataSetXmlTemplateQuery solution

```csharp
using System;
using System.Data;
using Microsoft.Data.SqlXml;

namespace FillDataSetXmlTemplateQuery
{
    class Program
    {
        private static string queryFileName = @"..\..\..\GetContactQuery.xml";
        private static int contactID = 10;

        static void Main(string[] args)
        {
            string oledbConnectString ="Provider=SQLOLEDB;Data Source=(local);" +
                "Integrated Security=SSPI;Initial Catalog=AdventureWorks;";

            // create the SQL XML command
            SqlXmlCommand command = new SqlXmlCommand(oledbConnectString);
            command.CommandType = SqlXmlCommandType.TemplateFile;
            command.CommandText = queryFileName;

            // set the contact ID parameter for the command
            SqlXmlParameter param = command.CreateParameter();
            param.Name = "@ContactID";
            param.Value = contactID;

            // create the SQL XML DataAdapter and fill the DataSet
            SqlXmlAdapter da = new SqlXmlAdapter(command);
            DataSet ds = new DataSet();
            da.Fill(ds);
```

Example 9-19. File: Program.cs for FillDataSetXmlTemplateQuery solution (continued)

```
        // output the Contact record retrieved
        foreach(DataRow row in ds.Tables[0].Rows)
            Console.WriteLine("ContactID = {0}\nFirstName = {1}\nLastName = {2}",
                row["ContactID"], row["FirstName"], row["LastName"]);

        Console.WriteLine("\nPress any key to continue.");
        Console.ReadKey();
    }
  }
}
```

The output is shown in Figure 9-12.

Figure 9-12. Output for FillDataSetXmlTemplateQuery solution

Discussion

The subsections in this discussion describe SQL XML Managed Classes and template queries.

SQLXML Managed Classes

The SQLXML Managed Classes expose SQLXML functionality from the Microsoft .NET Framework. They allow access to XML data from instances of Microsoft SQL Server 2000 or later. SQLXML Managed Classes consist of three classes:

SqlXmlCommand
> Represents a command to execute against the SQL Server database.

SqlXmlParameter
> Stores parameters used by the SqlXmlCommand object. The parameter is created using the CreateParameter( ) method of the SqlXmlCommand class.

SqlXmlAdapter
> Links the SQLXML managed classes to the disconnected ADO.NET DataSet class.

A description of the methods and properties of these classes are shown in Tables 9-7 through 9-10.

Table 9-7 describes the methods of the SqlXmlCommand class.

Table 9-7. SqlXmlCommand methods

Method	Description
ExecuteNonQuery( )	Executes a command that does not return a result or result set—for example, an updategram or DiffGram update.
ExecuteStream( )	Returns a query result set as a stream.
ExecuteToStream( )	Writes query result set to an existing stream.
ExecuteXmlReader( )	Returns the result set of the query as an XmlReader object.
CreateParameter( )	Creates a SqlXmlParameter object used to pass parameters to a command using the Name and Value properties.
ClearParameters( )	Clears SqlXmlParameter objects for a command.

Table 9-8 describes the properties of the SqlXmlCommand class.

Table 9-8. SqlXmlCommand properties

Property	Description
BasePath	The directory path used when specifying a relative path for an XSL file.
ClientSideXml	Whether the conversion of the result set occurs on the client (true) or server (false). The default is false.
CommandText	The text of the command to execute.
CommandType	The type of command to execute. Takes one of the following values from the SqlXmlCommandType enumeration:
	DiffGram Executes a DiffGram.
	XmlTemplate Executes an XML template.
	TemplateFile Executes an XML template file consisting of one or more SQL or XPath queries.
	Sql Executes a SQL command.
	UpdateGram Executes an updategram.
	XPath Executes an XPath command.
CommandStream	The stream to execute the command from.
Namespaces	The namespace for XPath queries.
OutputEncoding	The encoding for the stream returned by the command.
RootTag	The single root-level tag for XML output returned by the command.
SchemaPath	The name of the mapping schema file and its directory path, either absolute or relative.
XslPath	The name of the XSL file and its directory path, either absolute or relative.

The SqlXmlParameter class has no methods. Table 9-9 describes the properties of the SqlXmlParameter class.

Table 9-9. SqlXmlParameter properties

Property	Description
Name	The name of the parameter for an SqlXmlCommand object.
Value	The value of the parameter.

The SqlXmlAdapter class has no properties. Table 9-10 describes the methods of the SqlXmlAdapter class.

Table 9-10. SqlXmlAdapter methods

Method	Description
Fill	Fills a DataSet with the XML data retrieved from the SQL Server database.
Update	Updates the SQL Server database with the changes made to the DataSet.

For more information about the SQLXML Managed Classes, see the Microsoft SQLXML release documentation.

Template queries

A *template query* is an XML document containing one or more SQL queries or stored procedures to execute. Template queries, like stored procedures, promote code reuse, facilitate security, and encourage good design by encapsulating database-specific functionality.

Parameters for the query are identified by the <sql:param> tag with the name attribute used to specify the parameter name and the parameter default value optionally specified between the <sql:param> and <sql:param> tags. Parameter tags are enclosed within the <sql:header> tags. The example shows one parameter named ContactID without a default value:

```
<sql:header>
    <sql:param name="ContactID" />
</sql:header>
```

If the ContactID parameter had a default value of 10, the parameter would be defined as follows:

```
<sql:param name="ContactID">10</sql:param>
```

The SQL command text must be enclosed within <sql:query> tags:

```
<sql:query>
    SELECT
        ContactID, FirstName, LastName
    FROM
        Person.Contact
    WHERE
        ContactID = @ContactID
    FOR XML AUTO
</sql:query>
```

The query is a standard SQL command with the required FOR XML clause to return the result set as XML. The query could also execute a stored procedure with the EXEC or EXECUTE command followed by the name of the stored procedure and a list of parameter values as required.

The query in the previous example has a single parameter, ContactID, which is prepended with an at sign (@) when referred to in the query:

```
WHERE ContactID = @CustomerID
```

9.12   Using OpenXML to Update Multiple Changes to SQL Server

Problem

You need to update a SQL Server database with changes to multiple rows in a DataSet by executing a single stored procedure.

Solution

Use OpenXML with an XMLdocument representing a DataSet of the changes made.

Example 9-20 shows the T-SQL statement that creates the table UpdateUsingOpenXml used in this solution.

Example 9-20. T-SQL statement: Create table UpdateUsingOpenXml

```
USE AdoDotNet35Cookbook
GO
CREATE TABLE UpdateUsingOpenXml(
    Id int NOT NULL PRIMARY KEY,
    Field1 nvarchar(50) NULL,
    Field2 nvarchar(50) NULL)
```

The SQL statement creates the table UpdateUsingOpenXml with the schema shown in Table 9-11.

Table 9-11. UpdateUsingOpenXml schema

Column name	Data type	Length	Allow nulls?
Id	int	4	No
Field1	nvarchar	50	Yes
Field2	nvarchar	50	Yes

The T-SQL batch in Example 9-21 creates records in the table UpdateUsingOpenXml required by the solution.

Example 9-21. T-SQL batch to create records in table UpdateUsingOpenXml

```
USE AdoDotNet35Cookbook
GO

INSERT INTO UpdateUsingOpenXml VALUES (1, 'Field1.1', 'Field2.1');
INSERT INTO UpdateUsingOpenXml VALUES (2, 'Field1.2', 'Field2.2');
INSERT INTO UpdateUsingOpenXml VALUES (3, 'Field1.3', 'Field2.3');
```

The solution uses a single stored procedure named SycnUpdateUsingOpenXml that updates the table UpdateUsingOpenXml with the changes made to the DataSet passed in as an NText input parameter @data. The parameters @data and @datadeleted contain an XML representation of a DataSet containing all updated and added records and all deleted records, respectively. These parameters are parsed using the system stored procedure sp_xml_preparedocument that returns a handle that is subsequently used to access the parsed XML document. OpenXML is used to update, insert, and delete the DataSet changes made to UpdateUsingOpenXml. See Example 9-22.

Example 9-22. Stored procedure: SyncUpdateUsingOpenXml

```
USE AdoDotNet35Cookbook
GO

CREATE PROC SyncUpdateUsingOpenXml
    @data ntext = null,
    @datadelete ntext = null
AS

DECLARE @hDoc int

-- process updated and inserted records
IF @data IS NOT NULL
BEGIN
    EXEC sp_xml_preparedocument @hDoc OUTPUT, @data

    UPDATE UpdateUsingOpenXml
    SET
        UpdateUsingOpenXml.Field1 = XmlUpdateUsingOpenXml.Field1,
        UpdateUsingOpenXml.Field2 = XmlUpdateUsingOpenXml.Field2
    FROM
        OPENXML(@hDoc, 'NewDataSet/UpdateUsingOpenXml')
    WITH (
        Id int,
        Field1 nvarchar(50),
        Field2 nvarchar(50)
    ) XmlUpdateUsingOpenXml
    WHERE
        UpdateUsingOpenXml.Id = XmlUpdateUsingOpenXml.Id

    INSERT INTO UpdateUsingOpenXml
```

Example 9-22. Stored procedure: SyncUpdateUsingOpenXml (continued)

```
SELECT
    Id,
    Field1,
    Field2
FROM
    OPENXML(@hdoc, 'NewDataSet/UpdateUsingOpenXml')
WITH (
    Id int,
    Field1 nvarchar(50),
    Field2 nvarchar(50)
) XmlUpdateUsingOpenXml
WHERE
    XmlUpdateUsingOpenXml.Id NOT IN (SELECT Id from UpdateUsingOpenXml)

    EXEC sp_xml_removedocument @hDoc
end

-- process deleted records
IF @datadelete IS NOT NULL
BEGIN
    EXEC sp_xml_preparedocument @hDoc OUTPUT, @datadelete

    DELETE UpdateUsingOpenXml
    FROM
        UpdateUsingOpenXml INNER JOIN
    OPENXML(@hDoc, 'NewDataSet/UpdateUsingOpenXml')
    WITH (
        Id Integer,
        Field1 nvarchar(50),
        Field2 nvarchar(50)
    ) XmlUpdateUsingOpenXml
        ON UpdateUsingOpenXml.Id = XmlUpdateUsingOpenXml.Id

    EXEC sp_xml_removedocument @hDoc
END
```

The solution creates a DataSet containing the schema and data of the table UpdateUsingOpenXml and outputs the contents of the DataSet to the console. The ColumnMapping for each column is set to MappingType.Attribute. Changes are made to the data: the row with Id = 2 is deleted, the row with Id = 3 is modified, and a row is added with Id = 4. The changed DataSet contents are output to the console. A connection is created and a command for the stored procedure SyncUpdateUsingOpenXml is created. The stored procedure input parameters @data and @datadelete are given values of the added and modified records in the DataSet and the deleted records in the DataSet respectively. The stored procedure is executed to update the data source using OpenXML.

The C# code in *Program.cs* in the project SyncUpdateUsingOpenXml is shown in Example 9-23.

Example 9-23. File: Program.cs for UpdateUsingOpenXml solution

```csharp
using System;
using System.Data;
using System.Data.SqlClient;
using System.Xml;
using System.Text;
using System.IO;

namespace UpdateUsingOpenXml
{
    class Program
    {
        static void Main(string[] args)
        {
            string sqlConnectString = "Data Source=(local);" +
                "Integrated security=SSPI;Initial Catalog=AdoDotNet35Cookbook;";

            string sqlSelect = "SELECT * FROM UpdateUsingOpenXml";

            // Fill a DataSet with schema and data from table UpdateUsingOpenXml
            SqlDataAdapter da = new SqlDataAdapter(sqlSelect, sqlConnectString);
            da.TableMappings.Add("Table", "UpdateUsingOpenXml");
            DataSet ds = new DataSet();
            da.FillSchema(ds, SchemaType.Mapped);
            da.Fill(ds);

            // Output the original UpdateUsingOpenXml values to the console
            Console.WriteLine("---Original table---");
            foreach(DataRow row in ds.Tables["UpdateUsingOpenXml"].Rows)
                Console.WriteLine("Id = {0}\tField1 = {1}\tField2 = {2}",
                    row["Id"], row["Field1"], row["Field2"]);

            // Set columns in the XML representation to attributes
            foreach (DataColumn col in ds.Tables["UpdateUsingOpenXml"].Columns)
                col.ColumnMapping = MappingType.Attribute;

            // Modify the data in the table UpdateUsingOpenXml
            // Delete the row with Id = 2
            ds.Tables["UpdateUsingOpenXml"].Rows.Find(2).Delete();
            // Change Field2 value for row with Id = 3
            ds.Tables["UpdateUsingOpenXml"].Rows.Find(3).SetField<string>
                ("Field2", "Field2.3 (new)");
            // Add a new row with Id = 4
            ds.Tables["UpdateUsingOpenXml"].Rows.Add(
                new object[] { 4, "Field1.4", "Field2.4" });
            Console.WriteLine("\n-> Data in table UpdateUsingOpenXml modified.");

            // Output the modified UpdateUsingOpenXml values to the console
            Console.WriteLine("\n---Modified table---");
            foreach (DataRow row in ds.Tables["UpdateUsingOpenXml"].Rows)
            {
                if (row.RowState != DataRowState.Deleted)
                    Console.WriteLine("Id = {0}\tField1 = {1}\tField2 = {2}",
                        row["Id"], row["Field1"], row["Field2"]);
            }
```

```
            // Create the command for the synchronizing stored procedure
            SqlConnection connection = new SqlConnection(sqlConnectString);
            SqlCommand command =
                new SqlCommand("SyncUpdateUsingOpenXml", connection);
            command.CommandType = CommandType.StoredProcedure;

            // Handle inserted and updated records
            if (ds.HasChanges(DataRowState.Added | DataRowState.Modified))
            {
                StringBuilder sb1 = new StringBuilder();
                StringWriter sw1 = new StringWriter(sb1);

                ds.GetChanges(
                    DataRowState.Added | DataRowState.Modified).WriteXml(sw1,
                    XmlWriteMode.WriteSchema);
                command.Parameters.Add("@data", SqlDbType.NText);
                command.Parameters["@data"].Value = sb1.ToString();

                sw1.Close();
            }

            // Handle deleted records
            if (ds.HasChanges(DataRowState.Deleted))
            {
                StringBuilder sb2 = new StringBuilder();
                StringWriter sw2 = new StringWriter(sb2);

                // Get the DataSet containing the records deleted and call
                // RejectChanges() so that the original version of those rows
                // are available so that WriteXml() works.
                DataSet dsChange = ds.GetChanges(DataRowState.Deleted);
                dsChange.RejectChanges();
                dsChange.WriteXml(sw2, XmlWriteMode.WriteSchema);

                command.Parameters.Add("@datadelete", SqlDbType.NText);
                command.Parameters["@datadelete"].Value = sb2.ToString();

                sw2.Close();
            }

            // Execute stored procedure
            connection.Open();
            command.ExecuteNonQuery();
            connection.Close();
            Console.WriteLine("\n-> Changes synchronized with database.");

            // Accept changes in the DataSet
            ds.AcceptChanges();

            Console.WriteLine("\nPress any key to continue.");
            Console.ReadKey();
        }
    }
}
```

The output is shown in Figure 9-13.

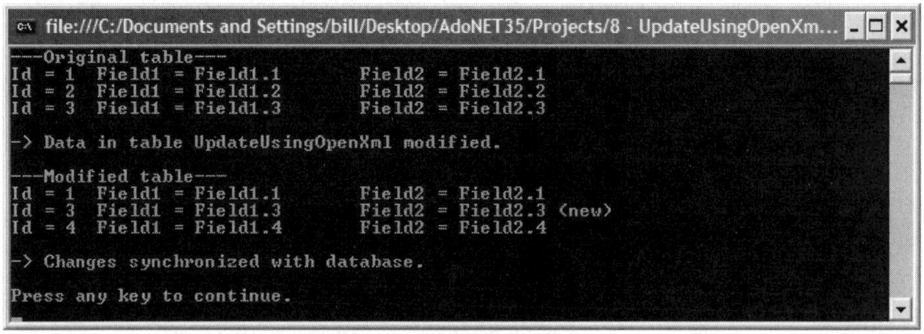

Figure 9-13. Output for UpdateUsingOpenXml solution

Figure 9-14 shows the data values in the table `UpdateUsingOpenXml` using SQL Server Management Studio after the `OpenXML` update.

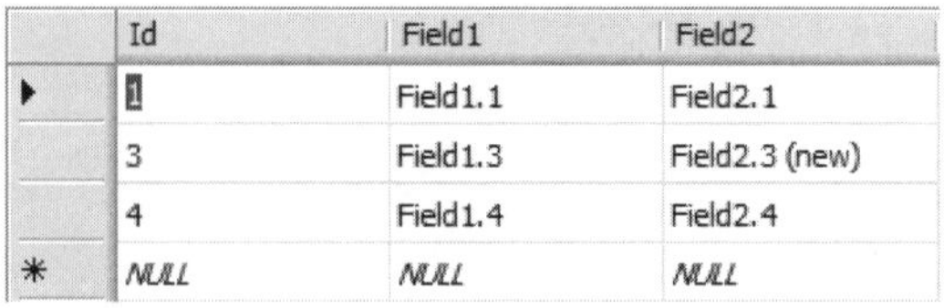

	Id	Field1	Field2
▶	1	Field1.1	Field2.1
	3	Field1.3	Field2.3 (new)
	4	Field1.4	Field2.4
*	*NULL*	*NULL*	*NULL*

Figure 9-14. Data in UpdateUsingOpenXml table after OpenXML update

Discussion

`OpenXML` provides a result set view of an XML document, allowing you to use the XML document in a T-SQL statement in the same way a result set provider such as a table or view is used.

The simple form of the `OpenXML` command is:

```
OPENXML(int iDoc, nvarchar rowPattern)
WITH (SchemaDeclaration)
```

The two input arguments are:

`iDoc`
: The document handle of the internal representation of an XML document created by using the system stored procedure `sp_xml_preparedocument`.

`rowPattern`
: The XPath query used to select the nodes in the XML document to be processed.

The argument for the WITH clause is:

SchemaDeclaration

The format of the result set. If not supplied, the results are returned in an *edge table* format representing the XML document structure in a single table.

The system stored procedure sp_xml_preparedocument reads XML as input text using the MSXML parser and returns a handle that you can use to access the internal representation of the XML document. The handle is valid for the duration of the connection to the SQL Server or until it is reset. The handle can be invalidated and the associated memory freed by calling the system stored procedure sp_xml_removedocument. The syntax of the sp_xml_preparedocument stored procedure is:

```
sp_xml_preparedocument hDoc OUTPUT, [xmlText], [xpathNamespaces]
```

Where:

hDoc

An integer parameter that returns a handle to the internal representation of the XML document.

xmlText

A text parameter that specifies the original XML document. The default value is null, which results in the return of a handle to an internal representation to an empty XML document.

xpathNamespaces

A text parameter that specifies the namespace declarations used in row and column XPath expressions in OpenXML. The default value is:

```
<root xmlns:mp="urn:schemas-microsoft-com:xml-metaprop">
```

The system stored procedure sp_xml_removedocument removes the internal representation of an XML document specified by a document handle obtained from the system stored procedure sp_xml_preparedocument and invalidates the handle. The syntax of the stored procedure is:

```
sp_xml_removedocument hDoc
```

Where:

hDoc

An integer parameter that returns a handle to the internal representation of the XML document.

For more information about the OpenXML command and the system stored procedures sp_xml_preparedocument and sp_xml_removedocuemnt, see Microsoft SQL Server Books Online.

CHAPTER 10

Optimizing .NET Data Access

10.0   Introduction

This chapter examines asynchronous processing, caching, paging, batching, and class-specific methods and techniques to improve application performance. Before optimizing any application, profile it to ensure that you have a good understanding of where the real bottlenecks are.

ADO.NET 2.0 introduces the ability to execute queries asynchronously. This lets you execute long-running T-SQL statements and both `DataReader` and `XmlReader` queries on a background thread, leaving the user interface responsive or letting you continue with other tasks. Recipe 10.2 shows how. You can execute multiple queries simultaneously, waiting for each or all to finish. Recipe 10.3 shows you how to do this.

A query can run asynchronously on background threads to improve application responsiveness and perceived performance by not blocking processing. This can also be used to give the user an opportunity to cancel a request that is taking too long. Recipes 10.4 and 10.5 shows how to use a background thread to run a query. Recipe 10.6 shows how to let the user cancel a query running on a background thread.

Caching data allows data to be retrieved once and saved in order to service subsequent requests for the same data. The load on the database server is reduced, potentially improving application performance. On the downside, cached data becomes less current (and less accurate) over time. The .NET Framework provides classes to allow both client- and server-side caching of data. On the client-side, caching requires few server-side resources, but increases network bandwidth required to move data back and forth with each round trip. Caching on the server-side consumes more network resources; however, it is less expensive in terms of bandwidth required. In either case, applications should be designed to retrieve the minimum data necessary to optimize performance and scalability. Recipe 10.7 shows how to use caching in an ASP.NET application.

Even if data is not cached, it can still become outdated. A timer can track the time that data was retrieved from the database in order to periodically refresh the data and thus present the data with a current view. Recipe 10.19 shows how to use the extended properties of a DataSet to automatically refresh the data a user sees. Recipe 10.20 uses notification classes introduced in .NET Framework 2.0, together with notification capabilities introduced in SQL Server 2005 to refresh a DataTable when data in the database changes.

SQL Server 2005 introduced user-defined types (UDTs). Recipe 10.16 shows you how to work with UDTs in your code.

This chapter also covers the following:

Paging

Paging is common in applications where a subset of a result set—a page—is displayed to the user. The way that paging is implemented affects both scalability and performance. .NET provides automatic paging in many Windows Forms and Web Forms controls; however, manual paging offers the best performance. This allows paging requirements to be met exactly, rather than automatically, which is the default. Recipe 10.8 shows a high-performance custom paging solution.

Moving large amounts of data

Storing binary large objects (BLOBs) in a database is becoming an increasingly viable option as vendors enhance database capabilities in response to demands that ubiquitous high-bandwidth has created for storing digital assets. Storing BLOBs in a database is simpler than other approaches because there is no need to synchronize database fields acting as pointers to an external repository such as the filesystem. BLOBs are easier to administer and are automatically backed up with the database. Built-in database functionality, such as full-text searching, can be used on BLOB fields, and it leverages tools already in the database rather than requiring external tools. Recipe 10.15 shows how to store and retrieve BLOBs in a SQL Server and Recipe 10.17 shows how to store and retrieve BLOBs in an Oracle database.

The DataSet is an in-memory database containing both relation and constraint objects to maintain the integrity of the data. These objects, can, however, slow performance when filling a DataSet with large amounts of data that have complex interdependencies and constraints. Turning off the constraints temporarily can sometimes improve performance in these situations, which Recipe 10.14 discusses.

Large amounts of data sometimes need to be loaded into a SQL Server database quickly. NET bulk load classes let you load XML data into SQL Server tables providing high performance when large amounts of data need to be inserted. Recipes 10.9 and 10.10 show how to do this.

Minimizing roundtrips and conversions

A `DataAdapter` makes a roundtrip to update the data source for every row that has been changed. In some situations, this can cause performance problems. You can batch these `DataAdapter` updates by handling `DataAdapter` events. Roundtrips are reduced and performance is improved. Recipe 10.18 shows how this is done.

`DataReader` typed accessor methods improve performance by eliminating type conversions when retrieving data from a `DataReader`. You can dynamically retrieve column ordinals at runtime and use them instead of column names to further improve performance when accessing data with a `DataReader`. Recipes 10.11 and 10.12 show how to use these techniques with a `DataReader`.

Debugging and optimizing

Visual Studio .NET supports debugging SQL Server stored procedures both in standalone mode and from managed code when called using the .NET provider for SQL server. This can help to optimize and troubleshoot stored procedures. Recipe 10.13 shows how to debug stored procedures from Visual Studio .NET. Recipe 10.21 shows how to retrieve runtime statistics from SQL Server.

Database independence

Applications often need to operate with different databases. Recipe 10.22 demonstrates the interfaces of ADO.NET connected classes, and the factory classes introduced in ADO.NET 2.0, which let you instantiate ADO.NET connected classes at runtime to write code that is provider and database independent.

10.1 Executing Multiple Commands on a Single Connection

Problem

You need to execute multiple commands using a single connection.

Solution

The solution creates a `DataReader` that contains the `SalesOrderID` and `TotalDue` fields for the top three records from the `Sales.SalesOrderHeader` table in `AdventureWorks` and iterates over and outputs these records to the console. For each record, a second `DataReader` retrieves the `ProductID` and `OrderQty` fields for the `SalesOrderID` from the `Sales.SalesOrderDetail` table—the same connection used for the first `DataReader` is used to create the second `DataReader`. The solution iterates over and outputs records from the `SalesOrderDetail` table in the second `DataReader`.

The C# code in *Program.cs* in the project `ExecuteMultipleCommandsSingleConnection` is shown in Example 10-1.

Example 10-1. File: Program.cs for ExecuteMultipleCommandsSingleConnection solution

```csharp
using System;
using System.Data.SqlClient;

namespace ExecuteMultipleCommandsSingleConnection
{
    class Program
    {
        static void Main(string[] args)
        {
            string sqlConnectString = "Data Source=(local);" +
                "Integrated security=SSPI;Initial Catalog=AdventureWorks;" +
                "MultipleActiveResultSets=true";

            SqlConnection connection = new SqlConnection(sqlConnectString);

            // create a DataReader with the top 3 sales header records
            SqlCommand cmdHeader = connection.CreateCommand();
            cmdHeader.CommandText =
                "SELECT TOP 3 SalesOrderID, TotalDue FROM Sales.SalesOrderHeader";
            connection.Open();
            SqlDataReader drHeader = cmdHeader.ExecuteReader();

            // Iterate over the reader with the SalesOrderHeader records
            while (drHeader.Read())
            {
                Console.WriteLine("SalesOrderID = {0}\tTotalDue = {1}",
                    drHeader["SalesOrderID"], drHeader["TotalDue"]);

                // Create a DataReader with detail for the sales order
                SqlCommand cmdDetail = connection.CreateCommand();
                cmdDetail.CommandText = "SELECT ProductID, OrderQty FROM " +
                    "Sales.SalesOrderDetail WHERE SalesOrderID=" +
                    drHeader["SalesOrderID"];

                // Iterate over the reader with the SalesOrderDetail records
                using (SqlDataReader drDetail = cmdDetail.ExecuteReader())
                {
                    while (drDetail.Read())
                        Console.WriteLine("\tProductID = {0}\tOrderQty = {1}",
                        drDetail["ProductID"], drDetail["OrderQty"]);
                    drDetail.Dispose();
                }
                Console.WriteLine();
            }

            connection.Close();

            Console.WriteLine("Press any key to continue.");
            Console.ReadKey();
        }
    }
}
```

The output is shown in Figure 10-1.

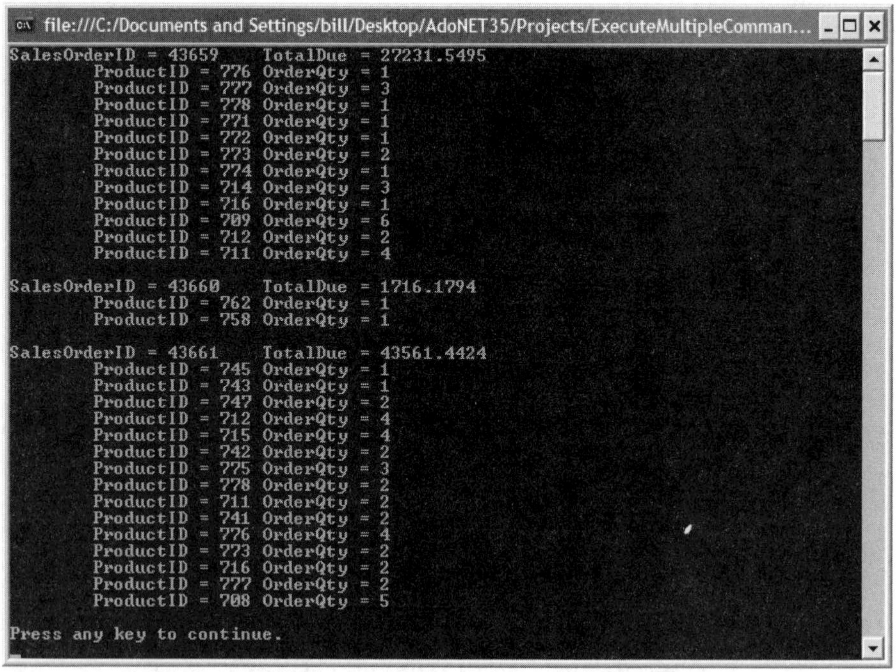

Figure 10-1. Output for ExecuteMultipleCommandsSingleConnection solution

Discussion

Multiple Active Result Sets (MARS) allows multiple commands to be executed on a single connection against a SQL Server 2005 and later database. Each command requires its own `SqlCommand` object and adds a session to the connection. You must enable MARS by setting the `MultipleActiveResultSets` key in the connection string to `true`.

10.2 Executing a SQL Statement Asynchronously

Problem

You need to execute a SQL statement asynchronously.

Solution

Use the `BeginExecuteNonQuery( )` method of the `Command` class. Two solutions are shown: one using a callback at query completion and the other using a timer to poll for completion.

The first solution uses the BeginExecuteNonQuery( ) method of the Command class to execute a command that asynchronously executes a T-SQL WAITFOR statement that instructs SQL Server to wait for five seconds and callback to the method HandleCallback( ) when the command completes. At the end of the five seconds, the callback method completes the execution of the T-SQL statement.

In the callback, the Command object is retrieved by casting the object returned by the AsyncState property of the IAsyncResult argument passed into the callback. The EndExecuteNonQuery( ) method of this Command object is called to finish the asynchronous execution of the command. The EndExecuteNonQuery( ) method returns either the number of rows affected for INSERT, UPDATE, and DELETE statements or –1 for all other types of statements—the same behavior as the ExecuteNonQuery( ) method.

The C# code in *Program.cs* in the project ExecuteAsyncSqlStatementCallback is shown in Example 10-2.

Example 10-2. File: Program.cs for ExecuteAsyncSqlStatementCallback solution

```
using System;
using System.Data.SqlClient;

namespace ExecuteAsyncSqlStatementCallback
{
    class Program
    {
        static void Main(string[] args)
        {
            string sqlConnectString =
                "Data Source=localhost;Integrated Security=SSPI;" +
                "Initial Catalog=AdventureWorks;Asynchronous Processing=true";
            string sqlSelect = "WAITFOR DELAY '00:00:05'";

            Console.WriteLine("(Press any key to exit.)\n");

            SqlConnection connection = new SqlConnection(sqlConnectString);
            SqlCommand command = new SqlCommand(sqlSelect, connection);

            connection.Open();
            // Start the async operation. The HandleCallback() method
            // is called when the operation completes in 5 seconds.
            command.BeginExecuteNonQuery(
                new AsyncCallback(HandleCallback), command);
            Console.WriteLine("[{0}] BeginExecuteNonQuery() called.",
                DateTime.Now);
            Console.WriteLine("[{0}] Waiting.", DateTime.Now);

            Console.ReadKey();
        }
```

Example 10-2. File: Program.cs for ExecuteAsyncSqlStatementCallback solution (continued)

```
        private static void HandleCallback(IAsyncResult asyncResult)
        {
            // get the original object
            SqlCommand command = (SqlCommand)asyncResult.AsyncState;

            // get and display the rows affected
            int rowsAffected = command.EndExecuteNonQuery(asyncResult);
            Console.WriteLine("[{0}] EndExecuteNonQuery() called.",
                DateTime.Now);
            Console.WriteLine("\nRows affected = {0}", rowsAffected);

            // close the connection
            command.Connection.Close();
        }
    }
}
```

The output is shown in Figure 10-2.

Figure 10-2. Output for ExecuteAsyncSqlStatementCallback solution

You can see from the output that the callback was called five seconds after the WAITFOR query was executed.

The second solution uses the BeginExecuteNonQuery( ) method of the Command class to execute a command that asynchronously executes a T-SQL WAITFOR statement that instructs SQL Server to simply wait for five seconds. A timer is used to poll the completion status of the query every second by checking the IsCompleted status of the IAsyncResult returned by the BeginExecuteNonQuery( ) method. When the command completes, the EndExecuteNonQuery( ) method of the Command object is used to finish the asynchronous execution of the command. The EndExecuteNonQuery( ) method returns either the number of rows affected for INSERT, UPDATE, and DELETE statements or –1 for all other types of statements—the same behavior as the ExecuteNonQuery( ) method.

The C# code in *Program.cs* in the project ExecuteAsyncSqlStatementPolling is shown in Example 10-3.

Example 10-3. File: Program.cs for ExecuteAsyncSqlStatementPolling solution

```
using System;
using System.Data.SqlClient;
using System.Timers;

namespace ExecuteAsyncSqlStatementPolling
{
    class Program
    {
        static IAsyncResult asyncResult;
        static SqlCommand command;

        static void Main(string[] args)
        {
            string sqlConnectString =
                "Data Source=(local);Integrated Security=SSPI;" +
                "Initial Catalog=AdventureWorks;Asynchronous Processing=true";
            string sqlSelect = "WAITFOR DELAY '00:00:05'";

            SqlConnection connection = new SqlConnection(sqlConnectString);
            command = new SqlCommand(sqlSelect, connection);

            connection.Open();
            // Start the async operation.
            asyncResult = command.BeginExecuteNonQuery();
            Console.WriteLine("[{0}] BeginExecuteNonQuery() called.",
                DateTime.Now);

            // Start a timer to check the results every 1000ms
            Timer timer = new Timer(1000);
            timer.Elapsed += new ElapsedEventHandler(timer_Elapsed);
            timer.Start();

            Console.WriteLine("\n---Begin polling---");

            Console.ReadKey();
        }

        static void timer_Elapsed(object sender, ElapsedEventArgs e)
        {
            Console.WriteLine("[{0}] Query complete = {1}",
                DateTime.Now, asyncResult.IsCompleted);
```

```
        if (asyncResult.IsCompleted)
        {
            // stop the polling and process the results
            ((Timer)sender).Stop( );

            Console.WriteLine("---End polling---");

            int rowsAffected = command.EndExecuteNonQuery(asyncResult);
            Console.WriteLine("\n[{0}] EndExecuteNonQuery( ) called.",
                DateTime.Now);
            Console.WriteLine("\nRows affected = {0}", rowsAffected);

            Console.WriteLine("\nPress any key to continue.");
        }
    }
  }
}
```

The output is shown in Figure 10-3.

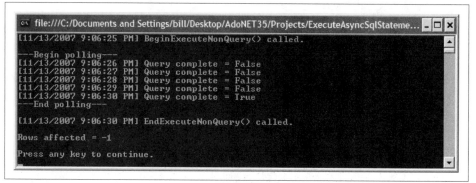

Figure 10-3. Output for ExecuteAsyncSqlStatementPolling solution

Discussion

ADO.NET 2.0 introduced the ability to execute queries asynchronously. This lets you execute long-running nonquery, DataReader, and XmlReader queries. Delegating the execution to a background thread lets you execute long-running tasks while leaving the user interface responsive or letting you continue with other tasks. The SqlCommand class has six methods that support asynchronous processing, described in Table 10-1.

Table 10-1. SqlCommand class methods for asynchronous processing

Asynchronous method	Description
BeginExecuteNonQuery	Starts the asynchronous execution of the T-SQL statement or stored procedure for the SqlCommand object. The method returns an IAsyncResult object that can be used to poll for or wait for results, or to invoke the EndExecuteNonQuery( ) method.
	Each call to a BeginExecuteNonQuery( ) method must be paired with the EndExecuteNonQuery( ) method that completes the operation.
	The method has two overloads:
| | ```
IAsyncResult BeginExecuteNonQuery( )
IAsyncResult BeginExecuteNonQuery(AsyncCallback callback,
Object stateObject)
``` |
	Where:
	callback The delegate invoked when the command execution has completed.
	stateObject A user-defined state object passed to the callback procedure. You retrieve this object in the callback method using the AsyncState property of the IAsyncResult callback argument.
EndExecuteNonQuery	Completes the asynchronous execution of the command started using the BeginExecuteNonQuery( ) method of the SqlCommand object. This method returns the number of rows affected by the command.
	The method signature is:
| | ```
int EndExecuteNonQuery(IAsyncResult asyncResult)
``` |
	Where:
	asyncResult The IAsyncResult returned from calling the BeginExecuteNonQuery( ) method.
BeginExecuteReader	Starts the asynchronous execution of the T-SQL statement or stored procedure for the SqlCommand object. The method returns an IAsyncResult object that can be used to poll for or wait for results, or to invoke the EndExecuteReader( ) method.
	Each call to a BeginExecuteReader( ) method must be paired with the EndExecuteReader( ) method that completes the operation.
	The method has four overloads:
| | ```
IAsyncResult BeginExecuteReader( )
IAsyncResult BeginExecuteReader(CommandBehavior behavior)
IAsyncResult BeginExecuteReader(AsyncCallback callback,
Object stateObject)
IAsyncResult BeginExecuteReader(AsyncCallback callback,
Object stateObject, CommandBehavior behavior)
``` |
	Where:
	callback The delegate invoked when the command execution has completed.
	stateObject A user-defined state object passed to the callback procedure. You retrieve this object in the callback method using the AsyncState property of the IAsyncResult callback argument.
	behavior A value from the CommandBehavior enumeration indicating options for statement execution and data retrieval.
```

Table 10-1. SqlCommand class methods for asynchronous processing (continued)

Asynchronous method	Description
EndExecuteReader	Completes the asynchronous execution of the T-SQL statement or stored procedure started using the BeginExecuteReader( ) method of the SqlCommand object. The command returns a SqlDataReader object that can be used to retrieve one or more result sets returned by the query.
	The method signature is:
	`SqlDataReader EndExecuteReader(IAsyncResult asyncResult)`
	Where:
	asyncResult
	The IAsyncResult returned from calling the BeginExecuteReader( ) method.
BeginExecuteXmlReader	Starts the asynchronous execution of the T-SQL statement or stored procedure for the SqlCommand object. The method returns an IAsyncResult object that can be used to poll for or wait for results, or to invoke the EndExecuteXmlReader( ) method.
	Each call to a BeginExecuteXmlReader( ) method must be paired with the EndExecuteXmlReader( ) method that completes the operation.
	The method has two overloads:

	`IAsyncResult BeginExecuteXmlReader( )`
	`IAsyncResult BeginExecuteXmlReader(AsyncCallback callback,`
	`   Object stateObject)`

	Where:
	callback The delegate invoked when the command execution has completed.
	stateObject A user-defined state object passed to the callback procedure. You retrieve this object in the callback method using the AsyncState property of the IAsyncResult callback argument.
EndExecuteXmlReader	Completes the asynchronous execution of the T-SQL statement or stored procedure started using the BeginExecuteXmlReader( ) method of the SqlCommand object. The command returns an XmlReader object that can be used to retrieve the XML data.
	The method signature is:
	`XmlReader EndExecuteXmlReader(IAsyncResult asyncResult)`
	Where:
	asyncResult The IAsyncResult returned from calling the BeginExecuteXmlReader( ) method.

The asynchronous command Begin/End pairs for the SqlCommand object work similarly to each other. The examples in this section that use one of the pairs can be transferred easily to one of the other pairs.

You must add the Asynchronous Processing=true attribute to the SQL Server connection string to use any of the asynchronous methods.

The IAsyncResult interface stores state information about the asynchronous operation and provides a synchronization object that lets threads get signaled when the operation completes. Table 10-2 lists the public properties exposed by the IAsyncResult interface.

Table 10-2. Public properties of IAsyncResult interface

Property	Description
AsyncState	Returns a user-defined object that contains information about or qualifies an asynchronous operation.
AsyncWaitHandle	Returns a WaitHandle object used to wait for an asynchronous operation to complete.
CompletedSynchronously	Returns a bool indicating whether the asynchronous operation completed synchronously.
IsCompleted	Returns a bool indicating whether the asynchronous operation has completed.

10.3 Executing Simultaneous SQL Statements Asynchronously

Problem

You need to execute multiple SQL statements simultaneously and process results when each statement completes or once all of the statements have completed.

Solution

Use the WaitAny( ) or the WaitAll( ) method of the WaitHandle class monitor. Both solutions are shown here.

The first solution creates an array of 10 Command objects that each execute a T-SQL WAITFOR statement that instructs SQL Server to wait for a random number of seconds between 1 and 10. The BeginExecuteNonQuery( ) method of the Command class is used to asynchronously execute each command in the array. The WaitHandle object for each Command object is retrieved using the AsyncWaitHandle property of the IAsyncResult returned by the BeginExecuteNonQuery( ) method. Each WaitHandle object is added to an array of WaitHandle objects corresponding to the Command array.

A loop is set up to process each of the 10 commands as they complete. Each iteration of the loop executes the WaitAny( ) method of the static WaitHandle class—the WaitAny( ) method takes a WaitHandle array argument of objects to wait to complete. When any command in the array completes, the EndExecuteNonQuery( ) method of that command is called to complete the command execution. The number of the command in the array and the number of records affected (0 in all cases for this example) are output to the console. Finally, the connection for the command is closed. The loop ends when all Command objects in the array have finished and have been processed.

The C# code in *Program.cs* in the project ExecSimultAsyncSqlStatementWaitAny is shown in Example 10-4.

Example 10-4. File: Program.cs for ExecSimultAsyncSqlStatementWaitAny solution

```csharp
using System;
using System.Data.SqlClient;
using System.Threading;

namespace ExecSimultAsyncSqlStatementWaitAny
{
    class Program
    {
        static void Main(string[] args)
        {
            string sqlConnectString =
                "Data Source=localhost;Integrated Security=SSPI;" +
                "Initial Catalog=AdventureWorks;Asynchronous Processing=true";

            Random rnd = new Random((int)DateTime.Now.Ticks);

            // create an array of commands with "n" members
            int n = 10;
            SqlConnection[] connection = new SqlConnection[n];
            SqlCommand[] command = new SqlCommand[n];
            string[] cmdText = new string[n];
            IAsyncResult[] asyncResult = new IAsyncResult[n];
            WaitHandle[] wh = new WaitHandle[n];

            Console.WriteLine("---COMMANDS START---");
            for (int i = 0; i < n; i++)
            {
                // each command waits randomly for between 1 and 10 seconds
                cmdText[i] = "WAITFOR DELAY '00:00:" + rnd.Next(1, 10) + "';";

                connection[i] = new SqlConnection(sqlConnectString);
                connection[i].Open();
                command[i] = new SqlCommand(cmdText[i], connection[i]);
                asyncResult[i] = command[i].BeginExecuteNonQuery();
                Console.WriteLine("[{0}] Command {1} started: {2}",
                    DateTime.Now, i, cmdText[i]);

                wh[i] = asyncResult[i].AsyncWaitHandle;
            }

            // wait for all processes to complete, outputting completion
            Console.WriteLine("\n---WAITANY()---");
            for (int i = 0; i < wh.GetLength(0); i++)
            {
                int index = WaitHandle.WaitAny(wh);
                int recAff = command[index].EndExecuteNonQuery(asyncResult[index]);
                Console.WriteLine(
                    "[{0}] Command {1} completed, records affected = {2}",
                    DateTime.Now, index , recAff);

                // Close the connection for the command
                connection[index].Close();
            }
```

Example 10-4. File: Program.cs for ExecSimultAsyncSqlStatementWaitAny solution (continued)

```
        Console.WriteLine("\nPress any key to continue.");
        Console.ReadKey();
    }
  }
}
```

The output is shown in Figure 10-4.

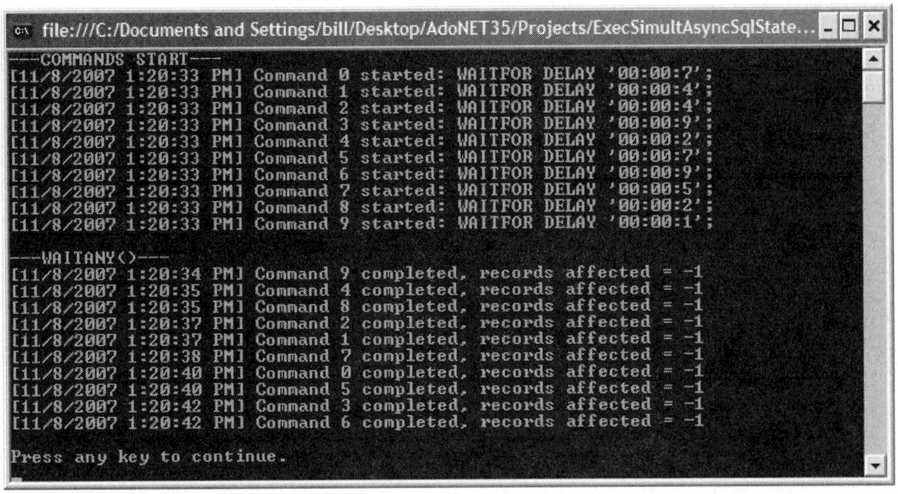

Figure 10-4. Output for ExecSimultAsyncSqlStatementWaitAny solution

You can see from the output that the commands are processed according from shortest to longest WAITFOR duration—in other words, they are processed in the order in which they complete.

The second solution creates an array of 10 Command objects that each execute a T-SQL WAITFOR statement that instruct SQL Server to wait for a random number of seconds between 1 and 10. The BeginExecuteNonQuery( ) method of the Command class is used to asynchronously execute each command in the array. The WaitHandle object for each Command object is retrieved using the AsyncWaitHandle property of the IAsyncResult returned by the BeginExecuteNonQuery( ) method. Each WaitHandle object is added to an array of WaitHandle objects corresponding to the Command array.

A loop is set up to process each of the 10 commands once they all complete. The WaitAll( ) method of the static WaitHandle class is executed—the WaitAll( ) method takes a WaitHandle array argument of objects to wait to complete. Processing continues when all commands in the array complete. Once all commands complete, a loop is set up to call the EndExecuteNonQuery( ) method for each command to complete the command execution. The number of the command in the array and the return value are output to the console. Finally, the connection for the command is closed.

The loop ends when all Command objects in the array have finished and have been processed.

The C# code in *Program.cs* in the project ExecSimultAsyncSqlStatementWaitAll is shown in Example 10-5.

Example 10-5. File: Program.cs for ExecSimultAsyncSqlStatementWaitAll solution

```csharp
using System;
using System.Data.SqlClient;
using System.Threading;

namespace ExecSimultAsyncSqlStatementWaitAll
{
    class Program
    {
        static void Main(string[] args)
        {
            string sqlConnectString =
                "Data Source=localhost;Integrated Security=SSPI;" +
                "Initial Catalog=AdventureWorks;Asynchronous Processing=true";

            Random rnd = new Random((int)DateTime.Now.Ticks);

            // Create an array of commands with "n" members
            int n = 10;
            SqlConnection[] connection = new SqlConnection[n];
            SqlCommand[] command = new SqlCommand[n];
            string[] sqlSelect = new string[n];
            IAsyncResult[] asyncResult = new IAsyncResult[n];
            WaitHandle[] wh = new WaitHandle[n];

            Console.WriteLine("---COMMANDS START---");
            for (int i = 0; i < n; i++)
            {
                // Each command waits for randomly between 1 and 10 seconds
                sqlSelect[i] = "WAITFOR DELAY '00:00:" +
                    rnd.Next(1, 10) + "';";

                connection[i] = new SqlConnection(sqlConnectString);
                connection[i].Open();
                command[i] = new SqlCommand(sqlSelect[i], connection[i]);
                asyncResult[i] = command[i].BeginExecuteNonQuery();
                Console.WriteLine("[{0}] Command {1} started: {2}",
                    DateTime.Now, i, sqlSelect[i]);

                wh[i] = asyncResult[i].AsyncWaitHandle;
            }

            // Wait for all processes to complete and output results
            Console.WriteLine("\n---WAITALL()---");
            bool result = WaitHandle.WaitAll(wh, -1, false);
            if (result)
```

Example 10-5. File: Program.cs for ExecSimultAsyncSqlStatementWaitAll solution (continued)

```
        {
            Console.WriteLine("[{0}] All commands completed successfully.\n",
                DateTime.Now);

            for (int i = 0; i < wh.Length; i++)
            {
                int recAff = command[i].EndExecuteNonQuery(asyncResult[i]);
                Console.WriteLine(
                    "[{0}] Command {1} completed, records affected = {2}",
                    DateTime.Now, i, recAff);

                connection[i].Close( );
            }
        }
        else
            Console.WriteLine("[{0}] Timeout error.", DateTime.Now);

        Console.WriteLine("\nPress any key to continue.");
        Console.ReadKey( );
        }
    }
}
```

The output is shown in Figure 10-5.

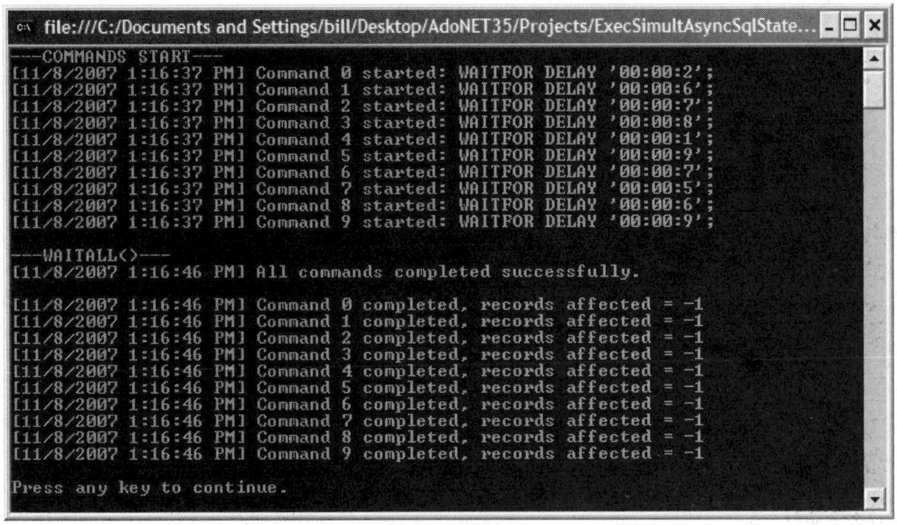

Figure 10-5. Output for ExecSimultAsyncSqlStatementWaitAll solution

You can see from the output that the commands are processed according to their create order after they all complete.

Discussion

The WaitAny( ) and WaitAll( ) static methods of the WaitHandle class monitor and wait for the completion of asynchronous operations.

The WaitAny( ) method waits for any of the asynchronous operations to complete or time out—you can process the results and continue to wait for the next operation to either complete or time out. The WaitAny( ) method has three overloads:

```
int WaitAny(WaitHandle[] waitHandles)
int WaitAny(WaitHandle[] waitHandles, int msTimeout, bool exitContext)
int WaitAny(WaitHandle[] waitHandles, TimeSpan timeout, bool exitContext)
```

Where:

waitHandles
> Array of WaitHandle objects for which to wait.

msTimeout
> Number of milliseconds to wait. −1 waits indefinitely.

timeout
> TimeSpan representing the length of time to wait. A TimeSpan value that represents -1 ms waits indefinitely.

exitContext
> Specifies whether to exit the synchronization domain before the wait.

WaitAny( ) returns an integer representing the index of the object in the array that satisfied the wait. A value is returned for each item in the array unless the WaitAny( ) method times out or fails.

The WaitAll( ) method waits for all of the processes in the array of WaitHandle instances to complete or time out before continuing. The WaitAll( ) method has three overloads:

```
bool WaitAll(WaitHandle[] waitHandles)
bool WaitAll(WaitHandle[] waitHandles, int msTimeout, bool exitContext)
bool WaitAll(WaitHandle[] waitHandles, TimeSpan timeout, bool exitContext)
```

Where the arguments are the same as for the WaitAny( ) method.

WaitAll( ) returns a Boolean value indicating whether all objects in the WaitHandle array returned a signal. A value is returned once all objects in the WaitHandle array have returned a signal or when the WaitAll( ) method times out.

For more information about asynchronous queries, and the BeginExecuteNonQuery( ) and EndExecuteNonQuery( ) methods of the Command class, see Recipe 10.2.

10.4   Creating a DataReader Asynchronously

Problem

You need to create a DataReader asynchronously.

Solution

Use the `BeginExecuteReader()` and `EndExecuteReader()` methods of the `Command` object.

The solution demonstrates two techniques to asynchronously create a `DataReader` and process it once its creation is complete. The first method uses a callback procedure to process the `DataReader` once it's complete. The second checks the status of the asynchronous operation and processes the `DataReader` once the status indicates it is complete.

The first solution is a Windows console application that uses an asynchronous data reader to get a result set containing all rows in the `Person.Contact` table in the `AdventureWorks` database. A `WAITFOR` T-SQL statement is used to delay the processing of the `SELECT` statement for five seconds to demonstrate the background processing of the query. After five seconds, the program executes the T-SQL statement to retrieve all rows into a `DataReader` object, and then calls the `HandleCallback()` callback to output the number of rows.

The C# code in *Program.cs* in the project `AsyncDataReaderCallback` is shown in Example 10-6.

Example 10-6. File: Program.cs for AsyncDataReaderCallback solution

```
using System;
using System.Data.SqlClient;

namespace AsyncDataReaderCallback
{
    class Program
    {
        static void Main(string[] args)
        {
            string sqlConnectString =
                "Data Source=localhost;Integrated Security=SSPI;" +
                "Initial Catalog=AdventureWorks;Asynchronous Processing=true";
            string sqlSelect = "WAITFOR DELAY '00:00:05';" +
                "SELECT * FROM Person.Contact;";

            Console.WriteLine("(Press any key to exit.)\n");
```

Example 10-6. File: Program.cs for AsyncDataReaderCallback solution (continued)

```
        SqlConnection connection = new SqlConnection(sqlConnectString);
        SqlCommand command = new SqlCommand(sqlSelect, connection);

        connection.Open( );
        // Start the async operation. The HandleCallback( ) method
        // is called when the operation completes in 5 seconds.
        command.BeginExecuteReader(
            new AsyncCallback(HandleCallback), command);
        Console.WriteLine("[{0}] BeginExecuteReader( ) called.",
            DateTime.Now);
        Console.WriteLine("[{0}] Waiting.", DateTime.Now);

        Console.ReadKey( );
    }

    private static void HandleCallback(IAsyncResult asyncResult)
    {
        // get the original object
        SqlCommand command = (SqlCommand)asyncResult.AsyncState;

        int rowCount = 0;
        // get the data reader returned from the async call
        using (SqlDataReader dr = command.EndExecuteReader(asyncResult))
        {
            // iterate over the reader
            while (dr.Read( ))
            {
                // do some work with the reader

                rowCount++;
            }
        }
        command.Connection.Close( );

        Console.WriteLine("[{0}] HandleCallbackCalled( )",
            DateTime.Now);
        Console.WriteLine("\n---RESULTS---");
        Console.WriteLine("Rows in Person.Contact: {0}", rowCount);
    }
    }
}
```

The output is shown in Figure 10-6.

The second solution uses an asynchronous data reader to get a result set containing all rows in the Person.Contact table in the AdventureWorks database. The solution polls the IAsyncResult interface using its IsComplete property to determine when the operation is complete. The example is similar to the previous example except that a timer is used to check the status of the asynchronous operation every second. The status is output to the console—false if the query is still running or true if it has completed. After completion, the time is stopped and the number of rows in the data reader returned from the query is displayed.

Figure 10-6. Output for AsyncDataReaderCallback solution

The C# code in *Program.cs* in the project `AsyncDataReaderPolling` is shown in Example 10-7.

Example 10-7. File: Program.cs for AsyncDataReaderPolling solution

```csharp
using System;
using System.Data.SqlClient;
using System.Timers;

namespace AsyncDataReaderPolling
{
    class Program
    {
        static IAsyncResult asyncResult;
        static SqlCommand command;

        static void Main(string[] args)
        {
            string sqlConnectString =
                "Data Source=(local);Integrated Security=SSPI;" +
                "Initial Catalog=AdventureWorks;Asynchronous Processing=true";
            string sqlSelect = "WAITFOR DELAY '00:00:05';" +
                "SELECT * FROM Person.Contact;";

            Console.WriteLine("(Press any key to exit.)\n");

            SqlConnection connection = new SqlConnection(sqlConnectString);
            command = new SqlCommand(sqlSelect, connection);

            connection.Open();
            // Start the async operation.
            asyncResult = command.BeginExecuteReader();

            // Start a timer to check the results every 1000ms
            Timer timer = new Timer(1000);
            timer.Elapsed += new ElapsedEventHandler(timer_Elapsed);
            timer.Start();

            Console.WriteLine("---Begin polling---");

            Console.ReadKey();
        }
```

Example 10-7. File: Program.cs for AsyncDataReaderPolling solution (continued)

```
        static void timer_Elapsed(object sender, ElapsedEventArgs e)
        {
            Console.WriteLine("[{0}] Query complete = {1}",
                DateTime.Now, asyncResult.IsCompleted);

            if (asyncResult.IsCompleted)
            {
                // stop the polling and process the results
                ((Timer)sender).Stop( );

                Console.WriteLine("---End polling---");

                ProcessResults( );
            }
        }

        private static void ProcessResults( )
        {
            int rowCount = 0;

            // Get the data reader returned from the async call
            using (SqlDataReader dr = command.EndExecuteReader(asyncResult))
            {
                // iterate over the reader
                while (dr.Read( ))
                {
                    // do some work with the reader

                    rowCount++;
                }
            }

            command.Connection.Close( );
            Console.WriteLine("\nRows returned: {0}", rowCount);
        }
    }
}
```

The output is shown in Figure 10-7.

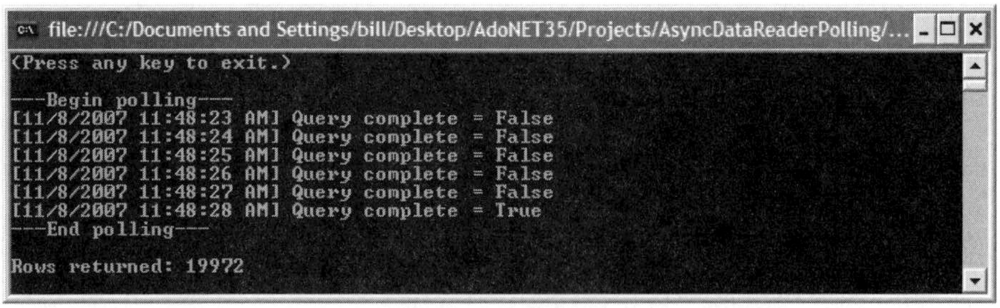

Figure 10-7. Output for AsyncDataReaderPolling solution

Discussion

For more information about asynchronous queries, and the `BeginExecuteReader()` and `EndExecuteReader()` methods of the `Command` class, see Recipe 10.2.

10.5 Filling a DataSet Asynchronously

Problem

Given some database queries that return large result sets and cause the calling application to be unresponsive, you need to make the application more responsive during the fill.

Solution

Create a background thread and use it to run a query to fill a `DataSet`.

The solution creates a thread invoking the `FillDataSet()` method that fills a `DataSet` with the `Sales.SalesOrderHeader` and `Sales.SalesOrderDetail` tables from the `AdventureWorks` database. The `FillDataSet()` method raises a `DateSetFilled` event that is handled in `Main()`. The `DataSetFilled` event handler calls the `Program_DataSetFilled()` method that displays some data from the filled `DataSet`.

The C# code in *Program.cs* in the project `AsyncFillDataSet` is shown in Example 10-8.

Example 10-8. File: Program.cs for AsyncFillDataSet solution

```
using System;
using System.Data;
using System.Data.SqlClient;
using System.Threading;

namespace AsyncFillDataSet
{
    // Define delegate
    public delegate void DataSetFilledEventHandler(
        object sender, DataSetFilledEventArgs e);

    // Define custom event arguments
    public class DataSetFilledEventArgs : EventArgs
    {
        private DataSet ds;

        public DataSetFilledEventArgs(DataSet filledDataSet)
        {
            this.ds = filledDataSet;
        }

        public DataSet FilledDataSet
```

Example 10-8. File: Program.cs for AsyncFillDataSet solution (continued)

```
        {
            get
            {
                return ds;
            }
        }
    }
}

class Program
{
    public static event DataSetFilledEventHandler DataSetFilled;

    protected static void OnDataSetFilled(DataSetFilledEventArgs e)
    {
        if (DataSetFilled != null)
            DataSetFilled(null, e);
    }

    static void Main(string[] args)
    {
        Console.WriteLine("(Press any key to exit.)\n");

        // Call Program_DataSetFilled( ) to handle DataSetFilled evnt
        Program.DataSetFilled +=
            new DataSetFilledEventHandler(Program_DataSetFilled);

        // Create the DataSet that will be filled
        DataSet ds = new DataSet( );
        Console.WriteLine("[{0}] Starting thread to fill DataSet.",
            DateTime.Now);

        // Create a thread that invokes FillDataSet( ) when started
        Thread thread = new Thread(FillDataSet);
        // Start the thread to fill the DataSet ds
        thread.Start(ds);

        // Indicate that the thread has returned control
        Console.WriteLine("[{0}] Returned to Main( ).", DateTime.Now);
        Console.ReadKey( );
    }

    private static void FillDataSet(object objDataSet)
    {
        string sqlConnectString = "Data Source=(local);" +
            "Integrated security=SSPI;Initial Catalog=AdventureWorks;";
        string sqlSelect = "SELECT * FROM Sales.SalesOrderHeader;" +
            "SELECT * FROM Sales.SalesOrderDetail;";

        // Cast the object argument to a DataSet
        DataSet ds = (DataSet)objDataSet;
```

Example 10-8. File: Program.cs for AsyncFillDataSet solution (continued)

```
            // Fill the DataSet with table and schema
            SqlDataAdapter da = new SqlDataAdapter(sqlSelect, sqlConnectString);
            da.TableMappings.Add("Table", "SalesOrderHeader");
            da.TableMappings.Add("Table1", "SalesOrderDetail");
            da.FillSchema(ds, SchemaType.Mapped);
            da.Fill(ds);

            // Create a relation between the tables.
            ds.Relations.Add("Header_Detail",
                ds.Tables["SalesOrderHeader"].Columns["SalesOrderID"],
                ds.Tables["SalesOrderDetail"].Columns["SalesOrderID"],
                true);

            // Raise event indicating the DataSet has been filled
            OnDataSetFilled(new DataSetFilledEventArgs(ds));
        }

        static void Program_DataSetFilled(object sender, DataSetFilledEventArgs e)
        {
            // Handle the event indicating that the DataSet is filled
            Console.WriteLine("[{0}] DataSet filled.\n", DateTime.Now);

            // Get the data set from the event arguments
            DataSet ds = e.FilledDataSet;

            // Output some of DataSet to the console.
            for (int i = 0; i < 3; i++)
            {
                DataRow rh = ds.Tables["SalesOrderHeader"].Rows[i];
                Console.WriteLine("ID = {0}\tDate = {1}\tTotal = {2}",
                    rh["SalesOrderID"], rh["OrderDate"], rh["TotalDue"]);

                foreach (DataRow rd in rh.GetChildRows("Header_Detail"))
                {
                    Console.WriteLine("\tOrderQty = {0}\tUnitPrice = {1}",
                        rd["OrderQty"], rd["UnitPrice"]);
                }
            }
        }
    }
}
```

The output is shown in Figure 10-8.

You can see from the output that the solution starts a thread to fill the DataSet, returns control to the following statement in Main( ), and handles the DataSetFilled event 11 seconds later by displaying some of the data in the DataSet.

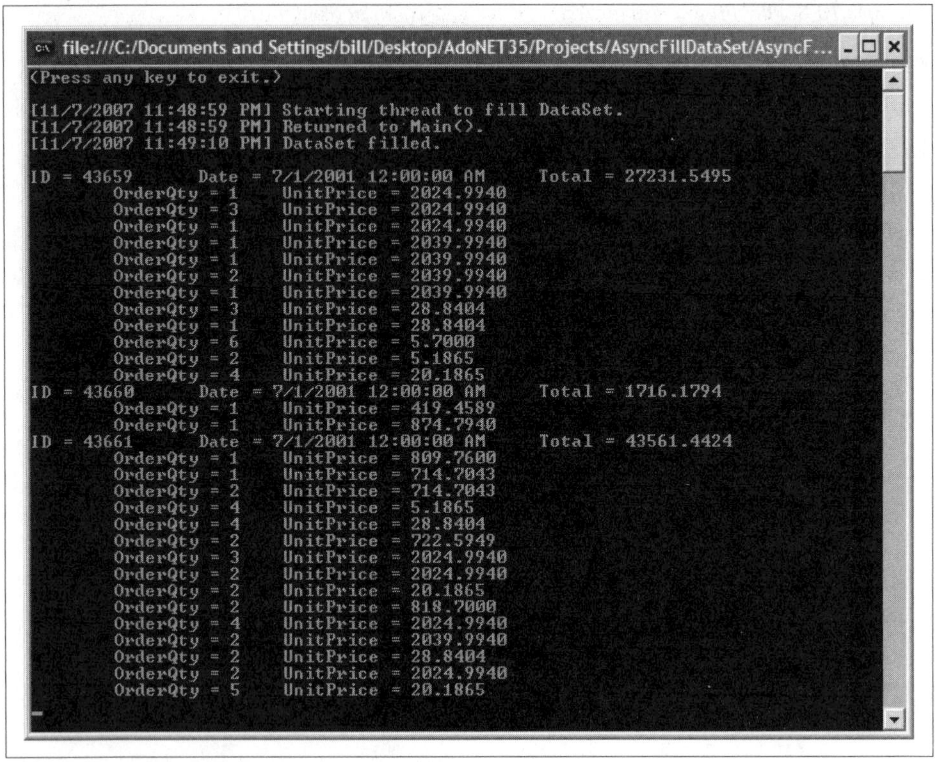

Figure 10-8. Output for AsyncFillDataSet solution

Discussion

When a synchronous call is made, the caller thread is blocked until the call completes. An asynchronous call returns immediately, freeing the calling thread to continue with its work while a new thread is created to run the method in parallel.

A new instance of a Thread is initialized using a constructor that takes a ThreadStart delegate argument, which references the method to be executed when the Thread starts executing. The Start( ) method of the Thread changes the state of the Thread to ThreadState.Running, allowing the operating system to schedule it for execution. Once it begins executing, the ThreadStart delegate supplied in the Thread constructor invokes its method.

Windows Form or control methods, such as a DataGrid, cannot be called on any thread other than the one that created the form or control because they are based on a single-threaded apartment (STA) model. Method calls from other threads must be marshaled to the creation thread. This can be done asynchronously by calling the BeginInvoke( ) method of the form, forcing the method to be executed on the thread that created the form or control.

10.6   Canceling an Asynchronous Query

Problem

Given a command running asynchronously on a background thread, you want to give the user the option to cancel the query if it is taking too long.

Solution

Use the Cancel( ) method of the Command object.

The solution first counts the number of records in the Sales.SalesOrderHeader table in AdventureWorks and outputs that number to the console. Next the solution creates a DataAdapter to fill a DataTable with the records from the Sales.SalesOrderHeader table in AdventureWorks. A new thread is created that invokes the IssueCommand( ) method when the thread starts, which in turn calls the Fill( ) method of the DataAdapter. A second thread is created that invokes the CancelMethod( ) when the thread starts, which in turn calls the Cancel( ) method of the Command object after a delay of 500 ms—enough time for a few records to fill the DataTable. The number of rows filled before the fill is canceled is output to the console.

The C# code in *Program.cs* in the project CancelCommand is shown in Example 10-9.

Example 10-9. File: Program.cs for CancelCommand solution

```
using System;
using System.Data;
using System.Data.SqlClient;
using System.Threading;

namespace CancelCommand
{
    class Program
    {
        private static SqlDataAdapter da;
        private static DataTable dt = new DataTable( );
        private static SqlCommand command;

        static void Main(string[] args)
        {
            Console.WriteLine("(Press any key to exit.)");

            string sqlConnectString =
                "Data Source=localhost;Integrated Security=SSPI;" +
                "Initial Catalog=AdventureWorks";

            string sqlCountText = "SELECT COUNT(*) FROM Sales.SalesOrderHeader";
            string sqlText = "SELECT * FROM Sales.SalesOrderHeader";

            // return the count of records in Sales.SalesOrderHeader
            SqlConnection connection = new SqlConnection(sqlConnectString);
```

Example 10-9. File: Program.cs for CancelCommand solution (continued)

```csharp
            command = new SqlCommand(sqlCountText, connection);
            connection.Open( );
            int rowCount = (int)command.ExecuteScalar( );
            connection.Close( );

            Console.WriteLine("\nCommand.ExecuteScalar( ): {0}", sqlCountText);
            Console.WriteLine("Rows in Sales.SalesOrderHeader = {0}", rowCount);

            // create a DataAdapter to fill a DataTable with all records in
            // Sales.SalesOrderHeader
            command = new SqlCommand(sqlText, connection);
            da = new SqlDataAdapter(command);

            // Create a thread to execute and cancel the command
            Thread tStart = new Thread(new ThreadStart(IssueCommand));
            Thread tCancel = new Thread(new ThreadStart(CancelCommand));
            tStart.Start( );
            tCancel.Start( );

            Console.ReadKey( );
        }

        static void IssueCommand( )
        {
            Console.WriteLine(
                "\nSQL command start -> DataAdapter.Fill( ): {0}",
                command.CommandText);

            try
            {
                da.Fill(dt);
            }
            catch (Exception ex)
            {
                Console.WriteLine("\nERROR:");
                Console.WriteLine("Type    = {0}", ex.GetType( ));
                Console.WriteLine("Message = {0}", ex.Message);
            }
        }

        static void CancelCommand( )
        {
            // Wait 500 ms before canceling to give fill a chance to start
            Thread.Sleep(500);

            // Cancel the command used by the DataAdapter to fill the table
            command.Cancel( );
            Console.WriteLine("\nSQL command cancel.", DateTime.Now);

            Console.WriteLine("\nDataTable.Rows.Count = {0}.", dt.Rows.Count);
        }
    }
}
```

The output is shown in Figure 10-9.

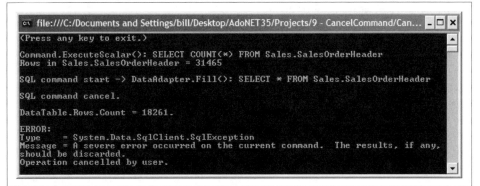

Figure 10-9. Output for CancelCommand solution

You can see from the output that the Sales.SalesOrderHeader table in AdventureWorks has 31,465 records and that the DataTable was filled with 18,261 records when the fill operation was canceled. The output also shows that a SqlException is raised as a result of the cancellation.

Discussion

The Cancel( ) method of the Command class tries to cancel the execution of the Command. An exception is not raised if the attempt to cancel the Command fails. Nothing happens if you call the Cancel( ) method on a Command that is not executing.

10.7   Caching Data

Problem

Given a Web Forms application that is performing poorly because it is repeatedly reading data that doesn't change very often, you need to cache the data to eliminate unnecessary queries and improve the performance.

Solution

Use the ASP.NET Cache class.

The solution has a Web Form that defines the data grid used to display the contents of a DataSet, a button to clear the cache, and a label that displays whether the data was retrieved from the cache or from the database. The C# code for the Web Forms page *Default.aspx* in the project CachingData is shown in Example 10-10.

Example 10-10. File: Default.aspx for CachingData solution

```
<%@ Page Language="C#" AutoEventWireup="true" CodeBehind="Default.aspx.cs"
    Inherits="CachingData.Default" %>

<!DOCTYPE html PUBLIC "-//W3C//DTD XHTML 1.0 Transitional//EN"
    "http://www.w3.org/TR/xhtml1/DTD/xhtml1-transitional.dtd">
<html xmlns="http://www.w3.org/1999/xhtml">
<head runat="server">
    <title>Untitled Page</title>
</head>
<body>
    <form id="form1" runat="server">
    <br />
    <asp:Button ID="clearCacheButton" runat="server" Text="Clear Cache"
        OnClick="clearCacheButton_Click" />
    <br />
    <asp:Label ID="cacheStatusLabel" runat="server" ForeColor="Green" />
    <br />
    <asp:GridView ID="departmentGridView" runat="server" AllowPaging="True"
        OnPageIndexChanging="departmentGridView_PageIndexChanging">
        <HeaderStyle Font-Bold="True"></HeaderStyle>
    </asp:GridView>
    </form>
</body>
</html>
```

The code-behind for the page checks the Cache for a DepartmentDataSet object. If there is no entry, a DataSet instance ds is loaded with the Person.Department table in AdventureWorks and inserted to the cache with an expiration time of 15 seconds. In either case, the source of the department data—cache or database—is displayed on the web page. If the DepartmentDataSet object exists in the Cache, it is cast to a DataSet and loaded into the DataSet instance named ds. The DataSet is bound to a DataGridView. In addition to a 15-second expiration, the clearCacheButton manually removes the DepartmentDataSet object from the Cache when it is clicked.

The C# code for the code-behind *Default.aspx.cs* in the project CachingData is shown in Example 10-11.

Example 10-11. File: Default.aspx.cs for CachingData solution

```
using System;
using System.Data;
using System.Data.SqlClient;
using System.Web.UI.WebControls;

namespace CachingData
{
    public partial class _Default : System.Web.UI.Page
    {
        private DataSet ds;
```

Example 10-11. File: Default.aspx.cs for CachingData solution (continued)

```csharp
protected void Page_Load(object sender, EventArgs e)
{
    // Load the data from database or cache and
    // display where the data came from.
    if (Cache["DepartmentDataSet"] == null)
    {
        LoadDataSet();
        cacheStatusLabel.Text = "DataSet retrieved from database.";
    }
    else
    {
        ds = (DataSet)Cache["DepartmentDataSet"];
        cacheStatusLabel.Text = "DataSet retrieved from cache.";
    }

    if (!Page.IsPostBack)
    {
        // When page is first opened, position to first grid page.
        departmentGridView.PageIndex = 0;
        BindDataGrid();
    }
}
private void LoadDataSet()
{
    string sqlConnectString = "Data Source=(local);" +
        "Integrated security=SSPI;Initial Catalog=AdventureWorks;";

    string sqlText = "SELECT * FROM HumanResources.Department";
    SqlDataAdapter da = new SqlDataAdapter(sqlText, sqlConnectString);
    ds = new DataSet();
    // Fill the Department table in the DataSet with all Department.
    da.Fill(ds, "Department");

    // Save the DataSet to the cache expiring in 15 seconds.
    Cache.Insert("DepartmentDataSet", ds, null,
        DateTime.Now.AddSeconds(15), System.TimeSpan.Zero);
}

private void BindDataGrid()
{
    // Bind the default view of the Department table to the grid.
    departmentGridView.DataSource = ds.Tables["Department"].DefaultView;
    departmentGridView.DataKeyNames = new string[] {"DepartmentID"};
    departmentGridView.DataBind();
}

protected void departmentGridView_PageIndexChanging(
    object sender, GridViewPageEventArgs e)
{
    // change the current page of the grid and rebind
    departmentGridView.PageIndex = e.NewPageIndex;
    BindDataGrid();
```

Example 10-11. File: Default.aspx.cs for CachingData solution (continued)

```
        }

        protected void clearCacheButton_Click(object sender, EventArgs e)
        {
            // Remove the cache when user presses "clear" button.
            Cache.Remove("DepartmentDataSet");
            cacheStatusLabel.Text = "Cache cleared.";
        }
    }
}
```

Figure 10-10 shows the application running.

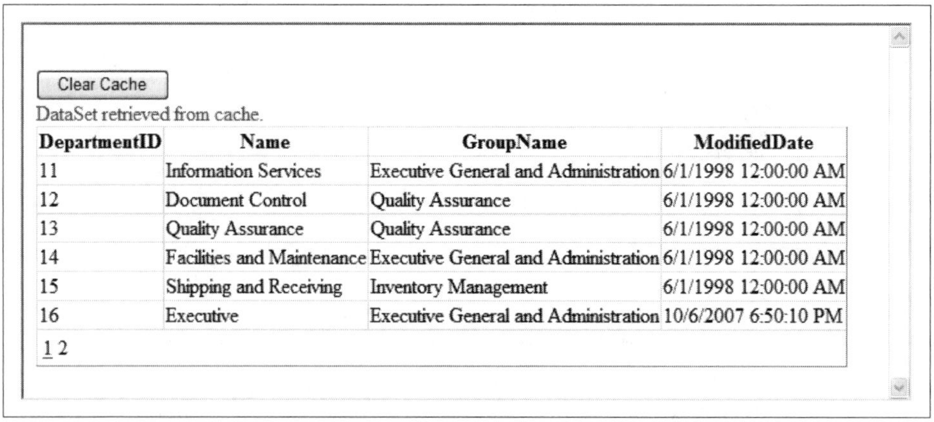

DepartmentID	Name	GroupName	ModifiedDate
11	Information Services	Executive General and Administration	6/1/1998 12:00:00 AM
12	Document Control	Quality Assurance	6/1/1998 12:00:00 AM
13	Quality Assurance	Quality Assurance	6/1/1998 12:00:00 AM
14	Facilities and Maintenance	Executive General and Administration	6/1/1998 12:00:00 AM
15	Shipping and Receiving	Inventory Management	6/1/1998 12:00:00 AM
16	Executive	Executive General and Administration	10/6/2007 6:50:10 PM
1 2			

Figure 10-10. Output for CachingData solution

Discussion

Data used by an application can be re-created in each roundtrip to the server or it can be cached and retrieved from the cache in subsequent page processing. Re-creating data tends to improve its accuracy; however, this can require significant additional processing. Caching data, on the other hand, uses more system resources, which can become a problem.

Data can be cached on the client—in the page using the view state—or on the server in a session state or application state variable or using a cache. Client-side caching uses no server resources for the cache, but requires network bandwidth to transmit the cached information back and forth with each roundtrip to the server. Server-side caching uses server-side resources but little bandwidth for caching. In either case, the amount of data cached should be minimized to optimize application performance and scalability.

ASP.NET implements a `System.Web.Caching.Cache` class to store objects that require a lot of server resources to create so that they do not have to be re-created each time they are needed. Instances of the Cache class are created for each application domain and remain active as long as the application domain remains active. When an application is restarted, its instance of the Cache class is re-created. You can programmatically access information about an instance of the Cache class through the Cache property of either the HttpContext object or the Page object.

Data is placed in a Cache object using key-and-value pairs. The Add( ) method is used to create an entry for a new key value that will fail if the key already exists, while the Insert( ) method will create either a new entry or overwrite an existing entry. The Remove( ) method is used to remove a key-and-value pair from the Cache object.

The Cache class allows an expiration policy to be established for items in the cache. Items can be set to expire at a specific time, called *absolute expiration*, or after not being accessed for a specific period of time, called *sliding expiration*. Items that have expired return a null value. Generally, the expiration policy is set so that data is cached only as long as it remains current.

Caching data can improve performance by reducing the number of trips between the server and the data source. Drawbacks of caching include server memory that is consumed by the cache and the data in the cache being out of sync with the data source.

10.8   Improving Paging Performance

Problem

Given an application that allows the user to page through a large result set in a data grid, you need to improve the performance of the paging.

Solution

Build a custom paging solution that overcomes the performance limitations of the overloaded Fill( ) method of the DataAdapter.

The solution uses a single stored procedure, which is shown in Example 10-12.

Page_Contact
>   Used to return 10 records from the Orders table of the Northwind database that correspond the first, last, next, or previous page, or a specific page. The procedure has the following arguments:

>   @PageCommand
>>   An input parameter that accepts one of the following values: FIRST, LAST, PREVIOUS, NEXT, or GOTO. This specifies the page of results to return to the client.

>   @FirstContactID
>>   An input parameter that contains the ContactID of the first record of the client's current page of Contact data.

@LastContactID

An input parameter that contains the ContactID of the last record of the client's current page of Orders data.

@PageCount

An output parameter that returns the number of pages, each of which contains 10 records, in the result set.

@CurrentPage

An output parameter that returns the page number of the result set returned.

Example 10-12. Stored procedure: Page_Contact

```
USE AdventureWorks
GO

CREATE PROCEDURE Page_Contact
    @PageCommand nvarchar(10),
    @FirstContactID int = null,
    @LastContactID int = null,
    @PageCount int output,
    @CurrentPage int output
AS
    SET NOCOUNT ON

    SELECT @PageCount = CEILING(COUNT(*)/10) FROM Person.Contact

    -- first page is requested OR previous page when the current
    -- page is already the first
    IF @PageCommand = 'FIRST' OR (@PageCommand = 'PREVIOUS' AND
        @CurrentPage <= 1)
    BEGIN
        SELECT TOP 10 *
        FROM Person.Contact
        ORDER BY ContactID

        SET @CurrentPage = 1

        RETURN 0
    END

    -- last page is requested or next page when the current
    -- page is already the last
    IF @PageCommand = 'LAST' OR (@PageCommand = 'NEXT' AND
        @CurrentPage >= @PageCount)
    BEGIN
        SELECT a.*
        FROM
            (SELECT TOP 10 *
            FROM Person.Contact
            ORDER BY ContactID DESC) a
        ORDER BY ContactID
```

Example 10-12. Stored procedure: Page_Contact (continued)

```
        SET @CurrentPage = @PageCount

        RETURN 0
    END

    IF @PageCommand = 'NEXT'
    BEGIN
        SELECT TOP 10 *
        FROM Person.Contact
        WHERE ContactID > @LastContactID
        ORDER BY ContactID

        SET @CurrentPage = @CurrentPage+1

        RETURN 0
    END

    IF @PageCommand = 'PREVIOUS'
    BEGIN
        SELECT a.*
        FROM (
            SELECT TOP 10 *
            FROM Person.Contact
            WHERE ContactID < @FirstContactID
            ORDER BY ContactID DESC) a
        ORDER BY ContactID

        SET @CurrentPage = @CurrentPage-1

        RETURN 0
    END

    IF @PageCommand = 'GOTO'
    BEGIN
        IF @CurrentPage < 1
            SET @CurrentPage = 1
        ELSE IF @CurrentPage > @PageCount
            SET @CurrentPage = @PageCount

        DECLARE @RowCount int
        SET @RowCount = (@CurrentPage * 10)

        EXEC ('SELECT * FROM
        (SELECT TOP 10 a.* FROM
        (SELECT TOP ' + @RowCount + ' * FROM Person.Contact ORDER BY ContactID) a
        ORDER BY ContactID DESC) b
        ORDER BY ContactID')

        RETURN 0
    END

    RETURN 1
```

The solution loads the schema for the Person.Contact table from the AdventureWorks database into a DataTable. Next, a DataAdapter is created to select records using the stored procedure Page_Contact to perform the custom paging through the DataTable, and to return the page count and current page for each call. The FIRST, NEXT, LAST, PREVIOUS, and GOTO paging operations are executed in turn, and partial results from the DataTable containing the specified page are output to the console in each case.

The C# code in *Program.cs* in the project ImprovePagingPerformance is shown in Example 10-13.

Example 10-13. File: Program.cs for ImprovePagingPerformance solution

```csharp
using System;
using System.Data;
using System.Data.SqlClient;

namespace ImprovePagingPerformance
{
    class Program
    {
        private static SqlDataAdapter da;
        private static DataTable dt;

        private static int currentPage;
        private static int firstOrderId;
        private static int lastOrderId;

        static void Main(string[] args)
        {
            string sqlConnectString = @"Data Source=(local);
                Integrated security=SSPI;Initial Catalog=AdventureWorks;";

            string sqlSelect = @"SELECT ContactID, FirstName, LastName
                FROM Person.Contact";

            // Get the schema .
            da = new SqlDataAdapter(sqlSelect, sqlConnectString);
            dt = new DataTable("Orders");
            da.FillSchema(dt, SchemaType.Source);

            // Create and configure the paging stored procedure.
            SqlConnection connection = new SqlConnection(sqlConnectString);
            SqlCommand command = new SqlCommand( );
            command.Connection = connection;
            command.CommandText = "Page_Contact";
            command.CommandType = CommandType.StoredProcedure;
            command.Parameters.Add("@PageCommand", SqlDbType.NVarChar, 10);
            command.Parameters.Add("@FirstContactID", SqlDbType.Int);
            command.Parameters.Add("@LastContactID", SqlDbType.Int);
            command.Parameters.Add("@PageCount", SqlDbType.Int).Direction =
                ParameterDirection.Output;
            command.Parameters.Add("@CurrentPage", SqlDbType.Int).Direction =
                ParameterDirection.InputOutput;
            da = new SqlDataAdapter(command);
```

```
        // Get the first page of records.
        Console.WriteLine("\n=> FIRST");
        GetData("FIRST");
        Console.WriteLine("\n=> NEXT");
        GetData("NEXT");
        Console.WriteLine("\n=> LAST");
        GetData("LAST");
        Console.WriteLine("\n=> PREVIOUS");
        GetData("PREVIOUS");
        Console.WriteLine("\n=> GOTO 1000");
        currentPage = 1000;
        GetData("GOTO");

        Console.WriteLine("\nPress any key to continue.");
        Console.ReadKey( );
    }

    static void GetData(string pageCommand)
    {
        da.SelectCommand.Parameters["@PageCommand"].Value = pageCommand;
        da.SelectCommand.Parameters["@FirstContactID"].Value = firstOrderId;
        da.SelectCommand.Parameters["@LastContactID"].Value = lastOrderId;
        da.SelectCommand.Parameters["@CurrentPage"].Value = currentPage;

        dt.Clear( );
        da.Fill(dt);

        if (dt.Rows.Count > 0)
        {
            firstOrderId = (int)dt.Rows[0]["ContactID"];
            lastOrderId = (int)dt.Rows[dt.Rows.Count - 1]["ContactID"];
        }
        else
            firstOrderId = lastOrderId = -1;

        int pageCount = (int)da.SelectCommand.Parameters["@PageCount"].Value;
        currentPage = (int)da.SelectCommand.Parameters["@CurrentPage"].Value;

        Console.WriteLine("\n---Person.Contact: Page {0} of {1}---",
            currentPage, pageCount);
        Console.WriteLine("Row\tID\tContact Name");
        Console.WriteLine("---\t--\t------------");
        OutputRow(1, dt.Rows[0]);
        OutputRow(2, dt.Rows[1]);
        Console.WriteLine("...");
        OutputRow(9, dt.Rows[8]);
        OutputRow(10, dt.Rows[9]);
    }

    static void OutputRow(int n, DataRow row)
    {
        Console.WriteLine("{0}\t{0}\t{1}, {2}", n, row["ContactID"],
            row["LastName"], row["FirstName"]);
```

Example 10-13. File: Program.cs for ImprovePagingPerformance solution (continued)

```
        }
    }
}
```

The output is shown in Figure 10-11.

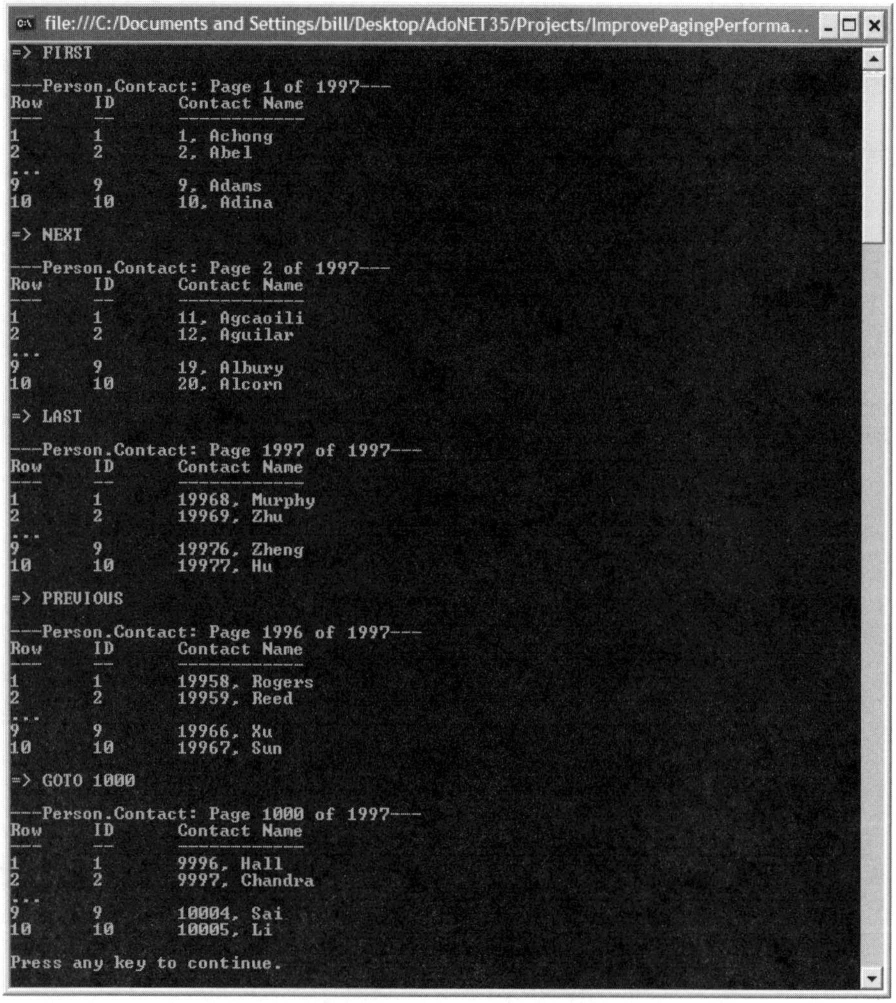

Figure 10-11. Output for ImprovePagingPerformance solution

Discussion

Overloads of the Fill( ) method of the DataAdapter allow a subset of data to be returned from a query by specifying the starting record and the number of records to return as arguments. This method should be avoided for paging through result sets—especially large ones—because it retrieves the entire result set for the query and subsequently discards the records outside of the specified range. Resources are used to process the entire result set instead of just the subset of required records.

The solution shows how to create a stored procedure that will return a result set corresponding to a page of data from a larger result set. The TOP and WHERE clauses are used together with the primary key (any unique identifier would do) and the sort order. This allows first, last, next, and previous paging. The goto paging is done by nesting SELECT TOP *n* statements with alternate ascending and descending sorts to get the subset of the records for the page specified. The goto select statement uses a dynamic SQL statement executed using the T-SQL EXEC command. This allows a variable number of top *n* records to be selected within the statement. The EXEC command could also be used to dynamically calculate the top records for all statements so that the number of records per page could be supplied as an input parameter to the stored procedure rather than hardcoded.

10.9 XML Bulk Loading with SQL Server

Problem

Given many records in an XML file that you need to add to a SQL Server database, you need to perform a bulk insert with optimal performance.

Solution

Perform a bulk insert and update using the XML bulk load functionality in Microsoft SQL Server.

The solution uses a table named Customers in the AdoDotNet35Cookbook database. The T-SQL statement to create the table follows:

```
USE AdoDotNet35Cookbook
GO

CREATE TABLE Customers(
    CustomerID nvarchar(5) NOT NULL PRIMARY KEY,
    CompanyName nvarchar(40) NULL,
    ContactName nvarchar(30) NULL,
    ContactTitle nvarchar(30) NULL,
    Address nvarchar(60) NULL,
    City nvarchar(15) NULL,
    Region nvarchar(15) NULL,
    PostalCode nvarchar(10) NULL,
    Country nvarchar(15) NULL,
    Phone nvarchar(24) NULL,
    Fax nvarchar(24) NULL
)
```

The solution uses an XML schema file that describes the XML data file. The schema file is named *Customers.xsd* and is shown in Example 10-14. The solution expects this file to be in the same directory as the solution file *BulkLoad.sln*.

Example 10-14. File: Customers.xsd

```xml
<xsd:schema xmlns:xsd="http://www.w3.org/2001/XMLSchema"
    xmlns:sql="urn:schemas-microsoft-com:mapping-schema">
    <xsd:element name="ROOT" sql:is-constant="true">
        <xsd:complexType>
            <xsd:sequence>
                <xsd:element ref="Customers" />
            </xsd:sequence>
        </xsd:complexType>
    </xsd:element>
    <xsd:element name="Customers" sql:relation="Customers">
        <xsd:complexType>
            <xsd:sequence>
                <xsd:element name="CustomerID" type="xsd:string"
                    sql:datatype="nvarchar(5)" />
                <xsd:element name="CompanyName" type="xsd:string"
                    sql:datatype="nvarchar(40)" />
                <xsd:element name="ContactName" type="xsd:string"
                    sql:datatype="nvarchar(30)" />
                <xsd:element name="ContactTitle"
                    type="xsd:string"
                    sql:datatype="nvarchar(30)" />
                <xsd:element name="Address" type="xsd:string"
                    sql:datatype="nvarchar(60)" />
                <xsd:element name="City" type="xsd:string"
                    sql:datatype="nvarchar(15)" />
                <xsd:element name="Region" type="xsd:string"
                    sql:datatype="nvarchar(15)" />
                <xsd:element name="PostalCode" type="xsd:string"
                    sql:datatype="nvarchar(10)" />
                <xsd:element name="Country" type="xsd:string"
                    sql:datatype="nvarchar(15)" />
                <xsd:element name="Phone" type="xsd:string"
                    sql:datatype="nvarchar(24)" />
                <xsd:element name="Fax" type="xsd:string"
                    sql:datatype="nvarchar(24)" />
            </xsd:sequence>
        </xsd:complexType>
    </xsd:element>
</xsd:schema>
```

The solution uses an XML file that contains the data to be loaded. The file is named *Customers.xml* and is partly shown in Example 10-15. The solution expects this file to be in the same directory as the solution file *BulkLoad.sln*.

Example 10-15. File: Customers.xml

```xml
<ROOT>
    <Customers>
        <CustomerID>ALFKI</CustomerID>
        <CompanyName>Alfreds Futterkiste</CompanyName>
        <ContactName>Maria Anders</ContactName>
        <ContactTitle>Sales Representative</ContactTitle>
        <Address>Obere Str. 57</Address>
        <City>Berlin</City>
        <PostalCode>12209</PostalCode>
        <Country>Germany</Country>
        <Phone>030-0074321</Phone>
        <Fax>030-0076545</Fax>
    </Customers>

<!--  . . .  -->

    <Customers>
        <CustomerID>WOLZA</CustomerID>
        <CompanyName>Wolski  Zajazd</CompanyName>
        <ContactName>Zbyszek Piestrzeniewicz</ContactName>
        <ContactTitle>Owner</ContactTitle>
        <Address>ul. Filtrowa 68</Address>
        <City>Warszawa</City>
        <PostalCode>01-012</PostalCode>
        <Country>Poland</Country>
        <Phone>(26) 642-7012</Phone>
        <Fax>(26) 642-7012</Fax>
    </Customers>
</ROOT>
```

The solution creates a bulk load object SQLXMLBulkLoad and sets the connection string and error log file for the object. The Execute( ) method of the SQLXMLBulkLoad object is used to bulk load the Customers data from the XML file into the Customers table in the AdoDotNet35Cookbook database. The Customers table must be empty prior to running this sample or a primary key constraint error will be raised and written to the error log.

The solution needs a reference to the SQLXML Bulk Load 4.0 COM object. Add a reference to the Microsoft SQLXML BulkLoad 4.0 Type Library from the COM tab in Visual Studio .NET's Add Reference Dialog. If it is not listed, browse for and add its DLL named *xblkld4.dll*—it should be in the directory *c:\Program Files\Common Files\System\Ole DB*. The SQLXML Bulk Load 4.0 library ships with SQL Server 2005. If unavailable, you can use version 3.0 of the library, which you can download from the Microsoft Download Center web site.

The C# code in *Program.cs* in the project BulkLoad is shown in Example 10-16.

Example 10-16. File: Program.cs for BulkLoad solution

```
using System;
using SQLXMLBULKLOADLib;

namespace BulkLoad
{
    class Program
    {
        [STAThread]
        static void Main(string[] args)
        {
            string oledbConnectString = "Provider=SQLOLEDB;Data Source=(local);" +
                "Initial Catalog=AdoDotNet35Cookbook;Integrated security=SSPI;";
            string dataFileName = @"..\..\..\Customers.xml";
            string schemaFileName = @"..\..\..\Customers.xsd";
            string errorLogFileName = @"..\..\..\BulkLoadError.log";

            SQLXMLBulkLoad4Class bl = new SQLXMLBulkLoad4Class();
            bl.ConnectionString = oledbConnectString;
            bl.ErrorLogFile = errorLogFileName;
            bl.KeepIdentity = false;

            Console.WriteLine("[{0}] Starting bulk load.", DateTime.Now);
            try
            {
                bl.Execute(schemaFileName, dataFileName);
                Console.WriteLine("[{0}] Bulk load completed.", DateTime.Now);
            }
            catch (Exception ex)
            {
                Console.WriteLine("[{0}] Error: {1}", DateTime.Now, ex.Message);
            }

            Console.WriteLine("\nPress any key to continue.");
            Console.ReadKey();
        }
    }
}
```

The output is shown in Figure 10-12.

Figure 10-12. Output for BulkLoad solution

Figure 10-13 shows partial data in the Customers table after the bulk copy.

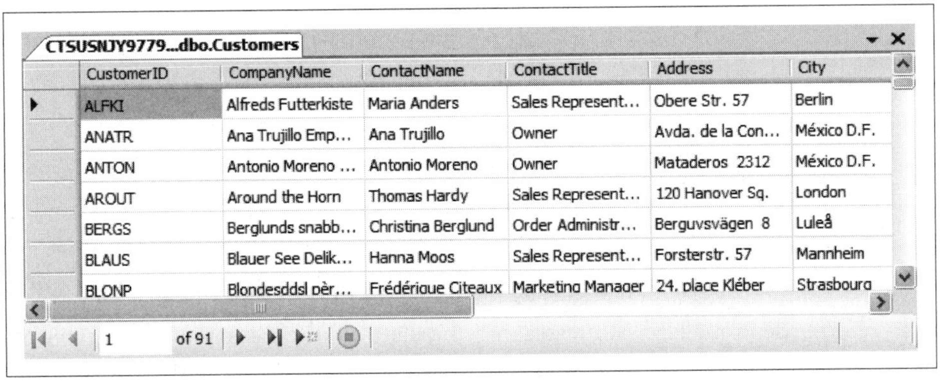

CTSUSNJY9779...dbo.Customers

CustomerID	CompanyName	ContactName	ContactTitle	Address	City
ALFKI	Alfreds Futterkiste	Maria Anders	Sales Represent...	Obere Str. 57	Berlin
ANATR	Ana Trujillo Emp...	Ana Trujillo	Owner	Avda. de la Con...	México D.F.
ANTON	Antonio Moreno ...	Antonio Moreno	Owner	Mataderos 2312	México D.F.
AROUT	Around the Horn	Thomas Hardy	Sales Represent...	120 Hanover Sq.	London
BERGS	Berglunds snabb...	Christina Berglund	Order Administr...	Berguvsvägen 8	Luleå
BLAUS	Blauer See Delik...	Hanna Moos	Sales Represent...	Forsterstr. 57	Mannheim
BLONP	Blondesddsl pèr...	Frédérique Citeaux	Marketing Manager	24, place Kléber	Strasbourg

1 of 91

Figure 10-13. Customers table after bulk copy

Discussion

The SQL Server XML Bulk Load component is used through COM Interop to bulk insert data contained in a XML document into a SQL Server database. This component controls the execution of a XML bulk load operation. The example defines an optional error logfile, where the default is an empty string meaning that no error log is created.

You can bulk load data into multiple parent-child tables at the same time, a feature that is not available in the `OpenXML` Transact-SQL extension.

For information about the XML Bulk Load component and its methods and properties, see the topic "XML Bulk Load [SQL Server]" in MSDN.

10.10 Bulk Copying with SQL Server

Problem

You need to bulk copy data into a SQL server table from another SQL Server table, or from an external file such as an XML file.

Solution

Use the `SqlBulkCopy` class.

The solution shows how to bulk copy data into a SQL Server table from two sources: a `DataReader` and an XML file.

Both solutions copy data into a table named `AddressExpand` in the database `AdoDotNet35Cookbook`. Execute the following T-SQL statement to create the table:

```
USE AdoDotNet35Cookbook
GO
CREATE TABLE AddressExpand(
    AddressID int NOT NULL PRIMARY KEY,
    AddressLine1 nvarchar(60) NOT NULL,
    AddressLine2 nvarchar(60) NULL,
    City nvarchar(30) NOT NULL,
    StateProvinceName nvarchar(50) NOT NULL,
    PostalCode nvarchar(15) NOT NULL,
    CountryRegionName nvarchar(50) NOT NULL )
```

The first solution creates a DataReader on the join of three tables in AdventureWorks that returns denormalized addresses for the data in the Person.Address table in AdventureWorks. A IDataReader instance is created for the query and used with the WriteToServer( ) method of the SqlBulkCopy class to perform the bulk copy into the AddressExpand table in the AdoDotNet35Cookbook database.

The C# code in *Program.cs* in the project BulkCopyDataReader is shown in Example 10-17.

Example 10-17. File: Program.cs for BulkCopyDataReader solution

```
using System;
using System.Data;
using System.Data.SqlClient;

namespace BulkCopyDataReader
{
    class Program
    {
        static void Main(string[] args)
        {
            string srcConnectString = "Data Source=(local);" +
                "Integrated Security=SSPI;Initial Catalog=AdventureWorks;";
            string destConnectString = "Data Source=(local);" +
                "Integrated Security=SSPI;Initial Catalog=AdoDotNet35Cookbook;";

            string sqlSelect = "SELECT AddressID, AddressLine1, AddressLine2, " +
                "City, sp.Name StateProvinceName, PostalCode, " +
                "cr.Name CountryRegionName FROM Person.Address a " +
                "JOIN Person.StateProvince sp " +
                "ON sp.StateProvinceID = a.StateProvinceID " +
                "JOIN Person.CountryRegion cr " +
                "ON cr.CountryRegionCode = sp.CountryRegionCode";

            string destTable = "AddressExpand";

            // get data from the source server using a data reader
            SqlConnection srcConn = new SqlConnection(srcConnectString);
            srcConn.Open( );

            SqlCommand command = new SqlCommand(sqlSelect, srcConn);
            IDataReader dr = command.ExecuteReader( );
```

Example 10-17. File: Program.cs for BulkCopyDataReader solution (continued)

```
        // connection to the destination server
        SqlConnection dstConn = new SqlConnection(destConnectString);
        dstConn.Open( );

        // bulk copy the  data to the destination table
        using (SqlBulkCopy bcp = new SqlBulkCopy(dstConn))
        {
            bcp.DestinationTableName = destTable;
            bcp.WriteToServer(dr);
        }

        // close connections
        dstConn.Close( );
        dr.Close( );
        srcConn.Close( );

        Console.WriteLine("Press any key to continue.");
        Console.ReadKey( );
    }
  }
}
```

Figure 10-14 shows the first few rows in the AddressExpand table in the AdoDotNet35Cookbook database after the bulk copy has completed.

AddressID	AddressLine1	AddressLine2	City	StateProvinceN...	PostalCode	CountryRegion...
1	1970 Napa Ct.	NULL	Bothell	Washington	98011	United States
2	9833 Mt. Dias Blv.	NULL	Bothell	Washington	98011	United States
3	7484 Roundtree...	NULL	Bothell	Washington	98011	United States
4	9539 Glenside Dr	NULL	Bothell	Washington	98011	United States
5	1226 Shoe St.	NULL	Bothell	Washington	98011	United States
6	1399 Firestone ...	NULL	Bothell	Washington	98011	United States
7	5672 Hale Dr.	NULL	Bothell	Washington	98011	United States

Figure 10-14. First few rows of AddressExpand table after bulk copy

The second solution uses an XML schema file that describes the XML data file. The schema file is named *AddressExpand.xsd* and is shown in Example 10-18.

Example 10-18. File: AddressExpand.xsd

```
<?xml version="1.0" standalone="yes"?>
<xs:schema id="NewDataSet" xmlns:xs="http://www.w3.org/2001/XMLSchema"
  xmlns:msdata="urn:schemas-microsoft-com:xml-msdata">
  <xs:element name="NewDataSet" msdata:IsDataSet="true"
    msdata:MainDataTable="AddressExpand" msdata:UseCurrentLocale="true">
    <xs:complexType>
      <xs:choice minOccurs="0" maxOccurs="unbounded">
        <xs:element name="AddressExpand">
```

Example 10-18. File: AddressExpand.xsd (continued)

```
        <xs:complexType>
          <xs:sequence>
            <xs:element name="AddressID" type="xs:int" minOccurs="0" />
            <xs:element name="AddressLine1" type="xs:string" minOccurs="0" />
            <xs:element name="AddressLine2" type="xs:string" minOccurs="0" />
            <xs:element name="City" type="xs:string" minOccurs="0" />
            <xs:element name="StateProvinceName" type="xs:string" minOccurs="0" />
            <xs:element name="PostalCode" type="xs:string" minOccurs="0" />
            <xs:element name="CountryRegionName" type="xs:string" minOccurs="0" />
          </xs:sequence>
        </xs:complexType>
      </xs:element>
    </xs:choice>
  </xs:complexType>
</xs:element>
</xs:schema>
```

The solution uses an XML file that contains the data to be loaded. The file is named *AddressExpand.xml* and is partly shown in Example 10-19.

Example 10-19. File: AddressExpand.xml

```
<?xml version="1.0" standalone="yes"?>
<DocumentElement>
  <AddressExpand>
    <AddressID>1</AddressID>
    <AddressLine1>1970 Napa Ct.</AddressLine1>
    <City>Bothell</City>
    <StateProvinceName>Washington</StateProvinceName>
    <PostalCode>98011</PostalCode>
    <CountryRegionName>United States</CountryRegionName>
  </AddressExpand>
  <AddressExpand>
    <AddressID>2</AddressID>
    <AddressLine1>9833 Mt. Dias Blv.</AddressLine1>
    <City>Bothell</City>
    <StateProvinceName>Washington</StateProvinceName>
    <PostalCode>98011</PostalCode>
    <CountryRegionName>United States</CountryRegionName>
  </AddressExpand>
  <AddressExpand>
    <AddressID>3</AddressID>
    <AddressLine1>7484 Roundtree Drive</AddressLine1>
    <City>Bothell</City>
    <StateProvinceName>Washington</StateProvinceName>
    <PostalCode>98011</PostalCode>
    <CountryRegionName>United States</CountryRegionName>
  </AddressExpand>
  <AddressExpand>
    <AddressID>4</AddressID>
    <AddressLine1>9539 Glenside Dr</AddressLine1>
```

Example 10-19. File: AddressExpand.xml (continued)

```
      <City>Bothell</City>
      <StateProvinceName>Washington</StateProvinceName>
      <PostalCode>98011</PostalCode>
      <CountryRegionName>United States</CountryRegionName>
    </AddressExpand>
    <AddressExpand>
      <AddressID>5</AddressID>
      <AddressLine1>1226 Shoe St.</AddressLine1>
      <City>Bothell</City>
      <StateProvinceName>Washington</StateProvinceName>
      <PostalCode>98011</PostalCode>
      <CountryRegionName>United States</CountryRegionName>
    </AddressExpand>
</DocumentElement>
```

The second solution creates a DataTable using the XML schema and data in the files *Customers.xsd* and *Customers.xml* described earlier in Recipe 10.9. The DataTable is used with the WriteToServer( ) method of the SqlBulkCopy class to perform the bulk copy into the AddressExpand table in the AdoDotNet35Cookbook database.

If you executed the first solution in this recipe, delete all records from the AddressExpand table before executing this second solution.

The C# code in *Program.cs* in the project BulkCopyXmlFile is shown in Example 10-20.

Example 10-20. File: Program.cs for BulkCopyXmlFile solution

```csharp
using System;
using System.Data;
using System.Data.SqlClient;

namespace BulkCopyXmlFile
{
    class Program
    {
        static void Main(string[] args)
        {
            // XML data and schema file
            string xmlDataFileName = @"..\..\..\AddressExpand.xml";
            string xmlSchemaFileName = @"..\..\..\AddressExpand.xsd";

            // connection string to destination database and table
            string destConnectString = "Data Source=(local);" +
                "Integrated Security=SSPI;Initial Catalog=AdoDotNet35Cookbook;";
            string destTable = "AddressExpand";

            // Create the DataTable and load the XML schema and data
            DataTable dt = new DataTable();
            dt.ReadXmlSchema(xmlSchemaFileName);
            dt.ReadXml(xmlDataFileName);
```

Example 10-20. File: Program.cs for BulkCopyXmlFile solution (continued)

```
                // connection to the destination server
                using (SqlConnection dstConn = new SqlConnection(destConnectString))
                {
                    dstConn.Open( );

                    // bulk copy the data to the destination table
                    using (SqlBulkCopy bcp = new SqlBulkCopy(dstConn))
                    {
                        bcp.DestinationTableName = destTable;
                        bcp.WriteToServer(dt);
                    }
                }

                Console.WriteLine("Press any key to continue.");
                Console.ReadKey( );
            }
        }
}
```

Figure 10-15 shows the `AddressExpand` table in the `AdoDotNet35Cookbook` database after the bulk copy has completed.

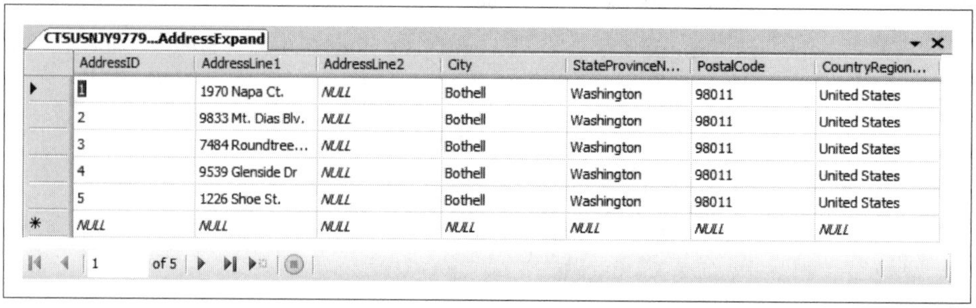

Figure 10-15. AddressExpand table after bulk copy

Discussion

The `SqlBulkCopy` class efficiently loads a SQL Server table with data from another source. This lets you write managed code with functionality similar to the command-prompt bulk copy utility bcp.exe. The `SqlBulkCopy` class can only write data to SQL Server tables. Any data source can be used, however, as long as the data can be loaded into a `DataTable` or accessed using a `DataReader`. The `SqlBulkCopy` class lets you perform single or multiple bulk copy operations, within a transaction if necessary.

The `SqlBulkCopy` class has four overloaded constructors:

```
SqlBulkCopy(SqlConnection conn)
SqlBulkCopy(string connectionString)
SqlBulkCopy(string connectionString, SqlBulkCopyOptions options)
SqlBulkCopy(SqlConnection conn, SqlBulkCopyOptions options, SqlTransaction tran)
```

Where:

conn

> A connection to the destination database. The connection is automatically closed at the end of the bulk copy operation.

connectionString

> A connection string to the destination database. The connection is automatically closed at the end of the bulk copy operation.

options

> One or a combination of values from the SqlBulkCopyOptions enumeration that specifies the data source rows that are copied to the destination. The SqlBulkCopyOptions enumeration is described in Table 10-3.

tran

> An existing transaction for the bulk copy operation to use.

Table 10-3. SqlBulkCopyOptions enumeration

Member	Description
Default	Use the default value for all options.
KeepIdentity	Preserve source identity values. The data destination determines the identity values if this option is not specified.
CheckConstraints	Check constraints while data is inserted. Constraints are not checked by default.
TableLock	Obtain a bulk update lock for the duration of the bulk copy operation. Row locks are used if this option is not specified.
KeepNulls	Preserve null values in the destination table. The data destination determines replacement for null values if this option is not specified.
FireTriggers	Fires insert triggers for inserted rows.
UserInternalTransaction	Each batch of the bulk copy operation is performed within a transaction.

The WriteToServer( ) method of the SqlBulkCopy class copies data from the source to the destination SQL Server table. The method has four overloads:

```
void WriteToServer(DataRow[] dataRows)
void WriteToServer(DataTable dataTable)
void WriteToServer(IDataReader dataReader)
void WriteToServer(DataTable dataTable, DataRowState dataRowState)
```

Where:

dataRows

> DataRow array that is the source of the data.

dataTable

> DataTable that is the source of the data.

dataReader

> DataReader that is the source of the data.

dataRowState

> Value from the DataRowState enumeration specifying the state of the rows that will be copied from the source.

Table 10-4 lists properties of the SqlBulkCopy class that control aspects of the bulk copy operation.

Table 10-4. SqlBulkCopy class properties

Property	Description
BatchSize	Number of rows in each batch sent to the server.
BulkCopyTimeout	Time in seconds after which the operation will time out.
ColumnMappings	A collection of SqlBulkCopyColumnMapping objects that define the mapping between source and destination columns.
DestinationTableName	Name of the destination SQL Server table in the database specified by the connection in the SqlBulkCopy class constructor.
NotifyAfter	Number of rows to process before generating a SqlRowsCopied notification event.

10.11 Improving DataReader Performance with Typed Accessors

Problem

You need to improve performance when accessing data from a DataReader.

Solution

Use DataReader typed accessors to improve performance by eliminating repeated boxing and unboxing of object data to and from .NET Framework data types.

The sample code measures the time to access data in a DataReader using three techniques: typed accessor, column ordinal, and column name. To ensure accuracy in each case, the routine reads all data from the DataReader 1,000 times and measures the total time in ticks, which are one-millisecond intervals.

The C# code in *Program.cs* in the project DataReaderTypedAccessors is shown in Example 10-21.

Example 10-21. File: Program.cs for DataReaderTypedAccessors solution

```
using System;
using System.Data;
using System.Data.SqlClient;
```

Example 10-21. File: Program.cs for DataReaderTypedAccessors solution (continued)

```
namespace DataReaderTypedAccessors
{
    class Program
    {
        static void Main(string[] args)
        {
            int loops = 1000;

            int contactID;
            string firstName;
            string middleName = null;
            string lastName;

            int startTick = 0;
            int elapsedTick;

            string sqlConnectString = "Data Source=(local);" +
                "Integrated security=SSPI;Initial Catalog=AdventureWorks;";

            string sqlSelect = "SELECT ContactID, FirstName, MiddleName, LastName " +
                "FROM Person.Contact";

            Console.WriteLine("---DataReader column value access timing test, " +
                "{0} iterations---\n", loops);

            SqlConnection connection = new SqlConnection(sqlConnectString);

            // Create the command and open the connection
            SqlCommand command = new SqlCommand(sqlSelect, connection);
            connection.Open();

            elapsedTick = 0;
            for (int i = 0; i < loops; i++)
            {
                // Create the DataReader and retrieve all fields for each
                // record using a typed accessor with a column ordinal
                using (SqlDataReader dr = command.ExecuteReader())
                {
                    startTick = Environment.TickCount;
                    while (dr.Read())
                    {
                        contactID = dr.GetInt32(0);
                        firstName = dr.GetString(1);
                        middleName = dr.IsDBNull(2) ? null : dr.GetString(2);
                        lastName = dr.GetString(3);
                    }

                    elapsedTick += Environment.TickCount - startTick;
                }
            }
```

```
        Console.WriteLine("Typed accessor: Ticks = {0}",
            elapsedTick);

        elapsedTick = 0;
        for (int i = 0; i < loops; i++)
        {
            // Create the DataReader and retrieve all fields for each
            // record using a column ordinal
            using (SqlDataReader dr = command.ExecuteReader())
            {
                startTick = Environment.TickCount;
                while (dr.Read())
                {
                    contactID = Convert.ToInt32(dr[0]);
                    firstName = Convert.ToString(dr[1]);
                    middleName = Convert.ToString(dr[2]);
                    lastName = Convert.ToString(dr[3]);
                }

                elapsedTick += Environment.TickCount - startTick;
            }
        }
        Console.WriteLine("Column ordinal: Ticks = {0}", elapsedTick);

        elapsedTick = 0;
        for (int i = 0; i < loops; i++)
        {
            // Create the DataReader and retrieve all fields for each
            // record using a column field name
            using (SqlDataReader dr = command.ExecuteReader())
            {
                startTick = Environment.TickCount;
                while (dr.Read())
                {
                    contactID = Convert.ToInt32(dr["ContactID"]);
                    firstName = Convert.ToString(dr["FirstName"]);
                    middleName = Convert.ToString(dr["MiddleName"]);
                    lastName = Convert.ToString(dr["LastName"]);
                }

                elapsedTick += Environment.TickCount - startTick;
            }
        }
        Console.WriteLine("Column name: Ticks = {0}", elapsedTick);

        Console.WriteLine("\nPress any key to continue.");
        Console.ReadKey();
    }
  }
}
```

The output is shown in Figure 10-16. Note that this code might take a minute to execute.

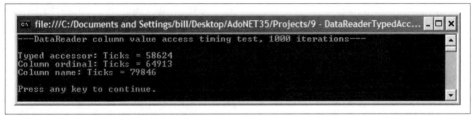

Figure 10-16. Output for DataReaderTypedAccessors solution

Discussion

You can access the data in a DataReader row using a column name, a column ordinal, or a typed accessor method such as GetInt32( ) and GetString( ). The typed accessor allows a column value to be accessed in its native data type, reducing the amount of type conversion required when retrieving a column value. When the underlying type is known, this reduces the type conversion effort required when retrieving the column value and thereby improves performance. For a list of typed accessor methods for SQL Server and OLE DB data providers, see Recipe 2.4.

Each typed accessor takes a single argument: the zero-based column ordinal of the column for which to retrieve the value. An IndexOutOfRangeException is raised if the ordinal value is not valid. An InvalidCastException is raised if the accessor method specifies an invalid cast. If the column might contain a nonexistent or missing value, call the IsDBNull( ) method prior to calling the typed accessor method to avoid raising an exception in case the column value is equivalent to DBNull.

Executing the solution shows the following relative performance when accessing DataReader column values using the different methods:

- A column ordinal is about 25 percent faster than a column name.
- A typed accessor method is about 10 percent faster than a column ordinal and 35 percent faster than a column name.

10.12 Improving DataReader Performance with Column Ordinals

Problem

You want to use column ordinals rather than column names to retrieve data from a DataReader to improve application performance and without hardcoding the ordinal values.

Solution

Enumerate the column ordinals using the GetOrdinal( ) method and use those values to retrieve data from the DataReader.

The solution uses a `DataReader` to retrieve and output the column ordinals for result set columns—ContactID, FirstName, and LastName—from the Person.Contact table in AdventureWorks. The solution then demonstrates three techniques to retrieve and output these fields for the first five rows in the Person.Contact table. The techniques used are index-based, .NET typed, and provider-specific typed.

The C# code in *Program.cs* in the project `DataReaderColumnOrdinals` is shown in Example 10-22.

Example 10-22. File: Program.cs for DataReaderColumnOrdinals solution

```
using System;
using System.Data;
using System.Data.SqlClient;

namespace DataReaderColumnOrdinals
{
    class Program
    {
        static void Main(string[] args)
        {
            int coContactID, coFirstName, coLastName;

            string sqlConnectString = "Data Source=(local);" +
                "Integrated security=SSPI;Initial Catalog=AdventureWorks;";

            string sqlSelect = "SELECT TOP 5 * FROM Person.Contact";

            SqlConnection connection = new SqlConnection(sqlConnectString);

            // Create the command and open the connection
            SqlCommand command = new SqlCommand(sqlSelect, connection);
            connection.Open();

            // Create the DataReader to retrieve column ordinals
            using (SqlDataReader drSchema =
                command.ExecuteReader(CommandBehavior.SchemaOnly))
            {
                // Get column ordinals for each field in the result set
                coContactID = drSchema.GetOrdinal("ContactID");
                coFirstName = drSchema.GetOrdinal("FirstName");
                coLastName = drSchema.GetOrdinal("LastName");
            }

            // Output column ordinals
            Console.WriteLine("---Column ordinals---");
            Console.WriteLine("ContactID = {0}, FirstName = {1}, LastName = {2}",
                coContactID, coFirstName, coLastName);

            Console.WriteLine("\n---Index-based accessor---");
            // Create the DataReader to retrieve data
            using (SqlDataReader dr = command.ExecuteReader())
```

```
        {
            while (dr.Read( ))
            {
                // Output fields using the column ordinals as accessors
                Console.WriteLine("{0}\t{1}, {2}",
                    dr[coContactID], dr[coLastName], dr[coFirstName]);
            }
        }

        Console.WriteLine("\n---.NET typed accessor---");
        // Create the DataReader to retrieve data
        using (SqlDataReader dr = command.ExecuteReader( ))
        {
            while (dr.Read( ))
            {
                // Output fields using the column ordinals as accessors
                Console.WriteLine("{0}\t{1}, {2}",
                    dr.IsDBNull(coContactID) ?
                        "NULL" : dr.GetInt32(coContactID).ToString( ),
                    dr.IsDBNull(coLastName) ?
                        "NULL" : dr.GetString(coLastName),
                    dr.IsDBNull(coFirstName) ?
                        "NULL" : dr.GetString(coFirstName));
            }
        }
        Console.WriteLine("\n---Provider-specific typed accessor---");
        // Create the DataReader to retrieve data
        using (SqlDataReader dr = command.ExecuteReader( ))
        {
            while (dr.Read( ))
            {
                // Output fields using the column ordinals as accessors
                Console.WriteLine("{0}\t{1}, {2}",
                    dr.IsDBNull(coContactID) ?
                        "NULL" : dr.GetSqlInt32(coContactID).ToString( ),
                    dr.IsDBNull(coLastName) ?
                        "NULL" : dr.GetSqlString(coLastName),
                    dr.IsDBNull(coFirstName) ?
                        "NULL" : dr.GetSqlString(coFirstName));
            }
        }

        connection.Close( );

        Console.WriteLine("\nPress any key to continue.");
        Console.ReadKey( );
    }
  }
}
```

The output is shown in Figure 10-17.

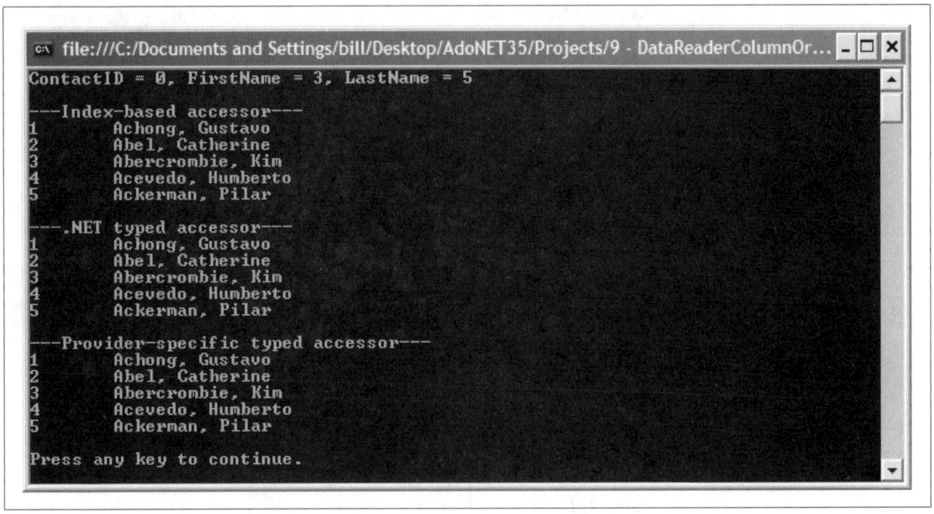

Figure 10-17. Output for DataReaderColumnOrdinals solution

Discussion

The GetOrdinal( ) method of the DataReader object gets the column ordinal for a specified column name. As discussed in Recipe 10.11, reading data from a DataReader is significantly faster using column ordinals instead of column names. The GetOrdinal( ) method can be used in the constructor to retrieve all column ordinals based on the column names. Column ordinals can then be used to read data from the DataReader to improve performance without having to code absolute column ordinal values.

The GetName( ) method of the DataReader takes a column ordinal and returns the column name.

10.13 Debugging a SQL Server Stored Procedure

Problem

Given an application that uses a SQL Server stored procedure that is causing errors, you need to debug the stored procedure.

Solution

Use Visual Studio .NET to debug SQL Server stored procedures (in both standalone mode and from managed code).

The solution provides a code sample to use during the discussion.

The C# code in *Program.cs* in the project DebugStoredProcedure is shown in Example 10-23.

Example 10-23. File: Program.cs for DebugStoredProcedure solution

```csharp
using System;
using System.Data;
using System.Data.SqlClient;

namespace DebugStoredProcedure
{
    class Program
    {
        static void Main(string[] args)
        {
            string sqlConnectString = "Data Source=(local);" +
                "Integrated security=SSPI;Initial Catalog=AdventureWorks;";

            string sqlSelect = "uspGetEmployeeManagers";

            // Create the connection
            SqlConnection connection = new SqlConnection(sqlConnectString);

            // Create the stored procedure command
            SqlCommand command = new SqlCommand(sqlSelect, connection);
            command.CommandType = CommandType.StoredProcedure;
            command.Parameters.Add("@EmployeeID", SqlDbType.Int).Value = 1;

            // Create the data reader
            connection.Open();
            SqlDataReader dr = command.ExecuteReader();

            // Output the result set
            Console.WriteLine("Level\tID\tEmp Name\tMgrID\tMgrName");
            while (dr.Read())
            {
                Console.WriteLine("{0}\t{1}\t{2}, {3}\t{4}\t{5}, {6}",
                    dr["RecursionLevel"], dr["EmployeeID"], dr["LastName"],
                    dr["FirstName"], dr["ManagerID"], dr["ManagerLastName"],
                    dr["ManagerFirstName"]);
            }

            Console.WriteLine("\nPress any key to continue.");
            Console.ReadKey();
        }
    }
}
```

The output is shown in Figure 10-18.

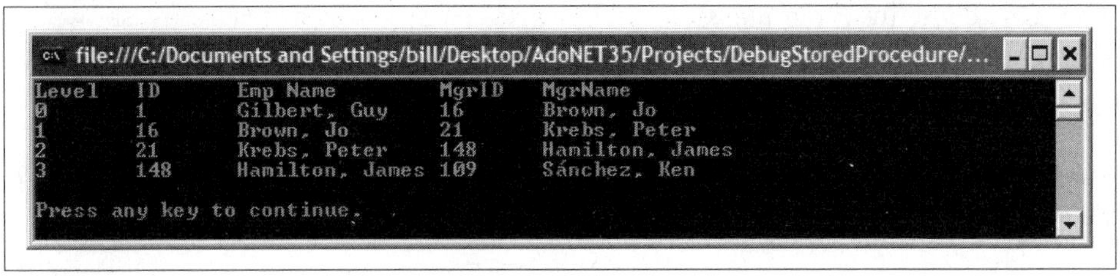

Figure 10-18. Output for DebugStoredProcedure solution

Discussion

You can debug a stored procedure in standalone mode and from managed code.

Debugging a stored procedure in standalone mode

You can debug a stored procedure in standalone mode from Visual Studio .NET Server Explorer by following these steps:

1. Open the Server Explorer window in Visual Studio .NET by selecting it from the View menu.

2. Create a connection to the database or select an existing connection.

3. Select and expand the node for the database that contains the stored procedure.

4. Expand the Stored Procedures node.

5. Right-click on the stored procedure to be debugged and select Step Into Stored Procedure from the pop-up menu.

6. If requested, supply the parameter values on the Run Stored Procedure dialog.

Alternatively, if the stored procedure is already open in a source window in Visual Studio .NET:

1. Right-click on the stored procedure to be debugged and select Step Into Stored Procedure from the pop-up menu.

2. If requested, supply the parameter values on the Run Stored Procedure dialog.

Debugging a stored procedure from managed code

Follow these steps to debug a stored procedure from managed code.

1. Open the project DebugStoredProcedure in Visual Studio.

2. You need to enable SQL Server debugging for the project. In the Solution Explorer window, select the project and right-click. Select Properties from the context menu to open the property sheet, as shown in Figure 10-19.

3. Select the Debug tab. Set Enable SQL Server debugging to true. Select File → Save Selected Items from the main menu to apply the changes. Close the property sheet.

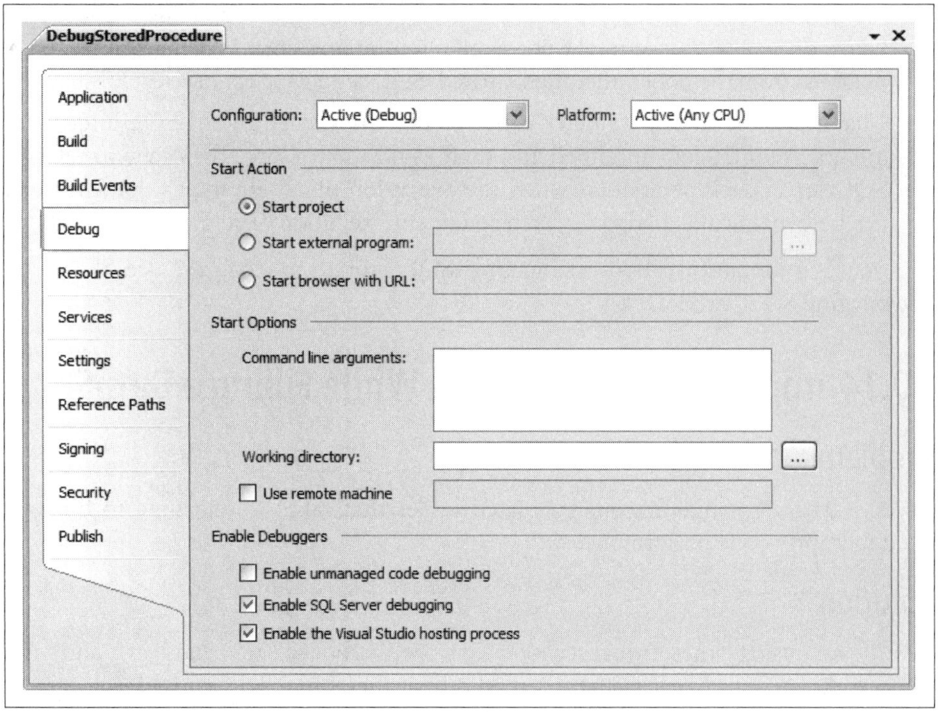

Figure 10-19. Debug properties

4. You also need to allow application debugging on the connection. Do this by right-clicking the connection in Server Explorer and checking Application Debugging on the context menu.

5. Open the stored procedure uspGetEmployeeManagers in the AdventureWorks database using Server Explorer. Set a breakpoint on the SET NO COUNT ON statement.

6. Select File → Debug from the main menu. Execution stops at the breakpoint added inside the stored procedure in the previous step.

There are some other significant limitations to SQL Server Debugging:

- It is not possible to debug SQL statements that are outside of a stored procedure.

- It is not possible to step into a stored procedure from managed or unmanaged code or into managed or unmanaged code from a stored procedure. Set a breakpoint at entry point in the stored procedure or in the re-entry point in the code as required. Alternatively, open the code or stored procedure and right-click on the line to break on. Select Run to Cursor from the shortcut menu to reach the desired line without setting a breakpoint.

- The database connection from your application must be established with the .NET data provider for SQL Server before debugging a mixed-language application. After that, you can open stored procedures and set breakpoints in the same way as for other applications.

- When connection pooling is enabled, debugging a stored procedure called from native or managed code might not work after the first time. When a connection is obtained from the pool rather than created, SQL debugging is not re-established.

- Changes to locals or parameter variables that are cached by the SQL interpreter are not automatically modified and there is no way to force the cache to refresh. SQL Server caches variables when the execution plan determines that they will not be dynamically loaded for each statement execution or reference.

For more information about debugging SQL stored procedures, see the topic "Debugging SQL" in MSDN.

10.14 Improving Performance While Filling a DataSet

Problem

Given a DataSet containing many related tables that takes a long time to fill, you need to improve the performance.

Solution

Investigate using the EnforceConstraints property of the DataSet and the BeginLoadData( ) and EndLoadData( ) methods of the contained DataTable objects to improve performance while filling a complex DataSet.

The solution measures the time it takes to fill a DataSet using a DataAdapter with all records in the Sales.SalesOrderHeader, Sales.SalesOrderDetail, and Sales.Customer tables, related in the DataSet. The fill times are measured for all four combinations of setting the EnforceConstraints property of the DataSet and using or not using the BeginLoadData( ) and EndLoadData( ) methods of the contained DataTable objects. Ten iterations are performed, and the total fill time for each combination is returned and displayed in ticks (one-millisecond intervals).

The C# code in *Program.cs* in the project ImprovePerformanceFillDataSet is shown in Example 10-24.

Example 10-24. File: Program.cs for ImprovePerformanceFillDataSet solution

```
using System;
using System.Data;
using System.Data.SqlClient;


namespace ImprovePerformanceFillDataSet
{
    class Program
    {
        private static DataSet ds = new DataSet();
        private static DataTable dtCustomer = new DataTable("Customer");
```

```csharp
private static DataTable dtHeader = new DataTable("Header");
private static DataTable dtDetail = new DataTable("Detail");
private static SqlDataAdapter daCustomer;
private static SqlDataAdapter daHeader;
private static SqlDataAdapter daDetail;

static void Main(string[] args)
{
    string sqlConnectString = "Data Source=(local);" +
        "Integrated security=SSPI;Initial Catalog=AdventureWorks;";

    string sqlSelectHeader = "SELECT * FROM Sales.SalesOrderHeader;";
    string sqlSelectDetail = "SELECT * FROM Sales.SalesOrderDetail;";
    string sqlSelectCustomer = "SELECT * FROM Sales.Customer";

    // define data adapters for the custoemr, header, and detail tables
    daCustomer = new SqlDataAdapter(sqlSelectCustomer, sqlConnectString);
    daHeader = new SqlDataAdapter(sqlSelectHeader, sqlConnectString);
    daDetail = new SqlDataAdapter(sqlSelectDetail, sqlConnectString);

    // create the header table schema and add to DataSet
    dtHeader = new DataTable("SalesOrderHeader");
    daHeader.FillSchema(dtHeader, SchemaType.Source);
    ds.Tables.Add(dtHeader);
    // create the detail table schema and add to DataSet
    dtDetail = new DataTable("SalesOrderDetail");
    daDetail.FillSchema(dtDetail, SchemaType.Source);
    ds.Tables.Add(dtDetail);
    // create the product table schema and add to DataSet
    dtCustomer = new DataTable("Customer");
    daCustomer.FillSchema(dtCustomer, SchemaType.Source);
    ds.Tables.Add(dtCustomer);

    // create data relations
    ds.Relations.Add("SalesOrderHeader_SalesOrderDetail",
        dtHeader.Columns["SalesOrderID"], dtDetail.Columns["SalesOrderID"],
        true);
    ds.Relations.Add("Customer_SalesOrderHeader",
        dtCustomer.Columns["CustomerID"], dtHeader.Columns["CustomerID"],
        true);

    int n = 10;
    Console.WriteLine("---{0} ITERATIONS. (ITERATION 0 DISCARDED)---", n);

    int ticks1 = 0;
    int ticks2 = 0;
    int ticks3 = 0;
    int ticks4 = 0;
    for (int i = 0; i <= n; i++)
    {
        Console.WriteLine("Iteration {0}.", i);
```

```
            ticks1 += FillDataSet(true, false);
            ticks2 += FillDataSet(false, false);
            ticks3 += FillDataSet(true, true);
            ticks4 += FillDataSet(false, true);

            // discard the first iteration
            if (i == 0)
                ticks1 = ticks2 = ticks3 = ticks4 = 0;
        }

        // output the results
        Console.WriteLine("\n---RESULTS---");
        Console.WriteLine("EnforceConstraints = true,  " +
            "Begin/EndLoadInit = false. Ticks = {0}", ticks1);
        Console.WriteLine("EnforceConstraints = false, " +
            "Begin/EndLoadInit = false. Ticks = {0}", ticks2);
        Console.WriteLine("EnforceConstraints = true,  " +
            "Begin/EndLoadInit = true.  Ticks = {0}", ticks3);
        Console.WriteLine("EnforceConstraints = false, " +
            "Begin/EndLoadInit = true.  Ticks = {0}", ticks4);

        Console.WriteLine("\nPress any key to continue.");
        Console.ReadKey();
    }

    private static int FillDataSet(bool enforceConstraints, bool loadData)
    {
        ds.Clear();

        // start the timer
        int startTick = Environment.TickCount;

        // set EnforceConstraints property
        ds.EnforceConstraints = enforceConstraints;

        if (loadData)
        {
            dtCustomer.BeginLoadData();
            dtHeader.BeginLoadData();
            dtDetail.BeginLoadData();
        }

        daCustomer.Fill(dtCustomer);
        daHeader.Fill(dtHeader);
        daDetail.Fill(dtDetail);

        if (loadData)
        {
            dtCustomer.EndLoadData();
            dtHeader.EndLoadData();
            dtDetail.EndLoadData();
        }
```

Example 10-24. File: Program.cs for ImprovePerformanceFillDataSet solution (continued)

```
        ds.EnforceConstraints = true;

        return Environment.TickCount - startTick;
    }
  }
}
```

The output is shown in Figure 10-20. Note that this code takes a few minutes to execute.

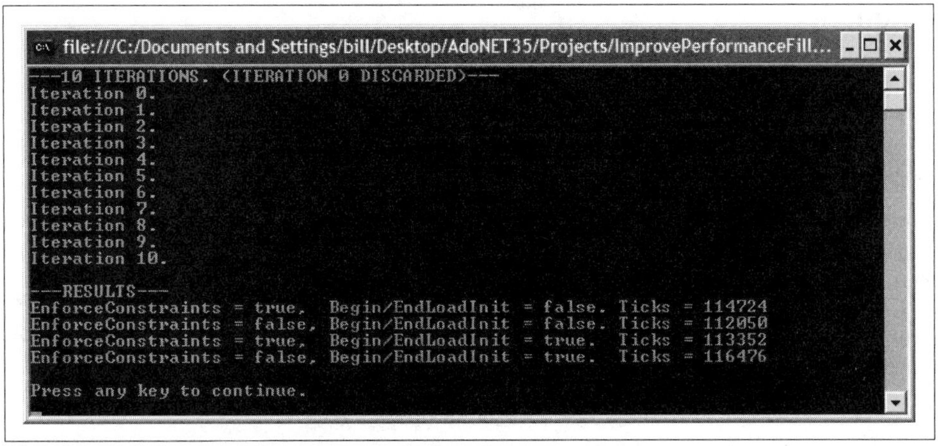

Figure 10-20. Output for ImprovePerformanceFillDataSet solution

Discussion

The EnforceConstraints property of the DataSet indicates whether constraint rules—unique and foreign key constraints—are verified when updating data in the DataSet.

Setting EnforceConstraints to false prior to loading data into a DataSet prevents the constraints on the DataSet from being validated when each row is added. Instead, when EnforceConstraints is set to true an attempt is made to enable the constraints. A ConstraintException is raised if the DataSet contains constraint violations.

The BeginLoadData( ) and EndLoadData( ) methods of the DataTable turn off notifications, index maintenance, and constraints while loading data using the LoadDataRow( ) method. These two methods must be called as each DataTable in the DataSet is loaded with data.

The output shows that the combinations of EnforceConstraints and Begin/EndLoadInit have little impact on the time it takes to load the DataSet using ADO.NET 3.5. This is a bit surprising because there was a significant performance difference running the same test using ADO.NET 1.0. The reason is that filling a DataSet is slowed by the time that the DataSet spends maintaining indexes and validating integrity constraints, allowing performance improvements to be realized by turning off this functionality while filling a DataSet and turning it back on once the DataSet is filled.

This solution gives you an easy approach to test the performance in your particular situation and determine whether a particular strategy is worth adopting.

10.15 Reading and Writing Large-Value Data with SQL Server

Problem

You need to read and write large-value data type values from and to a SQL Server database.

Solution

The solution shows how to store, retrieve, and output nvarchar(max), varbinary(max), and varchar(max) lengths and values from both a DataTable and a DataReader.

The solution uses the table ReadWriteLargeData in the database AdoDotNet35Cookbook. Execute the following T-SQL to create this table:

```
USE AdoDotNet35Cookbook
GO

CREATE TABLE ReadWriteLargeData(
    Id int NOT NULL PRIMARY KEY,
    NVarCharMaxField nvarchar(max) NULL,
    VarBinaryMaxField varbinary(max) NULL,
    VarCharMaxField varchar(max) NULL )
```

The C# code in *Program.cs* in the project ReadWriteLargeData is shown in Example 10-25.

Example 10-25. File: Program.cs for ReadWriteLargeData solution

```
using System;
using System.Data;
using System.Data.SqlClient;
using System.Text;
using System.Data.SqlTypes;

namespace ReadWriteLargeData
{
    class Program
    {
        static void Main(string[] args)
        {
            string sqlConnectString = "Data Source=(local);" +
```

Example 10-25. File: Program.cs for ReadWriteLargeData solution (continued)

```
        "Integrated security=SSPI;Initial Catalog=AdoDotNet35Cookbook;";

    string sqlSelect = "SELECT Id, NVarCharMaxField, VarBinaryMaxField, " +
        "VarCharMaxField FROM ReadWriteLargeData";

    // fill data with schema and data
    SqlDataAdapter da = new SqlDataAdapter(sqlSelect, sqlConnectString);
    SqlCommandBuilder cb = new SqlCommandBuilder(da);
    DataTable dt = new DataTable( );
    da.FillSchema(dt, SchemaType.Source);
    da.Fill(dt);

    // output schema info
    Console.WriteLine("---DataTable schema---");
    foreach (DataColumn col in dt.Columns)
        Console.WriteLine("ColumnName = {0}, DataType = {1}",
            col.ColumnName, col.DataType);

    // create some large test data
    StringBuilder sb1 = new StringBuilder( );
    for (int i = 0; i < 1000000; i++)
        sb1.Append("a");
    byte[] ba = new byte[1000000];
    for (int i = 0; i < 1000000; i++)
        ba[i] = 98;   // ASCII 'b'
    StringBuilder sb2 = new StringBuilder( );
    for (int i = 0; i < 1000000; i++)
        sb2.Append("c");

    // add a row to the table
    DataRow row = dt.NewRow( );
    row["Id"] = 1;
    row["NVarCharMaxField"] = sb1.ToString( );
    row["VarBinaryMaxField"] = ba;
    row["VarCharMaxField"] = sb2.ToString( );
    dt.Rows.Add(row);
    // update the data source
    da.Update(dt);
    Console.WriteLine("\n=> Added row using DataAdapter.Update( ).");

    // clear and reload the DataTable
    dt.Clear( );
    da.Fill(dt);
    Console.WriteLine("\n=> DataTable created.");

    // Create a row from the first row for easier reference
    DataRow row2 = dt.Rows[0];

    Console.WriteLine("\n---DataTable row---");

    Console.WriteLine("Id                        = {0}", row2["Id"]);
```

```
Console.WriteLine("NVarCharMaxField Length  = {0}",
    row2.Field<string>("NVarCharMaxField").Length);
Console.WriteLine("  Left 40 characters      = {0}",
    row2.Field<string>("NVarCharMaxField").Substring(0, 40));

Console.WriteLine("VarBinaryMaxField Length = {0}",
    row2.Field<byte[]>("VarBinaryMaxField").Length);
ASCIIEncoding ae0 = new ASCIIEncoding( );
string s0 = new string(
    ae0.GetChars(row2.Field<byte[]>("VarBinaryMaxField"), 0, 40));
Console.WriteLine("  Left 40 characters      = {0}", s0);

Console.WriteLine("VarCharMaxField Length    = {0}",
    row2.Field<string>("VarCharMaxField").Length);
Console.WriteLine("  Left 40 characters      = {0}",
    row2.Field<string>("VarCharMaxField").Substring(0, 40));

// create a DataReader
ASCIIEncoding ae = new ASCIIEncoding( );
using (SqlConnection connection =
    new SqlConnection(sqlConnectString))
{
    SqlCommand command = new SqlCommand(sqlSelect, connection);
    connection.Open( );
    SqlDataReader dr = command.ExecuteReader( );
    Console.WriteLine("\n=> DataReader created.");
    while (dr.Read( ))
    {
        // using SQL Server data type accessors
        SqlInt32 id1 = dr.GetSqlInt32(0);
        SqlString nvarCharMaxField1 = dr.GetSqlString(1);
        SqlBytes varBinaryMaxField1 = dr.GetSqlBytes(2);
        SqlChars varCharMaxField1 = dr.GetSqlChars(3);

        Console.WriteLine(
            "\n---DataReader row: SQL Server data type accessors---");

        Console.WriteLine("Id                       = {0}", id1);

        Console.WriteLine("NVarCharMaxField Length  = {0}",
            nvarCharMaxField1.ToString( ).Length);
        Console.WriteLine("  Left 40 characters      = {0}",
            nvarCharMaxField1.ToString( ).Substring(0, 40));

        Console.WriteLine("VarBinaryMaxField Length = {0}",
            varBinaryMaxField1.Length);
        byte[] b1 = new byte[40];
        varBinaryMaxField1.Read(0, b1, 0, 40);
```

```
                    // convert to characters to make readable
                    string s1 = new string(ae.GetChars(b1));
                    Console.WriteLine("  Left 40 characters      = {0}", s1);

                    Console.WriteLine("VarCharMaxField Length    = {0}",
                        varCharMaxField1.Length);
                    string s3 = new string(varCharMaxField1.Value, 0, 40);
                    Console.WriteLine("  Left 40 characters      = {0}", s3);

                    // using .NET data type accessors
                    int id2 = dr.GetInt32(0);
                    string nvarCharMaxField2 = dr.GetString(1);
                    byte[] varBinaryMaxField2 = new byte[40];
                    dr.GetBytes(2, 0, varBinaryMaxField2, 0, 40);
                    string varCharMaxField2 = dr.GetString(3);

                    Console.WriteLine(
                        "\n---DataReader row: .NET data type accessors---");

                    Console.WriteLine("Id                        = {0}", id2);

                    Console.WriteLine("NVarCharMaxField Length  = {0}",
                        nvarCharMaxField2.Length);
                    Console.WriteLine("  Left 40 characters      = {0}",
                        nvarCharMaxField2.Substring(0, 40));

                    byte[] b3 = new byte[dr.GetBytes(2, 0, null, 0, int.MaxValue)];
                    Console.WriteLine("VarBinaryMaxField Length = {0}",
                        b3.Length);
                    // convert to characters to make readable
                    string s2 = new string(ae.GetChars(varBinaryMaxField2));
                    Console.WriteLine("  Left 40 characters      = {0}", s2);

                    Console.WriteLine("VarCharMaxField Length    = {0}",
                        varCharMaxField2.Length);
                    Console.WriteLine("  Left 40 characters      = {0}",
                        varCharMaxField2.Substring(0, 40));

                }
            }

        Console.WriteLine("\nPress any key to continue.");
        Console.ReadKey();
        }
    }
}
```

The output is shown in Figure 10-21.

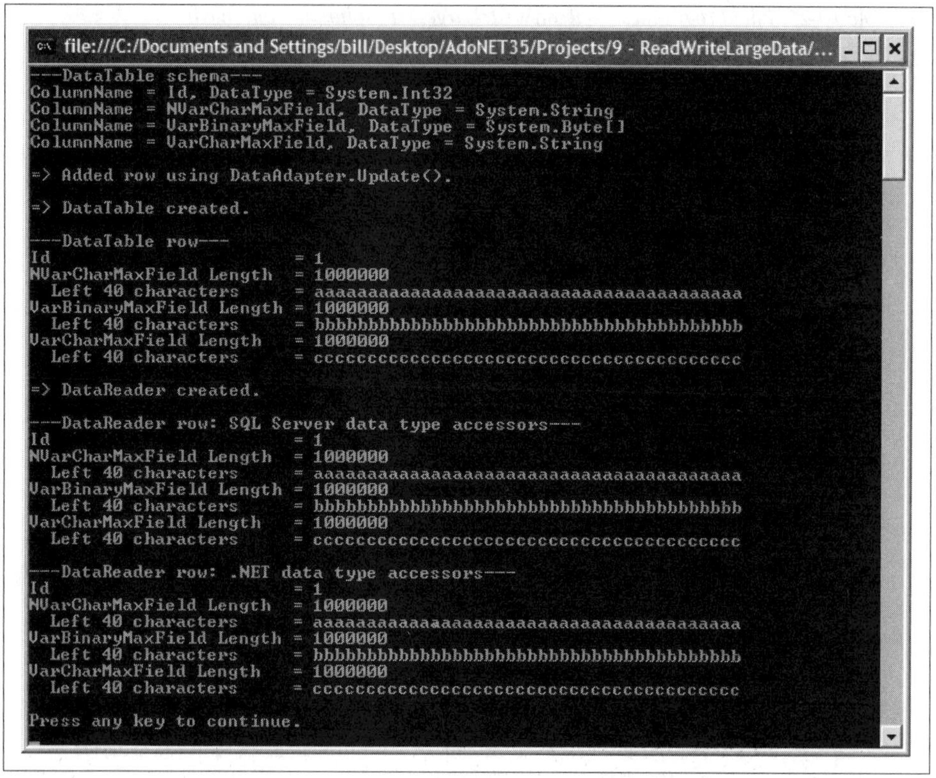

Figure 10-21. Output for ReadWriteLargeData solution

Discussion

SQL Server 2005 introduces the max specifier that extends the storage of the varchar, nvarchar, and varbinary data types. These new types—varchar(max), nvarchar(max), and varbinary(max)—are known collectively as *large-value data types*. These data types store up to $2^{31} - 1$ bytes of data. Large-value types behave similarly to their smaller versions—varchar, nvarchar, and varbinary—and let you work with large-character, Unicode, and binary data more efficiently and in ways not possible with the text, ntext, and image data types from earlier versions of SQL Server.

The SqlDataAdapter converts varbinary(max) data type values to byte arrays and converts nvarchar(max) and varchar(max) values to strings, making it easy to write and read these data types to and from a DataTable or DataSet. You need to be careful of the size of the values, however, so that you don't inadvertently retrieve a table with 10,000 10 MB BLOB values.

The SqlDataReader has a SQL typed accessor GetSqlBytes( ) that gets the value of a varbinary(max) data type as a SqlBytes object. The SQL typed accessors GetSqlString( ) and GetSqlChars( ) can be used to retrieve either an nvarchar(max) data value or a varchar(max) data value to a SqlString or SqlChars object.

Alternatively, the GetBytes( ) method of the SqlDataReader is a .NET typed accessor that can be used to retrieve a varbinary(max) data value to a byte array. The GetString( ) method of the SqlDataReader is a .NET typed accessor that can be used to retrieve an nvarchar(max) data value or a varchar(max) data value to a string.

 The ntext, text, and image classes are available in SQL Server 2005 and 2008 for backward compatibility—they will be removed in a future version. Instead, use nvarchar(max), varchar(max), and varbinary(max), respectively.

10.16 Reading and Writing a SQL Server User-Defined Type (UDT)

Problem

You need to retrieve the value of a user-defined type that you have created using a CLR routine from a SQL Server database.

Solution

The following example creates, registers, and uses a user-defined type that defines a point—the UDT is called Point. Follow these steps:

1. Enable CLR integration by following the instructions in the Introduction to Chapter 12, if necessary.

2. Create a new SQL Server project in Visual Studio and name it ClrPointType. Press the Cancel button to dismiss the New Database Reference dialog that is displayed.

3. Create a user-defined type item in the project. Name the item *Point.cs*.

The C# code in *Point.cs* in the project ClrPointType is shown in Example 10-26.

Example 10-26. File: Point.cs for ClrPointType solution

```
using System;
using System.Data.SqlTypes;
using Microsoft.SqlServer.Server;

[Serializable]
[Microsoft.SqlServer.Server.SqlUserDefinedType(Format.Native)]
public struct Point : INullable
{
    private bool isNull;
    private double x;
    private double y;

    public override string ToString()
```

Example 10-26. File: Point.cs for ClrPointType solution (continued)

```
{
    if (this.isNull)
        return "null";
    else
        return string.Format("(x, y) = ({0}, {1})", x, y);
}

public bool IsNull
{
    get
    {
        return isNull;
    }
}

public static Point Null
{
    get
    {
        Point p = new Point( );
        p.isNull = true;
        return p;
    }
}

public Point(double x, double y)
{
    this.x = x;
    this.y = y;
    isNull = false;
}

public static Point Parse(SqlString s)
{
    if (s.IsNull || s.Value.ToLower( ).Equals("null"))
        return Null;
    string[] sa = s.ToString( ).Split(',');
    if (sa.Length != 2)
        return Null;

    Point p = new Point( );
    try
    {
        p.x = double.Parse(sa[0]);
        p.y = double.Parse(sa[1]);
        return p;
    }
    catch (Exception)
    {
        return Null;
    }
}
```

Example 10-26. File: Point.cs for ClrPointType solution (continued)

```
    public double X
    {
        get { return x; }
        set { x = X; }
    }

    public double Y
    {
        get { return y; }
        set { y = Y; }
    }
}
```

1. Build the solution.

2. Register the assembly and create the aggregate function by executing the following T-SQL statement in SQL Server Management Studio, replacing <path> appropriately:

```
USE AdoDotNet35Cookbook
GO

CREATE ASSEMBLY ClrPointType
FROM '<path>\ClrPointType\bin\Debug\ClrPointType.dll'

GO

CREATE TYPE Point
EXTERNAL NAME ClrPointType
```

3. Next, create a table named PointTable that has a field of the UDT Point using the following T-SQL statement:

```
USE AdoDotNet35Cookbook
GO

CREATE TABLE PointTable(
    Id int NOT NULL PRIMARY KEY,
    PointField Point NOT NULL )
```

For more information about creating UDTs using CLR routines, see Recipe 12.5.

4. Finally, create a C# Windows console project named ReadWriteUdt that will use the Point UDT to read and write into the PointTable in the AdoDotNet35Cookbook table. The solution needs a reference to the ClrPointType assembly created in steps 1 through 4 of this solution—select the Browse tab when adding a reference, then locate and select *ClrPointType.dll*.

The C# code in *Program.cs* in the project ReadWriteUdt is shown in Example 10-27.

Example 10-27. File: Program.cs for ReadWriteUdt solution

```csharp
using System;
using System.Data;
using System.Data.SqlClient;

namespace ReadWriteUdt
{
    class Program
    {
        static void Main(string[] args)
        {
            string sqlConnectString = "Data Source=(local);" +
                "Integrated security=SSPI;Initial Catalog=AdoDotNet35Cookbook;";

            string sqlSelect = "SELECT * FROM PointTable";

            // Create and fill a DataTable
            SqlDataAdapter da = new SqlDataAdapter(sqlSelect, sqlConnectString);
            SqlCommandBuilder cb = new SqlCommandBuilder(da);
            DataTable dt = new DataTable();
            da.Fill(dt);

            // Add two rows
            DataRow row = dt.NewRow();
            row["Id"] = 1;
            row["PointField"] = new Point(1, 2);
            dt.Rows.Add(row);
            row = dt.NewRow();
            row["Id"] = 2;
            row["PointField"] = new Point(6, 9);
            dt.Rows.Add(row);
            da.Update(dt);
            Console.WriteLine("=> Rows added.");

            // Clear and reload DataTable
            dt.Clear();
            da.Fill(dt);

            // Output DataTable contents to console
            Console.WriteLine("\n---DATATABLE---");
            foreach (DataRow r in dt.Rows)
            {
                Point p1 = (Point)r["PointField"];
                Console.WriteLine("Id = {0}\tPoint.X = {1}\tPoint.Y = {2}",
                    r["Id"], p1.X, p1.Y);
            }
```

Example 10-27. File: Program.cs for ReadWriteUdt solution (continued)

```
        // Use a DataReader to read the data
        SqlConnection connection = new SqlConnection(sqlConnectString);
        SqlCommand command = new SqlCommand(sqlSelect, connection);
        connection.Open( );
        SqlDataReader dr = command.ExecuteReader( );

        // Output the DataReader result set
        Console.WriteLine("\n---DATAREADER---");
        while (dr.Read( ))
        {
            Point p2 = (Point)dr["PointField"];
            Console.WriteLine("Id = {0}\tPoint.X = {1}\tPoint.Y = {2}",
                dr["Id"], p2.X, p2.Y);
        }

        Console.WriteLine("\nPress any key to continue.");
        Console.ReadKey( );
    }
  }
}
```

The output is shown in Figure 10-22.

Figure 10-22. Output for ReadWriteUdt solution

Discussion

Once the assembly defining the UDT is added to the project, retrieving and using the UDT requires only that you cast the field retrieved from the DataTable or DataReader to the UDT.

To use a UDT as a parameter for a SqlParameter object for a SqlCommand object, specify the DbType as Udt from the SqlDbType enumeration. The UdtTypeName property of the SqlParameter class represents the fully qualified name of the UDT using the syntax database.schema_name.object_name.

10.17 Reading and Writing Oracle Large Data

Problem

You need to read and write large data type values from and to an Oracle database.

Solution

The solution shows how to store, retrieve, and output Oracle BLOB, CLOB, and NCLOB lengths and values from both a DataTable and a DataReader.

The solution uses a single table ReadWriteLargeData in the AdoDotNet35Cookbook schema. Execute the following SQL statement to create the table:

```
CREATE TABLE "ADODOTNET35COOKBOOK"."READWRITELARGEDATA" (
    "ID" INTEGER NOT NULL,
    "BLOBFIELD" BLOB,
    "CLOBFIELD" CLOB,
    "NCLOBFIELD" NCLOB,
    PRIMARY KEY ("ID") VALIDATE )
```

You need to add a reference to the System.Data.OracleClient assembly to the solution.

The C# code in *Program.cs* in the project ReadWriteLargeOracleData is shown in Example 10-28.

Example 10-28. File: Program.cs for ReadWriteLargeOracleData solution

```csharp
using System;
using System.Data;
using System.Data.OracleClient;
using System.Text;
using System.IO;

namespace ReadWriteLargeOracleData
{
    class Program
    {
        static void Main(string[] args)
        {
            string oracleConnectString = "Data Source=ORCL;" +
                "User Id=AdoDotNet35Cookbook;Password=password;";

            string sqlSelect = "SELECT ID, BLOBFIELD, CLOBFIELD, NCLOBFIELD " +
                "FROM ADODOTNET35COOKBOOK.READWRITELARGEDATA";

            // create DataTable and fill with schema and data
            OracleDataAdapter da =
                new OracleDataAdapter(sqlSelect, oracleConnectString);
            OracleCommandBuilder cb = new OracleCommandBuilder(da);
            DataTable dt = new DataTable();
            da.FillSchema(dt, SchemaType.Source);
            da.Fill(dt);
```

Example 10-28. File: Program.cs for ReadWriteLargeOracleData solution (continued)

```csharp
// output schema info
Console.WriteLine("---DataTable schema---");
foreach (DataColumn col in dt.Columns)
    Console.WriteLine("ColumnName = {0}, DataType = {1}",
        col.ColumnName, col.DataType);

// create some test large data
byte[] ba = new byte[1000000];
for (int i = 0; i < 1000000; i++)
    ba[i] = 97;  // ASCII 'a'
StringBuilder sb1 = new StringBuilder( );
for (int i = 0; i < 1000000; i++)
    sb1.Append("b");
StringBuilder sb2 = new StringBuilder( );
for (int i = 0; i < 1000000; i++)
    sb2.Append("c");

// add a row to the table
DataRow row = dt.NewRow( );
row["ID"] = 1;
row["BLOBFIELD"] = ba;
row["CLOBFIELD"] = sb1.ToString( );
row["NCLOBFIELD"] = sb2.ToString( );
dt.Rows.Add(row);

//// update the data source
//da.Update(dt);
Console.WriteLine("\n=> Added row using DataAdapter.Update( ).");

// clear and reload the DataTable
dt.Clear( );
da.Fill(dt);
Console.WriteLine("\n=> DataTable created.");

// Create a row from the first row for easier reference
DataRow row2 = dt.Rows[0];

Console.WriteLine("\n---DataTable row---");

Console.WriteLine("ID                          = {0}", row2["ID"]);

Console.WriteLine("BLOBFIELD Length  = {0}",
    row2.Field<byte[]>("BLOBFIELD").Length);
ASCIIEncoding ae0 = new ASCIIEncoding( );
string s0 = new string(
    ae0.GetChars(row2.Field<byte[]>("BLOBFIELD"), 0, 40));
Console.WriteLine("  Left 40 characters       = {0}", s0);

Console.WriteLine("CLOBFIELD Length  = {0}",
    row2.Field<string>("CLOBFIELD").Length);
Console.WriteLine("  Left 40 characters       = {0}",
    row2.Field<string>("CLOBFIELD").Substring(0, 40));
```

```
                Console.WriteLine("NCLOBFIELD Length = {0}",
                    row2.Field<string>("NCLOBFIELD").Length);
                Console.WriteLine("  Left 40 characters      = {0}",
                    row2.Field<string>("NCLOBFIELD").Substring(0, 40));

                // create a DataReader
                ASCIIEncoding ae = new ASCIIEncoding( );
                using (OracleConnection connection =
                    new OracleConnection(oracleConnectString))
                {
                    OracleCommand command = new OracleCommand(sqlSelect, connection);
                    connection.Open( );
                    OracleDataReader dr = command.ExecuteReader( );
                    Console.WriteLine("\n=> DataReader created.");
                    while (dr.Read( ))
                    {
                        //// using Oracle data type accessors
                        OracleNumber id1 = dr.GetOracleNumber(0);
                        OracleLob blobField1 = dr.GetOracleLob(1);
                        OracleLob clobField1 = dr.GetOracleLob(2);
                        OracleLob nclobField1 = dr.GetOracleLob(3);

                        Console.WriteLine(
                            "\n---DataReader row: Oracle data type accessors---");

                        Console.WriteLine("Id                       = {0}", id1);

                        Console.WriteLine("BLOBFIELD Length  = {0}",
                            blobField1.Length);
                        byte[] b1 = new byte[40];
                        blobField1.Read(b1, 0, 40);
                        // convert to characters to make readable
                        string s1 = new string(ae.GetChars(b1));
                        Console.WriteLine("  Left 40 characters      = {0}", s1);

                        Console.WriteLine("CLOBFIELD Length  = {0}",
                            clobField1.Length);
                        Console.WriteLine("  Left 40 characters      = {0}",
                            clobField1.Value.ToString( ).Substring(0, 40));

                        Console.WriteLine("NCLOBFIELD Length = {0}",
                            nclobField1.Length);
                        StreamReader sr = new StreamReader(nclobField1, Encoding.Unicode);
                        char[] c1 = new char[40];
                        sr.Read(c1, 0, 40);
                        string s3 = new string(c1);
                        Console.WriteLine("  Left 40 characters      = {0}", s3);

                        // using .NET data type accessors
                        int id2 = dr.GetInt32(0);
                        byte[] blobField2 = new byte[40];
                        dr.GetBytes(1, 0, blobField2, 0, 40);
```

```
                    string clobField2 = dr.GetString(2);
                    string nclobField2 = dr.GetString(3);

                    Console.WriteLine(
                        "\n---DataReader row: .NET data type accessors---");

                    Console.WriteLine("ID                        = {0}", id2);

                    byte[] b3 = new byte[dr.GetBytes(1, 0, null, 0, int.MaxValue)];
                    Console.WriteLine("BLOBFIELD Length   = {0}",
                        b3.Length);
                    // convert to characters to make readable
                    string s2 = new string(ae.GetChars(blobField2));
                    Console.WriteLine("  Left 40 characters    = {0}", s2);

                    Console.WriteLine("CLOBFIELD Length   = {0}",
                        clobField2.Length);
                    Console.WriteLine("  Left 40 characters     = {0}",
                        clobField2.Substring(0, 40));

                    Console.WriteLine("NCLOBFIELD Length = {0}",
                        nclobField2.Length);
                    Console.WriteLine("  Left 40 characters     = {0}",
                        nclobField2.Substring(0, 40));
                }
            }
            Console.WriteLine("\nPress any key to continue.");
            Console.ReadKey();
        }
    }
}
```

The output is shown in Figure 10-23.

Discussion

The OracleDataAdapter converts BLOB values to byte arrays and converts CLOB and NCLOB values to strings, making it easy to write and read these data types to and from a DataTable or DataSet. You need to be careful of the size of the values however so that you don't inadvertently retrieve a table with 10,000 10 MB BLOB values.

The OracleDataReader has the Oracle typed accessor GetOracleLob( ) method that gets the value of the specified column as an OracleLob object that represents an Large Object Binary (LOB) data type stored in an Oracle database. Alternatively, the GetBytes( ) method of the OracleDataReader is a .NET typed accessor that can be used to retrieve a BLOB to a byte array. The GetString( ) method of the OracleDataReader is a .NET typed accessor that can be used to retrieve a CLOB or an NCLOB into a string.

The three Oracle LOB types are described in Table 10-5.

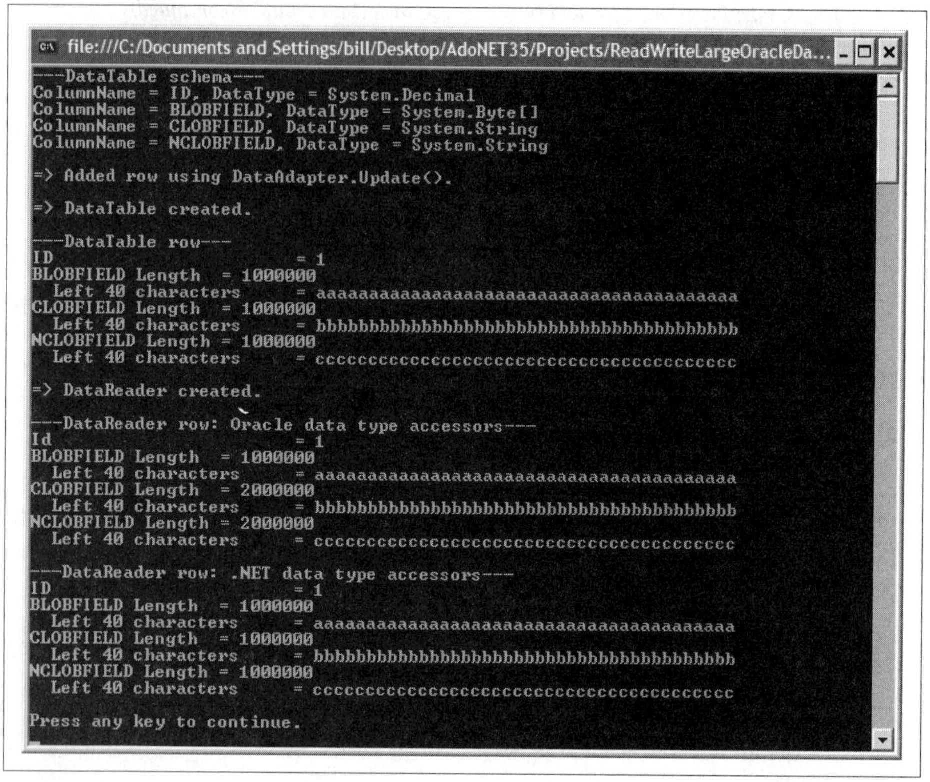

Figure 10-23. Output for ReadWriteLargeOracleData solution

Table 10-5. Oracle LOB data types

Data Type	Description
Blob	Oracle data type containing binary data with a maximum size of 4 GB. This data type maps to a `Byte` array.
Clob	Oracle data type containing character data based on the default character set of the server with a maximum size of 4 GB. This data type maps to a `String`.
NClob	Oracle data type containing character data based on the national character set of the server with a maximum size of 4 GB. This data type maps to a `String`.

The Oracle .NET data provider handles `CLOB` and `NCLOB` data as Unicode. Each character is therefore two bytes long.

10.18 Performing Batch Updates with a DataAdapter

Problem

When you use a `DataAdapter` to perform updates, it makes a separate round trip to the server for each row. You want to batch all of the updates into a single call to the server to improve performance.

Solution

In ADO.NET 1.0, a DataAdapter could only submit one pending change to a database at a time. ADO.NET 2.0 added support for sending batch updates using either a SqlDataAdapter or an OracleDataAdapter; as of ADO.NET 3.5, batch updates are not supported using the OleDbDataAdapter and the OdbcDataAdapter. Two solutions are demonstrated: one that uses the batch update capabilities of the DataAdapter introduced in ADO.NET 2.0 and another that is a custom approach. The custom approach can be used with ADO.NET 1.0 and with .NET data providers that do not support DataAdapter batch updates such as the OLE DB and ODBC data providers.

The first solution uses the batch update capabilities introduced in ADO.NET 2.0 to the DataAdapter class in both the SQL Server and Oracle data providers.

The solution uses a table named BatchUpdateAuto in the database AdoDotNet35Cookbook. The following T-SQL statement creates the table:

```
USE AdoDotNet35Cookbook
GO
CREATE TABLE BatchUpdateAuto(
    Id int NOT NULL PRIMARY KEY,
    Field1 nvarchar(50) NULL,
    Field2 nvarchar(50) NULL )
```

Add three records to the BatchUpdateAuto table by executing the following T-SQL batch:

```
USE AdoDotNet35Cookbook
GO

INSERT INTO BatchUpdateAuto VALUES (1, 'Field1.1', 'Field2.1');
INSERT INTO BatchUpdateAuto VALUES (2, 'Field1.2', 'Field2.2');
INSERT INTO BatchUpdateAuto VALUES (3, 'Field1.3', 'Field2.3');
```

The solution creates a DataAdapter and adds a CommandBuilder to it and handlers for the RowUpdating and RowUpdated DataAdapter events. Next, the three records from the BatchUpdateAuto table in the AdoDotNet35Cookbook database are retrieved into a DataTable using the DataAdapter and output to the console. Three modifications are made to the data in the DataTable: a record is modified, a record is deleted, and a record is inserted. The BatchUpdateSize property of the DataAdapter is set to 2 so that the three updates occur in two batches—a batch with two records and a batch with one. The Update( ) method of the DataAdapter is called and the progress is tracked by outputting information to the console in both the RowUpdating and RowUpdated event handlers. The DataTable after modifications is output to the console.

The C# code in *Program.cs* in the project BatchUpdateAuto is shown in Example 10-29.

Example 10-29. File: Program.cs for BatchUpdateAuto solution

```csharp
using System;
using System.Data;
using System.Data.SqlClient;

namespace BatchUpdateAuto
{
    class Program
    {
        private static DataTable dt;

        static void Main(string[] args)
        {
            string sqlConnectString = "Data Source=(local);" +
                "Integrated security=SSPI;Initial Catalog=AdoDotNet35Cookbook;";

            string sqlSelect =
                "SELECT Id, Field1, Field2 FROM BatchUpdateAuto";

            // Create the data adapter and command builder for update logic.
            SqlDataAdapter da = new SqlDataAdapter(sqlSelect, sqlConnectString);
            SqlCommandBuilder cb = new SqlCommandBuilder(da);

            da.RowUpdating += new SqlRowUpdatingEventHandler(da_RowUpdating);
            da.RowUpdated += new SqlRowUpdatedEventHandler(da_RowUpdated);
            // Create a DataTable and fill with schema and data
            dt = new DataTable();
            da.FillSchema(dt, SchemaType.Source);
            da.Fill(dt);

            // Output DataTable to console
            OutputTable();

            // Modify the data in the DataTable
            // --Update
            DataRow row = dt.Rows.Find(2);
            row["Field2"] += " (new)";
            // --Delete
            dt.Rows.Find(3).Delete();
            // --Insert
            dt.Rows.Add(new object[] { 4, "Field1.4", "Field2.4" });

            // Update the data source
            da.UpdateBatchSize = 2;
            da.Update(dt);

            // Output DataTable to console
            OutputTable();

            Console.WriteLine("Press any key to continue.");
            Console.ReadKey();
        }
```

Example 10-29. File: Program.cs for BatchUpdateAuto solution (continued)

```csharp
        static void da_RowUpdating(object sender, SqlRowUpdatingEventArgs e)
        {
            Console.WriteLine("\nDataAdapter.RowUpdating:\n{0}",
                e.Command.CommandText);
        }

        static void da_RowUpdated(object sender, SqlRowUpdatedEventArgs e)
        {
            Console.WriteLine("\nDataAdapter.RowUpdated: RecordsAffected = {0}",
                e.RecordsAffected);
        }

        private static void OutputTable()
        {
            Console.WriteLine("\n=> Output DataTable contents.");
            Console.WriteLine("\nID\tField1\t\tField2");
            Console.WriteLine("--\t------\t\t------");
            foreach (DataRow row in dt.Rows)
            {
                if (row.RowState != DataRowState.Deleted)
                {
                    Console.WriteLine("{0}\t{1}\t{2}", row["ID"],
                        row["Field1"], row["Field2"]);
                }
            }
            Console.WriteLine();
        }
    }
}
```

The output is shown in Figure 10-24.

As you can see from the output, two update batches were made—the first with two record updates and the second with the remaining record update.

The second solution is a custom solution that might form the basis for DataAdapter update batching in ADO.NET 1.0 or when using the OLE DB, ODBC, or other data providers that do not provide batch update support in the DataAdapter class.

The solution uses a table named BatchUpdateManual in the database AdoDotNet35Cookbook. The following T-SQL statement creates the table:

```sql
USE AdoDotNet35Cookbook
GO
CREATE TABLE BatchUpdateManual(
    Id int NOT NULL PRIMARY KEY,
    Field1 nvarchar(50) NULL,
    Field2 nvarchar(50) NULL )
```

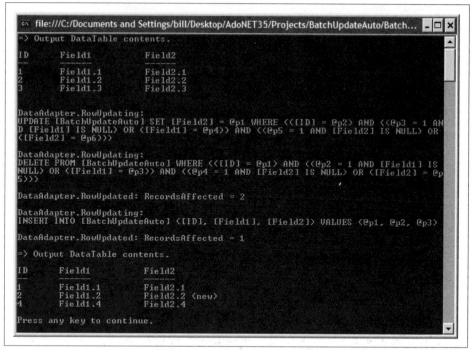

Figure 10-24. Output for BatchUpdateAuto solution

Add three records to the BatchUpdateManual table by executing the following T-SQL batch:

```
USE AdoDotNet35Cookbook
GO

INSERT INTO BatchUpdateManual VALUES (1, 'Field1.1', 'Field2.1');
INSERT INTO BatchUpdateManual VALUES (2, 'Field1.2', 'Field2.2');
INSERT INTO BatchUpdateManual VALUES (3, 'Field1.3', 'Field2.3');
```

The solution creates a DataAdapter and adds a CommandBuilder to it and a handler for the RowUpdating DataAdapter event. Next, the three records from the BatchUpdateAuto table in the AdoDotNet35Cookbook database are retrieved into a DataTable using the DataAdapter and output to the console. Three modifications are made to the data in the DataTable: a record is modified, a record is deleted, and a record is inserted.

The RowUpdating event handler intercepts the DataAdapter updates and constructs a single batched SQL statement that gets executed using the ExecuteNonQuery( ) method. The SQL command to be used to update the row by the DataAdapter is retrieved from the CommandText property of the Command object. The parameters for the Command are iterated over and each parameter variable in the update statement is replaced with the value for that parameter. Single quote delimiters are added around string type values.

Finally, the statement is added to a StringBuilder object and the Status property of the Command is set to UpdateStatus.SkipCurrent row so that the data source is not updated by the DataAdapter. Instead, the update is performed by executing the batch SQL statement created by this event handler.

The C# code in *Program.cs* in the project BatchUpdateManual is shown in Example 10-30.

Example 10-30. File: Program.cs for BatchUpdateManual solution

```csharp
using System;
using System.Data;
using System.Data.SqlClient;
using System.Text;

namespace BatchUpdateManual
{
    class Program
    {
        private static SqlDataAdapter da;
        private static DataTable dt;
        private static StringBuilder sb;

        private static string sqlConnectString = "Data Source=(local);" +
            "Integrated security=SSPI;Initial Catalog=AdoDotNet35Cookbook;";

        static void Main(string[] args)
        {
            string sqlSelect =
                "SELECT Id, Field1, Field2 FROM BatchUpdateManual";

            // Create the data adapter and command builder for update logic.
            da = new SqlDataAdapter(sqlSelect, sqlConnectString);
            SqlCommandBuilder cb = new SqlCommandBuilder(da);

            // Handle the RowUpdating event to batch the update.
            da.RowUpdating += new SqlRowUpdatingEventHandler(da_RowUpdating);

            // Create a DataTable and fill with schema and data
            dt = new DataTable();
            da.FillSchema(dt, SchemaType.Source);
            da.Fill(dt);

            // Output DataTable to console
            OutputTable();

            // Modify the data in the DataTable
            // --Update
            DataRow row = dt.Rows.Find(2);
            row["Field2"] += " (new)";
            // --Delete
            dt.Rows.Find(3).Delete();
            // --Insert
            dt.Rows.Add(new object[] { 4, "Field1.4", "Field2.4" });
```

Example 10-30. File: Program.cs for BatchUpdateManual solution (continued)

```
        // Update the data source
        UpdateDataSource( );

        // Output DataTable to console
        OutputTable( );

        Console.WriteLine("Press any key to continue.");
        Console.ReadKey( );
    }

    static void UpdateDataSource( )
    {
        // Create a new string builder
        sb = new StringBuilder( );

        // Update the data source using the DataAdapter
        Console.WriteLine("=> DataAdapter.Update( ) called.");
        da.Update(dt);

        // Check to see if there is a batched update to execute
        if (sb.Length > 0)
        {
            // Create a connection command with the aggregate update command.
            using (SqlConnection conn = new SqlConnection(sqlConnectString))
            {
                SqlCommand cmd = new SqlCommand(sb.ToString( ), conn);

                // Execute the update command.
                conn.Open( );
                cmd.ExecuteScalar( );
            }
            Console.WriteLine(
                "\n=> ExecuteScalar( ) called to udpate data source.");

            // Refresh the DataTable.
            dt.Clear( );
            da.Fill(dt);
            Console.WriteLine("\n=> DataTable reloaded.");
        }
    }

    static void da_RowUpdating(object sender, SqlRowUpdatingEventArgs e)
    {
        Console.WriteLine("\n=> RowUpdating event intercepted. Appending:");

        // Get the command for the current row update.
        StringBuilder sqlText =
            new StringBuilder(e.Command.CommandText.ToString( ));

        // Replace the parameters with values.
        for (int i = e.Command.Parameters.Count - 1; i >= 0; i--)
```

```
        {
            SqlParameter parm = e.Command.Parameters[i];
            if (parm.SqlDbType == SqlDbType.Char ||
                parm.SqlDbType == SqlDbType.NVarChar ||
                parm.SqlDbType == SqlDbType.NText ||
                parm.SqlDbType == SqlDbType.VarChar)
                // Quotes around the text-type fields
                sqlText.Replace(parm.ParameterName,
                    "'" + parm.Value.ToString() + "'");
            else
                sqlText.Replace(parm.ParameterName,
                    parm.Value.ToString());
        }
        // Add the row command to the aggregate update command.
        sb.Append(sqlText.ToString() + ";");

        Console.WriteLine("{0}.", sqlText);

        // Skip the DataAdapter update of the row.
        e.Status = UpdateStatus.SkipCurrentRow;
    }

    private static void OutputTable()
    {
        Console.WriteLine("\n=> Output DataTable contents.");
        Console.WriteLine("\nID\tField1\t\tField2");
        Console.WriteLine("--\t------\t\t------");
        foreach (DataRow row in dt.Rows)
        {
            if (row.RowState != DataRowState.Deleted)
            {
                Console.WriteLine("{0}\t{1}\t{2}", row["ID"],
                    row["Field1"], row["Field2"]);
            }
        }
        Console.WriteLine();
    }
  }
}
```

The output is shown in Figure 10-25.

Discussion

At the center of the custom approach is the fact that when a DataAdapter is used to update the data source with changes made to disconnected data in a DataSet or DataTable, a RowUpdating event is raised before the command to update each changed row executes. The event handler receives the SqlRowUpdatingEventArgs argument containing information about the event. Table 10-6 lists the properties of SqlRowUpdatingEventArgs used to access information specific to the event.

```
ox  file:///C:/Documents and Settings/bill/Desktop/AdoNET35/Projects/9 - BatchUpdateManual/...  _ □ ×
=> Output DataTable contents.

ID      Field1          Field2

1       Field1.1        Field2.1
2       Field1.2        Field2.2
3       Field1.3        Field2.3

=> DataAdapter.Update() called.

=> RowUpdating event intercepted. Appending:
UPDATE [BatchUpdateManual] SET [Field2] = 'Field2.2 (new)' WHERE ((IID] = 2) AND
  ((0 = 1 AND [Field1] IS NULL) OR ([Field1] = 'Field1.2')) AND ((0 = 1 AND [Fiel
d2] IS NULL) OR ([Field2] = 'Field2.2'))).

=> RowUpdating event intercepted. Appending:
DELETE FROM [BatchUpdateManual] WHERE ((IID] = 3) AND ((0 = 1 AND [Field1] IS NU
LL) OR ([Field1] = 'Field1.3')) AND ((0 = 1 AND [Field2] IS NULL) OR ([Field2] =
'Field2.3'))).

=> RowUpdating event intercepted. Appending:
INSERT INTO [BatchUpdateManual] ([ID], [Field1], [Field2]) VALUES (4, 'Field1.4'
, 'Field2.4').

=> ExecuteNonQuery() called to update data source. 3 rows affected

=> DataTable reloaded.

=> Output DataTable contents.

ID      Field1          Field2

1       Field1.1        Field2.1
2       Field1.2        Field2.2 (new)
4       Field1.4        Field2.4

Press any key to continue.
```

Figure 10-25. Output for BatchUpdateManual solution

Table 10-6. SqlRowUpdatingEventArgs properties

Property	Description
Command	Gets or sets the Command executed to perform the row update.
Errors	Gets errors raised by the .NET Framework data provider when the Command executes.
Row	Gets the DataRow that is being updated.
StatementType	Gets the type of SQL statement to execute to update the row. This is one of the following values: Select, Insert, Update, or Delete.
Status	Gets the UpdateStatus of the Command. This is one of the UpdateStatus enumeration values described in Table 10-7.
TableMapping	Gets the DataTableMapping object to use when updating.

The UpdateStatus is set to ErrorsOccurred when an error occurs while updating a row; otherwise it is set to Continue. UpdateStatus can be used to specify what to do with the current and remaining rows during an update. Table 10-7 describes the UpdateStatus enumeration values.

Table 10-7. UpdateStatus enumeration values

Value	Description
Continue	Continue processing rows.
ErrorsOccurred	Raise an error.
SkipAllRemainingRows	Do not update the current row and do not update the rows that have not yet been processed.
SkipCurrentRow	Do not update the current row. Continue processing with the next row.

To batch the update commands generated by the DataAdapter, the solution does the following in the RowUpdating event handler for each row updated:

- Gets the CommandText that will be used to update the row in the data source.
- Replaces the parameters in the CommandText with the parameter values applying required delimiters (for example, single quotes around string type values) to each value. Appends the result to the batch command text. Ensure that string, date, and other values as well as object names are properly delimited for your requirements.
- Sets the UpdateStatus of the Command to SkipCurrentRow so that the update for the row is not performed.

Once all of the rows have been processed, execute the assembled batch command text against the data source using the ExecuteScalar( ) method of a Command object.

Although this solution uses the CommandBuilder to generate the updating logic for the DataAdapter, the solution remains fundamentally the same if you use your own custom updating logic. One thing to keep in mind: the solution code iterates in reverse order through the parameters collection so that parameters are replaced correctly if there are more than nine parameters; if they were processed in forward order, parameter @p1 would cause the replacement for parameter @p10, @p11, and so on. When using custom updating logic, consider the potential problems that might occur if one parameter name is the start of another parameter name when replacing the parameters with the values in the DataRow.RowUpdating event handler.

Ensure that you set the AutoIncrementSeed and AutoIncrementStep properties prior to filling the DataTable; otherwise, the identity will not work properly.

10.19 Automatically Refreshing a DataTable Periodically

Problem

You need to automatically refresh a DataSet periodically.

Solution

Use extended properties and a timer.

The solution uses a table named AutoRefresh in the database AdoDotNet35Cookbook. The following T-SQL statement creates the table:

```
USE AdoDotNet35Cookbook
GO

CREATE TABLE AutoRefresh(
    Id int NOT NULL PRIMARY KEY,
    Field1 nvarchar(50) NULL,
    Field2 nvarchar(50) NULL )
```

Add three records to the AutoRefresh table by executing the following T-SQL batch:

```
USE AdoDotNet35Cookbook
GO

INSERT INTO AutoRefresh VALUES (1, 'Field1.1', 'Field2.1');
INSERT INTO AutoRefresh VALUES (2, 'Field1.2', 'Field2.2');
INSERT INTO AutoRefresh VALUES (3, 'Field1.3', 'Field2.3');
```

The solution creates a DataTable containing the schema and all records from the AutoRefresh table in the AdoDotNet35Cookbook database. A timer is set up to check whether the data needs to be refreshed based on the refresh time (every 15 seconds) stored in the ExtendedProperty of the DataTable. The data is refreshed if required, the ExtendedProperty updated to reflect the next refresh time, and the new data output to the console. A second timer is used to update the data in the data source after 10 seconds. The first refresh of the data after 15 seconds shows the updated data.

The C# code in *Program.cs* in the project AutoRefreshDataTable is shown in Example 10-31.

Example 10-31. File: Program.cs for AutoRefreshDataTable solution

```csharp
using System;
using System.Data;
using System.Data.SqlClient;
using System.Timers;

namespace AutoRefreshDataTable
{
    class Program
    {
        private static string sqlConnectString = "Data Source=(local);" +
            "Integrated Security=SSPI;Initial Catalog=AdoDotNet35Cookbook";

        private static DataTable dt;
        private static SqlDataAdapter da;

        // the refresh interval for the table in seconds
        private static int refreshInterval = 10;
```

```csharp
static void Main(string[] args)
{
    string sqlSelect = "SELECT * FROM AutoRefresh";

    Console.WriteLine("(Press any key to exit.)");

    // Create a DataTable and fill with schema and data.
    dt = new DataTable( );
    da = new SqlDataAdapter(sqlSelect, sqlConnectString);
    da.FillSchema(dt, SchemaType.Source);
    da.Fill(dt);

    // Set the refresh time for the data.
    dt.ExtendedProperties["RefreshTime"] =
        DateTime.Now.AddSeconds(refreshInterval);

    // Set up a timer to check if refresh required every 5 seconds
    Timer timerCheckRefresh = new Timer(5000);
    timerCheckRefresh.Elapsed +=
        new ElapsedEventHandler(timerCheckRefresh_Elapsed);
    timerCheckRefresh.Start( );

    // Set up a time to make a change to the data in 10 seconds
    Timer timerUpdateData = new Timer(10000);
    timerUpdateData.Elapsed +=
        new ElapsedEventHandler(timerUpdateData_Elapsed);
    timerUpdateData.AutoReset = false;
    timerUpdateData.Start( );

    OutputTable( );

    Console.ReadKey( );
}

static void timerUpdateData_Elapsed(object sender, ElapsedEventArgs e)
{
    string sqlBatch =
        "UPDATE AutoRefresh SET Field2 = 'Field2.2 (new)' WHERE Id = 2;" +
        "DELETE AutoRefresh WHERE Id = 3;" +
        "INSERT AutoRefresh VALUES (4, 'Field1.4', 'Field2.4');";

    using (SqlConnection connection = new SqlConnection(sqlConnectString))
    {
        SqlCommand command = new SqlCommand(sqlBatch, connection);
        connection.Open( );
        int rows = command.ExecuteNonQuery( );
        Console.WriteLine("[{0}] Data updated. {1} rows affected.",
            DateTime.Now, rows);
    }
}

static void timerCheckRefresh_Elapsed(object sender, ElapsedEventArgs e)
{
```

Example 10-31. File: Program.cs for AutoRefreshDataTable solution (continued)

```
        if (DateTime.Now > (DateTime)dt.ExtendedProperties["RefreshTime"])
        {
            Console.WriteLine("[{0}] Refreshing data.", DateTime.Now);
            // Refresh the data in the DataTable
            dt.Clear();
            da.Fill(dt);
            // Set the next refresh time for the data.
            dt.ExtendedProperties["RefreshTime"] =
                DateTime.Now.AddSeconds(refreshInterval);
            OutputTable();
        }
        else
        {
            Console.WriteLine("[{0}] Data refresh not required.", DateTime.Now);
        }
    }

    private static void OutputTable()
    {
        Console.WriteLine("\n[{0}] Output DataTable contents.", DateTime.Now);
        Console.WriteLine("\nID\tField1\t\tField2");
        Console.WriteLine("--\t------\t\t------");
        foreach (DataRow row in dt.Rows)
        {
            Console.WriteLine("{0}\t{1}\t{2}", row["ID"], row["Field1"],
                row["Field2"]);
        }
        Console.WriteLine();
    }
}
}
```

The output is shown in Figure 10-26.

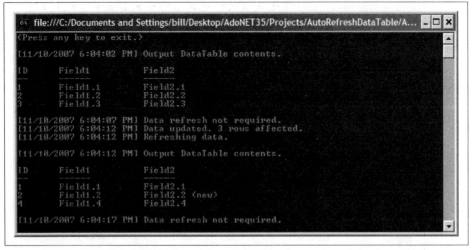

Figure 10-26. Output for AutoRefreshDataTable solution

Discussion

The `ExtendedProperties` property accesses a `PropertyCollection` of custom information for a DataSet, DataTable, DataColumn, DataRelation, or Constraint object. The `PropertyCollection` extends the `Hashtable` class to store information as a collection of key-and-value pairs. The extended property data must be stored as strings; otherwise, it will not be persisted when the data is written as XML. Add items to the collection using the `Add( )` method, remove them with the `Remove( )` method, and access them using the indexer in C# or the `Item( )` property in Visual Basic. For more information about members of the `PropertyCollection` class, see the MSDN Library.

There are three timers in Visual Studio .NET and the .NET Framework:

- The Windows-based timer `System.Windows.Form.Timer` (available on the Windows Form tab of the Toolbox) is designed for a single-threaded environment where UI threads are used for processing. This is the simplest timer to use but also the least accurate with an accuracy limited to 55ms.

- The thread timer `System.Threading.Timer` is a simple, lightweight timer that uses callback methods to periodically run a task on a separate thread. This timer can only be used programmatically. This timer is more accurate than the Windows-based timer.

  The thread timer specifies the method to execute when its time has elapsed. This delegate is specified when the `Timer` is constructed and cannot be changed. The method executes in a thread pool supplied by the system rather than in the thread that created the timer.

  When the thread timer is created, the *due time* (the time to wait before first execution of the method) and the *period* (the amount of time to wait between subsequent executions) are specified in the constructor. A due time of 0 results in the callback being invoked immediately; a due time of `Timeout.Infinite` results in the callback method never being invoked. You can change the behavior of the timer at any time by using the `Change( )` method.

- The server-based timer `System.Timers.Timer` (available on the Components tab of the Toolbox) is designed for use with worker threads in a multithreaded environment. This timer uses server ticks generated out-of-process and is the most accurate of the three.

  The server-based timer raises an `Elapsed` event when the interval specified by the `Interval` property elapses. The `Start( )` and `Stop( )` methods of the timer control whether the timer raises `Elapsed` events. If the AutoReset property is set to `false`, the `Elapsed` event is raised only once and the `Start( )` method must be called to start the count again. Calling the `Start( )` and `Stop( )` methods have the same effect as setting the `Enabled` property to `true` and `false`, respectively.

10.20 Automatically Refreshing a DataTable When Underlying Data Changes

Problem

You need to refresh a DataTable when the data in the underlying data source changes.

Solution

Use the SqlDependency class to create a query notification.

The solution uses a table named AutoRefreshChange in the database AdoDotNet35Cookbook. Execute the following T-SQL statement to create the table:

```
USE AdoDotNet35Cookbook
GO
SET ANSI_NULLS ON
GO
SET QUOTED_IDENTIFIER ON
GO
CREATE TABLE AutoRefreshChange(
    Id int NOT NULL PRIMARY KEY,
    Field1 nvarchar(50) NULL,
    Field2 nvarchar(50) NULL )
```

Add three records to the AutoRefreshChange table by executing the following T-SQL batch:

```
USE AdoDotNet35Cookbook
GO

INSERT INTO AutoRefreshChange VALUES (1, 'Field1.1', 'Field2.1');
INSERT INTO AutoRefreshChange VALUES (2, 'Field1.2', 'Field2.2');
INSERT INTO AutoRefreshChange VALUES (3, 'Field1.3', 'Field2.3');
```

SQL Server databases do not have Service Broker enabled by default, for security reasons. Enable Service Broker for the AdoDotNet35Cookbook database by executing the following T-SQL statement:

```
USE AdoDotNet35Cookbook
GO

ALTER DATABASE AdoDotNet35Cookbook SET ENABLE_BROKER
```

You can confirm that Service Broker is now enabled for the database by using the DATABASEPROPERTYEX function, as shown in the following T-SQL statement:

```
SELECT DATABASEPROPERTYEX('AdoDotNet35Cookbook', 'IsBrokerEnabled')
```

The function returns 0 for false and 1 for true.

The solution creates a Connection to the AdoDotNet35Cookbook database and a DataAdapter for the AutoRefreshChange table in that database. A SqlDependency object is created and associated with the select command of the DataAdapter. An OnChange event handler for the SqlDependency is added that is called when a change is made to the original data in the database. After the DataTable is filled, the contents are output to the console.

A timer is set up that changes, deletes, and adds a row in the AdoDotNet35Cookbook database after a delay of five seconds. Once the change is made, a query notification is sent causing the OnChange event handler for the SqlDependency object to be called. That method refreshes the DataTable and outputs its updated contents to the console.

The C# code in *Program.cs* in the project AutoRefreshDataTable is shown in Example 10-32.

Example 10-32. File: Program.cs for AutoRefreshDataTableChange solution

```
using System;
using System.Data;
using System.Data.SqlClient;
using System.Timers;
using System.Data.Sql;

namespace AutoRefreshDataTableChange
{
    class Program
    {
        private static string sqlConnectString = "Data Source=(local);" +
            "Integrated Security=SSPI;Initial Catalog=AdoDotNet35Cookbook";
        private static string sqlSelect =
            "SELECT ID, Field1, Field2 FROM dbo.AutoRefreshChange;";

        private static DataTable dt;

        static void Main(string[] args)
        {
            Console.WriteLine("(Press any key to exit.)");

            SqlDependency.Start(sqlConnectString);

            SqlConnection connection = new SqlConnection(sqlConnectString);
            SqlDataAdapter da = new SqlDataAdapter(sqlSelect, connection);

            // create the notification and handler
            SqlDependency sd = new SqlDependency(da.SelectCommand);
            sd.OnChange += new OnChangeEventHandler(sd_OnChange);

            // fill the DataTable using the DataAdapter with the notify command
            dt = new DataTable();
            da.Fill(dt);
```

Example 10-32. File: Program.cs for AutoRefreshDataTableChange solution (continued)

```csharp
            // output the contents of the DataTable
            OutputTable( );

            // Set up a time to make a change to the data in 5 seconds
            Timer timerChangeData = new Timer(5000);
            timerChangeData.Elapsed +=
                new ElapsedEventHandler(timerChangeData_Elapsed);
            timerChangeData.AutoReset = false;
            timerChangeData.Start( );

            Console.ReadKey( );

            SqlDependency.Stop(sqlConnectString);
        }

        static void timerChangeData_Elapsed(object sender, ElapsedEventArgs e)
        {
            // Make some changes to the DataTable using a NonQuery
            string sqlBatch =
                "UPDATE AutoRefreshChange SET Field2 = 'Field2.2 (new)' " +
                " WHERE Id = 2;" +
                "DELETE AutoRefreshChange WHERE Id = 3;" +
                "INSERT AutoRefreshChange VALUES (4, 'Field1.4', 'Field2.4');";

            using (SqlConnection connection = new SqlConnection(sqlConnectString))
            {
                SqlCommand command = new SqlCommand(sqlBatch, connection);
                connection.Open( );
                int rows = command.ExecuteNonQuery( );
                Console.WriteLine("[{0}] Data updated. {1} rows affected.",
                    DateTime.Now, rows);
            }
        }

        static void sd_OnChange(object sender, SqlNotificationEventArgs e)
        {
            // Output the change notification
            Console.WriteLine("[{0}] Data change notification: {1}. Refreshing data.",
                DateTime.Now, e.Info);

            // Refresh the data in the DataTable
            dt.Clear( );
            SqlDataAdapter da = new SqlDataAdapter(sqlSelect, sqlConnectString);
            da.Fill(dt);

            OutputTable( );
        }

        private static void OutputTable( )
        {
```

Example 10-32. File: Program.cs for AutoRefreshDataTableChange solution (continued)

```
            // output the contents of the DataTable, with a little formatting
            Console.WriteLine("\n[{0}] Output DataTable contents.", DateTime.Now);
            Console.WriteLine("\nID\tField1\t\tField2");
            Console.WriteLine("--\t------\t\t------");
            foreach (DataRow row in dt.Rows)
            {
                Console.WriteLine("{0}\t{1}\t{2}", row["ID"], row["Field1"],
                    row["Field2"]);
            }
            Console.WriteLine( );
        }
    }
}
```

The output is shown in Figure 10-27.

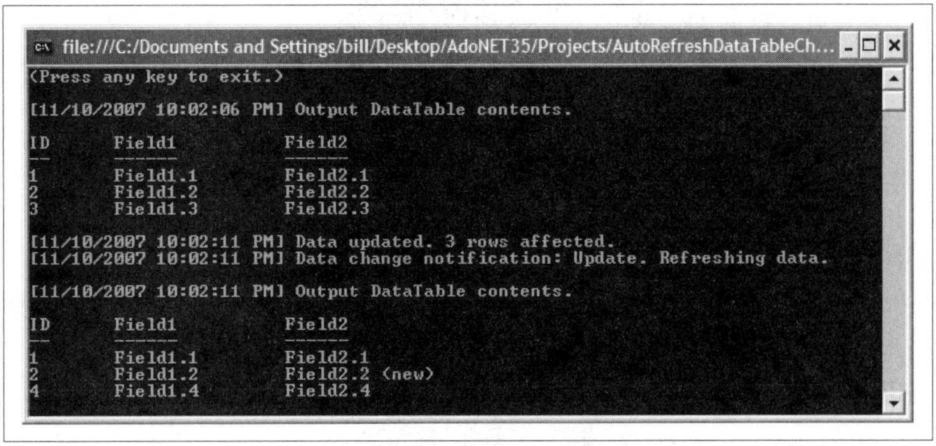

Figure 10-27. Output for AutoRefreshDataTableChange solution

Discussion

The SqlDependency class represents a query notification dependency between the application and an instance of SQL Server 2005 or later. The application receives notifications through the OnChange event handler. To use query notifications, you must:

- Use SQL Server 2005 or later.
- Enable query notifications for the database by setting the ENABLE_BROKER option.
- Connect to the database with a user ID that has adequate permissions.
- Associate a SqlDependency object with a SqlCommand object that has a valid SELECT statement.
- Provide the event handler to process the notification once received.

You must initialize SqlDependency by calling the static Start() method, passing an argument containing a connection string to the database. This establishes a dependency to the database. Prior to terminating the application, call the static Stop() method passing the same connection string as an argument for each dependency established.

There are two additional classes that provide query notification services:

- The SqlDependencyCache class establishes a relationship between the ASP.NET application Cache object and a SQL Server database or the results of a SQL Server query. Most ASP.NET applications should use this class, while most non-ASP.NET applications should use the SqlDependency class.

- The SqlNotificationRequest class provides lower-level access to query notification services than the SqlDepencency class. If you need more control over when notifications occur or you need to customize the notification message, use this class instead of the simpler SqlDependency class.

For more information about the SqlDependencyCache and the SqlNotificationRequest classes, consult MSDN.

10.21 Retrieving SQL Server Runtime Statistics

Problem

You want to get information about your connection to SQL Server, including bytes sent, bytes received, connection time, and execution time.

Solution

Use the RetrieveStatistics() method of the Connection class.

The solution creates a Connection and enables statistics by setting the EnableStatistics property of the Connection object to true. A DataAdapter is created and used to fill a DataTable with all records in the Person.Contact table in AdventureWorks. Statistics are retrieved into a dictionary using the RetrieveStatistics() method of the Connection object and then output to the console.

The C# code in *Program.cs* in the project RetrieveStatistics is shown in Example 10-33.

Example 10-33. File: Program.cs for RetrieveStatistics solution

```
using System;
using System.Data;
using System.Data.SqlClient;
using System.Collections;
```

Example 10-33. File: Program.cs for RetrieveStatistics solution (continued)

```
namespace RetrieveStatistics
{
    class Program
    {
        static void Main(string[] args)
        {
            string sqlConnectString = "Data Source=(local);" +
                "Integrated Security=SSPI;Initial Catalog=AdventureWorks";
            string sqlSelect = "SELECT * FROM Person.Contact";

            // open a connection and enable statistics
            using (SqlConnection connection = new SqlConnection(sqlConnectString))
            {
                connection.StatisticsEnabled = true;

                // do some work with the connection to generate statistics
                SqlDataAdapter da =
                    new SqlDataAdapter(sqlSelect, connection);
                DataTable dt = new DataTable( );
                da.Fill(dt);

                // get the statistics
                IDictionary d = connection.RetrieveStatistics( );
                // move the dictionary keys to an array
                string[] keys = new string[d.Count];
                d.Keys.CopyTo(keys, 0);

                // iterate over the dictionary displaying the key-value pair
                for (int i = 0; i < d.Count; i++)
                    Console.WriteLine("{0} = {1}", keys[i], (long)d[keys[i]]);
            }

            Console.WriteLine("\nPress any key to continue.");
            Console.ReadKey( );
        }
    }
}
```

The output is shown in Figure 10-28.

The output shows all of the statistics that the SQL Server data provider makes available. For a description of each statistic, see "Provider Statistics" in MSDN.

Discussion

The .NET Framework 2.0 added support for runtime statistics with the SQL Server data provider. Runtime statistics expose information about processing queries in the database.

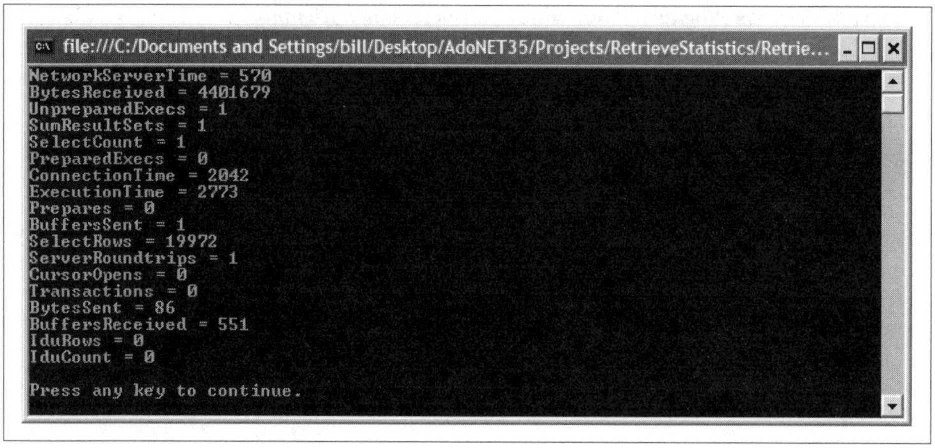

Figure 10-28. Output for RetrieveStatistics solution

You must enable statistics by setting the `StatisticsEnabled` property of the `SqlConnection` object to true after the connection has been created. Once statistics are enabled, they can be retrieved into an `IDictionary` instance using the `RetrieveStatistics()` method of the `SqlConnection` object. The values in the dictionary are the statistic counter values, and are all of the long data type. The .NET Framework 3.5 SQL Server data provider makes 18 statistics available. The `ResetStatistics()` method of the `SqlConnection` object resets the counters.

All statistics are gathered on a per-connection basis and are valid for the current point in time. If you continue using the connection after retrieving statistics, you have to retrieve statistics again to get the current values.

10.22 Writing Provider- and Database-Independent Code

Problem

You need to create a solution that can work with more than one data provider. The solution needs to use both connected classes, including `DataReader` objects, and disconnected classes, including `DataTable` objects, to both retrieve and update data.

Solution

Two solutions are given—one for ADO.NET 2.0 and later, and one for ADO.NET 1.1.

The first solution targets ADO.NET 2.0 and later uses data provider factories. This solution has two methods that use data provider factories to retrieve data as both a `DataReader` and `DataTable`:

GetDataTable( )

Takes provider invariant name, connection string, and select statement arguments and returns a DataTable.

GetDataReader( )

Takes provider invariant name, connection string, and select statement arguments and returns a DataReader.

The solution uses these methods to retrieve data using both the SQL Server data provider and the OLE DB data provider. Results are output to the console.

You can easily extend this solution to update a data source by using data provider factories to create a DbDataAdapter as shown in the GetDataTable( ) method. Call the Update( ) method of the DbDataAdapter, passing in a DataTable or DataSet object as an argument to update changes to the data source.

The C# code in *Program.cs* in the project WriteProviderIndependentCode is shown in Example 10-34.

Example 10-34. File: Program.cs for WriteProviderIndependentCode solution

```
using System;
using System.Data;
using System.Data.Common;

namespace WriteProviderIndependentCode
{
    class Program
    {
        static void Main(string[] args)
        {
            string sqlConnectString = "Data Source=(local);" +
                "Integrated security=SSPI;Initial Catalog=AdventureWorks;";
            string oledbConnectString = "Provider=SQLOLEDB;Data Source=(local);" +
                "Integrated Security=SSPI;Initial Catalog=AdventureWorks;";

            string sqlSelect = "SELECT TOP 5 ContactID, FirstName, LastName " +
                "FROM Person.Contact ORDER BY LastName";

            DataTable dt1 = GetDataTable(
                "System.Data.SqlClient", sqlConnectString, sqlSelect);
            OutputDataTable("SQL Server Data Provider", dt1);

            DataTable dt2 = GetDataTable(
                "System.Data.OleDb", oledbConnectString, sqlSelect);
            OutputDataTable("OLEDB Server Data Provider", dt2);

            DbDataReader dr1 = GetDataReader(
                "System.Data.SqlClient", sqlConnectString, sqlSelect);
            OutputDataReader("SQL Server Data Provider", dr1);
            dr1.Close( );
```

Example 10-34. File: Program.cs for WriteProviderIndependentCode solution (continued)

```
        DbDataReader dr2 = GetDataReader(
            "System.Data.OleDb", oledbConnectString, sqlSelect);
        OutputDataReader("OLEDB Server Data Provider", dr2);
        dr2.Close( );

        Console.WriteLine("\nPress any key to continue.");
        Console.ReadKey( );
    }

    static DataTable GetDataTable(string providerInvariantName,
        string connectString, string selectCommandText)
    {
        Console.WriteLine("\n=> Creating DataTable using {0}",
            providerInvariantName);

        // Create factory using the invariant name.
        DbProviderFactory f =
            DbProviderFactories.GetFactory(providerInvariantName);

        DbConnection connection = f.CreateConnection( );
        connection.ConnectionString = connectString;

        DbCommand selectCommand = connection.CreateCommand( );
        selectCommand.CommandText = selectCommandText;

        DbDataAdapter da = f.CreateDataAdapter( );
        da.SelectCommand = selectCommand;

        DataTable dt = new DataTable( );
        da.Fill(dt);

        return dt;
    }

    static void OutputDataTable(string providerType, DataTable dt)
    {
        Console.WriteLine("\n---DataTable Output [{0}]---", providerType);
        Console.WriteLine("ID\tContact Name");
        Console.WriteLine("--\t------------");
        foreach (DataRow row in dt.Rows)
        {
            Console.WriteLine("{0}\t{1}, {2}",
                row["ContactID"], row["LastName"], row["FirstName"]);
        }
    }

    static DbDataReader GetDataReader(string providerInvariantName,
        string connectString, string selectCommandText)
    {
        Console.WriteLine("\n=> Creating DbDataReader using {0}",
            providerInvariantName);
```

```
        // Create factory using the invariant name.
        DbProviderFactory f =
            DbProviderFactories.GetFactory(providerInvariantName);

        DbConnection connection = f.CreateConnection( );
        connection.ConnectionString = connectString;

        DbCommand selectCommand = connection.CreateCommand( );
        selectCommand.CommandText = selectCommandText;

        // Open the connection and return a data reader
        connection.Open( );
        return selectCommand.ExecuteReader(
            CommandBehavior.CloseConnection);
    }

    static void OutputDataReader(string providerType, DbDataReader dr)
    {
        Console.WriteLine("\n---DataTable Output [{0}]---", providerType);
        Console.WriteLine("ID\tContact Name");
        Console.WriteLine("--\t------------");
        while (dr.Read( ))
        {
            Console.WriteLine("{0}\t{1}, {2}",
                dr["ContactID"], dr["LastName"], dr["FirstName"]);
        }
    }
}
}
```

The output is shown in Figure 10-29.

The second solution, targeting ADO.NET 1.1 (although it can be used with ADO.NET 2.0 and later), uses interfaces that are inherited by .NET data provider connected classes to create provider-independent data access code. The solution also shows how to access provider-specific functionality.

The solution creates a method GetData( ), which is a .NET data provider-independent method that accepts provider-specific Connection and DataAdapter arguments through IDbConnection and IDbDataAdapter interface arguments. The interfaces are used to create an IDbCommand object, assign it to the data adapter using the IDbAdapter interface, and fill a DataSet with the TOP 10 records from the Person.Contact table in AdventureWorks. The solution shows how to identify the provider-specific Connection for the IDbConnection and add provider-specific logic, if required. The DataSet is returned to the caller.

The solution calls the GetData( ) method defined in the solution with the provider-specific SqlConnection and SqlDataAdapter and with OleDbConnection and OleDbDataAdapter arguments, and outputs the contents of the returned DataSet to the console.

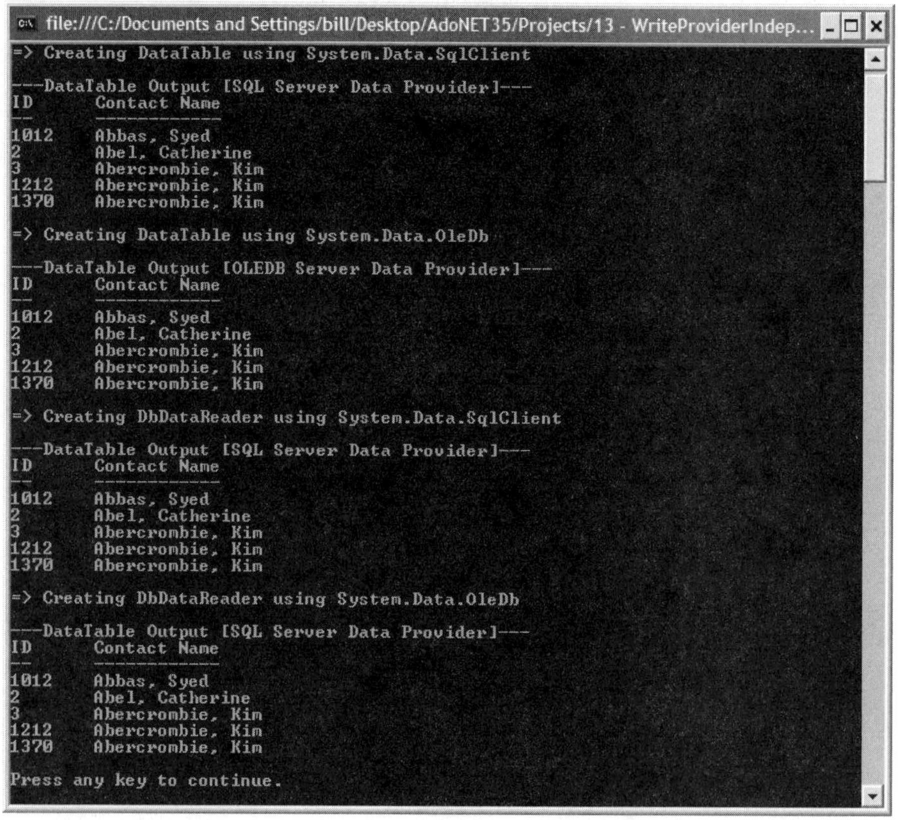

Figure 10-29. Output for WriteProviderIndependentCode solution

The C# code in *Program.cs* in the project DatabaseIndependentCode is shown in Example 10-35.

Example 10-35. File: Program.cs for DatabaseIndependentCode solution

```csharp
using System;
using System.Data;
using System.Data.SqlClient;
using System.Data.OleDb;

namespace DatabaseIndependentCode
{
    class Program
    {
        static void Main(string[] args)
        {
            string sqlConnectString = "Data Source=(local);" +
                "Integrated security=SSPI;Initial Catalog=AdventureWorks;";
            string oledbConnectString = "Provider=SQLOLEDB;Data Source=(local);" +
                "Integrated Security=SSPI;Initial Catalog=AdventureWorks;";
```

```csharp
            // Create a SQL Connection and DataAdapter.
            SqlConnection connSql = new SqlConnection(sqlConnectString);
            SqlDataAdapter daSql = new SqlDataAdapter();

            // Retrieve and output the data
            Console.WriteLine("=> Calling GetData() with System.Data.SqlClient");
            DataSet dsSql = GetData(connSql, daSql);
            Console.WriteLine("\n---SQL .NET Provider---");
            foreach (DataRow row in dsSql.Tables["Contact"].Rows)
                Console.WriteLine("ID = {0}\tName = {1}, {2}",
                    row["ContactID"], row["LastName"], row["FirstName"]);

            // Create a OLEDB Connection and DataAdapter.
            OleDbConnection connOleDb = new OleDbConnection(oledbConnectString);
            OleDbDataAdapter daOleDb = new OleDbDataAdapter();

            // Retrieve and output the data
            Console.WriteLine("\n=> Calling GetData() with System.Data.OleDb");
            DataSet dsOleDb = GetData(connOleDb, daOleDb);
            Console.WriteLine("\n---OLEDB .NET Provider---");
            foreach (DataRow row in dsOleDb.Tables["Contact"].Rows)
                Console.WriteLine("ID = {0}\tName = {1}, {2}",
                    row["ContactID"], row["LastName"], row["FirstName"]);

            Console.WriteLine("\nPress any key to continue.");
            Console.ReadKey();
        }

        private static DataSet GetData(
            IDbConnection connection, IDbDataAdapter da)
        {
            Console.WriteLine("=> GetData()");
            // Common connection, command, and data adapter code
            // Create the command and assign it to the IDbDataAdapter.
            IDbCommand cmd = connection.CreateCommand();
            cmd.CommandText = "SELECT TOP 10 * FROM Person.Contact";
            da.SelectCommand = cmd;
            // Add a table mapping.
            da.TableMappings.Add("Table", "Contact");

            // Fill the DataSet.
            DataSet ds = new DataSet();
            da.Fill(ds);

            // Identify provider-specific connection type and
            // process if and as necessary.
            if (connection is SqlConnection)
            {
                Console.WriteLine(
                    "=> Specific processing for SQL data provider.");
            }
            else if (connection is OleDbConnection)
```

Example 10-35. File: Program.cs for DatabaseIndependentCode solution (continued)

```
        {
            Console.WriteLine(
                "=> Specific processing for OLE DB data provider.");
        }

        return ds;
    }
  }
}
```

The output is shown in Figure 10-30.

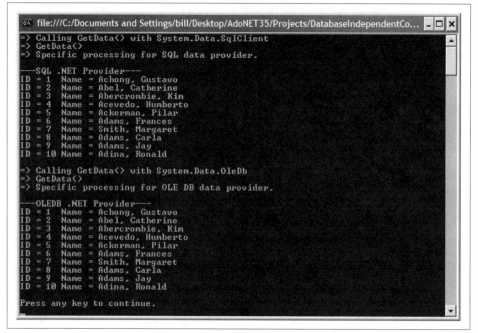

Figure 10-30. Output for DatabaseIndependentCode solution

Discussion

The following subsections discuss the solutions presented for ADO.NET 2.0 and later and for ADO.NET 1.1.

ADO.NET 2.0 and later

Data providers in ADO.NET 1.0 and 1.1 are a set of provider-specific classes that implement generic interfaces. These interfaces can be used to write code that is data provider-independent. For example, the data connection classes in the Microsoft SQL Server data provider (SqlConnection) and the Microsoft Oracle data provider

(OracleConnection) both implement the IDbConnection interface. Code based on the IDbConnection interface that is common to both classes, rather than a database-specific instance of a data provider, is independent of the data provider and therefore not dependent on the underlying database. The disadvantage of the interface approach is that you cannot use the interface to access any database-specific features implemented as members of the data provider class but not defined as part of the interface—the ChangeDatabase( ) method of the Oracle data provider, for example.

ADO.NET 2.0 introduces the *Common Model*, based on the *Factory* design pattern, which uses a single API to access databases that have different providers. Data provider factories let your code work with multiple data providers without choosing a specific provider. The factory class creates and returns a strongly typed, provider-specific object based on information in the request. This lets you write data provider-independent code and select the provider at runtime. Using the Common Model, it becomes easier to write an application to support multiple databases.

The DbProviderFactories class in the System.Data.Common namespace lets you retrieve information about installed .NET data providers. The static GetFactoryClasses( ) method returns a DataTable object containing information about the installed data providers that implement the abstract base class DbProviderFactory, with the schema described in Table 10-8.

Table 10-8. DataTable schema for GetFactoryClasses( ) method results

Column name	Description
Name	Data provider name.
Description	Data provider description.
InvariantName	A unique identifier for a data provider registered in machine.config in the <system.data><DbProviderFactories> element. For example, the invariant name for SQL Server is System.Data.SqlClient.
	The invariant name is used to programmatically refer to the data provider.
AssemblyQualifiedName	Fully qualified name of the data provider factory class—enough information to instantiate the object.

The providers returned by the GetFactoryClasses( ) method correspond to the DbProviderFactories element in *machine.config*, an example of which is shown in the following excerpt:

```
<system.data>
  <DbProviderFactories>
    <add name="Odbc Data Provider" invariant="System.Data.Odbc"
      description=".Net Framework Data Provider for Odbc"
      type="System.Data.Odbc.OdbcFactory,
      System.Data, Version=2.0.0.0, Culture=neutral,
        PublicKeyToken=b77a5c561934e089" />
    <add name="OleDb Data Provider" invariant="System.Data.OleDb"
      description=".Net Framework Data Provider for OleDb"
      type="System.Data.OleDb.OleDbFactory,
```

```
        System.Data, Version=2.0.0.0, Culture=neutral,
          PublicKeyToken=b77a5c561934e089" />
      <add name="OracleClient Data Provider" invariant="System.Data.OracleClient"
        description=".Net Framework Data Provider for Oracle"
        type="System.Data.OracleClient.OracleClientFactory, System.Data.OracleClient,
        Version=2.0.0.0, Culture=neutral, PublicKeyToken=b77a5c561934e089" />
      <add name="SqlClient Data Provider" invariant="System.Data.SqlClient"
        description=".Net Framework Data Provider for SqlServer"
        type="System.Data.SqlClient.SqlClientFactory, System.Data, Version=2.0.0.0,
        Culture=neutral, PublicKeyToken=b77a5c561934e089" />
      <add name="Microsoft SQL Server Compact Data Provider"
        invariant="System.Data.SqlServerCe.3.5"
        description=".NET Framework Data Provider for Microsoft SQL Server Compact"
        type="System.Data.SqlServerCe.SqlCeProviderFactory,
        System.Data.SqlServerCe, Version=3.5.0.0, Culture=neutral,
        PublicKeyToken=89845dcd8080cc91" />
    </DbProviderFactories>
  </system.data>
```

The static GetFactory( ) method of the DbProviderFactories class takes a single argument—either a DataRow object from the table returned by the GetFactoryClasses( ) method or a string containing the invariant name of the provider—and returns a DbProviderFactory instance for that data provider.

The DbProviderFactory class is an abstract base class that every ADO.NET 2.0 data provider must implement. DbProviderFactory is a data provider-independent class that provides a strongly typed object based on information supplied at runtime. The provider-specific classes derived from DbProviderFactory installed with .NET Framework 2.0 are listed in Table 10-9.

Table 10-9. Provider-specific classes derived from DbProviderFactory installed with .NET Framework 2.0

Factory class	Description
System.Data.Odbc.OdbcFactory	Used to create instances of ODBC provider classes.
System.Data.OleDb.OleDbFactory	Used to create instances of OLE DB provider classes.
System.Data.OracleClient.OracleClientFactory	Used to create instances of Oracle provider classes.
System.Data.SqlClient.SqlClientFactory	Used to create instances of SQL Server provider classes.

The DbProviderFactory class has public methods, listed in Table 10-10, that are used to create the provider-specific class instances.

Table 10-10. DbProviderFactory class public methods

Method	Description
CreateCommand()	Returns a DbCommand instance—the base class for strongly typed command objects.
CreateCommandBuilder()	Returns a DbCommandBuilder instance—the base class for strongly typed command builder objects.
CreateConnection()	Returns a DbConnection instance—the base class for strongly typed connection objects.
CreateConnectionStringBuilder()	Returns a DbConnectionStringBuilder instance—the base class for strongly typed connection string builder objects.
CreateDataAdapter()	Returns a DbDataAdapter instance—the base class for strongly typed data adapter objects.
CreateDataSourceEnumerator()	Returns a DbDataSourceEnumerator instance—the base class for strongly typed data source enumerator objects.
CreateParameter()	Returns a DbParameter instance—the base class for strongly typed parameter objects.
CreatePermission()	Returns a CodeAccessPermission instance—the base class for strongly typed code access permission objects.

Code written using factory classes is database-independent, with the exception of the invariant name of the provider and the connection string. These arguments would normally be retrieved from a configuration file or similar mechanism rather than hardcoded, to make the application truly database-independent.

ADO.NET 1.1

ADO.NET 1.1 does not provide a way to create provider-agnostic Connection or DataAdapter objects. Despite these limitations, you can still create code that is fairly provider-independent.

The IDbConnection and IDataAdapter interfaces are implemented by Connection and DataAdapter classes in .NET data providers. You can pass these provider-independent base classes as interface arguments instead of the provider-specific inherited classes. This allows applications that support multiple data providers by reusing common provider-independent code.

The provider-specific functionality of the classes is not available when the base interfaces are used. In this example, the is operator is used to identify the provider-specific class of the provider-independent interface. Branching logic can then be used to execute any code that might be required that is provider-specific.

Enumerating and Maintaining Database Objects

11.0 Introduction

This chapter describes techniques to get schema information and metadata from databases, manage database objects, and enumerate installed database providers and drivers.

There are many ways to get schema information and other information from a SQL Server database. Some of these techniques are:

- Catalog views were introduced in SQL Server 2005 and return information used by the SQL Server Database Engine. Microsoft recommends using catalog views because they provide the most general interface to catalog metadata and the most efficient way to get and present this information. All user-available catalog metadata is exposed through catalog views. Catalog views don't expose information about replication, backup, Database Maintenance Plan, or SQL Server Agent.

- SQL Server 2000 introduced *information schema views* that provide system-table independent access to SQL Server metadata. They provide an alternative to system stored procedures and conform to the SQL-92 Standard and are less tightly bound to the underlying database.

- System stored procedures can be used to get information about a SQL Server database and to perform a variety of administrative tasks.

- SQL Server Management Objects (SMO) was introduced in SQL Server 2005 and lets you programmatically manage and retrieve information about a SQL Server instance. SMO extends and supersedes SQL-DMO.

- SQL Server Distributed Management Objects (SQL-DMO) is a collection of objects that encapsulates SQL Server database and replication management. You can use SQL-DMO to automate SQL Server tasks, create and administer SQL Server objects, and install and configure replication.

Recipe 11.1 shows you two ways to enumerate SQL Server instances on your network using SMO.

The Connection class lets you find and retrieve metadata about the database for a connection—Recipe 11.2 shows you how. Recipe 11.3 shows how to use the SQL Server or OLE DB Connection classes, catalog views, and information schema views to retrieve database schema information.

Recipe 11.4 shows how to use both catalog views and the sp_helpconstraint system stored procedure to get default values for columns. Recipe 11.5 shows how to use a DataReader, a catalog view, and the sp_help system stored procedure to get the length of non-string columns.

The SQL SET statements alter session handling of current information. Recipe 11.6 shows how to retrieve the execution plan for a query.

Recipe 11.7 shows how retrieve only column metadata and not results when you execute a SQL Server command or stored procedure.

Data Definition Language (DDL) statements are used to manage objects in a SQL Server database—for example, adding or modifying objects such as databases, tables, indices, and views. You can execute a DDL statement through a .NET data provider to manipulate the database or catalog schema. Since DDL commands do not return a result set as a query does, these statements are executed using the ExecuteNonQuery( ) method of the Command object. Recipe 11.8 shows you how to use both a T-SQL DDL statement and SMO to create a new SQL Server database. Recipe 11.9 shows you how to use both a T-SQL DDL and SMO to create a new table in a SQL Server database.

Recipe 11.10 defines a method CreateDdlFromDataTable( ) that dynamically constructs a DDL statement from a DataTable schema that when executed creates a table in a SQL Server database. Recipe 11.11 uses both catalog views and information schema views to create relationships in a DataSet at runtime based on the relationships defined in the SQL Server database.

Recipe 11.12 shows you how to use ActiveX Database Objects Extensions for DDL and Security (ADOX) from .NET to create a new Microsoft Access database. You can use an OLE DB Connection object or ADOX to list the tables in a Microsoft Access database as shown in Recipe 11.13.

Recipe 11.14 shows you how to use the factory classes introduced in ADO.NET 2.0 to enumerate installed .NET data providers.

Every Windows system has OLE DB providers and ODBC drivers installed on it. You can examine the registry to get a list of which are installed. Recipe 11.15 does this for OLE DB providers while Recipe 11.16 does it for ODBC drivers. Recipe 11.15 also shows you how to use the OleDbEnumerator class and how to use an extended stored procedure to enumerate OLE DB providers.

Recipe 11.17 shows you how to programmatically change a SQL Server user password using the ChangePassword( ) method of the SqlConnection class, introduced in ADO.NET 2.0.

11.1   Enumerating SQL Servers

Problem

You need to get a list of SQL Servers available on the network.

Solution

Use either the `SmoApplication.EnumAvailableSqlServers()` method or the `SqlDataSourceEnumerator.Instance.GetDataSources()` method to retrieve details about each SQL Server on the network. The solution demonstrates both approaches. In each case the solution retrieves information about each available visible SQL Server and outputs those details to the console.

Both approaches use the SQL Server Browser service, which provides information about installed SQL Server instances. Start and stop the SQL Server Browser service using SQL Server Configuration Manager.

This solution needs a reference to the `Microsoft.SqlServer.Smo` assembly. You can download this assembly from Microsoft Download Center if it is not available on your computer.

The C# code in *Program.cs* in the project `EnumerateSqlServers` is shown in Example 11-1.

Example 11-1. File: Program.cs for EnumerateSqlServers solution

```csharp
using System;
using System.Data;
using System.Data.Sql;
using Microsoft.SqlServer.Management.Smo;

namespace EnumerateSqlServers
{
    class Program
    {
        static void Main(string[] args)
        {
            // Enumerate the SQL Servers using SMO
            DataTable dtSmo = SmoApplication.EnumAvailableSqlServers();
            Console.WriteLine(
                "---SmoApplication.EnumAvailableSqlServers()---");
            // Iterate over results and output results to console
            foreach (DataRow row in dtSmo.Rows)
            {
                foreach (DataColumn col in dtSmo.Columns)
                {
                    Console.WriteLine("{0} = {1}",
                        col.ColumnName, row[col.Ordinal]);
                }
                Console.WriteLine();
            }
```

```
            // Enumerate the SQL Servers using SqlDataSourceEnumerator
            DataTable dt =
                SqlDataSourceEnumerator.Instance.GetDataSources();
            Console.WriteLine(
                "---SqlDataSourceEnumerator.Instance.GetDataSources()---");
            // Iterate over results and output results to console
            foreach (DataRow row in dt.Rows)
                Console.WriteLine("ServerName = {0}\nInstanceName = {1}\n" +
                    "IsClustered = {2}\nVersion = {3}\n",
                    row["ServerName"], row["InstanceName"],
                    row["IsClustered"], row["Version"]);

            Console.WriteLine("Press any key to continue.");
            Console.ReadKey();
        }
    }
}
```

The output is shown in Figure 11-1.

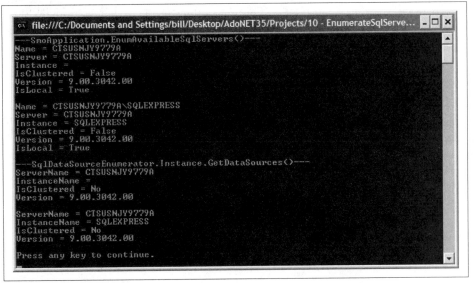

Figure 11-1. Output for EnumerateSqlServers solution

Discussion

The `SmoApplication.EnumAvailableSqlServers()` method enumerates a list of available and visible SQL Server instances into a `DataTable`. Two overloads allow the results to be filtered to the local instances or by machine name. The `SmoApplication` class represents a SQL Server Management Objects (SMO) application and is supported in .NET Framework 2.0 and later.

The `SqlDataSourceEnumerator.Instance.GetDataSources()` method also enumerates a list of available and visible SQL Server instances into a `DataTable`.

Neither method guarantees that the SQL Server instances being enumerated will respond in a timely manner. As a result, the returned list might not include all SQL Server instances and might be different on subsequent method calls. Server firewalls can also prevent either method from returning all instances.

11.2   Retrieving Database Metadata

Problem

You need to get schema information for the data source of a data connection.

Solution

Use the `GetSchema()` method of the `Connection` class.

The solution creates a connection to the `AdventureWorks` database. The following metadata information is retrieved and output to the console to demonstrate the three overloads of the `GetSchema()` method:

- Metadata collections for the connection
- Restriction collections for the connection
- Views in the Production schema

The C# code in *Program.cs* in the project `RetrieveDatabaseMetadata` is shown in Example 11-2.

Example 11-2. File: Program.cs for RetrieveDatabaseMetadata solution

```
using System;
using System.Collections;
using System.Data.SqlClient;
using System.Data;
using System.Data.Common;

namespace RetrieveDatabaseMetadata
{
    class Program
    {
        static void Main(string[] args)
        {
            string sqlConnectString = "Data Source=(local);" +
                "Integrated security=SSPI;Initial Catalog=AdventureWorks;";

            using (SqlConnection connection = new SqlConnection(sqlConnectString))
            {
                // Retrieve and output metadata collections
                connection.Open();
```

```
DataTable dt = connection.GetSchema(
    DbMetaDataCollectionNames.MetaDataCollections);
connection.Close( );

Console.WriteLine("---Metadata collections---");
foreach (DataRow row in dt.Rows)
    Console.WriteLine("{0}; {1}; {2}",
        row[0], row[1], row[2]);

// Retrieve and output restrictions
connection.Open( );
DataTable dtRestrictions =
    connection.GetSchema(DbMetaDataCollectionNames.Restrictions);
connection.Close( );

Console.WriteLine("\n---Restrictions--");
foreach (DataRow row in dtRestrictions.Rows)
    Console.WriteLine("{0} {1} {2} {3} {4}",
        row[0], row[1], row[2], row[3], row[4]);

// Retrieve and output Production views
Console.WriteLine("\n---Production views---");
connection.Open( );
string[] r = new string[] { null, "Production", null, "VIEW" };
DataTable dtTables = connection.GetSchema("Tables", r);
connection.Close( );

foreach (DataRow row in dtTables.Rows)
    Console.WriteLine("{0}.{1}.{2} {3}",
        row[0], row[1], row[2], row[3]);
    }

Console.WriteLine("\nPress any key to continue.");
Console.ReadKey( );
    }
  }
}
```

The output is shown in Figure 11-2.

Discussion

The schema discovery API introduced in ADO.NET 2.0 lets you programmatically find and return metadata about the database for a connection. The database-independent API exposes schema elements, including tables, columns, and stored procedures.

The first overload of the GetSchema( ) method of the DbConnectionClass takes no arguments and returns a DataTable containing information about metadata collections available for the connection. The DataTable three columns are described in Table 11-1.

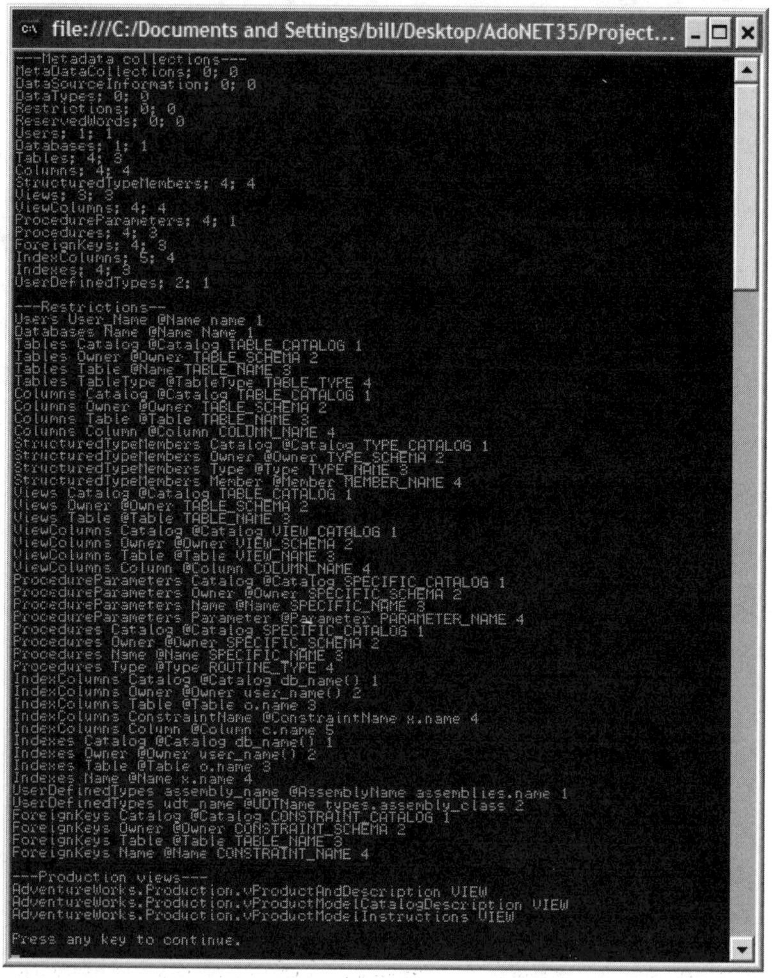

Figure 11-2. Output for RetrieveDatabaseMetadata solution

Table 11-1. Columns in DataTable object returned by GetSchema( )

Column name	Description
CollectionName	The metadata collection name.
NumberOfRestrictions	The maximum number of qualifiers for a metadata collection that can be used to restrict the scope of information returned.
NumberOfIdentifierParts	The maximum number of identifier parts.

The second overload of the GetSchema( ) method returns information about one of five categories of metadata as DataTable object. The overload takes an argument that specifies a CollectionName value returned from the GetSchema( ) method that takes no arguments or one of the values in the DbMetaDataCollectionNames class that provides constants to access five standard CollectionName values, as described in Table 11-2.

Table 11-2. DbMetaDataCollectionNames public fields

Collection name	Description
DataSourceInformation	Information about the database instance.
DataTypes	Information about data types that the database supports. This includes information about mapping data-source types to .NET Framework data types.
MetaDataCollections	List of metadata collections available.
ReservedWords	List of reserved words in the database.
Restrictions	Array of qualifiers for each metadata collection that can be used to restrict the scope of information returned. One value is returned per row with the position of the qualifier in the array specified by the RestrictionNumber column.

For example, the following statement returns metadata about the tables in the database:

```
DataTable dt = connection.GetSchema("Tables");
```

An extract from the result set follows.

TABLE_CATALOG	TABLE_SCHEMA	TABLE_NAME	TABLE_TYPE
AdventureWorks	dbo	AWBuildVersion	BASE TABLE
AdventureWorks	dbo	DatabaseLog	BASE TABLE
AdventureWorks	dbo	sysdiagrams	BASE TABLE
AdventureWorks	HumanResources	Department	BASE TABLE
...			
AdventureWorks	Sales	vSalesPerson	VIEW
AdventureWorks	Sales	vSalesPersonSales ByFiscalYears	VIEW
AdventureWorks	Sales	vStoreWith Demographics	VIEW

The third overload of GetSchema( ) takes two arguments: a string that specifies the collection name and a string array of restriction values as a second argument. Call the GetSchema( ) method with the DbMetaDataCollectionNames.Restrictions argument to get a valid list of restrictions for a metadata collection. There is one row per restriction—each restriction has a unique RestrictionNumber value. For example, for the Tables metadata collection in SQL Server, there are four restrictions.

Restriction name	Restriction default	Restriction ordinal
Catalog	TABLE_CATALOG	1
Owner	TABLE_SCHEMA	2
Table	TABLE_NAME	3
TableType	TABLE_TYPE	4

Continuing with the `Tables` metadata, the following code snippet uses restrictions to return information only for views in the `Production` schema:

```
string[] r = new string[] {null, "Production", null, "VIEW"};
DataTable dt = connection.GetSchema("Tables", r);
```

Support for `DbConnection.GetSchema()` is optional, so a data provider can choose to throw a `NotSupportedException`. There is no standard for the information returned when a metadata collection is queried—two providers can return different information (i.e., columns in the `DataTable` object) and support different restrictions.

11.3   Retrieving Database Schema Information from SQL Server

Problem

You need to retrieve database schema information from a SQL Server database.

Solution

Retrieve table schema information using the `GetSchema()` method of the `Connection` class, catalog views, information schema views, or the OLE DB .NET data provider `Connection` object. The solution demonstrates all four approaches.

For each approach, the solution retrieves a list of tables in the `AdventureWorks` sample database and outputs the first 10 tables to the console.

The C# code in *Program.cs* in the project `RetrieveDatabaseSchema` is shown in Example 11-3.

Example 11-3. File: Program.cs for RetrieveDatabaseSchema solution

```
using System;
using System.Data;
using System.Data.SqlClient;
using System.Data.OleDb;

namespace RetrieveDatabaseSchema
{
    class Program
    {
        static void Main(string[] args)
        {
            string sqlConnectString = "Data Source=(local);" +
                "Integrated security=SSPI;Initial Catalog=AdventureWorks;";

            string oledbConnectString = "Provider=SQLOLEDB;" +
                "Data Source=(local);Integrated Security=SSPI;" +
                "Initial Catalog=AdventureWorks";
```

Example 11-3. File: Program.cs for RetrieveDatabaseSchema solution (continued)

```csharp
DataTable dtSchema;
SqlDataAdapter da;

// Retrieve table list using Connection.GetSchema( )
SqlConnection conn = new SqlConnection(sqlConnectString);
conn.Open( );
dtSchema = conn.GetSchema("Tables");
conn.Close( );

Console.WriteLine(
    "---Top 10 tables names using Connection.GetSchema( )---");
for (int i = 0; i < 10; i++)
{
    Console.WriteLine("{0}.{1}.{2}",
        dtSchema.Rows[i]["TABLE_CATALOG"],
        dtSchema.Rows[i]["TABLE_SCHEMA"],
        dtSchema.Rows[i]["TABLE_NAME"]);
}

// Retrieve table list using catalog views
string sqlCV = "SELECT TOP 10 'AdventureWorks' CatalogName, " +
    "s.name SchemaName, t.name TableName " +
    "FROM sys.tables t JOIN sys.schemas s " +
    "ON t.schema_id = s.schema_id " +
    "ORDER BY CatalogName, SchemaName, TableName";

da = new SqlDataAdapter(sqlCV, sqlConnectString);
dtSchema = new DataTable( );
da.Fill(dtSchema);

Console.WriteLine(
    "\n---Top 10 tables names using catalog views---");
foreach (DataRow row in dtSchema.Rows)
    Console.WriteLine("{0}.{1}.{2}", row["CatalogName"],
        row["SchemaName"], row["TableName"]);

// Retrieve table list using INFORMATION_SCHEMA views
string sqlISV = "SELECT TOP 10 * " +
    "FROM INFORMATION_SCHEMA.TABLES " +
    "WHERE TABLE_TYPE = 'BASE TABLE' " +
    "ORDER BY TABLE_CATALOG, TABLE_SCHEMA, TABLE_NAME";

da = new SqlDataAdapter(sqlISV, sqlConnectString);
dtSchema = new DataTable( );
da.Fill(dtSchema);

Console.WriteLine(
    "\n---Top 10 table names using INFORMATION_SCHEMA.TABLES---");
foreach (DataRow row in dtSchema.Rows)
    Console.WriteLine("{0}.{1}.{2}", row["TABLE_CATALOG"],
        row["TABLE_SCHEMA"], row["TABLE_NAME"]);
```

```
                // Open an OLE DB connection and get the schema table
                OleDbConnection connection = new OleDbConnection(oledbConnectString);
                connection.Open( );
                dtSchema.Clear( );
                dtSchema = connection.GetOleDbSchemaTable(OleDbSchemaGuid.Tables,
                    new object[] { null, null, null, "TABLE" });
                connection.Close( );

                Console.WriteLine(
                    "\n---Top 10 table names using OleDbConnection.GetOleDbSchemaTable---");
                for (int i = 0; i < 10; i++)
                    Console.WriteLine("{0}.{1}.{2}", dtSchema.Rows[i]["TABLE_CATALOG"],
                        dtSchema.Rows[i]["TABLE_SCHEMA"], dtSchema.Rows[i]["TABLE_NAME"]);

                Console.WriteLine("\nPress any key to continue.");
                Console.ReadKey( );
            }
        }
}
```

The output is shown in Figure 11-3.

Discussion

The following subsections discuss the four approaches demonstrated in the solution.

Connection.GetSchema( ) method

ADO.NET 2.0 introduced the GetSchema( ) method of the Connection class that retrieves schema information from the database specified by the connection. The GetSchema( ) method has three overloads:

```
DataTable GetSchema( )
DataTable GetSchema(string collectionName)
DataTable GetSchema(string collectionName, string[] restrictionValue)
```

Where:

collectionName
    The name of the schema to return.

restrictionValue
    A set of restriction values for the requested schema.

The overload of GetSchema( ) that takes no parameters returns a DataTable containing information about the different available schemas, including Tables, Columns, Views, Procedures, and Indexes that can be accessed using the other two overloads of GetSchema( ). These two overloads that take parameters return a DataTable containing metadata for the specified schema. The solution retrieves and displays information from the Tables schema.

```
---Top 10 tables names using Connection.GetSchema()---
AdventureWorks.Production.ProductProductPhoto
AdventureWorks.Sales.StoreContact
AdventureWorks.Person.Address
AdventureWorks.Production.ProductReview
AdventureWorks.Production.TransactionHistory
AdventureWorks.Person.AddressType
AdventureWorks.Production.ProductSubcategory
AdventureWorks.Person.vAdditionalContactInfo
AdventureWorks.dbo.AWBuildVersion
AdventureWorks.HumanResources.vEmployee

---Top 10 tables names using catalog views---
AdventureWorks.dbo.AWBuildVersion
AdventureWorks.dbo.DatabaseLog
AdventureWorks.dbo.ErrorLog
AdventureWorks.dbo.sysdiagrams
AdventureWorks.HumanResources.Department
AdventureWorks.HumanResources.Employee
AdventureWorks.HumanResources.EmployeeAddress
AdventureWorks.HumanResources.EmployeeDepartmentHistory
AdventureWorks.HumanResources.EmployeePayHistory
AdventureWorks.HumanResources.JobCandidate

---Top 10 table names using INFORMATION_SCHEMA.TABLES---
AdventureWorks.dbo.AWBuildVersion
AdventureWorks.dbo.DatabaseLog
AdventureWorks.dbo.ErrorLog
AdventureWorks.dbo.sysdiagrams
AdventureWorks.HumanResources.Department
AdventureWorks.HumanResources.Employee
AdventureWorks.HumanResources.EmployeeAddress
AdventureWorks.HumanResources.EmployeeDepartmentHistory
AdventureWorks.HumanResources.EmployeePayHistory
AdventureWorks.HumanResources.JobCandidate

---Top 10 table names using OleDbConnection.GetOleDbSchemaTable---
AdventureWorks.dbo.AWBuildVersion
AdventureWorks.dbo.DatabaseLog
AdventureWorks.dbo.ErrorLog
AdventureWorks.dbo.sysdiagrams
AdventureWorks.HumanResources.Department
AdventureWorks.HumanResources.Employee
AdventureWorks.HumanResources.EmployeeAddress
AdventureWorks.HumanResources.EmployeeDepartmentHistory
AdventureWorks.HumanResources.EmployeePayHistory
AdventureWorks.HumanResources.JobCandidate

Press any key to continue.
```

Figure 11-3. Output for RetrieveDatabaseSchema solution

For more information about the GetSchema( ) method and the available collections and restrictions, see Recipe 11.2.

Catalog views

Catalog views were introduced in SQL Server 2005 and are used to return information used by the SQL Server Database Engine. Microsoft recommends using catalog views because they provide the most general interface to catalog metadata and the most efficient way to get and present this information. All user-available catalog metadata is exposed through catalog views. Catalog views don't expose information about replication, backup, Database Maintenance Plan, or SQL Server Agent.

Catalog views are defined within each database in a schema named sys. The metadata returned is limited to that which the user has permission to view. To access a catalog view, simply specify the fully qualified view name. In the solution, the view for the tables is accessed through the following syntax:

```
sys.tables
```

Table 11-3 categorizes the available catalog views and briefly describes the information exposed within each category.

Table 11-3. Catalog view categories

Category	Description
CLR Assembly	Assemblies, assembly files, assembly references
Database and Files	Backup devices, databases, database recovery status, database files, database mirroring, master files
Database Mirroring Witness	Database mirroring witnesses
Data Spaces and Full Text	Data spaces, destination data spaces, filegroups, full-text catalogs, full-text document types, full-text index catalog usages, partition schemes
Endpoints	Database mirroring endpoints, endpoints, web method endpoints, HTTP endpoints, service broker endpoints, SOAP endpoints, TCP endpoints, VIA endpoints
Extended Properties	Database extended properties
Linked Servers	Linked logins, remote logins, registered linked and remote servers
Messages (For Errors)	System-defined and user-defined error messages
Objects	Allocation units, assembly modules, check constraints, columns, computed columns, default constraints, events, event notifications, extended properties, foreign keys, foreign key columns, numbered procedures, numbered procedure parameters, objects, parameters, partitions, procedures, service queues, SQL entity dependencies, statistics, statistics columns, SQL language-defined modules
Partition Function	Partition functions, partition parameters, partition range values
Scalar Types	Assembly types, system and user-defined types
Schemas	Database schemas
Security	Database permissions, database principals, database role members, master key passwords
Service Broker	Conversation endpoints, conversation groups, remote service bindings, routes, service contracts, service contract message usages, service contract usages, service message types, service queue usages, services, transmission queue
Server-Wide Configuration	Server-wide configuration options, full-text languages, traces, trace categories, trace columns, trace events, trace event bindings, trace subclass values
XML Schemas (XML Type System)	Column XML schema usage, XML schema attributes, XML schema component placements, XML schema components, XML schema elements, XML schema facets, XML indexes, parameter XML schema collection usages, XML schema model groups, XML schema collections, XML schema namespaces, XML schema types, XML schema wildcard namespaces, XML schema wildcards

Information schema views

Information schema views were introduced in SQL Server 7.0 and provide system-table-independent access to SQL Server metadata. Although based on the sysobjects and syscomments system tables, the views allow applications to continue to work properly even if the system tables change. They provide an alternative to the system stored procedures that were previously used and are still available. The INFORMATION_SCHEMA views conform to the SQL-92 Standard. Information schema views do not contain any metadata specific to SQL Server 2005 or later.

Information schema views are defined within each database in a schema named INFORMATION_SCHEMA. The metadata returned is limited to that which the user has permission to view. To access an information schema view, simply specify the fully qualified view name. In the solution, the view for the tables is accessed through the following syntax:

```
INFORMATION_SCHEMA.TABLES
```

Table 11-4 lists the information schema views available in SQL Server.

Table 11-4. Information schema views

Name	Description
CHECK CONSTRAINTS	CHECK constraints
COLUMN_DOMAIN_USAGE	Columns that have a user-defined data type
COLUMN_PRIVILEGES	Columns with a privilege granted to or by the current user
COLUMNS	All columns
CONSTRAINT_COLUMN_USAGE	Columns that have a constraint defined on them
CONSTRAINT_TABLE_USAGE	Tables that have a constraint defined on them
DOMAIN_CONSTRAINTS	User-defined data types with a rule bound to them
DOMAINS	All user-defined data types
KEY_COLUMN_USAGE	Columns constrained as a key
PARAMETERS	All parameters for user-defined functions and stored procedures
REFERENTIAL_CONSTRAINTS	All foreign constraints
ROUTINE_COLUMNS	Columns returned by table-valued functions
ROUTINES	All user-defined functions and stored procedures
SCHEMATA	All databases
TABLE_CONSTRAINTS	All table constraints
TABLE_PRIVILEGES	Tables with a privilege granted to or by the current user
TABLES	All tables
VIEW_COLUMN_USAGE	Columns used in a view definition
VIEW_TABLE_USAGE	Tables used in a view
VIEWS	All views

The metadata returned will be limited to that which the user has permission to view. Like any other views, information schema views can also be joined in queries or participate in complex queries to extract specific information. For detailed information about the different views available, refer to SQL Server Books Online.

The solution shows how to retrieve table metadata using the INFORMATION_SCHEMA.TABLES view. It returns data as shown in Table 11-5.

Table 11-5. INFORMATION_SCHEMA.TABLES metadata

Column name	Data type	Description
TABLE_CATALOG	nvarchar(128)	Database name
TABLE_SCHEMA	nvarchar(128)	Table owner
TABLE_NAME	sysname	Table name
TABLE_TYPE	varchar(10)	Table type (either BASE_TABLE or VIEW)

The TABLES view is queried for all columns where the table type is BASE_TABLE in order to return only information about tables and not views.

OleDbConnection.GetOleDbSchemaTable( ) method

The GetOleDbSchemaTable( ) method of the OleDbConnection object returns schema information from a database as specified by a GUID value enumerated in the OleDbSchemaGuid class and detailed in Table 11-6.

Table 11-6. OleDbSchemaGuid public fields

Field	Description
Assertions	Assertions
Catalogs	Physical attributes and assertions for catalogs accessible from the data source
Character_Sets	Character sets
Check_Constraints	Check constraints
Check_Constraints_By_Table	Check constraints defined for a catalog
Collations	Character collations
Columns	Columns in tables and view
Column_Domain_Usage	Columns that are dependant on a domain defined in the catalog
Column_Privileges	Privileges on columns
Constraint_Column_Usage	Columns used by referential constraints, unique constraints, check constraints, and assertions
Constraint_Table_Usage	Tables used by referential constraints, unique constraints, check constraints, and assertions

Table 11-6. OleDbSchemaGuid public fields (continued)

Field	Description
DbInfoLiterals	Provider-specific literals used in text commands
Foreign_Keys	Foreign key columns
Indexes	Indexes
Key_Column_Usage	Columns constrained as keys
Primary_Keys	Columns that comprise primary keys
Procedures	Procedures
Procedure_Columns	Columns of row sets returned by procedures
Procedure_Parameters	Parameters and return codes of procedures
Provider_Types	Base data types supported by the .NET data provider for OLE DB
Referential_Constraints	Referential constraints
Schemata	Schema objects
Sql_Languages	Conformance levels, options, and dialects supported by the SQL implementation processing data
Statistics	Statistics
Tables	Tables and views
Tables_Info	Tables and views
Table_Constraints	Table constraints
Table_Privileges	Table privileges
Table_Statistics	Available statistics on tables
Translations	Defined character translations
Trustee	Trustee defined in the data source
Usage_Privileges	USAGE privileges on objects
Views	Views
View_Column_Usage	Columns in views
View_Table_Usage	Tables in views

In addition to taking the GUID schema argument, you can further restrict the results of the GetOleDbSchemaTable( ) through the second argument, which is an object array specifying column restrictions applied to the result columns in the order in which they are returned. In this example, the schema argument is Tables, which returns a four-column result set containing all tables and views in the database. The fourth column describes the table type; specifying TABLE as the fourth object in the restrictions object array limits the result set to user tables.

11.4   Retrieving Column Default Values from SQL Server

Problem

The DataColumn object exposes a Default property. While the FillSchema( ) method of the DataAdapter returns schema information, it does not include the default values for columns. You want to retrieve the default values of columns in a SQL Server table.

Solution

Retrieve default values using catalog views or the system stored procedure sp_ helpconstraint. The solution demonstrates both approaches.

For each approach, the solution retrieves and outputs default values for the columns in the HumanResources.Employee table in AdventureWorks.

The C# code in *Program.cs* in the project RetrieveColumnDefaultValueSqlServer is shown in Example 11-4.

Example 11-4. File: Program.cs for RetrieveColumnDefaultValueSqlServer solution

```
using System;
using System.Data;
using System.Data.SqlClient;

namespace RetrieveColumnDefaultValueSqlServer
{
    class Program
    {
        private static string schemaName = "HumanResources";
        private static string tableName = "Employee";

        static void Main(string[] args)
        {
            string sqlConnectString = "Data Source=(local);" +
                "Integrated security=SSPI;Initial Catalog=AdventureWorks;";
            string sqlSelect = "SELECT * FROM " + schemaName + "." + tableName;

            SqlDataAdapter da = new SqlDataAdapter(sqlSelect, sqlConnectString);
            DataTable dt = new DataTable( );
            da.FillSchema(dt, SchemaType.Source);

            // output column names and default values from the DataTable
            Console.WriteLine("---Column names and default values using " +
                "DataAdapter.FillSchema( )---");
            foreach (DataColumn col in dt.Columns)
                Console.WriteLine("{0} -> DefaultValue = {1}",
                    col.ColumnName, col.DefaultValue);
```

Example 11-4. File: Program.cs for RetrieveColumnDefaultValueSqlServer solution (continued)

```csharp
// get the column defaults from catalog views
string sqlDCV = "SELECT c.column_id, c.name, dc.definition " +
    "FROM sys.tables t " +
    "JOIN sys.default_constraints dc " +
    "ON t.object_id = dc.parent_object_id " +
    "JOIN sys.columns c " +
    "ON t.object_id = c.object_id " +
    "AND dc.parent_column_id = c.column_id " +
    "WHERE t.name = '" + tableName + "'";

SqlDataAdapter daDCV = new SqlDataAdapter(sqlDCV, sqlConnectString);
DataTable dtDCV = new DataTable();
daDCV.Fill(dtDCV);
dtDCV.PrimaryKey = new DataColumn[] {dtDCV.Columns["column_id"]};

// output column names and default values
Console.WriteLine(
    "\n---Column names and default values using catalog views---");
foreach (DataColumn col in dt.Columns)
{
    // find the default value for the column if it exists
    DataRow row = dtDCV.Rows.Find(col.Ordinal + 1);
    string defaultValue =
        row != null ? row["definition"].ToString() : null;
    Console.WriteLine("{0} -> DefaultValue = {1}",
        col.ColumnName, defaultValue);
}

// get the column defaults using the stored procedure sp_help
SqlConnection connectionSPH = new SqlConnection(sqlConnectString);
SqlCommand commandSPH =
    new SqlCommand("sp_helpconstraint", connectionSPH);
commandSPH.CommandType = CommandType.StoredProcedure;
commandSPH.Parameters.Add("@objname", SqlDbType.NVarChar, 776);
commandSPH.Parameters[0].Value = schemaName + "." + tableName;

SqlDataAdapter daSPH = new SqlDataAdapter(commandSPH);
DataSet dsSPH = new DataSet();
daSPH.Fill(dsSPH);
// Constraint information is in the second table returned by
// sp_helpconstraint
DataTable dtSPH = dsSPH.Tables[1];
// Delete the non-default constraints; rename defaults to column name
foreach (DataRow row in dtSPH.Rows)
{
    if (row["constraint_type"].ToString().StartsWith(
        "DEFAULT on column"))
    {
        // default constraint -- strip off the prefix leaving
        // only the column name
        row["constraint_type"] =
            row["constraint_type"].ToString().Substring(18);
```

```
            }
            else
                row.Delete( );
        }

        // set the primary key to the "constraint_type" column -- now the
        // column name
        dtSPH.PrimaryKey =
            new DataColumn[] { dtSPH.Columns["constraint_type"] };

        // output columns names and default values
        Console.WriteLine(
            "\n---Column names and default values using sp_help---");
        foreach (DataColumn col in dt.Columns)
        {
            // find the default value for the column if it exists
            DataRow row = dtSPH.Rows.Find(col.ColumnName);
            string defaultValue =
                row != null ? row["constraint_keys"].ToString( ) : null;
            Console.WriteLine("{0} -> DefaultValue = {1}",
                col.ColumnName, defaultValue);
        }

        Console.WriteLine("\nPress any key to continue.");
        Console.ReadKey( );
    }
  }
}
```

The output is shown in Figure 11-4.

Discussion

The following subsections discuss the two approaches demonstrated in the solution.

Catalog views

The sys.default_constraints catalog view contains a row for each object that is a default definition. The column default value is accessible through the definition column of the sys.default_constraints catalog view. The default values for the columns in a table are accessed using a query that joins the sys.table view (to specify the table) to the sys.columns view (to retrieve the columns for the table) to the sys.default_constraints view (to get the default value for each column).

For more information about catalog views, see the discussion in Recipe 11.3.

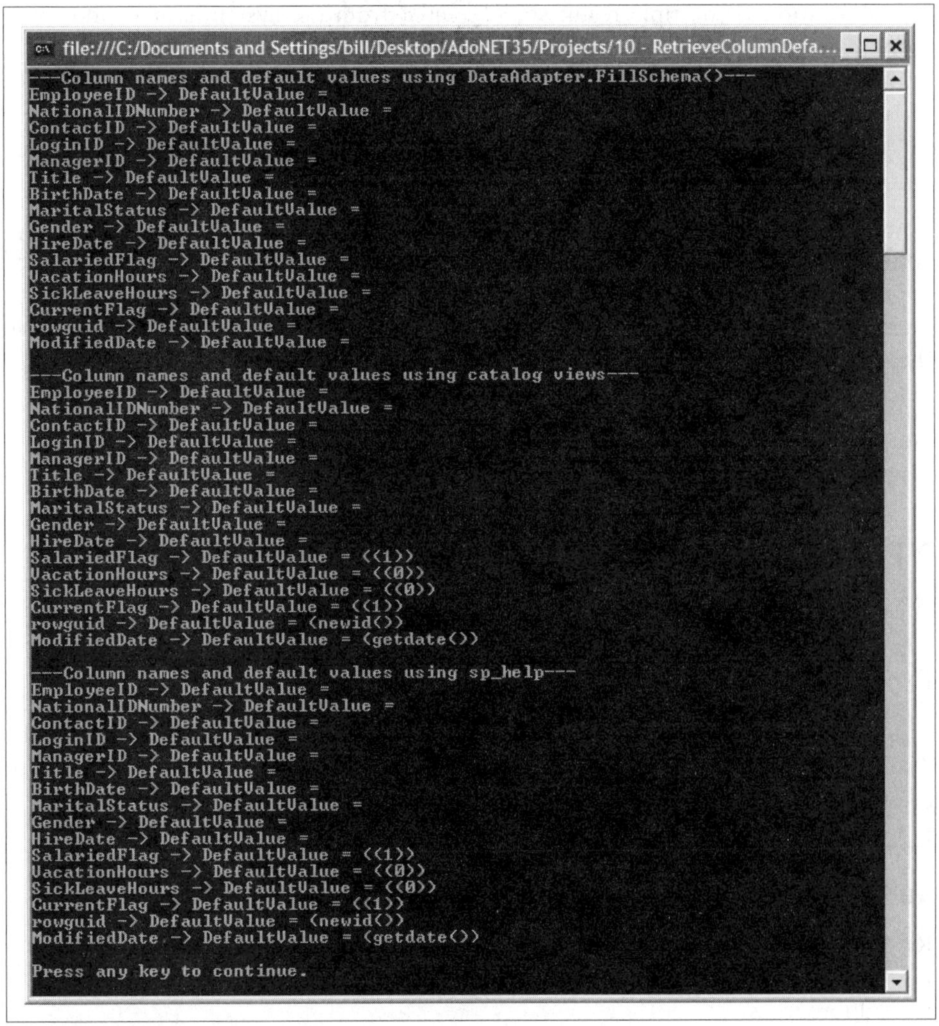

Figure 11-4. Output for RetrieveColumnDefaultValueSqlServer solution

sp_helpconstraint system stored procedure

The default value for a column in SQL Server is stored as a DEFAULT constraint. The system stored procedure sp_helpconstraint returns information about all constraints on a table. The procedure takes one mandatory parameter that specifies the table for which to return the constraint information.

The first column that the stored procedure returns is called constraint_type. As its name suggests, it specifies the type of constraint using the following pattern {constraint_type} [on column {column_name}].

In the solution, a multiple result set is created from the system stored procedure sp_helpconstraint specifying the HumanResources table in AdventureWorks. The second table contains the constraint information. The constraint_type column in the second table is examined for each row to determine whether it begins with the phrase DEFAULT on column indicating a default constraint. For default constraints, the column name is the string following the word column in the constraint_type column.

Once the default constraints have been identified, the overloaded constraint_keys column contains the default value for the column. The default value is surrounded by parentheses as well as delimiters for non-numeric fields—for example, single quotes by default in SQL Server for dates and strings, and an additional prefix N in the case of Unicode strings. These delimiters need to be stripped from the value before it can be assigned to the DefaultValue property for the column.

For more information about the sp_helpconstraint system stored procedure, see Microsoft SQL Server Books Online.

11.5 Determining the Length of Columns in a SQL Server Table

Problem

The FillSchema() method of the DataAdapter returns the correct length in the MaxLength property for string columns in a SQL Server database, but it returns –1 for the length of all other fields. You need to get the length of columns other than string type columns.

Solution

Retrieve table schema information using DataReader.GetSchematable() method, catalog views, or the system stored procedure sp_help. The solution demonstrates all three approaches.

For each approach, the solution retrieves size, precision, and scale for each column in the HumanResources.Employee table in the AdventureWorks sample database and outputs those values to the console.

The C# code in *Program.cs* in the project RetrieveColumnLengthSqlServer is shown in Example 11-5.

Example 11-5. File: Program.cs for RetrieveColumnLengthSqlServer solution

```
using System;
using System.Data;
using System.Data.SqlClient;

namespace RetrieveColumnLengthSqlServer
{
```

```csharp
class Program
{
    private static string schemaName = "HumanResources";
    private static string tableName = "Employee";

    static void Main(string[] args)
    {
        string sqlConnectString = "Data Source=(local);" +
            "Integrated security=SSPI;Initial Catalog=AdventureWorks;";
        string sqlSelect = "SELECT * FROM " + schemaName + "." + tableName;

        SqlDataAdapter da = new SqlDataAdapter(sqlSelect, sqlConnectString);
        DataTable dt = new DataTable( );
        da.FillSchema(dt, SchemaType.Source);

        // output column max length using DataAdapter.FillSchema( ) results
        Console.WriteLine("---Column names and length using " +
            "DataAdapter.FillSchema( )---");
        foreach (DataColumn col in dt.Columns)
            Console.WriteLine("{0} -> MaxLength = {1}",
                col.ColumnName, col.MaxLength);

        // get the column sizes using DataReader.GetSchemaTable( )
        SqlConnection connectionGST = new SqlConnection(sqlConnectString);
        SqlCommand commandGST = new SqlCommand(sqlSelect, connectionGST);
        connectionGST.Open( );
        SqlDataReader dr = commandGST.ExecuteReader( );
        DataTable dtGST = dr.GetSchemaTable( );
        connectionGST.Close( );
        // make the ColumnOrdinal the primary key
        dtGST.PrimaryKey = new DataColumn[] { dtGST.Columns["ColumnOrdinal"] };

        // output columns and sizes
        Console.WriteLine(
            "\n---Column names and sizes using DataReader.GetSchemaTable( )---");
        foreach (DataColumn col in dt.Columns)
        {
            // find the column sizes
            DataRow row = dtGST.Rows.Find(col.Ordinal);
            Console.WriteLine(
                "{0}\tMaxLength = {1}\tPrecision = {2}\tScale = {3}",
                col.ColumnName.PadRight(16), row["ColumnSize"],
                row["NumericPrecision"], row["NumericScale"]);
        }

        // get the column sizes from catalog views
        string sqlCS =
            "SELECT c.column_id, c.name, c.max_length, c.precision, c.scale " +
            "FROM sys.tables t " +
            "JOIN sys.columns c ON t.object_id = c.object_id " +
            "WHERE t.name = '" + tableName + "'";
```

```
        SqlDataAdapter daCS = new SqlDataAdapter(sqlCS, sqlConnectString);
        DataTable dtCS = new DataTable( );
        daCS.Fill(dtCS);
        dtCS.PrimaryKey = new DataColumn[] { dtCS.Columns["column_id"] };

        // output columns and sizes
        Console.WriteLine("\n---Column names and sizes using catalog views---");
        foreach (DataColumn col in dt.Columns)
        {
            // find the column sizes
            DataRow row = dtCS.Rows.Find(col.Ordinal + 1);
            if (row != null)
            {
                Console.WriteLine(
                    "{0}\tMaxLength = {1}\tPrecision = {2}\tScale = {3}",
                    col.ColumnName.PadRight(16), row["max_length"],
                    row["precision"], row["scale"]);
            }
        }

        // get the column sizes using the stored procedure sp_help
        SqlConnection connectionSPH = new SqlConnection(sqlConnectString);
        SqlCommand commandSPH = new SqlCommand("sp_help", connectionSPH);
        commandSPH.CommandType = CommandType.StoredProcedure;
        commandSPH.Parameters.Add("@objname", SqlDbType.NVarChar, 776);
        commandSPH.Parameters[0].Value = schemaName + "." + tableName;

        SqlDataAdapter daSPH = new SqlDataAdapter(commandSPH);
        DataSet dsSPH = new DataSet( );
        daSPH.Fill(dsSPH);
        DataTable dtSPH = dsSPH.Tables[1];

        dtSPH.PrimaryKey = new DataColumn[] { dtSPH.Columns["Column_name"] };

        // output columns names and sizes
        Console.WriteLine("\n---Column names and sizes using sp_help---");
        foreach (DataColumn col in dt.Columns)
        {
            // find the column sizes
            DataRow row = dtSPH.Rows.Find(col.ColumnName);
            Console.WriteLine(
                "{0}\tMaxLength = {1}\tPrecision = {2}\tScale = {3}",
                col.ColumnName.PadRight(16), row["Length"], row["Prec"],
                row["Scale"]);
        }

        Console.WriteLine("\nPress any key to continue.");
        Console.ReadKey( );
    }
  }
}
```

The output is shown in Figure 11-5.

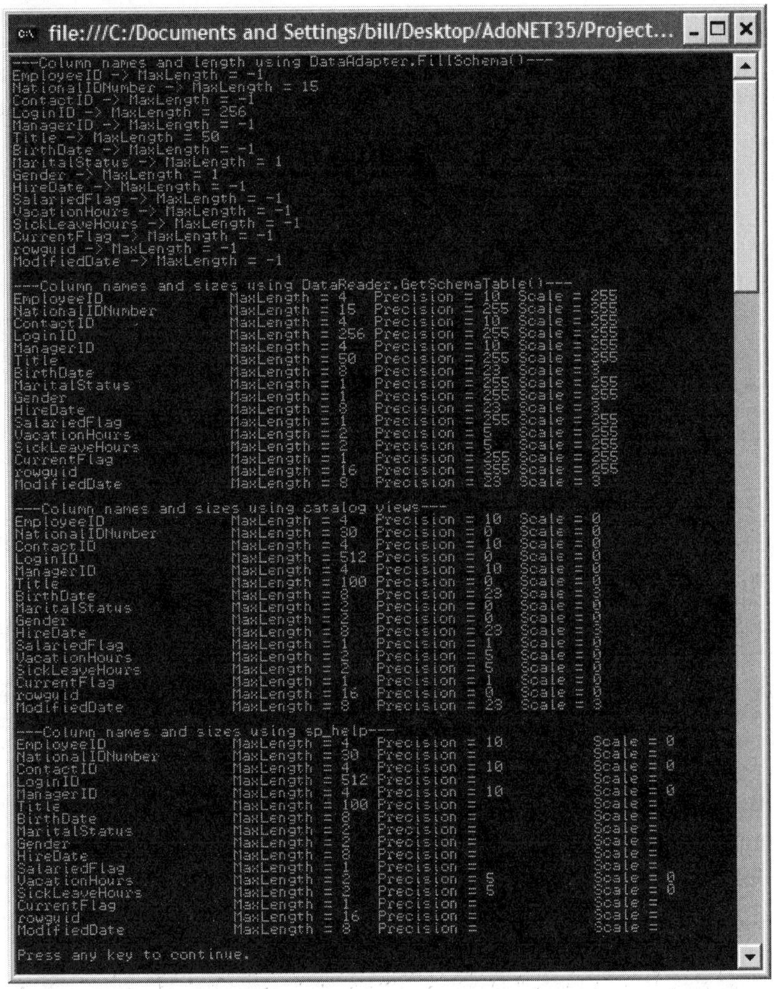

Figure 11-5. Output for RetrieveColumnLengthSqlServer solution

Discussion

The following subsections discuss the three approaches demonstrated in the solution.

DataReader.GetSchemaTable( )

The `GetSchemaTable( )` method of the `DataReader` returns column metadata. The method returns a `DataTable` containing values for column size (`ColumnSize`), precision (`NumericPrecision`), and scale (`NumericScale`). These values are null (255) for non-numeric columns.

For more information about the `GetSchemaTable( )` method, see the discussion for Recipe 6.4.

Catalog views

The `sys.columns` catalog view contains a row for each database column. The row includes values for the column size (`max_length`), precision (`precision`), and scale (`scale`). The size information for all columns in a table is accessed using a query that joins the `sys.table` view (to specify the table) to the `sys.columns` view (to retrieve the columns for the table).

The column length returned by the `sys.columns` catalog view is in bytes, meaning that Unicode data types (nchar, nvarchar, and ntext) report double the value of the `MaxLength` property of the column object, which indicates how many characters can be stored in the column. For example, the `NationalID` column reports a size of 30—the number of characters required to store nvarchar(15)—rather than the maximum string length 15.

For more information about catalog views, see Recipe 11.3.

sp_help system stored procedure

The system stored procedure `sp_help` returns, in addition to the length of all fields, the precision and scale of columns as appropriate.

The `sp_help` system stored procedure takes one optional parameter. When this parameter is the name of a table object, the result set returns data including the length, precision, and scale of each column in columns named `Length`, `Prec`, and `Scale`.

The column length returned by the `sp_help` is in bytes, meaning that Unicode data types (nchar, nvarchar, and ntext) report double the value of the `MaxLength` property of the column object, which indicates how many characters can be stored in the column. For example, the `NationalID` column reports a size of 30—the number of characters required to store nvarchar(15)—rather than the maximum string length 15.

For more information about the `sp_help` system stored procedure, refer to Microsoft SQL Server Books Online.

11.6 Retrieving a SQL Server Query Plan

Problem

You need to retrieve information about how query statements are executed by the SQL Server.

Solution

Use the `SET SHOWPLAN_TEXT` statement.

The sample code executes the SET SHOWPLAN_TEXT statement, using the ExecuteNonQuery( ) method of the Command object, to retrieve how query statements are executed by the SQL Server.

The C# code in *Program.cs* in the project RetrieveSqlServerQueryPlan is shown in Example 11-6.

Example 11-6. File: Program.cs for RetrieveSqlServerQueryPlan solution

```
using System;
using System.Data;
using System.Data.SqlClient;

namespace RetrieveSqlServerQueryPlan
{
    class Program
    {
        static void Main(string[] args)
        {
            string sqlConnectString = "Data Source=(local);" +
                "Integrated security=SSPI;Initial Catalog=AdventureWorks;";

            string sqlSelect = "SELECT * FROM Person.Contact WHERE " +
                "LastName LIKE 'A%' ORDER BY LastName, FirstName";

            SqlConnection connection =
                new SqlConnection(sqlConnectString);

            // Create and execute the command to retrieve the plan.
            SqlCommand command = new SqlCommand("SET SHOWPLAN_TEXT ON", connection);
            connection.Open( );
            command.ExecuteNonQuery( );

            // Create the command to get the plan for.
            command.CommandText = sqlSelect;

            // Retrieve the plan into DataReader.
            SqlDataReader dr = command.ExecuteReader( );

            // Iterate over all result sets and all rows to get plan.
            do
            {
                while (dr.Read( ))
                    Console.WriteLine(dr.GetString(0));
                Console.WriteLine( );
            } while (dr.NextResult( ));
            dr.Close( );

            // Create and execute the command to retrieve query results.
            command = new SqlCommand("SET SHOWPLAN_TEXT OFF", connection);
            command.ExecuteNonQuery( );
```

Example 11-6. File: Program.cs for RetrieveSqlServerQueryPlan solution (continued)

```
            connection.Close( );

            Console.WriteLine("\nPress any key to continue.");
            Console.ReadKey( );
        }
    }
}
```

The output is shown in Figure 11-6.

Figure 11-6. Output for RetrieveSqlServerQueryPlan solution

Discussion

The SQL SET statement alters current session handling of specific information. Table 11-7 describes the categories of SET statements.

Table 11-7. SET statement categories

Category	Description
Date and Time	Alters current session settings for handling of date and time data
Locking	Alters current session settings for handling SQL Server locking
Miscellaneous	Alters current session settings for miscellaneous SQL Server functionality
Query Execution	Alters current session settings for query execution and processing
SQL-92 Settings	Alters current session settings for using SQL-92 default settings
Statistics	Alters current session settings for displaying statistics
Transactions	Alters current session settings for handling SQL Server Transactions

When SHOWPLAN_TEXT (from the Query Execution category) is ON, SQL Server returns a result set containing detailed information about how the SQL statements are going to be executed, rather than actually executing the statements. Two result sets are returned for each statement, both containing a single column StmtText. The first result set contains the SQL statement while the second contains rows detailing the plan. For batch SQL statements, the result sets alternate between statement and plan for each statement in the batch.

SHOWPLAN_TEXT does not need to be explicitly set to OFF. It only affects the command issued subsequent to the statement in which it is SET ON, not all of the commands executed while the connection object is open.

SHOWPLAN_ALL returns more information about the plan than just the StmtText column but is turned on and off in the same way.

For more information about the SET statement, SHOWPLAN_TEXT, or SHOWPLAN_ALL, see the topic "SET statement" in Microsoft SQL Server Books Online.

11.7 Retrieving SQL Server Column Metadata Without Returning Data

Problem

You need to retrieve the column metadata from a SQL Server command or stored procedure without returning any data.

Solution

Use the SET FMTONLY ON statement.

The sample code creates and executes a query statement to retrieve only column metadata from the Person.Contact table in the AdventureWorks sample database. A new DataTable is created from this information.

The C# code in *Program.cs* in the project RetrieveSqlServerColumnMetadata is shown in Example 11-7.

Example 11-7. File: Program.cs for RetrieveSqlServerColumnMetadata solution

```
using System;
using System.Data;
using System.Data.SqlClient;

namespace RetrieveSqlServerColumnMetadata
{
    class Program
    {
        static void Main(string[] args)
        {
            string sqlConnectString = "Data Source=(local);" +
                "Integrated security=SSPI;Initial Catalog=AdventureWorks;";

            // Create the T-SQL statement to retrieve only the column schema.
            string sqlText = "SET FMTONLY ON;" +
                "SELECT * FROM Person.Contact;" +
                "SET FMTONLY OFF;";

            // Use a DataAdapter to fill the DataTable.
```

```
        SqlDataAdapter da = new SqlDataAdapter(sqlText, sqlConnectString);
        da.MissingSchemaAction = MissingSchemaAction.AddWithKey;
        DataTable dt = new DataTable( );
        da.Fill(dt);

        // Output partial column metadata to console
        foreach (DataColumn col in dt.Columns)
            Console.WriteLine(
                "Name={0}; DataType={1}; MaxLength={2}; AllowDBNull={3}",
                col.ColumnName, col.DataType, col.MaxLength, col.AllowDBNull);

        Console.WriteLine("\nPress any key to continue.");
        Console.ReadKey( );
    }
  }
}
```

The output is shown in Figure 11-7.

Figure 11-7. Output for RetrieveSqlServerColumnMetaData solution

Discussion

When SET FMTONLY is ON, no rows are processed or sent to a client when a SQL statement or stored procedure is executed; only metadata is returned to the client. The DataTable created is identical to one that would have been created if the SQL command used a WHERE clause that returned an empty result set. This lets you test the format of a query response without actually using a query.

Recipe 11.6 discusses the SQL SET statement in more detail.

For more information about the SET FMTONLY statement, see the topic "SET" in Microsoft SQL Server Books Online.

11.8 Creating a New SQL Server Database

Problem

You need to create a new database in your SQL Server.

Solution

Create the database using either SQL Management Objects (SMO) or using the CREATE DATABASE T-SQL data definition language (DDL) statement. The solution demonstrates both approaches.

The solution first uses SMO objects to create a new database called MySmoDatabase. Next, the solution executes a CREATE DATABASE T-SQL DDL statement to create a new database named MyDdlDatabase.

The solution needs a reference to the Microsoft.SqlServer.ConnectionInfo and Microsoft.SqlServer.Smo assemblies.

The C# code in *Program.cs* in the project CreateSqlServerDatabase is shown in Example 11-8.

Example 11-8. File: Program.cs for CreateSqlServerDatabase solution

```
using System;
using System.Data;
using System.Data.SqlClient;
using Microsoft.SqlServer.Management.Smo;

namespace CreateSqlServerDatabase
{
    class Program
    {
        static void Main(string[] args)
        {
            string sqlConnectString = "Data Source=(local);" +
                "Integrated security=SSPI;";

            // Use SMO to create a database
            Console.WriteLine("---Create database using SMO---");
            Server server = new Server("(local)");
            Database db = new Database(server, "MySmoDatabase");
            db.Create();
            Console.WriteLine("=> Database {0} created.", db.ToString());

            // DDL command text to create database, with minimal specification.
            string sqlText = "CREATE DATABASE MyDdlDatabase ON PRIMARY " +
                    "(NAME = MyDdlDatabase_Data, " +
                    "FILENAME = 'C:\\MyDdlDatabaseData.mdf') " +
                    "LOG ON (NAME = MyDdlDatabase_Log, " +
                    "FILENAME = 'C:\\MyDdlDatabaseLog.ldf')";
```

Example 11-8. File: Program.cs for CreateSqlServerDatabase solution (continued)

```
            // Use DDL to create a database.
            Console.WriteLine("\n---Create database using DDL---");
            Console.WriteLine("=> Executing command:\n{0}", sqlText);

            // Create a connection.
            SqlConnection connection = new SqlConnection(sqlConnectString);
            // Create the command to create the database.
            SqlCommand command = new SqlCommand(sqlText, connection);
            // Create the new database.
            connection.Open( );
            command.ExecuteNonQuery( );
            connection.Close( );
            Console.WriteLine("\n=> Database MyDdlDatabase created.");

            Console.WriteLine("\nPress any key to continue.");
            Console.ReadKey( );
        }
    }
}
```

The output is shown in Figure 11-8.

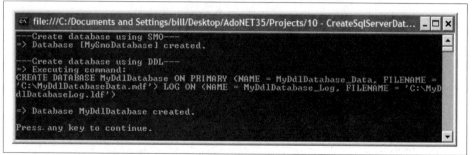

Figure 11-8. Output for CreateSqlServerDatabase solution

Discussion

The following subsections discuss the two approaches demonstrated in the solution.

SQL Management Objects (SMO)

SMO is a collection of objects designed for programming SQL Server management tasks. SMO is used to create databases, perform backups, create jobs, configure SQL Server, configure security, and many other administrative tasks.

The SMO Server class represents an instance of SQL Server and determines the connection to the physical SQL Server installation. The Server object is the topmost object in the SMO instance object hierarchy. A connection to a SQL Server instance is created when a Server object is instantiated.

The SMO Database class represents a SQL Server database, either system- or user-defined, on the SQL Server instance specified by the Server parameter in the Database class constructor and by the Parent property. In the solution, the database is created specifying the Server object set to (local) and the name of a new database MySmoDatabase. The Create( ) method of the Database object creates a new database with the properties defined by the Database object. Specify required database properties before calling the Create( ) method.

SMO is supported in .NET Framework 2.0 and later.

Database Definition Language (DDL)

There are two categories of SQL statements:

Database Definition Language (DDL)
> Used to manage all objects in the database, generally with CREATE, ALTER, and DROP statements to create, modify, and delete objects, respectively. Database objects are defined using DDL. These statements generally require DBA permissions to execute.

Database Management Language (DML)
> Used to manipulate—select, insert, update, and delete—data in the database objects.

The solution executes a DDL CREATE DATABASE statement to create a new database on a SQL Server.

You can programmatically drop the database by using the DROP DATABASE statement in a similar way. To drop the database created in the previous example, use the following code:

```
DROP DATABASE MyDdlDatabase
```

The DROP DATABASE statement will fail if the database is in use; therefore, it might be necessary to restart the SQL Server in order to drop the database. System databases—master, model, msdb, and tempdb—cannot be dropped.

For more information about the CREATE DATABASE statement, the DROP DATABASE statement, or DDL in general, see Microsoft SQL Server Books Online.

The solution for Oracle databases and other databases is similar to that shown for SQL Server, although the DDL syntax for each database varies slightly because of differences in database server capabilities and architecture. For more information about Oracle SQL syntax, see *Oracle in a Nutshell* by Rick Greenwald and David C. Kreines (O'Reilly).

11.9   Adding a Table to a SQL Server Database

Problem

You need to add a table to a SQL Server database.

Solution

Create the table using either SQL Management Objects (SMO) or using the CREATE TABLE T-SQL data definition language (DDL) statement. The solution demonstrates both approaches.

The solution first uses SMO to create a new database called MySmoTable. Next, the solution executes a CREATE TABLE T-SQL DDL statement to create a new database named MyDdlTable.

The solution needs a reference to the Microsoft.SqlServer.ConnectionInfo, Microsoft.SqlServer.Smo, and Microsoft.SqlServer.SqlEnum assemblies.

The C# code in *Program.cs* in the project AddTableSqlServerDatabase is shown in Example 11-9.

Example 11-9. File: Program.cs for AddTableSqlServerDatabase solution

```
using System;
using System.Data;
using System.Data.SqlClient;
using Microsoft.SqlServer.Management.Smo;
using Microsoft.SqlServer.Management.Common;

namespace AddTableSqlServerDatabase
{
    class Program
    {
        static void Main(string[] args)
        {
            // Use SMO to create a table and add it to the database
            Console.WriteLine("---Create database using SMO---");
            Server server = new Server("(local)");
            Database db = server.Databases["AdoDotNet35Cookbook"];
            // Create a new table
            Table table = new Table(db, "MySmoTable");
            // Create a column
            Column col = new Column(table, "MySmoTableId");
            col.DataType = DataType.Int;
            col.Nullable = false;
            col.Identity = true;
            col.IdentitySeed = 1;
            col.IdentityIncrement = 1;
            // Add the column to the table
            table.Columns.Add(col);
```

```
                // Create a primary key on the column
                Index index = new Index(table, "PK_MySmoTable");
                index.IndexKeyType = IndexKeyType.DriPrimaryKey;
                index.IndexedColumns.Add(new IndexedColumn(index, "MySmoTableId"));
                // Add the index to the table
                table.Indexes.Add(index);
                // Create the table
                table.Create();
                Console.WriteLine(
                    "\n=> Table {0} created in AdoDotNet35Cookbook database.",
                    table.ToString());

                // DDL statement to create a table with a single identity column
                string sqlText = "CREATE TABLE MyDdlTable " +
                    "(MyDdlTableId int NOT NULL IDENTITY(1,1) PRIMARY KEY CLUSTERED)";
                // Use DDL to add a table to the database.
                Console.WriteLine("\n---Add table using DDL---");
                Console.WriteLine("=> Executing command:\n{0}", sqlText);

                // Create a connection.
                string sqlConnectString = "Data Source=(local);" +
                    "Integrated security=SSPI;Initial Catalog=AdoDotNet35Cookbook;";
                SqlConnection connection = new SqlConnection(sqlConnectString);
                // Create the command to add the table
                SqlCommand command = new SqlCommand(sqlText, connection);
                // Add the table to the database.
                connection.Open();
                command.ExecuteNonQuery();
                connection.Close();
                Console.WriteLine(
                    "\n=> Table MyDdlTable created in AdoDotNet35Cookbook database.");

                Console.WriteLine("\nPress any key to continue.");
                Console.ReadKey();
            }
        }
    }
```

The output is shown in Figure 11-9.

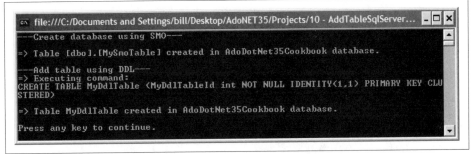

Figure 11-9. Output for AddTableSqlServerDatabase solution

Discussion

The following subsections discuss the two approaches demonstrated in the solution.

SQL Management Objects (SMO)

As mentioned in Recipe 11.8, SMO is a collection of objects designed for programming SQL Server management tasks. SMO is used to create databases, perform backups, create jobs, configure SQL Server, configure security, and many other administrative tasks.

The SMO Server class represents an instance of SQL Server and determines the connection to the physical SQL Server installation. The Server object is the topmost object in the SMO instance object hierarchy. A connection to a SQL Server instance is created when a Server object is instantiated.

The SMO Database class represents a SQL Server database, either system- or user-defined, on the SQL Server instance specified by the Server parameter in the Database class constructor and by the Parent property. In the solution, an existing database is accessed by specifying the Server object set to (local) and the name of the database AdoDotNet35Cookbook. A new table named MyTableSmo is created using the Table class, a column is added to it using the Column class, and an index is created using the Index class. Finally, the Create( ) method of the Table object creates the table.

SMO is supported in .NET Framework 2.0 and later.

Database Definition Language (DDL)

As mentioned in Recipe 11.8, there are two categories of SQL statements:

Database Definition Language (DDL)
> Used to manage all objects in the database, generally with CREATE, ALTER, and DROP statements to create, modify, and delete objects, respectively. Database objects are defined using DDL. These statements generally require DBA permissions to execute.

Database Management Language (DML)
> Used to manipulate—select, insert, update, and delete—data in the database objects.

The solution executes a DDL CREATE TABLE statement to create a new database on a SQL Server.

You can programmatically drop the table by using the DROP TABLE statement in a similar way. To drop the table created in the previous example, use the following code:

```
DROP DATABASE MyDdlTable
```

For more information about the CREATE TABLE statement, the DROP TABLE statement, or DDL in general, see Microsoft SQL Server Books Online.

The solution for Oracle databases and other databases is similar to that shown for SQL Server although the DDL syntax for each database varies slightly because of differences in database server capabilities and architecture. For example, the CREATE TABLE statement for Oracle is different because Oracle does not support identity columns and uses *sequences* instead (see Recipe 5.4 for more information about Oracle sequences). For more information about Oracle SQL syntax, see *Oracle in a Nutshell.*

11.10 Creating a Database Table from a DataTable Schema

Problem

You need to create a table in a database from an existing DataTable schema.

Solution

Use the CreateDdlFromDataTable( ) method shown in this solution.

The sample code contains creates a DataTable containing the schema from the Sales.SalesOrder table in the AdventureWorks sample database. The method CreateDdlFromDataTable( ) in the sample code is called which generates the T-SQL DDL to create the table from the DataTable schema. The NetType2SqlType( ) method is called by the CreateDdlFromDataTable( ) to map .NET data types to SQL Server types when building the DDL statement.

The C# code in *Program.cs* in the project CreateTableDdlFromDataTable is shown in Example 11-10.

Example 11-10. File: Program.cs for CreateTableDdlFromDataTable solution

```
using System;
using System.Data;
using System.Data.SqlClient;
using System.Text;
using System.Xml;

namespace CreateTableDdlFromDataTable
{
    class Program
    {
        static void Main(string[] args)
        {
            string schemaName = "Sales";
            string tableName = "SalesOrderHeader";

            string sqlConnectString = "Data Source=(local);" +
                "Integrated security=SSPI;Initial Catalog=AdventureWorks;";
```

Example 11-10. File: Program.cs for CreateTableDdlFromDataTable solution (continued)

```csharp
        // Fill a DataTable with the schema of the table.
        string sqlText = "SELECT * FROM " + schemaName + "." + tableName;
        SqlDataAdapter da = new SqlDataAdapter(sqlText, sqlConnectString);
        DataTable dt = new DataTable( );
        da.FillSchema(dt, SchemaType.Source);

        // Create the DDL that creates the table from the DataTable
        string sqlDdl =
            CreateDdlFromDataTable(schemaName, tableName, dt, sqlConnectString);
        Console.WriteLine("---START: DDL to create table {0}.{1}---",
            schemaName, tableName);
        Console.WriteLine(sqlDdl);
        Console.WriteLine("---END: DDL---");

        Console.WriteLine("\nPress any key to continue.");
        Console.ReadKey( );
    }

    private static string CreateDdlFromDataTable(string schemaName,
        string tableName, DataTable dt, String sqlConnectString)
    {
        // Drop the new table if it is already there.
        StringBuilder sqlDdl = new StringBuilder(
            "IF EXISTS (SELECT * FROM dbo.sysobjects WHERE id  = " +
            "object_id('[" + schemaName + "].[" + tableName + "]') " +
            "AND OBJECTPROPERTY(id, 'IsUserTable')  =  1)" +
            Environment.NewLine +
            "DROP TABLE [" + schemaName + "].[" + tableName + "];" +
            Environment.NewLine + Environment.NewLine);

        // Start building a command string to create the table.
        sqlDdl.Append(
            "CREATE TABLE [" + schemaName + "].[" + tableName + "] (" +
            Environment.NewLine);
        // Iterate over the column collection in the source table.
        foreach (DataColumn col in dt.Columns)
        {
            // Add the column.
            sqlDdl.Append("[" + col.ColumnName + "] ");
            // Map the source column type to a SQL Server type.
            sqlDdl.Append(NetType2SqlType(col.DataType.ToString( ),
                col.MaxLength) + " ");
            // Add identity information.
            if (col.AutoIncrement)
                sqlDdl.Append("IDENTITY ");
            // Add AllowNull information.
            sqlDdl.Append((col.AllowDBNull ? "" : "NOT ") + "NULL," +
                Environment.NewLine);
        }
        sqlDdl.Remove(sqlDdl.Length - (Environment.NewLine.Length + 1), 1);
        sqlDdl.Append(") ON [PRIMARY];" + Environment.NewLine +
            Environment.NewLine);
```

```csharp
            // Add the primary key to the table, if it exists.
            if (dt.PrimaryKey != null)
            {
                sqlDdl.Append("ALTER TABLE [" + schemaName + "].[" + tableName + "]" +
                    " WITH NOCHECK ADD " + Environment.NewLine);
                sqlDdl.Append("CONSTRAINT [PK_" + schemaName + "_" + tableName +
                    "] PRIMARY KEY CLUSTERED (" + Environment.NewLine);
                // Add the columns to the primary key.
                foreach (DataColumn col in dt.PrimaryKey)
                {
                    sqlDdl.Append("[" + col.ColumnName + "]," +
                        Environment.NewLine);
                }
                sqlDdl.Remove(sqlDdl.Length -
                    (Environment.NewLine.Length + 1), 1);
                sqlDdl.Append(") ON [PRIMARY];");
            }

            return sqlDdl.ToString();
        }

        private static string NetType2SqlType(String netType, int maxLength)
        {
            string sqlType = "";

            // Map the .NET type to the data source type.
            // This is not perfect because mappings are not always one-to-one.
            switch (netType)
            {
                case "System.Boolean":
                    sqlType = "[bit]";
                    break;
                case "System.Byte":
                    sqlType = "[tinyint]";
                    break;
                case "System.Int16":
                    sqlType = "[smallint]";
                    break;
                case "System.Int32":
                    sqlType = "[int]";
                    break;
                case "System.Int64":
                    sqlType = "[bigint]";
                    break;
                case "System.Byte[]":
                    sqlType = "[binary]";
                    break;
                case "System.Char[]":
                    sqlType = "[nchar] (" + maxLength + ")";
                    break;
                case "System.String":
                    if (maxLength == 0x3FFFFFFF)
                        sqlType = "[ntext]";
```

```
            else
                sqlType = "[nvarchar] (" + maxLength + ")";
            break;
        case "System.Single":
            sqlType = "[real]";
            break;
        case "System.Double":
            sqlType = "[float]";
            break;
        case "System.Decimal":
            sqlType = "[decimal]";
            break;
        case "System.DateTime":
            sqlType = "[datetime]";
            break;
        case "System.Guid":
            sqlType = "[uniqueidentifier]";
            break;
        case "System.Object":
            sqlType = "[sql_variant]";
            break;
        default:
            sqlType = "[not supported]";
            break;
    }

    return sqlType;
}
    }
}
```

The output is shown in Figure 11-10.

Discussion

The solution dynamically constructs a Data Definition Language (DDL) statement to create a table in a SQL Server database from the schema of a DataTable. The T-SQL statements generated are shown in Figure 11-10.

The first command—the DROP statement—is not strictly required and is included here so that the solution does not crash if it has been run previously. It might be more appropriate in your situation to check if the table already exists in the database, and if it does, abort execution since your table might contain important data. If that is the case, return the results of the EXISTS query to the calling application and use that to control whether the new table is created.

The second DDL command uses the CREATE TABLE statement to create the table in the database. The code iterates over the collection of the columns in the DataTable schema to retrieve the name and the maximum length of the column and whether the column is an identity column or allows null values. A method is called to map the .NET data types of the DataTable to SQL Server data types. This method does not

---

```
file:///C:/Documents and Settings/bill/Desktop/AdoNET35/Projects/CreateTableDdlFromData...
-----START: DDL to create table Sales.SalesOrderHeader-----
IF EXISTS (SELECT * FROM dbo.sysobjects WHERE id    = object_id('[Sales].[SalesOrd
erHeader]') AND OBJECTPROPERTY(id, 'IsUserTable')    = 1)
DROP TABLE [Sales].[SalesOrderHeader];

CREATE TABLE [Sales].[SalesOrderHeader] (
[SalesOrderID] [int] IDENTITY NOT NULL,
[RevisionNumber] [tinyint] NOT NULL,
[OrderDate] [datetime] NOT NULL,
[DueDate] [datetime] NOT NULL,
[ShipDate] [datetime] NULL,
[Status] [tinyint] NOT NULL,
[OnlineOrderFlag] [bit] NOT NULL,
[SalesOrderNumber] [nvarchar] (25) NULL,
[PurchaseOrderNumber] [nvarchar] (25) NULL,
[AccountNumber] [nvarchar] (15) NULL,
[CustomerID] [int] NOT NULL,
[ContactID] [int] NOT NULL,
[SalesPersonID] [int] NULL,
[TerritoryID] [int] NULL,
[BillToAddressID] [int] NOT NULL,
[ShipToAddressID] [int] NOT NULL,
[ShipMethodID] [int] NOT NULL,
[CreditCardID] [int] NULL,
[CreditCardApprovalCode] [nvarchar] (15) NULL,
[CurrencyRateID] [int] NULL,
[SubTotal] [decimal] NOT NULL,
[TaxAmt] [decimal] NOT NULL,
[Freight] [decimal] NOT NULL,
[TotalDue] [decimal] NULL,
[Comment] [nvarchar] (128) NULL,
[rowguid] [uniqueidentifier] NOT NULL,
[ModifiedDate] [datetime] NOT NULL
) ON [PRIMARY];

ALTER TABLE [Sales].[SalesOrderHeader] WITH NOCHECK ADD
CONSTRAINT [PK_Sales_SalesOrderHeader] PRIMARY KEY CLUSTERED (
[SalesOrderID]
) ON [PRIMARY];
-----END: DDL-----

Press any key to continue.
```

Figure 11-10. Output for CreateTableDdlFromDataTable solution

work perfectly because there is not a one-to-one mapping between .NET data types and SQL Server data types. Make the mapping decisions based on the requirements of your application. The mapping method also adds the field length for the DDL column description for string-type columns. For more information about mapping SQL Server data types to .NET Framework data types, see Recipe 2.4.

The third DDL command creates the primary key constraint on the newly constructed table. While single-column primary keys can easily be added to the CREATE TABLE command, the easiest way to handle compound keys is by using an ALTER TABLE statement with an ADD CONSTRAINT statement and PRIMARY KEY argument. Iterate over the collection of columns exposed by the PrimaryKey property of the table to add the columns to the command.

If you have a number of tables in a DataSet that you want to create in a database, you can iterate through the collection of DataRelation objects for the DataSet and use the ALTER TABLE statement with the ADD CONSTRAINT command and a FOREIGN KEY argument to add the table relations to the database.

For more information about DDL syntax, see Microsoft SQL Server Books Online.

11.11 Creating DataSet Relationships from SQL Server Relationships

Problem

You need to create relationships between DataTable objects within your DataSet at runtime based on the relationships that are defined in your SQL Server database.

Solution

Two approaches are shown—one that uses catalog views and one that uses information schema views—to create relationships automatically at runtime between the tables ParentTable and ChildTable. The T-SQL DDL that creates these tables is shown in Example 11-11.

Example 11-11. Create tables ParentTable and ChildTable

```
USE AdoDotNet35Cookbook
GO
-- Create the parent table
CREATE TABLE ParentTable(
    a int NOT NULL,
    b int NOT NULL,
    c int NOT NULL,
    d int NOT NULL,
  CONSTRAINT PK_ParentTable PRIMARY KEY CLUSTERED
  ( a ASC, b ASC )
)
GO
-- Create the child table
CREATE TABLE ChildTable(
    z int NOT NULL PRIMARY KEY,
    a int NOT NULL,
    b int NOT NULL,
)
GO
-- Create the relation between ParentTable and ChildTable
ALTER TABLE ChildTable
WITH CHECK ADD CONSTRAINT FK_ChildTable_ParentTable FOREIGN KEY(a, b)
REFERENCES ParentTable (a, b)
```

The first solution uses a query of the catalog views to get the relationships between the tables in the DataSet. DataRelation objects are created in the DataSet for the identified relationships.

The C# code in *Program.cs* in the project CreateRelationsFromSqlServerCV is shown in Example 11-12.

Example 11-12. File: Program.cs for CreateRelationsFromSqlServerCV solution

```
using System;
using System.Data;
using System.Data.SqlClient;
using System.Text;
using System.Collections;

namespace CreateRelationsFromSqlServerCV
{
    class Program
    {
        static void Main(string[] args)
        {
            string sqlConnectString = "Data Source=(local);" +
                "Integrated security=SSPI;Initial Catalog=AdoDotNet35Cookbook;";

            string[] schemaName = new string[] { "dbo", "dbo" };
            string[] tableName = new string[] { "ParentTable", "ChildTable" };

            // Add the tables to the DataSet.
            DataSet ds = new DataSet();
            SqlDataAdapter da;
            for (int i = 0; i < schemaName.Length; i++)
            {
                da = new SqlDataAdapter(
                    "SELECT * FROM " + schemaName[i] + "." + tableName[i],
                    sqlConnectString);
                da.Fill(ds, tableName[i]);
            }

            string sqlText = "SELECT fk.name ConstraintName, " +
                "fk.update_referential_action_desc UpdateRule, " +
                "fk.delete_referential_action_desc DeleteRule, " +
                "pt.name ParentTable, ct.name ChildTable, " +
                "pc.name ParentColumn, cc.name ChildColumn " +
                "FROM sys.foreign_keys fk " +
                "JOIN sys.tables pt ON fk.referenced_object_id = pt.object_id " +
                "JOIN sys.tables ct ON fk.parent_object_id = ct.object_id " +
                "JOIN sys.foreign_key_columns fkc " +
                "ON fk.object_id = fkc.constraint_object_id " +
                "JOIN sys.columns pc ON fkc.referenced_object_id = pc.object_id " +
                "  AND fkc.referenced_column_id = pc.column_id " +
                "JOIN sys.columns cc ON fkc.parent_object_id = cc.object_id " +
                "  AND fkc.parent_column_id = cc.column_id " +
                "ORDER BY ConstraintName, fkc.constraint_column_id";

            // Create the connection and command to retrieve constraint information.
            SqlConnection connection = new SqlConnection(sqlConnectString);
            SqlCommand command = new SqlCommand(sqlText, connection);
```

```
// Fill the DataReader with constraint information.
connection.Open( );
SqlDataReader reader = command.ExecuteReader( );

String prevConstraintName = "";
String constraintName = "";
String parentTableName = "";
String childTableName = "";
bool updateCascade = false;
bool deleteCascade = false;
String relationName = "";

// Arrays to store related columns from constraints in DataReader
ArrayList parentColsAL = new ArrayList( );
ArrayList childColsAL = new ArrayList( );
DataColumn[] parentCols;
DataColumn[] childCols;

DataRelation relation;

bool isRecord = false;
// Iterate over the constraint collection for the database.
do
{
    // Read the next record from the DataReader.
    isRecord = reader.Read( );

    // Store the current constraint as the previous constraint name
    // to handle multicolumn-based relations.
    prevConstraintName = constraintName;

    // Get the current constraint name.
    constraintName = isRecord ? reader["ConstraintName"].ToString( ) : "";

    // If the constraint name has changed and both tables exist,
    // create a relation based on the previous constraint column(s).
    if (prevConstraintName != "" &&
        constraintName != prevConstraintName &&
        ds.Tables.Contains(parentTableName) &&
        ds.Tables.Contains(childTableName))
    {
        // Create the parent and child column arrays.
        parentCols = new DataColumn[parentColsAL.Count];
        parentColsAL.CopyTo(parentCols);
        childCols = new DataColumn[childColsAL.Count];
        childColsAL.CopyTo(childCols);

        // Create the relation name based on the constraint name.
        relationName = prevConstraintName;

        // Create the relation and add it to the DataSet.
        relation = new DataRelation(relationName, parentCols, childCols,
            true);
```

```
                ds.Relations.Add(relation);
                // Set the cascade update and delete rules.
                relation.ChildKeyConstraint.UpdateRule =
                    updateCascade ? Rule.Cascade : Rule.None;
                relation.ChildKeyConstraint.DeleteRule =
                    deleteCascade ? Rule.Cascade : Rule.None;

                // Clear the parent and child column arrays for the previous
                // constraint.
                parentColsAL.Clear( );
                childColsAL.Clear( );

                Console.WriteLine("---New relationship created---");
                Console.WriteLine("Name: {0}", relation.RelationName);
                Console.WriteLine("ParentTable: {0}", relation.ParentTable);
                Console.WriteLine("ParentColumns:");
                foreach (DataColumn pcol in relation.ParentColumns)
                    Console.WriteLine("  {0}", pcol.ColumnName);
                Console.WriteLine("ChildTable: {0}", relation.ChildTable);
                Console.WriteLine("ChildColumns:");
                foreach (DataColumn ccol in relation.ChildColumns)
                    Console.WriteLine("  {0}", ccol.ColumnName);
                Console.WriteLine( );
            }

            if (isRecord)
            {
                // Store the current parent and child table names.
                parentTableName = reader["ParentTable"].ToString( );
                childTableName = reader["ChildTable"].ToString( );
                // Store the cascade update and delete for the current
                // constraint.
                updateCascade = (reader["UpdateRule"].ToString( ) ==
                    "CASCADE");
                deleteCascade = (reader["DeleteRule"].ToString( ) ==
                    "CASCADE");

                // Add the parent and child column for the current constraint
                // to the ArrayLists, if both parent and child are in DataSet.
                if (ds.Tables.Contains(parentTableName) &&
                    ds.Tables.Contains(childTableName))
                {
                    parentColsAL.Add(ds.Tables[parentTableName].Columns[
                        reader["ParentColumn"].ToString( )]);
                    childColsAL.Add(ds.Tables[childTableName].Columns[
                        reader["ChildColumn"].ToString( )]);
                }
            }
        } while (isRecord);

        // Close the DataReader and connection.
        reader.Close( );
        connection.Close( );
```

Example 11-12. File: Program.cs for CreateRelationsFromSqlServerCV solution (continued)

```
            Console.WriteLine("Press any key to continue.");
            Console.ReadKey();
        }
    }
}
```

The output is shown in Figure 11-11.

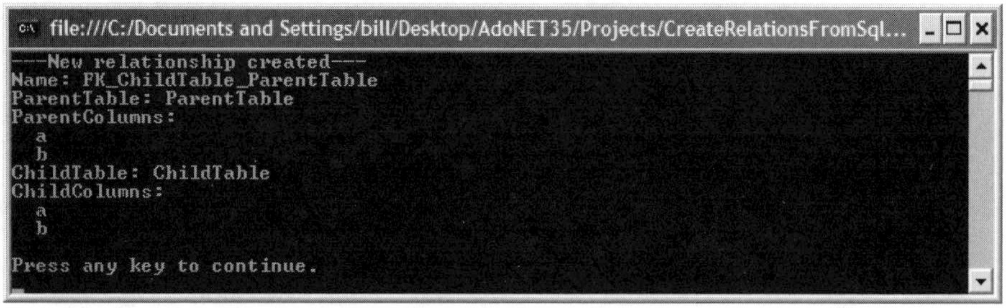

Figure 11-11. Output for CreateRelationsFromSqlServerCV solution

The first solution uses a query of information schema views to get the relationships between the tables in the DataSet. DataRelation objects are created in the DataSet for the identified relationships.

The code in *Program.cs* in the project CreateRelationsFromSqlServerISV is shown in Example 11-13.

Example 11-13. File: Program.cs for CreateRelationFromSqlServerISV solution

```
using System;
using System.Data;
using System.Data.SqlClient;
using System.Text;
using System.Collections;

namespace CreateRelationsFromSqlServerISV
{
    class Program
    {
        static void Main(string[] args)
        {
            string sqlConnectString = "Data Source=(local);" +
                "Integrated security=SSPI;Initial Catalog=AdventureWorks;";

            string[] schemaName = new string[] { "Sales", "Sales" };
            string[] tableName =
                new string[] { "SalesOrderHeader", "SalesOrderDetail" };

            // Add the Orders and Order Details tables to the DataSet.
            DataSet ds = new DataSet();
```

```csharp
SqlDataAdapter da;
for (int i = 0; i < schemaName.Length; i++)
{
    da = new SqlDataAdapter(
        "SELECT * FROM " + schemaName[i] + "." + tableName[i],
        sqlConnectString);
    da.Fill(ds, tableName[i]);
}

string sqlText =
    "SELECT rc.CONSTRAINT_NAME, rc.UPDATE_RULE, rc.DELETE_RULE, " +
    "kcuP.TABLE_NAME ParentTable, kcuC.TABLE_NAME ChildTable, " +
    "kcuP.COLUMN_NAME ParentColumn, kcuC.COLUMN_NAME ChildColumn " +
    "FROM INFORMATION_SCHEMA.REFERENTIAL_CONSTRAINTS rc " +
    "LEFT JOIN INFORMATION_SCHEMA.KEY_COLUMN_USAGE kcuP ON " +
    "rc.UNIQUE_CONSTRAINT_NAME = kcuP.CONSTRAINT_NAME " +
    "LEFT JOIN INFORMATION_SCHEMA.KEY_COLUMN_USAGE kcuC ON " +
    "rc.CONSTRAINT_NAME = kcuC.CONSTRAINT_NAME AND " +
    "kcuP.ORDINAL_POSITION = kcuC.ORDINAL_POSITION " +
    "ORDER BY rc.CONSTRAINT_NAME, kcuP.ORDINAL_POSITION";

// Create the connection and command to retrieve constraint information.
SqlConnection connection = new SqlConnection(sqlConnectString);
SqlCommand command = new SqlCommand(sqlText, connection);

// Fill the DataReader with constraint information.
connection.Open();
SqlDataReader reader = command.ExecuteReader();

String prevConstraintName = "";
String constraintName = "";
String parentTableName = "";
String childTableName = "";
bool updateCascade = false;
bool deleteCascade = false;
String relationName = "";

// Arrays to store related columns from constraints in DataReader
ArrayList parentColsAL = new ArrayList();
ArrayList childColsAL = new ArrayList();
DataColumn[] parentCols;
DataColumn[] childCols;

DataRelation relation;

bool isRecord = false;
// Iterate over the constraint collection for the database.
do
{
    // Read the next record from the DataReader.
    isRecord = reader.Read();
```

```
// Store the current constraint as the previous constraint name
// to handle multicolumn-based relations.
prevConstraintName = constraintName;

// Get the current constraint name.
constraintName = isRecord ? reader["CONSTRAINT_NAME"].ToString( ) : "";

// If the constraint name has changed and both tables exist,
// create a relation based on the previous constraint column(s).
if (prevConstraintName != "" &&
    constraintName != prevConstraintName &&
    ds.Tables.Contains(parentTableName) &&
    ds.Tables.Contains(childTableName))
{
    // Create the parent and child column arrays.
    parentCols = new DataColumn[parentColsAL.Count];
    parentColsAL.CopyTo(parentCols);
    childCols = new DataColumn[childColsAL.Count];
    childColsAL.CopyTo(childCols);

    // Create the relation name based on the constraint name.
    relationName = prevConstraintName;

    // Create the relation and add it to the DataSet.
    relation = new DataRelation(relationName, parentCols, childCols,
        true);
    ds.Relations.Add(relation);
    // Set the cascade update and delete rules.
    relation.ChildKeyConstraint.UpdateRule =
        updateCascade ? Rule.Cascade : Rule.None;
    relation.ChildKeyConstraint.DeleteRule =
        deleteCascade ? Rule.Cascade : Rule.None;

    // Clear the parent and child column arrays for the previous
    // constraint.
    parentColsAL.Clear( );
    childColsAL.Clear( );

    Console.WriteLine("---New relationship created---");
    Console.WriteLine("Name: {0}", relation.RelationName);
    Console.WriteLine("ParentTable: {0}", relation.ParentTable);
    Console.WriteLine("ParentColumns:");
    foreach (DataColumn pcol in relation.ParentColumns)
        Console.WriteLine("  {0}", pcol.ColumnName);
    Console.WriteLine("ChildTable: {0}", relation.ChildTable);
    Console.WriteLine("ChildColumns:");
    foreach (DataColumn ccol in relation.ChildColumns)
        Console.WriteLine("  {0}", ccol.ColumnName);
    Console.WriteLine( );
}
```

```
            if (isRecord)
            {
                // Store the current parent and child table names.
                parentTableName = reader["ParentTable"].ToString();
                childTableName = reader["ChildTable"].ToString();
                // Store the cascade update and delete for the current
                // constraint.
                updateCascade = (reader["UPDATE_RULE"].ToString() ==
                    "CASCADE");
                deleteCascade = (reader["DELETE_RULE"].ToString() ==
                    "CASCADE");

                // Add the parent and child column for the current constraint
                // to the ArrayLists, if both parent and child are in DataSet.
                if (ds.Tables.Contains(parentTableName) &&
                    ds.Tables.Contains(childTableName))
                {
                    parentColsAL.Add(ds.Tables[parentTableName].Columns[
                        reader["ParentColumn"].ToString()]);
                    childColsAL.Add(ds.Tables[childTableName].Columns[
                        reader["ChildColumn"].ToString()]);
                }
            }
        } while (isRecord);

        // Close the DataReader and connection.
        reader.Close();
        connection.Close();

        Console.WriteLine("Press any key to continue.");
        Console.ReadKey();
    }
  }
}
```

The output is shown in Figure 11-12.

Figure 11-12. Output for CreateRelationsFromSqlServerISV solution

Discussion

There is no ADO.NET data provider method that automatically returns information about table relationships that are defined in a database. To get the relation information, catalog or information views in SQL Server must be queried. These approaches are discussed in the following subsections.

Catalog views

The information required to reconstruct relationships between tables requires a query that pulls together information from three different information views—sys.foreign_keys, sys.tables, and sys.columns. The sys.foreign_keys view contains a row for each foreign key constraint in the database. The sys.tables view contains a row for each user-defined table. The sys.columns view contains a row for each column of objects such as tables and views that have columns.

The solution starts by loading a DataSet with two sets of tables ParentColumn and ChildColumn. Next, the query to retrieve the data relationship information is constructed. The SQL statement used is:

```
SELECT fk.name ConstraintName,
    fk.update_referential_action_desc UpdateRule,
    fk.delete_referential_action_desc DeleteRule,
    pt.name ParentTable, ct.name ChildTable,
    pc.name ParentColumn, cc.name ChildColumn
FROM sys.foreign_keys fk
JOIN sys.tables pt ON fk.referenced_object_id = pt.object_id
JOIN sys.tables ct ON fk.parent_object_id = ct.object_id
JOIN sys.foreign_key_columns fkc
    ON fk.object_id = fkc.constraint_object_id
JOIN sys.columns pc ON fkc.referenced_object_id = pc.object_id
  AND fkc.referenced_column_id = pc.column_id
JOIN sys.columns cc ON fkc.parent_object_id = cc.object_id
  AND fkc.parent_column_id = cc.column_id
ORDER BY ConstraintName, fkc.constraint_column_id;
```

This statement retrieves the constraint information needed to create the relations in the DataSet based on the schema information in the database. Specifically, the columns returned are shown in Table 11-8.

Table 11-8. Relation query columns

Column	Description
ConstraintName	Name of the constraint
UpdateRule	NO ACTION or CASCADE
DeleteRule	NO ACTION or CASCADE
ParentTable	Name of the parent table in the relationship
ChildTable	Name of the child table in the relationship
ParentColumn	Name of the column in the parent table
ChildColumn	Name of the column in the child table

For relationships that are based on more than one column, there will be more than one row in the result set that must be combined to create the DataRelation object in the DataSet. Notice that the statement groups the results that are returned by the constraint name, grouping all records related to a single relation. The result set is further ordered by the constraint_column_id field that defines the order of the columns in the relation. When iterating over the query results, if both the parent and child names are contained in the result set, a relationship has been identified and processing continues. For those relationships, the column names for the parent and child tables are loaded into arrays allowing relations based on multiple columns to be created.

Once all of the columns for a relation have been loaded (this is determined by a change in the constraint name and the names of the parent and child tables), the DataRelation is created in the DataSet based on the parent and child column names in the arrays. The update and delete cascade rules are set for the relation. Although not necessary, the sample names the relation based on the name of the constraint. Once the DataRelation is created, processing of the result set resumes with the remaining relations.

For more information about catalog views, see the discussion in Recipe 11.3.

Information schema views

The information necessary to reconstruct relationships between tables requires a query that combines information from two different information views, INFORMATION_SCHEMA.REFERENTIAL_CONSTRAINTS and INFORMATION_SCHEMA.KEY_COLUMN_USAGE, and requires two joins into the latter table to obtain required information for both unique and foreign key constraints. The REFERENTIAL_CONSTRAINTS table contains a row for each foreign key constraint in the database. The KEY_COLUMN_USAGE view contains one row for each row constrained as a key in the database.

The solution starts by loading a DataSet with two sets of tables ParentTable and ChildTable. Next, the query to retrieve the data relationship information is constructed. The SQL statement used is:

```
SELECT
    rc.CONSTRAINT_NAME, rc.UPDATE_RULE, rc.DELETE_RULE,
    kcuP.TABLE_NAME ParentTable, kcuC.TABLE_NAME ChildTable,
    kcuP.COLUMN_NAME ParentColumn, kcuC.COLUMN_NAME ChildColumn
FROM INFORMATION_SCHEMA.REFERENTIAL_CONSTRAINTS rc
LEFT JOIN INFORMATION_SCHEMA.KEY_COLUMN_USAGE kcuP ON
    rc.UNIQUE_CONSTRAINT_NAME = kcuP.CONSTRAINT_NAME
LEFT JOIN INFORMATION_SCHEMA.KEY_COLUMN_USAGE kcuC ON
    rc.CONSTRAINT_NAME = kcuC.CONSTRAINT_NAME AND
    kcuP.ORDINAL_POSITION = kcuC.ORDINAL_POSITION
ORDER BY rc.CONSTRAINT_NAME, kcuP.ORDINAL_POSITION
```

This statement retrieves the constraint information needed to create the relations in the DataSet based on the schema information in the database. Specifically, the columns returned are shown in Table 11-9.

Table 11-9. Relation query columns

Column	Description
CONSTRAINT_NAME	Name of the constraint
UPDATE_RULE	NO ACTION or CASCADE
DELETE_RULE	NO ACTION or CASCADE
ParentTable	Name of the parent table in the relationship
ChildTable	Name of the child table in the relationship
ParentColumn	Name of the column in the parent table
ChildColumn	Name of the column in the child table

For relationships that are based on more than one column, there will be more than one row in the result set that must be combined to create the DataRelation object in the DataSet. Notice that the statement groups the results that are returned by the constraint name, grouping all records related to a single relation. The result set is further ordered by the ORDINAL_POSITION field that defines the order of the columns in the relation. When iterating over the query results, if both the parent and child names are contained in the result set, a relationship has been identified and processing continues. For those relationships, the column names for the parent and child tables are loaded into arrays allowing relations based on multiple columns to be created.

Once all of the columns for a relation have been loaded (this is determined by a change in the constraint name and the names of the parent and child tables), the DataRelation is created in the DataSet based on the parent and child column names in the arrays. The update and delete cascade rules are set for the relation. Although not necessary, the sample names the relation based on the name of the constraint. Once the DataRelation is created, processing of the result set resumes with the remaining relations.

For more on information schema views, see the discussion in Recipe 11.3.

11.12 Creating a New Microsoft Access Database

Problem

You need to programmatically create a new Microsoft Access database.

Solution

Use ActiveX Database Objects Extensions for DDL and Security (ADOX) from .NET through COM Interop.

The solution calls the CreateAccessDatabase( ) method of the ADOX.Catalog class to create the Microsoft Access database.

The solution needs a reference to Microsoft ADO Ext. 2.8 (or later) for DDL and Security from the COM tab in Visual Studio .NET's Add Reference Dialog.

The C# code in *Program.cs* in the project `CreateAccessDatabase` is shown in Example 11-14.

Example 11-14. File: Program.cs for CreateAccessDatabase solution

```
using System;

namespace CreateAccessDatabase
{
    class Program
    {
        private static string fileName = @"..\..\..\MyDatabase.accdb";

        static void Main(string[] args)
        {
            string connectString =
                @"Provider=Microsoft.ACE.OLEDB.12.0;Data Source=" + fileName + ";";

            // Use ADOX to create the Access database.
            ADOX.Catalog cat = new ADOX.Catalog();
            cat.Create(connectString);
            cat = null;

            Console.WriteLine("Microsoft Access database {0} created.", fileName);

            Console.WriteLine("\nPress any key to continue.");
            Console.ReadKey();
        }
    }
}
```

The output is shown in Figure 11-13.

Figure 11-13. Output for CreateAccessDatabase solution

Discussion

ADO Extensions for DDL and Security (ADOX) extends the ADO objects and programming model with objects for schema creation and modification, and for security. ADOX is used to programmatically access and manipulate the objects in a database.

You can use ADOX from .NET through COM interop to create a new Microsoft Access database. Use the Create( ) method of the ADOX.Catalog object, passing a connection string for the new Access database name as the argument.

11.13 Listing Tables in an Access Database

Problem

You need a list of all tables in your Access database.

Solution

Use the GetOLEDBSchemaTable( ) method of the OleDbConnection class or ActiveX Database Objects Extensions for DDL and Security (ADOX).

The first approach uses the GetOLEDBSchemaTable( ) method to return schema information about user tables. These results are then displayed.

The C# code in *Program.cs* in the project ListAccessDatabaseTables is demonstrates the first approach and is shown in Example 11-15.

Example 11-15. File: Program.cs for ListAccessDatabaseTables solution

```
using System;
using System.Data;
using System.Data.OleDb;

namespace ListAccessDatabaseTables
{
    class Program
    {
        static void Main(string[] args)
        {
            string oledbConnectString =
                "Provider=Microsoft.ACE.OLEDB.12.0;Data Source=" +
                @"C:\Northwind 2007.accdb;";

            OleDbConnection connection = new OleDbConnection(oledbConnectString);
            connection.Open( );

            // Retrieve schema information for all tables.
            DataTable schemaTable =
                connection.GetOleDbSchemaTable(OleDbSchemaGuid.Tables,
                new object[] {null, null, null, "TABLE"});

            Console.WriteLine("---Tables, using GetOleDbSchemaTable( )---");
            foreach (DataRow row in schemaTable.Rows)
                Console.WriteLine("{0}", row["TABLE_NAME"]);

            connection.Close( );
```

Example 11-15. File: Program.cs for ListAccessDatabaseTables solution (continued)

```
            Console.WriteLine("\nPress any key to continue.");
            Console.ReadKey( );
        }
    }
}
```

The output is shown in Figure 11-14.

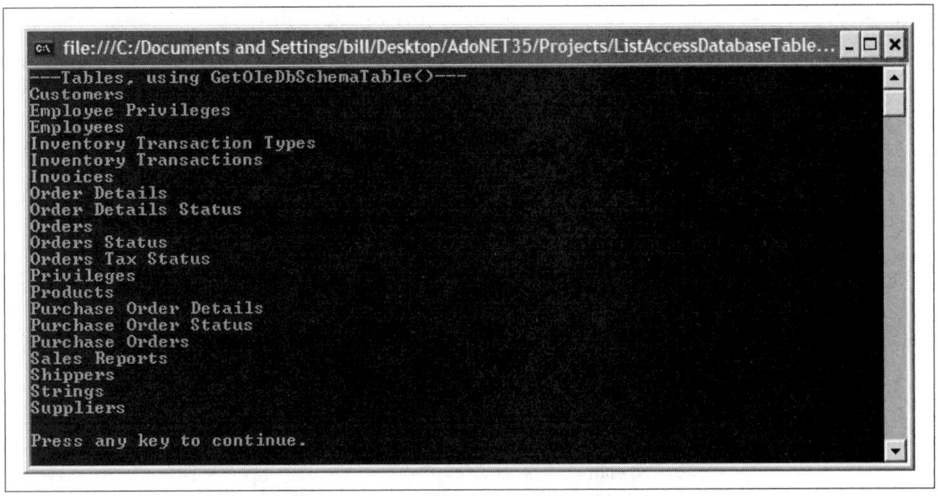

Figure 11-14. Output for ListAccessDatabaseTables solution

For the second approach, the solution needs a reference to the Primary Interop Assembly (PIA) for ADO provided in the file *ADODB.DLL*; select *adodb* from the .NET tab in Visual Studio .NET's Add Reference dialog. The solution also need a reference to Microsoft ADO Ext. 2.8 (or later) for DDL and Security from the COM tab in Visual Studio .NET's Add Reference dialog. The solution creates an ADOX `Catalog` object through COM interop. The `Tables` property of this object is used to access the collection of tables from which the name and other information is displayed.

The C# code in *Program.cs* in the project `ListAccessDatabaseTablesADOX` demonstrates the second approach and is shown in Example 11-16.

Example 11-16. File: Program.cs for ListAccessDatabaseTablesADOX solution

```
using System;
using System.Text;

namespace ListAccessDatabaseTables
{
    class Program
    {
        static void Main(string[] args)
        {
```

Example 11-16. File: Program.cs for ListAccessDatabaseTablesADOX solution (continued)

```
        string oledbConnectString =
            "Provider=Microsoft.ACE.OLEDB.12.0;Data Source=" +
            @"C:\Northwind 2007.accdb;";

        Console.WriteLine("---Tables with keys, using ADOX---");
        ADODB.Connection conn = new ADODB.ConnectionClass();
        conn.Open(oledbConnectString, "", "", 0);

        // Create an ADOX catalog object for the connection.
        ADOX.Catalog cat = new ADOX.Catalog();
        cat.ActiveConnection = conn;

        Console.WriteLine("\nTABLE\tKEY");
        Console.WriteLine("-----\t---");
        // Iterate over the collection of tables.
        foreach (ADOX.Table table in cat.Tables)
        {
            if (table.Type == "TABLE")
            {
                Console.WriteLine(table.Name);

                // Iterate over the collection of keys for the table.
                StringBuilder sb = new StringBuilder();
                foreach (ADOX.Key key in table.Keys)
                {
                    sb.Append("\t" + key.Name + " (");
                    // Iterate over the collection of columns for the key.
                    foreach (ADOX.Column col in key.Columns)
                    {
                        sb.Append(col.Name + ", ");
                    }
                    sb.Remove(sb.Length - 2, 2).Append(")\n");
                }
                Console.WriteLine(sb.ToString());
            }
        }

        cat = null;
        conn.Close();

        Console.WriteLine("\nPress any key to continue.");
        Console.ReadKey();
    }
}
```

The output is shown in Figure 11-15.

Discussion

The solution shows two approaches to get a list of tables in a Microsoft Access database.

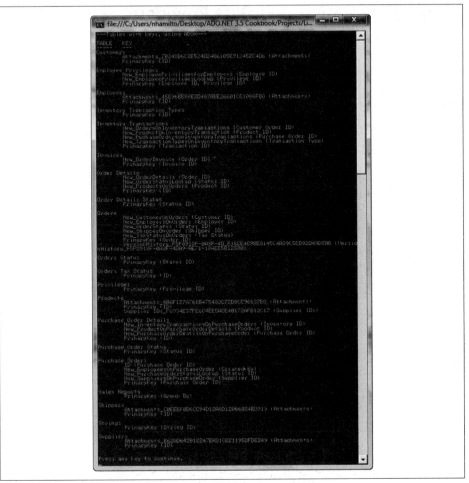

Figure 11-15. Output for ListAccessDatabaseTablesADOX solution

The first approach uses the GetOleDbSchemaTable( ) method of the OleDbConnection object. This technique is discussed in Recipe 11.3.

The second approach uses ADOX through COM interop. ADOX is an extension to the ADO objects and programming model that contains objects for schema creation and modification and for security. The OLE DB data provider fully supports ADOX while support with other data providers varies—see MSDN for more information.

ADOX has a Tables property that exposes a collection of Table objects in the database. The user tables are determined by iterating over the collection of tables and selecting only those tables where the Type property is TABLE. The Table object also exposes collections of Columns, Indexes, Keys, and Properties that can be used to further investigate the database. As an example, the sample code iterates over the collection of Keys in each table to get the list of both primary and foreign keys.

11.14 Enumerating .NET Data Providers

Problem

You need a list of .NET data providers installed on the machine running your code.

Solution

Use the static GetFactoryClasses( ) method of the DbProviderFactories class to return information about installed data providers.

The C# code in *Program.cs* in the project EnumerateDataProviders is shown in Example 11-17.

Example 11-17. File: Program.cs for EnumerateDataProviders solution

```csharp
using System;
using System.Data;
using System.Data.Common;

namespace EnumerateDataProviders
{
    class Program
    {
        static void Main(string[] args)
        {
            DataTable dt = DbProviderFactories.GetFactoryClasses( );
            foreach (DataRow row in dt.Rows)
                Console.WriteLine("{0}\n {1}\n {2}\n {3}\n",
                    row["Name"], row["Description"], row["InvariantName"],
                    row["AssemblyQualifiedName"]);

            Console.WriteLine("Press any key to continue.");
            Console.ReadKey( );
        }
    }
}
```

The output is shown in Figure 11-16.

Discussion

The static GetFactoryClasses( ) method of the DbProviderFactories class introduced in .NET Framework 2.0 returns a DataTable containing the information shown about all installed providers that implement the abstract base class DbProviderFactory. The schema of the DataTable is shown in Table 11-10.

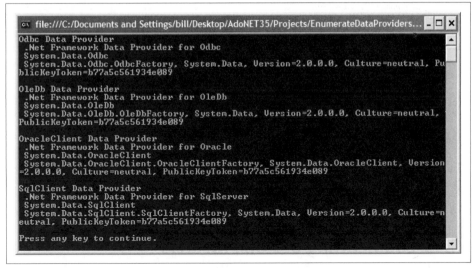

Figure 11-16. Output for EnumerateDataProviders solution

Table 11-10. Data provider information columns

Column name	Description
Name	Data provider name.
Description	Data provider description.
InvariantName	A unique identifier for a data provider registered in `machine.config` in the `<system.data><DbProviderFactories>` element. For example, the invariant name for SQL Server is `System.Data.SqlClient`.
	The invariant name is used to programmatically refer to the data provider.
AssemblyQualifiedName	Fully qualified name of the data provider factory class—enough information to instantiate the object.

The providers listed in Figure 11-16 correspond to the `DbProviderFactories` element in *machine.config*, shown in the following excerpt:

```
<system.data>
  <DbProviderFactories>
    <add name="Odbc Data Provider" invariant="System.Data.Odbc"
      description=".Net Framework Data Provider for Odbc"
      type="System.Data.Odbc.OdbcFactory,
      System.Data, Version=2.0.0.0, Culture=neutral, PublicKeyToken=b77a5c561934e089"
    />
    <add name="OleDb Data Provider" invariant="System.Data.OleDb"
      description=".Net Framework Data Provider for OleDb"
      type="System.Data.OleDb.OleDbFactory,
      System.Data, Version=2.0.0.0, Culture=neutral, PublicKeyToken=b77a5c561934e089"
    />
```

```
<add name="OracleClient Data Provider" invariant="System.Data.OracleClient"
  description=".Net Framework Data Provider for Oracle"
  type="System.Data.OracleClient.OracleClientFactory, System.Data.OracleClient,
  Version=2.0.0.0, Culture=neutral, PublicKeyToken=b77a5c561934e089" />
<add name="SqlClient Data Provider" invariant="System.Data.SqlClient"
  description=".Net Framework Data Provider for SqlServer"
  type="System.Data.SqlClient.SqlClientFactory, System.Data, Version=2.0.0.0,
  Culture=neutral, PublicKeyToken=b77a5c561934e089" />
<add name="Microsoft SQL Server Compact Data Provider"
  invariant="System.Data.SqlServerCe.3.5"
  description=".NET Framework Data Provider for Microsoft SQL Server Compact"
  type="System.Data.SqlServerCe.SqlCeProviderFactory,
  System.Data.SqlServerCe, Version=3.5.0.0, Culture=neutral,
  PublicKeyToken=89845dcd8080cc91" />
  </DbProviderFactories>
</system.data>
```

11.15 Enumerating OLE DB Providers

Problem

You need a list of the OLE DB providers installed on the machine running your code.

Solution

Use the `OleDbEnumerator.GetElements( )` method, the `OleDbEnumerator.GetEnumerator( )` method, a SQL Server extended stored procedure, or search the registry. The solution demonstrates these four approaches.

The first approach uses the `GetElements( )` method of the `OleDbEnumerator` class to retrieve a list of visible OLE DB providers and output them to the console.

The second approach uses the static `GetEnumerator( )` method of the `OleDbEnumerator` class to retrieve a list of OLE DB providers and output them to the console.

The third approach executes the extended stored procedure `xp_enum_oledb_providers`. The result set containing the installed OLE DB providers is output to the console.

In the fourth approach, the sample code uses the `Microsoft.Win32.Registry` class to examine the registry, identify OLE DB provider subkeys, and retrieve and display the OLE DB provider names from these subkeys.

The C# code in *Program.cs* in the project `EnumerateOleDbProviders` is shown in Example 11-18.

Example 11-18. File: Program.cs for EnumerateOleDbProviders solutions

```
using System;
using System.Data;
using System.Data.SqlClient;
using System.Data.OleDb;
using Microsoft.Win32;
```

Example 11-18. File: Program.cs for EnumerateOleDbProviders solutions (continued)

```csharp
namespace EnumerateOleDbProviders
{
    class Program
    {
        static void Main(string[] args)
        {
            // Enumerate OLE DB providers using GetElements( )
            OleDbEnumerator e = new OleDbEnumerator( );
            DataTable dt = e.GetElements( );
            Console.WriteLine(
                "---Using OleDbEnumerator.GetElements( ) (top 5)---");
            for (int i = 0; i < 5; i++)
                Console.WriteLine("{0} - {1}", dt.Rows[i]["SOURCES_NAME"],
                    dt.Rows[i]["SOURCES_DESCRIPTION"]);

            // Enumerate OLE DB providers using GetEnumerator( )
            Console.WriteLine(
                "\n---Using OleDbEnumerator.GetEnumerator( ) (top 5)---");
            OleDbDataReader dr =
                OleDbEnumerator.GetEnumerator(Type.GetTypeFromProgID("MSDAENUM"));
            int j = 0;
            while (dr.Read( ) && j++ < 5)
                Console.WriteLine("{0} - {1}",
                    dr["SOURCES_NAME"], dr["SOURCES_DESCRIPTION"]);

            // Enumerate OLE DB providers using xp_enum_oledb_providers
            Console.WriteLine(
                "\n---Using xp_enum_oledb_providers (top 5)---");
            string sqlConnectString = "Data Source=(local);" +
                "Integrated security=SSPI";
            SqlConnection connection =
                new SqlConnection(sqlConnectString);

            // create a command to execute the extended stored procedure to
            // retrieve OLE DB providers
            SqlCommand command =
                new SqlCommand("xp_enum_oledb_providers", connection);
            command.CommandType = CommandType.StoredProcedure;

            // create the DataReader
            connection.Open( );
            SqlDataReader rdr = command.ExecuteReader( );
            // iterate over the top 5 OLE DB providers in the DataReader
            for (int i = 0; i < 5; i++)
            {
                rdr.Read( );
                Console.WriteLine("{0} - {1}",
                    rdr["Provider Name"], rdr["Provider Description"]);
            }
            connection.Close( );

            // Enumerate OLE DB providers using the Windows registry
            Console.WriteLine("\n---Using registry (top 5)---");
```

Example 11-18. File: Program.cs for EnumerateOleDbProviders solutions (continued)

```
            // get the HKEY_CLASSES_ROOT/CLSID key
            RegistryKey keyCLSID =
                Registry.ClassesRoot.OpenSubKey("CLSID", false);
            // iterate through the collection of subkeys
            string[] keys = keyCLSID.GetSubKeyNames( );
            int count = 0;
            for (int i = 0; i < keys.Length && count < 5; i++)
            {
                // look for the OLE DB Provider subkey and
                // retrieve the value if found
                RegistryKey key = keyCLSID.OpenSubKey(keys[i], false);
                RegistryKey subKey = key.OpenSubKey("OLE DB Provider", false);
                if (subKey != null)
                {
                    Console.WriteLine("{0}",
                        subKey.GetValue(subKey.GetValueNames( )[0]));
                    count++;
                }
            }

            Console.WriteLine("\nPress any key to continue.");
            Console.ReadKey( );
        }
    }
}
```

The output is shown in Figure 11-17.

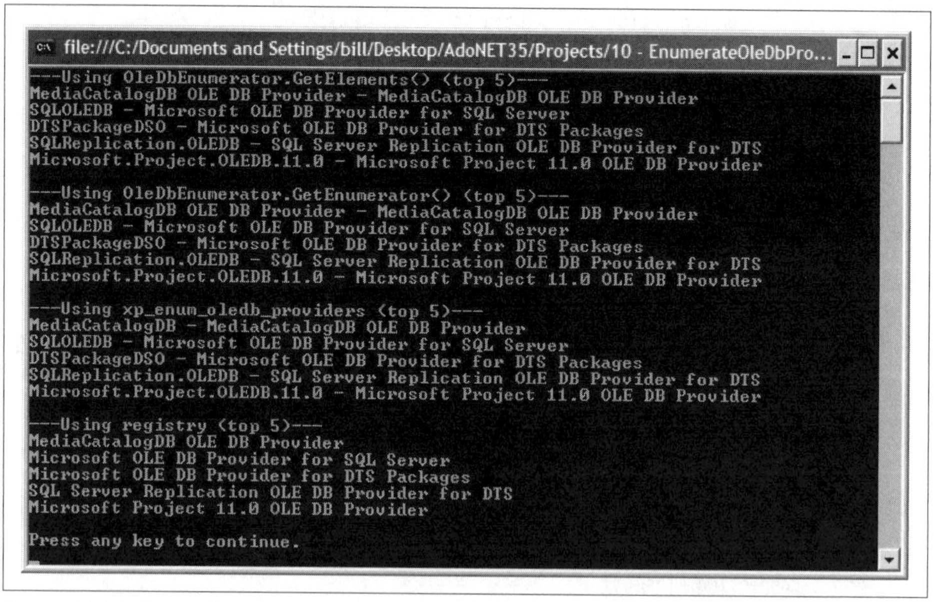

Figure 11-17. Output for EnumerateOleDbProviders solutions

Discussion

The following subsections discuss the four approaches demonstrated in the solution.

OleDbEnumerator.GetElements( ) method

The GetElements( ) method of the the OleDbEnumerator class returns a DataTable containing the information shown in Table 11-11 for all visible OLE DB providers. This method is available in .NET Framework 2.0 and later.

Table 11-11. OLE DB provider information columns

Column	Description
SOURCES_NAME	The name of the native OLE DB data source.
SOURCES_PARSENAME	Human-readable name that can be converted to a moniker using the native COM interface IParseDisplayName.
SOURCES_DESCRIPTION	Description of the native OLE DB data source.
SOURCES_TYPE	One of the following enumeration values: 0 (Binder), 1 (DataSource_MDP), 2 (DataSource_TDP), 3 (Enumerator).
SOURCES_ISPARENT	Indicates that the entry applies to the same enumerator on which GetSourcesRowset was called. This column applies only to enumerators.
SOURCES_CLSID	The class ID of the OLE DB data source.

OleDbEnumerator GetEnumerator( ) method

The static GetEnumerator( ) method of the OleDbEnumerator class uses a specific OLE DB enumerator (MSDAENUM component in the solution) to return an OleDbDataReader containing information shown in Table 11-11 about installed OLE DB providers. This method is available in .NET Framework 2.0 and later.

xp_enum_oledb_providers extended stored procedure

The extended stored procedure xp_enum_oledb_providers is available in SQL Server 7.0 or later. Executing the stored procedure against the master database returns a result set of all OLE DB providers installed on the SQL Server. The result set contains the information described in Table 11-12.

Table 11-12. xp_enum_oledb_providers result set

Column name	Description
Provider Name	Default value of the class ID (CLSID) key
Parse Name	Class ID (CLSID)
Provider Description	Name of the OLE DB provider

The SQL Server extended stored procedure xp_enum_oledb_providers does not list all installed OLE DB providers. Providers such as MSDataShape are excluded because they do not work as linked servers. Other providers, such as Microsoft Jet 3.51 OLE DB, are excluded because a later version of the provider is installed, for example Microsoft Jet 4.0 OLE DB.

Windows Registry

The fourth technique uses a registry scan and is necessary if SQL Server 7.0, or later, is not installed on the computer, although it can be used with later versions as well.

The .NET Framework classes that manipulate the registry are found in the Microsoft.Win32 namespace. The class IDs that represent OLE DB providers can be identified by the presence of a subkey OLE DB Provider in a class ID. So, to enumerate the OLE DB providers on a computer, iterate over all of the subkeys of the HKEY_CLASSES_ROOT\CLSID key and check for the presence of the OLE DB Provider subkey. The provider name returned by the SQL Server extended stored procedure is the default value for the ProgID subkey while the OLE DB provider name is the default value for the OLE DB Provider subkey.

11.16 Enumerating ODBC Drivers

Problem

You need a list of the ODBC drivers installed on the computer running your code.

Solution

Consult the registry.

The sample code uses the Microsoft.Win32.Registry class to display a list of all installed ODBC drivers.

The C# code in *Program.cs* in the project EnumerateOdbcDrivers is shown in Example 11-19.

Example 11-19. File: Program.cs for EnumerateOdbcDrivers solution

```
using System;
using Microsoft.Win32;

namespace EnuerateOleDbProviders
{
    class Program
    {
        static void Main(string[] args)
        {
```

Example 11-19. File: Program.cs for EnumerateOdbcDrivers solution

```
        // Get the HKEY_LOCAL_MACHINE\SOFTWARE\ODBC\ODBCINST.INI\ODBC Drivers key.
        RegistryKey keyLocalMachine = Registry.LocalMachine.OpenSubKey(
            @"SOFTWARE\ODBC\ODBCINST.INI\ODBC Drivers", false);

        // Retrueve and output the ODBC driver names
        string[] valueNames = keyLocalMachine.GetValueNames( );
        for (int i = 0; i < valueNames.Length; i++)
            Console.WriteLine("{0}", valueNames[i]);

        Console.WriteLine("\nPress any key to continue.");
        Console.ReadKey( );
    }
  }
}
```

The output is shown in Figure 11-18.

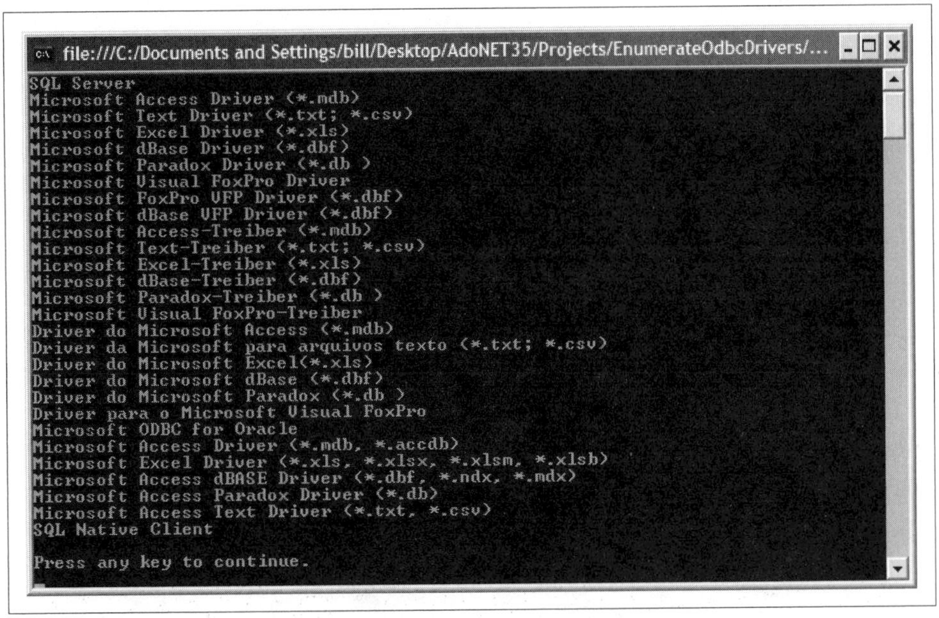

Figure 11-18. Output for EnumerateOdbcDrivers solution

Discussion

The .NET Framework classes that manipulate the registry are found in the Microsoft.Win32 namespace. The registry key HKEY_LOCAL_MACHINE\SOFTWARE\ODBC\ ODBCINST.INI\ODBC Drivers contains a value name for each installed ODBC driver.

11.17 Changing a SQL Server User Password

Problem

You need to programmatically change the existing password for the user specified in a connection string to SQL Server 2005 or later.

Solution

Use the ChangePassword( ) method of the SqlConnection class.

The solution uses the ChangePassword( ) method of the SqlConnection class to change the password for the user named sa (system administrator) and confirms the change by logging in with the new password.

The C# code shown in *Program.cs* in the project ChangeSqlServerUserPassword is shown in Example 11-20.

Example 11-20. File: Program.cs for ChangeSqlServerUserPassword solution

```
using System;
using System.Data;
using System.Data.SqlClient;

namespace ChangeSqlServerUserPassword
{
    class Program
    {
        static void Main(string[] args)
        {
            string password1 = "password";
            string password2 = "new-password";

            string sqlConnectString1 = "Data Source=(local);" +
                "uid=sa;pwd=" + password1 + ";Initial Catalog=AdventureWorks;";

            // Using password1 to connect, change the password to password2
            SqlConnection.ChangePassword(sqlConnectString1, password2);
            Console.WriteLine("Password changed to '{0}'.", password2);

            // Open a connection using the new password (password2)
            string sqlConnectString2 = "Data Source=(local);" +
                "uid=sa;pwd=" + password2 + ";Initial Catalog=AdventureWorks";
            using (SqlConnection conn = new SqlConnection(sqlConnectString2))
            {
                conn.Open( );
                Console.WriteLine("\nConnected with connect string:\n  {0}",
                    sqlConnectString2);
            }
            Console.WriteLine("\nDisconnected.");
```

Example 11-20. File: Program.cs for ChangeSqlServerUserPassword solution (continued)

```
        Console.WriteLine("\nPress any key to continue.");
        Console.ReadKey();
    }
  }
}
```

The output is shown in Figure 11-19.

Figure 11-19. Output for ChangeSqlServerUserPassword solution

Discussion

With SQL Server 2005 and later and with Windows Server 2003 and later, you can programmatically change the existing password for the user specified in a connection string using the ChangePassword( ) method of the SqlConnection class. The ChangePassword( ) method takes two arguments:

- A connection string containing the user ID and password. An exception will be thrown if integrated security is specified in the connection string.

- The new password.

The ChangePassword( ) method can be used to change an expired user password without administrator intervention. If the password has expired, calling the Open( ) method of the SqlConnection object raises a SqlException exception. If the password needs to be reset, the Number property of the SqlException object will be either 18487 (password expired) or 18488 (password must be reset before logging in).

SQL Server CLR Integration

12.0 Introduction

The .NET Framework Common Language Runtime (CLR) environment executes compiled code written in programming languages such as C# and Visual Basic. The code is compiled to a file, or *assembly*, that contains the compiled code and an assembly manifest. The manifest contains metadata about the assembly, including types, methods, and inheritance relationships. Code running within the CLR is called *managed code*.

The CLR provides services such as automatic garbage collection, security support, and runtime type checking. Because the compiled code is executed by the CLR rather than directly by the operating system, managed code applications are platform and language independent.

SQL Server 2005 and later versions host the CLR in the Database Engine. This is called *CLR integration*. CLR integration lets you create database objects such as functions, stored procedures, triggers, user-defined types (UDTs), and user-defined aggregate (UDA) functions in programming languages supported by the CLR. Managed code running in SQL Server-hosted CLR is referred to as a *CLR routine*.

Prior to SQL Server 2005, the main way that SQL Server was extended was using extended stored procedures that let you create external routines using programming languages such as C. Extended stored procedures are used like regular stored procedures, however, they can have performance problems such as memory leaks and can cause the server to become unreliable. CLR integration lets you extend SQL Server with the safety and reliability of T-SQL and with the flexibility of extended stored procedures.

Managed code uses code access security (CAS) to control what operations assemblies can perform. CAS secures the code running within SQL Server and prevents the code from adversely affecting the operating system or the database server. Generally, you should use T-SQL when the code in the routines primarily performs data access. CLR routines are best for CPU-intensive calculations and for supporting complex logic that would otherwise be difficult to implement using T-SQL. The components needed to develop CLR routines are installed with SQL Server 2005 and later.

Although these versions of SQL Server ship with the .NET Framework and command-line compilers for C# and VB.NET, as well as Business Intelligence Studio that lets you build Analysis Services and Reporting Services projects using the same IDE as Visual Studio, you need to install Visual Studio 2005 or later to create and compile CLR routines using the Visual Studio IDE.

CLR integration is turned off by default. Use the sp_configure system stored procedure to enable CLR integration, as shown here:

```
sp_configure 'clr enabled', 1
GO
RECONFIGURE
GO
```

The clr enabled server configuration option specifies whether .NET assemblies can be run by SQL Server (0 = do not allow; 1 = allow). The change takes effect immediately after sp_configure and RECONFIGURE are executed—the server does not need to be restarted. You need ALTER SETTINGS permissions at the server level to enable CLR integration.

Alternatively, you can use the SQL Server Surface Area Configuration tool to control whether CLR integration is enabled.

SQL Server CLR integration lets you build database objects using .NET languages. Once a .NET Framework assembly is registered with SQL Server, you can create CLR routines that can be used anywhere a T-SQL equivalent routine can be used. Table 12-1 describes the types of CLR routines you can build. The solutions in this chapter show you how to build each of these types of SQL Server CLR routines.

Table 12-1. Types of CLR routines

Database object	.NET Framework assembly type	Description
Scalar-valued function	Public static method	A UDF that returns a single value.
Table-valued function	Public static method	A UDF that returns a table as the result set.
Stored procedure	Public static method	A routine that returns tabular result sets and messages to the client, invokes DDL and DML statements, and returns output parameters.
User-defined aggregate function	Class or structure	A UDA function that operates on values in a set of rows and returns a scalar.
User-defined type	Class or structure	Complex data types complete with methods that extend the scalar type system in SQL Server.
Triggers (DML and DDL)	Public static method	A type of stored procedure that automatically runs when a DML or DDL event occurs.

SQL Server 2005 introduced new T-SQL statements to create and manage .NET assemblies and UDTs, and enhances other T-SQL statements to create and manage functions, stored procedures, triggers, and UDA functions created from CLR assemblies. These statements are briefly described in Table 12-2.

Table 12-2. New and changed T-SQL statements to support CLR integration

Scope	DDL statement	New .NET T-SQL statement	Description
.NET Framework assembly	CREATE ASSEMBLY	Yes	Loads assembly into SQL Server.
	ALTER ASSEMBLY	Yes	Changes a loaded assembly.
	DROP ASSEMBLY	Yes	Unloads an assembly from SQL Server.
User-defined aggregate function	CREATE AGGREGATE	Yes	Creates a UDA function in a SQL Server database from a UDA function implemented as a class in a .NET Framework assembly.
	DROP AGGREGATE	Yes	The assembly containing the class must first be registered in SQL Server with the CREATE ASSEMBLY T-SQL statement.
User-defined type	CREATE TYPE	No	Creates a UDT in a SQL Server database from a type implemented as a class or structure in a .NET Framework assembly.
			The assembly containing the class or structure must first be registered in SQL Server with the CREATE ASSEMBLY T-SQL statement.
	DROP TYPE	No	Removes a UDT from a SQL Server database.
Stored procedure	CREATE PROCEDURE	No	Creates a stored procedure in a SQL Server database from a CLR stored procedure implemented as a method in a .NET Framework assembly.
			The assembly containing the method must first be registered in SQL Server with the CREATE ASSEMBLY T-SQL statement.
	ALTER PROCEDURE	No	Changes a stored procedure previously created with the CREATE PROCEDURE T-SQL statement.
	DROP PROCEDURE	No	Removes a stored procedure from a SQL Server database.
User-defined function (scalar-valued or table-valued)	CREATE FUNCTION	No	Creates a UDF in a SQL Server database from a CLR UDF implemented as a method in a .NET Framework assembly.
			The assembly containing the method must first be registered in SQL Server with the CREATE ASSEMBLY T-SQL statement.
	ALTER FUNCTION	No	Changes a UDF previously created with the CREATE FUNCTION T-SQL statement.
	DROP FUNCTION	No	Removes a UDF from a SQL Server database.
Trigger	CREATE TRIGGER	No	Creates a DML or DDL trigger in a SQL Server database from a CLR trigger implemented as a method in a .NET Framework assembly.
			The assembly containing the method must first be registered in SQL Server with the CREATE ASSEMBLY T-SQL statement.
	ALTER TRIGGER	No	Changes a trigger previously created with the CREATE TRIGGER T-SQL statement.
	DROP TRIGGER	No	Removes a trigger from a SQL Server database.

For more information about assembly or CLR routine management, see SQL Server Books Online.

ADO.NET In-Process Extensions Supporting CLR Programming

ADO.NET has four main in-process functional extensions that are used when programming .NET Framework routines. The SqlContext object provides access to context information, to a SqlPipe object for sending results to the client, and to a SqlTriggerContext object that provides information about the operation that caused a trigger to fire. The fourth—the SqlDataRecord object—returns to the caller a custom result set from a stored procedure. These four extensions are discussed in the following subsections.

SqlContext object

Managed code is invoked in the server whenever a CLR routine is executed. Code running on the server executes in the context of the caller connection, so the CLR code needs access to the caller context. The SqlContext class in the Microsoft. SqlServer.Server namespace abstracts the context of the caller and provides access to the context components through its public static properties, described in Table 12-3.

Table 12-3. SqlContext public properties

Property	Return type	Description
IsAvailable	bool	Indicates whether the code executing is running inside SQL Server. If true, other members of SqlContext can be accessed. If false, all other properties will throw InvalidOperationException when accessed, and any attempts to open a connection using the context connection = true attribute in the connection string fail.
Pipe	SqlPipe	A path for messages and result sets to flow to the client.
TriggerContext	SqlTriggerContext	Provides access to information about the operation that caused a DML or DDL trigger to fire. Also provides a map of the updated columns.
		You can retrieve TriggerContext only within a CLR trigger.
WindowsIdentity	System.Security. Principal.WindowsIdentity	Provides access to an impersonation token representing the Windows identity of the caller if the client that initiated execution of the stored procedure or function connected to SQL Server using integrated authentication. null is returned if the caller was authenticated using SQL Server authentication and the code cannot impersonate the caller.
		The SQL Server process account is the context for all CLR code invoked inside of SQL Server. The impersonation token is used to let the code perform actions using the identity of the caller instead of the identity of the process account.
		Only assemblies marked with EXTERNAL_ACCESS or UNSAFE permission can access the WindowsIdentity property.

You obtain an in-process connection using the new connection context connection string keyword. For example:

```
SqlConnection conn = new SqlConnection("context connection=true")
```

SqlPipe object

Use the SqlPipe object to send messages and result sets from a CLR stored procedure to the calling client. The SqlPipe object cannot be directly instantiated. You obtain the SqlPipe object using the Pipe property of the SqlContext object within the body of a CLR routine. The SqlPipe class has the public properties and methods described in Table 12-4.

Table 12-4. SqlPipe public property and methods

Property	Description
IsSendingResults	Indicates whether the pipe is in the process of sending a result set, blocking it from use.
Method	
ExecuteAndSend( )	Executes a command specified as a SqlCommand object argument. The results are sent directly back to the client.
Send( )	Three overloads send one of the following to the client:
	• string (informational message—equivalent to T-SQL PRINT statement)
	• SqlDataRecord object (single-row result set)
	• SqlDataReader object (multiple-row result set)
SendResultsEnd( )	Marks the end of a custom result set from a stored procedure initiated by the SendResultsStart( ) method. Sets the SqlPipe object back to a state where other methods can be called on it. This method can be called only after SendResultsStart( ) is called.
SendResultsRow( )	Sends a row of data contained in a SqlDataRecord object to the client. This method can be called only after SendResultsStart( ) is called. Each row must conform to the SqlDataRecord argument describing the row that is supplied to the SendResultsStart( ) method.
SendResultsStart( )	Marks the start of a custom result set from a stored procedure. This method takes a SqlDataRecord argument to construct the metadata that describes the result set. All rows in the result set subsequently sent to the client using the SendResultsRow( ) method must conform to this metadata.

SqlTriggerContext object

The SqlTriggerContext class provides context information about the CLR DML or DDL trigger. The SqlTriggerContext object cannot be directly instantiated. You obtain the SqlTrigger object using the TriggerContext property of the SqlContext object within the body of a CLR trigger. The SqlTriggerContext class has the public properties and methods described in Table 12-5.

Table 12-5. SqlTriggerContext public properties and method

Property	Description
ColumnCount	The number of columns potentially affected by the UPDATE operation that caused the DML trigger to fire.
EventData	A SqlXml object containing XML describing the triggering operation for a DDL trigger.
TriggerAction	The type of action that caused the trigger to fire. This is one of the TriggerAction enumeration values.
Method	
IsUpdatedColumn( )	Indicates whether a column specified by its ordinal was modified by the UPDATE operation that caused the DML trigger to fire.

SqlDataRecord object

The SqlDataRecord class represents a single row of data together with its metadata. The class allows stored procedures to return custom result sets to the client using the Send( ) or SendResultsRow( ) methods of the SqlPipe object.

You instantiate a SqlDataRecord object by passing to the constructor a SqlMetaData object array that contains an element of metadata for each column in the row. Each SqlMetaData object defines a column name, column type, and possibly other column attributes. For example, the following code defines a SqlDataRecord containing two columns:

```
SqlMetaData[] md = new SqlMetaData[2];
md[0] = new SqlMetaData("intCol", SqlDbType.Int);
md[1] = new SqlMetaData("stringCol", SqlDbType.NVarChar, 50);
SqlDataRecord row = new SqlDataRecord(md);
```

The SqlDataRecord class has accessor methods that let you get and set column values. This is similar to a DataReader except that you can write column values in addition to reading them. For example, the following code fills the two columns in the SqlDataRecord object defined in the preceding example:

```
row.SetSqlInt32(0, 1);
row.SetSqlString(1, "Record 1");
```

Custom Attributes for CLR Routines

The .NET CLR is extended using attributes—descriptive keywords saved in the assembly metadata that provide additional information for programming constructs. The custom attributes used with SQL Server CLR routines are defined in the Microsoft.SqlServer.Server namespace. Table 12-6 describes custom attributes used with SQL Server CLR routines.

Table 12-6. Custom attributes for CLR routines

Attribute	CLR routine	Description
SqlFacet	UDT	Specifies details about the return type of a UDT.
SqlFunction	UDF	Indicates that the method should be registered as a UDF.
SqlMethod	UDT	Specifies the determinism and data access properties of methods in a UDT.
SqlProcedure	Stored procedure	Indicates that the method should be registered as a stored procedure.
SqlTrigger	Trigger	Indicates that the method should be registered as a trigger.
SqlUserDefinedAggregate	UDA	Indicates that the method should be registered as a UDA.
SqlUserDefinedType	UDT	Indicates that the class or structure should be registered as a UDT.

12.1   Creating a Stored Procedure

Problem

You need to create a CLR stored procedure.

Solution

The solution shows how to create four types of CLR stored procedures:

- A stored procedure that returns a result set
- A stored procedure that returns an output parameter, message, and return code
- A stored procedure that returns a dynamically created result set with a single row
- A stored procedure that returns a dynamically created result set containing multiple rows

The first solution is a CLR stored procedure that takes an input parameter @ShiftID and returns a result set of employees working that shift from the HumanResources.Employees table in AdventureWorks. Follow these steps:

1. Create a new SQL Server project in Visual Studio named ClrStoredProcedure.

2. Create a stored procedure item in the project; name it *SpEmployeesInShift.cs*.

3. The C# code in *SpEmployeesInShift.cs* in the project ClrStoredProcedure is shown in Example 12-1.

Example 12-1. Stored procedure: SpEmployeesInShift.cs

```
using System;
using System.Data;
using System.Data.SqlClient;
using System.Data.SqlTypes;
using Microsoft.SqlServer.Server;
```

Example 12-1. Stored procedure: SpEmployeesInShift.cs (continued)

```
public partial class StoredProcedures
{
    [Microsoft.SqlServer.Server.SqlProcedure]
    public static void SpEmployeeInShift(int shiftID)
    {
        using (SqlConnection conn = new SqlConnection("context connection=true"))
        {
            conn.Open( );
            SqlCommand cmd = new SqlCommand(
                "SELECT e.* FROM HumanResources.Employee e " +
                "JOIN HumanResources.EmployeeDepartmentHistory h " +
                "ON e.EmployeeID = h.EmployeeID " +
                "WHERE h.ShiftID = " + shiftID, conn);
            SqlContext.Pipe.ExecuteAndSend(cmd);
        }
    }
};
```

The SpEmployeeInShift( ) method implements the stored procedure and is annotated with the SqlProcedure attribute.

The tabular result set is returned to the client using the ExecuteAndSend( ) method of the SqlPipe object that executes a command and sends the tabular result set directly to the client. The method takes a single parameter that is a SqlCommand object associated with the context connection. Alternatively, you can send a tabular result set to the client using either the Send(SqlDataReader) or Send(SqlDataRecord) method of the SqlPipe object. The following line of code replaces the ExecuteAndSend( ) method used in this example with the Send(SqlDataReader) method:

```
SqlContext.Pipe.Send(cmd.ExecuteReader( ));
```

The Send( ) methods lets you manipulate the data before you send it to the client but is slightly slower because of additional overhead.

4. Build the solution.

5. Register the assembly and create the stored procedure by executing the following T-SQL statement in SQL Server Management Studio, replacing <path> appropriately:

```
USE AdventureWorks
GO

CREATE ASSEMBLY ClrStoredProcedure
FROM '<path>\ClrStoredProcedure\bin\Debug\ClrStoredProcedure.dll'
GO

CREATE PROCEDURE ClrSpEmployeeByShift
    @shiftID int
AS EXTERNAL NAME ClrStoredProcedure.StoredProcedures.SpEmployeeInShift
```

6. Execute the stored procedure from SQL Server Manager:

```
EXEC ClrSpEmployeeByShift @shiftID=1
```

Partial results are shown in Figure 12-1.

	EmployeeID	NationalIDNumber	ContactID	LoginID	ManagerID	Title	BirthD
1	1	14417807	1209	adventure-works\guy1	16	Production Technician - WC60	1972
2	2	253022876	1030	adventure-works\kevin0	6	Marketing Assistant	1977
3	3	509647174	1002	adventure-works\roberto0	12	Engineering Manager	1964
4	4	112457891	1290	adventure-works\rob0	3	Senior Tool Designer	1965
5	4	112457891	1290	adventure-works\rob0	3	Senior Tool Designer	1965
6	5	480168528	1009	adventure-works\thierry0	263	Tool Designer	1949
7	6	24756624	1028	adventure-works\david0	109	Marketing Manager	1965
8	6	24756624	1028	adventure-works\david0	109	Marketing Manager	1965
9	8	690627818	1071	adventure-works\ruth0	185	Production Technician - WC10	1946

Figure 12-1. Partial results for ClrSpEmployeeByShift stored procedure solution

The second solution shows how to build a CLR stored procedure that returns an output parameter, a message, and a return code. Follow these steps:

1. Add a stored procedure item to the existing project ClrStoredProcedure and name it SpOutputParameter_Message_ReturnCode.

2. The C# code in *SpOutputParameter_Message_ReturnCode.cs* in the project ClrStoredProcedure is shown in Example 12-2.

Example 12-2. Stored procedure: SpOutputParameter_Message_ReturnCode.cs

```
using System;
using System.Data;
using System.Data.SqlClient;
using System.Data.SqlTypes;
using Microsoft.SqlServer.Server;

public partial class StoredProcedures
{
    [Microsoft.SqlServer.Server.SqlProcedure]
    public static int SpOutputParameter_Message_ReturnCode(out int outVal)
    {
        outVal = 10;
        SqlContext.Pipe.Send("Test message.");
        return 5;
    }
};
```

Notice that the return value of the stored procedure is int rather than void and that it has output argument named outVal of data type int.

3. Build the solution.

4. Update the assembly registration in SQL Server and create the new stored procedure by executing the following T-SQL statement:

```
USE AdventureWorks
GO

ALTER ASSEMBLY ClrStoredProcedure
FROM '<path>\ClrStoredProcedure\bin\Debug\ClrStoredProcedure.dll'
GO

CREATE PROCEDURE ClrSpOutputParameter_Message_ReturnCode
    @outputVal int OUT
AS EXTERNAL NAME
    ClrStoredProcedure.StoredProcedures.SpOutputParameter_Message_ReturnCode
```

5. Execute the stored procedure:

```
DECLARE @returnCode int
DECLARE @outVal int

EXEC @returnCode = ClrSpOutputParameter_Message_ReturnCode @outVal OUTPUT

PRINT 'Return code = ' + CAST(@returnCode AS CHAR(5))
PRINT 'Output value @outVal = ' + CAST(@outVal AS CHAR(5))
```

Results are shown in Figure 12-2.

Figure 12-2. Output for SpOutputParameter_Message_ReturnCode stored procedure solution

The third solution shows how to build a CLR stored procedure that returns a result set containing a single row of data created dynamically by the stored procedure. Follow these steps:

1. Add a stored procedure item to the existing project ClrStoredProcedure and name it SpDynamicResultSet.

2. The C# code in *SpDynamicResultSet.cs* in the project ClrStoredProcedure is shown in Example 12-3.

Example 12-3. Stored procedure: SpDynamicResultSet.cs

```
using System;
using System.Data;
using System.Data.SqlClient;
using System.Data.SqlTypes;
using Microsoft.SqlServer.Server;
```

Example 12-3. Stored procedure: SpDynamicResultSet.cs (continued)

```
public partial class StoredProcedures
{
    [Microsoft.SqlServer.Server.SqlProcedure]
    public static void SpDynamicResultSet()
    {
        SqlMetaData[] md = new SqlMetaData[2];
        md[0] = new SqlMetaData("intCol", SqlDbType.Int);
        md[1] = new SqlMetaData("stringCol", SqlDbType.NVarChar, 50);
        SqlDataRecord row = new SqlDataRecord(md);
        row.SetSqlInt32(0, 1);
        row.SetSqlString(1, "Record 1");
        SqlContext.Pipe.Send(row);
    }
};
```

The method uses the SqlMetaData class to define the schema of the result set row. The row is created as an instance of the SqlDataRecord class. The row values are filled using the Set( ) methods of SqlDataRecord. The Set( ) methods take two arguments—an ordinal specifying the column number and the value. Finally, an overload of the SqlPipe.Send( ) method is used to return the instance of the SqlDataRecord class as the result set row.

You cannot extend this example to return a result set containing multiple rows since a new result set is returned each time the Send( ) method is called. The fourth solution in this section shows how to return a dynamically created result set containing multiple rows.

3. Build the solution.

4. Update the assembly registration in SQL Server and create the new stored procedure by executing the following T-SQL statement:

```
USE AdventureWorks
GO

ALTER ASSEMBLY ClrStoredProcedure
FROM '<path>\ClrStoredProcedure\bin\Debug\ClrStoredProcedure.dll'
GO

CREATE PROCEDURE ClrSpDynamicResultSet
AS EXTERNAL NAME
    ClrStoredProcedure.StoredProcedures.SpDynamicResultSet
```

5. Execute the stored procedure:

```
EXEC ClrSpDynamicResultSet
```

Results are shown in Figure 12-3.

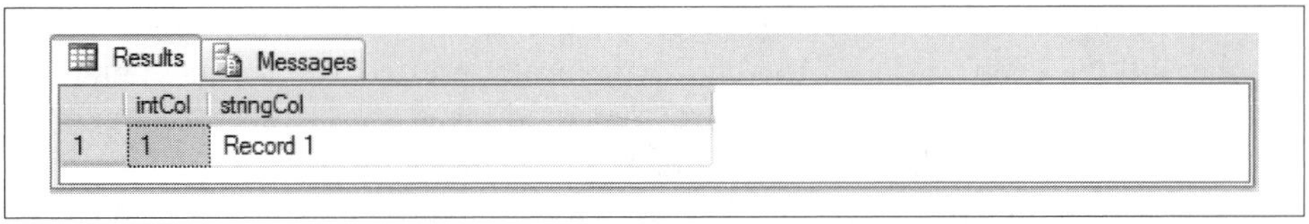

Figure 12-3. Results for SpDynamicResultSet_Result stored procedure solution

The fourth solution shows how to build a CLR stored procedure that returns a result set containing a two rows of data created dynamically by the stored procedure. Follow these steps:

1. Add a stored procedure item to the existing project ClrStoredProcedure and name it SpDynamicResultSet2.

2. The C# code in *SpDynamicResultSet2.cs* in the project ClrStoredProcedure is shown in Example 12-4.

Example 12-4. Stored procedure: SpDynamicResultSet2.cs

```csharp
using System;
using System.Data;
using System.Data.SqlClient;
using System.Data.SqlTypes;
using Microsoft.SqlServer.Server;

public partial class StoredProcedures
{
    [Microsoft.SqlServer.Server.SqlProcedure]
    public static void SpDynamicResultSet2()
    {
        // set up the meta data for the 2-column row
        SqlMetaData[] md = new SqlMetaData[2];
        md[0] = new SqlMetaData("intCol", SqlDbType.Int);
        md[1] = new SqlMetaData("stringCol", SqlDbType.NVarChar, 50);
        SqlDataRecord row = new SqlDataRecord(md);

        SqlContext.Pipe.SendResultsStart(row);

        // create and send five records
        for (int i = 1; i <= 5; i++)
        {
            row.SetSqlInt32(0, 1);
            row.SetSqlString(1, "Record " + i);
            SqlContext.Pipe.SendResultsRow(row);
        }

        SqlContext.Pipe.SendResultsEnd();
    }
};
```

The SendResultsStart( ), SendResultsRow( ), and SendResultsEnd( ) methods of the SqlPipe class are used to send dynamically created result sets containing multiple rows. The SendResultsStart( ) method takes a SqlDataRecord argument that it uses metadata from to infer the schema of the result set. The SendResultsRow( ) method is called for each row to return in the result set. It can be called any time after SendResultsStart( ) is called and before SendResultsEnd( ) is called marking the end of the result set.

3. Build the solution.

4. Update the assembly registration in SQL Server and create the new stored procedure by executing the following T-SQL statement:

```
USE AdventureWorks
GO

ALTER ASSEMBLY ClrStoredProcedure
FROM '<path>\ClrStoredProcedure\bin\Debug\ClrStoredProcedure.dll'
GO

CREATE PROCEDURE ClrSpDynamicResultSet2
AS EXTERNAL NAME
    ClrStoredProcedure.StoredProcedures.SpDynamicResultSet2
```

5. Execute the stored procedure:

```
EXEC ClrSpDynamicResultSet2
```

Results are shown in Figure 12-4.

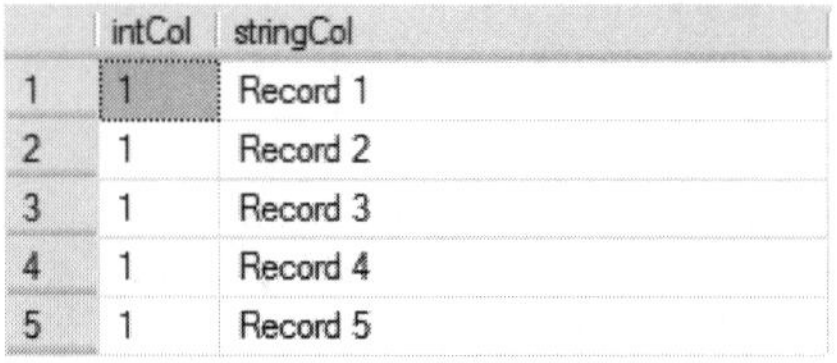

	intCol	stringCol
1	1	Record 1
2	1	Record 2
3	1	Record 3
4	1	Record 4
5	1	Record 5

Figure 12-4. Results for SpDynamicResultSet2 stored procedure solution

Discussion

Stored procedures are routines that return tabular result sets, messages, and output parameters to the client and invoke DML and DDL statements. A CLR stored procedure is implemented as a public static method of a class in a .NET Framework assembly. The method is either void or returns an integer that is the return code from the stored procedure. A method declared void implicitly returns a stored procedure return code of 0.

You identify a stored procedure by annotating the method that implements the stored procedure with the SqlProcedure attribute. The SqlProcedure attribute indicates that the method should be registered as a stored procedure. The SqlProcedure attribute has the following syntax:

```
SqlProcedure [ ( procedure-attribute [ ,... ] ) ]

procedure-attribute::=
   Name = "procedure name"
```

Where:

Name

Specifies the name of the stored procedure.

Arguments to the stored procedure method can be any native SQL Server data type that has an equivalent in managed code. CLR stored procedures can return information to the client as messages, tabular result sets, and output parameters. Send messages and tabular result sets using one of the Send( ) methods of the SqlPipe object or using the ExecuteAndSend( ) method of the SqlPipe object. Output parameters are arguments that are passed in the same way as other output arguments (i.e., using the out keyword in C#).

12.2   Creating a Scalar-Valued Function

Problem

You need to create a CLR scalar-valued function.

Solution

The solution creates a scalar-valued function that is a CLR stored procedure that returns the total for a specific sales order by summing the LineTotal values in the Sales.SalesOrderDetail table in AdventureWorks for a specified sales order ID. Follow these steps:

1. Create a new SQL Server project in Visual Studio and name it ClrScalarValuedFunction.

2. Create a user-defined function item in the project. Name the item *SumLineTotal.cs*.

3. The C# code in *SumLineTotal.cs* in the project ClrScalarValuedFunction is shown in Example 12-5.

Example 12-5. File: SumLineTotal.cs

```csharp
using System;
using System.Data;
using System.Data.SqlClient;
using System.Data.SqlTypes;
using Microsoft.SqlServer.Server;

public partial class UserDefinedFunctions
{
    [Microsoft.SqlServer.Server.SqlFunction(DataAccess = DataAccessKind.Read)]
    public static SqlMoney SumLineTotal(int salesOrderID)
```

Example 12-5. File: SumLineTotal.cs (continued)

```
{
    using (SqlConnection connection =
        new SqlConnection("context connection=true"))
    {
        connection.Open();
        SqlCommand cmd = new SqlCommand(
            "SELECT SUM(LineTotal) " +
            "FROM Sales.SalesOrderDetail " +
            "WHERE SalesOrderID=" + salesOrderID, connection);
        return (decimal)cmd.ExecuteScalar();
    }
}
};
```

Notice that the function returns data type SqlMoney and accepts an argument salesOrderID of data type int. The actual return value is decimal, which is compatible with the SQL Server Money data type. The function reads data from SQL Server, so the DataAccess property of the SqlFunction attribute is set to DataAccessKind.Read.

4. Build the solution.

5. Register the assembly and create the scalar-valued function by executing the following T-SQL statement in SQL Server Management Studio, replacing <path> appropriately:

```
USE AdventureWorks
GO

CREATE ASSEMBLY ScalarValuedFunction
FROM '<path>\ClrScalarValuedFunction\bin\Debug\ClrScalarValuedFunction.dll'
GO

CREATE FUNCTION udfSumLineTotal(@salesOrderID int)
RETURNS MONEY
AS EXTERNAL NAME ScalarValuedFunction.UserDefinedFunctions.SumLineTotal
```

6. Execute the scalar-valued function to return the line total sum for sales order with SaleOrderID = 43660 by executing the following T-SQL statement:

```
SELECT dbo.udfSumLineTotal(43660)
```

Results are shown in Figure 12-5.

Figure 12-5. Results for SumLineTotal scalar-valued function solution

Discussion

A scalar-valued function (SVF) is a user-defined function (UDF) that returns a single value. Scalar-valued functions can take arguments and return values of any scalar data type supported by SQL Server except rowversion, text, ntext, image, timestamp, table, or cursor. An SVF is implemented as a static method of a class in a .NET Framework assembly. The return value of the method must be compatible with the SQL Server data type that the method returns.

You identify a .NET SVF or table-valued function (TVF) by annotating the method where you implement the function with the SqlFunction attribute. In addition to indicating that the method should be registered as a function, the SqlFunction attribute can be used to define characteristics of the function. The SqlFunction attribute has the following syntax:

```
SqlFunction [ ( function-attribute [,...] ) ]

function-attribute::=
    IsDeterministic = {true | false}
  | DataAccess = { DataAccessKind.None | DataAccessKind.Read }
  | SystemDataAccess = { SystemDataAccessKind.None | SystemDataAccessKind.Read }
  | IsPrecise = { true | false }
  | FillRowMethodName = string
  | Name = string
  | TableDefinition = string
```

Where:

IsDeterministic

> Specifies whether the function always returns the same output values for the same set of input values and the same database state. This allows the server to do performance optimizations. The default value is false.

DataAccess = { DataAccessKind.None | DataAccessKind.Read }

> Specifies the type of data access the function requires if it accesses data on the local SQL Server or on a remote server if transaction integration is required. The DataAccess argument takes one of two values of the DataAccessKind enumeration:

DataAccessKind.None

> The function does not access data.

DataAccessKind.Read

> The function only reads data.

The DataAccess property should be set to DataAccessKind.Read if a T-SQL statement is executed inside a CLR SVF or TVF routine.

User-defined functions cannot insert, update, or delete data.

```
SystemDataAccess = { SystemDataAccessKind.None | SystemDataAccessKind.Read }
```
Specifies the type of data access the function requires if it accesses data stored in the system catalogs or virtual system tables. The `SystemDataAccess` argument takes one of the two values of the `SystemDataAccessKind` enumeration:

`SystemDataAccessKind.None`
> The function does not access data. This is the default value.

`SystemDataAccessKind.Read`
> The function only reads data.

`IsPrecise`
> Specifies whether the return value of the function depends on imprecise calculations involving single or double data types (`float` or `real` in SQL Server). This property is used to determine whether the computed columns using the function can be indexed. The default value is `false`.

`FillRowMethodName`
> Specifies the name of the method used by a table-valued function to fill a row of data in the table returned by the function. Fill row methods are discussed in Recipe 12.3.

`Name`
> Specifies the name with which the function should be registered in SQL Server.

`TableDefinition`
> Specifies the layout of the table returned by a table-valued function.

12.3   Creating a Table-Valued Function

Problem

You need to create a CLR table-valued function.

Solution

This solution creates, registers, and executes a table-valued function that returns a table containing the `Name`, `Length`, and `ModifiedDate` for each file in a specified directory. Follow these steps:

1. Create a new SQL Server project in Visual Studio and name it `ClrTableValuedFunction`.

2. Create a user-defined function item in the project. Name the item *ReadDirectoryFileInfo.cs*.

3. The C# code in *ReadDirectoryFileInfo.cs* in the project `ClrTableValuedFunction` is shown in Example 12-6.

Example 12-6. File: ReadDirectoryFileInfo.cs

```
using System;
using System.Data;
using System.Data.SqlClient;
using System.Data.SqlTypes;
using Microsoft.SqlServer.Server;
using System.Collections;
using System.IO;

public partial class UserDefinedFunctions
{
    [SqlFunction(FillRowMethodName = "FillRow", TableDefinition =
    "FileName nvarchar(256), Size int, DateModified datetime")]
    public static IEnumerator ReadDirectoryFileInfo(string path)
    {
        return new DirectoryLoader(path);
    }

    private static void FillRow(object obj, out SqlString fileName,
    out SqlInt64 fileLength, out SqlDateTime dateModified)
    {
        if (obj != null)
        {
            DirectoryEntry de = (DirectoryEntry)obj;
            fileName = de._fileName;
            fileLength = de._fileLength;
            dateModified = de._fileDateModified;
        }
        else
        {
            fileName = SqlString.Null;
            fileLength = SqlInt64.Null;
            dateModified = SqlDateTime.Null;
        }
    }
}

public class DirectoryLoader : IEnumerator
{
    // array that stores the directory entries
    private FileInfo[] fia;
    private int index = -1;
    public DirectoryLoader(string path)
    {
        string[] files = Directory.GetFiles(path);
        fia = new FileInfo[files.Length];
        for (int i = 0; i < files.Length; i++)
            fia[i] = new FileInfo(files[i]);
    }
```

Example 12-6. File: ReadDirectoryFileInfo.cs (continued)

```csharp
    public object Current
    {
        get
        {
            if (index != -1)
                return new DirectoryEntry(fia[index].Name,
                fia[index].Length, fia[index].LastWriteTime);
            else
                return null;
        }
    }

    public bool MoveNext()
    {
        if (index == fia.Length - 1)
            return false;
        index++;
        return true;
    }

    public void Reset()
    {
        index = -1;
    }
}

public class DirectoryEntry
{
    internal string _fileName;
    internal long _fileLength;
    internal DateTime _fileDateModified;
    public DirectoryEntry(string fileName, long fileLength,
    DateTime fileDateModified)
    {
        _fileName = fileName;
        _fileLength = fileLength;
        _fileDateModified = fileDateModified;
    }
};
```

The code contains three classes—UserDefinedFunctions, which implements the TVF, and two helper classes:

UserDefinedFunctions

> The method ReadDirectoryFileInfo( ) implements the TVF. It is annotated with the SqlFunction attribute described in Recipe 12.2 The SqlFunction attribute identifies the public method FillRow( ) as the method that SQL Server uses to map the current enumerator element to a row in the table that is returned from the TVF. The SqlFunction attribute also specifies the TableDefinition property, which defines the record in the table returned from the TVF.

DirectoryLoader

The enumerator that creates a collection of directory entries for a path specified as an argument to its constructor. The contents of the directory are stored in a FileInfo array named fia. The Current property of the enumerator returns a DirectoryEntry instance containing the filename, file length, and date modified.

DirectoryEntry

Defines a class used to store the current element in the directory enumerator.

Follow these steps:

1. Build the solution.

2. In SQL Server Management Studio, register the assembly and create the table-valued function by executing this T-SQL statement, replacing <path> appropriately:

```
USE AdoDotNet35Cookbook
GO

ALTER DATABASE AdoDotNet35Cookbook
SET TRUSTWORTHY ON
GO

CREATE ASSEMBLY ClrTableValuedFunction
FROM '<path>\ClrTableValuedFunction\bin\Debug\ClrTableValuedFunction.dll'
WITH PERMISSION_SET = EXTERNAL_ACCESS
GO

CREATE FUNCTION udfReadDirectoryFileInfo(@path nvarchar(256))
RETURNS TABLE
    (FileName nvarchar(256), Length bigint, DateModified datetime)
AS
EXTERNAL NAME ClrTableValuedFunction.UserDefinedFunctions.ReadDirectoryFileInfo
```

Notice that the assembly is registered with EXTERNAL_ACCESS permission set to allow it to access the filesystem.

3. Execute the table-valued function with the following T-SQL statement:

```
SELECT * FROM udfReadDirectoryFileInfo('c:\')
```

Results are shown in Figure 12-6.

	FileName	Length	DateModified
1	2006 Six Sigma Project Highlight.ppt	847872	2006-12-14 12:27:04.937
2	amlog.txt	267	2007-09-29 14:49:04.390
3	AUTOEXEC.BAT	0	2006-12-12 19:33:15.363
4	bar.emf	632	2007-04-24 22:42:41.320
5	BellSouthIW.re~	17839140	2007-02-16 12:33:15.340
6	boot.ini	211	2007-10-07 11:26:03.870
7	CONFIG.SYS	0	2006-12-12 19:33:15.363

Figure 12-6. Results for ReadDirectoryFileInfo table-valued function solution

Discussion

A table-valued function (TVF) is a UDF that returns a table. A TVF is implemented as a method of a class in a .NET Framework assembly that returns data as an IEnumerable or IEnumerator object. The columns of the return table cannot include timestamp columns or nonUnicode string data columns such as char, varchar, and text.

CLR TVFs are similar to their T-SQL counterparts—the main difference is that a T-SQL TVF temporarily stores results in an intermediate table, whereas a CLR TVF streams results back to the consumer. As a result, a T-SQL TVF supports constraints and unique indexes on the result set, whereas a CLR TVF can be consumed incrementally once the first row is available—the result set does not have to be fully materialized before returning values.

Enumerators

The IEnumerator interface supports simple iteration over a nongeneric collection. It is the base interface for all nongeneric enumerators. An enumerator can read the data in the underlying collection but cannot be used to modify the data. IEnumerator has one public property, Current, and two public methods, MoveNext( ) and Reset( ). Initially the enumerator is positioned before the first element in the collection.

- The Current property returns an object containing the current element in the collection. You must advance the enumerator from its initial position to the first element in the collection by calling MoveNext( ) before reading the value of the Current property. Reading the Current property when the enumerator is not positioned on an element in the collection (before the first element or after the last element) returns an InvalidOperationException.

- The MoveNext( ) method advances the enumerator to the next element in the collection. MoveNext( ) returns true if the enumerator was successfully advanced and false if the enumerator has passed the end of the collection.

- The Reset( ) method sets the enumerator to the initial position before the first element in the collection. The IEnumerable interface has a single method, GetEnumerator( ), which returns an IEnumerator object.

12.4   Creating an Aggregate Function

Problem

You need to create a CLR aggregate function.

Solution

This solution creates, registers, and executes a user-defined aggregate function that returns the sum of a SqlMoney column in a table. Follow these steps:

1. Create a new SQL Server project in Visual Studio and name it ClrAggregateFunction.

2. Create an aggregate item in the project. Name the item *SumMoney.cs*.

3. The C# code in *SumMoney.cs* in the project ClrAggregateFunction is shown in Example 12-7.

Example 12-7. SumMoney.cs

```csharp
using System;
using System.Data;
using System.Data.SqlClient;
using System.Data.SqlTypes;
using Microsoft.SqlServer.Server;

[Serializable]
[Microsoft.SqlServer.Server.SqlUserDefinedAggregate(Format.Native)]
public struct SumMoney
{
    private SqlMoney sum;

    public void Init()
    {
        sum = 0;
    }

    public void Accumulate(SqlMoney Value)
    {
        sum += Value;
    }

    public void Merge(SumMoney Group)
    {
        sum += Group.sum;
    }

    public SqlMoney Terminate()
    {
        return sum;
    }
}
```

4. Build the solution.

5. Register the assembly and create the aggregate function by executing the following T-SQL statement in SQL Server Management Studio, replacing <path> appropriately:

```
USE AdventureWorks
GO


CREATE ASSEMBLY ClrAggregateFunction
FROM '<path>\ClrAggregateFunction\bin\Debug\ClrAggregateFunction.dll'
GO


CREATE AGGREGATE udfSumMoney
    ( @Value money )
RETURNS money
EXTERNAL NAME ClrAggregateFunction.SumMoney
```

6. Execute the aggregate function on the Sales.SalesOrderHeader table in AdventureWorks:

```
SELECT dbo.udfSumMoney(SubTotal), dbo.udfSumMoney(TaxAmt),
    dbo.udfSumMoney(Freight), dbo.udfSumMoney(TotalDue)
FROM Sales.SalesOrderHeader
```

Results are shown in Figure 12-7.

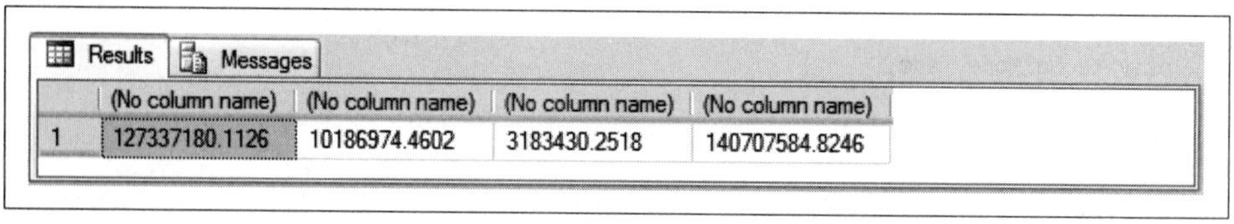

	(No column name)	(No column name)	(No column name)	(No column name)
1	127337180.1126	10186974.4602	3183430.2518	140707584.8246

Figure 12-7. Results for SumMoney user-defined aggregate function solution

Discussion

A user-defined aggregate (UDA) function returns a scalar result that is the result of a calculation on values in a set of rows. Examples of such functions include built-in SQL Server aggregate functions such as SUM, AVG, MIN, and MAX. A CLR UDA function is implemented as a structure or class in a .NET Framework assembly. A CLR UDA function can be invoked in T-SQL statements with the same rules that apply to system aggregate functions.

To implement a CLR UDA function, you have to write only the code that implements the accumulation logic—iteration over the result set and computing accumulated values are managed by the query processor. Specifically, you must implement an aggregation contract that defines mechanisms to save the intermediate state of the aggregation and to accumulate new values. This aggregation contract consists of four methods:

```
public void Init( )
```
Invoked once for each group that the query processor is aggregating to initialize the aggregate computation. This method should clean up previous uses of the instance, because the query processor can choose to reuse an instance of an aggregate class to compute aggregates for multiple groups.

```
public void Accumulate(input_type value)
```
The query processor invokes this method to accumulate aggregate values. The method is invoked for each value in the group being accumulated. The input_type argument is the managed SQL Server data type equivalent to the native SQL Server data type specified by the argument.

```
public void Merge(udagg_class value)
```
Used to merge a second instance of this aggregate class with the current instance. The query processor can invoke this method to merge partial computations of an aggregate on group partitions.

```
public return_type Terminate( )
```
Completes the aggregation and returns the result. The return_type is a managed SQL Server data type equivalent to the return_sqltype specified in the CREATE AGGREGATE T-SQL statement used to create the CLR aggregate function.

You identify a UDA function by annotating the implementing class with the SqlUserDefinedAggregate attribute, which indicates that a class should be registered as a UDA function. The SqlUserDefinedAggregate attribute has the following syntax:

```
SqlUserDefinedAggregate [ (aggregate-attribute [,...] ) ]

aggregate-attribute::=
  Format = {Native | UserDefined}
  IsInvariantToDuplicates = {true | false}
  IsInvariantToNulls = {true | false}
  IsInvariantToOrder = {true | false}
  IsNullIfEmpty = {true | false}
  | MaxByteSize = n
```

Where:

```
Format = {Native | UserDefined}
```
Specifies the serialization format for the type—either Native or UserDefined. Native serialization uses a simple algorithm to efficiently serialize the type. Native serialization is recommended for simple types containing only fields of the following types: bool, byte, sbyte, short, ushort, int, uint, long, ulong, float, double, SqlByte, SqlInt16, SqlInt32, SqlInt64, SqlDateTime, SqlSingle, SqlDouble, SqlMoney, and SqlBoolean.

Native serialization can also contain UDTs that use Native serialization. Native serialization has the following requirements:

- All the fields of the type must be *blittable*—data types that have a common representation in both managed and unmanaged memory and therefore do not need to be converted when passed between managed and unmanaged code. The following types from the System namespace are blittable: Byte, SByte, UInt16, Int32, UInt32, Int64, IntPtr, and UIntPtr. One-dimensional arrays of blittable types and formatted value types containing only blittable types are also blittable.

- The type must not specify the MaxByteSize property.

- The type must not have any fields that are not serialized.

UserDefined serialization controls the serialization through code and has the following requirements:

- You must specify the MaxByteSize property of the SqlUserDefinedAggregate attribute.

- The class or structure implementing the type must implement the Read( ) and Write( ) methods of the IBinarySerializable interface to read and write the byte stream.

IsInvariantToDuplicates

Specifies whether the aggregate is invariant to duplicates. For example, MAX and MIN are invariant to duplicates, and AVG and SUM are not.

IsInvariantToNulls

Specifies whether the aggregate is invariant to nulls. For example, MAX and MIN are invariant to nulls, and COUNT is not (since nulls are included in the count).

IsInvariantToOrder

Specifies whether the aggregate is invariant to the order of the values. Specifying true gives the query optimizer more flexibility in choosing an execution plan and can result in improved performance.

IsNullIfEmpty

Specifies whether the aggregate returns a null reference if no values are accumulated. Otherwise the value that the initialized value of the variable returned by the Terminate( ) method is returned.

MaxByteSize

The maximum size of the UDT instance. MaxByteSize must be specified if the Format property is set to UserDefined.

12.5 Creating a User-Defined Type

Problem

You need to create a CLR user-defined type.

Solution

The following example creates, registers, and uses a user-defined type that defines a polygon and implements a single method that returns the area of the polygon as a double. Follow these steps:

1. Create a new SQL Server project in Visual Studio and name it ClrType.

2. Create a user-defined type item in the project. Name the item *Polygon.cs*.

3. The C# code in *Polygon.cs* in the project ClrType is shown in Example 12-8.

Example 12-8. File: Polygon.cs

```csharp
using System;
using System.Data;
using System.Data.SqlClient;
using System.Data.SqlTypes;
using Microsoft.SqlServer.Server;

[Serializable]
[Microsoft.SqlServer.Server.SqlUserDefinedType(Format.Native)]
public struct Polygon : INullable
{
    private bool isNull;
    private int numberSides;
    private double sideLength;

    public override string ToString( )
    {
        if (this.isNull)
            return "null";
        else
            return string.Format("{0} sides each {1} units long",
                numberSides, sideLength);
    }

    public bool IsNull
    {
        get
        {
            return isNull;
        }
    }

    public static Polygon Null
    {
        get
        {
            Polygon p = new Polygon( );
            p.isNull = true;
            return p;
        }
    }
}
```

Example 12-8. File: Polygon.cs (continued)

```csharp
    public static Polygon Parse(SqlString s)
    {
        if (s.IsNull || s.Value.ToLower( ).Equals("null"))
            return Null;
        string[] sa = s.ToString( ).Split(',');
        if (sa.Length != 2)
            return Null;

        Polygon p = new Polygon( );
        try
        {
            p.numberSides = int.Parse(sa[0]);
            p.sideLength = double.Parse(sa[1]);
            if (p.numberSides > 2 && p.sideLength > 0)
                return p;
            else
                return Null;
        }
        catch (Exception)
        {
            return Null;
        }
    }

    public int NumberSides
    {
        get { return numberSides; }
        set
        {
            if (value > 2)
            {
                numberSides = value;
                isNull = false;
            }
            else
                isNull = true;
        }
    }

    public double SideLength
    {
        get { return sideLength; }
        set
        {
            if (value > 0)
            {
                sideLength = value;
                isNull = false;
            }
            else
                isNull = true;
        }
```

Example 12-8. File: Polygon.cs (continued)

```
    }

    [SqlMethod]
    public double Area( )
    {
        if (!isNull)
            return .25 * numberSides * Math.Pow(sideLength, 2) *
            (1 / Math.Tan(Math.PI / numberSides));
        else
            return 0;
    }

    [SqlMethod(IsMutator = true, OnNullCall = false)]
    public void SetValue(int numberSides, double sideLength)
    {
        if (numberSides > 2 && sideLength > 0)
        {
            this.numberSides = numberSides;
            this.sideLength = sideLength;
            this.isNull = false;
        }
        else
            isNull = true;
    }
}
```

The UDT is implemented as a struct marked with both a Serializable attribute and a SqlUserDefinedType attribute specifying Native serialization. A UDT must support both XML and binary serialization.

The UDT contains two private fields—numberSides and sideLength. The NumberSides and SideLength properties are used to get and set the value of these fields.

The UDT implements the IsNullable interface with the method IsNull( ), which simply returns the value of a private field, isNull, that keeps track of whether the polygon UDT is null. The UDT also implements the Null( ) method, which instantiates and returns a null instance of the Polygon UDT.

The UDT implements the required ToString( ) and Parse( ) methods. The ToString( ) method displays the value of the polygon as a string. The Parse( ) method converts a string to the Polygon UDT and is used by the SQL Server CONVERT and CAST functions.

The UDT implements two methods. The Area( ) method returns the area of the polygon. The SetValue( ) method changes the number of sides and the length of the sides in the Polygon UDT.

4. Build the solution.

5. Register the assembly and create the aggregate function by executing the following T-SQL statement in SQL Server Management Studio, replacing <path> appropriately:

```
USE AdoDotNet35Cookbook
GO

CREATE ASSEMBLY ClrType
FROM '<path>\ClrType\bin\Debug\ClrType.dll'

GO

CREATE TYPE Polygon
EXTERNAL NAME ClrType
```

6. Execute the following T-SQL statements that demonstrate the new Polygon type:

```
DECLARE @p Polygon
SET @p = CONVERT(Polygon, '5, 4.2')
PRINT @p.IsNull
PRINT @p.ToString()
PRINT @p.NumberSides
PRINT @p.SideLength
PRINT @p.Area()
SET @p.SetValue(7, 3)
PRINT @p.ToString()
PRINT @p.Area()
```

Results are shown in Figure 12-8.

Figure 12-8. Output for Polygon user-defined type solution

Discussion

In addition to supporting native and simple types as in previous versions of SQL Server, SQL Server lets you define CLR user-defined types (UDTs). This lets you extend the built-in data types and define complex data types. A CLR UDT can be used in all contexts where a SQL Server system type can be used.

A CLR UDT is implemented as a class in a .NET Framework assembly. You identify a CLR UDT by annotating the class that implements the UDT with the SqlUserDefinedType attribute, which indicates that a class should be registered as a UDT. The SqlUserDefinedType attribute has the following syntax:

```
SqlUserDefinedType [ ( udt-property [,...] ) ]

udt-property::=
    Format = { Native | UserDefined }
  | MaxByteSize= n
  | IsByteOrdered= { true | false }
  | ValidationMethod = string
  | IsFixedLength = { true | false }
  | Name = string
```

Where:

`Format = { Native | UserDefined }`

> The serialization format of the UDT. For more information about these two values, see the `Format` property for the `SqlUserDefinedAggregate` attribute in Recipe 12.4.

> If the UDT is defined in a class rather than a structure, and if the `Format` property is `Native`, a `StructLayout` attribute must be specified and set to `LayoutKind.Sequential`. This forces the members in the class to be serialized in the same order in which they appear in the class.

`MaxByteSize`

> Specifies the maximum size of an instance of the UDT between 1 and 8,000 bytes. You must specify `MaxByteSize` if the `Format` property is set to `UserDefined`.

> Do not specify `MaxByteSize` if the `Format` property is set to `Native`.

`IsByteOrdered`

> Specifies how binary comparisons are performed on the UDT by SQL Server. When `IsByteOrdered` is true, the UDT is ordered in the same way as its serialized binary representation and can be used to order the data. The following features are supported on the UDT column in a table when `IsByteOrdered` is true:

- Creating an index on the column
- Creating primary and foreign key constraints, and `CHECK` and `UNIQUE` constraints on the column
- Using the column in T-SQL `ORDER BY`, `GROUP BY`, and `PARTITION BY` clauses
- Using comparison operators in T-SQL statements on the column

`ValidationMethod`

> Specifies the method used to validate instances of the UDT when the data is deserialized from a binary value. The converted method returns a Boolean indicating whether the UDT instance is valid.

> The database engine automatically converts binary values to UDT values. The database engine prevents invalid values in the database by checking whether values are appropriate for the serialization format of the type and that the value can be deserialized. Default checking might be inadequate when, for example, UDT values are constrained by a value set or a range.

IsFixedLength

Specifies whether all instances of the UDT are the same length. If the IsFixedLength property is true, all instances of the UDT must have the length, in bytes, specified by the MaxByteSize property. The property is used only when the Format property is set to UserDefined.

Name

Specifies the name of the type.

When a field, method, or property is referenced as part of a query, the T-SQL type of the return value is inferred from the return type. The SqlFacet attribute can be used to return additional information about the return type of a nonvoid UDT expression—the SqlFacet attribute does not constrain the specific values that can be stored in the type. The syntax of the SqlFacet attribute is as follows:

```
SqlFacet[(facet-attribute [,...])]

facet-attribute::=
    IsFixedLength = { true | false }
  | MaxSize= { n }
  | Precision = { n }
  | Scale = { n }
  | IsNullable = { true | false }
```

Where:

IsFixedLength

Specifies whether the return type is a fixed length. IsFixedLength must be set to false if the MaxSize property is set to –1. The default value is false.

MaxSize

Specifies the maximum size of the return type in bytes for binary types and characters for character field types. The default is 4,000 for Unicode character types and 8,000 for binary types. The value –1 indicates a large character or binary type.

Precision

Specifies the precision (number of digits in the number) of the return type as a value from 1 to 38. This property is used only with numeric types. Scale must be specified if Precision is specified. The default value is 38.

Scale

Specifies the scale (number of digits to the right of the decimal point) of the return type as a value from 0 to 38. This property is used only with numeric types. Precision must be specified if Scale is specified. The default value is 0.

IsNullable

Indicates whether the value of the return type can be null. The default is true. The properties specified for the SqlFacet attribute must be compatible with the return type. Table 12-7 shows SqlFacet properties that can be specified for each return type.

Table 12-7. Allowable SqlFacet properties by return type

Type	IsFixedLength	MaxSize	Precision	Scale	IsNullable
SqlBoolean	N	N	N	N	Y
SqlByte	N	N	N	N	Y
SqlInt16	N	N	N	N	Y
SqlInt32	N	N	N	N	Y
SqlInt64	N	N	N	N	Y
SqlSingle	N	N	N	N	Y
SqlDouble	N	N	N	N	Y
SqlDateTime	N	N	N	N	Y
SqlMoney	N	N	N	N	Y
SqlGuid	N	N	N	N	Y
SqlDecimal	N	N	Y	Y	Y
SqlString	Y	Y	N	N	Y
SqlBinary	Y	Y	N	N	Y
SqlXml	N	N	N	N	Y
SqlBytes	Y	Y	N	N	Y
SqlChars	Y	Y	N	N	Y
SqlUtcDateTime	N	N	N	N	Y
SqlDate	N	N	N	N	Y
SqlTime	N	N	N	N	Y
Embedded UDTs	N	N	N	N	Y
string	Y	Y	N	N	Y
Byte[]	Y	Y	N	N	Y
Char[]	Y	Y	N	N	Y
decimal	N	N	Y	Y	N

You must do the following when you define a CLR UDT:

- Annotate the class with the SqlUserDefinedType attribute.
- Specify the Serializable attribute, indicating that the UDT can be serialized.
- Implement the System.Data.SqlTypes.INullable interface so that the UDT can recognize a null value. This means that the UDT must implement a static IsNull property that returns a Boolean indicating whether the instance of the UDT is null.
- Implement a public static property named Null that returns a null instance of the UDT.

- Implement public static ToString( ) and Parse( ) methods to convert to and parse from a string representation of the type. The Parse( ) method takes a single argument of type SqlString.

- Implement the IXmlSerializable interface if all public fields and properties are XML serializable or marked with the XmlIgnore attribute. The IXmlSerializable interface provides custom XML serialization and deserialization by explicitly defining how an object is serialized and deserialized by the XmlSerializer class. The IXmlSerializable interface has three methods: GetSchema( ), ReadXml( ), and WriteXml( ).

- Implement Read( ) and Write( ) methods if user-defined serialization is specified by implementing the IBinarySerialize interface.

A CLR UDT has the following restrictions:

- Public names cannot exceed 128 characters in length and must conform to SQL Server naming rules for identifiers.

- Only fields, properties, and methods defined in the type are callable from T-SQL. SQL Server is not aware of the inheritance hierarchy among UDTs.

- Members other than the class constructor cannot be overloaded.

- Static members must be declared either as constants or as read-only when the assembly permission is specified as SAFE or EXTERNAL_ACCESS.

The SqlMethod attribute is used to define characteristics of a UDT method or property. The syntax of the SqlMethod attribute is as follows:

```
SqlMethod [ ( method-attribute [ ,... ] ) ]

method-attribute::=
    function_attribute
  | IsMutator = { true | false }
  | OnNullCall = { true | false }
  | InvokeIfReceiverIsNull= { true | false }
```

Where:

function_attribute

The SqlMethod attribute inherits all properties of the SqlFunction attribute discussed in Recipe 12.2.

IsMutator

Specifies whether the method can modify the UDT instance. SQL Server looks for the IsMutator property of the SqlMethod attribute on void public methods in the UDT. If the IsMutator property is true on a void method, SQL Server marks the method as a mutator—a method that causes state change in the instance.

Mutator methods are not allowed in queries—their use is restricted to assignment statements or data modification statements. The default value of the IsMutator property is false.

OnNullCall

Specifies whether the method is evaluated if one or more null arguments are supplied. If false, the method returns null without evaluating the method if one or more of the arguments are null. If true, the method is evaluated regardless of whether arguments are null. The default value is true.

InvokeIfReceiverIsNull

Specifies whether SQL Server should invoke the method on a null reference. A value of true invokes the method on a null reference. The default value is false.

12.6 Creating a DML Trigger

Problem

You need to create a CLR DML trigger.

Solution

The solution uses two tables named Volume and VolumeAudit. Execute the following T-SQL batch to create the tables:

```
USE AdoDotNet35Cookbook
GO

CREATE TABLE Volume
(
    ID int NOT NULL,
    Length float NOT NULL,
    Width float NOT NULL,
    Height float NOT NULL,
    Volume float NOT NULL CONSTRAINT DF_Area_Area DEFAULT ((0)),
    CONSTRAINT PK_Volume PRIMARY KEY CLUSTERED
    (
        ID ASC
    )
)
GO

CREATE TABLE VolumeAudit
(
    Action varchar(50) NOT NULL,
    Description varchar(max) NOT NULL
)
```

The solution creates update, insert, and delete DML triggers that log updates, inserts, and deletes to a table named Volume. These events are logged to a table named VolumeAudit. The example then registers the triggers and shows the results of executing DML statements against the Volume table. Follow these steps:

1. Create a new SQL Server project in Visual Studio and name it `ClrDmlTrigger`.

2. Create a trigger item in the project. Name the item *VolumeTriggers.cs*.

3. The C# code in *VolumeTriggers.cs* in the project `ClrDmlTrigger` is shown in Example 12-9.

Example 12-9. File: VolumeTriggers.cs

```csharp
using System;
using System.Data;
using System.Data.SqlClient;
using Microsoft.SqlServer.Server;

public partial class Triggers
{
    [SqlTrigger(Target = "Volume", Event = "FOR INSERT")]
    public static void InsertTrigger()
    {
        using (SqlConnection conn = new SqlConnection("context connection=true"))
        {
            SqlDataAdapter da =new SqlDataAdapter("SELECT * FROM INSERTED",
                conn);
            DataTable dt = new DataTable();
            da.Fill(dt);

            SqlCommand cmd = new SqlCommand();
            cmd.Connection = conn;
            conn.Open();
            foreach (DataRow row in dt.Rows)
            {
                int id = (int)row[0];
                double length = (double)row[1];
                double width = (double)row[2];
                double height = (double)row[3];
                double volume = length * width * height;
                string audit = string.Format("ID = {0}, Length = {1}, " +
                    "Width = {2}, Height = {3}",
                    id, length, width, height);

                cmd.CommandText = "INSERT INTO VolumeAudit VALUES ('INSERTED', '" +
                    audit + "')";
                cmd.ExecuteNonQuery();

                cmd.CommandText = "UPDATE Volume SET Volume = " + volume +
                    " WHERE ID = " + id;
                cmd.ExecuteNonQuery();

                SqlPipe pipe = SqlContext.Pipe;
                pipe.Send("Row inserted: " + audit);
            }
        }
    }
}
```

Example 12-9. File: VolumeTriggers.cs (continued)

```csharp
[SqlTrigger(Target = "Volume", Event = "FOR UPDATE")]
public static void UpdateTrigger( )
{
    using (SqlConnection conn = new SqlConnection("context connection=true"))
    {
        SqlDataAdapter da = new SqlDataAdapter("SELECT * FROM DELETED",
            conn);
        DataTable dtDel = new DataTable( );
        da.Fill(dtDel);
        da = new SqlDataAdapter("SELECT * FROM INSERTED", conn);
        DataTable dtIns = new DataTable( );
        da.Fill(dtIns);

        SqlCommand cmd = new SqlCommand( );
        cmd.Connection = conn;
        conn.Open( );
        for (int i = 0; i < dtDel.Rows.Count; i++)
        {
            DataRow rowDel = dtDel.Rows[i];
            int delId = (int)rowDel[0];
            double delLength = (double)rowDel[1];
            double delWidth = (double)rowDel[2];
            double delHeight = (double)rowDel[3];
            double delVolume = (double)rowDel[4];
            string delAudit = string.Format("ID = {0}, Length = {1}, " +
                "Width = {2}, Height = {3}, Volume = {4}",
                delId, delLength, delWidth, delHeight, delVolume);

            DataRow rowIns = dtIns.Rows[i];
            int insId = (int)rowIns[0];
            double insLength = (double)rowIns[1];
            double insWidth = (double)rowIns[2];
            double insHeight = (double)rowIns[3];
            double insVolume = insLength * insWidth * insHeight;
            string insAudit = string.Format("ID = {0}, Length = {1}, " +
                "Width = {2}, Height = {3}, Volume = {4}",
                insId, insLength, insWidth, insHeight, insVolume);
                cmd.CommandText = "UPDATE Volume SET Volume = " + insVolume +
                " WHERE ID = " + insId;
            cmd.ExecuteNonQuery( );

            cmd.CommandText = "INSERT INTO VolumeAudit VALUES " +
            "('UPDATED', 'Original: " + delAudit + "; " + "New: " +
            insAudit + "')";
            cmd.ExecuteNonQuery( );

            SqlPipe pipe = SqlContext.Pipe;
            pipe.Send("Row updated: Original: " + delAudit + "; " + "New: " +
                insAudit);
        }
    }
}
```

Example 12-9. File: VolumeTriggers.cs (continued)

```csharp
[SqlTrigger(Target = "Volume", Event = "FOR DELETE")]
public static void DeleteTrigger( )
{
    using (SqlConnection conn = new SqlConnection("context connection=true"))
    {
        SqlDataAdapter da = new SqlDataAdapter("SELECT * FROM DELETED",
            conn);
        DataTable dt = new DataTable( );
        da.Fill(dt);
        SqlCommand cmd = new SqlCommand( );
        cmd.Connection = conn;
        conn.Open( );
        foreach (DataRow row in dt.Rows)
        {
            int id = (int)row[0];
            double length = (double)row[1];
            double width = (double)row[2];
            double height = (double)row[3];
            double volume = (double)row[4];
            string audit = string.Format("ID = {0}, Length = {1}, " +
                "Width = {2}, Height = {3}, Volume = {4}",
                id, length, width, height, volume);
            cmd.CommandText =
                "INSERT INTO VolumeAudit VALUES ('DELETED', '" + audit + "');";
                cmd.ExecuteNonQuery( );
            cmd.ExecuteNonQuery( );

            SqlPipe pipe = SqlContext.Pipe;
            pipe.Send("Row deleted: " + audit);
        }
    }
}
}
```

Each of the three triggers is marked with the SqlTrigger attribute that specifies the Volume table as the target of the trigger together with the event that causes each trigger to execute.

4. Build the solution.

5. Register the assembly and create the aggregate function by executing the following T-SQL statement in SQL Server Management Studio, replacing <path> appropriately:

```sql
USE AdoDotNet35Cookbook
GO

CREATE ASSEMBLY VolumeTriggers
FROM '<path>\ClrDmlTrigger\bin\Debug\ClrDmlTrigger.dll'
GO

CREATE TRIGGER VolumeInsertTrigger
ON Volume
FOR INSERT
```

```
AS
EXTERNAL NAME VolumeTriggers.Triggers.InsertTrigger
GO

CREATE TRIGGER VolumeUpdateTrigger
ON Volume
FOR UPDATE
AS
EXTERNAL NAME VolumeTriggers.Triggers.UpdateTrigger
GO

CREATE TRIGGER VolumeDeleteTrigger
ON Volume
FOR DELETE
AS
EXTERNAL NAME VolumeTriggers.Triggers.DeleteTrigger
GO
```

6. Execute the following T-SQL statements to insert two rows into the Volume table:

```
INSERT INTO Volume (ID, Length, Width, Height) VALUES (1, 2.2, 3.4, 5.7)
INSERT INTO Volume (ID, Length, Width, Height) VALUES (2, 6, 2, 5.4)
```

Results are shown in Figure 12-9.

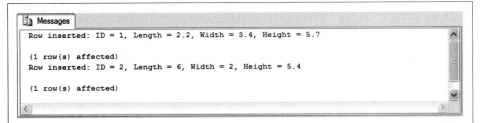

Figure 12-9. Output for VolumeTriggers CLR DML trigger solution

The output is generated by the following code in the insert DML trigger:

```
pipe.Send("Row inserted: " + audit);
```

Figure 12-10 shows the rows in the VolumeAudit table created by the DML triggers.

Action	Description
INSERTED	ID = 1, Length = 2.2, Width = 3.4, Height = 5.7
UPDATED	Original: ID = 1, Length = 2.2, Width = 3.4, Height = 5.7, Volume = 0; New: ID = 1, Length = 2.2, Width = 3.4, Height = 5.7, Volume = 42.636
INSERTED	ID = 2, Length = 6, Width = 2, Height = 5.4
UPDATED	Original: ID = 2, Length = 6, Width = 2, Height = 5.4, Volume = 0; New: ID = 2, Length = 6, Width = 2, Height = 5.4, Volume = 64.8
NULL	NULL

Figure 12-10. Results for VolumeTriggers CLR DML trigger solution

There are four records—two inserted by the insert DML trigger and two inserted by the update DML trigger when the insert DML trigger updates the Volume field.

Although the update trigger on the Volume table updates the Volume table, the query is not recursive as long as the RECURSIVE_TRIGGERS database option is set to OFF—this is the default. You can check the status of all database options by executing the following T-SQL statement:

```
SELECT * FROM sys.databases
```

The is_recursive_triggers_on column contains the setting of the RECURSIVE_TRIGGERS option for each database.

You can change the value of a database option using the ALTER DATABASE statement. For example, execute the following T-SQL statement to change the recursive trigger behavior for the AdoDotNet35Cookbook database to ON:

```
ALTER DATABASE AdoDotNet35Cookbook
SET RECURSIVE_TRIGGERS ON
```

7. Execute the following T-SQL statement to update the first of the two rows previously inserted into the Volume table:

```
UPDATE Volume
SET Length = 1, Width = 4, Height = 7.2
WHERE ID = 1
```

Results are shown in Figure 12-11.

```
Messages
Row updated: Original: ID = 1, Length = 2.2, Width = 3.4, Height = 5.7, Volume = 42.636;
            New: ID = 1, Length = 1, Width = 4, Height = 7.2, Volume = 28.8

(1 row(s) affected)
```

Figure 12-11. Output for VolumeTriggers CLR DML trigger update row

Figure 12-12 shows the row added to the VolumeAudit table by the update DML trigger.

Action	Description
INSERTED	ID = 1, Length = 2.2, Width = 3.4, Height = 5.7
UPDATED	Original: ID = 1, Length = 2.2, Width = 3.4, Height = 5.7, Volume = 0; New: ID = 1, Length = 2.2, Width = 3.4, Height = 5.7, Volume = 42.636
INSERTED	ID = 2, Length = 6, Width = 2, Height = 5.4
UPDATED	Original: ID = 2, Length = 6, Width = 2, Height = 5.4, Volume = 0; New: ID = 2, Length = 6, Width = 2, Height = 5.4, Volume = 64.8
UPDATED	Original: ID = 1, Length = 2.2, Width = 3.4, Height = 5.7, Volume = 42.636; New: ID = 1, Length = 1, Width = 4, Height = 7.2, Volume = 28.8
NULL	NULL

Figure 12-12. Results for VolumeTriggers CLR DML trigger update row

8. Execute this T-SQL statement to delete the two rows from the Volume table:

```
DELETE FROM Volume
```

Results are shown in Figure 12-13.

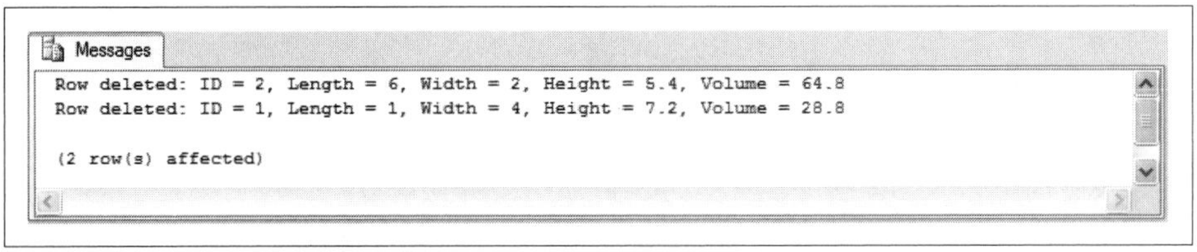

Figure 12-13. Output for VolumeTriggers CLR DML trigger delete rows

Figure 12-14 shows the rows added to the VolumeAudit by the delete DML trigger.

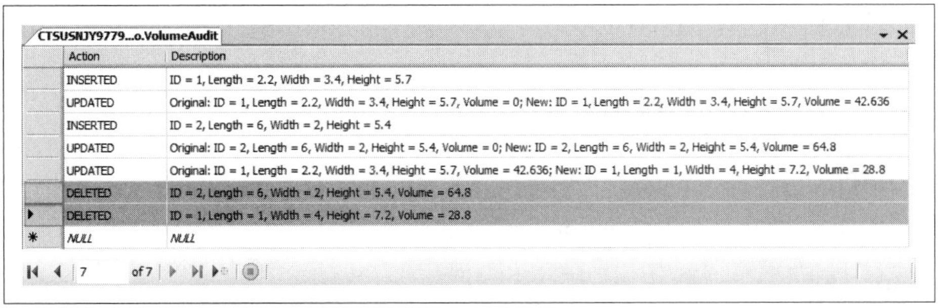

Figure 12-14. Results for VolumeTriggers CLR DML trigger delete rows

Discussion

A trigger is a type of stored procedure that executes automatically when an event occurs. SQL Server has two types of triggers:

Data Manipulation Language (DML) trigger
Executes when INSERT, UPDATE, and DELETE commands modify data in a table or view.

Data Definition Language (DDL) trigger
Executes in response to a DDL statement that is often used to make database schema changes. Examples include the CREATE, ALTER, and DROP statements.

A CLR trigger is implemented as a public static void method in a .NET Framework assembly. You identify a CLR DML trigger by marking the method that implements the trigger with the SqlTrigger attribute, which indicates that a method should be registered as a DML trigger. The SqlTrigger attribute has the following syntax:

```
SqlTrigger [ ( trigger-attribute [ ,... ] ) ]

trigger-attribute::=
    Target = "table-name"
  | Event = "trigger-type update-action [, ...]"

trigger-type::=
    FOR | AFTER | INSTEAD OF

update-action::=
    UPDATE | DELETE | INSERT
```

Where:

Target = "table-name"
> Specifies the table to which the trigger applies.

trigger-type
> Specifies the type of trigger.

update-action
> Specifies the DML action that activates the trigger—UPDATE, DELETE, or INSERT.

You can use the TriggerAction property of the SqlTriggerContext class instead of the SqlTrigger attribute. This is discussed in Recipe 12.7, next.

12.7   Creating a DDL Trigger

Problem

You need to create a CLR DDL trigger.

Solution

The solution creates a DDL trigger that executes when CREATE TABLE and DROP TABLE DDL statements are executed and logs the events to a table named Log.

The solution uses a single table named Log. Execute the following T-SQL statement to create the table:

```
USE AdoDotNet35Cookbook
GO

CREATE TABLE Log
(
    LogID int IDENTITY(1,1) NOT NULL,
    LogEntry varchar(max) NOT NULL,
    CONSTRAINT PK_Log PRIMARY KEY CLUSTERED
        ( LogID ASC )
)
```

Follow these steps:

1. Create a new SQL Server project in Visual Studio and name it ClrDdlTrigger.

2. Create a trigger item in the project. Name the item *LogTableActivityTrigger.cs*.

3. The C# code in *LogTableActivityTrigger.cs* in the project ClrDdlTrigger is shown in Example 12-10.

Example 12-10. File: LogTableActivityTrigger.cs

```
using System;
using System.Data;
using System.Data.SqlClient;
using Microsoft.SqlServer.Server;
```

Example 12-10. File: LogTableActivityTrigger.cs (continued)

```csharp
public partial class Triggers
{
    public static void LogTableActivityTrigger( )
    {
        SqlTriggerContext tc = SqlContext.TriggerContext;
        using (SqlConnection conn = new SqlConnection("context connection=true"))
        {
            conn.Open( );
            SqlCommand cmd = new SqlCommand( );
            cmd.Connection = conn;

            if (tc.TriggerAction == TriggerAction.CreateTable ||
                tc.TriggerAction == TriggerAction.DropTable)
            {
                cmd.CommandText = "INSERT INTO Log VALUES " +
                    "('" + tc.EventData.Value + "')";
                cmd.ExecuteNonQuery( );
            }
        }
    }
}
```

A single DDL trigger is defined in the Triggers class. The trigger checks the TriggerAction property of the SqlTriggerContext and then logs the EventData for the event that caused this trigger to fire. In this example, it is not necessary to check the trigger context, as all events for which the trigger is registered execute the same code to log the event. You could use the TriggerAction property to perform different actions for each of the different events that a DDL trigger is registered to handle.

4. Build the solution.

5. Register the assembly and create the aggregate function by executing the following T-SQL statement in SQL Server Management Studio, replacing <path> appropriately:

```sql
USE AdoDotNet35Cookbook
GO

CREATE ASSEMBLY ClrDdlTrigger
FROM '<path>\ClrDdlTrigger\bin\Debug\ClrDdlTrigger.dll'
GO

CREATE TRIGGER LogTableActivityTrigger
ON DATABASE
FOR CREATE_TABLE, DROP_TABLE
AS
EXTERNAL NAME ClrDdlTrigger.Triggers.LogTableActivityTrigger
```

6. Execute the following T-SQL statement to create and then drop a table named TestTable to demonstrate the DDL trigger:

```sql
USE AdoDotNet35Cookbook
GO
```

```
CREATE TABLE TestTable
(
    TestID int NOT NULL,
    CONSTRAINT PK_TestTable PRIMARY KEY CLUSTERED
    ( TestID ASC )
)
GO

DROP TABLE TestTable
GO
```

Table 12-8 shows the Log table that now contains two rows detailing the DDL CREATE_TABLE and DROP_TABLE events.

Table 12-8. Log table

LogID	LogEntry

1	`<EVENT_INSTANCE>`
	`  <EventType>CREATE_TABLE</EventType>`
	`  <PostTime>2007-11-03T17:25:45.407</PostTime>`
	`  <SPID>52</SPID>`
	`  <ServerName>CTSUSNJY9779A</ServerName>`
	`  <LoginName>CTSUSNJY9779A\bill</LoginName>`
	`  <UserName>dbo</UserName>`
	`  <DatabaseName>AdoDotNet35Cookbook</DatabaseName>`
	`  <SchemaName>dbo</SchemaName>`
	`  <ObjectName>TestTable</ObjectName>`
	`  <ObjectType>TABLE</ObjectType>`
	`  <TSQLCommand>`
	`    <SetOptions ANSI_NULLS="ON" ANSI_NULL_DEFAULT="ON"`
	`      ANSI_PADDING="ON" QUOTED_IDENTIFIER="ON"`
	`      ENCRYPTED="FALSE" />`
	`    <CommandText>CREATE TABLE TestTable`
	`      (`
	`        TestID int NOT NULL,`
	`        CONSTRAINT PK_TestTable PRIMARY KEY CLUSTERED`
	`        ( TestID ASC )`
	`      )`
	`    </CommandText>`
	`  </TSQLCommand>`
	`</EVENT_INSTANCE>`

2	`<EVENT_INSTANCE>`
	`  <EventType>DROP_TABLE</EventType>`
	`  <PostTime>2007-11-03T17:25:45.827</PostTime>`
	`  <SPID>52</SPID>`
	`  <ServerName>CTSUSNJY9779A</ServerName>`
	`  <LoginName>CTSUSNJY9779A\bill</LoginName>`
	`  <UserName>dbo</UserName>`
	`  <DatabaseName>AdoDotNet35Cookbook</DatabaseName>`
	`  <SchemaName>dbo</SchemaName>`
	`  <ObjectName>TestTable</ObjectName>`
	`  <ObjectType>TABLE</ObjectType>`
	`  <TSQLCommand>`
	`    <SetOptions ANSI_NULLS="ON" ANSI_NULL_DEFAULT="ON"`
	`      ANSI_PADDING="ON" QUOTED_IDENTIFIER="ON"`
	`      ENCRYPTED="FALSE" />`
	`    <CommandText>DROP TABLE TestTable</CommandText>`
	`  </TSQLCommand>`
	`</EVENT_INSTANCE>`

Discussion

A trigger is a type of stored procedure that executes automatically when an event occurs. SQL Server has two types of triggers:

Data Manipulation Language (DML) trigger
> Executes when INSERT, UPDATE, and DELETE commands modify data in a table or view.

Data Definition Language (DDL) trigger
> Executes in response to a DDL statement that is often used to make database schema changes. Examples include the CREATE, ALTER, and DROP statements.

A CLR trigger is implemented as a method of a class in a .NET Framework assembly.

A CLR trigger is implemented as a public static void method in a .NET Framework assembly. Instead of using the SqlTrigger attribute as described in Recipe 12.6 to define events for which a DDL trigger executes, the SqlTriggerContext is used to get context information about the trigger. This SqlTriggerContext class cannot be instantiated directly—call the TriggerContext property of the SqlContext class to get an instance.

The SqlTriggerContext class has a TriggerAction property that indicates the action that caused a trigger to fire. For DML triggers, the value can be TriggerAction.Update, TriggerAction.Insert, or TriggerAction.Delete. There are many DDL trigger actions—see Microsoft SQL Server Books Online for a complete list.

What's New in ADO.NET Since Version 1.0

ADO.NET is a set of classes that gives .NET applications access to relational, XML, and application data. The classes let you connect to data sources such as SQL Server and Oracle, as well as to data sources exposed through OLE DB and ODBC, and XML data. After you connect to these data sources, the ADO.NET classes let you retrieve, manipulate, and update data.

This appendix describes the new functionality, support, and features in ADO.NET since version 1.0.

ADO.NET 2.0

ADO.NET 2.0 was released as part of the release of .NET Framework 2.0. This section provides an overview of both new features in ADO.NET 2.0 and of significant changes and enhancements in ADO.NET 2.0 since ADO.NET 1.0.

Data Provider Enumeration and Factories

Data providers in ADO.NET 1.0 and 1.1 are a set of provider-specific classes that implement generic interfaces. These interfaces can be used to write code that is data provider-independent. For example, the data connection classes in the Microsoft SQL Server data provider (SqlConnection) and the Microsoft Oracle data provider (OracleConnection) both implement the IDbConnection interface. Code based on the IDbConnection interface that is common to both classes, rather than a database-specific instance of a data provider, is independent of the data provider and therefore not dependent on the underlying database. The disadvantage of the interface approach is that you cannot use the interface to access any database-specific features implemented as members of the data provider class but not defined as part of the interface—the ChangeDatabase( ) method of the Oracle data provider, for example.

ADO.NET 2.0 introduces the *Common Model*, based on the *Factory* design pattern, which uses a single API to access databases having different providers. Data provider factories let your code work with multiple data providers without choosing a specific provider. The factory class creates and returns a strongly typed, provider-specific object based on information in the request. This lets you write data provider-independent code and select the provider at runtime. Using the Common Model, it becomes easier to write an application to support multiple databases.

The DbProviderFactories class in the System.Data.Common namespace lets you retrieve information about installed .NET data providers. The static GetFactoryClasses() method returns a DataTable object containing information about the installed data providers that implement the abstract base class DbProviderFactory, with the schema described in Table A-1.

Table 0-1. DataTable schema for GetFactoryClasses() method results

Column name	Description
Name	Data provider name.
Description	Data provider description.
InvariantName	A unique identifier for a data provider registered in machine.config in the <system.data><DbProviderFactories> element. For example, the invariant name for SQL Server is System.Data.SqlClient.
	The invariant name is used to programmatically refer to the data provider.
AssemblyQualifiedName	Fully qualified name of the data provider factory class—enough information to instantiate the object.

The following console application uses the DbProviderFactories class to get information about the installed data providers:

```
using System;
using System.Data;
using System.Data.Common;

class Program
{
    static void Main(string[] args)
    {
        DataTable dt = DbProviderFactories.GetFactoryClasses();
        foreach (DataRow row in dt.Rows)
        {
            Console.WriteLine("{0}\n\r  {1}\n\r  {2}\n\r  {3}\n\r",
                row["Name"], row["Description"], row["InvariantName"],
                row["AssemblyQualifiedName"]);
        }

        Console.WriteLine("Press any key to continue.");
        Console.ReadKey();
    }
}
```

The output is shown in Figure A-1.

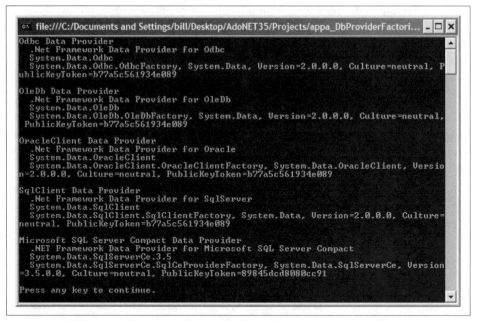

Figure A-1. Information about installed data providers

The providers listed in Figure A-1 correspond to the DbProviderFactories element in *machine.config*, shown in the following excerpt:

```
<system.data>
  <DbProviderFactories>
    <add name="Odbc Data Provider" invariant="System.Data.Odbc"
      description=".Net Framework Data Provider for Odbc"
      type="System.Data.Odbc.OdbcFactory,
      System.Data, Version=2.0.0.0, Culture=neutral, PublicKeyToken=b77a5c561934e089"
    />
    <add name="OleDb Data Provider" invariant="System.Data.OleDb"
      description=".Net Framework Data Provider for OleDb"
      type="System.Data.OleDb.OleDbFactory,
      System.Data, Version=2.0.0.0, Culture=neutral, PublicKeyToken=b77a5c561934e089"
    />
    <add name="OracleClient Data Provider" invariant="System.Data.OracleClient"
      description=".Net Framework Data Provider for Oracle"
      type="System.Data.OracleClient.OracleClientFactory, System.Data.OracleClient,
      Version=2.0.0.0, Culture=neutral, PublicKeyToken=b77a5c561934e089" />
    <add name="SqlClient Data Provider" invariant="System.Data.SqlClient"
      description=".Net Framework Data Provider for SqlServer"
      type="System.Data.SqlClient.SqlClientFactory, System.Data, Version=2.0.0.0,
      Culture=neutral, PublicKeyToken=b77a5c561934e089" />
    <add name="Microsoft SQL Server Compact Data Provider"
      invariant="System.Data.SqlServerCe.3.5"
      description=".NET Framework Data Provider for Microsoft SQL Server Compact"
      type="System.Data.SqlServerCe.SqlCeProviderFactory,
      System.Data.SqlServerCe, Version=3.5.0.0, Culture=neutral,
      PublicKeyToken=89845dcd8080cc91" />
```

```
    </DbProviderFactories>
  </system.data>
```

The static GetFactory( ) method of the DbProviderFactories class takes a single argument—either a DataRow object from the table returned by the GetFactoryClasses( ) method or a string containing the invariant name of the provider—and returns a DbProviderFactory instance for that data provider.

The DbProviderFactory class is an abstract base class that every ADO.NET 2.0 data provider must implement. DbProviderFactory is a data provider-independent class that provides a strongly typed object based on information supplied at runtime. The provider-specific classes derived from DbProviderFactory installed with .NET Framework 2.0 are listed in Table A-2.

Table A-2. Provider-specific classes derived from DbProviderFactory installed with .NET Framework 2.0

Factory class	Description
System.Data.Odbc.OdbcFactory	Used to create instances of ODBC provider classes
System.Data.OleDb.OleDbFactory	Used to create instances of OLE DB provider classes
System.Data.OracleClient.OracleClientFactory	Used to create instances of Oracle provider classes
System.Data.SqlClient.SqlClientFactory	Used to create instances of SQL Server provider classes

The DbProviderFactory class has public methods, listed in Table A-3, that are used to create the provider-specific class instances.

Table A-3. DbProviderFactory class public methods

Method	Description
CreateCommand( )	Returns a DbCommand instance—the base class for strongly typed command objects
CreateCommandBuilder( )	Returns a DbCommandBuilder instance—the base class for strongly typed command builder objects
CreateConnection( )	Returns a DbConnection instance—the base class for strongly typed connection objects
CreateConnectionStringBuilder( )	Returns a DbConnectionStringBuilder instance—the base class for strongly typed connection string builder objects
CreateDataAdapter( )	Returns a DbDataAdapter instance—the base class for strongly typed data adapter objects
CreateDataSourceEnumerator( )	Returns a DbDataSourceEnumerator instance—the base class for strongly typed data source enumerator objects
CreateParameter( )	Returns a DbParameter instance—the base class for strongly typed parameter objects
CreatePermission( )	Returns a CodeAccessPermission instance—the base class for strongly typed code access permission objects

The following console application shows how to create an instance of the SqlClientFactory class and use it to output the top 10 rows from the Person.Contact table in AdventureWorks:

```
using System;
using System.Data;
using System.Data.Common;

class Program
{
    static void Main(string[] args)
    {
        string sqlConnectString = "Data Source=(local);" +
            "Integrated security=SSPI;Initial Catalog=AdventureWorks;";
        string sqlSelect = "SELECT TOP 10 FirstName, LastName, EmailAddress " +
            "FROM Person.Contact ORDER BY LastName";

        // create factory using the invariant name
        DbProviderFactory f =
            DbProviderFactories.GetFactory("System.Data.SqlClient");

        DbConnection connection = f.CreateConnection();
        connection.ConnectionString = sqlConnectString;

        DbCommand command = connection.CreateCommand();
        command.CommandText = sqlSelect;

        DataTable dt = new DataTable();
        DbDataAdapter da = f.CreateDataAdapter();
        da.SelectCommand = command;
        da.Fill(dt);

        foreach (DataRow row in dt.Rows)
            Console.WriteLine(row[0] + ", " + row[1] + ", " + row[2]);

        Console.WriteLine("\nPress any key to continue.");
        Console.ReadKey();
    }
}
```

The output is shown in Figure A-2.

The code is database-independent, with the exception of the invariant name of the provider and the connection string, highlighted in the preceding example. These arguments would normally be retrieved from a configuration file or similar mechanism rather than hardcoded, to make the application truly database independent.

The ConfigurationManager class in the System.Configuration namespace provides access to application configuration information. The ConnectionStrings() method returns a ConnectionStringSettingsCollection instance containing the connection strings for the application, each one corresponding to a named connection string in the <connectionStrings> section of the application configuration file.

Figure A-2. Output for SqlClientFactory example

This example shows how to retrieve a connection string from the configuration file. First create a new console application project in Visual Studio .NET. Select Add → New Item → Application Configuration File to add a new application configuration file named *App.config*. Add a connection string to the file—the following snippet shows the completed configuration file with the connection string named MyConnection highlighted:

```
<?xml version="1.0" encoding="utf-8" ?>
<configuration>
  <connectionStrings>
    <add name="MyConnection"
      connectionString="Data Source=(local);Integrated Security=SSPI;
      Initial Catalog=AdventureWorks"
      providerName="System.Data.SqlClient" />
  </connectionStrings>
</configuration>
```

Note that the connectionString attribute should be on a single line in the actual *App.config* file.

The following code retrieves the connection string from the configuration file. You need to add a reference to the System.Configuration assembly to compile and execute this example:

```
using System;
using System.Collections;
using System.Data.SqlClient;
using System.Configuration;

class Program
{
    static void Main(string[] args)
    {
        // get the configuration string from the .config file
        Configuration c =
            ConfigurationManager.OpenExeConfiguration(ConfigurationUserLevel.None);

        ConnectionStringsSection css = c.ConnectionStrings;
        for (int i = 0; i < css.ConnectionStrings.Count; i++)
        {
```

```
                Console.WriteLine("Connection string {0}: {1}", i + 1,
                    css.ConnectionStrings[i].Name);
                Console.WriteLine("  {0}\n", css.ConnectionStrings[i]);
            }

            Console.WriteLine("Press any key to continue.");
            Console.ReadKey();
        }
    }
```

The output is shown in Figure A-3.

Figure A-3. Output for retrieving configuration strings from application configuration file example

Two connection strings are retrieved. The first is the default string defined in the *Machine.config* file, as shown in the excerpt that follows:

```
<connectionStrings>
  <add name="LocalSqlServer"
    connectionString="data source=.\SQLEXPRESS;Integrated Security=SSPI;
    AttachDBFilename=|DataDirectory|aspnetdb.mdf;User Instance=true"
    providerName="System.Data.SqlClient" />
</connectionStrings>
```

DbConnectionStringBuilder is a helper class used to construct provider-specific connection strings. You supply the connection string name-value pairs to the Add( ) method and retrieve the connection string using the ConnectionString property. You could change the previous example so that it constructs the connection string using the connection string builder, and then assign it to the ConnectionString property of the connection with the following code:

```
using System;
using System.Data;
using System.Data.Common;
using System.Data.SqlClient;

class Program
{
    static void Main(string[] args)
    {
        // build the connection string
        DbConnectionStringBuilder csb = new DbConnectionStringBuilder();
        csb["Data Source"] = "(local)";
        csb["Integrated Security"] = "SSPI";
        csb["Initial Catalog"] = "AdventureWorks";
```

```
        // create a connection using the connection string
        SqlConnection conn = new SqlConnection();
        conn.ConnectionString = csb.ConnectionString;

        // output the connection string
        Console.WriteLine("ConnectionString:\n  {0}", csb.ConnectionString);

        Console.WriteLine("\nPress any key to continue.");
        Console.ReadKey();
    }
}
```

The output is shown in Figure A-4.

Figure A-4. Output for DbConnectionStringBuilder example

Data Provider Enhancements

ADO.NET 2.0 introduces new features and enhancements to .NET Framework data providers, which are used to connect to data sources, execute commands, retrieve data, and update data. The following subsections describe the key changes.

Asynchronous processing

ADO.NET 2.0 supports asynchronous programming for data retrieval. This lets you delegate long-running data-processing tasks to a background thread while allowing the user interface to remain responsive. Standard asynchronous processing techniques include callbacks, wait handles, and polling. The SqlCommand class has six methods that support asynchronous processing, described in Table A-4.

Table A-4. SqlCommand class methods for asynchronous processing

Asynchronous method	Description
BeginExecuteNonQuery()	Starts the asynchronous execution of the T-SQL statement or stored procedure for the SqlCommand object. The method returns an IAsyncResult object that can be used to poll for or wait for results, or to invoke the EndExecuteNonQuery() method.
	Each call to a BeginExecuteNonQuery() method must be paired with the EndExecuteNonQuery() method that completes the operation.
EndExecuteNonQuery()	Completes the asynchronous execution of the T-SQL statement or stored procedure started using the BeginExecuteNonQuery() method of the SqlCommand object. The command returns the number of rows affected by the command.

Table A-4. SqlCommand class methods for asynchronous processing (continued)

Asynchronous method	Description
BeginExecuteReader()	Starts the asynchronous execution of the T-SQL statement or stored procedure for the SqlCommand object. The method returns an IAsyncResult object that can be used to poll for or wait for results, or to invoke the EndExecuteReader() method.
	Each call to a BeginExecuteReader() method must be paired with the EndExecuteReader() method that completes the operation.
EndExecuteReader()	Completes the asynchronous execution of the T-SQL statement or stored procedure started using the BeginExecuteReader() method of the SqlCommand object. The command returns a SqlDataReader object containing one or more result sets.
BeginExecuteXmlReader()	Starts the asynchronous execution of the T-SQL statement or stored procedure for the SqlCommand object. The method returns an IAsyncResult object that can be used to poll for or wait for results, or to invoke the EndExecuteXmlReader() method.
	Each call to a BeginExecuteXmlReader() method must be paired with the EndExecuteXmlReader() method that completes the operation.
EndExecuteXmlReader()	Completes the asynchronous execution of the T-SQL statement or stored procedure started using the BeginExecuteXmlReader() method of the SqlCommand object. The command returns an XmlReader object.

The asynchronous command Begin/End pairs for the SqlCommand object work similarly. The examples in this section that use one of the pairs can be transferred easily to one of the other pairs.

You must add the Asynchronous Processing=true attribute to the SQL Server connection string to use any of the asynchronous methods.

The IAsyncResult interface stores state information about the asynchronous operation and provides a synchronization object that lets threads get signaled when the operation completes. Table A-5 lists the public properties exposed by the IAsyncResult interface.

Table A-5. Public properties of IAsyncResult interface

Property	Description
AsyncState	Returns a user-defined object that contains information about or qualifies an asynchronous operation
AsyncWaitHandle	Returns a WaitHandle object used to wait for an asynchronous operation to complete
CompletedSynchronously	Returns a bool indicating whether the asynchronous operation completed synchronously
IsCompleted	Returns a bool indicating whether the asynchronous operation has completed

The following Windows console application uses an asynchronous data reader to get a result set containing all rows in the Person.Contact table in the AdventureWorks database. A WAITFOR T-SQL statement is used to delay the processing of the SELECT statement for five seconds to demonstrate the background processing of the query. After five seconds, the program executes the T-SQL statement to retrieve all rows into a DataReader object, and then calls the HandleCallback() callback to output the number of rows:

```
using System;
using System.Data.SqlClient;

class Program
{
    static void Main(string[] args)
    {
        string sqlConnectString =
            "Data Source=localhost;Integrated Security=SSPI;" +
            "Initial Catalog=AdventureWorks;Asynchronous Processing=true";
        string sqlSelect = "WAITFOR DELAY '00:00:05';" +
            "SELECT * FROM Person.Contact;";

        SqlConnection connection = new SqlConnection(sqlConnectString);
        SqlCommand command = new SqlCommand(sqlSelect, connection);

        connection.Open();
        // Start the async operation. The HandleCallback() method
        // is called when the operation completes in 5 seconds.
        command.BeginExecuteReader(
            new AsyncCallback(HandleCallback), command);
        Console.WriteLine(
            "BeginExecuteReader() called at: {0}", DateTime.Now);

        Console.WriteLine("\n(Waiting. Press any key to exit.)");
        Console.ReadKey();
    }

    private static void HandleCallback(IAsyncResult asyncResult)
    {
        // get the original object
        SqlCommand command = (SqlCommand)asyncResult.AsyncState;

        int rowCount = 0;
        // get the data reader returned from the async call
        using (SqlDataReader dr = command.EndExecuteReader(asyncResult))
        {
            // iterate over the reader
            while (dr.Read())
            {
                // do some work with the reader

                rowCount++;
            }
        }

        command.Connection.Close();

        Console.WriteLine(
            "\nHandleCallbackCalled() at: {0}", DateTime.Now);
        Console.WriteLine("Rows in Person.Contact: {0}", rowCount);
    }
}
```

The output is shown in Figure A-5.

Figure A-5. Output for HandleCallback() example

The next example polls the IAsyncResult interface using its IsComplete property to determine when the operation is complete. This example is similar to the previous one except that a timer is used to check the status of the asynchronous operation every second. The status is output to the console—false if the query is still running or true if it has completed. After completion, the time is stopped and the number of rows in the data reader returned from the query is displayed.

```
using System;
using System.Data.SqlClient;
using System.Timers;

class Program
{
    static IAsyncResult asyncResult;
    static SqlCommand command;

    static void Main(string[] args)
    {
        string sqlConnectString =
            "Data Source=(local);Integrated Security=SSPI;" +
            "Initial Catalog=AdventureWorks;Asynchronous Processing=true";
        string sqlSelect = "WAITFOR DELAY '00:00:05';" +
            "SELECT * FROM Person.Contact;";

        SqlConnection connection = new SqlConnection(sqlConnectString);
        command = new SqlCommand(sqlSelect, connection);

        connection.Open();
        // Start the async operation.
        asyncResult = command.BeginExecuteReader();

        Console.WriteLine("(Waiting. Press any key to exit.)\n");

        // Start a timer to check the results every 1000ms
        Timer timer = new Timer(1000);
        timer.Elapsed += new ElapsedEventHandler(timer_Elapsed);
        timer.Start();

        Console.WriteLine("---Begin polling---");

        Console.ReadKey();
    }
```

```
static void timer_Elapsed(object sender, ElapsedEventArgs e)
{
    Console.WriteLine("[{0}] Query complete = {1}",
        DateTime.Now, asyncResult.IsCompleted);

    if (asyncResult.IsCompleted)
    {
        // stop the polling and process the results
        ((Timer)sender).Stop();

        Console.WriteLine("---End polling---");

        ProcessResults();
    }
}

private static void ProcessResults()
{
    int rowCount = 0;

    // Get the data reader returned from the async call
    using (SqlDataReader dr = command.EndExecuteReader(asyncResult))
    {
        // iterate over the reader
        while (dr.Read())
        {
            // do some work with the reader

            rowCount++;
        }
    }

    command.Connection.Close();
    Console.WriteLine("\nRows returned: {0}", rowCount);
}
}
```

The output is shown in Figure A-6.

Figure A-6. Output for polling IAsyncResult example

The callback and polling techniques shown in the preceding examples are useful when you are processing one asynchronous operation at a time. The *wait* model lets you process multiple simultaneous asynchronous operations. The wait model uses the AsyncWaitHandle property of the IAsyncResult instance returned from the BeginExecuteNonQuery( ), BeginExecuteReader( ), or BeginExecuteXmlReader( ) method of the SqlCommand object.

The WaitAny( ) and WaitAll( ) static methods of the WaitHandle class monitor and wait for the completion of asynchronous operations. The WaitAny( ) method waits for any of the asynchronous operations to complete or time out—you can process the results and continue to wait for the next operation to either complete or time out. The WaitAll( ) method waits for all of the processes in the array of WaitHandle instances to complete or time out before continuing.

The following console application demonstrates using the WaitAny( ) method for asynchronous command processing:

```
using System;
using System.Data.SqlClient;
using System.Threading;

namespace appa_WaitAny
{
    class Program
    {
        static void Main(string[] args)
        {
            string sqlConnectString =
                "Data Source=localhost;Integrated Security=SSPI;" +
                "Initial Catalog=AdventureWorks;Asynchronous Processing=true";

            Random rnd = new Random((int)DateTime.Now.Ticks);

            // create an array of commands with "n" members
            int n = 10;
            SqlConnection[] connection = new SqlConnection[n];
            SqlCommand[] command = new SqlCommand[n];
            string[] cmdText = new string[n];
            IAsyncResult[] asyncResult = new IAsyncResult[n];
            WaitHandle[] wh = new WaitHandle[n];

            for (int i = 0; i < n; i++)
            {
                // each command waits randomly for between 1 and 10 seconds
                cmdText[i] = "WAITFOR DELAY '00:00:" + rnd.Next(1, 10) + "';";

                connection[i] = new SqlConnection(sqlConnectString);
                connection[i].Open( );
                command[i] = new SqlCommand(cmdText[i], connection[i]);
                asyncResult[i] = command[i].BeginExecuteNonQuery( );
```

```
            wh[i] = asyncResult[i].AsyncWaitHandle;
        }

        // wait for all processes to complete, outputing completion
        for (int i = 0; i < n; i++)
        {
            int index = WaitHandle.WaitAny(wh);
            int result = command[index].EndExecuteNonQuery(asyncResult[index]);
            Console.WriteLine("Completed command " + index +
                ": " + command[index].CommandText);
            connection[index].Close();
        }

        Console.WriteLine("\nPress any key to continue.");
        Console.ReadKey();
    }
  }
}
```

The preceding example creates an array of 10 WAITFOR T-SQL statements of random duration between 1 and 10 seconds and displays a line to the console as each of them completes. The output is shown in Figure A-7.

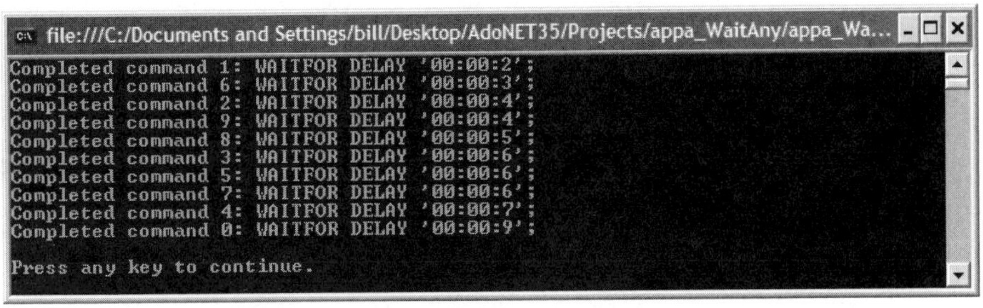

Figure A-7. Output for WaitAny() method example

The *wait all* model waits for the completion of all processes. The method returns true if every element in the WaitHandle array receives a signal within the timeout time span (in this example, 20,000 milliseconds, or 20 seconds). Otherwise, false is returned.

The following console application demonstrates using the WaitAll() method for asynchronous command processing:

```
using System;
using System.Data.SqlClient;
using System.Threading;

class Program
{
    static void Main(string[] args)
```

```csharp
    {
        string sqlConnectString =
            "Data Source=localhost;Integrated Security=SSPI;" +
            "Initial Catalog=AdventureWorks;Asynchronous Processing=true";

        Random rnd = new Random((int)DateTime.Now.Ticks);

        // Create an array of commands with "n" members
        int n = 10;
        SqlConnection[] connection = new SqlConnection[n];
        SqlCommand[] command = new SqlCommand[n];
        string[] sqlSelect = new string[n];
        IAsyncResult[] asyncResult = new IAsyncResult[n];
        WaitHandle[] wh = new WaitHandle[n];

        Console.WriteLine("[{0}] Begin.", DateTime.Now);
        for (int i = 0; i < n; i++)
        {
            // Each command waits for randomly between 1 and 10 seconds
            sqlSelect[i] = "WAITFOR DELAY '00:00:" +
                rnd.Next(1, 10) + "';";

            connection[i] = new SqlConnection(sqlConnectString);
            connection[i].Open();
            command[i] = new SqlCommand(sqlSelect[i], connection[i]);
            asyncResult[i] = command[i].BeginExecuteNonQuery();

            wh[i] = asyncResult[i].AsyncWaitHandle;
        }

        // Wait for all processes to complete and output results
        Console.WriteLine("[{0}] Waiting.", DateTime.Now);
        bool result = WaitHandle.WaitAll(wh, 20000, false);
        if (result)
        {
            for (int i = 0; i < n; i++)
            {
                int recAff = command[i].EndExecuteNonQuery(asyncResult[i]);
                connection[i].Close();
            }
            Console.WriteLine("[{0}] Completed all commands successfully.",
                DateTime.Now);
        }
        else
            Console.WriteLine("[{0}] Timeout error.", DateTime.Now);

        Console.WriteLine("\nPress any key to continue.");
        Console.ReadKey();
    }
}
```

The preceding example creates an array of 10 WAITFOR T-SQL statements of random duration between 1 and 10 seconds and displays a line to the console indicating when all of them have completed. The output is shown in Figure A-8.

Figure A-8. Output for WaitAll( ) method example

See MSDN for more information about the WaitAny( ) and WaitAll( ) methods.

Support for SQL Server notifications

SQL Server 2005 and later with ADO.NET 2.0 and later let you ask for a notification if executing the same command to retrieve data would generate a different result set. This happens, for example, if another user has changed the data since the current user fetched it. This capability is built on top of the new queuing functionality introduced in SQL Server 2005. The two classes that support notifications are SqlDependency and SqlNotificationRequest. A discussion and example of each follows.

Both examples use a table called Contact. Create the table and add two records to it with the following T-SQL batch:

```
USE AdoDotNet35Cookbook
GO

CREATE TABLE Contact(
    ID int NOT NULL PRIMARY KEY,
    FirstName varchar(50) NOT NULL,
    LastName varchar(50) NOT NULL )
GO

INSERT INTO Contact (ID, FirstName, LastName) VALUES (1, 'John', 'Doe');
INSERT INTO Contact (ID, FirstName, LastName) VALUES (2, 'Jane', 'Smith');
```

SQL Server databases do not have Service Broker enabled by default, for security reasons. Enable Service Broker for the AdoDotNet35Cookbook database by executing the following T-SQL statement:

```
USE AdoDotNet35Cookbook
GO

ALTER DATABASE AdoDotNet35Cookbook SET ENABLE_BROKER
```

You can confirm that Service Broker is now enabled for the database by using the DATABASEPROPERTYEX function, as shown in the following T-SQL statement:

```
SELECT DATABASEPROPERTYEX('AdoDotNet35Cookbook', 'IsBrokerEnabled')
```

The function returns 0 for false and 1 for true.

The SqlDependency class lets you create an object to detect changes in the query result. In this example, you create a SqlDependency instance. You then register to receive notifications of changes to the result set through the OnChanged event handler. Follow these steps:

1. Create a SqlConnection object and a SqlCommand object with the query that you want to monitor for changes.

2. Create a SqlDependency object and bind it to the SqlCommand object.

3. Subscribe an event handler to the OnChanged event of the SqlDependency object.

4. Execute the SqlCommand object using any Execute( ) method.

The following example shows how to monitor and handle notifications using the SqlDependency class. For notifications to be successful, you must specify the database owner as part of the table name and a list of columns in the query—specifying all columns using an asterisk (*) will not work.

```
using System;
using System.Data.SqlClient;

namespace appa_SqlDependency
{
    class Program
    {
        static void Main(string[] args)
        {
            string sqlConnectString =
                "Data Source=(local);Integrated Security=SSPI;" +
                "Initial Catalog=AdoDotNet35Cookbook;";

            // create the connection and the command to monitor for changes
            SqlConnection connection = new SqlConnection(sqlConnectString);
            SqlCommand command = new SqlCommand(
                "SELECT ID, FirstName, LastName FROM dbo.Contact", connection);

            // create the SqlDependency object and bind it to the command
            SqlDependency d = new SqlDependency(command);
            d.OnChange += new OnChangeEventHandler(d_OnChange);
            SqlDependency.Start(sqlConnectString);

            Console.WriteLine("Press any key to end.");
            Console.WriteLine("\n[{0}] Notification handler configured.",
                DateTime.Now);
```

```
        // create the DataReader
        connection.Open( );
        SqlDataReader dr = command.ExecuteReader( );
        while (dr.Read( ))
        {
            // process the DataReader row
        }
        dr.Close( );

        Console.ReadKey( );

        connection.Close( );
    }

    static void d_OnChange(object sender, SqlNotificationEventArgs e)
    {
        Console.WriteLine("\n[{0}] SqlDependency.OnChange event",
            DateTime.Now);
        Console.WriteLine("  Source = " + e.Source);
        Console.WriteLine("  Type =   " + e.Type);
        Console.WriteLine("  Info =   " + e.Info);
    }
  }
}
```

Run the example and, while it is running, add a row to the Contact table. The output is shown in Figure A-9.

Figure A-9. Output for SqlDependency event example

The SqlNotificationRequest class lets you execute a command so that SQL Server generates a notification when query results change. Unlike the SqlDependency class, once the notification is created, you do not have to maintain the SqlNotificationRequest object. You simply query your queue for notifications as you need to. This model is particularly useful in a disconnected environment.

You must first create a queue and a service to receive the notification messages, as shown in the following T-SQL statement:

```
USE AdoDotNet35Cookbook
GO

CREATE QUEUE ContactQueue
```

```
CREATE SERVICE ContactNotification
  ON QUEUE ContactQueue
  ([http://schemas.microsoft.com/SQL/Notifications/PostQueryNotification]);

CREATE ROUTE ContactQueueRoute
  WITH SERVICE_NAME = 'ContactNotification', ADDRESS = 'LOCAL';
```

This T-SQL block does three things:

- Creates a queue named ContactQueue to hold Service Broker messages.
- Creates a service named ContactNotification used by Service Broker to deliver messages to the ContactQueue queue in the SQL Server database.
- Creates a route used by Service Broker to route messages to the correct SQL Server for the service.

After setting up the queue, service, and route, you need to bind a SqlNotificationRequest object to the SqlCommand object containing your query. This means that when a T-SQL statement is executed, SQL Server keeps track of the query and sends a notification to the SQL Server queue specified in the notification request if a change is detected.

To do this, build a console application to create the notification as follows:

```
using System;
using System.Data.SqlClient;
using System.Data.Sql;

namespace appa_SqlNotificationRequest
{
    class Program
    {
        static void Main(string[] args)
        {
            string sqlConnectString = "Data Source=(local);" +
                "Integrated Security=SSPI;Initial Catalog=AdoDotNet35Cookbook;";
            string sqlSelect = "SELECT ID, FirstName, LastName FROM dbo.Contact";

            SqlConnection connection = new SqlConnection(sqlConnectString);
            SqlCommand command = new SqlCommand(sqlSelect, connection);

            // create the SqlNotificationRequest and bind to the command
            SqlNotificationRequest nr = new SqlNotificationRequest();
            nr.UserData = Guid.NewGuid().ToString();
            nr.Options = "Service=ContactNotification; " +
                "Local Database=AdoDotNet35Cookbook";
            nr.Timeout = Int32.MaxValue;
            command.Notification = nr;
            Console.WriteLine("Notification handler configured.");

            // create a data reader
            connection.Open();
            SqlDataReader dr = command.ExecuteReader();
            while (dr.Read())
```

```
        {
            // ... do some work with the data reader
        }

        Console.WriteLine("\nPress any key to end.");
        Console.ReadKey();

        connection.Close();
    }
  }
}
```

The output is shown in Figure A-10.

Figure A-10. Output for SqlNotificationRequest example

When you run the example, SQL Server creates a new query-notification subscription. Any changes to the data that affect the results of the query SELECT ID, FirstName, LastName FROM dbo.Contact produce a notification.

While the example is running, add a record to the contact table using SQL Management Studio. The notifications are delivered to the ContactNotification service. The ContactNotification service uses the queue ContactQueue to store the notifications. You can retrieve those messages by using the following T-SQL statement:

```
SELECT * FROM ContactQueue
```

As the example shows, you must specify three properties for the SqlNotificationRequest object:

UserData
> The application-specific identifier for the notification

Options
> The Service Broker service name where the notification messages are posted

Timeout
> The length of time, in seconds, that SQL Server waits for a change to occur before timing out

Multiple Active Result Sets

Multiple Active Result Sets (MARS) allows multiple commands to be executed on a single connection against a SQL Server 2005 and later database. Each command requires its own SqlCommand object and adds an additional session to the connection.

You must enable MARS by setting the `MultipleActiveResultSets` key in the connection string to true.

The following console application queries AdventureWorks and returns the top three sales order headers and the sales order details for each header. A single connection is used with two command objects to create the DataReader objects:

```
using System;
using System.Data.SqlClient;

namespace appa_MARS
{
    class Program
    {
        static void Main(string[] args)
        {
            string sqlConnectString = "Data Source=(local);" +
            "Integrated Security=SSPI;Initial Catalog=AdventureWorks;" +
            "MultipleActiveResultSets=true";
            string sqlSelectHeader =
                "SELECT TOP 3 SalesOrderID, TotalDue FROM Sales.SalesOrderHeader";

            // Open a connection
            SqlConnection conn = new SqlConnection(sqlConnectString);
            conn.Open();

            // Create a DataReader over the top 10 sales header records
            SqlCommand cmdHeader = conn.CreateCommand();
            cmdHeader.CommandText = sqlSelectHeader;

            using (SqlDataReader drHeader = cmdHeader.ExecuteReader())
            {
                while (drHeader.Read())
                {
                    int salesOrderID = (int)drHeader["SalesOrderID"];
                    Console.WriteLine("SalesOrderID = {0}\tTotalDue = {1}",
                        salesOrderID, drHeader["TotalDue"]);

                    string sqlSelectDetail = "SELECT ProductID, OrderQty FROM " +
                        "Sales.SalesOrderDetail WHERE SalesOrderID=" + salesOrderID;

                    // Create a DataReader with detail for the sales order
                    SqlCommand cmdDetail = conn.CreateCommand();
                    cmdDetail.CommandText = sqlSelectDetail;
                    using (SqlDataReader drDetail = cmdDetail.ExecuteReader())
                    {
                        while (drDetail.Read())
                            Console.WriteLine("\tProductID = {0}\tOrderQty = {1}",
                                drDetail["ProductID"], drDetail["OrderQty"]);
                        drDetail.Dispose();
                    }
                    Console.WriteLine();
                }
```

```
            }

            conn.Close();

            Console.WriteLine("Press any key to continue.");
            Console.ReadKey();
        }
    }
}
```

The output is shown in Figure A-11.

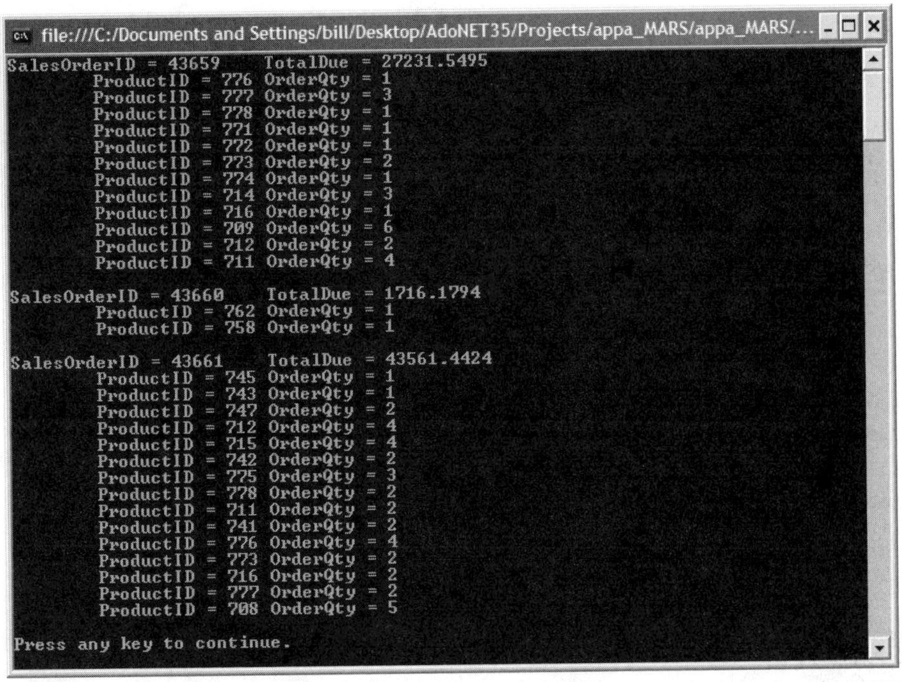

Figure A-11. Output for MARS example

Bulk copy

Bulk copy is a high-performance mechanism for transferring large amounts of data
into a SQL Server database table or view. In ADO.NET 2.0, you can bulk copy data
into SQL Server from either a DataTable or DataReader object using the new
SqlBulkCopy class in the System.Data.SqlClient namespace. This class supports both
single and multiple bulk copy operations within either dedicated (by default) or
existing transactions.

Table A-6 describes the key methods and properties of the SqlBulkCopy class.

Table A-6. Key methods and properties of the SqlBulkCopy class

Constructors	Description

`SqlBulkCopy(SqlConnection conn)`
`SqlBulkCopy(string connString)`
`SqlBulkCopy(string connString,`
`SqlBulkCopyOptions options)`
`SqlBulkCopy(string connString,`
`SqlBulkCopyOptions options,`
`SqlTransaction tx)`
	Creates a new instance of the `SqlBulkCopy` class, where:
	
	conn
	   A `SqlConnection` instance.
	
	connString
	   A SQL Server connection string.
	
	options
	   Bitwise flag that specifies options for the `SqlBulkCopy( )` method from the `SqlBulkCopyOptions` enumeration. See MSDN for more information.
	
	tx
	   An existing transaction (as a `SqlTransaction` object) in which the bulk copy takes place.

Properties	
`BatchSize`	The number of rows in each batch sent to the server. The default is 0, indicating that the rows are written in a single batch.
`BulkCopyTimeout`	Number of seconds for the bulk copy to complete before it times out.
`ColumnMappings`	A collection of `SqlBulkCopyColumnMapping` objects that defines the mapping of columns from the source data object to the destination table.
`DestinationTableName`	The name of the destination table on the server.
`NotifyAfter`	The number of rows to process before generating a notification event. The default is 0, indicating that notifications are not sent.
Methods	
`Close( )`	Closes the `SqlBulkCopy` instance.
`WriteToServer( )`	Copies all rows in the data source object (`DataReader` or `DataTable`) to the destination table.

In general, an application performs the following steps to bulk copy data:

1. Retrieve the data to copy into a `DataTable` or `DataReader` object.

2. Connect to the destination database server.

3. Create and configure the `SqlBulkCopy` object.

4. Call the `WriteToServer( )` method of the `SqlBulkCopy` object.

5. Call the `Close( )` method of the `SqlBulkCopy` object or dispose of the `SqlBulkCopy` object.

The following example copies all rows in the `Person.Address` table in the `AdventureWorks` database to a new table called `Address` (without a schema) in the `AdoDotNet35Cookbook` database. Follow these steps:

1. Create a SQL Server database called `AdoDotNet35Cookbook` if you haven't already created it.

2. Execute the following T-SQL command to create the `Address` table in the `AdoDotNet35Cookbook` database:

```
USE AdoDotNet35Cookbook
GO

CREATE TABLE Address(
    AddressID int NOT NULL PRIMARY KEY,
    AddressLine1 nvarchar(60) NOT NULL,
    AddressLine2 nvarchar(60) NULL,
    City nvarchar(30) NOT NULL,
    StateProvinceID int NOT NULL,
    PostalCode nvarchar(15) NOT NULL,
    rowguid uniqueidentifier ROWGUIDCOL  NOT NULL,
    ModifiedDate datetime NOT NULL)
```

3. Create a Windows console application named BulkCopy.

4. Copy the following code into *Program.cs*. Change the connection strings if necessary:

```
using System;
using System.Data;
using System.Data.SqlClient;

class Program
{
    static void Main(string[] args)
    {
        string srcConnectString = "Data Source=(local);" +
            "Integrated Security=SSPI;Initial Catalog=AdventureWorks;";
        string destConnectString = "Data Source=(local);" +
            "Integrated Security=SSPI;Initial Catalog=AdoDotNet35Cookbook;";

        string sqlSelect = "SELECT * FROM Person.Address";

        // get data from the source server using a data reader
        SqlConnection srcConn = new SqlConnection(srcConnectString);
        srcConn.Open();

        SqlCommand command = new SqlCommand(sqlSelect, srcConn);
        IDataReader dr = command.ExecuteReader();

        // connection to the destination server
        SqlConnection dstConn = new SqlConnection(destConnectString);
        dstConn.Open();

        // bulk copy the  data to the destination table
        using (SqlBulkCopy bcp = new SqlBulkCopy(dstConn))
        {
            bcp.DestinationTableName = "Address";
            bcp.WriteToServer(dr);
        }

        // close connections
        dstConn.Close();
        dr.Close();
        srcConn.Close();
```

```
            Console.WriteLine("Press any key to continue.");
            Console.ReadKey();
        }
    }
```

5. Execute the application. The rows from the Person.Address table in the
AdventureWorks database are bulk copied into the Address table in the
AdoDotNet35Cookbook database, as shown in Figure A-12.

AddressID	AddressLine1	AddressLine2	City	StateProvinceID	PostalCode	rowg
1	1970 Napa Ct.	NULL	Bothell	79	98011	9aadc
2	9833 Mt. Dias Blv.	NULL	Bothell	79	98011	32a54
3	7484 Roundtree...	NULL	Bothell	79	98011	4c506
4	9539 Glenside Dr	NULL	Bothell	79	98011	e5946
5	1226 Shoe St.	NULL	Bothell	79	98011	fbaff9
6	1399 Firestone ...	NULL	Bothell	79	98011	febf8:
7	5672 Hale Dr.	NULL	Bothell	79	98011	0175a

1 of 19614   Cell is Read Only.

Figure A-12. Address table in AdoDotNet35Cookbook database after bulk copy

If the column names in the source and destination table do not match, you need to
map the columns by using the SqlBulkCopyColumnMapping class. Each
SqlBulkCopyColumnMapping instance defines a map between a column in the bulk copy
source and the destination. Add the mapping instances by using the Add( ) method of
the ColumnMappings property of the SqlBulkCopy object before calling the
WriteToServer( ) method.

For example, if you change the name of the address line fields from AddressLine1 and
AddressLine2 to AddressLine1a and AddressLine2a, you must add the following mapping code before you call the WriteToServer( ) method:

```
bcp.ColumnMappings.Add(
  new SqlBulkCopyColumnMapping("AddressID", "AddressID"));
bcp.ColumnMappings.Add(
  new SqlBulkCopyColumnMapping("AddressLine1", "AddressLine1a"));
bcp.ColumnMappings.Add(
  new SqlBulkCopyColumnMapping("AddressLine2", "AddressLine2a"));
bcp.ColumnMappings.Add(
  new SqlBulkCopyColumnMapping("City", "City"));
bcp.ColumnMappings.Add(
  new SqlBulkCopyColumnMapping("StateProvinceID", "StateProvinceID"));
bcp.ColumnMappings.Add(
  new SqlBulkCopyColumnMapping("PostalCode", "PostalCode"));
bcp.ColumnMappings.Add(
  new SqlBulkCopyColumnMapping("rowguid", "rowguid"));
bcp.ColumnMappings.Add(
  new SqlBulkCopyColumnMapping("ModifiedDate", "ModifiedDate"));
```

Mappings can be specified by ordinal or column name, but all mappings must be specified in the same way. If the ColumnMapping collection is not empty, every column must be mapped whether their names match or not.

The SqlBulkCopy class supports transactions that are dedicated to the bulk copy operation, and can also use existing transactions. Dedicated transactions are used by default, as shown in the preceding example. The bulk copy is committed or rolled back automatically.

You can perform a bulk copy within an existing transaction, making the bulk copy part of the transaction together with other operations. This Windows application is similar to the previous example. It performs a bulk copy within a transaction. It also uses a DataTable object as the data source instead of a DataReader object:

```
using System;
using System.Data;
using System.Data.SqlClient;

class Program
{
    static void Main(string[] args)
    {
        string srcConnectString = "Data Source=localhost;" +
            "Integrated Security=SSPI;Initial Catalog=AdventureWorks;";
        string destConnectString = "Data Source=localhost;" +
            "Integrated Security=SSPI;Initial Catalog=AdoDotNet35Cookbook;";

        string sqlSelect = "SELECT * FROM Person.Address;";

        SqlConnection srcConn = new SqlConnection(srcConnectString);
        SqlCommand cmd = new SqlCommand(sqlSelect, srcConn);
        SqlDataAdapter da = new SqlDataAdapter(cmd);
        DataTable dt = new DataTable( );
        da.Fill(dt);

        // connection to the destination server
        SqlConnection dstConn = new SqlConnection(destConnectString);
        dstConn.Open( );

        // create the transaction on the destination connection
        SqlTransaction tx = dstConn.BeginTransaction( );
        Console.WriteLine("Transaction started.");
        try
        {
            // ... do some work using the transaction (tx)

            // bulk copy the  data to the destination table within
            // the transaction (tx)
            using (SqlBulkCopy bcp =
                new SqlBulkCopy(dstConn, SqlBulkCopyOptions.Default, tx))
```

```
            {
                bcp.DestinationTableName = "Address";
                bcp.WriteToServer(dt);
            }

            tx.Commit();
            Console.WriteLine("Transaction committed.");
        }
        catch
        {
            tx.Rollback();
            Console.WriteLine("Transaction rollback.");
        }

        dstConn.Close();

        Console.WriteLine("\nPress any key to continue.");
        Console.ReadKey();
    }
}
```

The output is shown in Figure A-13.

Figure A-13. Output for transacted SqlBulkCopy example

Support for new SQL Server large-value data types

SQL Server 2005 introduced *large-value data types*—varchar(max), nvarchar(max), and varbinary(max)—which allow storage of values up to $2^{31} - 1$ bytes in size. These types simplify working with large object (LOB) data—working with large-value data types is the same as working with the smaller-value data types (varchar, nvarchar, and varbinary). Large-value data types can be used as column types and as variables, and they can be specified as input and output parameters without special handling. You can return a large-value data type in a SqlDataReader object or use a large-value data type to fill a DataTable object using a SqlDataAdapter object.

The limitations of the large-value data types are as follows:

- A sql_variant type cannot contain a large-value data type.
- A large-value data type cannot be specified as a key column in an index or used as a partitioning key column.

Support for SQL Server user-defined types

SQL Server 2005 introduced user-defined types (UDTs). These extend SQL Server data types by letting you define both custom data structures containing one or more data types and objects containing one or more data types together with behaviors. UDTs can be used everywhere that SQL Server system data types can be used, including as variables or arguments or in column definitions.

You can create a UDT by using any language supported by the .NET Common Language Runtime (CLR). UDTs are defined as a class or structure—data is exposed as fields or properties, whereas behaviors are defined by methods.

Once a UDT is compiled into a .NET assembly, you must register the assembly in SQL Server by using the CREATE ASSEMBLY T-SQL statement. You must then create the UDT in SQL Server by using the CREATE TYPE T-SQL statement before you can use the UDT.

Support for snapshot isolation in transactions

SQL Server 2005 introduced support for *snapshot isolation* row locking. When snapshot isolation is enabled, updated row versions for each transaction are maintained in the tempdb system database. Each transaction is identified by a unique transaction sequence number, which is recorded together with the updated row versions. A transaction works with the most recent row versions having transaction sequence numbers prior to the sequence number of the current transaction—transaction sequence numbers that are greater than the current transaction sequence number indicate that the transactions occurred after the current transaction started, and thus are ignored. The result is that all queries in the transaction see a consistent view of the database at the moment the transaction started. No locks are acquired, which allows multiple simultaneous transactions to execute without blocking or waiting. This improves performance and significantly reduces the chance of a deadlock. Snapshot isolation uses optimistic concurrency—if an attempt is made to update data that has been modified since it was last read, the transaction will roll back and an error will be raised.

You can reduce the chance of update conflict by using locking hints in a T-SQL statement or at the beginning of a transaction. For example, the UPDLOCK hint locks rows selected in a statement and blocks attempts to update them before the statement completes. Hints should be used sparingly—excessive hints might suggest a problem with the application design.

Snapshot isolation is explicitly enabled for each database by setting the ALLOW_TRANSACTION_ISOLATION option to ON. You also need to set the READ_COMMITTED_SNAPSHOT option to ON to allow access to versioned rows under the default READ_COMMITTED isolation level. If the READ_COMMITTED_SNAPSHOT option is set to OFF, you must explicitly set the isolation level when initiating a transaction, as shown in the following code snippet:

```
SqlTransaction tx = conn.BeginTransaction(IsolationLevel.Snapshot);
```

Database mirroring support

Database mirroring lets you keep an up-to-date copy of a database on a standby server. The two copies of the database provide high availability and redundancy—if the primary database fails, the mirror can quickly be promoted to take its place. The .NET Data Provider for SQL Server implicitly supports database mirroring on SQL Server 2005 and later. Once the SQL Server database has been configured, database mirroring is automatic and is transparent to the developer.

SQL Server 2005 and later also supports explicit database mirroring. The SqlConnection object supports the Failover Partner parameter in the connection string. This lets the client application specify the name of the failover partner server. In this way, the client application can transparently attempt to establish a connection with the mirror database if the principal database is unavailable.

The name of the active server for the current connection is always available through the DataSource property of the SqlConnection instance—this property is updated when a connection is switched to the mirror server in response to a failover event.

Server enumeration

The GetDataSources( ) method of the SqlDataSourceEnumerator class enumerates active instances of SQL Server 2000 and later that are installed on your local network. The results are returned in a DataTable object with the columns shown in Table A-7.

Table A-7. DataTable schema for GetDataSources( ) method results

Column name	Description
ServerName	Name of the SQL Server.
InstanceName	Name of the server instance. This value is blank if the server is running as the default instance.
IsClustered	Indicates whether the server is part of a cluster.
Version	The version number of the server.

The following console application uses the SqlDataSourceEnumerator object to enumerate SQL Server instances:

```
using System;
using System.Data;
using System.Data.Sql;

class Program
{
    static void Main(string[] args)
    {
        DataTable dt = SqlDataSourceEnumerator.Instance.GetDataSources( );
        foreach (DataRow row in dt.Rows)
        {
```

```
            Console.WriteLine("ServerName = {0}\nInstanceName = {1}" +
                "\nIsClustered = {2}\nVersion = {3}\n",
                row["ServerName"], row["InstanceName"],
                row["IsClustered"], row["Version"]);
        }

        Console.WriteLine("Press any key to continue.");
        Console.ReadKey();
    }
}
```

The output looks similar to Figure A-14.

Figure A-14. Output for SqlDataSourceEnumerator example

The static Instance property of the SqlDataSourceEnumerator class returns an instance of the enumerator that is used to retrieve information about SQL Server instances.

Support for retrieving provider statistics in SQL Server 2005 and later

The .NET Framework Data Provider for SQL Server supports runtime statistics that expose information about processing queries in the database.

You must enable statistics by setting the StatisticsEnabled property of the SqlConnection object to true after the connection has been created. Once statistics are enabled, they can be retrieved into an IDictionary instance using the RetrieveStatistics() method of the SqlConnection object. The values in the dictionary are the statistic counter values, and are all of the long data type. The ResetStatistics() method of the SqlConnection object resets the counters. All statistics are gathered on a per-connection basis.

The following console application creates a connection, enables statistics, does a bit of work by filling a DataTable object using a data adapter, and iterates over the dictionary to output the name-value pair for each counter in the dictionary:

```
using System;
using System.Data;
using System.Data.SqlClient;
using System.Collections;

class Program
{
```

```
static void Main(string[] args)
{
    string sqlConnectString = "Data Source=(local);" +
        "Integrated Security=SSPI;Initial Catalog=AdventureWorks";
    string sqlSelect = "SELECT * FROM Person.Contact";

    // open a connection and enable statistics
    using (SqlConnection connection = new SqlConnection(sqlConnectString))
    {
        connection.StatisticsEnabled = true;

        // do some work with the connection
        SqlDataAdapter da =
            new SqlDataAdapter(sqlSelect, connection);
        DataTable dt = new DataTable();
        da.Fill(dt);

        // get the statistics
        IDictionary d = connection.RetrieveStatistics();
        // move the dictionary keys to an array
        string[] keys = new string[d.Count];
        d.Keys.CopyTo(keys, 0);

        // iterate over the dictionary displaying the key-value pair
        for (int i = 0; i < d.Count; i++)
            Console.WriteLine("{0} = {1}", keys[i], (long)d[keys[i]]);
    }

    Console.WriteLine("\nPress any key to continue.");
    Console.ReadKey();
}
}
```

The output is shown in Figure A-15.

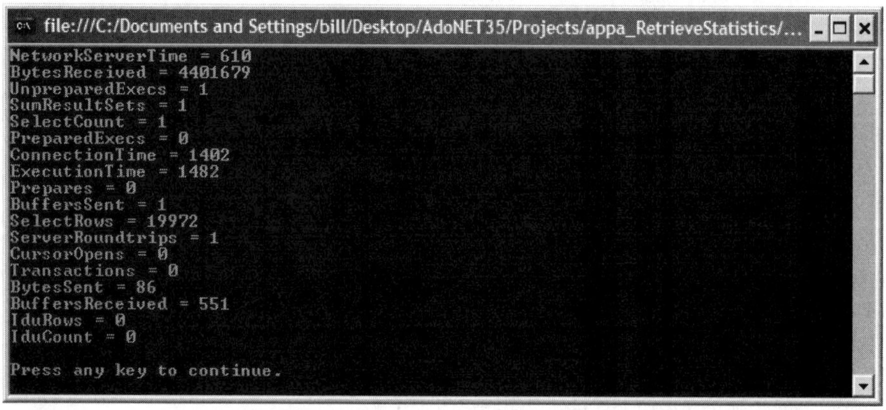

Figure A-15. Output for retrieving provider statistics example

See MSDN for a complete discussion of the available statistics.

Change password support

When using SQL Server 2005 with Windows Server 2003 (or more recent versions of either), you can programmatically change the existing password for the user specified in a connection string.

This example changes the password for login TestUser. First, create the user login in SQL Server Management Studio by right-clicking Security → Logins in Object Explorer and selecting New Login from the context menu. In the Login-New dialog box:

- Select the General page on the left side of the dialog box.
- Enter TestUser in the "Login name" listbox.
- Select the SQL Server Authentication radio button.
- Enter password in both the Password and Confirm Password listboxes.
- Uncheck the "Enforce password policy" checkbox.
- Select User Mapping on the left side of the dialog box.
- Check the AdventureWorks checkbox in the "Users mapped to this login" panel.
- Click the OK button to create the user.

Create a new console application, replace *Program.cs* with the following code, and execute the example:

```
using System;
using System.Collections.Generic;
using System.Text;
using System.Data.SqlClient;

class Program
{
    static void Main(string[] args)
    {
        string oldConnectString = "Data Source=(local);" +
            "uid=TestUser;pwd=password;Initial Catalog=AdventureWorks";

        SqlConnection.ChangePassword(oldConnectString, "password2");
        Console.WriteLine("Password changed to 'password2'.");

        // open a connection
        string newConnectString = "Data Source=(local);" +
            "uid=TestUser;pwd=password2;Initial Catalog=AdventureWorks";
        SqlConnection conn = new SqlConnection(newConnectString);
        conn.Open();
        Console.WriteLine("Connected with new password.");
        conn.Close();

        Console.WriteLine("Connection closed.");

        Console.WriteLine("\nPress any key to continue.");
        Console.ReadKey();
    }
}
```

The output is shown in Figure A-16.

Figure A-16. Output for change password example

The ChangePassword( ) method of the SqlConnection class takes two arguments:

- A connection string containing the user ID and password. An exception will be thrown if integrated security is specified in the connection string.
- The new password.

The ChangePassword( ) method can be used to change an expired user password without administrator intervention. If the password has expired, calling the Open( ) method of the SqlConnection object raises a SqlException exception. If the password needs to be reset, the Number property of the SqlException object will be either 18487 (password expired) or 18488 (password must be reset before logging in).

Schema discovery

The schema discovery API introduced in ADO.NET 2.0 lets you programmatically find and return metadata about the database for a connection. The database-independent API exposes schema elements, including tables, columns, and stored procedures.

The data connection exposes five categories of metadata through the GetSchema( ) method of the DbConnection class. This returns a DataTable object containing the metadata. It takes one of the five metadata collection names from the DbMetaDataCollectionNames class described in Table A-8.

Table A-8. DbMetaDataCollectionNames public fields

Collection name	Description
DataSourceInformation	Information about the database instance.
DataTypes	Information about data types that the database supports. This includes information about mapping data-source types to .NET Framework data types.
MetaDataCollections	List of metadata collections available.
ReservedWords	List of reserved words in the database.
Restrictions	Array of qualifiers for each metadata collection that can be used to restrict the scope of information returned. One value is returned per row with the position of the qualifier in the array specified by the RestrictionNumber column.

The following example retrieves and outputs the available metadata collections:

```
using System;
using System.Data;
using System.Data.SqlClient;
using System.Data.Common;

class Program
{
    static void Main(string[] args)
    {
        string sqlConnectString = "Data Source=(local);" +
            "Integrated Security=SSPI;Initial Catalog=AdventureWorks";

        SqlConnection conn = new SqlConnection(sqlConnectString);

        conn.Open();
        DataTable dt = conn.GetSchema(
            DbMetaDataCollectionNames.MetaDataCollections);
        conn.Close();

        foreach (DataRow row in dt.Rows)
        {
            Console.WriteLine("{0}; {1}; {2}",
                row[0], row[1], row[2]);
        }

        Console.WriteLine("\nPress any key to continue.");
        Console.ReadKey();
    }
}
```

The output is shown in Figure A-17.

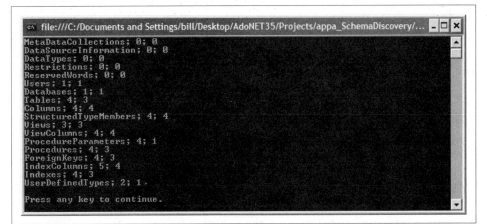

Figure A-17. Output for GetSchema() method example

The `DataTable` object returned from the `GetSchema()` method has three columns, as described in Table A-9.

Table A-9. Columns in DataTable object returned by GetSchema()

Column name	Description
CollectionName	The metadata collection name
NumberOfRestrictions	The maximum number of qualifiers for a metadata collection that can be used to restrict the scope of information returned
NumberOfIdentifierParts	The maximum number of identifier parts

An overload of the `GetSchema()` method takes the metadata collection name (one of the `CollectionName` values returned by the `GetSchema()` method) as an argument. For example, the following statement returns metadata about the tables in the database:

```
DataTable dt = conn.GetSchema("Tables");
```

An extract from the result set follows.

TABLE_CATALOG	TABLE_SCHEMA	TABLE_NAME	TABLE_TYPE
AdventureWorks	dbo	AWBuildVersion	BASE TABLE
AdventureWorks	dbo	DatabaseLog	BASE TABLE
AdventureWorks	dbo	sysdiagrams	BASE TABLE
AdventureWorks	HumanResources	Department	BASE TABLE
...			
AdventureWorks	Sales	vSalesPerson	VIEW
AdventureWorks	Sales	vSalesPersonSalesByFiscalYears	VIEW
AdventureWorks	Sales	vStoreWithDemographics	VIEW

Another overload of `GetSchema()` takes a string array of restrictions as a second argument. Call the `GetSchema()` method with the `DbMetaDataCollectionNames.Restrictions` argument to get a valid list of restrictions for a metadata collection. There is one row per restriction—each restriction has a unique `RestrictionNumber` value. For example, for the `Tables` metadata collection in SQL Server, there are four restrictions.

Restriction name	Restriction default	Restriction number
Catalog	TABLE_CATALOG	1
Owner	TABLE_SCHEMA	2
Table	TABLE_NAME	3
TableType	TABLE_TYPE	4

Continuing with the `Tables` metadata, the following code snippet uses restrictions to return information only for views in the `Production` schema:

```
string[] r = new string[] {null, "Production", null, "VIEW"};
DataTable dt = conn.GetSchema("Tables", r);
```

Support for DbConnection.GetSchema() is optional, so a data provider can choose to throw a NotSupportedException. There is no standard for the information returned when a metadata collection is queried—two providers can return different information (i.e., columns in the DataTable object) and support different restrictions.

Disconnected Class Enhancements

ADO.NET 2.0 introduced new features and enhancements for working with disconnected data. These changes affect both retrieving and updating data. The following subsections describe the key changes.

DataSet and DataTable enhancements

The new DataTableReader class lets you iterate over the rows in a DataTable object in a read-only, forward-only manner much like a regular DataReader. The DataTableReader object returns the rows and columns in the same order as in the underlying DataTable object. The DataTableReader returns only the current version of the row in the DataTable object—rows marked for deletion are skipped over. The data in the underlying DataTable object can be modified or deleted while the DataTableReader object is active, and the DataTableReader object will maintain its position and validity.

The DataTableReader object has an overloaded constructor—one takes a DataTable object as an argument and the other takes a DataTable[] object as an argument. The DataTableReader object can also be constructed by calling the CreateDataReader() method of the DataTable or DataSet class. For multiple tables, the tables appear in the same order in which they exist in the DataTable array or DataSet object. The NextResult() method of the DataTableReader object advances to the next result set if one exists.

The following console application creates a DataTable object containing all rows in the Person.Contact table in AdventureWorks, creates a DataTableReader object, and writes the first and last name for each person to the console window:

```
using System;
using System.Data;
using System.Data.SqlClient;

class Program
{
    static void Main(string[] args)
    {
        string sqlConnectString = "Data Source=(local);" +
            "Integrated Security=SSPI;Initial Catalog=AdventureWorks";

        string sqlSelect = "SELECT TOP 10 * FROM Person.Contact";

        // open a connection
        SqlConnection conn = new SqlConnection(sqlConnectString);
```

```
        // create a DataTable and fill with Person.Contact data
        SqlCommand command = conn.CreateCommand();
        command.CommandText = sqlSelect;
        DataTable dt = new DataTable();
        SqlDataAdapter da = new SqlDataAdapter(command);
        da.Fill(dt);

        // create a DataTableReader
        DataTableReader dtr = dt.CreateDataReader();

        // iterate over the rows in the DataTableReader and output
        // the first name and last name for each person
        while (dtr.Read())
            Console.WriteLine("{0} {1}", dtr["FirstName"], dtr["LastName"]);

        Console.WriteLine("\nPress any key to continue.");
        Console.ReadKey();
    }
}
```

The output is shown in Figure A-18.

Figure A-18. Output for CreateDataReader() method example

Batch processing with the DataAdapter

The DataAdapter class in ADO.NET 2.0 and later lets you group insert, update, and delete operations on a DataSet object or a DataTable object, instead of sending one row at a time to the server. This reduces round trips and typically results in performance gains. The SQL Server and Oracle providers support batch updates.

The UpdateBatchSize property of the DataAdapter object specifies the number of rows to be sent in each batch. If the UpdateBatchSize property is set to 0, the DataAdapter object uses the largest batch size that the database server can handle. Extremely large batches can negatively affect performance—the size of the batch should be tuned for your environment before deploying an application.

When batching updates, the UpdatedRowSource property of the DataAdapter object UpdateCommand, InsertCommand, and DeleteCommand properties must be set to the value UpdateRowSource.None or UpdateRowSource.OutputParameters. The values UpdateRowSource.FirstReturnedRecord and UpdateRowSource.Both are both invalid.

When updating rows using the DataAdapter object with batch processing disabled, the RowUpdating and RowUpdated events are raised for each row processed. When batch processing is enabled, the RowUpdating event occurs for each row processed, while the RowUpdated event is raised only once—after the batch is processed. Because the RowUpdated event is raised only once for all rows in the batch, its Row property is null. Instead, you can use the CopyToRows() method of the RowUpdatedEventArgs object to copy the processed rows to a DataRow array, where you can access them.

ADO.NET 3.5

ADO.NET 3.5 is the third major release of ADO.NET after ADO.NET 2.0 and was introduced together with the .NET Framework 3.5.

As a bit of background, the previous version of the .NET Framework—version 3.0—is a superset of .NET Framework version 2.0 with the addition of four major new components:

- Windows Communication Framework (WCF)
- Windows Presentation Framework (WPF)
- Windows Workflow Foundation (WF)
- Windows CardSpace (WCS)

There was no new version of ADO.NET released in .NET Framework 3.0.

This section provides an overview of new features in ADO.NET 3.5.

LINQ

Language-Integrated Query (LINQ) is a technology introduced in .NET Framework 3.5 that let you express queries directly in programming languages rather than as string literals in the application code. C# 3.0 and Visual Basic 9.0 introduce language extensions that implement LINQ—compilers for these languages ship with .NET Framework 3.5.

LINQ provides standard query and update mechanisms that can potentially support any type of data store, thereby unifying the syntax for querying any data source. LINQ creates a unified programming model for working with objects, relational data, and XML data with LINQ providers that let you access these data sources with LINQ.

LINQ to Objects

> Provides query capabilities over in-memory data collection objects that implement IEnumerable or IEnumerable<T> including user-defined Lists, Arrays, Dictionaries, and .NET collections.

LINQ to ADO.NET

> Provides query capabilities over any enumerable ADO.NET object. LINQ to ADO.NET consists of two related LINQ technologies:
>
> - LINQ to DataSet provides LINQ query capabilities into DataSet objects.
> - LINQ to SQL manages relational data as objects by mapping and brokering the data models of a relational database to the object model of a programming language.

LINQ to XML

> Provides query and document modification capabilities for XML data. It provides similar functionality to XPath queries and the document modifications capabilities of the Document Object Model (DOM) in a more strongly typed manner.

The following subsections provide a brief overview of LINQ queries and a description of LINQ to ADO.NET.

LINQ queries

A *query* is an expression that retrieves data from or updates data in a data store. Different query languages have been developed for different types of data stores—for example, SQL for relational databases, and XQuery for XML. LINQ simplifies creating queries for different data stores by providing a common model for accessing data in different data stores and formats. You write query expressions using a declarative syntax introduced in C# 3.0 and in Visual Basic 9.0. The same coding pattern is used to query and transform data in diverse stores, including relational databases, ADO.NET DataSet objects, XML data, and .NET collections.

Although a LINQ query looks somewhat like a SQL statement, it is structured differently. Instead of specifying the fields to return like you would with a SQL statement, you specify the data source first in a LINQ query. This isn't arbitrary—in C# and VB it is necessary to declare a variable before it is used. This ordering also lets Intellisense work with LINQ queries.

A LINQ query operation requires three steps: obtain a data source, create a query, and execute the query. A brief introduction to LINQ query operators used to create a LINQ query follows:

- You specify the data source using a from clause in C# (From clause in Visual Basic). The from clause is called a generator. In addition to the data source, the generator specifies a range variable that serves the same purpose as the iterator in a foreach loop (although no iteration actually takes place). The compiler can infer the type of the range variable from the context so there is no need to specify type explicitly.

- The join clause in C# (Join clause in Visual Basic) is used to combine multiple data sources into a single source for a query—similar to an INNER JOIN in T-SQL. In addition to explicitly using a LINQ join clause, you can access related items through collections exposed as properties of foreign keys.

- The where clause in C# (Where clause in Visual Basic) is used to filter the results returned by a LINQ query—similar to a WHERE clause in T-SQL. The filter takes the form of a Boolean expression that uses optional OR (||) and ADD (&&) operators to exclude non-non-matching elements from the source.

- The orderby clause in C# (Order By clause in Visual Basic) is used to sort the data returned by the LINQ query—similar to the ORDER BY clause in T-SQL. The orderby clause specifies a comma-delimited list of fields to sort by. The default comparator for each field is used as the basis of the sort. The default ascending clause is used to sort the results in the normal order, while the descending clause is used to sort the results in the reverse order.

- The group clause in C# (Group By in Visual Basic) groups the results returned based on a specified key—similar to the GROUP BY clause in T-SQL. The group clause specifies a comma-separated list of fields to group by. The results are returned as a set of nested lists corresponding to the grouping specified.

- The select clause in C# (Select in Visual Basic) specifies the elements that the query returns from the data source—similar to the T-SQL SELECT statement. You can select multiple from a source object in one of two ways: define a named type, and create and initialize it within the select clause, or create and initialize an anonymous type in the select clause.

A simple example follows that uses LINQ to query a string array. The example creates a string array containing seven colors, executes a LINQ query over the array to locate colors that are five or fewer characters long, and outputs the resulting colors in ascending order to the console:

```
using System;
using System.Linq;

class Program
{
    static void Main(string[] args)
    {
        string[] colors = {"Red", "Orange", "Yellow", "Green",
                    "Blue", "Indigo", "Violet"};
```

```
            var colorQuery = from color in colors
                             where color.Length <= 5
                             orderby color
                             select color;

        foreach (string s in colorQuery)
            Console.WriteLine(s);

        Console.WriteLine("\nPress any key to continue.");
        Console.ReadKey();
    }
}
```

The results are shown in Figure A-19.

Figure A-19. Output for LINQ query of array example

The first line sets up the data source—a string array of colors. The array implicitly supports IEnumerable<T>, allowing it to be used as a data source for a LINQ query.

The second line creates the query. This query has four clauses: from, orderby, where, and select. The from clause specifies that the data source is the array colors and that the color is the range variable representing each successive element in the source as it is traversed. The query is stored to a query variable named colorQuery. The query variable and range variable are strongly typed—in this case, the compiler infers the types from the data source. In the case of the query variable, the var keyword indicates an anonymous type and instructs the compiler to infer the type of the query variable at compile time. The where clause uses the Length property of the color range variable to select only colors where the length of the colors array element <= 5 characters. The orderby clause sorts the result set in ascending order. Finally, the select clause instructs the query to return the range variable color. You could return the uppercase of the colors by rewriting the select clause as select color.ToUpper().

The third line uses a foreach loop to execute the query. A query variable stores the query and not the result set returned by the query—the query is not actually executed until you iterate over the query variable using either a foreach loop (or by calling the MoveNext() method of the query). The results of the query are returned through the iteration variable of the foreach loop—in this case s. The third line iterates over the query colorQuery to execute it, the results are returned in the foreach loop iterator s, and each value of s is written to the console.

LINQ to ADO.NET lets you query over enumerable ADO.NET objects using the LINQ programming model. As mentioned previously, LINQ to ADO.NET is made up of two technologies: LINQ to DataSet and LINQ to SQL. The following sections discuss these two technologies.

LINQ to DataSet

The DataSet is the standard object used in ADO.NET to work with disconnected data from a variety of data sources and optionally update the data source at a later time with changes made working in disconnected mode. Despite its extensive capabilities, the DataSet object has limited query capabilities—these capabilities include basic filtering and sorting through the Select( ) method of the DataSet. Other methods can be used to navigate the hierarchy of related parent and child tables within the database. Complex queries either need to be created new, or use complex programming that performs poorly, tends to be error prone, and frequently results in business logic being hardcoded in layers of the application where it does not belong.

LINQ to DataSet lets you query DataSet objects using LINQ queries. Additionally, Visual Studio developers benefit from Intellisense and compile-syntax checking. LINQ to DataSet also lets you easily add flexible solutions to support tasks such as generic reporting and analysis.

A LINQ to DataSet query is shown in the following example. A discussion follows.

```
using System;
using System.Data;
using System.Data.SqlClient;
using System.Linq;

class Program
{
    static void Main(string[] args)
    {
        string connectString = "Data Source=(local);" +
            "Integrated security=SSPI;Initial Catalog=AdventureWorks;";

        string sqlSelect = "SELECT * FROM Production.Product; " +
            "SELECT * FROM Production.ProductInventory;";

        // Create the data adapter to retrieve data from the database
        SqlDataAdapter da = new SqlDataAdapter(sqlSelect, connectString);
        // Create table mappings
        da.TableMappings.Add("Table", "Product");
        da.TableMappings.Add("Table1", "ProductInventory");
        // Create and fill the DataSet
        DataSet ds = new DataSet( );
        da.Fill(ds);
```

```
// Create the relationship between the Product and
// ProductInventory tables
DataRelation dr = ds.Relations.Add("Product_ProductInventory",
            ds.Tables["Product"].Columns["ProductID"],
            ds.Tables["ProductInventory"].Columns["ProductID"]);

DataTable product = ds.Tables["Product"];
DataTable inventory = ds.Tables["ProductInventory"];

var query = from p in product.AsEnumerable()
            join i in inventory.AsEnumerable()
                on p.Field<int>("ProductID") equals
                    i.Field<int>("ProductID")
            where p.Field<int>("ProductID") < 100
            select new
            {
                ProductID = p.Field<int>("ProductID"),
                Name = p.Field<string>("Name"),
                LocationID = i.Field<short>("LocationID"),
                Quantity = i.Field<short>("Quantity")
            };

foreach (var q in query)
{
    Console.WriteLine("{0} - {1}: LocationID = {2} => Quantity = {3}",
        q.ProductID, q.Name, q.LocationID, q.Quantity);
}

Console.WriteLine("\nPress any key to continue.");
Console.ReadKey();
    }
}
```

The output is shown in Figure A-20.

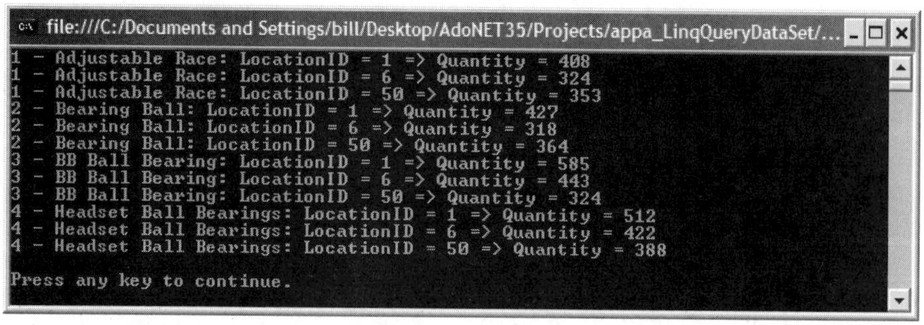

Figure A-20. Output for LINQ query of DataSet example

The first step in a LINQ query is to obtain a data source. With LINQ to DataSet, this means that you need to fill a DataSet object from the data source. You do this using the DataAdapter object (the only way before LINQ) or by using LINQ to

SQL discussed in the next section. The DataSet is filled with the Production.Product and Production.ProductInventory tables from AdventureWorks, and a relationship is created between the tables.

The second step is to create a LINQ query. This example uses a cross-table query—a query against two related tables. In LINQ, this done using join clause to specify the elements being related. The select clause returns four fields—ProductID, Name, LocationID, and Quantity—in the result set.

The example sets up a relationship between the Product and ProductInventory tables in the DataSet. This lets you eliminate the join clause in the query. The query in the following code is equivalent to that shown in the preceding example. The query eliminates the explicit join clause and adds a nested from clause. The GetChildRows() method of the range variable p accesses the related records in the ProductInventory table:

```
var query = from p in product.AsEnumerable()
            where p.Field<int>("ProductID") < 100
            from i in p.GetChildRows("Product_ProductInventory")
            select new
                {
                    ProductID = p.Field<int>("ProductID"),
                    Name = p.Field<string>("Name"),
                    LocationID = i.Field<short>("LocationID"),
                    Quantity = i.Field<short>("Quantity")
                };
```

The final step uses a foreach loop to execute the query. As mentioned, a query variable stores the query and not the result set returned by the query—the query is executed when you iterate over the query variable using either a foreach loop (or by calling the MoveNext() method of the query). The results of the query are returned through the iteration variable of the foreach loop—in this case q. The loop outputs the four fields in the query result set to the console.

LINQ to SQL

LINQ to SQL provides a runtime infrastructure that lets you manage relational data as objects. In LINQ to SQL you set object properties and execute object methods instead of issuing database commands. LINQ to SQL translates LINQ to SQL objects to SQL queries and sends them to the database for processing. Once processed, LINQ to SQL translates the results back to LINQ objects that you can work with programmatically.

The first step to use LINQ to SQL is to create an object model that represents the database in terms of the programming language. You can create an object model using the Object Relational Designer (O/R Designer), which is a graphical tool hosted in Visual Studio, or using the SQLMetal Tool, which is a command-line utility. This discussion is limited to the O/R Designer. For more information about SQL-Metal, see Microsoft Visual Studio documentation.

The O/R Designer generates a LINQ to SQL object model from a relational database. It provides a visual design surface for creating LINQ entity classes (tables and columns) and associations (relationships) from the objects in a database. The O/R Designer can also map stored procedures and functions to DataContext methods. The O/R Designer supports only 1:1 mapping from an entity class to a database table or view.

The O/R Designer generates either C# or Visual Basic source code that you add to your Visual Studio project. Alternatively, you can generate an external XML file—this approach keeps mapping metadata separate from your application code.

Follow these steps to use the O/R Designer to generate a simple C# object model:

1. Open Visual Studio and create a console application named LinqToSql.

2. Right-click the project in the Solution Explorer pane and select Add → New Item… from the context menu to open the Add New Item dialog. Select the Linq to SQL file template in the Data category. Change the Name to *MyDataClasses.dbml*. Click the Add button to close the Add New Item dialog. The empty design surface for the new *dbml* file appears, representing the DataContext that you will configure next. LINQ to SQL files have the extension *.dbml*.

3. In Server Explorer, right-click on the Data Connections node and select Add Connection from the context menu to open the Add Connection dialog. Complete the dialog to create a connection to the AdventureWorks database on your SQL Server. Click OK to close the dialog and create the connection.

4. Expand the new data connection in the Data Connections node. Drag the Product (Production) table from the table subnode onto the O/R Designer design surface to create the entity class Product—the new class contains properties corresponding to columns in the Product table. Next, drag the ProductInventory (Production) table onto the design surface to create the entity class ProductInventory. Notice that an association (relationship) is automatically created between the two entities based on the database metadata. The design surface is shown in Figure A-21.

5. Build the project.

6. Open the Data Sources pane by selecting Data → Show Data Sources from the main menu. Click the Add New Data Source link to open the Data Source Configuration Wizard dialog. Select Object as the data source type. Click Next.

7. Expand the LinqToSql node. Navigate to and select the Product class. Click Next. Click Finish to confirm that you want to add the Product entity class. The Product and its related ProductInventory classes are added to the Data Sources pane, as shown in Figure A-22.

8. Next, create the LINQ to SQL query to return data from the Product table using the Product entity class. The completed C# code for *Program.cs* is shown in the following example:

```
using System;
using System.Linq;
```

```
namespace LinqToSql
{
    class Program
    {
        static void Main(string[] args)
        {
            MyDataClassesDataContext dc =
                new MyDataClassesDataContext();

            var products = from row in dc.Products
                           where row.ProductID < 100
                           select row;

            foreach (Product p in products)
                Console.WriteLine(p.ProductID + ": " + p.Name);

            Console.WriteLine("\nPress any key to continue.");
            Console.ReadKey();
        }
    }
}
```

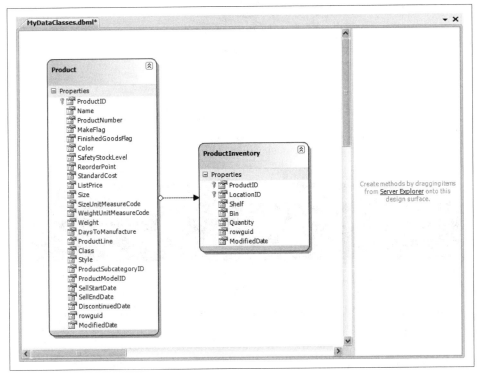

Figure A-21. O/R Designer design surface

The output is shown in Figure A-23.

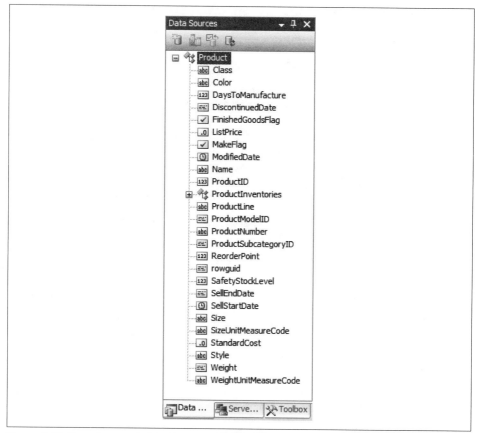

Figure A-22. Data Sources dialog after adding LINQ to SQL data source

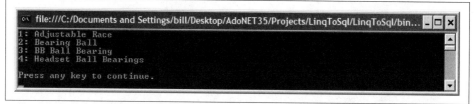

Figure A-23. Output for LINQ to SQL example 1

An instance of `MyDataClassesDataContext` is created. This class inherits from `DataContext`—the LINQ to SQL class that contains methods and properties that connect the database to the LINQ to SQL entity classes mapped to the database. The LINQ query retrieves all of the rows in the `Products` table where the `ProductID` < 100 into the query variable `products`. The `ProductID` and `Name` fields are output to the console.

9. Alternately, we can return a type from the query that contains a subset of the data in each row. The query in the following code snippet returns a type containing the ProductID and Name. These are output in the foreach loop, which iterates over the inferred type variable p—the output is the same as the previous example:

```
var products = from row in dc.Products
               where row.ProductID < 100
               select new
                   {
                       ProductID = row.ProductID,
                       ProductName = row.Name
                   };
foreach (var p in products)
    Console.WriteLine(p.ProductID + ": " + p.ProductName);
```

10. The association created by the O/R Designer lets you navigate to the related ProductInventory records for each Product. These records are accessed through the ProductInventories property of Product that exposes the related collection for each Product record. This is shown in the foreach loop:

```
foreach (var p in products)
{
    Console.WriteLine("{0}: {1}", p.ProductID, p.Name);
    // iterate over the collection of ProductInventory records
    foreach (var pi in p.ProductInventories)
        Console.WriteLine("    {0} = {1}", pi.LocationID,pi.Quantity);
}
```

The output is shown in Figure A-24.

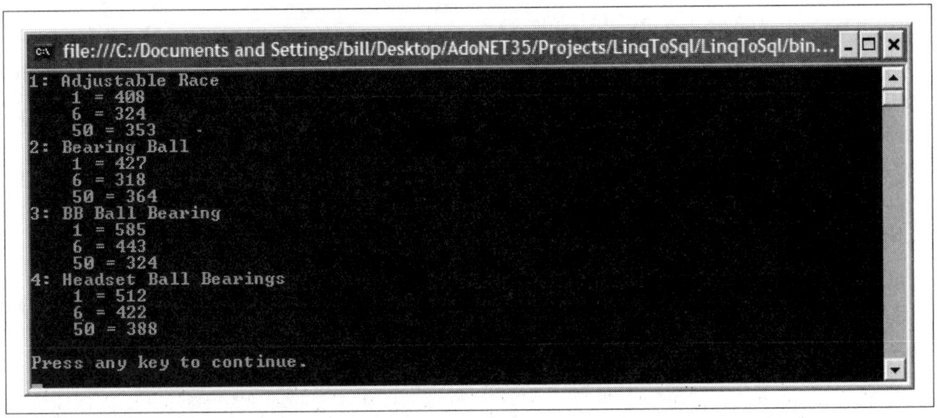

Figure A-24. Output for LINQ to SQL query example 2

11. You can also explicitly join tables in a LINQ query using the join clause. The following example returns the same results as in the previous example using an explicit join:

```
var query = from p in dc.Products
            join pi in dc.ProductInventories
                on p.ProductID equals pi.ProductID into pis
            where p.ProductID < 100
            select new { Product = p, Inventories = pis };

foreach (var q in query)
{
    Console.WriteLine("{0}: {1}", q.Product.ProductID, q.Product.Name);
    // iterate over the collection of ProductInventory records
    foreach (var pi in q.Inventories)
        Console.WriteLine("    {0} = {1}", pi.LocationID, pi.Quantity);
}
```

The Products entity class is joined to the ProductInventories entity class on the
ProductID. The select clause returns a new type (inferred by the compiler) containing a Product and the associated (related) ProductInventory objects. The
foreach loop performs a nested iteration over the query variable to return the
same results as the previous example.

Table-Valued Parameters

SQL Server 2008 supports table-valued parameters. Table-valued parameters let you
marshal multiple rows of data from a client application to a SQL Server in a single trip
without special server-side logic to process the data. Column values in table-valued
parameters can be accessed using standard T-SQL statements or using CLR routines.
You cannot pass table-valued parameters to user-defined functions. Table-valued
parameters are read-only by SQL Server.

In ADO.NET, table valued parameters can be populated with DataTable, DataReader,
and System.Collections.Generic.IList<SqlDataRecord> objects. You must set the
data type of the parameter to the Structured value of the SqlDbType enumeration. If
you pass the table-valued parameter to a parameterized SQL statement, you need to
specify the previously created type in the SQL Server through the TypeName property
of the Parameter object.

Index

We'd like to hear your suggestions for improving our indexes. Send email to *index@oreilly.com*.

O

O/R (Object Relational) Designer, 216, 222, 917
  generating C# object model, 918
Object data type, 266
object model, 216
  C#, 918
  LINQ to SQL, 222, 918
Object Relational Designer (see O/R Designer)
objects, relational data as, 222
OCI (Oracle Call Interface), 26
ODBC, 1
  connecting Oracle databases, 27
  connecting to an ODBC data source, 29
  connection pooling, 53
    counters, 64
    support by the driver manager (DM), 50
  connection to SQL Server database, 16
  data types and accessors for .NET data provider, 82
  drivers installed on Windows, 765
  enumerating drivers, 826–827
  monitoring connection pooling, 59
  performance monitoring, 62–64
  Programmer's Reference, 50
  providers compatible with ODBC.NET data provider, 31
OdbcConnection class, 31
OdbcDataReader class, 30
OdbcFactory class, 762
OLE DB, 1, 224
  Access Database Engine (ACE) driver, 305
  accessing Excel as a data source, 228
  ADOX support, 819
  batch query and FillSchema() method, 171
  COMPUTE BY statement from Command object, 261
  connecting Oracle databases, 27
  connecting to a data source, 28
  connecting to password-protected Access database, 33
  connection pooling, 52
  connection strings in UDL files, 10
  connection to a text file, 40
  connection to Access database, 32
  connection to Excel workbook, 38
  connection to SQL Server database, 16

Data Shaping Service, 266
  data types and accessors for .NET data provider, 81
  Excel as a data source, 228
  executing SHAPE command, 264
  Jet 4.0 or later, 297
  listing providers, 822–826
  positional parameter markers, 184
  providers on Windows systems, 765
  resource pooling, 49
  Shape language, Data Shaping Services, 236
  SQL Server, accessing data from heterogeneous sources, 243
OLE DB Jet provider, accessing text files, 222
OLE DB Service Component, displaying data Link Properties dialog box, 56
OLE DB Services attribute, 52
OleDbCommand class, 261
OleDbConnection class, 29, 816
  GetOleDbSchemaTable() method, 365, 778, 819
OleDbDataAdapter class, 226
  key/index information for Excel Workbooks, 305
OleDbEnumerator class
  GetElements() method, 822, 825
  GetEnumerator() method, 822, 825
OleDbFactory class, 762
OleDbSchemaGuid class, 778
OleDbTransaction class, 455
OnDataRowUpdated event, 485
one-to-many relationships between parent and child records, 182
OnRowUpdated event (DataAdapter), 297
OnRowUpdating event, 485
OPEN XML, 609
Open() method, SqlConnection class, 829
OPENDATASOURCE function, 242, 244
OPENROWSET function, 242, 244
OpenXML, 651–657
  OPENXML command, 656
  Transact-SQL extension, 699
optimistic concurrency, 496
optimization
  caching and application performance, 688
  SQL stored procedures, 660, 712–716
  (see also performance)
OR (||) operator, 213

About the Author

Bill Hamilton creates solutions using .NET and Java technologies. Over the past 15 years, he has provided consulting services ranging from strategic planning and inception through design, development, and implementation of enterprise-scale solutions. He specializes in the health care, professional services, financial services, retail, and manufacturing industries. He is the author of the highly praised *Programming SQL Server 2005* and *ADO.NET in a Nutshell*, and he also writes for the Microsoft Developer Network. You can email Bill at *bill.hamilton@element14.com*.

Colophon

The animal on the cover of *ADO.NET 3.5 Cookbook*, Second Edition, is a white spoonbill (*Platelea leucorodia*), also called the common or Eurasian white spoonbill, named for its large, spatulate bill. Spoonbills feed by wading through the shallow waters of their marshy habitats, moving their partly opened bills from side to side to filter out mud and water. When the sensitive nerve endings inside their bills detect an edible morsel, they snap them shut. A spoonbill's typical diet includes insects, larvae, small crustaceans, and tiny fish.

Mature white spoonbills are about 85 centimeters long from the tips of their tails to the tips of their bills, and their wingspans average 125 centimeters. As the name suggests, white spoonbill feathers are a creamy white. During breeding season, however, adults develop yellow patches on their breasts, faces, and bills.

White spoonbills are found in northeast Africa and much of Europe and Asia. They nest in trees and reed beds, typically in large colonies and sometimes with other bird species in the *Threskiornithidae* family, such as herons and storks. Males gather nesting materials, and females weave these sticks and reeds into shallow, bowl-shaped nests. Females generally lay a clutch of three to four eggs per year and share incubation duties with their mates.

Although the white spoonbill is an endangered species, conservation efforts have led to a slow increase in population in some areas, particularly in northwestern Europe. Loss of breeding sites due to land clearance and pesticide use are the main threats to the white spoonbill's survival.

The cover image is from *Bewick's British Birds*. The cover font is Adobe ITC Garamond. The text font is Linotype Birka; the heading font is Adobe Myriad Condensed; and the code font is LucasFont's TheSans Mono Condensed.

Related Titles from O'Reilly

.NET and C#

ADO.NET Cookbook

ADO.NET 3.5 Cookbook, *2nd Edition*

ASP.NET 2.0 Cookbook, *2nd Edition*

ASP.NET 2.0: A Developer's Notebook

Building an ASP.NET Web 2.0 Portal

C# 3.0 in a Nutshell, *3rd Edition*

C# Cookbook, *2nd Edition*

C# Design Patterns

C# in a Nutshell, *2nd Edition*

C# Language Pocket Reference

Exchange Server 2007 Administration: The Definitive Guide

Head First C#

Learning ASP.NET 2.0 with AJAX

Learning C# 2005, *2nd Edition*

Learning WCF

MCSE Core Elective Exams in a Nutshell

.NET and XML

.NET Gotchas

Programming Atlas

Programming ASP.NET, *3rd Edition*

Programming ASP.NET AJAX

Programming C#, *4th Edition*

Programming MapPoint in .NET

Programming .NET 3.5

Programming .NET Components, *2nd Edition*

Programming .NET Security

Programming .NET Web Services

Programming Visual Basic 2005

Programming WCF Services

Programming WPF, *2nd Edition*

Programming Windows Presentation Foundation

Programming the .NET Compact Framework

Visual Basic 2005: A Developer's Notebook

Visual Basic 2005 Cookbook

Visual Basic 2005 in a Nutshell, *3rd Edition*

Visual Basic 2005 Jumpstart

Visual C# 2005: A Developer's Notebook

Visual Studio Hacks

Windows Developer Power Tools

XAML in a Nutshell

O'REILLY®

Our books are available at most retail and online bookstores.

To order direct: 1-800-998-9938 • *order@oreilly.com* • *www.oreilly.com*

Online editions of most O'Reilly titles are available by subscription at *safari.oreilly.com*